# Principles of Conservation Biology

# Principles
# of
# Conservation
# Biology

Gary K. Meffe
University of Georgia's Savannah River Ecology Laboratory

C. Ronald Carroll
Institute of Ecology, University of Georgia

and Contributors

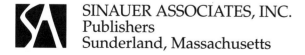
SINAUER ASSOCIATES, INC.
Publishers
Sunderland, Massachusetts

**THE COVER**

Skamania County, Washington. The border between industry-owned forest (right) and the Gifford Pinchot National Forest, 1990, illustrating the effects of clear-cutting, a predominant method of logging worldwide. Since this photograph was taken, much of the National Forest has also been clear-cut. Photograph by Daniel Dancer.

**PRINCIPLES OF CONSERVATION BIOLOGY**

© 1994 by Sinauer Associates, Inc.

All rights reserved.

This book may not be reproduced in whole or in part for any purpose whatever without permission from the publisher. For information address Sinauer Associates, Inc., Sunderland, MA 01375 U.S.A.

**Library of Congress Cataloging-in-Publication Data**

Meffe, Gary K.
    Principles of conservation biology / Gary K. Meffe, C. Ronald Carroll and contributors.
        p.    cm.
    Includes bibliographical references.
    ISBN 0-87893-519-3
    1. Biological diversity conservation.   2. Ecosystem management.   3. Nature conservation.   I. Carroll, C. Ronald (Carl Ronald), 1941– .   II. Title.
  QH75.M386   1994
  333.95'16—dc20                                  93–48913
                                                          CIP

Printed in U.S.A.

6 5 4 3

*To the students of conservation biology, in whose collective hands the future of biodiversity rests, and to the pioneers of the field, upon whose shoulders we stand.*

# Contents in Brief

# Contents

# Contributing Chapter Authors

**J. Baird Callicott,** Department of Philosophy, University of Wisconsin, Stevens Point

**Blair Csuti,** College of Forestry, University of Idaho, Moscow

**John B. Dunning,** Institute of Ecology, University of Georgia, Athens

**William R. Jordan III,** The Arboretum, The University of Wisconsin, Madison

**James A. MacMahon,** College of Science, Utah State University, Logan

**Norman Myers,** Meadlington, Oxford, England

**Richard B. Norgaard,** Energy and Resources Group, University of California, Berkeley

**Reed F. Noss,** College of Forestry, University of Idaho, Moscow; and Fisheries and Wildlife, Oregon State University, Corvallis

**Gordon H. Orians,** Department of Zoology, University of Washington, Seattle

**Stuart L. Pimm,** Department of Zoology, University of Tennessee, Knoxville

**H. Ronald Pulliam,** Institute of Ecology, University of Georgia, Athens

**Steven Viederman,** Jesse Smith Noyes Foundation, New York

# Preface

The field of conservation biology is a new, rapidly growing, and swiftly changing endeavor, a product of the calamitous decline of biodiversity formally recognized by the scientific community in the 1970s. The field grew in the 1980s from an amalgam of disciplines but until the fall of 1993 no textbook existed to guide its new practitioners. This is the second textbook in the field, and the first at a more advanced level.

The two primary authors initially undertook this project several years ago on their own, but soon realized that two people cannot comprehensively and fairly represent the broad interests of conservation biology without input from others. If conservation biology is the study and protection of biological diversity, then diversity in its presentation is surely appropriate. Thus, after a period of retrenchment, the project moved forward with a new concept: to recruit the best minds available in the field to strengthen certain topics and provide insight in areas for which we lacked expertise. In addition to recruiting authors for nine chapters (see the Brief Contents that precede this Preface), we also invited a number of individuals to provide 11 case studies based on their experiences in conservation, and we asked more than 50 people to write essays on pertinent topics. If there is strength in diversity, then you have it in front of you.

The book proceeds in four parts. Part I introduces the philosophical, ethical, and biological framework upon which all conservation must be built. A strong ethical standard is a prerequisite for success in any venture, and lack of ethical direction is a root cause of many of the problems we face in conservation today. We paraphrase conservation biologist and ethicist Phil Pister, who has said that training people in any field without also providing an ethical foundation is like launching missiles without guidance systems. They will certainly take off and do *something,* but we really do not know what. The discussion on ethics is followed by an exploration of definitions and roles of species and populations in conservation, which also has strong bearing on legal aspects of protection. Part I finishes with two chapters that define biodiversity and its local and global patterns, causes, and dynamics, and focuses on patterns and causes of biodiversity losses.

Part II presents two chapters on the population level. First, the genetic basis of conservation is examined, including discussion of the importance and losses of genetic diversity, and management approaches to its conservation. We then discuss demographic processes of populations, emphasizing mechanisms of population regulation, dynamics of populations, and the importance of linking the population and landscape levels in conservation.

Part III focuses on system-wide issues. The implications of species interactions and community influences on conservation are discussed by examining the keystone species concept, mutualistic interactions, and the effects of invasive species on communities. We then move to a dominant global problem in conservation, habitat fragmentation, exploring various concepts of fragmentation and its effects on biota. This sets the stage for a discussion of the design of nature reserves, a major challenge in conservation biology.

The eight chapters in Part IV build on the foundation of the previous parts, and address practical applications and human concerns in conservation. First, two chapters on the theory and practice of management ask why management is necessary, explain different types and levels of management, and discuss management priorities and external threats to management plans. This is followed by a series of management case studies written by individuals experienced in management issues ranging from working with endangered species to managing conservation units. We then explore one particular management approach, habitat restoration and mitigation of habitat loss. Although it is not a substitute for protection of natural areas, restoration ecology can potentially reclaim some degraded and destroyed areas and make them ecologically valuable again. Conservation biology is then melded with economics and politics in the next chapter. If the political and economic arenas are not modified to recognize long-term problems associated with biodiversity losses and global environmental change, then even the best biological knowledge will have little effect.

One of the greatest potentials for progress in conservation is within the political and economic realms. The way this can happen is to understand how policy is developed and how science influences that process. The next chapter deals with these topics, setting the groundwork for a series of case studies on sustainable development by people who have been in the thick of such projects. Sustainable development is considered by many to be the best hope for both conservation of biodiversity and a reasonable standard of living for much of the world. Others fear it is an excuse for continued global exploitation. Finally, we look at future prospects and directions of conservation biology, and address some of the most pressing problems and possible solutions.

We emphasize that this book is incomplete, in the sense that no single work can possibly cover all relevant aspects of conservation biology. The field is nearly limitless in scope, and the serious student must pursue literature far beyond the materials covered here. In particular, we highly recommend regular reading of the journal *Conservation Biology* for cutting-edge reports in the field. Conservation biology literature is growing rapidly, and numerous outstanding works are available; many of these are listed at the ends of each chapter, as suggestions for further reading. Each chapter also includes a series of discussion questions, which we hope will be the basis for a participatory classroom exercise. Many of the questions have no easy answer, but reflect real world problems that conservation biologists must grapple with daily. It is never too soon to be exposed to these practical and difficult issues.

We encourage teachers and students alike to respond with comments that might improve future editions of the text. You are the users of this material, and you must tell us what you like and dislike about it.

Finally, a message about *commitment.* Conservation requires more than good intentions, scientific insight, and wishful thinking: it requires money. Consequently, one-third of royalties from this textbook will be donated by the authors and the publisher to two major conservation organizations plus the Organization for Tropical Studies, in hopes of turning student book costs into actual conservation gains. We challenge other authors and publishers in ecological and conservation fields to also give something back to the systems about which they write. It will make a tangible difference if that commitment becomes the norm of conservation publishing.

# Acknowledgments

A book like this cannot be completed without a tremendous intellectual and logistic support network of people and institutions. First, we thank the University of Georgia and the Savannah River Ecology Laboratory for logistical support and the time necessary to complete this project, which was considerable. In particular, Director Michael Smith, Division Head Ronald Chesser, and Research Manager Laura Janecek at SREL deserve thanks for their patience, understanding, and encouragement. Numerous students and colleagues helped in many ways, from discussions, to suggesting graphics, to reviewing bits and pieces, to taking up the research workload when writing and editing were in full swing. This includes Lehr Brisbin, Beverly Collins, Justin Congdon, Anne Dix, Marion Dobbs, Greg Eckert, Dean Fletcher, Whit Gibbons, Frank Hensley, Carol Hoffman, Chuck Jagoe, Chuck Lydeard, J. Vaun McArthur, Margaret Mulvey, Jim Novak, Joe Pechmann, John Pinder, Gene Rhodes, David Scott, Becky Sharitz, Joel Snodgrass, Steve Weeks, and David Wilkins. We greatly appreciate the University of Georgia's first cohort in the graduate program in Conservation Ecology and Sustainable Development, for being constructive critics and "guinea pigs" when we tried out the first chapter drafts in the classroom. Special thanks go to Carol Ercolano for repeated and rapid help with word processing and other assorted chores, and Aline DeLaperriers and especially Jan Hinton for production of graphics. Ms. Hinton's extraordinary efforts were single-handedly responsible for keeping graphics, and thus the book, on schedule, and keeping the authors' reliance on analgesics and antacids to a minimum.

Numerous individuals served as chapter reviewers, and we thank the following for their insights and suggestions: William Ascher, Susan Bratton, James Brown, Peter Brussard, Ronald Chesser, Edward Connor, Douglas Futuyma, Ed Grumbine, Robert Holt, Susan Harrison, James Johnson, W. L. Minckley, Peter Morin, Margaret Mulvey, Barry Noon, Elliott Norse, David Orr, Thomas Parker, Eric Pianka, Steward Pickett, Margaret Race, Peter Raven, Mark Sagoff, Michael Scott, Daniel Simberloff, Beryl Simpson, Stephen Viederman, David Wilcove, and David Woodruff. Special recognition goes to Martha Groom of the University of Washington, who read the entire manuscript and made countless improvements. She greatly strengthened several chapters with her broad background and up-to-the-minute knowledge, and we only wish we could have incorporated more of her insights.

Finally, the people at Sinauer Associates make book publishing an absolute delight. We have never been associated with a finer, more professional, and more caring bunch, and we especially thank Kathaleen Emerson, Andy Sinauer, and Christopher Small for their guidance, patience, and good humor, and Norma Roche for impressive copy editing.

# Personal Acknowledgments

GKM: I wish to recognize the major mentors in my career, Jim Collins, W. L. Minckley, and Bob Vrijenhoek, for their influences on my thinking and professional development, and Phil Pister, who has been a constant source of ethical guidance for conservationists. My students and technicians have been remarkably patient with me during writing, and I hope to once again give them the attention they deserve. My parents, Mary and the late Edward Meffe, provided the moral foundation of values, fairness, and simple decency that must be at the center of true conservation. There is no greater gift. Finally, this book literally would not have been completed were it not for the efforts of my wife and best friend, Nancy Meffe. Despite a challenging personal workload she was always there to sympathize, encourage, and kick butt, and always had the keen perception to know which one was needed at the time. Our regular evening walks and discussions made this work possible, bearable, and enjoyable, and I owe her a great debt of gratitude.

CRC: I wish to thank my major advisor, Dan Janzen, for teaching me how to "see" nature, and my colleagues in the Organization for Tropical Studies for their delightful intellectual companionship. I wish to thank my parents, Maxine and Henry Carroll, for always encouraging my interest in nature and accepting the occasional critter that colonized the household. Finally, I want to thank my wife, Carol A. Hoffman, for her constant support, insight (personal and otherwise), and willingness to pick up the slack at home on the frequent occasions when my schedule collapsed.

Gary K. Meffe, Aiken, South Carolina
C. Ronald Carroll, Athens, Georgia
March 1994

# Principles of Conservation Biology

# I

# Introductory Concepts

# 1

# What Is Conservation Biology?

*When the last individual of a race of living things breathes no more,*
*another heaven and another earth must pass before such a one can be again.*

*William Beebe*

## Environmental Problems and Human Population Growth

The natural world is a far different place now than it was 10,000 years ago, or even 100 years ago. Every natural ecosystem on the planet has been altered by humanity, some to the point of collapse. Vast numbers of species have gone prematurely extinct, natural hydrologic and chemical cycles have been disrupted, billions of tons of topsoil have been lost, genetic diversity has eroded, and the very climate of the planet may have been disrupted. What is the cause of such vast environmental change? Very simply, the cumulative impacts of 5.5 billion people (Figure 1.1), a number growing by 95 million each year (260,000 per day), have stressed the ecological support systems of the planet past their powers of resilience. As a consequence, biological diversity (**biodiversity**, for short), the grand result of evolutionary processes and events tracing back several billion years, is itself at stake and rapidly declining. One of the many species suffering the consequences of ecological destruction is *Homo sapiens*, the perpetrator of it all.

The seeming inevitability of human population growth outstripping our planet's resources can easily lead to a feeling of helplessness and apathy in the face of so much destruction. However, there are three points that should provide reason for optimism. First, there are instances of countries significantly lowering their population growth rates, and doing so in a short period of time. Examples include Costa Rica, Cuba, Mexico, Venezuela, and Thailand. Some, such as Hungary and West Germany, have even had periods of negative growth in the past few decades.

Second, the destruction of biodiversity today is due not so much to numbers of people per se, but to where they live and what they consume. In developing countries the expansion of highly commercialized agriculture and forestry has displaced the rural poor into city slums or onto steep hillsides and other ecologically fragile areas. In the industrialized world, the wealthy

**Figure 1.1** Estimated global human population size from the last Ice Age to the present, illustrating the exponential nature of human population growth since the Industrial Revolution. Note that the human population took hundreds of thousands of years to reach 2 billion, but then more than doubled in 40 years. (Modified from various sources.)

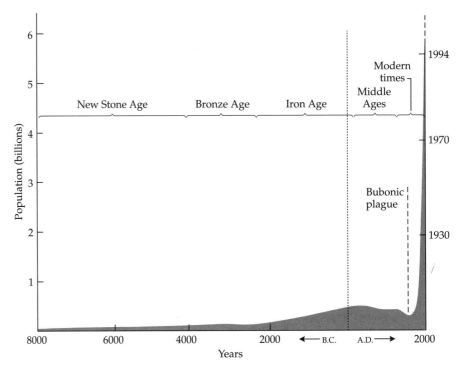

consume a disproportionate share of the global resources. These patterns are reversible.

Third, and this is the key, birth rates are high where family survival depends on being successful in an unskilled and uneducated labor pool, that is, where there are strong economic incentives for large families. The corollary is that education and the appropriate kinds of economic development can greatly reduce population growth rates.

The many ways that human population growth rates can be humanely reduced have several features in common: gender equity, access to education, equitable distribution of rural income, and rural economies based on other than simple exploitation of natural resources. The take-home message is that we must think broadly about conservation. The **stewardship** of natural biodiversity requires that a strong link be forged between conservation biology and environmentally **sustainable development**.

The field of **conservation biology** is a response by the scientific community to this biodiversity crisis. It is a new, synthetic field that applies the principles of ecology, biogeography, population genetics, economics, sociology, anthropology, philosophy, and other theoretically based disciplines to the maintenance of biological diversity throughout the world. It is new in that it is a product of the 1980s, although its roots go back centuries. It is synthetic in that it unites traditionally academic disciplines such as population biology and genetics with the applied traditions of game and forest management and allied fields. It is most of all challenging and imperative, in that it is motivated by human-caused global changes that have resulted in the greatest episode of mass extinction since the loss of the dinosaurs, 65 million years ago.

Environmentally, we are at the most critical point in the history of humanity, and the current population of students and professionals has a unique place in that history: of the hundreds of thousands of human generations that ever existed, no previous generation has had to respond to possible annihilation by humans of a large percentage of the species diversity on the planet. Unless humanity acts quickly and in a significant way, the next generation will not have this opportunity. We are it, and conservation biology is, in every sense of the word, a "crisis discipline" (Soulé 1985, and discussed below). One of the major developments needed in conservation is a shift from a reactive analysis of each crisis to a proactive science that permits us to anticipate developing crises and to prepare scientifically grounded contingency plans.

Many would ask, "What's so new about conservation biology? People have been doing conservation for decades, even centuries." This is true, but the "new" conservation biology differs in at least three ways. First, it now includes, and has been partially led by, major contributions from theoretically oriented academicians, whose ecological and genetic models are being applied to real-world situations. The unfortunate and false dichotomy of "pure" and "applied" research is finally breaking down, as the academic researcher and the resource manager have joined intellects, experience, and perspectives to address local to global conservation problems.

Second, much of traditional conservation was rooted in an economic, **utilitarian** philosophy whose primary motivation was to maintain high yields of selected species for harvest. Nature was seen as providing benefits to people, mostly from Western nations, through highly visible, selected components such as deer, trout, grouse, or timber, and was managed for maximization of a single or a few species, a small subset of the huge diversity of nature. The "new" conservation biology views all of nature's diversity as important and having inherent value. With this perspective, management has been redirected toward stewardship of the world's biodiversity and natural ecosystems, rather than toward single species. Three detailed perspectives on the "new" conservation biology are offered in essays in this chapter from academic (Stanley A. Temple), government agency (Hal Salwasser), and nongovernmental organization, or NGO (Kathryn S. Fuller), viewpoints.

---

## ESSAY 1A

*An Academic Perspective:*
# The Role of the University in Conservation Biology

Stanley A. Temple, University of Wisconsin

---

Conservation biology was largely conceived in academia, and academic scientists have continued to play a major role in guiding its development. The generally recognized vision for conservation biology features at least four characteristics that have encouraged an academic bias: a focus on biological diversity, an expectation of scientific rigor, a focus on multidisciplinary and interdisciplinary approaches, and innovative practical measures for dealing with the biodiversity crisis. Because conservation biology focuses on understanding and conserving biodiversity, rather than on selected utilitarian species, academic prevalence in the field seems inevitable. The scope of biodiversity topics is so broad that no other institution outside of academia encompasses a wide enough range of specialists to cover the territory. Only in universities does one find such a broad array of geneticists, population biologists, ecologists, social scientists, philosophers, resource economists, and other disciplinarians who share an interest in and concern for biodiversity.

In contrast, government conservation agencies and private conservation groups tend to harbor a narrower range of specialists among their ranks, and the collective diversity of their interests may be too limited to provide expertise in all aspects of conservation biology. Conservation agencies have typically targeted specific categories of biological resources for attention (forests, fisheries, wildlife, rangeland) rather than biodiversity. Even the network of subjects that these government bureaus collectively cover leaves enormous gaps because they may provide minimal attention to elements of the biota that are "non-resources." Conservation organizations also specialize, though recently some have expanded their missions to encompass biodiversity. Still, their collective staffs are far smaller and more narrowly focused than academic departments.

Conservation biology has always regarded itself as a field in which the usual criteria of scientific rigor should be imposed. Search for new generalizations from theoretical models that explain widespread patterns, use of the scientific method to test hypotheses generated from these models, and publication of findings in peer-reviewed journals where they can be critically evaluated by the scientific community are important traits of academic science. The credibility that attends this approach has allowed conservation biologists to gain a general level of respect within the scientific community that previously had not been extended to many scientists who worked in conservation fields.

How rigorous has conservation biology proven to be? The report card is mixed. Although the field emerged with a body of useful theory already in hand (such as the equilibrium theory of island biogeography and its various manifestations), there have been few new theoretical contributions, in contrast to many tests and validations of existing models. This has led some scientists to question whether conservation biology, as a synthetic field, has actually generated any principles of its own or instead just borrows extensively from other disciplines.

Conservation biology aims to encourage collaborative work among specialists from many disciplines who share an interest in biodiversity. Ideally, these collaborations result in interdisciplinary problem-solving, and most recognized centers of excellence in conservation biology have tried to foster an interdisciplinary approach. An academic bias again results because universities are the home of many of the potential collaborating disciplines.

When incorporating conservation biology into the academic bureaucracy, most institutions have opted to create new administrative units in conservation biology rather than to introduce biodiversity as a conspicuous issue in many existing units. Because these units include individuals from a broad array of disciplines, one of the consequences of this approach will be a new generation of conservation biologists who are trained as broadly versed generalists, rather than as disciplinary specialists, who can think and work well in an interdisciplinary mode. This situation contrasts sharply with the training of the first generation of leaders in the field, who had no specific training in conservation biology but typically focused on a particular aspect of conservation. Although the next generation of conservation biologists may be well-equipped to promote more interdisciplinary work, their educational backgrounds may also reduce the likelihood of new scientific breakthroughs.

Conservation biology stresses the importance of generating new scientifically sound approaches to solving the complex web of problems that have created the biodiversity crisis. Producing innovations is a central mission of university scientists, whereas applying such research is often the challenge for nonacademic scientists. Often self-described as a mission-oriented, crisis-driven group, conservation biologists in academia have a heavy responsibility to make their research applicable and to venture forth from the Ivory Tower environment and make their findings available to the decision makers and managers who will actually implement strategies for preserving biodiversity in the real world.

Relations between academics and practitioners can be awkward, and there were early hints of disharmony in conservation biology. The new breed of conservation scientists in academia was initially perceived by some in the conservation establishment as arrogant, out-of-touch, and unwilling to work cooperatively with practitioners. Whether justified or not, this initial reaction hampered progress, and there are still old-guard conservationists who are threatened by the ascendancy of conservation biology and remain antagonistic to it. There are also some academics who do remain arrogant and out of touch. This unfortunate divisiveness may be one of the most serious handicaps associated with conservation biology's academic roots, and one that all conservation biologists should try hard to dispel. Fortunately, the barriers are crumbling and their dissolution should be encouraged by all parties.

The urgent and lofty goals of conservation biology can only be achieved if all members of the conservation community work together on biodiversity issues. As a university scientist who has been closely involved with conservation biology, I have fluctuated between enthusiasm for, and concern over the academic bias in the field. Despite occasional apprehension, I continue to believe that conservation biology's development and on-going evolution have been well served by its academic roots. Working closely with colleagues in conservation agencies and organizations, academic scientists will continue to have a vital role to play in preserving biological diversity.

---

The "new" conservation biologist recognizes that diverse and functioning ecosystems are critical not only to maintenance of the few species we harvest, but also to perpetuation of the nearly limitless variety of life forms of which we know little or nothing. The conservationist realizes that intact and functioning ecosystems are also important as life-support systems for the planet, and are critical to our own continued survival and well-being as a species (Odum 1989).

Third, conservation biology fully recognizes and embraces the contributions that need to be made by nonbiologists to conservation of biodiversity. In particular, the social sciences, economics, and political science may ultimately have more impact on real advances or losses in conservation than the biological sciences. Unless major changes can be made in the way that humanity does business with the natural world, and in humanity's destructive patterns of population growth and resource consumption, it would appear that much of our biological knowledge of conservation will be rendered useless under the sheer weight of the human presence.

A goal of conservation biology is to understand natural ecological systems well enough to maintain their diversity in the face of an exploding human population that has fragmented, simplified, homogenized, and destroyed many ecosystems to the point that contemporary species extinction rates are estimated to be 1000 to 10,000 times higher than the normal **background extinction rate** expected in the absence of human influences (Wilson 1989). Thus, conservation biology tries to provide the basis for intelligent and informed management of highly disrupted ecosystems.

In 1965, the ecologist G. Evelyn Hutchinson described the natural world as an "ecological theater" serving as a stage for the "evolutionary play." Perhaps no better metaphor sums up the mission of conservation biology: *to retain the actors in that evolutionary play and the ecological stage on which it is performed*. Conservation biology strives to maintain the diversity of genes, populations, species, habitats, ecosystems, and landscapes, and the processes normally carried out by them, such as natural selection, biogeochemical cycling, photosynthesis, energy transfer, and hydrologic cycles. It is a dynamic play, with players and action on many different spatial and temporal scales, old actors disappearing and new ones arriving. But the play ultimately comes down to one thing: dynamic evolutionary processes in a changing ecological background. Conservation biology attempts to keep those normal evolutionary processes working within a functioning ecological setting.

## A Brief History of Conservation Biology

The global effort to conserve and protect the natural environment is a recent phenomenon, though efforts to conserve economically important natural resources have a long history. Although we may think of environmental destruction as a product of recent times—and certainly the scale of recent destruction is unprecedented—significant environmental degradation has always accompanied humankind. Humans may have been responsible for the extinction of most of the large mammal fauna of North America shortly after human colonization from Asia about 11,000 years ago (Martin and Klein 1984). According to what has been termed the "blitzkrieg" hypothesis (Martin 1973), mastodons, camels, tapirs, glyptodonts, giant ground sloths, and many other species may have been hunted to extinction shortly after human colonization of the continent.

In the classical Greek period, Aristotle commented on the widespread destruction of forests in the Baltic region. At the same time in southern Asia, forests were felled to meet the growing need for timber to build trading ships to serve expanding mercantile centers such as Constantinople (now Istanbul). The barren landscapes that we associate with much of Turkey, Syria, Iraq, and Iran are unnatural deserts resulting from massive exploitation of fragile woodlands. Indeed, this part of Asia had been known in earlier times as the "land of perpetual shade." The Mediterranean region of Italy and Greece was likewise heavily wooded before human settlement.

Diamond (1992) argues that virtually wherever humans have settled, environmental destruction has been the rule; he and others (e.g., Redford 1992) largely debunk the notion of the "noble savage," primitive but wise peoples who had great concern for natural resources. Many, if not most, societies have had some lasting, destructive impact on the natural world. However, some societies have certainly minimized their environmental influences and lived in a more sustainable fashion than most.

In the humid tropics, early agrarian societies dealt with declining resources by moving when yields began to drop and local game became scarce, an option no longer available in today's crowded world. Some of these shift-

**Figure 1.2** Highly diverse agro-forestry systems, such as the Dammar system from Indonesia, can be found in many tropical regions. This photograph shows a similar agroforestry system from southeastern Mexico. It is known locally as a "huerto," or tree-garden. These traditional agroforestry systems of mixed, cultivated perennials may be structurally similar to old, second-growth natural forests and contain nearly as many tree species on a per-hectare basis. (Photograph by C. R. Carroll.)

ing cultivators practiced, and some still practice, forms of conservation management. In many tropical regions, complex tree gardens helped stabilize land use (see Carroll 1990 for examples), and some shifting cultivators practiced a kind of management of natural succession. Today, in "Dammar" agroforestry in Sumatra, for example, natural forest plots are converted over a period of 10–20 years into complex modified forests based primarily on dammar (*Shorea javanica*), a tree that is tapped for resins, and other economically important native trees (Mary and Michon 1987). The plots are structurally similar to natural successional plots and likely help support the regional biodiversity. Although we may think of conservation management as a modern Western notion, there are many such examples of management of natural resources to be found in other cultures (Figure 1.2).

We would be remiss if we failed to point out the fragility of these traditional systems in the modern, interconnected global marketplace. To continue with the Dammar example, the practice is disappearing for two unexpected reasons. First, the establishment of Burkit National Park appropriated a major portion of Dammar forestry land and put severe constraints on the use of the remaining land. In particular, the long fallow period needed became increasingly difficult to accommodate. Second, a growing urban market created great demand for rice and, to a lesser extent, coffee and cloves. In response to these two factors, Dammar agroforestry has been largely replaced by dryland rice and coffee cultivation.

In Europe, conservation efforts were largely devoted to private game management and maintenance of royal preserves and private manor lands. Until the 18th and 19th centuries, little notice was given to problems of the **commons,** the public lands. As a consequence, exploitation of these common-use resources led to the deforestation of most of Europe by the early 18th century. This occurred even earlier in Great Britain, where many of the native forests were destroyed by the 12th century (McKibben 1989); the demand for charcoal to supply home heating and industrial needs led to virtual elimination of the remaining public forests by the late 18th century. Similarly, in Asia, conservation efforts were game-oriented and largely restricted to the private lands of the privileged. An artist's early rendition of a forest and pastoral scene in China juxtaposed against a later photograph of the same place, which depicted an eroded and barren landscape, is said to have been the telling argument made to the Theodore Roosevelt administration by forester Gifford Pinchot in his successful campaign to establish the U.S. Forest Service in 1905.

---

## ESSAY 1B

*A Government Agency Perspective:*
# Conservation Biology and the Management of Natural Resources

Hal Salwasser, University of Montana (formerly U.S. Forest Service)

---

In the closing decades of the 19th century, the concept of conservation was developed and promoted as an ethical relationship between people, land, and resources. It meant wise use of lands and resources so as not to destroy their capacity to serve future generations. Its champions were men such as William Hornaday, Theodore Roosevelt, George Bird Grinnell, and Gifford Pinchot. They were sportsmen, lovers of the outdoors, and political activists, the progressive thinkers of their time. The result of their zeal was the start of national conservation laws, government agencies to manage lands and resources in the public trust, and the great systems of national parks, forests, wildlife refuges, and public lands that now encompass about one-third of the land area of the United States.

The ideals of conservation can be traced back to Henry David Thoreau, George Perkins Marsh, and landscape artists of the mid-1800s. The philosophical roots go even further back to Native American beliefs and ancient cultures from other lands. What is significant about the period of the late 1800s in the United States is that the philosophy, ideals, and action to conserve natural resources came together in a set of government policies, public institutions, and social commitment.

Yet almost immediately, the conservation movement diverged along pragmatic utilitarian and romantic preservationist lines, a split in perspectives that to some extent continues to this day. Natural resource disciplines such as forestry, range management, wildlife management, and fisheries, along with their respective government agencies, arose from the utilitarian roots. Wilderness advocacy and its public agents arose from the preservation roots. Eventually, The Nature Conservancy, a nongovernmental conservation organization, emerged from the scientific discipline of ecology. The field of endeavor now called Conservation Biology shares common roots with these contemporary resource disciplines and their government agencies. It also shares with them a wide array of aims and methods.

One example of the common roots and shared aims of conservation biology and natural resource management comes from the opening sentence of the first article in the first issue of the first volume of the *Journal of Wildlife Management*: "In the new field of conservation biology, few life history phenomena have occasioned more comment than the heavy percentages of nest failures for many species of birds thus far studied." (Errington and Hamerstrom 1937). The discipline described is now known as Wildlife Management. From the start it recognized conservation biology as its scientific basis. As an aside, nest failures of birds are still a perplexing subject of both old and new traditions in conservation biology.

Some 40 years after Errington and Hamerstrom published their article, a new discipline was forming under the title of Conservation Biology. It confused a lot of people in government agencies and academia who thought all along that they were conservation biologists. But there must have been a need or the new field would not have emerged. The need was to compensate for a weakness in applied conservation disciplines that focused most of their attention on the continued productivity of already common or productive plants and animals. Conservation Biology has its current focus on population viability of all native plant and animal species, many of them uncommon, and on biological diversity in general. Beyond counterbalancing the weakness in applied conservation disciplines, however, Conservation Biology has more in common with traditional conservation fields than it has differences with them.

For those intent on finding differences between the values and aims of Conservation Biology and Wildlife Management, for example, a review of the preface in that 1937 issue of the *Journal of Wildlife Management* might be useful. The officers of The Wildlife Society stated their policy in unequivocal terms: "Management along sound biological lines means management according to the needs and capacities of the animals concerned, as related to the environmental complex in which they are managed. It does not include the sacrifice of any species for the benefit of others, though it may entail the reduction of competing forms where research shows this is necessary. It consists largely of enrichment of environment so that there shall be maximum production of the entire wildlife complex adapted to the managed areas. Wildlife management is not restricted to game management, though game management is recognized as an important branch of wildlife management. It embraces the practical ecology of all vertebrates and their plant and animal associates. While emphasis may be placed on species of special economic importance, wildlife management along sound biological lines is also part of the greater movement for conservation of our entire native fauna and flora." (Bennitt et al. 1937). This statement, if extended to fisheries, forestry, recreation, and range management, would put conservation biology squarely in a role as the foundation science for resource management and the agencies that carry it out.

While conservation biology is not entirely new, Conservation Biology is. As an organized discipline, it is about 15 years old. But still it is not exactly clear what role the discipline will play in resource management and government programs. These are the perspectives of one who had a hand in the birthing of Conservation Biology out of a need to implement federal policies to better protect biological diversity and out of a desire to obtain a broader set of concepts, theories, and methods than traditional conservation disciplines had provided.

First, let's retreat to the dictionary for some help. For most speakers of the English language, *conservation* means the care and protection of resources so as to prevent loss or waste. It includes actions that government agencies call preservation, restoration, enhancement, recycling, extending useful life, and sustained-yield management. *Biology* is the body of scientific knowledge and methods that deals with the origin, history, physical characteristics, life processes, and habits of plants and animals. Thus a "common-folks" definition for conservation biology would be the application of biology to the care and protection of plants and animals to prevent their loss or waste. This is a broad field for conservation biology, certainly broader than a focus on just the scarce elements of a flora and fauna.

This broad view of conservation biology is consistent with how I suspect Errington, Hamerstrom, and probably Aldo Leopold might have seen it: the

basic biological sciences that underpin the applied conservation fields of forestry, wildlife management, fisheries, nature protection, and so on. These basic sciences would include genetics, physiology, population biology, natural history, and ecology. Because conservation entails more than biology, other sciences or disciplines are necessary complements to Conservation Biology, such as economics, geography, history, sociology, and philosophy.

The issue now facing Conservation Biology is this: will it become the foundation of biological sciences that supports conservation of plant and animal diversity and productivity? Or will it become another subspecialty that focuses on preservation of the scarcer parts and processes of biological diversity? Both would be legitimate outcomes. Both are needed. But the latter would leave it to another synthetic field to form the foundation needed by all the subdisciplines of biological conservation.

The polarized rhetoric swirling around Conservation Biology's role in issues such as endangered species, old-growth forests, landscape fragmentation, and biological diversity during the latter decades of the 20th century seems to indicate that Conservation Biology is destined for the rank of a new subspe-

cialty. I hope this is not the case.

Conservation Biology sits on the horns of a dilemma. It can become the foundation of biological sciences that serves the broad spectrum of conservation in both public and private sectors. Or, it can become a special part of the framework of biological conservation, that part dealing with rare elements and processes. There are significant implications to how the practitioners of Conservation Biology decide to resolve this dilemma. The choice still exists, but it won't for much longer. I would like to see Conservation Biology become a foundation of biological sciences for conservation rather than just a subdiscipline for preservation of the rare elements of diversity. I would like to see it embrace the full spectrum of aims and methods in biological conservation, from preservation of natural systems and their diversity to sustainable management to produce the natural resources upon which all human life depends. But regardless of how the field evolves, the world of biological management programs is better off because Conservation Biology came into being in the 1980s. We needed the new perspectives and methods it brought to conservation, and they will continue to be useful for a long time to come.

## Conservation in the United States

Conservation in the continental United States has had a somewhat unusual history. Europeans colonizing America found a landscape that, by comparison with a highly exploited Europe, must have seemed pristine. Aboriginal peoples had exploited natural resources and driven some species to extinction, but their low population densities and lack of technologies for widespread devastation prevented wholesale destruction. American Indians apparently made extensive use of fire to manage lands for both agriculture and game. Some historians argue that Atlantic coastal lands cleared by Indians became important colonization sites for European settlers and helped them survive their first winters (Russell 1976).

During the colonial period, North American forests were extensively exploited for lumber, ship masts, naval stores (gum and turpentine), and charcoal for heating. Huge tracts were cleared for agriculture. Demand for forest products in Europe and domestic demand by a rapidly growing population were eagerly met by exploiting the seemingly endless forests. Later, forests were again called upon to provide lumber for vast railroad networks and building construction as the nation expanded westward. In coastal areas, salt marshes were harvested for salt hay (*Spartina*) to feed cattle before the opening of the prairies to grain farming.

The value of forests as an economic resource was not the only philosophical perspective held by the colonists, however. Religious attitudes of some groups, especially the Puritans, held that the forest was the abode of the devil. This is perhaps not an unfamiliar attitude even today, for many children's stories place witches, trolls, and goblins in deep, dark forests, and many otherwise reasonable adults are more frightened in a remote forest than in the heart of a large city with high murder rates.

Thus, the forests were beset by increasing economic demands and were perceived to be endless and vaguely evil—hardly a nourishing environment for conservation. Conservation did, of course, develop in North America, but it required several centuries after initial European colonization to become firmly established. Perhaps it was necessary first to develop a significant population whose livelihood was not intimately tied to forest exploitation.

American conservation efforts can be traced to three philosophical movements, two of the 19th century and one of the 20th (Callicott 1990). The **Romantic-Transcendental Conservation Ethic** derived from the writings of Ralph Waldo Emerson and Henry David Thoreau in the East, and John Muir in the West. Emerson and Thoreau were the first prominent North American writers to argue, in the mid-1800s, that nature has uses other than human economic gain. Specifically, they spoke of nature in a quasi-religious sense, as a temple in which to commune with and appreciate the works of God. Nature was seen as a place to cleanse and refresh the human soul, away from the tarnishings of civilization. This was the philosophical and aesthetic position that Muir used as he argued for a national movement to preserve nature in its wild and pristine state, and condemned its destruction for material and economic gain. John Muir's movement flourishes today in the form of many citizen conservation groups; his direct organizational legacy is the Sierra Club.

This noneconomic view was countered by the so-called **Resource Conservation Ethic**, made popular by the forester Gifford Pinchot at the turn of the 20th century. His was an approach to nature based in the popular utilitarian philosophy of John Stuart Mill and his followers. Pinchot saw only "natural resources" in nature and adopted the motto, "the greatest good of the greatest number for the longest time" (Pinchot 1947). Nature, to Pinchot, was an assortment of components that were either useful, useless, or noxious to people. Note the **anthropocentric** valuing of nature, not because it is part of "God's design" (as per the Romantic-Transcendentalists), but because natural resources feed the economic machine and contribute to the material quality of life. Pinchot (1947) once stated that "the first great fact about conservation is that it stands for development."

Pinchot's approach to conservation stressed equity—a fair distribution of resources among consumers, both present and future—and efficiency, or lack of waste. This led to adoption of the **multiple-use** concept for the nation's lands and waters, which is the current mandate of the U.S. Forest Service and Bureau of Land Management. Under multiple use, many different uses of the land are attempted simultaneously, such as logging, grazing, wilderness preservation, recreation, and watershed protection. Because a market economy may or may not be efficient and has little to do with equity, governmental regulation or outright public ownership of resources was deemed necessary to develop and enforce conservation policy (see Essay 12D for a discussion of the contradictions inherent in "multiple use management").

These two movements thus created a schism, with the Preservationists (Muir, Emerson, Thoreau) advocating pure wilderness and a spiritual appreciation for nature, and Conservationists (Pinchot) adopting a resource-based, utilitarian view of the world. A third movement, born of this century, emerged with the development of evolutionary ecology. This **Evolutionary-Ecological Land Ethic** was developed by Aldo Leopold in his classic essays, published as *A Sand County Almanac* (1949), and in other writings. Leopold was educated in the Pinchot tradition of resource-based conservation, but later saw it as inadequate and scientifically inaccurate. The development of ecology and evolution as scholarly disciplines conclusively demonstrated that nature was not a simple collection of independent parts, some useful and others to be discarded, but a complicated and integrated system of interdependent processes and components, something like a fine Swiss watch. There are really only a few parts of a watch that appear to be of direct utility to its owner, namely, the hour, second, and minute hands (back when watches had hands). However, proper functioning of these parts depends on dozens of unseen components that must all function well and together. Leopold saw ecosystems in this context, and this is the context in which modern ecology first developed. This **equilibrium** view has been replaced by a dynamic, **nonequilibrium** ecological perspective (discussed below). Nevertheless, the Leopold land ethic remains as the philosophical foundation for conservation biology.

Although the Evolutionary-Ecological view of the world, updated by the nonequilibrium perspective, is the most biologically sensible and comprehensive approach to conservation, much of modern conservation is based on various mixtures of these three philosophies. The Resource Conservation Ethic of the late 19th century is still the dominant paradigm followed by public resource agencies such as the U.S. Forest Service, under which U.S. forest tracts are seen as economic resources to be managed for multiple human use (Figure 1.3). The Romantic-Transcendental Conservation Ethic, though more typically without the overt religious rationale of its early proponents, is the basis for activism by many private conservation organizations throughout the world, whose goals are to save natural areas in a pristine state for their inherent value. This difference has resulted in repeated confrontations among so-called "special interest groups."

Leopold's Evolutionary-Ecological Land Ethic is the best informed and most firmly grounded of any approach to nature and should serve as the philosophical basis for most decisions affecting biodiversity. It is the only system that can provide even moderately useful predictions about our effects on the natural world, but it is still only part of the total decision-making process; the economic, spiritual, and social needs of people must also be met. It is curious that management decisions concerning natural areas can be made without recourse to evolutionary ecology, yet this still routinely happens in many resource agencies. Similarly, it would be a fruitless, counterproductive, and ethically suspect exercise to base comprehensive land use

**Figure 1.3** The deeply rooted multiple-use paradigm of the U.S. Forest Service is reflected in the irony of this sign in Aiken County, South Carolina, and the virtually clearcut forest in the background. The Resource Conservation Ethic that has dominated most public resource agencies demands that forests and other natural areas be treated as economic resources to be managed for human gain. True "protection" for biodiversity often is not an option. (Photograph by G. K. Meffe.)

**Figure 1.4** An example of a mixed natural and human landscape in South Carolina. This aerial photograph shows patches of natural areas of various sizes interspersed with human-dominated activities such as agriculture and housing. (Photograph courtesy of Savannah River Ecology Laboratory.)

decisions solely on evolutionary ecology without regard to the people who will be affected.

Most natural areas today are remnant patches of formerly contiguous habitats in landscapes dominated by human economic endeavors (Figure 1.4). The biological activity within any one of these natural areas is strongly dependent on what happens outside its boundaries. Any long-term security for a natural area will come about only when it is accepted as an integral and contributing part of broader economic and development planning. Just as the Evolutionary-Ecological Land Ethic grew out of traditional disciplines to meet the emerging crises in biodiversity, so also are the traditional disciplines of resource economics and anthropology giving rise to new interdisciplinary views, sometimes called "ecological economics" and "ecological anthropology," views that stress long-term environmental sustainability.

### Modern Conservation Biology: A Synthesis

The time is ripe to replace both the extreme Romantic Preservationist and the exploitative utilitarian philosophies of the 19th century with a balanced approach that looks to an ethic of stewardship for philosophical guidance, and a melding of natural and social sciences for theory and practice. This new context is necessary for conservation biology to flourish and make contributions to a sustainable biosphere.

By the 1960s and 1970s, it was becoming painfully obvious to many ecologists that prime ecosystems throughout the world, including their favorite study sites, were disappearing rapidly. Biodiversity, the outcome of millions of years of the evolutionary process, was being carelessly discarded, and, in some cases, willfully destroyed. Previous conservation efforts, while focusing on important components of nature such as large vertebrates, soils, and water, still had not embraced the intricacies of complex ecosystem function and the importance of all the "minor," less charismatic, biotic components such as insects, nematodes, fungi, and bacteria. It was time to change this attitude.

Early attempts at moving in this direction included Raymond Dasmann's *Environmental Conservation* (1959) and David Ehrenfeld's *Biological Conserva-*

**Figure 1.5** The first issue of the journal *Conservation Biology*, published in May 1987. (Photograph courtesy of E. P. Pister.)

*tion* (1970). These books helped to lay the groundwork for today's conservation biology by melding good evolutionary ecology with human resource use, and providing a vision of where modern conservation should go.

In 1980, Michael Soulé and Bruce Wilcox published a seminal work entitled *Conservation Biology: An Evolutionary-Ecological Perspective*, in which they presented conservation in this new light. This was quickly followed by Frankel and Soulé's (1981) *Conservation and Evolution*, another attempt to draw attention to evolution as a basis for conservation decisions. This lesson was further driven home in 1983 with Schonewald-Cox et al.'s *Genetics and Conservation: A Reference for Managing Wild Animal and Plant Populations*, which specifically addressed the short- and long-term genetic (and thus evolutionary) health of managed populations. Shortly thereafter, in 1985, the Society for Conservation Biology was formed, a large membership rapidly grew, and a new journal, *Conservation Biology* (Figure 1.5), was developed to complement existing journals such as *Biological Conservation* and *The Journal of Wildlife Management*. Thus, in little more than a decade, the thrust and outlook of international conservation had dramatically changed, and continues to change as conservation science matures.

The students of conservation biology today should be excited to know that they are still "getting in on the ground floor." The science of conservation is still developing and needs many bright minds to determine its future directions. Anyone who thinks that much of the science has already been done, and that there is little room left for contributions, does not yet understand the challenges of conservation biology; hopefully, the following chapters will set that record straight.

## ESSAY 1C

*A Nongovernmental Organization Perspective:*
## The Role of Science in Defining Conservation Priorities for Nongovernmental Organizations

Kathryn S. Fuller, World Wildlife Fund

The proposition that science should play a key role in setting conservation priorities seems self-evident: after all, where would conservation *be* without ecology? Isn't science the foundation of the environmental movement?

Science indeed lies at the heart of conservation, but the relationship is complex. Understanding how science contributes to conservation requires us to reexamine our notions of both endeavors, to reconcile ecology with disciplines that would once have seemed completely alien to it.

A crucial part of that process has been the emergence of conservation biology. As might be expected, this effort to conserve biological diversity by wedding the disciplines of ecology, genetics, and practical wildlife management has prompted dissent, some of it from wildlife managers who have worked for years without benefit—or, many of them would argue, *need*—of scientific

oversight. It is clear that conservationists need to build more bridges between these managers and the scientists now entering the field, simply because both sides have much to learn from each other.

Some dissenters claim that conservation biology is simply the latest in a series of gimmicky cross-disciplines, aimed at dazzling foundations with gaudy new academic packages. Nothing could be further from the truth. Conservation biology is here to stay because it looks at long-standing fieldwork through the prisms of new theoretical frameworks, and thus creates a synergy of enormous potential power. The proper question is not whether conservation biology is just a passing fad, but rather, what do we *do* with this new hybrid? How do we tap its potential?

There are two answers to this question. First, science no longer exclusively sets the boundaries of conservation. This

is due in part to the uniquely multidisciplinary nature of modern conservation, which is the product of years of evolving philosophy and practice. My own organization, World Wildlife Fund (WWF), is a useful case study in this evolution. When we began in 1961, we concentrated our efforts on individual species, animals like the Arabian oryx, the rhinoceros, and the giant panda, our organization's symbol. We emphasized scientific research and hands-on fieldwork.

Achieving genuine long-term conservation, however, requires a broader approach. Initially, that meant looking not just at species but at their habitats. That, in turn, led us toward the humans who interact with those habitats and the connection between human poverty and resource destruction. Now, every day, WWF addresses itself to what is perhaps conservation's bitterest irony: some of the world's poorest people struggle to survive alongside the world's greatest natural treasures. Beyond the borders of parks live people desperate for cropland and firewood. Adjacent to herds of wildlife in Africa are villagers without an adequate source of protein. And around the world is a vastly increasing new category of refugees, fleeing not tyrants but a deteriorating environment.

Clearly, unless we can help ease the economic burdens that drive people to overexploit their natural resources, we can never hope to arrest the environmental degradation of the developing world. So WWF seeks ways to marry the preservation of biological diversity with environmentally sound economic development.

This transition from "pure" conservation to one that integrates conservation and development means we can no longer closet ourselves behind laboratory doors. We must delve into areas unfamiliar to conservationists, such as anthropology, sociology, economics, and political science. And, recognizing that the best-designed projects will fail without ongoing funding, we must take on the role of conservation financiers, brokering debt-for-nature swaps and creating new financial mechanisms to leverage our limited resources into lasting change.

Given all this, it might be easy to go on and say that science has less of a claim on today's conservation agenda, fighting for attention as it is with the fields of economics and politics. But that would be a mistake. Because the second answer to the question of science's role in conservation is this: science is more critical than ever. If we posit ourselves as architects, then science is the foundation of our edifice, the base from which we use various tools—sustainable development, conservation finance—to structure something strong and enduring.

In a way, science is not just foundation but continuing illumination, telling us where we need to go and how to get there. How, for instance, do we help people in the developing world improve their quality of life in sustainable ways unless we give them viable models of development? This is where science plays a role. Already, we are seeing exciting and promising new sustainable-use techniques at work in our tropical forests: harvesting of non-timber products like fruits, seeds, medicinal plants, and wild game; agroforestry methods that combine traditional crops with multiple-purpose trees; restoration ecology and watershed protection.

Science can and must contribute to the fruitful mélange of ideas currently circulating in the field. Without science's help, we cannot hope to tackle the truly forbidding problems facing our planet today—problems that in fact were first identified by scientists: global warming, ozone depletion, fragmentation and degradation of habitat, and perhaps foremost of all, the loss of biological diversity.

We can only guess at the number of species on this planet. Some estimates put the number at 50 million or more, but with millions still to be identified, most of this is highly educated guesswork. What we do know is that we are losing species at an almost unimaginable rate. The renowned biologist E. O. Wilson says we are on the brink of a catastrophic extinction of species—of a kind unseen since the demise of dinosaurs 65 million years ago.

When confronted with mass extinctions on this scale, the inevitable temptation is to throw up one's hands and ask, "Where to begin?" Again, this is where science comes in. Science can tell us where to begin our path, and equally important, it can help correct our path while we forge it. Science also provides the kind of foresight that every conservation organization desperately needs—the ability to look ten, twenty years in the future and figure out where we need to be.

Of course, setting conservation priorities for our planet will never be simple or straightforward. As a start, we know that most of today's mass extinctions are taking place in the tropical forests, which contain at least half of all earth's species and are being depleted faster than any other ecological community. Tropical forests are in fact the crucible of modern conservation. Knowing this only takes us so far, however, since it still leaves us with billions of acres of forest to somehow incorporate into our planning. But scientists at WWF and elsewhere are working to identify key natural areas featuring exceptional concentrations of endemic species and facing exceptional degrees of threat. By concentrating efforts in those areas where the needs and the potential payoffs are greatest, conservationists can respond in a more informed and systematic way to the challenge of preserving biodiversity.

Science can be a partner in that effort, anchoring the economic and political exigencies of modern conservation in intellectual bedrock. Conservation biology can rise to the moment, expanding its temporal and spatial reach to fully incorporate today's conservation challenges. Although foundations and endowments encourage scientists to think in small and discrete terms, the problems confronting us are so massive that scientists must scale their thinking accordingly. The need for solid science to inform decisive action by nongovernmental organizations and other groups has never been so great.

## Guiding Principles for Conservation Biology

Three principles or themes that serve as working **paradigms** for conservation biology will appear repeatedly throughout this book (Table 1.1). A paradigm is "the world view shared by a scientific discipline or community" (Kuhn 1972), or "the family of theories that undergird a discipline" (Pickett et al. 1992). A paradigm underlies, in a very basic way, the approach taken to a discipline, and guides the practitioners of that discipline. We believe these three principles are so basic to conservation practice that they should permeate all aspects of conservation efforts and should be a presence in any endeavor in the field.

*Principle 1: Evolutionary Change.* The population geneticist Theodosius Dobzhansky once said, "Nothing in biology makes sense except in the light

**Table 1.1**
Three Guiding Principles of Conservation Biology

| | |
|---|---|
| **Principle 1:** | Evolution is the basic axiom that unites all of biology. (The evolutionary play.) |
| **Principle 2:** | The ecological world is dynamic and largely nonequilibrial. (The ecological theater.) |
| **Principle 3:** | The human presence must be included in conservation planning. (Humans are part of the play.) |

of evolution." Evolution is indeed the single principle that unites all of biology; it is the common tie across all areas of biological thought. Evolution is the only reasonable mechanism able to explain the patterns of biodiversity that we see in the world today; it offers an historical perspective on the dynamics of life. The processes of evolutionary change are the "ground rules" for how the living world operates.

Conservationists would do well to repeatedly recall G. E. Hutchinson's metaphor, "the ecological theater and the evolutionary play," discussed above. Because conservation issues all lie within the biological arena, evolution should guide their solution. Answers to conservation problems must be developed within an evolutionary framework; to do otherwise would be to fight natural laws, a foolish approach that could eventually destroy the endeavor.

The genetic composition of most populations is likely to change over time, whether due to drift in small populations, immigration from other populations, or natural selection (discussed in Chapter 6). From the perspective of conservation biology, the goal is not to stop genetic (and thus evolutionary) change, not to try and conserve the *status quo*, but rather to ensure that populations may continue to respond to environmental change in an adaptive manner.

*Principle 2: Dynamic Ecology.* The ecological world, the "theater" of evolution, is a dynamic, largely nonequilibrial world. The classic paradigm in ecology for many years was the "equilibrium paradigm," the idea that ecological systems are in equilibrium, with a definable stable point such as a "climax community." This paradigm implies closed systems with self-regulating structure and function, and embraces the popular "balance of nature" concept. Conservation under this paradigm would be relatively easy: simply select pieces of nature for protection, leave them undisturbed, and they will retain their species composition and function indefinitely and in balance. Would that it were so simple!

The past several decades of ecological research have taught us that nature is dynamic (Pickett et al. 1992). The old "balance of nature" concept may be aesthetically pleasing, but it is inaccurate and misleading; ecosystems or populations or gene frequencies may appear constant and balanced on some temporal and spatial scales, but other scales soon reveal their dynamic character. This principle applies to ecological structure, such as the number of species in a community, as well to as evolutionary structure, such as characteristics of a particular species. Conservation actions based on a static view of ecology or evolution will misrepresent nature and be less effective than those based on a more dynamic perspective.

The contemporary dominant paradigm in ecology (Botkin 1990) recognizes that ecological systems are generally not in dynamic equilibrium, at least not indefinitely, and have no stable point. Regulation of ecological

(A)

(B)

(C)

(D)

**Figure 1.6** Nonequilibrial processes play a major role in most ecosystems. Surface disturbances by bison create openings or "wallows" in prairies (A). Hurricanes and other storms open gaps in both temperate (B) and tropical (C) forests. Wave action (D) and tidal changes on rocky shorelines open up disturbance patches. (A, courtesy of Jerry Wolfe; B, Congaree Swamp, South Carolina after Hurricane Hugo, 1989, by Rebecca Sharitz; C, lower montane forest in Costa Rica, by C. R. Carroll; D, coral rock in the Dominican Republic, Caribbean Sea, by Michael C. Newman.)

structure and function is often not internally generated; external processes, in the form of natural disturbances such as fires, floods, droughts, storms, earth movement, and outbreaks of diseases or parasites are frequently of overriding importance. Indeed, we now know that biodiversity in ecosystems as different as prairies, temperate and tropical forests, and the intertidal zone are maintained by nonequilibrial processes (Figure 1.6). Ecosystems consist of patches and mosaics of habitat types, not of uniform and clearly categorized communities.

It is important to understand that our emphasis on nonequilibrial processes does not imply that species interactions are ephemeral or unpredictable, and therefore unimportant. Communities are not chaotic assemblages of species; they do have structure. Embedded within all communities are clusters of species that have strong interactions, and in many cases, these interactions have a long evolutionary legacy. Nevertheless, this does not mean that community structure is invariant and that species composition does not change at some scale of space and time. Change at some scale is a universal feature of ecological communities.

Conservation within this paradigm focuses on dynamic processes and physical contexts. An important research goal for conservation biologists is to understand how the interplay between nonequilibrial processes and the hierarchy of species interactions determines community structure and biodiversity. Ecosystems are open systems with fluxes of species, materials, and energy, and must be understood in the context of their surroundings. A further implication is that conservation reserves cannot be treated in isolation, but must be part of larger conservation plans whose design recognizes and accounts for spatial and temporal change. This principle is further developed in Botkin (1990), Pickett et al. (1992) and Petraitis et al. (1989).

*Principle 3: The Human Presence.*  Humans are and will continue to be a part of both natural and degraded ecological systems, and their presence must be included in conservation planning. Conservation efforts that attempt to wall off nature and safeguard it from humans will ultimately fail. As discussed in principle 2, ecosystems are open to the exchange of materials and species, and to the flux of energy. Because nature reserves are typically surrounded by lands and waters intensively used by humans, it will be impossible to isolate the reserve completely from these outside influences. There is simply no way to "protect" nature from human influences, and those influences must be taken into account in planning efforts. Indeed, isolating reserves carries its own liability in terms of increased extinction probabilities and gene losses for many species.

On the positive side, there are benefits to be gained by explicitly integrating humans into the equation for conservation. First, people who have been longtime residents in the region of a reserve often know a great deal about local natural history. This "indigenous knowledge" can be useful in developing reserve management plans (see Essay 11C), and local residents can play important roles on reserve staffs as, for example, guards and environmental educators. Second, reserves should be "user friendly" in order to build public support. Two ways to achieve this are through zoning that allows limited public access to portions of the reserves with established nature trails, and through bringing ecological knowledge about the reserve into formal and informal educational programs. Most cultures take pride in their natural heritage, and a critical mission for all conservation ecologists is to build upon that pride through public education. If people do not perceive that the reserve has any value to them, they will not support it.

Finally, native human cultures are a historical part of the ecological landscape and have an ethical right to the areas where they live. Aboriginal and tribal peoples from alpine to tropical regions have existed for millennia in their local systems, and to displace them in the name of conservation is simply unethical. Furthermore, they themselves add other types of diversity, cultural and language diversity, which the earth is rapidly losing. Impoverishment of indigenous human cultures and languages is as large a problem as is impoverishment of other levels of biological diversity. What's more, some of these cultures have developed sustainable methods of existence that can serve as models for modern sustainable development.

We must equally recognize that indigenous cultures have the right to control their destiny. We would be hopelessly naive to imagine that indigenous cultures can remain unchanged and unaffected by outside influences. What we can do is understand their internal systems of values and their knowledge of local natural resources, and then try to work with them toward the twin goals of conservation of biodiversity and sustainable economic development.

We must also incorporate problems of modern cultures into conservation, for they will have the largest influences on resource use. Many conservationists feel that the only realistic path to conservation in the long term is to ensure a reasonable standard of living for all people. Of course, this involves achieving greater equity among peoples, with less disparity between the "haves" and the "have-nots." In part, this will involve convincing some to accept lower standards of living so that others may climb out of desperate poverty, with the result that all will have lesser impact on biodiversity. This will not be an easy task. It will also involve attention to a number of other issues, such as birth control, revised concepts of land ownership and use, education, health care, empowerment of women, and so forth.

### Some Postulates of Conservation Biology

Of course, the foundation of conservation biology is much broader than these three principles. For example, Michael Soulé, a cofounder of the Society for Conservation Biology, listed four postulates and their corollaries that characterize value statements relevant to conservation biology (Soulé 1985). Like the principles listed above, these postulates help to define the ethical and philosophical foundations for this field. Soulé's first postulate is that *diversity of organisms is good.* Humans seem to inherently enjoy diversity of life forms (called **biophilia** by E. O. Wilson [1984]), and seem to understand that natural diversity is good for our well-being and that of nature. A corollary of this postulate is that untimely extinction (that is, extinction caused by human activities) is bad. His second postulate, *ecological complexity is good,* is an extension of the first, and "expresses a preference for nature over artifice, for wilderness over gardens." It also carries the corollary that simplification of ecosystems by humans is bad. The third postulate, *evolution is good,* has already been discussed above, and carries the corollary that interference with evolutionary patterns is bad. The final postulate is that *biotic diversity has intrinsic value,* regardless of its utilitarian value. This postulate recognizes inherent value in nonhuman life, regardless of its utility to humans, and carries the corollary that destruction of diversity by humans is bad. This is perhaps the most fundamental motivation for conservation of biodiversity.

These postulates can be and have been debated, as can any philosophical position that, by definition, cannot be founded on an entirely objective, scientific basis. Nevertheless, they are explicitly or implicitly accepted by many, both in and out of the conservation profession. Aspects of these arguments will be further pursued in the next chapter.

## Some Characteristics of Conservation Biology

Conservation biology has some unusual characteristics not associated with many other sciences. These partly result from the daunting nature of the problem of how to preserve the evolutionary potential and ecological viability of a vast array of biodiversity. Some of the uniqueness of conservation biology also stems from basic conflicts between the complexity, dynamics, and interrelationships of natural systems, and humankind's propensity to try to control, simplify, and conquer those systems.

### A Crisis Discipline

Soulé (1985) labeled conservation biology a "crisis discipline," with its relationship to the larger field of biology analogous to surgery's relation to physiology, or that of war to political science (or, we suppose, AIDS to epidemiology). In such crisis disciplines, action must often be taken without complete knowledge, because to wait to collect the necessary data could mean inaction that would destroy the effort at hand. Such immediate action requires working with available information with the best intuition and creativity one can muster, while tolerating a great deal of uncertainty. This, of course, runs counter to the way that scientists are trained, but is nonetheless necessary given the practical matters at hand. These problems are discussed further in Chapter 16.

Conservation biologists are often asked for advice and input by government and private agencies regarding such issues as design of nature reserves, potential effects of introduced species, propagation of rare and endangered species, or ecological effects of development. These decisions are usually politically and economically charged and cannot wait for detailed studies that take months or even years. The "expert" is expected to provide quick, clear, and unambiguous answers (which is, of course, generally impossible), and is looked upon askance if such answers are not there, or seem counterproductive to short-term economic gain. This is a major challenge for conservation biologists, who must walk a fine line between strict scientific credibility, and thus conservatism and possibly inaction, versus taking action and providing advice based on general and perhaps incomplete knowledge, thereby risking their scientific reputations.

### A Multidisciplinary Science

No single field of study prepares one to be a conservation biologist, and the field does not focus on input from any single area of expertise. It is an eclectic, broad discipline, to which contributions are needed from fields as different as molecular genetics, biogeography, philosophy, landscape ecology, policy development, sociology, population biology, and anthropology. This multidisciplinary nature is illustrated in Figure 1.7, in which the overlapping fields of natural and social sciences contribute to the special interdisciplinary identity of conservation biology.

Several features of this conceptualization of conservation biology are of note. First is the melding of the formerly "pure" fields of population biology and ecology with the "applied" field of natural resource management. The historical distinction between these disciplines is beginning to blur, and practitioners in these areas are working together toward a common goal. Second is the need for a strong philosophical basis and input from the social sciences. Because the need for conservation in the first place is the direct result of human intervention into natural systems, concern for humanistic viewpoints is vital for reducing present and future confrontations between human expansion and the natural world. Finally, this conceptualization illustrates that conservation biology is a holistic field because protection involves entire ecosystems, and multidisciplinary approaches and cooperation among disparate groups will be the most successful approach.

**Figure 1.7** The interdisciplinary nature of conservation biology merges many traditional fields of natural and social sciences. The list of relevant subdisciplines and interactions shown is not meant to be exhaustive.

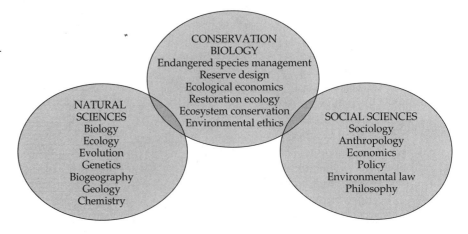

A strong cross-disciplinary perspective is desirable and necessary for success in conservation. A conference held in 1989 that included several global resource agencies outlined their collective vision of the training necessary for their future conservation employees (Jacobson 1990). The interests of these agencies were less in narrow, disciplinary skills than in "real-world" problem-solving abilities. These included "(1) cross-disciplinary breadth as well as disciplinary depth; (2) field experience; (3) language and communications skills; and (4) leadership skills, especially a mix of diplomacy and humility" (Jacobson 1990). A broad, liberal education and an ability to communicate across disciplines, combined with strength within a specialized area, is probably an ideal combination for success and real contributions in conservation biology.

### An Inexact Science

Ecological systems are complex, often individualistic, and currently unpredictable beyond limited generalities. The public, and even other scientists, often do not appreciate this and cannot understand why ecologists are such uncertain folks who hedge their bets and will not provide a simple answer to an environmental problem. The reason is, of course, that there usually *is* no simple answer. Ecological systems are complex, their dynamics are expressed in probabilities, **stochastic** influences may be strong, and many significant processes are nonlinear. *Uncertainty is inherently part of ecology and conservation.*

Thus, the conservation biologist often faces a credibility gap, not because he or she is incompetent, or because the field is poorly developed, but because even the simplest of ecosystems is far more complicated than the most complex of human inventions, and most people have not the slightest notion that this is the case. This gap can easily be exploited by representatives of special interest groups, such as lawyers, engineers, and developers, all of whom are used to dealing with concrete situations that can be easily quantified, and a "bottom line" extracted. There is never an easy bottom line in ecology, and we can only hope to educate others to that fact, rather than be forced to develop meaningless and dangerous answers that have no basis in reality. The conservation biologist must think "probabilistically" and understand the nature of scientific uncertainty. Consequently, conservationists should include safety margins in the design of management and recovery strategies, as does an engineer in the design of a bridge or an aircraft.

### A Value-Laden Science

Science is supposed to be value-free. It is presumably completely objective and free from such human frailties as opinions, goals, and desires. Because science is done by humans, however, it is never value-free, but is influenced by the experiences and goals of the scientists, although they typically will not admit that. "Too many teachers, managers, and researchers are trapped by the Western positivist image of science as value-free; . . . Biologists must realize that science, like everything else, is shot through with values. Sorting out the norms behind positions is the initial step of critical thinking" (Grumbine 1992). This idea of value-laden science has been called "postmodern science" and is discussed in depth in Chapter 16 and Essay 18A.

Unlike many other areas of science, conservation biology is "mission-oriented" (Soulé 1986); its goal clearly is to conserve natural ecosystems and biological processes, and there is nothing value-free about it. However, the methodology used to obtain information and put it into action must be good, objective science; if not, all credibility will quickly be lost. Nevertheless, conservation biologists should not delude themselves into thinking that their science is value-neutral. The value is clearly defined: natural systems and biological diversity are good and should be conserved.

### A Science with an Evolutionary Time Scale

In contrast to traditional resource management, whose currency includes maximum sustained yields, economic feasibility, and immediate public satisfaction with a product, the currency of conservation biology is long-term viability of ecosystems and preservation of biodiversity *in perpetuity*. A conservation biology program is successful not when more deer are harvested this year, or even when more natural areas are protected, but when a system retains the diversity of its structure and function over long time periods, and when the processes of evolutionary adaptation and ecological change are permitted to continue. If there is a common thread running throughout conservation biology, it is the recognition that evolution is *the* central concept in biology, and has played and should continue to play *the* central role in nature.

### A Science of Eternal Vigilance

The price of ecosystem protection is eternal vigilance. Even "protected" areas may be destroyed in the future if they contain resources that are deemed desirable enough by powerful groups or individuals. A case in point is the United States' Arctic National Wildlife Refuge, an area set aside for its ecological significance, but repeatedly under pressure to be opened up for oil extraction as world political affairs affect the price and availability of oil. What appears secure today may well be exploited tomorrow for transitory resource use, and the conservation biologist must continually be protective of natural areas. Natural ecosystems can easily be destroyed, but they cannot be created, and at best only partially restored.

## A Final Word

Throughout this book you may find cases of seeming opposites or contradictions in our messages. It may seem that at one point we advise letting natural processes occur and at another suggest interventionist management. We will recognize nonequilibrial processes in general, but then discuss deterministic processes that can reach equilibrium in particular cases. This is not done to confuse you. Ecological systems are complex, and situations are often unique. What makes sense in one system or circumstance will be inapplicable in another. Idiosyncrasies abound, as do conflicting demands. Conservation scenarios need to be defined and pursued individually, and not be part of an automatic, "cookbook" approach. The message is that conservation biology is not easy, but it is not hopelessly complicated either, and much research and application remains to be done. Above all, it can provide exciting and unparalleled career opportunities for students interested in solving real-world problems. The world's biodiversity desperately needs bright, energetic, and imaginative students who feel they can make a difference. And they certainly can, and must.

## Summary

Exponential human population growth in the last few centuries has affected the natural world to the extent that massive alteration of habitats and associated biological changes threaten the existence of millions of species and basic ecosystem processes. The field of conservation biology developed during the last 15 years as a response of the scientific community to this crisis. The "new" conservation biology differs from traditional resource conservation in being motivated not by utilitarian, single-species issues, but by the need for conservation of entire systems and all their biological components and processes.

Conservation practices have a varied history around the world, but generally have focused on human use of resources. In the United States, two value systems dominated resource conservation early in the 20th century. The Romantic-Transcendental Conservation Ethic of Emerson, Thoreau, and Muir recognized that nature has inherent value and should not simply be used for human gain. The Resource Conservation Ethic of Pinchot was based on a utilitarian philosophy of the greatest good for the greatest number of people; most resource agencies in the United States and elsewhere follow this view. Aldo Leopold's Evolutionary-Ecological Land Ethic developed later, and is the most biologically relevant perspective, recognizing the importance of ecological and evolutionary processes in producing and controlling the natural resources we use. Much of modern conservation biology has grown from and is guided by Leopold's land ethic.

Three overriding principles should guide all of conservation biology. First, evolution is the basis for understanding all of biology, and should be a central focus of conservation action. Second, ecological systems are dynamic and nonequilibrial; change must be a part of conservation. Finally, humans are a part of the natural world and must be included in conservation actions.

Conservation biology has some unusual characteristics not always found in other sciences. It is a crisis discipline that requires multidisciplinary approaches. It is an inexact science that operates on an evolutionary time scale. It is a value-laden science that requires long-term vigilance to succeed. It also requires of its practitioners innovation, flexibility, multiple talents, and an understanding of the idiosyncrasies of ecological systems, but offers outstanding career challenges and rewards.

## Suggestions for Further Reading

Gore, A., Jr. 1992. *Earth in the Balance: Ecology and the Human Spirit.* Penguin Books, New York. A stunningly good grasp of global environmental crises is shown by the Vice President of the United States. A better account of biodiversity problems and potential solutions written by a nonscientist cannot be found.

Grumbine, R. E. 1992. *Ghost Bears: Exploring the Biodiversity Crisis.* Island Press, Washington, D.C. An outstanding summary of the biodiversity crisis written in the context of old-growth forests of the Pacific Northwest, and encompassing ethics, law, environmental policy, and activism. A very broad, "real-world" perspective of the challenges facing biodiversity conservation.

Soulé, M. E. (ed.). 1986. *Conservation Biology: The Science of Scarcity and Diversity.* Sinauer Associates, Sunderland, MA. Already a classic, this book laid much of the groundwork for the science of conservation biology. It contains 25 chapters written by scientists who helped define modern conservation biology.

Western, D. and M. Pearl (eds.). 1989. *Conservation for the Twenty-First Century.* Oxford University Press, New York. An outstanding follow-up to the Soulé text that presents a broader perspective of conservation. In addition to biological issues, it includes much information on management of parklands, global issues, human value systems, and planning and legislation in conservation.

Wilson, E. O. 1992. *The Diversity of Life.* Belknap Press of Harvard University Press, Cambridge, MA. This is an excellent overview of the biodiversity crisis, in easily understood terms, spanning the gene to ecosystem level of concern. It also covers basic concepts such as evolutionary change, extinction, and speciation, all described in an engaging style.

# 2

# Conservation Values
# and Ethics

*It is inconceivable to me that an ethical relation to land can exist without love,
respect, and admiration for land, and a high regard for its value. By value,
I of course mean something far broader than mere economic value;
I mean value in the philosophical sense.*

*Aldo Leopold, 1949*

## The Value of Biodiversity

Conservation biologists often treat the value of biodiversity as a given. To
many laypeople, however, the value of biodiversity may not be so obvious.
Since conservation efforts require broad public support, the conservation biologist should be able to articulate fully the value of biodiversity. Why
should we care about—that is, value—biodiversity?

Environmental philosophers customarily divide value into two main
types, expressed by alternative pairs of terms: **instrumental** or **utilitarian** as
opposed to **intrinsic** or **inherent**. Instrumental or utilitarian value is the
value that something has as a means to another's ends. Intrinsic or inherent
value is the value that something has as an end in itself. The intrinsic value
of human beings is rarely contested. The intrinsic value of nonhuman natural entities and nature as a whole has been the subject of much controversy.
Perhaps because the suggestion that nonhuman natural entities and/or nature as a whole may also have intrinsic value is so new and controversial,
some prominent conservationists (e.g., Myers 1983) have preferred to provide a purely utilitarian rationale for conserving biodiversity. The view that
biodiversity has value only as a means to human ends is called anthropocentric (human-centered). On the other hand, the view that biodiversity is valuable independently of its use to human beings is called nonanthropocentric
(not human-centered).

### Instrumental Value

The anthropocentric instrumental (or utilitarian) value of biodiversity may
be unequivocally divided into three basic categories: goods, services, and information. The psycho-spiritual value of biodiversity is possibly a fourth

**Table 2.1**
Four Categories of the Instrumental Value
of Biodiversity

| Category | Examples |
| --- | --- |
| **Goods** | Food, fuel, fiber, medicine |
| **Services** | Pollination, recycling, nitrogen fixation, homeostatic regulation |
| **Information** | Genetic engineering, applied biology, pure science |
| **Psycho-spiritual** | Aesthetic beauty, religious awe, scientific knowledge |

kind of anthropocentric utilitarian value (Table 2.1).

First, goods. Human beings eat with, heat with, build with, and otherwise consume many other living beings. But only a small fraction of all life-forms have been investigated for their utility as food, fuel, fiber, and other commodities. Many potential food plants and animals may await discovery. And it is possible that many of these could be grown on a horticultural or agricultural scale, as well as harvested in the wild, adding variety at least to the human diet, and possibly even saving us from starvation if conventional crops fail due to incurable plant diseases or uncontrollable pests (Vietmeyer 1986a,b). Fast-growing trees, useful for fuelwood or making charcoal, or for pulp or timber, may still be undiscovered in tropical forests. New organic pesticides may be manufactured from yet-to-be screened or discovered plants (Plotkin 1988). The medicinal potential of hitherto undiscovered and/or unassayed plants and animals seems to be the most popular and persuasive rationale of this type for preserving biodiversity. Vincristine, extracted from the Madagascar periwinkle, is the drug of choice for the treatment of childhood leukemia (Farnsworth 1988). Discovered in the late 1950s, it is the most often cited example of a recent and dramatic cure for cancer manufactured from a species found in a place where the native biota is now threatened with wholesale destruction. Doubtless many other hitherto unscreened, perhaps even undiscovered, species might turn out to have equally important medical uses—if we can save them.

The degree to which conservationists rely on the possibility that potential medicines may be lost if we allow species extinction to grind on is revealing. It reflects the reverence and esteem in which medicines are held in contemporary Western culture—a culture, it would seem, of hypochondriacs. Spare no expense or inconvenience to save them, if unexplored ecosystems may harbor undiscovered cures for our diseases! According to Meadows (1990), "some ecologists are so tired of this line of reasoning that they refer wearily to the 'Madagascar periwinkle argument.' . . . [Those] ecologists hate the argument because it is both arrogant and trivial. It assumes that the earth's millions of species are here to serve the economic purposes of just one species. And even if you buy that idea, it misses the larger and more valuable ways that nature serves us."

Which brings us to the second point, services. Often overlooked by people who identity themselves first and foremost as "consumers" are the services performed by other species working diligently in the complexly orchestrated economy of nature (Meadows 1990). Green plants replenish the atmosphere with oxygen and remove carbon dioxide. Certain kinds of insects, birds, and bats pollinate flowering plants, including many agricultural species. Fungal and microbial life-forms in the soil decompose dead organic material and play a key role in recycling plant nutrients. Rhizobial bacteria turn atmospheric nitrogen into usable nitrate fertilizer for plants. If the **Gaia hypothesis** (Lovelock 1988) is correct, the earth's temperature and the salinity of its oceans are organically regulated. The human economy is a subsystem of the economy of nature and would abruptly collapse if any of these and other major service sectors of the larger natural economy were to be disrupted.

Third, information. The mindless loss of species "uncared for and unknown"—in the words of Darwin's contemporary and codiscoverer of evolution by natural selection, Alfred Russell Wallace (1863)—has been compared to setting fire to sections of a vast library and burning books that no one has read. Each is a storehouse of information. Desirable characteristics encoded in isolatable genes and transferable, by means of gene splicing, to edible or medical resources, may be "burned up" with the "volume" in which they could once be found. Genetic information, in other words, is a potential economic good. Such information also has another utility, more difficult to express. Meadows (1990), however, captures it nicely:

> Biodiversity contains the accumulated wisdom of nature and the key to its future. If you ever wanted to destroy a society, you would burn its libraries and kill its intellectuals. You would destroy its knowledge. Nature's knowledge is contained in the DNA within living cells. The variety of genetic information is the driving engine of evolution, the immune system for life, the source of adaptability.

According to Wilson (1985), approximately 1.7 million species have been formally named and described. Based upon the most conservative recent estimate of the total, between 5 and 10 million, that means that only about 20% of the planet's species are known to science (Gaston 1991). Based upon more liberal recent estimates of the total, more than 30 million, the number known to science could represent only about 5% (Erwin 1988). Imagine the loss to science if, as Raven (1988) predicts, 25% of the world's life-forms, due to the destruction of much of their moist tropical habitat, become extinct in the coming quarter century, before they can even be scientifically named and described.

The vast majority of these threatened species are not vascular plants or vertebrate animals; they are insects (Wilson 1985). The reason that Erwin (1988) suspects that there may be so many species of invertebrates is that so many may be endemic or host-specific. Most of these unknown insects at risk of extinction would probably prove to be useless as human food or medicine—either as whole organisms, as sources of chemical extracts, or as sources of gene fragments—nor would many likely play a vital role in the functioning of regional ecosystems (Ehrenfeld 1988). Though it may be difficult to so callously view such a tragedy, we may account their loss, nevertheless, in purely utilitarian terms—as a significant loss of a potential nonmaterial human good, namely, pure human knowledge of the biota.

Fourth, psycho-spiritual resources. Aldo Leopold (1953) hoped that, through science, people would acquire "a refined taste in natural objects." A beetle, however tiny and ordinary as beetles go, is as potentially beautiful as any work of fine art. And natural variety—a rich and diverse biota—is something Soulé (1985) thinks nearly everyone prefers to monotony. Wilson (1984) finds a special wonder, awe, and mystery in nature, which he calls "biophilia," and which for him seems almost to lie at the foundations of a religion of natural history. To be moved by the beauty of organisms and whole, healthy ecosystems, to experience a sense of wonder and awe in the face of nature's inexhaustible marvels is to become a better person, according to Norton (1987).

If from the point of view of the value of information—genetic and otherwise—the mindless destruction of biodiversity is like book burning, then from the point of view of natural aesthetics and religion, it is like vandalizing an art gallery or desecrating a church. There has been little doubt expressed that the value of pure scientific knowledge is anthropocentric. And the aesthetic and spiritual value of nature is often understood to be a highfalutin kind of utilitarian value. Ehrenfeld (1976), for example, thinks that aesthetic and spiritual rationales for the conservation of biodiversity are "still rooted in the homocentric, humanistic world view that is responsible for bringing the natural world, including us, to its present condition." Nevertheless, the beauty and sanctity of nature has sometimes been accounted an intrinsic, not an instrumental, value. According to Sagoff (1980), for example, "we enjoy an object because it is valuable; we do not value it merely because we enjoy it. . . . Esthetic experience is a perception, as it were, of a certain kind of worth."

### Intrinsic Value

Unlike instrumental value, intrinsic value is not divisible into various categories. Discussion of intrinsic value has focused on two other issues: the sorts of things that may possess intrinsic value, and whether intrinsic value exists objectively or is subjectively conferred.

In response to mounting concern about human destruction of nonhuman life, some contemporary philosophers have broken with Western religious and philosophical tradition and attributed intrinsic value, by whatever name, to the following: robustly conscious animals (Regan 1983); **sentient** animals (Warnock 1971); all living things (Taylor 1986); species (Callicott 1986; Rolston 1988; Johnson 1991); biotic communities (Callicott 1989); ecosystems (Rolston 1988; Johnson 1991) and evolutionary processes (Rolston 1988). Leopold attributed "value in the philosophical sense"—by which he could only mean what philosophers call "intrinsic value"—to "land," defined as "all of the things on, over, or in the earth" (Callicott 1987b). Soulé (1985) categorically asserts that "biotic diversity has intrinsic value"; and Ehrenfeld (1988) categorically asserts that "value is an intrinsic part of diversity."

Environmental philosophers who claim that intrinsic value exists objectively in human beings and other organisms reason as follows. In contrast to a machine, such as a car or a vacuum cleaner, an organism is "autopoietic," that is, self-organizing and self-directed (Fox 1990). A car is manufactured, in other words; it does not grow up, orchestrated by its own DNA. And a car's purposes—to transport people and to confer status on its owner—are imposed on it from a source outside itself. Machines do not have their own goals or purposes, as organisms do—neither consciously chosen goals nor genetically determined goals. What are an organism's self-set goals? They may be many and complex. For us human beings they may include everything from winning an Olympic gold medal to watching as much television as possible. All organisms, however, strive (usually unconsciously and in an evolutionary sense) to achieve certain basic predetermined goals—to grow, to reach maturity, to reproduce (Taylor 1986).

Interests, thus, may be intelligibly attributed to organisms, but not to machines. Having ample sunlight, water, and rich soil is in an oak tree's interest, though the oak tree may not be actively interested in these things, just as eating fresh vegetables may be in a child's interest, though the child may be actively interested only in junk food. One may counter that, by parity of reasoning, getting regular oil changes is in a car's interest, but since a car's ends or purposes are not its own, being well maintained is not in its own interest, but in the interest of its user, whose purposes it serves exclusively. Another way of saying that ever striving and often thriving organisms have interests is to say that they have a good of their own. But *good* is just an older, simpler word meaning pretty much the same thing as *value*. Hence to acknowledge that organisms have interests or goods of their own is to acknowledge that they have what philosophers call intrinsic value.

One problem with objective intrinsic value, thus understood, is that it seems limited to individual organisms. Conservationists, however, are not professionally concerned with the welfare of specimens, but with the preservation of species, the health and integrity of ecosystems, and evolutionary and ecological processes (Soulé 1985). Johnson (1991) attributes interests to species, based on the controversial claim by Ghiselin (1974) and Hull (1976, 1978) that species are best conceived not as taxa, but as individuals protracted in space and time. He also attributes interests to ecosystems, claiming that they are superorganisms. But such a conception of ecosystems has fallen so far out of fashion in ecology that Johnson can cite no contemporary ecologists to support his claim. Rolston prudently avoids basing his attribution of intrinsic value to species and ecosystems on either obsolete or suspect scientific ideas. He argues that since a basic evolutionary "goal" of an organism is to reproduce its species, that therefore its species is one of its primary goods. Species evolved, however, not in isolation, but in a matrix of ecosystems. Therefore, Rolston (1988) concludes, ecosystems also have intrinsic value. Evolutionary processes, going all the way back to the Big Bang, produced beings with goods of their own; thus they too, Rolston reasons, have intrinsic value.

More strictly observing the classic distinction between objective "facts" and subjective values, some environmental philosophers argue that all value, including intrinsic value, is subjectively conferred (Callicott 1986; Elliot 1992): no conscious subjects, no value. *Value*, they think, is (or should be) used as a verb, not a noun. In this view, something has instrumental value if it is valued for its utility, while something has intrinsic value if it is valued (verb transitive) for its own sake. Subjects, at least those capable of the intentional, conscious act of valuing, value themselves intrinsically. But some conscious subjects, among them human beings, are quite capable of intrinsically valuing other human beings, other living things, species, ecosystems, and ecological and evolutionary processes. Science has revealed that we human beings are kin to all other species and are members of biotic as well as human communities (Leopold 1949). Thus, according to Callicott (1992), other species and the hierarchically ordered biotic communities and ecosystems to which we human beings belong are—no less than our fellow human beings and our hierarchically ordered human communities—the sorts of entities that we should value intrinsically.

Intrinsic and instrumental value are not mutually exclusive; many things may be valued both for their utility and for themselves. Employers, for example, may value their employees in both ways. Similarly, intrinsically valuing biodiversity does not preclude appreciating the various ways in which it is instrumentally valuable.

Norton (1991) argues that, by claiming that biodiversity has intrinsic value (or is intrinsically valuable), some environmental philosophers and conservation biologists have actually done more harm than good for the cause of conservation. Why? Because the intrinsic value issue divides conservationists into two mutually suspicious factions: anthropocentrists versus nonanthropocentrists. The latter dismiss the former as "shallow resourcists"; and the former think that the latter have gone off the deep end. If biodiversity is valuable because it ensures the continuation of ecological services,

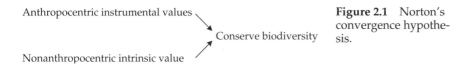

Anthropocentric instrumental values

Conserve biodiversity

Nonanthropocentric intrinsic value

**Figure 2.1** Norton's convergence hypothesis.

represents a pool of potential resources, satisfies us aesthetically, inspires us religiously, and makes better people out of us, the practical conclusion is the same as if we attributed intrinsic value to it: we should conserve it. Instrumentally valuing biodiversity and intrinsically valuing it "converge" on identical conservation policies, in Norton's view (Figure 2.1); thus, we don't really need to appeal to the intrinsic value of biodiversity to ground conservation policy. Hence, Norton (1991) argues, the controversial and divisive proposition that biodiversity has intrinsic value should be abandoned. A wide and long anthropocentrism, he thinks, is an adequate value package for conservation biology.

Attributing intrinsic value to biodiversity, however, makes a practical difference in one fundamental way that Norton seems not to have considered. If biodiversity's intrinsic value were as widely recognized as is the intrinsic value of human beings, would it make much difference? All forms of natural resource exploitation that might put it at risk would not be absolutely prohibited. After all, recognizing the intrinsic value of human beings does not absolutely prohibit putting people at risk when the benefits to the general welfare (or "aggregate utility") of doing so are sufficiently great. For example, in 1990, soldiers from the United States and other industrial nations were sent into combat, and some were killed or wounded, not to protect themselves and their fellow citizens from imminent annihilation, but to secure supplies of Middle Eastern petroleum and to achieve geopolitical goals.

Rather, if the intrinsic value of biodiversity were widely recognized, then sufficient justification would have to be offered for putting it at risk—just as we demand sufficient justification for putting soldiers at risk by sending them to war. The practical difference that attributing intrinsic value to biodiversity makes is to shift the burden of proof from conservationists who are trying to protect it to those whose actions might jeopardize it (Figure 2.2). Fox (1993) puts this point clearly and forcefully:

> Recognizing the intrinsic value of the nonhuman world has a dramatic effect upon the framework of environmental debate and decision-making. If the nonhuman world is only considered to be instrumentally valuable then people are permitted to use and otherwise interfere with any aspect of it for whatever reasons they wish. If anyone objects to such interference then, within this framework of reference, the onus is clearly on the person who objects to justify why it is more useful to humans to leave that aspect of the world alone. If, however, the nonhuman world is considered to be intrinsically valuable then the onus shifts to the person who wants to interfere with it to justify why they should be allowed to do so.

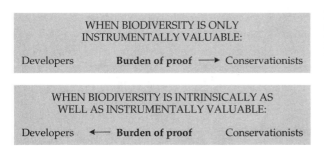

WHEN BIODIVERSITY IS ONLY INSTRUMENTALLY VALUABLE:

Developers        **Burden of proof** ⟶ Conservationists

WHEN BIODIVERSITY IS INTRINSICALLY AS WELL AS INSTRUMENTALLY VALUABLE:

Developers   ⟵   **Burden of proof**        Conservationists

**Figure 2.2** Burden of proof according to instrumental and intrinsic value systems.

## Monetizing the Value of Biodiversity

**Monetizing** the value of biodiversity is a technical task for economists. Here, only the basic ways of putting a dollar value on biodiversity and the philosophical issues raised by the prospect of doing so can be discussed. It might seem that only the instrumental value of biodiversity is subject to expression in monetary terms. Some environmental economists, accordingly, explicitly endorse a strict anthropocentrism (Randall 1986). However, as we shall see, even the intrinsic value of biodiversity can be taken into account in an economic assessment of conservation goals.

Some endangered species have a market price: notoriously, elephants for their tusks; rhinoceroses for their horns; baleen whales for their meat, bone, and oil; and Bengal tigers for their pelts. In some cases—the blue and sperm whales, for example—their monetary value is the only reason the species are threatened with extinction. In other cases—the Bengal tiger and the mountain gorilla, for example—habitat destruction is also a factor in their endangerment. Myers (1981), however, suggests that taking advantage of their monetary value may be the key to conserving many species. An alternative perspective is provided by Holmes Rolston in Essay 2A.

## ESSAY 2A
# Our Duties to Endangered Species

Holmes Rolston III, Colorado State University

Few persons doubt that we have obligations *concerning* endangered species, because persons are helped or hurt by the condition of their environment, which includes a wealth of wild species, currently under alarming threat of extinction. Whether humans have duties directly *to* endangered species is a deeper question, important in both ethics and conservation biology, in both practice and theory. Many believe that we do. The U.N. *World Charter for Nature* states, "Every form of life is unique, warranting respect regardless of its worth to man." The *Biodiversity Convention* affirms "the intrinsic value of biological diversity." Both documents are signed by well over a hundred nations. A rationale that centers on species' worth to persons is anthropocentric; a rationale that includes their intrinsic and ecosystem values is naturalistic.

Many endangered species have no resource value, nor are they particularly important for the usual humanistic reasons: scientific study, recreation, ecosystem stability, and so on. Is there any reason to save such "worthless" species? A well-developed environmental ethics argues that species are good in their own right, whether or not they are "good" for anything. The duties-to-persons-only line of argument leaves deeper reasons untouched; such justification is not fully moral and is fundamentally exploitive and self-serving on the part of humans, even if subtly so. Ethics has never been very convincing when pleaded as enlightened self-interest (that one ought always to do what is in one's intelligent self-interest).

An account of duties to species makes claims at two levels; one is about facts (a scientific issue, about species); the other is about values (an ethical issue, involving duties). Sometimes, species can seem simply made up, since taxonomists regularly revise species designations and routinely put after a species the name of the "author" who, they say, "erected" the taxon. If a species is only a category or class, boundary lines may be arbitrarily drawn, and the species is nothing more than a convenient grouping of its members, an artifact of taxonomists. No one proposes duties to genera, families, orders, or phyla; biologists concede that these do not exist in nature.

On a more realistic account, a biological species is a living historical form, propagated in individual organisms, that flows dynamically over generations. A species is a coherent, ongoing, dynamic lineage expressed in organisms, encoded in gene flow. In this sense, species are objectively there—found, not made, by taxonomists. Species are real historical entities, interbreeding populations. By contrast, families, orders, and genera are not levels at which biological reproduction takes place. Far from being arbitrary, species are the real survival units.

This claim—that there are specific forms of life historically maintained over time—does not seem fictional, but rather is as certain as anything else we believe about the empirical world, even though at times scientists revise the theories and taxa with which they map these forms. Species are not so much like lines of latitude and longitude as like mountains and rivers, phenomena objectively there to be mapped. The edges of such natural kinds will sometimes be fuzzy, and to some extent discretionary (see Chapter 3). One species will slide into another over evolutionary time. But it does not follow from the fact that speciation is sometimes in progress that species are merely made up, rather than found as evolutionary lines.

At the level of values and duties, an environmental ethics finds that such species are good kinds, and that humans ought not, without overriding justification, cause their extinction. A consideration of species offers a biologically based counterexample to the focus on individuals—typically sentient and usually persons—so characteristic of Western ethics. In an evolutionary ecosystem, it is not mere individuality that counts. The individual represents, or re-presents anew, a species in each subsequent generation. It is a token of an entity, and the entity is more important than the token. Though species are not moral agents, a biological identity—a kind of value—is here defended. The dignity resides in the dynamic form; the individual inherits this, exemplifies it, and passes it on. The possession of a biological identity reasserted genetically over time is as characteristic of the species as of the individual. Respecting that identity generates duties to species.

The species is a bigger event than the individual, although species are always exemplified in individuals. Biological conservation goes on at this level too, and, really, this level is the more appropriate one for moral concern, a more comprehensive survival unit than the organism. When an individual dies, another one replaces it. Tracking its environment over time, the species is conserved and modified. With extinction, this stops. Extinction shuts down the generative processes in a kind of superkilling. It kills forms (species) beyond individuals. It kills collectively, not just distributively. To kill a particular plant is to stop a life of a few years or decades, while other lives of such kind continue unabated; to eliminate a particular species is to shut down a story of many millennia, and leave no future possibilities.

Because a species lacks moral agency, reflective self-awareness, sentience, or organic individuality, some hold that species-level processes cannot count morally. But each ongoing species represents a form of life, and these forms are, on the whole, good kinds. Such speciation has achieved all the planetary richness of life. All ethicists say that in *Homo sapiens* one species has appeared that not only exists but ought to exist. A naturalistic ethic refuses to say this exclusively of one late-coming,

highly developed form, but extends this duty more broadly to the other species—though not with equal intensity over them all, in view of varied levels of development.

The wrong that humans are doing, or allowing to happen through carelessness, is stopping the historical gene flow in which the vitality of life lies. A shutdown of the life stream is the most destructive event possible. Humans ought not to play the role of murderers. The duty to species can be overridden, for example, with pests or disease organisms. But a *prima facie* duty stands nevertheless. What is wrong with human-caused extinction is not just the loss of human resources, but the loss of biotic sources. The question is not: What is this rare plant or animal good for? But: What good is here? Not: Is this species good for my kind, *Homo sapiens?* But: Is *Rhododendron chapmanii* a good of its kind, a good kind? To care about a plant or animal species is to be quite nonanthropocentric and objective about botanical and zoological processes that take place independently of human preferences.

Increasingly, we humans have a vital role in whether these stories continue. The duties that such power generates no longer attach simply to individuals or persons, but are emerging duties to specific forms of life. The species line is the more fundamental living system, the whole, of which individual organisms are the essential parts. The species too has its integrity, its individuality, and it is more important to protect this than to protect individual integrity. The appropriate survival unit is the appropriate level of moral concern.

A species is what it is, inseparable from the environmental niche into which it fits. Particular species may not be essential in the sense that the ecosystem can survive the loss of individual species without adverse effect. But habi-

tats are essential to species, and an endangered species typically means an endangered habitat. Integrity of the species fits into integrity of the ecosystem. Endangered species conservation must be ecosystem-oriented. It is not preservation of *species* that we wish, but the preservation of *species in the system.* It is not merely *what* they are, but *where* they are that we must value correctly.

It might seem that for humans to terminate species now and again is quite natural. Species go extinct all the time. But there are important theoretical and practical differences between natural and anthropogenic extinctions. In natural extinction, a species dies when it has become unfit in its habitat, and other species appear in its place. Such extinction is normal turnover. Though harmful to a species, extinction in nature is seldom an evil in the system. It is rather the key to tomorrow. The species is employed in, but abandoned to, the larger historical evolution of life. By contrast, artificial extinction shuts down tomorrow because it shuts down speciation. One opens doors, the other closes them. Humans generate and regenerate nothing; they only dead-end these lines. Relevant differences make the two as morally distinct as death by natural causes is from murder.

On the scale of evolutionary time, humans appear late and suddenly. Even more lately and suddenly they increase the extinction rate dramatically. What is offensive in such conduct is not merely senseless loss of resources, but the maelstrom of killing and insensitivity to forms of life. What is required is not prudence, but principled responsibility to the biospheric earth. Only the human species contains moral agents, but conscience ought not be used to exempt every other form of life from consideration, with the resulting paradox that the sole moral species acts only in its collective self-interest toward all the rest.

---

According to modern economic theory, what is necessary for transforming a species' market price from a conservation liability into a conservation asset is to take it out of a condition that economists call a "commons" and "enclose" it. *Enclosing* here does not mean literally building a fence around a species population; it means, rather, assigning rights to cull it. A wild species that has a market value is subject to overharvesting when property rights to it cannot be legitimately asserted and enforced. This leads to the **tragedy of the commons** (Hardin 1968), discussed in Chapter 18. If a resource can be owned (either privately or publicly) and property rights to it can be enforced, then the species will be conserved, so the theory goes, since the owner will not be tempted to "kill the goose that lays the golden egg."

Or will he, she, or it? Other factors, such as species' reproductive rates and growth rates in relationship to interest rates, discount rates, and so on, confound this simple picture (discussed in Chapter 15). As Hanemann (1988) points out, "the interest rate level, the nature of the net benefit function and its movement over time, and the dynamics of the resource's natural growth process combine to determine the optimal intertemporal path of exploitation. . . . Other things being equal, the higher the interest rate at which future consequences are discounted, the more it is optimal to deplete the resource now."

The blue whale is a case in point. The International Whaling Commission effectively encloses whale populations, despite occasional poaching, by allotting species harvest quotas to whaling nations (Forcan 1979). Clark (1973) concludes, however, that it would be more profitable to hunt blue whales to complete extinction and invest the proceeds in some other industry than to wait for the species population to recover and harvest blue whales at sustainable levels indefinitely. Clark does not recommend this course of action. On the contrary, his point is that market forces alone cannot always be made to further conservation goals.

The idea of conserving economically exploitable threatened species by enclosing and sustainably harvesting them may work well enough in conserving species with relatively high reproductive and growth rates (such as ungulates), but may not work at all well in conserving species that have relatively low reproductive and growth rates (such as whales). Hence, enlisting the market in the cause of conservation must be done very carefully on a case-by-case basis.

Potential goods—new foods, fuels, medicines, and the like—have no market price, obviously, since they remain unknown or undeveloped. To destroy species willy-nilly, however, before they can be discovered and examined for their resource potential is to eliminate the chance that a desirable commodity will become available in the future. Hence, biodiversity may be assigned an "option price," defined as "the amount people would be willing to pay in advance to guarantee an option for future use" (Raven et al. 1992). The option price of any given undiscovered or unassayed species may be very small, since the chance that a given species may prove to be useful is also probably very small (Ehrenfeld 1988). But added together, the option prices of the million or more species currently threatened with wholesale extinction might be quite formidable.

The market confers a dollar value on biodiversity in other ways than the price of the actual and potential goods that nature affords. People pay fees to visit national parks, for example, and to hike in wilderness areas. Such fees—no less than the price of vincristine or of wildebeest steaks—express the value of a bit of biodiversity in money. But often, since user fees are usually low, the true monetary value of the psycho-spiritual "resource" is underexpressed by those fees alone. Subsidies provided from local, state, and federal tax revenues might also be factored in when assessing the monetary value of a psycho-spiritual resource. The money people spend—for such things as gasoline, food, lodging, and camping equipment—to get to a particular spot and visit it may be credited to the resource by employing the "travel cost method" (Peterson and Randall 1984; see also Case Study 3 in Chapter 17). "Contingent valuation," in which people are polled and asked what they would be willing to pay for the opportunity to enjoy a certain experience— say, to hear wolves howling in Yellowstone National Park in the United States—is also used to calculate the dollar value of psycho-spiritual resources (Peterson and Randall 1984).

Economists now even recognize—and of course attempt to monetize—the "existence value" of biodiversity (Randall 1988). Some people take a modicum of satisfaction in just knowing that biodiversity is being protected even if they have no intention of consuming exotic meats or personally enjoying a wilderness experience. Existence value has a price. One way to ascertain it would be to calculate the amount of money sedentary people actually contribute to conservation organizations such as The Nature Conservancy or the Rainforest Action Network. Further, economists now also recognize "bequest value," the amount people would be willing to pay to assure that future generations of *Homo sapiens* will inherit a biologically diverse world (Raven et al. 1992).

Accurately monetizing the value of the often free or underpriced recreational, aesthetic, intellectual, and spiritual utility of nature is more often attempted than monetizing the value of the services provided to the human economy by the economy of nature. In part this may simply reflect the level of ecological literacy among economists, who may be growing adept at "shadow pricing" (as contingent valuation is sometimes called) psycho-spiritual resources. As occasional ecotourists and consumers of outdoor recreation, they can readily understand these resources, but the niceties of pollination, nutrient cycling, and the like may remain a mystery. Their neglecting to quantify the value of the service sector of the economy of nature may also reflect the fact that so far, most vital services performed for us free of charge by other species are not scarce, and economists only calculate prices for those things that are.

Meadows hints at one way of monetizing natural services: "How would you like the job," she asks (1990), "of pollinating trillions of apple blossoms some sunny afternoon in May? It's conceivable maybe that you could invent a machine to do it, but inconceivable that the machine could work as elegantly and cheaply as the honey bee, much less make honey on the side." The value of nature's service economy could be monetized by calculating the cost of replacing natural services with artificial ones. Put in terms of scarcity and option, what would be the cost of employing human labor or machines to pollinate plants, if—because of present economic practices, such as excessive use of insecticides—pollinating organisms were to become vanishingly scarce?

Ehrenfeld (1988) notes, however, that, just as many species have little potential value as goods, many species are likely to have little importance in the service sector of the economy of nature: "The species whose members are the fewest in number, the rarest, the most narrowly distributed—in short, the ones most likely to become extinct—are obviously the ones least likely to be missed by the biosphere. Many of these species were never common or ecologically influential; by no stretch of the imagination can we make them out to be vital cogs in the ecological machine."

Some philosophers and conservation biologists strenuously object to the penchant of economists for reducing all value to monetary terms (Sagoff 1988; Ehrenfeld 1988). Some things have a price, others have a dignity. And, as a familiar matter of fact, we have attempted to exclude from the market certain things that we believe have a dignity—things, in other words, to which we attribute intrinsic value. Indeed, one possible motive for claiming that biodiversity has intrinsic value is to exclude it from economic valuation, and thus to put it beyond the vagaries of the market. We have, for example, attempted to take human beings off the market by outlawing slavery, and attempted to take sex off the market by outlawing prostitution. Why not take intrinsically valuable biodiversity off the market by outlawing environmentally destructive human activities?

Sagoff (1988) argues that we have two parallel and mutually incommensurable systems for determining the value of things: the market and its surrogates on the one hand and the ballot box on the other. As private individuals, most of us would refuse to sell our parents, spouses, or children at any price. And as citizens united into polities, we may refuse to trade biodiversity for any "benefit" projected in a benefit-cost analysis. Indeed, the United States Endangered Species Act of 1973 is a splendid example of a political decision to take biodiversity off the market.

Economists counter that we must often make hard choices between such things as the need to bring arable land into production and saving the habitat of endangered species (Randall 1986). While we may like to believe, piously and innocently, that intrinsically valuable people are literally priceless, the value of a human life is not uncommonly monetized. The dollar value of a human life, for example, might be reflected by the amount that an automobile insurance company pays a beneficiary when a customer kills another person in an accident, or by the maximum amount, prorated, that an industry is willing to pay (or is required by law to pay) to protect the health and safety of its employees. Similarly, recognizing the intrinsic value of biodiversity does not imply that it cannot be priced. The only way we can make informed choices is to express the entire spectrum of natural values from "goods" and "services" to "existence" in comparable terms: dollars.

The Endangered Species Act was amended in 1978 to create a high-level interagency committee, the so-called "God Squad," which could allow a project that put a listed species in jeopardy of extinction to go forward if its economic benefits were deemed sufficiently great. This legislation affirms that we do indeed have two incommensurable systems of determining value—the one economic and the other political. It also affirms the original political decision to exempt biodiversity from being routinely monetized and traded off for greater economic benefits. But it acknowledges that politically and economically determined values often clash in the real world. And it provides that when the opportunity cost of conserving biodiversity exceeds an unspecified threshold, the God Squad can allow economic considerations to override the general will of the citizens of the United States, democratically expressed through their Congressional representatives, that the nation's extant native species be conserved, period.

Bishop (1978) formalizes the reasoning behind the God Squad amendment to the U.S. Endangered Species Act. He advocates the safe minimum standard (SMS) approach, an alternative to the practice of aggregating everything from the market price to the shadow price of biodiversity, plugging it into a benefit-cost analysis (BCA), and choosing the economically most efficient course of action. Instead, the SMS assumes that biodiversity has incalculable value and should be conserved unless the cost of doing so is prohibitively high. As Randall (1988) explains,

> Whereas the . . . BCA approach starts each case with a clean slate and painstakingly builds from the ground up a body of evidence about the benefits and costs of preservation, the SMS approach starts with a presumption that the maintenance of the SMS for any species is a positive good. The empirical economic question is, "Can we afford it?" Or, more technically, "How high are the opportunity costs of satisfying the SMS?" The SMS decision rule is to maintain the SMS unless the opportunity costs of doing so are intolerably high. In other words, the SMS approach asks, how much will we lose in other domains of human concern by achieving the safe minimum standard of biodiversity? The burden of proof is assigned to the case against maintaining the SMS [Figure 2.3].

As noted in the previous subsection of this chapter, the practical effect of

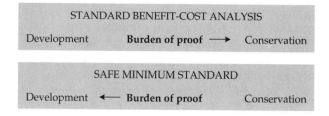

**Figure 2.3** Burden of proof according to the standard BCA and the SMS approaches.

recognizing the intrinsic value of something is not to make it inviolable, but to shift the burden of proof, the onus of justification, onto those whose actions would adversely affect it. Since the safe minimum standard approach to monetizing the value of biodiversity shifts the burden of proof from conservationists to developers, it tacitly acknowledges, and incorporates into economic appraisal, biodiversity's intrinsic value.

## Conservation Ethics

According to Leopold (1949), ethics, biologically understood, constitutes "a limitation on freedom of action." Ethics, in other words, constrains self-serving behavior in deference to some other good (Table 2.2).

### Anthropocentrism

In the Western religious and philosophical tradition, only human beings are worthy of ethical consideration. All other things are regarded as mere means to human ends. Indeed, anthropocentrism seems to be set out in no uncertain terms at the beginning of the Bible. Man alone is created in the image of God, is given dominion over the earth and all the other creatures, and finally, is commanded to subdue the whole creation. White (1967) claimed that because Jews and Christians believed, for many centuries, that it was not only their God-given right, but their positive religious duty, to dominate all other forms of life, science and an eventually aggressive, environmentally destructive technology developed uniquely in Western civilization.

As Norton (1991) has shown, an effective conservation ethic can be constructed on the basis of traditional Western anthropocentrism. Ecology has revealed a world that is far more systemically integrated than the biblical authors could have imagined. Subduing nature has untoward ecological consequences. An anthropocentric conservation ethic would require individuals, corporations, and other interest groups to fairly consider how their actions directly affecting the natural environment indirectly affect

**Table 2.2**

Types of Western Environmental Ethics

|  | Anthropocentrism | Judeo-Christian Stewardship | Biocentric | Ecocentric |
|---|---|---|---|---|
| Intrinsic value | Human beings | Species/creation as a whole | Individual organisms | Species, ecosystems, biosphere |
| The value of nature | Instrumental | Holistic-intrinsic | Individualistic-intrinsic | Holistic-intrinsic |
| "Man's" place in nature | Lord and master | Caretaker | One among equals | Plain member and citizen |

other human beings. Logging tropical forests, for example, may make fine hardwoods available to wealthy consumers, turn a handsome profit for timber companies, employ workers, and earn foreign exchange for debt-ridden countries. But it may also deprive indigenous peoples of their homes and traditional means of subsistence and people everywhere of undiscovered resources, valuable ecosystem services, aesthetic experience, and scientific knowledge. And unchecked, logging may leave future generations of human beings a depauperate world (creating what is called intergenerational inequity). Thus, logging and other environmentally destructive types of resource development may be judged unethical without any fundamental change in the framework of traditional Western moral thought.

### The Judeo-Christian Stewardship Conservation Ethic

Stung by the allegation that the Judeo-Christian worldview was ultimately responsible for bringing about the contemporary environmental crisis, some environmentally concerned Christians and Jews challenged White's (1967) interpretation of biblical environmental attitudes and values (Barr 1972). After all, God pronounced everything that He created to be "good," during the five days before He created human beings. Thus, God appears to have conferred intrinsic value on every kind of creature, not just on humanity. Indeed, the text suggests that God intended His creation to be replete and teeming with life:

> And God said, Let the waters bring forth abundantly the moving creature that hath life, and fowl that may fly above the earth in the open firmament of heaven. And God created great whales, and every living creature that moveth, which the waters brought forth abundantly, after their kind, and every winged fowl after his kind: and God saw that it was good. And God blessed them, saying, Be fruitful and multiply, and fill the waters in the seas, and let fowl multiply in the earth (Genesis 1:20–22).

Further, "dominion" is an ambiguous notion. Just what does it mean for "man" to have dominion over nature? White (1967) argues that in the past, at least, Jews and Christians took it to mean that people should exercise a despotic reign over nature. Later in Genesis, however, God put Adam (who may represent all human beings) in the Garden of Eden (which may represent all of nature) "to dress it and to keep it" (Genesis 2:15). Our "dominion," this suggests, should be that of a responsible caretaker—a steward—rather than that of a tyrant. But what about "man" alone being created in the image of God? That could be taken to confer unique responsibilities, not unique privileges, on human beings. As God cares for humanity, so we who are created in the image of God must care for the earth.

The Judeo-Christian Stewardship Environmental Ethic is especially elegant and powerful. It also exquisitely matches the ethical requirements of conservation biology. The Judeo-Christian Stewardship Environmental Ethic confers objective intrinsic value on nature in the clearest and most unambiguous of ways: by divine decree. But intrinsic value devolves upon species, not individual specimens. For it is clear that during His several acts of creation God is creating species, "kinds," not individual animals and plants—whales, in other words, not specifically the one that swallowed Jonah or the one named Moby Dick. Thus, it is species, not individual specimens, that God pronounces good. Hence, human beings may freely use other living things as long as we do not endanger their species—as long, in other words, as we do not compromise the diversity of the creation. As Ehrenfeld (1988) points out, the Judeo-Christian Stewardship Environmental

Ethic makes human beings directly accountable to God for conserving biodiversity: "Diversity is God's property, and we, who bear the relationship to it of strangers and sojourners, have no right to destroy it."

## Traditional Non-Western Environmental Ethics

Christianity is a world religion, but so are Islam and Buddhism. Other major religious traditions, such as Hinduism and Confucianism, while more regionally restricted, nevertheless claim millions of devotees. Ordinary people are powerfully motivated to do things that can be justified in terms of their religious beliefs. Therefore, distilling environmental ethics from the world's living religions is extremely important for global conservation. The well-documented effort of Jewish and Christian conservationists to formulate the Judeo-Christian Stewardship Environmental Ethic in biblical terms suggests an important new line of inquiry: How can effective conservation ethics be formulated in terms of other sacred texts? Callicott (1994) offers a comprehensive survey, but to provide even a synopsis of that study would be impossible in this chapter. However, a few abstracts of traditional non-Western conservation ethics may be suggestive.

Muslims believe that Islam was founded in the seventh century A.D., by Allah (God) communicating to humanity through the Arabian prophet, Mohammed, who regarded himself to be in the same prophetic tradition as Moses and Jesus. Therefore, since the Hebrew Bible and the New Testament are earlier divine revelations underlying distinctly Muslim belief, the basic Islamic worldview has much in common with the basic Judeo-Christian worldview. In particular, Islam teaches that human beings have a privileged place in nature, and, going further in this regard than Judaism and Christianity, that indeed, all other natural beings were created to serve humanity. Hence, there has been a strong tendency among Muslims to take a purely instrumental approach to the human-nature relationship. As to the conservation of biodiversity, the Arabian oryx was hunted nearly to extinction by oil-rich sheikhs armed with military assault rifles in the cradle of Islam. But callous indifference to the rest of creation in the Islamic world is no longer sanctioned religiously.

Islam does not distinguish between religious and secular law. Hence, new conservation regulations in Islamic states must be grounded in the Koran, Mohammed's book of divine revelations. In the early 1980s, a group of Saudi scholars scoured the Koran for environmentally relevant passages and drafted *The Islamic Principles for the Conservation of the Natural Environment.* While reaffirming "a relationship of utilization, development, and subjugation for man's benefit and the fulfillment of his interests," this landmark document also clearly articulates an Islamic version of stewardship: "he [man] is only a manager of the earth and not a proprietor, a beneficiary not a disposer or ordainer" (Kadr et al. 1983). The Saudi scholars also emphasize a just distribution of "natural resources," not only among members of the present generation, but among members of future generations. And as Norton (1991) has argued, conservation goals are well served when future human beings are accorded a moral status equal to that of those currently living. The Saudi scholars have even found passages in the Koran that are vaguely ecological. For example, God "produced therein all kinds of things in due balance" (Kadr et al. 1983).

Ralph Waldo Emerson and Henry David Thoreau, thinkers at the fountainhead of North American conservation philosophy (discussed in Chapter 1), were influenced by the subtle philosophical doctrines of Hinduism, a major religion in India. Hindu thought also inspired Arne Naess's (1989) contemporary "Deep Ecology" conservation philosophy. Hindus believe that at the core of all phenomena there is one and only one Reality or Being. God, in other words, is not a supreme Being among other lesser and subordinate beings, as in the Judeo-Christian-Islamic tradition. Rather, all beings are a manifestation of the one essential Being, called *Brahman*. And all plurality, all difference, is illusory or at best only apparent.

Such a view would not seem to be a promising point of departure for the conservation of biological diversity, since the actual existence of diversity, biological or otherwise, seems to be denied. Yet in the Hindu concept of *Brahman*, Naess (1989) finds an analogue to the way ecological relationships unite organisms into a systemic whole. However that may be, Hinduism unambiguously invites human beings to identify with other forms of life, for all life-forms share the same essence. Believing that one's own inner self, *atman*, is identical, as an expression of *Brahman*, with the selves of all other creatures leads to compassion for them. The suffering of one life-form is the suffering of all others; to harm other beings is to harm oneself. As a matter of fact, this way of thinking has inspired and helped motivate one of the most persistent and successful conservation movements in the world, the Chipko movement, which has managed to rescue many of India's Himalayan forests from commercial exploitation (Guha 1989b; Shiva 1989).

Jainism is a religion with relatively few adherents, but a religion of great influence in India. Jains believe that every living thing is inhabited by an immaterial soul, no less pure and immortal than the human soul. Bad deeds in past lives, however, have crusted these souls over with *karma*-matter. *Ahimsa* (noninjury of all living things) and asceticism (eschewing all forms of physical pleasure) are parallel paths that will eventually free the soul from future rebirth in the material realm. Hence, Jains take great care to avoid harming other forms of life and to resist the fleeting pleasure of material consumption. Extreme practitioners refuse to eat any but leftover food prepared for others, and carefully strain their water to avoid ingesting any waterborne organisms—not for the sake of their own health, but to avoid inadvertently killing other living beings. Less extreme practitioners are strict vegetarians and own few material possessions. The Jains are bidding for global leadership in environmental ethics. Their low-on-the-food-chain and low-level-of-consumption lifestyle is held up as a model of ecological right livelihood (Chappel 1986). And the author of the *Jain Declaration on Nature* claims that the central Jain moral precept of ahimsa "is nothing but environmentalism" (Singhvi, n.d.).

Though now virtually extinct in its native India, Buddhism has flourished for many hundreds of years elsewhere in Asia. Its founder, Siddhartha Gautama, first followed the path of meditation to experience the oneness of Atman-Brahman, and then the path of extreme asceticism in order to free his soul from his body—all to little effect. Then he realized that his frustration, including his spiritual frustration, was the result of desire. Not by obtaining what one desires—which only leads one to desire something more—but by stilling desire itself can one achieve enlightenment and liberation. Further, desire distorts one's perceptions, exaggerating the importance of some things and diminishing the importance of others. When one overcomes desire, one can appreciate each thing for what it is.

When the Buddha realized all this, he was filled with a sense of joy, and he radiated loving-kindness toward the world around him. He shared his enlightenment with others, and formulated a code of moral conduct for his followers. Many Buddhists believe that all living beings are in the same predicament: we are driven by desire to a life of continuous frustration. And all can be liberated if all can attain enlightenment. Thus Buddhists can regard other living beings as companions on the path to Buddhahood and *nirvana.*

Buddhists, no less than Jains and Christians, are assuming a leadership role in the global conservation movement. Perhaps most notably, the Dalai Lama of Tibet is the foremost conservationist among world religious leaders. In 1985, the Buddhist Perception of Nature Project was launched to extract and collate the many environmentally relevant passages from Buddhist scriptures and secondary literature. Thus, the relevance of Buddhism to contemporary conservation concerns could be demonstrated and the level of conservation consciousness and conscience in Buddhist monasteries, schools, colleges, and other institutions could be raised (Davies 1987). Bodhi (1987) provides a succinct summary of Buddhist environmental ethics: "With its philosophic insight into the interconnectedness and thoroughgoing inter-dependence of all conditioned things, with its thesis that happiness is to be found through the restraint of desire, with its goal of enlightenment through renunciation and contemplation and its ethic of non-injury and boundless loving-kindness for all beings, Buddhism provides all the essential elements for a relationship to the natural world characterized by respect, care, and compassion."

One-fourth of the world's population is Chinese. Fortunately, traditional Chinese thought provides excellent conceptual resources for a conservation ethic. The Chinese word *tao* means *way* or *road*. The Taoists believe that there is a *Tao*, a Way, of nature. That is, natural processes occur not only in an or-derly but also in a harmonious fashion. Human beings can discern the *Tao*, the natural well-orchestrated flow of things. And human activities can either be well adapted to the *Tao*, or they can oppose it. In the former case, human goals are accomplished with ease and grace and without disturbing the natural en-vironment; but in the latter, they are accomplished, if at all, with difficulty and at the price of considerable disruption of neighboring social and natural sys-tems. Capital-intensive Western technology, such as nuclear power plants and industrial agriculture, is very "unTaoist" in esprit and motif.

Modern conservationists find in Taoism an ancient analogue of today's countermovement toward appropriate technology and sustainable develop-ment. The great Mississippi Valley flood of 1993 is a case in point. The river system was not managed in accordance with the *Tao*. Thus, levees and flood walls only exacerbated the big flood when it finally came. Better to have lo-cated cities and towns outside the flood plain and allowed the mighty Mis-sissippi River occasionally to overflow. The rich alluvial soils in the river's floodplains could be farmed in dryer years, but no permanent structures should be located there. That way, the floodwaters could periodically spread over the land, enriching the soil and replenishing wetlands for wildlife, and the human dwellings on higher ground could remain safe and secure. Per-haps the officers of the U.S. Army Corps of Engineers should study Taoism. We can hope that their counterparts in China will abandon newfangled Mao-ism for old-fashioned Taoism before going ahead with their plans to contain, rather than cooperate with, the Yangtze River.

The other ancient Chinese religious worldview is Confucianism. To most people, Asian and Western alike, Confucianism connotes conservatism, ad-herence to custom and social forms, filial piety, and resignation to feudal in-equality. Hence, it seems to hold little promise as an intellectual soil in which to cultivate a conservation ethic. Ames (1992), however, contradicts the re-ceived view: "There is a common ground shared by the teachings of classical Confucianism and Taoism . . . Both express a 'this-worldly' concern for the concrete details of immediate experience rather than . . . grand abstractions

**Table 2.3**
Types of Traditional Non-Western Conservation Ethics

|  | Islam | Hinduism | Jainism | Buddhism | Taoism | Confucianism |
|---|---|---|---|---|---|---|
| Source of value in nature | External *Allah* (God) | Internal *Atman-Brahman* | Internal Soul (*jiva*) | Internal Buddha-nature | Emergent The *Tao* (Way) | Emergent Relational |
| Human attitude toward nature | Respect for creation is respect for Creator | Identification, self-realization | *Ahimsa* (noninjury) | Loving-kindness, solidarity | Harmony, cooperation | Interrelated, interdependent |
| Conservation practicum | Conserve resources for future generations | Conserve trees and other beings that manifest *Atman-Brahman* | Low on the food chain  Low level of consumption | Still desires, reduce consumption, contemplate nature | Adapt human economy to nature's economy | Conserve nature to preserve human society |

and ideals. Both acknowledge the uniqueness, importance, and primacy of particular persons and their contributions to the world, while at the same time expressing the ecological interrelatedness and interdependence of this person with his context."

From a Confucian point of view, a person is not a separate immortal soul temporarily residing in a physical body; a person is, rather, the unique center of a network of relationships. Since his or her identity is constituted by these relationships, the destruction of one's social and environmental context is equivalent to self-destruction. Biocide, in other words, is tantamount to suicide.

In the West, since individuals are not ordinarily conceived to be robustly related to and dependent upon their context—not only for their existence but for their very identity—then it is possible to imagine that they can remain themselves and be "better off" at the expense of both their social and natural environments. But from a Confucian point of view, it is impossible to abstract persons from their contexts. Thus, if *context* is expanded from its classic social to its current environmental connotation, Confucianism offers a very firm foundation upon which to build a contemporary Chinese conservation ethic.

The tenets and conservation implications of these various non-Western religions are summarized in Table 2.3. Essay 2B by Susan Bratton further explores the role of religion in conservation.

## ESSAY 2B
# Monks, Temples, and Trees
## The Spirit of Diversity

Susan P. Bratton, University of North Texas

A Buddhist monk bends over and carefully waters a small seedling in the temple garden. There are others of its kind nearby. Older, taller trees shade the sanctuary paths with their fan-shaped leaves, and produce a crop of edible nuts each year. The monk looks at the little ginkgo and reflects that he never has seen one growing on its own in the surrounding mountains. Only in the temple gardens and their environs has the ginkgo survived, at least in his region of China.

From a venerable lineage, datable to the lower Jurassic, *Ginkgo biloba* is the only known remaining species of an entire division of vascular plants, the Ginkgophyta. Often called a "living fossil," the modern shade tree is little different from the ginkgos of the early Cretaceous period. *Ginkgo* is also a taxon that may or may not exist in the wild. One of the largest "seminatural" populations, at Tian Mu Shan, is near the Kaishan temple, and thus may have been under partial human protection, if not management, for centuries. Over the last several thousand years, Buddhist monks have probably slowly replaced the ginkgo's natural dispersal agents, such as leopard cats, *Felis bengalensis*, and helped preserve the species for posterity (del Tredici et al. 1992).

Our contemporary technocratic and scientifically oriented society often mistakenly considers religion to be either uninterested or uninformed when it comes to protection and management of the natural world. We also assume that if religion is interested, it is the more "primitive" religions and those that practice magic that attempt to relate to or manipulate wild nature, while the great religions of the world—particularly the "peoples of the book," Judaism, Christianity, and Islam—are too theological and other-worldly to concern themselves with the various small pieces that make up the cosmos. The truth is, religious values have often helped to protect natural diversity, and religion remains one of the most important wellsprings of human concern for other species. E. O. Wilson has suggested that science alone cannot protect biodiversity; other cultural values must be called on as well.

Science attempts to understand the world through objective comparison. The various elements in the environment become "other," or differentiated from the scientist, who makes a conscious effort to distance herself from the phenomena she is observing. Religion, in contrast, establishes relationship or identification with the "other." The shaman becomes an intermediary with nature and links the village with the surrounding forests and their creatures; the Buddhist monk works in the temple garden and increases his spiritual understanding of the cosmos as a whole; the Hebrew psalmist sees the glory of God in the diversity of the wild and praises divine wisdom for placing the stork in the cedars and for maintaining both birds and forests with water gushing from mountain springs. Religion has a freedom of symbolic and aesthetic expression inappropriate to science. Religion can speak *with* nature, science can only speak *about* it.

Religion forwards the preservation of natural diversity in several different ways. The first is by providing ethical and social models for living respectfully with nature. For most cultures, religion is a primary means of defining right and wrong. The Koyukon of Alaska, for example, do not separate the natural and the spiritual world, and explain the spiritual power residing in nature through Distant Time stories about the evolution of the cosmos. Since nature has spiritual power, it commands respect and is included in the religious code of morality and etiquette. The Koyukon avoid waste in food harvest and take only what they can use from their fragile far-northern lands. They do not kill female waterfowl preparing to nest, nor do they take young animals. They fear retribution in the form of bad luck if they violate taboos or are disrespectful of the animals they hunt, so their husbandry of natural resources is tightly tied to an animist worldview (Nelson 1983). Other religions with very different notions of the otherworldly may have rather similar rules. The Hebrew scriptures, with their one transcendent God, forbid removal of a mother bird from her nest.

Secondly, religion often provides direct protection for wild and cultivated plants and animals. Many cultures have holy places, including mountains, which humans may approach only for religious purposes, if at all. Rivers or forests may be sacred environs, where wildlife and vegetation are not to be disturbed. Sites are sometimes set aside specifically to protect taxa that have medicinal value or are utilized in religious ritual. Taboos or special religious significance can prevent the killing of individual wildlife species. Buddhism, one of the most abstract and philosophical of all religions, has protected numerous organisms, from gingkos to cranes to monkeys, resident on the grounds of its temples. Some early Christian monks would not allow the native oak forests to be cleared from around their monasteries. St. Francis of Assisi instructed his followers to leave the borders of a cultivated garden unweeded to provide space for wildflowers, so that the blossoms, in their beauty, could praise the creator God.

Even our contemporary wilderness areas in the United States are, among other purposes, supposed to preserve and protect "spiritual values."

Lastly, religion ties the nonhuman residents of the cosmos to the divine or to the overall meaning of human existence. This gives the biota a value that science alone cannot provide. The saffron-robed initiate caring for the temple landscape sees each individual creature as beautiful in itself and beautiful in its interrelationship with its neighbors. The trees, the small clump of flowers, the rock and the sand, become more than xylem and chloroplasts, or feldspar and quartz. For the dedicated practitioner, the sanctity of the environment is an inspiration and a blessing. The spiritual realization of the Buddhist, in turn, blesses the environment (14th Dalai Lama 1992). In early and medieval Christianity, where love and compassion were key values and holiness was fervently pursued, the monks and desert ascetics often cared for wildlife, healing animals with injuries and even rescuing them from hunters. The early Christians thought animals could recognize the pure of heart, and that even wild lions and wolves would show affection for the great saints.

The religious myths and stories that teach us about the importance of other species are often so basic that we, in our human-dominated, industrial world, miss the critical message. Take, for example, the tale of Noah's ark. Noah did not save the animals just to be nice. Noah saved the animals because humans need the animals—all the animals, not just the domestic and the edible. Also, in the Genesis original, it is God who instructs Noah to build the ark. The great God of Israel wanted the animals rescued, and put Noah to a great deal of trouble during a very damp climatic period to accomplish this. God had created the animals in wondrous diversity and in marvelous order, and had blessed them as both good and beautiful well before the Garden of Eden was an official mailing address. When the animals march onto the ark according to their kinds, it is divine organization that is being honored, and when Noah saves them all, not just a few, it is the glory of divine handiwork that is being preserved (Bratton 1992). Modern conservation biology can perhaps take a lesson from this.

## Biocentrism

Before the advent of environmental ethics, moral philosophers in the Western tradition granted moral standing to human beings and human beings alone, not by appeal to a mystical property, such as the image of God, but by appeal to an observable trait, such as rationality or linguistic ability. Because only people, they argued, can reason or speak, only people are worthy of ethical treatment. In the 18th century, Immanuel Kant (1959), for example, argued that human beings are intrinsically valuable ends because we are rational, while animals (and other forms of life) are only instrumentally valuable means because they are not. Contemporary environmental philosophers have attempted to construct a nonanthropocentric environmental ethic without appeal to mystical religious concepts such as God, the Tao, or the universal Buddha-nature. Some have done so by arguing that reason and linguistic ability are inappropriate qualifications for moral standing, and that other observable traits are more appropriate.

Singer (1975) and Regan (1983) exposed classic Western anthropocentric ethics to the following dilemma: if the qualification for ethical standing—or "criterion for moral considerability," as it is more technically called—is pitched high enough to exclude nonhuman beings, then it will exclude as well those human beings who also fail to measure up. Human infants, the severely retarded, and the profoundly senile are not rational. If, following Kant, we make rationality the criterion of moral considerability, then these human "marginal cases" may be treated just as we treat nonhuman beings who fail to meet it. They may become, for example, unwilling subjects of painful medical tests and experiments; they may be hunted for sport; or they may be made into dog food. No one would want that to happen. To consistently avoid it, Singer and Regan argue, we must lower the criterion for moral considerability. But if it is pitched low enough to include the human marginal cases, then it will also include a number of nonhuman animals. Singer follows Kant's 18th century contemporary, Jeremy Bentham, and argues that sentience, the capacity to experience pleasure and pain, ought to be the criterion for ethical standing.

Goodpaster (1978) first took the step from animal liberation to biocentric (literally "life-centered") environmental ethics. From a biological point of view, sentience, he argued, evolved not as an end in itself, but as a means to animals' survival. Hence if there is something morally relevant about sentience, how much more morally relevant is that which sentience evolved to serve—namely, life. Moreover, all living things, as explained earlier in this chapter, have a good of their own, and therefore interests. That fact too, according to Goodpaster, ought to entitle all living things to ethical standing.

Taking a more extreme view, Taylor (1986) argues that all living things are of equal "inherent worth" (Figure 2.4). Apart from the ethically problematic and practically impossible task of according equal moral consideration to each and every living thing, Taylor's pure and extreme biocentrism has little relevance to conservation biology, which, once more, is not concerned with the fate of specimens but of species, ecosystems, and evolutionary processes.

As modified by Rolston (1988), however, biocentrism may address the concerns of conservation biologists and hence may represent a viable conservation ethic. Rolston agrees with Taylor that all living things have intrinsic value (or inherent worth) and thus should enjoy moral standing. But he does not agree that all living things are equal. To the baseline intrinsic value that organisms possess by virtue of having interests and a good of their own, Rolston adds a value "bonus," as we might think of it, for being sentient; and he

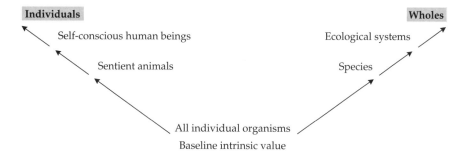

**Figure 2.4** Taylor's biocentrism, in which all individual organisms have equal intrinsic value, and Rolston's, in which the baseline intrinsic value at the level of individual organisms is augmented by sentience and self-consciousness; that is, organisms incur increasing intrinsic value for sentience and self-consciousness. Rolston also provides a parallel valuation scheme for "wholes," species, and ecosystems.

adds an additional value bonus for being rational and self-conscious. Hence, sentient animals have more intrinsic value than insentient plants, and human beings have more intrinsic value than sentient animals (Figure 2.4). Rolston's biocentrism thus better accords with our intuitive sense of a value hierarchy than does Taylor's, since in Rolston's version, the life of a human being is more valuable than that of a white-tailed deer, and that of a deer more valuable than that of a jack pine. And, as noted earlier in this chapter, Rolston also provides intrinsic value, or something similar to it—a value "dividend" as we might think of it—for species, ecosystems, and their evolutionary processes. He argues, therefore, that we have a moral duty to preserve them as well. The development of biocentric and ecocentric philosophies in a historical framework is further explored in Essay 2C by Roderick Nash.

## ESSAY 2C

*An American Perspective*
# Discovering Radical Environmentalism in our Own Cultural Backyard
## From Natural Rights to the Rights of Nature

Roderick Frazier Nash, University of California at Santa Barbara

The search for philosophical foundations for ecocentrism and radical environmentalism have led to ancient Asian religions, pre-Christian Druidic rituals, and Native American cosmologies. Much can be learned—and certainly much inspiration gained—from these attempts to relate humans to nature respectfully and responsibly. But are these belief systems the most promising platform for environmental reform, indeed paradigm change, in the modern American context?

The problem is that mainstream Americans cannot easily think like Indians, Druids, or Taoists; for better or for worse, we march to the beat of a different cultural drummer. But we do have one powerful ideal with which to change paradigms. It is as American as apple pie, and it could provide the motivation to save the planet and us along with it.

Natural rights liberalism is the most potent concept in the history of American thought. It was present before the

American experiment, in 1215, when a handful of English nobles presented a Magna Carta to their king, challenging the exclusivity of the royal definition of rights. The message was straightforward: we are members of this society and we want rights too. By 1776 England's American colonies had expanded the meaning of natural rights considerably. Now "all men" were thought to be endowed with them, and the colonists felt strongly enough about them to fight a war for independence.

Granted that the Jeffersonian sense of "men" was severely limited. Red men, black men, and female men were not yet regarded as full members of the moral community. But the spirit of 1776 was extremely volatile. One of its most dramatic extensions resulted in a huge paradigm change: the abolition of slavery. Beginning in the 1830s, a handful of "radical" American reformers determined to extend basic American natural rights ideals to blacks. The campaign struck one of the most sensitive chords in the American mind: the rights of an oppressed minority to liberation. By 1865 the moral circle had widened and all slaves were legally free.

Today we see in the environmental movement remarkable growth of another "radical" idea: nature has rights that humans should respect. **Deep ecologists** call for the liberation of land and nonhuman life from ownership and abuse. There are appeals for the end of

*earth* slavery. Echoing the Abolitionists' cry, "No Compromise with Slave Holders!", Earth First! proclaims, "No Compromise in Defense of Mother Earth!" The Boston Tea Party of 1773 and John Brown's 1859 raid on Harper's Ferry, Virginia on behalf of slaves inspire environmental radicals. The arresting implication of this parallel is that the slavery issue was not educated or legislated away; it took a civil war and cost a million lives. Will the implementation of environmental ethics also involve conflict?

It is important to acknowledge that the extension of ethics to include nature is not even a simple *conceptual* task. Colonists and slaves, after all, were human; Spotted Owls and wild rivers are not. Classic natural rights are individual-oriented: *every* human has them. This spells trouble in the human relationship to nature. Are we to refrain from *any* impact on our environment?

Can we never kill *anything* to eat? Few rational people think so; clearly there must be differences in moral behavior. But for increasing numbers of people it does make sense to say that all the species that share the planet with us have rights to exist and pursue their lives in their own way. Some feel that ecosystem processes have intrinsic value and a claim to freedom from the tyranny often imposed by human civilization.

Already we have legislation such as the Endangered Species Act of 1973, which gives legal protection to nonhuman existence rights. We also have national park and wilderness acts, which protect nonliving things and ecological processes. From this starting point, it is plausible that American morality can once again expand. This time we could move from natural rights to the rights of nature.

### Ecocentrism

For sound philosophical as well as temperamental reasons, those conservation biologists with nonanthropocentric sympathies have gravitated to the Aldo Leopold Land Ethic in their search for a fitting conservation ethic. Leopold was himself a conservation biologist; indeed he was, perhaps, the prototype of the breed (Meine 1992). Further, the Leopold Land Ethic is not based on religious beliefs, nor is it an extension of the ethical paradigm of classic Western moral philosophy. It is grounded, rather, in evolutionary and ecological biology. Hence, all nonanthropocentric conservation biologists, irrespective of religious or cultural background, will find the Leopold Land Ethic intellectually congenial.

In *The Descent of Man*, Darwin tackled the problem of the evolutionary origins and development of ethics. How could "limitations on freedom of action" possibly have arisen through natural selection, given the universal "struggle for existence" (Leopold 1949)? In a nutshell, Darwin (1904) answered as follows. Social organization enhances the survival and reproductive efficiency of many kinds of organisms. Among mammals, parental and filial affections, having spilled over to other close kin, bound individuals into small social units, such as packs, troops, and bands. When one mammal—*Homo sapiens*—acquired the capacity for reflection and speech, behaviors that were conducive to social integrity and stability were dubbed "good" and those that were antisocial were dubbed "bad." Or, as Darwin (1904) wrote, "No tribe could hold together if murder, robbery, treachery, &c., were common; consequently such crimes within the limits of the same tribe, 'are branded with everlasting infamy.'" Once originated, ethics developed apace with the growth and development of society. According to Darwin (1904),

> As man advances in civilization, and small tribes are united into larger communities, the simplest reason would tell each individual that he ought to extend his social instincts and sympathies to all the members of the same nation though personally unknown to him. This point being once reached, there is only an artificial barrier to prevent his sympathies extending to the men of all nations and races.

Here, at the end of the 20th century, we have finally reached the point that Darwin could only envision in the middle of the 19th: a universal ethic of human rights. But, also during the 20th century, ecology discovered (actually rediscovered, since many tribal peoples seem to have represented their natural environments in analogous terms) that human beings are not only members of various human communities—from the familial clan to the family of man—but members of a "biotic community" as well.

From Darwin we may learn that "all ethics so far evolved rest upon a single premise: that the individual is a member of a community of interdependent parts" (Leopold 1949); and from Leopold, that ecology now "simply enlarges the boundaries of the community to include soils, waters, plants, and animals, or collectively: the land." If whenever a new community came to be recognized in the past, "the simplest reason would tell each individual that he ought to extend his social instincts and sympathies," Leopold argues, then the same "simplest reason" ought to kick in again, now that ecology informs us that we are members of a biotic community.

Though it has been altogether forgotten in Western moral philosophy over the last 200 years, human ethics has always had a strong holistic aspect. That is, human beings have felt that they had duties and obligations to their communities as such, as well as to individual members of those communities. About this, Darwin (1904) was emphatic: "actions are regarded by savages, and were probably so regarded by primeval man, as good or bad, solely as they obviously affect the tribe, not that of the species, nor that of the individual member of the tribe. This agrees well with the belief that the so-called moral sense is aboriginally derived from the social instincts, for both relate at first exclusively to the community."

Influenced by Darwin, Leopold also gave his land ethic a decided holistic cast: "In short, a land ethic," he writes, "changes the role of *Homo sapiens* from conqueror of the land community to plain member and citizen of it. It implies respect for his fellow-members and also respect for the community as such" (Leopold 1949). Indeed, by the time Leopold came to write the summary moral maxim, or "golden rule," as we might like to think of it, of the land ethic, he seems to have forgotten about "fellow-members" altogether and only mentions the "community as such": "A thing is right when it tends to preserve the integrity, stability, and beauty of the biotic community. It is wrong when it tends otherwise."

Staunch apologists for the rugged individualism characteristic of Western moral philosophy during the last two centuries have charged that the land ethic leads to "environmental fascism"—the subordination of the rights of individuals, including human individuals, to the good of the whole (Aiken 1984; Regan 1983). They have a point where nonhuman animals are concerned. The land ethic would permit—nay, even require—killing animals, such as feral goats or rabbits, that pose a threat to populations of endangered floral species or to the general health and integrity of biotic communities. But Leopold, following Darwin, represented the land ethic to be an ethical "accretion"—that is, an addition to, not a substitute for, our long-standing human-to-human ethics.

That human beings have recently become members of national and international communities does not mean that we are no longer members of more ancient and more narrowly circumscribed social groups, such as extended families, or that we are relieved of all the moral duties and responsibilities that attend our active family, clan, and civic affiliations (Figure 2.5). Similarly, our realization that we are also members of a biotic community does not mean that we are relieved of all the moral duties and responsibilities that attend our membership in the full spectrum of human communities.

**Figure 2.5**  The various communities to which human beings belong, and how these communities are hierarchically ordered in the Leopold Land Ethic. The smallest and most intimate community is the family; the largest is the multispecies biotic community. In general, duties and obligations related to the communities at or closer to the center historically have taken precedence over duties and obligations to those at or closer to the perimeter. But we must also consider the gravity, or weight, of our duties and obligations to these communities, as well as their proximity, when they come into conflict with one another.

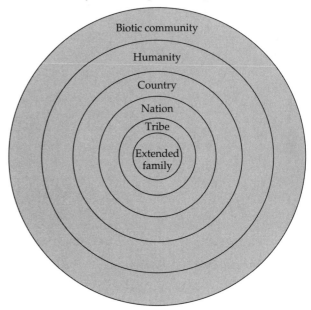

**Community membership in the Leopold Land Ethic**

This defense of the Leopold Land Ethic against the charge that it promotes environmental fascism leads to the charge that it is a "paper tiger," an ecocentric environmental ethic without "teeth." For if we must fully acknowledge all our ancient and modern human duties and obligations as well as our more recently discovered environmental ones, how can we ever justify sacrificing human interests to conserve nonhuman species and ecosystems?

Fortunately, all human-environment conflicts are not life and death issues. We rarely face a choice between killing human beings and conserving biodiversity. Rather, most choices are between human lifestyles and biodiversity. For example, Japanese and other consumers of whale meat are not asked to lay down their lives to save the whales, only to change their dietary preferences. To save forests we don't have to commit suicide; we can save them simply by using less lumber and paper and by recycling what cellulose we must extract. All human interests are not equal. We should be prepared to override less important human interests for the sake of the vital interests of other forms of life, and for ecological health and integrity.

In addition to Leopold's "golden rule," referred to above, five "commandments" can be abstracted from Leopold's exposition of the land ethic:

1. Thou shalt not extirpate or render species extinct.
2. Thou shalt exercise great caution in introducing exotic and domestic species into local ecosystems.
3. Thou shalt exercise great caution in extracting energy from the soil and releasing it into the biota.
4. Thou shalt exercise great caution in damming or polluting watercourses.
5. Thou shalt be especially solicitous of predatory birds and mammals. (Callicott 1987a).

We might to want add a sixth commandment concerning genetic diversity or the maintenance of minimum viable populations, but these commandments, as far as they go, still make good conservation sense. Leopold, however, penned the land ethic at mid-century. Ecology then represented ecosystems as tending toward a static equilibrium, and portrayed disturbance and perturbation as abnormal and destructive (Odum 1953). In light of recent doubts about the very existence of "biotic communities" that persist as such through time (Brubaker 1988), and in light of the shift in contemporary ecology to a more dynamic paradigm (Botkin 1990), we might want to revise the land ethic's summary moral maxim. One hesitates to edit Leopold's elegant prose, but, risking that impertinence, a more up-to-date golden rule of the land ethic might read as follows:

> A thing is right when it tends to protect the health and integrity of ecosystem and evolutionary structure and processes. It is wrong when it tends otherwise.

## Summary

Conservation biology, a crisis discipline, is driven by the *value* of biodiversity. But why should people value biodiversity? Philosophers have distinguished two basic types of value, instrumental and intrinsic. Biodiversity is instrumentally valuable for the *goods* (e.g., actual and potential food, medicine, fiber, and fuel), *services* (e.g., pollination, nutrient cycling, oxygen production), *information* (e.g., practical scientific knowledge, a genetic library), and *psycho-spiritual satisfaction* (e.g., natural beauty, religious awe, pure scientific knowledge) that it provides for intrinsically valuable human beings. Biodiversity may also be intrinsically valuable—valuable, that is, as an end in itself, as well as a means to human well-being. Like ourselves, other forms of life are self-organizing beings with goods of their own. And we human beings are capable of valuing other beings for their own sakes, as well as for what they do for us.

In order to compare its value with the value of other things, economists have attempted to *monetize* both the instrumental and intrinsic value of biodiversity. Philosophers have also based *conservation ethics* on the value of biodiversity. If biodiversity is only instrumentally valuable to human beings, its destruction by one party in pursuit of personal gain may be harmful to another—in which case, the destruction of biodiversity may be immoral. If biodiversity also has intrinsic value its destruction may be doubly immoral.

The Bible recognizes the intrinsic value of other species (God declared them to be "good"). Accordingly, contemporary Jewish and Christian theologians have formulated a Judeo-Christian Stewardship Conservation Ethic. Many other world religions are also developing distinct conservation ethics based on their scriptures and traditions. The Aldo Leopold Land Ethic is not based on any religion, but on contemporary evolutionary and ecological biology. From an evolutionary point of view, human beings are kin to all other forms of life, and from an ecological point of view, human beings are "plain members and citizens" of the "biotic community." According to Leopold, these general scientific facts generate ethical obligations to our "fellow voyagers in the odyssey of evolution," to "fellow-members of the biotic community," and to that "community as such."

## Questions for Discussion

1. Should conservation biologists explain the value of biodiversity to the general public in purely instrumental (or utilitarian) terms or should they also offer reasons for thinking that biodiversity also has intrinsic (or inherent) value?

2. How should a conservation biologist trying to save a rare, endangered

plant species, such as Furbish's lousewort, respond to the question, "What good is it?"

3. Suppose a conservation biologist answered this question with another, "What good are you?" What sort of reflection would the conservation biologist be inviting the person who posed the first question to engage in? How would you answer the question, "What good are you?" Could your answer to this question be transposed to the question "What good is Furbish's lousewort?"

4. Suppose a developer wants to build a dog track outside Houston, Texas in the last remaining habitat of the Houston toad. If nonhuman species have only instrumental value, should the toad's habitat be saved? If nonhuman species have intrinsic value, could any development proposal that usurped its habitat be morally justified?

5. Would the existence of a legal international market in ivory help or hurt efforts to conserve African elephants?

6. Should conservation biologists campaign to take biodiversity off the market and say, in effect, "Not for sale at any price," or should we try to show that the dollar value of biodiversity exceeds the dollar value of the lumber, electricity, beef, or what-have-you, whose production contributes to the erosion of biodiversity?

7. How does the understanding of human nature and the place of human beings in nature set out in Genesis in the Bible compare with the understanding of human nature and the place of human beings in nature forthcoming from science?

8. Suppose a population of weedy sentient animals, say feral goats, is threatening a plant species endemic to an island with extinction. What ethical concerns should a conservation biologist take into account before proposing a course of action?

9. If, in Rolston's biocentrism, the life of a white-tailed deer is more intrinsically valuable than that of a jack pine, would it also follow that the life of a gray squirrel is more intrinsically valuable than the life of a 1000-year-old redwood tree? Is the life of a human being more intrinsically valuable than that of a 1000-year-old redwood tree? Why?

10. Suppose your brother is a logger or millworker in the Pacific Northwest. As a conservation biologist, should you support a moratorium on all logging of old-growth forests in the region, or do family obligations require you to be more concerned about your brother's lifestyle and livelihood?

## Suggestions for Further Reading

Callicott, J. B. (ed.). 1987. *Companion to A Sand County Almanac*. University of Wisconsin Press, Madison. Essays by biographers, historians, literary critics, scientists, and philosophers sketch Leopold's life and the natural history of Wisconsin's sand counties. They analyze his classic work on conservation values and ethics, interpret his land ethic, and trace its impact on conservation policy and practice.

Callicott, J. B. 1994. *Earth's Insights: A Multicultural Survey of Ecological Ethics*. University of California Press, Berkeley. Global conservation efforts can succeed only if they are consistent with and motivated by the deepest beliefs of people all over the world. Sketched in this book are conservation values and ethics grounded in Judaism, Christianity, Islam, Hinduism, Buddhism, Taoism, Confucianism, and the worldviews of selected Pacific, North American, African, and Australian indigenous peoples.

Krutilla, J. and A. Fisher. 1985. *The Economics of Natural Environments: Studies in the Valuation of Commodity and Amenity Resources*. Revised ed. Resources for the Future, Washington, D.C. This volume provides a straightforward account of methods of monetizing the values of natural environments used by neoclassical economists.

Leopold, A. 1949. *A Sand County Almanac, and Sketches Here and There*. Oxford University Press, New York. Leopold is often called a "prophet" because he was a quarter-century ahead of his time in formulating a nonanthropocentric conservation philosophy and environmental ethic. This slender volume of essays is often called "the Bible of the contemporary conservation movement," and is a "must-read" for any serious student of conservation.

Norton, B. G. 1991. *Toward Unity among Environmentalists*. Oxford University Press, New York. The "convergence hypothesis"—the idea that the full spectrum of ideas about the instrumental and intrinsic values of nature converge on the same environmental policies—is here set out and championed.

Rolston, H. III. 1988. *Environmental Ethics: Duties to and Values in the Natural World*. Temple University Press, Philadelphia. The dean of the new field of environmental ethics provides a sustained defense of the objective intrinsic value of nature from which he derives our duties and obligations to conserve biodiversity.

Sagoff, M. 1988. *The Economy of the Earth: Philosophy, Law, and the Environment*. Cambridge University Press, Cambridge. Sagoff's collected essays provide a critique of methods of monetizing the values of natural environments used by neoclassical economists. Some value questions, Sagoff argues, belong in the political realm, not the economic.

# The Species in Conservation

*In all probability more paper has been consumed on the questions of the nature and definition of the species than any other subject in evolutionary and systematic biology.*

*E. O. Wiley, 1978*

One of the main players in conservation, conceptually, biologically, and legally, is the species. Most people have a conception of an entity called the species, and understand that there is a great deal of global diversity at that level, much of which is being lost. Biologists have focused on the species level for centuries, and have developed systems for naming, cataloging, and comparing species. Many of our conservation efforts, from fund-raising to recovery programs to reserve design, dwell on species. Species are the focus of some of the most powerful conservation legislation in the world, including the U.S. Endangered Species Act (ESA) and the Convention on International Trade in Endangered Species (CITES).

Because of its central role in all of conservation, we will explore in this chapter some implications of a species focus. Conservation biologists should develop an understanding of the species category, the biological importance of variation within species, the vagueness of and different perspectives of species concepts, and especially, an appreciation for the ecological and evolutionary values of species and populations.

One of the clear distinctions we hope to draw is between biological and legal definitions of species. Legislation drives much of the emphasis on species as a unit of conservation, yet it is often difficult to define species biologically. Even if we can, other levels of biological organization, from populations to landscapes, may be more significant or more practical units of concern in various situations.

## Views on Species

To the uninitiated, it may seem a simple thing to define a species; after all, most of us have an intuitive feel for species of animals and plants and can identify and name many species, seemingly with great confidence. The species is far from easy to delineate, however, and in fact many different species definitions and concepts exist among biologists, which we discuss below.

Much of the **species problem**—the ambiguity of the species category—stems from the fact that the biological world is a continuum of organization, from atoms and molecules, through cells, organ systems, and individuals, to populations and species, to communities, ecosystems, and landscapes. Cut-off points that separate categories within this continuum are often fuzzy, or are determined by the particular needs of a research or policy question. Consider something apparently as clear as an individual organism; surely there should be no ambiguity at that level. Yet, what exactly is an "individual" in a vegetatively reproducing plant that covers a hectare as a population of separate shrubs sprouting from spreading roots originating from one seed? What is an "individual" in a planarian worm, after it is split down the middle and two living physical entities result? How about a lizard that reproduces asexually, resulting in exact genetic replicas of itself?

Similarly, the species category is often ambiguous. Although definitions vary (below), we may generally think of species as consisting of naturally occurring groups of individuals that can interbreed and that have a common evolutionary history. The species really represents a level of evolutionary discontinuity, but how discontinuous must two populations or individuals be in order to be of different species? (Note that this concept is equally valid if inverted: the species can represent a level of evolutionary continuity. How continuous must two populations or individuals be to be considered the same species?) It is obvious that a Mallard Duck (*Anas platyrhynchos*) is evolutionarily discontinuous with a Downy Woodpecker (*Dendrocopos pubescens*), but what about its relationship to the Mexican Duck (*Anas diazi*), with which it sometimes interbreeds? What about subspecies? How discontinuous are they, and what does their category really mean, biologically and legally? To answer such questions, we need to examine the various ways of looking at the problem of defining species.

### Typological versus Populational Thinking

There are two major ways in which species have been viewed historically, which are reflections of two major schools of philosophical thought. The **typological** approach views species as categorical entities, distinct and somewhat clearly differentiated (Figure 3.1A). This outlook originated with the typological perspective of the Greek philosopher Plato, who maintained that all physical objects in our world represent an "eidos," an eternal and changeless ideal or perfect "type"; any variations about that ideal are merely unfortunate imperfections of the material world.

The typological view was adopted by early biologists, including Linnaeus, the father of our present system of Latin binomial nomenclature (genus and species), and was largely, although not completely, accepted through the middle of the 19th century. It was manifested in the prevailing view of the time that species are immutable creations of God and occur in a fixed number. This view blended nicely with the "balance of nature perspective," also popular at the time, that nature was a finely tuned, divinely engineered machine with perfectly fitting and unchanging parts. Early taxonomists therefore viewed individual variation as unimportant and even annoying, and species, subspecies, and races were named as though they were discrete and invariant units. The distinctness and fixity of species are central features of the typological perspective.

The **populational** or evolutionary view, in contrast, focuses directly on

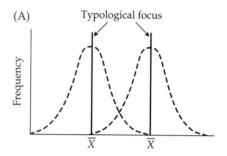

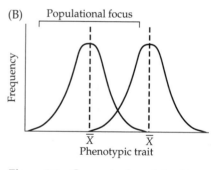

**Figure 3.1** Conceptual models of typological and populational species concepts. (A) In the typological view, the essence of the species is represented by the mean. Variance around the mean is considered "noise" and therefore unimportant. (B) In the populational view, the essence of the species includes the distribution of the trait, and the mean is simply one statistical descriptor. There is no perfect "type," and species may even grade into one another, with no clear gap. In each figure conceptualization, the perceived reality of the species is represented by a solid line; a dotted line represents the perceived less important aspect.

variation within species. This perspective recognizes that a category such as the species is a group of individuals that collectively express genetic, morphological, physiological, and behavioral variation, and that this variation is not unimportant and annoying, but is in fact the basis of evolutionary change and adaptation (Figure 3.1B). Within-species variation in the populational view is not seen as an unfortunate deviation from a perfect type, but the result of genetic differences among, and environmental influences upon, individuals. Ernst Mayr (1959) summarized the typological/populational dichotomy clearly when he said, "For the typologist, the type (*eidos*) is real and the variation an illusion, while for the populationist the type (average) is an abstraction and only the variation is real. No two ways of looking at nature could be more different."

In its classic manifestation, the typological perspective results in a "pattern analysis" of species (Rojas 1992). Species are treated as nonhistorical entities, and their delineations are based on the statistical distribution of measurable characters, with no assumptions made about the historical (evolutionary) processes that caused these patterns. The populational perspective results in a "process analysis" of species, in which observed patterns are seen as the result of historical events and dynamic change—real processes—and causal analyses of patterns are offered. Evolutionary events in this perspective operate at the level of localized populations, which are the functional ecological and evolutionary units.

Virtually all contemporary biologists reject classic typological thinking and accept the populational view of species. They recognize the importance of diversity within species and the potential for genetic, morphological, physiological, or behavioral diversification among populations. They recognize that most measurable characteristics of living things vary to some degree, and that much of the variation is genetically based and of evolutionary importance (Futuyma 1986).

**Geographic variation** is a common type of variation in most species and is an important part of species concepts. Geographic variation consists of measurable divergence among different populations in characters such as color, body size, protein structure, behavior, egg size, or any other measurable trait. The degree of divergence varies, but is typically greater in geographically more distant populations or those living under very dissimilar ecological conditions (Figure 3.2). Well-marked, consistent differences in a character among populations, such as differences in plumage in birds, scale counts in fish, or color patterns in butterflies, are often the basis for subspecies designations, regardless of their biological importance. Less obvious

**Figure 3.2** Individuals of different populations of the rock pocket mouse (*Perognathus intermedius*), illustrating geographic variation in coat color, presumably a result of different habitats and substrates. The two specimens on the left are from Socorro County, New Mexico, which has darker soils, and the two on the right are from Yuma County, Arizona, which has lighter soils. (Specimens courtesy of Smithsonian Institution; photograph by G. K. Meffe.)

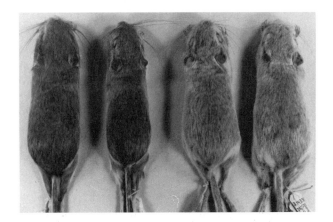

but perhaps more important differences in other characters relevant to natural selection may go unrecognized and thus unheralded.

Geographic populations that clearly differ in the *mean state* of a particular character may nevertheless have within-population *variation* in that character such that some individuals overlap with other populations, which further blurs population variation. In other words, an individual from one population (or subspecies) may resemble more closely the mean of another population (or subspecies) than that of its own. Many degrees of mean character divergence and overlap may thus be found among populations, confusing the picture, and making determination of species boundaries difficult.

Geographic variation is an important element in the study of evolutionary processes and the practice of conservation biology because it often reflects local adaptation, and is a first step toward the process of **speciation,** the development of new species. It is itself a form of biological variation worthy of protection and perpetuation.

Recognition of such biologically relevant variation within the species category raises important conservation questions. For example, how much of within-species variation is (or can be) conserved in species-level protection? How can we choose how much within-species diversity to protect? Is the species the appropriate unit on which to focus? To answer questions such as these, we need to look more closely at various species concepts.

## Species Concepts

It should be obvious by now that the nature and definition of species is an area fraught with difficulty, and one which has the potential to bog us down and obstruct our progress toward more pressing questions in conservation. Nevertheless, we must pay heed to species concepts, as they have great bearing on how we approach conservation and what we ultimately conserve. The way species are defined can affect our perceptions of how many species there might be, their importance relative to populations, and their dynamics over time.

Many biologists argue that the species is the only nonarbitrary taxonomic category, and most would agree that subspecies, genera, families, and other categories are purely artificial constructs (Futuyma 1986). Yet even the species has many definitions, on which there is no universal agreement.

Definitions presented in introductory biology textbooks form the first and perhaps most lasting impressions most students obtain of the "species" issue, yet these definitions illustrate disparities in use of the term. For example, Campbell (1987) defined a species as "a particular kind of organism, its members possessing similar anatomical characteristics and having the ability to interbreed." Keeton (1972) called a species "the largest unit of population within which effective gene flow occurs or could occur." Kirk (1975) defined a species as "a group of related individuals that are actually or potentially capable of interbreeding; a group of organisms constituting a single gene pool." Each of these definitions has merit and each has problems, but they collectively indicate that the species concept is not a universally defined and agreed-upon biological entity.

It is important to realize that species designations are nothing more than testable hypotheses, based upon the best information currently available. Species designations are temporary, and may change when better information becomes available; that is, the hypothesis may be rejected in the future. The main argument over the species question is how these hypotheses are tested, the type of information used, how it is used, and the philosophical framework chosen.

There are several biological bases upon which species concepts may be developed, such as morphological discontinuity, reproductive isolation, patterns of ancestry and descent, genetic cohesion, and ecological adaptation. In part, these differences arise because the various concepts are sometimes used for different purposes (Endler 1989). Our intent here is not to go into the details and relative merits of the various species concepts, or to settle species issues, but to present some major species concepts as an illustration of the complexity of the topic, and as a preamble to further discussion relative to conservation.

Of the many species concepts in use today, three receive the most attention. The **biological species concept** (BSC), or "isolation concept," has been a central focus since 1942 and perhaps remains the most popular view among zoologists. It defines species as "groups of actually or potentially interbreeding populations, which are reproductively isolated from other such groups" (Mayr 1942). Because the essential criterion is reproductive isolation, or conversely, the ability to reproduce and therefore exchange genetic material, this is a genetically based definition. Mayr (1969) explained that, under this concept, a species has three separate "functions": it forms a reproductive community, is an ecological unit, and comprises a genetic unit consisting of a large, intercommunicating gene pool.

Despite modifications to the definition in recent years (Mayr 1982), the BSC has received criticism and has fallen out of favor with some. For one thing, it is often operationally difficult to determine reproductive isolation if the "species" are not **sympatric** (i.e., do not occur together and have the opportunity to interbreed). Reproductive isolation becomes trivial if the two forms live 1000 km apart and never come into contact. So, although defined on the basis of reproductive isolation, in practice species are largely judged on a surrogate measure, morphological criteria; these are assumed to provide evidence of reproductive community versus reproductive isolation, but this correlation is often hard to test (Donoghue 1985). Thus, practically speaking, the BSC is defined by one set of criteria (reproductive isolation), but the practicing taxonomist often finds this difficult and uses another set of criteria (generally, morphology) as evidence for reproductive isolation.

Because the definition is based on reproductive isolation and genetic exchange, the BSC has further limitations. It is inapplicable to asexual species and "chronospecies" (species that are defined by changes through time, such as fossil taxa), and is often difficult to apply to microorganisms and plants, in which natural hybridization and genetic introgression (infiltration of the genes of one species into another) among recognized "species" is common, and species are found in all stages of divergence (Grant 1957).

The **phylogenetic species concept** (PSC) is another popular concept today, and is sometimes called the **cladistic** species concept. This concept argues that classification should reflect the branching, or cladistic, relationships among species or higher taxa, regardless of their degree of genetic relatedness. The relationships among taxa are described in a **cladogram,** which is an estimate or hypothesis of the true genealogical relationship among the species or higher taxa. In the phylogenetic method, a species is defined as "the smallest diagnosable cluster of individual organisms within which there is a parental pattern of ancestry and descent" (Cracraft 1983). The species is an irreducible, or basal, unit distinct from other such units.

The PSC definition is based on the concept of shared derived characters, called **synapomorphies.** If two or more individuals or populations share a derived character (defined as a unique character not found in other, more distantly related groups), then they are thought to be more closely related

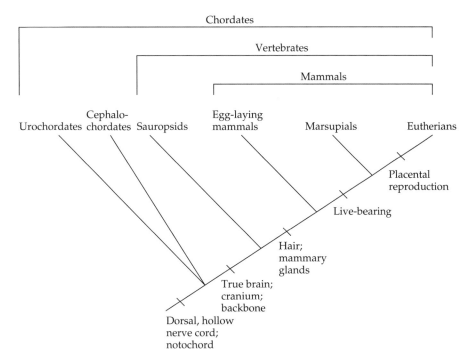

**Figure 3.3** A simple cladogram, using some chordates as an example. A series of synapomorphic characters sequentially separates the different chordate groups. A more detailed phylogenetic analysis could separate down to the species level. (Note that, for simplicity, not all vertebrate groups are shown.)

than individuals or populations lacking that character. For example (Figure 3.3), all chordates have a dorsal hollow nerve cord and a notochord, which separate chordates from all other animal groups. However, these are common characters within the group (i.e., all chordates have the character) that do nothing to further determine relationships among them, so other characters must be explored. Within the chordates, vertebrates have a true brain, a cranium, and a backbone, which are unique characters that the other chordates (urochordates and cephalochordates) do not possess. Within the vertebrates, hair and mammary glands are found only in mammals, thus clearly separating them from their closest relatives, the sauropsids (reptiles and birds). Other unique characters, such as live-bearing and placental reproduction, further separate the mammals. This sort of analysis, if carried out at finer levels, eventually separates species.

It is important to realize that a synapomorphy is a relative term and depends on the particular taxonomic level of interest. For example, the presence of a backbone is a synapomorphy of vertebrates when compared with other chordates; however, within the vertebrates, presence of a backbone does nothing to further determine relationships among vertebrate taxa, so we must search for other characters that vary within the group. Hair and mammary glands are synapomorphic characters of mammals, and clearly separate them from other vertebrates, but *within* the mammals, they are not synapomorphic (are **plesiomorphic**), because all mammals have these characters. Other characters, unique to various mammal groups, must be found for further separation of taxa.

The PSC definition is based on the conviction that evolution "results in a hierarchy of **monophyletic** groups . . . and that classifications should reflect genealogical relationships accurately and unambiguously at all levels" (Donoghue 1985). A monophyletic group ". . . is one that contains all and only the descendants of a particular common ancestor [plus the ancestor]. It is a group wherein every member is more closely related (in a strictly genealogical sense) to every other member than to any organisms classified outside the group" (Donoghue 1985). Evidence for monophylies (which define ancestral-descendant relationships) is provided by synapomorphic characters, which may be morphological, genetic, behavioral, biochemical, or any other measurable characteristic of an organism. In the above example, mammals are monophyletic in that they all possess hair and mammary glands; within mammals, eutherians are monophyletic because they all undergo placental reproduction.

Adoption of a phylogenetic species concept would result in the elevation of subspecies to full species in many groups, and recognition of individual populations with even small character differences as species. There are no subspecific designations in a PSC; geographically distinct populations that a BSC proponent would call subspecies would be full species under the PSC, even if the populations interbreed where their ranges meet. Cracraft (1992), for example, applied the phylogenetic species concept to the birds of paradise (family Paradisaeidae) and described 90 species, up from 40–42 species proposed using the biological species concept, which also included about 100 subspecies. Such application of the PSC presumably accurately reflects actual evolutionary relationships and pathways.

The **evolutionary species concept** (ESC) defines a species as "a single lineage of ancestral descendant populations of organisms which maintains its identity from other such lineages and which has its own evolutionary tendencies and historical fate" (Wiley 1978, modified from Simpson 1961). A species is viewed here as an evolutionary entity with historical, rather than reproductive ties, and is based on phenetic (physical trait) cohesions and discontinuities; in that way it is similar to the phylogenetic concept. It emphasizes that a species can be held together as a unit of evolution by developmental, genetic, and ecological constraints. Templeton (1989) pointed out several practical problems with the evolutionary concept: there is no guidance as to which traits are more relevant, and several traits may give contradictory information; there is a problem in judging what constitutes a "common" evolutionary fate; and it is not a mechanistic definition because it deals only with the results of evolutionary cohesion, and not the mechanisms responsible.

A variety of other species concepts have been used, which we will not discuss in detail, but present to illustrate the diversity of approaches to the species problem, and also the conceptual overlap among them. A modification of the typological approach is the **phenetic** school of taxonomy, based on numerical measurements of individuals and mathematical analysis of morphological discontinuities. The phenetic approach argues that the best classification system is based on the overall pattern of similarity and difference among individuals or groups, based on as many characteristics as possible, regardless of actual ancestral relationships. This concept is rarely used today.

The **ecological species concept** (Van Valen 1976) considers a species to be "a lineage (or a closely related set of lineages) which occupies an adaptive zone minimally different from that of any other lineage in its range and which evolves separately from all other lineages outside its range." An adaptive zone is defined as the resource space plus predators and parasites.

The **recognition species concept** (Paterson 1985) is essentially a corollary of the BSC. It defines species as a field for gene recombination with reproductive mechanisms facilitating gene exchange; in the BSC, mechanisms that prevent gene exchange among dissimilar individuals are emphasized.

The **cohesion species** is a relatively new concept introduced by Templeton (1989) in which a species is defined as "the most inclusive population of individuals having the potential for phenotypic cohesion through intrinsic cohesion mechanisms." The cohesion concept emphasizes mechanisms (such as gene flow and natural selection) that result in species cohesion, rather than isolation.

Two relevant philosophical perspectives that further complicate species concepts deserve mention. **Nominalists** question the very existence of species as real and natural entities, claiming that only individuals exist and species are artificial mental constructs without objective existence. Charles Darwin was perhaps a nominalist, or at least felt that the species concept had been confused and used in arbitrary ways. He wrote, "I look at the term species as one arbitrarily given, for the sake of convenience, to a set of individuals closely resembling each other, and it does not essentially differ from the term variety which is given to less distinct and more fluctuating forms" (1859).

Although most modern biologists would disagree, there are contemporary adherents to the nominalist view (e.g., Levin 1979) and it is not without its appeal, at least for some groups such as plants. Ehrlich and Holm (1963), for example, wrote, ". . . the idea of good species . . . is a generality without foundation—an artifact of the procedures of taxonomy. These procedures require that distinct clusters be found and assigned to some level in a hierarchy—subspecies, species . . . and so on." Ehrlich (1961) stated that, ". . . *at least at the present level of knowledge,* the prevalence of the clearly defined species is a myth" [italics original].

Contrasted with the nominalist philosophy is the **pluralist** suggestion that species concepts should vary with the taxa under consideration and that we should consider more than one species definition. Thus, Scudder (1974) suggests existence of paleospecies, sibling species, morphospecies, hybrid species, and a host of other types that arise in different ways or apply to different biological situations.

The particular species concept favored may indeed depend on the particular biota in question. This is based less on biological differences than on historical legacies: some species definitions were developed by individuals with expertise in particular taxa, and convention has followed those definitions. For example, the biological species concept was championed by an ornithologist, Ernst Mayr; birds seemed to fit the definition well because so much was known about their individual biologies, and because breeding groups were often clearly delineated. In contrast, plant species provide many examples in which the use of the biological species concept is ambiguous or contradictory. Much more than animals, plants may form fertile hybrids between species, may develop new self-perpetuating varieties through **polyploidy** (multiplication of chromosome numbers), and may form asexual species. The problem of species identification and definition is further developed for freshwater mussels in Essay 3A by James Williams and Margaret Mulvey.

## ESSAY 3A
# Recognition of Freshwater Mussel Taxa
## A Conservation Challenge

James D. Williams, National Biological Survey, and
Margaret Mulvey, Savannah River Ecology Laboratory

The most diverse freshwater mussel fauna in the world occurs in North America. Currently, 281 species and 16 subspecies belonging to two families, Unionidae and Margaritiferidae, are recognized (Turgeon et al. 1988). They inhabit aquatic systems ranging from small ponds to lakes and from cold upland streams to warm and turbid lowland rivers. The greatest mussel diversity is found in the Tennessee, Cumberland, and Mobile River drainages of the southeastern United States.

Mussels were once a common component of freshwater ecosystems throughout most of the central and eastern United States. The decline of freshwater mussels parallels that of other freshwater organisms that have experienced gradual, but continuous, losses. The earliest threats, during the late 1800s, resulted from excessive commercial harvest of shell for the pearl button industry (Smith 1899). Dams, pollution, and siltation continue to plague mussel populations, but the introduction and spread of nonindigenous mollusks, especially Asiatic clams (*Corbicula fluminea*) and zebra mussels (*Dreissena polymorpha*), have intensified threats. During the past three decades there has been a precipitous decline of mussels both in numbers of individuals and in species diversity. Williams et al. (1993) reported 21 mussel species, 7.1% of the United States fauna, as possibly extinct, 77 species (20.6%) as endangered, and 43 species (14.5%) as threatened. With the present trajectory we will witness the demise of this widespread and diverse fauna during the next 20 years.

## Defining Mussel Species: What's in a Name?

Uncertainties in defining and delineating species, discussed in this chapter, are well illustrated with freshwater mussels. Almost all American freshwater mussels were described in an 80-year period between 1820 and 1900, mostly by a single conchologist, Isaac Lea (1827–1874). He was a wealthy individual, and all of his descriptions were accompanied by detailed drawings illustrating variations in shape, thickness, and color that he observed in the shell. Isaac Lea did almost no fieldwork, and specimens on which he based his descriptions were gifts, trades with fellow conchologists, or purchases from collectors. His lack of field experience left him with no concept of the morphological variation that existed in populations of mussels. Like many early naturalists, he had a typological concept of species, which resulted in the description of more than 1000 new "species" of mussels. Of the 297 U.S. taxa recognized today, more than 115 were described by Isaac Lea.

In the early 1900s biologists began to assemble large museum collections of mussels from throughout the central and eastern United States, which provided an opportunity to evaluate variation within and among mussel popula-

tions. As they examined the variation exhibited by this new material, researchers were unable to distinguish many of the "species" of mussels described by conchologists during the 1800s. No longer were they seeing distinct morphotypes, but rather parts of a larger, continuously variable morphology. An example of this problem is illustrated by three taxa described by Isaac Lea from the Mobile River drainage (Figure A). Considered alone, these three taxa are separable based on the shape, degree of inflation, and sculpturing of the shell. However, considered with individuals from geographically and ecologically intermediate areas, they were found to morphologically grade into one another. Currently, these forms are treated as a single, highly variable species, *Quadrula asperata*.

To determine the validity of some of the described taxa, research into the factors affecting shell morphology has been undertaken. Earlier in this century, characteristics of the shell, including shape, color, and thickness, were compared among populations of the same species in different environments. Grier (1920) compared the shell morphology of populations of several species from the upper Ohio River and Lake Erie, and found those from Lake Erie to be more inflated and thinner-shelled than those from the Ohio River. Ortmann (1920) compared populations of the same species from small headwater streams and downstream in large river habitats, and found that shells were more inflated (obese), shorter, and less sculptured in riverine habitats than in the smaller headwater streams. In a similar study, Ball (1922) reported that factors other than stream size (discharge) entered into determination of

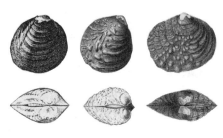

**Figure A**   Three taxa originally described as distinct species, *Unio keineriana* (left), *Unio asperatus* (center), and *Unio cahabensis* (right), and subsequently considered to represent a single species, *Quadrula asperata*.

the degree of shell obesity.

Results of these early studies and others (see Eagar 1978; Balla and Walker 1991) suggest that variation in shell morphology reflects the interaction of numerous environmental and genetic factors; thus, shell morphology alone is often insufficient for species identification. Recognition of ecophenotypic variation led to synonymy of many of the older names. In an extreme example, Johnson (1970) listed 102 synonyms for the widespread *Elliptio complanata*. Recent work with *Elliptio* has revisited some of these 102 taxa and argued for their recognition (Davis and Mulvey, 1993); these recent studies incorporate enzyme electrophoresis and multivariate analysis of shell morphology and anatomy. This shifting taxonomy of freshwater mussels reflects both changes in our concept of species, and the application of new methods to problems of species identification.

Although phenotypic variation may confuse the taxonomy of mussel "species," such variation reflects the interaction of environmental and genetic factors and is the basis of evolution and adaptation. We now recognize that delineation of mussel taxa should include shell morphology, soft tissue anatomy, ecology, and genetics. We also recognize that, for most taxa, this will not be easy.

In the task of species conservation we are frequently faced with the question of what to protect. Rarely does one have the opportunity to protect portions of all populations of a species; this necessarily leads to prioritization of populations and geographic areas that need to be protected. In determining priorities for species conservation one should consider the morphologic, genetic, ecological, and behavioral variation of the species in question. In the absence of population genetics data for mussels we can turn to the morphological data. For example, in the case of *Quadrula asperata*, conservation efforts should, at a minimum, include the extremes of morphological variation (see Figure A).

Protection of species at the population level, including the full array of morphological and genetic diversity, is essential to the long-term survival of species. This is especially critical in species such as freshwater mussels, where the very nature of species definitions is in question and changes with new information. Saving all the pieces seems a prudent course of action.

Oaks provide a good example of confusion in species definitions. Oaks often form reproductively viable hybrid populations and one might question whether the parental species should be called "species" at all. *Quercus alba* and *Q. stellata* are known to form natural hybrids with 11 other oak species in the eastern United States. It might be argued that, if these oaks cannot tell each other apart, why should biologists impose different species names on them? However, Whittemore and Schaal (1991) provide some assurance for retaining species identities, at least under the BSC, despite such seemingly fluid species boundaries. They analyzed variation of chloroplast and nuclear DNAs among 16 species of eastern white oaks. Although maternally inherited chloroplast genes were freely exchanged between species, the distribution of nuclear genes appeared to follow species patterns. These results are consistent with other work that indicates strong separation of white oak species based on genetic and morphological traits. Even though oaks appear to exchange genes and form reproductively viable hybrids, the species remain distinct and form at least partially closed gene pools.

Furthermore, it is worth noting that many examples of viable hybrid formation in nature occur when historically isolated species are brought into contact through climate change, landscape transformation, or transport by humans beyond their historic boundaries. Oaks were absent from eastern deciduous forests during most of the Pleistocene, and in many places their co-occurrence is no older than 100 generations (Davis 1983). There are numerous other examples of fertile hybrids forming when once-isolated species of plants or animals are rapidly thrust into contact, usually as a consequence of the way humans quickly and drastically modify landscapes.

In closing this section on species concepts, we reemphasize that species are not fixed entities. If it were possible to inventory all species in the world every million years or so, each of our time windows would show species going extinct, new species appearing, and the rates of additions and subtractions changing over time. And at every inventory, including today's, we would find species in various stages of formation and decline.

From this omniscient perspective we would see that the ranges of some species are discontinuous, and that comparison of a species in two parts of its range might indicate genetic, morphological, or behavioral differences. When the differences are slight, we may simply say that the same species is found in disjunct populations. When the differences are large, we may recognize the beginnings of a new species, an **incipient species.** In a survey of our inventory we might also find a continuum extending from species with highly connected populations to species that are spatially highly fragmented and disjunct. Within the latter group, we would find reason to argue that in some cases the disjunct populations are so different that they should be distinguished as two or more new species. By so doing we would be making a judgment that the species now exists in two or more largely closed gene pools, which now have independent evolutionary pathways. That we see such variation in species formation does not invalidate concepts of species; it only reinforces the fact that the species, whether as a gene pool in various stages of closure or as a diagnosable cluster of individuals with common ancestry, is a unit of continual evolutionary change.

## The Species and Conservation

### How Do Species Concepts Affect Conservation Efforts?

Adoption of different species concepts could alter the way we define, and thus conserve, species, but would that have any real effect on conservation of biodiversity? We will examine two of the current species concepts in primary use and ask how their perspectives affect species conservation.

The biological species concept has been the reigning species concept for about half a century, and its use is deeply engrained throughout much of biology; it has resulted in the present estimates of 5 to 30 million species extant today (Wilson 1988; see also Essay 4B). The BSC has also been adopted de facto in much of conservation with respect to both biological and legal aspects of species protection. The focus of the BSC is on species and subspecies as distinct entities; there is less emphasis on populations and ecological functions within these broader categories, although the Endangered Species Act does recognize endangered or threatened populations of vertebrates.

How would adopting a phylogenetic species concept affect conservation? The PSC would result in more recognized species than at present (McKitrick and Zink 1988) because many currently recognized subspecies or distinct populations would be elevated to species status (Figure 3.4). These new species would be distinguished based on genealogical relationships and derived character states, rather than major morphological gaps or genetic isolation. This would better reflect evolutionary history and more appropriately recognize the unique evolutionary pathways traveled. However, the PSC does raise the possibility that any character difference, even a single molecular marker or minor morphological trait unique to a population, could mark it as a unique phylogenetic species, begging the question of where one stops in the quest to differentiate forms. Biologically trivial differences among individuals, such as number of facial hairs in primates or variation in striping patterns in zebras, could designate species differences.

**Figure 3.4** Distribution of the various named subspecies of the racer (*Coluber constrictor*), a common snake of North America. Each of the subspecies would probably be designated a full species under the PSC. (Modified from Conant 1975.)

Under the PSC, some presently endangered species would undoubtedly be split into several. Populations of species not presently endangered because they are widespread and abundant at some localities might attain endangered status as new species, if split under a phylogenetic system. However, single populations or subspecies of vertebrates can already be legally

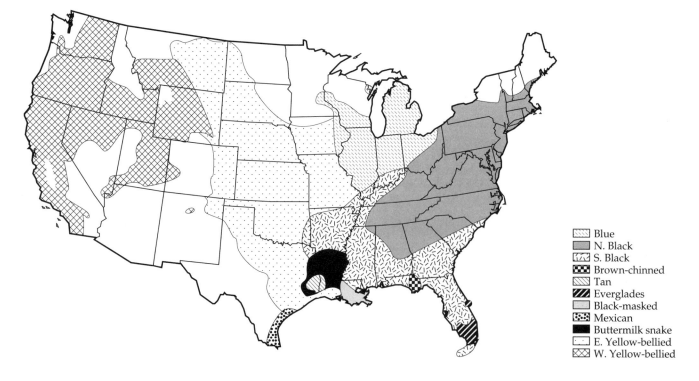

| | |
|---|---|
| ▨ | Blue |
| ▦ | N. Black |
| ▨ | S. Black |
| ▨ | Brown-chinned |
| ▨ | Tan |
| ▨ | Everglades |
| ▨ | Black-masked |
| ▨ | Mexican |
| ■ | Buttermilk snake |
| ▨ | E. Yellow-bellied |
| ▨ | W. Yellow-bellied |

recognized as endangered (U.S. Fish and Wildlife Service 1988) even if the remainder of the species is secure (as in the cases of the southern Bald Eagle, Florida panther, and San Francisco garter snake), so this change would only affect plants and invertebrates.

Although the PSC would result in more species, and perhaps greater recognition of populational diversity (because many populations would be raised to species level), it would not necessarily lead to better conservation of biodiversity. First, a PSC would only change the level of the problem. Instead of being concerned with endangered populations, we would be concerned with those populations newly defined as endangered species. With sorely inadequate funding for existing endangered species (Campbell 1991), a potential severalfold increase in their number created by a new definition could result in a strong political backlash against their legal protection.

Second, from a biological perspective, the present definition of endangered species places local species recovery efforts within the context of other populations and the species at large; there are strong linkages among populations involved in recovery. If each of those present populations became endangered "species," they could be treated in isolation as distinct entities (Figure 3.5). This by itself might increase the chances of local extinction and loss of diversity (Chapters 6–10).

On the other hand, in order to protect a population of an endangered species in practice, one must essentially prove that loss of that population would jeopardize survival of the species at large. Listing of smaller units, as per the PSC approach, would expedite protection of these populations. Obviously, with respect to conservation actions, there is no species definition that emerges as overtly superior.

## Conserve Diversity, Not Latin Binomials

Regardless of the species concept used in conservation, there is need for greater emphasis on the protection of variation within the species category. The critical evolutionary and ecological functional unit is not necessarily the species, but the population. As Williams (1966) stated, the species is "a key taxonomic and evolutionary concept but has no special significance for the study of adaptation. It is not an adapted unit and there are no mechanisms that function for the survival of the species." The local population is where responses to environmental challenges occur, where adaptations arise and where genetic diversity is maintained and reshuffled each generation.

From a conservation perspective, the species category can provide a false sense of security. A wide-ranging taxon may consist of many genetically isolated or semi-isolated populations that play different functional roles in different systems. However, the species concept implies that all conspecific populations, by being the same entity, play the same adaptive roles in all environments. This is not always the case. For example, some plant populations have evolved different levels of metal tolerance in different habitats (Antonovics et al. 1971), and could not easily be interchanged. Guppies (*Poecilia reticulata*) in Trinidad streams have very different genetically based color patterns, clutch sizes, and offspring sizes depending on whether they occur in streams with or without predaceous fishes (Reznick and Bryga 1987; Reznick et al. 1990). Some plant species have markedly different genetically based growth forms in low- and high-elevation ecosystems (Clausen et al. 1940). Such genetically based **plasticity** in life history characters is probably a pervasive feature of most organisms (Figure 3.6) but is underappreciated and virtually unexplored in the conservation realm.

Another problem is that the ecological function of each population may

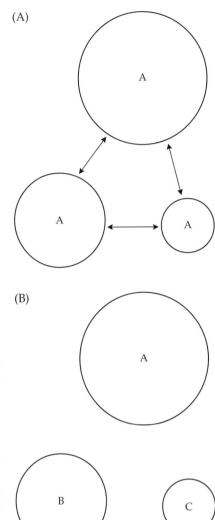

(A)

(B)

**Figure 3.5** Schematic diagram of relationships among endangered entities under two species definitions. (A) The present approach, using the biological species concept. The arrows represent the connection and potential genetic exchange among endangered populations of species A. (B) A modified approach, using the phylogenetic species concept. The three "populations" are now considered species (A, B, C) and are managed in isolation, with no genetic exchange.

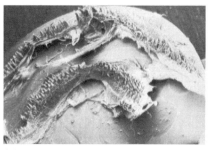

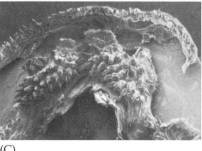

(A)

(B)

(C)

**Figure 3.6** Phenotypic plasticity in *Ambystoma tigrinum*, the tiger salamander. (A) The individual on top is a normal form, that on the bottom is a cannibalistic form (note the broader head) induced by a dense larval environment. The electron micrographs show teeth of the normal (B) and cannibalistic (C) form. (Photographs courtesy of James P. Collins.)

be independent of other populations of the species, but this is not recognized when they are all lumped together under one name. If a population of a bee is lost from a river basin due to pesticides, for example, it does no good to the flowers depending on that bee for pollination that the "species" still exists elsewhere. The bee was performing a particular role in that particular system and is no longer there; unless recolonization from elsewhere can occur, this population extinction is as important functionally to that local system as if the entire species were destroyed. *Population persistence within each local system is more important than simple overall species persistence.*

A species approach to conservation also results in an overly optimistic assessment of retention of biodiversity. A species can continue to exist even if many of its populations are destroyed. Those lost populations represent a decline in biodiversity if they contained unique genetic or phenotypic traits, but the species approach tells us that diversity has not been lost because our species count remains unchanged. (Note that the PSC approach to defining species would reduce or eliminate this problem). In fact, we have been losing much more global biodiversity, in the form of populations, than heretofore recognized (Figure 3.7), and the biodiversity problem is far worse than species-level loss would indicate.

A case in point is loss of crop genetic diversity throughout the world (discussed in Chapter 6). Many of the original, wild, localized races of domesticated grains or vegetable crops are extinct or exist tenuously in remote areas of the world. The genetic diversity contained in those populations could prove valuable to our modern crops by providing the genetic basis for disease resistance or other traits relevant to agricultural production. In these cases, the species are by no means endangered, but biodiversity in the form of select individual populations has been and is being lost.

Losses of countless populations of even common species have eroded population diversity and variation, and have eliminated the diverse roles played by those populations. This was addressed by Ehrlich (1986) who said ". . . *species* extinction is only one part of the problem. At least in the temperate zones, it is the smaller part. There the disappearance of parts of species—subspecies, ecotypes, and genetically distinct populations—is much more threatening to the functioning of ecosystems. Numbers of such infraspecific units worldwide are even more difficult to estimate than those of species, but almost certainly there are billions."

### Is the Species Category Useful to Conservation?

The answer to this question is an emphatic yes and no. The species category *is* useful in that it identifies entities for legal attention and assessment of the problem. We can count species (although we have thus far done a terrible job; see Essay 4B) and determine how individual species are doing over time. There is also public support for species; most people can identify better with the loss of a species than with the loss of a population or erosion of genetic diversity.

On the other hand, the species, as discussed above, is a conventional breakpoint on a larger biological continuum. The species contains a great deal of hidden diversity in the form of local adaptations and genetic information (discussed in Chapter 6). A species focus by itself also does not directly address the larger problem of habitat and ecosystem loss, which is the real driving force in extinction (although one part of the U.S. Endangered Species Act does recognize critical habitat). A piecemeal, species-driven approach to conservation draws attention to only one part of the biodiversity crisis; a more comprehensive perspective must also be taken.

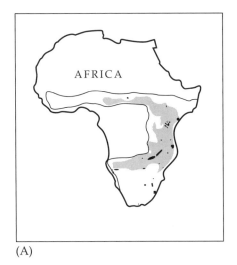

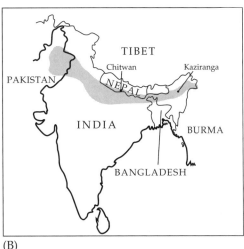

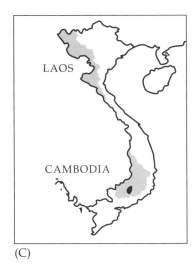

(A)  (B)  (C)

**Figure 3.7** Present and former distributions of three species of rhinoceros, showing loss of populational diversity and retreat to a few refuges. (A) The black rhinoceros (*Diceros bicornis*), showing historical distribution (black outline), distribution in 1900 (shaded area), and distribution in 1987 (black areas). (B) The greater one-horned rhinoceros (*Rhinoceros unicornis*), formerly distributed across the shaded area, is now reduced to two populations at Chitwan and Kaziranga reserves. (C) The Javan rhinoceros (*Rhinoceros sondaicus*), showing historical (shaded) and present (black) distributions. (A, from Ashley et al. 1990; B, from Dinerstein and McCracken, 1990; C, from Santiapillai 1992.)

## Taxonomic Problems in Conservation

One improvement that can be made irrespective of species concept is better taxonomy and greater recognition of the role of systematics and phylogenetic relationships in conservation (Wilson 1985; see Essay 3B by Melanie Stiassny). In particular, the broadest possible data set should always be employed in the designation of species. The recent availability of information from molecular genetics is a case in point. Because the speciation process is ultimately a genetic divergence between populations through time (or conversely, genetic cohesion within a group), consideration of genetic data along with other data sets such as morphology, behavior, and distribution seems warranted when determining species boundaries. The molecular genetic constitution of biota may sometimes be more conservative and may more accurately reflect true evolutionary relationships, including divergence. We encourage inclusion of such data in taxonomic aspects of conservation.

Furthermore, morphology by itself can mislead due to sexual dimorphism, phenotypic plasticity, or intense selection on particular characters (Avise 1989). In some cases, biologists have described two species only to later find that they were males and females, or different color or shape morphs, of the same species. In other cases, especially in insects, morphologically similar or indistinguishable individuals have been shown genetically to be different species (Dobzhansky 1970); these are **cryptic** or **sibling species.** The mosquito vector of yellow fever, *Aedes aegypti*, is part of such a complex of sibling species. Its affinity for visiting buildings made it an important disease vector, but control programs were ineffective as long as it was not separated from species that had very different foraging behaviors. Once those species differences were recognized, and the behavioral differences realized, control was possible.

Ignorance of genetic relationships, and taxonomic difficulties in general, can hinder conservation efforts. For example, the tuatara (Figure 3.8) is a large, lizard-like animal that is the only surviving representative of an entire order (Rhynchocephalia) of reptiles, and occurs only on islands off the coast of New

(A)

(B)

**Figure 3.8** Two species of tuatara, both adult males. (A) *Sphenodon punctatus* from Stephens Island, New Zealand. (B) *Sphenodon guentheri* from North Brother Island, New Zealand. (Photographs courtesy of Allison Cree.)

Zealand. Three species were named in the 19th century, one of which is now extinct. One of the remaining species, *Sphenodon guentheri,* was ignored by protective legislation dating back to 1895 because it was morphologically similar to *S. punctatus,* the most abundant species; *S. guentheri* was subsequently reduced to subspecies status. Consequently, *S. guentheri* was not considered unique and most populations were lost; it now occurs only on one island. Recent genetic data indicate that *S. guentheri* is a distinct species, and highly divergent genetically from other populations (Daugherty et al. 1990). Unfortunately, this information comes too late for special efforts to protect any but that single remaining population. However, genetic techniques can help in clarification of taxonomic difficulties in many other taxa and thereby aid in the identification of critical genetic groupings to guide conservation efforts.

## ESSAY 3B
## Systematics and Conservation

Melanie L. J. Stiassny, American Museum of Natural History

There is a growing recognition of the vital role that museums and museum-based taxonomic research must play in the biodiversity crisis. Clearly, we need to know what is out there, where it is, how much there is of it, and how endangered it is. Without this very basic information no inventories of threatened areas, endangered species lists, or programs for rational planning are possible. Taxonomic and biogeographic analysis, two major components of systematic biology, also clearly are fundamental elements of conservation biology. However, there is another aspect to

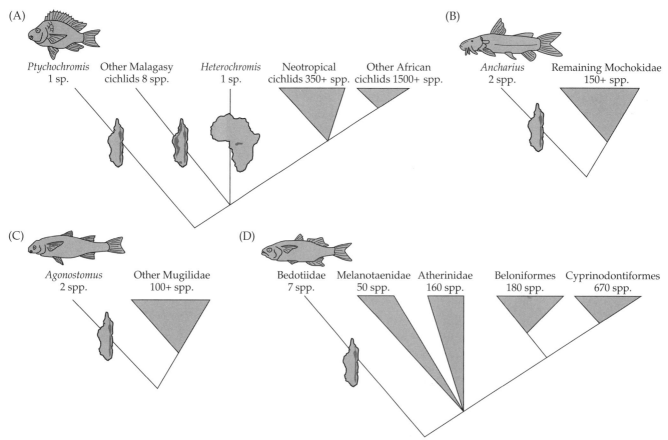

**Figure A**   Phylogenetic relationships of (A) the Cichlidae, (B) the Mochokidae, (C) the Mugilidae, and (D) the Atherinomorpha. Insets indicate geographic distributions of basal taxa restricted to the eastern coastal forests of Madagascar. (Modified from Stiassny and De-Pinna, in press.)

systematic biology that has yet to be fully integrated into conservation biology: phylogenetic analysis.

Phylogenetic analysis is essentially concerned with the reconstruction of evolutionary history. By interpreting the distribution of the intrinsic properties of organisms (characters), the composition and interrelationships of lineages are determined and depicted in the form of branching diagrams. Phylogenetic trees portray the genealogical relationships and sequence of historical events uniting taxa, and form the baseline for virtually all comparative evolutionary studies. The potential role of phylogenetics in conservation biology has only begun to be addressed.

Recently a number of different indices encoding notions such as "phylogenetic uniqueness," "higher taxon richness," "taxonomic dispersion," "taxonomic distinctiveness," and "phylogenetic diversity" have been developed to incorporate phylogenetic information into the evaluation of conservation priorities (May 1990; Vane-Wright 1991; Williams et al. 1991, in press; Nixon and Wheeler 1992; Faith 1992; Crozier 1992). The advantage of these measures over simple comparative estimates of species numbers (species richness) is that they incorporate information about genealogical relationships and weighted measures of the phylogenetic uniqueness of the taxa involved. When viewed from this perspective it is clear that not all species contain equivalent information, and there may be strong phylogenetic arguments for conservation prioritization of some taxa over others.

With a well-resolved phylogenetic tree for a group of organisms, many different measures pertinent to conservation issues can be derived. But sadly, for most groups, we are a long way from having such sound phylogenetic data, and lack the trees necessary for analysis. Practically speaking, for some groups this lack of phylogenetic resolution poses little problem; most biologists would agree with a high priority being given to saving, for example, *Sphenodon* (the tuatara), the last surviving member and sister group of the entire Lepidosauria (some 5800 species of worm lizards, snakes, and lizards), or *Latimeria chalumnae* (the coelacanth), a sister group to more than 21,450 species, including all of the tetrapods. The loss of these taxa would be particularly poignant as it would represent the loss of the last living vestige of their lineage. Clearly, if there were hundreds of extant

species of *Sphenodon* the issue would be more complex; it is the marked asymmetry in species numbers between sister groups that emerges as a key factor.

A review of current taxonomic literature indicates that many groups exhibit such high-level phylogenetic asymmetry; that is, the basal sister taxon to a diverse and species-rich group has contrastingly low species numbers. Frequently, these basal groups also have extremely restricted geographic distributions, and these two features render them particularly vulnerable to environmental pressures. Numerous examples of this asymmetry occur among teleost fishes. And in freshwater groups, a heterogeneous assemblage representing more than 25% of all extant vertebrates, the association of low species numbers and restricted geographic distribution in basal groups is particularly striking. Phylogenetic data can be used to strengthen arguments for

broad regional conservation plans; for example, the eastern coastal forest of Madagascar is recognized as an area harboring a concentration of basal taxa of considerable phylogenetic importance (Figure A). This particular proposal is similar to highlighting an area of extreme species endemism as a priority conservation region but this need not always be the case (Stiassny 1992).

Basal taxa have importance by virtue of the unique comparative information they contain, which is in a sense complementary to that of the entire membership of their more species-rich sister groups. Perhaps even more important, they are of critical significance when, as is frequently the case, the precise intrarelationships of their sister group are unknown. By virtue of their position, the phylogenetic relevance of basal groups can be appreciated at three levels: (1) character state changes in these taxa can influence hypotheses of

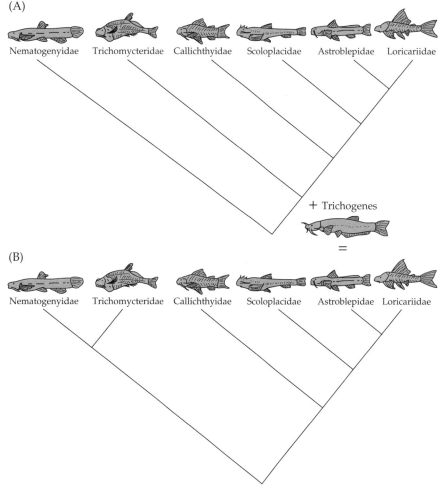

**Figure B** (A) Traditional view of loricarioid relationships. (B) The single most parsimonious scheme after character distributions in *Trichogenes* are introduced into the matrix. (Modified from Stiassny and DePinna, in press.)

relationships among the remaining members of their lineage, regardless of the states observed in more distant outgroups and in more phylogenetically derived taxa; (2) in certain instances knowledge of character states in these basal groups can introduce character conflicts that lead to the proposal of a particular phylogenetic hypothesis; (3) they can sometimes provide the only possible evidence for understanding the evolution of certain character transitions.

A study by Stiassny and DePinna (in press) shows that inclusion of a single species, *Trichogenes longipinnis* (the basal member of the Trichomycteridae, restricted to a small creek between Rio de Janeiro and São Paulo, and escaping discovery until the early 1980s) in an analysis of relationships among loricarioid catfishes results in a major shift of phylogenetic hypotheses for that large group (Figure B). Not only does the discovery of *T. longipinnis* allow correct resolution of the relationships of a group of well over 1000 species, it enables us to understand the evolution of certain osteological characters within that group. While few conservationists are going to be overly concerned about understanding the evolution of obscure fish bones, what is true for such bones is also true for our understanding of other biological features. The inclusion of *Trichogenes*, a single basal taxon, has a major impact on our understanding of character evolution, and these characters can in turn be of profound importance to the ecology or functional biology of the whole group. Clearly, the loss of this species is not commensurate with the loss of "just another" of the numerous other loricarioid species, and it is phylogenetic analysis that indicates why this is the case.

In the face of a profound crisis of biodiversity, biologists are confronted with the onerous task of allocating conservation priorities. If there were some absolute biological criterion by which to judge the relative value of a given species or community against another, perhaps the problem would not seem so acute, but no such criterion exists. In an ideal world we could argue for saving everything, but our world is far from ideal. The rachet of extinction clicks faster each day, and our resources seem to diminish in inverse proportion. The potential role of phylogenetic analysis in helping to define and elaborate our understanding of biodiversity and its conservation is only just beginning to be explored, but already promises to be of considerable importance.

## Species and the Law: The ESA and CITES

We indicated earlier that biological and legal definitions or concepts of species do not necessarily coincide perfectly, and that legal definitions really are more critical because they form the basis for species protection and recovery actions. The United States Endangered Species Act (ESA) and the Convention on International Trade in Endangered Species (CITES) are major global biodiversity protection statutes that focus primarily on the species category.

The Endangered Species Act, Public Law 93-205, became effective on December 28, 1973, and is "the most far-reaching wildlife statute ever adopted by any nation" (Reffalt 1991). The stated purpose of the ESA is to "provide a means whereby the ecosystems upon which endangered species and threatened species depend may be conserved, [and] to provide a program for the conservation of such endangered species and threatened species" (USFWS 1988). The ESA is thus ecosystem oriented, but the particular ecosystems protected are determined by which species are deemed to be in danger of extinction. That, in turn, depends in part on how "species" is legally defined.

According to the ESA, "species" is defined to include "any *subspecies* of fish or wildlife or plants, and any *distinct population segment* of any species of vertebrate fish or wildlife which interbreeds when mature" (USFWS 1988; emphases added). In this definition, subspecies of any endangered biota receive legal recognition, as do "distinct populations" of vertebrates. This immediately raises the question of what constitutes "distinctness," a critical aspect of the definition that could offer special protection to unique entities; the difficulties of an objective definition of that term will be addressed in Chapter 6.

The ESA definition thus offers protection to endangered and threatened species, and recognizes some degree of within-species diversity in the form of subspecies and selected distinct populations. A species is deemed to be **endangered** if it is in imminent danger of extinction throughout all or a significant portion of its range. A **threatened** species is one that is likely to become endangered in the foreseeable future. Both of these terms recognize that the species is the functional unit of concern, and that extinction is the threat to be avoided.

Although there is no specific reference to genetic diversity, the historical

(A)

(B)

(C)

(D)

**Figure 3.9** The U.S. Endangered Species Act has had many clear success stories in species that are recovering or are stable thanks to its legal and habitat protection. Examples include (A) the American alligator (*Alligator mississippiensis*), (B) the Bald Eagle (*Haliaeetus leucocephalus*), (C) the relict trillium (*Trillium reliquum*), and (D) the Wood Stork (*Mycteria americana*). (A, B, and D, courtesy of David Scott; C, courtesy of Trip Lamb.)

development of the ESA indicates that genetics was in fact a motivation in species protection (Waples 1991). House Resolution 37, a forerunner of the ESA, stated that ". . . it is in the best interests of mankind to minimize the losses of genetic variations. The reason is simple: they are potential resources. They are keys to puzzles which we cannot yet solve, and may provide answers to questions we have not yet learned to ask" (H.R. Rept. 412, 93rd Congress, 1st sess., 1973). However, this astute observation is not overtly reflected in the actual legal statutes.

Is the ESA working as an effective piece of legislation that protects biological diversity at the species level? Most certainly it has been effective within the scope of its intentions to conserve species. There have been some clear successes for the ESA (Figure 3.9): the American alligator has recovered to the point of no longer being on the list, the Bald Eagle is increasing in numbers, and Whooping Cranes and black-footed ferrets remain with us in part because of efforts legislated by the ESA (U.S. Department of the Interior 1990). Even among those species not recovering, it is likely that many would have been lost were it not for legal protection and implementation of recovery efforts.

However, we must also ask whether the broader category of biodiversity has been well served by legislation centered on species. Species protection carries with it a degree of legislated habitat protection. Indeed, within the language of the ESA, destroying the habitat of an endangered species is legally equivalent to destroying the species itself. The ESA includes provisions to conserve "the ecosystems upon which endangered species and threatened species depend" by designating and listing **critical habitat** when a species is listed. Critical habitat is defined as specific areas within the species' range with physical or biological features either (1) essential to conservation of the species, or (2) which may require special management considerations or protection (USFWS 1988). "Habitat" varies according to species, and could range from small patches of grassland, set in a matrix of housing developments, for endangered butterflies, to entire and uninterrupted watersheds for grizzly bears. However, there is no systematic ecosystem-level protection by the ESA, nor does critical habitat refer to more than localized, short-term survival requirements.

At the other end of the diversity spectrum, within-species diversity may be protected by subspecific designations, or by determination of particularly critical individual populations. However, this depends on good taxonomy and recognition of distinct clusters of variation within the species category. For invertebrates and plants, individual populations are not recognizable for protection, so a subspecific designation must have been made in order to protect within-species diversity. Such a designation depends on the particular characters selected by individual taxonomists, and whether they were "lumpers" or "splitters." Where one taxonomist (a splitter) may assign many subspecific designations to a species, another (a lumper) may be inclined to group geographic variation into a smaller number of subspecies based on stricter criteria. Within-species legal protection by the ESA may then come down to the choice of the particular taxonomist (Murphy 1991).

One of the criticisms leveled against the ESA by its opponents is that too much protection has been offered in recent years to subspecies and populations, causing undue economic strain. Calls have been made for revision of the ESA to make only full species subject to protection. This was highlighted by the former U.S. Secretary of the Interior, Manuel Lujan, Jr., in reference to the endangered Mount Graham red squirrel (*Tamiasciurus hudsonicus grahamensis*) of Arizona, when he stated, "Nobody's told me the difference between a red squirrel, a black one or a brown one. Do we have to save every subspecies?" (Sward 1990). In addition to demonstrating a profound ignorance of biodiversity and evolutionary processes by the highest conservation officer in the land, the statement reflects a general public perception that subspecies and populations are not very important and interfere with economic progress. However, a survey of all 492 listings or proposed listings of plants and animals from 1985 to 1991 (Wilcove et al. 1993) indicates that 80% were full species, 18% were subspecies, and only 2% were distinct populations. Obviously, species-level taxonomy is still driving endangered species legislation.

The international legislation, CITES, also focuses on species as the category of concern, with even less attention paid to within-species diversity. The goal of CITES is "to regulate the complex wildlife trade by controlling species-specific trade levels on the basis of biological criteria" (Trexler and Kosloff 1991). It includes all species "threatened with extinction which are or may be affected by trade" (CITES, Appendix I). Again, species and extinction are the criteria of concern, but subspecies and geographic criteria are not specifically mentioned. Rather, the statute is based on endangered species lists and laws developed in individual countries. Thus, a particular species may be legally captured and traded from one country, but not another. For example, leopards (*Felis pardus*) may legally be taken from Somalia, but not from Kenya.

The disparities between biological and legal aspects of species protection that frequently arise are further discussed in Essay 3C by Stephen O'Brien on the hybrid policy of the U.S Fish and Wildlife Service. Lawyer Daniel Rohlf provides yet another perspective on legal aspects of biodiversity protection in Essay 3D.

## ESSAY 3C
# When Endangered Species Hybridize
## The U.S. Hybrid Policy

Stephen J. O'Brien, National Institutes of Health

Taxonomy, the systematic classification of plants and animals, had little relevance beyond academic institutions before the mid-1970s. Species were grouped according to morphological types into genera, genera into families, families into orders, and so on. Systematic uncertainties had little relevance to everyday life, and taxonomic resolution was limited. When taxonomic distinctions became the basis for legal protection afforded by the Endangered Species Act of 1973, this innocence was lost forever. Disagreements over taxonomic status fueled legal assaults on the Act, and misclassifications led to inappropriate conservation measures resulting in losses of some species. Even today, with vastly improved molecular methods for discriminating taxonomic groups, there remains considerable confusion about the units of conservation that the Endangered Species Act was designed to protect.

A recent example of the turbulence caused by taxonomic blurs involves the so-called "hybrid policy" of the U.S. Fish and Wildlife Service (USFWS). Originally formulated as a series of official memoranda from the Office of the Solicitor (legal counsel of the USFWS) in the early 1980s, this policy led to assaults on species protection by special interest groups seeking to evade the Endangered Species Act. With the advantage of 20/20 hindsight, our chronicle provides a fascinating glimpse of how the best of policymakers' intentions fell short and left open the door for legal challenge as well as nearly causing the suppression of important biological information collected to benefit endangered species.

To understand the chronology, we need to look back to the mid-19th century, when Charles Darwin first taught us about his remarkable theory of natural selection. *On the Origin of Species* is filled with discussions of distinct species and recognizable divisions below the species level; Darwin called them races, we usually call them subspecies. Darwin wrote an entire chapter on "hybridism" in which he pointed out that most species, when crossed, produced sterile hybrids. This observation, plus a rich experience in studying

natural history, prompted the noted ornithologist Ernst Mayr to formulate the biological species concept (BSC), based on reproductive isolation, in 1942.

The BSC replaced the "typological species" concept of Linnaeus and Lyell, which defined a species as a class of organisms that differed from other species by constant diagnostic characters, primarily morphological. Mayr argued that the BSC has the advantage of being less subjective because organisms themselves achieve (or failed to achieve) isolation, while the typological concept required an arbitrary selection of phenotypic characters by the taxonomist. The typological species concept would fail particularly in recognizing "sibling species," groups of reproductively isolated but morphologically indistinguishable species that occur in nature.

The whole issue of species concepts comes into sharp focus when one looks at the charge of the U.S. Endangered Species Act. The law extends legal protection to three categories of taxa: species, subspecies, and certain vertebrate populations. (As of this writing there are over 600 U.S. species and over 500 foreign species listed as endangered; some 3500 candidates await classification!) The USFWS loosely defined "species," I suspect, to accommodate anticipated taxonomic uncertainty about the status of certain groups and to avoid being constrained by a tight academic definition, and seemed to embrace the BSC because of its mention of "species that interbreed in nature." This did make sense, until the issue of hybrids appeared. What should be the status of the offspring of an endangered species and a nonlisted species? A series of tortuous internal memoranda from the Office of the Solicitor (the legal arm of the USFWS) over the next few years, dealing with the hybridization of Dusky Seaside Sparrows, southern Selkirk Mountain caribou, sea otters, and other species, ruled with the force of legal precedent that hybrids between listed "species" did not merit protection. These opinions gradually evolved into an adopted hybrid "policy" that precluded hybrids from habitat protection, from hunting protection, and from federal expenditures on their behalf.

Again this seemed sensible because interspecies hybrids would conceivably compete with "pure" species for habitat and natural resources.

The trouble with this logic began to surface when the tools of molecular genetics were applied to endangered taxa. Studies of molecular population genetics uncovered strong evidence that certain endangered groups were composed of different genetic stocks, revealing that they were descended from recently admixed ancestors. A tiny relict population of Florida panthers, an endangered puma subspecies, was shown to be a mix of historic panthers and recent immigrants from a captive stock derived from Florida and a South American puma subspecies. Wolves in certain populations carry genetic material from coyotes, proving that under certain natural conditions wolves and coyotes will interbreed. A genetic analysis of the endangered red wolf (the group went extinct in the wild in the 1970s), revealed mitochondrial DNA genotypes indistinguishable from coyote or gray wolf genotypes. Since there was no unique "red wolf" genotype, results suggested that red wolves might simply be genetic mixes of wolves and coyotes. Strictly interpreted, the molecular data from each of these taxa would imperil continued protection if the "hybrid policy" was invoked. Those of us who had collected the genetic data were in an untenable position: publish the results and reveal a legal loophole for adversaries of endangered species protection, or suppress the data outright.

Faced with this dilemma, I asked Professor Mayr to work with me to address the hybrid issue in the context of the BSC, since it was this species concept upon which these opinions and precedents were originally based. Our conclusions and recommendations for revising the USFWS position on hybrids appeared as an editorial in *Science* (March 1991). Here is what we said.

First, the ESA definition of "species" designated for protection listed three entities: species, subspecies, and populations. The consequences of hybridization or gene flow between each were different and they should be treated differently. If we were to adhere to the BSC (which we prefer over alternative species concepts even though we recognize its limitations), then we note that species will occasionally hybridize in nature and can be hybridized in captivity without being a threat to the overall species integrity. The BSC acknowledges natural occurrence of hybrid individuals or even hybrid zones (for which there are now over 100 described examples), but recognizes these genetic exchanges as dead ends that do not disintegrate the genetic integrity of the species. This means that occasional hybridizations between species are natural (almost common) events, do not threaten species integrity, and should not imperil species protection.

The subspecies category is a different story. Mayr originally defined a subspecies as "a geographically defined aggregate of local populations which differs taxonomically from other subdivisions of the species." Members of a subspecies share a unique geographic range, a group of phylogenetically concordant phenotypic characters, and a unique natural history relative to other subdivisions of the species. Because they are below the species level, different subspecies are reproductively compatible.

There are four possible fates for a subspecies. A subspecies could: (1) evolve over time into a "proper" species, a scenario Darwin suggested by calling races "incipient species"; (2) go extinct; (3) change gradually to become one or more new subspecies; and (4) physically connect with another subspecies, undergo gene flow, and produce a new mixed subspecies. The last possibility is as natural as the other three because subspecies are by definition not yet reproductively isolated species; yet, the USFWS hybrid policy strictly interpreted continued production of "hybrids" as threatening to species integrity.

If subspecies are below the species level, can we argue that they are worth saving? We believe so, for the following reasons. First, all subspecies have the potential to become new species, and it is that potential we need to conserve. Second, subspecies in an isolated geographic locale gradually accumulate adaptive genetic variation in response to natural selection. These are compelling reasons for affording hybrids protection.

In December 1990, just after our essay was accepted for publication, the USFWS withdrew the hybrid policy permanently. To date, there is no replacement, although the agency has decided it will revisit the issue, this time with more input from the conservation and scientific communities. The lesson here is that as technology develops, so also should our conservation policies, with a constant focus on protection of threatened taxa. Historic precedence may be the gold standard of jurisprudence, but it can fail as new scientific data become available. Most scientists, conservationists and government officials share the common goal of species preservation, but taxonomic uncertainties and uncritical adherence to precedent can thwart these important concerns.

### How Will Environmental Degradation Affect Speciation?

Speciation is a term for various processes by which new species form. The BSC would contend that speciation consists of development of reproductive (and thus genetic) isolation among populations, which subsequently results in independent evolutionary pathways. The PSC or ESC would argue that speciation consists of cohesion of distinct evolutionary lines, independent of other lines. Regardless of the species concept used, the processes by which speciation occurs may vary among taxa and ecological situations. These processes are most easily discussed in context of the BSC.

Several models of geographic modes of speciation have been offered. The most widely accepted model is **gradual allopatric speciation** (Figure 3.10A), in which a population is geographically split by a physical barrier (e.g., a mountain range, a river, a lava flow) and the resultant subpopulations diverge genetically or morphologically to the extent that reproduction between them would be impossible if they were reunited (Mayr 1942). Actual reproductive isolation may develop through a variety of isolation mechanisms (Table 3.1). It should be emphasized that reproductive isolation does not cause, but is a result of, divergence.

For populations that diverged because they were isolated completely, there would not be specific selection to reinforce traits that prevent interbreeding. Species formed **allopatrically** become reproductively isolated only as a byproduct of the accumulated differences in their respective genomes and phenotypes. As we said earlier, populations that have been isolated for relatively short periods of time and have therefore diverged only slightly are sometimes called incipient species; they have not gone very far down the path to speciation. When these partially differentiated populations come into secondary contact, they may interbreed in the contact zone, and if their offspring on the average have no reproductive disadvantage compared with either parent (are not selected against), much of the distinctness of the populations may be lost through gene exchange. Sometimes such hybrid populations in contact zones

**Table 3.1**
Reproductive Isolation Mechanisms Considered in the
Biological Species Concept

**A. Premating isolation mechanisms**

1. Seasonal and habitat isolation (potential mates do not meet)
2. Behavioral isolation (potential mates meet but do not mate because of behavioral differences)
3. Mechanical isolation (copulation is attempted but transfer of sperm is unsuccessful)

**B. Postmating isolation mechanisms**

1. Gametic mortality (sperm transfer occurs but ovum is not fertilized)
2. Zygote mortality (ovum is fertilized but zygote dies)
3. Hybrid inviability (zygote produces an $F_1$ hybrid of reduced viability)
4. Hybrid sterility ($F_1$ hybrid is fully viable but partially or completely sterile or produces deficient $F_2$)

From Mayr 1963.

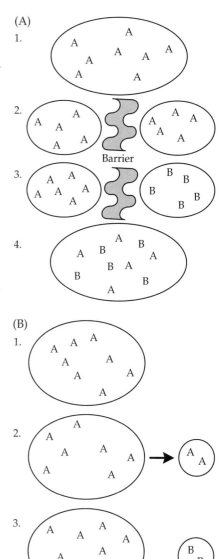

**Figure 3.10** (A) Allopatric model of speciation. 1. The original species (A) covers a contiguous range. 2. Upon establishment of a barrier within the range, the species now consists of two isolated populations. 3. One population (now B) diverges in some characteristic(s) that prevent interbreeding of the two forms. Both populations also could have diverged. 4. If the barrier disappears, the two populations (now species) may again be sympatric but will not interbreed. (B) The founder or quantum model of speciation. 1. The original species in its contiguous range. 2. Some founders form a new colony, isolated from the original range. 3. The colony (now B) diverges in some character(s) and is reproductively isolated from the parent colony.

can be stable over long periods. Hybrids between two species of the neotropical butterfly *Heliconius,* for example, are thought to have persisted in a narrow contact zone for at least 2000 generations (Turner 1971).

However, when the isolated species have diverged so much that hybrids are inferior to either parent, then natural selection may result in the evolution of traits that reinforce the reproductive isolation of the species. In the absence of other events, these species will continue to evolve separateness, close their gene pools, and eventually be distinguishable as species.

A variant of the gradual allopatric model is the **founder model** (Mayr 1963), also called **quantum speciation** because it occurs so quickly. In this model (Figure 3.10B), a small and isolated population—perhaps only a few colonists on an island, for example—undergoes rapid and massive genetic change due to random **genetic drift** or homogeneous selective pressures on a small gene pool, resulting in a substantial, rapid genetic change. Because of the small population size, speciation may be quite rapid.

Other speciation models abound (see Otte and Endler 1989), but it is not critical that we explore them all here. Suffice it to say that speciation is a creative part of biodiversity, and is a dynamic process that may be at work subtly at all times. How might global environmental changes affect speciation processes?

We envision two different scenarios of speciation in light of environmental change. Both are a result of extensive habitat fragmentation, a common process and one that will undoubtedly continue in the foreseeable future (discussed in Chapter 9). The first scenario is that habitat fragmentation, by increasingly isolating small populations, will offer greater opportunities for local speciation events, according to the quantum speciation model. Recurrent isolation of small populations in small habitats could result in local genetic change, leading to reproductive isolation and rapid speciation events (Figure 3.11).

The second, and much more likely, scenario involves the same physical setting but a different outcome. Increased habitat fragmentation, although setting the stage for potential speciation, also sets the stage for rapid local extinctions. Extinction probabilities increase greatly in small populations (Chapters 5, 6, 7, and 9), and extinction often occurs in a matter of years or

**Figure 3.11**    Two scenarios of future speciation patterns based on habitat fragmentation. In both scenarios, a formerly contiguous species (A) is split into many small populations in fragmented habitats. In scenario 1, quantum speciation occurs in these habitat fragments, resulting in several new species (B–E). In scenario 2, local extinction occurs more quickly than speciation, and no new species evolve, but several populations go extinct.

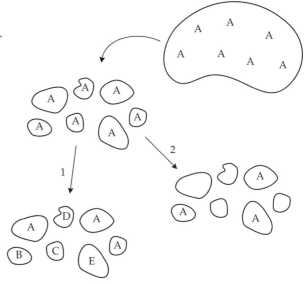

decades. Since speciation typically takes orders of magnitude longer, it is more likely that fragmentation into small populations will favor local extinction rather than local speciation (Figure 3.11). Additionally, the sheer magnitude of loss of biological materials and habitats should also decrease opportunities for speciation. Thus, we speculate that environmental degradation will reduce speciation events, increase extinction events, and result in impoverished biodiversity at the species level.

## ESSAY 3D
# Law and Protection of Biodiversity

Daniel J. Rohlf, *Lewis and Clark College*

The dictionary defines "law" as both a rule of human conduct and a principle stating something that always works in the same way under the same conditions, such as a "law of nature." The fundamental insights of Muir and Leopold essentially merged these definitions; they argued that instead of acting as if we are above the dictates of the natural world, humans should see themselves as fellow members of the earth's biotic community. But moving legal systems toward this ideal requires far more than simply adding an endangered species act to the statute books or signing an international convention on biodiversity. Providing effective legal protections for biodiversity demands a synthesis of social structure, policy, and regulation. Most important from the standpoint of a conservation biologist, the fuel for this process is an understanding of the biotic community and our place in this community.

Our ability to control our own be-

havior, even through law, is as yet quite limited. For example, a vast number of stringent environmental laws and treaties are really paper tigers because governments lack the ability or will to enforce them. More significantly, individuals, communities, and even entire countries often have little choice but to ignore laws and treaties. An immediate worldwide agreement to ban clearing of tropical forests, for example, would in reality do little to alter the behavior of exponentially increasing numbers of landless (and hungry) farmers, or of countries scrambling to service huge foreign debts. In sum, no government or treaty can simply legislate biodiversity protection; we must first structure our society so as to make adherence to such protections possible.

In countries with advanced legal systems and a citizenry whose basic needs are consistently met, the structure and degree of legal protections of biodiversity become policy issues. Legisla-

tive bodies allocate resources and formulate laws dealing with biodiversity according to their perceptions of costs and benefits, as well as their gauge of public sentiments. The U.S. Endangered Species Act, for example, reflects this deliberative process. In the initial section of the Act, Congress recognized that imperiled species have "esthetic, ecological, educational, historical, recreational, and scientific value to the Nation and its people." However, in funding appropriations, American lawmakers consistently relegate the chronically underfunded endangered species program to a level far below items such as military research. This reflects a policy decision by Congress of the relative social importance of biodiversity protection.

Even assuming policy consensus in placing high priority on conserving biodiversity, however, laws aimed at protecting this resource can successfully achieve their goals only if they are biologically sound in both structure and implementation. In other words, even the most stringent legal protections for biodiversity will fail if they are not written and implemented in a manner consistent with how the physical world works. Two opposite examples illustrate this idea. The U.S. Forest Service's regulation supposedly protecting viable populations of all native species within national forests has proven to be relatively ineffective because the regulation's definition of the term "viable population" is so muddled as to be of little practical use in gauging a target level of habitat protection. On the other hand, unlike many harvest management schemes, the Convention for the Conservation of Antarctic Marine Living Resources explicitly protects ecosystem integrity by restricting harvest of Antarctic marine species to a level that managers determine will produce no adverse effects on the target species or on other species dependent on the target species.

Finally, governments occasionally attempt to manipulate law in order to hide controversial policy decisions behind a veil of science. Former president George Bush, for instance, sought to reverse his pledge to safeguard wetland habitats. To avoid the appearance of breaking a political promise, the Bush administration attempted to eliminate protection for wetlands by restrictively defining the areas considered wetlands. Though the Administration framed its proposal in terms of updating the scientific definition of wetlands, the clear aim was to implement a policy that lifted federal protection on vast areas of important habitat.

It is critical for conservation biologists to understand the process of facilitating, structuring, and implementing legal protection for biodiversity because they have the power to substantially influence this process. They gain this power through generating information about biodiversity and its value to society. It is difficult to overstate the value of such information. Without data demonstrating the importance of maintaining biodiversity, social and policy changes necessary to stem its erosion will not occur. Also, increasing understanding of ecosystems and their constituent elements will enable creation of biologically sound regulatory schemes that effectively protect biodiversity. Information also plays a key role in implementing these regulatory schemes. Many laws that affect biodiversity require resource managers to base their decisions on the best scientific information available, virtually guaranteeing researchers that their data will be used in on-the-ground decision making. Finally, biologists can expose policy decisions masquerading as science.

Conservation biologists' principal challenge, therefore, is to direct their research so as to influence the process of creating and implementing effective legal protections for biodiversity. Doing so requires knowledge of the social, policy, and legal dimensions of this process, as well as careful, unbiased scientific research. With the hemorrhage of biodiversity we currently face, conservation biologists cannot content themselves with merely adding to the general body of scientific knowledge; they must provide knowledge that *counts* in decision-making forums. Such focused research is needed on both overarching questions and on site-specific projects: more empirical information on the importance of biodiversity will encourage policy decisions favoring biodiversity protection, just as more information on the biodiversity impacts of a development proposal will improve managers' ability to gauge whether the project is consistent with the public interest and existing legal standards. In providing this information, conservation biologists play a vital role in bringing human laws closer to natural laws.

## If There Are 30 Million Or So Species, Can Conservation Be Based on a Species Approach?

Species will always need to be part of the larger conservation equation. Loss of species diversity is more obvious and quantifiable than, say, loss of genetic or habitat diversity, and the human populace can readily identify with species loss. Even habitat or landscape approaches to conservation ecology (Parts III and IV of this book) depend on understanding species biology. The design of nature reserves, for example (Chapter 10), may rely on knowledge of species-area relationships, life history requirements of particular species, or the minimum number of individuals of a species necessary to avoid major loss of genetic diversity.

The focus on species in conservation has largely centered on vertebrates, especially birds and large mammals. They are visible, dominant parts of our natural environments, and, for better or worse, extract more sympathy from the public than do most plants or insects (Kellert 1984). They can serve as "flagship" or "charismatic" species (Figure 3.12) that draw financial support more easily than do stinging insects or obscure mussels, and by so doing serve to protect habitat and other species under the "umbrella" of their large habitat requirements.

The individual species approach has also had tangible success stories to tell, some of which were mentioned earlier in this chapter. These successful efforts serve to increase support for conservation programs at all levels. However, the single-species approach can also backfire. The snail darter (*Percina tanasi*), because of its endangered species status, held up construc-

(A)

(B)

(C)

(D)

**Figure 3.12** The public often responds positively to "flagship" or "charismatic" endangered species, creating political support for protection of other species and their ecosystems. Typical flagship vertebrates in the United States include (A) the California Condor (*Gymnogyps californianus*), (B) the Florida panther (*Felis concolor*), (C) the black-footed ferret (*Mustela nigripes*), and (D) the grizzly bear (*Ursus horribilis*), shown here eating a potentially endangered species or race of salmon. (A, photograph by Ron Garrison © San Diego Zoo; B, courtesy of Chris Belden; C, Dean Biggins; D, David Scott.)

tion of the Tellico Dam in Tennessee (Figure 3.13), and the ESA received much criticism and scrutiny as a result. The Northern Spotted Owl (*Strix occidentalis caurina*) is perceived as having negative effects on the timber industry in California, Oregon, and Washington because of its protected status and consequent limitations on logging in its old-growth habitat. In cases such as these, the species may be the legal issue, but the larger biological issue is ecosystem protection. That point is often lost in the struggle, and the public *perception* is that obscure and "worthless" species block economic progress.

Because of confrontations between single species and economic interests, the species approach, by itself, remains open to attack. The species may be perceived as an enemy of economic development, and can come to be regarded as trivial in comparison with human interests. The larger issues of habitat protection and erosion of biodiversity tend to be lost in the fray; the true focus in these cases should be the habitat and ecosystem of which the species is but one part, and the ecological and evolutionary processes that result in biological diversity.

Although we argue that species should always be a part of the conservation scene, a species-by-species approach will not make much headway in the bigger picture. Regardless of whether there are 5 million or 30 million or 100 million species on the planet, and regardless of how "species" is defined, a single-species approach can secure only a minuscule fraction of overall biological diversity. Such security assumes that we even know how many species there are, what they are, and where they are, which of course we do not. We *do* know that the major diversity patterns, and the major losses of species diversity are among invertebrates, primarily insects, and primarily in the tropics (Wilson 1987, 1992). Much of this diversity is endemic to small regions and is lost through habitat destruction. Given that we do not know what or where most of these species are, or anything about their natural histories, a species-by-species approach, by itself, is impractical in the bigger picture; it must be combined with habitat and ecosystem protection.

However, a species-oriented conservation agenda would certainly benefit by a more systematic, global approach. Because species are distributed nonrandomly (diversity is concentrated in certain areas), their conservation could follow these patterns. For example, 25% of bird species are found in

5% of the world's land area; protection of 14 of 90 studied localities in Thailand would conserve all hawkmoth species in that country; 16% of the land area of South Africa, if properly selected, would protect 95% of vascular plant species of the region (Georgiadis and Balmford 1992). Such examples indicate that identification and protection of certain relatively small areas can have disproportionate positive effects on conservation efforts. These "hot spots" of diversity are discussed in great detail in Chapter 5.

A large-scale, ecosystem-level approach has also been promoted by any number of conservation ecologists (numerous papers in Hudson 1991), and even by some politicians (Gore 1992; Scheuer 1993). This affords perhaps the best hope for biodiversity conservation at any biological level. For example, former U.S. Representative James Scheuer (1993) stated, "We need to become proactive and holistic in our policies and move toward an integrated, multispecies and ecosystem approach to land use and conservation. The issue isn't endangered species per se but endangered ecosystems. Our goal should become the management of ecosystems for the sustainable use of biological resources and the conservation of biodiversity."

An ecosystem protection act would of course be difficult politically. Just defining ecosystems and their boundaries would be a major task; defining such boundaries is ecologically undesirable because there generally are no boundaries, but boundaries likely would be required legally. Securing the necessary land and changing land use practices to be consistent with ecosystem protection would be another challenge. However, such actions seem inevitable if real protection of biodiversity is to occur. Grumbine (1992) offered four ecosystem management goals to start us on this path:

1. To protect enough habitat for viable populations of all native species in a given region.
2. To manage at regional scales large enough to accommodate natural disturbances (fire, wind, climate change, etc.).
3. To plan over a period of centuries so that species and ecosystems may continue to evolve.
4. To allow for human use and occupancy at levels that do not result in significant ecological degradation.

Protection of large habitats or landscapes, and of connections among them via habitat corridors, holds the most promise for stemming the tide of modern extinctions that began with the spread of industrial humanity. This approach is manifested in the United States in a largely grassroots effort, called the Wildlands Project, whose mission "is to help protect and restore the ecological richness and native biodiversity of North America through the establishment of a connected system of reserves" (Foreman et al. 1992). Setting aside and connecting large tracts of land seems to be the best way to conserve not only species but their ecosystems and the ecological processes they undergo (Noss 1992). Although fraught with difficulties, such an approach may be the best opportunity to stem the tide of species loss and general ecosystem collapse. Such issues will be discussed in greater detail in several chapters that follow.

(A)

(B)

**Figure 3.13** (A) The snail darter (*Percina tanasi*), and (B) Tellico Dam on the Little Tennessee River in Tennessee. This fish was the focal point of a long conflict between enforcement of the U.S. Endangered Species Act and perceived economic progress. The fish's presence blocked the building of the dam until its protection was exempted by the Endangered Species Committee, also known as the "God Squad." (Photographs courtesy of David A. Etnier.)

## Summary

The species is a conceptual, biological, and legal focus in conservation, but the species as a biological unit is not a clear and unambiguous entity because species are part of a larger continuum of biological organization. The so-called species problem (i.e., What is a species?) is underlain by two fundamentally different views of species. The typological view sees species as fixed, unchanging entities, within which variation is unimportant. The populational view understands species as highly variable and changing over time, with no clear boundaries, and is the only accepted perspective today. The major species concepts of today include the biological, phylogenetic, and evolutionary; all have advantages and disadvantages. Regardless of the particular concept used, it is important to remember that species are dynamic, changing entities containing a great deal of populational variation that is relevant to conservation efforts. Biological diversity at all levels, rather than Latin binomials, should be the emphasis of conservation.

The U.S. Endangered Species Act and the Convention on International Trade in Endangered Species are two powerful legislative packages for protection of biological diversity based on species. Although both have been successful, and are critical for continued protection of species and their habitats, they should probably be supplemented by broader approaches that explicitly protect ecosystems. With anywhere between 5 million and 100 million species on the planet, a species-by-species approach will fall short of the biodiversity protection actually needed to prevent expansive extinctions.

## Questions for Discussion

1. The predominant view of the world today among biologists is populational. Is it then realistic to even try to delineate all that variation in terms of species, which tends to be a typological concept?

2. Frequently conflicting information is provided by morphological and genetic data relative to species designations. Should one data set take priority over the other? Can they be reconciled?

3. Programs such as the U.S. Endangered Species Act are chronically underfunded, and much of the limited money goes toward a few high-profile species such as California Condors, grizzly bears, Florida panthers, and other large birds and mammals, while groups such as fishes, amphibians, reptiles, insects, mollusks, and plants, which represent much more diversity, go underfunded or are ignored. Discuss the biological, political, economic, and legal implications of switching funding toward these "low-profile," but diverse, groups.

4. We do not know the number of species on earth to within even an order of magnitude. Programs have been suggested that would develop species inventories, country by country, throughout the world. Discuss some practical problems that would need to be overcome to make headway in this attempt.

5. Referring back to Question 4, are species inventories necessary for good conservation? Do we really need to know all the details to protect diversity? Discuss how having such information would aid the protection process.

6. We indicated that ecosystem-level legal protection might be a good way to protect diversity of species and ecological processes. Discuss some practical problems and difficulties that would need to be overcome before we could realistically expect an "Endangered Ecosystems Act."

## Suggestions for Further Reading

Kohm, K. A. (ed.). 1991. *Balancing on the Brink of Extinction: The Endangered Species Act and Lessons for the Future.* Island Press, Washington, D.C. A collection of papers dealing with various aspects of the U.S. Endangered Species Act, including its history, various perspectives on the Act, legal aspects, and various supplementary approaches to conservation.

Mayr, E. 1976. *Evolution and the Diversity of Life.* Belknap Press of Harvard University Press, Cambridge, MA. A collection of original essays by the person responsible for the biological species concept. Many of these essays deal with speciation, theories of systematics and classification, species concepts, and biogeography.

Otte, D. and J. A. Endler (eds.). 1989. *Speciation and Its Consequences.* Sinauer Associates, Sunderland, MA. Otte and Endler give us an outstanding, contemporary collection of chapters by numerous authors dealing with the complex and controversial topic of biological speciation. Various speciation models and species concepts are presented.

Rohlf, D. J. 1989. *The Endangered Species Act: A Guide to Its Protections and Implementation.* Stanford Environmental Law Society, Stanford, CA. A comprehensive guide to legal aspects of the U.S. Endangered Species Act written by a lawyer but understandable by scientists and laypeople.

Rojas, M. 1992. The species problem and conservation: what are we protecting? *Conserv. Biol.* 6:170–178. Rojas presents a comprehensive discussion of the species problem in conservation, and of differences between typological and evolutionary (populational) approaches to the species in conservation.

# Global Biodiversity I
## Patterns and Processes

*The most wonderful mystery of life may well be the means by which it created so much diversity from so little physical matter. The biosphere, all organisms combined, makes up only about one part in ten billion of the earth's mass. It is sparsely distributed through a kilometer-thick layer of soil, water, and air stretched over a half billion square kilometers of surface.*

E. O. Wilson, 1992

Biodiversity can refer to a broad extent of types and levels of biological variation. Units of biodiversity range from the genetic variability within a species, to the biota of some selected region or the globe, to the number of evolutionary lineages and the degree of distinctness among them. There is no one "correct" level at which to measure and analyze biodiversity because different scientific issues and practical problems find their focus at different levels. These various levels of biodiversity are best understood in a hierarchical fashion, an analysis promoted by Reed Noss in Essay 4A.

## The Levels of Biodiversity

### Genetic Diversity

Genetic variation is the ultimate source of biodiversity at all levels. The number of genes found in organisms ranges over more than three orders of magnitude, although not all of those genes code for products. Even with a small average number of **alleles,** or variant forms, per gene, the possible number of combinations is enormous, much larger than the number of individuals present in the species. This genetic variability is the material upon which the agents of evolution act.

Recent advances in molecular biology provide the tools needed to measure the amount of genetic variability present in living organisms. Measurements of variability within local populations are important for testing theories about the nature of the forces acting on genetic variation that are responsible for evolutionary change. Such knowledge has important practical applications in, for example, designing captive breeding programs for rare species so as to reduce deleterious effects of inbreeding, or determining the best sources of individuals for reestablishing populations in areas from which they have been exterminated. Measurements of the amount of genetic difference among species are important for determining rates of evolution and for establishing phylogenetic relationships among organisms.

## ESSAY 4A
# Hierarchical Indicators for Monitoring Changes in Biodiversity

Reed F. Noss, University of Idaho and Oregon State University

Biodiversity and how to save it is the subject matter of conservation biology. If you have read this far in this book, or even skimmed its pages, two things about biodiversity should be clear: (1) it is complex, and (2) it is always changing. How on earth can a conservation biologist or land manager deal with this mess?

First, we need to make some sense of the complexity of nature. We can dissect the biodiversity concept into meaningful components, and yet retain some idea of how they all fit together, by appealing to hierarchy theory. There are several kinds of hierarchies in nature, including the familiar levels of biological organization (such as genes, populations, species, communities), hierarchies of space and time, and hierarchies of rates. There are also ethical hierarchies; for instance, many people care about the suffering of individual animals but some also care about the loss of species, ecosystems, and biomes. All of these hierarchies are nested; that is, higher levels enclose lower levels and, to a great extent, constrain their behavior. A tree is part of a forest stand, the stand is part of a landscape, the landscape is part of a physiographic region, and so on. If the physiographic region is inundated by a volcanic flow, everything nested within it also goes.

Biodiversity is not just species diversity. A comprehensive approach to biodiversity conservation must address multiple levels of organization and many different spatial and temporal scales. Most definitions of biodiversity recognize its hierarchical structure, with the genetic, population–species, community–ecosystem, and landscape levels considered most often. Each of these levels can be further divided into compositional, structural, and functional components. Composition includes the genetic constitution of populations, the identity and relative abundances of species in a natural community, and the

kinds of habitats and communities distributed across the landscape. Structure includes the sequence of pools and riffles in a stream, downed logs and snags in a forest, and the vertical layering and horizontal patchiness of vegetation. Function includes the climatic, geologic, hydrologic, ecological, and evolutionary processes that generate biodiversity and keep it forever changing.

Change is universal, but some kinds

of change threaten biodiversity. Changes in climate, changes in disturbance regime (such as fire suppression, or conversely, increases in ignitions), introductions of novel chemicals into the environment, and species introductions or deletions are all changes likely to degrade native biodiversity. These kinds of changes happen naturally, but often occur faster and are of greater magnitude with human activity. In order to have

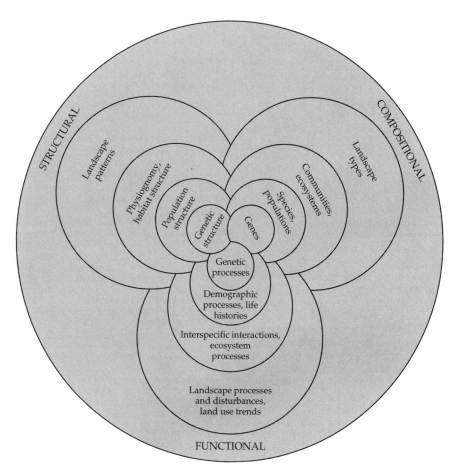

**Figure A**   Compositional, structural, and functional attributes of biodiversity at four levels of organization. (From Noss 1990.)

any chance of protecting biodiversity against the onslaught of these factors, we must have early warning of change; hence the need for monitoring. Because biodiversity is multifaceted and hierarchical, those indicators that we select as targets for monitoring should represent all of this complexity. Otherwise, something might fall through the cracks.

Land managers are familiar with the use of *indicator species,* often selected to represent a suite of species with similar habitat requirements. As a well-known example, the Northern Spotted Owl (*Strix occidentalis caurina*) was selected by managers of national forests in the Pacific Northwest as a surrogate for all other species associated with old-growth forests. However, the use of indicator species has encountered problems, including biased selection criteria, false assumptions about species–habitat relationships, unwarranted extrapolations from one species to others, and flawed design of monitoring programs. But species will continue to be useful as indicators, particularly if we focus on those most sensitive to human activities and those that play pivotal roles in their ecosystems. For example, change in the abundance of woodpeckers may warn us of possible changes in populations of other species that use woodpecker cavities. But we should not carry our extrapolations too far. The idea of one species representing all others that share a similar habitat is not ecologically realistic.

Indicators for monitoring biodiversity must consist of much more than a set of indicator species. Because biodiversity is distributed hierarchically, so too should indicators be. A framework for selecting biodiversity indicators might follow a nested hierarchy of compositional, structural, and functional elements (Figure A). A monitoring program should select a broad range of indicators that correspond to critical management questions, such as: Are populations of rare species being maintained in sizes and distributions that assure long-term demographic and genetic viability? Are natural structure and species composition of the community being maintained? Is the configuration of the landscape adequate to permit normal movements of organisms? Using the example of a managed forest landscape, some measurable indicators that might help answer such questions are listed in Table A. Only with such a comprehensive approach will conservation biologists be able to track changes in biodiversity and obtain the information they need to preserve it.

**Table A**
Hierarchical Indicators for Monitoring Biodiversity

**GENETIC**
*Composition*
- Allelic diversity
- Presence/absence of rare alleles

*Structure*
- Heterozygosity
- Phenotypic polymorphism

*Function*
- Symptoms of inbreeding depression or genetic drift (reduced survivorship or fertility, abnormal sperm, reduced resistance to disease, morphological abnormalities or asymmetries)
- Inbreeding/outbreeding rate
- Rate of genetic interchange between populations (measured by rate of dispersal and subsequent reproduction of migrants)

**POPULATION–SPECIES**
*Composition*
- Absolute and relative abundance, density, basal area, cover, importance value for various species

*Structure*
- Sex ratio, age distribution, and other aspects of population structure for sensitive species, keystone species, and other special interest species
- Distribution and dispersion of special interest species across the region

*Function*
- Population growth and fluctuation trends of special interest species
- Fertility, fecundity, recruitment rate, survivorship, mortality rate, individual growth rate, and other individual and population health parameters
- Trends in habitat components for special interest species (varies by species)
- Trends in threats to special interest species (depends on life history and sensitivity of species in relation to land use practices and other influences)

**COMMUNITY–ECOSYSTEM**
*Composition*
- Identity, relative abundance, frequency, richness, and evenness of species and guilds (in various habitats)
- Diversity of tree ages or sizes in community (stand)
- Ratio of exotic species to native species in community (species richness, cover, and biomass)
- Proportions of endemic, threatened, and endangered species

*Structure*
- Frequency distribution of seral stages (age classes) for each forest type and across all types
- Average and range of tree ages within defined seral stages
- Ratio of area of natural forest of all ages to area in clear-cuts and plantations
- Abundance and density of snags, downed logs, and other defined structural elements in various size and decay classes

- Spatial dispersion of structural elements and patches
- Foliage density and layering (profiles), and horizontal diversity of foliage profiles in stand
- Canopy density and size, dispersion of canopy openings
- Areal extent of each disturbance event (e.g., fires)

*Function*
- Frequency, intensity, return interval, or rotation period of fires and other natural and anthropogenic disturbances
- Cycling rates for various key nutrients (e.g., N, P)
- Intensity or severity of disturbance events
- Seasonality or periodicity of disturbances
- Predictability or variability of disturbances
- Human intrusion rates and intensities

**LANDSCAPE**
*Composition*
- Identity, distribution, richness, and proportions of patch types (such as forest types and seral stages) across the landscape
- Total amount of late successional forest interior habitat
- Total amount of forest patch perimeter and edge zone

*Structure*
- Patch size frequency distribution for each seral stage and forest type, and across all stages and types
- Patch size diversity index
- Size frequency distribution of late successional interior forest patches (minus defined edge zone, usually 100–200 m)
- Forest patch perimeter:area ratio
- Edge zone:interior zone ratio
- Fractal dimension
- Patch shape indices
- Patch density
- Fragmentation indices
- Interpatch distance (mean, median, range) for all forest patches and for late successional forest patches
- Juxtaposition measures (percentage of area within a defined distance from patch occupied by different habitat types, length of patch border adjacent to different habitat types)
- Structural contrast (magnitude of difference between adjacent habitats, measured for various structural attributes)
- Road density (mi/mi$^2$ or km/km$^2$) for different classes of road and all road classes combined

*Function*
- Disturbance indicators (see above)
- Rates of nutrient, energy, and biological transfer between different communities and patches in the landscape

**Intraspecific Diversity**

Intraspecific diversity has both within-population and between-population genetic components. The nature and extent of such differences is of both theoretical and practical interest. Within populations, the potential rate of evolutionary change is proportional to the amount of available genetic variability. For individuals in those populations, **heterozygosity** is believed to confer fitness benefits; conversely, loss of heterozygosity is believed to lead to reductions in **fitness.** Therefore, the study of within-population genetic variability is a central focus of evolutionary research. Between-population variability is the result primarily of adaptations of populations to local ecological conditions. Locally adapted populations of a widespread species may have particular genes or gene combinations critical for viability in those particular areas. If those populations become extinct, individuals transplanted from other populations may have difficulty surviving in those areas. The nature and extent of between-population genetic variability reveals much about the evolutionary history of populations and processes of speciation. The theoretical and practical importance of intraspecific genetic diversity is treated in greater detail in Chapter 6.

**Species Richness**

The number of species of organisms present in an area—**species richness**—is an important component of biodiversity. If species are weighted by some measure of their importance, such as their abundance, productivity, or size, we speak of **species diversity.** The most frequently used indices of diversity are the Shannon-Wiener index,

$$H' = -\Sigma\, p_i \ln(p_i)$$

and the Simpson index,

$$D = \frac{1}{\Sigma\, p_i^2}$$

in both of which $p_i$ represents the fractional abundance (or biomass or productivity) of the $i^{\text{th}}$ species.

   Indices of diversity and species richness are both commonly used in ecological and conservation biology studies because each gives useful information not provided by the other. Ecologists commonly use diversity measures to assess the adverse effects of pollution and other types of environmental disturbances. Typically an ecological community subjected to stresses experiences losses of species and increases in abundances—and hence dominance—of a few species. Weighted diversity indices quantify these shifts in relative abundances, and an examination of the nature of the changes often yields clues as to their causes. Understanding causes is essential for the design of management plans that can counteract the changes and restore the systems to their former states.

   Conservation biologists usually use unweighted measures of species richness because the many rare species that characterize most biotas are often of greater interest than the more common ones that dominate weighted indices of diversity. In addition, accurate estimates of population densities on geographic scales are seldom available. Therefore, the remainder of this chapter will concentrate on patterns in number of species. Also, species lists are the only type of information that is available for most areas.

   Approximately 1.5 million living and 300,000 fossil species have been described and given scientific names (Table 4.1). Estimates of the actual num-

**Table 4.1**
Numbers of Species Living Today

| Kingdom | Phylum (Division) | Number of described species | Estimated number of species | Percent described |
|---|---|---|---|---|
| Monera | Viruses and bacteria[a] | | | |
| Protista | | 100,000 | 250,000 | 40.0 |
| Fungi | Eumycota | 80,000 | 1,500,000 | 5.3 |
| Plantae | Bryophyta | 14,000 | 30,000 | 46.7 |
| | Tracheophyta | 250,000 | 500,000 | 50.0 |
| Animalia | Porifera | 5,000 | | |
| | Cnidaria | 10,000 | | |
| | Ctenophora | 100 | | |
| | Platyhelminthes | 25,000 | | |
| | Nemertea | 900 | | |
| | Gastrotricha | 500 | | |
| | Kinorhyncha | 100 | | |
| | Priapulida | 16 | | |
| | Entoprocta | 150 | | |
| | Nematoda | 20,000 | 1,000,000 | 2.0 |
| | Rotifera | 1,800 | | |
| | Annelida | 75,000 | | |
| | Arthropoda | 1,250,000 | 20,000,000 | 5.0 |
| | Mollusca | 100,000 | 200,000 | 50.0 |
| | Sipuncula | 250 | | |
| | Echiura | 150 | | |
| | Pogonophora | 145 | | |
| | Ectoprocta | 5,000 | | |
| | Phoronida | 70 | | |
| | Brachiopoda | 350[b] | | |
| | Hemichordata | 100 | | |
| | Chateognatha | 100 | | |
| | Echinodermata | 7,000 | | |
| | Chordata | 40,000 | 50,000 | 80.0 |

Data from Andersen 1992; Hawksworth 1991a; Trüper 1992; Vickerman 1992; World Conservation Monitoring Centre 1992.
[a]Numbers for viruses and bacteria are omitted because species limits are poorly defined and essentially unknown in these groups.
[b]26,000 fossil species described

ber of living species vary widely because they are based on incomplete and indirect evidence. Current estimates of the total number of living species range from 10 million to as high as 50 million or more (May 1988; Wilson 1992). In other words, we do not know within an order of magnitude the number of living species. Thus, a large fraction of the species likely to be exterminated during the next century will disappear before they have been named, much less understood ecologically. Essay 4B, by Peter Raven and E. O. Wilson, explores this problem in more detail.

The immense richness of viruses, bacteria, protists, and unicellular algae is largely uncatalogued today. There are few studies of viruses except for those that attack people, domesticated plants and animals, and the organisms we study scientifically. How many types attack, for example, non-crop plants and insects is totally unknown, as is the number of marine forms.

## ESSAY 4B
# A 50-Year Plan for Biodiversity Surveys[1]

Peter H. Raven, Missouri Botanical Garden, and
E. O. Wilson, Harvard University

In the wake of the 1992 "Earth Summit" in Rio de Janeiro, it should be evident why biological systematics, hitherto regarded as "little science," is badly in need of growing large—and soon. The roughly 1.5 million species of living organisms known to date are probably fewer than 15% of the actual number, and by some estimates could be fewer than 2%. The Linnaean shortfall reaches from supposedly well known groups to the most obscure, as illustrated by the following examples:

- Eleven of the 80 known living species of cetaceans (whales and porpoises) have been discovered in this century, the most recent in 1991; at least one more undescribed species has been sighted in the eastern Pacific but not yet collected.

- One of the largest shark species, the megamouth, constituting the new family Megaschasmidae, was discovered in 1976 and is now known from five specimens.

- During the past decade, botanists have discovered three new families of flowering plants in Central America and southern Mexico; one, a remarkable relict, is a forest tree, frequent at middle elevations in Costa Rica.

- The most recent new animal phylum, the Loricifera, was described from the meiobenthos in 1983; many additional new species in the group have since come to light.

- The great majority of insects in the canopy of tropical rain forests, possibly in excess of 90% in some groups, remains unknown.

- Although only 69,000 species of fungi have been described thus far, a leading specialist estimates that the world total is 1.5 million or more.

- Although the number of bacterial species recognized by microbiologists is about 4000, the huge majority in existence remain incommunicado and hence undiscovered, because their culturing requirements are unknown. DNA matching can circumvent this difficulty. Recent studies in

Norway indicate the presence of 4000–5000 species in a single gram of beech forest soil and a comparably large but different array in a gram of nearby marine sediment.

Clearly, progress over the past 250 years toward an overall knowledge of the earth's prodigious biodiversity has been very slow. Close attention to this problem might be postponed for the delectation of future generations, except for two compelling circumstances. On the positive side, biodiversity represents a potential source of wealth in the form of new crops, pharmaceuticals, petroleum substitutes, and other products. If used wisely, wild species will also continue to provide essential ecosystem services, from the maintenance of hydrologic cycles to the nitrification of soils. On the negative side, biodiversity is disappearing at a rapid rate, primarily due to habitat destruction. Tropical deforestation alone is reducing species in these biomes by half a percent per year, as estimated by the conservative models of island biogeography. This figure is likely to be boosted many times when the impact of pollution and exotic species is determined and factored in. Coral reefs, the marine equivalent of rainforests in magnitude of diversity, are also in increasing trouble.

There is growing recognition of the need for a crash program to map biodiversity in order to plan its conservation and practical use. With up to a fifth or more of the species of all groups likely to disappear over the next 30 years, as human populations double in the warmer parts of the world, we are clearly faced with a dilemma. But what is the best way to proceed?

Some systematists have urged initiation of a global biodiversity survey, ultimately aimed at full identification and biogeography of all species. Others, noting the shortage of personnel, funds, and above all, time, see the only realistic hope to lie in overall inventories of those groups that are relatively well known now, including flowering plants, vertebrates, butterflies, and a few others. In order to accomplish this second objective as early as possible, it would be necessary to survey transects across

broad geographic areas, and to examine a number of carefully selected sites in great detail. A reasonable number of specialists is available to begin this task, and with adequate funding it could be completed in a decade. The results would reveal a great deal about patterns of endemism, including the existence of hot spots, those parts of the world believed to contain the largest numbers of endangered species. They could be applied directly to problems of economic development, land use, science, and conservation. Meanwhile, adequate numbers of specialists could be trained and preparations made to deal with all of the remaining groups of organisms. The aim would be to gain a reasonably accurate idea of the representation of the best-known groups on earth while attempting complete inventories of all the global biota over the course of the next 50 years. As most of the tropical forests of the world are likely to be reduced to less than 10% of their original extent during this half century, adequate planning is of the essence. The results from inventories should be organized in such a way as to apply directly to the development of new crops, sustainable land use, conservation, and the enhancement of allied disciplines of science.

In order to propel systematics into its larger role foreordained by the biodiversity crisis, its practitioners need to formulate an explicitly stated mission with a timetable and cost estimate. In the approach outlined above, the 50-year period could be viewed as a series of successive 10-year plans. As each decade approaches an end, progress to that point could be assessed and new directions for the next decade identified. Momentum in the enterprise will result in economies of scale. Costs per species will fall as new methods for collecting and distributing specimens are invented and procedures for storing and accessing information approved. Costs are moreover not simply additive when new higher taxa are added, but instead fall off on a per-species basis. For example, entomologists could collect nematodes on the insects they collect, while identifying these hosts for the nematologists—and vice versa. Multiple groups can be collected by mass sampling of entire habitats, and then distributed to systematists specializing on individual taxa.

The results of inventorying, as opposed to the costs, are not just additive but multiplicative. As networks of expertise and monographing grow, ecologists, population biologists, biochemists and others will be drawn into the enterprise. It is also inevitable that genome descriptions similar to those now planned for the human species and *Drosophila* will feed into the database. Molecular biology is destined to fuse with systematics.

Applied systematics can develop collaterally with basic studies, as is being demonstrated by the organization of the Instituto Nacional de Biodiversidad (INBio) in Costa Rica (see Case Study 2 in Chapter 17). Chemical prospecting, the search for new natural products, is readily hooked onto inventories. So is screening for species and gene complexes of special merit in agriculture, forestry, and land reclamation.

Fully 80% of the earth's terrestrial biodiversity is likely to occur in the tropics, where only a few groups of organisms can be described as reasonably well known at present. Aside from the roughly 170,000 flowering plants and 30,000 vertebrates, only about 250,000 species of all groups appear to have been described thus far. With estimates of the remainder ranging from 8 million to 100 million, one can readily appreciate the magnitude of the task at hand, and the fact that the few hundred systematists available are woefully inadequate to complete the task while most of the species are still in existence. We require, in fact, a wholly new approach to this great problem in order to be able to provide even an outline of the nature and occurrence of these species.

Abdus Salam has estimated that some 6% of the world's scientists and engineers live in developing countries, with a rapidly increasing share of 77% of the world's population, 15% of the world's wealth (GDP), and perhaps 20% of the world's use of industrial energy. A net sum amounting to tens of billions of dollars flows annually from these countries to the rich, industrial parts of the world. These relationships must be taken into account if our common objective is to chart the outlines of global biodiversity, use it for humanity's benefit, understand it scientifically, and preserve an intelligently selected sample of it for the future.

We believe that the best strategy for approaching this task is the implementation of national biological surveys throughout the world, conceived like INBio, and set up as management strategies for each nation's biodiversity. Such operations will expedite the increased understanding, efficient use (assisted by biotechnology transfer), and conservation, both in nature and ex situ, of as many organisms as possible. They will allow the people of every nation to see themselves as benefiting from their own biodiversity, while preserving it for their own purposes.

[1]Reprinted with permission and modified from *Science* 1992, 258:1099–1110. Copyright 1992 by the AAAS.

---

Similarly, the bacteria and protists that live in soils or attack invertebrates have scarcely been examined. Terrestrial algal species, especially those living on bark and rocks, have been little studied; the existence of very small marine species, living in interstitial spaces in the ocean floor, was not recognized until 1980. All estimates of the number of species in these groups are crude guesses at best.

About 70,000 species of fungi have been described, but the total number living today almost certainly exceeds one million. For example, the 12,000 fungal species described in Britain is about six times the number of native vascular plants described for the same area. If there are, on average, six fungal species for each vascular plant species worldwide, the number of fungal species would be approximately 1.6 million (Hawksworth 1991a). The global ratio could be much higher or lower than the one in Britain, but we have little else upon which to base estimates.

Taxonomists believe that the number of species of nematodes is very large because millions of individuals may be present in $1 \ m^3$ of soil or mud, and more than 200 species have been reported in samples of just a few cubic centimeters of coastal mud (Poinar 1983). Nonetheless, almost nothing is known about species ranges and rates of species turnover geographically, so global estimates are very uncertain.

Approximately 30,000 species of mites have been described, but, because knowledge of tropical mite faunas is extremely poor, the actual number of living species could easily exceed 1 million. Nearly 1 million species of insects, the world's most speciose group of organisms, have been described, but this is certainly a small fraction of the total. Most of the insects collected by fogging the canopies of tropical trees, for example, are members of undescribed species (Erwin 1991).

Thus, the earth is a relatively unexplored planet biologically. Not only are most living species still undescribed, but very little is known about the life history and ecological relations of most of the species that have been named. The rate of description of new species today is higher than it ever has been, but the rate is nonetheless quite inadequate to accomplish a reasonable inventory prior to the likely extinction of many of the species.

### Richness of Higher Taxa

The distinctness of evolving lineages is an important component of biodiversity. The higher taxonomic categories (orders, classes, phyla) of the universally used Linnaean biological classification system provide rough measures of distinctness of lineages. By this measure, marine biodiversity is much higher than terrestrial biodiversity even though there are far fewer species of marine than of terrestrial organisms. Of the 32 extant phyla of multicellular animals, for example, 31 are marine, and 14 of these are exclusively marine. From this perspective, preservation of marine biodiversity is more important than might be suggested simply by comparing the numbers of species in marine and terrestrial environments. Diversity in marine systems is further discussed by Elliott Norse in Essay 4C.

---

## ESSAY 4C
## Uncharted Waters
### Conserving Marine Biological Diversity

Elliott A. Norse, Center for Marine Conservation

In a movie from my youth, *The Beast from 20,000 Fathoms*, a gigantic reptile terrorizing New York is confronted by a minuscule (and short-lived) policeman firing his service revolver. The clear lesson: a big task needs commensurate tools.

Maintaining life on our planet is a task of unequaled magnitude, but conservation needs and efforts are poorly matched. Too few resources are devoted to protecting anything, and the crumbs that *do* go to conservation are sliced in peculiar ways. States spend far more on boosting populations of species that a small segment of the population enjoys hooking and shooting than on conserving "nongame" species. Many more scientist-years, journal articles, and TV programs are devoted to conserving vertebrates than to the more than 99% of species that are not so closely related to us. Most research and hands-on conservation work occurs in nations whose biological diversity was relatively modest even before it was further reduced by industrial development, while there are few conservation biologists and institutions in biotically rich developing nations where wholesale loss is still preventable.

These disparities are reasonably well known. A less appreciated one is the scant conservation effort applied to the realm constituting over 99.5% of the biosphere: the sea. Covering more than twice the area of the terrestrial realm in a permanently inhabited layer (average depth: ~4000 meters) more than 100 times thicker, the sea is the least protected part of the biosphere.

The lack of protection would be unimportant if estuaries, coastal waters, and the ocean basins were not both biologically diverse and seriously threatened. The sea is rich in species; recent evidence (Grassle and Maciolek 1992) suggests that the number of undescribed species in the deep sea might be roughly comparable to the number in tropical forests. However, marine and terrestrial patterns of taxonomic diversity are quite different. Land is inhospitable to most multicellular life-forms except fungi, bryophytes, vascular plants, a few invertebrate phyla, and tetrapod vertebrates. The sea, in contrast, hosted the evolution of all animal phyla, and is still inhabited by 31 of the 32 that are extant (all but the Onychophora). Indeed, 14 animal phyla are *exclusively* marine, including echinoderms, lamp shells, and arrow worms; other algal and animal phyla, such as brown algae and sponges, are almost exclusively so. The few successful "themes" that colonized land, particularly insects, have diversified into dazzlingly speciose variations, but in a more fundamental sense the sea has higher taxonomic diversity.

The sea also has higher ecosystem diversity. Like the land, the sea has forests, grasslands, deserts, montane and insular ecosystems, caves and hot springs; however, it also has three phases—solid, liquid, and gaseous—not just two. The ecosystems without terrestrial analogues—the sea-air interface, the underside of pack ice, the water column—are home to life-forms, including pleuston, plankton, and nekton, that are entirely or largely absent on land. Marine ecosystems have the highest measured primary production (northeastern Pacific intertidal kelp beds), but they also have vast inhabited spaces in which there is no autochthonous primary production. Moreover, some deep-sea marine ecosystems are based wholly on chemosynthesis, not photosynthesis.

Marine biological diversity is threatened at the genetic, species, and ecosystem levels. Losses of genetic diversity are unquantified and are known mainly as anecdotal accounts of local population extinction. Documented modern species extinctions are few, with the first extinction of an invertebrate reported only recently (Carlton et al. 1991). Destruction of marine ecosystems is documented mainly for conspicuous mangrove forests and coral reefs. Yet, at all three levels, there is ample reason to believe that documented losses are but a tiny fraction of what has actually disappeared, or will in coming decades.

Five driving forces jeopardize marine life: (1) there are too many people; (2) we consume too much; (3) our institutions degrade, rather than conserve, biodiversity; (4) we do not have the knowledge we need; and (5) we do not value nature enough. These, in turn, drive the five proximate threats to marine biological diversity: (1) overexploitation; (2) physical alteration; (3) pollution; (4) introduction of alien species; and (5) global atmospheric change (Norse 1993). Thus, the list of threats is the same in the sea and on land, although the relative importance of the factors differs somewhat. The significance of overexploitation and pollution in the sea, although usually underestimated, has long been recognized, but few people realize the importance of the other three. For example, there has been little research on effects of physical alterations such as bottom trawling or diversion of riverine flow on marine species and ecosystems.

Some aspects of marine conservation differ little from terrestrial conservation. Marine ecosystems are heterogeneous, and certain areas merit special attention, including areas of high diversity, high endemism, or high productivity, spawning areas that serve as sources of recruits, nursery grounds, migration corridors, and stopover points. As on land, large species with low fecundity are at special risk, and endangerment, phyletic distinctness, or ecological importance can be criteria for establishing priorities for species conservation.

However, distinctive aspects of the sea have profound implications for conservation. The spatial scale of marine patterns and processes is generally much larger. Time scales are different; for example, dominant marine primary producers can have doubling times of days, rather than months or years as on land. Mineralized nutrients, however, might not be taken up by primary producers for centuries, rather than years or less. Life histories and dispersal mechanisms are markedly different; a substantial fraction of marine species have the potential to disperse passively across hundreds of kilometers. As a result, the question of population sources and sinks (discussed in Chapter 7) may be more important in the sea than on land. Marine species are under very different legal regimes than are terrestrial species, a fact that often overshadows biological considerations in their conservation. And conservation remedies can differ markedly: for example, unlike terrestrial and freshwater species, ex situ conservation of marine species will be insignificant for the foreseeable future.

Perhaps the greatest difference between terrestrial and marine biodiversity conservation is that so much less is known about the sea. There are, for example, no marine analogues to the Bailey, Küchler, and Udvardy geographic ecosystem classification schemes used to determine gaps in protected area coverage on land. Marine conservation biology lags terrestrial conservation biology by about 20 years. It lacks central paradigms, graduate training programs, and substantial dedicated funding. Unless this changes, the task will continue to dwarf the tools we have for protecting marine biological diversity.

The preservation of evolutionarily distinct lineages above the level of species is important for a number of reasons. First, the evolutionary potential of life depends upon the variety of evolving lineages, not just the number of species. Lineages that have been evolving separately for long periods of time have many unique genes and gene combinations that would be lost were those lineages to become extinct. Second, these lineages are storehouses of information about the history of life. Scientists can read and interpret this information with increasing accuracy using modern molecular methods. Third, the integrated functioning of ecosystems depends upon the variety of species in them. For example, microorganisms have more diverse mechanisms for obtaining energy from the environment and are able to decompose a wider variety of substances than multicellular organisms can. Without microorganisms, ecosystems would be unable to provide, at high rates, such goods and services to humankind as absorbing and breaking down pollutants, storing and cycling nutrients, forming soils, and maintaining soil fertility. The numbers and kinds of fuels, construction materials, and medicines we obtain from nature depend upon the evolutionary distinctness of species. And finally, the aesthetic benefits we receive from nature are strongly correlated with the variety of living organisms with which we interact. No matter how many species of beetles there may be, they cannot substitute aesthetically for mammals, fishes, corals, or butterflies.

## Ecosystem and Biome Diversity

Attempts to classify large ecological units consisting of all of the species living together in a region have a long and complicated history. Plants have been used extensively in terrestrial ecological classification systems because they dominate the structure of those communities and are much easier to sample than are animals. Alexander von Humboldt (1806) classified vegetation into groups on the basis of the shapes of the dominant plants, such as spruce-tree shape or palm shape. In 1874 de Candolle proposed a classification of plant communities based on life-forms because he believed that life-forms were determined by climate. More complicated schemes of describing life-forms of plants and characterizing plant communities by the relative dominance of plants with different shapes have been developed (Raunkaier 1934; Dansereau 1951; Halle et al. 1978). Köppen (1884) went even further by using plant life-form distribution to define climates. Holdridge's (1967) widely used life zone system, on the other hand, is based entirely upon climatic variables.

Although ecological communities clearly grade into one another, recognition of major divisions has proven to be useful for ecological discourse. Most textbooks divide the world into **biomes,** the largest ecological units, on the basis of the dominant vegetation. In tropical regions, biomes are divided along precipitation gradients (rainforest, evergreen seasonal forest, dry forest, thorn woodland, desert scrub, and desert) and elevational gradients (rainforest, montane rainforest, cloud forest, elfin woodland, páramo). At temperate latitudes, commonly recognized biomes along a moisture gradient are mesophytic forest, woodland, tallgrass prairie, shortgrass prairie, and desert (Figure 4.1). With increasing latitude, mesophytic forests become conifer-dominated boreal forests and eventually tundra. Finer divisions of biomes into ecosystem types use the same types of information, but also use data on drainage, soil type, slope, and species composition to identify units. All such classifications are arbitrary, but if properly constituted, they identify ecological units that are useful for comparative purposes.

Preservation of the variety of the earth's biomes is necessary for preservation of species. Without sufficient quantities of their natural habitats, species become extinct in the wild. Captive propagation can, and does, serve a role in keeping species alive for short periods until they can be reintroduced into the wild. But captive propagation is of little ultimate use if there are no suitable sites into which to reintroduce the species. Managing species in zoos and botanical gardens is expensive, and an animal in a cage or a plant in a garden is not a fully functioning member of its species.

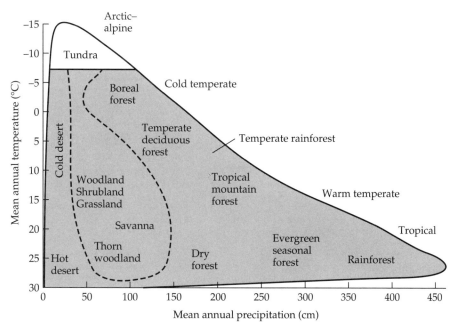

**Figure 4.1** Biomes and climate. Distributions of the major biomes are plotted on axes of mean annual temperature and mean annual precipitation. Within the region bounded by the dashed lines, factors such as seasonality of drought, fire, and grazing strongly affect which type of vegetation is present. (Modified from Whittaker 1970.)

Also, ecosystems can provide the environmental goods and services upon which human life depends only if well-functioning systems are distributed over most of the surface of the earth. This requires a rich variety of ecosystems because the combinations of species that can perform as an integrated ecosystem change with environmental conditions. Deciduous trees cannot adequately replace conifers in boreal environments, nor can conifers function well in the regions dominated by deciduous forests. Finally, the richness of our aesthetic experiences depends upon the richness of biomes as well as the richness of species.

## Patterns of Species Richness

The earth is not uniform, and neither is the distribution of organisms across its surface. Some important general patterns in the geographic distribution of species richness have been discovered, but much remains unknown, in large part because the inventory of living organisms is so incomplete. Also, the distributions of species are best known for temperate regions, where most taxonomists and ecologists live and work. Tropical regions, where most of the world's species live, are extremely poorly known biologically.

### Species Richness over Geologic Time

The fossil record, though very incomplete, provides a rough measure of trends in species richness during the history of life on earth (Table 4.2). Cellular life in the form of bacteria evolved about 3.5 billion years ago (Bya); eukaryotic or-

**Table 4.2**
The Geological Time Scale

| Era | Period | Epoch | Mya[a] |
|---|---|---|---|
| Cenozoic | Quaternary | Recent (Holocene) | 0.01 |
| | | Pleistocene | 2.0 |
| | Tertiary | Pliocene | 5.1 |
| | | Miocene | 24.6 |
| | | Oligocene | 38.0 |
| | | Eocene | 54.9 |
| | | Paleocene | 65.0 |
| Mesozoic | Cretaceous | | 144 |
| | Jurassic | | 213 |
| | Triassic | | 248 |
| Paleozoic | Permian | | 286 |
| | Carboniferous | | 360 |
| | Devonian | | 408 |
| | Silurian | | 438 |
| | Ordovician | | 505 |
| | Cambrian | | 570 |
| Pre-Cambrian | Vendian | | 670 |
| | Sturtian | | 800 |

[a]Millions of years from the beginning of the period or epoch to the present. From Futuyma 1986.

ganisms probably evolved about 2 Bya. About 30 taxa have been described from these early biotas, and although many more species must have lived then, paleontologists agree that species richness was low during the first 2 billion years of earth's existence. During the late Precambrian, the richer Ediacarian fauna, consisting of strange frond- and disc-shaped soft-bodied animals and some forms that appear to be arthropods and echinoderms, evolved. The first real explosion of biodiversity took place during the early Cambrian period. As many as 100 phyla of organisms may have evolved during the Cambrian, of which only 32 survive today. Thus, as measured by the number of animal phyla, life was more diverse during the Cambrian period than at any time since (Gould 1989).

The fossil record for marine invertebrates with hard skeletons is good enough to provide a general picture of the number of evolutionary lineages present at different times in the past. The Cambrian explosion was followed, about 60 million years later, by the extensive radiation of the Paleozoic fauna. Following the Permian mass extinction, the modern fauna evolved, and species richness has increased steadily throughout the Mesozoic and Cenozoic eras to a maximum today (Figure 4.2). Approximately 40,000 species of marine invertebrates lived in the Paleozoic and Mesozoic eras, a number that increased to about 250,000 in the late Cenozoic era. The fossil record of terrestrial animals is much poorer, especially among such speciose groups as insects, which fossilize poorly. The fossil record of vertebrates, particularly mammals, is much better, and it indicates that richness, as measured by the

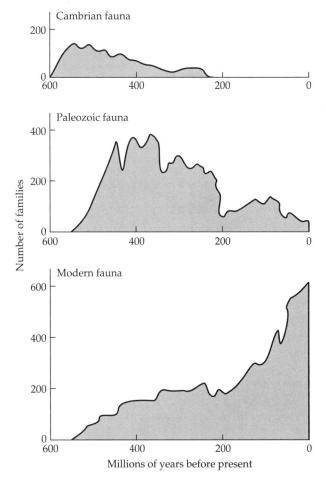

**Figure 4.2** The number of families of animals in lineages that arose during the three major evolutionary "explosions," illustrating species richness in the major evolutionary faunas. Important elements of the Cambrian fauna include trilobites, brachiopods, monoplacophorans, and eocrinoids. Important components of the Paleozoic fauna include several lineages of echinoderms, anthozoans, graptolites, ostracods, and cephalopod mollusks. (Modified from Sepkoski 1984.)

**Figure 4.3**  Terrestrial plant species richness. Ferns, gymnosperms, and angiosperms have, in turn, dominated the world's flora. (Modified from Signor 1990.)

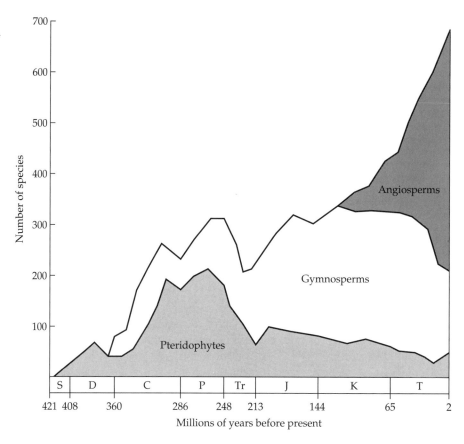

number of orders, is slightly higher today than at any previous time in the history of life on Earth.

Terrestrial vascular plants appeared in the late Ordovician or early Silurian and increased rapidly during the Devonian, when seed-bearing plants first appeared. Species richness has continued to increase overall, but the number of species of ferns and gymnosperms has decreased, while the number of species of angiosperms has increased dramatically (Figure 4.3).

### Local Species Richness

To describe the complex spatial patterns of biodiversity, ecologists and biogeographers have found it useful to divide species richness into four major components: point richness; alpha ($\alpha$-) richness; beta ($\beta$-) richness; and gamma ($\Upsilon$-) richness. **Point richness** refers to the number of species that can be found at a single point in space; $\alpha$**-richness** refers to the number of species found in a small, homogeneous area; $\beta$**-richness** refers to the rate of change in species composition across habitats; and $\Upsilon$**-richness** concerns changes across larger landscape gradients. A high $\beta$-richness means that the cumulative number of species recorded increases rapidly as additional areas along some environmental gradient are censused. Species may also drop out rapidly along such gradients, resulting in a high rate of species turnover.

Alpha-richness is characterized by several widespread patterns. These patterns are characteristic of most taxa, are statistically very different from random patterns, and are strongly correlated with physical environmental variables. First, for most higher taxonomic categories, there are many more species in tropical regions than in higher-latitude communities. For example, Arctic waters have about 100 species of tunicates, 400 species are known

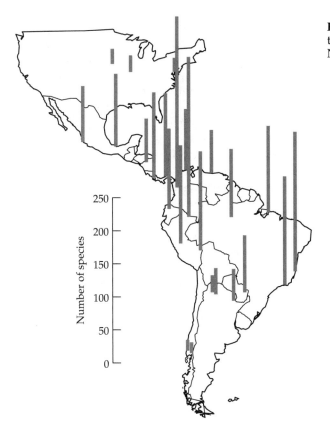

**Figure 4.4** Tree species richness in the New World. Plotted are total numbers of species recorded in small areas scattered over North, Central, and South America. (Modified from Gentry 1988.)

from temperate waters, and more than 600 species inhabit tropical seas. The average number of ant species found in local regions increases from about 10 at 60° north latitude to as many as 2000 in equatorial regions. Greenland hosts 56 species of breeding birds, New York 105, Guatemala 469, and Colombia 1395. The numbers of species of trees recorded at selected sites in the New World are illustrated in Figure 4.4. There are, however, exceptions to these latitudinal patterns; in some orders and families the number of species is greatest at mid- or high latitudes. Examples include marine algae, coniferous trees, bees, salamanders, penguins, and waterfowl.

Second, the richness of species in most taxa is positively correlated with the structural complexity of the ecological community. Structurally simple habitats, such as the open ocean, grasslands, and cold deserts, generally support fewer species of organisms than structurally more complex communities, such as forests and coral reefs. In most terrestrial environments, plants provide the major components of the physical structure within which the activities of all other organisms are carried out. Coral reefs serve the same function in marine environments. Structurally complex communities have a greater variety of microclimates, a greater variety of resources, a larger number of ways in which to exploit those resources, and more places in which to find shelter from predators and the physical environment.

Third, among many ecosystems there is a positive correlation between productivity and the number of species found in the system. Total production is determined primarily by temperature, moisture, and soil fertility. The highest terrestrial production is found in regions with high rainfall and year-round warm temperatures. Production drops with elevation because of lowered temperatures. In many areas of the world, the amount of precipitation determines total production. As a result, species richness typically is in-

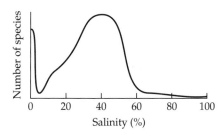

**Figure 4.5** Estimated species richness of aquatic invertebrates living in waters of different salinity throughout the world. The two peaks correspond to fresh water (< 2%) and seawater (30%–40%). (Modified from Kinne 1971.)

versely correlated with elevation (unless compensated by increasing rainfall). In arid and semiarid regions, annual production can be predicted fairly accurately from the amount and distribution of precipitation. Marine production is limited primarily by the nutrients available in surface waters. Production is highest in coastal regions, where nutrient-rich waters upwell, and lowest in the open ocean (Koblentz-Mishke et al. 1970; Bunt 1975).

There are, however, conspicuous exceptions to the generalization that more productive ecosystems harbor more species. For example, some extremely productive systems, such as salt marshes, sea-grass beds, and hot springs, are relatively species-poor. Most such systems are distributed as relatively small, fragmented patches whose physical environments differ strikingly from those of the surrounding dominant ecosystems. Therefore, special adaptations are required for ecological success in these environments. Such special adaptations are less likely to evolve in relation to rare than to common habitat types. Evolutionary biologists believe that the combination of major physical environmental differences and isolation of the patches results in fewer species of organisms evolving adaptations to these unusual environments. For the same reason, species adapted to the more common surrounding environments are less likely to "spill over" into these rare habitat types. At a broader scale, this evolutionary phenomenon is illustrated by the richness of species as a function of salinity. Both fresh water and seawater are widely distributed, but waters of intermediate salinity and waters that are more saline than the oceans are rare. The species richness of aquatic invertebrates throughout the world parallels this pattern (Figure 4.5).

The importance of the prevalence of a habitat type for the richness of species it supports is demonstrated vividly by the floras of outcrops of serpentine rocks. Soils derived from serpentine have such high levels of nickel, chromium, iron, and magnesium that individuals of most plant species grow very poorly on them. In regions where serpentine outcrops are small and scattered, constituting a very small fraction of the landscape, serpentine soils support scrubby, open, species-poor vegetation with many endemic species (Kruckeberg 1985). However, in areas such as South Africa, where serpentine outcrops are a dominant landscape feature, serpentine soils support vegetation that is richer in species than that growing on other soil types (Terborgh 1973).

Fourth, island communities are poorer in species than comparable mainland communities. In general, the number of species found on islands is positively correlated with island size and topographic diversity, and negatively correlated with distance from the mainland source of immigrants. Low species richness on islands is attributed to low colonization rates, high extinction rates (because populations are usually small and subject to decimation by local catastrophes and stochastic variation), and lack of certain types of resources typically provided by species that are poor dispersers across ocean barriers (MacArthur and Wilson 1967). Also, island communities have experienced extremely high extinction rates of species during recent centuries, primarily because of human introduction of mammalian predators (mammals other than bats disperse poorly across ocean barriers) and mainland diseases.

### Regional Turnover of Species Richness

One of the first ecological relationships to be established empirically was the relationship between area and number of species (Arrhenius 1921). This relationship is commonly expressed using a power function of the form

$$S = cA^z$$

(A)

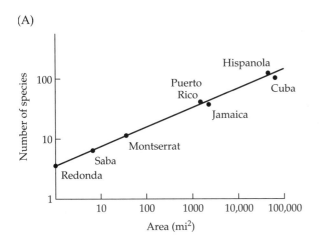

(B)

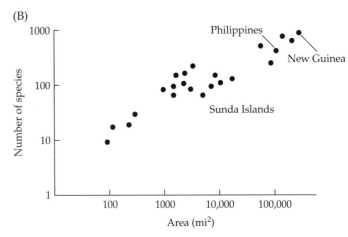

**Figure 4.6** Relationship between area and number of species on islands of various sizes. (A) The number of species of amphibians and reptiles found on selected islands in the West Indies. (B) The number of land and freshwater bird species on the Sunda Islands, the Philippines, and New Guinea. These islands are close to the Asian continent, and many were connected to the mainland during glacial periods. Therefore, many of the larger islands are relatively species-rich. (Modified from MacArthur and Wilson 1967.)

where $S$ = the number of species, $A$ = area, and $c$ and $z$ are constants fitted to the data. On a logarithmic scale, this relationship plots as a straight line where $c$ is the $y$-intercept and $z$ is the slope of the line (Figure 4.6). Analysis of species–area relationships in many groups of organisms reveals that most values of $z$ are between 0.20 and 0.35. For a while, some ecologists argued that the narrow range of $z$ values was a simple statistical consequence of the lognormal distribution of species abundances (May 1975), but it became evident that a much wider range of $z$ values is possible even if species abundances are lognormally distributed. The regular relationship between the size of an area and the number of species it supports, which is most readily observed using island data, was a key empirical generalization in the development of the theory of island biogeography (MacArthur and Wilson 1967). This relationship will appear repeatedly throughout this book.

The rate at which the species composition of communities changes across environmental gradients is determined by the sizes of species ranges and the extent to which species are habitat specialists. The ranges of tropical species are much less well known than the ranges of their temperate counterparts but it appears that, on average, terrestrial tropical species have smaller ranges than species of higher latitudes. It is also well established that many species have narrower altitudinal ranges on the slopes of tropical mountains than on temperate mountains. There is some evidence that tropical species may, on average, be more specialized dietarily than their temperate counterparts but much more research is needed to establish the degree to which this is true and the dimensions along which the specialization has evolved (Beaver 1979; Marquis and Braker 1994).

An intimate relationship exists between local and regional species richness; in general, they are positively correlated. For example, the number of gall wasp species found locally on a particular species of oak in California is positively correlated with the total number of gall wasps known to feed on that oak species throughout its entire range (Figure 4.7). Similarly, the more species of birds found on an island, the greater the number of species found in a single habitat on that island.

Species turnover rates have been extensively studied among birds of Mediterranean-type ecosystems (Cody 1975). Chile, which is isolated from the remainder of South America by extremely arid deserts to the north and very high mountains to the east, has both a low number of bird species and a low β-richness; that is, most of the species have ranges that encompass a broad variety of habitat types. South Africa and California are not well iso-

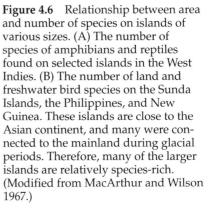

**Figure 4.7** Interactions between local and regional species richness. The number of species of cynipid gall wasps found locally on an oak species is strongly correlated with the number of cynipids recorded from throughout the range of that oak species. The solid line connects points at which local and regional richness are equal. (Modified from Ricklefs 1987; Data from Cornell 1985.)

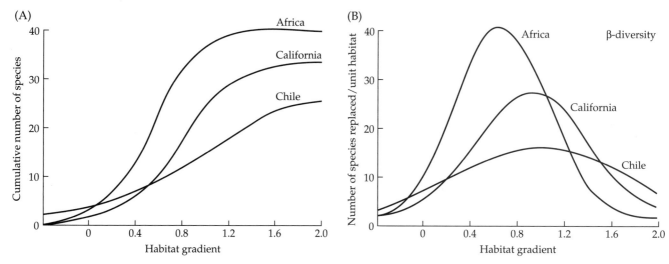

**Figure 4.8** Species turnovers along habitat gradients. (A) Species accumulation curves for birds across habitat gradients in Mediterranean vegetation (from dry scrub to woodland) in southern Africa, California, and Chile. (B) The differentials of the curves in (A) give the rate of species turnover across the gradient. (Modified from Cody 1975.)

lated from the remainder of their respective continents, but southern Africa is surrounded by much larger semiarid areas than is California. Consequently, both species-accumulation and species-turnover curves are higher in the more arid portions of the habitat gradient from very dry scrub to woodland in Africa than in California or Chile (Figure 4.8).

A species that is found in a particular region and nowhere else is said to be **endemic** to that region. However, what constitutes a region is ill-defined. All species are, as far as we know, endemic to earth. At the opposite extreme, some species are restricted to single desert springs (see Figure 5.2), small islands, or isolated mountaintops. Regions with many endemic species are the result of one or more major events that caused the ranges of many taxa to be fragmented at approximately the same place. Causes of such geographic isolation, commonly called **vicariance**, include continental drift, mountain building, and sea level rises. Following such isolation, many taxa may undergo evolutionary radiations in the same general locality. Vicariance due to continental drift has been extremely important in generating the high degrees of endemism found in the biotas of Madagascar, Australia, New Guinea, and New Caledonia. Owing to their isolation, islands often have high proportions of endemic species, but, given that islands often have relatively impoverished biotas, high endemism often is not associated with high species richness.

Biogeographers recognize 18 areas of unusually high endemism, commonly referred to as **hot spots**. These areas contain about 49,950 endemic plant species, 20% of the world's total, in 746,400 km$^2$, only 0.5% of the world's land area. They are also rich in endemics in other taxa (Table 4.3). This topic is pursued in greater depth in the next chapter.

Patterns of endemism differ greatly among taxa (see Table 4.3). Thus, both the Cape region of South Africa and southwestern Australia have extremely high numbers of endemic plant species but very few endemic mammals or birds. These differences arise because the area required for speciation differs widely among taxa. Plants speciate in much smaller areas than do vertebrates. However, there are strong correlations of patterns of endemism among mammals, birds, and reptiles, all of which require relatively large areas for speciation.

An inevitable and important corollary of patterns of species richness is that areas with high α-richness inevitably have many rare species. For example, a tropical wet forest in South America or Southeast Asia may harbor be-

**Table 4.3**
Numbers of Endemic Species in Some "Hot Spot" Areas

| Region | Area (km²) | Vascular plants | Mammals | Reptiles | Amphibians |
|---|---|---|---|---|---|
| Cape region (South Africa) | 134,000 | 6000 | 16 | 43 | 23 |
| Upland western Amazonia | 100,000 | 5000 | — | — | ca. 70 |
| Atlantic coast of Brazil | 1,000,000 | 5000 | 40 | 92 | 168 |
| Madagascar | 62,000 | 4900 | 86 | 234 | 142 |
| Philippines | 250,000 | 3700 | 98 | 120 | 41 |
| North Borneo | 190,000 | 3500 | 42 | 69 | 47 |
| Eastern Himalayas | 340,000 | 3500 | — | 20 | 25 |
| Southwestern Australia | 113,000 | 2830 | 10 | 25 | 22 |
| Western Ecuador | 27,000 | 2500 | 9 | — | — |
| Colombian Chocó | 100,000 | 2500 | 8 | 137 | 111 |
| Peninsular Malaysia | 120,000 | 2400 | 4 | 25 | 7 |
| California Floristic Province | 324,000 | 2140 | 15 | 25 | 7 |
| Western Ghats (India) | 50,000 | 1600 | 7 | 91 | 84 |
| Central Chile | 140,000 | 1450 | — | — | — |
| New Caledonia | 15,000 | 1400 | 2 | 21 | 0 |

Data from Myers 1988, 1990; World Conservation and Monitoring Centre 1992.
*Note:* Original area of rainforest only is given for the tropical regions.

tween 300 and 400 species of trees per square kilometer, whereas a temperate forest harbors an order of magnitude fewer. However, the number of trees per hectare is roughly the same in tropical and temperate forests. It follows that most of the tree species in tropical forests must be present at very low densities. Many of those species are probably more abundant elsewhere, but some species evidently are present only at low densities throughout their ranges.

## What Are the Limits to Species Richness?

The fact that species richness has continued to increase throughout evolution, despite setbacks by mass extinction events, suggests that whatever limits to species richness may exist have not yet been reached on a global scale. Nevertheless, because all regional biotas contain many more species than are found in any single locality or habitat type, there are evidently limits to species richness in ecological time, whatever may happen over millennia. Therefore, both evolutionary and ecological processes must be included in any analysis of the causes of and limits to species richness.

### Evolutionary Limits to Species Richness

Large numbers of new evolutionary lineages originated three times during the history of life. The first such event, known as the Cambrian explosion, took place about half a billion years ago. The second, about 60 million years later, resulted in the Paleozoic fauna. Biodiversity was greatly reduced 300 million years later by the great Permian extinctions, which were followed by the Triassic explosion that led to our modern biota. Although all three of these explosions resulted in many new species, they were qualitatively very different. Virtually all major groups of living organisms appeared in the Cambrian period, along with a number of phyla that subsequently became extinct. The Paleozoic and Triassic explosions greatly increased the number of families, genera, and species, but no new phyla of organisms evolved.

The most commonly accepted theory for the differences among these explosions is that, unlike the other two explosions, the Cambrian explosion took place in a world that contained few species of organisms, all of them small. Therefore, the ecological setting was favorable for the evolution of many different life-forms and body plans. Many types of organisms were able to survive initially in this world, but as competition intensified and new types of predators evolved, many forms became extinct. The earth was also relatively poor in species at the times of both of the later explosions, but the species that were present included a wide array of body plans and life-forms. They may have preempted the opportunities for the evolution of strikingly new life-forms.

Two factors appear to be primarily responsible for the continued rise in species richness over evolutionary time. One is the increasing provinciality that accompanied the breakup of Pangaea and, later, Gondwanaland. At the time of breakup, many species probably had distributions covering much of the huge continental landmass. Following the separation, evolution on each of the new continents produced many new species that were continental endemics. Much of the Cenozoic era increase in numbers of species appears to be due to provincialization. Thus, South America, Africa, and Southeast Asia are all rich in species, but they share few species in common because they have been separated from one another for so many millions of years.

The second major factor contributing to species richness is the increasing number of species within ecological communities. For example, late Cenozoic era communities appear to have had about twice as many species in them as did earlier communities, primarily because organisms in later communities were more diverse in their ways of living. In the earlier communities, most organisms lived on or near the surface of bottom sediments. Later there were many more burrowing forms, species able to move actively around on the surface, and species able to swim in the water column. The number of species living together also increased as a result of finer adaptations to particular environmental conditions and ways of exploiting the environment made possible by minor variations in morphology, physiology, and behavior. A perusal of any museum tray of insect specimens can provide a quick overview of the kinds of subtle variations in morphology that have contributed so much to the richness of insect species.

On land, the richness of vascular plants increased dramatically with the evolution of the angiosperms and their complicated interactions with animals during reproduction and dispersal of seeds. The evolution of flight probably also contributed to the great diversity of both insects and birds by allowing better exploitation of the third dimension on land.

More than 99% of the species that have ever lived on earth are extinct. There have been extinctions at all times throughout the history of life, but rates have changed dramatically. Paleontologists distinguish between "normal" or "background" extinction rates and the much higher rates associated with mass extinctions (Sepkoski and Raup 1986). The first of six mass extinctions, at the end of the Cambrian period, destroyed about half of the known animal families. At the end of the Devonian period, 345 million years ago (Mya), another 30% of animal families became extinct. The catastrophe at the close of the Permian period affected both marine and terrestrial organisms. In the oceans, trilobites declined to extinction and brachiopods almost became extinct. On land, the trees that formed the great coal forests became extinct, as did most lineages of amphibians. At the end of the Triassic period, about 180 Mya, nearly all ammonites and approximately 80% of reptile species vanished. At the end of the Cretaceous period, 65 Mya, dinosaurs, large reptiles, and a large fraction of marine lineages disappeared. The current mass extinction, promulgated by human expansion over the planet, initially exterminated large mammals and island species, but if current trends continue, organisms of all sizes and lineages will be seriously affected.

Following each of the previous mass extinctions, biodiversity rapidly expanded again, mostly by the evolution of new families, genera, and species. As we have seen, species richness has continued to increase until very recently, and it might well have continued to increase had *Homo sapiens* not arrived on the scene, armed with the tools of modern technology. The time to recover former richness was measured in millions of years, but the fossil evidence does not suggest that any limits to the number of species that the earth could support have yet been reached.

## Ecological Limits to Species Richness

A number of ecologically based hypotheses to explain patterns of species richness have been proposed (Pianka 1966). Some, but not all of them, are mutually exclusive, and there is no reason to believe that any one hypothesis can explain all patterns of richness. As mentioned previously, most of the geographic patterns of species richness are correlated with patterns in the physical environment that set the stage upon which all biological interactions take place.

*Productivity Hypotheses.* Higher productivity results in higher numbers of individuals and, hence, an opportunity to divide resources among a larger number of species. If high productivity is combined with moist tropical conditions, such that organisms devote relatively little energy to maintaining their temperatures and moistures at appropriate levels, even more energy is potentially available for augmenting populations and species (Connell and Orias 1964). This hypothesis is attractive because of its logical simplicity and the broad correlations between productivity and species richness along latitudinal and altitudinal gradients. Support for the hypothesis is provided by studies showing that there is a strong correlation between realized annual evapotranspiration, a measure of energy available to plants, and tree species richness in North America (Currie and Paquin 1987). Similarly, Gentry (1988) demonstrated a strong correlation between plant species richness in Neotropical forests and absolute annual precipitation, a variable strongly positively correlated with productivity.

However, the relationship between productivity and species richness continues to be controversial. One reason for this, already discussed, is that many of the world's most productive systems, such as estuaries, sea-grass beds, and hot springs, are species-poor. Conversely, plant species richness is higher in semiarid regions with nutrient-deficient soils than in similar areas with richer soils. For example, the remarkably rich plant communities of the Cape region of South Africa (fynbos) and the extreme southwestern corner

**Figure 4.9** Numbers of species of *Eucalyptus* and *Acacia* in southwestern Australia. Notice how many species in these two genera can be found living in close proximity. Similar patterns are found among many other genera of plants in southwestern Australia. (Modified from Lamont et al. 1984.)

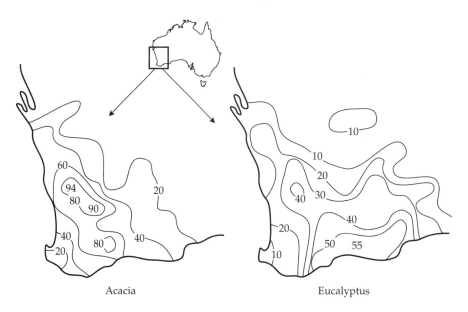

Acacia          Eucalyptus

of Australia (Figure 4.9) are found on highly infertile soils (Kruger and Taylor 1979; Bond 1983; Rice and Westoby 1983; Cody 1986). Nitrogen levels in these soils, derived from ancient sandstones (Bettenay 1984), are an order of magnitude lower than in California and Chile (Specht and Moll 1983), which have fewer species.

Ecologists are still investigating why there is an inverse correlation between soil fertility and plant species richness, but evidence suggests that soil infertility itself is a major contributor to this pattern because it favors abilities to exploit slightly different microhabitats more efficiently (Tilman 1982, 1985). Fynbos vegetation is remarkably variable in leaf morphology (Cody 1986) and growth phenology (Kruger 1981), and these differences are probably correlated with a corresponding diversity of carbon-fixing strategies. In addition, the low palatability of leaves of plants growing on nutrient-poor soils results in a rapid accumulation of flammable biomass, leading to high frequencies of fires in these summer-dry climates.

Frequent fires favor either serotinous (fire-released) seed capsules or rapid burial of seeds. Ants move seeds relatively short distances compared with birds, but they usually bury them. Also, ants pick up and move seeds that offer much smaller rewards than those required to attract birds. Australia, a continent with notoriously poor soils, has the highest proportion of plants with ant-dispersed seeds of any continent (Berg 1975; Westoby et al., 1991) and has unusually high ant species richness (Andersen 1983; Greenslade and Greenslade 1984). Ant-dispersed seeds are also common in South African fynbos (Milewski and Bond 1982). In combination, these factors could result in very high α-species richness and unusually high β-species richness. Species richness on a scale of one hectare is higher in southwestern Australia than it is in rainforests, even though the latter accumulate more species at slightly larger scales (Figure 4.10).

*Structural Hypotheses.* Because plants provide the physical structure within which most other activities take place, it is not surprising that species richness in some taxa is correlated with the structure of the plant community. The animal groups whose richness most strongly reflects the structure of the plant community are those that exploit the environment in three dimensions. Such a relationship is well established for birds, for example, beginning with

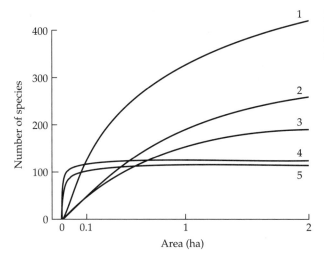

**Figure 4.10** Plant species richness in Borneo and in southwestern Australia. Curves 1, 2, and 3 represent trees >10 cm in diameter in mixed forests in Borneo. Curves 4 and 5 are for plots in southwestern Australia. (Modified from Lamont et al. 1984.)

the pioneering work of Robert MacArthur, who first demonstrated a strong correlation between bird species diversity and foliage height diversity in a number of plant communities (MacArthur and MacArthur 1961; MacArthur 1964). This relationship has been tested on all continents and in many different vegetation types and found to be generally true, although the precise details of the relationships differ among continents, between temperate and tropical regions, and between mainlands and islands. Similarly, the richness of species of web-building spiders is positively correlated with heterogeneity in heights of the tips of vegetation to which such spiders attach their webs (Greenstone 1984).

In contrast, there is no consistent relationship between vegetation structure and lizard species richness in hot deserts in North America, Africa, and Australia (Pianka 1986). The study sites on the three continents were chosen to control for vegetation structure. Low, small-leaved shrubs dominated all sites, and the genus *Atriplex* was an important element at all sites. Despite these similarities, the number of lizard species in African deserts averages twice that in North America, and Australian deserts are about twice as rich as African ones (Table 4.4). The main differences are due to non-lizardlike lizards and nocturnal species. Only one nocturnal lizard is found at the North American sites, whereas there are four nocturnal species at the African and eight at the Australian desert sites. Mammal-like species (the monitors) and wormlike species add to the richness of Australian desert lizard faunas. These differences relate primarily to the long-term evolutionary history of deserts on the three continents, not to any differences in today's vegetation (Pianka 1986).

*Competition/Predation Hypotheses.* The relative importance of competition and predation in shaping ecological communities is highly controversial. It is likely to continue to be so for some time because relationships among these factors are highly complex and difficult to measure. Competition could be expected to reduce α-richness whenever intense competition resulted in the loss of species from ecosystems. The same process could, however, increase α-richness if competition resulted in finer habitat segregation among species. Predation can act to increase species richness if predators prey preferentially upon competitive dominants, thereby preventing competitive exclusion. A well-known example is the increase in species richness in rocky intertidal communities of the Pacific coast of North America resulting from selective predation by the sea star *Pisaster ochraceus* on the com-

**Table 4.4**
Numbers of Species of Lizards in Three Hot Deserts

| Mode of life | North America | | Africa | | Australia | |
|---|---|---|---|---|---|---|
| | Mean | % | Mean | % | Mean | % |
| Diurnal | 6.3 | 86 | 8.2 | 56 | 17.0 | 60 |
|   Ground-dwelling | 5.4 | 74 | 6.3 | 43 | 15.4 | 54 |
|     Sit-and-wait | 4.4 | 60 | 2.3 | 16 | 5.3 | 18 |
|     Widely foraging | 1.0 | 14 | 4.0 | 27 | 10.1 | 36 |
|   Arboreal | 0.9 | 12 | 1.9 | 13 | 2.7 | 9 |
| Nocturnal | 1.0 | 14 | 5.1 | 35 | 10.3 | 36 |
|   Ground-dwelling | 1.0 | 14 | 3.5 | 24 | 7.6 | 27 |
|   Arboreal | 0 | 0 | 1.6 | 11 | 2.7 | 9 |
| Subterranean | 0 | 0 | 1.4 | 10 | 1.2 | 4 |
| All ground-dwelling | 6.4 | 88 | 9.8 | 67 | 23.0 | 78 |
| All arboreal | 0.9 | 12 | 3.5 | 24 | 5.4 | 18 |
| All lizard species | 7.4 | 100 | 14.7 | 100 | 29.8 | 100 |

Data from Pianka 1986.
*Note:* Semiarboreal species are assigned half to arboreal and half to ground-dwelling categories.

petitively dominant mussel *Mytilus californianus* (Paine 1974). On the other hand, predation can reduce species richness by preventing especially vulnerable species from living in an area. Experimental evidence exists for all of these outcomes, but how often, and where these forces exert their influence is unknown (Orians and Kunin 1991).

Several excellent reviews of the competition literature have been carried out, spawned by a heated debate about the importance of interspecific competition in natural communities. Connell (1975, 1983) and Schoener (1983) both reviewed existing field experiments on the subject. Connell used a narrowly defined group of studies under strict criteria, whereas Schoener used a broader sample of studies. They both used their surveys to test a number of hypotheses, including one advanced by Hairston, Smith, and Slobodkin (1960). Hairston et al. observed that the world is green and that dung, detritus, and dead bodies rarely accumulate; therefore, they reasoned, green plants and decomposers must commonly compete for food. Herbivores, on the other hand, especially those that eat the foliage of plants rather than "plant products" such as seeds, pollen, or nectar, seldom exhaust their resources and must, therefore, be limited by their predators. These predators must, in turn, be limited by their own food supply. Schoener found support for this hypothesis in both terrestrial and freshwater environments but only weak support among marine studies. Connell, on the other hand, found no support for the hypothesis among the cases he analyzed. These differences indicate how sensitive conclusions from literature surveys are to the specific criteria used to make the evaluations.

Some researchers have hypothesized that many organisms are held at such low population densities that competition rarely occurs (Connell 1975), but other researchers have suggested that competition occurs primarily during unusually hard times when resources are scarce, called "competitive crunches" (Wiens 1977). Which of these two scenarios applies depends upon

**Table 4.5**
Relative Abundance and Habitat Distribution of Land Birds on Caribbean Islands and Panama[a]

| Locality | Number of species (regional richness) | Average number of species per habitat (local richness) | Habitats per species | Relative abundance per species per habitat | Relative abundance per species per habitat, times number of habitats | Relative abundance of all species together across all habitats |
|---|---|---|---|---|---|---|
| Panama | 135 | 30.2 | 2.01 | 2.95 | 5.93 | 800 |
| Trinidad | 108 | 28.2 | 2.35 | 3.31 | 7.78 | 840 |
| Jamaica | 56 | 21.4 | 3.43 | 4.97 | 17.05 | 955 |
| St. Lucia | 33 | 15.2 | 4.15 | 5.77 | 23.95 | 790 |
| St. Kitts | 20 | 11.9 | 5.35 | 5.88 | 31.45 | 629 |

Data from Cox and Ricklefs 1977.
[a]The table indicates that each habitat in Panama contains more species, but the species are, on average, restricted to fewer habitats than are island species.

whether low population densities are caused by harsh physical conditions or by scarcity of consumable resources.

Indirect evidence of the role of competition in structuring ecological communities is provided by the fact that when many species coexist within a region, each lives in a smaller number of habitats than in areas where there are fewer species (MacArthur et al. 1966). These relationships are most readily seen in island communities, where those species present often attain higher population densities than they or closely related species attain on the mainland, and often expand into habitats they do not occupy on the mainland (Table 4.5). Together these processes of density compensation and habitat expansion (or compression) are collectively referred to as **ecological release.**

Predation can serve as a source of disturbance, especially when it acts upon sessile or space-limited prey species that otherwise dominate available space. Intermediate levels of such disturbance (see Figure 10.3) should result in greater diversity than do either very high or very low levels (Connell 1978; Abugov 1982). Predation should augment species richness where other sources of disturbance are few, but it should reduce species richness when exogenous disturbance is high. However, among marine environments, exposed rocky intertidal zones subjected to periodic desiccation, rain-induced osmotic stress, wave shear, and surf-propelled flotsam face higher background disturbance regimes than protected intertidal habitats, benthic mud habitats, or rocky subtidal habitats. Nonetheless, predators have been demonstrated to increase species richness in most studies in the rocky intertidal and in about half of the studies in the rocky subtidal, but only rarely in studies of benthic mud communities.

*Stability Hypothesis.* The stability hypothesis was originally advanced by Sanders (1968, 1969) who observed that productive estuaries and continental shelves in most latitudes have few species of benthic animals, but that the cold, dark, unproductive floor of the deep sea is very species-rich. Sanders suggested that the deep sea supported many species because its environments were highly predictable and stable and had been so for millennia. Research stimulated by Sanders' data has confirmed that the deep oceans support a rich array of organisms, nearly all of which are dependent upon organic detritus falling from sunlit waters near the surface. Current researchers believe that a combination of factors is needed to explain this unexpected deep-sea species richness; among these factors are the relatively constant levels of temperature, salinity, and oxygen concentration, and the lack of major disturbances. Also, the large size of the oceans and the lack of major barriers to dispersal results in a large species pool from which colonists can be drawn. In addition, food resources are patchily distributed, and the main disturbances are local ones caused by the feeding, burrowing, and mound-building activities of animals (Grassle 1989, 1991). These activities create a patchiness similar to that produced by tree-falls in terrestrial environments. They should create conditions suitable for many different species.

*Time Hypothesis.* Even though patterns of species richness can be explained in terms of one or more processes acting in ecological time, this does not preclude a role for more slowly acting processes that influence species richness patterns over much longer time frames. Indeed, the popularity of Sanders' hypothesis is, in part, attributable to its apparent ability also to account for high species richness in tropical areas. Ecologists were aware that the temperate zones had been subjected to massive disturbances during the Pleistocene, but it was generally believed that the tropics had been stable for extremely long time periods. Therefore, the tropics might have more species because of the long time over which species had accumulated, combined with low extinction rates in those stable environments. By comparison, high-latitude environments, which had undergone a major shuffle during glacial advances, were still accumulating species following retreat of the glaciers.

This hypothesis was fully stated in 1878 by Alfred Russel Wallace:

> The equatorial zone, in short, exhibits to us the result of a comparatively continuous and unchecked development of organic forms; while in the temperate regions there have been a series of periodical checks and extinctions of a more or less disastrous nature, necessitating the commencement of the work of development in certain lines over and over again. In the one, evolution has a fair chance; in the other, it has had countless difficulties thrown in its way. The equatorial regions are then, as regards their past and present life history, a more ancient world than that represented by the temperate zones, a world in which the laws which have governed the progressive development of life have operated with comparatively little check for countless ages, and have resulted in those wonderful eccentricities of structure, of function, and of instinct—that rich variety of colour, and that nicely balanced harmony of relations which delight and astonish us in the animal productions of all tropical countries.

More recent evidence, however, reveals that tropical regions have not been stable. Not only are there well-marked wet and dry seasons there today, but precipitation patterns and temperatures changed dramatically concurrently with glacial advances at high latitudes. For example, long pollen records from Africa reveal that regions that today are wet tropical forests were covered with dry woodland or grassland at the time of the last glaciation (Livingstone 1975; Livingstone and van der Hammen 1978). In South America, temperatures dropped in equatorial regions, and the Amazonian rainforest was broken into isolated patches separated by deciduous forest or savanna (Prance 1982). Indeed, some authors attribute the extremely high species richness in many groups of forest organisms in South America to rapid speciation in isolated forest fragments during dry glacial periods (Haffer 1969; Simpson and Haffer 1978; Prance 1982). Alternate expansions and contractions of forests are also believed to account for the diversity of some groups of Australian organisms, such as *Eucalyptus* (Pryor and Johnson 1971) and birds (Keast 1961).

The ecological interactions that appear, in combination with physical environmental factors, to determine today's patterns of species richness might set absolute limits to species richness. On the other hand, they might change over time to allow more species to be accommodated. Are there limits to the number of species, limits that can exert major influences on the composition of a given ecological community? Is there a critical limit to overlap in resource use that will prevent more species from being accommodated unless dramatic changes occur in the nature of available resources? Does the chemical warfare between plants and herbivores set limits to species richness or does it offer possibilities for more species? Are there limits to the size of mimicry systems and do mimicry systems allow more species to be accommodated in ecosystems than would be possible without them? Is there reason to believe that the richness-generating interactions between plants and their pollinators and between plants and their seed dispersers have been exhausted? These questions cannot be answered with any assurance today but research on these and related questions is under way.

## The Future of Biodiversity Studies

The incomplete state of our knowledge of the identities, taxonomic relationships, and distributions of the vast majority of the world's organisms means that the primary work of cataloging biodiversity is yet to be done. How this inventory should be carried out is the subject of much debate. Some biologists recommend initiation of an intense global survey, aimed at the discovery and classification of all species. Others, pointing to the shortage of people, funds, and time, believe that the only realistic hope lies in the rapid recognition and preservation of those threatened habitats that contain the largest numbers of endemic species, relegating the inventory task to a lower immediate priority. Wilson (1992) strongly advocates a mixed strategy that combines global surveys designed to achieve a complete biodiversity inventory in 50 years with quicker attention to hot spots (see Essay 4B). He envisions a three-level strategy. The first level is a Rapid Assessment Program (RAP) that would investigate, within the next few years, poorly known ecosystems that might turn out to be unidentified hot spots. RAP teams would be formed, consisting of experts on groups such as flowering plants, reptiles, mammals, birds, fishes, and butterflies that are well enough known to be inventoried quickly and accurately. These groups would then serve as proxies for the entire biota. (There is a fuller discussion of RAP in Essay 5B).

The next level proposed by Wilson is the BIOTROP approach, patterned after the Neotropical Biological Diversity Program of the University of Kansas and a consortium of other North American universities. The goal of this approach is to establish research stations in areas believed to be major hot spots or to contain multiple hot spots. Inventories and ecological studies would then be carried out across latitudes and elevations in the regions surrounding the stations. The third level, with a time frame of 50 years, would combine the inventories from RAP and BIOTROP with monographic studies of many groups of organisms to provide a more complete picture of global biodiversity and its distribution.

Whatever approach is taken by society, it will require much more effort than has been invested in biodiversity studies during recent decades. Not only is the scope of the untapped wealth residing in biodiversity unappreciated, but the importance of inventorying biodiversity and understanding ecological relationships among species has not been sufficiently appreciated. It is doubtful that humans can devise a sustainable future without a more complete knowledge of biodiversity. Even the very notion of biodiversity will be modified as our knowledge grows. For example, Lincoln Brower, in Essay

4D, introduces the concept of an "endangered biological phenomenon," in which a species will likely survive, but some spectacular aspect of its life history, such as a mass annual migration, is in jeopardy of disappearing.

## ESSAY 4D

# A New Paradigm in Conservation of Biodiversity
## Endangered Biological Phenomena

Lincoln P. Brower, University of Florida

Much of conservation research focuses on describing diminishing species diversity and on understanding the processes that lead species to small populations, and thence to extinction. Here, I discuss endangered biological phenomena, a newly developed conservation theme recently introduced by Brower and Malcolm (1991). *An endangered phenomenon is a spectacular aspect of the life history of an animal or plant species involving a large number of individuals that is threatened with impoverishment or demise; the species per se need not be in peril, rather, the phenomenon it exhibits is at stake.*

Examples of endangered phenomena include the ecological diversity associated with naturally flooding rivers, the vast herds of bison of the North American prairie ecosystems, the synchronous flowering cycles of bamboo in India, the 17-year and 13-year cicada emergence events in eastern North America, entire indigenous fish faunas of the African Rift Valley lake ecosystems, and scores of current animal migrations. Instances of the latter include seasonal migrations of the African wildebeest and North American caribou, the billion individuals of 120 songbird species that migrate from Canada to Neotropical overwintering areas, and the nearly obliterated migrations of numerous species of whales.

There are two principal biological reasons why animal migrations are endangered by human activities. First, migrant species move through a sequence of ecologically distinct areas, any one of which may become an Achilles' heel. Second, population aggregation or bottlenecking occurs during certain times of the year, making the animals especially vulnerable. The major impact on migrating animals is from accelerating habitat modification throughout the world. Even when problems are recognized, mitigation is difficult because of different policies and enforcement abilities in the different countries the ani-

mals occupy during different parts of their life history cycles. The extraordinary migration and overwintering behavior of the monarch butterfly, both in eastern and western North America, has become such an endangered phenomenon.

The monarch butterfly, *Danaus plexippus* (L.), is a member of the tropical subfamily Danainae, which contains 157 known species (Ackery and Vane-Wright 1984). It is alone in its subfamily for having evolved an extraordinary spring and fall migration (Figures A and B) that allows it to exploit the abundant *Asclepias* (milkweed) food supply across

the North American continent. Here it has become one of the most abundant butterflies in the world. Remarkably, and in contrast to vertebrate migrations, the monarch's orientation and navigation to its overwintering sites is carried out by descendants three or more generations removed from their migrant forebears. Its fall migration is completely inherited, with no opportunity for learned behavior. This, together with the vastness of the migration and overwintering aggregations, constitutes a unique biological phenomenon.

Two migratory populations of the monarch occur in North America. The

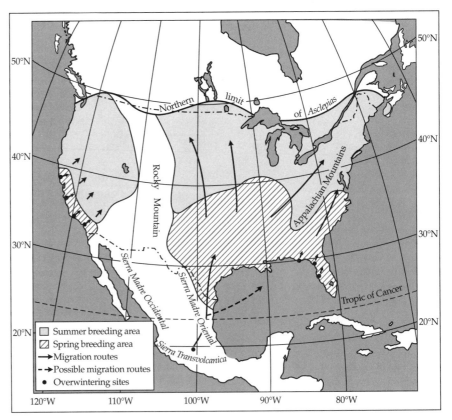

**Figure A** Spring migrations of the eastern and western populations of the monarch butterfly in North America. (From Brower and Malcolm 1991.)

larger one occurs east of the Rocky Mountains and undoubtedly represents the stock from which the smaller western North American migration evolved. Both migrations are threatened because the monarch's aggregation behavior during winter concentrates an entire species gene pool into several tiny and vulnerable geographic areas.

***Threats to the Western Population.*** Monarchs that breed west of the Rocky Mountains migrate in the fall to about 40 known overwintering sites in California. All of these are within a few hundred meters of the Pacific Ocean, which moderates the climate and prevents the butterflies from freezing.

Because of the exorbitant value of coastal real estate in California, all colonies on privately owned land are in a tenuous position. Moreover, several of the sites protected in city, county, or state parks are rapidly deteriorating. Four factors contribute to this: benign neglect ignores ecological succession and tree senescence, which results in failure of the sites to provide protection against winter winds; trees on unprotected land adjacent to parks are subject to cutting, again leading to wind invasion; humans cause soil compaction, erosion, and vegetational deterioration; and there are conflicting policies over native versus exotic plant management.

The people of California are reacting to these threats. For example, the city of Pacific Grove managed, by a remarkable 67% vote, to purchase the most famous of all California overwintering habitats. However, the sheer magnitude of the problem is indicated by the fact that Pacific Grove had to appropriate $1.4 million to buy the 2.5-acre parcel of land. The earlier passage of California Proposition 70 in 1988, which appropriated $2 million to purchase monarch habitat, thus palls in the face of economic reality. A more creative approach is needed in order to acquire, protect, and manage a substantial number of the coastal overwintering habitats.

***Threats to the Eastern Population.*** The eastern population breeds over a much larger area east of the Rocky Mountains and is probably at least 10,000 times larger than the western population. Beginning in late August, monarchs migrate to central Mexico, where they overwinter for more than 5 months in high-altitude fir forests in the Sierra Transvolcanica, about 90 km west of Mexico City. Here the butterflies coalesce by the tens of millions into dense and stunningly spectacular aggregations that festoon up to 5 ha of forest (Figure C). The butterflies, effectively in cold storage, remain sexually inactive until the approach of the vernal equinox.

Survivors from the Mexican overwintering colonies begin migrating northward in late March to lay their eggs on sprouting milkweed plants (*Asclepias* spp.) along the Gulf Coast. These 8-month-old remigrants then die, and their offspring, produced in late April and early May, continue the migration northward to Canada. Over the summer, two or three more generations are produced. Toward the end of August, butterflies of the last summer generation are in reproductive diapause, and the cycle begins anew as these monarchs instinctively migrate southward to the family overwintering grounds in Mexico.

To date, ten overwintering areas have been discovered in the states of Michoacan and Mexico on a few isolated mountain ranges at elevations from 2900 to 3400 m. The five largest and least disturbed of these occur in an astoundingly small area of 800 km². This elevational band occupies a summer fog belt and is dominated by boreal

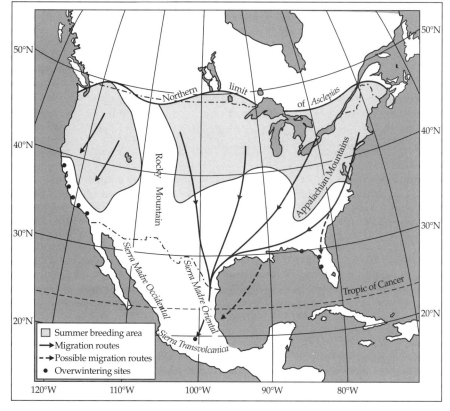

**Figure B**   Fall migrations of the eastern and western populations of the monarch butterfly in North America. (From Brower and Malcolm 1991.)

**Figure C**   Dense overwintering clusters of the monarch butterfly on the trunk of an *Abies religiosa* fir tree in the Sierra Chinqua colony, Michoacan, Mexico, on 18 January 1985. (From Calvert and Brower 1986.)

forests that probably are a relict ecosystem of the Pleistocene. By clustering in this cool and moist environment, individual monarchs are able to survive in a state of reproductive inactivity until the resurgence of the North American milkweed flora the following spring.

Because the monarch's specialized overwintering sites are limited to such a small area in Mexico, the eastern North American migratory phenomenon is now threatened with extinction and likely will be destroyed within 15 years if drastic measures are not implemented immediately. The following briefly summarizes some of the problems and what must be done to prevent the loss of this endangered phenomenon.

Until recently, human impact on the high-altitude fir forests has been less than that on other forest ecosystems in Mexico. However, in the past 15 years, human population growth and commercial logging have accelerated at an alarming pace. Negative developments include: (1) major commercial harvesting of trees, involving thinning and clear-cutting; (2) expansion of villages up the mountainsides, which in turn has led to (3) an increased frequency of fires associated with forest clearing for planting corn and oats; (4) legal and illegal removal of logs and firewood; (5) an increase in localized charcoal manufacturing in pits dug within the *Abies* forest; (6) purposeful setting of fires in the forest to kill and cure young trees for use in local home construction; (7) forest lepidopteran pests that have recently invaded some areas of the *Abies* ecosystem, probably due to the stress caused by thinning and deforestation at lower altitudes; (8) spraying of *Bacillus thuringiensis*, an organic pesticide, which has been initiated and considered for widespread use without adequate knowledge of its potential effect on the monarchs; and (9) increasingly heavy visitor impact upon the vegetation within and surrounding the overwintering colonies, even though the government is developing tourist control policies.

A major problem for monarchs in Mexico is that political and administrative difficulties arise in implementing conservation laws because the forests are under a mosaic of control by local, state, and federal governmental entities. The federal and state governments of Mexico must pass, coordinate, and enforce major new legislation in order to solve this problem. Time is running out.

Because the probability of a species' extinction is inversely proportional to the number of its refuges, prudence argues that all major overwintering mountain areas in Mexico should be preserved. An unrecognized incentive to do this is that protection of the higher montane slopes that host the fir forest as well as the monarchs will automatically preserve the hydrological resources of the area.

Unlike the Passenger Pigeon or Carolina Parakeet, we will not lose the monarch butterfly as a species, because numerous nonmigratory populations will persist in its tropical range. However, its spectacular North American migrations will soon be destroyed if extensive overwintering habitat protection and management in Mexico and California is not successfully implemented. The impending fate of this unusual insect is an omen for the entire world biota, warning us that we must incorporate the concept of endangered biological phenomena into our 21st century plans for conserving biodiversity.

Once a reasonably complete inventory of the biota of a region, or significant components of it, has been achieved, a monitoring program should be established. Such a program should be designed to detect trends in biodiversity and to identify impending problems to which attention should be directed. Without such a program, society cannot know whether its efforts to preserve biodiversity are succeeding, or where and why they are failing.

The relationship between area and species richness has major practical implications for the location, design, and management of parks and reserves established and maintained to preserve biodiversity. There is increasing evidence that even the largest parks and reserves are too small to maintain viable populations of those species with the largest areal requirements (discussed in Chapter 10). Many of the national parks of the United States have already lost their largest mammal species, and the trend continues (Newmark 1987). Therefore, additional studies of the species–area relationship and its causes are essential for informed management of reserves. Meanwhile, existing knowledge of species–area relationships is being used to establish reserves, a notable example being the megareserve system of Costa Rica (see Figure 13.18), which is designed to preserve about 80% of the biodiversity of the country over the long term. Each megareserve includes natural areas and areas managed for economically valuable products. Some of them remain the homes of indigenous people who continue to use the environment in their traditional ways. The largest of the Costa Rican reserves, Talamanca Biosphere Reserve, is a mosaic of more than 500,000 hectares and includes three national or international parks, a large biological reserve, five Indian reservations, and two large forest reserves (Figure 4.11).

Talamanca is part of the UNESCO Man and the Biosphere (MAB) program of worldwide Biosphere Reserves. Reserves are nominated by the na-

**Figure 4.11** The mountainous La Amistad International Park is part of the Talamanca Biosphere Reserve of southern Costa Rica and northern Panama. This Biosphere Reserve contains some of the richest biodiversity in all of Central America. At least 263 species of amphibians and reptiles and 400 species of birds have been recorded in the reserve. (Photograph by C. R. Carroll.)

tional MAB committee of the country concerned. The nomination is reviewed by the MAB Bureau, and if accepted, the reserve is formally designated part of the MAB network. Some Biosphere Reserves cross national boundaries and are, therefore, international; such is the case with La Amistad International Park, within Talamanca. Biosphere Reserves serve a range of objectives which include research, monitoring, training, education, and conservation. Many Biosphere Reserves include indigenous human populations that continue to utilize the area in ways that maintain the functional integrity of the ecological systems. The "ideal" Biosphere Reserve contains an undisturbed core area surrounded by peripheral zones which permit increasing levels of human-caused disturbances. However, few existing reserves actually have this structure. These reserves are discussed more fully in Chapters 10 and 17.

On a theoretical level, biodiversity studies continue to be needed to resolve the many uncertainties surrounding the historical and present-day ecological processes that determine today's patterns of biodiversity. Modern molecular techniques that enable systematists to develop soundly based phylogenies are being combined with biogeographic studies to provide a more complete picture of the history of the distribution of life on earth than has previously been available. Processes operating over ecological time frames are increasingly being studied using manipulative experiments in which restricted areas are defaunated, particular species are removed, or species are introduced. Many "natural experiments" are being conducted from which ecological insight may be gained: volcanic eruptions that eliminate the biotas of islands; the massive inadvertent movement of species around the world by human travel; deliberate introductions for agricultural, aesthetic, or pest control purposes; and habitat fragmentation by conversion of natural landscapes to those dominated by highly modified communities that are managed to channel most of their productivity to human uses. Such scenarios provide opportunities to examine the results of manipulations over longer time frames than is possible with investigator-initiated experiments.

Studies of the influences of human activities on species distributions and species richnesses are adding rapidly to our understanding of the roles of the varied processes that interact to cause the patterns of biodiversity on earth that so fascinate us today. This knowledge is also being used to attempt to reduce the rates of species extinctions and to restore landscapes so that they can continue to support the array of species originally found in them.

## Summary

Biodiversity is a term that refers to the variety of living organisms, their genetic diversity, and the types of ecological communities into which they are assembled. The number of species—species richness—found in different areas is the measure of biodiversity commonly used in conservation biology, both because accurate information on abundance typically is not available and because rare species are often of great conservation interest. About 1.5 million living and 300,000 fossil species have been described, but estimates of the total number of living species range from 10 million to as high as 50 million or more. Although species richness is higher on land than in the oceans, 31 of the 32 extant animal phyla are marine, and 14 are exclusively marine.

Cellular life in the form of bacteria evolved about 3.5 billion years ago, and eukaryotic organisms about 2 billion years ago. The first major explosion of biodiversity took place in the early Cambrian period, and except during mass extinctions, the number of species has increased since then. More species are probably alive today than at any other time in the history of life, even though some taxa had more species in the past than they do today. The causes of increasing species richness over evolutionary time include the breakup of the continents and the evolution of more diverse body plans that enabled animals to burrow, swim, and fly.

Several broad patterns characterize the distribution of species today. Among most taxa, more species live in tropical regions than at higher latitudes. Species richness is also positively correlated with structural complexity. On land, structure is provided primarily by vascular plants, whereas in many marine communities, animals such as corals generate most structure. In general, there is a positive correlation between productivity and species richness, but there are conspicuous exceptions. Some highly productive systems, such as salt marshes, sea-grass beds, and hot springs, are species-poor. Conversely, plant species richness is extremely high in some unproductive semiarid regions with poor soils. Island communities are poorer in species than comparable mainland communities at all latitudes.

Areas that have experienced long geographic isolation and which have great topographic relief often support many endemic species. Biogeographers recognize 18 of these "hot spots," which collectively contain about 20% of the world's plant species in only 0.5% of the world's land area. Some of these areas are also regions of high endemism of animal species, but others, such as southwestern Australia and the Cape region of Africa, have relatively few endemic animals. These areas are too small to have permitted in situ speciation of most taxa of larger animals. In addition to productivity and structural complexity, species diversity is influenced by competitive interactions and predation. Formerly it was believed that stability favored high species richness, but more recent evidence suggests that moderate levels of disturbance enhance local species richness.

The state of knowledge of earth's biodiversity is so poor that the primary work of cataloging biodiversity has yet to be done. Resources currently devoted to this task are inadequate, especially given the rate at which species are becoming extinct. Better information on biodiversity, its distribution, and its causes is needed for informed management of the earth's biotic resources.

## Questions for Discussion

1. Indices of species diversity that are weighted by abundance, biomass, or productivity have been used frequently by ecologists, but seldom by conservation biologists. For what purposes might conservation biologists wish to use weighted indices instead of simple lists of species?

2. Given that millions of species have yet to be described and named, how should the limited human and financial resources available for taxonomic research be allocated? Should attention be concentrated on poorly known taxa? Should efforts be directed toward areas threatened with habitat destruction so that species can be collected before they are eliminated? Should major efforts be directed toward obtaining complete "all-taxa" surveys of selected areas? How should these decisions be made?

3. The history of life has been punctuated by six episodes during which extinction rates were very high. If extinction is a normal process, and if life has diversified after each of the previous mass extinctions, why should we be worried about the prospect of high extinction rates during the coming century? How does the current extinction spasm differ from previous ones?

4. Many conservation efforts are directed at particular local areas harboring rare species or having high species richness. Why is concentrating only on local problems insufficient as an effective conservation strategy? Why is local species richness dependent, in part, upon regional species richness? How can we find out which processes dominate the interactions between local and regional species richness?

5. For which animal taxa would you expect species richness to be most positively correlated with plant community structure? Mammals? Amphibians? Insects? Why?

6. Evidence gathered by many ecologists suggests that intermediate levels of disturbance often act to increase the number of species found in an area. What are the implications of this finding for investigations in conservation biology and management of reserves?

7. How can biologists determine whether there are limits to the number of species that can be supported in local areas? What type of research could determine whether the global number of species is still increasing (or would have increased had humans not intervened)?

## Suggestions for Further Reading

Brown, J. H. and A. C. Gibson. 1983. *Biogeography.* Mosby, St. Louis. The best textbook on biogeography. It describes both the history of the distribution of life and the current patterns of distributions of organisms and the theories to account for them.

MacArthur, R. H. and E. O. Wilson. 1967. *The Theory of Island Biogeography.* Princeton University Press, Princeton, NJ. The classic book that launched the modern experimental study of causes of patterns of species richness. It lays out the basic species–area relationships and the patterns of species diversity on islands.

Myers, N. 1983. *A Wealth of Wild Species.* Westview Press, Boulder, CO. An engaging account of the ways in which humans benefit from the use and enjoyment of other organisms.

Prance, G. H. (ed.). 1982. *The Biological Model of Diversification in the Tropics.* Columbia University Press, New York. A set of essays that analyzes why the tropics are the home of so much of the earth's biological richness.

World Conservation and Monitoring Centre. 1992. *Global Biodiversity: Status of the Earth's Living Resources.* Chapman & Hall, London. A storehouse of information on biodiversity. Intended as a sourcebook of data and analysis rather than a book to be read cover to cover.

# 5

# Global Biodiversity II
## Losses

*The worst thing that can happen during the 1980s is not energy depletion, economic collapse, limited nuclear war, or conquest by a totalitarian government. As terrible as these catastrophes would be for us, they can be repaired within a few generations. The one process ongoing in the 1980s that will take millions of years to correct is the loss of genetic and species diversity by the destruction of natural habitats. This is the folly that our descendants are least likely to forgive us.*

E. O. Wilson, 1985

In the previous chapter you learned about patterns of biodiversity and some of the processes that result in those patterns. The extent of biodiversity—the tremendous wealth of genetic, species, and ecosystem diversity—should by now be evident. But those biological riches, the information and entities that constitute our biosphere, are individually and collectively in grave danger of major degradation or outright loss. This chapter will address the problem of biodiversity losses.

## Overview of Mass Extinctions

There is much evidence that we are in the opening phase of a **mass extinction** of species (Ehrlich and Ehrlich 1981; Wilson 1988a, 1989, 1992; Western and Pearl 1989; Club of Earth 1990; Myers 1990a,b; Raven 1990; Soulé 1991). A mass extinction can be defined as an exceptional decline in biodiversity that is substantial in size and global in extent, and affects a broad range of taxonomic groups over a short period of time (Jablonski 1986; Sepkoski 1988). In this sense, the present mass extinction—if it remains unchecked by conservation action of appropriate scope and scale—could rival and conceivably surpass in extent any of the great mass extinction episodes of the prehistoric past.

As discussed in Chapter 4, there are other forms of biodiversity, notably genetic and ecosystem diversity, and their losses will be addressed in this chapter. But the biggest and most readily recognized form of biodepletion lies with species extinctions, and this will be our prime focus.

The evidence for a mass extinction of species is as follows. Earth's stock of species is widely estimated to total a minimum of 10 million (Ehrlich and Ehrlich 1981; Club of Earth 1990; May 1992b; Wilson 1992). Some scientists, notably Erwin (1991), believe the true total could well be 30 million, possibly 50 million, and conceivably 100 million. Of the conservative number of 10 million species, about 90% are usually considered to be terrestrial (Raven et al. 1993), and of these, some 80%, or 7.2 million, are believed to occur in the tropics (Stevens 1989), with more than two-thirds of them, or roughly 5 million, in tropical forests of various sorts, ranging from very wet to quite dry forests and thorn scrub (Ricklefs and Schluter 1993).

As we shall see, tropical forests are not only the richest biome biotically, they are also the biome where habitat depletion is occurring fastest—not only outright destruction but gross degradation and fragmentation, resulting in the loss of many ecosystem functions, including food webs. So this biome is the prime locus of mass extinction, and hence the main focus of this chapter.

But the reader should bear in mind—and we emphasize the point—that several other biomes are ultrarich biotically and likewise undergoing depletion. The marine realm, with its estimated one million species or so, has traditionally been viewed as biotically depauperate in comparison with the terrestrial realm. But recent research suggests the true total on just the ocean floor, mostly made up of mollusks, crustaceans, and polychaete worms, could be as high as 10 million (Grassle 1991; Grassle et al. 1991; Ray and Grassle 1991; for a dissident view, proposing only half a million species, see May 1992a). There is also a qualitative aspect: whereas land habitats feature 11 phyla (only one of which is limited to land), the seas are home to 32 phyla, 14 of which are found nowhere else. A deep sea area no bigger than two tennis courts has been found to contain 798 species representing 14 phyla, a higher-taxon diversity that could not remotely be matched on land (Grassle and Maciolek 1992; see also Essay 4C).

Coral reefs are often richer in species per unit area than are tropical forests, and they are undergoing widespread degradation. They cover about 600,000 km$^2$, or only 0.2% of the oceans' surface (tropical moist forests cover 7.5 million km$^2$, or 6% of land surface), yet in this limited expanse they may well contain one-third of the oceans' fish species. As many as 93% of coral reefs have already been damaged and possibly 5–10% destroyed by human activity, and at the present depletion rate a full 60% could be lost within 20–40 years (Dubinsky 1990; Fujita et al. 1992). But major habitat losses are not confined to tropical forests or marine systems. Examples of severe losses of other habitat types around the world are listed in Table 5.1.

Similarly, freshwater ecosystems feature exceptional concentrations of certain taxa, as well as high rates of endemism, and are rapidly being degraded. For example, the three main East African Rift Valley lakes (Victoria, Tanganyika, and Malawi) harbor almost 1000 cichlid fish species (about the same number of fishes found in all of North America and Europe), the great bulk of them endemic; Lake Victoria has already lost at least 200 of its 300 cichlids, making this the largest vertebrate mass extinction of the modern era (Baskin 1992; Kauffman 1992; Goldschmidt et al. 1993). Most of this loss is due to the intentional introduction of a single species, the Nile perch (*Lates niloticus*), a voracious predator (Figure 5.1). Many North American freshwater fish species are likewise endangered or are already extinct (Miller et al. 1989; Williams et al. 1989; Minckley and Deacon 1991), and many are at extreme risk due to their ultrarestricted distribution; for example, the Devil's Hole pupfish has a global habitat totaling a few square meters (Figure 5.2), dependent on groundwater stability in a desert that is under constant pressure for development.

**Figure 5.1**   The Nile perch (*Lates niloticus*), an introduced species in Lake Victoria, is responsible for the extinction of numerous endemic species of cichlids. (Photograph courtesy of John N. Rinne.)

**Figure 5.2**   Devil's Hole, Nye County, Nevada, home of the Devil's Hole pupfish (*Cyprinodon diabolis*). This deep, water-filled fissure in the rocks encompasses the entire range of this species, and may represent the most restrictive distribution of any vertebrate in the world. (Photograph by G. K. Meffe.)

**Table 5.1**

Examples of Major Nonforested Habitat Types, Their Original Extent, and
Percentage Remaining

| Country or region | Habitat type | Original extent (km$^2$) | Percent remaining | Reference |
|---|---|---|---|---|
| North America | Tallgrass prairie | 1,430,000 | 1 | WRI 1991 |
| Sri Lanka | Thorn scrub | 19,800 | 25 | MacKinnon and MacKinnon 1986b |
| United Kingdom | Heathland | 1,432 | 27 | Nature Conservancy (UK) 1984 |
| Nigeria | Mangrove | 24,440 | 50 | MacKinnon and MacKinnon 1986a |
| Paraguay | Chaco | 320,000 | 57 | Redford et al. 1990 |
| South Africa | Fynbos | 75,000 | 67 | Mooney 1988 |

From Groom and Schumaker 1993.

But let us return to tropical forests and consider again the higher estimates for the planetary spectrum of species, between 30 million and 100 million. Since many of the additional species are thought to live in tropical
moist forests, the true planetary total is not a matter of mere academic speculation. These forests are where habitats are being lost fastest and where the
great bulk of extinctions is occurring. So if the real total is at least 30 million
species, the extinction rate will surely be twice as high as the rate postulated
on a basis of only 10 million species. But for the sake of caution and conservatism, let us accept a total of 10 million species. At least half of these species
live in tropical moist forests (see Figure 5.6), even though remaining forests
of this type now cover only 6% of earth's land surface, an expanse equivalent
to the continental United States.

According to the latest calculations of Myers (1989, 1992a,b), these forests
are being destroyed at a rate of at least 150,000 km$^2$ per year. Globally, rates
of loss of forest cover of all types vary greatly by continent (Figure 5.3), but
the inarguable trend is toward severe losses. "True" deforestation rates are
difficult to pin down, and have been a matter of some controversy (discussed in Box 5A). With regard to tropical forests, controversy surrounded
separate estimates for 1980 deforestation rates worked out by Myers and by
the main United Nations agency concerned with tropical forests, the Food
and Agriculture Organization (FAO). Now, the FAO (1993) has estimated
that deforestation in 1991 was 134,000 km$^2$—a figure only 11% lower than
Myers's estimate.

In addition to outright destruction of forests, an expanse at least as large
is being grossly disrupted through logging and slash-and-burn conversion to
pasture and cropland (Figure 5.4), with resultant degradation and impoverishment of ecosystems and their species' life-support systems. Recent information from the Amazonian region of Brazil, based on satellite data, shows
that not only are forests being lost outright, but the remaining forests are
highly degraded through edge effects and isolation (a concept discussed in
detail in Chapter 9), which greatly increases the total negative effects on biodiversity (Table 5.2).

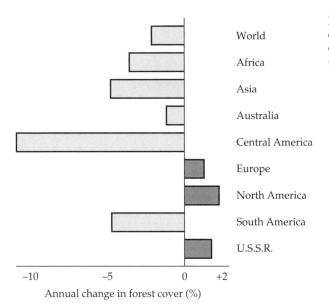

**Figure 5.3** Estimates of average annual rates of change in forest cover around the world for the period 1977–1989. Deforestation is estimated as the amount of forest converted to nonforest use. (Modified from WRI 1992.)

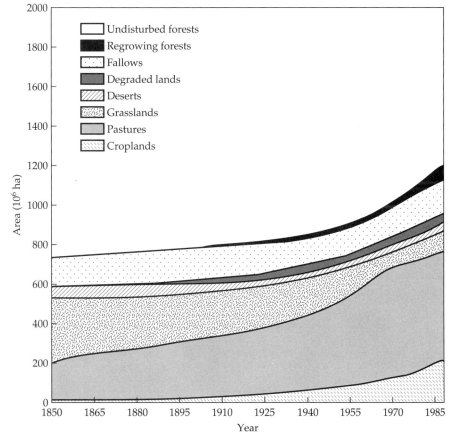

**Figure 5.4** Changes in land use in Latin America from 1850 to 1985. Note the increase in pastures and croplands, and the losses of undisturbed forests and grasslands. (From Houghton et al. 1991.)

# BOX 5A
# Quantifying Patterns of Deforestation
Martha J. Groom, University of Washington

Landscape change is one of the foremost threats to both biodiversity and sustainability of human development. Although it is clear that the pace of landscape alteration has increased in recent decades, the details of the patterns and processes underlying habitat loss are poorly known. We need detailed information on the effects of landscape change throughout the world in order to interpret how habitat losses may affect biodiversity and human development. Patterns of forest loss are generally better quantified than losses in nonforested habitats, yet data limitations abound here as well. Unfortunately, the comparability among deforestation estimates is often low due to differences in the methods and definitions used by researchers.

Estimates of deforestation rates vary tremendously both for global and regional totals (Table A) and for single countries (Figure A). There is often profound disagreement over deforestation statistics largely because they have very real political consequences. Statistics on deforestation are influential in both conservation and development policy, af-

fecting the design of national or multinational agreements to preserve the environment as well as allocation of funding for development programs (Groom and Schumaker 1993). Recent treaties on biodiversity and limitations on greenhouse emissions signed in 1992 at the Earth Summit in Rio de Janeiro suggest that deforestation estimates may soon have significant political consequences for individual countries. Such estimates can be used to indicate how well a country is preserving its biodiversity, as well as in calculating a country's total contribution to global greenhouse gas emissions. Countries may be pressured to reduce forest conversion if available estimates of deforestation are too high (Monastersky 1993). Yet, because the data available for evaluating landscape change are so few, it is inevitable that disagreements will occur. Understanding some of the reasons that the statistics vary can help us interpret them better.

Differences in the definitions and assumptions used in quantifying both the forests' original extent and how much forest has been converted to another

land use are the primary reasons deforestation statistics have varied so widely. There are many different types of forest, and different authors may include all or just one or a few types in their calculations. The broadest classification is "closed" versus "open" forest, which refers to whether or not trees cover a sufficiently high proportion of the area to prevent a continuous grass layer from growing. Open forests may be more commonly degraded by low levels of human use (such as timber gathering) than closed forests, although closed forests may often be more sensitive to less direct forms of degradation, such as edge effects. Some of the earliest data on deforestation did not include gross disruption of forests (FAO 1981), and thus underestimated global forest losses. More recent reports usually include separate estimates for open and closed forests (FAO 1988; Myers 1989). Information on forest losses at this scale is mostly used to evaluate conservation needs on a country-by-country basis, or in modeling efforts to monitor change (Schneider 1993).

To evaluate whether particular habitats are in critical need of protection, it is necessary to make finer distinctions among habitat types in reports of deforestation and other forms of landscape change (Groom and Schumaker 1993). There are many vegetational associations, each of which may harbor characteristic suites of species. To the extent that we can distinguish among different habitat types, we can begin to evaluate where habitat losses have been concentrated, and thus begin to set our conservation priorities. Table B shows a more detailed breakdown of forest losses in three countries. It is clear that some forest types are severely threatened (such as dry deciduous forests in Costa Rica and tropical pine forests in Thailand), while others may be relatively intact

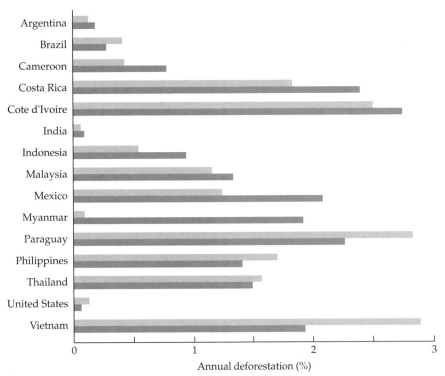

**Figure A**   Two different estimates of annual deforestation rates for 15 countries. Dark bars: data adapted from FAO 1980 and 1990 estimates (WRI 1992, Table 17.1); light bars: data taken from several independent country-based estimates made between 1980 and 1991 (WRI 1992, Table 19.1). Methods used for the latter are not uniform. (From Groom and Schumaker 1993.)

**Table A**
Tropical Forest Area and Reported Deforestation Rates Listed by Country

| Country | Total forest area (km²) | Percent of world total | 1970s | | Late 1980s | | | |
|---|---|---|---|---|---|---|---|---|
| | | | Deforestation rate (km²) (FAO) | Percent of world total | Deforestation rate (km²) (Myers) | Percent of world total | Deforestation rate (km²) (WRI) | Percent of world total |
| Brazil | 3,562,800 | 30.7 | 13,600 | 19.7 | 50,000 | 36.1 | 80,000 | 48.4 |
| Indonesia | 1,135,750 | 9.8 | 5,500 | 8.0 | 12,000 | 8.7 | 9,000 | 5.4 |
| Zaire | 1,056,500 | 9.1 | 1,700 | 2.5 | 4,000 | 2.9 | 1,820 | 1.1 |
| Peru | 693,100 | 6.0 | 2,450 | 3.6 | 3,500 | 2.5 | 2,700 | 1.6 |
| Columbia | 464,000 | 4.0 | 8,000 | 11.6 | 6,500 | 4.7 | 8,200 | 5.0 |
| India | 460,440 | 4.0 | 1,320 | 1.9 | 4,000 | 2.9 | 15,000 | 9.1 |
| Bolivia | 440,100 | 3.8 | 650 | 1.0 | 1,500 | 1.1 | 870 | 0.5 |
| Papua New Guinea | 337,100 | 2.9 | 210 | 0.3 | 3,500 | 2.5 | 220 | 0.1 |
| Venezuela | 318,700 | 2.7 | 1,250 | 1.8 | 1,500 | 1.1 | 1,250 | 0.8 |
| Burma | 311,930 | 2.7 | 920 | 1.3 | 8,000 | 5.8 | 6,770 | 4.1 |
| Others[a] | 2,829,930 | 24.4 | 33,300 | 48.3 | 44,100 | 31.8 | 39,610 | 23.9 |
| Total | 11,610,350 | 100.0 | 68,900 | 100.0 | 138,600 | 100.0 | 165,400 | 100.0 |

From Skole and Tucker 1993.
[a]Sixty-three other countries

(such as tropical montane evergreen forests in Thailand and montane rainforests in Costa Rica).

There are many ways to delineate habitat types, but our strongest limits here may primarily be technical. We must rely on aerial and satellite images if we are to evaluate landscape change on anything other than a local scale. However, these images are often too coarse to allow us to distinguish many forest types (see below). Obviously, in the interests of obtaining estimates of changes on broad scales, we have to sacrifice detailed knowledge of where our losses are concentrated.

Similarly, differences in what authors decide constitutes a loss of forest and how those losses are estimated greatly influence deforestation statistics (Houghton et al. 1991). Most commonly, authors differ on whether land used for commercial forestry should be considered a loss. From the perspective of biodiversity, even low-intensity forestry, such as selective logging, often causes local extinctions (Johns 1985; Myers 1989). Commercial logging may cause smaller changes in geochemical processes or ecosystem function than other land uses, although differences from primary forests are detectable (Jordan 1986).

Clearly, forestry will have negative effects on species, communities, and ecosystems. What is not clear is how large these negative effects are relative to those associated with other changes in land use. There may be somewhat

**Table B**
Habitat Loss by Forest Type in Thailand, Madagascar, and Costa Rica

| Forest type | Original extent (km²) | Percent lost |
|---|---|---|
| **Thailand** | | |
| Lowland rainforest | 12,027 | 84 |
| Tropical semi-evergreen forest | 88,799 | 51 |
| Tropical pine forest | 4,222 | 93 |
| Montane deciduous forest | 144,500 | 77 |
| Tropical montane evergreen forest | 9,331 | 10 |
| Forest over limestone | 200 | 0 |
| Freshwater swamp | 1,250 | 63 |
| Monsoon forest | 6,794 | 79 |
| Mangrove forest | 2,223 | 69 |
| Dry deciduous forest | 219,451 | 81 |
| Total | 507,267 | 74 |
| **Madagascar** | | |
| Lowland rainforest | 80,729 | 85 |
| Lowland rainforest/grassland | 21,875 | 80 |
| Moist montane forest | 45,312 | 80 |
| Mixed montane forest | 3,646 | 70 |
| Montane forest/secondary grassland | 121,354 | 70 |
| Dry deciduous forest | 51,875 | 85 |
| Dry deciduous forest/grassland | 198,875 | 70 |
| Deciduous thicket | 38,125 | 85 |
| Thicket/secondary grassland | 31,250 | 70 |
| Mangrove forest and swamp | 2,170 | 40 |
| Total | 595,211 | 75 |
| **Costa Rica** | | |
| Dry deciduous forest | 3,733 | >99 |
| Lowland moist forest | 9,903 | >99 |
| Lowland wet forest | 11,517 | 78 |
| Premontane moist forest | 3,659 | >99 |
| Premontane wet forest | 12,005 | 81 |
| Premontane rainforest | 4,341 | 50 |
| Lower montane moist forest | 127 | >99 |
| Lower montane wet forest | 925 | 86 |
| Lower montane rainforest | 3,576 | 35 |
| Montane wet forest | 38 | >99 |
| Montane rainforest | 1,165 | 32 |
| Total | 50,990 | 79 |

From Groom and Schumaker 1993.

more agreement that the effects of small-scale or temporary land uses can be transient (Lovejoy and Shubart 1980), but these uses often lead to more destructive ones (Uhl and Buschbacher 1985), and thus some authors feel they should be monitored (Myers 1989; Groom and Schumaker 1993). Those who choose not to delineate between primary forest and lands subjected to commercial forestry or shifting cultivation do so either because they believe the differences between these land uses are not large enough to be a primary focus of concern, or because it is too difficult to distinguish between these types of land use in satellite images. Because different landscape alterations have different consequences, it is likely that the finer the distinctions we can make, the better we will be able to set conservation priorities or define development policy.

There is much promise for improving our estimates of the patterns of landscape change through the use of satellite imagery (Figure B). For example, a recent study of Landsat images of the Brazilian Amazon has provided the most accurate estimates to date of the extent of forest loss in that region (Skole and Tucker 1993). Using fairly high resolution images, Skole and Tucker have not only quantified deforestation, but have estimated the amount of area that may be affected by edge influences or isolation (see Table 5.2). Currently, there are plans by NASA and the FAO to analyze large numbers of satellite images from across the tropics to obtain more accurate data on the status of tropical forests (Monastersky 1993).

Although satellite imagery presents the most promising avenue for estimat-ing and monitoring landscape change in a consistent and relatively detailed manner, it is important to keep in mind the limitations of satellite data. First, the images themselves and the facilities needed to interpret them are expensive (each image can cost as much as $4000, although costs may go down: Rough-garden et al. 1991). Second, not all land uses can be distinguished, particularly different types of low-intensity forestry, and secondary versus primary forest. Until extensive field verification of the actual vegetation is made, the number of habitat types that can be distiguished will be limited. Third, the extensive cloud cover in many tropical areas can often severely reduce the number of usable images (see Figure B), although some scanners can penetrate cloud layers. Finally, the use of satellite data cannot tell us anything about the effects of the changes we see—that is, losses of species and disruption of ecosystem processes are invisible to a satellite's sensors (Groom and Schumaker 1993).

Despite the methodological difficulties, it is important to continue our progress toward greater accuracy in deforestation estimates. Some of our progress will depend on the availability of satellite images and our ability to interpret the large amounts of data they make available. The rest will come from seeking uniformity in methodology, clarity in definitions and assumptions used, and providing fine-scale categorization of deforestation by habitat and by current land use as much as is possible. These statistics will ultimately be the most powerful for use in planning conservation and development strategies.

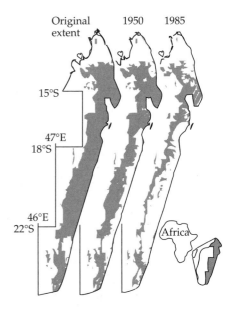

**Figure B**   Distribution of rainforest in eastern Madagascar from before human colonization to modern times. Note the progressive loss of both overall forest cover and large blocks of forest. (From Green and Sussman 1990.)

But in the interests of being cautious and conservative again, let us consider only the first form of habitat loss, outright destruction of forests. The current loss of 150,000 km$^2$ per year represents 2% of remaining forests. The annual loss increased by 89% during the 1980s, and if present patterns and trends of forest destruction persist with still more acceleration in the annual rate, the current amount of 2% may well double again by the year 2000 or shortly thereafter.

A current annual 2% rate of forest destruction does not mean that 2% of the forests' species are disappearing as well. Many species have wide distributions, sometimes extending across hundreds of thousands of square kilometers. Equally to the point, and by strong contrast with the situation outside tropical forests, many other species have highly restricted ranges, with their entire populations confined to just a few tens of thousands of square kilometers (Gentry 1992). A large number of cloud forest plants in tropical Latin America are endemic to isolated sites smaller than 10 km$^2$ (Gentry 1992). In tropical forests of South America, 440 bird species (25% of the total) have ranges of less than

**Table 5.2**
Forest Land (km$^2$) Deforested, Isolated, and Influenced by Edge Effects in
the Brazilian Amazon in 1978 and 1988[a]

| State | Deforested | Isolated | Edge effects | Total |
|---|---|---|---|---|
| **1978** | | | | |
| Acre | 2,612 | 18 | 4,511 | 7,141 |
| Amapá | 182 | 0 | 368 | 550 |
| Amazonas | 2,300 | 36 | 6,498 | 8,834 |
| Maranhão | 9,426 | 705 | 13,120 | 23,251 |
| Mato Grosso | 21,134 | 776 | 25,418 | 47,328 |
| Pará | 30,449 | 2,248 | 49,791 | 82,488 |
| Rondônia | 6,281 | 991 | 17,744 | 25,016 |
| Roraima | 196 | 4 | 812 | 1,012 |
| Tocantins | 5,688 | 337 | 6,584 | 12,609 |
| Total | 78,268 | 5,115 | 124,846 | 208,229 |
| **1988** | | | | |
| Acre | 6,369 | 405 | 23,686 | 30,460 |
| Amapá | 210 | 1 | 689 | 900 |
| Amazonas | 11,813 | 474 | 36,392 | 48,679 |
| Maranhão | 31,952 | 2,123 | 28,147 | 62,222 |
| Mato Grosso | 47,568 | 2,542 | 71,128 | 121,238 |
| Pará | 95,075 | 6,837 | 116,669 | 218,581 |
| Rondônia | 23,998 | 2,408 | 52,345 | 78,751 |
| Roraima | 1,908 | 1 | 5,236 | 7,145 |
| Tocantins | 11,431 | 1,437 | 6,760 | 19,628 |
| Total | 230,324 | 16,228 | 341,052 | 587,604 |

From Skole and Tucker 1993.
[a]Note the tremendous increase in all categories in this 10-year span. Data were compiled using
satellite imagery.

50,000 km$^2$, in contrast to 8 species (2% of the total) with similarly restricted
ranges in the United States and Canada (Terborgh and Winter 1980).

Such small, localized areas of endemism are unusually susceptible to unnoticed and large-scale extinctions. On a single forested ridge, Centinela, in
the western Andes of Ecuador, there used to be as many as 90 endemic plant
species. Although no comprehensive scientific check has been made, one can
realistically assume on the basis of plant/animal relationships elsewhere that
the same habitat contained tens of times as many endemic animal species
(mainly invertebrates). In the 1980s, the ridge's forest was cleared for agriculture, and the 90 plant species, plus their associated animal species, were
summarily eliminated (Dodson and Gentry 1991). In the words of E. O. Wilson (1992):

> Its name deserves to be synonymous with silent hemorrhaging of biological di-
> versity. When the forest on the ridge was cut a decade ago, a large number of
> rare species were extinguished. They went just like that, from full healthy pop-
> ulations to nothing, in a few months. Around the world such anonymous ex-
> tinctions—call them "centinelan extinctions"—are occurring, not open wounds
> for all to see and rush to stanch but unfelt internal events, leakages from vital
> tissue out of sight.

A detailed analysis of more subtle processes leading to local extinctions is
presented by James Karr in Essay 5A.

## ESSAY 5A

# Extinction of Birds on Barro Colorado Island

James R. Karr, University of Washington

If rates of biodiversity loss are to be slowed, then we need a better understanding of the ecological and demographic processes involved in local extinction. Understanding how extinction actually occurs on a local scale may enable us to take appropriate actions to minimize probabilities of losing particular components of the biota. Birds on an island in Panama offer some important clues to local extinction processes.

The avifauna of Barro Colorado, a small hilltop in central Panama, existed for thousands of years with limited human influence. That changed, first, during the l9th century, when the eastern half of Barro Colorado was cleared for small subsistence farms, and, second, between 1903 and 1914, when construction of the Panama Canal dammed the Chagras River and flooded the lowlands around Barro Colorado. As a result, the hilltop became a 15 km² land-bridge island (Barro Colorado Island, or BCI) isolated from nearby lowland forest. Designation of BCI as a biological reserve in 1923, along with growing interest in tropical biology, created an ideal situation for the interplay of theory, experiment, and observation.

One of the results of studies on BCI is that we know it now supports fewer species of birds than do nearby mainland forests. The most recent compilation lists 375 bird species known from BCI in this century, with 209 species known to breed on the island. Since its isolation early in the century, many bird species have disappeared from BCI, apparently due to two factors: successional loss of second-growth habitats (32 species), and island effects (50–60 species), including ecological truncation (differential loss of large and specialized species). During 24 years of fieldwork in the forests of central Panama, I asked several questions about these extinction processes.

*Are species lost at random?* I classified all resident land birds of the mainland (called the Pipeline Road area, or PR) according to their food habits, vegetation stratum used for foraging, and habitat affinity (dry, wet, or foothill forest). By comparing the distribution of species in the mainland source fauna with the list of species missing from BCI, I could determine if the missing species were a random subset of the

mainland fauna. The distributions did not differ as a function of food habits, but striking differences were found for both foraging stratum and forest type. Among the strata, high rates of loss occurred for ground (2.4×) and undergrowth (1.4×) species, while canopy species had extinction rates lower than expected at random (0.4×). Among the primary habitats, dry forest species had low extinction rates (0.1×), while foothill species had high extinction rates (3.7×). Clearly, the forest species missing from BCI are not a random set of species relative to the presumed source fauna on the nearby mainland (Karr 1982).

*Are certain demographic attributes associated with extinction?* Extinction of species on a land-bridge island occurs when a population is no longer able to maintain itself and recolonization from the nearby mainland is not possible. In 1979, I initiated a long-term study of central Panama birds to evaluate the role of demographic attributes in the extinction process. Birds at PR were captured, banded with uniquely numbered aluminum bands, and released. Using statistical models for open populations, I estimated demographic parameters such as mean annual survival rate and population size for 25 species of forest undergrowth birds on the mainland (Karr 1990). Mean annual survival rates for the 8 species missing from BCI were significantly lower than those for the 17 species still present on BCI. When the species are arrayed in sequence of their time of disappearance from BCI, survival rate seems to indicate not only which species are at greatest risk, but also the sequence of their loss from BCI.

*Why are undergrowth species especially at risk?* A common explanation for the high loss of terrestrial and undergrowth species on BCI is predation; high densities of small to medium-sized predators expose nests and adults to high predation rates. Reintroduction of an extinct species, the Song Wren, began with a period of successful reproduction on BCI followed by a population decline, probably due to high predation rates. Two experimental studies of nest predation on BCI and PR also showed higher nest predation rates on BCI than at PR.

*Does risk of nest predation vary*

*among undergrowth species?* Sieving (1992), who noted that 8 of 12 bird species in the terrestrial insectivore guild are now extinct on BCI, tested the hypothesis that interspecific variation in nest design and placement underlies differential avian extinction on the island. She selected five terrestrial insectivores for intensive study—two that are extinct and three that persist on BCI. Handmade mimics of their nests containing quail eggs were placed in forest undergrowth in microhabitats appropriate to the nests of each species. Losses of eggs to predators were higher on BCI than on the mainland. Predation rates varied between BCI-extinct and BCI–persistent species, but paradoxically, loss rates of BCI-extinct species were lower than loss rates for BCI-persistent species. Sieving then showed that those absolute rates were less important than the relative change in predation rates from mainland to island; that is, proportionate increases in predation rates were higher for BCI-extinct species (100%) than for species that persisted (30%).

Apparently, species with "safer" nests on the mainland have a reduced ability to renest, and thus are unable to compensate for the higher predation rates on BCI. Over evolutionary time, species-specific rates of nest loss associated with nest design and placement may determine clutch replacement capability and patterns of differential extinction for these species on BCI.

Studies of avian extinctions on BCI provide insight about the number, identity, and attributes of species susceptible to local extinction. Extinction of birds on BCI is nonrandom at species and guild levels, and can be attributed to numerous factors, including ecological truncation and differential loss of species of undergrowth and foothill forest. In addition, demographic attributes such as adult survival rate and population variability, life histories that balance susceptibility to nest loss due to predation with clutch replacement capability, and the local and regional habitat mosaic also interact in complex ways to vary the risk of extinction among species. The importance of the landscape mosaic demonstrates that strategies for siting nature preserves should consider more than just reserve size.

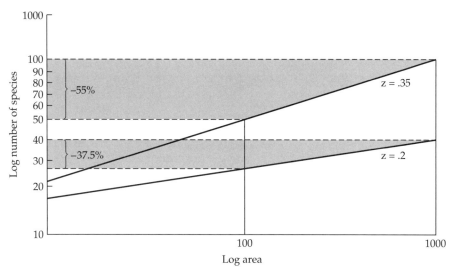

**Figure 5.5** Species–area relationships based on the equation $S = cA^z$, with $c = 10$ and $z = 0.2$ or $0.35$. Note that a 90% decrease in area, from 1000 to 100 ha, would result in a predicted loss of from 37.5% to 55% of the species, depending on the particular value of $z$. Greater $z$ values (steeper species–area relationships) imply greater species losses per unit area.

How shall we translate a 2% annual rate of forest destruction into an annual species extinction rate? One analytic path is revealed by the species–area relationship and the theory of island biogeography, introduced in Chapter 4, a well-established theory with supporting empirical evidence drawn from on-the-ground analyses around the world (MacArthur and Wilson 1967; Case and Cody 1987; Ricklefs 1990; Shafer 1991). The theory states that the number of species in a given area increases as the $z^{th}$ power of area, where $z$ generally ranges between 0.2 and 0.35. (Recall from Chapter 4 that $S = cA^z$; the model is also discussed in greater detail in Chapter 9 and presented in Figure 9.6). This species–area relationship also means that the number of species declines as area is lost. So when a habitat loses 90% of its original extent, it can no longer support, as a very rough average, about 50% of its original species (Figure 5.5).

How likely is this estimate to be correct? It depends critically upon the status of the remaining 10% of habitat. If this relict expanse is split into many small pieces (as is often the case with remnant tracts of tropical forests), a further "islandizing effect" comes into play, reducing the stock of surviving species still more. It is not clear how severe this additional depletion can be. Quality of remaining habitat independent of size is also important. Wilson (1992) suggests that the 50% can readily be reduced to 40%, more generally to 30%, sometimes to 20%, and occasionally even to 10%. Similarly, if most species concerned occur in small, local endemic communities, the percentage loss of species can readily approach the percentage loss of area. On the other hand, if the species are largely widespread and not endemic to narrow regions, less than a 50% loss with 90% habitat reduction could occur. So the 90%/50% species–area calculation for extinctions could be a minimum estimate, a reasonable estimate, or could overestimate losses, depending on specific circumstances. The estimates are also a function of the taxa involved. Certain taxa are more able than others to overcome habitat loss: for example, some birds and butterflies can disperse more readily than can other species.

The broadest application of island biogeography to tropical deforestation and species extinctions has been presented by one of the authors of the original theory, E. O. Wilson (1989, 1992). He has calculated that, on the basis of a 1% annual deforestation rate (as was supposed to be the case at the time of his analysis in the late 1980s), tropical forests have been losing between 0.2% and 0.3% of their species per year. Wilson further supposed that tropical forests contain only 2 million species, so he calculated that the annual tropical forest loss has amounted to somewhere between 4000 and 6000 species per year. But as we have seen, the annual forest destruction rate is now 2%, and the species stock is more realistically taken to be at least 5 million species (possibly 6, and conceivably 10 or 15 times as many). Using Wilson's analytic model, this means that the annual species loss in tropical forests is somewhere between 20,000 and 30,000 per year, or between 50 and 80 per day. Wilson has in fact subsequently refined his earlier estimate upward in light of more recent and substantive data, postulating an annual loss of 27,000 species, or around 75 per day in tropical forests alone (Wilson 1992).

Note, moreover, and as Wilson has repeatedly emphasized, that these are optimistic calculations. If we employ a more "realistic" reckoning, and qualitatively incorporate a number of other bioecological factors such as diseases, alien introductions, and overhunting, the annual total could become a good deal larger. The annual extinction rate in tropical forests alone means that we are witnessing a rate far above that of the "natural" rate of extinctions before the advent of the human era, considered to be perhaps one species every 4 years (Raup 1991a,b). So the present global extinction rate is roughly 100,000 times higher than the background rate.

A skeptic may ask, if extinctions are occurring in large numbers right now, why are they not individually documented? How much solid evidence is there? To this, the pragmatic scientist responds that it is far easier to demonstrate that a species exists than that it does not. To achieve the first, all one has to do is to find a few specimens. To achieve the second with absolute certainty, one must search every last locality of the species' range before being finally sure. This is all right for the purist, but unfortunately we live in a world without sufficient scientists, funding, and above all, time to undertake a conclusive check. Given that we are witnessing a mass extinction of exceptional scope, should it not be sufficient to make a best-judgment assessment of what is going on, and in cases of uncertainty ("Has the species finally disappeared or is it still hanging on?"), assume that a species that has not been seen for decades is in fact extinct until it is proven to be extant?

This is the case for large numbers of species. Recall the 90 endemic plant species of the Centinela ridge, where outright deforestation has eliminated all natural vegetation. Yet the plants have not officially been declared extinct; conservation organizations generally require that a species fail to be recorded for 50 years before it can be designated *in memoriam*. In Peninsular Malaysia, a 4-year search for 266 known species of freshwater fish turned up only 122, less than half, yet they are all officially regarded as still in existence (Mohsin and Ambok 1983). In Lake Victoria, two-thirds of the former stock of 300 haplochromine fish species, all but one of them endemic, have not been seen for years; even though they are not yet "officially" extinct, this species extinction spasm must rank as the greatest single extinction episode of vertebrate species in modern times (Ogutu-Ohwayo 1990; Baskin 1992). Dozens more such instances can be cited even though we have scarcely made a start on documenting the situation overall (Wilson 1992).

Above all, it should be borne in mind that we are dealing with the irreversible loss of unique life forms. It is not always possible to detail the precise survival status of tens of thousands of threatened plant species and millions of animal species. In light of the irreversibility and uniqueness involved, perhaps the burden of proof (recall Figure 2.3) should be shifted onto the shoulders of the skeptics, who should be asked to prove that a species still exists, rather than the reverse.

This raises a key question concerning species extinctions that also applies to many other environmental issues: what is "legitimate scientific caution" in the face of uncertainty? Uncertainty can cut both ways. Some observers may object that in the absence of conclusive evidence and analysis, it is appropriate to stick with low estimates of species extinctions on the grounds that they are more "responsible." But what about asymmetry of evaluation? A low estimate, ostensibly "safe" because it takes a conservative view of limited evidence, may fail to reflect the real situation just as much as does an "unduly" high estimate. In a situation of uncertainty where not all parameters can be quantified to conventional satisfaction, let us not become obsessed with what can be counted if that is to the detriment of what counts. Undue caution can readily become recklessness, and it will be better for us to find we have been roughly right than precisely wrong.

So much for the current extinction rate. What of the future? Through detailed analysis backed by abundant documentation, Wilson (1992) concludes that we face the prospect of losing 20% of all species within 30 years and 50% or more thereafter. Another long-standing expert in this area, Peter Raven (1990), calculates that one–sixth of all plant species, and, by implication, of all animal species, occur in the tropical forests of just three countries, Colombia, Ecuador, and Peru, and that these three countries appear likely to lose virtually all their forest cover within another 3 decades at most. Hence, their species communities will be largely eliminated. Based on a further and more extensive calculation, Raven believes that half of all species exist in tropical forests that will be reduced to less than one-tenth of their present expanse within the same 3 decades ahead. So in accord with island biogeography, Raven concludes—and he stresses that this is a conservative prognosis—that one-fourth of all plant species are likely to be eliminated during the next 30 years, and "fully half of total species may disappear before the close of the 21st century." These estimates have been endorsed by the Club of Earth (1990), which comprises scientists with abundant field biology experience and with a collective total of several hundred years of professional endeavor. The estimates are also in line with those of a good number of other analysts (Myers 1986, 1990a,b; Diamond 1989; May 1992b).

Of course, the calculations leading to extinction rate estimates are only as good as the assumptions and data that go into them. Actual estimates of species losses, like estimates of habitat losses, vary greatly. Box 5B discusses this issue and compares some of the extinction estimates that have been proposed, showing the variation involved. Regardless of the precision of these various estimates, the message is clear: large numbers of species are already going extinct, and still larger numbers will go extinct unless prevailing patterns of habitat destruction stop, and are eventually reversed.

## BOX 5B
## Quantifying the Loss of Species Due to Tropical Deforestation

Martha J. Groom, University of Washington

Estimates of how many species are being lost through habitat destruction are hampered by our ignorance of the total number of species and their distribution, and the patterns of habitat loss (see Box 5A). In addition, our ignorance of the effects of deforestation on species also limits our ability to predict extinctions due to habitat loss and degradation. Currently, the estimates for species loss vary enormously (Table A), primarily because authors choose different baseline estimates of (1) the number of species present in the world (commonly between 10 and 30 million), (2) the proportion that reside in tropical forests (between 25% and 70%), (3) the shape of the relationship between habitat loss and extinction, and (4) the rate and extent of habitat loss (between 0.5% and 2% annual global deforestation).

The difficulties of estimating the number of species in the world and in tropical forests were discussed in the previous chapters. In particular, the uncertainty over insect diversity, because the potential number of undescribed insect species is so large, can have an enormous effect on estimates of species loss. Further, the distribution of centers of endemism throughout the tropics, and the extent to which these areas are protected from deforestation can bias estimates in either direction. The problems of estimating habitat loss were discussed in detail in Box 5A. The accuracy of forest loss estimates themselves, as well as what types of habitat alterations are included, will affect species loss estimates. Extinction estimates will be influenced by the inclusion of specific effects—for example, the effects of habitat degradation accompanying deforestation, or of fragmentation or isolation of habitats.

Degraded forests will lose species, but not as rapidly or as entirely as forests destroyed outright. Thus, inclusion of lesser forms of habitat disturbance, such as fragmentation, will tend to bias estimates of species losses upward, whereas exclusion of these forms of disturbance will bias estimates downward. Most frequently, losses due to habitat degradation are not included in extinction estimates (e.g., Wilson 1992). Similarly, as cleared areas of forest recover, they will be able to support more species (but not, of course, those that went extinct because of the forest clearing). Thus, whether areas of recov-

ering forest are included in estimates of the amount of disturbed habitat will influence extinction estimates, which usually ignore forest recovery.

We probably know the least about the shape of the relationship between habitat loss and extinctions. Generally, most authors have to choose a relationship fairly arbitrarily, either set directly as a level of extinction per area of habitat loss or set indirectly using a species–area curve (see main text). For example, Wilson (1988a) assumes that about 50% of tropical forest species are so localized in their distribution that they will go extinct following local deforestation, and that another 50% are broadly enough distributed to still be represented in undisturbed areas of forest. Thus, Wilson sets his extinction rate estimate to 50% species loss/area lost (so if there are 94 species in 100 ha deforested, Wilson would estimate that 47 extinctions occurred as a result). The use of species–area curves for tropical forest species produces nearly as arbitrary an estimate since there are no empirically derived extinction curves for all tropical species. It is the slope ($z$) of these curves that most strongly influences the prediction of species loss for a given loss of area. Consequently, most authors examine a range of $z$ values in their estimates, and in most cases choose their value

from the range between 0.20 and 0.35 (which is where most empirically calculated $z$ values fall: see Figure 5.5). It is important to remember that the use of species–area curves may be inaccurate, primarily because they apply to the equilibrium number of species that should persist in a given habitat area; however, they are being used to predict losses in scenarios of disequilibrium. Estimates based on species–area curves therefore are likely to underestimate losses due to the degradation that accompanies deforestation.

Compounded, all these sources of uncertainty in extinction estimates can lead to extremely large errors (Simberloff 1986). Nonetheless, it is indisputable that a large extinction event is occurring. Indeed, despite the variety of ways in which these estimates were calculated, all are chilling: at minimum, 10% of all the world's species are likely to go extinct in the next decade. It may be critical to obtain more precise estimates of losses in particular circumstances, and from this discussion some of the ways in which we can do this should be clear, but imprecision of estimates and need for "further study" should not be used as an excuse for inaction. The crucial point is that these figures constitute a strong signal that we cannot ignore.

**Table A**
Some Estimates of Global Species Loss Due to Tropical Deforestation, and Their Assumptions

| Extinction estimate | Assumptions | | | Source |
| | Total no. species (millions)/percent tropical | Tropical forest loss | Extinction/area lost | |
| --- | --- | --- | --- | --- |
| 1 species/hr by 2000 | 5–10/40%–70% | 245,000 km²/yr | 50% of species extinct when 10% area left | Myers 1979 |
| 33%–50% of all species between 1970 and 2000 | 3–10/25% | 12.3% deforestation between 1980 and 2000 | Concave curve[a] | Lovejoy 1980 |
| 1 million species by 2000 | 3–10/70% | >200,000 km²/yr | 50% of species extinct when 10% area left | NRC/Meyers 1980 |
| 1 million species by 2000 | 5/40% | 33% of remaining forests destroyed by 2000 | 50% of species in area will go extinct | Myers 1985 |
| 10% of all species by 2000; 25% of all species by 2015 | 4–5/50% | 2% deforestation/yr | 50% of species in area will go extinct | Raven 1988 |
| 17,500 species/yr | 10/50% | 0.7% deforestation/yr | 50% of species in area will go extinct | Wilson 1988a |
| 8.8% of all species by 2000 | 3–10/25% | 12.3% deforestation between 1980 and 2000 | Same as Lovejoy 1980 | Lugo 1988 |
| 5%–15% of all species between 1990 and 2020 | 10/>50% | 0.8% deforestation/yr | Species–area curve; $z = 0.15, 0.35$ | Reid and Miller 1989 |
| 10%–38% of all species between 1990 and 2020 | 10/>50% | 1.6% deforestation/yr | Species–area curve; $z = 0.15, 0.35$ | Reid and Miller 1989 |
| 27,000 species/yr | 10 in tropical rainforests | 1.8% deforestation/yr | Species–area curve; $z = 0.15$ | Wilson 1992 |

[a]Corresponds to curve D in Figure 1, p. 329 of Lovejoy 1980.

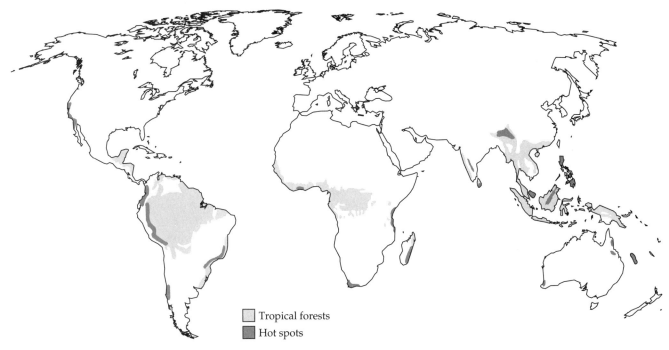

Tropical forests

Hot spots

**Figure 5.6** The extent of tropical forests ca. 1950, and the 18 global "hot spots" of biodiversity so far identified. These hot spots, mostly in tropical systems, contain a disproportionately high level of species diversity in very small areas.

## Critical Regional Losses: Hot Spots of Extinction

The calculations above represent a generalized mode of estimating the present extinction rate in tropical forests. This method is applied at the biome level, making next to no allowance for local circumstances. Fortunately, we have a parallel set of calculations at the local level, in the form of a "hot spots" analysis relating to areas that feature exceptional concentrations of species with extraordinary levels of endemism, and face exceptional threat of imminent habitat destruction (Myers 1988, 1990a).

The analysis reveals that 14 hot spots occur in tropical forests: Madagascar, the Atlantic coast of Brazil, western Ecuador, the Colombian Chocó, the uplands of western Amazonia, the eastern Himalayas, Peninsular Malaysia, northern Borneo, the Philippines, New Caledonia, Côte d'Ivoire, Tanzania, the western Ghats in India, and southwestern Sri Lanka (Figure 5.6; see also Table 4.3). Their collective expanse is less than the size of California, and constitutes less than 5% of remaining undisturbed forests. They contain more than 37,000 endemic plant species, or 15% of all plant species, in less than 311,000 km$^2$, or just 0.2% of the earth's land surface.

Four other hot spots occur in Mediterranean biomes: California, central Chile, the southern tip of South Africa, and southwestern Australia (Figure 5.6). They contain 12,720 endemic plant species in a collective expanse of 435,700 km$^2$, or 0.3% of the earth's land surface. Adding the two sets of hot spots together, we find that 50,000 endemic plant species, or a full 20% of all plant species, face severe threat of habitat destruction in 746,700 km$^2$, or a mere 0.5% of the earth's land surface (Myers 1990a).

The hot spots also contain a still higher, though unquantified, proportion of the earth's animal species (Myers 1988, 1990a). Species–area inventories in diverse sectors of tropical forests, among other biomes, suggest there are at least 40 animal species for every plant species, assuming a minimum planetary total of all species of 10 million. If the planetary total is in fact 30 million (it could conceivably be a good deal higher), and accepting that virtually all the additional species are animal species, then the 18 hot spots described contain a minimum of 2 million endemic animal species—threatened just as much as are the plant species.

Five of the hot spots have already lost 90% or more of their original habitat expanse, and the rest are expected to lose 90% within the opening decade or two of the next century at the latest, if recent land use trends continue even without acceleration. If we apply the 90%/50% species–area relationship, these areas will lose at least half of their species within the foreseeable future. Some have surely lost a good share already. This means that in these areas alone, a greater mass extinction than any since the demise of the dinosaurs 65 million years ago has probably already occurred.

Hot spots occur elsewhere, though as yet they have not been documented and analyzed in any detail. The most prominent of such localities are in certain wetlands (including swamps, rivers, and lakes), coral reefs, and montane environments. According to a preliminary and exploratory appraisal by Myers, these additional hot spots may well constitute the sole habitats of at least 5% of all plant species and a still higher proportion of animal species. In turn, this means that at least one-fourth of all species are confined to hot spots. Suppose we accept, in line with the assessments presented above, that in the absence of conservation efforts of sufficient scope and scale, we should anticipate the demise of one-half of all species within the foreseeable future. The hot spots analysis shows that we can make a substantial dent in the overall problem simply by safeguarding a handful of top-ranked biodiversity areas.

The analytic strategy based on hot spots is supported by recent research on birds (Bibby et al. 1992). As many as 2609 species, or one-fourth of the earth's 9000-plus bird species, are confined to just 2% of the earth's land surface. They are located in 221 endemic bird areas (EBAs) with a maximum expanse of 50,000 km$^2$; more than three-fourths of them are in the tropics, notably in tropical forests. These areas also accommodate 70% of all bird species recognized to be threatened or endangered, and are also vitally important for the conservation of large numbers of species of plants, mammals and other vertebrates, and insects and other invertebrates. If these EBAs lost 90% of their habitats, and the remaining 10% were to be completely protected, we would still witness the eventual demise of half their bird species, well over 1000 species and more than 10% of the world's avifauna. Fortunately, half of the species are found in just 46 EBAs, lending themselves to hot spots treatment for strategic planning on the part of conservationists.

The protection of hot spots obviously should be a high global priority. But how are biodiversity protection priorities set in general? How do we face the awesome task of protecting so much diversity that is being lost so quickly? How is the information gathered? Such issues are addressed in Essay 5B, by Russell Mittermeier and Adrian Forsyth.

## Patterns of Species Vulnerability

So far we have looked at entire communities of species at risk. Let us now consider three categories of species that appear to be unduly vulnerable to extinction.

### Rare Species

In *On the Origin of Species* (1859), Charles Darwin observed that "rarity is the attribute of a vast number of species in all classes, in all countries." Indeed, in most biotas studied, many, and sometimes the majority, of species are to

## ESSAY 5B

# Setting Priorities for Biodiversity Conservation
## One Organization's Approach

Russell A. Mittermeier and Adrian B. Forsyth, Conservation International

Maintenance of biological diversity is now recognized in many circles as the single highest conservation priority of our time. Biological diversity is our living natural resource base, our biological capital in the global bank. Unfortunately, although interest in the global environment is growing, and more resources are being made available, we still have only a tiny fraction of the resources, both human and financial, to get the job done. Consequently, we have to put available resources to use in the best possible ways, applying them to areas containing the highest concentrations of diversity and areas at immediate risk of disappearing. To do this effectively, we need priority-setting methodologies based on the best scientific information available.

In several ways, Conservation International has placed a great deal of emphasis on priority setting. We have done it at a global level, refining Norman Myers' concept of "threatened hot spots," 18 areas around the tropics that together occupy only 0.5% of the land surface of the planet, and yet may hold a third or more of all terrestrial species diversity and a much higher percentage of the diversity at greatest risk. We have done it with the "major tropical wilderness areas" concept, which recognizes the value of the last few major blocks of undisturbed tropical forest. We have done it with the "megadiversity country" concept, highlighting the importance of the political entities that harbor the largest chunks of global biodiversity. And we are now looking at a series of global priority-setting exercises for other major categories of ecosystems, such as deserts, dry forests, savannas, wetlands, Mediterranean biomes, and marine systems.

As the next step down in the "hierarchy of priority setting," we have focused on the regional workshop concept, in which a group of experts on a threatened hot spot, a major wilderness area, or a key country get together for

several weeks and pool their information using the most up-to-date mapping data and computerized Geographic Information Systems. The maps and other material emerging from such an exercise are powerful planning tools and can often serve to catalyze action in a way that goes beyond the actual data that they provide.

All of the above priority-setting exercises make use of the best available information (both published, and in the minds of the world's biodiversity experts) to provide the soundest scientific underpinning for the hard conservation choices that need to be made in the next few years. Inevitably, many information gaps exist simply because the field of biodiversity conservation is a new one and the amount of actual fieldwork that has been conducted is still minimal relative to the size of the priority areas identified. Although the 18 hot spots thus far identified occupy only 0.5% of the land surface of the planet, they still cover several hundred thousand square kilometers, only a tiny fraction of which has been properly inventoried. To fill some of the gaps in our knowledge and to refine our data base, Conservation International (CI) created the Rapid Assessment Program (RAP) in 1989.

RAP is a biological inventory program designed to provide the information necessary to catalyze conservation action and improve biodiversity protection. The purpose of RAP is to quickly collect, analyze, and disseminate information on poorly known areas that are potentially important biodiversity conservation sites. RAP works by assembling teams of top-notch tropical biologists and host country scientists to generate first-cut, on-the-ground assessments of the biological value of different sites.

The core members of the RAP team are four of the world's most experienced field biologists, representing more than 100 years of accumulated field time. They are combined with a

number of other scientists who together examine an area's species diversity, its degree of endemism, the uniqueness of the ecosystem, and the degree of risk of extinction on a national and global scale. As a conservation tool, RAP provides a primarily qualitative assessment and precedes long-term scientific inventory and research by establishing the relative importance of the site in question in regional and global terms. This unique tool helps us further refine our conservation strategies.

We recognize the fundamental importance of long-term field studies at key sites and are actively involved in promoting such work. However, we believe that the tremendous time pressure under which we are operating makes it essential that we have this capacity for top-quality rapid assessment of as many unknown or poorly known ecosystems as possible in order to efficiently direct conservation activities. This is the principle role of the CI RAP team.

It is important to point out that, while the program is conducted under the auspices of Conservation International, its results are for the international conservation community at large. We readily make available all reports in draft form both to the host governments of the countries being surveyed and to any other interested scientists and organizations. The ultimate purpose of the RAP team is to generate the best possible conservation action on behalf of our planet's biological diversity, that legacy of life that is so critical to us all.

The priority-setting exercises discussed here are not a form of triage. The biological resources of all nations are valuable to them, and worthy of being conserved and used sustainably. By setting priorities, we are merely facing reality by suggesting that levels of investment be at least roughly proportional to the richness and uniqueness of different ecosystems and the degree of threat under which they exist.

some degree rare. That is, a few species tend to be very common and dominate the biota, many more species are at an intermediate range of abundance, and a few species are very rare. This pattern is illustrated in Table 5.3

**Table 5.3**
Estimated Total Populations of Fish Species by Abundance Categories in Owego Creek, New York

| Abundance class | Species |
|---|---|
| >100,000 | *Cottus bairdi* |
| 10,001–100,000 | *Rhinichthys atratulus, Rhinichthys cataractae, Campostoma anomalum, Catostomus commersoni* |
| 1,001–10,000 | *Etheostoma olmstedi, Notropis cornutus, Semotilus margarita, Exoglossum maxillingua, Semotilus atromaculatus, Notropis hudsonius, Notropis procne, Hypentelium nigricans, Noturus insignis* |
| 101–1,000 | *Pimephales notatus, Salvelinus fontinalis, Percina peltata, Salmo trutta, Clinostomus elongatus, Notropis rubellus* |
| 11–100 | *Semotilus corporalis, Fundulus diaphanus, Notropis analostanus, Ictalurus nebulosus, Cottus cognatus, Pimephales promelas* |
| ≤10 | *Lepomis auritus* |

From Sheldon 1987.
*Note:* Depending on criteria of rarity, about one-half of these species could be considered rare.

for fish species of Owego Creek in central New York, where about one-half the fauna may be said to be rare. In general, rarity should make a species more vulnerable to both natural and human-induced extinction.

But rarity is not a simple concept. A species may be rare in at least seven different ways, based on different distributional patterns (Rabinowitz et al. 1986). A species may be rare because of a highly restricted geographic range, because of high habitat specificity, because of small local population size, or because of various combinations of these characteristics (Table 5.4). Thus, for example, a species may be distributed across an entire continent (broad geographic range), be a habitat generalist (low habitat specificity), and yet be rare because it occurs at extremely low densities (small local population size) wherever it is found. Similarly, a species may be locally superabundant, but be rare because it occurs in very specialized habitats that are geographically restricted.

Different types of rarity make species vulnerable to different extinction processes. For example, a locally abundant species that only occurs at one location (such as the Devil's Hole pupfish, discussed earlier, or many other highly endemic species) is extremely vulnerable to local stochastic events or intentional habitat destruction. A broadly distributed species that exists at low population sizes may weather such events quite well, but be more vulnerable to loss of genetic diversity and inbreeding (discussed in Chapter 6). A broadly distributed habitat specialist, such as a wetland annual, is vulnerable to any broad actions that influence its particular habitat, such as pollution, reduced rainfall, or climate change.

Human-caused rarity may be more devastating than natural rarity if the species is not adapted to having low numbers. Bighorn sheep (*Ovis canadensis*) of North America (Figure 5.7), which probably numbered as many as 2 million before European settlers arrived, now total only 5000 or so, living in small, widely scattered populations. Due to a lifestyle that induces each herd to sense a strong attachment to its traditional range, the species is not inclined to colonize new territory, not even former habitat. Because the

**Figure 5.7** The bighorn sheep (*Ovis canadensis*), one of the examples of rarity that makes a species more vulnerable to extinction. Populations of the bighorn have been made very small by human activities, making the species more vulnerable to extinction due to small population size. (Photograph by David Scott.)

**Table 5.4**
Seven Forms of Species Rarity, Based on Three Distributional Traits

| Geographic range | Large | | Small | |
|---|---|---|---|---|
| Habitat specificity | Broad | Restricted | Broad | Restricted |
| Somewhere large | Common | Locally abundant over a large range in a specific habitat | Locally abundant in several habitats but restricted geographically | Locally abundant in a specific habitat but restricted geographically |
| Everywhere small | Constantly sparse over a large range and in several habitats | Constantly sparse in a specific habitat but over a large range | Constantly sparse and geographically restricted in several habitats | Constantly sparse and geographically restricted in a specific habitat |

Modified from Rabinowitz et al. 1986 and Holsinger 1993.

bighorn sheep is an exceptionally conservative creature, it now seems almost predestined to remain rare (Geist 1971).

Humans have also been known to drive very abundant species to or near extinction: witness the Passenger Pigeon, Carolina Parakeet, and bison of North America. Their former patterns of abundance did not prevent declines to extinction for the first two and near-extinction for the latter. Once driven to rarity, even once-abundant species are vulnerable.

There are still other ways of becoming rare. The giant sequoia (*Sequoia gigantea*) of California was rare long before humans arrived on the scene. The tree has a restricted geographic range because it is a "relict" species, left over after geoecological change eliminated related species. The California Condor (*Gymnogyps californianus*) formerly had a broad geographic range, but its range contracted several centuries ago coincident with climate changes, and it became rare; its specialized lifestyle leaves it particularly vulnerable to further human disruption of its habitat. Many other species were historically common and broadly distributed, but have become rare because of human influences.

There is a lengthy list of taxa that are even more restricted to small areas. An Arizona cactus survives in a valley less than 10 km long. The El Segundo blue butterfly (*Euphilotes battoides allyni*) lives in only a few hectares at the end of a runway at the Los Angeles airport. In Northern California, a critically imperiled butterfly, Lange's Metalmark (*Apodemia mormo langei*), is confined to an 8 ha patch of sand dunes. The Laysan Teal (*Anas laysanensis*) inhabits the marshy shores of a 5 km$^2$ lagoon on a Hawaiian island. Numerous species of fish, amphibians, and invertebrates occur in one or a few springs in desert regions. Rarity in all these cases lends itself to extinction.

Rarity is especially a key characteristic of large numbers of tropical forest species (Elton 1973; Gilbert 1980; Janzen 1975). As previously noted, many species are confined to small areas, sometimes hardly more than a few hundred square kilometers on an isolated ridge or in a single valley, and many have specialized lifestyles. Such species are particularly vulnerable to extinction through habitat disruption or destruction.

(A)

(B)

(C)

**Figure 5.8**  Long-lived species are vulnerable to extinction for a number of reasons, including (A) over-exploitation, such as African elephants (*Loxodonta africana*), or (B) habitat destruction, such as many sea turtles, including this Pacific ridley (*Lepidochelys olivacea*). Other species restricted to small, stable but isolated habitats (C), such as these plants on a granite outcrop, are also especially vulnerable. (A, photograph © M. P. Kahl/DRK Photo; B, by C. R. Carroll; C, by Robert Wyatt.)

Thus, rarity of all types, be it natural or human-induced, is cause for special concern. This is even reflected in legal protection; almost by definition, most species listed under the U.S. Endangered Species Act are rare in some way. One of the keys to successfully stemming the tide of broad-scale extinctions is to act *before* species become rare, while they, and their habitats, are still common. This is one of the motivations behind setting aside lands and waters for conservation purposes; it not only protects the rare species, but should prevent the common species from becoming rare.

### Long-Lived Species

Long-lived species typically have a suite of life history characteristics well suited to long-term predictability, but not conducive to rapid response to a human-disturbed world, let alone to population recovery in such a world. These characteristics include delayed sexual maturity (often one or more decades), low fecundity, reliance on high juvenile survivorship, and cessation of reproduction and protection of the adult phenotype when times are bad. Together, they mean that long-lived species have great difficulty responding to environmental changes that reduce their populations; that is, they cannot easily "bounce back" from major population declines because their reproductive rates are so low and they take so long to mature. In short, they are closely adjusted to the long-term capacity of their habitats to support them—a fine strategy for a stable world, but unsuited to a world experiencing abundant disruptions at the hands of humans.

These unfortunates in our modern world include species that are overexploited (e.g., whales, rhinoceroses, elephants), and species that are losing critical habitat (e.g., great apes, nestling sea turtles, some freshwater turtles, many cranes, and other large birds). They also include many others that are restricted to small, stable habitats and suffer local extinction (Figure 5.8).

If, through whatever cause, a long-lived species loses a large proportion of its numbers, it may prove unable to build up its population again, no matter what protective measures are provided (see Essay 7A and Case Study 2 in Chapter 13). Because these species are particularly vulnerable to extinction due to their life history characteristics, their populations should be closely monitored and their habitats accorded special protection. One of the unique conservation problems with this group is that population declines may take many years to be noticeable simply because individuals live so long. Consequently, particular attention should be paid to population age structure and recruitment of juveniles into the population. Thus, special conservation action is needed to safeguard long-lived species while their numbers are still well above what would be acceptable levels for other types of species.

## Keystone Species

In its most general sense, a **keystone species** (or, more commonly, a group of species) is one that makes an unusually strong contribution to community structure or processes. A keystone species may be a major predator, whose presence limits the abundance of prey and thereby reduces their competitive interactions; a unique food source, such as species groups of figs and palms that fruit during seasons of fruit scarcity for tropical frugivores; or a species that maintains critical ecosystem processes, such as nitrogen-fixing bacteria or phosphorus-mobilizing fungi. The concept of keystone species will be discussed in greater detail in Chapter 8; their critical feature for our purposes here is that the removal of keystone species can make many other members of the community vulnerable to extinction.

While some individual taxa may function as keystone species, it is more common that sets of species will function in that regard. For example, the set of insectivorous tropical birds that feed by gleaning caterpillars off leaf surfaces may function, in aggregate, as a keystone species. The removal of any one of these bird species in a tropical forest may have little effect on the abundance and diversity of lepidopterans or their host plants. However, elimination of the set of species or a large fraction of the set may have major effects on caterpillars and plants.

The goal of analyzing keystone species for any community is to determine membership in the *minimal* set of species that has disproportionate effects on the rest of the community and to focus our conservation efforts on those sets. It would be vastly impractical if not impossible to imagine a conservation plan that would apply to all seed dispersers in a tropical forest. However, it is reasonable and productive to think of specific conservation plans for the small set of critically important keystone species that disperse large seeds, and then to embrace the many species of animals that disperse small seeds in a more general plan of habitat conservation.

Unfortunately, there are major gaps in our understanding of keystone species. We have only a rudimentary knowledge of which sets of species are keystone in particular communities, and even less knowledge about the ecology of these critically important species. Therefore, an important research priority in conservation is to identify keystone species and to understand how to conserve them. A corresponding policy priority is the creation of appropriate legislation to accord keystone species special protection.

An example of a keystone species "set" is tropical trees that produce large, oil-rich seeds, such as the family Lecithydaceae. A familiar example of this tree family is the Brazil nut tree, whose nuts are widely harvested in Amazonia as a source of cash (Figure 5.9). The huge tree is pollinated solely by an iridescent bee, a member of the euglossine subfamily. Likewise, the tree's nut depends for its germination on a sharp-toothed rodent, the agouti, which chews and softens the large woody pod before eating and dispersing the seeds inside (or simply leaving them free to germinate). So this towering tree requires, for its reproductive system, the services of a high-flying bee that pollinates flowers in its crown, and a forest-floor rodent that disperses its seeds. Of the two creatures, the euglossine bee appears to be the more important in that it also pollinates, among many other plants, orchids—and in turn, these plants often supply prime sources of food to sundry other insects, which pollinate other plants, and so on. The Brazil nut tree may be regarded as a keystone species in the sense that it provides a critical or pivotal food source in its large oil-rich seeds.

In another sense, we can view the euglossines as a different kind of keystone species, one known as a **mobile link species.** Because these euglossine

**Figure 5.9**   A Brazil nut tree, an example of a set of keystone species; in addition to its ecological role, the tree is widely used as a cash crop by humans. (Photograph by Chris Miller.)

bees are specialist pollinators of many species of orchids, aroids, and bromeliads, as well as pollinators of Brazil nuts and other trees, the reproductive success of these plants depends on the services provided by the bees. Thus, the success of all these plants is "linked" by the mobility of their specialist pollinators. Furthermore, plant hosts, by virtue of supplying food to extensive associations of mobile links, have been termed **keystone mutualist species** (Gilbert 1980; Terborgh 1986, 1988).

Many other cash crops, after the pattern of the Brazil nut tree, are pollinated by obligate insects, bats, or birds. Tiny midges and thrips pollinate rubber and cocoa; certain bees and other hymenopterans pollinate passion fruit and cucurbits; flies pollinate cashew, mango, and cola nut; nocturnal moths and bats pollinate calabash, kapok, and balsa trees; and hummingbirds pollinate wild pineapple. All of these specialized pollinator relationships form part of larger food webs, often with their own mobile links and keystone mutualists.

This concept of pivotal linkages within tropical forest ecosystems can be extended to thousands of plants that, through their nectar, pollen, and fruits supply critical support for multitudes of insects, mammals, and birds; an outstanding example is figs, with their 800 species worldwide, mostly in tropical forests. If, as a result of human disturbance of forest ecosystems, a keystone mutualist is eliminated, the loss may lead to that of several other species. Still more to the point, these additional losses may, in certain circumstances, trigger a cascade of linked extinctions. Eventually, a series of forest food webs could become unraveled. Developed as they are through the coevolution of plants and animals that have sustained each other through ever more complex relationships, these food webs can steadily become destabilized from the start to the finish of their workings, with "shatter effects" throughout their ecosystems. Thus, we see the exceptional intricacy of the tropical forest's fabric of life, in which interdependency is critical. When human incursion causes the severing of a few threads, the damage can ultimately lead to a rending of the fabric from top to bottom.

## Genetic Losses

There is more to the biotic crisis than extinction of species in large numbers: there is also biodepletion within species. While little reflected in many conservation strategies, this loss will add a further dimension to the depauperization of the spectrum of life on earth. Clearly, a species cannot supply a full array of environmental services such as nutrient cycling, soil formation, disease resistance, or climate regulation (Ehrlich and Ehrlich 1981) if it has lost much of its genetic variability and the ecological adaptability that encompasses. The loss of genetic diversity is dealt with in great detail in Chapter 6; here we provide only a brief discussion.

Every species represents the outcome of evolutionary processes that have generated a unique amalgam of genetic variability. The individuals that make up a species are genetically differentiated, due to the high levels of genetic polymorphism across many of the gene loci. Moreover, some species are exceptionally numerous. So biodiversity, properly understood, comprises the sum of all variants constituting the genomes of all organisms on earth. In turn, this means that the total number of species is not the only standard by which we should evaluate the abundance and diversity of life; genetic variation within species represents another major level of biological diversity.

While intraspecific genetic differences may appear slight, they can be quite pronounced: consider, for example, the variation manifested in the many races of dogs or the specialized types of wheat developed by breeders. Yet even this gives only a crude picture. A typical bacterium may contain about 1000 genes, certain fungi 10,000, and many flowering plants and a few animals 400,000 or even more (Hinegardner 1976). While many of these genes may not be expressed, their numbers provide some sense of the potential for genetic variation.

Within this context of the planet's genetic variability, we can recognize that biological depletion applies not only to species themselves, but to subspecies, races, and populations. A given species may consist of hundreds of genetically distinct populations. Many species are far from threatened—indeed they flourish with unprecedented numbers—but their gene pools have been sorely reduced through elimination of most of their populations. An example is wheat, a species that totals trillions of individuals every growing season; yet the wild and primitive-cultivar relatives of modern commercial wheat have disappeared to the extent that the great bulk of the species' genetic variability has already been lost, and most of the rest is severely threatened (Yeatman et al. 1984).

Much the same applies to virtually all our leading crops and to our breeds of domestic livestock. Yet we know all too little about how far the biological depletion has proceeded, or how soon it may reach a threshold of critical genetic impoverishment beyond which a domesticated species loses its capacity to adapt to new diseases and other environmental threats (Soulé 1987). Most of our agricultural crops have very little remaining genetic diversity and are susceptible to disease and pest infestations.

The key to resisting such problems is the genetic diversity residing in wild stocks. Like biodiversity hot spots, certain areas of the world are especially critical as centers of crop genetic diversity because they either contain the wild ancestors of our domesticated crops, or hold concentrations of modern agricultural germ plasm. Twelve of these regions have been identified: Mexico–Guatemala; Peru–Ecuador–Bolivia; southern Chile; Brazil–Paraguay; the United States; Ethiopia; Central Asia; the Mediterranean region; India–Burma; Asia Minor; Thailand–Malaya–Java; and China (Witt 1985). Particular regions, often very small areas, within these countries hold the key to crop genetic diversity because the wild ancestors of agricultural crops originated there, may still occur there, and are a reservoir of genetic diversity. Such areas are critical to continued, let alone expanded, crop production (Witt 1985), yet they are being lost at a rapid rate.

## Habitat Fragmentation and Degradation

Of course, not all natural habitats are going to be destroyed outright within the immediate future. Species will also be eliminated via a "fragmentation effect," caused by the breakup of extensive habitats into small, isolated patches that are too limited to maintain their species stocks into the indefinite future. This phenomenon has been widely analyzed through the theory of island biogeography, and appears to be strongly supported by empirical evidence, albeit with a good number of variations on the general theme (MacArthur and Wilson 1967; Williamson 1981; Case and Cody 1987; Wilcove 1987).

Suppose, for instance, that the rainforests of Borneo, an expanse of roughly 500,000 km$^2$, were to be preserved as they remain today. If the remaining forest comprised a single large block, or even ten 50,000-km$^2$ blocks, that would be far preferable to the more likely case of a mosaic of forest patches, few of them larger than 20,000 km$^2$, due to broad-scale fragmentation in the recent past. Because of fragmentation, a sizable loss of species would still ensue, no matter how well we might preserve the myriad forest fragments.

Not only will fragmentation cause long-term loss of species, but so will the related factor of dynamic inertia in environmental degradation—especially degradation that has already occurred. Through dynamic inertia, this degradation will continue to exert an increasingly adverse effect well into the future, no matter how vigorously we try to resist the process: much potential damage is already "in the pipeline." An obvious example is acid rain, which will keep on inflicting injury on biotas by reason of pollutants already deposited though not yet causing apparent harm. Similarly, many tropical forests will suffer desiccation through climatic changes induced by deforestation that has already taken place. Desertification will keep on expanding its impact through built-in momentum. Ozone-destroying CFCs now in the atmosphere will continue their work for a whole century even if we were to cease releasing them immediately. There is potentially enough global warming in store through past greenhouse gas emissions to cause significant climate change no matter how much we seek to slow it, let alone halt it.

In light of this ongoing degradation of the biosphere, let us suppose, for the sake of argument, that in the year 2000 the whole of humankind were to be removed from the face of the earth in one fell swoop. Because of the many environmental perturbations already imposed, with effects persisting for many subsequent decades, gross biospheric impoverishment would continue and thus serve to eliminate further large numbers of species in the long term (Myers 1990a).

To consider specifics, note Simberloff's (1986) calculations concerning Amazonia. If deforestation continues at recent rates until the year 2000 (it is likely to accelerate in much of the region), but then halts completely, we should anticipate an eventual loss of about 15% of the plant species of Amazonia. Were the forest cover to be ultimately reduced to those areas now set aside as parks and reserves, we should anticipate that 66% of plant species will eventually disappear, together with almost 69% of bird species and similar proportions of other major categories of animal species.

On top of these main causes of species extinction (habitat disruption and destruction, plus widespread fragmentation), there are still further sources of biodiversity depletion—notably one that is hardly ever considered, yet possesses the capacity to generate perhaps the greatest problem of all: the issue of synergistic interactions between long-standing problems. We shall now turn to this critical question.

## Synergistic Interactions

The main mechanisms of extinction tend to be studied in isolation from one another. We know much less and understand even less still about the dynamic relationships between discrete mechanisms. Yet, **synergistic interactions** are unusually significant. For instance, a biota's tolerance of one stress tends to be lower when other stresses are in operation. A plant that experiences water stress is unduly prone to the adverse effects of hot weather and thereby suffers more in the heat than would a plant enjoying normal growth and full vigor.

When we consider the likely outcome of several extinction mechanisms operating at once, we can reasonably surmise that many of their effects will serve to amplify one another. This means that synergisms, working collec-

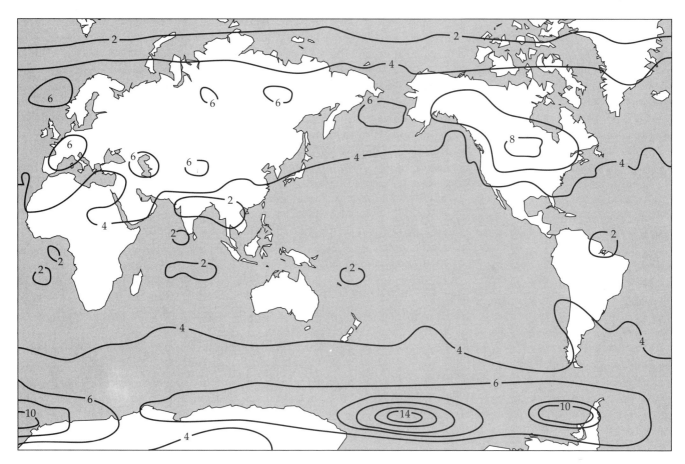

**Figure 5.10** An example of a predicted global warming scenario. Each contour line represents a 2°C increase. Higher temperature increases are expected at higher latitudes. These increases could interact in synergistic ways with a multitude of other human activities and result in great ecological upheaval. (Modified from Manabe and Wetherald 1987.)

tively and with compounding effects on one another, surely will lead to an ultimately larger-scale extinction episode. In the more immediate term, they may cause the episode to be compressed in time, especially in the early phases. It all means that the large-scale elimination of species may occur even sooner than many observers anticipate. Indeed, the synergistic connection could well prove to be a major, if not the predominant, phenomenon at work during the impending extinction spasm (Myers 1986, 1992c). To the extent that we can discern some of its possible workings, we shall start to better understand some potential patterns and processes as the spasm works itself out, and be better able to anticipate and prevent some of them.

Especially damaging in its synergized impact will be global climate change. For many species, a few degrees of temperature change, or slight changes in rainfall pattern, make a difference between survival and extinction—and these changes will be unusually harmful for those many species that will already be stressed through other human activities. As the planet warms, higher temperature profiles will move from the equator toward the poles (Figure 5.10), and rainfall patterns will change. Vegetation, trying to adapt by following the temperature and moisture changes, will meet with limited success. For one thing, climatologists project that changes will not only be large, but will emerge very suddenly compared with previous climate changes (Intergovernmental Panel on Climate Change 1990, 1992). At the end of the last Ice Age, when the glaciers covering much of North America retreated, trees and other plants followed the ebbing ice northward. But they moved at a rate of only 50 km or so per century. The sudden arrival of greenhouse warming will require communities of plants and animals to migrate at a rate ten times faster. Many species will find it impossible to achieve this, and they will die out, or their ranges will be severely restricted.

Those species that can make a quick transition will encounter a further problem. In the past, they have enjoyed a "free run," with only geographic obstacles—mountains, rivers and the like—blocking their paths. This time they will find their way blocked by farmlands, cities, and other paraphernalia of human communities, which are "development deserts" for wild species. To a migrating forest, an urban sprawl may present a bigger barrier than a mountain range. Formerly, species could at least follow cooler climates up a mountain slope; now, how will they navigate around urban sprawls?

Nor will present networks of parks and reserves provide much help, because protected areas have been set up to reflect natural conditions that are fast disappearing. Thus, a rainforest park might soon start to desiccate into woodland, leaving its rainforest species high and dry. A desert reserve might be overcome by moister conditions to which its species are not adapted. In each case, the protected area's biota will seek refuge elsewhere. But they will find themselves thwarted by the protected area's boundaries and the alien, human-dominated lands beyond. What was once a sanctuary will become a trap. Moreover, all this will arise because many more species will be threatened through other causes than is the case today. Global climate change will exert a reinforcing effect far greater than if it operated in isolation.

Further complicating the effects of global change is the likelihood that the changes will not be simple shifts in the mean temperature or precipitation. Rather, in addition to average changes, there will be, at least in some regions, increases in the variability of temperature and precipitation (Schneider 1993). One reason for this increase in variability is that many of the mechanisms involved in climate change are nonlinear. As a simple example, the rate of evaporation is exponentially related to water temperature. Because of such nonlinear behavior, plants and animals will face greater climate uncertainty and extremes.

In these several respects, then, we should direct special attention to synergistic interactions. Yet we are far from recognizing, let alone documenting and analyzing, the most prevalent manifestations of synergisms in the natural world today (Ehrlich 1986; Odum 1993). Still less have we attempted a methodical assessment of the ways in which multiple synergisms will affect the outlook for biodiversity.

## The Problem of Stressed Biotas

There is still another way in which the current mass extinction could generate greater impact. It lies with the possibility that many of earth's biotas today may have been "stressed" by events that occurred in the late Pleistocene. If this is the case, certain species, or rather communities of species, may be unduly prone to extinction. For want of a better term, they may lack long-term "ecological resilience" or "survival capacity."

The evidence, minimal though it is, lies in the fact that a mini-mass extinction started to overtake the earth's biotas during the late Pleistocene. After very long periods of steadily growing biodiversity (Signor 1990), there was a marked decline starting some 30,000 years ago and continuing until about 1000 years ago. Whether through human overhunting or climatic change, or both, the large mammal fauna of several entire regions—notably North and South America, Oceania, and Madagascar—lost more than 100 genera, including 70% of large North American mammals (Martin and Klein 1984). Following this species extinction spasm, there has been continuing elimination of vertebrate species (plus some plant species), albeit not on as spectacular a scale as in the late Pleistocene episode. The present mass extinction then began in roughly the middle of this century for tropical moist forests and earlier for other regions; these recent eliminations are almost entirely due to human activities. We have no idea how many associated species—especially invertebrate species—have been lost, but they must be quite numerous.

According to this scenario, today's biodiversity had already become somewhat depauperate before the arrival of the unprecedentedly severe human impact of the Industrial Age. Many surviving biotas have surely been adversely affected along the way, at least through depletion of their subspecies and populations (Kauffman and Walliser 1990). As we have seen, large numbers of species must have lost much of their genetic variability—hence much of their ecological adaptability—leaving them all the more vulnerable to summary extinction.

In short, the present mass extinction may have had origins in events long past. It would be more than difficult to determine how far today's biotas have been not only impoverished but also subjected to stress in the manner postulated. How should we define and document the stressing factors involved? What criteria could we invoke to evaluate the processes at work, let alone their present-day outcome? Thus far, the overall question has received scant substantive attention, despite the possibly potent significance for the capacity of today's biotas to resist extinction pressures.

## The Future of Evolution: A Process at Risk

Regrettably, mass extinction of species is far from the whole story concerning the current biotic crisis; also at risk are certain processes of evolution itself. In fact, the most serious repercussion of the species extinction spasm will probably lie with the eventual disruption of the course of evolution, insofar as speciation processes will have to work with a greatly reduced pool of species, populations, and genetic variability. Remarkably, this dimension of the biotic crisis has received virtually no attention from biologists. A computer check of *Evolution* and similar journals showed that hardly a single article in recent years makes even a passing reference to the notion that we could be at a crossroads in evolution's course. On the contrary, one could gain the impression that biological research is proceeding as if in a world that features virtually no significant change—even though the perturbations of the next few decades will surely leave an impoverishing impact on evolution's course for at least 5 million years, possibly several times longer.

The forces of natural selection can work only with the "resource base" available. If that base is drastically reduced, the result could be disruption of the creative capabilities of evolution, persisting far into the future. Given what we can discern from the geologic record, the "bounce-back" time is likely to be protracted. After the late Cretaceous crash 65 million years ago, some 50,000 to 100,000 years elapsed before there started to emerge a set of diversified and specialized biotas; a further 5 to 10 million years went by before there were bats in the skies and whales in the seas. In the case of coral reefs, which suffered more severely than most other biomes, there was a 10-million-year hiatus before a fresh community of reef-building species became established. Following the crash of the late Permian, when marine invertebrates lost roughly half their families, it took as much as 20 million years before the survivors could establish even half as many families as they had lost (Jablonski 1986, 1991; Raup 1988, 1991b).

But the evolutionary outcome this time around could prove yet more drastic (Myers 1990b). The critical factor lies with the likely loss of key environments. Not only do we appear set (in the absence of greatly expanded conservation efforts) to lose most, if not virtually all, tropical forests, but there is also progressive depletion of tropical coral reefs, wetlands, estuaries, and other ecosystems with an exceptional abundance and diversity of species and unusual complexity of ecological workings. These environments have served in the past as preeminent "powerhouses" of evolution, meaning that they have produced more species than other environments. It has long been believed (Darlington 1957; Mayr 1982) that virtually every major group of vertebrates and many other large categories of animals originated in spacious zones with warm, equable climates. It has likewise been supposed that the rate of evolutionary diversification—whether through proliferation of species or through emergence of major new adaptations—has been greatest in the tropics, especially in tropical forests (Stanley 1981; Stenseth 1984). In addition, tropical species, especially tropical forest species, appear to persist for only brief periods of geologic time, which implies a high rate of evolution.

Furthermore, the current mass extinction will surely apply across most, if not all, major categories of species. This is almost axiomatic if extensive environments are eliminated wholesale. So the result will contrast sharply with the end of the Cretaceous, when not only placental mammals survived (leading to the adaptive radiation of mammals, eventually including humans), but also birds, amphibians, crocodiles, turtles, squamates, and many other non-dinosaurian reptiles. In addition, the present extinction spasm looks likely to eliminate a sizable share of terrestrial plant species, at least one-fifth within the next half century and a good many more within the following half century. During most mass extinction episodes of the prehistoric past, by contrast, terrestrial plants survived with relatively few losses for the most part (Hickey 1984; Knoll 1984; Traverse 1988). They have thus supplied a resource base on which evolutionary processes could start to generate replacement animal species forthwith. If this biotic substrate is markedly depleted within the foreseeable future, the restorative capacities of evolution will be diminished all the more.

At the same time, of course, a mass extinction episode could trigger an outburst of speciation in a few categories of species. As discussed in Chapter 3, a certain amount of "creative disruption" in the form of habitat fragmentation can readily lead to splitting off of populations, followed by differentiation and termination of interbreeding, so that a population becomes distinctive enough to rank as a new race, then a subspecies, and finally a species. Note the case of Lake Nabugabo, for instance, a recent "offshoot" of Lake Victoria in East Africa, which has led to the development of six species of *Haplochromis* cichlids. Also fostering speciation is the introduction of new food resources and other materials into existing species' habitats, as has occurred in the case of bananas in Hawaii, leading to the emergence of several moth species of the genus *Hydylepta*, all of which are obligate feeders on banana plants.

Equally important, mass extinction will leave a multitude of niches vacant, allowing a few species to expand and then to diversify. Through these forms of creative disruption, we can discern incipient speciation in, for instance, the House Sparrow and the coyote in the United States, both of which have developed several distinctive races, even subspecies, in short order.

Of course, the main point is that a marked acceleration of speciation through these processes will not remotely match the rate and extent of extinctions. Whereas extinction can occur in just a few decades, and sometimes in a year or less, the time required to produce a new species is much longer. It takes decades for outstandingly capable contenders such as certain insects, centuries to millennia for many other invertebrates, and hundreds of thousands to millions of years for most mammals.

Among the reduced stock of species that survives the present extinction episode will surely be a disproportionate number of opportunists. These species rapidly exploit newly vacant niches (by making widespread use of food resources), are generally short-lived with short generation times, feature high rates of population increase, and are adaptable to a wide range of environments. All of these traits enable them to exploit new environments and to make excellent use of disturbances and "boom periods"—precisely the attributes that enable opportunistic species to prosper in a human-disrupted world. Examples of such species include the House Sparrow, the European Starling, the housefly, rabbits, rats, and other "pest" species, together with many "weedy" plants. Not only are these species harmful to humans' material needs, but they foster a homogenization of biotas by squeezing out less adaptable species. The House Sparrow in North America is usurping the niches of bluebirds, wrens and swallows, while the Herring Gull in northwestern Europe is adversely affecting the rarer terns.

While generalist species are profiting from the coming crash, specialist species, notably predators and parasites, will probably suffer disproportionately higher losses. Not only are their lifestyles specialized, but their numbers are also typically much smaller. Because specialist predators and parasites are often the creatures that keep down the populations of generalists, there may be little to hold pests in check. Today, probably less than 5% of all insect species deserve to be called pests (Pimentel 1991). But if extinction patterns tend to favor such species, the outcome could soon be a situation in which pests increase until their natural enemies can no longer control them. In short, our descendants could find themselves living in a world with a "pest and weed" ecology.

Overall, the prospect is that in the wake of the present extinction spasm, there will not be a mere hiatus in evolutionary processes. Rather, our distant descendants may find that many evolutionary developments that have persisted throughout the Phanerozoic could be suspended, if not terminated. To cite the vivid phrasing of Soulé and Wilcox (1980), "Death is one thing, an end to birth is something else."

The impending upheaval in evolution's course could rank as one of the greatest biological revolutions of palaeontological time. In scale and significance, it could equal the development of aerobic respiration, the emergence of flowering plants, or the arrival of limbed animals. But whereas these three departures of life's course rank as advances, the prospective depletion of many evolutionary capacities will rank as a profound setback.

In short, the future of evolution should be regarded as one of the most challenging problems that humankind has ever encountered. Yet evolutionary biologists seem to have given scant attention to this unique challenge—or indeed to the unprecedented opportunity for research into evolution in an incipient state of extreme turmoil. Surely there is a broad scope for innovative inquiry at a time when life's abundance and diversity on earth seem poised for an exceptionally profound upheaval.

## Concluding Thoughts

It is becoming obvious that we are in the opening phase of a mass extinction of species, especially in tropical forests. If, through lack of conservation responses of sufficient scope and scale, this mass extinction is allowed to proceed unchecked, it could eliminate half of all species within the foreseeable future of the next century or so. The same biodepletive processes will also leave many surviving species with grossly reduced populations and genetic variability, and thus diminished environmental adaptability. Still more important, the species-extinction spasm will have an impoverishing effect on evolution's capacity to generate stocks of replacement species, causing a hiatus that could well extend for five million years, possibly several times longer.

All this presupposes that we shall fail to do a better job of preserving biodiversity. Whatever the dismal character of the prognosis presented in this chapter, it is far from inevitable that we face a mass extinction of the full scope delineated. After all, prediction is not destiny. True, our best efforts will fail to save sizable numbers of species, since the processes of habitat depletion have generated too much momentum to be halted in short order. But there is still time, though barely, for us to save species in their many millions—provided we immediately come to grips with the challenge.

Humankind is the sole species in the whole of life's course with the capacity to eliminate other species in large numbers. It is also unique in that it possesses the power to save species in large numbers. Fortunately, we still have time, minimal though it may be, to turn an unprecedented problem into an unrivaled opportunity. But that time will run out soon after the year 2000, after which the processes of habitat depletion will have worked up so much momentum that they will be difficult to stem, let alone halt, without much greater expense and with far less chance of success. The time during the rest of this decade amounts to little more than 2000 days. We lose 1% of our maneuvering room with every 3 weeks that go by.

## Summary

As a result of human activities and overpopulation, we are now witnessing a global mass extinction spasm. Species-rich biotas are being destroyed at high rates, especially in tropical lowland forests, but also in other tropical environments, coral reefs and other marine environments, freshwater lakes, Mediterranean biomes, and many other areas. In the process, biological diversity, including genetic, species, and ecosystem diversity, is in sharp decline. Estimates of habitat and species loss vary greatly, due to the difficulties of gathering accurate data over broad expanses and the use of a variety of models and assumptions. Predictions of future losses also vary, but all unquestionably point to extinctions of sizable percentages of life-forms, most of which are unknown at this time. One of the easiest and most efficient ways of stemming this loss is protection of 18 identified "hot spots" of diversity, small areas of the earth that contain exceptionally high concentrations of species diversity found nowhere else.

Not all species are equally vulnerable to extinction. Rare species and long-lived species are especially vulnerable. Additionally, keystone species or sets of species typically support many other species that are reliant on them. If these keystones are lost, the vulnerability of their many dependent species is high, and cascading extinctions are likely.

Species losses are only one component of biodiversity losses. Genetic diversity—the basis for evolutionary change and adaptation—and population diversity—the result of local adaptations—are also being lost at high rates.

This may be especially critical with respect to loss of crop genetic diversity, which forms the basis for agricultural production for the human population. Most of the world's major crops and domestic animals have quite narrow levels of genetic variation, and the wild ancestors of many of these species are extinct or headed in that direction. As a result of this biotic impoverishment, the human sustenance base is increasingly vulnerable to pests, diseases, and changing environments, frequently without the genetic diversity needed to adapt.

In addition to outright habitat destruction, fragmentation and degradation of habitats is yet another threat to biodiversity, as it may intensify biodepletive effects. Creating ever smaller chunks of forest exposes the remaining habitats to edge effects, invasive species, and other ills that accelerate extinctions. Synergistic processes (interactions among many different stresses) are poorly understood and are also likely to accelerate extinctions. In particular, global climate changes are certain to add to and complicate all the other problems leading to extinctions. On top of that, parts of the world's biota may still be under stress from changes in the late Pleistocene period, which resulted in the loss of many large vertebrates, among hosts of other species. In other words, these biotas may be entering the modern mass extinction already vulnerable.

All of this will result in risk to certain processes of evolution itself. The actual course of evolution may be disrupted, as speciation processes will be working with a reduced pool of species, populations, and genetic variation. The events of the next few decades could have an impoverishing effect on evolution's course that will be felt for several million years, and could radically change the history of life on earth.

## Questions for Discussion

1. Should our aim be solely to preserve a maximum number of species, or should we give differential emphasis to higher taxa such as families and orders, even if this goal conflicts with the first? Remember that we cannot do everything, if only because conservation resources—especially time—are in ever shorter supply in relation to the challenge.

2. Regardless of your answer to Question 1, should our sole aim be to preserve a maximum amount of biodiversity? Or—in light of what we know about food webs and ecosystem stability—should we seek to safeguard ecological processes?

3. Following from Question 2, recall that the most depauperizing effect of the present mass extinction could well be its disruption of the future course of evolution. Consequently, should our predominant conservation strategies be geared to safeguarding evolutionary processes? If so, would this mean that we should give less attention to species that are "evolutionary dead ends" since they will not produce new species for millions of years? Notable examples of such "dead ends" include the whales, the rhinos, the elephants, the great apes, and certain other long-lived species. Should we not direct greater emphasis to those species that, by reason of their far more rapid turnover of population stocks, supply more of a "resource base" for natural selection to work on, notably the insects and other invertebrates?

4. If conservation biologists accept that the biotic crisis demands a strong, action-oriented response, what does this imply in practical terms? Should they engage not only in on-the-ground efforts to save strategic habitats, but strive to bring the matter to the attention of political leaders and policymakers? Or should they stick to what they are best at, their scientific

disciplines, and leave politicking to others? Or should they expand their expertise from, for example, the flow of energy through ecosystems, to include the flow of influence through the corridors of power?

5. What does all of this say about the boundaries of conservation biology as a discrete discipline? Is it a certain sort of biology, strictly a life-sciences affair? Or should it give equal prominence to social sciences such as economics, political science, law, and ethics?

6. In two or three decades' time, your children or other youngsters may ask you a question along the lines of, "When the biodiversity crisis became apparent in its full scope during the early 1990s, what did you do about it?" What will your answer be?

## Suggestions for Further Reading

Davis, S. and seven others. 1986. *Plants in Danger: What Do We Know?* International Union for Conservation of Nature and Natural Resources, Gland, Switzerland. We probably know more about plants—their numbers, distribution, conservation status, and the like—than any other major taxon. This book presents country-by-country documentation and assessment, with all the vital statistics.

Ehrlich, P. R. and A. H. Ehrlich. 1981. *Extinction: The Causes and Consequences of the Disappearance of Species.* Random House, New York. A first-rate and eminently accessible account of how and why we are triggering a mass extinction of species—and how and why we need to stem it forthwith. Containing an abundance of hard science, the text is illuminated with a host of anecdotal insights, making the book a fine introduction to the mass extinction field for the neophyte and expert alike.

Elliott, D. K. (ed.). 1986. *Dynamics of Extinction.* John Wiley and Sons, New York. Curiously enough, we know little about the actual mechanisms of extinction in its final phases. What happens to a species when its numbers are brought below a critical level, what processes of ecological equilibration start to operate, how does demographic stochasticity work on the ground? A book you will return to time and again.

Myers, N. 1979. *The Sinking Ark.* Pergamon Press, Oxford. The first detailed account of the species extinction spasm that is overtaking the biosphere. Looks especially at social science factors that unwittingly promote extinction of species and populations, and erosion of their genetic base.

Myers, N. 1992. *The Primary Source: Tropical Forests and Our Future.* (expanded ed.). W. W. Norton, New York. A synoptic review and analysis of the biome that is richest biotically and the most threatened through habitat depletion. A detailed account of what is at stake for us all in tropical forests, with a comparative assessment of deforestation rates, the main agents of deforestation, and what we can do to safeguard this, the principal locus of mass extinction.

Raven, P. H. 1990. The politics of preserving biodiversity. *BioScience* 40:769-774. A fine account of the "social science" aspects of biodiversity. Raven should know: he is a past president of the American Institute of Biological Sciences and the current home secretary of the National Academy of Sciences.

Soulé, M. E. (ed.). 1987. *Viable Populations for Conservation.* Cambridge University Press, New York. Biodiversity exists within species as well as among species. This is the book that will bring readers up to speed on the crucial factors of genetic variability, especially as concerns key issues such as the critical minimum gene pool size of populations.

Wilson, E. O. and F. Peter (eds.). 1988. *Biodiversity.* National Academy Press, Washington, D.C. This book contains 57 chapters by front-rank authors in the biodiversity arena. If you are looking for the best expertise on the basic biology, evolution, genetics, economics, ethics, and philosophy of biodiversity, you will find it here. If you have just one biodiversity book by your bedside, make it this one.

Wilson, E. O. 1992. *The Diversity of Life.* Belknap Press of Harvard University Press, Cambridge, MA. Far and away the finest book on biodiversity generally: what biodiversity consists of, where it is primarily located, how fast it is disappearing, what we are losing thereby, and what we can do to better safeguard it. Informative, illuminating, and highly readable—a wonderful combination by the guru of biodiversity.

# II

# Population-Level Concerns

# 6

# Genetics

## Conservation of Diversity within Species

*Wild species must have available a pool of genetic diversity if they are to survive environmental pressures exceeding the limits of developmental plasticity. If this is not the case, extinction would appear inevitable.*

*O. H. Frankel, 1983*

As indicated in Chapter 5, contemporary extinction rates are, or will soon be, as high as any that have ever occurred on earth. This unrestrained loss of species is accompanied by a more subtle but no less important process, the loss of genetic diversity. When a population or species disappears, all of the genetic information carried by that population or species is lost. When a contiguous population is fragmented through habitat destruction, and many small, isolated populations result, genetic diversity within each will decay over time. In the words of Thomas Foose (1983), "Gene pools are becoming diminished and fragmented into gene puddles."

But why be concerned with something as detailed as genetic diversity when bigger problems such as large-scale habitat destruction, global warming, toxic wastes, and the spread of exotic species threaten wholesale destruction of ecological systems? Certainly, massive destruction of tropical rainforest, for example, does not lend itself to genetic solutions. Species in those systems will go extinct through loss of habitat, and all the genetic diversity in the world will not save them (other than, perhaps, genetically based human intelligence). Those situations of mass destruction require different approaches, at different scales (see chapters in Parts III and IV). However, there are many conservation challenges that require the guidance and direction that genetic data, collected and interpreted within the constructs of sound genetic theory, can provide. Rhinoceroses, grizzly bears, Pacific salmon, desert fishes, Siberian tigers, African elephants, and many other species are all benefiting from the input of geneticists (Figure 6.1).

(A)

(B)

**Figure 6.1**   Many species around the world are beginning to benefit from inclusion of genetic information in their management plans. These include (A) various species of rhinoceros, including the white rhinoceros (*Ceratotherium simum*); (B) Przewalski's horse (*Equus przewalskii*) from the Dzungarian Basin of Mongolia, Kazakhstan, and China; (C) numerous fish species, such as the Sonoran topminnow (*Poeciliopsis occidentalis*) from Arizona; and (D) the Red-cockaded Woodpecker (*Picoides borealis*) of the southeastern United States. (A, photograph © San Diego Zoo; B, by Ron Garrison © San Diego Zoo; C, by John N. Rinne; D, by Walker Montgomery.)

(C)

(D)

## Why Genetics?

There are at least three biological reasons to believe that genetics can be the basis of an important and critical area of conservation biology. First, the **Fundamental Theorem of Natural Selection** (Fisher 1930) tells us that the rate of evolutionary change in a population is proportional to the amount of genetic diversity available. When genetic diversity in a population decreases, the rate and scope of potential evolutionary change in that population in response to environmental challenges is reduced. Essentially, loss of genetic diversity reduces future evolutionary options.

Second, there is a consensus among population geneticists that **heterozygosity,** or high genetic variation within populations, is positively related to fitness. Heterozygosity at single or multiple **gene loci** (single-locus and multi-locus heterozygosity, respectively) may confer fitness advantages upon individuals. This will be discussed in greater detail below, but for now we will say that reduced individual heterozygosity may lead to lower fitness.

Finally, the global pool of genetic diversity represents all of the information for all biological processes on the planet. Every biochemical product, every growth pattern, every instinctive behavior, every color morph is encoded in a genetic "library" of unimaginable global extent. Wilson (1985) has calculated that the billion bits of genetic information carried in the DNA of a single house mouse, if translated into equivalent English text, would fill nearly all editions of the *Encyclopedia Britannica* printed since 1768. Loss of such diversity likely will decrease the ability of organisms to respond to environmental change, and will also discard biological information potentially useful to humans, such as crop genetic diversity or valuable biochemicals. In essence, we are losing the "blueprints" of life.

Throughout this text we promote the evolutionary paradigm for conservation, which means that genetics should be prominent in its practice. Evolution is the single most unifying organizational concept in all of biology, and it should play a prominent role in conservation as well. Vrijenhoek (1989b) even called for an "evolutionary conservation ethic," which would place a long-term, evolutionary perspective at the heart of conservation. The role of evolution perhaps is most evident with respect to genetic conservation, but permeates all aspects of the field. Consequently, we encourage all students of conservation biology to develop a solid foundation of evolutionary knowledge, including genetics, and apply that mindset to conservation. As Ehrenfeld (1991) so aptly put it, "The biosphere is a system, or a set of systems, with many millions of elements that are changing in time and are affected by myriad local irregularities and discontinuities and by countless historical singularities. As yet, there is no single comprehensive theory besides evolution that takes it all in. Quite possibly there never will be."

The basic problem linking genetics to conservation is that small populations, whether in the wild or in captivity, tend to lose genetic variation over time. This loss of variation may well increase the probability of population extinction or reduce opportunities for future adaptation through evolutionary change. Because habitat fragmentation and destruction will continue to produce small, isolated populations of plants and animals, and because by the time many species are recognized as threatened or endangered, they are, almost by definition, in small and isolated populations, understanding the genetic consequences is vital to good management and recovery efforts. The basic thrust of conservation genetics, the message to take from this chapter, is to maintain genetic diversity and thus preserve options for future evolution.

Before proceeding further, we state two important caveats for the remainder of this chapter. First, we assume the student has a working knowledge of basic (Mendelian) genetics and at least a rudimentary knowledge of population genetics. This includes, but is not limited to, patterns of inheritance, basic molecular genetic structure and function (DNA and chromosome structure), the meaning of **Hardy-Weinberg equilibrium,** and the concept of **natural selection.** If the student lacks this background, we recommend consulting a good introductory genetics text before proceeding, or other writings such as Chapter 2 in Wilson and Bossert (1971), or Chambers (1983).

The second caveat is that entire books have been written on conservation genetics, and the field has a large literature. The application of genetics to conservation is also a young endeavor, with advances made quickly and arguments generated (though often not resolved) easily. We can provide only a basic introduction to the topic, and encourage the serious student to pursue more advanced topics in other texts or the original literature, such as Frankel and Soulé (1981), Schonewald-Cox et al. (1983), relevant chapters in Soulé (1986), and especially in more recent works such as Ryman and Utter (1987) and Falk and Holsinger (1991).

## Genetic Variation: What Is It and Why Is It Important?

A species' pool of genetic diversity exists at three fundamental levels: genetic variation within individuals (heterozygosity), genetic differences among individuals within a population, and genetic differences among populations. Each level is a genetic resource of potential importance to conservation, so each must be understood relative to the others.

### Variation within Individuals

Heritable genetic variation is the basis for evolutionary change and is essential if natural selection is to operate. With the exception of identical twins and clones, every individual of a species is genetically unique. This is easily seen by looking around a college classroom: some resemblances may occur, but every individual is distinguishable from every other. Some of this **phenotypic,** or physically expressed, variation is due to variation in the **genotype,** or the genetic constitution, and some is due to **environmental modifications,** such as differences in nutritional history or hair stylists.

**Quantitative genetics** describes this relationship between an organism's phenotype, its genotype, and environmental influences as

$$V_p = V_g + V_e + V_{ge}$$

where $V_p$ is overall phenotypic variation among individuals, $V_g$ is variation due to genotype (usually multi-locus), $V_e$ is variation due to environmental influences, and $V_{ge}$ is variation due to genetic–environmental interactions. A particular physical or behavioral character may be due entirely to genotype (such as eye color), to environment (such as loss of a limb to an accident), or, more likely, a combination of both (such as skin color as an interaction between racial background [genetics] and recent exposure to sunlight [environment]). This is the essence of the age-old "nature versus nurture," or genetics versus environment, debate, an argument about whether genetics or environment is more important as the basis for characteristics (usually in the context of humans). The answer, of course, is usually "both." Suffice it to say here that genetic variation is important at the level of the individual because it forms part of the basis for its phenotype.

At any particular gene **locus** there are two **alleles,** or copies of the gene inherited from the two parents. At the *population* level, each locus may be said to be either **monomorphic** (both copies of the allele are always the same; there is no variation at that locus) or **polymorphic** (there are multiple types of alleles at that locus). For any particular *individual,* any polymorphic locus may be either **homozygous** (two copies of the same allele) or **heterozygous** (two different alleles); monomorphic loci, of course, are always homozygous. The overall level of heterozygosity, or the proportion of gene loci in an individual that contain alternative forms of alleles, is one measure of individual genetic diversity.

Rarely can we directly document alleles, however. Instead, we can more easily determine allele products, such as enzymes encoded by gene loci. A technique called **electrophoresis** is typically used to estimate the genetic constitution of individuals at selected gene loci. In electrophoresis, a tissue sample such as blood, muscle, or liver is homogenized and placed in a gel medium, through which is passed an electric current. All of the enzymes and other proteins in the sample migrate various distances through the gel based on their relative sizes and electric charges, which are unique to each. When a protein-specific stain is applied to the gel, the locations of the particular forms of that enzyme (called **allozymes**) are revealed. In this way, one can determine the presumptive alleles carried by the individual responsible for the allozymes present, and infer the genotype of that individual.

The significance of within-individual variation measured by techniques such as electrophoresis is that greater heterozygosity may correlate with higher individual fitness, a topic to be addressed below. The ultimate origin of such genetic variation is **mutations,** but within-individual variation is produced each generation by recombination during sexual reproduction.

What is the value of a focus on individual genetic variation? First, the individual is the level upon which natural selection acts. Genetic variation at the individual level can reflect the action of selection, or can indicate low levels of diversity relevant to conservation. Second, the individual is the level at which genetic problems such as inbreeding occur; this will be discussed below. Third, knowledge of individual genotypes may be important in some captive breeding programs, when mating schemes are developed that attempt to maximize genetic diversity of offspring. Finally, genetic variation is always measured in individuals, but then summed over populations and compared at that higher level. Rarely do we direct our conservation efforts solely toward individuals; more typically, populations or species are the units of concern. Consequently, we must understand genetic variation of groups, variation both within and among populations.

## Variation within Populations

Population-level genetic variation consists of the types of alleles present and their frequencies across all members of a population considered together (the **gene pool**). Both the conservationist and the population geneticist are interested in the structure of that variation—how much there is and how it is distributed over space and time. The causes of change are of particular interest to the conservation biologist, who generally wishes to minimize major losses of genetic variation or changes in its natural distribution.

Genetic variation at the population level is described by the types and frequencies of alleles present, and the particular combination of alleles (genotypes). Consider, for example, the gene locus that encodes for an enzyme called phosphoglucomutase (PGM) in the club moss *Lycopodium lucidulum*, a primitive plant (Table 6.1). This locus has three possible alleles in this species, called *a*, *b*, and *c*. In four populations in New York and Connecticut, there occur major differences in the presence and frequencies of these alleles. One Connecticut population has alleles *b* and *c*, another has

**Table 6.1**
Gene Frequencies at Five Polymorphic Loci in the Club Moss *Lycopodium lucidulum*

| Locus | Allele | Woodridge, CT | Litchfield, CT | Binghamton, NY | New Lebanon, NY |
|-------|--------|---------------|----------------|----------------|-----------------|
| PGI-2 | | | | | |
| | *a* | 0.68 | 1.00 | 1.00 | 0.75 |
| | *b* | 0.32 | 0.00 | 0.00 | 0.25 |
| G6PD-1 | | | | | |
| | *a* | 0.93 | 1.00 | 0.82 | 0.91 |
| | *b* | 0.07 | 0.00 | 0.18 | 0.09 |
| G6PD-2 | | | | | |
| | *a* | 1.00 | 1.00 | 0.50 | 1.00 |
| | *b* | 0.00 | 0.00 | 0.50 | 0.00 |
| PGM | | | | | |
| | *a* | 0.00 | 0.00 | 0.50 | 0.00 |
| | *b* | 0.86 | 1.00 | 0.50 | 1.00 |
| | *c* | 0.14 | 0.00 | 0.00 | 0.00 |
| LGGP-1 | | | | | |
| | *a* | 0.50 | 0.50 | 1.00 | 1.00 |
| | *b* | 0.50 | 0.50 | 0.00 | 0.00 |

From Levin and Crepet 1973.

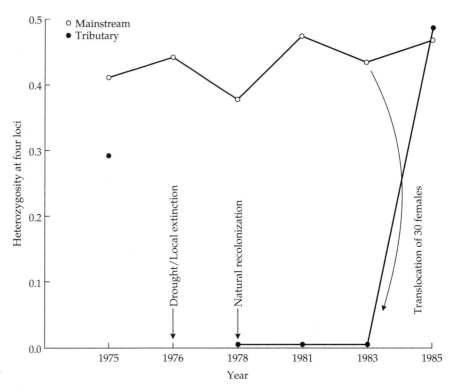

**Figure 6.2**  Example of gene frequency change due to local extinction and a founder event in a natural population of *Poeciliopsis monacha*, a small desert fish of Sonora, Mexico. Heterozygosity at four loci from fish in a small tributary dropped from near 0.3 in 1975 to zero after a drought and local extinction. Natural recolonization by presumably few individuals resulted in zero heterozygosity from 1978 through 1983, while heterozygosity in an adjacent mainstream population remained high. Translocation (gene flow) of 30 fish to the tributary population from the mainstream population restored heterozygosity in 1985. (Modified from Vrijenhoek 1989a.)

only *b*; one New York population has only *a* and *b*, and the other has only *b*. Each population may thus be described by the types (*a, b, c*) and frequencies of occurrence of these alleles. With measurements across a broad spectrum of gene loci (Table 6.1), patterns often emerge that distinguish populations genetically.

Gene frequencies within a population generally change over time, due to selection, random processes such as **genetic drift,** or immigration from or emigration to other populations, called **gene flow** (Figure 6.2). It is these changes in gene frequencies, and especially loss of alleles, that are often of concern to the conservation biologist, and these will be discussed in detail below.

### Variation among Populations

Species rarely exist as single, randomly interbreeding, or **panmictic,** populations. Instead, genetic differences typically exist among populations; these geographic genetic differences are an important component of overall genetic diversity.

To understand among-population variation, consider a hypothetical species consisting of three populations (Figure 6.3). Genetic diversity in this species consists of within-population diversity (mean individual heterozygosity level within a population) and among-population divergence (mean genetic differences among geographic locations). A simple genetic model of this diversity is

$$H_t = H_p + D_{pt}$$

where $H_t$ = total genetic variation in the species, $H_p$ = average diversity within populations, or average local heterozygosity, and $D_{pt}$ = average divergence among populations across the total species range (Nei 1973, 1975). Divergence may arise among populations both from random processes (founder effects, genetic drift, demographic bottlenecks, and mutation, discussed below) and from local selection.

The critical point is that a species' total genetic variation may be partitioned into component parts: within-versus among-population diversity. With that approach, one can determine how variation is spatially distributed and thus define areas of particular conservation interest. For example, Stangel et al. (1992) found that the endangered Red-cockaded Woodpecker (*Picoides borealis*) in the southeastern United States had an overall mean allozyme heterozygosity level of 0.078 (or 7.8%), which is within the typical range of values for most bird species that have been sampled. Of the total genetic variation measured, 14% consisted of among-population differentiation, and 86% was mean genetic diversity (heterozygosity) within populations. The among-population component for these woodpeckers is higher than for most other bird species examined, whose vagility typically results in high genetic exchange and thus little local genetic differentiation. These woodpeckers are more site-specific than many birds, and consequently local populations tend to diverge genetically. Conservation programs for this species should therefore protect both components of genetic diversity in order to retain the maximum amount of variation and maintain a natural population genetic structure. We will return to this topic in detail when we discuss management of genetic diversity in nature.

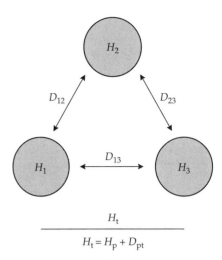

**Figure 6.3** Partitioning of total genetic diversity, $H_t$, into within- and among-population variation. This schematic represents a species with three populations, each with some level of within-population heterozygosity ($H_1$, $H_2$, and $H_3$); mean heterozygosity is $H_p$. Among-population divergence ($D_{12}$, $D_{23}$, and $D_{13}$) is represented by the arrows between populations; mean divergence is $D_{pt}$.

### The Fitness Consequences of Variation

We stated earlier that genetic diversity is the basis for a species' evolutionary flexibility and responsiveness to environmental change. Let us now elaborate by looking at first, the association between genetic diversity of individuals (heterozygosity) and their fitness, and second, the importance of among-population genetic divergence.

An individual's **fitness** is defined by its lifetime reproductive success relative to other individuals in the population. In genetic terms, fitness is measured as the proportion of the next generation's gene pool represented by the individual's genotype. Fitness is thus a *relative* term, measured against the performance of all other individuals in the gene pool. Fitness is extremely difficult to measure in nature (Endler 1986), but characters that likely contribute to fitness (*fitness correlates*), such as size, fecundity, growth rate or metabolic efficiency, may often be quantified. An important question, then, is whether these fitness correlates are related to heterozygosity. If so, then preservation of as much genetic diversity as possible is a matter of high conservation priority.

Many population geneticists agree that heterozygosity enhances fitness-related characteristics. The evidence for this is good (e.g., Figure 6.4, and summarized in Mitton and Grant 1984, and Allendorf and Leary 1986), although there are counter-examples (Zouros and Foltz 1987) and cautionary guides (Hedrick and Miller 1992).

Although high heterozygosity may appear to be good, not all species or populations have high levels of heterozygosity and there is no standard, "ac-

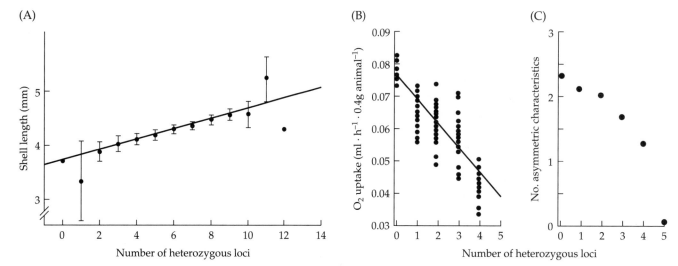

**Figure 6.4**  Three examples of correlations between heterozygosity level and a fitness-related character. (A) Growth rate in the coot clam *Mulinia lateralis* over a two-week period after collection as larvae. (B) Oxygen consumption in the American oyster (*Crassostrea virginica*); low consumption indicates greater metabolic efficiency. (C) Morphological asymmetry in rainbow trout (*Oncorhynchus mykiss*); greater asymmetry indicates less developmental stability. (A, from Koehn et al. 1988; B, from Koehn and Shumway 1982; C, from Leary et al. 1983.)

ceptable" level. Typical heterozygosity levels vary greatly among taxonomic groups, and heterozygosity may simply reflect the recent demographic history of the population. Measured values from natural populations range from 0 to over 0.3 (0 to > 30%). Mean measured values are about 0.07 for plants, 0.11 for invertebrates, and 0.05 for vertebrates, with a great deal of variance around each mean (Nevo 1978). Thus, expectations of heterozygosity levels vary greatly, and a low level does not necessarily indicate an anomaly. However, *loss* of heterozygosity in a population, especially over just a few generations, may indicate real problems.

The mechanism(s) that may translate higher heterozygosity into higher fitness are not clearly understood. In some cases, higher fitness may be due to **overdominance** at a single locus or multiple loci, wherein the heterozygous genotype is superior to either homozygote. This is clearly the case for the locus encoding the β chain of human hemoglobin in Africa. Two doses of the normal allele make the subject susceptible to malaria, a common parasitic disease in some areas. An alternative allele, in homozygous form, leads to severe anemia through sickling of red blood cells (sickle-cell anemia). A heterozygous individual, however, is protected from malaria and is only mildly anemic; the heterozygote clearly has higher fitness than either homozygote in a malarial environment. In other cases, higher fitness may derive not from individual heterozygous loci, but by lethal or sublethal recessive alleles being masked by alternative alleles. That is, homozygosity at these loci would be lethal, or would at least reduce fitness. This is particularly a problem in inbreeding, discussed below.

An oft-cited example of a correlation between low heterozygosity and low fitness (at least in captivity) is the South African cheetah (*Acionyx j. jubatus*). Fifty-five cheetahs from several populations examined had no detectable genetic diversity at 47 allozyme loci (*H* = 0.0%), low heterozygosity (*H* = 1.3%) of 155 soluble proteins, and no diversity in the major histocompatibility complex (O'Brien et al. 1983, 1985). These animals were so genetically uniform that skin tissue transplants were routinely accepted among all individuals; their immune systems could not distinguish between themselves and other individuals because they were virtually identical genetically. It was claimed that the animals had difficulty breeding in captivity, there were high rates of infant mortality in both wild and captive populations, males had sperm counts 10 times lower than related cat species and

70% morphologically abnormal sperm, and the species was especially susceptible to an epizootic coronavirus under zoo conditions. Both genetic diversity and fitness in captivity in these populations are thus low.

However, the story is not without controversy, as is often the case in conservation. O'Brien and his colleagues attributed the low heterozygosity in cheetahs to multiple demographic bottlenecks, but this conclusion has been criticized by Pimm (1991) and others as unsupported and unrealistic. Also, there is evidence that male cheetahs in zoos, despite abnormal sperm, can fertilize females with high efficiency and produce normal offspring (Lindburg et al. 1993). Additionally, there is a problem of cause and effect, as there is no "control" group with which to compare these cheetahs. Do cheetahs have poor reproductive performance because of low genetic diversity, or low diversity because of a history of poor reproductive performance? Some have suggested that poor performance in captivity is merely due to poor husbandry (Caro 1993). Caro and Laurenson (1994) presented convincing evidence that low population densities and poor recruitment in the wild are due to heavy predation on juveniles, rather than lack of genetic diversity. However, regardless of the cause, the fact remains that the cheetah has little measurable genetic variation, and, at least in some cases, low fitness correlates in captivity.

Regardless of its actual fitness effects, heterozygosity is often higher at larger population sizes (Figure 6.5). This implies that small populations tend to lose heterozygosity over time, which is an argument for maintaining larger populations, and thus larger reserves, wherever possible. This topic will be revisited repeatedly in this and other chapters.

A cautionary note is in order relative to heterozygosity estimates for small populations of wild organisms. Low heterozygosity per se does not necessarily mean that a demographic bottleneck has occurred or that the population is in genetic danger. Sherwin et al. (1991) studied a small, endangered and isolated population of the eastern barred bandicoot (*Perameles gunnii*), a marsupial, in southeastern Australia. No genetic variation was detected at 27 loci, suggesting an effect of small population size. However, two large "control"

**Figure 6.5** Relationships between heterozygosity level and population size in two species. (A) *Halocarpus bidwillii*, a coniferous tree from New Zealand (*r* = 0.94). (B) The Red-cockaded Woodpecker (*Picoides borealis*) from the southeastern United States (*r* = 0.48). (A, from Billington 1991; B, data from Stangel et al. 1992.)

(A)

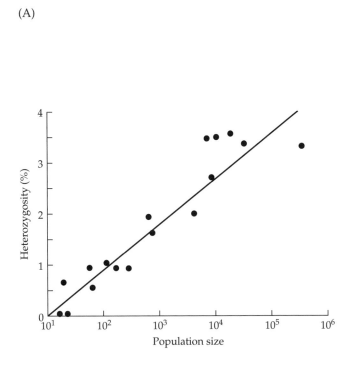

(B)

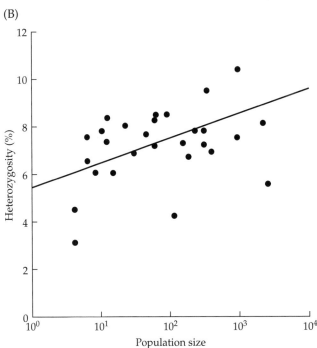

populations on Tasmania also had no variation at those loci, indicating that recent population size alone cannot account for the paucity of genetic diversity in this species. Too often, control populations for comparison are lacking.

Among-population divergence may also play a critical role in local fitness and population survival, for two reasons. First, populations may be locally adapted, due to long-term interaction of their genetic systems with the biotic and abiotic environments of the region. Local adaptation is common, and readily seen in many plant and animal populations; it may even lead to speciation (Chapter 3). Second, so-called **coadapted gene complexes** may arise in local populations (discussed in Essay 6A by Alan Templeton). These are gene combinations with a long history together in a population, and are thought to work particularly well in combination. For both of these reasons, among-population divergence should be considered for its potential importance as a component of overall genetic diversity, contributing to local uniqueness and evolutionary adaptability.

# ESSAY 6A
# Coadaptation, Local Adaptation, and Outbreeding Depression

Alan R. Templeton, Washington University, St. Louis

When individuals of an animal or plant species from different geographic areas are brought together, as in captive breeding or translocation programs, they often hybridize with one another. Outbreeding depression occurs if these hybrids, or the offspring of the hybrids, have reduced fertility and/or survival abilities. There are two main causes of outbreeding depression: coadaptation and local adaptation. Coadaptation results when a local population evolves a gene pool that is internally balanced with respect to reproductive fitness. For example, the process of gamete formation normally requires a matched set of chromosomes (with the exception of the sex chromosomes). However, if the two sets of chromosomes differ in number or structure, fertility problems are possible. This type of coadaptation is illustrated by a reduction in fertility that occurred during captive breeding of the owl monkey, *Aotus trivirgatus* (de Boer 1982). It turned out that animals from different geographic populations had been mixed and that these local populations had different chromosome types. By pairing animals with similar chromosome types, successful reproduction was restored.

The second major cause of outbreeding depression is local adaptation. The geographic range of many species encompasses a variety of environmental conditions. Under such conditions, local populations often adapt to their regional environment, particularly if dispersal among populations is limited.

Hybridization between individuals from different local populations often results in individuals that are not adapted to any or to the wrong local environment. For example, ibex (*Capra ibex*) became extinct locally in the Tatra Mountains of Czechoslovakia through overhunting. Ibex were then successfully transplanted from nearby Austria, which had a similar environment. However, some years later, a decision was made to augment the Tatra ibex population by importing animals from Turkey and the Sinai, areas with a much warmer and drier climate. The introduced animals readily interbred with the Tatra herd, but the resulting hybrids rutted in the early fall instead of the winter (as the native Tatra and Austrian ibex did), and the resulting kids of the hybrids were born in February, the coldest month of the year. As a consequence, the entire population went extinct (Greig 1979).

The problem of local adaptation is inherent in all translocation programs, which by definition involve the movement of organisms from one location to another. If the translocation program also involves moving organisms from more than one location to a common place, the problem of coadaptation is also present. Both local adaptation and coadaptation were factors in the reintroduction of collared lizards (*Crotaphytus collaris*) in the Missouri Ozarks.

Most collared lizards live in the deserts of the American Southwest. The Ozark populations therefore represent both a geographic and ecological extreme for the species as a whole. Although there are no true deserts in the Ozarks, the collared lizards can live in glades—open, rocky habitats characterized by a hot, dry microclimate. One of the few trees that can invade these hot, dry glades is the juniper, *Juniperus virginiana*. Prior to European settlement, the Ozarks were subjected to frequent fires that prevented junipers from becoming established in the glades. After European settlement, the suppression of fires has caused many former glades to become completely shaded over by junipers, leading to the extirpation of many glade inhabitants. As the role of fire in the Ozarks has become appreciated, fire regimes have been deliberately reestablished to restore glade habitat. The glade flora has returned remarkably well with little or no need for reintroductions. However, collared lizards will not disperse through even a few hundred yards of forest, so once extirpated from a glade, they are incapable of natural recolonization. Consequently, there was a need for reintroduction of collared lizards as part of a general glade community restoration program.

An examination of past reintroduction programs indicates that the probability of a self-sustaining reintroduced population increases with increasing geographic proximity of the site of origin of the propagules to the site of release (Griffith et al. 1989). Such a strategy minimizes the dangers of local adaptation. Local adaptation was a real danger for the Ozark collared lizards, which inhabit an ecological extreme for the species as a whole and which display many unique adaptive traits not found in their southwestern relatives (Templeton 1994). Therefore, all lizards obtained for the reintroduction program were captured from other Ozark glades whose habitats had not yet degenerated to the point of causing local extinction. Although this strategy minimized the problems associated with local adaptation, it accentuated the danger of coadaptation. The remaining glade populations are small in size, so only a handful of lizards could be collected from any single glade without endangering the natural glade population. This meant that releases into restored glades would have to involve lizards caught from several different natural glade populations. Moreover, molecular genetic surveys revealed that the different natural glade populations are genetically distinct from one another with little or no genetic contact, making the possibility of coadaptation even more likely. Despite the risk of coadaptation, it was decided to go ahead with a mixed release program.

The decision to accept the risk of coadaptation was based on an evolutionary consideration. Natural populations are the products of evolutionary change, and as long as they retain genetic variation, they will continue to evolve. Reintroduced populations are no exception. Hence, evolutionary

change, and the factors that promote it or retard it, must be incorporated into strategic decision making. In general, when compromises must be made, genetic diversity and the potential for evolutionary change should always have priority over other considerations. We are simply not wise enough to anticipate all the challenges a reintroduced population will face. If natural or released populations have the potential for evolutionary change, they can evolve solutions to problems such as outbreeding depression or environmental change; without it, their adaptive flexibility is lost. We should never forget that the earth's biodiversity is the product of past evolution and is not, nor has it ever been, static. Hence, conservation programs should try to conserve processes (such as evolution) that affect living organisms and ecosystems rather than conserving the current status quo of the living world.

Mixing lizards from different glades would maximize their genetic variation, and hence they should be capable of overcoming outbreeding depression through evolutionary change, just as captive populations have been able to overcome inbreeding depression through evolutionary change (Templeton and Read 1984). To see if this was the case, and to monitor the success of the release program, a blood sample was taken from each lizard prior to release and scored with molecular genetic surveying techniques. After release, each population has usually been resampled

once a year to monitor its success, to gather individual size and growth rate data, and to obtain blood samples from lizards born into the reintroduced population for genetic monitoring.

In terms of the primary goal (to establish self-sustaining genetically variable populations), the program has been completely successful: all six populations released between 1984 and 1989 still existed as of 1993, and are highly genetically variable. The genetic markers also allow individuals to be ranked in their degree of hybridity (the extent to which their ancestry represents mixtures of founders from different glades). By coupling hybrid rankings with data on adult size, growth rates, and reproductive success, the hypothesis of an outbreeding depression can be tested. The data are still being gathered, but preliminary analyses indicate no outbreeding depression. However, regardless of the ultimate outcome, valuable lessons will be learned.

Given the rate at which biodiversity is being lost, management decisions often have to be made with incomplete scientific knowledge. Conservation programs should be implemented in a manner that aids in the management of biodiversity as well as in finding answers to questions about biodiversity that can be generalized to other conservation needs. In this respect, reintroduction programs should be regarded and designed as both management programs and scientific experiments simultaneously.

## Loss of Genetic Variation

If genetic variation is important to fitness and adaptive change, then its loss should be of serious concern to conservationists. The central problems in conservation genetics are loss of genetic diversity in small populations and change in the distribution of this diversity among populations. Loss of diversity can result in reduced evolutionary flexibility and decline in fitness, either from expression of deleterious recessive alleles or loss of overdominance. Change in the distribution of diversity can destroy local adaptations or break up coadapted gene complexes (outbreeding depression). Both problems can lead to a poorer "match" of the organism to its environment, reducing individual fitness and increasing the probability of population or species extinction. A major concern of conservation biologists at the population level should be to maintain as much natural genetic variation as possible, in as near a natural geographic distribution as possible, so that evolutionary and ecological processes may be allowed to continue. To do this, we need to understand how genetic variation is lost, both within and among populations.

Reduced genetic diversity within populations may arise from four factors that are a function of population size: founder effects, demographic bottlenecks, genetic drift, and the effects of inbreeding. However, it is not the census size ($N_c$), or absolute number of individuals, that is relevant, but the so-called **genetically effective population size** ($N_e$), and we must describe that concept first.

An "idealized population" is one in which every individual has an equal probability of contributing genes to the next generation. It is typically conceived as a large, randomly mating population with nonoverlapping generations, a 1:1 breeding sex ratio, even progeny distribution among females, and no selection occurring. Since real populations never meet these criteria, but population genetic models are based on such idealized populations, corrections must be made in the sizes of real populations in order to use these models. Such a correction is the genetically effective size ($N_e$), which is typically smaller, and often much smaller, than the census size ($N_c$). $N_e$ is defined as "the size of an idealized population that would have the same amount of inbreeding or of random gene frequency drift as the population under consideration" (Kimura and Crow 1963).

An analogy with the "wind chill factor" is helpful in understanding $N_e$. A winter day of 2°C will feel colder if there is a 20 km/hr wind than if the wind is calm. The *effective* temperature is reduced by wind; it is *as though* the actual temperature were lower than it really is, due to the chilling effect of wind. Similarly, the effective size of a population, in a genetic sense, may be substantially lower if breeding sex ratios are uneven, or reproductive success among females is uneven, or the population has undergone a major decline in size. The *effective* size of the population is reduced by these features; it is *as though* the actual population size were lower than it really is, due to the effects just mentioned. $N_e$ takes into account who is actually breeding and how many offspring they are contributing to the next generation.

Mathematically, $N_e$ is affected by sex ratio of the breeders in the following way:

$$N_e = (4N_m \cdot N_f) / (N_m + N_f)$$

where $N_m$ and $N_f$ are the numbers of successfully breeding males and females, respectively. For example, a census population of 500 would have an $N_e$ of 500 (at least with respect to sex ratio) if they all bred and there was a 50:50 sex ratio: $N_e = (4 \cdot 250 \cdot 250)/(250 + 250) = 500$. However, if 450 females bred with 50 males, $N_e = (4 \cdot 50 \cdot 450)/(50 + 450) = 180$; the genetically effective population size in this case is only 36% of the census size due to few males participating in breeding. Or, if there were only 114 breeding females and 63 breeding males, and the remaining 323 individuals were immature, $N_e$ would be about 162. This relationship can produce some surprising results. For example, one male breeding with four females results in an $N_e$ (3.2), not much less than one male breeding with nine females (3.6) (Seal 1985). Obviously, breeding systems and population structure are important concerns in effective population size and conservation of genetic diversity.

$N_e$ is also strongly affected by the distribution of progeny among females (family size), and is estimated as

$$N_e = 4N_c / (\sigma^2 + 2)$$

where $\sigma^2$ = variance in family size among females. Higher variance results in a smaller $N_e$, which makes intuitive sense: if one female should produce the majority of offspring in a population (and thus higher variance), her genes would be disproportionately represented in the next generation. The effects of progeny distribution on $N_e$ are clearly demonstrated in Table 6.2. Interest-

**Table 6.2**
Effects of Variance in Number of Progeny among Females ($\sigma^2$) on Genetically Effective Population Size ($N_e$)

| $\sigma^2$ | $N_c{}^a$ | $N_e$ | $N_e/N_c$ |
|---|---|---|---|
| 0 | 100 | 200 | 2.0 |
| 1 | 100 | 133 | 1.3 |
| 2 | 100 | 100 | 1.0 |
| 5 | 100 | 57 | 0.57 |
| 10 | 100 | 33 | 0.33 |

[a]In all cases, the census population size ($N_c$) = 100.

ingly, $N_e$ can actually be *twice* $N_c$ if the variation in progeny distribution is zero, because all alleles are equally represented in the next generation, and $N_e$ is actually a measure of allelic representation.

Large population fluctuations also reduce $N_e$, because every time a population crashes to a small size, it experiences a demographic bottleneck (discussed below). The harmonic mean of population sizes in each generation provides an estimate of $N_e$:

$$1/N_e = 1/t\,(1/N_1 + 1/N_2 + \cdots + 1/N_t)$$

where $t$ = time in generations. A single population crash can produce a large reduction in $N_e$.

Unfortunately, there are no theories or equations that simultaneously handle multiple deviations from the ideal situation. Influences of bottlenecks, skewed sex ratios, and family sizes cannot at present be simultaneously estimated by these models. However, the important point is that, due to properties associated with sex ratio, family size, and population fluctuations, $N_e$ is nearly always significantly smaller than the census population size. $N_e$ in a management scenario is discussed in Essay 6B by Fred Allendorf.

## ESSAY 6B
# Genetically Effective Sizes of Grizzly Bear Populations

Fred W. Allendorf, University of Montana

The fragmentation and isolation of populations is of increasing concern in management of endangered species. Loss of genetic variation in isolated populations of large mammals is especially serious because of their low population densities and large spatial requirements. Thus, even the largest protected reserves may be too small to maintain genetically viable populations of large mammals.

The most useful concept for estimating the expected rate of loss of genetic variation in isolated populations is effective population size ($N_e$). Knowledge of $N_e$ allows prediction of the expected time when reduced genetic variation is likely to threaten continued existence of an isolated population. In spite of agreement about the importance of effective population size for making management decisions, considerable confusion persists about its estimation in natural populations. This is especially true for large mammals because of their complex demographics and numerous departures from the genetically "ideal" population.

Well-known studies with domestic animals have shown that loss of genetic variation has a variety of harmful effects on development, reproduction, survival, and growth rate. Studies with a variety of species in zoos indicate that similar effects probably occur in wild populations of animals (Ralls and Ballou 1986). For example, natural populations of lions (*Panthera leo*) that have lost genetic variation through recent population bottlenecks have more developmentally abnormal sperm and lower testosterone concentrations than adjacent populations that have not lost genetic variation through a bottleneck (Wildt et al. 1987).

The rate of loss of genetic variation generally has been measured by change in average heterozygosity per individual per locus ($H$). Heterozygosity is expected to be lost at a rate of $1/2N$ per generation in the theoretical "idealized" population of equal numbers of males and females that are all equally likely to contribute a sperm or egg to the next generation (Wright 1969). However, as described in the main text, a wild population of $N$ individuals will lose heterozygosity much faster than $1/2N$ due to unequal sex ratios, fluctuations in population size, and nonrandom reproductive success, resulting in a smaller genetically effective population size ($N_e$).

A variety of methods provide estimates of $N_e$ under different violations of the assumptions of the ideal population (Wright 1969), but several problems restrict the application of these estimations to wild populations. First, these formulas cannot be combined to estimate rate of loss of genetic variation in a wild population in which all of the assumptions are simultaneously violated. Second, many of the parameters needed to estimate $N_e$ with these formulas are virtually impossible to estimate in wild populations. Finally, most populations do not consist of a single, randomly mating group. Existing formulas for estimating $N_e$ have not been designed to incorporate the effects of gene flow between geographically separated local populations.

In 1975, the U.S. Endangered Species Act declared the grizzly bear (*Ursus arctos horribilis*) to be a threatened species. The number of grizzly bears in the contiguous 48 states has declined from an estimated 100,000 in 1800 to less than 1000 at present. Similarly, the range of the species within this area is now less than 1% of its historical range. The current verified range of the grizzly bear is approximately 5 million ha in six separate subpopulations in four states (Servheen 1985). The range reduction isolated subpopulations because continuous habitat was divided and movement corridors disappeared. Population decline accelerated because these isolated subpopulations were small and subject to stochastic demographic influences.

An estimation of the rate of loss of genetic variation in grizzly bear subpopulations is needed to determine population sizes necessary to maintain genetically viable subpopulations. Moreover, it is also important to determine what management actions can be taken to reduce loss of genetic variation in the remaining subpopulations. Current estimates of **minimum viable population size** (MVP) for the grizzly bear are based upon a comprehensive series of computer simulations of demographic structure (Shaffer and Sampson 1985); recovery targets for some of the six subpopulations are less than 100 individuals, a size that will lose genetic variation at a rate likely to decrease fitness if the subpopulations are isolated.

We have developed a simulation model to estimate effective population size (Harris and Allendorf 1989). The model is a discrete-time, stochastic computer program that follows the history and kinship of each individual. Values of life history parameters used in the simulations were taken from studies of grizzly bear populations in Montana, Wyoming, and British Columbia.

Our results indicate that the effective population size of grizzly bears is approximately 25% of census size (Allendorf et al. 1991). Thus, even fairly large isolated subpopulations, such as the 200 or so bears in Yellowstone National Park, are vulnerable to the harmful effects of loss of genetic variation. A moderate decrease in genetic variation in

this population may decrease reproductive rates, further reducing population size, which would further accelerate the rate of loss of genetic variation. The population could thus enter an "extinction vortex" (Gilpin and Soulé 1986).

Exchange of bears among currently isolated subpopulations is likely to be required to decrease the rate of loss of genetic variation. We therefore extended our simulations to determine the amount of gene flow needed to reduce this loss to a more acceptable level. The introduction of only two unrelated bears each generation greatly reduced the rate of loss of genetic variation (Figure A). This agrees with analytic results that have shown that even one migrant per generation is expected to limit genetic divergence

among subpopulations (Wright 1969).

Our results support the notion that even large and protected reserves are too small to maintain viable populations of large mammals if they are isolated. Genetically viable populations can only be maintained in such reserves by artificial gene flow among reserves. However, even if all available isolated reserves are genetically connected, there is insufficient habitat available for many species (Ralls and Ballou 1986). A combination of protected natural habitat preserves and ex situ preservation in zoos will become necessary for many species. Zoos will allow an increase in the total number of animals to be maintained and can also serve as sources of individuals to be used in gene exchange programs.

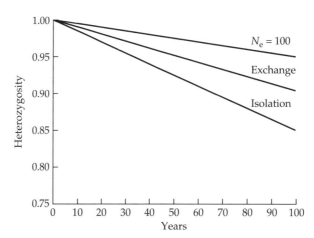

**Figure A** Expected rate of loss of heterozygosity in a population of 100 grizzly bears. The top line shows the expected rate of loss if the population behaved as an ideal population of 100 individuals. The bottom line shows the rate of loss estimated by computer simulations in an isolated population of 100 bears. The middle line shows the effect of introducing 2 unrelated bears every generation (10 years) into the population of 100 bears.

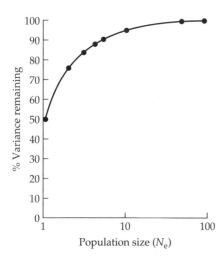

**Figure 6.6** Average percentage of genetic variance remaining after bottlenecks of various sizes in a theoretical, idealized population.

After this digression into genetically effective population size, we can now return to the question of loss of genetic diversity within populations. There are several closely related mechanisms by which small populations lose genetic diversity.

First, a **founder effect** occurs when a few individuals establish a new population, the genetic constitution of which depends upon the genetics of the founders. If the founders are not representative of the parent population, or if only a few founders are involved, then the newly established population is a biased representation of the larger gene pool from which it came, and may have lower overall genetic diversity.

Second, a **demographic bottleneck** occurs when a population experiences a severe, temporary reduction in size. One result is that the genetic variability of all subsequent generations is contained in the few individuals that survive the bottleneck and reproduce, the same phenomenon that occurs in the founder effect. Some genetic variability will be lost in the process, the magnitude of the loss depending on the size of the bottleneck and the growth rate of the population afterward. The proportion of genetic diversity remaining from one generation to the next is $1 - (1/2N_e)$; this proportion can range from 0.5 (50% variation) with an $N_e$ of 1 (the gametes of one individual carry, on average, 50% of the genetic diversity of the population), to near 1.0

(100%) with a large $N_e$, say of 1000. The predicted relationship between population size and remaining genetic variation is shown in Figure 6.6. Generally, a bottleneck rarely has severe genetic or fitness consequences if population size quickly recovers in a generation or two.

Third, **genetic drift** is a random change in gene frequencies in small populations, attributable to sampling error. That is, in small populations, by chance alone some alleles will not be "sampled" or represented in the next generation. Mathematically, genetic drift simply represents a chronic bottleneck that results in repeated loss of variability and eventual fixation of loci (loss of alleles). The proportion of variance retained is estimated by $[1 - (1/2N_e)]^t$, where $t$ is the number of generations at that population size. Whereas a single-generation bottleneck of moderate size, say 10–50, may not severely reduce genetic diversity (Figure 6.6), a prolonged bottleneck of the same size, resulting in genetic drift, can have greater effects (Figure 6.7).

Population genetics theory tells us that perhaps more important than depletion of quantitative genetic variation by founder events, demographic bottlenecks, or genetic drift, is loss of rare alleles from the population. However, empirical support for this idea is not abundant. We do know that rare alleles contribute little to overall genetic variation, but they may be important to a population during infrequent or periodic events such as abnormal temperatures or exposure to new parasites or pathogens, and can offer unique responses to future evolutionary challenges. The expected number of alleles, $E_{(n)}$, remaining at a locus each generation is estimated as

$$m - \sum_{1}^{j} \left(1 - p_j\right)^{2N_e}$$

where $m$ = the original number of alleles, and $p_j$ is the frequency of the $j$th allele (from Denniston 1978). The loss of alleles from drift is demonstrated in Table 6.3, in which rare alleles are seen to be lost rapidly from small populations, even though much of overall genetic diversity would be retained.

Fourth, **inbreeding,** or mating of individuals related by common ancestry, is a potentially serious problem whose probability of occurrence increases in smaller populations if mating occurs at random (i.e., if mating with relatives is not actively avoided). Empirically, there is no absolute measure of inbreeding; the level of inbreeding is measured relative to a base population. The expected increase of inbreeding per generation, $\Delta F$, is expressed, once again, as $1/2N_e$ if panmixia prevails. Inbreeding results in a predictable increase in homozygosity, and may be manifested in **inbreeding depression,** such as reduction in fecundity, offspring size, growth, or survivorship (Figure 6.8), changes in age at maturity, and physical deformities (Falconer 1981). Data from domesticated animals indicate that a $\Delta F$ of 10% will result in a 5%–10% decline in individual reproductive traits such as clutch size or survival rates; in aggregate, total reproductive attributes may decline by 25% (Frankel and Soulé 1981).

Not all inbreeding is cause for alarm. Many natural populations have apparently experienced low levels of inbreeding for many generations with no ill effects. In these cases, it is thought that slow inbreeding has given selection an opportunity to purge the population of deleterious recessive alleles. Rapid inbreeding, however, can be damaging to a population, especially if it has little history of prior inbreeding. Inbreeding depression may therefore be more prevalent in a species or population with historically large population sizes that now occurs in small populations, than in historically small populations.

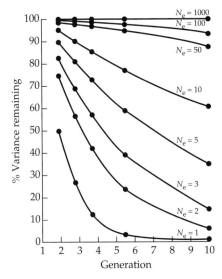

**Figure 6.7** Average percentage of genetic variance remaining over 10 generations in a theoretical, idealized population at various genetically effective population sizes ($N_e$). Variation is lost randomly through genetic drift.

**Table 6.3**

The Loss of Rare Alleles as a Function of Population Size

| $N_e$ | No. alleles remaining |
|---|---|
| 1000 | ~8.00 |
| 100 | 7.81 |
| 10 | 3.86 |
| 5 | 2.69 |
| 1 | 1.35 |

*Note:* In this hypothetical example, a large population starts with 8 alleles, 7 of which are rare. Original allele frequencies are 0.80, 0.07, 0.03, 0.03, 0.02, 0.02, and 0.01. The average number of remaining alleles after one generation at various effective population sizes is shown.

**Figure 6.8** The effects of inbreeding on juvenile mortality in captive populations of mammals. Each point compares the percentage of juvenile mortality for offspring of inbred and noninbred matings. The line indicates equal levels of mortality under the two breeding schemes. Points above the line represent higher mortality from noninbred matings; points below the line, higher mortality from inbred matings. The distance of a point from the line indicates the strength of the effect of level of inbreeding. (From Ralls and Ballou 1983.)

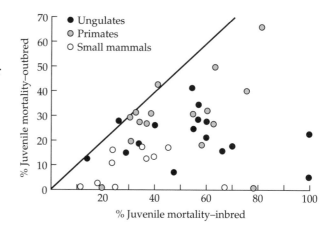

The fundamental point in this section is that small, isolated populations—which describes many threatened and endangered species—will lose some percentage of their original genetic diversity over time, approximately at the rate of $1/2N_e$ per generation. A population of 1000 will retain 99.95% of its genetic diversity (assuming lack of selection) in a generation, while a population of 50 will retain only 99.0%. Such losses of diversity may seem small, but are magnified over many generations. After 20 generations, the population of 1000 will still retain over 99% of its original variation, but the population of 50 will retain less than 82%. Small populations over a prolonged period are thus to be avoided in conservation programs whenever possible. This is particularly evident in captive breeding programs.

Loss of among-population genetic diversity occurs when historically divergent and isolated populations experience an artificially high rate of gene flow with other populations through human actions. This would typically occur when plants or animals are moved, intentionally or inadvertently, by people, or when new movement corridors are created. The uniqueness of formerly isolated populations may then be diminished or lost, as may their local adaptations and coadapted gene complexes.

It is important to remember that the total amount of genetic variation in a species ($H_t$) is a function of within-population diversity ($H_p$) and among-population divergence ($D_{pt}$), as described earlier. Simply looking at $H_t$ does not provide a clear picture of the condition of genetic diversity, as overall diversity can be a complicated balance between the two individual components. For example, decreasing $D_{pt}$ by homogenizing populations through gene flow will probably increase $H_p$, keeping $H_t$ constant. However, an important component of genetic diversity, population uniqueness, may be lost in the process. Generally, an increase in one component of diversity results in a decline in the other, and this can be a complicating problem in management.

## Management of Genetic Variation in Natural Populations

If evolution is the unifying feature and driving force of natural systems, then the primary goal of genetic management in nature should be to allow continued evolutionary change in the populations and species of concern. By definition, evolution is dynamic, and change is expected. Ecological systems are dynamic, and generally are not at equilibrium (Chapter 1). The best way to "manage" such dynamic, changing systems is to permit and allow for change—a conservationist rather than a preservationist approach. The status quo is inappropriate to long-term conservation at any level, including genetics. Rather, a fluid, evolutionary perspective will allow populations to continually adapt to inevitably changing conditions.

## Time Scales of Concern

Genetic conservation actions should be compatible with three conservation goals, on three time scales of concern: maintenance of viable populations in the short term (extinction avoidance), maintenance of the ability to continue adaptive evolutionary change, and maintenance of the capacity for continued speciation.

The first level of concern, avoidance of population extinction, has a time scale of days to decades and is the first and most obvious goal of conservation. If this goal is not met, then further goals are automatically denied. Of course, some populations repeatedly undergo extirpation and recolonization cycles, exemplified by "weedy" or "fugitive" species, and local extinction is a natural part of their dynamics. Such is the case of early successional plant species in forests, which appear only when light gaps are opened by treefalls (Collins et al. 1985). The type of population extinction to be avoided, however, is that which is not part of the natural system dynamics, probably does not have a recolonization source, and is usually caused, directly or indirectly, by human action.

Since all environments change, and change is being accelerated by humans, genetic management must also maintain the ability of populations and species to genetically adapt, or evolve. "Locking" a population or species into a genetic configuration from which it cannot easily escape, as through inbreeding or genetic drift in small populations, is poor longer-term management. This concern has a time scale of decades to millennia.

Finally, speciation is the creative part of biodiversity, as extinction is the annihilating part. The potential for continued speciation must be maintained, especially now that extinction rates are so exceedingly high. To consider only short-term, preservationist goals is to adopt a narrow perspective and ignore the larger picture of the human role in earth's history. Retention of the ability to continue to speciate is the ultimate goal of conservation, although its time scale, tens of thousands or more years, makes it difficult to appreciate.

## Units of Conservation

Given the importance of genetic variation to short-term fitness, continued adaptation, and the speciation process, a difficult and practical question confronts the resource manager: What are the units of genetic conservation? What, in fact, should we conserve? Even casual reflection reveals that we cannot save every population, every morphological variant, every unique allele. How do we determine and define the biologically significant units within a species worthy of attention?

To answer these questions, we must return to our underlying premise that our main goal in conservation is to conserve evolutionary potential, which of course requires genetic diversity; this should be done irrespective of taxonomic status. Consequently, the population seems the most reasonable level at which genetic conservation should take place. The population, rather than the species, is the ecologically and evolutionarily functional unit. The population is where genetic changes take place over generations, and is where local adaptive change occurs. Natural geographically and genetically isolated populations are of particular interest, as they have the greatest potential for speciation. To conserve only at higher levels, such as species, overlooks important dynamics and attributes of individual populations and risks

**Figure 6.9**  An illustration of a metapopulation. Each circle is a local population, with the circle size indicative of relative population size. Solid arrows indicate regular and free gene flow; dashed arrows indicate occasional or irregular gene flow.

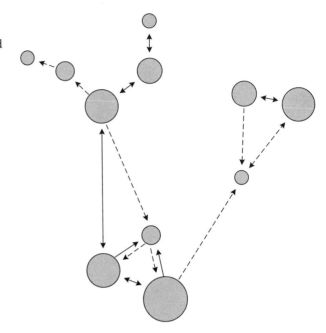

the loss of critical genetic diversity and local ecological function. On the other hand, to work below the level of populations in the wild, say with alleles, is impractical at best, a micromanagement approach that is probably counterproductive in a larger, dynamic system.

If we accept the population as the reasonable unit of conservation, the problem then becomes how to define a population. The population geneticist has a ready answer—the **deme,** or local, randomly interbreeding group of individuals, is a good and worthy unit of protection. Unfortunately, the deme is often of greater theoretical than practical utility, as it is difficult or impossible to clearly delineate in the wild. How does one define the borders of reproductive isolation for a Michigan beech forest or a fan coral in the Caribbean? Also, a continuum of population types exists, from those that are clearly isolated (such as aquatic plants or animals in desert springs, or birds on small oceanic islands) to those that clearly have genetic exchanges with similar groups in other geographic regions.

Many populations, in fact, may really be members of **metapopulations**—networks of populations that have some degree of intermittent or regular gene flow among geographically separate units (Figure 6.9). For example, the Bay checkerspot butterfly (*Euphydryas editha bayensis*) in California exists in many distinct habitat patches; individuals may move among patches, creating gene flow and recolonizing patches where populations have gone extinct (Ehrlich and Murphy 1987; Harrison et al. 1988). Such metapopulation structures are likely to become even more common as habitat fragmentation splits large populations into smaller units that manage to retain some gene flow. When we speak of populations, then, we mean anything from a single, clearly isolated unit to a complex network of units with some degree of gene flow. Metapopulations will be discussed in greater detail in the next chapter.

Perhaps you can see that we are facing a problem inherent in many aspects of biology: that of trying to define breakpoints in a continuum, where breakpoints may not exist. This was discussed in Chapter 3, in the context of defining species; it cannot objectively and absolutely be done, and we must accept some "fuzziness" as a result. Populations exist along a continuum from totally isolated units to those that experience regular and high gene flow with similar units. In trying to define a population we must realize that most populations probably experience some level of gene flow with other populations, and that we will usually not find clear breaks. The best we can do is try to identify units that seem to have some ecological and evolutionary significance.

If we define our goal as protecting biological diversity within the species level, there are many potential ways to identify conservation units. For example, distinct phenotypes, such as different butterfly color morphs or distinct banding patterns in land snails, could qualify as conservation units. Long-term geographic isolation, such as that found in Galápagos tortoises or in fishes or snails in desert springs, would certainly qualify the populations as reasonable conservation units. Even geographic distance, in the absence of clear isolation, could be used to assign conservation unit status, protecting extremes of a species' geographic range. If populations occur under very different selective regimes that produce distinct life histories or behaviors, they could be considered as conservation units. Basically, any biologically relevant characteristics could help to distinguish conservation units within the species level.

The U.S. Endangered Species Act addresses the question of a conservation unit in a more rigorous, legalistic sense, and provides further guidance. The definition of a "species" in the Act includes "any *distinct population segment* of any species of vertebrate fish or wildlife which interbreeds when mature" (emphasis added). The phrase "distinct population segment" is rather indistinct, of course, and federal agencies have struggled to find a consistent approach to interpreting "distinct."

A suggested solution (Waples 1991) says a population is distinct if it represents an **Evolutionarily Significant Unit** (ESU) of the biological species. An ESU is in turn defined as a population that (1) is reproductively isolated from other conspecific population units, and (2) represents an important component in the evolutionary legacy of the species. Note that use of the term "significant" is somewhat unfortunate, because it could be interpreted to imply that other units are "insignificant," and can be dispensed with. That is not the case. Virtually any biological unit, down to the single individual, has the *potential* to be evolutionarily significant. However, the ESU approach tries to identify levels of biological organization that presently appear to be of greatest importance because of their distinctness.

Adoption of the ESU definition may be satisfying conceptually because it recognizes the evolutionary role, importance, and fate of populations, rather than just species. However, it is difficult operationally for two reasons. The first part of the definition essentially defines a deme, which we already noted is difficult or impossible to delineate in nature. The second part requires a subjective assessment of the population of concern relative to other populations of the species, which are equally undefined under the first part of the definition. However, as discussed next, an expansion of the simple genetic model presented in Figure 6.3 may offer a reasonable solution to these problems and allow adoption of the ESU approach in a functional, as well as conceptual sense.

### Hierarchical Gene Diversity Analysis

One approach to more rigorously defining ESUs in a genetic sense is called a **hierarchical gene diversity analysis,** and it is based on the fact that species consist of a spatially hierarchical genetic structure. Our task is to partition overall genetic diversity into within-population and among-population components (the latter of which can be further subdivided, as shortly will be explained) and determine where biologically significant breaks in genetic diversity occur. At the lowest level of the hierarchy, interbreeding individuals within a population are genetically most similar. As we move through the hierarchy, greater genetic differences occur among more geographically separated or otherwise distinct populations (i.e., poor dispersers), until there may be very large genetic differences between populations strongly isolated by physiography or geographic distance. This genetic hierarchy in fact extends beyond species; under the biological species concept, different, closely related species simply represent very large genetic gaps, which are sometimes crossed in hybridization.

A genetic hierarchy exists because the divergence component of diversity ($D_{pt}$) can be subdivided, based on any biologically meaningful *geographic* hierarchy in the distribution of the species. That is, populations of a species exhibit various levels of genetic divergence from other populations, based on the amount of gene flow among populations. Populations that are geographically proximate, and that experience regular gene flow, will be more similar genetically than populations that are geographically further apart and experience less or no gene flow. A species can thus be visualized as having a spatial genetic architecture. The species consists of a collection of populations, with a hierarchical genetic structure based on the degree of genetic similarity among them. In turn, this is a function of geography and levels of gene flow.

Consider a hypothetical species with eight sampled populations and geographic relationships as shown schematically in Figure 6.10. The number of lines necessary to travel from one population to another is an indication of their geographic proximities. There are four levels of geographic structure in this example that are potentially reflected in genetic structure. Total genetic diversity ($H_t$) will occur as average heterozygosity of the eight populations ($H_p$), plus genetic divergence between pairs of adjacent populations ($D_{12}$), plus genetic divergence among the four groups of two populations ($D_{23}$), plus genetic divergence among the two groups of four populations ($D_{34}$).

**Figure 6.10**   A schematic diagram demonstrating a hierarchical genetic structure of a species. The eight populations (A–H) may be grouped at different levels according to some objective geographic criterion. Level 1 in this hierarchy is mean heterozygosity within each population ($H_p$). The first level of divergence ($D_{12}$) is the mean genetic divergence between pairs of geographically adjacent populations. Divergence may also occur among the four pairs of two populations ($D_{23}$) and the two pairs of four populations ($D_{34}$).

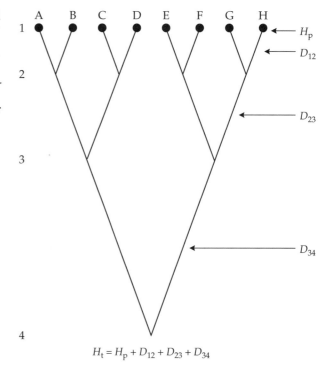

$$H_t = H_p + D_{12} + D_{23} + D_{34}$$

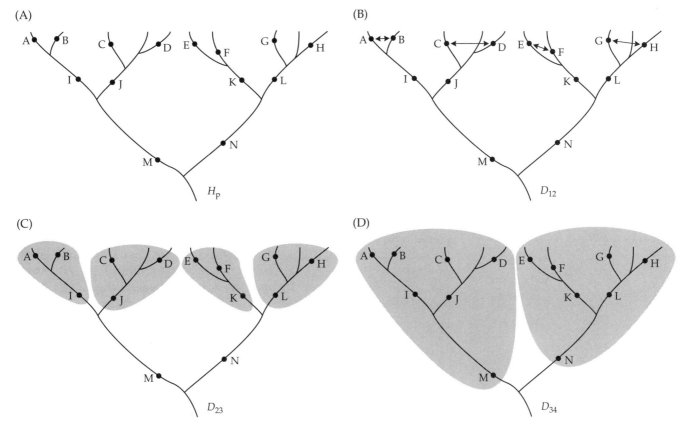

**Figure 6.11** A genetic hierarchy in stream organisms based on an objective stream order classification, using 14 sampling sites distributed across the drainage. Total genetic diversity ($H_t$) may be partitioned into (A) heterozygosity within populations ($H_p$), (B) mean divergence among populations taken in different first-order streams ($D_{12}$), (C) mean divergence among populations taken in different second-order streams ($D_{23}$), and (D) mean divergence of populations taken in different third-order streams ($D_{34}$).

Perhaps the clearest example of a geographic (and thus genetic) hierarchy involves riverine species, since rivers form a geographic structure with a natural hierarchy. River headwaters are called first-order streams, which combine to form second-order streams. Third-order streams consist of two or more second-order streams, and so forth. Consider, then, a species of fish (or plant or benthic invertebrate) that is found in a river drainage, for which 14 sites are sampled, as in Figure 6.11. The relevant questions for genetic conservation are: (1) What is a reasonable breeding unit of concern? and (2) How distinct (evolutionarily significant) are different breeding units? The task is first to distinguish reasonable breeding units and then to determine what level of genetic divergence represents evolutionary significance. Since streams are geographically hierarchical, they provide a natural basis for defining genetic structure.

Total genetic diversity in this case consists of average heterozygosity across all populations ($H_p$), plus average divergence between populations in first-order within second-order streams ($D_{12}$), plus average divergence among populations in second-order within third-order streams ($D_{23}$), plus average divergence among populations in third-order within fourth-order streams ($D_{34}$). Divergence could also occur among populations in different watersheds across the total range of the species ($D_{wt}$), or at any other reasonable level in a hierarchy.

Three hypothetical examples (Table 6.4) illustrate how genetic diversity might be partitioned in a species such as this, and how that information could be used to define an evolutionarily significant unit. For simplicity, the heterozygosity ($H_p$) or within-population component of diversity is constant (70%) in all three cases. In the first example, 17.7% of genetic diversity occurs

**Table 6.4**

Hypothetical Examples of Possible Genetic Hierarchies in Stream Fishes

| Level of diversity | Diversity (%) | | |
| --- | --- | --- | --- |
| | Example 1 | Example 2 | Example 3 |
| $H_p$ | 70.0 | 70.0 | 70.0 |
| $D_{12}$ | 17.7 | 0.2 | 0.6 |
| $D_{23}$ | 11.1 | 22.3 | 1.3 |
| $D_{34}$ | 1.2 | 7.5 | 28.1 |

as the average divergence among populations in different first-order streams ($D_{12}$). This large number indicates that fish in different first-order streams experience some reproductive isolation and are the ESUs. That is, individual, local breeding units in each headwater stream have high genetic divergence from similar breeding units in other headwater streams, and need to be managed as evolutionarily significant units. Divergence (11.1%) also occurs among second-order streams, but management at the lower level of first-order streams would automatically maintain divergence at the level of second-order streams.

In the second example, essentially no genetic divergence occurs at the level of first-order streams (there is so much gene flow among fish in connected first-order streams that there is no detectable genetic divergence at that level), but over 22% of genetic diversity occurs as average divergence among fish in different second-order streams. In this case, fish in different second-order streams would be a reasonable ESU for management.

In the third example, significant divergence does not occur until the level of third-order streams; different populations *within* third-order systems are not genetically structured. Because there is little divergence among first- or second-order streams, probably due to high mobility and gene flow throughout the system, any group of fish from any point within the third-order level of the hierarchy fairly represents the entire system. However, fish from different third-order streams are very different and should be treated as ESUs.

The question arises as to what constitutes "significant" genetic differentiation worthy of recognition and protection. There is no easy answer, and each conservation program must determine what is "significant" genetic differentiation for its particular circumstance. This determination should be guided by biological understanding of the system. For example, the cheetah may have extremely low, nearly undetectable levels of genetic diversity. However, what little among-population diversity remains, even if it represents a tiny percentage of overall variation, may be very critical to protect. In a highly variable species, that same small percentage of among-population divergence may be unimportant by comparison. There are no cutoffs or rules of thumb here; understanding the biology of the organism and the ecology of the system is the best way to decide upon reasonable levels of genetic differentiation for identifying conservation units.

To date, real-world data are rarely as clear and comprehensively collected as the hypothetical example presented. Echelle (1991) compiled hierarchical genetic data for numerous fish species of western North America. The data (Table 6.5) allowed genetic diversity to be partitioned into only three levels: within-population diversity ($H_p$), divergence among samples within drainages ($D_{sd}$) and divergence between drainages ($D_{dt}$). (Note that the subscripts can freely change to reflect the particular situation. There is nothing set about the subscripts used, or the levels of diversity addressed). Echelle found a great deal of variation among these species in their hierarchical patterns of genetic diversity. Some, such as *Xyrauchen texanus* (razorback sucker) and *Cyprinodon bovinus* (Leon Springs pupfish), had nearly all of their genetic variation represented as within-population heterozygosity. Others, such as *Oncorhynchus clarki henshawi* (cutthroat trout) and *Gambusia nobilis* (Pecos gambusia) had a large proportion of their diversity represented as divergence among samples within drainages. Finally, some had appreciable variation between drainages, such as *O. clarki lewisi* (another cutthroat trout subspecies) and *C. macularius* (desert pupfish).

These data are of limited value because of incomplete geographic sampling; they are therefore only rough approximations of a hierarchical distrib-

**Table 6.5**
Distribution of Genetic Diversity in Endangered and Threatened Fishes of Western North America

| Taxon | P/L | $H_p$ | $D_{sd}$ | $D_{dt}$ |
|---|---|---|---|---|
| **Salmonidae (trout and salmon)** | | | | |
| *Oncorhynchus nerka* | 18/26 | 94.4 | 3.1 | 2.5 |
| *O. apache* | 5/35 | 90.5 | 9.5 | — |
| *O. clarki bouvieri* | 8/46 | 96.3 | 3.7 | — |
| *O. clarki henshawi* | 15/35 | 55.5 | 44.5 | — |
| *O. clarki lewisi* | 103/29 | 67.6 | 15.7 | 16.7 |
| *O. mykiss* | 38/16 | 85.0 | 7.7 | 7.3 |
| *O. gilae* | 4/35 | 86.4 | 13.6 | — |
| **Catostomidae (suckers)** | | | | |
| *Catostomus discobolus yarrowi* | 3/45 | 54.8 | — | 45.2 |
| *C. plebeius* | 5/45 | 92.9 | — | 7.1 |
| *C. plebeius* (second study) | 4/27 | 11.3 | — | 88.8 |
| *Xyrauchen texanus* | 2/21 | 98.9 | 1.1 | — |
| **Cyprinodontidae (killifishes)** | | | | |
| *Cyprinodon bovinus* | 5/28 | 98.6 | 1.4 | — |
| *C. elegans* | 7/28 | 89.2 | 10.8 | — |
| *C. macularius* | 3/38 | 70.1 | — | 29.9 |
| *C. pecosensis* | 6/28 | 92.3 | 7.7 | — |
| *C. tularosa* | 3/28 | 81.0 | 19.0 | — |
| **Poeciliidae (livebearers)** | | | | |
| *Gambusia nobilis* | 16/24 | 48.4 | 51.6 | — |
| *Poeciliopsis o. occidentalis* | 10/25 | 59.3 | 40.7 | — |
| **Cichlidae (cichlids)** | | | | |
| *Cichlosoma minckleyi* | 3/13 | 97.7 | 2.3 | — |
| *C. minckleyi* (second study) | 3/27 | 94.6 | 5.4 | — |
| **Cottidae (sculpins)** | | | | |
| *Cottus confusus* | 16/33 | 53.9 | 46.1 | — |

Modified from Echelle 1991.
*Note:* P/L = numbers of populations/gene loci surveyed; percentage of total genetic diversity measured is separated into heterozygosity within populations ($H_p$), divergence among samples within drainages ($D_{sd}$), and divergence among drainages ($D_{dt}$). Dash indicates data not measured at that level in the hierarchy.

ution of diversity. Also, they were collected by entire drainages rather than by stream order, and thus may not be fine-grained enough to determine ESUs. Nevertheless, we can see that for some species, local populations contain virtually all of the genetic diversity in the species. From a solely genetic perspective (ignoring for the moment ecological, demographic, or other factors of relevance to conservation decisions), one population will contain most of the genetic variation in the species. In other cases, strong geographic divergence (either within or between drainages) occurs, indicating the need to conserve multiple units in order to capture representation of the species' genetic diversity. More comprehensive data sets than these would allow more detailed genetic analyses and better estimation of units of conservation.

*Distance as a Genetic Hierarchy.* Both the contrived example and the western fish data involved clear geographic hierarchies (stream structure) upon which the genetic hierarchy could be based. If no obvious geographic hierarchy exists, however, this approach may still be used, with distance as the hierarchical unit. In this case, individuals would be sampled across part

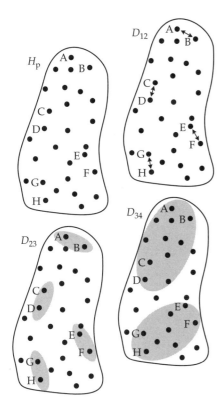

**Figure 6.12** A genetic hierarchy based on geographic distance. In this example, eight populations (A–H) of oak trees are sampled across a landscape containing no obvious geographic structure. Total genetic diversity may be partitioned as in previous examples: mean heterozygosity ($H_p$) within all eight populations, plus mean divergence of adjacent populations taken at distances of, say, 100 m ($D_{12}$), plus divergence among groups of populations at a greater distance, say 1 km ($D_{23}$), plus divergence across groups over larger distances, say 10 km ($D_{34}$).

or all of their range of occurrence, and different distances between samples would be the structuring unit (Figure 6.12). For example, oak trees in an oak woodland might have no obvious geographic structure other than distance. This would not deter a hierarchical analysis because trees in closer proximity likely form more cohesive genetic units than trees farther apart, since gene flow (pollen dispersal) will probably be higher among closer trees. Divergence is more likely to occur at further distances, and the hierarchical approach can detect this. In this case, the hierarchical approach might consider distances of, say, 0.1 km, 1 km, and 10 km as the hierarchical units, and then determine at which level significant genetic divergence occurs.

The actual hierarchical partitioning of the genetic data is accomplished through an analysis called "*F* statistics"; further details of such analyses are beyond the scope of this book, and should be pursued elsewhere (Hartl and Clark 1990 provide a good, general overview; more detailed presentations may be found in some of the original literature, such as Crow and Kimura 1970; Nei 1975; and Wright 1978).

***The Data Needed for a Hierarchy.*** The data to be used in defining conservation units can be anything reliably quantifiable that has variation. Morphological or behavioral data can be used, but these are subject to environmental modifications of the underlying genetic base. More typically, allozyme electrophoresis is used as a reliable, fairly inexpensive, and relatively easy procedure. The data generated, allozyme frequencies, are a direct function of genetic constitution and are not modified by the environment. Other genetic data may also be useful in defining conservation units, including karyotype analysis (inspection of chromosome structure), mitochondrial DNA (mtDNA) analysis, and DNA sequencing.

A technique known as polymerase chain reaction (PCR) can be quite useful in conservation studies because it can produce large quantities of DNA (a process called amplification) from tiny and even degraded samples, such as skin particles, hair, bone, epithelial cells in urine, or remains in gut contents of predators. Once amplified, the DNA can be analyzed by other means to acquire genetic data.

## Biogeographic Models of Gene Flow

As we have said, undisturbed populations in the wild have some degree of genetic population structure based on biogeographic patterns. A single population or metapopulation exists somewhere along a spectrum of isolation and gene flow, from an extreme of complete isolation and no genetic exchange with other populations, to the opposite extreme of free genetic exchange among populations. These structures have important implications for genetic management, because the natural biogeographic structure has often been altered by human actions, and may seriously affect fitness and local adaptation. These management implications will be addressed after a brief discussion of divergence and gene flow.

Populations diverge from one another as a function of genetic drift, mutation, and local selection. Drift can be particularly effective in small populations, and is an inverse function of $N_e$. Countering the effects of these various divergent forces is gene flow via dispersal and reproduction (often expressed as migration rate, *m*, the proportion of individuals exchanged among populations per generation), which tends to homogenize populations and increase within-population variation.

The level of genetic divergence between two populations is the product of $N_e$ and *m*. If $N_e$ is small, populations will tend to diverge as a result of random genetic drift, and high rates of migration (*m*) are needed to prevent di-

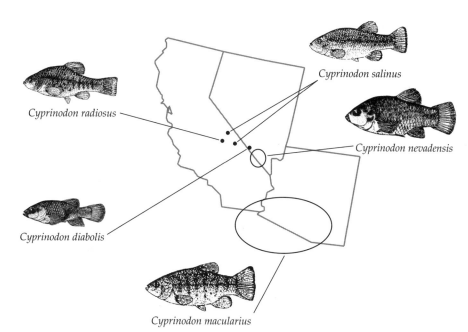

*Cyprinodon radiosus*

*Cyprinodon salinus*

*Cyprinodon nevadensis*

*Cyprinodon diabolis*

*Cyprinodon macularius*

**Figure 6.13** Pupfishes of the southwestern American deserts, an example of local population differentiation and speciation through genetic isolation. These five closely related species have apparently been isolated for at least 10,000–12,000 years, since the end of the Pleistocene. They have differentiated in their respective drainages or single habitats into different forms, recognizable as species. The habitat of two pupfishes, *Cyprinodon diabolis* and *C. radiosus,* are shown in Figure 5.2 and Figure 11.11, respectively.

vergence. If $N_e \cdot m$ is greater than 1, local populations will tend not to diverge significantly relative to the types of alleles present (Allendorf 1983). For example, a pair of populations with a mean $N_e$ of 1000 and an $m$ of 0.01 (average of one individual exchanged per hundred generations) would not significantly diverge by chance alone, since $N_e \cdot m = 10$. However, a pair of smaller populations, with a mean $N_e$ of 100 and the same rate of gene flow, would diverge, since $N_e \cdot m = 1$; random genetic drift would be greater in the smaller populations, and a higher rate of gene exchange (such as $m = 0.02$) would be needed to prevent divergence. Of course, strong local selection can influence divergence as well (Endler 1973).

Some populations or species in nature have existed for long periods in strong or complete isolation from other gene pools, and have diverged through genetic drift or selection (Figure 6.13). Notable examples include numerous species in the Galápagos Islands (Lack 1947; Levinton and Bowman 1981), and fishes and snails in isolated desert springs (Minckley and Deacon 1991). In these cases, natural movement among islands or springs was historically rare or nonexistent ($m \approx 0$), and strong divergence occurred. $H_p$ is expected to be low and $D_{st}$ high in such cases; virtually all of the total genetic diversity ($H_t$) in such a species could be due to the divergence component. The management implication in this scenario is that the separation of these naturally isolated populations should be maintained. This makes intuitive, as well as genetic, sense; no credible biologist would casually move finches or tortoises among the islands of the Galápagos, for example, without extraordinary justification.

Contrasted with this isolated, "island" model is the typical hierarchical model, in which genetic exchange occurs among populations in a hierarchical fashion. In this case, local populations may be only partially isolated from other gene pools, with some probability of gene flow among them. Geographically proximate populations would, on average, more frequently experience gene flow ($m$ would be higher) than would more geographically distant populations. Genetic "connectedness" is then a function of geographic structure and spatial scale.

Most endangered species will not experience the equilibrium conditions implicit in a hierarchical model, however. By their very nature of being endangered or of special concern, their genetic structure has probably been altered, populations have been lost, and remaining populations are dangerously small and fragmented. Habitat destruction, blockage of migratory routes, drying or diversion of waterways, clear-cutting, urbanization, and other human activities isolate populations that normally would experience gene exchange with other populations. Such induced fragmentation and isolation will lead to loss of heterozygosity and divergence from other populations where gene exchange previously occurred. Leberg (1991), for example, found that Eastern Wild Turkey (*Meleagris gallopavo silvestris*) populations in Arkansas, Kentucky, Tennessee, and Connecticut were fragmented and had gone through bottlenecks because of human activity. Genetic divergence among populations (10.2%) was among the highest recorded for birds, and much higher than for turkey populations that had not experienced known bottlenecks. He attributed this divergence to human activity, including management manipulations.

Scenarios such as the Wild Turkey situation may call for the manager to simulate natural gene flow by artificial means: by moving individuals among now-isolated populations where gene flow once occurred before it was interrupted by human actions. The management challenge in the hierarchical model is to determine former rates and directions of gene flow among populations and try to mimic those rates in the face of human disturbance. The age and sex ratios of translocated individuals should match the natural history of the species, and care should be taken to not introduce parasites or pathogens in the process. This management prescription is in direct contrast to the island model, in which case the manager should not induce gene flow, but in fact should protect the normal isolation of populations. But where natural gene flow has historically occurred and has been interrupted by humans, management should emphasize continuance of gene flow near the historical level.

The natural genetic structure of a species, and its normal rates of gene flow, may be inferred from geography, historical records, knowledge of the biology of the species, and genetic information derived from a hierarchical analysis (Slatkin 1987; Meffe and Vrijenhoek 1988). Assuming that the value obtained for the divergence component ($D_{pt}$) of total genetic variation ($H_t$) reflects a balance between the divergent influences of genetic drift and the convergent influences of gene flow, then the effective migration rate historically experienced can be roughly estimated as

$$D_{pt}/H_t = 1/(4N_e m + 1)$$

(modified from Crow and Kimura 1970).

Thus, in a species in which the divergence component of genetic variation is 3%, $0.03 = 1/(4N_e m + 1)$; rearranging, $4N_e m + 1 = 33.3$, and $N_e m \approx 8.1$. In other words, an average of 8 reproductive individuals per generation must move among the populations to maintain a divergence level of 3%. Compare that with the situation of a high $D_{pt}$, such as 35%. In that case, $0.35 = 1/4N_e m + 1$; $4N_e m + 1 = 2.86$, and $N_e m = 0.46$; on average, less than 1 reproductive individual should be moved among the populations every other generation to maintain that level of divergence.

Echelle et al. (1987) studied four species of pupfishes in the Chihuahuan Desert region of New Mexico and Texas, and their data are amenable to calculating historical migration rates. These four species span a range of geo-

**Table 6.6**
Estimated Historical Rates of Gene Flow among Populations of Four
Species of Western North American Pupfishes

| Species | Distribution | $D_{pt}{}^{a}$ | $N_e m$ |
|---------|--------------|------|------|
| *Cyprinodon bovinus* | A single, ~ 8 km-long section of spring-fed stream | 1.4% | 17.6 |
| *C. pecosensis* | 600–700 km of mainstream Pecos River | 7.7% | 3.0 |
| *C. elegans* | Spring-fed complex of canals and creek, with partial isolation | 10.8% | 2.1 |
| *C. tularosa* | Two isolated springs and associated creek in extremely arid area | 19.0% | 1.1 |

Modified from Echelle et al. 1987.

$^{a}D_{pt}$ is the proportion of total genetic diversity attributable to divergence among populations. The more isolated populations have a higher $D_{pt}$ and consequently a lower estimated rate of gene flow.

graphic distribution and isolation, and their estimated migration rates reflect this (Table 6.6). The geographically most isolated species (*Cyprinodon tularosa*) has the lowest estimated migration rate based on genetic data, while the highest estimated migration rate occurs in *Cyprinodon bovinus*, which occurs along a single drainage system that is at least occasionally connected when flooded.

In this section we have presented some simplified analyses of very complicated genetic situations. Such analyses are for illustrative purposes, to demonstrate basic principles, and should not be taken as the final word in genetic management. We caution that effective genetic management programs for species in the wild should not be approached lightly; they require a good understanding of the biology and distribution of the species in question, comprehensive genetic data collected and analyzed properly, and proper models for predicting rates of change of gene diversity and heterozygosity. However, complex genetic models are no substitute for sound biological knowledge, including basic natural history.

In some cases, genetic data for a hierarchical analysis are difficult to obtain, or there is no detectable genetic variation in the data. Large mammals, such as cheetahs, polar bears, or white rhinoceroses, may be especially prone to these problems. In such cases, the manager must do the best job possible with what is available and rely on historical records of distribution, inferences from the species' biology, or genetic knowledge from similar species. Genetics is only one aspect of a broader management picture, and provides only one type of data.

### Depths of Evolutionary Separation

The hierarchical gene diversity approach discussed throughout this chapter can not only outline the overall genetic structure of a species and estimate historical rates of gene flow, but can also help to discriminate "deeper" or older evolutionary separations from "shallower" or more recent divergences that have lesser evolutionary significance (Figure 6.14). This is possible because the degree of genetic separation between two populations is thought to correlate with the time since physical separation, and is used as a sort of

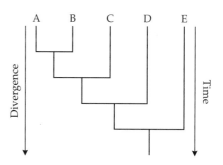

**Figure 6.14** A schematic demonstration of deep versus shallow evolutionary separations. Level of genetic divergence and time both increase toward the bottom. Population E is the most divergent; all else being equal, that level of divergence should receive priority protection before other levels of (more recent) divergence.

molecular genetic "clock." Because genetically based changes in protein structure are known to occur on a somewhat regular basis in evolutionary time, evolution of protein structure has been used as a calibrated standard for the time since separation between populations (Maxson and Wilson 1974; Sarich 1977); more genetic changes mean a longer ("deeper") evolutionary separation. There have been critiques of this approach due to difficulties in accurately standardizing the "clock," but the basic premise is that greater genetic change between two entities indicates a longer evolutionary separation.

This is a phenetic approach, which measures degree of genetic divergence among various species, populations, or any taxonomic level of interest. A phylogenetic (cladistic) approach (Chapter 3) in which unique character states would identify groups of interest would also work. In that case, older, more primitive groups would be those with the fewest evolutionary novelties (in this case, genetic changes). More detailed discussions of selection of taxa for conservation based on uniqueness and evolutionary separation may be found in Vane-Wright et al. (1991), Crozier (1992), and Faith (1992).

This theme of evolutionary depth has been especially well elucidated by John Avise and his colleagues (Avise et al. 1987; Avise 1989; Avise and Ball 1990), who are strong proponents of using molecular genetic data to determine **phylogeographic** relationships within species and to identify the deepest evolutionary separations. They argue that, because we cannot save every variant, the older lineages, all else being equal, should receive conservation priority, since they represent major branches. The newer, "minor" separations probably do not have as deeply rooted adaptations or as long histories in their present habitats and should receive attention only after the deeper lineages are secure.

Greater evolutionary depth will often correspond to major geographic separation in genetic structure, tying this concept back to the hierarchical gene diversity analysis. For example, a small, livebearing desert fish, the Sonoran topminnow (*Poeciliopsis occidentalis*), was found to exist in three major geographic groupings, based on allozyme studies and a hierarchical gene diversity study (Vrijenhoek et al. 1985). These three groups, two of which had already been recognized as subspecies, were estimated roughly to have been separated for periods ranging from 1.7 to 4.3 million years. These three major genetic groups should be the primary foci for genetic conservation and should receive priority attention, because within-group differentiation is much smaller by comparison. More genetic information would be lost if one of these three major groups went extinct than if an equivalent number of populations distributed across the species range went extinct.

Such major genetic groups can often be identified in species of conservation interest and should be the primary concern for genetic management. For example, Bischof (1992) used mtDNA to show that African elephants have a highly subdivided population structure. Unique genetic types exist in eastern and southern African regions, but there was also evidence of gene flow among regions, indicating the importance of migration corridors among reserves (see Chapter 10).

### "Cookbook Prescriptions" in Genetic Conservation

Before we leave the topic of management of genetic variation in nature, let us examine standardized prescriptions and "cookbook" methodologies for management of diversity at genetic or other levels. It is tempting for a manager of any system to rely on developed, reliable procedures that produce a predictable outcome. The need for detailed knowledge of each system in order to make management decisions is an unwelcome message for many managers, because it demands more of their limited resources and involves less certainty. Unfortunately, biological systems are so complex and individualistic that at least some detailed knowledge of the specific system of concern is necessary for reasonable management; generalities are dangerous and destabilizing to a management scheme (Ehrenfeld 1991). Consequently, we caution against management approaches that rely on quantitative rules of thumb and cookbook procedures.

For example, early discussions of conservation of genetic diversity in small populations included the so-called "50/500 rule," which stated that a genetically effective population size ($N_e$) of at least 50 individuals is necessary for conservation of genetic diversity in the short term (several generations) and to avoid inbreeding depression, and an $N_e$ of 500 is needed to avoid serious genetic drift in the long term (Franklin 1980; Soulé 1980). These may in fact be reasonable order-of-magnitude estimates of minimum numbers needed, based on simple genetic models, but they may also mislead in many cases (Lande 1988).

Such a rule as the 50/500 ignores demographic, ecological, and behavioral considerations. For example, many more than 50 or 500 individuals may be necessary in colonially breeding species that require large numbers to reproduce successfully, or in species that depend on large groups to feed successfully. The passenger pigeon became extinct earlier this century not because populations slowly dwindled to very low numbers and then disappeared because of genetic decline, but because the species needed hundreds or thousands of individuals for its breeding colonies. When population sizes fell below these large, threshold numbers, the last populations of the species rapidly disappeared, even though genetically viable numbers remained (Brisbin 1968).

On the other hand, the 50/500 rule may discourage conservation attempts in situations where less than the prescribed population size is available. Smaller populations may be "written off" as a likely loss because of small numbers, yet they may be doing well and be worthy of attention. Some populations of desert fishes, for example, may have existed at population sizes of several hundred or less for many generations and have thrived (Deacon and Deacon 1979). Yet, a genetic rule of 500 would dictate that they are not worth conservation efforts because they are doomed to extinction through genetic deterioration. Likewise, Pére David's deer (*Elaphurus davidianus*) and Przewalski's horse (*Equus przewalski*) both recovered from population sizes of less than 20 (Woodruff 1989). A suggestion was made, and then rejected, that conservation efforts for the Orange-bellied Parrot (*Neophema chrysogaster*) of Australia be abandoned because fewer than 200 individuals remained (Brown et al. 1985). These examples raise interesting questions (Pimm 1991). Can a large population lose genetic variation? Perhaps that happened with the African cheetah, and it did not go through a demographic bottleneck. Why do some small populations not lose genetic variation? Why do some populations with low genetic variation seem to thrive anyway?

The point is that strict *quantitative* rules should generally be avoided, or at least be applied with a great deal of caution, because historical and ecological factors for each species may make it more or less prone to losses of genetic diversity and the problems those losses cause. Every ecological scenario has the potential to be unique, and other data, such as natural history, biogeography, or demography, should be acquired whenever possible to assess the case before management decisions are made. There are no easy fixes to most conservation problems.

**Table 6.7**
Qualitative Guidelines for Genetically Based Conservation Practices

1. Large genetically effective population sizes are better than small ones because they will lose genetic variation more slowly.

2. The negative effects of genetic drift and inbreeding are inversely proportional to population size. Thus, avoid managing for unnaturally small populations.

3. Management of wild populations should be consistent with the history of their genetic patterns and processes. For example, historically isolated populations should remain isolated unless other concerns dictate that gene flow must occur. Gene flow among historically connected populations should continue at historical rates, even if that calls for assisted movement of individuals.

4. Low genetic diversity per se is not cause for alarm, because some species historically have low diversity. However, sudden and large losses of diversity in natural or captive populations are always cause for concern.

5. Avoid artificial selection in captivity. This is best done by keeping breeding populations in captivity for as few generations as possible, and also by simulating wild conditions as nearly as possible.

6. After a population crash, encourage rapid population growth to avoid a prolonged bottleneck.

7. Avoid possible outbreeding depression caused by breeding distantly related populations if other choices are available.

8. Avoid inadvertent introductions of exotic alleles into wild or captive populations.

9. Harvesting of wild stocks (hunting, fishing) can select for genetic changes which can affect the future evolution of the population or species. For example, culling the largest individuals can select for earlier maturity at smaller body sizes. Thus, avoid selection in harvesting wild stocks.

10. Maintenance of genetic diversity in captive stocks is no substitute for genetic diversity in the wild. Technological mastery over the genome should not be used as an excuse to overexploit or destroy species or populations in the wild.

*Qualitative* rules are another matter, and a number of good genetic guidelines have emerged based on our current knowledge (Table 6.7). These are not based on strict quantitative rules, but are consensuses on reasonable approaches to genetic conservation.

## Other Uses of Genetic Information in Conservation

Much of this chapter discussed two major uses of genetic data in conservation of populations and species in the wild. The primary discussion emphasized ways of describing the quantity and geographic distribution of genetic variation in species, employing a hierarchical gene diversity analysis. That same approach was shown to be useful in estimating historical levels of gene flow among populations, information that could determine whether artificial gene flow is necessary to retain natural geographic patterns of genetic diversity. There are several other conservation uses to which genetic data may be put, and we discuss these now.

Electrophoretic or other genetic data may be used to identify unique gene pools worthy of special protection. This is particularly true with reference to identification of unique alleles present in one population but absent in others. Such a scenario could dictate that special efforts be made to protect a population with unique genetic attributes. Echelle et al. (1989) studied 16 populations of a small endangered fish, the Pecos gambusia (*Gambusia nobilis*) from its four remaining, widely separated locations in the Pecos River

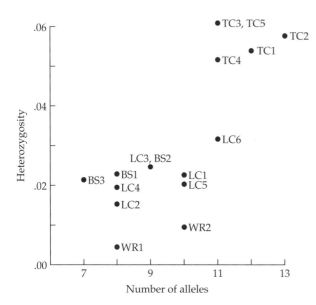

**Figure 6.15** Heterozygosity plotted against number of alleles in the population for 16 populations of the Pecos gambusia (*Gambusia nobilis*) from Texas and New Mexico. The five Toyah Creek (TC) populations have the highest diversity and are the most divergent from other populations (BS, LC, and WR). (From Echelle et al. 1987.)

system in New Mexico and Texas. They found that populations from a drainage called Toyah Creek had the highest heterozygosity and allelic diversity, and were the most divergent of all the populations (Figure 6.15). This group of fish should receive particular conservation attention, as it contains more genetic diversity than fish from other regions, and also has unique alleles that would be lost if these populations went extinct.

Genetic data can also make important contributions to taxonomic questions. Traditional taxonomies are usually based on morphological data, which may accurately reflect evolutionary relationships, or may be misleading due to local adaptations and plasticity. Genetics can help to clarify relationships and guide conservation efforts toward truly divergent or unique taxa. Such analyses are discussed in Essay 6C by John Avise.

Genetic data are also critical throughout all aspects of captive breeding programs (see Essay 6D by Oliver Ryder). Captive breeding occurs at one end of a continuum of genetic concerns, from large, wild populations that require no genetic management, to smaller, fragmented wild populations that may require manipulations to maintain genetic diversity, to the captive situation, which is the ultimate in genetic management. The genetic principles used with small populations in the wild are the same when applied to populations in captivity, but are even more germane, since captive populations tend to be very small, individuals tend to be related, and the entire population may be genetically characterized. Genetic data can guide selection of parental stocks, and the structure of controlled breedings, and can monitor overall genetic variation and loss in captivity.

## The Limitations of Genetics in Conservation

Genetic information at the population and species levels can provide important specific guidance for management and recovery programs, as well as an overall philosophical perspective of the primacy of evolutionary dynamics in life's processes. Genetics does have limitations, however, and will not be the savior of biodiversity. The application of genetics to conservation problems is a young science that is still developing; we have much to learn, and we must be realistic about the limitations. Habitat availability and biological interactions and processes should be the primary focus of conservation

## ESSAY 6C
# A Rose Is a Rose Is a Rose

John C. Avise, University of Georgia

In the final analysis, biodiversity reflects genetic heterogeneity. Thus, the concerns of conservation biology ultimately represent concerns about the erosion and loss of genetic diversity. As discussed in this chapter and Chapter 3, this genetic diversity is arranged hierarchically, from the family units, extended kinships, and geographic population structures within species, to a graded scale of genetic differences among reproductively isolated taxa that separated phylogenetically at various depths in evolutionary time. Unfortunately, traditional taxonomic characters (the visible phenotypes of organisms) are not an infallible guide to the underlying genetic subdivisions. In the last three decades, evolutionists have acquired a new set of tools that can be employed to assess genetic diversity more directly, at the level of proteins and even the genes themselves. In general, these various molecular assays can be of service to conservation biology by contributing to the characterization of genetic diversity at any level of the biological hierarchy.

What's in a name? A "Dusky Seaside Sparrow" by any other name is just as melanistic. Nonetheless, nomenclatural assignments inevitably shape our perceptions of how the biotic world is partitioned, and hence the biological units toward which conservation efforts may be directed. In the case of the Dusky Seaside Sparrow, this dark-plumaged population near Cape Canaveral, Florida, was described in the late 1800s as a species (*Ammodramus nigrescens*) distinct from the other Seaside Sparrows (*Ammodramus maritimus*) common along the Atlantic and Gulf coasts of North America. Although the dusky later was demoted to subspecies status, the nomenclatural legacy stemming from the original taxonomic description prompted continued special focus on this recognized form. Thus, in the late 1960s, when the population crashed due to changing land use practices, the dusky was listed formally as "endangered" by the U.S. Fish and Wildlife Service. Despite last-ditch conservation efforts, the Dusky Seaside Sparrow went extinct in 1987.

The point of relating this sad story involves an unexpected footnote. After the natural death of the last known dusky (in captivity), molecular analyses of DNA isolated from its tissues revealed an exceptionally close genetic relationship to other Atlantic coast Seaside Sparrows, but a deep phylogenetic distinction of all Atlantic coast populations from Gulf of Mexico populations, likely due to the effects of ancient (Pleistocene) population separations (Avise and Nelson 1989). Thus, the traditional taxonomy for the seaside sparrow complex (upon which management efforts were based) apparently had failed to capture the true genetic relationships within the group, in two respects: (1) by giving special emphasis to a presumed biotic partition that proved to be shallow evolutionarily; and (2) by failing to recognize a deeper phylogeographic subdivision between Atlantic and Gulf coast populations. This finding from molecular genetics should not be interpreted as evidence of heartlessness over the loss of the dusky. All population extinctions are regrettable, particularly in this age of accelerated habitat loss. The extinction of the dusky population is to be mourned, but perhaps we can be consoled by the knowledge that it is survived by close genetic relatives elsewhere along the Atlantic coast. Furthermore, the discovery of a deep and previously unrecognized phylogenetic subdivision between Atlantic and Gulf coast forms of the seaside sparrow should be paramount in any conservation plans for the remaining populations.

Many taxonomic assignments in use today were first proposed in the last century, often from limited phenotypic information and preliminary assessments of patterns of geographic variation. How adequately these traditional assignments summarize biological diversity remains to be determined, through continued systematic reevaluations to which molecular approaches can contribute. As with the Seaside Sparrows, past errors of phylogenetic commission and omission may be anticipated, at least occasionally. Another example involves pocket gophers in the southeastern United States. An endangered population referable to *"Geomys colonus"* in Camden County, Georgia,

first described in 1898, has proven upon molecular reexamination to represent merely a local variant of the widespread *G. pinetis* (Laerm et al. 1982). In these same genetic assays (which involved comparisons of proteins, DNAs, and chromosome karyotype), a deep but previously unrecognized phylogeographic split was shown to distinguish the pocket gophers of eastern Georgia and peninsular Florida from those to the west.

Inadequate taxonomy also can kill, as exemplified by studies of the tuatara lizards of New Zealand, discussed in Chapter 3. This complex has been treated as a single species by government and management authorities, despite the fact that molecular (and morphological) appraisals have revealed three distinct groups (Daugherty et al. 1990). Official neglect of this described taxonomic diversity may unwittingly have consigned one form of tuatara (*Sphenodon punctatus reischeki*) to extinction, whereas another form (*S. guentheri*) has survived to this point only by good fortune. As noted by Daugherty et al. (1990), "Taxonomies are not irrelevant abstractions, but the essential foundations of conservation practice."

In other cases, molecular reappraisals of endangered forms may bolster the rationale for special conservation efforts directed toward otherwise suspect taxa. For example, recent molecular appraisals of the endangered Kemp's ridley sea turtle (*Lepidochelys kempi*) showed that this "species" (which had a controversial taxonomic history) does indeed fall outside the range of genetic variability exhibited by assayed samples from its more widespread congener, *L. olivacea* (Bowen et al. 1991).

These examples illustrate but a few of the many ways that molecular genetic methods can contribute to the assessment of biodiversity, and hence to the implementation of conservation programs. Ironically, even as these exciting molecular methods for reexploring the biological world are being developed, the biota to which they might be applied are vanishing at an unprecedented rate through the direct and indirect effects of the human population explosion.

## ESSAY 6D

# Ex Situ Conservation and the Conservation Role of Zoological Parks and Aquariums

Oliver A. Ryder, San Diego Zoo

In response to consensus predictions concerning species extinctions, habitat reduction, and depletion of biological diversity, humankind is faced with the problem of managing diminishing resources vital for future generations. Under these circumstances, and in the face of acknowledged uncertainty concerning future environments, future technologies, and the perspectives held by future generations, strategies for conserving biodiversity and preserving options for the future have been elaborated in many circles. Clearly, the maximum amount of biological diversity can be conserved through long-term conservation of landscapes that collectively encompass diverse ecosystems and the variety of species residing therein.

Some habitats, however, are so greatly diminished or degraded that the remnant populations of many species are at unacceptably high risks of extinction. For many other species, insufficient knowledge exists to make a factual determination about the extent of extinction risks. For such species, ex situ conservation, including germ plasm banking, DNA collections, collections of frozen viable cells, and living collections managed for retention of genetic diversity can contribute to the strategic goal of conservation of biological diversity.

Of the various ex situ options, arguably the one of most direct relevance to conservation of species in situ is the maintenance of self-sustaining populations of vertebrate and invertebrate species in the world's zoos and aquari-

ums. Currently, these "living gene banks" are increasingly carefully managed in order to meet long-term goals for maintenance of species' genetic variation. The Species Survival Plans of the American Association of Zoological Parks and Aquariums (in North America) and the Europäisches Erhaltungszucht Programm (in Europe) act to increase the relevance of ex situ populations to the conservation of a species' gene pool. Increasingly, opportunities exist to link ex situ and in situ conservation efforts through application of technologies developed with captive populations in support of populations in the wild and through reintroduction of captive-bred animals into appropriate habitats.

One of the greatest benefits of captive populations is the role they play in public education. More people visit zoos and aquariums each year in the United States than attend all professional football, baseball, hockey, and basketball games combined. Increasingly, this zoogoing public can provide a constituency for conservation action at the regional, national, and global levels. Educating the public about animals and the ecosystems in which they reside provides an opportunity to increase public concern and support for in situ conservation activities. In the future, the perceived dichotomy between in situ and ex situ conservation efforts will become increasingly blurred.

The fundamental and applied knowledge needed for making informed decisions about conservation management does not exist for many species. Inves-

tigations made feasible by studies of captive populations have provided significant information contributing to efforts to recover many species and remove them from the endangered and threatened listing categories. For example, DNA fingerprinting studies of captive California condors have shed light on the population structure of the pre-existing wild population. Noninvasive endocrine assessment can contribute to an understanding of the behavioral ecology of wild populations. Studies on the systematics and population genetics of many species can help conservation managers to interpret the evolutionary placement of taxa and inform decisions in which knowledge of phylogenetic significance or uniqueness plays a role.

For some species, reintroduction from captive populations is a possibility. Clearly, if no effort has been made to establish a self-sustaining captive population, then reintroduction is impossible and extinction of populations in the wild will be a finality. Efforts currently under way suggest that, under appropriate circumstances, even large mammals may be translocated and/or reintroduced to restore missing components of a formerly more diverse ecosystem.

In the end, we will save what we value. The ability of zoos and aquariums to acquaint the public with the richness and diversity of animal life-forms, in addition to their role in providing ex situ populations for conservation, research, and reintroduction, is a recognized component of strategic efforts to conserve the world's biological diversity.

everywhere. If the habitat is not available, and materials and energy do not flow through an ecosystem, then maintenance of genetic diversity will ultimately degrade to an exercise in ex situ care. Without suitable ecosystems and dynamic ecological processes, genetic diversity in isolation may be nearly worthless.

There are limitations to genetic conservation on a purely logistic level as well. First, many genetic techniques are not cheap, are not easily learned, and can be misused or misapplied. The techniques require experience and sophisticated laboratory equipment. Thus, ad hoc or casual genetic analyses are not recommended; established laboratories with experienced investigators should be consulted.

Second, plant or animal tissues must be obtained and properly treated. For many techniques this means fresh or frozen samples from many individuals. This may be easy for pine trees or bumblebees, but difficult for ibex or condors. The investigator often has to get to remote field sites, find the organisms, capture and handle them, obtain samples, and return the samples to the laboratory in undegraded condition. In some cases, obtaining tissues simply may be impractical.

Third, sampling often necessitates killing individuals, or at least capturing and handling them to obtain tissues. Obviously, killing is legally or morally prohibited for many endangered species. Fortunately, new techniques are being developed that allow nondestructive sampling of body tissues: these may use scales or slime from fish (Robbins et al. 1989) or hair from mammals, or even epithelium recovered from their feces (Woodruff 1993). Regardless, genetic data are often difficult and expensive to gather.

There is also a danger of genetic conservation taking the focus off of larger, regional and global issues and sinking into esoteric details of genetic analysis. Genetics should be approached as a "fine-tuning" of management procedures, after the "coarse-tuning" of habitat availability has been done satisfactorily. If the ecosystem remains functional, viable reserves are planned or in place, pollution is not an immediate threat to life, and so forth, then attention should be paid to genetic issues. Genetics will play a pivotal role in specific circumstances, such as small isolated populations on real or habitat islands, small numbers of charismatic vertebrates such as large and rare predators or ungulates, salmon stocks exploited by humans, and captive rearing in zoos, botanical gardens, and aquariums. However, a genetic approach will not save the biological diversity being lost daily in tropical forests, or the coral reefs being killed by coastal development. Wholesale habitat destruction is a problem on a different level that cuts across genetic boundaries, and for which solutions are more economic and political than biological (Chapters 15 and 16).

Woodruff (1992) stated this concisely when he said:

> Genetic factors do not figure among the four major causes of extinction (the Evil Quartet): overkill, habitat destruction and fragmentation, impact of introduced species, and secondary or cascade effects (Diamond 1989). Thus, although genetic factors are major determinants of a population's long-term viability, conservationists can do more for a threatened population in the short-term by managing its ecology. Ecological management is the cheapest and most effective way of conserving genetic diversity.

## Summary

Because evolution is the central concept in biology, and population genetics is a central feature of evolution, genetics plays an important role in modern conservation biology. Genetic variation provides the raw material from which adaptation proceeds, and is critical to continued evolutionary change. This variation occurs at three levels: within individuals, within populations, and among populations. Loss of variation may have negative fitness consequences and prevent adaptive change in populations. Loss of variation occurs in small populations through founder effects, genetic drift, and inbreeding; among-population differentiation is eroded when isolated populations experience gene flow by human movement of organisms.

Management of genetic variation in nature should proceed with immediate (months, years), moderate (decades, centuries) and long-term (millennia) time scales in mind. The appropriate units of conservation for a given species may be based on any reasonable biological criteria that identify separate populations. Genetically, conservation units may be defined through a hierarchical gene diversity analysis, which apportions the total genetic diversity of a species into within- and among-population components, the latter in a geographically hierarchical fashion. This biogeographic scenario is important in determining natural population genetic structure and probable historical levels of gene flow among populations. This methodology also allows estimation of the relative depths of evolutionary separation of geographic groups; the older separations should receive priority conservation action. Such approaches are not rote, and require analysis of individual circumstances; "cookbook" prescriptions for genetic management should be avoided, or at least applied with extreme caution.

Genetics may also be used for identification of unique gene pools in need of special protection, for taxonomic clarification of declining species, and in management of captive propagation efforts. The role of genetics in conservation biology does have its limits, however. Genetics should be viewed as "fine-tuning" to be done after the "coarse-tuning" of habitat protection has been accomplished. For the long term, habitat availability must receive top priority, or gene conservation will degrade to museum curation of a genetic library.

## Questions for Discussion

1. Consider an island population of outcrossing land snails that has been naturally isolated from mainland populations for tens of thousands of years. Human activities have further isolated this population into many small units, each of which has lost most of its original heterozygosity. Should mainland individuals be introduced to the island to increase heterozygosity levels? What are the pros and cons of such a suggestion? What are some other factors to consider?

2. The golden toad (*Bufo periglenes*) is a rare toad species of the mountains of Costa Rica that has not been seen in several years and may be extinct. Suppose four males and two females are suddenly found and brought into captivity for breeding. Because the eggs are externally fertilized, you have the freedom to devise various breeding schemes. Discuss some possible breeding schemes and their likely outcomes with respect to genetic diversity.

3. Recall the case of the Dusky Seaside Sparrow (Essay 6C), in which John Avise argued that, despite the recognizable color differences of this subspecies, genetic information indicated no strong basis for separate conservation efforts (i.e., the subspecies was not genetically differentiated from other so-called subspecies). If this information had been known several years sooner, when several duskies were still alive, should conservation efforts for the subspecies have been abandoned? Are there other reasonable criteria for protection that should take priority over genetics, or at least be considered as well?

4. Let us continue with the extinct Dusky Seaside Sparrow. Was it a reasonable idea to attempt hybridization of the last individuals of this subspecies with other subspecies in an effort to preserve some remnant of the gene pool? Is there a point at which we should abandon efforts to save the last remnants of a gene pool?

5. Conservation efforts could focus, among other things, on either uniqueness or high diversity. That is, at the genetic, or species, or habitat or even ecosystem levels, choices could be made between protecting diversity and

protecting uniqueness. Where should priorities lie? Is there a ready answer to this question?

6. It is sometimes stated that moving individuals among habitats to restore natural levels of genetic diversity is an interventionist strategy that should be avoided because we are "tinkering with evolution." Discuss this issue.

7. Genetic information can sometimes have biopolitical consequences. For example, Boone et al. (1993) found that there was no genetic basis for recognition of four subspecies of cotton mice (*Peromyscus gossypinus gossypinus, P. g. megacephalus, P. g. palmarius,* and *P. g. anastasae*) in the southeastern United States, although there was a great deal of both within- and among-population diversity and most populations were somewhat differentiated. His data argue that subspecific status is unwarranted, but this could also remove habitat protection for one habitat, Cumberland Island, because its protection was based on the presence of this endangered subspecies. How should such genetic information be handled with respect to the legal consequences for habitat protection?

8. Consider a species of small rodent that is extinct in the wild but which exists in eight small (5–12 each) zoo populations around the world. Habitat restoration at one site now makes reintroduction to the wild possible. Using genetic approaches, how would you design an optimal breeding program for reintroduction of offspring of these rodents to the restored habitat? (See also Haig et al. 1990.)

9. Can zoos, hatcheries, and similar ex situ species sanctuaries harbor enough specimens to provide the genetic diversity their species need to survive until they can be reestablished in the wild?

## Suggestions for Further Reading

Falk, D. A. and K. E. Holsinger. (eds). 1991. *Genetics and Conservation of Rare Plants.* Oxford University Press, New York. As the title implies, this multiauthored volume focuses on the genetic diversity of plants. The 14 chapters cover topics relative to the population biology and genetics of rare plants, problems in sampling their genetic variation, management of rare plant collections, and strategies for protecting their genetic diversity.

Hartl, D. L. and A. G. Clark. 1990. *Principles of Population Genetics,* 2nd ed. Sinauer Associates, Sunderland, MA. This is a very good textbook on the basics of population genetics, offering more advanced topics than is possible here. A great "next step" for the serious student who wants to better understand population genetics and then apply it to species conservation.

Orians, G. H., G. M. Brown, Jr., W. E. Kunin and J. E. Swierzbinski. (eds.). 1990. *The Preservation and Valuation of Biological Resources.* The University of Washington Press, Seattle. The rather cryptic title of this book hides the fact that much of it deals with conservation of genetic diversity. Interesting perspectives on ex situ and in situ gene conservation, measures of genetic uniqueness, ecological uniqueness, and valuation of genetic resources are offered by a number of authors. Each chapter is accompanied by one or more commentaries and a summary of discussions that ensued at the workshop that resulted in this book.

Ryman, N. and F. Utter (eds.). 1987. *Population Genetics and Fishery Management.* University of Washington Press, Seattle. One of the oldest forms of resource management is fisheries biology. This book explains for fisheries managers (although it is applicable to many management scenarios) both the basic and advanced topics relative to genetics in a fisheries resource.

Schonewald-Cox, C. M., S. M. Chambers, B. MacBryde and L. Thomas (eds.). 1983. *Genetics and Conservation: A Reference for Managing Wild Animal and Plant Populations.* Benjamin/Cummings, Menlo Park, CA. This is a classic reference that was among several that initiated broad concern for conservation of genetic diversity. Twenty-five papers by experts in various aspects of genetic diversity lay out the principles and problems in the field.

# 7

# Demographic Processes
## Population Dynamics on Heterogeneous Landscapes

*In looking at Nature it is most necessary to . . . never forget that every single organic being around us may be said to be striving to the utmost to increase its numbers.*

*Charles Darwin, 1859*

Few topics have attracted the attention of ecologists more than fluctuations in the numbers of plants and animals through time and their variation in abundance through space. Understanding population fluctuations, and thus population conservation, requires understanding the links between demographic processes—birth, death, immigration, and emigration—and the environments in which populations exist.

Some ecologists have been particularly impressed by the relative constancy of populations while others have been impressed with their extreme variation. The former usually postulate an "equilibrium" population size and explain the observed equilibrium by reference to density-dependent factors, which prevent populations from getting either too small or too large. On the other hand, those impressed by the magnitude of population fluctuations usually see the world as consisting of many local subpopulations, each of which has a high probability of extinction due to the unpredictable nature of factors that operate independently of population density. Given the great diversity of organisms and environments and the fact that most ecologists study only a few species in a few places, there is little surprise in such diversity of opinions.

Organisms clearly vary with regard to both their susceptibility to the vicissitudes of nature and the duration of their life spans in relation to the frequency of natural disturbances. Organisms also vary in the extent to which they live their lives in one location or experience a wide variety of environmental conditions in different locations. These facts alone account for much of the difference between species regarding the extent to which populations fluctuate in time and space. An entire generation of rotifers or thrips may experience an unusual cold spell that reduces reproduction and increases mortality, while in the next generation conditions may be optimal for the species. Individual whales and sequoias, on the other hand, experience thousands of separate cold and warm fronts, and the whales of one generation are quite likely to experience an average environment something like that experienced by the whales of other generations. Accordingly, whales and sequoias are much less likely to fluctuate wildly in population size than are thrips, and even if they did fluctuate as much, an ecologist observing them over the course of his or her career would be less likely to record the fluctuations.

Unfortunately, much of the theory of population ecology, particularly as it is presented at the undergraduate level, has been based on the fallacious notion that all organisms in a population experience more or less the same environmental conditions. A more modern point of view is that every organism exists as part of an open population in a heterogeneous landscape, and that different individuals in the same population experience different conditions for a variety of reasons, the most obvious of which is that they live in different places. Even if they live in similar habitats, they may experience vastly different conditions because similar patches of the same habitat are often out of phase with one another with regard to availability of essential resources or other environmental conditions. Furthermore, organisms may move from one habitat patch to another, resulting in an interdependence of the dynamics of the subpopulations in various patches. Accordingly, conservationists must concern themselves with the spatial and temporal scales over which animals move and their environments change.

This chapter covers a variety of concepts that allow one to study and understand the demography and dynamics of natural populations on various temporal and spatial scales. It is only by viewing populations from these several perspectives at once that one can both appreciate the enormous complexities of population abundance and distribution and begin to organize and understand that complexity. This understanding is an essential prerequisite to developing a practical theory of population ecology that can aid in conserving biological diversity.

## What Is Population Demography?

Demography embodies the intrinsic factors that contribute to a population's growth or decline, including natality (especially the birth rate associated with different age classes of individuals within the population) and mortality (especially juvenile and adult survivorship). Rates of dispersal between populations (immigration into and emigration out of habitat patches) are also components of demography. These four factors, *Birth, Immigration, Death,* and *Emigration,* are often referred to as the "BIDE factors." The sex ratio of the breeding population and the age structure (the proportion of the population found in each age class) are also considered demographic factors because they contribute to birth and death rates.

These demographic factors are studied together because they are the means by which populations can respond to short-term changes in their environments. Other population attributes, such as the age of first breeding, are more difficult to alter in response to short-term stimuli, and are more likely to change in response to long-term changes in an organism's environment. These long-term attributes are often referred to as life history characteristics, and their value to conservation biology is discussed in Essay 7A by Justin Congdon and Arthur Dunham.

## ESSAY 7A
# Contributions of Long-Term Life History Studies to Conservation Biology

Justin D. Congdon, Savannah River Ecology Laboratory and
Arthur E. Dunham, University of Pennsylvania

Life history studies can contribute to the conceptual basis of conservation biology by identifying the range of feasible suites of life history trait values that can exist within a given life history. Suites of feasible life history trait values are combinations of values that are physically and genetically possible; they are known to presently exist in some organisms. In the many cases in which trait values of a target species are not known, they can be estimated from well-studied organisms with similar suites of life history traits.

Making informed estimates of life history trait values requires an understanding of life history traits in general and how they coevolve, as well as reasonably complete life history data on a range of organisms. The ability to place realistic boundaries on trait values is extremely important in cases in which decisions may be based on projections from population modeling (Crouse et al. 1987), or when a conflict exists between harvesting and conserving a target species.

A case in point is sea turtle conservation and management programs aimed at stabilizing and restoring sea turtle populations (Frazer 1992). At present, it is technologically impossible to obtain complete sea turtle life history data, almost all of which are obtained from hatchlings and adult females at nesting beaches. Age of females at sexual maturity is estimated from minimum ages of females at nesting beaches; clutch frequency and survivorship of adult females is estimated from the return rates of females to nesting beaches (Frazer 1983). All of the above estimates are based on the assumption that the vast majority of females show strict nest beach fidelity. Data on males are virtually nonexistent.

Without the empirical foundation that can only be provided by long-term life history studies, the permutations of assumed life history trait values for species like sea turtles are infinite. Although values of 3 to 30 years have been suggested for age at maturity in sea turtles as a group, it is unlikely that all values in this range are equally probable. If we are constrained only to data

from sea turtles, opinions about probable ages at maturity remain without empirical boundaries. Presently, only existing studies of other long-lived organisms can provide life history data that are empirically sufficient to resolve some conflicting opinions about life history trait values of sea turtles and approaches to sea turtle conservation (Frazer 1992).

To illustrate the importance of associations of life history trait values in long-lived organisms, we created a set

of graphs from life history data on common snapping turtles (*Chelydra serpentina*) on the University of Michigan's E. S. George Reserve. The relationship between juvenile and adult survivorship was determined for low (0.2, Figures A1 and A3) and high (0.8, Figures A2 and A4) nest survivorships, which might represent a worst- and best-case scenario for a sea turtle nesting beach. In one set of simulations, age at maturity was allowed to vary from 15 to 30 years of age (Figures A1 and A2), with

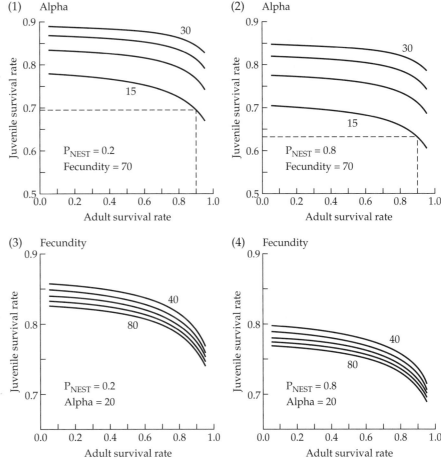

**Figure A** The relationship between adult and juvenile survival rates with $P_{NEST}$ (probability of nest survival) set at 0.20 (1, 3) or 0.80 (2, 4). In (1) and (2) alpha (age at sexual maturity) varies between 15 and 30 years, and in (3) and (4) fecundity (annual production of female producing eggs) varies between 40 and 80. In all simulations, isoclines are produced where the population is stable ($r = 0$) for each combination of life history trait values. Values above or below isoclines represent increasing or decreasing populations, respectively.

fecundity fixed at 70 eggs annually, a value close to that reported for loggerhead sea turtles (Frazer 1984). In another set of simulations, fecundity was allowed to vary from 40 to 80 eggs, with age at maturity fixed at 20 years (Figures A3 and A4). These simulations result in a set of isoclines at which the intrinsic rate of increase ($r$) of the population is 0 (the population is stable); values above or below an isocline represent increasing or decreasing populations, respectively.

From Figures A1 and A2, it is obvious that, regardless of whether or not nest survivorship is high due to conservation efforts, age at maturity has a substantial effect on the levels of juvenile survivorship required to maintain a stable population. From Figures A3 and A4 it is also apparent that annual fecundity can double at either nest survival level, but juvenile survival rates still must exceed 70% to maintain a stable population. Under all conditions, lowering of adult survival levels (such as through harvest or accidental killing in shrimping nets) exacerbates the problem by increasing the already high required juvenile survival with even higher ones. Therefore, conservation efforts aimed at increasing nest survival and head-starting young juveniles are probably doomed to failure without a concomitant reduction in mortality of adults and juveniles.

Because all five species of sea turtles found in waters off the United States are listed as endangered or threatened by the Endangered Species Act of 1973, their populations are already substantially reduced from historical levels. Efforts should and are being made to reduce existing sources of mortality and to prevent new sources of mortality being imposed on any age classes of sea turtles. A potential new source of mortality to young juvenile sea turtles is a proposal to harvest *Sargassum* (a floating brown alga), where juveniles live (Coston-Clements et al. 1991). The potential effects of *Sargassum* harvest on survival rates of juveniles are unknown, but it seems unlikely that harvesting can be undertaken without some level of increase in juvenile mortality. If age at maturity of sea turtles is set at 15 years, and survivorship of adults is 0.9, average juvenile survivorship cannot fall below 0.68 (Figure A1) or 0.63 (Figure A2) annually, with low and high nest survival, respectively. Thus, examination of Figure A can only lead to the conclusion that any increase in juvenile mortality will almost certainly have serious consequences for stable populations of sea turtles and potentially catastrophic consequences for populations that are already declining.

The combination of life history modeling and a long-term life history study of freshwater turtles at the University of Michigan's E. S. George Reserve has documented that in long-lived organisms, both juvenile and adult survival must be high to maintain a stable population. Since life history traits of age at first reproduction and longevity positively covary across many taxa (Charlesworth 1980; Charnov 1990), it is almost certain that all long-lived organisms, such as sea turtles, sharks, some bony fishes, tortoises, and freshwater turtles, delay sexual maturity. In addition, the whole range of trait values that make up a long-lived organism's life history combine to limit their ability to respond to increased mortality. They exist in populations that, when compared with shorter-lived organisms, require both high adult and juvenile survivorship. Thus, populations of long-lived organisms have limited abilities to respond to chronic increases in juvenile mortality and even lesser abilities to respond to increased mortality through commercial harvest of juveniles or adults (Congdon et al. 1993). Data obtained from long-term life history studies of species that are not of direct conservation concern are a resource that can contribute to developing concepts and solving problems related to management and conservation practices.

In this section we provide an example of the importance of demographic factors in a conservation strategy; other examples will follow when specific demographic topics are discussed. The Hawaiian monk seal (*Monorchus schauinslandi*), which is found in the northwestern Hawaiian Islands, has been in a population decline for several decades. The seals rest and give birth on the beaches of the mostly uninhabited islands. When the U.S. Coast Guard established stations on some of the islands, the seals shifted their activities to islands away from the Guard personnel, and the population began to decline precipitously (Figure 7.1). The Hawaiian monk seal was declared endangered in 1976 because of this population decline, and steps were taken to reverse the trend (Gerrodette and Gilmartin 1990).

The seals' decline was puzzling because the beaches they used were unchanged by the military presence, and the adults were not being killed or harassed by the Coast Guard personnel. The only effect on the species was that some of the Guard's recreational activities on the beaches caused the seals to move to previously unused beaches on other islands. Demographic studies revealed that juvenile survivorship on these alternative islands was drastically lower than on the original beaches. The shape of the new islands allowed waves to pass completely over the sandy beaches at high tide, sweeping the young seal pups into the sea, where large numbers of sharks were waiting. The original beaches did not have a problem with large waves, and so the young seals, which are poor swimmers, did not suffer high mortality there.

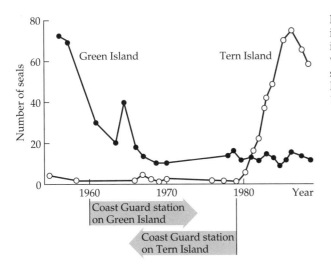

**Figure 7.1**  Total number of Hawaiian monk seals recorded during monitoring efforts at two islands in the northwestern Hawaiian Islands. Seals stayed away from Green Island and Tern Island while U.S. Coast Guard stations were present. During this time, seals used other islands where juvenile survivorship was very low, causing a population crash. (From Gerrodette and Gilmartin 1990.)

Few offspring were produced during the years that the seals were restricted to the alternative islands, and therefore adults lost through normal mortality were not replaced, causing the population to become both smaller and older. When the Coast Guard personnel modified their behavior, the Hawaiian monk seals returned to their original "hauling out" beaches, juvenile survivorship increased, and the population began to recover. Gerrodette and Gilmartin (1990) point out that simple population counts through monitoring programs failed to identify the seals' problem. It took a demographic analysis to uncover the low survivorship of juveniles and the resulting lack of recruits into the population. Correcting this demographic problem proved to be the key to the recovery process for this endangered species.

## Mechanisms of Population Regulation

Conservation biologists are interested in why some species are rare, and what keeps them so. Thus, conservationists are concerned with the factors that might regulate population size. A population can be said to be regulated if it has the tendency to increase when rare and to decline when common. The concept of population regulation is closely tied to that of density dependence. Howard and Fiske (1911) introduced the distinction between "catastrophic mortality factors" that kill a constant proportion of a population independent of its density and "facultative mortality factors" that kill an increasing proportion of the population as density is increased. The same idea is now embodied in the distinction between density-independent and density-dependent factors affecting population growth, though density dependence can refer to birth rates as well as to death rates. **Density-independent factors** influence birth and/or death rates in a manner independent of population density, while the intensity of **density-dependent factors,** by definition, changes with population density (Figure 7.2).

For density-dependent factors to regulate population growth, either per capita mortality must increase or per capita natality must decline as population density increases. Although there are a myriad of factors that can, in theory, contribute to density-dependent changes in mortality and natality, most of these can be grouped into several categories or mechanisms of population regulation. Among the most prominent are the following:

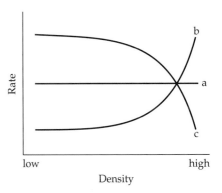

**Figure 7.2**  A demonstration of density-independent (a) and density-dependent (b and c) population responses. In the case of density-independent responses (a), density has no influence on a given parameter, such as mortality or birth rate. In the case of density dependence, a parameter such as mortality may increase at higher densities (b), while other parameters, such as clutch size or individual growth rate may decrease at higher densities (c). The particular shapes of the response curves, of course, would vary greatly among taxa and environments.

- Increased mortality or decreased natality due to a shortage of resources
- Increased mortality due to increased predation, parasitism, or disease
- Increased mortality or decreased natality due to increased intensity of intraspecific social interactions

Of all of the density-dependent mechanisms that could lead to population regulation, the increased shortage of resources at high population densities is probably the most investigated. Many examples exist, ranging from the limitation of population growth in aquatic algae due to reduction of available nutrients at high algal densities, to the control of wolf populations due to reduction in deer or caribou abundance. The essential point is that, in each case, reduction in the resource (such as food, shelter, or space) is due to the presence and activity of large numbers of the resource consumer.

Mortality due to disease, parasitism, or predation may commonly increase as the density of potential victims increases. Probably the best-known case of disease-related population regulation is the control of introduced rabbits by the *Myxoma* virus in Australia. In 1859, about 25 European rabbits were released from captivity in southeastern Australia. By the turn of the next century hundreds of millions of rabbits occupied an area in excess of 3 million km$^2$, and rabbits had become a major pest in Australian agricultural lands. In 1950 an effort was initiated to control the rabbits through the introduction of a virulent form of the myxoma virus, which is transmitted primarily by mosquitoes. The disease spread rapidly, devastating the rabbit population over large areas by 1954. Thereafter, the incidence of the disease also declined. In the following decades there were various periods of recovery of the rabbits followed by subsequent outbreaks of the virus; however, during this time the virulence of the virus also declined, resulting in less dramatic oscillations in both rabbit and virus populations.

There is no doubt that social behavior can play a direct role in regulating some animal populations, although in most, and perhaps all cases, social behavior interacts with resource shortage, disease, and predation to determine population size. In general, social behavior regulates access to resources such as food, cover, and breeding sites, and thereby affects survival and reproduction. Dominance interactions, for example, may give dominant individuals greater access to concentrated food resources, increasing the mortality risks of subordinates. Dominant individuals may also have better access to cover, forcing subordinate individuals to areas where predation risks are higher. In the former case, starvation due to limited access to food is the proximate cause of mortality, and in the second case, predation due to lack of access to cover or refuge sites is the proximate cause of mortality. In both cases, however, social behavior influences the fraction of the population dying, and thereby plays a key role in regulating population size.

Occasionally, density and social behavior have the opposite effect in that birth rates may increase or death rates may decrease at high densities. For instance, in some organisms high population densities are required to stimulate courtship and breeding activity. This stimulation, called an "Allee effect," may cease and breeding may be halted if the population drops below some required density (Allee et al. 1949).

The above examples emphasize the facultative nature of the regulating factors whereby per capita mortality increases or per capita natality declines with increasing population density. Many mortality factors act independently of population density; that is, the magnitude of mortality or natality does not depend on population density per se. For example, in the northern United States, winter ranges of many bird species are defined by severe winter weather

(Root 1988). A series of unusually cold years will greatly decrease population densities in a region, regardless of the birds' densities during the previous summer. These population declines are therefore density independent.

Davidson and Andrewartha (1948a,b) investigated the causes of outbreaks of populations of *Thrips imaginis,* a major pest on apples in Australia. In moist areas, such as irrigated suburban residential areas, these thrips persist even during dry years, but in drier habitats, food supplies decline in midsummer, causing a catastrophic crash in the numbers of thrips. Although the crashes in thrip numbers occur following the peak of thrip populations in midsummer, there is no evidence for a density-dependent regulating mechanism, because the decline in food availability is due to an extrinsic factor, dry weather, rather than being due to the activity of the thrips per se. In other words, the food does not disappear because of overexploitation by thrips, but rather because of the dry weather, which is unaffected by the density of thrips.

It must be kept in mind that populations can be regulated by more than one factor, and that the simultaneous effects of several factors working in concert may be responsible for population change. A recent analysis of the extinction of *Trilepidea adamsii,* a New Zealand mistletoe, cited the interaction of both density-independent and density-dependent factors as critical components of the events leading to extinction of the plant (Norton 1991). The mistletoe was never widespread, so the extensive habitat destruction (a density-independent factor) that took place in New Zealand probably limited the plant to a few locations. Overcollecting by botanists and grazing by an introduced opossum were density-dependent forces that further reduced the species until it disappeared. (Scientific collecting is density dependent because as a species becomes more rare, specimens become more valuable, and field collectors may put a special effort into finding and gathering the last few individuals; of course, this also hearkens back to the discussion of ethics in Chapter 2.) This added pressure may have eliminated the few remaining *Trilepidea* populations.

## A Hierarchical Approach to Population Regulation

Most models of population dynamics project future population sizes based on current population size and per capita birth and death rates. Some population models and studies go further by attempting to incorporate the causal factors that determine birth and death rates. Although the latter approach is sometimes described as incorporating the mechanisms of population regulation, there are mechanisms of population regulation that operate at more than one level in a hierarchy of causation. Thus, population regulation must be viewed as a hierarchical process.

An example of this view comes from studies of population fluctuations in granivorous birds such as sparrows. Typically, these studies have looked for regulatory factors by relating sparrow birth and death rates to spatial and temporal variations in food supply. All other things being equal, the survival of sparrows during winter is highest when and where seed production has been greatest. Unfortunately, all other things are rarely equal, and, in the case of sparrows, not only food supply but also habitat availability varies dramatically from year to year. Sparrows live primarily in early successional habitats, and the availability of such habitats depends on a complex of factors ranging from the decisions of farmers to abandon land to the rate of old-field succession. Year-to-year variation in the abundance of wintering sparrows in the southeastern United States may depend less on how much food is available in each patch of habitat than on how habitat availability is affected by factors such as the influence of the global economy on the price of soybeans and the decisions made by farmers.

As stated above, the population dynamics of animals needs to be viewed as a hierarchical process. In the case of the wintering sparrows, local factors such as food supply affect sparrow populations at one level, while regional patterns of agriculture affect habitat availability for the sparrows at a very different level. To make population projections, one needs to know how many individuals there are, what habitats they occupy, and the characteristic birth and death rates for individuals in those habitats. A purely empirical model can be constructed based on population size and distribution and on habitat-specific demography. Such a model can be used to project future population sizes as long as (1) the habitat-specific birth and death rates do not change, and (2) the fraction of the population in each habitat type does not change.

This type of model can be used to examine the various hierarchical levels of population regulation. The model can incorporate factors such as food supply, competition, disease, and predation that influence population growth by affecting birth and death rates within the habitats where individuals occur. Such a model is called a "mechanistic" model, and provides a "lower" or "individual-level" explanation of the phenomenon of population growth since it emphasizes factors operating within small-scale patches. These are the factors that ecologists have emphasized in population studies (Hassell 1978; Pulliam 1983; Werner et al. 1983).

There is, however, a "higher level" of explanation consisting of all those factors operating at larger spatial and temporal scales, such as the factors that determine the availability of suitable habitat. In the case of overwintering sparrows just discussed, the factors influencing availability of suitable habitat are at least as important in determining population dynamics as are the individual level factors. Broad-scale geographic factors, such as land use and climate change, operate at a "landscape level," beyond the habitats where the population currently resides and often over relatively long periods of time. Factors at this landscape level determine the amount and location of suitable habitat for each particular species. Figure 7.3 illustrates this hierarchical approach. A complete explanation of past trends or a projection of future trends requires an understanding of both the "lower-level" factors determining birth and death rates within habitats and the "higher-level" factors determining regional trends in habitat availability. To understand the population dynamics of species of interest, conservationists will therefore need to be concerned with environmental factors that operate at a variety of spatial scales. The next few sections discuss several key concepts that link populations to these higher-level factors.

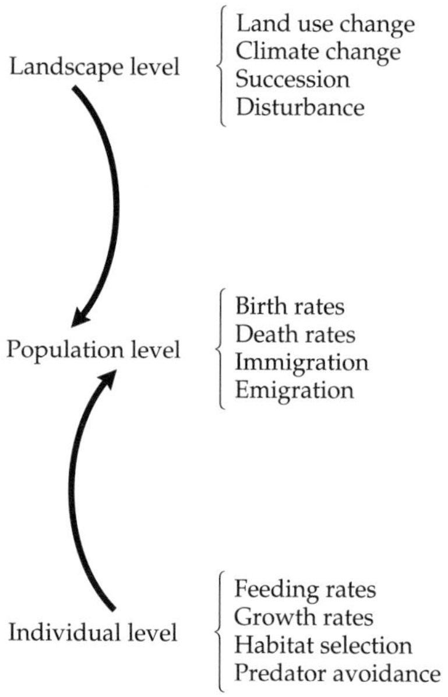

## Habitat-Specific Demography

### Sources and Sinks

In many populations, individuals occupy habitat patches of differing quality. Individuals in highly productive habitats are successful in producing offspring, while individuals in poor habitats may suffer poor reproductive success or survival. The fate of a population as a whole may depend on whether the reproductive success of individuals in the good habitats outweighs the lack of success by individuals in the poor areas. The concept that population dynamics may depend on the relative quality of good and poor habitats is called **source and sink dynamics,** and recently has been recognized as an important idea in conservation biology.

| Landscape level | Land use change<br>Climate change<br>Succession<br>Disturbance |
| Population level | Birth rates<br>Death rates<br>Immigration<br>Emigration |
| Individual level | Feeding rates<br>Growth rates<br>Habitat selection<br>Predator avoidance |

**Figure 7.3** Population dynamics must be understood as resulting from a hierarchy of processes affecting populations at different levels. Landscape-level changes in the availability of habitat determine how much suitable habitat exists for a given species. The availability of suitable habitat and the behavior and physiology of individual organisms combine to influence the dynamics of populations.

Good habitats are called **sources,** and are defined as areas where local reproductive success is greater than local mortality (see Box 7A for a more complete definition of sources and sinks). Populations in source habitats produce an excess of individuals, who must disperse outside their natal patch to find a place to settle and breed. Poor habitats, on the other hand, are areas where local productivity is less than local mortality. These areas are called **sinks** because, without immigration from other areas, populations in sink habitats inevitably spiral "down the drain" to extinction. The terms "sources" and "sinks" are also used to describe the populations found in these habitats: **source populations** are those found in source habitats, and **sink populations** are those found in sink habitats.

Population ecologists are establishing that many species have both source and sink populations (see Pulliam 1994 for a recent review). The excess individuals produced by source populations can disperse to sink habitat patches and maintain the populations found in these poorer habitats. A population

## BOX 7A
# The Theory of Sources and Sinks

The population dynamics of an organism can be strongly influenced by the abundance and location of suitable habitat. The approach taken here is to attempt to understand how demography relates to habitat suitability and to relate population dynamics to the characteristics of real landscapes, including the location of suitable habitat. Consider a population of organisms living in a seasonal environment, consisting of a nonreproductive season or "winter" and a reproductive or breeding season. If the population has $n_T$ individuals at the end of the winter, just prior to the onset of the reproductive season, and if none of the adults die during the breeding season, and each adult produces an average of $b$ offspring, then at the end of the breeding season there will be $n_T + bn_T$ individuals alive (Pulliam 1988). Furthermore, if adults survive the nonbreeding season with probability $P_A$ and juveniles survive with probability $P_J$, then at the beginning of the next breeding season the population size will be

$$n_{T+1} = P_A n_T + P_J bn_T = n_T (P_A + bP_J)$$

Let $\lambda = P_A + bP_J$. Lambda ($\lambda$) is the finite rate of increase for the population and gives the number of individuals at the beginning of year $T + 1$, per individual at the beginning of year $T$. The annual finite rate of increase ($\lambda_t$) can vary from year to year as the survival rates and/or reproductive rates vary. The geometric mean, $\bar{\lambda} = (\lambda_1 \lambda_2 \cdots \lambda_t)^{1/t}$ of

the rates over a sequence of $t$ years characterizes the growth rate of the population in the sense that $n_t = n_0 \bar{\lambda}^t$. Accordingly, if the long-term mean $\bar{\lambda}$ is less than 1.0, the population will decline, and if it exceeds 1.0, the population will grow. Obviously, the population cannot grow forever, so for a population that does not go extinct or become infinitely abundant, the long-term mean $\bar{\lambda}$ must be close to 1.0.

The mean finite rate of increase ($\bar{\lambda}$) can also be used to describe spatial variation in population growth rates. In this case, we refer to the habitat-specific rate of increase and calculate $\bar{\lambda}$ based on the birth and death rates that apply in a specific habitat or patch of habitat (Pulliam 1988). This concept of habitat-specific growth rate is complicated by dispersal. If each patch of habitat were isolated from all others, then the value of $\bar{\lambda}$ calculated for any one habitat would be the growth rate experienced by the population in that habitat. However, if habitats are connected, the growth rate experienced by the entire interconnected population is given by the weighted average across all habitats; that is, different parts of the population are growing at different rates.

Some habitats are clearly more suitable than others. Consider the simple case in which there are two habitats of different quality, and migration between them. Habitat 1 is the better habitat, called the source, and here reproduction exceeds mortality, so that the habitat-specific growth rate, $\bar{\lambda}_1$, is greater than

1.0. In habitat 2, the sink, mortality exceeds reproduction, so $\bar{\lambda}_2$ is less than 1.0. Assume that the subpopulation in the source grows at the rate $\bar{\lambda}_1$ until it reaches a maximum size ($n_1^*$), which represents the maximum number of breeding individuals that can be accommodated in the source. Once the source has reached its maximum size, there are $\bar{\lambda}_1 n_1^*$ individuals at the end of each nonbreeding season; of this total only $n_1^*$ can remain to breed, and the remaining $n_1^*(\bar{\lambda}_1 - 1)$ must emigrate from the source habitat into sink habitat (Pulliam 1988).

In the absence of immigration, the sink subpopulation would soon disappear, because each year there would be fewer individuals than the year before. However, with the steady immigration of $n_1^*(\lambda_1 - 1)$ individuals from the source habitat, the sink population will grow to an equilibrium population of $n_2^* = n_1^*(\lambda_1 - 1)/(1 - \lambda_2)$. Note that $\lambda_1 - 1$ is the per capita reproductive surplus in the source habitat and $1 - \lambda_2$ is the per capita reproductive deficit in the sink habitat. Clearly, if the reproductive surplus in the source is much larger than the reproductive deficit in the sink, the sink habitat will contain far more individuals than the source habitat, despite the fact that the sink subpopulation is dependent on emigration from the source for its very existence. In other words, most of the individuals in a local population may exist in habitat which cannot maintain the population (Pulliam 1988).

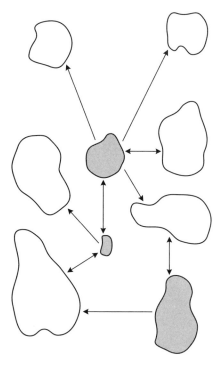

**Figure 7.4**  A schematic example of a metapopulation structure affected by source and sink patches. In this case, a few source habitats (shaded) provide excess individuals, which emigrate to and colonize sink habitats (open). The sink habitats may be spatially larger than the sources, and may even have higher population densities, but their populations would quickly go extinct were it not for the presence of the source habitats. Arrows indicate directions of movement of individuals.

that consists of several subpopulations linked together by immigration and emigration is called a **metapopulation** (Figure 7.4); this concept was introduced in Chapter 6 and is discussed more fully later in this chapter. Metapopulation is a broader term than sources or sinks because in metapopulations the demographic rates may or may not be the same in different patches of habitat. Sources and sinks are a special case of metapopulations in which some patches (sources) are substantially better than others (sinks). Metapopulations have been recently described in systems as diverse as Scandinavian crickets, desert grasses in Israel, and Spotted Owls in the western United States.

Several results from studies of source and sink dynamics have broad implications for conservation biology. First, theoretical models of sources and sinks have shown that a small proportion of the total population may be located in the source habitat. For instance, using demographic parameters that are reasonable for many natural populations, Pulliam (1988) showed that as little as 10% of a metapopulation may be found in source habitat and still be responsible for maintaining the 90% of the population found in the sink. Such relationships may greatly affect the ability of conservationists to identify critical habitats for endangered species. Until recently, critical habitats were defined as the places where a species was most common. Source habitat, however, is defined by demographic characteristics—habitat-specific reproductive success and survivorship—not population density. Source habitats could easily (and mistakenly) be ignored if conservationists only concentrated on preserving habitat where a species was most common, not where it was most productive. If source habitats are not protected in a conservation plan, obviously the whole metapopulation could be threatened.

An example of the utility of considering source–sink dynamics in conservation is Wootton and Bell's (1992) analysis of the population dynamics of the Peregrine Falcon (*Falco peregrinus*) in California. Wootton and Bell modeled this population as two subpopulations (northern and southern California) linked by dispersal. Their analysis suggests that the northern population acts as a source for the smaller southern population. The regional management strategy for this species includes the release of captive-reared young, and is aimed primarily at the southern population, which Wootton and Bell show to be a sink. Management efforts would be more productive if they were directed at stabilizing and increasing the northern source population rather than the southern sink population.

Another major implication of the source–sink concept concerns reserve design. Pulliam and Danielson (1991) showed with a source–sink model that adding habitat to a reserve can actually result in a smaller metapopulation if most of the additional land is sink habitat. Individuals dispersing within the reserve may settle in the unproductive sink patches if the available source patches are too hard to find—in essence, the available source patches become lost in a sea of sink. Recent studies using a metapopulation model developed for Spotted Owls predict just such a problem with some reserve designs proposed for this species in the Pacific Northwest. These researchers have proposed that Spotted Owl reserves should have "hard boundaries"; that is, the reserves should be separated from similar-looking sink habitat, so that dispersing birds will not settle in unproductive territories (McKelvey et al. 1993).

Determining which habitats are sources and which are sinks requires a great deal of knowledge about the natural history of organisms. One needs to know the birth and death rates of individuals in each habitat type, details of dispersal behavior, and other aspects of the organism's life history. Without such knowledge, it is impossible to design a conservation plan that considers realistic population dynamics. Studies to obtain such basic information will be critical in the planning of management and conservation strategies that incorporate the natural variability found in most populations.

## Metapopulation Concepts

Levins (1969) introduced the concept of the metapopulation to describe a collection of subpopulations of a species, each occupying a suitable patch of habitat in a landscape of otherwise unsuitable habitat. Levins demonstrated that the fraction of suitable habitat patches occupied at any given time represents a balance of the rate at which subpopulations go extinct in occupied patches and the rate of colonization of empty patches (see Hanski 1989). The rate of local extinction depends largely on conditions within a patch and the stochastic (or random) nature of the dynamics of small populations. The rate of colonization of empty patches, on the other hand, depends on the dispersal ability of the species and the location of suitable patches in the landscape.

The subpopulation in each patch can fluctuate in size, and when a subpopulation is very small, local extinction can be prevented by occasional immigrants that arrive from neighboring patches. This has been termed the **rescue effect** by Brown and Kodric-Brown (1977), who argue that this is often a major factor in maintaining small populations. The rescue effect may also be important in maintaining high levels of species diversity because poor competitors will not be excluded from patches by locally well adapted species if the populations of the poorer competitors are maintained through immigration (Stevens 1989).

Conservation biologists are using metapopulation models to describe the structure of populations that are found scattered across isolated patches, and that are threatened or otherwise of management interest. In many of these metapopulation analyses, the goal is to identify particular subpopulations, habitat patches, or links between patches that are critical to maintenance of the overall metapopulation. Beier (1993) provides an excellent example of this type of analysis in his study of the cougar (*Felis concolor*) population of the Santa Ana Mountains of southern California. Beier used radiotelemetry data to show that the cougars formed a series of semi-isolated populations found mostly in small mountain ranges linked by riparian corridors (Figure 7.5). A

(A)

(B)

**Figure 7.5**   The use of riparian habitat (A) as corridors was shown to be a crucial element in the maintenance of a viable population of cougars (B) in southern California. (A, photograph by John B. Dunning; B, by Rick and Nora Bowers.)

metapopulation simulation model showed that the overall population in the region was heavily dependent on movement by individual cats through the corridors to colonize empty areas. Beier's analysis showed that any loss of habitat (and corresponding decrease in population size) in this region would greatly increase the chance of extinction for the entire metapopulation.

Beier looked at the importance of specific patches of habitat and corridors in maintaining the metapopulation. One corridor in the northern part of the study area linked a 150 km² patch (8% of the total area) with the rest of the region. When the study was published, this corridor was slated for development by the city of Anaheim. Beier's analysis demonstrated that loss of this corridor would mean that the northern habitat patch would be unoccupied due to lack of immigrants, and that the cougar population as a whole would suffer greatly. Because the metapopulation model identified the importance of this corridor, the development plan is being modified to leave the corridor intact.

There has been much debate about how the number, size, and arrangement of suitable sites influences population persistence. Much of this controversy can be illustrated by what has come to be known as the SLOSS debate. SLOSS is an acronym for "Single Large Or Several Small" and refers to whether conservation reserves are best designed as one big block of protected land or as several smaller reserves. The SLOSS debate has been mostly concerned with the effect of reserve design on the diversity of species protected, but the SLOSS logic can also be applied to the viability of a metapopulation by focusing on the two contradictory ways in which distance between suitable sites influences population persistence. If several populations are close to one another, migration between them may be common, and thus metapopulation persistence may be promoted. On the other hand, sites close to one another are more likely to experience the same environmental conditions, such as the same floods, disease outbreaks, or other disturbances. This negative aspect of proximity leads to shortened metapopulation persistence by increasing the correlation between the dynamics of local populations, and thereby increasing the likelihood that all local populations will go extinct at once.

There is no single answer to the SLOSS debate because the number, size, and location of habitat patches affect different species differently. Likewise, there is "no single 'magic' population size that guarantees the persistence of populations" (Thomas 1990). Extinction is best described as a probabilistic phenomenon: the larger the number of populations and the larger the size of each population, the lower the probability of extinction. For good dispersers, broadly separated sites that are close enough to permit adequate dispersal between them, yet far enough apart to experience different environmental conditions, might maximize population persistence. On the other hand, this arrangement might lead to the rapid extinction of a species with poor dispersal ability because no exchange of individuals among sites would be possible.

## Population Viability Analysis

Models of factors contributing to population viability are proving to be valuable additions to the conservationist's toolbox. The study of the ways in which habitat loss, environmental uncertainty, demographic stochasticity, and genetic factors interact to determine extinction probabilities for individual species has been termed **Population Viability Analysis,** or PVA (Soulé 1987; Shaffer 1990). Although PVA is a relatively new approach, a number of excellent studies have demonstrated its utility (e.g., Ehrlich and Murphy 1987; Marcot and Holthausen 1987; Murphy et al. 1990; Menges 1990; Stacey and Taper 1992). Our discussion of PVA is enhanced by Mark Shaffer, one of its developers, in Essay 7B.

As far as we know, all populations eventually go extinct. Very large populations may last for hundreds, thousands, or even millions of generations, while small populations are much more vulnerable to extinction. Shaffer (1981, 1987) lists the following four categories of factors that influence the likelihood of population extinction:

1. Demographic uncertainty (also called demographic stochasticity)
2. Environmental uncertainty
3. Natural catastrophes
4. Genetic uncertainty (including the founder effect, genetic drift, and inbreeding)

We discuss the first three of these below; the fourth category, genetic uncertainty, was treated at length in Chapter 6.

**Demographic uncertainty** is usually taken to mean uncertainty resulting from the effects of random events on the survival and reproduction of individuals. An extremely skewed sex ratio is an example of an unusual demographic event that could occur in a small population. For example, the Dusky Seaside Sparrow (*Ammodramus maritimus nigrescens*) was doomed to extinction in 1980 when the last six known individuals all happened to be males (Kale 1983). **Environmental uncertainty** usually refers to unpredictable events, such as "changes in weather, food supply, and the populations of competitors, predators and parasites" (Shaffer 1987). One way of appreciating the distinction between these two categories is to think of demographic stochasticity as referring to the variation experienced at the individual level, given a mean population mortality rate and/or rate of reproduction. Environmental uncertainty, on the other hand, refers to temporal and spatial variation in these mean rates. Even where different subpopulations are subject to the same mean rate, some subpopulations will, by chance, experience more mortality or reproduction than others during a particular interval of time. The final category of extinction factors to be considered in this chapter is **natural catastrophes.** These can be defined as extreme cases of environmental uncertainty, such as hurricanes or large fires. Catastrophes are usually short in duration, but widespread in their impact.

Demographic uncertainty, environmental uncertainty, and natural catastrophes are convenient labels for various forms of variation that influence the demographic process and thereby contribute to extinction probability. The lines between these categories are, however, somewhat arbitrary. For example, natural catastrophes such as floods, droughts, and fires are distinguished by their brief durations and strong impacts, and by their infrequent occurrence. What constitutes a flood or drought, however, is not always clear; accordingly, arbitrary definitions based on expected frequency are often used (i.e., "a 50-year flood"). A "catastrophe" that is repeated frequently may become part of the normal level of environmental uncertainty to which organisms must adapt.

As a general rule, genetic and demographic uncertainty are important factors affecting the viability of only very small populations (< 50 individuals). Environmental uncertainty and catastrophes can also affect the viability of much larger populations. Conservationists working with endangered species often must deal with the combined effects of all four factors, since many endangered species, especially large vertebrates, exist in small populations. The recovery plans for many endangered species usually set two goals for establishing viable populations: (1) create multiple populations, so that a single catastrophic event cannot wipe out the whole species, and (2) increase the size of each population to a level at which genetic, demographic, and normal environmental uncertainties are less threatening. This can be very difficult to do, especially with species that currently exist in a single small population, or are found in a single unique habitat patch.

A number of authors have suggested general guidelines for establishing viable population sizes (e.g., Gilpin and Soulé 1986). Populations of 10 to 50 individuals are often said to be too small because they result in rapid loss of genetic variability or because they are too prone to extinction by a single natural catastrophe. Populations of 1000 to 10,000 individuals, on the other hand, are often said to be adequate to ensure long-term persistence. Such numbers can, however, at best be viewed as very general guidelines. The evolutionary record tells us that populations of 10,000 or more will almost certainly go extinct eventually, even though the expected persistence time is very long. Also, populations that appear to be safe for many years may suddenly decline if they are subject to threshold responses (see Box 7B). Any attempt to estimate a population's viability must be done in the context of social goals and political realities, and with an understanding that any predictions are made in a context of uncertainty.

## Box 7B
# Thresholds of Population Responses

Researchers and policymakers concerned about species extinction normally worry about very rare organisms. It is generally agreed that species whose total population has declined to just a few individuals are the most likely to go extinct in the immediate future. The history of human exploitation of plants and animals tells us, however, that common species, even abundant ones, can suffer huge population declines that threaten the species with extinction. The Passenger Pigeon (*Ectopistes migratorius*) was one of the most abundant birds in North America in the early 1800s. A century of overhunting and habitat destruction caused the bird to decline until the huge populations suddenly crashed over the span of a few decades. The Passenger Pigeon became extinct in the early 1900s, when the last few individuals died in zoos (Blockstein and Tordoff 1985). Similarly, overexploitation by humans has caused the collapse of a number of fisheries of formerly abundant species such as the Pacific anchovy and the Atlantic striped bass. Why have these common species declined so precipitously?

Part of the explanation of sudden population crashes lies in the nonlinear nature of population change. Populations do not always follow smooth trajectories such as those mapped in Figure 7.2. Under some circumstances, populations will exhibit **threshold responses,**

dramatic changes in population size over short periods of time. Because threshold responses make it particularly difficult to design strategies for managing populations over time, it is important for conservation biologists to consider such population responses in their investigations. Lande (1987) developed a general metapopulation model for territorial species that is useful in the study of thresholds of population change. In the discussion below, we use this to model one kind of population threshold response. We consider how far habitat loss and land use change might proceed before there is any significant effect on the fraction of suitable sites that are occupied by a territorial species.

Lande (1987) considered metapopulation dynamics on a large landscape divided into many sites, each the size of one territory. In his model, the landscape consists of two habitat types (suitable and unsuitable) with a fraction $h$ of the sites being suitable and a fraction $u = 1 - h$ being unsuitable. In the Lande model, the suitable and unsuitable sites are considered to be randomly interspersed. The model considers females only, assuming that females can always find a mate.

In the Lande metapopulation model, juveniles are assumed to inherit their mother's site with probability $e$; if they fail to inherit their natal site, they must disperse, in which case they can search

up to $m$ tracts (potential territories) before perishing. A juvenile survives only if she finds an unoccupied, suitable site, and the probability of doing this is

$$1 - (1 - e)(u + \hat{p}h)^m$$

where $\hat{p}$ is the proportion of the territories already occupied. Juvenile mortality during dispersal is thus density-dependent, because as population size increases, more of the suitable sites are already occupied and juveniles have a lessened chance of finding a suitable unoccupied site before perishing.

Lande calculates the "conditional" lifetime reproductive success of those females that live to find a suitable territory. The product of this conditional reproductive success and the probability of a dispersing juvenile female finding an unoccupied, suitable territory gives the expected lifetime reproductive success, $R_0$, which according to the Lotka-Euler equation equals unity for a stationary population. Accordingly, Lande solves the equation $R_0 = 1.0$ for the value of $\hat{p}$ in order to get the equilibrium proportion of suitable territories occupied.

The utility of metapopulation models can be easily demonstrated by simplifying the Lande expression for the probability of a dispersing juvenile finding an unoccupied, suitable site before perishing. Lande assumes that dispersing juveniles search both suitable and unsuitable sites. This is probably a realistic assumption if suitable and unsuitable sites look the same superficially and must be explored in detail in order to differentiate them. In some cases, however, such as might be the case for suitable forest intermixed with unsuitable fields, potentially unsuitable sites may be so obvious that the dispersing female need not waste her limited number of searches on finding them. The female still must search for an unoccupied site, so the probability of finding an unoccupied site before perishing becomes $1 - (1 - e)\hat{p}^m$.

The probability $(1 - e)$ of not inheriting the natal territory depends on when the juveniles disperse. If, for example, juveniles disperse in the fall when their parents are sure to still be alive, this probability reduces to unity. These simplifying assumptions make it easy to solve for the equilibrium proportion of suitable sites occupied by setting the finite rate of increase equal to unity as follows:

$$\lambda = P_A + bP_j \left[1 - (1 - e)\hat{p}^m\right] = 1.0$$

and solving for $\hat{p}$, the equilibrium proportion of suitable sites occupied.

The above equation can be solved for the equilibrium proportion of suitable sites occupied. According to the model, all other things being equal, the equilibrium population size declines linearly as the proportion of the entire landscape that is suitable declines (Figure A1). The decline of population size with decreasing reproductive success or decreasing survivorship is, however, nonlinear and may indeed be very abrupt (Figure A2). This is because for high values of $m$, virtually all suitable sites are found, so equilibrium population size remains about the same so long as the same amount of suitable habitat is available and $\lambda$ does not fall below 1.0.

Pulliam (1992) gives a hypothetical example based on this model in which the equilibrium population stays steady and then abruptly declines as the proportion of agricultural land in the landscape increases (Figure B). The example assumes that birds in territories next to

agricultural plots are exposed to high levels of pesticide residues in the food they feed their young and, as a result, have lower reproductive success. Thus, as a greater proportion of the landscape becomes agricultural, the average reproductive success decreases. At some point the reproductive success drops so low that $\bar{\lambda}$ is less than 1.0, and the population abruptly goes extinct. If the ability of dispersing juveniles to find suitable sites is high (large $m$), the proportion of suitable sites occupied is essentially a step function, abruptly declining from near 100% to 0%.

Such abrupt declines in populations may be difficult to predict because the problem may well go undetected until a critical threshold is reached. Such threshold responses could apply to a variety of situations, including habitat loss, exposure to toxins, and habitat fragmentation. Since catastrophic population collapse has been documented in a number of real-world situations, such as the Passenger Pigeon and the commercial fisheries mentioned above, threshold responses are a major unsolved problem facing conservationists. Models such as Lande's are useful tools for studying population threshold responses.

(1)

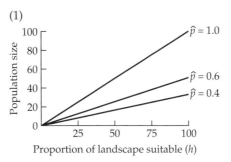

(2)

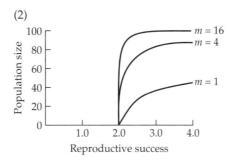

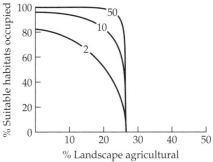

**Figure A** Population size depends on both the fraction of the landscape that is suitable and the demography of the species within suitable patches of habitat. In most cases, population size will increase linearly as the proportion of the landscape that is suitable increases. In Figure A1, $\hat{p}$ refers to the fraction of suitable sites occupied at demographic equilibrium. Population size can change abruptly with changes in demographic factors such as survival probability and reproductive success. In Figure A2, $m$ refers to the dispersal ability of the species; higher values of $m$ imply that the species is a better disperser and can therefore find a larger fraction of suitable sites.

**Figure B** If reproductive success or survival depends on landscape structure, population size can change abruptly as landscape features change. In this example, suitable habitat patches that are adjacent to agricultural land where pesticides are used are characterized by low reproductive success. Consequently, as the fraction of the landscape in agriculture increases and a greater fraction of other habitat patches abuts agricultural land, reproductive success declines. When reproductive success reaches the threshold necessary to balance mortality, the fraction of suitable habitat patches occupied (and therefore the population size) declines abruptly. The numbers on the three lines refer to relative dispersal ability ($m$), as discussed above.

Most published PVAs to date have combined field studies on important demographic parameters with simulation modeling of the possible effects of various extinction factors. Generally, the object of the analyses is to generate a prediction of the probability that a population will go extinct in a given

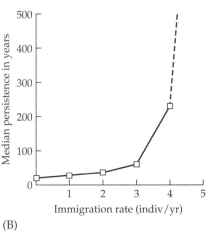

(A)    (B)

**Figure 7.6** Small populations of Acorn Woodpeckers are found in isolated oak canyons (A) in New Mexico. (B) A population viability model showed that these populations could persist only if some immigration between populations occurred. Persistence times of populations increased quickly as the average number of immigrants per population increased. (A, photograph by John B. Dunning; B, from Stacey and Taper 1992.)

number of years (e.g., "a 95% probability of extinction within 1000 years"). Murphy et al. (1990) have proposed that two different styles of PVA will be needed for different types of organisms. Organisms with low population densities that are restricted to small geographic ranges (most endangered large vertebrates, for example) will require a PVA that includes analysis of the genetic and demographic factors that affect small populations. This is the style of PVA that has been done most frequently to date. Smaller organisms, such as most threatened invertebrates, have a different set of problems. They frequently are restricted to a few habitat patches, but within those patches small organisms can reach high population densities. For these species, Murphy et al. (1990) propose that PVAs will need to emphasize environmental uncertainty and catastrophic factors.

Stacey and Taper (1992) provide an example of a PVA for a nonendangered bird, the Acorn Woodpecker (*Melanerpes formicivorus*), which is found in the oak woodlands of the western United States and Mexico (Figure 7.6). This species is normally found in small, isolated populations scattered across large regions. Stacey and Taper developed a simulation model to predict the effect of environmental uncertainty on the viability of individual woodpecker populations. In the simulations, when total isolation was imposed, most of the populations went extinct within 20 years. With a small amount of migration between populations, however, most of the simulated populations lasted more than 1000 years. At their New Mexico study sites, Stacey and Taper have records showing that small woodpecker populations have survived for over 70 years, suggesting that migration must be important in maintaining these natural populations.

In general, population viability cannot be assessed by focusing on a single patch of suitable habitat and the organisms living in it. Most organisms live in islands of suitable habitat embedded in a larger landscape. As the Acorn Woodpecker study demonstrated, there is often an exchange of individuals among suitable habitat patches in the landscape. Because the populations in the various patches are linked by the movement of dispersing individuals, the fates of the populations are interconnected. Studies of population viability of most organisms will therefore need to consider the importance of factors that link subpopulations within a metapopulation (see The Landscape Approach, below).

# ESSAY 7B
# Population Viability Analysis
## Determining Nature's Share

Mark L. Shaffer, The Wilderness Society

Until the human population stabilizes, a major challenge for conservation biology is to determine nature's share of the landscape. We must know how much land, and in what patterns, will allow natural dynamics to maintain the diversity of life in a global ecosystem that is already dominated by humankind. Population viability analysis is the branch of conservation biology that seeks to determine nature's share by understanding the relationship of habitat and species survival.

Since humankind began hunting, we have understood the importance of habitat *type* in determining the distribution and abundance of a species: you do not hunt for pronghorns in alpine meadows. Game management, both archaic and modern, extended this recognition to the equal importance of habitat *quality*. It reflects an understanding that there are degrees of habitat suitability for any species, and these are reflected in overall population features, such as abundance, fecundity, or average size. In fact, the very basis for modern game management is maintenance of habitat type and manipulation of habitat quality to achieve desired levels of distribution and abundance.

Over the past 30 years, studies of biogeography, particularly of island biotas, have shown us that habitat *quantity* is as fundamental to the survival of a species as is habitat type or quality. In other words, having the proper type of habitat, even of high quality, may not assure species survival unless there is enough of it.

In just the last 5 years, the controversy over the Spotted Owl and old-growth forests in the Pacific Northwest has taught us that habitat *pattern* is also crucial in determining a species' fate. Not only must we maintain the proper habitat of good quality in sufficient amounts, but that habitat must be arranged in an appropriate pattern across the landscape.

Like physicists searching for a grand unified theory explaining how the four fundamental forces (strong nuclear force, weak nuclear force, electromagnetism, and gravity) interact to control the structure and fate of the universe, conservation biologists now seek their own grand unified theory explaining how habitat type, quality, quantity, and pattern interact to control the structures and fates of species. Population viability analysis (PVA) is the first expression of this quest.

PVA seeks to determine how the likelihood of extinction changes in response to changes in habitat type, quality, quantity, and pattern. In a world with a fixed land area and a growing human population, competition for land use can only intensify. If land must be set aside from development to maintain habitat for certain species, how much land is enough?

The roots of PVA trace back to MacArthur and Wilson's (1967) island biogeography theory. In seeking to explain the relatively low species diversity of island biotas, they proposed that the number of species on an island at any time represented a balance between immigration of species to the island and extinction of species already present. Smaller islands had fewer species, in part, because they could support only smaller populations, and smaller populations should have higher extinction rates.

Given the pace at which modern civilization is fragmenting natural landscapes, it was not long before conservationists saw the similarity between an island and a stand of old-growth timber in a sea of clear-cuts, or a patch of coastal sage scrub in a sea of subdivisions. And it was not long before they began to examine the reasons why smaller populations should have higher extinction rates (Soulé and Wilcox 1980; Shaffer 1981; Gilpin and Soulé 1986). Population viability analysis was born.

The reason small populations are fragile, it turns out, is because of chance events. Chance operates at several levels that affect the likelihood of extinction. Chance plays a role in determining when individuals die, how many offspring they have or whether they can find suitable mates (called demographic stochasticity). Chance affects the weather, which affects the food supply and helps determine the rates of survival and fecundity (environmental stochasticity). Periodic major catastrophes such as floods, fires, and hurricanes can also be viewed as chance events; at least they are unpredictable (natural catastrophes). Chance even affects the genetic makeup of populations through genetic drift (genetic stochasticity).

All of these four chance factors become more important as population size gets smaller. Moreover, they can interact to reinforce one another's negative effects and draw small populations into what have been termed "extinction vortices" (Gilpin and Soulé 1986).

Among the earliest attempts to determine what all this means in real numbers for a real species was my work (Shaffer 1983) on the grizzly bear (*Ursus arctos horribilis*). Using very detailed data collected over a 12-year period in Yellowstone National Park and environs by John and Frank Craighead and their colleagues, I constructed a quantitative model of grizzly bear population dynamics that kept track of individual bears and incorporated the effects of chance events. The results demonstrated that if you want a grizzly bear population to have a 95% chance of persisting for a century, you have to have enough habitat to support 70–90 bears. If you want a higher probability of survival (say 99%), or the same probability but over a longer period of time (say 200 years), you must save even more habitat to support a larger, more durable population.

Although the above analysis was incomplete in that it did not include an assessment of the genetic effects of small population size or the impacts of natural catastrophes, it nonetheless captured the essence of what a PVA should be, namely, a data-based, quantitative assessment of the relationship between the likelihood of extinction and the amount of habitat available to a species.

Fifteen years, and at least 28 PVAs (Boyce 1992) later, we have made significant progress in understanding extinction dynamics. We better understand the threats to small populations and how these threats can interact to pull such populations toward extinction. And we are beginning to understand the geometry of extinction, how the loss and fragmentation of natural habitats can so dilute them across the landscape that they no longer support many of the species dependent on them. Efforts to devise a credible strategy for conserving the Spotted Owl have led to the first PVA for a true metapopulation (Thomas et al. 1990). This is a data-based, (partially) quantitative assessment of the relationship between the likelihood of owl extinction and both the amount *and* pattern of old-growth forest maintained across the landscape of the Pacific Northwest.

Still, we cannot say how much natural habitat is enough to perpetuate nature's diversity of species, for several reasons. First, the theoretical basis for assessing population viability is still developing. There is no single model of population dynamics sophisticated enough to simultaneously incorporate all classes of chance events. But even if

our theory were perfect, we know virtually nothing of the details of the life histories of the vast majority of species. Conservation biology operates in a model-rich but data-poor world, and the tub of species we need to know something about is filling rapidly: The Nature Conservancy has identified 9000 species native to the United States that may be at some risk of extinction.

How then to proceed? One of the major lessons of 20 years of the Endangered Species Act is that we should focus our efforts on conserving natural habitats and ecosystems, and not on attempting to rescue one endangered species at a time. Similarly, we should not attempt a quantitative PVA for every threatened or endangered

species. Instead, we need to concentrate our efforts on those species indicative of natural systems, species whose own area requirements for viability provide some index of the area requirements of the systems that support them. These will likely be top carnivores: large-bodied, long-lived, slowly reproducing species at the top of their ecosystem's food chain. If we can come to understand their requirements for viability, we will have gone a long way toward understanding the appropriate spatial requirements of the ecosystems that support them. In this way, PVA can assist in the quantification of landscape ecology, and in designing land use patterns that allow for perpetuation of overall biodiversity.

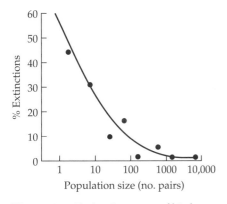

**Figure 7.7** Extinction rates of bird species as a function of population size on the California Channel Islands. Plotted is the percentage of populations in various size classes that became extinct during the study. (From Jones and Diamond 1976.)

**Figure 7.8** The checkerspot butterfly (*Euphydryas editha*) is the focus of one of the best long-term studies of metapopulation dynamics. See also Figures 9.15 and 10.12. (Photograph by P. R. Ehrlich.)

## Empirical Studies of Population Persistence

Thomas (1990) points out that, whereas estimates of population viability based on theoretical models are quite uncertain, a number of studies of real populations give us guidelines about population persistence. For example, Thomas refers to the extinctions of birds in the California Channel Islands over an 80-year period (Jones and Diamond 1976; Figure 7.7). Of populations on islands with fewer than 10 breeding pairs, 39% went extinct during the 80-year period, but only about 10% of the populations numbering between 10 and 100 pairs went extinct in the same time. Only one population numbering between 100 and 1000 went extinct, and no populations exceeding 1000 pairs went extinct. Thomas also refers to a study of birds on islands around the British coastline by Pimm et al. (1988), which found that populations of 1 or 2 pairs had a mean time to extinction of 1.6 years, populations of 3 to 5 pairs had a mean time to extinction of 3.5 years, and populations of 6 to 12 pairs had a mean time to extinction of 7.5 years. Thus, even among very small populations (1–12 pairs), the time to extinction increased with population size.

The above examples refer to persistence times of isolated populations receiving few or no immigrants. A number of studies have shown that the local populations of a metapopulation may often go extinct, but studies directly relevant to the persistence time of metapopulations per se are extremely rare. One of the best studies of metapopulation dynamics is the long-term study of checkerspot butterflies (*Euphydryas editha*, Figure 7.8) near Jasper Ridge in northern California, briefly mentioned in Chapter 6 (Ehrlich et al. 1980; Ehrlich and Murphy 1987; Murphy et al. 1990).

Checkerspot butterflies are found in scattered serpentine grasslands around the San Francisco Bay area, and such grassland habitat has been declining rapidly due to development. Ehrlich and Murphy (1987) point out that the butterflies at Jasper Ridge live in distinct demographic units or subpopulations despite the fact that the serpentine grassland habitat in which they occur is "essentially continuous" at Jasper Ridge and "uninterrupted by barriers to the butterfly's flight." The local demographic units are sufficiently connected by individual movement that they are likely part of the same genetic population. Ehrlich and Murphy describe the situation as a metapopulation that is "subdivided into groups that occupy clusters of habitat patches and interact extensively." More to the point, the demographic units fluctuate in size more or less independently of one another and are subject to local extinction and recolonization.

Although the checkerspot butterfly exists at a variety of locations in the San Francisco Bay area, not all populations are equal in their ability to resist environmental perturbations. The total population at Jasper Ridge is small, ranging from less than ten to a few hundred individuals. Such small populations are too small to maintain themselves indefinitely, particularly during periods of prolonged drought. Other populations are much larger and may persist through even the worst of environmental conditions. Murphy et al. (1990) review evidence that local populations in marginal areas frequently go extinct and are repopulated by emigration from nearby "reservoir" or source habitats. While the small population at Jasper Ridge may go extinct occasionally, Murphy et al. (1990) conclude that the metapopulation should be resilient to extinction because of the presence of the large reservoir subpopulation.

Although animals are generally thought to be better dispersers than plants, many plant species may also exist in metapopulations characterized by frequent local extinction and recolonization. One of the best studies of plant metapopulation dynamics is the work of Menges (1990, Menges et al. 1986) on Furbish's lousewort (*Pedicularis furbishiae*, Figure 7.9). This herbaceous perennial species is endemic to the Saint John River Valley in northern Maine, and lives in very unstable habitat patches along the riverbanks. Menges describes this lousewort as inhabiting "a disturbance/successional niche" defined by hydrology and vegetation response. The species is a poor competitor and seems to do best in low sites characterized by nonwoody vegetation, frequent flooding and springtime ice scour.

Menges and his colleagues measured habitat-specific demographic variables and concluded that in the absence of catastrophic disturbance, the wetter, early-successional sites can maintain viable populations. However, this system is characterized by catastrophic events that lead to local extinction due to ice scour and bank slumping. Menges developed a model incorporating much of the known biology of the species and its response to such catastrophic events, and concluded that local population extinction probability was high even at the best of sites. Thus, "individual *P. furbishiae* populations are temporary features of the riverine ecosystem," and metapopulation viability "depends on a positive balance between new populations and extinction" (Menges 1990).

**Figure 7.9** Furbish's lousewort is found in small isolated populations that are often destroyed by natural catastrophes. (Photograph by Sue Gawler.)

## The Landscape Approach

Individuals of the same species living in relatively close proximity to one another may experience quite different physical and biotic environments, even to the extent that some may not be able to survive and reproduce while others do very well. At spatial scales substantially larger than what one individual encounters, the landscape experienced by a population represents a mosaic of good and bad places for the species. The growth, or lack thereof, of the population is determined not only by the quality of the individual microsites occupied, but also by the spatial and temporal distribution of suitable and unsuitable microsites or patches of habitat.

Increasingly, conservationists are adopting the landscape perspective when designing management plans and analyzing the environmental factors affecting species of interest (Noss 1983). Conservation strategies must recognize that organisms move over heterogeneous landscapes, and therefore that saving a single patch of "critical habitat" will rarely be enough to maintain a population. Researchers working with aquatic systems were among the first to realize this principle, since a river or lake cannot be considered protected if the watershed that feeds the system is not included in the management plan. Similarly, recognition of concepts such as source–sink dynamics requires conservationists and land managers to adopt a landscape perspective. In many areas, this broader perspective requires planners to consider the landscape patterns and land use strategies outside of the land unit (park, forest district, county) that the planners work with directly (Noss 1983). Even in a region as large as Yellowstone National Park, wildlife managers are realizing that their management strategies must cut across artificial political and agency boundaries to establish a regionwide conservation plan (Turner et al. 1994; see also Case Study 6 in Chapter 17).

How is this landscape perspective developed and applied in the field? First, we must define what is meant by a landscape. A landscape is a mosaic of habitat patches across which organisms move, settle, reproduce, and eventually die (Forman and Godron 1986). The size of a landscape depends on the organism. A field or woodlot that is a single patch of relatively uniform quality for a bird or mammal may, at the same time, be a mosaic of patches of quite different quality for individual nematodes or shrubs. For any species, the landscape containing a population can, in principle, be mapped as a mosaic of suitable and unsuitable patches. These maps are the basic tool of the landscape ecologist. Each map is specific to the habitat requirements of one species and must be done at a scale appropriate to that organism. In general, the scale must be fine enough to resolve the areas occupied by individuals over significant portions of their lifetimes (Turner 1989; Turner et al. 1989).

In order to map the patches of suitable habitat for a particular species, one must have a set of criteria for drawing the habitat boundaries. Following Elton (1949) and Andrewartha and Birch (1984), a habitat boundary is chosen by an ecologist to circumscribe a "certain homogeneity with respect to the sort of environments it might provide for animals" (Andrewartha and Birch 1984). In managed landscapes, drawing habitat boundaries is usually simplified by the strong contrasts between habitats subjected to different management histories. For example, a pine plantation is clearly discernible from a neighboring old field or deciduous woodlot. In landscapes less dominated by human activities, habitat boundaries are often "softer" and more arbitrary.

Suitable sites for a particular species are often distributed as isolated patches embedded in a matrix of unsuitable habitat. Figure 7.10 provides an example of this type of landscape, showing suitable habitat for Bachman's Sparrow (*Aimophila aestivalis*), a species of management interest to the U.S. Forest Service. This bird is found on pinelands where timber is harvested.

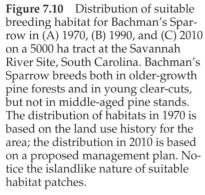

**Figure 7.10** Distribution of suitable breeding habitat for Bachman's Sparrow in (A) 1970, (B) 1990, and (C) 2010 on a 5000 ha tract at the Savannah River Site, South Carolina. Bachman's Sparrow breeds both in older-growth pine forests and in young clear-cuts, but not in middle-aged pine stands. The distribution of habitats in 1970 is based on the land use history for the area; the distribution in 2010 is based on a proposed management plan. Notice the islandlike nature of suitable habitat patches.

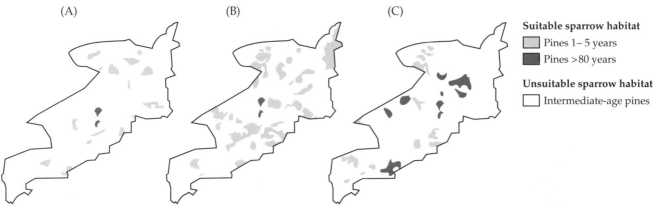

(A)   (B)   (C)

**Suitable sparrow habitat**

☐ Pines 1–5 years

■ Pines >80 years

**Unsuitable sparrow habitat**

☐ Intermediate-age pines

The maps in Figure 7.10 show distributions of suitable habitat on a 5000-ha tract of timberland at the Savannah River Site, a U.S. Department of Energy facility in South Carolina. At the Savannah River Site the sparrow is found in two habitats: frequently burned old-growth pine stands, and very young pine clear-cuts. Both of these habitat types have the appropriate vegetative structure and are therefore suitable breeding sites for this species (Dunning and Watts 1990). Hardwood stands and pine stands between 5 and about 80 years of age are unsuitable for Bachman's Sparrows. Figure 7.10B shows the distribution of suitable sites on the study area in 1990. Figure 7.10A shows the probable distribution of suitable sites 20 years earlier (1970) based on the known land use history of the area, while Figure 7.10C shows the projected distribution of suitable sites 20 years in the future (2010) based on a proposed management plan for the site. The maps indicate that the locations of suitable habitat patches change for this species on a relatively short time scale (20 years = 4–6 sparrow generations).

A number of factors that influence the location of suitable habitat for Bachman's Sparrow are quite general in that they influence the location of habitat for many terrestrial species. Factors such as soil type, topography, and vegetative cover all provide information on the suitability of a site for a particular species, and all of these factors can be readily mapped. For the Bachman's Sparrow, soil type and topography influence the rate at which seedling trees grow and, therefore, the ages of pine stands that have vegetation profiles suitable for the sparrow. In addition, time since disturbance, successional status, and management history may provide additional information on the suitability of a site. Knowledge of these factors improves our ability to map out suitable habitat patches for a species.

The combination of factors determining site suitability will be different for every species. Such information alone will not be enough to determine unambiguously the presence or absence of a species, but it can often be used to categorize habitats as suitable versus unsuitable, and in some cases to assign a probability of occupation. As discussed in the next section, a landscape map based on the number and location of suitable sites under existing or proposed land use patterns can be an invaluable tool for species management.

### Spatially Explicit Models

Metapopulation models of the sort discussed earlier are very general conceptual models that do not attempt to incorporate the complexities of real landscapes. As Levins (1966) pointed out, general models typically offer general insights, but they are neither very precise nor very realistic. One of the primary themes of both conservation biology and landscape ecology is that details, such as the geometry of habitat patches in a landscape, can influence population trends and extinction probabilities. Metapopulation models make very unrealistic assumptions about the dispersal behavior of individuals and do not reflect the complexity of real landscapes. Whereas such models are useful for gaining general insights into population dynamics, they are not as well suited for managing particular species on particular landscapes. In contrast, spatially explicit models of the sort discussed below are well suited for incorporating realistic details of particular species and landscapes but, because they are so specific, the conclusions reached from them cannot always be generalized to other species and landscapes.

**Spatially explicit population models** incorporate the actual locations of organisms and suitable patches of habitat, and explicitly consider the movement of organisms among such patches. The *Mobile Animal Population*, or MAP, is a class of spatially explicit population simulation models (Pulliam et al. 1992; Liu 1992) that simulate habitat-specific demography and the dispersal behavior of organisms on computer representations of real landscapes. In MAP models the landscape is represented as a grid of cells, each of which is the size of an individual territory of the species being simulated (e.g., 2.5 ha for Bachman's Sparrow or 1000 ha for the Spotted Owl; see map inserts in Figure 7.12). Clusters of adjacent cells represent the size and location of forest tracts in the landscape; these tracts are assumed to be relatively uniform in terms of suitability for the species of interest. MAP models contain subroutines that specify forest management practices, succession, and, in some cases, the growth rates of tree species. Thus, such a model can depict current landscape structure and project the landscape structure in the future based on a management plan specifying a harvest and replanting schedule. Other management activities such as thinning or burning stands, which might influence stand suitability, can be easily incorporated into MAP models. The most realistic MAP models are run on landscape maps generated by **geographic information systems** (GIS), which incorporate the actual distribution of habitat patches in a region. Whereas most MAP models run on landscapes of less than 10,000 ha, MAP models can simulate landscape change and population dynamics over 100,000 ha or more.

Analyses using MAP models have proven valuable in a variety of conservation situations. For example, BACHMAP, a MAP model developed specifically for Bachman's Sparrow, is being used to determine how forest management practices may influence the population viability of the sparrow in pine forests in the southeastern United States. One analysis using BACHMAP demonstrated that aspects of a management plan designed to improve habitat for one endangered species (the Red-cockaded Woodpecker) may cause a short-term decline in the sparrow's numbers, thus potentially creating a second species requiring management intervention. MAP models can become innovative tools for avoiding this type of unintended effect during the design of management plans (see Box 7C).

## Box 7C
## Conservation of Nontarget Species in Managed Landscapes
### The Role of Population Models

Traditionally, wildlife management has focused on the preservation of single species. For many decades, public land management emphasized game animals or other species with economic importance. In more recent years, additional attention has shifted to threatened and endangered species. Single-species management, however, also affects dozens of nontarget species found in the same habitats. Such nontarget effects are rarely assessed prior to implementation of the management actions. As conservationists call for greater emphasis on management for biodiversity, it has become increasingly important to develop tools that allow one to assess the effects of a specific management strategy on a wide variety of organisms.

One potential tool for this purpose is population simulation models linked to maps that capture the complexity of real-world landscapes. With such models, the responses of many different organisms, including both target and nontarget species, to a specific landscape change can be modeled and assessed. Such an approach requires (1) a population model that is flexible enough to reflect the life history and behavior of species of interest, (2) realistic landscape maps, usually created through a geographic information system (GIS), and (3) habitat-specific information on the species' distribution and demography to parameterize the model.

One group of models that fits this description is the MAP models, designed to model *Mobile Animal Populations* in complex landscapes (Pulliam et al. 1992). One MAP model has been developed to model the population dynamics of Bachman's Sparrow, a declining species of management interest in the southeastern United States. Conservationists have used this model to determine how this species may be affected by management strategies designed to preserve populations of the endangered Red-cockaded Woodpecker, which is found in some of the same habitats as Bachman's Sparrow.

Bachman's Sparrow is found in pine woodlands that contain a dense ground cover of grasses and forbs as well as relatively open understories with few shrubs (Dunning and Watts 1990). These conditions are found in the oldest of mature pine forests (> 80 years old) or in early successional habitats such as 1–5 year-old clear-cuts. Mature pine forest managed for the Red-cockaded Woodpecker usually provides adequate habitat for Bachman's Sparrow. In many areas, patches of habitat suitable for the sparrow (either mature forest or clear-cuts) are found only as isolated islands embedded in a landscape of unsuitable habitat (see Figure 7.10).

Populations of the sparrow have declined since the 1930s to the point where the species is absent over much of its former range. Even where it is still reasonably common, the sparrow is locally distributed and absent from many patches of seemingly suitable habitat. This population decline, and the absence of the bird from many areas, may be related to the scattered distribution of suitable habitat patches, if the sparrows find it difficult to find and colonize unoccupied territories in isolated clear-cuts or mature stands. We analyzed landscape change and the population dynamics of the Bachman's Sparrow using BACHMAP, a MAP model parameterized for the sparrow. In this analysis, we used landscape maps that reflect the complex habitat mosaics of the Savannah River Site (SRS), a large region of pine forest in South Carolina managed by the U.S. Forest Service for timber production and wildlife conservation.

We have used our MAP model to study the current management strategies at the SRS and their effect on nontarget organisms. The U.S. Forest Service has developed a 50-year Operation Plan that sets management strategies for meeting wildlife goals for the SRS. The Operation Plan is a model for multiple species management, because it lists target goals for over 42 species at the SRS. A majority of the specific management practices described in the Op-

eration Plan, however, deals specifically with the endangered Red-cockaded Woodpecker, because the Endangered Species Act dictates that the needs of the woodpecker be given priority. We modeled the Operation Plan to determine how Bachman's Sparrow, a nontarget species of most of the specified management strategies, would fare under the Operation Plan.

Our studies have suggested that many aspects of management have a strong effect on the sparrow. For example, mature pine forest is now a rare habitat type in most areas of southern pine timberlands. Our simulations suggest, however, that it can be a very important habitat for the sparrows. Simulations that included a small amount of mature forest in the landscape almost always supported at least a small sparrow population. Without the mature forest patches, the sparrow populations often suffered extinction, even if a relatively large amount of clear-cut habitat was available (Pulliam et al. 1992). The mature forest acted as a source habitat that produced dispersers that would colonize the surrounding clear-cut habitat. As has been suggested in analytical models of source and sink habitats, a small population in a source habitat patch may be critical for supporting a much larger sink population (Pulliam 1988).

Our simulations suggest that in general the sparrow would benefit from the changes specified in the Operation Plan. To benefit the woodpecker, which is restricted to mature pine forest stands, the Operation Plan proposed increasing the overall age of the SRS forest. Since Bachman's Sparrows also use mature forest,

over the long term these changes should result in a large increase in the sparrow population. Over the first 1–2 decades of the Operation Plan, however, our simulations suggest that the sparrow population will decline to a dangerously low level. This decline reflects the decrease in suitable habitat caused by the low numbers of clear-cuts created while the forests are allowed to age.

Thus, the Operation Plan as modeled may have some unintended negative effects on the sparrow, despite the fact that the sparrow shares a major habitat type—mature pine forest—with the main target species of the Plan. Several additional measures that the Forest Service has initiated may increase the amount of suitable habitat during these first few decades, which may help counter the negative effect on the sparrow population that we saw in our simulations. In particular, our simulations show that one management program, if expanded, would greatly increase the sparrow population. This program manages middle-aged pine stands (50–70 years old) in a manner that generates the ground vegetation found in mature pine habitat, and therefore provides suitable habitat for the sparrow in a wider variety of pine age classes. A series of MAP models, each parameterized for other nontarget species, would give the managers of the SRS a research tool that could be used to test the effects of the Operation Plan on a wide variety of species. Population simulation models linked to GIS landscape maps should prove to be increasingly valuable tools for land managers and conservation biologists in the future.

A spatially explicit model developed for Yellowstone National Park has been used to show that wintering herds of bison and elk respond to the local patterns of habitat diversity caused by large-scale fires (Turner et al. 1994; Figure 7.11). The 1988 fires at Yellowstone, although dramatically large and well publicized, proved to be well within the range of disturbance to which the herds could respond. Spatially explicit population models developed for the Spotted Owl (McKelvey et al. 1993) have also proven to be valuable conservation tools (Figure 7.12). Much of the current conservation plan for the owl in the Pacific Northwest has been tested using the Spotted Owl model (Verner et al. 1992; McKelvey et al. 1993). An analysis of Spotted Owl populations in southern California using the spatially explicit Spotted Owl model has identified the owl populations in the San Gabriel and San Bernardino Mountains as being critical to the viability of the entire southern California metapopulation (Verner et al. 1992).

Spatially explicit models provide land managers with a new tool for predicting how management plans and land use changes may affect species of management concern. While some spatially explicit models are sufficiently

**Figure 7.11** GIS map of part of Yellowstone National Park, showing the distribution of burned and unburned forest after the fires in 1988. Burned patches are oriented NE–SW due to prevailing winds during the fires. A spatially explicit model of this region showed that bison and elk herds were able to respond effectively to the new distributions of habitats caused by the fires. (From Turner et al., unpublished manuscript.)

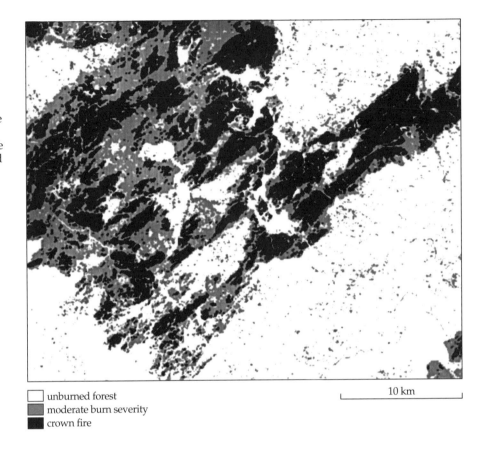

☐ unburned forest
▨ moderate burn severity
■ crown fire

10 km

well developed and parameterized to be used in conservation and management, for most species the relevant population parameters are not known, and several years of concentrated fieldwork would be required to collect the large amount of data needed to parameterize the models.

## Summary

An understanding of the fluctuations in numbers of natural populations and the application of this understanding to the conservation of species must be firmly based on an understanding of the factors influencing spatial and temporal variability in population demography. All populations exist in heterogeneous landscapes and different individuals experience different conditions depending on when and where they are located. Some locations (termed "sources") are highly productive and produce an excess of individuals that often populate less productive locations ("sinks"), where local mortality exceeds reproduction. In some cases, sink populations may be larger than the source populations that support them. Accordingly, great care must be exercised in the design of nature reserves to identify and protect source habitats.

Population viability depends not just on the quality of local patches of habitat, but also on the number and location of patches and the amount of movement between them. The dispersal mode of a population is a key factor in determining its viability. In many cases population dynamics must be studied at the level of many local patches of habitat, and population models must incorporate immigration and emigration explicitly. Metapopulation models that consider the dynamics of many interacting subpopulations in a habitat mosaic demonstrate that the fraction of a landscape suitable for a

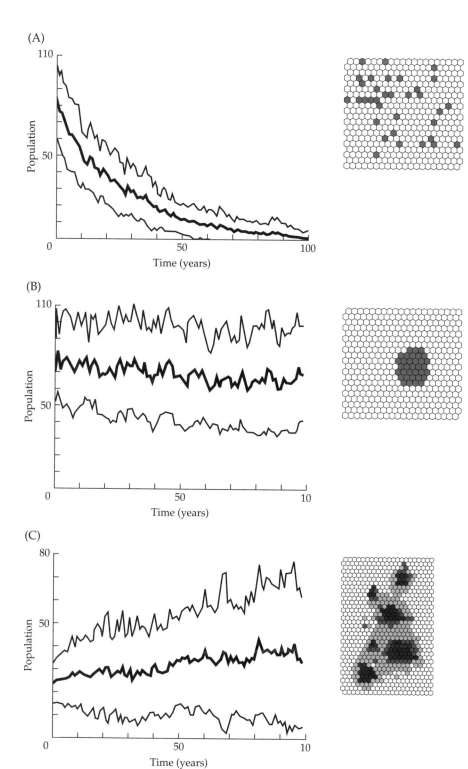

**Figure 7.12** Results of a simulation model for Spotted Owls that varied only the configuration of suitable and unsuitable habitat; all other population parameters were held constant. All results are based on 30 simulations; the heavy line in each graph is the mean population response, and the thin lines are one standard deviation from the mean. (A) Suitable habitat is randomly scattered. (B) Suitable habitat is arrayed in one large block. (C) Clusters of suitable habitat are surrounded by marginal habitat (buffers). (From McKelvey et al. 1993.)

given species and the magnitude of dispersal between suitable patches are critical components of population viability. Unlike metapopulation models, spatially explicit population models consider the exact location of habitat patches and can incorporate detailed behavioral information about how dispersing individuals locate suitable habitat. Spatially explicit models can be useful tools for testing specific conservation strategies in a given region, while metapopulation models are more useful for testing general landscape influences using hypothetical populations.

A number of theoretical models are now available for quantitative analysis of population viability and extinction probability. These models should be viewed as useful additions to the collection of tools available for understanding the dynamics of natural populations. The more realistic models are, however, very data hungry and are only as good as the natural history insights and field studies that support them.

## Questions for Discussion

1. Traditionally, population studies have been done at a local scale on homogeneous populations. Recently there has been a shift toward landscape studies. What are some of the advantages of working at the landscape scale? Are there any disadvantages?

2. In a paper discussed in this chapter, Davidson and Andrewartha showed that thrip populations decline precipitously in dry summers when food is in short supply. Does this necessarily mean that thrips are food-limited or that they are regulated in a density–dependent manner? What further evidence would be required to demonstrate density-dependence?

3. In the late 1960s, Furbish's lousewort came to national attention when a dam was proposed for the St. John River in Maine. This dam would have eliminated floods and ice scour in the river valley, thus eliminating the creation of new habitat patches for this plant. How would this have affected the lousewort's population dynamics? Can you think of any management actions that might be taken to mitigate the dam's impact?

4. How could management designed to improve conditions for an endangered species actually have negative effects on other species? Do you know of any cases in which this has actually occurred or might occur in the future? What could a land manager do to prevent this situation from occurring?

5. Why is it necessary to consider population regulation from a hierarchical perspective? Can you think of a real population where different factors at the local and the regional scales limit population growth? How could policies in effect at a regional scale make it difficult to manage populations by manipulating local factors?

6. This chapter emphasizes that conservationists must consider habitat quality as well as habitat quantity when managing for threatened organisms. What is meant by habitat quality and how would land managers measure and/or improve it?

7. Many recent studies on local populations of migratory birds have found that birth rates are lower than expected, and, in some cases, that local birth rates are not as high as local death rates. Does this necessarily mean that the local populations are about to go extinct? How would this finding influence your attitude toward the need to preserve other habitats in the local area and the region?

8. Murphy et al. (1990) argued that small organisms face different kinds of extinction threats than do large endangered vertebrates. Why is this so? Why are different kinds of population viability analyses necessary for these different groups of organisms?

# Suggestions for Further Reading

Andrewartha, H. G. and L. C. Birch. 1984. *The Ecological Web.* University of Chicago Press, Chicago and London. This book presents an excellent overview of how resources, mates, predators, and other hazards influence population dynamics. Andrewartha and Birch view the environment of an organism as "everything that might influence its chance to survive and reproduce." The book is a good beginning source for readers who want more information on the topic of population regulation.

Dunning, J. B., D. J. Stewart, B. J. Danielson, B. R. Noon, T. Root, R. H. Lamberson and T. Stevens. 1994. Spatially-explicit population models: Current forms and future uses. *Ecol. Appl.* in press. Most population models do not consider space explicitly and, therefore, do not incorporate the ways in which the dynamics of populations might change as the relative shapes and positions of habitat patches change. This paper presents a summary of how spatially explicit models are being used to further our understanding of the role of spatial location in determining population processes. The paper emphasizes how such models are being used in conservation and management applications.

Gilpin, M. E. and M. E. Soulé. 1986. Minimum viable populations: Processes of species extinction. In M. E. Soulé (ed.). *Conservation Biology: The Science of Scarcity and Diversity.* Sinauer Associates, Sunderland, MA, pp. 19–34. A conceptual model for understanding and studying population viability. In this chapter, Gilpin and Soulé started many people thinking about the causes of extinction and how one might study them. Gilpin and Soulé argue that many species are threatened because they experience a specific combination of life history traits and environmental conditions (called an "extinction vortex") that makes the species susceptible to extinction. One has to recognize the kinds of threats that a given species is likely to experience before one can design a plan to protect that species.

Hanski, I. and M. E. Gilpin. 1991. Metapopulation dynamics: Brief history and conceptual domain. *Biol. J. Linn. Soc.* 42:3–16. This paper provides a brief history of the metapopulation concept and presents a survey of metapopulation terminology. The paper also reviews a number of studies that have been conducted on single-species and multispecies metapopulations and relates those studies to conservation issues.

Pulliam, H. R. 1988. Sources, sinks, and population regulation. *Am. Nat.* 132:757–785. Although the idea of source and sink habitats had been described previously, this paper was the first to analyze the consequences of sources and sinks for population dynamics. Pulliam proposed that many organisms live in sink habitat where local reproduction is insufficient to balance local mortality. Large sink populations might be common in nature, being maintained by immigration from very productive source habitats. The paper also discusses the implications of sources and sinks for the study of population conservation.

Shaffer, M. L. 1981. Minimum population sizes for species conservation. *BioScience* 31:131–134. This paper was one of the first to discuss the concept of a minimum population size necessary to maintain viability. Schaffer proposed that the probability of population extinction could be analyzed by focusing on the interaction of four factors: demographic uncertainty, environmental stochasticity, natural catastrophes, and genetic uncertainty.

We also suggest the following papers by the researchers who have developed the analytical and spatially explicit models for Spotted Owls. These papers help describe the theory and data underlying the models and their results, and discuss how these models can be used in today's political environment:

Noon, B. and C. Biles. 1990. *J. Wildl. Mgmt.* 54:18–27. (Analytical modeling attempt to see if owl populations are declining.)

Murphy, D. and B. Noon. 1992. *Conserv. Biol.* 2:3–17. (Description of use of models in the Pacific Northwest political and management arena.)

Verner, J. et al. 1992. *The California Spotted Owl: A Technical Assessment of Its Current Status.* U.S. Forest Service General Technical Report PSW-GTR-133. (Complete description of databases and modeling efforts for the California subspecies.)

# III

# System-Level Concerns

# 8

# Community-Level Conservation

## Species Interactions, Disturbance Regimes, and Invading Species

*A thing is right when it tends to preserve the integrity, stability,*
*and beauty of the biotic community. It is wrong when it tends otherwise.*

*Aldo Leopold, 1949*

Much of conservation, and much of our previous discussion, deals with single species and their welfare. The Endangered Species Act, CITES, genetic conservation, and ex situ preservation in zoos, aquariums, and arboretums all deal with the species as a unit. However, species must ultimately exist in natural settings, within functioning communities and ecosystems, interacting with other species and the abiotic environment. Conservation must therefore also focus on species interactions and the systems within which these interactions occur.

The very nature of the problem with which we are dealing—loss of and protection of biodiversity—dictates that we consider collections of interacting species and not just properties and declines of single species. By definition, bio*diversity* ultimately means working at the community and ecosystem levels and dealing with the effects of species declines and losses on other species and on interactive processes. Unfortunately, the principles of community ecology are less certain than some other areas of ecology and evolution, and their application to conservation problems is less well developed. Consequently, we will focus less specifically on community ecology in conservation in this chapter, and more on particular and critical species interactions.

Although some mention has been made in previous chapters of species interactions and system-wide conservation, in this chapter we will explore those topics in greater depth. In particular, we will examine the roles of keystone species, mutualisms, disturbance regimes, and the effects of invading species. We will also explore patterns of community-level changes over ecological and evolutionary time to search for lessons useful in understanding the effects of contemporary changes affecting conservation efforts.

## Critical Species Interactions

Not all species in a community are equal in their contributions to community structure and processes, and not all interactions are vital. Some community members or species interactions are especially critical because they affect many other species, process materials out of proportion to their numbers or biomass, or have particularly strong links to other species or even other systems. In contrast, some species may be quite removable from, or substitutable in, a community, with little to no effect on its structure or function. Conservation biologists should identify and focus research on those species or interactions that are especially critical to community dynamics. We will discuss three classes of such interactions here.

### The Role of Keystone Species

Some species, because of their trophic position, production of food resources, or other interactions, play a disproportionately large role in community structure, and are called keystone species. We began to develop the idea of keystone species in Chapter 5, and will explore it further here. A classic example of a keystone species is the sea star *Pisaster ochraceus*, which preys on invertebrate communities in the rocky intertidal zone along the North American Pacific coast. By conducting exclusion experiments in which sea stars were removed, Paine (1966, 1969) found that species richness of mussels, barnacles, snails, and other rocky shore inhabitants decreased from 15 with sea stars present to 8 without them. Sea star predation apparently kept densities of all species low, but especially those of the competitive dominant, a mussel (*Mytilus californianus*) which, in the absence of predation, usurped a larger proportion of limiting space and thus excluded several other species. Consequently, *Pisaster* is known as a keystone predator.

The sea otter (*Enhydra lutris*, Figure 8.1), which preys on sea urchins (*Strongylocentrotus droebachiensis*) in large numbers, appears to be another keystone predator. When sea otter populations declined in the 20th century through fur trapping and removal by fishermen, sea urchin populations expanded greatly and grazed heavily on algae and kelp. In some places, they effectively destroyed entire kelp forests, which in turn lowered the diversity of the other plants and animals in that habitat (Estes and Palmisano 1974). Reintroduction of sea otters reversed this situation, and kelp beds recovered (Krebs 1988).

Terborgh (1986) described another type of keystone species, a keystone food resource. The tropical forests of Central and South America are not bountiful and constant Gardens of Eden, as they are often portrayed. The diverse mammal assemblages of such regions, including many species of primates, bats, birds, and marsupials, depend on a diverse collection of fruits and seeds for much of their caloric intake. There is usually about a 3-month period in the year when production drops to or below the level of consumptive demands, and most mammals must migrate or expand their diets. Figs, nectar, and miscellaneous fruits, representing less than 1% of plant species diversity, appear to be keystone resources because they sustain nearly the entire frugivore community through this period of scarcity. Without these few plant resources, the frugivore community would have a much more difficult time surviving this period.

**Figure 8.1**   The sea otter is a keystone species that controls abundance of sea urchins, which in turn prevents overgrazing of kelp beds. (Photograph © Stephen J. Krasemann/DRK Photo.)

**Figure 8.2** Beavers fundamentally change the characteristics of aquatic systems, thus acting as keystone species through habitat modification. This particular beaver dam and lodge in northwestern New Jersey flooded a large tract of land, killing streamside trees and creating a lake environment. (Photograph by G. K. Meffe.)

Another type of keystone species is a habitat modifier. Examples include the beaver (*Castor canadensis*) and the African elephant (*Loxodonta africana*). Beavers turn free-flowing, barrier-free streams into sluggish ponds and lakes, and create impediments to movement by fishes (Figure 8.2). Beaver dams change not only flow rate, but a myriad of other habitat characteristics, including nutrient dynamics, sedimentation rates, channel geomorphology, and biogeochemical cycles (Naiman et al. 1986); they also change habitat availability for terrestrial and amphibious species, and can kill large expanses of terrestrial forests, at the same time creating opportunities for aquatic or semiaquatic species.

The African elephant is an herbivore that browses on a variety of woody plants, supplemented by grasses. When feeding on shrubs, or small to large trees, the elephants strip bark and branches, and sometimes uproot and trample entire trees. Dense woodlands can be transformed by elephant feeding into woodland-grasslands or even open grasslands (Figure 8.3). These areas may support more grazing ungulates, but are then more susceptible to fire, which further favors grasses over woody plants. This keystone browser thus can change the major plant features of entire landscapes.

Yet another type of keystone species includes inconspicuous and even microscopic members of ecosystems whose biological processes are critical to the functioning of larger, more evident species. For example, mycorrhizal fungi are often associated with the roots of many species of trees and enhance the plant's ability to extract soil minerals (Harley and Smith 1983). The fungi are critical to the growth and productivity of the trees, and may also protect the roots from infections by producing antibiotics. In the tropics, many trees are obligately dependent on mycorrhizal fungi, and the absence of appropriate fungi in the soil after large agricultural or natural disturbances may greatly retard reforestation (Janos 1980). Such fungi are no less important in temperate zones, especially for gymnosperm trees (Marks and Kozlowski 1973). Bacteria, tiny invertebrates, and algae and fungi all exist in soils and break down and decompose dead matter that would otherwise build up and remain unavailable to living species. The great cycles of nature would literally shut down were it not for these inconspicuous but keystone species (Wilson 1987).

Removal, addition, or change of population size of keystone species locally can have wide-ranging effects on other species, on processes and interactions, and even on landforms. As we have seen, in many cases keystone species are large, predaceous, or otherwise of direct interest to humans. In other cases they may be small and inconspicuous; they can even be rare and

**Figure 8.3** Elephants greatly alter their environments and can change a forested area into a grassland. In Tsavo National Park, Kenya, elephants have stripped bare all large vegetation within the park, which is separated by a road, a railroad, and two fire breaks for a non-park area. By creating a more barren landscape, elephants are acting as a keystone species. (Photograph by D. B. Botkin.)

only a minor part of the biomass. Regardless, the nature of keystone species' effects is such that they typically play a part in trophic interactions—as predators on competitive dominants, mutualists such as pollinators and mycorrhizal fungi, major dispersers of seeds, herbivores that change vegetative conditions for other grazers, or decomposers of dead matter. It is these trophic relations that are largely responsible for the structure of natural communities and ecosystems; disrupting this structure can have repercussions far beyond the immediate and obvious interactions involved.

Despite the apparently clear relations of some putative keystone species to their communities, the concept presents some problems in its application to conservation (Mills et al. 1993). First, it is not rigorously defined; the keystone concept can mean different things to different people. Second, there is a range in the strength of the keystone species' effects, and manipulation of combinations of a few non-keystone species could have the same or greater effects than manipulating the apparent keystone species. Third, a focus simply on protection of keystone species could fail to protect other species of interest or the system at large. Clearly, protection of a few keystones, even if we knew what they were, would not guarantee successful system conservation.

Thus, Mills et al. (1993) argue that "the complexity of ecological interactions and ignorance of them militates against the application of the keystone-species concept for practical management recommendations . . . Instead, we advocate the study of interaction strengths and subsequent application of the results into management plans and policy decisions." We agree with this assessment; as we said earlier in this chapter, conservation biologists should focus their research on identifying and understanding the strongest interactions in communities, regardless of what we call them. Throughout this book we will continue to refer to "keystone" species and resources, but with the caveat that the term will simply refer to species and resources that have a disproportionate effect on the rest of the community. Thus, related terms, such as "mobile links" in Chapter 5, may be used for particular circumstances, but the point remains that conservation biologists need to identify and focus on the most significant interactions.

### Mutualisms

**Mutualistic** relationships, a particular type of keystone process in which two or more species benefit from an interaction, can be an especially important conservation interest. For example, many angiosperms must be pollinated by a particular species of insect (a mobile link; see Chapter 5), and have evolved elaborate mechanisms to attract specific insects and thereby ensure that pollen is transferred to other individuals (Figure 8.4). Likewise, seed dispersal is a critical function for many plants, and some have evolved elabo-

**Figure 8.4** Euglossine bees are important, specialized tropical pollinators of orchids, aroids, and other plants. (A) Euglossine bees visiting an aroid plant. Because individual plants are visited repeatedly by the same bee, these bees act as "mobile link mutualists." (B) Orchid pollen sacs (pollenia) adhere to the backs of bees. (Photographs by C. R. Carroll.)

(A)

(B)

(A)

(B)

**Figure 8.5**   Numerous mechanisms have evolved for efficient dispersal of seeds. Some seeds, such as this Acacia (A), are attractive to birds, which ingest the seeds and later pass them. Other seed types are attractive to mammals, such as this agouti (B). (Photographs by D. H. Janzen and Winifred Hallwachs.)

rate mechanisms to disperse their seeds by means of animals (Figure 8.5). The very existence of fruit is attributable to the plant's need for seed dispersal. Legumes and their nitrogen-fixing bacteria in root nodules are another example of a plant mutualism.

Animals can form mutualistic relationships with other animals as well. A classic example is parasite pickers, which remove parasites from other species. Some birds are known to clean parasites from the bodies of rhinoceroses or other large mammals, and wrasses (small marine fishes) set up "cleaning stations," where large, often predaceous fishes come to be relieved of their parasites (Feder 1966; Snelson et al. 1990). A different type of animal mutualism is a nesting association. Some stream fish species spawn in the nests built by other species, and may help to fan the eggs and reduce predation rates on both species (Wallin 1989).

Because they affect more than one species, and often incorporate a critical function with far-reaching community effects, mutualisms should be identified and maintained whenever possible. It is easy to see that the loss of a seemingly insignificant species such as an insect could have much larger ramifications for the community as a whole if the insect is involved in a critical mutualism. For example, loss of a pollinator could lead to local extinction of a flowering annual, which could then lead to loss of other insects that may be associated with that annual; loss of a seed food resource for small mammals would reduce prey availability for snakes and birds; and so forth. The importance of tightly coevolved species interactions is further elaborated by Douglas Futuyma in Essay 8A.

## ESSAY 8A
# The Evolution and Importance of Species Interactions

Douglas J. Futuyma, State University of New York, Stony Brook

Charles Darwin, a great thinker and an outstanding naturalist, remarked in *On the Origin of Species* that in England, red clover is pollinated exclusively by bumblebees (or humblebees, as they are called in England), that "the number of humblebees in any district depends in a great measure upon the number of field-mice, which destroy their combs and nests,"and that since "the number of mice is largely dependent, as every one knows, on the number of cats . . . It is quite credible that the presence of a feline animal in large numbers in a district might determine, through the intervention first of mice and then of bees, the frequency of certain flowers in that district!"

Darwin's perception of the complex interactions among the species in a community has been thoroughly substantiated. The abundance of every species is influenced by that of other species, which serve as its food, as mutualists, predators, parasites, or competitors, or which create its habitat or influence it indirectly though such interventions as Darwin described. Consequently, substantial changes in the abundance of one species will often threaten the extinction of others.

Although some effects are obvious, such as those of exotic predators, other species interactions are more subtle, yet still fragile. Many of these have their origin in two evolutionary phenomena—the evolution of specialization and the coevolution of species—which often go hand in hand.

All species are ecologically specialized in one way or another, sometimes to an extraordinary degree. The koala eats only *Eucalyptus* leaves, for example, and some snakes eat only crayfish or termites or other snakes. Specialization reaches its apogee in many parasites that attack only one or a few related species of hosts, and in herbivorous insects. The majority of the more than half million species of herbivorous insects have diet restrictions like that of the Colorado potato beetle, which will feed only on potato and a few closely related plants, and will starve to death if confined to any other plant. Related species of insects often feed on related plants; for example, larvae of each of the 60 or more species of Neotropical butterflies in the tribe Heliconiini feed only on particular species of passionflowers (Passifloraceae). Thus, much the same feeding habit has been retained throughout the time it has taken for the ancestral heliconiine to give rise to all these species.

This long-term restriction in diet has persisted in some groups of insects for at least 40 million years, which suggests that the insects may have little potential for adapting to different kinds of plants. In my laboratory, we are studying genetic variation in several species of specialized leaf beetles, to determine whether they have the genetic potential for evolving changes in their willingness to feed on, or in their capacity to grow and survive on, plants other than their natural hosts. In some instances, they do have such a capacity, but in most cases we find no evidence

that they could adapt even to plants that are the normal hosts of closely related species of beetles. A species that feeds only on ragweed, for example, shows no hint of a genetic potential to feed on goldenrod, a member of the same family that is the host of several species in the same beetle genus. An obvious conservation implication of this work is that loss of plant species could easily result in simultaneous losses of specialized insect species.

Coevolution is the process of reciprocal adaptation among interacting species. All kinds of ecological interactions may coevolve, but I shall cite examples only of mimicry and mutualism.

The heliconiine butterflies, mentioned above, are famous for their mimetic color patterns. They are distasteful to birds, and advertise their unpalatability by bright coloration that is recognized by birds that learn, after one unpleasant experience, not to attack them. Individuals of each of two or more unpalatable species gain advantage from possessing the same color pattern, since they then profit from the birds' experience with any of the other species. In tropical America, several species of heliconiines have an almost identical orange and black tiger-striped pattern, evolved independently in several evolutionary lineages; moreover, the same pattern has evolved in some distasteful ithomiine butterflies—a quite unrelated group—as well as in some other butterflies that are palatable, but gain protection from resemblance to the distasteful "models."

Mutualism is an ecological interaction in which each of two (or more) species profits by using the other as a resource. (It would be better called "reciprocal exploitation," because neither species is doing the other an altruistic favor.) Often the interactions are highly specialized. A spectacular example is provided by the more than 900 species of figs (*Ficus*) throughout the tropics and the tiny wasps (Agaonidae) that pollinate them. The astonishing fact is that almost every fig species is pollinated by only one species of wasp, which uses only one species of fig. It appears likely that the specificity of this interaction is responsible for the origin of new pairs of associated species, for if

a genetic variant of one fig species were to be visited exclusively by a wasp variant that responds exclusively to that fig, it would form the basis of a new reproductively isolated species.

The biology of the fig/wasp interaction is extraordinary. The tiny fig flowers are enclosed within a hollow structure (syconium) with an opening that is occluded by scales that differ in form among fig species. The scales apparently prevent the wrong species of wasp from entering. In most fig species, the syconium contains male flowers and both short and long female flowers. The female wasp enters, bringing with her pollen, held in special structures, which she then actively places on the female flowers' stigmas. She inserts an egg into each of many female flowers, but her ovipositor can reach the ovaries of only the short flowers, and it is in these that the larvae develop. Seeds develop only from long flowers, in which a wasp egg does not hatch. The female wasp dies, and her offspring emerge and mate within the syconium. The males die within, but the females gather pollen from the male flowers and then emerge to repeat the cycle.

Space does not permit exploration of the many fascinating questions about evolution that the fig/wasp system raises. But we should note that this exquisite coadaptation of species to each other has far-reaching ecological and conservation effects. It has caused the evolution of an extremely diverse group of plants. In many tropical forests, figs of various species are abundant, and are extremely important resources for birds, bats, monkeys, various other mammals, and even fish, which all feed on the fruit. Wasps about 1 mm long, which no one but an entomologist would notice unless he or she already knew about them, are fundamentally important components—perhaps keystone species—of many tropical communities. The long history of evolution, often of small, obscure species, has given rise to intricate interactions on which the structure of many communities depends. Conservation of these communities is dependent on the retention of these myriad species interactions.

## Indirect Effects and Diffuse Interactions

One salient feature of keystone predators is that their indirect interactions with non-prey species can be very strong; their presence in a community can have far-reaching effects, even on species they do not consume. These indirect effects, though less obvious than predation, may be critical to community structure and thus be of conservation interest. Examples of such interactions are legion: two, one involving birds and one involving fishes, should suffice to illustrate this type of interaction.

Throughout its range in North America, the Peregrine Falcon, a predator on other birds, declined in abundance for several decades in this century due to pesticide effects on its reproduction. Recovery beginning in the 1970s restored the species to some of its former range. On Tatoosh Island, Washington, Peregrine Falcon abundance increased from the late 1970s throughout the 1980s. Paine et al. (1990) studied the falcon and other native birds on the island during this period. They found that some species of birds, especially two species of auklets, declined after falcons increased, as a result of predation, a direct interaction. However, other species increased in abundance. In particular, Pelagic Cormorants (*Phalacrocorax pelagicus*) and Common Murres (*Uria aalge*) increased significantly in the few years after falcons became abundant, even though murres are subject to low levels of falcon predation. Paine et al. (1990) attributed these increases, as well as slight increases in Black Oystercatcher (*Haematopus bachmani*) abundance, to the effects of falcons on Northwestern Crows (*Corvus caurinus*). Crows formerly were major egg and nest predators on various bird species, but falcons both preyed directly on crows and suppressed their nest-raiding activities. Thus, a direct predatory effect of falcons on crows resulted in an indirect effect on other species, and an increase in their abundance.

In prairie streams of Oklahoma, an herbivorous minnow called the stoneroller (*Campostoma anomalum*) heavily grazes algae wherever it occurs and keeps algal growth on rock substrates to a minimum. The stoneroller in turn is preyed upon by largemouth (*Micropterus salmoides*) or spotted (*M. punctulatus*) bass, very effective fish predators. The natural distribution of these fishes is often complementary in pools of a given stream; stonerollers are found in pools without bass, either because they leave when bass appear, or because they are eaten by the bass. In stoneroller pools, algae is typically cropped very closely, but algal growth is luxuriant in bass pools (Power and Matthews 1983; Power et al. 1985). Experimental manipulations of predator and prey fishes confirms this scenario: if a bass is tethered in a pool with stonerollers, algae grows luxuriantly within the range of the bass, because stonerollers avoid that area, but is cropped heavily just outside the range of the bass. Bass addition to pools containing stonerollers soon results in heavy growth of algae (Figure 8.6). Thus, the direct predator–prey interaction be-

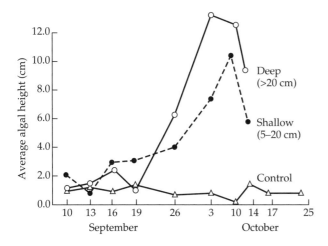

**Figure 8.6** Algal standing crops in an experimental pool (to which bass were added) and a control pool (with no bass and only the algivore *Campostoma anomalum*) in a small stream in Oklahoma. The addition of bass inhibits or stops algal grazing by the herbivore, allowing algae to recover from heavy herbivory. This phenomenon is an indirect interaction between bass and algae. (From Power et al. 1985.)

**Table 8.1**
Classes of Possible Keystone and Mutualistic Interactions and the Potential Results of Their Losses

| Class | Effects of losses |
|---|---|
| Top carnivores | Increases in abundances of prey species and smaller predators; overgrazing and overbrowsing |
| Large herbivores and termites | Habitat succession and decrease in habitat diversity |
| Habitat modifiers | Disappearance of habitat features |
| Pollinators and other mutualists | Reproductive failure of certain plants |
| Seed dispersers | Recruitment failure of certain plants |
| Plants providing essential resources during scarcity | Local extinction of dependent animals |
| Parasites and pathogenic microorganisms | Population explosions of host species |
| Mutualists with nutritional and defensive roles for their hosts | Increased predation, disease, and dieback of plants |

Modified from Soulé and Kohm 1989.

(A)

(B)

(C)

**Figure 8.7**   A typical successional sequence from Hutchison Memorial Forest in central New Jersey. (A) The field in this photograph is 2 years old and dominated by herbaceous species. (B) A 10-year-old field, with some woody species and a higher overall diversity. (C) An older forest stand eventually results from the successional process. (Photographs by S. T. A. Pickett.)

tween bass and stonerollers indirectly controls algal distribution and abundance. Again, an indirect interaction influences community structure.

We conclude this section on critical species interactions by reiterating our warning that not every species interaction is crucial, its loss dooming the community. We know from numerous population or species extinctions that many species can be removed from a system without overriding harm to the remainder of the community. However, some species are especially important because of the central role they play in community processes, and their loss could have a cascading effect. It is one of the challenges of conservation biology to identify these critical interactions and ensure that they are maintained.

A summary of critical keystone and mutualistic interactions, and the potential effects of their losses, is presented in Table 8.1. We will take a closer look at the results of the removal of certain types of species in the discussion of species introductions below.

## Community Changes in Ecological Time: Disturbance Regimes and Invasive Species

### The Importance of Disturbance Regimes

Much of the early historical development of theoretical ecology was premised on the comfortable notion that population dynamics and species interactions were at, or at least very near, an equilibrium state. In this view, nature could ultimately be understood if we only knew the appropriate deterministic rules that controlled ecology. More recently, theoretical and empirical interest has shifted away from purely deterministic viewpoints to place much more emphasis on the roles of various kinds of disturbances, patch dynamics (see Essay 9B), and other stochastic processes.

When one speaks of disturbance, of course, ecological succession immediately comes to mind. **Succession** is the familiar textbook process by which an abandoned agricultural field eventually returns to mature forest (Figure 8.7), or a coral reef rebuilds after destruction by a hurricane. The older literature described succession as an innate characteristic of a community; that is, the "natural state" of a community was defined by what was perceived to be the last, or "climax," stage of succession. A deciduous forest would therefore be called an "oak–hickory forest" (representing the apparent climax condition) rather than being named for an association more characteristic of a recent disturbance, such as a "black locust–black cherry" or "sumac–elderberry" forest, even though the latter may be common. Indeed, forests and many other communities tend to be labeled by the association that appears under conditions of least disturbance.

In contrast, current thought emphasizes the dynamics of disturbance patches in both space and time, rather than just the duration of a patch. In this perspective, the characteristic biodiversity of a forest is a product of patch dynamics generated by particular disturbance regimes. Thus, as we emphasize throughout this book, nature does not keep a tidy house. A perception of nature in disequilibrium is much closer to reality than a "balance of nature" perspective. A celebrated question in ecology is, "What determines the number of species?" The research agenda associated with this enduring question now includes attempts to understand the interplay between deterministic and stochastic processes, and the effects of the scale, intensity, and frequency of these processes.

In ecology, there is always a creative tension between, on the one hand, theorists and analytical modelers who wish to simplify nature and explore general processes, and on the other hand, the field ecologists and simulation modelers who focus on complexity in nature. This is particularly apparent in the body of research that addresses disturbance regimes. At one extreme, disturbance regimes can be generalized simply by allowing some parameter of mortality to vary. At the other extreme, every disturbance patch and event, from pocket gopher mounds and ant hills to landslides, is seen as having its unique natural history (Figure 8.8).

In conservation biology, the focus should be clear. Disturbance regimes are important to the extent that they influence probabilities of extinction and colonization, and, thereby, the patterns of biodiversity in the landscape. It is clear that at least some kinds of disturbances greatly influence biodiversity, and often the effects are strongly influenced by scale, intensity, and frequency (see discussion of "intermediate disturbance hypothesis" in Chapter 10). For example, we noted that in tropical forests many trees are obligately associated with mycorrhizal fungi. If soil does not contain the fungi, the germinating seeds of these obligate species cannot survive or compete with other species. A small soil disturbance patch, such as from a fallen tree, may retain, or quickly regain, its fungal inoculum. However, large soil disturbances may lose the fungal inoculum and regain it only very slowly. Thus, biodiversity will be maintained if soil disturbances are small, but will decline in large disturbances.

Fire frequency and intensity provides another example. As will be discussed in Essay 12E, a forest will respond very differently to low-intensity fires than to intense fires, and the effects of frequent fires will be different than those of infrequent ones. The role of the conservation ecologist then, is to understand how systems respond to different types of disturbances and how the responses are influenced by changes in scale, intensity, and frequency. Because disturbance regimes are often important to the maintenance of biodiversity, conservation managers, especially of small areas where the disturbance regime may not occur naturally, may need to mimic natural disturbance regimes as part of their management plan. We will discuss the diffi-

(A)

(B)

(C)

**Figure 8.8** Every type of disturbance patch, no matter how small, has relevance to the local ecology. Shown here are three types of soil disturbance patches. (A) A large atta ant colony in Costa Rica; (B) a gopher tortoise burrow, with newly hatched tortoises moving from their nest into their mother's burrow; and (C) a tip-up mound from a tree blow-down. (Photographs by C. R. Carroll.)

culties of implementing disturbance regimes in Chapters 11 and 12, but here introduce the point that the role of disturbance regimes in conservation ecology should be an area of priority research.

Many of our conservation problems are associated with loss of the most mature stages of succession, such as old-growth forests in the northwestern United States, or mature tropical lowland forests in many regions of the world, which may take many hundreds of years to reach a mature state. "Resetting" of these areas to earlier successional stages reduces the temporal and spatial diversity of habitat available, and many species associated with more mature successional stages cannot survive in the extensive earlier stages that are created. Likewise, agriculture arrests the successional process at the earliest stages, and replaces even that naturally low diversity with a monoculture (at least in temperate zones) that is harvested each year. A major challenge of conservation is to retain both later successional stages and a mix of all successional types within a landscape, not to retain ecosystems as static and unchanging.

### Species Invasions

A particular concern for native communities and species of conservation interest is the introduction of species beyond their native ranges. Known variously as "exotics," "aliens," "invaders," "non-natives," or "nonindigenous species," there are many examples of disastrous invasions by such species that resulted in losses of native species, changes in community structure and function, and even alterations of the physical structure of the system (Mooney and Drake 1986; Drake et al. 1989). However, not all species invasions result in disaster, and fortunately so, because there are few areas that remain free of non-native species. In some cases, the use of exotics can actually have positive conservation value; this perspective, a minority opinion, is elaborated in Essay 8B by Ariel Lugo.

---

## ESSAY 8B
# Maintaining an Open Mind on Exotic Species

Ariel E. Lugo, Institute of Tropical Forestry, Puerto Rico

*To consider only the invading species themselves in developing management programs or in recommending regulatory actions is tantamount to curing symptoms and not disease.*

                                    *J. J. Ewel, 1986*

Several reasons are given for the success of exotic species. They may do well because they are freed from natural enemies, competitors, and parasites. Consequently, a common strategy of control programs is to introduce organisms from the native habitats of target exotic plants to harm them; that is, eliminate exotics by introducing more exotics! Exotic species may also find little competition in the ecosystems they invade; empty niches may be available to exotics, which thus have little effect on the invaded ecosystem. The success of exotics has

also been attributed to their being aggressive colonizers, fast growing, and highly fecund. However, Ewel (1986) noted that "species invasions often reflect the conditions of the community being invaded rather than the uniquely aggressive traits of the invader."

I subscribe to Ewel's point of view. When a good match is made between the genome of any species and the environmental conditions that support its growth, the result can be explosive population increases. This is why organisms that are rare in their natural habitats may suddenly become weedy in a new situation. The water hyacinth (*Eichhornia crassipes*) is fairly inconspicuous in its natural Amazonian habitats, but exhibits explosive growth in the slow-moving, highly eutrophic waters of artificial canals and reservoirs in

Florida. Experiments show that it cannot grow as well when subjected to oligotrophic waters or fast flow. Close observation of successful exotic organisms usually yields similar results.

### Ecological Functions and Services of Exotic Species

I have studied monoculture plantations of exotic trees in Puerto Rico and compared them with native forests of similar age. My studies include 73 comparisons of structure, composition, and function of these ecosystems. I cannot find a single comparison that suggests an ecological anomaly in the forests dominated by exotic species. These ecosystems function like native forests, with differences mostly in the magnitude of rates and state variables (i.e., biomass and other structural features).

No negative effects have been detected in the water cycle, accumulation of carbon and nutrients, or in any other site condition. Claims to the contrary, such as those leveled against *Eucalyptus* trees, cannot be substantiated when evaluated critically.

I have also found that native plant species grow and develop under canopies of exotic species established in degraded sites, including some where succession was arrested prior to planting exotics. Native birds are attracted to and use the native species understory of these exotic tree plantations. For these reasons, I and others have suggested that exotic species can be important tools for land rehabilitation and restoration of biological diversity in damaged sites where natural succession is arrested. For example, Vitousek and Walker (1989) documented nitrogen enrichment in nitrogen-poor lava flows in Hawaii by the exotic tree *Myrica faya*. The greater availability of soil nitrogen where the exotic occurs favors the entire ecosystem and results in higher productivity. One would expect that higher productivity would eventually result in a greater capacity to fix carbon, circulate nutrients, and support more species.

## Will Exotic Species Dominate the World?

The dominance of exotic species on the landscape will be a function of the degree of human modification of the environment. In general, human activity fragments the landscape, favors establishment of exotic species, increases environmental heterogeneity, may cause species extinctions, and may augment the total number of species on the landscape. The Pacific Islands are instructive because they represent a worst-case scenario of the effects of intensive human activity on small land areas isolated from sources of biotic replenishment. In these islands, particularly the Hawaiian chain, isolation allowed the evolution of a highly diverse and endemic suite of organisms, originally exposed to merely a slow rate of invasion by exotic species.

Humans greatly accelerated that rate and in the process transformed the flora and fauna of the Pacific Islands. The process has been ongoing for some 2000 to 4000 years, and the results have been staggering in terms of species extinctions and transformation of biotic composition. The number of species across all taxonomic groups has increased from about 9000 to 12,000, but

many see this trend as an erosion in global biodiversity because endemic forms are lost while pantropical weeds replace them. There is certainly truth to this argument, but it is not entirely accurate because many exotic species are neither weedy nor pantropical. Some may be rare and endangered species that find refuge in another, more favorable location and then become weedy. In Puerto Rico, for example, *Delonix regia* is a common naturalized species in danger of extinction in its native Madagascar habitat.

Species–area curves help to illustrate the size/isolation issue. I compared the density of species on two Caribbean Islands with that of the Hawaiian Islands (Table A). If the area and plant species density values of the Hawaiian Islands are used to estimate the numbers of plant species expected in Cuba and Puerto Rico (same latitude as Hawaii), the results underestimate the actual number of species on the two Caribbean islands. This means that when area is corrected for, the density of species in the Caribbean is much higher than in the Hawaiian Islands. Part of this higher species density in the Caribbean is caused by the islands being closer to sources of propagules, but part is also explained by the Caribbean islands being six times older than the Hawaiian Islands. Could this mean that the Hawaiian Islands have a greater capacity to absorb additional plant species than do Caribbean islands? The age of islands, as well as their degree of isolation, influences the density of species and invadability of their communities. In Hawaii, exotic species are the likely invaders of plant communities because they are actively transported from a large reservoir of genetic material (the whole world), while the native species evolve slowly and are constrained by founder effects.

I would expect that in the absence of significant climate change, environments that today support high species richness will do so in the future, but the species composition may be different. And we should not forget that the forces of evolution are not suspended for exotic species. One could argue that the enrichment of islands with exotic genomes provides fuel for the evolutionary process and greatly increases adaptive possibilities. This is particularly important in light of human-induced changes in the atmosphere, climate, geomorphology, and other environmental conditions.

The change in species composition taking place in the world today is not a chaotic process; it is a process that is responding to fundamental changes in the conditions of the planet. Age-old ecological constraints such as time, energetics, biotic factors, growth conditions, and opportunity are at play, regulating which species are successful and which are not in a specific location. Human activity generates the environmental change that powers the response of organisms through adaptation, evolution, or formation of new groupings of species and communities.

## Management Strategies for a Changing World

I have highlighted contradictions in the way we deal with biodiversity issues in general and exotic species in particular. Even in Hawaii, where there is great concern about the degree of exotic species invasions and their potentially negative effects, the government actively and successfully introduces hundreds of insect species for agricultural pest control. We correctly worry about the negative effects of human activity, but forget that this activity started thousands of years ago at a time when people depended directly on the environ-

## Table A

Predicted and Actual Number of Plant Species in Cuba and Puerto Rico Using the Species–Area Relationship for the Hawaiian Islands ($S = cA^z$).

| Island | Area (km²) | $z$ | Predicted number of plant species | Actual number of flowering plant species |
|---|---|---|---|---|
| Cuba | 70,750 | 0.30 | 3100 | 6000 |
| Hawaii | 16,640 | — | — | 1750–2350 |
| Puerto Rico | 8960 | 0.30 | 1600 | 2200 |

*Note:* The $z$ value is that for Hawaiian plants. Consideration of only fern species results in 143 species in Hawaii and 408 species in Puerto Rico.

ment for survival. Even then, exotics were introduced and perhaps countless numbers of species were driven to extinction. I do not point these things out to excuse introductions of species nor to condone driving species to extinction. But we must maintain an open mind and analyze the issue of exotic species introductions and management as an intrinsic and continuous process in a world where our own species is a main driver of change.

It is in our power to take actions to mitigate the negatives of our activities and to enhance the positives. Actions that may help are learning to manage and control environmental change, recognizing when conditions are obviously beyond our control, avoiding condemning species because of successional stage or ecological function, improving our capacity to manage biotic resources, concentrating human activity to allow more space for native ecosystems, and encouraging environmental heterogeneity as a mechanism to maximize biodiversity. One thing is clear: the world will continue to change and become less familiar to those that walked on it or wrote about it centuries ago.

We face several critical questions in understanding invading species in a conservation context. What are the particular characteristics of invading species and invaded communities that determine the outcomes of such floral and faunal changes? Are there general rules by which the effects of such invasions can be predicted? Should some species cause more concern than others? Should there be special planning to eradicate some species if they establish a population? Or, if the invader cannot be eliminated, can it be managed to minimize its effects? Similar arguments arise when we consider the species that may be lost from communities due to invasions. We lack the resources to save everything, so which species are most important?

This section argues that the effects of invasions depend a great deal on which species and which communities are involved. Some species are more likely to invade than others, and some species are more likely to be lost from a community than others (general patterns are summarized in Table 8.2). This means that conservation biologists need to identify the important invaders or important native species that will be vulnerable. The major questions we will ask are:

1. Which species are most likely to invade communities?
2. Which native species are communities most likely to lose?
3. Which species, once they do invade, will cause extensive extinctions of native species?
4. Which native species extinctions will lead to many further losses of species and change in community structure?

We will address each of these four questions in turn and argue that each has two sides. The answers depend both on the natural history of the species that may invade or be lost—their physiology, behavior, genetics, and ecology—and on community characteristics, especially the role of potential competitors with, and predators on, the invading species.

*Which Species Introductions Succeed?* Not all introduced species succeed. We are not even aware of many of the accidental introductions that have failed (the successes are obvious), but there have been enough deliberate introductions to provide some records of failures. Fishes, birds, and mammals have been introduced for sport, plants and birds for aesthetics, and insects for biological control of pests. Typically, the majority of introductions fail. Across various invertebrate and vertebrate taxa, success rates of >50% are rare, 10%–40% are common, and, in some groups, any success is unusual (Lawton and Brown 1986).

Chance clearly plays a role, for repeated attempts with the same species in the same place are often necessary for success. Game bird biologists have successfully introduced seven species of pheasants, quail, and their relatives into the United States, but even under optimal circumstances, most of these introductions fail (Pimm 1991). Similarly, the starling introduced in New York's Central Park in 1891, has spread to most of North America, but sev-

**Table 8.2**
Some Generalized Characteristics of Invasive Species
and Invadable Communities

---

**Characteristics of successful invaders**
    High reproductive rate, pioneer species, short generation time
    Long-lived
    High dispersal rates
    Single-parent reproduction (i.e., gravid or pregnant female can colonize)
    Vegetative or clonal reproduction
    High genetic variability
    Phenotypically plastic
    Broad native range
    Habitat generalist
    Broad diet (polyphagous)
    Human commensal

**Characteristics of invadable communities**
    Climatically matched with original habitat of invader
    Early successional
    Low diversity of native species
    Absence of predators on invading species
    Absence of native species morphologically or ecologically similar to invader
    Absence of predators or grazers in evolutionary history ("naive" prey)
    Absence of fire in evolutionary history
    Low-connectance food web
    Anthropogenically disturbed

**Characteristics of communities likely to exhibit large invasion effects**
    Simple communities
    Anthropogenically disturbed communities

---

Modified from Lodge 1993.
*Note:* The list is not exhaustive, nor is every characteristic critical in a given situation. These are merely generalized trends, with many exceptions.

eral introductions before 1891 failed (Long 1981).

Deciding which introductions are likely to succeed and which are likely to fail requires application of a wealth of autecological information. We should know, for example, whether the species can tolerate the physical conditions of the new habitat. Indeed, we should ask how important is a match between, say, the climate of the potential new home and the existing one; for plants, a similar photoperiod can also be important. (Many introduced species do *not* show a good match in the climate of their old and new homes.) We should know how well the species can fare when it is at low density. Can it find mates? Can it reproduce quickly to overcome low numbers? Is it vulnerable to the genetic problems of inbreeding that haunt small populations? Will biological interactions with competitors, diseases, or predators prevent the species from invading? In any given case it may not be critical to have detailed answers to all these questions, but any particular question may be critical to an invasion's success or failure.

The role of competition in determining which species can invade has been of interest for a long time. Elton (1946) suggested that communities might be structured by competition. If so, there should be fewer representatives of each genus in any given community than expected at random because species in the same genus, by being ecologically similar, would tend to exclude each other through competition. Elton's competitive exclusion idea was extended to morphological similarity by Lack (1947). Competition is

**Figure 8.9**  Two species of mud snails (*Hydrobia ulvae* [open circles] and *H. ventrosa* [filled circles]) tend to be the same size where allopatric (A), but diverge in size where sympatric (B). Shown are means plus and minus one standard deviation for several different localities. The phenomenon of size separation is thought to be due to competition for limited resources, and is called character displacement. (From Fenchel 1975.)

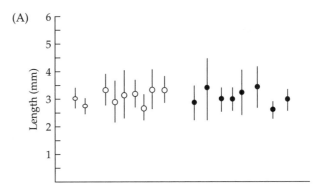

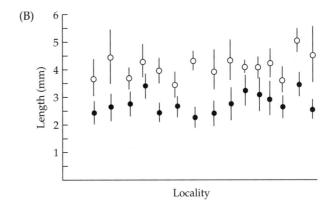

proposed to be more intense between species that are similar, for they are more likely than dissimilar species to share essential resources. This is often reflected in morphology: body size or shape of a critical character may be divergent where two species co-occur, but more similar where they do not (Figure 8.9). Taxonomic or morphological similarity between invader and resident thus is more likely when there are more resident species, and sufficiently intense competition can prevent species introductions. Some of the most direct evidence of invasions being more difficult in species-rich communities comes from studies of introduced birds on islands (Moulton and Pimm 1983, 1985, 1986, 1987; Moulton 1985, 1993).

What is the role of predation in species invasion? Obviously, a native predator, if it preys on the invader, will make it harder for the invader to succeed, but nature can be more complex than this. Predators may also make it easier for a species to invade if the predator feeds heavily on resident species and so reduces their competitive effects on the invader. There is no universal answer to this question.

***Which Species Are Most Likely To Go Extinct?***  This may be the easiest question to answer. Rarity is by far the best predictor of the chance of extinction (Diamond 1984a,b; Pimm 1991), in large part because species numbers vary so much. Among Hawaiian birds, for example, there are some species with fewer than ten individuals, and others with millions (Scott et al. 1986). Whatever other factors are important, a species six orders of magnitude more abundant than another is going to be less threatened.

Abundance is not the only factor, of course. Species differ in their risks of extinction at a given small population size (Pimm et al. 1988). Species also differ greatly in how much their numbers vary from year to year. Some species vary by only a factor of two over 20 years, others by four orders of

(A)

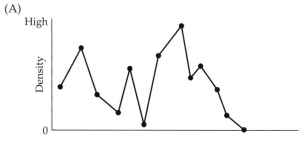

(B)

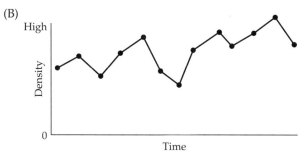

Time

**Figure 8.10** A highly variable population (A) has a higher likelihood of extinction than a population with lower variation (B), simply because it approaches low numbers (or zero) more frequently. At that low point, it is more vulnerable to extinction due to demographic or genetic stochasticity, or to environmental variation (see Chapter 7.)

magnitude over the same interval (Pimm 1991). Other things being equal, greater variability in population size may lead to greater risk of extinction (Figure 8.10).

What makes some species vary more than others? Environmental variability, the diversity of predators that exploit the species, the species' degree of trophic specialization (monophagy, polyphagy), and its life history characteristics all contribute. An extended discussion of these effects is provided by Pimm (1991).

***Which Invaders Will Cause Extensive Extinctions of Native Species?***
Not all alien species cause damage, and Simberloff (1981) has suggested that only a few do. However, the evidence for severe damage in particular instances is compelling, and there are many cases of communities devastated by alien plants and animals (Pimm 1991). Some of the best examples are native fishes of North American deserts that are extinct as a result of introductions of predatory exotic fishes (Minckley and Deacon 1991).

Are there repeat offenders or just vulnerable communities? Are some species the ecological equivalent of Ghengis Khan, wreaking ecological havoc wherever they invade? Are there species whose introductions should always be avoided and others that are never a problem? Or does the outcome depend on the community into which the species is introduced?

Two mosquitofish species (*Gambusia affinis* and *G. holbrooki*) of eastern and central North America are notorious for their devastating effects as exotic species in a variety of different community types (Courtenay and Meffe 1989). These small (< 5 cm), harmless-looking, guppylike fish are documented to have caused species reductions or extinctions (through their predatory habits) in a variety of community types (springs, ponds, lakes, slow rivers) when introduced in Australia, Europe, Asia, Africa, western North America, and especially on oceanic islands (reviewed in Courtenay and Meffe 1989; Arthington and Lloyd 1989). Several dozen species of fish (including large predators and game species) and numerous species of invertebrates have been negatively affected or extirpated after mosquitofish introductions. The outcome seems little affected by the community type or native species involved.

(A)

(B)

(C)

**Figure 8.11** A number of invasive species have repeatedly been shown to be successful colonists and a major challenge to native communities. These include species such as (A) zebra mussels (shown growing on a native mussel, *Leptodea fragilis*), (B) kudzu overgrowing a native forest in southeastern United States, and (C) Africanized honey bees who took over a Wood Duck nest box in Costa Rica. (A, photograph by D. W. Schloesser; B and C, by C. R. Carroll.)

In a major review of introduced mammals and birds, Ebenhard (1988) recorded 59 introductions of domestic cats (*Felis domesticus*). A majority of these (38, or 64%) had detrimental effects, including extinctions of native prey populations. This percentage should be contrasted with that for all predator introductions: 32%. Cats are thus twice as likely to cause damage as are other introduced predators. The story is more complicated than this, however. Thirty-five of 49 (71%) introductions of cats to islands had detrimental effects, while only 3 of 10 (30%) introductions to mainlands, or islands once connected to mainlands, had such effects. Island communities are particularly vulnerable to introduced predators. The figure of 30% introductions is still about three times the average for all mammalian predators introduced to mainlands (9%). Quite clearly, cats have an unusual potential to create problems, and they, along with the mosquitofishes just discussed, are a good example of a species whose introduction should always be avoided. Other examples of invasive species with a track record of severe impacts include rats, goats, zebra mussels, fire ants, and plants such as kudzu (Figure 8.11). So yes, there are repeat offenders whose introductions should always be avoided.

***Which Native Species Extinctions Will Result in Further Losses of Species and Change in Community Structure?*** Which species can we not afford to lose? Are there some species whose presence in a community is crucial? That is, if we do not make special efforts on their behalf, might we lose species that play keystone roles in maintaining the composition of the ecological community?

In practice, some species get much more protection than others, but not always for well-justified ecological reasons. Their protection may arise because they are large, feathered, or furred, and they capture the public's imagination more than the small and the scaled. Although they may not always be known as critical species to their communities, large species typically require more space than small species, thus their protection may protect other species or the community at large. Protect the Spotted Owl of old-growth forests of the Pacific Northwest, and nearly 200 other species are protected under its umbrella. But there are species that are important for reasons other than their size or public appeal; these are classes of species whose loss will cause extensive **secondary extinctions.**

The community consequences of particular species introductions and extinctions depend critically on which species are removed and the patterns of trophic interactions. Computer models of the process of removing species demonstrate several possibilities. Removing a plant species from the base of a simple food chain destroys the entire community (Figure 8.12A). However, the loss of one of several plant species used by a polyphagous herbivore in a more complex community (Figure 8.12C) would cause few or no extinctions because the herbivore is not so dependent on one species. Similar rules apply one trophic level up when contrasting polyphagous and monophagous predators. These effects are obvious and well known. Less obvious are the effects of removing species from the tops of food chains.

Removing a predator species that preys on a monophagous herbivore (Figure 8.12B) probably leaves the plant the herbivore eats at a lower density, but the plant is likely to survive; it is unlikely that an herbivore would eliminate its sole food base before it too became extinct. In a more complex community (Figure 8.12D), the predator's absence may lead to the herbivore exterminating all but one resistant plant species, which then regulates the herbivore's numbers.

In short, secondary extinctions are most likely when plants are removed from trophically simple communities. In more complex communities, the remaining species have alternative food supplies. Yet, secondary extinctions are more likely in complex communities than in simple ones following the loss of top predators because cascading extinctions from upper trophic levels can propagate more widely in complex communities (see Pimm 1991 for a detailed explanation).

These principles have simple extensions to discussions involving competitors. Removing the predator of a species that competes with many other species may cause many changes (see keystone predators, above). Removing a predator of a species that competes more locally may have fewer effects.

What kinds of introduced species are likely to cause the greatest community changes? We can predict the effects of introduced species from these conclusions about species removals. Adding an herbivore to an island lacking predators may be equivalent to removing the herbivore's predator in the herbivore's native community. Highly polyphagous introduced species are likely to cause more damage than monophagous species, just as predator removals are more severe when their prey are polyphagous. A parallel argument suggests that polyphagous predators should cause more damage if they are introduced into areas containing no competitors or diseases.

Finally, the combination expected to produce the most profound changes will be the introduction of polyphagous herbivores without their predators into relatively simple communities. Without predators, these herbivores may attain high densities, their generalized feeding habits may exterminate many species of plants, and the removal of a few plant species may cause the collapse of entire food chains. Oceanic islands invaded by goats often fall under this worst-case scenario.

To see how these various ideas about invaders and invaded communities apply, let us consider several examples of additions and subtractions of species, which will together present several sides of the invasion story.

***The Brown Tree Snake on Guam.*** We start with the case of the brown tree snake, *Boiga irregularis* (Figure 8.13), which is accused of exterminating all the forest birds on Guam, an island in the Mariana Islands of the western Pacific. Our conservation interest here is whether special efforts are needed to prevent *Boiga* from spreading from Guam to the Hawaiian Islands of the central Pacific, the most remote archipelago on the planet. To answer that, we need to first establish what *Boiga* has done on Guam, and then try to understand the unique species and community characteristics of Hawaii that might have bearing on this question.

The brown tree snake's native range is from Australia north through New Guinea to the Solomon Islands. It arrived in Guam after World War II, probably in a military transport, and eventually spread across the entire island, remaining at low densities for two decades. Birds started disappearing from the middle of Guam in the early 1960s. At about the same time, the snakes appeared in large numbers—some well-fed in chicken coops, others reduced to carbon on power poles (surrogate trees!) after short-circuiting insulators and causing blackouts. Savidge (1987) noticed that ten species of forest birds followed a similar pattern of decline: the birds were gone from the forests on southern Guam by the late 1960s, and one by one, species were lost progressively further north (Figure 8.14). In early 1983, ecologists found all ten species in one small patch of tall forest beneath a cliff line on the northern tip of the island. By 1986, they had disappeared from this area as well.

There was considerable debate about the causes of the decline in Guam's birds. Some scientists argued that pesticides were to blame, and others be-

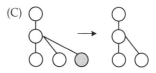
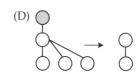

**Figure 8.12** The effects of species removals depend on the complexity of the food web and the species' position in the web. (A) A plant removed from the bottom of a simple food chain causes the entire food chain to be lost. (B) A predator removed from the same food chain may have no effect. In contrast, a plant lost from a more complex web may have little effect (C), but a predator lost from the same web may release its herbivore prey and so lead to the loss of several species of plants (D). (From Pimm 1991.)

**Figure 8.13** The brown tree snake, *Boiga irregularis,* the cause of loss of 10 bird species on Guam, and a potential threat to Hawaii. (Photograph by Gordon H. Rodda.)

**Figure 8.14**    Map of Guam showing the spread of *Boiga* and the loss of forest bird species. *Boiga* colonized the southern part of the island after World War II, and progressively spread from there, as indicated by the arrows. Each box lists the number (out of a possible 10) of forest bird species found at that location in the year indicated. For 1986, the surveys were incomplete, and those numbers are in parentheses. (Modified from Savidge 1987.)

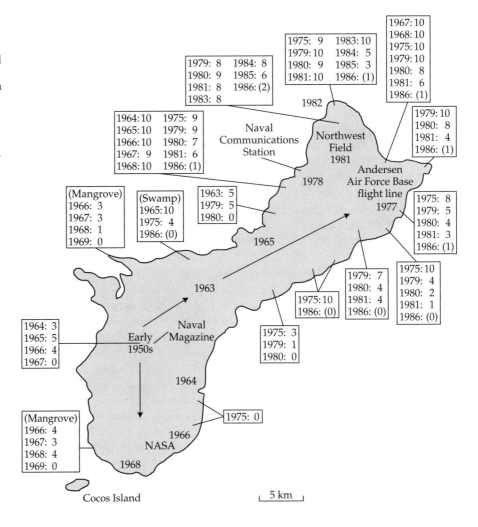

lieved that avian diseases might be at fault. The native species might be susceptible to diseases carried by introduced birds or domesticated chickens and pigeons. Introduced birds might be directly responsible by competing with or harassing native species. There was also the familiar list of introduced rats, cats, and other mammals.

Not only did the forest birds decline, but the fairy tern stopped nesting on the island. However, on the small island of Cocos, a few hundred meters off the south coast of Guam (Figure 8.14) where there are no *Boiga*, it remains abundant. The terns' decline on Guam ruled out pesticides, because it nests in trees but feeds on oceanic fish, which would not be affected by pesticides. It is also a highly mobile species; were it declining on Guam from disease, the population on Cocos would also have been infected. The cumulative evidence indicates that *Boiga* has driven ten bird species to extinction on Guam by predation; two of these species and one distinctive subspecies lived nowhere else. Four more bird species are so rare that their survival is unlikely.

Will *Boiga* colonize Hawaii in the coming decades and cause similar destruction? *Boiga* made it from the Solomons to Guam; the snake can survive far longer than the 8-hour plane ride from Guam to Hawaii, and dead *Boiga* have already appeared on airfields in Hawaii. *Boiga* can certainly reach Hawaii, but can it increase in numbers from a few founding stowaways, and can it devastate? Small populations run high risks of extinction from chance events (discussed in Chapters 6 and 7): individuals may not find mates; for species producing few young, there is a chance that those individuals will be of the same sex; inbreeding in small founder populations may quickly take its toll; all individuals may die early in the invasion for completely independent reasons. These factors make up the demographic and genetic accidents unavoidable at very low numbers, as discussed in Chapter 7, but they quickly become unimportant as the population increases in size. Every population not arriving in force must run this gauntlet of demographic accidents, but many succeed quite well. With *Boiga*, a female could arrive already gravid and lay a clutch of a dozen eggs (Cogger 1979). Thus, a single female could initiate a successful invasion.

Of course, invading species must also be able to survive the physical environment of their new home. Interestingly, a bad match between the climates of old and new homes may not prevent success; some species readily adapt to different conditions and climate in their new homes. The lush, tropical forests in lowland Hawaii house a community of introduced birds, many of which are from temperate climates. In the case of *Boiga*, the physical environment of Hawaii is similar to that of Guam and appears quite suitable for the snake.

Whether an alien succeeds or not also depends on the welcome afforded it by the community's established species. Do they provide it with prey or do they prey on the alien? Do they compete with it by feeding on species that the alien also may feed upon? Do they harbor reservoirs of diseases fatal to the alien, or does it carry diseases fatal to them?

The nearest continent to Hawaii, North America, is more than 4000 km away, and consequently few species arrived on the islands naturally; there is only one native terrestrial mammal (a bat) and no native reptiles or amphibians. There were once about 100 species of passerine birds, but they descended from just four colonizations (a crow, a finch, a flycatcher, and a honeyeater). Of the plants, only about 10% are found elsewhere; the remainder are endemic. Thus, the Hawaiian Islands are too remote to have native snakes that could be competitors, predators, or hosts of fatal diseases. Yet they are home to many native and introduced birds and introduced lizards on which the snake could feed; the large numbers of introduced birds in disturbed habitats around airfields and ports could provide *Boiga* with abundant prey. The community setting thus seems favorable to *Boiga*.

Oddly enough, the only enemy for *Boiga* may be another introduced species. Over a century ago, the small Indian mongoose was introduced to Hawaii to control rats. That effort was a conspicuous failure, perhaps because rats are nocturnal while the mongoose is diurnal. (Ecological insight has rarely been a close partner of deliberate species introductions.) The mongoose is an aggressive and generalized predator that might prey on *Boiga*, and this could prevent the snake's establishment. However, this is a slim hope at best, and we cannot bet the ecological future of Hawaii on such good fortune. Prevention of establishment of *Boiga* offers the best chance of not repeating the Guam tragedy on Hawaii.

The evidence all points to *Boiga* being able to colonize Hawaii and damage its ecological communities. It has managed to exterminate one avifauna already, and its natural history and the features of the Hawaiian ecological communities make a successful invasion and subsequent damage quite likely. Thus, we conclude that *Boiga* is more likely to succeed than other species and more likely to cause harm if it establishes itself. Any conservationist would strongly recommend that special measures be taken to first prevent and then seek out and eliminate potential immigrants like *Boiga*.

(A)                                                                    (B)

**Figure 8.15** The American chestnut tree, *Castanea dentata,* formerly dominant in the eastern deciduous forest of North America, was nearly removed from the forests by chestnut blight. (A) A second-growth stand of chestnuts near Voluntown, Connecticut, in 1910 shows the former dominance of this species. (B) By 1922, near Oxford, Pennsylvania, large stands of the tree were dying from blight. (Photographs courtesy of the Connecticut Agricultural Experiment Station and S. L. Anagnostakis.)

***The Loss of the American Chestnut Tree.*** The American chestnut (*Castanea dentata*) was once an important component of the deciduous forests of eastern North America. It ranged from Georgia in the south and Illinois in the west to as far north as Maine. In some forests it made up more than 40% of the overstory trees (Krebs 1985). Yet in the early part of this century, chestnuts were driven almost to extinction by a fungal disease, chestnut blight, first noticed in an area near New York City (Figure 8.15). The species now survives only as rare, small individuals, which become infected and die as they mature. The fungus is thought to have been introduced on nursery stock from Asia, where it is endemic. It is found on other species of trees but appears to kill only chestnuts. Our interest is the fate of the animal communities that depended on chestnuts. Many species might have been expected to use chestnuts, and we might expect many animal extinctions.

Despite the numerical importance of chestnuts, there have been no extinctions of terrestrial vertebrates in eastern North America due to the chestnut's decline. Seven species of Lepidoptera (moths and butterflies) apparently fed exclusively on chestnuts (Opler 1978) and all of them are now possibly extinct. Forty-nine other species of Lepidoptera fed on chestnuts, but the tree made up only part of their diets. Hence, only 12% of Lepidoptera reported to have fed on chestnuts were so specialized that they may have become rare or extinct. None of these seven species supported very specialized species of insect predators, so the chestnut food web is probably like the one shown in Figure 8.12C; most of the herbivores were polyphagous and the web is fairly resistant to the removal of one of its plant species. Thus, the American chestnut tree was lost with very few known effects on animal species.

***The Loss of Trees and Birds in Hawaii.*** The contrast of the American chestnut experience with that of the loss of Hawaiian trees is striking. About half of the bird species of Hawaii went extinct after the islands' discovery by Polynesians over a millennium ago. Approximately half of the remaining bird species went extinct after Europeans colonized Hawaii in the early 1800s, and about half of those remaining are now endangered (Freed et al. 1988). These patterns of extinctions and survival are closely tied to plant species extinctions.

Two families of nectarivores are of particular interest. Three of the five endemic meliphagid species are extinct, and the other two are probably extinct. One meliphagid, the Hawaii O'o, and two related species of drepani-

(A)

(B)

(C)

dids, the Black Mamo and I'iwi, have peculiar nectar-feeding bills (Figure 8.16); the first two are extinct, and the third is extinct on two islands, very rare on a third, and has declined on others. All these extinctions may have followed the destruction of important nectar-producing plants by introduced goats and pigs. A native hibiscus, *Hibiscadelphus*, a rich source of nectar, is now exceedingly rare. Many of the native lobelliods (such as the genera *Trematolobellia* and *Clermontia*) have clearly evolved to be pollinated by the three drepanidids; they have corollas that fit their unusual beaks (Figure 8.17). Some of this remarkable plant radiation is extinct, and other parts are very rare; at least one species has only one individual remaining in the wild.

Some surviving Hawaiian birds also seem to be unusually specialized species and are threatened as a consequence. Another rare drepanidid is the 'Akiapola'au, an insectivore, which feeds in forests of large koa trees. The koa forest is being lost because the trees are felled for their attractive wood. A granivore, the Palila, is endangered because it depends almost exclusively on the seeds of one tree, the mamane, which is declining because of introduced goats and sheep. The ranges of frugivorous thrushes in Hawaii are declining because the loss of a small number of fruiting species may prevent the thrushes from having a year-round food supply (van Riper and Scott 1979). Thus, in contrast to the loss of the American chestnut tree, most of whose herbivores were polyphagous, the loss of various Hawaiian trees is having a much more devastating effect on their specialized feeders.

***Species Invasions: A Summary.*** We wish to summarize four features of the arguments presented relative to species invasions. First, all species introductions and losses are not equal. Second, which species invade will depend on the particular characteristics of individual species and the potential host community. Which species have major effects once they have invaded will also depend on these characteristics.

Third, decisions about which species invasions are likely to be important and which communities are likely to be vulnerable require a very broad range of ecological expertise, and may be quite complicated. Problems in conservation biology frequently do not fit easily into the small pigeonholes (physiological ecology, avian community ecology, and so forth) our academic training creates. Interdisciplinary thinking is often necessary to understand these problems.

Finally, conservation biologists have to make decisions based on what we know now. Experiments may be impossible for many reasons, including lack of time. We must often choose priorities using knowledge of surrogate systems. The recommendation to pay special attention to the potential introduc-

**Figure 8.16**  A meliphagid and two drepanidids in Hawaii are all specialized as nectar feeders. The Hawaii O'o (A) and Molokai Black Mamo (B) are extinct. The I'iwi (C) is extinct on Lanai and Molokai and endangered on Oahu, but survives elsewhere. These birds' declines and extinctions may be a result of losses of the nectar-producing plants that constituted their food sources. (A and B, photographs by Bishop Museum; C, by Jaan Lepson.)

**Figure 8.17**  *Trematolobelia kauaensis* is an example of the Lobeliacae, a family that experienced adaptive radiation on Hawaii. Many of these species, which were pollinated by nectar-feeding birds and provided major foods for those birds, are now extinct. The plant extinctions were likely caused by depredations of introduced pigs and goats, and in turn may have caused various bird extinctions. (Photograph by Stuart L. Pimm.)

tion of *Boiga* to Hawaii has only a little to do with what we know about the snake in its native range. It is based more on what we know about introductions of species in general, on the effects of this particular introduction elsewhere, and particularly, about the vulnerability of islands to exotics.

Often, the evidence we must marshal is less than satisfactory, yet the conservation implications may be huge. For example, few if any stories of secondary extinctions are better than anecdotes. But we cannot afford to ignore the possibility of secondary extinctions just because it is hard to collect compelling data and impossible to perform experiments. The problems are immediate, and the science will be driven by them and not by taxonomic or methodological preferences.

## Community Changes in Evolutionary Time

We have seen that losses of keystone species or mutualists, or additions of exotic species, can have drastic, negative effects on communities, and that disturbance regimes are an important factor in determining levels of biodiversity. But how unexpected are changes in species composition in the long-term picture of ecological communities? Is it that unusual for species to drop out of or be added to a community? What are the long-term patterns, and what can they tell us about conservation of ecological communities? To answer such questions, we must examine communities over longer periods of time.

In addition to the normal, short-term community changes that occur in ecological time and can be observed even within the lifetime of a single conservationist, long-term changes, over thousands to tens or hundreds of thousands of years, can shed further light on community patterns and processes relevant to conservation. For example, are communities stable and predictable over the longer haul? Do species associations and interactions remain constant over centuries? Do communities respond as a unit to global changes such as glacial advances and retreats? Or, does community composition change over these longer time periods, with species being lost as other species spread, and with fluid associations and interactions over time?

Evidence over both longer-term (millions of years) and shorter-term (tens of thousands of years) evolutionary time indicates that many plant and animal communities are in fact quite fluid and have changed appreciably throughout their histories. Addressing first the longer term, we know that diversity of marine invertebrates (Bambach 1986) and terrestrial plants (Knoll 1986) has increased over many millions of years (see also Chapter 4). In the case of marine organisms, this took the form of an increase in the number of guilds, as new methods of predation or new ways of exploiting a particular environment developed, rather than a packing of existing guilds more tightly. As species of coral reef organisms disappeared over about 10 million years, reef structure did not collapse, but community structure changed. Thus, community structure, and therefore species interactions in these systems do not remain stagnant or tend toward a status quo, but change over longer-term evolutionary time.

The shorter-term geologic record contains even better evidence for the impermanence of community structure. Davis (1986) and Delcourt and Delcourt (1987) analyzed records of pollen deposition in Quaternary (from 2 million years ago) and Holocene (from 10,000 years ago) plant communities in North America. There were time lags of decades to centuries in responses of some plant species to climatic changes such as glaciation, meaning that some species in a community shifted distribution before others. Conse-

**Figure 8.18** The northward range expansion of maple (*Acer*) in eastern North America from glacial refuges in the southern Mississippi Valley during the Holocene period. Lines represent thousands of years before present when maples first appeared at that point along the advancing front. The shaded area is the present range of *Acer*. (From Davis 1981.)

quently, forest communities that are similar today may have quite different temporal histories, and a given species may have been in place for very different lengths of time in different locations (Figure 8.18).

In New Hampshire, for example, maple (*Acer* spp.) arrived 9000 years ago, hemlock (*Tsuga canadensis*) 7500 years ago, and beech (*Fagus grandifolia*) 6500 years ago. In Wisconsin, maple arrived 7000 years ago and hemlock and beech only 2000 years ago. Beech arrived before hemlock in central Michigan, but hemlock preceded beech in northern Michigan. Oak–hickory communities in southern Michigan have existed 5000 years longer than those in Connecticut (Davis 1981). The point is, contemporary plant communities may have very different histories of association depending on their locations, and thus different histories of species interactions. These communities are not necessarily set in any particular configuration of species combinations; if certain species are added or removed, the communities will likely continue to function normally. As stressed earlier, though, the question is: *which* species can be added or lost without major repercussions to the rest of the community?

Delcourt and Delcourt (1987) likewise indicated that contemporary North American temperate forests must be better understood in the context of long-term changes. In particular, because 90% of the Quaternary period has been glaciated, temperate zone plant communities have been shaped by conditions very different from what we see today. Vegetational dynamics in eastern North America range from a long-term equilibrium to alternating periods of equilibrium and disequilibrium, to continual disequilibrium. For example, low latitude forests have maintained the greatest integrity and stability in a dynamic equilibrium throughout the last 20,000 years. Mid-latitude forests were in one dynamic equilibrium state during glaciation, but shifted to a new equilibrium after glacial retreat. Postglacial forests at high latitudes were initially in disequilibrium, but tended toward an equilibrium in more recent times. In the Pacific Northwest, Douglas fir forests began domination of that area only about 10,000 years ago, and their old-growth forests have existed for only 5000 to 7000 years (Brubaker 1988). The species of a particular contemporary forest thus may have a relatively long period of association under relatively constant conditions, or may be a more recent phenomenon affected by disturbance and environmental change.

Animals show similar patterns of community change in the long term. Graham (1986) indicated that there were some 22 glaciations of the Northern Hemisphere during the last million years, during which northern and montane mammal species moved southward and downslope, respectively. Many arctic mammals occurred in presently temperate regions of the United States and Europe (Figure 8.19), and temperate species moved toward the tropics. In reference to these movements, Graham addressed the question of how old ecological communities are today. He concluded that distributional shifts during the Quaternary period were not wholesale, community-level movements, but individual species responses to environmental changes. Species migrated in different directions at different times and

**Figure 8.19**   An example of change in geographic distribution of a small mammal after glacial periods. The Greenland collared lemming (*Dicrostonyx groenlandicus*) was found as far south as West Virginia during the late Pleistocene, but occurs today only in boreal regions. (From Graham 1986.)

for different distances, thereby changing community structure at any location. There was great intermingling of mammalian faunas at different times, with no modern analogues for some of these communities. In some cases, arctic and boreal faunas mixed with temperate faunas rather than displacing them. Modern mammalian communities in regions affected by glaciation are geologically young, less than 10,000 years old.

Van Devender's (1986) studies of packrat middens in the Chihuahuan Desert of North America confirm these patterns. Vegetation in that region changed in the late Pleistocene (starting about 11,000 years ago) from pinyon–juniper–oak woodland to oak–juniper woodland to desert grassland, and finally to Chihuahuan Desert scrub about 4000 years ago. The stashes of seeds and animal parts left by packrats indicate that many present desert animals lived in the same general places in the late Pleistocene, but in different habitats; they did not tightly associate with particular plant communities, but switched to new ones as plant communities changed. These changes, however, would have occurred slowly compared with patterns of contemporary habitat destruction and alteration.

Of course, not all communities have changed so drastically over evolutionary time. Some, such as the deeper parts of the oceans are presumably more stable, having been little affected by sea level changes during glacial advances and retreats. Similarly, tropical regions may have had a longer period of associations, again having been disrupted less by global climatic change (although there is evidence of significant changes in community composition [Colinvaux et al. 1989]). Because of these possibly longer-term associations, such communities may have developed stronger coevolutionary relationships, and may be more cohesive units than more recently formed communities.

What does the age of a community association tell us about conservation efforts and policy? What does knowledge of an association's age tell us about the importance of retaining the system and species interactions intact? Older communities, those that have existed in something like their present states for longer periods, may be more vulnerable to outside disturbance and change than are younger systems. These older communities may have had time to develop more and tighter interspecific interactions such as mutualisms, and individual species may be more dependent upon such interactions. For example, there are many intricate and highly specific pollination and seed dispersal systems in tropical forests, more so than in temperate or boreal regions. If such systems are disturbed by humans, the disruption may have greater consequences than similar changes in temperate regions.

This is not to say that communities at higher latitudes, or those that regularly receive natural disturbances, can be freely disturbed by humans and not be affected. Rather, such communities may be more resistant or resilient to anthropogenic disturbance than are the more complex communities of the tropics or the more stable communities of the deep oceans. But the picture is more complicated than that. Regions with low rates of productivity, such as tundra and deserts, are famous for the effects of even minor disturbances, such as wheel tracks from early pioneers, remaining visible for many decades or even centuries afterward. Productivity therefore must also be considered when estimating possible damage to a community from an artificial disturbance.

Understanding the short- and long-term historical changes evident in many communities makes their conservation today even more challenging. Contemporary biotic changes such as species additions and deletions are superimposed upon a dynamic and somewhat uncertain evolutionary history.

We know that species composition changes over time, but we usually do not understand the local causes and effects of such change. It would be easier to conserve contemporary systems if they were historically stable and unchanging; we could simply (at least in theory) strive to maintain native species compositions as we find them, or as we suspect them to have been before the influence of humans. However, ecological and evolutionary history tells us that there is no set endpoint for biotic composition of these communities. What constitutes a "natural" northern temperate forest or dry savanna? Because their species compositions have changed over time, there is no clear target for contemporary conservation.

What we can do is realize that these historical changes typically occurred over much greater time periods than the changes being imposed on natural systems by humankind. Slow climatic changes over centuries, set in a completely wild matrix, afford ecological systems opportunities to gradually adjust to change, while eliminating a pollinator by pesticides over one month, or introducing a novel predator in one season, does not. The human-directed influences throughout the world that are changing species interactions and community compositions are merely one more in a series of ecological insults for which the evolutionary history and genetic variation of species has not prepared them. Minimizing such influences is clearly a reasonable conservation goal.

## Summary

By definition, conservation of bio*diversity* must ultimately reach beyond the species level and consider communities and ecosystems. Knowledge of a community's particularly critical components and strong interactions such as keystone species and mutualisms, can focus and guide conservation actions. A species may be a keystone component typically because of some aspect of its trophic ecology, such as being an important predator, changing habitat structure through foraging efforts, or providing a critical food resource. Mutualisms create critical links among species, such as pollination or seed dispersal, that perform a function that may be critical to continued community composition.

Changes occur in communities over ecological time for a variety of reasons, but especially relevant to conservation are natural disturbance regimes and the introduction of exotic species. Virtually all natural communities experience a normal disturbance regime, such as fire, flooding, drought, herbivory, or storm damage. Understanding the scale, frequency, and intensity of natural disturbances is critical to conservation at the community level. Continuance of normal disturbance regimes at appropriate scales should be encouraged, and new, artificial disturbances should be avoided. An especially devastating type of new disturbance is invasive species. Many examples exist of the destructive effects of both plant and animal invasions. Their success depends on the characteristics of both the particular invader and the particular communities invaded, and is difficult to predict a priori. All species introductions to and losses from communities are not equal with respect to their community effects; some may be quite benign, while others can devastate.

Long-term studies of ecological communities over evolutionary and geological time shed more light on community conservation. Many communities, especially in temperate zones, have been dynamic over spans of thousands of years, and some may be relatively new communities in evolutionary time. Species additions to or deletions from communities in evolutionary time are often independent; that is, many communities do not seem to be cohesive, tightly woven units that remain together over time, but assemblages of species that continually enter and leave the picture. These types of communities may be less susceptible to human disturbance than are communities with long-term associations that have evolved complicated species interactions. Thus, the changes wrought by humans on natural communities are superimposed upon a historical dynamism in many cases, making conservation more difficult, but providing another perspective on ecological change that should be incorporated into management efforts.

## Questions for Discussion

1. How might you determine whether a particular species is a keystone species in a given area? What are the sorts of approaches you might use?

2. If species X is determined to be a keystone species in reserve Y, is that good evidence that it is also a keystone species in reserve Z, or outside of any reserves?

3. How could you determine what factors are important in predisposing a particular invasion to success or failure? What types of data for the species and the system would help you out?

4. If climatic change over evolutionary time repeatedly has caused shifts in species ranges and community structures, why should we be concerned with conservation of these communities today? Aren't the human-induced changes simply another form of the disturbance that natural communities have had to deal with for eons?

5. We stated that not all species interactions in a community are equal. How might you evaluate which interactions in a given community have disproportionately large effects?

6. Following up on Question 5, should we work harder to prevent a species' extinction if it is shown to be a strong interactor? That is, should a species' role in a community have bearing on ultimate conservation efforts at preventing its untimely extinction?

## Suggestions for Further Reading

Cody, M. L. and J. M. Diamond (eds.). 1975. *Ecology and Evolution of Communities.* Belknap Press of Harvard University Press, Cambridge, MA. An early synthesis of the community ecology perspective. This collection of papers by the leading community ecologists of the day covers important questions in the evolution of abundance and diversity patterns and community structure.

Diamond, J. and T. J. Case (eds.). 1986. *Community Ecology.* Harper & Row, New York. An excellent overview of issues in community ecology by a large group of authors. This book covers topics in experimental methods in ecology, species introductions and extinctions, the relevance of spatial and temporal scales, equilibrium and nonequilibrium communities, various forces structuring communities, and various types of communities.

Drake, J. A., H. A. Mooney, F. di Castri, R. H. Groves, F. J. Kruger, M. Rejmanek and M. Williamson (eds.). 1989. *Biological Invasions: A Global Perspective.* John Wiley & Sons, New York. A very comprehensive review of biological invasions around the world. Topics cover a variety of ecosystems and numerous species and concepts. This book provides an excellent overview of biological invasions.

Pickett, S. T. A. and P. S. White (eds.). 1985. *The Ecology of Natural Disturbance and Patch Dynamics.* Academic Press, Orlando, FL. This is a seminal work that stimulated the current interest in and awareness of disturbances and patches in ecological systems. Twenty-one chapters cover a broad array of disturbance topics relative to plants and animals.

Pimm, S. L. 1991. *The Balance of Nature? Ecological Issues in the Conservation of Species and Communities.* University of Chicago Press, Chicago. This is a good compilation of a large amount of information regarding community ecology and conservation. Pimm reviews such topics as community resilience, temporal variation of species and the environment, extinctions, food web structure, species introductions, and the vast and complex experimental and observational literature on communities.

Strong, D. R., Jr., D. Simberloff, L. G. Abele and A. B. Thistle. 1984. *Ecological Communities: Conceptual Issues and the Evidence.* Princeton University Press, Princeton, NJ. This collection of papers covers many of the highly contentious issues in community ecology, and challenges some of the earlier concepts regarding community patterns and stability. It also emphasizes the more rigorous, experimental approaches to understanding community structure and function.

# 9

# Habitat Fragmentation

*A natural community that occurs as a central portion of a larger regional habitat will contain numerous rare species that rely on the larger system for existence. As progressively more of the surrounding area is allocated to other uses, the distinctiveness of the habitat island patch is accentuated. As the habitat island becomes progressively more isolated from surrounding vegetation of similar form, the rare species are quickly lost.*

*Larry D. Harris, 1984*

Alteration of habitats by human activity is the greatest threat to the richness of life on Earth. The most visible form of habitat alteration is direct habitat removal, as when a forest is clear-cut, a wetland is drained, a stream is dammed to create a reservoir, or a remnant prairie is converted to a shopping mall. However, if we step back and view the broader landscape, as from a mountain peak or an airplane, the most striking pattern is often **fragmentation** of a once continuous natural landscape.

Habitat fragmentation has two components: (1) reduction of the total amount of a habitat type, or perhaps of all natural habitat, in a landscape; and (2) apportionment of the remaining habitat into smaller, more isolated patches (Harris 1984; Wilcove et al. 1986; Saunders et al. 1991). Although the latter component is fragmentation in the literal sense, it usually occurs in tandem with widespread deforestation or other habitat reduction. In managed landscapes, such as national forests, there are ways that vegetation can be removed (temporarily or permanently) without fragmenting the remaining vegetation (Franklin and Forman 1987; Harris and Silva-Lopez 1992). In some cases, a landscape may be more "shredded" than fragmented (see Essay 9B by Peter Feinsinger). However, the end result of human settlement and resource extraction in a landscape is often a patchwork of small, isolated natural areas in a sea of developed land (Figure 9.1).

Studies in many regions have documented local extinctions, shifts in composition and abundance patterns to favor weedy species, and other forms of biotic impoverishment in fragmented landscapes (Burgess and Sharpe 1981; Noss 1983; Harris 1984; Wilcox and Murphy 1985; Saunders et al. 1991). Thus, fragmentation has become a major subject of research and debate in conservation biology. In this chapter, we review some differences be-

**Figure 9.1** Changes in wooded area of Cadiz Township, Green County, Wisconsin, during the period of European settlement. Shaded area represents the amount of land in forest in each year. (From Curtis 1956.)

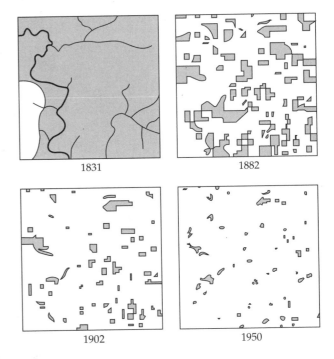

tween fragmented landscapes and naturally heterogeneous landscapes, island biogeography and species–area relationships, and biological consequences of fragmentation. We conclude with recommendations for countering fragmentation, leading into the following chapter on reserve design.

## Fragmentation and Heterogeneity

A superficial view of fragmentation portrays a large area of homogeneous habitat being broken up into small, isolated pieces. Thus, the forest in Figure 9.1 is shown as uniformly gray. But the apparent homogeneity of these forest patches is an artifact of graphic art. If we zoom in and map forests at higher resolution (see Figures 9.2 and 9.3), we see that they are far from uniform. In fact, virtually all landscapes are mosaics at one scale or another (see Essay 9A by Steward Pickett). At a landscape scale of analysis (a few kilometers across), the distribution of vegetation types typically corresponds to changes in elevation and slope aspect. This is vividly displayed in mountainous regions, such as the Smoky Mountains (Figure 9.2), but is also true in relatively flat landscapes such as the southeastern coastal plain of the United States. An eleva-

**Figure 9.2** Topographic distribution of vegetation types on an idealized west-facing slope in the Great Smoky Mountains National Park. Vegetation types: BG, beech gap; CF, cove forest; F, Fraser fir; GB, grassy bald; H, hemlock; HB, heath bald; OCF, chestnut oak–chestnut; OCH, chestnut oak–chestnut heath; OH, oak–hickory; P, pine forest and heath; ROC, red oak–chestnut oak; S, spruce; SF, spruce–fir. (From Whittaker 1956.)

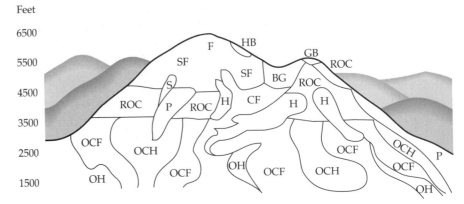

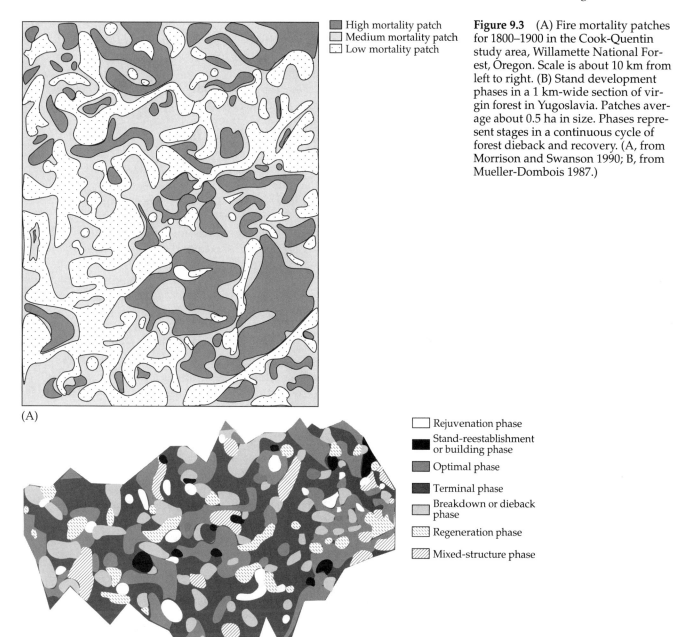

High mortality patch
Medium mortality patch
Low mortality patch

(A)

(B)

Rejuvenation phase
Stand-reestablishment or building phase
Optimal phase
Terminal phase
Breakdown or dieback phase
Regeneration phase
Mixed-structure phase

**Figure 9.3** (A) Fire mortality patches for 1800–1900 in the Cook-Quentin study area, Willamette National Forest, Oregon. Scale is about 10 km from left to right. (B) Stand development phases in a 1 km-wide section of virgin forest in Yugoslavia. Patches average about 0.5 ha in size. Phases represent stages in a continuous cycle of forest dieback and recovery. (A, from Morrison and Swanson 1990; B, from Mueller-Dombois 1987.)

tion gradient of only a few meters in Florida may lead through a progression of longleaf pine (*Pinus palustris*) and turkey oak (*Quercus laevis*) on dry sand-hills, down through flatwoods with longleaf pine, then slash pine (*P. elliottii*) on wetter sites, and sometimes pond pine (*P. serotina*) on the wettest sites. Slopes may have seepage bogs grading down into shrub swamps. This gradient-aligned vegetation pattern is a product of fire interacting with the slope–moisture gradient (Wolfe et al. 1988; Noss and Harris 1990).

Natural disturbances create considerable heterogeneity in forests and other vegetation. The "grain" of a landscape is determined largely by the spatial scale of disturbance, that is, by the size and distribution of disturbance-generated patches. Relatively large disturbances, such as extensive fires, create a coarse-grained pattern (Figure 9.3A), whereas canopy gaps caused by death and fall of individual trees or small groups of trees create fine-grained patterns (Figure 9.3B). Because a given area will be affected by many different kinds and scales of disturbance, several grains of pattern may be overlaid on one another, increasing the diversity of the horizontal pattern. Furthermore, disturbances are typically patchy in time as well as space, so that new disturbances occur in some areas while previously disturbed sites are recovering. This continuously changing pattern has been called a space–time mosaic (Watt 1947) or shifting mosaic (Bormann and Likens 1979). Ecologists generalize that natural disturbances, especially when of moderate intensity or intermediate frequency of occurrence, increase the diversity of habitats, microhabitats, and species in an area.

The patterns portrayed in Figures 9.2 and 9.3 are examples of natural patchiness or horizontal complexity. Every landscape is patchy at one scale or another, and often at many scales, though some landscapes are obviously more patchy than others (Forman and Godron 1986). As a consequence of patchiness, habitat quality for species varies spatially, and many species may be distributed as metapopulations, systems of local populations linked by dispersal (discussed in Chapters 6 and 7). Because patches of habitat suitable to a species are often spatially separated, the persistence of a metapopulation is tied to the efficiency of dispersal by individuals or propagules from one patch to another (see Figures 6.9 and 7.4). If connections between the patches are broken, disrupting dispersal, metapopulations may be destabilized.

Dispersal is more likely to maintain metapopulations in naturally patchy landscapes than in formerly continuous landscapes fragmented by human activity (den Boer 1970; Hansson 1991). The metapopulation model also suggests that habitat patches currently unoccupied may be critical to survival, because they represent sites for possible recolonization. Establishing small populations on vacant patches may help prevent downward spirals in metapopulations (Smith and Peacock 1990). Although the classic model of metapopulations as sets of populations persisting in a balance between local extinction and colonization is too simplistic to depict the many types of population spatial structure found in nature (Harrison 1991), the basic model of spatially distinct population units connected by occasional dispersal seems to have considerable generality.

Recognizing that conservation biology is a value-laden science, and that conservation biologists place high value on diversity, it is easy to conclude that patchiness is "good." Old-growth forests, for example, have been of interest to ecologists and conservationists in part because they are so heterogeneous. With trees of many ages, and canopies that are tall and uneven, old-growth forests have higher rates of gap formation than do younger stands (Clebsch and Busing 1989; Lorimer 1989). High levels of habitat heterogeneity, expressed horizontally and vertically, contribute to high species diversity.

But if patchiness is good, then why is fragmentation caused by humans perceived as bad? Surely fragmentation creates a patchy landscape; superficially, at least, the patterns in Figures 9.1, 9.2, and 9.3 are similar. Are conservation biologists just being misanthropic? Or are there fundamental differences between naturally patchy landscapes and fragmented landscapes? What precisely are these differences? These are not trivial questions. Answering them may allow the design of land use plans and management practices that mimic natural processes and patterns and thereby maintain biodiversity; failing to answer them will likely lead to further biotic impoverishment.

The differences between naturally patchy and fragmented landscapes are only beginning to be explored scientifically. We can hypothesize that the following three distinctions are of major ecological significance:

1. A naturally patchy landscape has rich internal patch structure (lots of tree-fall gaps, logs, and different layers of vegetation), whereas a fragmented landscape has simplified patches, such as parking lots, cornfields, clear-cuts, and tree farms with trees all of the same species and size.
2. Largely because of (1), a natural landscape has less contrast (less pronounced structural differences) between adjacent patches than does a fragmented landscape, and therefore potentially less intense edge effects.
3. Certain features of fragmented landscapes, such as roads and various human activities, pose specific threats to population viability.

We will attempt to shed light on these differences below in explaining how fragmentation threatens biodiversity. But we must admit at the outset that the mechanisms underlying the differences in the viability of populations in natural and fragmented landscapes are still largely inferred, not proven. Fragmentation is not simply the creation of habitat islands. There are many degrees and scales of fragmentation. It is a process with unpredictable thresholds, not simply an either/or condition.

## The Fragmentation Process

In terrestrial ecosystems, fragmentation typically begins with gap formation or perforation of the vegetative matrix. For a while, the matrix (that is, the most common habitat type) remains as natural vegetation, and species composition and abundance patterns may be little affected (Figure 9.4). But as the gaps get bigger or more numerous, they eventually become the matrix. The connectivity of the original vegetation has been broken. By analogy, if the holes in Swiss cheese become much bigger than the cheese, the block of cheese collapses.

Because fragmentation is a complex process involving many variables, no two landscapes are likely to show identical trajectories of change. Each landscape at any point in time will have its own unique structure, though landscapes in a given region subjected to the same kind of development or resource exploitation may have very similar patterns. Ecologists have suggested a number of measures of landscape structure, including fractal dimension (a measure of patch size and shape complexity), contagion (the positive or negative association between patch types), and other spatial statistics (O'Neill et al. 1988; Turner 1989; Mladenoff et al. 1993). Although the relevance of these statistics to conservation questions has not been firmly established, time series analysis of change in landscape pattern, as measured by various spatial statistics, can be related to changes in species composition and other expressions of biodiversity, and provides a powerful monitoring approach (Noss 1990).

The point in the fragmentation process at which biological integrity declines dramatically is usually not known, as few fragmentation studies have been conducted over a long enough period. In the Wisconsin sequence (see Figure 9.1), for example, the matrix shifted from forest to farmland sometime between 1831 and 1882. Is this when the avifauna changed from predominately forest species to largely edge species, or did that happen sometime later as forest species failed to reproduce successfully and edge species invaded? Site tenacity in birds is one of many factors that may create time lags in response to fragmentation and other disturbances. Individuals may return to a site where they have bred successfully in the past, long after the habitat has been altered (Wiens 1985). In fragmentation studies, researchers may see

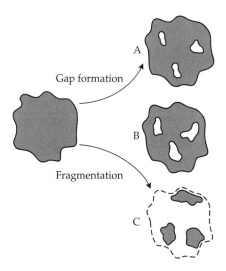

**Figure 9.4** A fragmentation sequence begins with gap formation or perforation of the landscape (A). Gaps become bigger or more numerous (B) until the landscape matrix shifts from forest to anthropogenic habitat (C). (From Wiens 1989.)

the final outcome of fragmentation without observing the process. Alternatively, they may observe the process, but not the long-term consequences.

As we discuss the consequences of fragmentation in the remainder of this chapter, bear in mind that the process can occur at many different spatial and temporal scales and in any kind of habitat. Essentially, fragmentation is the "disruption of continuity" in pattern or processes (Lord and Norton 1990). At a broad biogeographic scale, regions that were once connected by wide (many kilometers) expanses of natural habitat may now be isolated by agriculture; the severance of such biogeographic corridors may take place over hundreds of years. The occasional interchanges that once took place between the faunas and floras of these regions are now precluded, with unknown evolutionary consequences. What if there had been no Bering Land Bridge or Isthmus of Panama? Migration of species in response to climate change, which in the past occurred over hundreds of kilometers (Davis 1981), may not be possible when regions are heavily fragmented (Peters and Darling 1985).

At an intermediate scale, the kind of landscape fragmentation portrayed in Figure 9.1 typically takes place over decades; this is the scale at which effects of fragmentation have usually been studied. Although sometimes we arrive too late to observe mechanisms leading to species loss, intensive field studies of populations and communities in regions currently being fragmented may teach us a great deal.

At a finer scale, the internal fragmentation of once pristine natural areas by roads, trails, power lines, fences, canals, vegetation removal by livestock, and other human-related activities has not been well studied, but it has potentially dramatic effects on native biodiversity and ecological processes. Lord and Norton (1990) discussed structural fragmentation of short-tussock grasslands in New Zealand by grazing and other disturbances, which was followed by invasion of naturalized plants. They concluded that ecosystem functioning is more likely to be disrupted at finer scales of fragmentation, although the organisms affected are smaller and the overall process is less noticeable to human observers.

## ESSAY 9A
# Mosaics and Patch Dynamics

Steward T. A. Pickett, Institute of Ecosystem Studies, New York Botanical Garden

Mosaics are patterns composed of smaller elements, like the tile or glass works that reached an artistic zenith during the Byzantine Era. One of the marvels of such mosaics is that in spite of being made of individual bits fixed in place by mortar, the best works seem animated and lively. It is ironic that a static entity can suggest such motion and liveliness.

Like mosaic art, most of the landscapes in which we must practice conservation are composed of smaller elements—individual forest stands, lakes, hedgerows, shrubland patches, highways, farms, or towns. Because the time scale of human observation is short rel-

ative to many landscape changes, people have often assumed mosaic landscapes to be static, with unchanging bits of nature and culture cemented into place.

Most often, landscape mosaics have been looked at only from the perspective of specific elements in them, rather than as an entire array that might interact. The focus may be on a stand of a rare plant, or the breeding ground of an unusual animal. The local spatial scale of observation is linked to a tacit assumption that the status of a particular population, community, or ecosystem can be understood by studying a particular patch in a mosaic. The conditions

in adjoining or distant elements of the mosaic have been ignored.

Ecologists have learned, however, that these two assumptions often do not hold in the real world. First, virtually all landscapes are in fact dynamic. Although the mosaics of art only *seem* to vibrate and shimmer, mosaic landscapes *do* in fact change. Bormann and Likens (1979) coined the phrase "shifting mosaic" to label the insight that landscapes are dynamic. Landscapes may change in two ways. First, the individual elements, or patches, may arise, change size or shape, or disappear. For example, new patches may arise through logging, lightning fires, turning of prairie sod for farming, conversion of a farm to a suburb, or reforestation. Examples of changes in patch shape include encroachment of a forest into a field, or the spread of a bog into a pond. Second, the structure, function, or composition of individual patches may change. For instance, the species composition, and hence the rate of nutrient cycling, in an ecosystem may change as a result of succession. Patch dynamics is the term that incorporates all these fluid possibilities.

The second incorrect assumption about mosaics is that the elements act separately from one another. As ecologists began to look longer and more mechanistically at the dynamics of the specific sites they studied, it became increasingly clear that organisms, materials, and other influences can flow between systems, even when there are distinct boundaries between them. Thus, mammal populations in a forest may rely on food from outside the forest, certain insect populations may be maintained by migration, and some forest successions can be driven primarily by seed input rather than species interactions at the site. It is safer to assume that ecological systems in a mosaic landscape are open, rather than closed and isolated.

These changes within landscapes and fluxes among patches are crucial to conservation. Conservation strategies and tactics that ignore these two dynamic aspects of landscapes are doomed to failure. This conclusion is all the more germane in landscapes where humans, with their great mobility, energy subsidies, and insertions of novel organisms and materials into systems, are dominant influences. It is also important to realize that the dynamics of a landscape may reflect specific human behaviors and land uses, either now or in the past. So the dynamics of landscapes are in reality a complex mixture of human effects and natural effects such as land use, disturbance, and succession.

Successful conservation requires knowing what the patches are, how they change, and how they are affected by fluxes from outside the target area (or even the region). There may be important fluxes that have been halted or reversed by human activities in the landscape. Or there may be important population, community, or ecosystem processes within the site that no longer occur naturally. Conservation requires not only choosing areas in which the processes that are responsible for the existence of a conservation target are intact, but also compensating for natural or anthropogenic processes that no longer occur. Conservation is, in a sense, active maintenance of patch dynamics.

Some of the most important insights for conservation to arise from modern ecology concern the need to treat ecological systems, be they populations, communities, or ecosystems, as open to outside influences, and to manage systems to maintain the dynamics that created them. All landscapes in which we practice conservation should be treated as shifting and interconnected mosaics. The smaller or more delicate the target for conservation, the more critical the patch dynamic view becomes.

## Insularization and Area Effects

Rapid settlement of regions such as the midwestern United States (see Figure 9.1) left behind scraps of the original vegetation as habitat fragments. The analogy with islands, though imperfect, was easy to make. Biogeographers have long known that as the area of any insular habitat declines, so does the number of species it contains. In 1855 the Swiss phytogeographer Alphonse de Candolle predicted that "the breakup of a large landmass into smaller units would necessarily lead to the extinction or local extermination of one or more species and the differential preservation of others" (cited and translated in Browne 1983). This statement may be the first written recognition of the potential negative effects of habitat fragmentation on biodiversity (Harris and Silva-Lopez 1992).

Recognition of a relationship between species number and land area goes back further, and is one of the great empirical generalizations of biogeography (see Chapter 4). Apparently the first recorded mention of a species–area effect was by Johann Reinhold Forster, a naturalist on Captain Cook's second tour of the Southern Hemisphere in 1772–1775. Forster noted that "islands only produce a greater or lesser number of species, as their circumference is more or less extensive" (Forster 1778, in Browne 1983). Subsequent studies have confirmed the species–area effect for many groups of islands and have extended the effect to "habitat islands" in terrestrial landscapes. More generally, a species–area relationship exists for sample plots of vegetation within continuous habitats, but the slope is less steep than for islands (Figure 9.5). On islands or in insular habitats, a tenfold decrease in habitat area typically cuts the number of species by about half (Darlington 1957).

What are the causes of the species–area relationship? This question has been long debated. As with most natural phenomena, many scientists have sought single causes for the relationship between species richness and area,

(A)

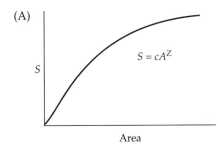

$S = cA^Z$

*S*

Area

(B)

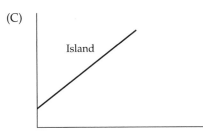

Log *S*

Log *S* = Log *c* + *z* log *A*

Log area

(C)

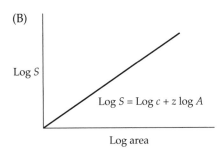

Island

(D)

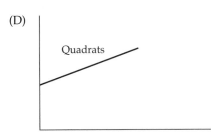

Quadrats

**Figure 9.5** A schematic diagram of the species–area relationship. Shown on an arithmetic plot (A), species richness (*S*) increases rapidly with increasing area, then levels off. A log–log plot (B) linearizes the relationship. The slope of the relationship is steeper for islands or other isolated habitats (C) than for sample quadrats within extensive habitats (D). (From Harris 1984.)

although the phenomenon is almost certainly multicausal. The most straightforward explanation in many cases is habitat diversity. As area increases, so does the diversity of physical habitats and resources, which in turn support a larger number of species (Williams 1943; Lack 1976). Several studies have concluded that habitat diversity is better than area as a predictor of species diversity (Power 1972; Johnson 1975), though other studies have concluded that area itself, or some unrecognized factor correlated with area, is more important (Johnson and Raven 1973; Johnson and Simberloff 1974; Harner and Harper 1976). Disentangling the effects of area, habitat diversity, and other factors that contribute to species richness has proven difficult. Simberloff (1991) concluded that "probably, on all but very small sets of sites, the majority of the species–area relationship is accounted for by the fact that larger sites, on average, have more habitats than small ones." Studies showing that area and habitat diversity are both important for increasing species richness suggest that nature reserves should be both large and naturally heterogeneous (Freemark and Merriam 1986).

Although habitat diversity frequently provides the best explanation for species–area relationships, other phenomena are often at work. Possibly we could ignore biology and consider sampling theory. In a statistical population of many individuals of both rare and common species, larger samples would be expected to yield more species. Thus, passive sampling may be an appropriate null hypothesis for biological factors (Connor and McCoy 1979). Among biological explanations, species richness might increase with area because the size of populations increases, thus reducing the probability of extinction (Preston 1960, 1962). We know from studies and models of population viability that large populations are less likely than small ones to go extinct due to various stochastic processes (see Chapters 6 and 7). All populations fluctuate through time; a small population is more likely to fluctuate down to zero.

A small island or nature reserve may be smaller than the territory or home range of a single individual of some species. For example, a cougar (*Felis concolor*) is unlikely to find enough to eat even within areas as large as a few thousand hectares; annual home ranges for cougars in southern California average about 450 km² for males and 155 km² for females (P. Beier, personal communication). Large carnivores and other wide-ranging animals are typically among the species most threatened by habitat fragmentation, in part because small areas fail to provide enough prey, but also because these animals are vulnerable to mortality due to humans and vehicles when they attempt to travel through fragmented landscapes (Harris and Gallagher 1989). Other species, for reasons not entirely understood, avoid settling in small tracts of seemingly suitable habitat. Studies in the eastern United States confirmed that many songbird species are "area-sensitive" and usually breed only in tracts of forest many times larger than the size of their territories (Figure 9.6). Similarly, studies of grassland birds on prairie remnants in Missouri showed that several species occur only on fragments larger than 10 ha, even though their territories are much smaller (Samson 1983).

The most famous and controversial explanation for the species–area relationship is the equilibrium theory of island biogeography (MacArthur and Wilson 1963, 1967). MacArthur and Wilson, though recognizing the role of habitat diversity in controlling species occurrence, suggested an ultimate explanation: the number of species on an island represents a balance between immigration and extinction (Figure 9.7). Over a period of time, species continually go extinct on an island, but other species immigrate to the island from the mainland or other islands. Islands near the mainland experience higher rates of immigration than remote islands because the dispersal distance is shorter. Large islands contain larger populations and consequently suffer lower rates of extinction. Size may affect immigration rates as well, as larger islands stand a higher chance of intercepting dispersing individuals. Islands close to an immigration source can also be expected to have lower extinction rates, as declining populations can be bolstered by immigrants of the same species—a rescue effect (Brown and Kodric-Brown 1977). Therefore, equilibrium theory predicts that large, "near" islands will contain the most species, all else being equal.

The effect of isolation on diversity was noticed by Forster (1778, in Browne 1983), who observed that the number of species common to islands and continents decreased as islands became more distant from the mainland. However, Forster and other biogeographers of the time failed to recognize that inadequate dispersal was responsible for the absence of many species on islands, particularly distant ones. Forster attributed the depauperate condition of islands to peculiarities of their physical environments. Charles Darwin was among the first to recognize that species on islands had arrived from the continents, many of them subsequently differentiating into new species (Browne 1983).

A common distinction in island biogeographic studies is between oceanic and **land-bridge islands** (MacArthur 1972). Land-bridge islands were connected to each other or to continents during the Pleistocene, when sea level was as much as 100 m lower than today. Presumably, at that time, land-bridge islands contained numbers of bird species similar to those in areas of equal size on the mainland. Since becoming isolated, these islands apparently lost species over time, a phenomenon called **relaxation,** with some species being more extinction-prone than others (Diamond 1972; Terborgh

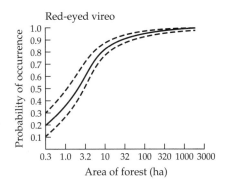

**Figure 9.6** Probability of four species of common forest-interior Neotropical migrant birds nesting in United States mid-Atlantic forests of various sizes, based on point counts. Dotted lines indicate 95% confidence intervals. (From Robbins et al. 1989.)

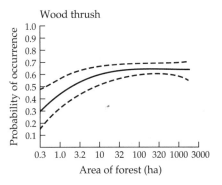

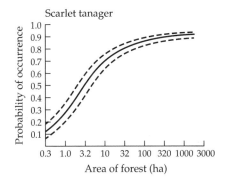

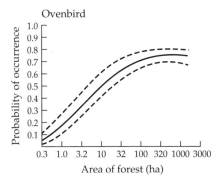

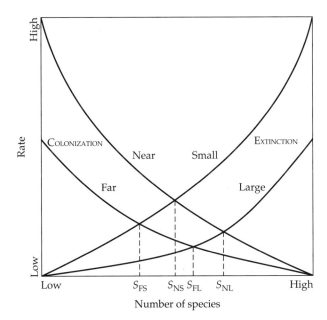

**Figure 9.7** Predicted species richness on an island, represented as a balance between rate of colonization (immigration) to the island and rate of extinction, according to the equilibrium theory of island biogeography (MacArthur and Wilson 1967). In this model, colonization is affected mainly by island distance from the mainland (near or far); extinction is affected by island size. Species richness corresponds to the intersection of the colonization and extinction curves. The greatest number of species is predicted to occur on islands that are near and large ($S_{NL}$). (From Wilcox 1980.)

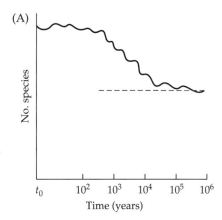

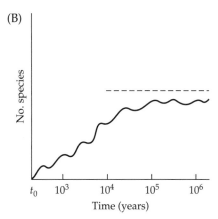

**Figure 9.8**  Predicted species richness over time for land-bridge islands (A) and oceanic islands (B). Land-bridge islands were once part of a large land area and contained more species than they could retain after their isolation by rising sea level; the decline in species richness after isolation is known as "relaxation." Oceanic islands, often of volcanic origin, are slowly colonized by long-distance dispersal, so species richness builds gradually to an equilibrium level. (From Harris 1984.)

1974; Faaborg 1979). However, equilibrium species richness on land-bridge islands is typically higher than on similar-sized oceanic islands that were never connected to larger land bodies (Figure 9.8; Harris 1984). The analogy between land-bridge islands and terrestrial habitat patches isolated by development of the surrounding landscape was persuasive and spawned a series of papers proposing rules for the design of nature reserves (Terborgh 1974; Willis 1974; Diamond 1975; Wilson and Willis 1975; Diamond and May 1976). Unfortunately, the usefulness of land-bridge island analogies for conservation was marred by, among other problems, the weak evidence for relaxation being strongly related to island size (Abele and Connor 1979; Faeth and Connor 1979).

Island biogeography can be studied at several levels of biological organization. The response variable in the classic equilibrium model—species number—is a community-level property and not necessarily the most appropriate variable for conservation planning in fragmented landscapes. Subdivision or fragmentation of habitats may increase species richness (Burkey 1989), but often favors weedy species (those that thrive in areas disturbed by humans) over more sensitive ones (Noss 1983). Thus, population-level considerations of extinction and colonization are often more important than species number (Haila 1990). Density-dependent models of population persistence show that fragmentation may greatly increase extinction risk (Burkey 1989). In studying the overall effects of fragmentation and other human activities on biodiversity, it is generally wise to consider multiple levels of organization; for example, genetic, population, community, and landscape.

Island biogeographic theory has sometimes been supported by empirical studies and sometimes not. Often, researchers claiming support for the theory have failed to consider alternative or null hypotheses. The reserve design rules offered by Diamond, Terborgh, Willis, and others have been challenged as idiosyncratic and having many exceptions. Half of them do not even follow directly from island biogeographic theory (Simberloff and Abele 1976, 1982; Margules et al. 1982; Simberloff 1991). But despite problems with the theory and its uncritical application to reserve design, island biogeography has led to major advances in conservation. Above all, the theory expanded the focus of scientists and conservationists to landscapes—to collections of sites, not just single sites—and got them thinking about the potential effects of habitat area and isolation on biodiversity. Considering the problem of habitat fragmentation, it would be difficult to think of a more meaningful contribution.

## Biological Consequences of Fragmentation

Some effects of fragmentation on biodiversity have been conspicuous; others have been subtle and indirect. Some have occurred almost immediately after the initial disturbance, whereas others have developed over decades or are still unfolding. Fragmentation of some regions, such as the Georgia Piedmont (Turner and Ruscher 1988; Odum 1989), has been partially reversed through abandonment of agriculture and maturation of second-growth forests. However, fragmentation of other regions, such as the Pacific Northwest, Florida, and much of the tropics, continues. Most deforestation in Central America has occurred since 1950 and is increasing in rate (Hartshorn 1992).

As suggested earlier, the effects of fragmentation can be seen at several levels of biological organization, from changes in gene frequencies within populations to continent-wide changes in the distributions of species and ecosystems. At the species level, there are essentially three options for persistence in a highly fragmented landscape. First, a species might survive or even thrive in the matrix of human land use; a number of weedy species worldwide fit this description. Second, a species might survive in a fragmented landscape by maintaining viable populations within individual habitat fragments; this is an option only for species with small home ranges or otherwise modest area requirements, such as many plants and invertebrates. Many of these species can meet all of their life history requirements within the boundaries of a single fragment, barring major environmental change.

A third way to survive in a fragmented landscape is to be highly mobile. A mobile species might integrate a number of habitat patches, either into individual home ranges or into an interbreeding population. The Pileated Woodpecker (*Dryocopus pileatus*) has demonstrated adaptation to fragmented landscapes, particularly in eastern North America. Foraging individuals now travel among a number of small woodlots in landscapes that were formerly continuous forest, often using wooded fencerows as travel corridors (Whitcomb et al. 1981; Merriam 1991). White-footed mice (*Peromyscus leucopus*) and chipmunks (*Tamias striatus*) maintain populations in fragmented landscapes only when dispersal between woodlots, aided by fencerow corridors (Figure 9.9), is great enough to balance local extinctions (Fahrig and Merriam 1985; Henderson et al. 1985). A species incapable of pursuing one or more of these three options is bound for eventual extinction in a fragmented landscape.

### Initial Exclusion

One of the most rapid and obvious effects of fragmentation is elimination of species that occurred only in the portions of the landscape destroyed by development. Many rare species are endemics with very narrow distributions, occurring in only one or a few patches of suitable habitat. Recall the loss of up to 90 species of plants on the Centinela Ridge in Ecuador (Chapter 5) when that small patch of forest was destroyed by loggers (Gentry 1986). Similarly, Cerro Tacarcuna is a mountain on the Panama-Colombia border that supports at least 71 species of angiosperms (24% of its flora) that are "extremely endemic"; that is, they have a range of only 5–10 km$^2$, and could easily be lost through fragmentation (Gentry 1986). In Colombia and Ecuador, existing national parks do not include the ranges of most of the bird species unique to those countries (Terborgh and Winter 1983). If habitat outside the parks is eliminated, these species will also be lost by exclusion unless they are capable of moving rapidly to suitable habitat elsewhere. Eventually, as habitat destruction continues, suitable habitat may not be available anywhere.

### Barriers and Isolation

Isolation of habitats by movement barriers is an effect of fragmentation as important as reduction in habitat size. Species that are restricted to certain kinds of habitat may depend on a constellation of habitat patches in relatively close proximity, if no single patch is large enough to meet the needs of individuals or groups (Figure 9.10). As noted earlier, the viability of metapopulations may depend on movement of individuals between patches being great enough to balance extirpation from local patches. Also, many animal species require a mix of different habitats with distinct resources—for example, food patches, roost sites, and breeding sites—in order to meet their life history requirements (Figure 9.11). If these critical areas become separated by barriers, populations may decline rapidly to extinction.

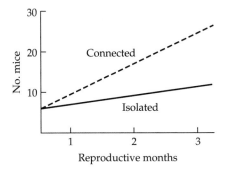

**Figure 9.9** Isolated woodlots in a fragmented landscape are predicted by simulation models to have lower rates of population growth than woodlots connected by fencerow corridors. These predictions were verified by studies of white-footed mice in southern Ontario. (From Merriam 1991, based on Fahrig and Merriam 1985.)

**Figure 9.10**  A constellation of separate habitat patches may be critical to the survival of individuals or populations. If a species requires resources in the shaded habitat patches, site A will be preferable to site B. Although no single patch is large enough by itself to support a population, the close grouping of patches in site A provides sufficient resources within the accessible part of the landscape (circle). In contrast, site B consists of one small, isolated patch and will not support a population. If human activities create impenetrable barriers to movement between the patches in site A, that site will no longer be superior to site B. (From Dunning et al. 1992.)

**Figure 9.11**  Many animals require a suite of different habitats or resources to meet life history needs. If a species requires nonsubstitutable resources found in two habitat types (shaded and open), regions of the landscape where the two habitats are in close proximity (site A) will support larger populations than regions where one habitat type is rare (site B). However, as in the example in Figure 9.10, barriers between habitat patches will destroy any advantage of site A. (From Dunning et al. 1992.)

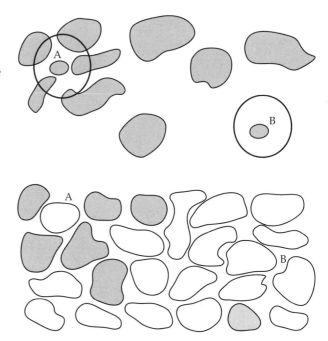

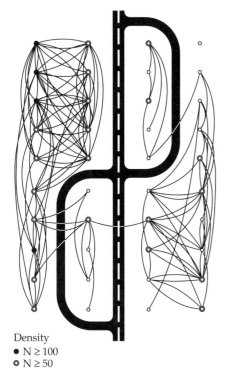

Density
- ● N ≥ 100
- ◉ N ≥ 50
- ○ N ≥ 20

**Figure 9.12**  Roads can be significant barriers to the movement of small vertebrates and invertebrates. In this example, populations of the forest-dwelling carabid beetle *Abax ater* were almost completely divided by a road and even by parking loops. Lines represent movements of marked beetles between capture and recapture points. (Modified from Mader 1984.)

What constitutes a movement barrier is highly species-specific; a hedgerow that is a barrier to the movement of some species will be a corridor to others. Unfortunately, very little information exists on the qualities of suitable dispersal habitat or on barriers for various species. Species- and habitat-specific dispersal studies are essential for gaining a better understanding of fragmentation effects. However, what we do know suggests that human-created structures and habitats—roads, urban areas, agricultural fields, clearcuts—can greatly inhibit the movements of many kinds of animals and, potentially, plants (especially those dispersed by animals).

One significant type of barrier in many landscapes is roads. Habitat fragmentation is usually accompanied, and augmented, by road building. To the extent that individual animals hesitate to cross roads, roads fragment populations into smaller demographic units that are more vulnerable to extinction. A study in southeastern Ontario and Quebec found that several species of small mammals rarely ventured onto road surfaces when the road clearance (distance between road margins) exceeded 20 m (Oxley et al. 1974). In Oregon, dusky-footed woodrats (*Neotoma fuscipes*) and red-backed voles (*Clethrionomys occidentalis*) were trapped at all distances from an interstate highway right-of-way, but never in the right-of-way itself, suggesting that these rodents did not cross the highway (Adams and Geis 1983). In Germany, several species of carabid beetles and two species of forest rodents rarely or never crossed two-lane roads (Figure 9.12); even a narrow, unpaved forest road, closed to public traffic, served as a barrier (Mader 1984). Another study found that roads and railroads inhibited normal movements of lycosid spiders and carabid beetles; although crossings were rare, longitudinal movements along these barriers were stimulated (Mader et al. 1990).

Road clearances can be barriers in a wide variety of habitat types. In a study of the effects of a highway on rodents in the Mojave Desert (Garland and Bradley 1984), only one white-tailed antelope squirrel (*Ammospermophilus leucurus*), out of 612 individuals of eight rodent species captured and 387 individuals recaptured, was ever recorded as having crossed the

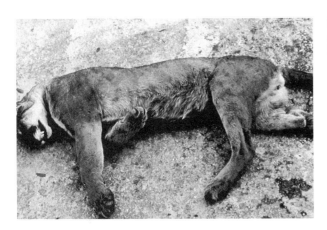

**Figure 9.13** A road-killed Florida panther. Automobile collisions are the largest single source of mortality for Florida panthers. (Photograph by R. C. Belden.)

road. A 9-year study in a Kansas grassland found that very few prairie voles (*Microtus ochrogaster*) and cotton rats (*Sigmodon hispidus*) ever crossed a dirt road 3 m wide that bisected a trapping grid (Swihart and Slade 1984). Many other studies have documented the barrier effects of roads, even for animals as large as black bears (*Ursus americanus*) (Brody and Pelton 1989). In the latter study, the frequency at which bears crossed roads of any type varied with traffic volume. An interstate highway was the most significant barrier, and bears that attempted to cross it were often killed. Roads are the largest source of mortality for endangered Florida panthers (Figure 9.13).

The long-term effects of roads and other dispersal barriers on population dynamics and genetic structure are generally unknown. Effects of isolation are usually only inferred. Low rates of genetic interchange between populations (on the order of one successful migrant per generation) appear sufficient to prevent inbreeding depression and other genetic problems in many cases (see Chapter 6). However, a German study found that separation of populations of common frogs (*Rana temporaria*) by highways reduced the average heterozygosity and genetic polymorphism of local populations (Reh and Seitz 1990). A Canadian study of white-footed mice failed to find any significant effects of road barriers on genetic structure, but hypothesized that such effects could be important in cases in which roads are absolute barriers (Merriam et al. 1989).

Although inbreeding depression and genetic drift may increase extinction risk in small, isolated populations, in other cases fragmentation may increase the among-population component of genetic diversity (Simberloff and Cox 1987; Simberloff 1988). As discussed in Chapter 6, the creation of fragmented distributions and population bottlenecks by human activities has apparently increased genetic differentiation among populations of Wild Turkeys (*Meleagris gallopavo*) in three regions of the eastern United States (Leberg 1991). However, these increases in among-population genetic diversity due to fragmentation could be offset in the long run by the erosion of genetic diversity within the family of populations that were once connected.

Barrier effects are both relative and cumulative. A city block can be expected to be more of a barrier to most forest species than a cornfield, which will be more of a barrier than a pine plantation. The cumulative effects of many barriers are probably what finally extinguishes populations in many cases. In a multiple-species context, the landscape matrix in which habitat islands are embedded is better seen as a "filter" than as a barrier. The matrix will allow individuals of some species, but not of others, to pass through. In-

**Figure 9.14** Natural or artificial barriers to movement are perhaps better understood as filters, because individuals of some species will cross them but others will not. The Columbia River defines range limits for some species and subspecies of terrestrial animals because it is an essentially permanent barrier to movement. For other species, such as most birds, the river is only a partial barrier at most. However, logging and urban development in lowland areas of western Oregon and Washington have created a "bottleneck," or area of restricted interchange, for forest species such as the Northern Spotted Owl (*Strix occidentalis caurina*) that once crossed the river. It is unknown whether interchange presently occurs between Spotted Owl populations in the two states. (Photograph by B. Csuti.)

dividual features, such as a river or a highway, are also filters because individuals of some species, but not others, cross them (Figure 9.14).

The amount of structural contrast between habitat fragments and the matrix in which they exist is one measure of fragmentation (Harris 1984); that is, as the landscape around fragments is progressively altered, the functional isolation of those fragments increases. A structurally rich matrix may serve as marginal habitat for some species and buffer population fluctuations; it may also encourage dispersal among patches. However, a low-contrast matrix could be dangerous in situations in which habitat selection is imperfect and individuals are drawn to low-quality (sink) habitats (see Chapter 7). Individuals dispersing from habitat patches could settle in the matrix, but then fail to survive or reproduce. For example, Northern Spotted Owls (*Strix occidentalis caurina*) usually nest in old-growth forests, but occasionally nest in younger forests, including second growth. Available data suggest that reproduction is poor in the latter habitats. In such cases, it may be better to surround habitat fragments with highly dissimilar habitat, for example, to surround old growth with pastures. The presence of old-growth species in a managed forest matrix may give the impression that these species are not dependent on old growth; but once old-growth source populations are eliminated, populations in the matrix may disappear rapidly.

However, for many species, as the landscape matrix departs more and more from natural habitat, isolation increases as individuals are less willing or able to travel from one patch of natural habitat to another. This process is a very common one, and occurs when the intensity of development or resource extraction increases in a landscape. Landscape-scale studies are needed that measure birth and death rates in different habitats, as well as dispersal among those habitats. Only then can we say with assurance which kinds of matrix are optimal for a network of natural areas.

Although the examples above come from terrestrial ecosystems, as these have been better studied with regard to fragmentation, human-created barriers also fragment aquatic habitats. Dams, for example, not only block access of migratory fishes to upstream areas, but also prevent recolonization of stream segments by any species whose local populations have been extinguished due to natural or human causes (Moyle and Leidy 1992). The flattened musk turtle (*Sternotherus depressus*) has been lost from over half of its range in the Warrior River Basin of Alabama because habitat modification of stream and river channels has fragmented suitable habitat. The remaining populations are small and isolated, and therefore at high risk of extinction (Dodd 1990).

## Crowding Effect

When an area is isolated by destruction of the surrounding natural habitat, population densities of mobile animal species may initially increase in the fragment as animals are displaced from their former homes. This packing phenomenon has been called a "crowding on the ark" and has been described for tropical (Leck 1979) and temperate (Noss 1981) forest reserves. The initial rise in population densities in these isolated fragments is followed by collapse. The crowding effect has been convincingly demonstrated in tropical forest patches in the Minimum Critical Size of Ecosystems Project in the Amazonian forest of Brazil (Lovejoy et al. 1986). In this study, the capture rate of understory birds in an isolated 10-ha fragment more than doubled in the first few days following its isolation, but rapidly fell in subsequent days. Longer-term crowding effects are likely in many cases, but not proven. The subsequent biological consequences of crowding effects are not known.

## Local and Regional Extinctions

Metapopulation dynamics suggest that even once-common species are not immune to the effects of widespread habitat alteration and fragmentation. When local populations become isolated, they face a higher probability of extinction. For example, the Middle Spotted Woodpecker (*Dendrocopos medius*) is a sedentary forest species with poor powers of dispersal. A population in Sweden, isolated since about 1950, remained relatively stable at 15–20 pairs from 1967–1974, then declined rapidly to extinction in the period 1975–1983. The proximate causes of extinction were mortality from cold weather and, more importantly, reproductive failures due to reduced fecundity, probably related to inbreeding depression (Pettersson 1985). The White-backed Woodpecker (*Dendrocopos leucotos*) has gone extinct in parts of Sweden where habitat fragmentation has resulted in a low density of suitable habitat patches; recolonization of vacated patches in such areas is too low to maintain the metapopulation (Carlson and Aulen 1992).

What kinds of species are most vulnerable to local and regional extinction following habitat fragmentation? Consideration of life histories suggests some hypotheses about relative vulnerability to fragmentation. Among the categories of species predicted to be most vulnerable are the following:

*Naturally Rare Species.* Terborgh and Winter (1980) concluded that rarity is the best predictor of population vulnerability. But there are many potential reasons why a particular species is rare (Rabinowitz et al. 1986; Chapter 5). Some plants and animals are rare because humans have driven them to that condition; other species are rare naturally. Two major categories of naturally rare species are (1) species with limited or patchy geographic distributions, and (2) species with low population densities. Some species, of course, fall into both categories. The first includes narrowly endemic species, which fragmentation may eliminate by initial exclusion. The second category includes animals with large territories or home ranges (see below).

*Wide-Ranging Species.* Some animals, such as large carnivores and migratory ungulates, roam a large area in the course of their daily or seasonal movements. Even rather large fragments may not provide enough area for viable populations of these species; thus, they must travel widely and will often attempt to move even in heavily fragmented landscapes. In so doing, they encounter roads and other sources of mortality. As discussed above (see Figure 9.11), animals of heterogeneous landscapes, such as amphibians and other species that depend on distinct habitats for different phases of their life cycles, also are vulnerable to roads and other barriers. Resplendent Quetzals (*Pharomachrus mocinno*), which require fruits from spatially separated habitats at different times of the year, cannot maintain year-round populations in small reserves; if reserves are isolated by fragmentation, Quetzals cannot migrate to track fruiting schedules and will go extinct (Wheelright 1983).

*Nonvagile Species.* Species with poor dispersal abilities may not travel far from where they were born, or may be stopped by barriers as seemingly insignificant as a two-lane road or clear-cut. Many insects of old-growth forests are flightless and are poor dispersers (Moldenke and Lattin 1990). Clear-cuts are substantial barriers to carrion and dung beetles in Amazonian forests being fragmented by pasture development (Klein 1989). Perhaps surprisingly, some species of birds have very low colonizing abilities and will not cross areas of unsuitable habitat (Diamond 1975; Opdam et al. 1984; van Dorp and Opdam 1987). Without the occasional arrival of immigrants to provide a rescue effect and bolster genetic diversity, populations of nonvagile species may not persist long in habitat fragments. Variation in dispersal ability has been shown to be a critical determinant of survival for mammals in fragmented tropical forests in Queensland, Australia (Laurance 1990).

*Species with Low Fecundity.* A species with low reproductive capacity cannot quickly rebuild its population after a severe reduction caused by any number of factors. These species may be prone to genetic deterioration because they are unable to recover adequate levels of genetic variation after large losses. As an example, Neotropical migrant birds often have low reproductive potential in comparison with permanent resident species, which perhaps is one factor responsible for their decline in fragmented eastern forests (Whitcomb et al. 1981).

*Species Dependent on Patchy or Unpredictable Resources or Otherwise Highly Variable in Population Size.* Species with specialized habitat or resource requirements are often vulnerable to extinction, especially when those resources are unpredictable in time or space. When resources fluctuate seasonally or annually, species dependent on those resources also fluctuate. Populations may also fluctuate in response to weather extremes or other variation in the physical environment. Whatever the cause, population variability predisposes species to extinction. The higher the level of fluctuation, the greater the chance of extinction (Karr 1982; Pimm et al. 1988). Drought years, for instance, often cause population crashes of wading birds, amphibians, and other species dependent on ephemeral wetlands. Reductions in fruit or mast abundance due to drought will affect frugivorous and mast-dependent animals. Habitat fragmentation makes such species vulnerable in two ways: by reducing the number of sites that contain critical resources, and by isolating suitable sites and making them harder to find.

Studies of metapopulation dynamics in the Bay checkerspot butterfly (*Euphydryas editha bayensis*) suggest that local extinction is frequent on small patches of serpentine grassland, to which the species is now restricted due to fragmentation of the original, more extensive native grassland (Figure 9.15; see also Chapter 7). Persistence of the metapopulation is heavily dependent

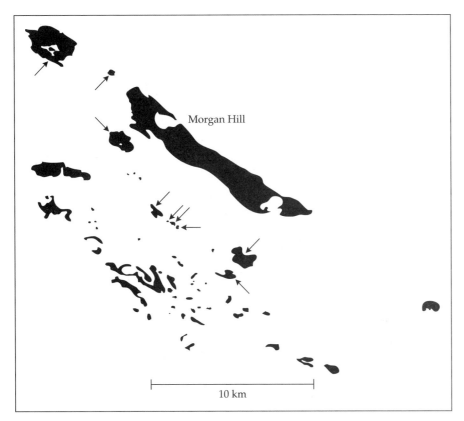

**Figure 9.15** Habitat for the Bay checkerspot butterfly (*Euphydryas editha bayensis*) metapopulation is fragmented due to natural and anthropogenic factors. The black areas represent the butterfly's serpentine grassland habitat. Of the small patches of grassland, only those closest to the large Morgan Hill population (denoted by arrows) are usually occupied, suggesting that this butterfly is a poor disperser. Extinctions in small patches are apparently common and can be reversed only when isolation is minimal. (From Harrison et al. 1988.)

on dispersal from a source population to recolonize vacated patches. Because the species is a relatively poor disperser, stepping-stone habitat patches that reduce isolation may be important (Murphy and Weiss 1988). However, only those patches of suitable habitat closest to the large source population were found to be occupied by Bay checkerspots (Harrison et al. 1988).

*Ground Nesters.* Nesting on or near the ground is another life history trait ill suited to ecological conditions in fragmented landscapes. Ground-nesting birds and other animals are highly vulnerable to various "opportunistic mesopredators" that abound in landscapes with high ratios of edge to interior habitat (Wilcove 1985; see below). On the other hand, ground nesting birds seem less susceptible than shrub nesters to brood parasitism by Brown-headed Cowbirds (Robinson 1992b).

*Interior Species.* Some species simply avoid habitat edges. They occur only in the interior of forests, prairies, or other habitats, and will be absent from small habitat patches with little or no true interior habitat. In a hardwood forest in northern Florida, four breeding bird species showed significantly reduced densities within 50 m of the forest edge (Noss 1991). Harris and Wallace (1984) found that isolated northern Florida hardwood forests smaller than 30 ha lack many of the birds characteristic of this community. Forest interior birds in the eastern Usambara Mountains of Tanzania are more vulnerable to extinction in fragmented landscapes than are edge species, perhaps because they avoid crossing large clearings; populations are therefore easily isolated (Newmark 1991). In some cases, populations of forest interior birds in habitat fragments are lower than might be estimated from counts of singing males. In Missouri, about 75% of territorial male Ovenbirds (*Seiurus aurocapillus*) in forest fragments were unmated, compared with 25% in larger sites (Gibbs and Faaborg 1990).

*Species Vulnerable to Human Exploitation or Persecution.* Some species are actively sought by people for food, furs, medicine, pets, or other uses, whereas other species, such as snakes and large predators, may be killed on sight. Most habitat fragments are readily accessible to humans due to high edge–interior ratios and the ubiquitous presence of roads. In traveling between habitat fragments, animals may be visible and easily killed or collected by people. The Iberian lynx (*Felis parinda*), the most endangered carnivore in Europe, is declining because fragmentation of its habitat has increased human access and has led to high levels of illegal trapping, road mortality, and hunting with dogs (Ferreras et al. 1992).

For purposes of comparison, studies of fragmentation should concentrate on species predicted to be vulnerable due to the kinds of traits reviewed above, as well as on related species with different life histories. Land managers might also concentrate monitoring and conservation efforts on vulnerable species. Knowing more about the autecology of such species will be fundamental to conservation success (Simberloff 1988).

## Edge Effects

The structural contrast between habitat islands and the landscape matrix is an indicator not only of isolation, but also of **edge effects.** The outer boundary of any habitat island is not a line, but rather a zone of influence that varies in width depending on what is measured. Sunlight and wind impinge on a forest island from the edge and alter the microclimate. Edge zones are usually drier and less shady than forest interiors, favoring shade-intolerant, xeric plants over typical mesic forest plants. In southern Wisconsin forests, edge zones of shade-intolerant vegetation may extend 10–15 m into a forest on the east, north, and south sides, and up to 30 m on the west side (Ranney et al. 1981). In Douglas fir (*Pseudotsuga menziesii*) forests of the Pacific Northwest, increased rates of blowdown, reduced humidities, and other physical edge effects may extend two to three tree-heights, or over 200 m, into a forest (Harris 1984; Franklin and Forman 1987; Chen and Franklin 1990). These physical edge effects have been shown to increase growth rates, elevate rates of mortality, reduce stocking density, and differentially affect regeneration of conifer species in old-growth forests up to 137 m from clear-cuts in Washington and Oregon (Chen et al. 1992). Elevated rates of canopy and subcanopy damage, as well as proliferation of disturbance-adapted plants, occurred up to 500 m from edges of tropical forest fragments in Queensland, Australia (Laurance 1991).

Biological communities and ecological processes may change substantially as a result of edge effects. Climatic edge effects may explain why dung and carrion beetle communities in 1-ha and 10-ha forest fragments in Brazil contain fewer species, sparser populations, and smaller beetles than do comparable areas within intact forest (Klein 1989). The drier conditions in small fragments, which are largely edge habitat, may lead to increased fatal desiccation of beetle larvae in the soil. Loss of beetles results in reduced decomposition rates of dung and probably other "ripple effects" throughout the ecosystem (Klein 1989).

In some cases, animals are attracted to edge, which functions as an "ecological trap" (Gates and Gysel 1978). Many passerine birds were attracted to a field–forest edge in Michigan and nested at greater densities near the edge than in the forest interior. However, birds nesting near the edge suffered higher rates of nest predation and brood parasitism by Brown-headed Cowbirds, and as a result had greatly reduced fledging success (Gates and Gysel 1978). Cowbird parasitism can be significant for at least 200 m into a forest from an edge and is a major reason for the decline of forest birds in heavily fragmented landscapes (Brittingham and Temple 1983). Increased rates of nest predation by jays (e.g., *Cyanocitta cristata*), crows (*Corvus brachyrhynchos*), raccoons (*Procyon lotor*), opossums (*Didelphis marsupialis*), foxes (e.g., *Vulpes fulva*), squirrels (*Sciurus* spp.), skunks (*Mephitis mephitis*), and other opportunistic predators may extend up to 600 m from an edge in eastern North America (Figure 9.16). Similar problems have been observed in Swedish forest fragments (Andren and Angelstam 1988). Furthermore, predation and parasitism edge effects are not limited to forests. A study of birds in tallgrass prairie fragments in Minnesota found higher rates of nest predation in small fragments, in areas close to wooded edges, and in vegetation that had not recently burned. Rates of brood parasitism by cowbirds were also higher near wooded edges (Johnson and Temple 1990).

Some studies have failed to confirm the ecological trap hypothesis with regard to nest predation (Ratti and Reese 1988). Nest predation in agricultural landscapes in central Spain was found to be lower in farmland than in forest patches, perhaps because small specialist predators "packed" into small remnant forest patches (Santos and Tellaria 1992). In heavily fragmented landscapes dominated by disturbed lands, such as southern Illinois, edge effects may not be observed because the remaining patches of natural habitat are saturated with nest predators and brood parasites. Cowbirds saturate even the largest available tracts (ca. 2000 ha) and even areas more than 800 m from edges (Robinson 1992a). In such situations, nesting success of forest birds may be so low that the entire region is a population sink. Persistence of forest interior birds in such landscapes is tenuous and may depend on immigration from landscapes with greater forest cover and better reproductive rates (Temple and Cary 1988; Robinson 1992b).

The matrix surrounding habitat patches in terrestrial landscapes clearly distinguishes these patches from real islands; disturbed lands may pose far greater threats than water. A study in Maine found that large forest patches bordered on at least one side by water had lower nest predation rates than did small tracts surrounded completely by land (Small and Hunter 1988). Generally, the greater the structural contrast between adjacent terrestrial habitats, the more intense the edge effects. However, Janzen (1983) found that problems with weedy species invading natural disturbance sites in pristine forests in Costa Rica were greater when the forests were surrounded by successional habitats rich in weeds than when they were surrounded by croplands and heavily grazed pastures. Janzen (1986) found invasion of weedy plant species and various human disturbances at least 5 km into a forest. In Maryland, nest predation rates are higher in woodlots surrounded by suburbs than in woodlots surrounded by agriculture, probably because garbage and other food subsidies in suburban landscapes encourage proliferation of opportunistic predators (Wilcove 1985).

Deleterious edge effects contradict the message, often promoted by wildlife managers, that edge habitat benefits wildlife. One popular wildlife textbook urged managers to "develop as much edge as possible" because "wildlife is a product of the places where two habitats meet" (Yoakum and Dasmann 1971). It is true that most terrestrial *game* animals in the United States are edge-adapted, as are many animals characteristic of urban and intensive agricultural landscapes (Noss 1983). Forest fragmentation, some of it intentional for the production of game, has increased deer densities so much in the upper Midwest that regeneration of several tree species is at risk because of heavy browsing (Alverson et al. 1988). The game-management bias of many wildlife biologists may have blinded them to the negative effects of

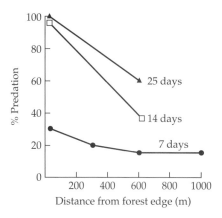

**Figure 9.16**  Percentage of experimental nests (quail eggs) preyed upon as a function of distance from forest edge. Graph shows losses after 7, 14, and 25 days. Results indicate that edge-related predation extends 300–600 m into the forest. (From Wilcove et al. 1986.)

**Figure 9.17**   A comparison of breeding success of fragmentation-sensitive birds in two forest fragments with similar total areas but vastly different core areas (forest interior). Fragment A is entirely edge habitat (light); fragment B contains 20 ha of core habitat (dark). Of 16 species known to be sensitive to fragmentation, none bred in fragment A, and 6 bred in fragment B. (From Temple 1986.)

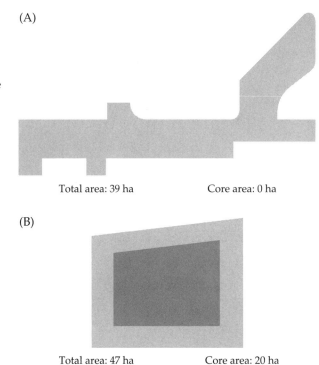

(A)

Total area: 39 ha          Core area: 0 ha

(B)

Total area: 47 ha          Core area: 20 ha

edge in fragmented landscapes. Increased interest in nongame wildlife, which constitutes a far greater proportion of the biota than game species, has coincided with concern about deleterious edge effects.

The pervasiveness of edge effects implies that habitat patches below a certain size will lack the true interior or "core" habitat that some species require. If 600 m is determined to be the penetration distance of significant nest predation, then a circular reserve smaller than 100 ha (250 acres) will be all edge (Wilcove et al. 1986). Using a conservative, two tree-height edge width of 160 m, patches of old-growth Douglas fir forest in the Pacific Northwest smaller than 10 ha (25 acres) are all edge; a landscape that is 50% cutover in a typical checkerboard harvest system contains no true interior forest habitat (Franklin and Forman 1987). Temple (1986) assumed a 100-m edge width for forest fragments in south-central Wisconsin. Sixteen bird species were found to be sensitive to fragmentation in this landscape, breeding less frequently or not at all in smaller sites. In a comparison of two forest fragments, one without any core habitat (due to its shape) lacked successful breeding by interior birds. The other fragment, of similar total area but with a core area of 20 ha (50 acres), contained successful breeding pairs of 6 of the 16 fragmentation-sensitive bird species (Figure 9.17).

### Changes in Species Composition

The edge effect studies reported above suggest that species composition and abundance patterns will change in fragmented landscapes. For example, birds characteristic of forest interior habitats may be unable to maintain their populations in landscapes where edge is abundant; instead, the landscape may gradually become dominated by edge-adapted species not in great need of conservation. Species composition is altered in fragmented landscapes because some species are more vulnerable than others to reduced area, increased isolation, edge effects, and other factors that accompany the fragmentation process.

Species loss from fragmented habitats, then, may follow a predictable and deterministic sequence (Patterson 1987; Blake 1991). In studying habitat patches of various sizes, a pattern of **nested subsets** (not to be confused with "nesting" for reproduction) in the distribution of species is often observed (Figure 9.18). A nested subset is a geographic pattern in which larger habitats contain the same subset of species found in smaller habitats, but add new species to that subset. Thus, a set of the most common species is found in all habitat sizes from smallest to largest, but progressively larger habitats add subsets of species found only in larger areas.

Boreal mammals and birds on mountain ranges in North America's Great Basin, which are natural habitat islands, show a nested distribution pattern that may be a consequence of selective extinction of area-dependent species on smaller islands. In this case, extinctions occurred in the same basic sequence throughout the region, despite considerable variation in extinction rates (Cutler 1991).

Distribution of bird species among woodlots in agricultural landscapes is typically nonrandom; species found in small woodlots are also found in the larger sites. In east-central Illinois, the most highly nested pattern was found for species requiring forest interior habitat for nesting, and for species that migrate to the Neotropics (Blake and Karr 1984; Blake 1991). A similar nonrandom pattern, with all species occupying large patches but many species not occurring in small patches, has been documented for birds in Swedish lakes and many other temperate communities (Nilsson 1986). Studies of birds in the Wheatbelt of Western Australia documented loss of many species in small habitat remnants since isolation (Saunders 1989), a relaxation effect predictable from island biogeographic theory. Such results support previous suggestions that although a collection of small sites may harbor more species, large sites are needed to maintain populations of species sensitive to human disturbance. Recognizing that "conservation strategy should not treat all species as equal but must focus on species and habitats threatened by human activities" (Diamond 1976), an optimal conservation strategy in most cases would avoid fragmentation of large natural areas.

Nested species distribution patterns do not always have straightforward explanations. There can be other reasons for nested subsets besides a predictable sequence of extinctions as habitats are progressively fragmented. An examination of nestedness from the perspective of individual species showed that different kinds of factors, most related to habitat requirements, were responsible for occurrence patterns of different species (Simberloff and Martin 1991). Moreover, most studies suggesting loss of bird species from small forest fragments have failed to test the null hypothesis that bird assemblages in small patches are simply "samples" from the larger regional pool of bird species.

A study of breeding birds in forest fragments in the southern taiga of Finland confirmed predictions from the null model that the location of breeding pairs varies randomly among fragments from year to year, and that the pattern of species additions with increasing sample size is similar to that expected for random sampling (Haila et al. 1993). Thus, local turnover of species in small fragments may represent simple changes in territory locations from year to year, rather than true "extinctions" and "recolonizations." These studies do not, in our view, negate the evidence that fragmentation is harmful. However, they suggest a need for greater experimental rigor, so that the true effects of fragmentation can be separated from statistical artifacts.

The addition of species to fragmented landscapes is as important to consider in conservation strategy as is species loss. Many of the species that in-

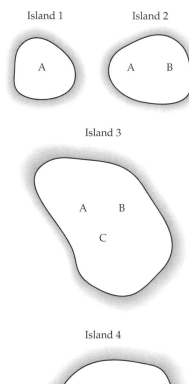

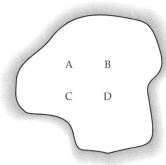

**Figure 9.18** Hypothetical nested subset distribution of species on islands of different sizes. The letters A through D represent different species. Species are added in a predictable sequence with increasing island size and number of habitats. The largest island contains all four species. (From Cutler 1991.)

vade fragmented landscapes are exotics. Increases in the number of species at a local scale due to invasions by weedy or exotic species are often accompanied by declines in diversity at a regional or global scale as sensitive native species are progressively lost, even though overall species richness may remain the same or even increase. As cosmopolitan species invade more and more regions, regional biotas are homogenized and lose their distinctness—a "mongrelization" of the global landscape. This process of homogenization is one of the most prominent forms of biotic impoverishment worldwide.

Fragmentation generally increases the rate of exotic species invasion, often through creation of disturbed habitats through which exotics travel rapidly. For example, many fungal diseases of trees, exotic plants, and exotic insect pests are known to disperse and invade natural habitats in the western United States via roads and vehicles (Schowalter 1988). Sometimes habitat fragments can be relatively resistant to invasion. Patches of old-growth forest in Indiana had alien plants along their edges, but forest interiors were virtually free of aliens (Brothers and Springarn 1992). The dense wall of vegetation that developed along the edges of fragments in this study was thought to discourage invasion by reducing interior light levels and wind speeds.

### The Problem of Climate Change

Fragmentation is a threat to biodiversity even in a relatively stable world. If we add the phenomenon of rapid climate change, then we have perhaps the most ominous of all potential threats to biodiversity. Species migrating in response to climate change have always had to cope with dispersal barriers such as rivers, lakes, mountain ranges, and desert basins. The additional set of barriers created by human activities will make migration all the more difficult (Peters and Darling 1985). New climates will render reserves set aside to protect certain species or communities unsuitable for them. Weeds may dominate many fragments.

Even natural rates of climate change threaten species restricted to fragments surrounded by inhospitable habitat. The increased rates of change predicted with greenhouse warming may eliminate all but the most vagile species as they fail to track shifting climatic conditions (see Chapter 10). High-elevation and high-latitude habitats may be lost entirely. Although wide habitat corridors and artificial translocations of populations northward and upslope may help some species in some areas, these solutions will not suffice for whole communities, especially if climate change is as rapid as predicted.

## ESSAY 9B
## Habitat "Shredding"

Peter Feinsinger, University of Northern Arizona

When modern-day humans convert a landscape and reduce the original habitat to a small fraction of its former area, the term "habitat fragmentation" is most commonly employed. This label conjures up an image of circumscribed islands of natural habitat jutting from an advancing sea of agriculture or other form of land development, isolated by quite inhospitable terrain from one another and from the nearest unconverted "continent." The insularization analogy is compelling and powerful, with the result that most work on habitat remnants and nature reserves assumes, implicitly or explicitly, that these are configured as islands. For example, MacArthur and Wilson used a fragmentation example (1967; reprinted in this chapter as Figure 9.1) to lead off their classic treatise on island biogeography.

Even the debate surrounding very different physical layouts—corridors and networks—now treats these as means of connecting remnant habitats of greatest concern, assumed to be islandlike, rather than as entities themselves of conservation interest. The island analogy also underlies models of the genetic and demographic consequences of small population size (Chapters 6 and 7). The observation that "nature is patchy" generates many potent ecological concepts, such as metapopulations, source–sink topographies, dispersal–diffusion processes, and landscape mosaics. When these concepts are used to model events on landscapes of conservation concern, again we often assume that natural habitat in such landscapes is insularized. And for many landscapes the assumption is valid (Figure A).

Other configurations are possible, however. In Latin America, and I suspect in other regions, it is often difficult to find landscapes that fit the image of insularization well enough for the island analogy and its corollaries to be applied with a clear conscience. Graphic examples abound, though, of "habitat shredding." Along many advancing agricultural frontiers, and even in some stabilized agricultural landscapes, land use practices *shred* the original habitat into long, narrow strips (Figure B) rather than fragmenting it into two-dimensional isolates. Shreds of native vegetation snake along watercourses or ridges, survive on disputed boundaries between different landholders, persist as buffers between different crops, or serve as cheap (if rather ineffective) fences for cattle pasture. Shreds may be several meters wide or several hundred, encompassing hectares or thousands of hectares. Typically, shreds are not isolates; they connect directly with the as-yet-unconverted habitat (which may itself be a protected reserve) that persists beyond the invasion front. Some shreds protrude as simple peninsulas, others link with one another in complex networks, and a few, corridorlike, run into a second large tract at the far end, although this last is rare.

Does it really make a difference to the biota, or to its investigators, whether habitats are fragmented or shredded? *Yes!* In shredded landscapes, populations of native plants and animals do not necessarily languish in isolated, two-dimensional patches; rather, they are tentacles extending from a corpus that still resides in unconverted habitat, probing the converted countryside. The key questions are not about who persists despite low population size for how long in which sizes of fragments; they are about which populations extend outward for what distance along which sorts of shreds. Long and narrow, shreds may be "all edge." Thus, edge effects and the interaction of a shred's contents with its landscape context are of paramount importance (Forman and Godron 1986). The investigator's focus must of necessity broaden beyond the focus on contents alone that often characterizes studies of fragments.

**Figure A** A fragmented landscape: Islands of "chaco serrano," a dry subtropical thorn forest, surrounded by cattle pastures and forage crops, in Tucumán Province, Argentina. (Photograph by Peter Feinsinger.)

**Figure B** A shredded landscape: "Selva basal," a wet subtropical forest invaded by citrus groves and sugarcane fields, in Tucumán Province, Argentina. (Photograph by Peter Feinsinger.)

Metapopulation models, landscape mosaic metaphors, and other "nature is patchy" concepts do not fit the shred configuration well. Instead, shredded landscapes may demand that ecologists develop new or modified models of population dynamics, demography, dispersal, and genetics, or that they apply the principles of landscape ecology (Forman and Godron 1986). Most importantly, the conservation consequences of shredded habitats may differ significantly from those of fragmented habitats.

So, what questions might conservation ecologists ask of shredded landscapes? Here are a few; I trust that readers will be able to generate many additional ones.

At the population level:

> For a given plant or animal species, what demographic changes occur along a shred?
> What genetic structure characterizes the tentacular demes occupying shreds, as compared with demes

in the intact habitat? Genetically speaking, are shred populations robust or decaying?

At the community level:

What changes in species composition occur along a peninsular shred from base to tip? Who drops out, who appears, where do these changes occur, and why?

What is the nature of species replacement (if any) along the shred? Is there a one-for-one replacement of natives by robust opportunists and exotics, or is there a monotonic shift in species richness?

What happens to community function, structure, and dynamics? For example, do guild structure, life-form spectrum, community-level plant phenology, and internal disturbance regimes remain fairly constant, or do these attributes change with distance along the shred?

Does the nature of species interactions change along a shred, and if so, what are the consequences to the interactors? For example, might pollination of native flora depend on animal populations centered in habitat beyond the invasion front, and thus decline along the shred's length? In contrast, might seed predation levels respond most directly to exposure to edge, and thus remain quite constant throughout the shred's length?

At the landscape level (see also discussions in Forman and Godron 1986):

Are edge effects constant along the length of a shred?

How do edge effects vary with the shred's context? For example, what differences exist among the edge effects exerted by neighboring habitat consisting of (1) unimproved cattle pasture, (2) improved cattle pasture, (3) crops of various kinds with various levels of treatment with fertilizers and pesticides, (4) variously treated shrub or tree plantations, (5) second growth of various ages and consistencies?

What sorts of interchange occur between the shred's contents and its context, and how do these vary with different contexts? Do animals native to the shredded habitat exploit, on a daily or seasonal basis, resources in the context? Do animals resident in the context exploit resources in the shred?

Do shreds merely absorb exotics from nearby converted landscapes, or do shreds spray the converted landscapes with propagules of native species?

Are shreds doomed to decay, to fade into the species composition of the converted landscape, or might they serve as reservoirs of native species for eventual restoration of that landscape?

How do shreds themselves affect the ecology of their context? Aside from effects on physical attributes such as hydrology and nutrient flow, how do shreds affect their agricultural context regarding weed control, arthropod herbivores, natural enemies of herbivores, or pollinators of animal-pollinated crop plants?

What might shredded habitats tell us about corridor design?

Thus, what role might shreds, and various shred configurations, play in the management of converted landscapes?

In short, shredded habitats invite empirical study and modeling in their own right as ecologically interesting and significant landscape features along agricultural frontiers, in the Neotropics at least. They should arouse conservation concern as possible refuges for native species, as corridors for or barriers to exotics, and as potential reservoirs of native species for future restoration of their surroundings. Shreds' manifest potential for interchange with the developed lands surrounding them suggests a potentially critical role for them in landscape management. But how much do we really know about the ecology of shreds and their role in conservation? Aside from extensive work in European landscapes, summarized by Forman and Godron (1986), very little (which has enabled me to speculate shamelessly here). Need a research topic? Think "shreds."

This essay is not intended to disparage the "nature is patchy" perspective, an approach that has tremendous explanatory and predictive power for most landscapes and a metaphor that has guided most of this author's own research career. Many converted landscapes may fit the island analogy well, and others that now display shreds may be doing so only temporarily, as a transitional phase on the way to true insularization. Nevertheless, rather than accepting without question the island analogy, conservation ecologists working at population or community levels should allow landscapes themselves to instruct them as to which metaphor—islands, shreds, or yet another—best fits the current layout of remnant habitats, and then ask the questions most appropriate to that layout.

## Conclusions and Recommendations

This chapter has reviewed evidence that fragmentation occurs at many spatial scales and may have a variety of short-term and long-term effects. Some species benefit from fragmentation, whereas many others are at increased risk of extinction. Global biodiversity can be maintained in part by devoting conservation resources to those species and ecosystems most at risk, and by controlling or reversing the processes that place them at risk. However, species not currently at great risk from fragmentation must also be addressed in conservation planning, lest continued habitat alteration change their status to rare and make conservation more difficult. There is also a tremendous need to develop effective management strategies for landscapes that are already fragmented, including management of the internal dynamics of remnant natural areas and the external influences on those areas.

Strategies for countering fragmentation follow logically from consideration of the fragmentation process and its effects, discussed above. Because fragmentation causes a reduction in the size of natural areas and isolation of remaining areas in a sea of unsuitable habitat, corrective action should include maintenance or restoration of large, intact land units interconnected across regional landscapes. Where circumstances prohibit establishment of truly large reserves, biodiversity can be well served by land use practices— for example, clustered developments and reduced road building—that minimize fragmentation and optimize connectivity of similar natural habitats. Connectivity must be defined functionally as the potential for movement or genetic interchange of target species or, on a broader scale, migration of floras and faunas.

Large interconnected nature reserves are not the only solution to the fragmentation problem. Entire landscapes, including private and multiple-use public lands, should be managed in ways that minimize destruction and isolation of natural habitats. Opportunities to reduce and reverse fragmentation abound on public lands in the United States. Unfortunately, fragmentation continues on these lands. Between 1972 and 1987, average forest patch size in two ranger districts of the Willamette National Forest, Oregon, decreased by 17%, the amount of forest–clear-cut edge doubled, and the amount of forest interior at least 100 m from an edge declined by 18% (Ripple et al. 1991). In the Olympic National Forest, Washington, more than 87% of the old growth in 1940 was in patches larger than 4000 ha; in 1988, only one patch larger than 4000 ha remained, and 60% of the old growth was in patches smaller than 40 ha in size. Of the remaining old growth in 1988, 41% was within 170 m of an edge (Morrison 1990). Stopping destructive management of public lands is an essential ingredient of conservation strategy in the United States.

Some recommendations for maintaining biodiversity in fragmented landscapes (or those in danger of being fragmented) follow from the information presented in this chapter:

1. Conduct a landscape analysis. Determine the pattern of habitats and connections, and relate these to the needs of native species in the landscape. Where are the major, unfragmented blocks of habitat? Can natural connections between habitats be maintained or restored?
2. Evaluate the landscape of interest in a larger context. Does it form part of a critical linkage of ecosystems at a regional scale? What is the significance of this landscape to conservation goals at regional, national, and global scales?
3. Avoid any further fragmentation or isolation of natural areas. Developments, resource extraction activities, and other land uses should be clustered so that large blocks of natural habitat remain intact. In planning reserves, emphasize large areas whenever possible.
4. Minimize edge effects around remnant natural areas. This can be done by establishing buffer zones with low-intensity land use. Be careful, however, not to produce population sinks that lure sensitive species out of reserves and into areas where mortality is greater or reproduction is reduced.
5. Identify traditional wildlife migration routes and protect them. Steer human activities away from critical wildlife movement areas.
6. Maintain native vegetation along streams, fencerows, roadsides, power line rights-of-way, and other remnant corridors in strips as wide as possible, in order to minimize edge effects and human disturbances.

7. Minimize the area and continuity of artificially disturbed habitats dominated by weedy or exotic species, such as roadsides, in order to reduce the potential for biological invasions of natural areas.

## Summary

Fragmentation, the loss and isolation of natural habitats, is one of the greatest threats to regional and global biodiversity. Whereas natural disturbances and other processes create heterogeneous landscapes rich in native species, human land uses often create islands of natural habitat embedded in a hostile matrix. Such fragmentation reduces or prevents normal dispersal, which is critical to long-term population viability for many species, and increases edge effects and other threats.

Fragmentation acts to reduce biodiversity through four major mechanisms. First, because remaining fragments represent only a sample of the original habitat, many species will be eliminated by chance (initial exclusion). Second, the modified landscape in which fragments exist is often inhospitable to many native species, thus preventing normal movements and dispersal (isolation). Third, small fragments contain fewer habitats, support smaller populations of native species that are more susceptible to extinction, and are less likely to intercept paths of dispersing individuals (island-area effect). Finally, climatic influences and opportunistic predators and competitors from the disturbed landscape penetrate into fragments, reducing the core area of suitable habitat (edge effects). Many terrestrial game animals in North America are adapted to habitat edges and thrive in fragmented landscapes, which has encouraged wildlife managers to promote edge habitat at the expense of sensitive species of habitat interiors.

Eight kinds of species are identified that are especially vulnerable to the effects of fragmentation: rare species, species with large home ranges, species with limited powers of dispersal, species with low reproductive potential, species dependent on resources that are unpredictable in time or space, ground-nesting species, species of habitat interiors, and species exploited or persecuted by people. One of the most ominous effects of habitat fragmentation may not become apparent for decades or centuries: the inability of species in isolated fragments to track changes in habitat conditions related to changing climate.

Some strategies for countering fragmentation are available: (1) do not fragment intact wildlands and other natural areas, few of which remain in most regions; (2) minimize road construction, clearing of vegetation, and creation of other barriers to dispersal; (3) maintain or restore wide habitat corridors or other forms of functional connectivity between natural areas; and (4) minimize creation of artificial dispersal corridors (such as weedy roadsides) that encourage proliferation of exotic species.

## Questions for Discussion

1. Lake Gatun was formed when the Panama Canal was built in 1914, creating the 17-km$^2$ Barro Colorado Island (see Essay 5A). Since then, careful observations have documented a 25% decline in the island's avifauna. Speculate on the reasons for this decline.

2. The Northern Spotted Owl, an obligate resident of old-growth coniferous forests in the Pacific Northwest, is thought to be sensitive to high temperatures, feeds on small mammals (many of them arboreal), and is subject to predation by the Great Horned Owl, a habitat generalist. Old-growth

forests within the range of the Northern Spotted Owl once covered 60%–70% of the region, but have been reduced by 90%. How might different approaches to forest management affect the long-term viability of Spotted Owl populations?

3. Much of southern California was once covered by coastal sage scrub, a vegetation type dominated by California sagebrush, buckwheat, and herbaceous sages of the genus *Salvia*. A number of species endemic to this vegetation type, including the California Gnatcatcher (federally listed as threatened) and many plant species, have been proposed for listing. Development, mostly residential, has destroyed nearly 90% of this habitat. How might future developments or other land uses be controlled to protect biodiversity in coastal sage scrub?

4. Many species of small vertebrates and invertebrates are sensitive to the barrier effects of roads, refusing to cross even two-lane roads in some cases. Larger animals, including endangered species such as the Florida panther, are vulnerable to roadkill. How might these kinds of problems be corrected?

5. Recent population models suggest that the grizzly bear in the northern Rocky Mountains may require about 30 million acres of wilderness habitat for long-term viability. Yellowstone Park, for comparison, is only 2.2 million acres (Essay 6B). Thus, habitat fragmentation at a regional scale is a threat to grizzly bear survival. The grizzly bear is vulnerable to human encounters, many related to livestock production or road access by poachers. Housing subdivisions are also being constructed in grizzly bear habitat. How might conservation strategy address these regional fragmentation problems? What kinds of information—biological and otherwise—might be used to determine necessary reserve sizes, linkage widths, and management guidelines?

6. The longleaf pine–wiregrass ecosystem was once the dominant vegetation of the Southeastern Coastal Plain of the United States, but has declined by 98% since European settlement. The dominant plants of this ecosystem depend on frequent (2–5-year intervals) low-intensity ground fires that control invading hardwoods and other competitors, and maintain the characteristic open structure of the ecosystem. Fire suppression, in addition to logging, has been a major reason for the decline of this ecosystem. How might habitat isolation by roads, agriculture, and urbanization contribute to this decline?

7. Suppose you are the manager of a small (20-ha) forested nature reserve in the midwestern United States. What kind of management would you consider to reduce edge effects and maintain ecological integrity in this reserve? What variables (biotic and abiotic) would you monitor to determine whether or not management is effective?

## Suggestions for Further Reading

Burgess, R. L. and D. M. Sharpe (eds.). 1981. *Forest Island Dynamics in Man-Dominated Landscapes.* Springer-Verlag, New York. This text was the first book-length treatment of fragmentation problems. The chapters, by a number of prominent authors, focus on island-area effects, edge effects, and other problems in small fragments of eastern North American deciduous forest. Most of the studies reported were carried out in southeastern Wisconsin or Maryland.

Harris, L. D. 1984. *The Fragmented Forest: Island Biogeography Theory and the Preservation of Biotic Diversity.* University of Chicago Press, Chicago. Larry Harris won considerable acclaim with this book on fragmentation problems and potential solutions in the western Cascades of Oregon. More than any book before and virtually any since, this book spells out the advantages of taking a "Big Picture" approach to conservation by looking at landscapes and regions instead of only at individual sites.

MacArthur, R. H. and E. O. Wilson. 1967. *The Theory of Island Biogeography.* Princeton University Press, Princeton, NJ. This book, now a classic, formally presented and explored the idea that the number of species on an island was dependent on its size, distance from the mainland, and biogeographic history. Although the equilibrium theory proposed here remains controversial, this book stimulated more research in conservation than did any other work in history.

Noss, R. F. 1987. Protecting natural areas in fragmented landscapes. *Natural Areas J.* 7:2–13. This article reviews threats to biodiversity in fragmented landscapes and offers an approach for designing regional reserve networks composed of core areas, buffer zones, and corridors. Case studies are presented for southern Ohio and Florida. The basic model developed here has since been proposed for many regions.

Saunders, D. A., R. J. Hobbs and C. R. Margules. 1991. Biological consequences of ecosystem fragmentation: A review. *Conserv. Biol.* 5:18–32. This review of the literature on fragmentation problems starts with the observation that most fragmentation research to date has provided little of practical value to managers. After reviewing the literature on physical and biotic effects of fragmentation, the authors conclude that research and management should focus on controlling external influences on fragments and that an integrated approach to management of whole landscapes is needed.

Soulé, M. E. and D. Simberloff. 1986. What do genetics and ecology tell us about the design of nature reserves? *Biol. Conserv.* 35:19–40. In addition to being an excellent review of the general literature in conservation biology, this paper reconciles the two opposing viewpoints of the SLOSS (single large or several small reserves) controversy: multiple reserves in different habitats and regions will sample more species, but each reserve should ideally be large enough to maintain viable populations and maintain normal ecosystem processes.

Wilcove, D. S., C. H. McLellan and A. P. Dobson. 1986. Habitat fragmentation in the temperate zone. pp. 237–256 In M. E. Soulé (ed.), *Conservation Biology: The Science of Scarcity and Diversity.* Sinauer Associates, Sunderland, MA. Wilcove and co-authors present one of the most concise and comprehensive treatments of problems arising from habitat fragmentation, with emphasis on temperate forests. The model presented suggests that further fragmentation of even heavily fragmented regions may lead to rapid species loss, and that insularization can cause extinctions independent of habitat reduction. The advantages of large reserves, close reserves, and circular reserves are underscored.

# 10

# The Design of Conservation Reserves

*It is from the earth that we must find our sustenance; it is on the earth that we must find solutions to the problems that promise to destroy all life here.*

*Justice William O. Douglas*

The last several millennia have seen the earth transformed from an expanse of contiguous habitats, interrupted only by natural barriers or localized natural disturbances, to a patchwork of natural, human-modified, and thoroughly destroyed habitats. As explained in Chapter 9, habitat modification and degradation on many scales has fragmented natural areas into habitat patches separated by highways, cities, agricultural fields, plantation forests, mines, railroads, deforested wastelands, and countless other barriers. Because this trend will continue in the foreseeable future, conservation efforts must proceed with the understanding that only a small, critical fraction of the world's habitats may survive as natural or seminatural areas. This makes it all the more crucial that stewardship of these remaining areas be undertaken in a responsible and biologically sound manner through good reserve design.

Protection of habitat in reserves is a recent phenomenon, dating back only about a century, although habitat was indirectly protected for millennia as hunting reserves and for other amusements of royalty. Many of the original reserves in the United States, including Yosemite, Glacier, Yellowstone, and Grand Canyon National Parks, were created not to protect biological resources, but as geological attractions and for their aesthetic appeal (Figure 10.1). Sequoia and Kings Canyon National Parks were established not to protect the giant sequoia trees, but rather to protect the watershed serving the large agricultural interests in California's Central Valley. Many existing reserves, therefore, do not effectively capture critical biotic regions, nor are they designed in a manner conducive to biological conservation. Conspicuously missing, for example, at least in the United States, are protected natural areas of highly productive flatlands, including native prairies. Generally, reserves are remnants of low net productivity lands that have marginal agricultural value.

(A)

(B)

(C)

(D)

**Figure 10.1**   Many of the large, attractive natural reserves in the United States, such as (A) Grand Canyon, (B) Death Valley National Monument, (C) Kings Canyon, (D) Yosemite, and other national parks, were created as geological attractions and for their aesthetic appeal. Consequently, they may not be especially effective in biological conservation. (Photographs A and B, by G. K. Meffe; C, by C. R. Carroll; D, by Art Wolfe.)

Today, about 4.25 million km² (about half the size of the United States), or about 2.8% of the world's land surface, is protected in reserves worldwide (Western 1989). For many of these reserves, though, protection is nominal at best: they exist on planning maps but do not function in their intended sense because of continued destructive land uses such as poaching, mining, agriculture, and logging. The goal recommended by the International Union for Conservation of Nature and Natural Resources (IUCN) is preservation of a cross-section of all major ecosystems, and calls for 13 million km², or 8% to 10% of the earth's surface (Western 1989). How these areas are selected and protected is of utmost importance.

This chapter will not specifically address theory of reserve design, because much of that has been covered, directly or indirectly, in the previous chapters on biodiversity, genetics, demography, communities, and habitat fragmentation. We will instead build on information from those chapters to explore real-world issues in reserve design. Many of the issues, problems, and opportunities associated with conservation reserves are foretold in Essay 10A, by Philippe Cohen, who describes a mid-sized reserve in the Mojave Desert of California.

The phrase "reserve design" is actually something of a misnomer. There are increasingly small probabilities that conservationists will have the luxury of actually "designing" reserves. Perhaps it remains a possibility in the Amazon basin and when deciding how to clear-cut much of the small remaining old-growth forests in the United States. However, in most cases the reality is that conservation interests will take what they can get, and work within the constraints of what is available, regardless of any optimal theoretical designs that may or may not be accepted at the time.

For example, several years and great intellectual energies were spent on a debate over **"SLOSS"**—the acronym for "Single Large Or Several Small." The debate asked whether, given limited money, time, and personnel, it would in general be a better practice to develop one large reserve or several small reserves *of the same total size.* The debate raged for years with no clear resolution. Rather than probing the details of this debate, which is now largely relegated to historical interest (Soulé and Simberloff 1986), we will let it serve as a reminder that sound reserve design is a more complicated issue than simply adopting a general principle that, even if agreed upon, would rarely present itself as a real-world decision to be made.

Given that conservationists will seek and accept whatever reserves they can acquire, the key questions focus more on how to convince the human populace that large reserves are needed, and how to manage internal dynamics of and external threats to reserves once acquired. No longer at issue is whether bigger reserves are better; we knew all along that, *all else being equal,* bigger reserves hold more species, better support wide-ranging species, and have lower extinction rates than small reserves. The problems are more complicated than that. We must instead determine what other physical and biological features are important in supporting viable populations, communities, or functioning ecosystems at given localities.

## ESSAY 10A
# University of California Granite Mountains Reserve

Philippe Cohen, Stanford University

The East Mojave Desert is characterized by numerous isolated mountains with a high degree of endemism and many Pleistocene remnant populations. To the degree that endemism is a measure of biodiversity, the East Mojave appears to be one of the biologically richest deserts in the world. Consequently, special efforts are required to maintain and manage these unique biological resources in reserves.

The Granite Mountains Reserve (GMR), part of the University of California Natural Reserve System, was developed for just such a mission. It is located in the most geologically, climatically, and biologically diverse portion of the Mojave Desert, within the East Mojave National Scenic Area. GMR captures much of the eastern Mojave Desert's diversity: it encompasses 3630 ha and an elevational range of 1100–2061 m.

Ideally and uniquely located at the crossroads of three of the four North American deserts, GMR's biodiversity is correspondingly rich, displaying strong affinities to the Mojave, Sonoran, and Great Basin Deserts. About 43% of

plant taxa have affinities with Sonoran Desert assemblages, 21% are distinctly Mojavean, and 14% Great Basin (MacMahon 1979; Thorne et al. 1981). Recognizing the scientific and resource value of such habitats in the eastern Mojave Desert, the University of California acquired GMR from 1978–1987 through a series of purchases and a joint management agreement with the Bureau of Land Management (BLM). Of the 3630 ha making up GMR, about 75% is public land managed jointly with BLM.

Preservation of this large and diverse area of desert habitat has coincided with several other trends, including accelerating loss and degradation of desert habitats, a burgeoning human population in areas surrounding the East Mojave, and a growing demand for pure and applied research in arid zones stemming from global warming and increasing desertification of the planet. Given the rich biodiversity of the site and the benefits associated with preserving the habitat, one would imagine that the creation of GMR involved a clear, planned vision concerning the

size, shape, and location of the reserve and field station. This is not the case.

While the history surrounding acquisition and formation of GMR bespeaks a clear commitment to conservation of biodiversity, the actual boundaries of the reserve are primarily a function of acquisition opportunities. Although the location and setting of GMR appear well suited for conserving biological resources, specifically defined conservation objectives were not the driving force behind the final determination of its size and shape.

Maximizing reserve size has been the major strategy employed in the formation of GMR. This has obvious benefits, not the least of which is an opportunity to manage and preserve valuable desert habitats and include a matrix of habitat types historically exposed to different intensities of land use. The latter is significant because it opens the door for research in restoration of arid lands through manipulation of heavily impacted habitats. Nearby, relatively pristine habitats can act as comparative baselines. Additional benefits of large

reserve size include decreasing the likelihood of insularization and minimizing
the influences of habitat fragmentation.
Wilderness Study Areas constitute
buffers on three of the four sides of
GMR, further enhancing its value as a
reserve. All these advantages are directly or indirectly attributable to a
strategy of maximizing reserve size. In
addition, the size of GMR allows for a
management plan that designates five
land use classifications for promoting
research and education without adversely affecting important habitats, as
follows:

1. *Applied Research*: lands subject to
   direct manipulation of habitat
   and biological resources. These
   lands have experienced the effects of past cattle grazing and
   other human activities.
2. *Education*: lands set aside primarily for field class use—typically
   campground areas and limited
   residential facilities.
3. *Habitat Preservation*: unique or
   pristine habitats with priority
   given to basic research. Direct
   manipulation by research activities is strictly regulated; it is the
   responsibility of researchers to
   prove that their activities will not
   adversely affect the habitat.
4. *Facilities Development*: areas
   where new facilities are being
   developed; these coincide with
   habitat already severely affected
   by past human activity.
5. *Research Natural Area*: lands managed under a joint management
   agreement between the University of California and the Bureau
   of Land Management for investigation of natural patterns and
   processes.

While GMR's location and size have
many strengths, there are shortcomings
to the approach used in its creation. The
reserve's design is primarily a result of
the historical and political realities encountered in creating it, rather than the
use of specifically defined conservation
objectives. Historical antecedents of
land ownership provided most of the
driving force behind reserve shape and
size. Hence, some important habitat
types are not represented in GMR.

These shortcomings became more
evident once management of the reserve as a productive field station began in earnest. For instance, important
biological considerations such as endemism, corridors between habitat
types, distribution of riparian habitat,
and the location of sensitive species
were not an explicit part of boundary
establishment for the reserve. Despite
these shortcomings, the strategy of
maximizing reserve size ameliorates
some of these concerns.

While conservation of biological
resources is an important objective of
GMR, a major focus is to promote research and educational use. Hence,
management considerations extend beyond preservation and maintenance of
pristine habitats. From a research perspective, access to habitats reflecting
various stages of degradation from human-induced damage is often as important as the presence of pristine habitats.

Management of GMR means balancing the value of any given research
question against the effects the research
might have on reserve habitats. For instance, while a restoration project is
confined to already disturbed habitat,
the effects of a research design might
extend beyond the boundaries of the already disturbed habitat. Clearly, to address such problems, judgments about

the importance, relevance and interest
of the proposed project are required,
which makes it important that multidisciplinary risk assessments be conducted
to evaluate the potential effects of such
efforts. Field stations and other natural
areas will face these sorts of issues with
increasing frequency as restoration and
climatic change research become more
critical.

As a research site, GMR must also
supply facilities for research. This provides an additional opportunity, albeit
not often considered: to learn how to
supply facilities that are environmentally responsive, thereby exemplifying
ecologically sustainable architecture.
The importance of minimizing effects
on surrounding habitats has been central to the design and construction of
new research facilities. The effort to
construct low-impact, "sustainable"
buildings has resulted in unique facilities that have become a research project
in their own right.

There is a natural and unavoidable
tension between the need for conserving habitats and the requirements associated with studying them. Field stations such as GMR play an essential
role in trying to reconcile that tension in
the hope that future generations will
have greater knowledge and better
tools for properly managing and maintaining the earth's ecosystems. Efforts
to preserve habitats without providing
the means for studying them are destined to ultimately mismanage them.
While GMR is valuable for the habitats
and species it seeks to preserve, its most
important long-term contributions will
most likely be in the opportunities it
provides for studying, understanding,
and more effectively managing ecosystems found outside its boundaries.

## Considerations and Goals of Reserve Design

As you have already seen, the prevailing paradigm of ecology well into the
1970s was the equilibrium, "balance of nature" perspective. Ecological systems were thought to have a stable-point equilibrium such as a predictable
climax state, and to be structurally and functionally complete and self-regulating. Most species populations within an ecosystem were relatively stable
from year to year, and kept each others' numbers in check. If disturbed from
a given physical configuration, a climax ecosystem would return to it (Figure
10.2A). The conservation implications of this paradigm included the notions
that (1) a particular unit of nature is conservable by itself in a reserve; (2)
such units will maintain themselves in a stable and balanced configuration;
and (3) if disturbed, the system will return to its former, balanced state (Pickett et al. 1992). Under this paradigm, reserves would likely succeed as long

as they were locked up and protected from human influences. If only it were that easy!

As we have repeatedly emphasized, the last two decades have witnessed a shift in the prevailing paradigm toward a new worldview, stimulated by empirical contradictions with the equilibrium perspective (e.g., Botkin and Sobel 1975), by recognition of the prevalence and effects of natural disturbances in ecological systems (Sousa 1984), and by a change in scale of focus, from very coarse-scaled to finer-scaled views (Pickett et al. 1992). This "nonequilibrium" paradigm (Figure 10.2B) indicates that ecological systems are rarely at a stable point, are open to exchange of materials and energy from their surroundings, are not internally self-regulating, and are very much influenced by periodic disturbances that affect their internal structure and function. It is a perspective that emphasizes processes, dynamics, and context, rather than endpoint stability.

The definition of "disturbance," and what actually constitutes a disturbance in a given community, has been debated. Useful definitions include those of White and Pickett (1985), who defined a disturbance as "any relatively discrete event in time that disrupts ecosystem, community, or population structure and changes resources, substrate availability, or the physical environment," and Petraitis et al. (1989), who included under disturbance any "process that alters the birth and death rates of individuals present in the patch."

One of the most important concepts in the study of disturbance, and one relevant to conservation reserves, is the **intermediate disturbance hypothesis** (Connell 1978), which states that maximum species richness in many systems will occur at an intermediate intensity and frequency of natural disturbance (Figure 10.3). This is because high disturbance levels allow persistence of only those species that are disturbance-adapted, while low disturbance levels allow competitive dominance by some species, causing local extinction of others. However, many species can coexist and persist at intermediate levels of disturbance, especially if patches of different disturbance types and intensities exist.

The conservation implications of this nonequilibrium paradigm include the following: (1) a particular unit of nature is not easily conservable as a reserve in isolation from its surroundings; (2) reserves will not maintain themselves in a stable and balanced configuration; and (3) reserves will incur natural disturbances (as well as human disturbances) and are likely to change state as a result (Pickett et al. 1992). The nonequilibrium paradigm tells us that reserves will not succeed simply by being locked up and protected from humans; disturbances and influences from surrounding areas and from human societies will affect reserves, resulting in changing species compositions and changing rates and directions of natural processes. This dynamism needs to be accommodated in reserve design.

Application of the nonequilibrium paradigm makes conservation in reserves more difficult, because reserves must be able to incorporate often unpredictable magnitudes and directions of change and still maintain species diversity and ecological processes. Regardless of the difficulties associated with this perspective, to the best of our current knowledge this appears to be how natural systems function, and reserve design must operate under this paradigm. *The nonequilibrium paradigm should be the underlying model and motivation for all decisions affecting selection and management of conservation reserves.*

In very large reserves these nonequilibrium processes largely develop from naturally occurring disturbance regimes, and may add to habitat and species diversity. However, as the sizes of reserves decrease, disturbances

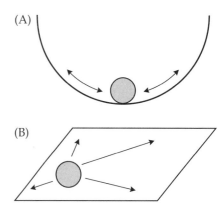

**Figure 10.2** Conceptual models of (A) equilibrium and (B) nonequilibrium ecological systems. If disturbed, the equilibrium system eventually returns to its original state, but the nonequilibrium system can assume a new state. The latter perspective also more explicitly recognizes the importance of external disturbances.

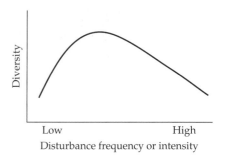

**Figure 10.3** Model of the intermediate disturbance hypothesis. Species diversity is lowest at high and low levels (frequencies or intensities) of disturbance, and highest at an intermediate level. (Modified from Connell 1978.)

may become destructive to diversity, and intervention through management may become necessary. For example, a tree blowdown in a small reserve of, say, 100 ha, may allow colonization by exotic species from adjacent areas off the reserve. Mechanical removal of those colonists and planting of native species may become necessary. There are great conceptual and practical difficulties in finding relevant types and levels of management that mimic natural processes; these are discussed in detail in Chapters 11 and 12.

### Goals of Reserves

The purpose of conservation reserves should be to retain the diversity of biological elements and ecological processes inherent in nature that would otherwise be lost through continuing habitat degradation. This being the case, it is important to realize that reserves are often relatively small, remnant parts of larger ecosystems, strongly influenced by a matrix of variously modified and perturbed systems surrounding them. Even rather large reserves are influenced by external events at local to global scales.

Nature reserves are typically developed for one or more of three primary biological motivations (Soulé and Simberloff 1986). First is the preservation of large and functioning ecosystems. Large expanses may be protected for their local and global "ecosystem services" (Ehrlich and Mooney 1983), principally watersheds for flood control and water recharge, as occurred in Sequoia and Kings Canyon National Parks. Complete, functional units such as intact watersheds are most desirable as primary, critical resources to be set aside for their free ecosystem services to both humans and nature (Figure 10.4).

A second motivation for nature reserves is to preserve biodiversity. This reserve strategy will focus on areas of high species richness, such as tropical rainforests or coral reefs, or unique areas with high rates of endemism, such as Madagascar or some desert regions or other extreme or unique environments (one such reserve, Ash Meadows, is the topic of Essay 10E, later in this chapter).

**Figure 10.4**  The Coweeta watershed of North Carolina, a Long-Term Ecological Research (LTER) site, is an example of the type of a complete, functional unit that should be protected in reserves. (Photograph courtesy of USDA Forest Service.)

(A)

(B)

(C)

**Figure 10.5** Conservation reserves are often motivated by single-species protection. The protected species are often large, high-profile vertebrates, such as (A) the African elephant (*Loxodonta africana*), (B) the giant panda (*Ailuropoda melanoleuca*), or (C) the Bengal tiger (*Panthera tigris*). (A, photograph by Art Wolfe; B, by Ron Garrison © San Diego Zoo; C, by E. R. Degginger.)

Finally, reserves are also developed to protect particular species or groups of species of special interest. These are typically either severely endangered species or taxa otherwise of high visibility, and include the California Condor, African elephants, rhinoceroses, pandas, or large carnivores such as tigers or jaguars (Figure 10.5). In the process, many other species and entire ecosystems will be preserved as a secondary benefit under the "umbrella" of these high-visibility, so-called "charismatic" vertebrates, which invariably require large expanses. As discussed in Chapter 3, for example, current laws in the United States recognize endangered species but not endangered ecosystems. However, because the protected plants or animals are an integral part of their ecosystems, their habitats are also protected by law, as are other species inhabiting those areas. A visible case in point is protection of old-growth forests in the Pacific Northwest through legal protection of Northern Spotted Owls (*Strix occidentalis caurina*) and Marbled Murrelets (*Brachyramphus marmoratum*).

These three reserve types are not mutually exclusive, of course. A reserve designed to protect a single, high-profile species may also protect an intact ecosystem (although not necessarily); likewise, an ecosystem reserve will likely protect a large amount of diversity. Ideally, the more a reserve can protect at all three levels, the more desirable and successful it will be.

An additional motivation for reserves, which we will not directly address here, but which nevertheless can have important effects on habitat use and preservation, is perpetuation of plants or animals for harvest. In particular, great quantities of wetlands have been protected by waterfowl hunting groups as duck habitat, some estuaries are protected as fish and invertebrate nurseries, and forest tracts are often managed for improvement of deer, quail, or turkey habitat, or for eventual logging. Although these efforts are motivated by concerns for single- or multiple-species harvest rather than biodiversity or ecosystem function, they still have positive influences on broader aspects of conservation, if for no other reason than precluding development in these areas.

However, if a reserve is managed too intensively for one species, then biodiversity in general may decline, or particular aspects of diversity may be lost. For example, large predators that are thought (usually erroneously) to compete with hunters for game species may be purposely eliminated, and game densities may become so high that they damage their habitat. Forests managed for low plant species diversity or low structural diversity, which may favor a particular game species or may benefit logging, also tend to support lower diversities of vertebrates than do high-diversity, multispecies stands (Pianka 1967; Cody 1975).

### Concerns in Reserve Design

There are three major classes of concern in the development of conservation reserves, and they require disciplinary integration. First and perhaps foremost are the biological considerations we have just discussed—the siting of reserves for protection of ecological processes, an intact biota, or a special, identified subset of a biota. These goals require consideration of the location, size, and shape of the reserve, its connections and spatial relationships with other natural areas, population sizes needed to maintain critical species, local colonization and extinction dynamics of the biota at large, ecological dynamics within the reserve, and threats posed by land uses surrounding the reserve.

The second concern is for the reserve's anthropological or cultural effects. Wherever possible, a biological reserve should not disrupt the traditional, sustainable cultures of indigenous peoples, and should be compatible with cultural norms of local societies (Figure 10.6). This is recommended both because of ethical considerations common to all human societies, and because it is less likely to cause strife and resentment, and thus failure of the reserve. Social support for a reserve by local people, paying visitors, and the general public will greatly enhance its chances for success.

Finally, reserve design needs to work within the political and economic constraints and realities present at local to global levels; if those constraints seem unreasonable, they must be modified through public education or, at times, court action. There are usually trade-offs to be made with, and battles to be fought against, competing interests for land. Land and its products are

**Figure 10.6** The traditional, sustainable cultures of indigenous peoples should be considered in the design of any nature reserve. The reserve should be compatible with traditional and sustainable cultural norms of local societies. Shown here are the Chief and Chieftess of the Ecuadorian Siona people. As elders, they are the principal repositories of indigenous knowledge, and can have great bearing on the success or failure of a reserve. (Photograph by Eduardo Asanza.)

and will continue to be limiting resources for an expanding global human population, and conflicts will arise among groups with diametrically opposed viewpoints concerning land use. The more these conflicts can be defined, understood, and minimized at the outset, the easier it will be to maintain successful reserves.

## Six Critical Issues in Reserve Success

Wilcox and Murphy (1985) summarized the problems and challenges facing conservation reserves when they said, "Habitat fragmentation is the most serious threat to biological diversity and is the primary cause of the present extinction crisis." Fragmentation of natural habitat in a matrix of degraded or inhospitable urban, industrial, and agricultural lands is the common pattern of human land use. This fragmentation results in habitat loss, isolation of remaining habitat, strong influences from the new matrix, and creation of edges exposed to that matrix.

There are at least six critical issues to be considered in developing and maintaining successful conservation reserves that have a chance of functioning ecologically despite this habitat fragmentation. All of these hearken back to the basic premise that ecological systems are dynamic and nonequilibrium, and they tell us that successful reserves will be selected and managed on that basis. Species will go extinct in reserves despite our best efforts, and plant and animal community structure will change over time within reserves—that is the essence of natural systems. Reserves must be designed to accommodate those changes rather than to resist natural change. Ideally, this is done by creating reserves of the largest size possible, by including spatial and temporal heterogeneity, by considering the geographic context of the reserve, by connecting reserves on a regional basis, by considering natural landscape elements, and by creating zones of different uses within reserves.

### Reserve Size

Larger reserves are better for maintenance of individual species, biodiversity, and ecological functions than are smaller reserves, for at least two reasons. First, the basic species–area relationship (Chapters 4, 5, and 9) tells us that larger reserves capture a greater number of the species within a region than do smaller reserves. More species are thus protected by larger reserves. Second, the persistence of individual species in a reserve may depend on the size of the reserve; some species, especially large vertebrates, tend to be lost from smaller reserves. However, persistence varies greatly by taxon and life history characteristics. Many species will persist with no problem in smaller reserves—witness the success of gray squirrels (*Sciurus carolinensis*) in eastern North American city parks—whereas other species disappear in decades from our largest protected wilderness areas (discussed below). It is the latter type of species that is usually of concern relative to reserve size.

Reserve size needed may also vary as a function of the habitat quality of the area. That is, reserve size may be partly a surrogate for a critical amount or type of resources. A reserve with low-quality resources for a target species may need to be larger than another reserve with higher-quality resources, simply to accommodate the number of individuals needed to maintain a viable population.

Much of the concern for extinctions of large vertebrates in reserves comes from analyses of Minimum Viable Populations (MVP), a concept discussed in Chapter 7. This approach to conservation reserve design addresses individual species and their long-term probability of population persistence in reserves of various sizes. Its goal is to maintain viable populations of selected species, usually large vertebrates, over long periods of time in the face of likely biotic and abiotic challenges, and to identify the population sizes, and thus reserve sizes, necessary to do this. (Note that the goal is not to maintain a *minimum* number, but to identify a population size below which extinction is likely, and then maintain populations well above that size). This is done through a Population Viability Analysis (PVA), "a structured, systematic, and comprehensive examination of the interacting factors that place a population or species at risk" (Shaffer 1990). The serious practical difficulties involved in actually applying PVA in reserve management are discussed in Chapter 7, and reviewed by Boyce (1992).

In general, large-bodied, low-density, upper-trophic-level species with large individual ranges need a greater area to maintain viable populations in the long term than do smaller-bodied, higher-density, lower-trophic-level species with smaller ranges. For plants, larger areas are required to support species that are obligate outcrossers rather than facultative selfers; larger areas are also needed for species that are disturbance specialists or that require forest "gaps" than for habitat generalist species. Among animals, large mammals and birds generally require larger reserves than other animal or plant taxa, and carnivores require larger reserves than herbivores (Figure 10.7). Thus, much of the concern regarding reserve size has centered on mammals.

The loss of large animals from even a large area is illustrated by changes that have occurred in Florida's large mammalian fauna in the last few centuries (Harris and Atkins 1991). Florida supported 11 species of large mammals (> 5 kg) until 200 years ago: bison, manatee, black bear, monk seal, white-tailed deer, key deer, Florida panther, red wolf, bobcat, otter, and raccoon. Three of these species, the monk seal, the bison, and the red wolf, are locally or globally extinct (largely though hunting and predator control); three others, the manatee, the Florida panther, and the key deer, have been so reduced that they are federally listed as endangered; and three more, the black bear, the bobcat, and the otter, are listed as threatened species by Florida or are species listed by the Convention on International Trade in Endangered Species (CITES). Only the white-tailed deer and the raccoon (two

**Figure 10.7** Population sizes supported by reserves of various sizes around the world for small and large herbivores and large carnivores. (From Schonewald-Cox 1983.)

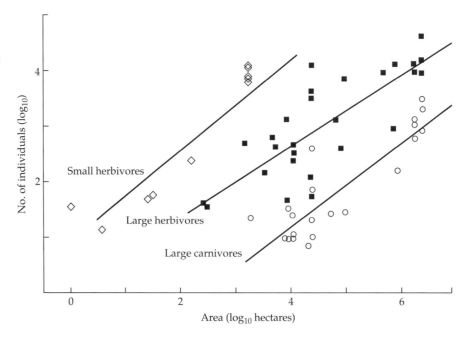

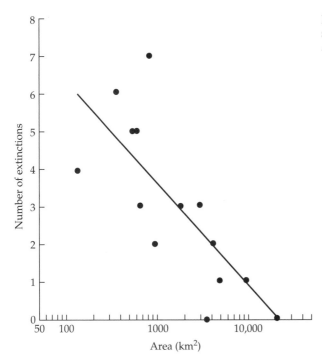

**Figure 10.8** Naturally caused extinctions that occurred after reserve establishment as a function of park area in 14 western North American national parks. (From Newmark 1987.)

habitat generalists, an herbivore and an omnivore, respectively) are doing well in Florida.

Newmark (1987) reported on cases of natural extinctions of mammals in 14 western North American national parks over a period of 43–94 years after park establishment. He found a strong negative relationship between park size and extinction (Figure 10.8): the largest parks had few or no extinctions, whereas the smallest parks had up to seven mammalian species disappear since legal protection of the park less than a century ago. Picton (1979) also found that loss of large mammal species from isolated mountain ranges in the northern Rocky Mountains was a function of habitat size (Figure 10.9). It is clear from these data that many of our reserves are simply not large enough to maintain viable populations of large vertebrates indefinitely without management intervention.

The danger of small reserve size was given further credence by the modeling exercises of Belovsky (1987). His mathematical extinction models indicate that from 0% to 22% of current parks worldwide can be expected to support the largest mammalian carnivore species (10–100 kg) for 100 years; none of these species are expected to persist for 1000 years. Large herbivores have slightly better prospects; from 4% to 100% of reserves should allow persistence for 100 years, and 0% to 22% for 1000 years. For persistence in evolutionary time ($10^5$–$10^6$ years), Belovsky estimates that reserves of $10^6$ to $10^9$ km$^2$ are needed for large mammals (>50 kg). However, the majority of all reserves worldwide are under $10^5$ km$^2$ (Frankel and Soulé 1981).

Grumbine (1990) summed up thoughts on reserve size with the following: "The assumption that our current parks and preserves are in any meaningful sense protecting large, wide-ranging native mammals has little factual basis. For most areas (100,000 ha or less) this lack of protection seems to include the short term (decades). For the long term (centuries), it is likely that all current reserves are incapable of supporting minimum viable populations of large carnivores and herbivores." Likely, at least, without active management.

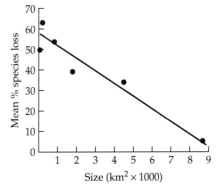

**Figure 10.9** Percentage loss of large mammal species since European settlement as a function of area of isolated ranges in the northern Rocky Mountains. (From Harris 1984; data from Picton 1979.)

Another concern related to reserve size is maintenance of genetic diversity of reserve species, discussed more fully in Chapter 6. The smaller populations maintained in smaller reserves will contain less genetic diversity and be more subject to genetic stochasticities with negative effects on population viability. These smaller populations are more likely to suffer loss of heterozygosity from genetic drift or founder effects, are more likely to experience inbreeding, and are more likely to go extinct from random demographic influences (Lande 1988).

Reserve size also has implications for the expected degree of edge effects, addressed in Chapter 9. Smaller reserves have a greater edge-to-volume ratio, thereby increasing edge effects and decreasing the amount of true interior habitat. This shift can make the reserve more vulnerable to invasion by exotic and edge species, and subject it to edge environmental influences such as higher or lower temperature extremes and increased winds (Saunders et al. 1991).

Finally, larger reserves are more likely to be able to accommodate disturbances, either natural or anthropogenic. All of a small reserve of several hundred hectares, for example, could be affected by a fire or hurricane, and its residents left with no suitable habitat patches. This happened in 1938 in Harvard Forest, when all of the mature timber was blown down in a single hurricane (White and Bratton 1980). A reserve of hundreds of thousands of hectares, by comparison, is more likely to have some patches unaffected by the same disturbance, leaving appropriate habitat available. This topic of heterogeneity is pursued more fully in the next section. The need for large reserves is discussed further in Essay 10B by Brent Danielson.

---

## ESSAY 10B

# A Justification for the Conservation of Large Reserves

Brent J. Danielson, Iowa State University

The bulk of efforts in conservation biology are directed toward preserving the current diversity of species, often applied to one species at a time. As the scope of the declining diversity problem becomes more apparent, this approach has become the ultimate ecological juggling act. As with any other form of juggling, the ecological juggler cannot keep an ever-increasing number of species going indefinitely. So recently, the emphasis has been shifting to the conservation of communities, loosely defined here as a collection of species coupled by direct and/or indirect interactions. This shift is at least partially a practical matter: an intact community may retain the ecological integrity necessary to support each individual species with little or no external management, thereby relieving us of the bulk of our ecological baby-sitting chores.

But there are at least two good reasons why simply identifying and protecting individual communities is, by it-self, insufficient. Fortunately, there is a solution, albeit an initially costly one, and it involves increasing the ecological, and thus spatial, scale of our conservation efforts. Here, I outline these two major problems and explain how they can be dealt with through the creation of very large refuges.

The first problem with simple community-based conservation is that communities are dynamic. Under the community-based method, individual representative communities are preserved by a judicious "cookie-cutter" method that forms relatively small (often on the scale of a few hundred to a few thousand hectares) and isolated refuge communities. The philosophy is that, if we create enough of them, we will manage to have most, if not all species represented somewhere in the new landscape of isolated refugia. Initially, this may be possible. But it is a blind leap of faith to hope that the species will continue to persist indefinitely within these refugia. Paleo-ecologists have shown conclusively that, in fact, communities are not stable entities unto themselves over the long term (Graham 1986; Hunter et al. 1988). Even over shorter time scales, communities can be quite dynamic (Gee and Giller 1987). Natural community dynamics will result in species being lost from each community as the result of interspecific interactions, stochastic variation in population abundances, or the cumulative biotic and abiotic changes in the environment within these small fragments. Thus, even if we get all the extant species into at least one "cookie-cutter" refuge, there is little reason to believe that we will have a long-term solution to the maintenance of biotic diversity.

By way of contrast, a large region, with its many semi-independent communities, will still experience a turnover of species within each community. However, because the communities exist in a larger fabric, within which dispersal between communities is reasonably likely, each species will also be able to colonize new areas while becoming locally extinct in others, thereby maintaining the original level of regional diversity.

A system of small refugia interconnected by dispersal corridors has been put forward as an alternative solution. Nevertheless, even with a high degree of connectedness, the degree of dispersal is likely to be severely restricted for many species. There are several other problems with the corridor concept, but by far the most severe, in my opinion, is that each corridor and the connected refugia can be constructed at the appropriate spatial scale for only a few species. Clearly, a diverse community of species requires a diversity of spatial scales. What may be an entire landscape to a population of voles is not more than a patch to the individual hawk that hunts the voles. In a large contiguous reserve, each species is free to function at its own spatial scale, yet continues to interact with species that are functioning at different spatial scales. While a system of corridors is probably better than no corridors, it is nonetheless, far from ideal when the entire range of species is considered.

Theoretically, it may be possible for us to artificially substitute for natural dispersal and colonization by actively moving individual species among the set of small refugia. This not only assumes that we can actually learn to mimic the natural rates of local colonization and extinction for each species, but also brings us back to the single-species approach, returning conservation to the ecological baby-sitting situation that we are attempting to avoid.

The second reason to opt for the preservation of large regions is that it is here that evolution can best produce the new adaptations and even new species that will eventually inhabit the new ecological landscapes that are continually arising. When a species exists in many different communities, it is subject to different selective pressures. Most of the microevolution that occurs in these situations will have no appreciable effect on a species' evolutionary future, but some will, and in which communities this will occur, we cannot even make an informed guess. Of course, this localized evolution may occur within a small refuge, but without omniscient foresight, we can rarely distinguish the adaptation from the maladaptation. So, how would we know which types of new variation we should actively spread to other refugia, and which to keep isolated? In a large refuge, we do not have to recognize anything. Large refuges that retain their ecological integrity will also retain their evolutionary integrity; natural selection, operating among as well as within individual populations and communities, will make the necessary choices for us.

Furthermore, some adaptations may not be possible in small refuges. Consider a species strongly affected by anthropogenic climatic change. It might adapt to utilize other habitats, but only if such habitats are available to it. Under changing conditions, the strength of the associations between species can change as well. If there is a sufficient pool of other species available in nearby communities, new interspecific interactions may evolve, leading to novel biotic communities. How likely is this type of evolution in small isolated refugia? And how scientifically and economically capable are we of artificially intervening in ways that will compensate for this isolation? If a long-term solution to the conservation of natural systems is to be successful, we will have to allow these sorts of evolutionary changes to take place.

It may be argued that it is impractical to create the large refugia that are required for ecological and evolutionary integrity. However, it is likely that the allegedly more practical small reserves will ultimately be much more costly in any currency you wish to name. Thus, I recommend that we aim high, for solutions with the greatest potential for long-term ecological and evolutionary self-sufficiency.

## Heterogeneity and Dynamics

Spatially and temporally heterogeneous areas are generally superior to homogeneous areas as conservation reserves if the goal is to maintain high biological diversity. This principle stems from the observation that nature is dynamic and changes over time and space through biotic and abiotic disturbance. Spatial heterogeneity of habitat "patches" within a reserve accommodates disturbances better than does a homogeneous reserve by offering species a diversity of habitat types at any given time. If a particular habitat patch is altered or destroyed by disturbance, or if it undergoes succession and becomes unsuitable for a given species, then other appropriate patches may be available for colonization within the reserve.

Patches are perhaps best discussed in terms of $\alpha$ and $\beta$ diversity (Chapter 4). A single habitat patch supports a particular group of species at any point in time and has an $\alpha$-, or within-patch, diversity. Species differences among different patch types constitute $\beta$-diversity. High overall diversity in a reserve may arise from $\alpha$-diversity, $\beta$-diversity, or both.

The presence or absence of a species in a given habitat patch is a function of local colonization and extinction rates in that patch for that species. Overall patch diversity is then a function of colonization and extinction dynamics across the pool of species. Because conservation reserves are typically the last bastion for many species, probability of colonization from external sources may be reduced or eliminated. In that case, extinction dynamics become the dominant force in species diversity for that reserve, and species di-

**Figure 10.10** Most landscapes consist of habitat patches created by various natural processes, including disturbances, resulting in a patchwork of habitat types, such as this area along the Savannah River in South Carolina. (Photograph courtesy of Savannah River Ecology Lab.)

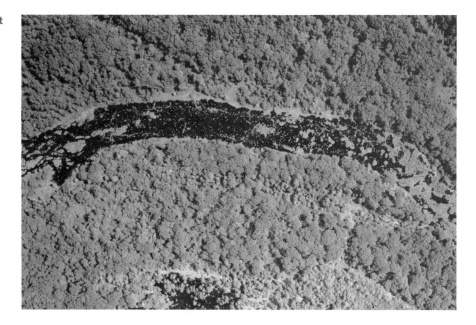

versity will ultimately decline. In order to retain species, then, rather than depending on recolonization from external sources, the reserves themselves need to provide the source areas. Thus, the need for internal heterogeneity of patches in a reserve.

This emphasis on heterogeneity within reserves (or **patch dynamics**) was developed by Pickett and Thompson (1978), who stressed the importance of internal dynamics of habitat patches in maintaining overall diversity. Habitat patches in a landscape are created by disturbance regimes, which result in a patchwork of habitat types of different sizes, shapes, successional stages, and persistence times (Figure 10.10). Types of natural disturbances that create habitat patches include fires, storm treefalls, and insect damage in forests; wave action on marine shorelines; floods and droughts in streams; and herbivory and soil disruption by mammals in grasslands. Each of these disturbances modifies or destroys some component of the existing biota, creating a habitat patch of an earlier successional stage. Anthropogenic disturbances, often of greater size or intensity than natural disturbances, also create patches (Figure 10.11).

The internal structure of the reserve, including species composition, population densities and dispersions, and organic geometry, is defined by the disturbance pattern and longevities of the patches. A reserve is thus a mosaic of patches of various sizes and ages, and diversity depends partly on the dynamics of these patches. Patches change through time, new patches are created by disturbance, and spatial relationships among patches change.

The patch dynamics perspective does not mean that reserves should be chopped up into many small patches. Rather, the natural disturbance regime and the resultant size and frequency of disturbance patches must be ascertained, as well as successional patterns for the landscape. Ideally, then, the size of reserve necessary to include the various natural patch types can be determined. The types of disturbance, their usual magnitude and frequency, and the typical responses of the biota are requisite information. It is also important to understand and incorporate rare but extensive disturbances, such as hurricanes or monsoon floods, into reserve design—those severe disturbances that may occur at frequencies of once in hundreds to thousands of

**Figure 10.11** Anthropogenic disturbances, such as this clear-cut in an old-growth forest in Washington State, create new types of patches on the landscape. (Photograph by G. K. Meffe.)

years, but which can have drastic consequences for a reserve based on "normal" magnitudes of disturbance.

Pickett and Thompson (1978) recommended that reserve size be based on a **minimum dynamic area,** which is the smallest area with a complete, natural disturbance regime. This would maintain internal recolonization sources and minimize extinction by maintaining a complete diversity of patches at any given time. Such a minimum dynamic area can only be determined by empirical knowledge of each system; it could vary, for example, from perhaps tens of hectares in a rocky shoreline community to hundreds of thousands of hectares in a lowland rainforest, but in any case should be considerably larger than the largest disturbance patch, including rare and extreme disturbances.

Another empirical fact argues for habitat heterogeneity in reserves. A review of the conservation literature suggests that many, perhaps most, species in nature may exist not as single or isolated populations, but as groups of populations, or metapopulations, in different habitat patches (see Chapters 6, 7, and 9 for detailed discussions). Metapopulation structure may indeed be widespread, but too few studies have been conducted to provide much insight into just how common it is. As you will see in the discussion that follows, an assumption of metapopulation structure has important implications for the management and design of conservation areas. Determining the existence of metapopulation structures (through studies of population structure and movements) and their distribution among taxonomic groups and in different environmental conditions should be a high research priority in conservation biology. When metapopulation structure exists, then interactions occur among the populations in a metapopulation through movement among habitat patches, which affects genetic structure of individual populations, habitat patch occupancy, and recolonization of patches after local extinction.

Metapopulations have important implications for patch dynamics and heterogeneity of reserves. When similar habitat patches are spatially separated across a reserve, individual species may have a metapopulation structure, with populations occurring in different suitable patches. The patch dynamics perspective assumes that dispersal among similar successional patches is possible, countering local extinction processes. In order for patch dynamics to work, of course, multiple habitat patches need to exist and to be accessible to metapopulations of species appropriate to each patch type. That is, reserves need to be internally heterogeneous.

Murphy et al. (1990) point out that the metapopulation perspective may be more critical for "small" biota, such as annual plants, invertebrates, and small vertebrates, than for the megavertebrates championed as the "umbrella" species under which everything else will be protected. This is because these smaller species, with short generation times, small body sizes, high rates of population increase, and, sometimes, high habitat specificity, are more vulnerable to localized density-independent environmental factors than are the megavertebrates. Thus, a large, local population of a threatened butterfly, for example, such as the Bay checkerspot (*Euphydryas editha bayensis*) in California (discussed in previous chapters), may be lost because of annual variations in temperature or rainfall that would not affect even sparse populations of vertebrates (Figure 10.12). A metapopulation structure, with repeated patches inhabited by this species, may have kept the Bay checkerspot from going globally extinct in the face of numerous local extinctions (Ehrlich and Murphy 1987). It is important to note also that, although small-bodied species may be more directly influenced by environmental disturbances than are large-bodied species, the higher rate of population growth found in small-bodied species also means that they recover from perturbations more quickly (Minckley et al. 1991).

The emphasis on habitat heterogeneity in reserve design is an outgrowth of the realization of the importance of processes, rather than just patterns, in ecological systems. A patch dynamics approach fosters continuation of natural processes and change in a reserve, which means that disturbance events should generally not be controlled or eliminated. In fact, lack of disturbance may be a problem.

One of the important questions in reserve management is how to ensure that disturbance regimes are maintained (see Chapters 11 and 12). For terrestrial communities, the role of fire provides an instructive case in point. In large, intact forests, fires were usually the result of lightning strikes, and occurred rather frequently, but at low intensity (Heinselman 1973). In preindustrial societies fires were sometimes used to manage habitat for game pro-

**Figure 10.12** Size changes in three populations of the Bay checkerspot butterfly (*Euphydryas editha bayensis*) southeast of San Francisco, California. Numbers of the combined metapopulation are shown at left; the separate population dynamics are shown at right. Note the extinctions and recolonization in area G. (From Ehrlich and Murphy 1987.)

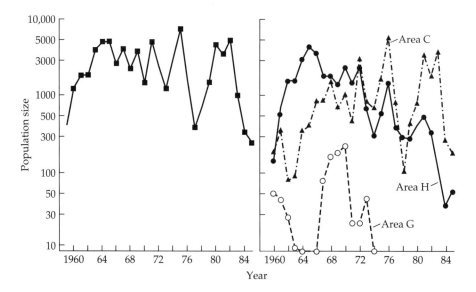

duction or to clear small areas for agriculture. Under these conditions, fires tended to be small and patchy, thereby creating an important disturbance regime or patch dynamic. Today, unless prescribed fires are explicitly used to manage habitats, fires tend to be suppressed and thus rare, but extensive and intensive when they do occur, as in the 1989 Yellowstone National Park fires, which covered thousands of hectares and destroyed large forest stands. Under such conditions, fire is less an agent of disturbance and patch dynamics than an agent of large-scale habitat conversion.

When patch heterogeneity must be generated through management, the goal should be kept clearly in mind. If the goal is to maintain the characteristic biodiversity of the region, then management should be used to mimic the magnitude, frequency, and spatial scale of natural processes that generate patch heterogeneity. However, management of heterogeneity simply to maximize numbers of species per se would result in transforming a landscape into a mosaic of edges and patches, and would perhaps make it more vulnerable to invasion by exotic species (Hobbs and Huenneke 1992).

### Context

Biodiversity in reserves is influenced both by the patch dynamics within reserves and by the context of the larger landscape, which must be considered at multiple scales. At the within-reserve scale, each patch type is spatially located in the context of other patch types. Patch inhabitants must be able to move among similar patches and recolonize new patches if metapopulation structure is to continue. Some species also may use different patch types seasonally or at different life history stages, and must be able to find those patches within the larger context of the reserve. For example, elk must have access to low-elevation winter grazing and to high mountain meadows during summer. Some salamanders develop as larvae in ponds but spend their adult lives in a terrestrial "patch."

At a larger scale, the entire reserve functions in the context of a surrounding, nonreserve landscape (Figure 10.13), which can have critical consequences, both positive and negative, for the reserve. Biological reserves are dynamic, with extensive movements by plants and animals, as well as material transport and energy flux, occurring within and among habitats. Consequently, the boundaries or edges of reserves have received a great deal of attention, and may be critical factors in the protection of interior habitat, because edges determine the dynamics of immigration and emigration. The landscape surrounding reserves also requires attention. It may be a combination of urban, suburban, industrial, or agricultural/forestry lands, offering a mixture of threats ranging from domestic plants and animals to crop monocultures to pathogens and severe pollution.

The importance of edges in reserve success was emphasized in a boundary model developed by Schonewald-Cox and Bayless (1986). This model recognizes that the administrative boundary of a reserve is often designated by political or legal, rather than ecological considerations, within the constraints of previous land ownership and conflicting public demands. This legal boundary then acts as a filter, controlling human activities within and outside of the reserve, and will often differ from natural, ecological boundaries or edges, which control biological and physicochemical events.

The administrative boundary will typically result in the creation of a generated edge, a false edge that is the result of the effects of greater protection within a reserve and lesser protection outside (Figure 10.14). The generated edge may be close to or far from the legal boundary; if deep within the reserve, it reduces the effective reserve size. These various boundaries and

**Figure 10.13** Satellite image of the U.S. Department of Energy's Savannah River Site in South Carolina, adjacent to the Savannah River. Note how this 780 km$^2$ area of largely forested lands (dark circle) stands out from the surrounding region of heavy agricultural use and suburban development. (Photograph courtesy of Savannah River Ecology Lab.)

**Figure 10.14**  Boundary model of a reserve, illustrating natural ecological edges and generated edges created by an ecologically artificial administrative boundary. (Modified from Schonewald-Cox and Bayless 1986.)

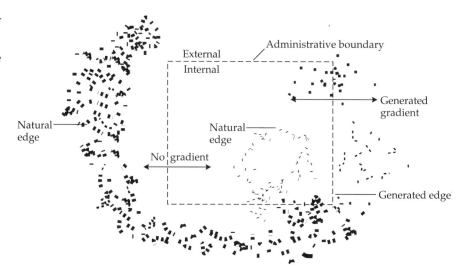

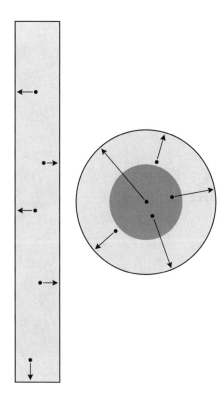

**Figure 10.15**  A schematic diagram showing the relationship between area and edge in two "reserves" of the same area. In the rectangular reserve, there is no true interior habitat; all points are close to an edge (light shading). In the circular reserve, there is some true interior habitat (dark shading).

edges create gradients that affect movements into and out of the "legal" reserve, and thus affect population dynamics, community structure, and ecosystem function.

The incongruity of the legal and biotic boundaries of reserves was explored for the eight largest reserves or reserve assemblages in western North America by Newmark (1985). He compared the identified legal boundaries with the biotic boundaries, which he determined by watershed locations and the estimated areas needed to maintain viable populations of the nonflying mammals with the largest home ranges. Newmark found that seven of the eight reserves have biotic boundaries larger than their legal boundaries by factors of 1.2 to 9.6 for MVPs of 50, and 6 to 96 for MVPs of 500. Seven of the eight reserves also have legal boundaries smaller than the simple minimum area requirements of one or more mammalian species. This approach reinforces the earlier message that even our largest North American reserves are too small to maintain some species in perpetuity, and emphasizes the conservation significance of semiwild public and private lands that may surround reserves as a buffer.

The **area/perimeter ratio** of a reserve is important when considering reserve boundaries (Buechner 1987); if the ratio is low (as in small or elongated reserves with proportionately more perimeter length per unit of interior area), then the average distance from interior points to the boundary is small, and interior species, those requiring undisturbed habitat away from edges, would presumably do poorly. If the ratio is large, then the interior is farther removed from edge influences (see Chapter 9). A lower area/perimeter ratio also means that more management, and thus more energy, money, and time, is necessary to maintain the interior characteristics of a reserve. From an edge perspective, a more circular reserve, with a higher area/perimeter ratio, would be preferable to an elongated reserve (Figure 10.15).

There is another critical point to be made here. A narrow reserve with no core habitat is less sensitive to further habitat loss because the area is already essentially all edge habitat. In contrast, a circular reserve with core habitat can be strongly affected by even small habitat losses because they bring edge effects further into the core (Figure 10.16). For example, inholdings in large natural areas can have effects much larger than their area might suggest simply because they extend edge effects into core areas.

The boundary model encourages the creation of buffers around reserves to increase available habitat (even if suboptimal) and to decrease exposure to adverse conditions from the developed world. The buffers could have some limited exploitative function, such as selective timber harvest, hunting, or low-density development, and still function in a protective role. If the generated edge forms within a buffer rather than within the reserve, then it is an added positive feature.

Context must also consider human intervention, both direct and indirect, legal and illegal. Direct intervention includes activities such as legal harvest (hunting, logging), poaching, industrial and agricultural activities, mining, and urban and suburban development, and raises a number of questions in each instance. For example, will a proposed or existing reserve be encroached upon by new development? If so, how will drainage patterns change? What are the likely effects of domestic animals on the reserve? What types of cultivated plants are likely to escape into the reserve? Will adjacent agricultural activities affect the reserve through use of fertilizers and pesticides? Will industrial expansion affect the reserve through increased air and water pollution or legal or illegal dumping of wastes? Mitigation of these adverse effects is the concern of reserve management (Chapters 11 and 12); however, as we discuss below, reserves can be designed to minimize some of these risks using buffers and zoning.

Indirect human influences can affect reserves as well, and include regional and global changes such as production of acid rain, global climate change, and regional land use activities. These effects are less subject to control or mitigation, but should nevertheless be considered in reserve selection and management. For example, are regional land use activities so heavily urban that it is unlikely that a reserve can effectively function as other than a green space for human use? If so, then monies should not be devoted to unrealistic goals of species preservation. Is acid rain so intense that continuous neutralization of lakes will be necessary to maintain fish populations? If so, then perhaps resources should focus on other species more likely to persist under such conditions.

Janzen (1983, 1986) has been especially adamant about the context of reserves. He argues that mainland "insular" reserves are in fact not at all insular, but are under constant threat from the surrounding landscape and all of its evils, both natural and anthropogenic, a problem he calls the "eternal external threat." Such evils include pesticides, fire (or lack of it), local or global climate modification, migration of reserve animals into surrounding areas, movement of animals and plants (especially alien species) into the reserve from adjacent areas, and energy subsidy for reserve residents from outside of the system. Unfortunately, most of the biotic movement and subsidy will be from successional species of disturbed habitats or species from croplands, which will invade reserves from edges inward. The smaller the reserve, the greater the effect of the surrounding habitat as a source of problems, and the greater the need for habitat buffers that minimize habitat differences between the core reserve and adjacent areas.

The invasion of a reserve by species from surrounding, "unbuffered" lands is clearly illustrated by a study of a natural tree-fall gap in a 10-ha patch of original forest surrounded by old pastures and secondary successional forest in Santa Rosa National Park, in northwestern Costa Rica (Janzen 1983). Nearly all the plant species that grew after creation of this 124-m² gap came from second-growth vegetation of anthropogenic origin outside of the park, from a minimum of 60 m away. This patch will presumably not regenerate as primary forest, but will form a long-lasting patch of disturbance veg-

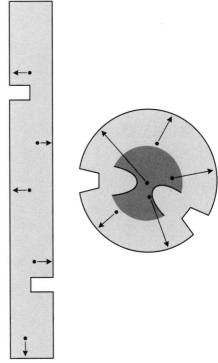

**Figure 10.16**　The same hypothetical reserves from Figure 10.15, with small pieces of edge habitat destroyed. In the rectangular reserve, little real effect is realized, because the reserve was previously all edge. In the circular reserve, the new habitat loss extends edge habitat far into the core, effectively reducing the size of the core reserve.

etation uncharacteristic of the mature forest of this region. More important, perhaps, than the loss of species in the gap is that species interactions and processes inherent in the original vegetation will be altered. Insolation levels will change, soil moisture and drainage may be altered, nutrient cycling will be different from that in the surrounding forest, and coevolved relationships among the biota will be disrupted. Attention to context, including incorporation of a buffer zone, could have significantly reduced these unnatural effects of this natural disturbance.

### Connecting Fragmented Habitats

As you saw in Chapter 9, human activities around the planet have created widespread habitat fragmentation and isolation in virtually every ecosystem type. Because these activities are a major contributor to loss of biodiversity, it makes intuitive sense that reconnection of habitats would be a major step toward solving that problem. This is the basis for the idea of connecting reserves through corridors, or strips of habitat connecting otherwise isolated habitat patches. Corridors have been promoted as important features of reserve design that allow movement, and thus recolonization, among high-quality habitats.

Corridors may be necessary even across small disturbance areas, as species differ greatly in dispersal capabilities. A nocturnal mammal, for example, may have no problem traversing a 100-m-wide clear-cut, whereas a forest-interior bird or a diurnal snake may find it an insurmountable barrier. A given corridor may actually serve as a selective filter, allowing movement by some species and blocking movement of others (Noss 1991).

There are two major categories of need for wildlife corridors. The first is for species that require corridors for periodic migrations among different habitat types used for breeding, birthing, feeding, or roosting (Soulé 1991). Such movements might range from annual migrations of large herbivores between summer and winter grazing areas, to daily movements of birds between feeding and roosting sites. The second category is permanent immigration and emigration of individuals among habitat patches in a metapopulation context, allowing gene flow and recolonization after local extinction.

Noss (1991) discussed three types of wildlife corridors needed at different spatiotemporal scales, because specific problems exist at different scales of both time and space, and at different levels of biological organization. The particular scale of concern for a given situation depends on the biota involved and the conservation goals. The **fencerow scale** connects close habitat patches, such as woodlots, using narrow rows of appropriate habitat, such as trees or shrubs, for the movement of small vertebrates, such as mice, chipmunks, or passerine birds (Figure 10.17). This is a very localized scale for movement among small patches. These corridors are entirely "edge" habitat and thus are not useful for habitat interior species.

The second type of corridor functions at the **landscape mosaic scale.** These are usually broader and longer corridors that connect major landscape features rather than small woodlots (Figure 10.18). They may function for daily, seasonal, or more permanent movement of interior as well as edge species, and result in a landscape-level mosaic of reserves. This type of corridor would include large strips of forest that connect otherwise separate reserves, riparian forests along streams, or habitats that follow natural gradients or topographic features such as mountainous ridges.

The **regional scale** is the largest corridor scale, and connects nature reserves in regional networks (Figure 10.19). This last type of corridor is further discussed below and in Essay 10C, by Reed Noss.

**Figure 10.17**  A fencerow corridor in northeastern Georgia. Such fencerow corridors connect small habitat patches such as woodlots, and may be effective for movement of small vertebrates. These corridors are entirely "edge" habitat and are not at all effective for habitat interior species. (Photograph by G. K. Meffe.)

**Figure 10.18** A strip corridor, in this case a riparian forest along the Río Tempisque in Costa Rica (center of photo). Strip corridors are broader and longer than fencerow corridors and connect major landscape features. Strip corridors can promote daily or seasonal movements of interior and edge species, and create a landscape level mosaic of reserves. (Photograph by C. R. Carroll.)

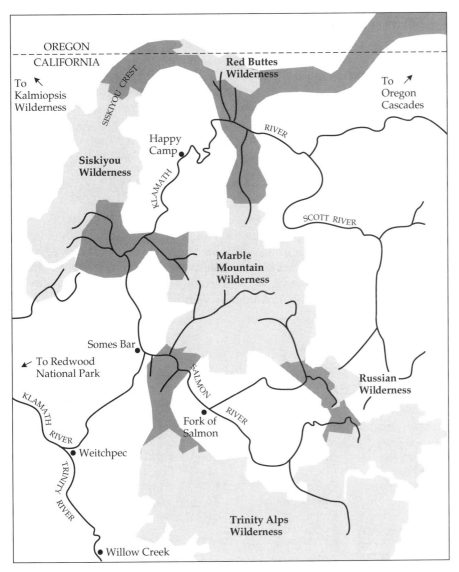

**Figure 10.19** Proposed corridors (dark shading) that would connect various wilderness areas (light shading) into a regional mosaic in the Klamath area of northern California/southern Oregon. Arrows show directions of other nearby wilderness areas. (From Pace 1991.)

The benefits of corridors can be high (Noss 1987), even though corridor inclusion has potential costs, and corridors may not be desirable in all situations (discussed below). Because fragmentation is one of the greatest threats to biodiversity, countering its effects through reconnections of prime habitats should be considered whenever possible. One of the best arguments for corridors is that the original landscape was largely interconnected, but then fragmented by human actions; reconnection will move the situation slightly back toward the original state (Noss 1987). Corridors should be considered on an individual basis for each reserve, and included or rejected on the basis of data pertinent to each system.

If corridors are desirable for a given situation, what design should they take? Again, there is no set answer, and only an empirical approach tailored to each situation, combined with generalized knowledge about the biology of the species involved, will suffice. The solution will depend partly on what types of biota are to be preserved and their mobilities, the distance between reserves to be connected, how likely it is that human interference will occur in the corridors, availability of corridor habitat, and other factors unique to each situation. Corridors may be as simple and mundane as a hedgerow, a power-line cut, or a highway median of pine trees that allows movements of birds and small mammals. Such simple corridors, consisting of all edge habitat, are called **line corridors.** In contrast, **strip corridors** are broader, and contain some interior habitat with intact and functioning communities, such as a swath of tropical forest several hundred meters wide. Ideally, such corridors would be large enough to experience their own patch dynamics.

Riparian zones in particular can serve as excellent strip corridors in many cases and protect important habitat at the same time. Especially in more arid areas, many species are drawn to riparian areas from upland zones, and are at least periodically dependent on the resources there. Riparian strips can also connect highland and mountain habitat with the lowlands and thereby provide for elevational migrations. However, riparian corridors are not the answer to all problems in connectivity. They will not serve as corridors, for example, for upland species that avoid mesic conditions.

Reserves that are farther apart may require wider corridors in order to be effective (Harrison 1992), because larger, wide-ranging animals such as some mammalian predators require interior habitat in order to travel very far. One cannot expect a grizzly bear to travel many kilometers among reserves in a corridor 50 m wide. Knowledge of average home range sizes for individuals or groups can help in estimating necessary minimum widths for corridors (Table 10.1).

**Table 10.1**
Estimates of Minimum Corridor Widths Based on Average Female or Pack Home-Range Sizes in Several Mammals

| Species | Location | Minimum width (km) | Source |
|---|---|---|---|
| Wolves | Minnesota | 12.0 | Nowak and Paradiso (1983) |
| Wolves | Alaska | 22.0 | Ballard and Spraker (1979) |
| Black bears | Minnesota | 2.0 | Rogers (1987) |
| Mountain lions | California | 5.0 | Hopkins et al. (1982) |
| Bobcats | South Carolina | 2.5 | Griffith and Fendley (1982) |
| White-tailed deer | Minnesota | 0.6 | Nelson and Mech (1987) |
| Dwarf mongoose | Tanzania | 0.6 | Rood (1987) |

From Harrison 1992.

Soulé (1991) warned that the quality and effectiveness of corridors need to be considered, and not just their size, shape, and position. This means that the objective of the corridor, usually in terms of viability of specific target species, needs to be clearly stated at the outset. A corridor that does not function in its intended way can actually be detrimental by serving as a "death trap" or "sink corridor" that pulls individuals away from source areas and exposes them to increased mortality but does not effectively deliver them to the intended reserve.

Lindenmayer and Nix (1993) studied corridor use by marsupials in Australia and provided evidence for Soulé's warning; they found that more than home range and minimum corridor width were important in corridor use. Additional factors influencing corridor use included the larger landscape context of the site, habitat structure (such as number of trees with hollows or size of stream in the corridor), and the social structure (solitary/colonial; monogamous/polygamous), diet, and foraging patterns of the target species. Thus, an important point is that each corridor design should be the result of a detailed ecological analysis.

Noss and Harris (1986) point out that conservation strategies that focus on individual reserves while ignoring the larger landscape are unrealistic for several reasons: (1) isolated reserves are static, and do not effectively deal with continuous and expected biotic change within reserves; (2) they are focused on the *content* of individual reserves rather than the *context* of entire landscapes; (3) they emphasize populations and species rather than the systems in which they occur and interact; and (4) the strategies are oriented toward high species diversity rather than toward maintaining the natural and characteristic diversity of the area.

Noss and Harris (1986) proposed an approach to regional reserve design called "Nodes, Networks, and MUMs." A **node** is an area with an unusually high conservation value; for example, a region with high species diversity, high endemism, or that contains critical resources, such as breeding or feeding grounds for a species of particular interest. The criteria for selection of nodes can span the entire range of the biological hierarchy, from genetics to ecosystems. Nodes also may be dynamic, moving in space in response to environmental change, and must be permitted to track shifting environments through time.

Individual nodes will rarely, if ever, be large enough to maintain and protect all the biodiversity within their borders indefinitely, however. That was demonstrated earlier with North American large mammals, and East (1981) has also argued that large herbivores and carnivores in African savanna reserves will not persist for long in their current configuration. Consequently, **networks** of reserves need to be developed by connecting the various nodes through corridors of suitable habitat. These corridors connect the nodes into a landscape scheme that allows flow of species, genes, energy, and materials among them.

Multiple-use modules, or **MUMs,** as proposed by Harris (1984), consist of a central, well-protected core area surrounded by buffer zones of increasingly heavy use by humans farther from the central core. The core would be inviolable, allowing no development or avoidable human impacts, whereas the buffer zones would be used for human endeavors ranging from bird-watching and backpacking near the core, to hunting, logging, and low-density residential development farther from the core. Management of all areas, however, would be consistent with preservation of the core or node. This approach resolves conflicts between "hands-on" conservation/management and "hands-off" preservation through zoning of individual components, further discussed below. An example of a MUM network for northern Florida and southern

**Figure 10.20** An example of a proposed multiple use module (MUM) network in southern Georgia and northern Florida. The various nodes (existing protected areas) could be connected by proposed riparian and coastal corridors. (From Noss and Harris 1986.)

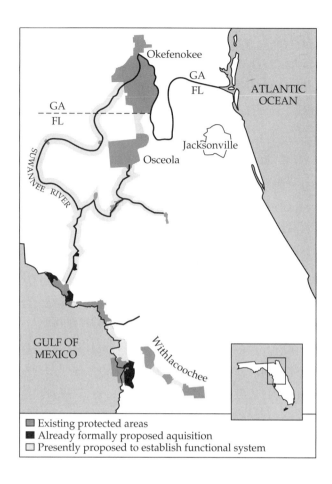

Existing protected areas
Already formally proposed aquisition
Presently proposed to establish functional system

Georgia was proposed by Noss and Harris (1986) (Figure 10.20). Interestingly, they note that the major impediment to development of MUMs is not lack of money, but lack of cooperation among federal, state, and local land-management and regulatory agencies, and private landowners.

*Corridors: A Caveat.* We have just discussed the conservation role of corridors in largely favorable terms, while at the same time calling for more empirical studies. There are good reasons to expect that corridors, if designed properly, can enhance population viability in fragmented and otherwise isolated habitats. However, there are important "real-world" considerations that urge caution. First, the empirical basis for our confidence in corridors is poorly developed. Most of the studies on corridors have simply demonstrated whether or not the organisms in question can be found there. We do not know how often existing putative corridors are really used for movement between major habitat patches, or the probability of mortality should an individual attempt to disperse. Experimental studies testing efficacies of corridors are virtually nonexistent. Second, the establishment of new corridors, especially of extensive systems designed to facilitate the movement of many species, requires the commitment of resources that might otherwise be used to enlarge existing reserves or buy new ones. If fixed acreages are to be set aside, then inclusion of corridors could reduce the size of core areas for reserves.

The real utility of corridors remains to be demonstrated both as a general principle and in specific cases. Even if corridors seem to work generally, every case of planned corridor use should involve some assessment of the likelihood of real contributions of corridors to reserve success. These themes are discussed further in Simberloff and Cox (1987) and Simberloff et al. (1992).

# ESSAY 10C
# Creating Regional Reserve Networks

Reed F. Noss, University of Idaho, and Oregon State University

In the early days of land conservation, biology played a small role in the selection of parks and other reserves. People were interested in geological wonders and scenic features, places to hike or picnic, watersheds to safeguard water quality and supply, and overall aesthetics. Wildlife was sometimes considered for viewing purposes, but seldom from a biological standpoint. Areas considered for protection usually had to contain little timber or other extractable resources, an anthropocentric tradition that continues today.

When biology finally came into the conservation equation, in the 1920s and 1930s in the United States, the emphasis was on preservation of representative plant communities, and occasionally on protection of rare species. Small reserves were eventually established by The Nature Conservancy and by state and federal natural areas programs for the protection of such sites. The meaning of preservation then was pure and very static; lines were drawn around natural areas and managers strived to keep them forever in the condition in which they were set aside. Although the need for large reserves to represent whole ecosystems, replete with large carnivores, was noted early (for example, Shelford 1933; Kendeigh et al. 1950–1951), practical difficulties usually precluded such designs, as they still do today.

We now know that small, isolated reserves, while valuable for some purposes, are difficult to manage and will seldom maintain the species and communities for which they were established, even with considerable management effort. Smaller populations are more vulnerable to extinction, so while a small reserve might be suitable for plants, many invertebrates, and small vertebrates, it will not suffice for larger animals. Moreover, external influences extend across boundaries of reserves. The microclimate near a forest edge is usually drier, brighter, and has greater temperature fluctuations than that deep in the forest. Exotic plants and animals, ranging from dandelions to domestic cats, invade across reserve boundaries, sometimes outcompeting or preying heavily on native species. Deer and other herbivores that now lack natural

predators build large populations and inhibit regeneration of native trees, shrubs, and herbs, plants that might otherwise do fine in a small reserve. The biotic community in a small reserve is vulnerable, especially when the surrounding land is altered radically.

A new approach to land conservation takes a broader view, one focused on whole landscapes and regions, and on time scales ranging from decades to millennia. This new approach is also highly ambitious. No longer is our goal merely the protection of a few rare species or outstanding examples of plant communities, but rather to represent ecosystem variation across environmental gradients, to maintain viable populations of all native species, and to sustain ecological and evolutionary processes. Perhaps above all, the land conservation system must be adaptable to change. Organisms must be able to move in response to disturbances and climate change, and to interact genetically with other populations to which they were once connected. This new approach will not usually be achievable in the short term; hence the need for expanded horizons. But the sooner such an effort is begun, the more likely it will ultimately be accomplished.

Biodiversity conservation at a regional scale has essentially four options: (1) more reserves; (2) bigger reserves; (3) interconnected reserves; or (4) better management of the multiple-use lands or seminatural matrix that often surrounds reserves. These options are not mutually exclusive alternatives, but complementary components of an overall strategy. The emphasis given to each option will vary from landscape to landscape, but each region will require a pluralistic strategy if all elements of its biodiversity are to be maintained over time. A model for a regional reserve network (Figure A) shows reserves connected by corridors and buffered by multiple-use lands. Designs for such systems are cropping up in region after region in North America, initiated by local, grassroots action but guided by an overall strategy called The Wildlands Project, an attempt to link conservation biologists with activists (Foreman et al. 1992, Noss 1992).

Perhaps the most controversial and misunderstood component of the regional reserve network model (Figure A) is connectivity. The thesis in support of connectivity is that a system of reserves may be united into a whole that is greater than the sum of its parts. Although no single reserve will be likely to maintain a viable population of species with large area requirements, a network of linked reserves may provide for such species. This reasoning is difficult to argue against. Single reserves capable of supporting viable populations of wolves, wolverines, grizzly bears, or cougars might have to be 2–10 million ha in size, or perhaps even larger (Schonewald-Cox 1983; Hummel 1990; Noss 1992). Not many opportunities re-

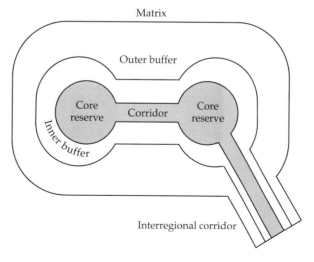

Matrix

Outer buffer

Core reserve

Corridor

Core reserve

Inner buffer

Interregional corridor

**Figure A**  A regional reserve network, consisting of core reserves, connecting corridors or linkages, and buffer zones. Only two core reserves are shown, but a real system might contain many reserves. Inner buffer zones would be strictly protected, while outer zones would allow a wider range of compatible human uses. In this example, an interregional corridor connects the system to a similar network in another region.

main for establishing reserves of this size. Of course, many regions lack large carnivores today because they have been hunted to extinction. Bringing these species back is a legitimate long-range conservation goal. Even if we consider much smaller animals, such as songbirds, hundreds or thousands of hectares may be necessary to maintain populations (Whitcomb et al. 1981). A connected system of large reserves, buffered from the harsh influences of intensively used lands, seems necessary to meet broad biodiversity conservation goals.

Arguments against corridors have been voiced, and there may be instances in which corridors, particularly narrow ones, do more harm than good. For example, a narrow corridor may be entirely edge habitat and could encourage the proliferation of pests, which could then invade reserves. But connectivity need not rely on distinct corridors; for many species, it might be provided by a well-managed landscape matrix. This is partly a scale issue. At a regional scale, corridors might constitute whole watersheds or mountain ranges. Thus, the corridors in a regional network, such as one proposed for Florida (see Figure 10.20) might be miles wide and contain many habitat types and land ownerships, yet be managed for low road density and retention of adequate security cover for wildlife. These corridors would serve to allow natural movements of wide-ranging species, such as the Florida panther and black bear, and to provide opportunities for multi-species migration northward and away from the coasts as climate warms and sea level rises. The core reserves in this model would be centered on "hot spots" or "nodes" of diversity in the landscape, such as centers of endemism, complemented by areas selected to represent a full range of ecosystem types and physical habitat gradients. Roadless areas and other undeveloped sites would also be protected, as such sites are exceedingly rare nowadays and provide security to species sensitive to human disturbance.

The most difficult remaining questions for design and implementation of regional reserve networks include the following:

1. What constitutes adequate dispersal habitat, or conversely, a dispersal barrier, for various species?
2. What kinds of land uses in the various zones (core reserves, buffer zones, and corridors) are compatible with conservation objectives, including protection and recovery of species most sensitive to human activities?
3. What proportion of a given region must be devoted to these zones in order to meet conservation objectives?
4. How can human population and resource use be reduced enough to allow large areas to be devoted to low-intensity uses?
5. How can people be led to appreciate the value of biodiversity and wild areas for their own sake?

While we ponder and seek answers to these questions, some interim management priorities are clear: stop destruction of natural and near-natural habitats everywhere, instead concentrating development in areas already degraded; dramatically reduce road construction and seek closure and revegetation of unnecessary roads; initiate ecological restoration projects, both short-term and long-term, concentrating on critical sites in proposed regional networks; and educate the public about what it takes to restore the full richness of life.

### Natural and Modified Landscape Elements

Landscape elements are the "basic, relatively homogeneous, ecological elements or units" (Forman and Godron 1986) that make up the overall landscape (Figure 10.21). *Natural* landscape elements include features such as drainage basins, ridges, ecotones, salt marshes, slopes, canyons, habitat peninsulas, or any other identifiable piece of natural landscapes. *Modified* landscape elements include roads and highways, agricultural fields, timberlands, industrial zones, and cities. Natural and modified landscape elements should be identified at the outset in reserve design and incorporated, accounted for, or excluded as appropriate. As a general rule, a diversity of natural landscape elements (i.e., habitat patches) will enhance the conservation value of reserves, and modified elements will detract from it.

Inclusion of the entire extent of a particular natural element, rather than a portion, permits control and protection of the entire unit. For example, a reserve or system of reserves that includes an entire drainage basin is preferable to one in which part of the basin is out of the reserve, especially upstream from it. In the former case, reserve management has control over activities within the whole basin; in the latter case, the reserve is subject to upstream events, such as pollution or stream modification, outside of the control of reserve managers.

Exclusion of modified landscape elements cannot always be accomplished, and reserve design must incorporate such elements at the outset and determine how to minimize their detrimental effects. For example, a major highway may run through a proposed reserve, effectively cutting it in two, or creating a population sink via highway mortality. An upstream sewage

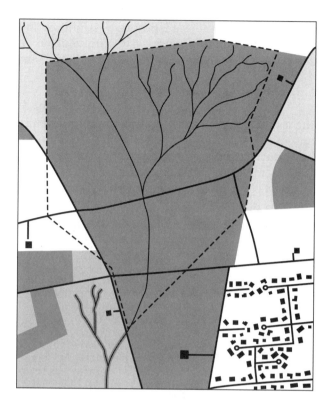

**Figure 10.21**   A schematic diagram showing various natural and modified landscape elements in and around a newly created reserve. The reserve is denoted by the dashed line. The dark shading is primary forest, light shading is second-growth forest, and white areas represent present or former agricultural fields. Dwellings are indicated by black squares, roads by solid black lines. Note that both natural and modified landscape elements are contained within and outside of the reserve.

treatment facility may be dumping secondary effluents into a river that runs through a downstream reserve, reducing the quality of water through eutrophication. In cases such as these, the problematic element must first be identified, and then its effects reduced as much as possible. This effort could include measures to minimize the effects (such as highway underpasses for wildlife, or installation of tertiary treatment facilities), or mitigation measures elsewhere to create replacement for habitat reduced or lost through the activity.

The above are examples of point-source problems, discrete problems at identifiable locations. Analysis of landscape elements must also consider nonpoint-source avenues of impact, which may be more difficult to control. For example, chemical pesticides, nutrients, and invasive species are not confined by reserve boundaries; typically, as agricultural and timber production intensifies, chemical leakage and invasion of natural areas by weedy plants, animals, and pathogens also increases (Carroll 1991). Furthermore, agricultural crops near reserves may become important food resources for a subset of reserve animals and thereby distort their effect on other populations. Such species include food generalists such as raccoons and corvids (crows and jays) in the temperate zone, whose enhanced populations seriously threaten nesting bird species (Wilcove et al. 1986), or granivorous birds (e.g., quelea and parakeets), rodents, bandicoots, and other generalists in the tropics. Insects on crops may also cause expansion of populations of generalist predators and parasitoids that may then invade natural habitats and attack the much smaller and potentially more vulnerable populations of insects in natural systems, as Howarth (1985) has shown in Hawaii.

Use of landscape elements around natural areas is rarely constant and, hence, the influence of surrounding land use on natural areas also changes. Patterns change in response to technology, external markets, population growth and decline, war, government policies, land degradation, and other socio-economic factors. The complexity of these land use possibilities and historical changes makes it difficult to determine the extent to which contemporary biological patterns are the product of purely biological processes or are strongly influenced by a particular history of resource exploitation. To use African elephants as an example, Caughley (1976) argued that Zambian elephants have natural long-term population cycles. Abel and Blaikie (1986) countered with the argument that apparent long-term elephant population cycles were really the consequences of hunting pressure and agricultural land use changes that were, in turn, greatly influenced by 18th and 19th century slave and ivory trade. Thus, modified landscape elements and changing land use near reserves may affect elephant populations within reserves. Further perspectives on landscapes in conservation reserves are provided by Richard Forman in Essay 10D.

## ESSAY 10D

# Designing Landscapes and Regions to Conserve Nature

Richard T. T. Forman, Harvard University

Future biodiversity depends largely on success in designing landscapes in places such as New Jersey and China. Today, nine-tenths of the land shows a significant human imprint, and the global human population still doubles about every generation. Tropical mega-reserves are desirable, but it is unwise to count entirely on their survival. Rather, I believe we must design whole landscapes and regions that mesh humans and nature, including biodiversity. Several key issues are outlined here, but all focus on the central attribute of land, namely, the spatial arrangement of elements in a mosaic.

If you are a physician who keeps people's livers working, you would like to know how liver cells function. But if given a choice, you would prefer to know how livers are connected to the heart, lungs, intestine, and brain, because a live liver depends on a living body. So it is in protecting species. You would like to know the fine-scale details of genetics and demography, but success depends more on understanding the broad-scale configuration of ecosystems and land use within a landscape or region.

### Spatial Elements of Landscapes

A patch-corridor-matrix paradigm, in which every point is within a patch, a corridor, or the background matrix, provides generality for use in a forested, arid, agricultural, suburban, or any other landscape (Forman and Godron 1986; Forman 1993).

*Patch Size and Number.* Large patches of natural vegetation are essen-tial for protecting aquifers, habitat interior species, large-home-range species, natural disturbance regimes, and sources of species dispersing through corridors and the matrix. Small patches act as stepping-stones for dispersal across the landscape, decrease wind/water flows and erosion in the matrix, and occasionally provide habitats for small-patch-restricted species. In short, large patches provide several major benefits, and small patches provide minor, supplementary benefits (Forman 1993).

How many large patches are needed to protect the species of a particular landscape? We do not know, but apparently more than three large patches of a habitat type are generally required (Forman et al. 1976; Game and Peterken 1984; Margules and Austin 1992).

*Boundaries and Patch Shape.* Nature provides a rich assortment of landscape boundaries that have major effects on species use and movement. The most common natural boundary types are (1) curvilinear (with lobes and coves) and (2) a strip of mosaic; less common are (3) straight and (4) self-similar fractal boundaries. Yet civilization geometricizes the land; hard straight lines replace the soft curves of nature. The ecological effects of this process may be large. For example, plant colonization patterns, herbivore browsing, and wildlife movement and usage are strongly affected by the curvilinearity and cove sizes in a boundary (Hardt and Forman 1989; Forman and Moore 1991).

The literature agrees that round patches are the ecologically optimum shape for reserves based on edge/center ratios, yet this may not always be true. Based only on species conservation, a patch should provide (1) a large core and interior area, (2) dispersal of species from the patch to the matrix and other patches, (3) a "drift-fence effect" to aid in recolonization of the patch, and probably other functions. Many useful shapes are possible, and the optimum will reflect a balance among the functions provided (Forman 1993).

*Corridors and Networks.* Wooded strips, where habitat was formerly continuous in a landscape, play key roles as species habitats, conduits, and barriers, in controlling wind erosion, and in creating a landscape grain or mesh size. Stream and river corridors normally are the most important strips because of their numerous ecological roles, and their ecologically based minimum width varies markedly along the corridor system. Species also move along stepping-stones, which are equivalent to corridors with major gaps. The enhancement of movement requires continuous suitable habitats not squeezed too tightly by unsuitable habitats. The key steps in implementing corridor and stepping-stone systems for species conservation are to determine the optimum locations, types, and designs. Corridors often form dendritic or rectilinear networks that provide optional routes for species movement (Forman 1992, 1993).

*Context.* Adjacency or juxtaposition effects are familiar; examples include seeds blowing into an oasis, and herbivores moving from woodlots to clearings. But how are the species in a patch affected by the number of adjacent habitats? Or the number of adjacent habitat types? Or the size of adjacent habitats? To answer such questions we could compare a woodlot surrounded by, for example, cropland, versus cropland and marsh, versus four types, versus *n* types.

The landscape mosaic surrounding a patch or corridor normally contains a variety of ecosystem types, each with its own species pool. Each local ecosystem in the mosaic is a source, as well as a sink, for species. In addition, resistances to movement across a landscape vary from low to high. Thus, the equilibrium island biogeographic theory is of only tangential use on land, since the central mosaic attribute of landscapes swamps the model assumption of islands in a homogeneous, inhospitable matrix. Only portions of an ecomosaic theory have solidified as yet (Turner and Gardner 1991; Forman 1993), but they are highly useful in understanding and planning the landscapes and regions around us.

**Landscape Change and Planning**

In the mosaic dynamics of landscape changes such as deforestation, suburbanization, or desertification, an ecologically optimum pattern or mosaic sequence of landscape change may exist, and is worth a search. If successful, one could pinpoint the worst element, or the best element, to change at any point along the sequence.

For example, forest cutting of dispersed patches was studied to understand its effect on biodiversity, windthrow, fire ignition, game populations, and other parameters in a whole landscape (Franklin and Forman 1987; Hansen et al. 1992). In comparing the mosaic sequence progressing from 100% forest through a 50% checkerboard pattern to 0% forest, ecologically important thresholds were detected. The dispersed-patch cutting sequence is highly detrimental ecologically, compared with several other cutting patterns considered. Indeed, a limited number of mosaic sequences may describe almost all types of landscape change (Forman 1993).

To attain the support required for sustained species protection, two or three major ecological objectives should be concurrently addressed. Thus, a large reserve protects both biodiversity and an aquifer. A stream corridor enhances fish populations, mineral nutrient absorption, and biodiversity. If a community or a farmer has a soil erosion problem, planting a row of exotic shrubs helps. But an ecologist would combine erosion control and biodiversity, planting rows of several native species with roots and canopies at different levels, which in turn provide food and cover for diverse animals over the year.

A sustainable environment is an area in which ecological integrity (including biodiversity) and basic human needs are concurrently maintained over generations (Forman 1990). Saving species depends on designing sustainable landscapes and regions. Aggregating land uses in large patches, maintaining small outliers in fine-grained areas, and providing connectivity for species movement are ready handles for wise planning, management, and policy.

## Buffer Zones

The overall reserve design should include **zoning** to influence land use activities around reserves and make them more compatible with the conservation goals of the reserves. This helps to avoid conflicts between various user groups and may be the only way to secure a reserve in the first place, due to fears of exclusionary wilderness use. Through a carefully planned zoning approach, a conservation reserve system can allow for habitat and species protection, experimental scientific research (including manipulations), human habitation and development, and limited use of natural resources.

A zoning approach might proceed as follows (Figure 10.22). A reserve system should have a central core area consisting of a protected natural area that is subject only to nondestructive activities such as ecological monitoring, photography, hiking, and bird-watching. Often, these cores may already exist within established national parks or monuments, wilderness areas, or state wildlife areas. Surrounding or adjoining the core is a buffer zone, which may be a mix of public and private lands in which activities compatible with protection of the central core are allowed; these could include manipulative research, education, habitat rehabilitation, ecotourism, and traditional, low-impact land use, including sustained harvest of natural crops such as nuts or mushrooms. Outside of the buffer zone, and lacking distinct boundaries, would be a transition area, which would typically include human settlements and associated activities such as fishing, forestry, agriculture, and other sustainable economic pursuits consistent with protection of the core area. Transition areas may extend indefinitely and link several reserve systems in the region.

It may seem intuitively obvious that the vegetation and other community characteristics of buffer zones should resemble those of the protected natural areas they surround. However, there are situations in which the transition

**Figure 10.22**   A schematic diagram of a zoned reserve system, showing the possible spatial relationship between a core area, a buffer zone, and a transition area. Human activities in each zone should be appropriate to the goal of that zone and especially to the protection of the reserve core.

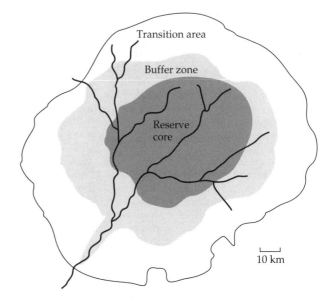

from core reserve to buffer zone should be abrupt, and the buffer zone habitat very different from that of the core reserve. Whether to have an abrupt or a gradual transition in the buffer zone needs to be considered on a case-by-case basis. If vulnerability to fire is severe, then eliminating highly combustible weedy and second-growth vegetation around forested reserves may be important. Where the protection of ground-nesting birds in the reserve is an important management goal, it may be useful to surround the reserve with habitat unsuitable for generalist predators. Where the reserve is fragmented and vulnerable to invasion from exotic species, it may be important to create buffer habitat that excludes those weedy species that are likely to be successful colonists of the fragmented reserve.

## The Problem of Certain Change and Uncertain Direction

Despite our most careful planning and prediction efforts, biological, cultural, economic, and political changes will affect conservation reserves over the long term. These changes will occur over and above the dynamic changes expected in biological systems, as discussed repeatedly to this point. Flexibility then becomes a key to reserve success. Although many changes cannot be predicted with respect to extent or direction, some classes of changes are more likely and can be included in reserve design. A good example is global climate change.

All indications point toward an average global warming trend of several degrees over the next century through accumulation of so-called "greenhouse gases" produced by humanity (Grover 1990; Kareiva et al. 1992). These gases, including $CO_2$, methane, and chlorofluorocarbons, trap infrared energy as it reradiates into space from earth, increasing the temperature of the lower atmosphere. The thermal increase will also likely be accompanied by changes in rainfall patterns, soil conditions, and sea levels. In some regions, the frequency of extreme events such as droughts may rise, increasing the ecological effects of environmental stochasticity. Such changes portend major effects on species and communities in reserves (Peters and Darling 1985; Gates 1993).

Past global climate changes, such as those that occurred repeatedly in the coming and going of ice ages, offer clues to the expected effects of human-induced global warming. Latitudinal shifts in community types and species ranges of hundreds of kilometers were typical of global warming and cooling of only a few degrees, the same magnitude that is predicted for our present warming scenario. When average global temperatures were only 2–3°C higher than at present during Pleistocene interglacials, manatees occurred in New Jersey, tapirs and peccaries foraged in Pennsylvania, and Osage oranges grew in southern Canada (Dorf 1976). This indicates that major changes can be expected in the imminent greenhouse warming.

A great deal of habitat would likely be altered and made unsuitable for existing species in a global warming scenario. For example, a model based on biogeographic species–area relationships in montane small mammals (McDonald and Brown 1992) predicts loss of 9%–62% of the species currently inhabiting 19 isolated mountain peaks in the Great Basin of the western United States. This estimate was based on areal habitat loss expected in a 3°C temperature rise. Such boreal species would have no place higher and colder to go during a warming event.

The impact of global changes on conservation reserves may be great, and should be considered at the outset and planned for wherever possible. Species whose entire ranges are confined to reserves with little altitudinal variation are likely to experience climatic changes beyond their tolerance levels and could be in danger of global extinction if other populations are not available for recolonization. Additionally, species in reserves are often remnant populations with reduced genetic diversity, living in isolated areas with little chance for movement to new regions outside the reserve. Climate change would only place further pressures on such species, including physiological stress and changes in competitive, predatory, mutualistic, or parasitic interactions (Peters and Darling 1985). The lowered genetic diversity of small reserve populations would reduce their likelihood of responding to added challenges through selective change (Chapter 6). Certain types of species or habitats are more likely to be affected by global climate change than others (Peters and Darling 1985); these are summarized in Table 10.2.

The implications of global climate change for reserve function are profound, and increased management of reserves will be necessary because of it. For example, individual animals or plants may need to be transported among reserves in response to altered climate or rainfall patterns, or natural disturbances in reserves (such as fire) may need to be simulated. Consequently, design of reserves should anticipate climate change. One approach might be to locate reserves near the present northern limits of the ranges of critical species, rather than at the southern ends, which will only become warmer and less likely to support the desired species (Figure 10.23). Reserves located in an area of maximum heterogeneity of topography and soil types will increase the "choices" of the biota; especially important will be access to a range of elevations and permanent water sources.

Maximization of the number and size of reserves will also increase the likelihood of species survival. Connections of reserves through corridors, especially north-south oriented or high-low elevation corridors, would allow movement of species in response to changing conditions. Long north-south corridors would, of course, be costly and politically difficult to establish, but not insurmountably so. In the United States, national forests are already largely arrayed in north-south strips along the Appalachian, Rocky, and Cascade Mountain ranges; better connections among them would help to address the global warming scenario. Riparian forests frequently offer north-south habitat, and we should look more closely into the role of riparian

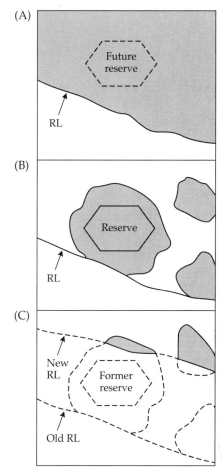

**Figure 10.23** Schematic diagram of a reserve relative to latitudinal changes in temperatures. Shaded regions show suitable remaining habitat for a given species. The range limit of the species (RL) moves north as a result of global climate change (A–C), making the reserve ineffective. (From Peters and Darling 1985.)

**Table 10.2**
Types of Species and Communities Most Likely to Be Affected
by Global Climate Change

| Type | Prediction |
|---|---|
| 1. Peripheral populations | Populations near the edge of the species' range would be more likely affected by range shifts due to warming. |
| 2. Geographically localized species | Local endemics would be unlikely to have populations in areas of suitable habitat after a range shift due to climate change. |
| 3. Genetically impoverished species | Species or populations with low genetic diversity may lack the variability necessary to adapt to changing climatic or habitat conditions. |
| 4. Specialized species | Specialized species generally are less tolerant of environmental change and often require a narrow range of conditions. |
| 5. Poor dispersers | Sedentary or less mobile species would have difficulty spreading their distributions into newly created suitable habitat during climate change. |
| 6. Annual species | Complete reproductive failure in one year by an annual species spells local extinction. Such failure is more possible during climate change in annual than in perennial species. |
| 7. Montane and alpine communities | Species distributions would shift to higher elevation during global warming, occupying smaller areas with smaller populations, making them more vulnerable to extinction. Species originally at the highest elevations would have nowhere higher to go. |
| 8. Arctic communities | Temperature increases in arctic regions are expected to be greater than in equatorial areas, and those communities may undergo greater stress. |
| 9. Coastal communities | It is expected that upwelling patterns in coastal areas will be altered, and that sea levels will rise, flooding coastal habitat. Both events will stress coastal communities, which will likely not be able to follow rising waters inland due to human development. |

Modified from Peters and Darling 1985.

corridors in the siting of new reserves. Finally, buffers around reserves with flexible zoning retain options to shift reserve boundaries in the future in response to climate changes.

## Anthropological and Cultural Implications of Reserve Design

A conservation reserve may be doomed to eventual failure, regardless of its biological soundness, if its planning does not consider and include the needs and desires of people. An exclusively preservationist approach, which locks

**Figure 10.24** The Guanacaste project is a major effort to rehabilitate and restore a 75,000-ha dry tropical forest in northwestern Costa Rica. This area was degraded over the last three centuries, but natural systems are being reconstituted through a cooperative effort with local residents. Shown here is a degraded dry forest. (Photograph by C. R. Carroll.)

nature away for safekeeping, only causes increased conflict between people and nature, and can backfire to the detriment of the protected area. Planned and controlled inclusion of people in the reserve will ensure greater cooperation with, and more positive attitudes of people toward, the reserve.

For example, since 1986, Daniel Janzen and Winifred Halwachs of the University of Pennsylvania have been working with Costa Rican colleagues in an effort to rehabilitate and restore a 75,000-ha dry tropical forest in Guanacaste National Park in northwestern Costa Rica (Figure 10.24). Degraded over the last three centuries by agriculture, ranching, and alteration of natural fire patterns, the natural communities that existed in the pre-colonization state are being recreated (Allen 1988). Doing this, however, requires more than knowledge of the regional biology.

The project is based on a philosophical approach called "biocultural restoration," which incorporates local people into all aspects of the reserve's development and protection. The idea is to embed biological understanding and appreciation in the local culture through education about, and interaction with, the park. Early on, Janzen and Halwachs realized that an important reward for local people is an intellectual understanding of their environment and the complexities of the world around them, recreating an understanding of the land that their grandparents had, but which they may have lost in the modern world.

The goal of the project is to create a "user-friendly" park that contributes to the quality of daily life of the people. This is accomplished by making Guanacaste a "living classroom" through formal educational programs, encouraging independent exploration of the area, and creating apprenticeships in the areas of ecological research or law enforcement. Some local farms are being purchased, but the former owners are allowed to remain there and work toward restoration or protection. A family that formerly raised cattle may now be involved in raising and managing a dry tropical forest. Once the forest is restored they may be trained as park guards and own land nearby. The formula for such a project is strictly "home-grown" and not an accepted textbook model (there is no such thing). Such formulas need to be developed independently in each case according to the local situation and needs of the people and wildlife. Nevertheless, the general approach used in the Guanacaste National Park restoration project is a good model to adopt elsewhere, and we will return to it in Chapter 14 when we discuss restoration.

At least three "user" groups need to be considered in reserve design. First and foremost are local residents who are already established in the region, perhaps having been there for centuries. Every effort should be made to allow continuation of their normal mode of life, including *sustainable* use of natural resources. If lifestyle modifications are necessary to meet the biological goals of the reserve (such as stopping poaching or illegal timber cutting), these need to be introduced in a cooperative, rather than confrontational, manner; voluntary adoption is much more likely to succeed than will enforced changes. Implementation of such modifications will typically require educational and economic programs, and any other assistance necessary to smooth the transition with minimal interruption of traditional lifestyles.

If local land use patterns are not sustainable, then conflict may be a necessary requisite to good reserve management. This is evident in current conflicts between loggers and conservationists over remaining old-growth forests in the western United States, for example. The (recent) traditional use of the land, clear-cutting of forests whose trees are 200 to over 1000 years old, is clearly not sustainable and must be altered if any forests are to remain as reserves. Likewise, corporate-style agriculture, in which large expanses of land are cleared, tilled, and sprayed with chemical fertilizers and pesticides, may be incompatible with conservation reserves. In cases such as these, there may be no alternative to direct conflict over land use. The reasonable approach is to help residents make necessary changes in their lifestyles and livelihoods.

The second "user" group is the population at large, whether local (tribal, city, county), regional (state), national, or international. This population must be supportive of reserves to ensure the necessary long-term funding and to provide the political base to resist development contrary to the biological interests of the reserve. If citizen support is lacking, it is unlikely that a reserve or reserve system will be able to resist developmental incursion for any extended period.

Finally, the needs of visitors must be included in reserve design, as they will often be a major source of revenue and public support for the reserve. Even if the local constituency does not initially support a particular reserve, those opinions may change if economic benefits of tourism are realized in the local area. Ecotourism is a developing industry worldwide; its use should be considered whenever its presence would not interfere with the ecological aspects of the park (see Case Study 4 in Chapter 17).

Most people seem to have an inherent positive attitude toward natural areas and nature in general (termed **biophilia** by Wilson [1984]), and will work toward their protection if they understand the value of the system, and if conflicts between conservation and economic utilization are minimized. The key is to identify and alleviate these conflicts during the planning stages of a reserve through active inclusion of the various user groups. They know the area, and they will be affected by the outcome of reserve design; communication and cooperation with such people is not only pragmatic, but ethically proper.

Many examples exist of failures of reserves to either preserve native biodiversity or to protect indigenous cultures because the needs of people were not adequately considered in the original planning. If it is seen as inhibiting the welfare of local inhabitants, or if their needs are not met elsewhere, a reserve will usually be exploited for its resources in an unsustainable manner (see Case Study 3 in Chapter 17). For example, when banana plantations closed in southwestern Costa Rica, one of the few opportunities left for the displaced workers was to become part of illegal gold mining efforts in nearby Corcovado National Park. The mining caused serious damage to the terrestrial, and especially the aquatic, ecosystems, contaminating rivers with silt and mercury (Tangley 1988). Unemployment and hunger are strong motivators to exploit whatever resources are available, regardless of their designated level of protection. A reserve will only be protected from exploitation when local economies are sound and people's basic needs are satisfied.

Long-established cultures have been destroyed by development of well-intended biological reserves that ignored or did not meet the needs of the people. It may be argued that this anthropological loss is every bit as devastating as losses of biodiversity. One African tribe was displaced from its ancestral homeland in creation of the Kidepo National Park in Uganda; its culture soon disintegrated (Turnbull 1972). The Waliangulu people of Kenya, traditional elephant hunters, likewise suffered cultural disintegration when the Tsavo National Park was established (Murrey 1967). The Vedda society of Sri Lanka broke down due to a development project to expand rice production, together with creation of the Madura Oya National Park, established to mitigate the effects of the rice project on wildlife. This 2000-year-old culture of hunter-gatherers has shown no tendency to take up rice cultivation, and their knowledge of sustainable existence in tropical forests is being lost with their societal collapse (Burgess 1986, in Dasmann 1988).

Fortunately, negative examples such as these are countered by positive examples of reserve development in which the welfare of indigenous peoples was included in the planning. For example, the economic value of wildlife is being used in Zimbabwe to the benefit of local people. Some 200 local conservation councils control wildlife use on private lands and are overseen by the national government to ensure protection of rare and endangered species (Dasmann 1988). The local communities benefit from the sale of wildlife products such as meat and hides, and are therefore motivated to protect the resource as their own. Communal lands are controlled by the national government, with economic benefits still going to local communities.

A different problem was addressed in a World Wildlife Fund project on the western slopes of the Andes in Colombia, an area of high biological diversity. A 1600-ha ranch was purchased for protection of a forested plateau. However, the ranch was subject to degradation by probable development in the surrounding area. Adjacent to the ranch lived the Awa/Cuayquer people, who traditionally employed sustainable land use practices consistent with biodiversity protection. To protect the ranch forest, a reserve system was created that included zoning outside the central core, with protected, manipulative, and administrative zones. These zones were established in consultation with the Awa/Cuayquer, and provided for the satisfaction of their basic needs, including programs in education, nutrition and health, and agroecology. Strong community support developed for the reserve system, which included Awa/Cuayquer land (Dasmann 1988).

Through programs such as these, natural biodiversity is more likely to be protected, and traditional cultures, which often enjoy sustainable and low-impact lifestyles, are served as well. Bullying of any culture, from Peruvian Indians to American ranchers, will never serve the best interests of conservation. Confrontation is often unavoidable, but should be approached with an understanding and appreciation of the local culture, with every attempt made to accommodate their concerns and fears.

(A)

(B)

(C)

(D)

**Figure 10.25** The results of multiple uses of public lands in the United States. Activities such as off-road vehicles (A), clear-cutting (B), geothermal energy extraction (C), and cattle grazing (D) all degrade public lands. In reserves that serve multiple functions biodiversity protection may be a minor aspect of a larger and more environmentally destructive agenda. (Photographs A and D, courtesy of Bureau of Land Management; B, by Barry R. Noon; C, by Edwin P. Pister.)

## Political and Economic Constraints on Reserve Design

Up to this point in our discussion of reserve design, we have focused on biological or anthropological considerations. Now we will introduce some political realities into the discussion. The issues raised in this brief section are explored in more detail in the following chapters, and are illustrated in a real-world scenario in Essay 10E, by Jack Williams.

Conservation biology can tell us some of the ecological and genetic trade-offs that will result from choosing one design feature over another, but conservation biologists will usually not decide the final configuration of a reserve. For publicly owned reserves, such as state and federal parklands, decisions on reserves and conservation in general are part of the larger political/economic/sociological landscape, and are made within a much broader context than biological expediency. Even privately owned reserves are subject to political and economic issues. Reserves may serve multiple functions as do National Forest lands and the range and desert lands of the Bureau of Land Management in the United States. In these reserves, mining, timber harvest, grazing, hunting and fishing, and off-road vehicle recreation are just some of the more prominent uses (Figure 10.25); conservation of biodiversity is only part of a crowded agenda for these multiple-use reserves. In some countries, even national parks may be exploited for minerals, timber, and game. The Organic Act of 1917, which established the National Park Service in the United States, permits restricted grazing in U.S. national parks.

With the exception of the National Park Service, the management authority for publicly controlled reserves in the United States seldom comes from a single agency; usually multiple agencies are involved. Protection of wetlands on the east coast may jointly involve the Army Corps of Engineers, the Environmental Protection Agency, the Fish and Wildlife Service, the National Park Service, and numerous state and local agencies. The agency authorized to take action within reserves is usually not the same agency that principally controls activities on lands adjacent to the reserve. This can create special difficulties for reserve management. In the western United States, for example, the national parks, which are managed by the Department of the Interior, are usually surrounded by National Forest lands controlled by the Department of Agriculture or by lands controlled by the Bureau of Land Management, or by state-owned lands. Logging activities, mineral mining, petroleum extraction, and power plant operations in these adjacent lands can cause serious pollution in the air and water of reserves.

Air pollution and energy extraction on public lands are considered to be the two most important external threats to United States national parks. Oil-fired power plants, smelters, and even distant metropolitan areas create severe air pollution and impaired visibility in Grand Canyon National Park (Figure 10.26); oil and gas extraction on public lands adjacent to Glacier National Park are considered to be the park's most serious external threat (Freemuth 1991).

The many forms that reserves can take, in terms of ownership, management authority, and use, can create serious obstacles to achieving conservation goals. Usually, these problems are tackled in an ad hoc fashion through various management programs. It would be far better if these problems could be ameliorated during the process of designing the reserve. For example, land exchanges between public agencies are common and can be used during establishment of a reserve to reduce the number of agencies involved in reserve operations and authority. Earlier in this chapter we discussed a major problem in conservation: many reserves may be too small to support

(A)

(B)

(C)

viable populations of the species they are supposed to protect. In the United States it is possible to greatly increase the effective sizes of reserves, especially in western states, by aggregating or connecting (through habitat corridors) adjacent or nearby lands controlled by different public agencies. For example, many western national parks are surrounded by national and state forest lands or lands controlled by the Bureau of Land Management. If the agencies involved would develop compatible conservation goals and management programs, the total conservation areas would be greatly expanded. As Grumbine (1990) remarks, "To preserve biodiversity in national parks, national forests, or anywhere else, we can no longer afford fragmentation in our management efforts any more than we can afford habitat fragmentation in natural ecosystems."

**Figure 10.26** Air pollution in Grand Canyon National Park, Arizona, as shown in a fixed camera at the Desert View Watchtower on three different days; visibility is (A) 303 km, (B) 156 km, and (C) zero. Visibility can change daily as a result of air pollution from copper smelters and power plants in the region, and smog from metropolitan areas such as Los Angeles. (Photographs courtesy of U.S. National Park Service.)

## ESSAY 10E

# Pupfish, Politics, and Preserve Management in the Arid Southwest

Jack E. Williams, Bureau of Land Management

The desert oasis named Ash Meadows has been the scene of many battles over land and water use. Endangered fish—mostly species of pupfish—have been the focal point of concern. One pivotal battle between the diminutive Devil's Hole pupfish (*Cyprinodon diabolis*) and agricultural interests intent on withdrawing water from the aquifer that supplies the only spring habitat of the species, was ultimately decided in the United States Supreme Court. On 7 June 1976, the Court upheld a lower court ruling for a permanent injunction on groundwater pumping until a safe water level for the pupfish could be established. During the court proceedings, the fate of the pupfish became the rallying cry for both conservationist and development interests (Figure A). Now, almost two decades later, and despite numerous endangered species listings and the creation of a National Wildlife Refuge at Ash Meadows, questions still remain concerning the survival of the Devil's Hole pupfish and the area's many other endemic species.

Ash Meadows, located along the Nevada–California border approximately 145 km northwest of Las Vegas, consists of dozens of crystal-blue springs, wetlands, and alkaline uplands surrounded by the Mojave Desert. With 26 endemic taxa of fishes, springsnails, aquatic insects, and plants within the 94.7-km² oasis, it is the smallest area with such a rich and specialized flora and fauna in the United States (Deacon and Williams 1991).

As in most preserves, protection of Ash Meadows has come in fits and starts. On 17 January 1952, President Harry S. Truman declared 16 ha around Devil's Hole as a disjunct portion of Death Valley National Monument. The natural values of Devil's Hole received further protection through court rulings during the 1970s. The major breakthrough for protection of the entire Ash Meadows area, however, came in June of 1984, when 5154 ha was acquired with the help of The Nature Conservancy and designated by Congress as the Ash Meadows National Wildlife Refuge. This halted plans for a large commercial and residential develop-

(A)

(B)

**Figure A** Preserves protecting species such as the Devil's Hole pupfish typically provoke visible responses on both sides of the development/conservation debate. (Photographs by Edwin P. Pister.)

ment, but not before some spring systems were drained and ditched and their flows diverted to create reservoirs. Some areas within the refuge boundary remain privately owned, while others are managed by the Bureau of Land Management.

During the 1940s, early investigations of Ash Meadows' unique fauna found numerous populations of introduced bullfrogs and crayfish already established. Introduction of nonnative species has continued to be a problem at Ash Meadows. During the 1960s, an illegal tropical fish farm provided the source for a wide variety of exotic species that flourished in the warm spring waters. Large populations of introduced mosquitofish (*Gambusia affinis*) and sailfin mollies (*Poecilia latipinna*) persist in many areas. Largemouth bass (*Micropterus salmoides*) have been introduced into reservoirs and have invaded springpools, where they prey on the native pupfish and speckled dace.

How are the problems of introduced species and groundwater management to be handled? Introduced species such as mosquitofish are notoriously hard to control in areas like Ash Meadows, with its many interconnected waterways.

Chemical treatment has been tried, but the effects of such control efforts on nontarget species, such as tiny native springsnails, can be severe. Removal of groundwater from areas outside Ash Meadows also may have long-term negative consequences by reducing springflows within Ash Meadows. With deep groundwater throughout much of the state slowly flowing from northeast to southwest, proposals by the city of Las Vegas to buy ranches and pump their groundwaters for municipal uses are cause for concern.

These issues are not easily resolved by the National Wildlife Refuge system, which traditionally has focused on waterfowl production and hunting. Even fishing activities on the refuge's reservoirs may conflict with protection of the endemic spring-dwelling species because of the likelihood of introducing and managing for predatory fishes, such as largemouth bass. Restoration of natural springs, their outflows, and desert wetlands may conflict with desires for improved vehicle access, recreational facilities, and our tendency to intensively manage landscapes. And, as with the groundwater concerns, we are finding that ecosystem boundaries seldom conform to the administrative boundaries of the preserve.

To date, many urban and agricultural centers of the arid West have flourished with little regard for water consumption rates or impacts on native biota. There are better alternatives for meeting the growing urban needs for western water than tapping our already depleted surface and groundwaters. Professor James Deacon of the University of Nevada, Las Vegas, has questioned why society should spend billions of dollars on new water projects, when it would be cheaper and environmentally more sound to "get serious about retrofitting Las Vegas for water efficiency [and] then get serious about converting agriculture in the Colorado River basin to water efficiency and use the savings for urban needs—in both Nevada and California."

Water use, whether surface waters on the refuge or groundwater from outside, will continue to garner political attention. How society responds to these issues may be the ultimate court case for the Devil's Hole pupfish as well as other members of the Ash Meadows community.

---

We usually think of politics and economics as forces acting to limit the size of reserves. Sometimes, though, reserves may be expanded in order to meet political and economic objectives. Transnational reserves, so-called "peace parks," may be established as part of a larger foreign policy agenda. Glacier International Peace Park connects Glacier National Park in the United States with Banff and Waterton Lakes National Parks in Canada. In Central America, two peace parks are under development, one on the Atlantic watershed between Nicaragua and Costa Rica, and the other connecting Costa Rica's La Amistad National Park with Panama's proposed Boca del Toro National Park.

The most obvious situation in which economic considerations can lead to expanded reserve design is where lands protect critical economic resources. In Venezuela, it was discovered that Oilbirds were important seed dispersers of trees in forested watersheds that border important shipping channels for petroleum tankers. To provide long-term protection of the watershed forest, and thereby reduce erosion and landslides that would damage shipping lanes, a small reserve containing cave nest sites for Oilbirds was expanded to include large watersheds. There is still considerable opportunity for development of additional reserves in watersheds and catchment basins that provide irrigation and drinking water. In such cases, the design of the reserve will not only be based on conservation science, but will also be part of the larger planning effort for economic development.

## Summary

The selection and development of conservation reserves should be conducted under a nonequilibrium paradigm that recognizes the dynamism of natural systems and the importance of natural and anthropogenic disturbance to their ecology. Biological motivations for reserves include ecosystem protection, conservation of biodiversity, and protection of selected target species. However, biological motivations are not the only concerns in reserve design; anthropological or cultural effects, as well as political and economic influences must also be considered.

Within the biological arena, at least six critical issues should be considered in reserve design: reserve size; heterogeneity and ecological dynamics within the reserve; the physical context of the reserve; connections of the reserve to other reserves or natural areas; the landscape elements, both natural and modified, that will influence the success of the reserve; and accommodation of different human activities. All of this must be conducted with some degree of flexibility due to the uncertainty of change. For example, global climate change over the next century is quite likely, but the specific directions of changes and their effects on particular reserves are less certain.

Reserves are unlikely to meet their conservation goals if the human presence is not included in their planning. Anthropological and cultural considerations include concern for traditional peoples in and around reserves. Sustainable practices should be continued and included in reserve design; nonsustainable practices that conflict with conservation reserves will need to be changed through education and other support. Reserve success would be enhanced by political and economic practices congruent with conservation objectives. In particular, multiple-agency mandates that do not work at cross purposes with each other and with conservation objectives are more likely to enhance reserve goals than will fragmented agencies working in opposition.

## Questions for Discussion

1. The metapopulation concept is central to reserve design, particularly with respect to connected networks of reserves. Yet, data relevant to metapopulations are rare. Discuss the possible characteristics of plant and animal populations that might predispose them to having a metapopulation structure.

2. Discuss how presence or absence of a metapopulation structure would affect the desirable levels of patchiness and spatial connections within a reserve.

3. Many reserves are developed at least partly to protect a visible and popular segment of the biota, such as tigers, elephants, or coral reefs. Develop arguments that might be used to convince legislators and the local populace that developing reserves to protect the following is in the public interest: (a) endemic snails in springs on western United States grazing lands; (b) a diverse but mostly unknown assemblage of beetles in a Bornean forest; (c) wading birds in a Japanese wetland to be drained for a corporate headquarters; and (d) six endemic mussel species in a Virginia river under heavy recreational and industrial use.

4. Information on the utility of corridors is too limited for us to confidently prescribe many expensive corridors connecting habitats or reserves; yet the concept seems reasonable. Discuss how you might collect data or design experiments to test the efficacy of corridors in reserve design.

5. How might you go about determining the minimum dynamic area for a particular reserve and disturbance regime?

6. Discuss some problems and approaches that might be used in establishing a reserve for a large carnivore in an area with mixed cultural values and multiple land ownership.

## Suggestions for Further Reading

Forman, R. T. T. and M. Godron. 1986. *Landscape Ecology.* John Wiley & Sons, New York. Forman and Godron produced this first textbook on landscape ecology several years ago, but it remains a definitive work. It defines landscape ecology, outlines its principles, emphasizes dynamics, and discusses management at the landscape scale.

Hudson, W. E. (ed.). 1991. *Landscape Linkages and Biodiversity.* Island Press, Washington, D.C. Hudson has put together a strong grouping of papers touting the benefits of linked landscapes in conservation. The collection presents a broad perspective on biological and political aspects of linkages in landscapes.

Kareiva, P. M., J. G. Kingsolver and R. B. Huey (eds.). 1992. *Biotic Interactions and Global Change.* Sinauer Associates, Sunderland, MA. This is a rich compilation of 29 chapters on global climate change, including patterns and determinants of change, physiological, population, evolutionary, and community responses, habitat fragmentation and landscape change, and community research on global change.

Pickett, S. T. A. and J. N. Thompson. 1978. Patch dynamics and the design of nature reserves. *Biol. Conserv.* 13:27–37. This is a classic paper central to the idea that heterogeneity and patches are important in development of conservation reserves. A "must read" for a heterogeneity perspective.

Shafer, C. L. 1990. *Nature Reserves: Island Theory and Conservation Practice.* Smithsonian Institution Press, Washington, D.C. This book is a thorough overview of the design of nature reserves from the perspective of island biogeography theory. Because of its focus on island theory, the book is limited in its scope for reserve design, but is thorough with respect to that area.

# IV

# Practical Applications and Human Concerns

# 11

# Management to Meet Conservation Goals

## General Principles

*Applied ecology is difficult, but not impossible. Action has to be taken, but the problems cannot be solved by off-the-shelf answers. Solutions will require intellectual and empirical depth well beyond what is now available, as well as commitment, money, organization, and work. Most significantly, applied ecology requires rethinking the basis of how ecological problems and their solutions are approached. It is almost too late to start, but tomorrow is even later.*

L.B. Slobodkin and D.E. Dykhuizen, 1991

### Why Is Management Necessary?

In Chapter 1 we said that conservation biology was a crisis discipline. A species is threatened with extinction and something must be done quickly. An aggressive invader establishes itself in a sensitive natural environment and a program for eradication must be developed and implemented. Cattle are carrying disease into a population of desert bighorn sheep and some intervention is necessary. Heavy metals from urban runoff are contaminating a stream that is the only water source for a large wetland reserve, and funds must be found for diverting the stream and drilling wells to supply the wetland with groundwater. These are examples of the immediate crises that occupy much of the professional lives of conservation managers. They are, however, symptoms of more systemic and larger problems. As we argue throughout this book, conservation biology will remain a crisis discipline until we stop parasitizing the natural environment in order to maintain ever-expanding economies and human populations.

Not only are there many different kinds of crises, but the contexts in which the crises occur also vary. For example, wildfires can be essential natural processes when they occur at the right frequency and intensity, and a disaster otherwise. Wildfires are more acceptable in remote wilderness areas than they are in more heavily visited natural areas. This is true even when park visitors accept the idea that fire is an essential natural process for maintaining the ecosystem that supports the animals and plants they find so appealing.

Crises in conservation take many forms, and good management, in equally varied forms, is the appropriate response. Because there are so many different challenges, all of which are strongly influenced by the environmental and social context in which they occur, management is an eclectic set of approaches. There is no theoretical base specific to conservation management, though good management approaches have a strong dependency on the wealth of theoretical and empirical studies in biology. There is no particular field of training that prepares one to be a good conservation manager; management approaches have changed over several decades, and continue to evolve. The history of wildlife conservation management, elaborated by Curt Meine in Essay 11A, elegantly demonstrates that we have come a long way in our understanding of and appreciation for diverse natural systems, and that we have developed a more sophisticated and sound philosophy toward biological diversity.

The basic theme of this chapter is that conservation management, while critically important, is only a set of tools and approaches whose usefulness and appropriateness are measured by the extent to which they contribute to long-term conservation of natural patterns and processes. Because management is very often an intervention to reverse or mitigate the negative consequences of human activities, managers must be more than good biologists. Indeed, good management requires a blending of many skills beyond those learned in biology classes (Figure 11.1). There is a real need for managers to have training and experience in economic and humanistic fields such as ecological economics, sociology, anthropology, and philosophy, and to meld all these types of knowledge to develop a more complete vision of the management world. As conservation managers we may not be able to reorder national or international priorities for environmental stewardship and protection, though we should all work toward that goal. However, we can take more proactive approaches to management and thereby anticipate problems before they become crises. Much of this chapter and the next provides guidance for developing these proactive approaches for conservation management.

In our view, management is bad, or at least woefully inadequate, when it is seen as an end in itself, as a technological "fix." However, management

**Figure 11.1** Conservation management is a complicated mix of biological, economic, and humanistic concerns. Some expertise in each of the three major axes of concern is desirable in a manager, although detailed expertise in all areas is unusual. Some aspects of management, such as risk assessment or restoration ecology, involve mixes of skills from all three axes.

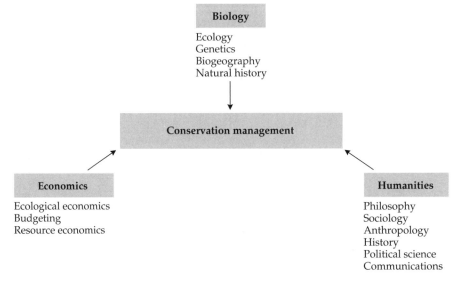

that is logically linked to long-term solutions, to stewardship of the environment, can provide the critical intervention needed to conserve biodiversity. Thus, elaborate breeding programs to maintain genetic diversity in captive populations of endangered species have limited usefulness if they are conceived as ends in themselves. But management of captive populations can become a valuable management option when it is part of a larger effort to restore and protect natural habitats so that the endangered species can be released into the wild with a greater chance for survival and a capacity to adapt to environmental change.

By the time you have reached this chapter, you should be thoroughly disabused of the romantic notion that nature seeks a balance and that everything would be just fine if we would only stop interfering with natural processes. For those still unconvinced, we pose the following questions: Do we really need to manage natural areas and their populations? Why can't nature take care of its own? To begin to address these questions, we must understand that across the globe human actions have, directly and indirectly, seriously undercut the self-sustaining and natural regenerative capacity of many ecological systems. This has led to a number of serious problems that require direct management, such as the following:

- Because management areas are frequently too small to support all of the species they might once have held, intervention management is necessary to maintain populations at viable levels.
- Similarly, protected areas are often too small to contain the normal patterns of disturbance that generate important processes of resource diversity. Management frequently must simulate those disturbances.
- Protected areas are often so fragmented and isolated that natural migration is unable to balance local extinctions. Under these conditions, managers may have to translocate individuals between management areas.
- Protected areas are typically surrounded by hostile anthropogenic environments that produce invasive species (weeds, diseases, and generalist predators) and degrading processes (siltation and pollution). Management must minimize or remove such influences.
- Some protected areas are under direct pressure for development, for release of their natural resources for human use, or for use as agricultural lands to feed rapidly increasing and desperately poor human populations.

Many of the crises that we face arise from the extreme pace and extent of change in a human-oriented and technology-dominated world. The rapid changes that occur daily force conservation managers to act quickly, often to head off disasters in the very near to distant future.

It is important to remember that natural systems, even those remote from humanity, change: they are dynamic rather than constant. For example, relative species abundances and even absolute species composition in a particular habitat can change over periods as short as a few years (Figure 11.2). This temporal change in biodiversity may be purely a reflection of natural processes of local extinction and colonization, making it more difficult to determine whether management is working. On top of this natural variation, however, are the pervasive intrusions of human activities into natural systems. The pre-agricultural natural landscape of 10,000 years ago has been replaced by a highly fragmented and human-dominated landscape where natural areas are few, often degraded, and isolated. Consequently, local

(A)

(B)

**Figure 11.2** Habitats can change greatly from year to year, even without catastrophic events, as demonstrated by these two photographs of a central Texas prairie in spring in two different years. (A) The prairie habitat in one year is rich in spring wildflowers. (B) In the same habitat a year later, few wildflowers appear. Slight variation in spring rainfall apparently resulted in a nearly complete failure of the spring wildflowers, with subsequent declines in solitary bee populations. (Photographs by C. R. Carroll.)

extinction rates of native species can be high, colonization rates low, and rates of invasion by exotics greatly increased.

In such a context, a laissez-faire or passive approach to protection without active management would lead, in many cases, to rapid rates of local extinction, to increased probability that some species would become extinct, and to further habitat degradation. In Chapter 10, we described one way to mitigate the effects of these external threats: innovative land use planning that creates systems of reserves by providing corridors for migration and compatible land uses around protected areas. In this chapter we focus on the complement to reserve design; that is, once the protected area is defined, how we can best manage it to preserve natural processes, habitat heterogeneity, resources, and thereby, biodiversity. Conservation management scenarios certainly go well beyond reserve management, and examples will be discussed in the case studies in Chapter 13. Here, we simply use reserves to focus on the types of decisions and dilemmas that resource managers typically face.

To return to our questions, yes, nature can "take care of its own," but only if the ecosystem is sufficiently large and intact, and the surrounding landscape not too intrusive. Because some level of management seems generally necessary, the earlier questions should be recast: "In order to achieve given conservation goals, what is the minimum level of management required?"

## ESSAY 11A
# Conservation Biology and Wildlife Management in America
## A Historical Perspective

Curt Meine, International Crane Foundation

"All through college I was trained to create edge, edge, and more edge. Now all I'm hearing is that edge is bad!" The words were those of a district-level wildlife manager in the U.S. Forest Service. He and two dozen colleagues were attending an agency-sponsored continuing education program designed to keep them up to date on innovations in habitat management. But after several

days of patient participation, this agency veteran could no longer contain his confusion. What he was hearing (this was 1989) and what he had been told in college (perhaps 20 years before) simply did not jibe.

His exasperation revealed much, not only about recent changes in the way edge effects were viewed, but about longer-term changes within (and sur-

rounding) the field of wildlife management generally. The immediate source of his confusion could be surmised. Likely none of his college instructors had explained—perhaps they did not realize themselves—the origins and development of the edge effect concept and its application in wildlife management. None cautioned that the creation of edge habitat was a management tool, the appropriate and effective use of which (like that of all tools) was a function of timing, location, and ecological context. None recounted how, in the 1930s, maximization of edge habitat was seen as a progressive technique in the then-new field of game management, and was used to restore game populations in a midwestern landscape that, after decades of intensive agricultural development, retained little edge, little cover of any kind, and only incidental remnants of its originally extensive biotic communities. None foresaw how the too-eager use of this tool, especially in forest settings, could have detrimental effects on interior-dwelling species.

But the manager's complaint revealed a still deeper frustration. Beyond concerns about the proper application of this or that technique, he was confronting the rapidly changing role and context of wildlife management as it entered the 1990s. The reconsideration of edge effects has been only one outward sign of a more basic reappraisal of means and ends in the effort to conserve, in the face of intensified human impacts, wild places and the flora and fauna they contain. The emergence of conservation biology itself, with its special emphasis on protection and maintenance of biological diversity, is another important indicator of this reappraisal.

Seen from one angle, conservation biology directly challenges many of the assumptions and priorities that have guided wildlife management for five decades. These include the profession's heavy emphasis on a narrow range of species, especially game animals and those select few (usually higher vertebrates) with obvious economic, aesthetic, or symbolic value; a tendency to adopt single-species approaches in research and management, and to underestimate the importance of broader, system-wide approaches; education and training programs that stress the development of technical skills while downplaying conceptual clarity and intellectual flexibility; and a relatively rigid disciplinary framework that carries over from the classroom to the agency department—and ultimately to the landscape. These tendencies, though, are not unique to wildlife management, but find analogous expression within agriculture, forestry, range management, fisheries management, and other resource-related professions.

The roots of conservation biology lie in many fields, within and beyond the sciences proper. Wildlife management is only one, but its contributions have been disproportionate. It was the arena in which biological knowledge and ecological principles were first applied in a systematic manner to the conservation of organisms and their natural habitats. As such, it played a leading role in advancing conservation beyond the point where success was measured solely in human economic terms (whether that measure was board feet produced, deer "harvested," fingerlings released, acre-feet retained, or tourists admitted). In this, it helped initiate the process—still far from complete—that would redefine conservation as the effort to protect, manage, and restore healthy and diverse ecosystems. Seen from this perspective, conservation biology represents not so much a radical departure from the past, but a further stage in conservation's continual evolutionary process. Along the way, it has given "traditional" wildlife management the opportunity to return to its roots, and to revise and reaffirm many of its founding (if sometimes neglected) principles.

At the time of its own emergence as a distinct profession in the 1930s, wildlife management itself represented a significant departure from conservation's status quo. As Aldo Leopold noted in his seminal text *Game Management* (1933), "the thought was that restriction of hunting could 'string out' the remnants of the virgin supply [of game animal populations] and make them last a longer time. . . . Our game laws . . . were essentially a device for dividing up a dwindling treasure." Leopold introduced the idea, profound in its implications, that populations of wild animals and plants could best be perpetuated through the active study, protection, and, where necessary, restoration of their habitats. He called upon science "to furnish biological facts" and "to build on them a new technique by which the altruistic idea of conservation can be made a practical reality."

Some sense of how this new approach transformed wildlife conservation in America can be gained by summarizing several key developments in the crucial decade of the 1930s.

- In 1930, virtually all of those involved in the management (as distinguished from the *study* or *protection*) of wild animal populations focused on game species. In 1936, the one-word term "wildlife" came into common usage, signaling the broadened purview of the field. By 1940, "wildlife" was standard terminology, and included for many not just "non-game" vertebrates, but invertebrates and plants as well.

- Prior to 1930, "management," such as it was, entailed mainly captive breeding programs, persecution of predatory species, tighter legal restrictions on hunting, and essentially ad hoc creation of refuges and sanctuaries. By 1940, the basic shift in approach was complete, and primary emphasis was placed on the provision of suitable habitat.

- In 1930, understanding of the science of ecology was confined to a select few, mainly within academia. By 1940, ecology was the cornerstone of wildlife management.

- In 1930, there existed no textbooks, journals, or professional organization devoted exclusively to the emerging field. By 1940, it had its text (Leopold's *Game Management*), its journal (the *Journal of Wildlife Management*), and its professional society (The Wildlife Society).

- In 1930, one could count on one hand the number of research projects set up specifically "to furnish biological facts" relevant to the conservation of wildlife. By 1940, a national system of financial and institutional support for wildlife research (the Cooperative Wildlife Research Unit program) had been established.

- In 1930, opportunities to study wildlife management were virtually nonexistent, confined (at best) to an occasional lecture in a forestry or agriculture class. By 1940, courses and whole departments devoted to wildlife management were in place in dozens of universities (particularly the nation's land-grant universities).

- And perhaps most significantly, in 1930 few appreciated the connections between wildlife ecology and management, other basic and applied sciences, and economics, philosophy, and other fields. By 1940, at least the first inklings of the broad implications of conservation were being heard, spurred on in no small part by the new generation of "wildlifers."

Even as wildlife management was securing these professional footholds, its conceptual foundation continued to broaden. During these years of ferment, the focus had expanded well beyond Leopold's (1933) original aim of "making land produce sustained annual crops of game for recreational use." The shift toward the more inclusive term "wildlife" reflected not just an interest in a wider spectrum of species, but a deeper realization of the pervasive importance of the science of ecology. Leopold himself saw this clearly. In a 1939 address to a joint meeting of the Society of American Foresters and the Ecological Society of America, he described ecology as "a new fusion point for all the natural sciences." He noted that ecology challenged traditional notions of utility, even as it highlighted the basic importance of biological diversity. "No species," he proposed, "can be 'rated' without the tongue in the cheek. The old categories of 'useful' and 'harmful' have validity only as conditioned by time, place, and circumstance. The only sure conclusion is that the biota as a whole is useful, and biota includes not only plants and animals, but soils and waters as well" (Leopold 1939).

Leopold was by no means alone in this realization. In every field of natural resource management there were "dissenters" (to use Leopold's term) who came to the same conclusions: that an understanding of natural phenomena and human environmental impacts could be gained not simply through dividing reality up into smaller and smaller bits—the method of reductionist science—but by attending to the connections and relationships in nature at various scales of time and space. For the conservation professions this had important practical implications. One could not simply manage soils, or trees, or game animals, or any other "resource" as discrete entities; one had to treat as well the ecological processes that kept the system as a whole healthy. And this meant that, departmental and disciplinary labels notwithstanding, integration was essential to all conservation work.

This line of thinking would endure even the tumult of World War II. As an inherently integrative endeavor, wildlife management was partially immune to the postwar trend toward hyperspecialization. Through the 1950s, there was close, active, and regular interaction among academic ecologists, other biologists, and the applied wildlife management programs in the universities and the state and federal governments (Wagner 1989).

By the end of the 1950s, however, even wildlife management began to suffer from "hardening of the categories." As Wagner (1989) notes, new directions in the underlying sciences "would send academic ecology and applied wildlife management down somewhat different paths and dissolve the close association of previous decades." And in the ensuing decades, these widening gaps—between theoretical and applied scientists, between scientists and managers, between departments in the agencies and universities—would make consensus ever more difficult, even as threats to the biota, at all geographic scales, intensified. In short, the "glue" that first allowed wildlife management to come together and stick together—an expanding appreciation of biological diversity and ecosystem processes, broad training in the natural sciences, collaborative research projects, and integrated approaches to resource management—was allowed to break down. For a generation, fragmentation would become increasingly evident, not only in the modern landscape, but in the modern mindscape (Cooperrider 1991).

The quickening pace of environmental degradation and biological impoverishment in the 1960s and 1970s would outstrip the ability of the various conservation-related sciences, acting in isolation, to respond. In a world beset by complex, large-scale, interrelated environmental concerns, including deforestation, air and water pollution, global climate change, human population growth, and misguided international development projects, wildlife management as generally practiced seemed less and less relevant or responsive.

The newly energized environmental movement sought to confront these trends through ambitious conferences, management programs, and legislative initiatives at the national and international level. Yet, these measures alone could not reverse the trends. Ultimately, conservation goals could only be attained through understanding and changing the entrenched patterns of resource use that threatened plant and animal populations, degraded their habitats, and disrupted the functioning of ecosystems. This was, in many ways, the proper domain of wildlife management, but in order to respond, the profession has had to rethink its priorities, broaden its mission, and reintegrate itself with the other resource management professions (Meine 1992). For many within wildlife management, that process has in fact gone on under the name of conservation biology.

The rise of conservation biology has all but inevitably provoked defensiveness on the part of some in the "traditional" conservation fields. But it has also allowed many—from the agency head to the district-level wildlife manager—to step beyond, and return to, their respective areas of expertise with a deeper sense of their professional roots, their shared goals, and the special contribution they can make to the common cause. Conservation biology treats the world not as a disaggregated collection of specialties, but as an interconnected whole to which each of the specialties can bring emphasis, insight, and perspective. In this, it is not so much a challenge to wildlife management as a fulfillment of the conservation vision to which wildlife management has always given so much. As wildlife management redefines its own future role accordingly, it can take justifiable pride in its historic efforts to promote what Leopold (1933) called "that new social concept toward which conservation is groping."

## Five Basic Principles of Good Conservation Management

To find our way through the maze of all possible management options, it is critical that we operate from basic, scientifically grounded principles of management. Any good ecological manager could, and should as a matter of practice, articulate a list of management principles and corollaries that guide them in making management decisions. We give priority to the following five principles of conservation management, although others could certainly be added.

1. Critical ecological processes must be maintained.
2. Goals and objectives must come from a deep understanding of the ecological properties of the system.
3. External threats must be minimized and external benefits maximized.
4. Evolutionary processes must be conserved.
5. Management must be adaptive and minimally intrusive.

### Principle 1: Critical Ecological Processes Must Be Maintained

We need to move beyond a species-by-species approach to management and instead think in terms of maintaining ecological processes. We can appreciate the limitations of a species-based management approach by remembering that even small management areas contain hundreds to thousands of species, and that the number of possible ways that species may directly interact in a community is calculated as $[n \times (n–1)]/2$ (Figure 11.3). Thus, 4 species can have 6 possible interactions $[(4 \times 3)/2]$; 10 species can have 45 possible interactions, and 100 species can have nearly 5000 possible interactions. Consequently, structure can be complex in even a simple community, and when multiple and indirect interactions are added, we face a bewildering array of complexity.

It should be apparent that management plans cannot be created, much less put into effect, for every species in a management area. So what is to be done? There are two common, and not necessarily mutually exclusive, tactics: one is to focus on key species, and the other is to focus on habitat or ecosystem processes. In **key species management,** plans are developed for just a few species that, for various reasons, are thought to be important. Typically, these are species that are highly visible, are relatively large ("charismatic megafauna"), are aggressive exotics, or are particularly characteristic of the environment represented by the reserve. The conservation management of these species, when they are chosen judiciously, can serve as a larger "umbrella" of protection for many other species. For example, in central California the focus might be on approaches to expand remnant native perennial grasses while eliminating alien annual grasses. In the Greater Yellowstone Ecosystem, the grizzly bear (*Ursus horribilis*) is central to much management planning; maintaining habitat of sufficient quality and size to support a viable grizzly bear population will also support most of the species characteristic of the northern Rocky Mountains. In East Africa, the need to accommodate the long-distance migrations of large ungulates, and thus maintain their habitats, is a major concern.

The other common management approach is to emphasize important ecological processes; this is sometimes referred to as **habitat** or **ecosystem management.** There is a potentially long menu of ecological processes important in maintaining the characteristic biodiversity of any given management area. Disturbance processes such as fires, floods, or windstorms, spatial processes such as migration, and temporal processes such as seasonal food abundance constitute just a small list of the more obvious candidate processes. However, selection of the right process to manage and its implementation at the appropriate scale, frequency, and intensity is far more difficult.

Consider the use of fire as a disturbance process in southeastern pine savannas. Imagine that you are responsible for a 500-ha reserve in northern Florida that consists of 90% upland longleaf pine savanna and 10% small patches of hardwoods. How often should you burn the uplands? What is the best time of year? Should you burn at night for a low-temperature burn or during the day for a hotter burn? Should you burn the entire uplands at one

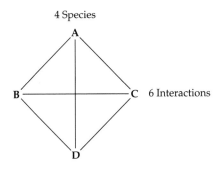

4 Species

6 Interactions

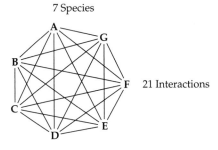

7 Species

21 Interactions

**Figure 11.3** Illustration of the possible numbers of species interactions in systems with 4 and 7 species. The possible number of direct interactions is calculated as $[n(n–1)]/2$, and increases rapidly in real communities.

time or burn in patches? How large should the patches be? What ratio of fire-tolerant pinelands to fire-sensitive hardwoods do you want? What are the consequences of creating firebreaks; i.e., can the firebreaks act as another kind of disturbance that might encourage weedy species, or might firebreaks act as barriers that inhibit movement of native species? These are the types of questions that need to be wrestled with in management of disturbance processes. We will have more to say about ecological processes later in this chapter and in Chapter 12. The use of fire as a management tool, in particular, is considered in more detail in Essay 12E.

### Principle 2: Goals and Objectives Must Come from an Ecological Understanding of the System

Making the right decisions about biodiversity and the appropriate processes to maintain depends on having well-defined management goals and objectives that are derived from a deep understanding of the ecological properties of the system. You cannot properly manage a system that you do not understand. The statement seems obvious but the literature is replete with examples of management strategies gone awry because they were based on faulty or incomplete ecological knowledge.

Along the southern and central California coast, for example, chaparral, the characteristic vegetation of coastal slopes (Figure 11.4), is maintained by a winter rainfall regime and periodic fires. To protect highways and streams, annual ryegrass is planted on hillsides to prevent erosional runoff from bare soil following fires. The use of ryegrass seems to work in regions of low rainfall, but problems arise in higher rainfall regimes, where the rye grass sod can become saturated and sections can tear free, causing large land slips. Furthermore, the grass inhibits germination of the normal post-fire chaparral vegetation and slows the regeneration process. And in some places, ryegrass appears to support large populations of pocket gophers, which, through their root browsing, can also inhibit regeneration of chaparral vegetation.

The very complexity of ecological systems makes them difficult to understand through observational and experimental approaches alone. Thus, computer modeling has become an important tool for management. Computer

**Figure 11.4** Chaparral shrub vegetation along the southern California coast (A) is a unique habitat that is maintained by frequent fires. It is under extreme pressure from urban development, both directly from land conversion (B) and indirectly through fire suppression. (Photographs by C. R. Carroll.)

(A)

(B)

models, of course, are only as good as the information used to create them. A model built on bad or incomplete biology of the system will be useless, or worse, misleading. However, models, especially simulation models, that are based on good fieldwork and that have biological parameters with reasonable ranges can provide important insight into the behavior of complex systems.

Management of complex ecological systems bears some methodological similarity to the management of complex industrial systems (Ehrenfeld 1991). Both systems are highly interactive, structured, and (should be) adaptive to environmental change. An important, perhaps defining, characteristic of the management of complex systems is that you cannot take action on one item without affecting others. Solutions cannot simply maximize single entities, but must optimize sets of interdependent entities. Consequently, the mathematics of complex systems emphasizes approaches such as multi-objective programming, optimization modeling, and analytic hierarchy processes (see Essay 11B by Linda Joyce and John Hof).

---

## ESSAY 11B
# Multiple Objectives in Planning
### Economic and Ecological Solutions

Linda A. Joyce and John G. Hof
Rocky Mountain Forest and Range Experiment Station, Fort Collins, Colorado

Resource management has almost always been characterized as a "multiple-objective" problem because of the wide variety of resources and outputs that derive from forests and rangelands. Historically, the trade-offs between different resources or outputs have typically been measured in economic terms (costs and benefits) and analyzed using mathematical techniques such as linear programming. Recently, however, societal values have shifted the focus of resource management from economic to ecological objectives.

These ecological analyses have typically utilized simulation techniques, as opposed to mathematical programming approaches. As long as ecological analyses were applied to strictly predictive questions (involving what "will" happen), these simulations have been appropriate and effective. But if management objectives are to become more ecological, then analyses will have to address prescriptive questions that involve what "should" be done. In particular, with multiple ecological objectives, a manager will typically want information on the trade-offs between ecological considerations.

For example, a manager may be concerned about water quality, deer habitat, elk habitat, and overall biodiversity. In a finite environment, all of these cannot be maximized simultaneously. Water quality might depend on total forest cover, while the best deer habitat might be a mosaic of fields and second-growth forest. Elk may require a mix of forest and meadowlands, and the prescription for overall biodiversity is largely undefined. In determining an optimal combination of these resources, it is important to recognize that gains in one resource may come at the expense of another resource. A simulation model may not be able to identify efficient combinations of these "outputs" such that each is maximized subject to the levels of the others.

If biodiversity or multispecies populations are to be objectives for forest management, then the consequences of management actions need to be quantitatively tied to these objectives so that trade-offs can be examined. For example, Hof and Raphael (1993) examined the problem of determining habitat (forest age class) distributions to optimize viability of 92 terrestrial wildlife species. The criteria for optimizing viability of species were specified as three different objective functions. In the first approach, the objective was to maintain the highest number of species possible. In the second approach, the objective was to maximize the evenness of abundance. In the third approach, the objective was to maximize the joint probability of viability across all species. Forest age-class distributions resulting from these mathematical programs differed among the three objective functions, indicating the importance of identifying the ecological objective of management: different objectives suggest very different solutions.

Ecologists are beginning to realize the considerable difficulties in modeling mobile or spatially sensitive resources such as wildlife. It is also clear that traditional economic analyses do not adequately capture the spatial dimension so important to ecological objectives. Hof and Joyce (1992) formulated a nonlinear programming model in which the spatial requirements of wildlife species were used as criteria to maximize the population numbers of different wildlife species and the amount of timber production. The purpose of this model was to develop a spatial layout of wildlife habitat and timber harvest on a landscape. Trade-offs between the physical layout of habitat for different species and different population sizes of each species were explored by varying the values for each species and timber within the objective function.

In this formulation, four criteria important to wildlife were accounted for: edge, the juxtaposition of different habitat types for cover versus feeding, dispersal distance, and minimum patch size. The landscape was initially a uniform, mature forest stand, and the optimization model searched for the optimal layout of habitat patches (uncut forest stands) subject to these spatial criteria. Edge was computed as the perimeter around forest stands adjacent to harvested areas. Some species require forage from one type of habitat and cover from another, and will use these types only to the degree that they are adjacent. Thus, the model accounted for population responses to the area of harvested stands that buffered mature forest stands. Ensuring access to all parts of the landscape may also be important; thus, the farther forest stands were from one another on the landscape, the lower the dispersing population level in the model. Finally, size often influences the suitability of habitat patches. Depending upon the species, a threshold was established in the model for the minimum usable size of habitat patch. Many species will be influenced by more than one of these determinants, and the formulation assumed that a given species' population was determined by the most limiting of the habitat factors.

Such approaches are initial, exploratory efforts. Resource analysts and ecologists have little experience in specifying ecological objectives such as biodiversity. The temporal dimension is critical in developing a sustainable management system, and as yet, no trade-off analysis has simultaneously examined the spatial and temporal dimension. Furthermore, the spatial requirements of many wildlife species remain to be specified. Questions such as total dispersal distance through specific types of habitats are known with little certainty, even for intensively studied species.

Our point is that ecological analyses must be capable of analyzing trade-offs in order to support management decisions based on ecological objectives, just as economic analyses have historically focused on trade-offs to support management decisions based on economic objectives. Adapting mathematical programming procedures to the new ecological objectives is not trivial and will require much interdisciplinary effort. However, focusing on trade-offs and identification of ecological objectives will greatly facilitate communication between conservation biologists and resource managers.

Compared with systems engineers who are making sophisticated analytical advances in the industrial environment, ecologists who deal with the management of natural systems are novices, but this industrial analogy has its limits. A factory is complicated, but the tasks of every person and machine are specified, the system is largely predictable, and the kinds of outputs are few. By contrast, the ecological functions and species interactions of the plants and animals that make up natural systems are only partly known, the system is largely unpredictable, the outputs are highly diverse, and the species members come and go. We do not suggest that ecological managers should become systems engineers or engage in highly analytical operations research, but simply that (1) they should not attempt to manage for just one thing; (2) they should be vigilant for the specter of unintended consequences of management; and (3) there is a role for modeling in complex decision making, and that role is primarily to clarify thinking and to identify nonintuitive possibilities.

### Principle 3: External Threats Must Be Minimized and External Benefits Maximized

Because the management area will most likely be embedded in a landscape dominated by human activities, we must pay particular attention to two questions: (1) how can we shelter the management area from negative outside influences such as pollutants? (2) how can the management area benefit from potentially positive outside influences, such as semi-wildlands that form a buffer zone around the management area?

Land-based natural reserves may be metaphorically described as "islands of natural habitat," but they differ ecologically from real oceanic islands in several ways. The most important difference is that, unlike oceanic islands, land-based reserves are surrounded by landscapes that produce invasive species, degradative pollutants, and intrusive processes (Figure 11.5). Thus, as Janzen (1986) cautions, reserves are faced with the "eternal external threat." On the positive side, land outside the conservation area can possibly be used to ameliorate three serious problems: boundary effects, small size, and fragmentation.

***Boundary effects.*** Boundary effects occur in the transition zone between the management area and the outside world (Figure 11.6). By definition, this

**Figure 11.5** A habitat "island" surrounded by external influences. The San Joaquin Freshwater Marsh of the Natural Reserve System of the University of California (right of center at top) is one of few remaining naturally-occurring freshwater marshes in southern California and is completely surrounded by the city of Irvine. (Photograph courtesy of the California Natural Reserve System.)

**Figure 11.6**  The boundary of a small (45 ha) reserve near North Augusta, South Carolina, showing the severe edge effect that can influence species and processes in the reserve. In this case, a powerline cut has created the sharp boundary. (Photograph by G. K. Meffe.)

is the zone where influences from outside have a significant effect on management goals. In the ideal situation, boundary effects may be limited to a narrow edge. For example, populations of forest birds that nest on or near the ground may be depressed by scavengers and generalist predators, such as raccoons and opossums, that occur commonly near edges bordering agricultural lands, but will not venture far into interior habitat. Other boundary effects may penetrate deeply into the conservation area, as, for example, when agrochemicals are carried into a stream that enters the reserve. And of course, in small reserves, the entire area may be affected.

An important role for managers is to minimize the depth of negative boundary effects. There is no general recipe for doing this because the agents that cause the boundary effects are so varied. If you are concerned about raccoon and opossum predation, then you may wish to reduce edge habitat by maximizing the discontinuity between reserve and non-reserve, for example, by maintaining a low grass buffer around a forest reserve. On the other hand, you may be concerned with the susceptibility of forest-dwelling birds to the effects of aerial drift from pesticides used on nearby agricultural fields. In this case you may decide to create a larger boundary area of early successional vegetation as a buffer between the fields and forest-dwelling birds.

In many cases, the conservation manager will need to work with the owners and managers of land surrounding the reserve to reduce negative impacts that may come from their land use practices. The following three examples illustrate this need.

In United States deserts, ranchers hold federal grazing allotments that permit them to stock public lands with cattle (Figure 11.7). The cattle range widely and may use springs near protected reserves, springs that may be important for animals of the reserve as well. Reserve managers might work with local ranchers or, more commonly, with federal agencies such as the Bureau of Land Management to provide drinking troughs for cattle while fencing off sensitive natural springs to protect them from contamination and trampling by cattle.

**Figure 11.7**  Public lands in the United States, from deserts to mountains, are used for cattle grazing under an allotment scheme that sets the number of head of cattle that can be grazed. Cattle frequently damage and despoil desert springs, streams, and range habitat. (Photograph by E. P. Pister.)

In reserves located near urban centers, problems from trespassing and petty vandalism can be severe, and simply erecting higher fences and posting more "No Trespassing" signs may be inadequate. In these circumstances, good community relations assume great importance, and encouraging schools and private conservation organizations to use the reserve for environmental education is a major means of improving community relations. Managers should always look for appropriate ways to use their reserves for public education, because establishment of environmental education programs is important for promoting local understanding of the reserve and its purpose. Also, problems with vandalism are more likely to get attention from local law enforcement officials if the reserve provides important services to the community.

In the southeastern United States, much of the forested land is privately held and used for timber. Thus, privately held upland pine forest constitutes most of the southeastern pine ecosystem. In this region, conservation of pine forest must involve cooperative agreements with the families and corporations that own most of the pinelands. Recently, for example, Georgia-Pacific, one of the largest timber companies and landowners in the Southeast, agreed to a conservation plan to protect the endangered Red-cockaded Woodpecker, which nests in cavities in large pines on Georgia-Pacific lands. These woodpeckers must be protected on private timberlands, because it is doubtful that sufficient protected habitat exists to ensure their survival.

Traditional or "indigenous" rights create special management problems, but sometimes unique opportunities as well. In some places, local people have long traditions of using reserve lands for hunting, fur trapping, fishing, and gathering medicinal plants. Sometimes these traditional uses long predate establishment of the protected reserve, as, for example, harvesting of saguaro cactus fruits in Arizona desert reserves by Pima Indians, harvesting of medicinal plants in eastern Ecuadorian national parks by Siona Indians, and harvesting of ginseng plants (used in oriental medicine) and mushrooms by longtime residents of the southern Appalachian Mountains. There are some ambiguous cases and gray areas, but generally it is easy to distinguish between long-term traditions of land use that should be continued, if they do not jeopardize the conservation objectives of a reserve, and irresponsible poaching that should be stopped.

Long-term residents often have considerable indigenous knowledge about natural resources that could be useful to management. In particular, families that have lived in a region for several generations may have important information about how the natural landscape and land uses have changed over long periods. You may learn, for example, that 40 years ago extraction of hemlock trees for the tanbark industry was intense in one part of an eastern forest but absent in other hemlock forests; such information may help to explain the current spatial pattern of hemlock and rhododendron thickets. In some reserves, such as Guanacaste, Corcovado, Braulio Carillo, and other national parks in Costa Rica, local residents have been hired by the Park Service, at least in part for their natural history knowledge of the area. The value of such indigenous knowledge systems is the topic of Essay 11C by Mark Plotkin and Adrian Forsyth. One should not overly romanticize the value of long-term residents, though. Sometimes they, as individuals or organized groups, are simply hostile to the reserve, and legal restraints may be required to prevent damage to the reserve through arson, poaching, vandalism, and the like.

*Effective reserve size.* Management areas are often small with respect to the resource needs of the species they contain. This is especially true for

# ESSAY 11C

# Retaining Indigenous Knowledge Systems as a Management Tool

Mark J. Plotkin and Adrian Forsyth
Conservation International

The philosopher-naturalist Laurens Van der Post recently remarked that the most damning legacy of colonialism has been its relentless tendency to separate tropical peoples from their land and culture. "The great mistake people make is in thinking about the aboriginal races in South Africa—the Bushmen and Hottentots and the like—as primitive peoples. They were actually very sophisticated societies and cultures with immense awareness and very important values."

The sophistication of many indigenous cultures is most evident in their agricultural systems. Over 200 years ago, a Jesuit priest in lowland Bolivia, Francisco Eder, noted that an extraordinary irrigation system in the local savannas, which had been devised in pre-Columbian times, still supported an enormous population of Mojeno Indians. Thanks to the influence of the Padre and his cohorts, as well as introduced diseases, this Amerindian agricultural system was abandoned, and the savannas that once fed the teeming local populace today are covered with a scrub vegetation supporting a few mangy cows.

The chinampa system, developed in pre-Columbian Mexico, remains in use, albeit in a much more restricted range than it once covered. Usually constructed in swampy or lacustrine environments, chinampas consist of garden plots created by building small islands using layers of vegetation and mud. The surrounding waters seep in and provide the necessary moisture, while mud scooped up from canals around the plot is periodically added as fertilizer to the garden on top of the island. According to Jim Nations of Conservation International, chinampas not only produce food and other useful crops year-round, they do not deplete the soil or require artificial fertilizers or pesticides.

A similar system is now being studied in the altiplano of northwestern Bolivia. Alan Kolata of the University of Chicago had long been intrigued by a series of ridges and depressions in this remote region that seemed to indicate some form of agricultural system that involved raised planting beds sur-

rounded by canals. The local Aymara Indians, however, employed no such system. Kolata and his colleagues worked with the Aymaras to dig a series of raised beds surrounded by ditches; the results were a crop yield seven times greater than the local average.

Here we see three different fates for three independently evolved agricultural systems: the Mojeno system has been lost, the chinampa system still exists, and the altiplano system would have remained lost if it had not been for an intrepid anthropologist and his indigenous colleagues. How many other equally valid and possibly even more productive systems have completely disappeared without a trace? The superiority complex that drives outsiders from Western societies to want to replace "primitive" systems with ill-suited ones developed on foreign soils continues to this day: the Indonesian government is currently trying to get tribal peoples in highland New Guinea to forgo their traditional and highly productive agricultural system based on sweet potatoes or sago palms, and replace it with rice, an inappropriate crop. This colonial attitude comes from cultural biases and a lack of understanding.

Yet, the problem we face is not just loss of agricultural systems themselves, but extinction of cultivar diversity as well. Indigenous agricultural systems typically contain many different varieties of a single crop, much as a farmer in the industrialized world may grow several different types of corn: one to feed his family, another to feed his animals, still another to make popcorn, and another to sell as a cash crop. The Amerindian farmer in the Amazon usually cultivates distinct varieties of cassava for the production of bread, beer, meal, porridge, and whatever other end products he desires. The Tirio Indians of northeastern Amazonia have at least 15 varieties of cassava in their gardens, while other tribes like the Machiguenga of Peru may cultivate several dozen. Time and again, these often obscure varieties from indigenous gardens are crossed with commercial varieties to increase yield and increase resistance to

pests and diseases. A barley plant from Ethiopia was crossbred with barley in California, providing resistance to the lethal yellow dwarf virus, which threatened an industry worth $160 million per year. The yield of cassava in Africa has been increased tenfold because of disease resistance provided by cassava from the Amazon. And scientists have recently found that a variety of sunflower being cultivated by the Havasupai Indians in the American Southwest offers resistance to a blight attacking sunflower crops in the Old World.

The late economic botanist Edgar Anderson once stumbled across an Indian garden in Guatemala that initially seemed more of a rat's nest than a productive agricultural plot. It was only after careful study that he realized how much more sophisticated than the botanist was the farmer:

> In terms of our American & European equivalents the garden was a vegetable garden, an orchard, a medicinal plant garden, a rubbish heap, a compost heap, and a bee-yard. There was no problem of erosion though it was at the top of a steep slope; the soil surface was practically all covered and apparently would be during most of the year. Humidity would be kept up during the dry season and plants of the same sort were so isolated from one another by intervening vegetation that pests and diseases could not readily spread from plant to plant . . . It is frequently said by Europeans and European Americans that time means nothing to an American Indian. This garden seemed to me a good example of how an Indian, when we look more than superficially into his activities, is budgeting his time more efficiently than we do. The garden was in continuous production but was taking only a little effort at any one time . . . I suspect that if one were to make a careful study of such an American Indian garden, one would find it more productive than ours in terms of pounds of vegetables and fruit per man-hour per square foot of ground. Far from saying time means nothing to an Indian, I would suggest that it means so much more to him that he does not wish to waste it in profitless effort as we do.

At a time when there are ever more mouths to feed on this planet, we suggest that Anderson's admonition to look more closely at the form and function of indigenous systems is advice worth following. Modern management techniques often overlook and disparage these indigenous systems, which are based on centuries of in situ sustainable existence, in favor of high-tech but often inappropriate and expensive systems that fail. We can learn a great deal about environmental management (and humility) from such cultures. This was succinctly summarized by anthropologist David Maybury Lewis, who said, "It's an irony that while tribal peoples with few resources strive mightily to keep their ties to the earth, we, with huge resources, strive mightily to leave it behind. We need no more power for the children to live another thousand years. We need the old wisdoms of the last one hundred thousand, those wisdoms that lie at the common fundament of all humanity. Wisdom of the different, yet common family. Wisdom of the different, yet common myths. Wisdom of the different, yet common home."

large-bodied species, species with long generation times, large predatory vertebrates, and highly migratory species. For these species, the area required to maintain a minimum viable population may greatly exceed the actual size of the reserve (see Chapter 7 on population dynamics and Chapter 10 on reserve design for extended discussions of this problem).

Semi-wild lands around a reserve could increase the effective size of the reserve. The game reserve system of East Africa provides a good illustration. The core reserves act as refuges for large game animals, but the mixed agricultural fallow and brush lands that surround the reserves are important grazing and hunting grounds for game and other wild animals. In the United States, protected natural reserves are commonly surrounded by public and private semi-wild lands, some examples of which include multiple-use national and state forest lands, Army Corps of Engineers lands around lakes and reservoirs, Bureau of Land Management lands in the western states, and large portions of state and national parks and monuments.

***Habitat corridors.*** The expansion of human-dominated landscapes has increasingly fragmented and isolated natural habitats. One of the most active debates in the conservation community concerns the advantages and disadvantages of reconnecting fragmented habitats. Because the conservation of fragmented habitats was extensively treated in Chapters 9 and 10, we simply remind you here of some of the salient points.

First, the habitat corridors that may have to be established to connect habitat patches should facilitate movement between patches and minimize mortality within the corridors. The corollary is that the corridors should be designed so that they are not misinterpreted by the species as resident habitat. This is important because the high edge-to-interior ratio of corridors may enhance the density of generalist predators and scavengers, and the longer a species takes to move through a corridor, the greater the risk of mortality. Therefore, managers need to understand, for each species, what is perceived as an acceptable environment for migration versus what is seen as acceptable for longer-term residency. For example, some birds, such as vireos of North American deciduous forests or bellbirds of Neotropical forests, that are normally restricted to forest interiors may move through corridors made up of second-growth forest but are unlikely to regard them as suitable habitat for residency. Similar reasoning applies to the use of corridors to facilitate movement of animal-dispersed plants.

Second, reconnecting existing habitat patches may be cheaper than protection of large habitat blocks through outright purchase, but there are still real costs to be paid. Corridors may have to extend long distances and cross significant barriers such as highways. The engineering required to assist migrants in crossing these barriers may be expensive, and the right solutions are not always obvious. Indeed, it is easy to find crossings that are used by habitat generalists such as white-tailed deer; that is, the solution is easy for species that probably do not need connected habitat in order to maintain viable population densities. But, how would you engineer a highway crossing for pine martens, arboreal predators that seldom leave the tree canopy to cross open ground? If barrier crossings are not adequately designed, a corridor can become a death trap.

## Principle 4: Evolutionary Processes Must Be Conserved

Species should not be protected as though they were static museum pieces, but rather as participants in evolutionary processes. We asserted in previous chapters that two fundamental objectives of conservation biology are (1) keeping populations large enough to ensure against stochastic causes of extinction, and (2) ensuring that species retain sufficient genetic diversity to permit adaptation to changing environments. The two objectives are related in that small populations are more likely to lose genetic diversity through chance processes and are also more vulnerable to stochastic environmental events. Obviously, a reserve manager cannot maintain the optimal mix of genes (who could predict what it should be?), but ecological conditions can be maintained that will favor maintenance of genetic diversity at reasonable levels. And in general, the processes that increase population size will also favor increased genetic diversity. Chapters 6 and 7 discuss the significance of genetics and demography to conservation issues and explain the influences that environmental and demographic factors have on the likelihood that a species will go extinct.

Typically, genetic management of a species is not explicitly included in a management plan until its populations have declined to some precariously low level. Thus, by the time genetics becomes a management issue, much diversity will likely already have been lost, and managers may have to deal with additional genetic problems such as inbreeding depression. For these reasons, Templeton (1990) reminds us that "rather than establish captive populations as acts of desperation, it is better to establish them as "insurance policies" when the natural populations are still sufficiently large to contain much genetic diversity."

It is commonly said that genetic diversity in outbreeding animals and plants is best retained when the species is distributed in subdivided populations with low levels of gene exchange between them—that is, in a metapopulation structure. However, under some circumstances, genetically effective population size may be reduced in subdivided populations, thereby leading to losses in local genetic variation (see, for example, Gilpin and Hanski 1991). The lack of agreement among theorists over the relationship between the spatial structure of populations and genetic variation implies that much more empirical work needs to be done. This need is reinforced when we realize that probably very few species that have spatially structured populations meet the criteria for traditional metapopulation structure; for example, asynchronous dynamics among the subpopulations and sufficient dispersal to allow for recolonization. Therefore, a major contribution that managers of protected areas can make is to encourage long-term studies of population and genetic dynamics in the field.

## Principle 5: Management Must Be Adaptive and Minimally Intrusive

Insofar as possible, management should be gentle and minimally intrusive. Because environmental conditions may change and new problems will arise, management should also be adaptive; that is, it should remain flexible in order to meet new contingencies, rather than stubbornly adhering to a written plan simply because it has survived a bureaucratic maze and is supported by "headquarters." As a corollary to the general attributes of good management discussed above, contingency plans should be included in the event that the original strategy fails to work. The following question should be applied to every management plan: If the plan fails, will the biotic community be worse off than if the plan had not been executed? If the answer seems to be "yes," then special attention should be given to contingency plans to minimize negative effects on the biotic community.

Often, management decisions have to be made quickly and without benefit of complete field data. To help managers explore the probable consequences of management decisions, computer models are frequently used to analyze the consequences of alternative decisions. An important role exists for computer modeling—especially simulation models—in management: it allows us to explore the potential consequences of different management plans before they are actually or fully implemented. Thus, computer-assisted decision making can help reduce the risks involved in management decisions. For example, habitat management may involve the use of disturbance regimes, such as prescribed burning, and modeling can provide insight into the advantages of one disturbance pattern over another. The simulation of fire behavior, species tolerances to fire, and dispersal processes can be combined to show how different patterns of habitat heterogeneity can be produced by prescribed burning.

Recent work by Wootton and Bell (1992) on the viability of, and management strategies for, Peregrine Falcon (*Falco peregrines*) populations shows how computer models can provide important counterintuitive insight. Wootton and Bell developed a deterministic population model that incorporated the spatial structuring of falcon populations in California. The model projections provided a good fit to current population estimates and yielded important information about management strategies. First, they found that southern (sink) populations were unlikely to remain viable unless individuals were continually reintroduced from northern (source) populations (Figure 11.8). Second, sensitivity analysis (that is, identification of aspects of the model sensitive to even small changes in input values) suggested that management to improve adult survival would contribute more to population viability than would improving fledgling success. Third, northern populations were most likely to reach highest densities and, through migration, make the greatest contribution to overall population size. This work suggests that the most effective plan would emphasize management to improve adult survival and core habitat protection for northern populations.

Such insight into population viability is not necessarily possible through empirical observation, and can be of great assistance in management deci-

**Figure 11.8** Predicted population trajectories of northern (source) and southern (sink) populations of the Peregrine Falcon in California, generated from computer population models. Modeling indicated that migration among populations has little effect on the northern population, but is critical to the survival of the expansive southern population in California. (From Wootten and Bell 1992.)

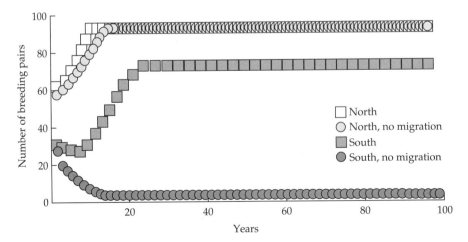

sions. However, the computer will not replace biological intuition and past experience in the system, nor relevant information from other systems. Modeling and simulation is merely one more tool to help the manager make informed decisions about a system.

The use of these five principles in management, along with other relevant knowledge, may be demonstrated by looking at one pervasive conservation problem, the control of invasive species.

## Management Principles in Practice: Controlling Invasive Species

The objectives or goals of any management plan must be clearly defined and unambiguous, and an objective method for evaluating success must be developed. Consider, as a realistic example, the kinds of questions and issues that might arise during development of a management plan for controlling exotic species in the Everglades National Park and Big Cypress Swamp, Florida. Sometimes an exotic successfully invades a seemingly natural and intact habitat, but more often than not, successful invasions depend on some habitat alteration.

A case in point is the Everglades system, where urban and agricultural water diversions have seriously reduced the supply of water, allowing successful invasion by a number of exotic plant species. The course of management could range from no action, simply monitoring populations of potentially invasive species and watching for negative effects, to a program of complete eradication. With all of the principles, especially principle 5 (management should be adaptive and minimally intrusive) in mind, the manager would ask questions such as, "Will my attempts to control the invasive species cause other kinds of damage? Does the eradication program pose an unacceptable risk to the natural community and habitat?" In the real world of limited budgets and competing demands, a manager will also have to ask, "Will eradication be so costly that other priority programs would suffer?" For example, the only affordable way to eliminate two exotic plant species, the Australian melaleuca (*Melaleuca quinquinervia*) and the Brazilian pepper shrub (*Schinus terebrinthinus*), might require extensive use of an herbicide; the manager might then decide that the effects of contaminating the wetlands would be worse than the effects of the exotic, and consider mechanical or hand removal as an alternative (Figure 11.9).

**Figure 11.9**  Several exotic plant species have successfully invaded Everglades National Park, and have become a serious management problem. (A) The melaleuca is a small tree from Australia. Here, several clumps of adult trees are surrounded by a heavy density of seedlings. (B) A solid forest of exotic Brazilian pepper shrub. (Photographs by Don C. Schmitz.)

(A)

(B)

An important point particularly relevant to this example is the difference between proximate and ultimate courses of action. Melaleuca and the Brazilian pepper shrub each have colonized about 45,000 ha in Florida, but neither species can tolerate extended submergence of their seedlings. They are successful invaders because the hydrology of the wetlands has been drastically altered by water diversion for agriculture and urban needs. The proximate course of action, removal of the invasive plants, is premised on the assumption that the cause of the invasive process will not be altered. Thus, the problem is likely to recur. The ultimate course of action would address the fundamental cause of the problem; in this case, the solution might be restoring the natural hydrology of the ecosystem (Principles 1, 2, and 3). Good management approaches, as is the case in the Everglades and Big Cypress, will include both proximate and ultimate courses of action. All too often, symptoms of problems are treated in management, without the underlying causes being identified or addressed (Meffe 1992).

Some exotic species are so widespread and well established that, for all practical purposes, managers may have to accept them as part of the community. In North America, this is particularly true for some exotic game birds and fishes, such as the Ring-necked Pheasant (*Phasianus colchicus*), brown trout (*Salmo trutta*), and common carp (*Cyprinus carpio*). In some habitats in North America, notably the interior valley grasslands of California, most of the biomass of annual plants is comprised of exotic species (Figure 11.10).

A manager of a central California grassland reserve may believe that Ring-necked Pheasants have only a trivial effect on the natural system and elect to exclude them from active management. On the other hand, considerable evidence would suggest that annual non-native grasses are seriously disrupting critical ecological processes (Principle 1), for example, by competing with native plants for nitrogen and water, and that active management is necessary. By studying the ecophysiology of native perennial and exotic annual grasses, the manager may conclude that implementing a fire regime at the right time might provide a growth advantage to the native perennials while reducing seed production in the non-native annuals. Thus, a management plan would arise from a deep understanding of the ecological proper-

**Figure 11.10**  Virtually all of the grasses in this coastal valley in California are non-native annuals. The native perennial grasses have been displaced. (Photograph by C. R. Carroll.)

ties of the system (Principle 2). However, because some uncertainty may exist, the cautious manager would test the plan on a series of small experimental plots before implementing it on a large scale. That is, the manager would follow Principle 5, by keeping the management adaptive and minimally intrusive. Our five principles of good management do not tell you what to do in any particular situation, but they will provide guidance, a mindset, to help you make the right decision.

## Different Scales of Management

Management may be focused at different environmental scales (Table 11.1) ranging from individual populations through landscapes of interconnected ecosystems. The scale at which an observation is made or an experiment conducted may very well influence the results. Therefore, the kind of ecological information needed for development of good management plans, and successful implementation of those plans, may be sensitive to both temporal and spatial scales. For example, on small plots of a few hectares, Least Flycatchers (*Empidonax minimus*) are competitively superior to American Redstarts (*Setophaga ruticilla*). Yet on a regional scale, the two species are positively associated (Sherry and Holmes 1988). If a management plan for these species were based solely on small-plot studies, coexistence of the species might seem to be an impossible objective, and the factors that promote coexistence at the larger landscape scale might be missed. As discussed in Chapter 7, management actions need to recognize the importance of the landscape habitat mosaic to population dynamics and the ecological mechanisms that link population dynamics to spatial patterns.

Many species require access to different components of the landscape, and determining the best methods for maintaining and protecting such multiple habitat use is a major challenge for conservation biologists. Most field biologists can recite lists of species that require access to more than one habitat type. Very often species use different parts of their environment during seasonal migration and reproduction and to meet the special requirements of different life stages. Their movements range from short distances, as with species having different microhabitat requirements, to very long distances, as with migratory birds.

In addition to these rather deterministic uses of the landscape there are also spatial patterns that are the consequence of population growth and dispersal. As populations grow and optimal habitats become saturated, suboptimal, less-preferred habitats are colonized more rapidly. The spatial configuration of optimal and sub-optimal habitats creates source–sink relationships that are important in the population dynamics of many species (see Chapter 7). Box 11A

## Table 11.1
Examples of Management at Different Environmental Scales

| Scale | Management example |
|---|---|
| Population | Population vulnerability analysis leading to estimates of minimum viable population densities |
| Habitat | Using prescribed burning to maintain natural patterns of vegetation heterogeneity |
| Landscape | Protecting riparian wetlands against pollution from agrochemicals by developing vegetation buffers between agricultural fields and wetlands |

provides some examples to illustrate the generality of multiple habitat use and the diversity of taxa involved. The point of these examples is to emphasize that management research should include protection of the various components of the landscape that are actually used by the species, and that sometimes this will involve management beyond the borders of the protected land.

## Box 11A
## Examples of Species Using Multiple Habitats

### Long-Distance Migrators

**1.** *Lepidoptera.* Many tropical Lepidoptera use deciduous forests during the wet season, both as adults and as larvae, but move to tropical wet forests at the beginning of the dry season. In northwestern Costa Rica, the larvae of saturniids (royal moths) and sphingids (hawkmoths) spend the wet months feeding on leaves in the dry forest of Santa Rosa National Park. At this time, these larvae are important food for the young of many insectivorous birds. Toward the end of the wet season, adults migrate across the central mountains to wet Atlantic lowlands (Janzen 1986). Populations of these lepidopterans, and thus the reproductive success of many birds in the deciduous forest, are critically dependent on the spatial linkage of intact wet and dry forest. Some temperate zone lepidoptera migrate long distances as well. The best-known case is the eastern United States population of the monarch butterfly as discussed in Essay 4D.

**2.** *Birds and Bats.* Many of the most familiar passerine birds of the temperate zone (warblers, orioles, tanagers, redstarts, vireos) as well as hawks, waterfowl and many other kinds of birds, spend half the year or more in the tropics. Less well appreciated is the long-

distance migration of some bats. There is considerable debate among conservation biologists concerning the ultimate cause of the observed decline in many songbird populations. Whatever the primary causes, it is clear that some measure of habitat protection in both the tropical and the temperate zone parts of their ranges is necessary.

### Short-Distance Migrators

**1.** *Lepidoptera.* At a smaller scale, nonmigratory tropical lepidoptera of dry forests spend the dry season in riparian forests in a state of reproductive diapause. Destruction of riparian forests, or even excessive grazing of the understory by cattle, can greatly affect butterfly populations. Temperate zone lepidoptera, such as many of the swallowtails, feed on nectar as adults but require forests as sources of larval food. For these species, fragmented forests will support higher densities than will large intact forests.

**2.** *Birds.* Even within a region there are critical migrational patterns. For example, fruit- and nectar-feeding birds often have altitudinal migrations that track the seasonal changes in their food supply. Quetzals and bellbirds of the Neotropics are just two of many species that breed at high elevations and then

descend to lower elevations. Thus, the destruction of even a small band of mid-elevational forest can have a major effect on such species.

**3.** *Ungulates.* Elk, mule deer, mountain sheep, and other temperate zone ungulates often use high mountain meadows and slopes for breeding and foraging, and move to lower elevations when winter sets in. Management to meet the habitat needs of these animals can conflict with the grazing needs of cattle and sheep, and where domestic stock and wild ungulates use common grazing lands, transmission of diseases such as "blue tongue" can occur. In this case, management not only requires that a migration route be protected, but that common use of grazing lands by cattle and wild ungulates be regulated.

**4.** *Fishes.* Within streams some fish use different habitats for foraging and breeding. Fish known as darters provide good examples. *Etheostoma* darter species in the subgenus *Ozarka* forage and live in rivers but move into ephemeral seepage streams for breeding. Clearly, the protection of species in this subgenus, some of which are classified as "species of special concern," would require the protection of lands that drain into the seepage streams.

## Living with Uncertainty and Risk

Managers often have to take quick action to reduce the ecological risk arising from some hazard. Frequently, decisions must be made before all the information is available, or when the quality of some of the information is suspect. California Fish and Game biologist Phil Pister once saved an entire species, the endangered Owens pupfish (*Cyprinodon radiosus*), by collecting them in buckets and coolers when he discovered their single habitat (Figure 11.11) rapidly drying up (Pister 1993). He was forced to take action although there was considerable uncertainty and risk, both biological and political. He literally held the evolutionary fate of the entire species in his hands as he carried them in buckets across the desert, with no contingency plan, and where tripping over a rock could mean extinction of the species. A large part of a manager's responsibility is identification of ecological risk before it reaches

**Figure 11.11** The single native habitat of the Owens pupfish, *Cyprinodon radiosus*. The fish nearly went extinct in August 1969 when the habitat dried up because of unexplained reduction in spring flow combined with unusually high evapotranspiration rates on hot afternoons. The species was rescued only through unplanned, unapproved action by a California Fish and Game biologist. (Photograph by E. P. Pister.)

such a crisis stage, and, keeping the five principles of good conservation management in mind, development of risk management plans to minimize the negative consequences.

In the most general sense, ecological risk assessment involves estimating the likelihood that an identified hazard will have a negative effect, and estimating the ecological consequences of that negative effect. A typical example might involve the risk of damage to a lake ecosystem if a particular pesticide were applied to agricultural lands in the lake watershed. Generally, risk assessment has two phases. The first involves identifying the risk, the environment in which it occurs, and the size and distribution of the sources of the hazard. The second phase is assessment of how the recipient environment will be exposed to the causal agents and what the environmental effects will be for various exposure regimes. The information from risk assessment is then integrated into a decision analysis process that typically includes cost–benefit and other economic analyses and policy studies. Essay 11D by Lynn Maguire provides a fuller exploration of the important area of decision and risk analysis.

## ESSAY 11D
# Decision Analysis in Conservation Biology

Lynn A. Maguire, Duke University

Suppose that the manager of a tiger reserve in India has been successful at controlling poaching within the reserve, and the tiger population has increased to the point where tigers sometimes leave the reserve, causing trouble in adjacent villages, where they are often killed. The manager suspects that the reserve may be too small to maintain a stable, self-contained tiger population and worries that continuing the present management strategy may lead to high levels of human/tiger conflicts and a declining tiger population.

One solution to this problem might be intensive management of the reserve's tigers, adding and removing tigers of certain ages and sexes to maintain a stable population within the reserve and to minimize human/tiger conflicts. Because tigers have a complex social system, such intervention might backfire, causing increased mortality from territorial disputes and infanticide. In addition, moving tigers will be very expensive. How can the manager satisfy demands from conservationists for protection of tigers, demands from politicians for protection of people, and demands from everyone for financial efficiency?

This problem embodies dilemmas typical of conservation decisions: there are multiple interest groups with many, sometimes conflicting, objectives; the outcomes of alternative management actions are far from certain, and any decision may have serious consequences. Are there any ways to improve on unguided intuition when facing such dilemmas?

Decision analysis, a structured way of analyzing decisions under uncertainty, can help. The first step is to identify the decision maker and her objectives: in this case, the reserve manager, who must improve tiger population status, minimize conflicts between tigers and humans, and minimize financial costs. The next step is to propose alternatives: continuing to protect the reserve under the present strategy, or actively adding and removing tigers. The next is to identify uncertain events that could affect how each management alternative might turn out. Whether or not the reserve *is* too small to maintain a viable tiger population will determine whether the tiger population is stable or declining and whether the level of conflict is high or low. Whether or not mortality increases will determine tiger population status under the "add and remove" alternative. The alternatives, uncertain events, and verbal descriptions of possible outcomes for all three decision objectives can be shown graphically on a decision tree (Figure A).

Sometimes just this structured description of the problem can help clarify the dilemma and suggest a solution; for many problems, a more quantitative analysis is helpful. Which alternative is better depends on *how likely* it is that the reserve is too small or that intervention will increase mortality, *how much* better it is to have a declining population with low levels of conflict than a declining population with high levels of conflict, and *how much* more money you are willing to spend to improve tiger status and minimize conflict. Resolving the dilemma requires a quantitative representation of the decision maker's beliefs about the facts of the matter and the preferences she has for different outcomes.

Beliefs about facts include estimates of the probabilities of the uncertain events that can affect outcomes, and predictions of the consequences of all the possible combinations of management actions and uncertain events. Sometimes there are historical observations (such as weather records) that can be used to estimate the probabilities of uncertain events directly. More often, lack of historical data and unique features of the current situation necessitate using **Bayesian statistics** to combine evidence from empirical data, theoretical models, and expert judgment. Structured questioning techniques have been developed to quantify a decision maker's intuition about uncertain events, or "subjective probabilities"; in this particular case, we will suppose that the decision maker assigns a probability of 0.4 to the likelihood that the re-

serve is too small to maintain a viable tiger population.

Quantifying the verbal descriptions of outcomes requires the decision maker to specify observable criteria for measuring how well each decision objective is met, e.g., population growth rate as a measure of population status, number of human/tiger conflicts per year as a measure of conflict, and dollars as a measure of financial cost. Models of tiger population/habitat relationships and of tiger/human interactions might be used to predict population growth rates and rates of conflict under the two scenarios, "reserve too small" and "reserve OK," and similarly, under the two intervention alternative, "increased mortality" and "OK."

These predictions may not accurately reflect the decision maker's preferences among outcomes; she may not think that 200 tigers are twice as good as 100 and half as good as 400. "Utility" measures relative preferences among outcomes, often on a scale of 0 to 1. Using a structured questioning technique, the decision maker can be guided from the verbal descriptions of tiger population status and human/tiger conflicts to a numerical value that combines these two criteria (leaving financial cost separate for now). Suppose the decision maker considers a stable population with low conflict the best outcome (utility = 1); a declining population with high conflict the worst (utility = 0); and, with the help of structured questions, finds that a declining population with low conflict has an intermediate utility value of 0.4.

To analyze the decision quantitatively, the decision maker applies a decision rule; maximizing expected utility is a common one, but others are possible. First, she calculates expected utility for each alternative by multiplying the utility of each outcome by its probability. For "protect reserve," the expected utility is (0.4)(0) + (0.6)(1) = 0.6; for "add and remove," the expected utility is 0.64. The action with higher utility, "add and remove," is preferred, but not by much.

The next step is to take account of any other criteria, in this case, financial cost: is it worth an extra $300,000 to improve expected utility (representing tiger population status and human/tiger conflict) from 0.6 to 0.64? Sometimes the answer to such tradeoff questions is obvious. If not, there are again structured sets of questions that can help the decision maker articulate her willingness to trade

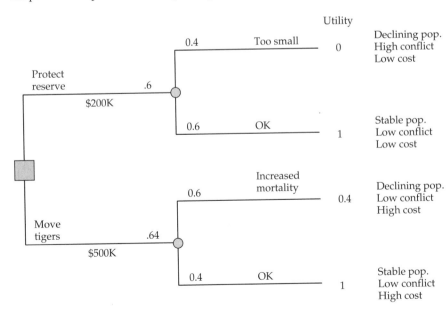

**Figure A**   An example of a decision tree.

additional dollars for improved population status and/or reduced conflict.

One advantage of imposing a quantitative structure on a decision problem is the ability to see how sensitive the choice of action is to changes in probability or utility values. If the probability of increased mortality under the "add and remove" option were 0.7, instead of 0.6, the expected utility of this option would be 0.58, instead of 0.64, and the "protect reserve" option would be superior for all objectives. Sensitivity analysis identifies which components of a problem have the greatest effect on choice of action, guiding further analysis and research. Sensitivity analysis can also be used to represent the views of different decision makers, or different interest groups, who may not share the beliefs or values of the reserve manager, pointing out where disagreements about facts or values do or do not lead to disagreements about actions.

Decision analysis addresses some of the major difficulties of conservation decisions in the following ways: (1) the structured framework helps the decision maker describe the problem accurately and make full use of available information; (2) making uncertainties explicit helps the decision maker use subjective, as well as objective, information about probabilities rationally, a task that is difficult in intuitive decision making; (3) identifying specific decision objectives, measurement criteria, and utility scores makes the value structure used by the decision maker explicit and open to scrutiny; (4) an explicit decision rule guides the choice of action; and, (5) the explicit and graphical format of decision analysis aids communication and negotiation when conservation decisions are in dispute.

**Figure 11.12** An agricultural landscape in southwestern Honduras. Erosion from these fragile slopes contributes large silt loads to downstream estuaries and shrimp ponds. (Photograph by C. R. Carroll.)

To further illustrate the process, consider comprehensive evaluation of an agricultural project in the Pacific coastal zone of Honduras (Figure 11.12). Multinational lending institutions such as the World Bank and the Inter-American Development Bank require impact assessments as part of their lending requirements. In the river bottoms of this region, melons for the United States and European market are an important commercial crop. Because U.S. and European consumers demand cosmetically perfect melons, large amounts of pesticides are used in their production. Imagine that the government of Honduras requests international credit to build irrigation systems for export melon production. Part of the environmental risk assessment would involve concern over the possible transport of agricultural chemicals into rivers that drain into estuaries of the economically and ecologically important Bay of Fonseca. This bay borders three countries, contains one of the largest intact mangrove ecosystems along the Pacific coast, and is the locale of an important export shrimp mariculture industry (Figure 11.13). Further analysis would include determining the fate and transport of the chemicals and their likely ecological effects on aquatic populations.

**Figure 11.13** A commercial shrimp pond in Honduras. Silt from eroding farmland and pesticides from commercial export farming threaten the shrimp production industry. (Photograph by C. R. Carroll.)

A cost–benefit analysis might be conducted that would weigh the benefits of increased agricultural productivity and sales against potential losses to estuarine-based fisheries and shrimping, or the cost of cleanup should chemical pollution occur. It is unlikely, however, that biodiversity losses (or, for that matter, human health) would be included in the cost–benefit analysis, except possibly as a comment in the text. If a decision to proceed with the irrigation project were made, it might incorporate a risk management approach to minimize the environmental effects. For example, policies might be developed so that economic incentives or governmental regulation would favor minimal use of toxic chemicals or prohibit those known to affect aquatic ecosystems. In its classic form, cost–benefit analysis does not include nonmarket "goods." In other words, if the costs and benefits cannot be expressed in monetary units, they are not included in the analysis. Obviously, the classic form of cost–benefit analysis does not count losses in natural biodiversity as part of the "cost."

The process of risk assessment and risk management has become much more inclusive in recent years. We must now develop risk assessment and management approaches that explicitly incorporate the protection of biodiversity and cultural integrity of native peoples. This will not be an easy transformation because cost–benefit analysis grew out of a need to make market-based investment decisions. Attempts to find ecologically meaningful surrogate units for market value in cost–benefit analyses have so far been unsatisfactory (Chapter 2). Most of these surrogate measures, such as "willingness to pay" or "maximum travel to visit," treat natural areas and biodiversity protection as if they were amusement parks; that is, their "value" is determined by how much people are willing to pay for their existence or by what they are willing to give up in order to ensure their continuance (see Chapter 17).

The illogic of assigning some measurement of value to biodiversity is perhaps made more apparent by considering an analogy. Just as extinction is forever, so is the loss of a classic painting. We can assign a transaction value to the painting, that is, how much money one museum would demand from another in order to be willing to sell the painting. We could even assign a kind of societal value to the painting by asking art lovers how far they would be willing to travel to view the painting or what maximum admission price they would be willing to pay. In these ways, we would have a quantitative assessment of value. However, suppose some wealthy madman wanted to buy the painting so that he could burn it? One would hope that, under those circumstances, a museum would be unable or unwilling to assign a market value to the painting. So it is with attempts to assign a monetary value to the loss of biodiversity.

## Four Causes of Uncertainty

Conservation management decisions are premised on an analysis of costs of planning and implementation, and on ecological trade-offs; the former is measured in money or time and effort, and the latter in biological units that are not easily specified, and are almost always nonmarket values. However, the limitations of the analysis are set more by various sources of uncertainty in the system's ecology than by inabilities to define homogeneous units for costs and benefits. The causes of uncertainty must be explicitly understood in order to minimize risk. Our focus will include the following four principal sources of uncertainty (other than investigator error and poor data collection): environmental stochasticity, indirect effects, nonindependent effects of stresses, and extrapolation from incomplete knowledge.

*Environmental stochasticity.* Environmental stochasticity introduces uncertainty that is characteristic of the kind of environmental change being measured, the taxa involved, the ecosystem, and the scale at which measurements are made. For example, a large storm can uproot individual trees in a forest. At the scale of meters, near an affected tree, the influence of this stochastic event would be large and exist for a long time. On a larger scale, the entire forest, the event may have minimal spatial and temporal influence. In streams flowing through the forest there may be no influence beyond a temporary increase in runoff. Stochasticity in this type of storm event would generate moderate to high uncertainty in studies of tree species, but little uncertainty in studies of aquatic species. Very often, computer models can be used to explore the significance of stochastic effects on management plans. For example, the introduction of environmental stochasticity did not influence the threshold for extinction in computer-modeled population dynamics of the Northern Spotted Owl (McKelvey et al. 1993).

*Indirect effects.* Indirect effects may involve species that are not directly affected by a particular stress. For example, when a pesticide eliminates a predator, its loss may influence the population densities of the predator's normal prey, as well as those of competitors of the prey species. The resurgence of secondary pests in agricultural fields following pesticide treatments is a very common example of this phenomenon. Indirect effects will be likely when particularly important species, such as strong interactors and keystone species (see Chapter 12), are removed.

*Nonindependent effects.* Nonindependent effects of stresses, such as synergisms between different toxic chemicals, may introduce errors when the effects of stresses are estimated separately. For example, heavy metals are toxic to fish, but the joint toxicity of two metals such as copper and zinc can be greater than their independent additive toxicities (Lewis 1978; Finlayson and Verrue 1982). Another illustration of nonindependence is the effects of stress events that occur so frequently that the system cannot recover in the short interims between stresses; these are sometimes referred to as "cumulative time effects." For example, the frequency of fires of human origin can be so high that even classic fire climax communities such as chaparral can be degraded.

*Cumulative space effects.* Cumulative space effects can occur when management units cannot be treated independently of other management units or private lands. The obvious example, and one that has been discussed frequently throughout this book, is that of fragmented forests. As fragmentation increases, the survival of species in each patch is increasingly dependent on immigration between patches. This importance of cumulative space effects is an argument for pursuing management of fragmented habitats at the scale of landscapes. Cumulative effects are often ignored in management planning, but the cost of ignoring them can be high.

Extrapolation is often made from limited measurements at a lower level of biological organization in order to estimate an effect occurring at a higher level. For example, life history studies of individual populations are sometimes used to estimate effects at the level of communities. This problem introduces uncertainty when reductionist studies are used to understand the behavior of larger systems. The most common form that this extrapolation takes is the use of so-called **indicator species** as surrogates for the community or even the ecosystem. For example, the Northern Spotted Owl (*Strix occidentalis caurina*) requires large tracts of old-growth forest in the Pacific Northwest, and has sometimes been called an indicator species for high-quality old-growth forest habitat. But this would only be true for very large forest patches. The owl would be a poor surrogate for the many species, such as voles, that also flourish in small patches of old-growth forest. Using the occurrence of the owl as an indicator of habitat quality would underestimate the conservation value of high-quality, small forest patches; use of voles as indicators of high-quality habitat for large mobile vertebrates would likewise result in error. Good management planning explicitly recognizes these sources of uncertainty and develops policy priorities to minimize their magnitude and effects.

Uncertainty and risk will always be a central part of conservation management. It cannot be avoided, largely because ecological systems are so inherently complex and dynamic, and because the forms of human influences on systems are so diverse. There is always the danger in management of "paralysis by overanalysis"—doing nothing because of continued uncertainty. Such a non-decision is in fact a decision—to do nothing. This may be the correct decision in many cases, but that decision should be made overtly, after careful analysis of all the information at hand, not covertly by default and inaction. Conservation management inherently will always have some risk and some uncertainty, and indeed some mistakes will be made. However, reliance on general ecological and evolutionary principles, combined with knowledge of the system at hand, and divorced from biologically unsound bureaucratic pressures, should result in good management policy decisions in most cases.

## Cultural Context of Management Decisions

Much of the biota of conservation concern may use parts of the landscape outside of the area of legal protection. The recovery of black-footed ferrets, for example, requires cooperation from private landowners because the ferrets' only prey, prairie dogs, and the best habitats, are on private ranchlands. Furthermore, as discussed in Chapter 10, fully protected areas are usually too small to provide all the resources needed to maintain populations above their critical minimum sizes. Under these conditions, gene flow and immigration of individuals from outside the protected area are necessary to buffer legally protected populations against vulnerability to extinction and genetic losses.

Increasingly, interactions with those who control semi-wild and other rural lands around protected areas, both positive and negative, are essential parts of population and community management. Conservation ecologists frequently find themselves working with landowners, recreational interests, stockmen, foresters, and governmental agencies ranging from local municipalities to the federal level. These interactions are enormously time-consuming but essential to conservation action. Unfortunately, conservationists seldom have the appropriate training in the social or political sciences to effectively communicate with individuals and groups representing such diverse interests and agendas. These kinds of interactions are vitally important social and economic dimensions of conservation management, and we strongly encourage students of conservation to include appropriate social science courses, such as rural sociology and cultural anthropology, in their academic training.

For ecologists working within their own countries, the need to deal effectively and preemptively with conflict is reason enough to include the social sciences in their training and to develop good collaborations with appropriate social science researchers. When ecologists tackle conservation projects in cultural contexts very different from their own, such as development of reserves that include the protection of indigenous peoples, such training is even more critical, and ecology becomes only one of many useful perspectives.

Extractive reserves in Brazil and game management areas in East Africa are just two prominent examples of situations calling for these skills. In Brazil there are two general kinds of extractive reserves: one provides protection for indigenous cultures and the other protects traditional extractive activities, principally latex extraction for rubber and harvest of wild populations of brazil nuts (Figure 11.14). In both cases the local people can be rich sources of information about resource management and natural history. Game management in East Africa also must include the needs and lifestyles of indigenous peoples, for several reasons. They have historically hunted many of these game species and understand their ecologies, and they are also affected by protection programs that cause large vertebrates to raid their agricultural crops. Whether in Brazil, Africa, or elsewhere, talents for communicating with and understanding people from other cultures will pay great dividends for conservation programs.

Whether we are talking about Indians living in a Brazilian rainforest reserve, fishermen harvesting crabs from a coastal marsh in Maryland, cattle ranchers in Wyoming, or hikers along the Appalachian Trail, the same general principle applies: because people are integral parts of the system, and because their economic interests and livelihoods are tied to the land, they must also be integral to any process of conflict resolution regarding conservation goals and objectives.

**Figure 11.14** A Brazilian rubber tapper in the Amazon Basin. Rubber tappers who extract raw latex from wild rubber trees are carrying out a possibly sustainable use of tropical forests, and their concerns and needs should be incorporated into any conservation management plans for the area. (Photograph courtesy of National Archives.)

## Summary

It is important for conservation managers to move beyond an ad hoc approach to management, where each day brings new and unexpected problems, to a more systematic approach that allows them to identify and anticipate management needs. Although it is certainly not an exhaustive list, we identified and discussed five principles of good conservation management that will help managers develop a more systematic approach to decision making and planning. By building these principles into management plans, as discussed in the next chapter, managers can anticipate and prevent many crises. These principles are:

1. Critical ecological processes must be maintained.
2. Goals and objectives must come from a deep understanding of the ecological properties of the system.
3. External threats must be minimized and external benefits maximized.
4. Evolutionary processes must be conserved.
5. Management must be adaptive and minimally intrusive.

We illustrated how these principles could be applied to a particular, and important, management issue, the control of invasive species.

Other general concerns of conservation management include the different scales of management, the uncertainty and risk of management decisions, and the need to make decisions in the right cultural context. Choosing the right scale of management decisions can be critical to the success of the program. For example, management of individual populations may not be successful if the metapopulation structure at the scale of landscapes is not considered.

Uncertainty and risk are inherent in conservation management. Understanding the contributions of sources of uncertainty and risk, such as environmental stochasticity, nonindependent effects, and cumulative effects, is essential to good management planning.

Finally, conservation decisions usually involve more than simply the biology of endangered species or the conservation of natural habitats. Decisions usually involve human affairs within and outside of protected areas. Therefore, the long-term success of conservation management will strongly depend on public support, and management decisions need to be made in the appropriate cultural context.

## Questions for Discussion

1. Imagine you are the director of a 500-ha private reserve owned by a local conservation organization. The reserve is on an isolated mountain located in the Mojave Desert of California at an elevation of about 1000 m. The reserve was established to protect a small herd of desert bighorn sheep. Additionally, you have a use agreement to manage 15,000 ha of public multiple-use land that surrounds your private reserve. The public land includes several springs that contain water in years of average or greater rainfall, but only one has continual flow in drought years. Ranchers have been given grazing allotments on the public land to stock cattle at densities of one head per five ha. Identify the critical management issues from your perspective. Identify the critical management issues from the perspective of a cattle rancher. Discuss possible means for resolving conflicts. How might you make use of the "cultural knowledge" of the ranchers? Are there, perhaps, more environmentally benign ways to raise cattle? What information would you need in order to develop a management plan for the protection of the bighorn sheep?

2. When an exotic (alien) species has survived in an area for a long time it is often said to have become "naturalized." The implication is that the species should now be considered as a permanent part of the biota. What are some "naturalized" species in your area? Why do you think that exotic plants are more likely to become "naturalized" than exotic animals? How would you develop a research agenda to determine whether or not a "naturalized" species poses a threat to the community?

3. Many exotic plants and animals are brought into new environments, either intentionally or accidentally, yet very few become established in the wild. For any particular taxon (e.g., a plant family), discuss attributes that might make it a successful invader. Review the major exotic species in your area. Do they have identifiable attributes that contribute to their success as invading species? Pick one and develop a risk management plan for its control.

4. Do you think that economic cost–benefit analysis has any place in conservation ecology? What can you offer in its place to assist the decision-making process?

5. Suppose you are the lead manager for the Spotted Owl in Oregon. You understand that the owl needs large expanses of old-growth forest to survive. You also understand that the larger issue is protection of those few remaining forests, and that the owl is the most powerful legal means to do so. The owl is not popular among loggers, whose livelihoods depend on those forests; in fact, many loggers would like to kill owls to open up more logging opportunities. Discuss the relevant management issues from the perspective of ecosystem protection, endangered species protection, and economic viability of the region.

## Suggestions for Further Reading

Chase, A. 1986. *Playing God in Yellowstone: The Destruction of America's First National Park.* Atlantic Monthly Press, Boston. This is a devastating, though one-sided, critique of national park management. It should be read in conjunction with Keiter and Boyce (1991), listed below.

Fiedler, P. L., R. Leidy, R. D. Laven, N. Gershenz and L. Saul. 1993. The contemporary paradigm in ecology and its implication for endangered species conservation. *Endangered Species Update* 10:7–12. This article contains a good discussion of the rationale of and some approaches for managing ecological processes.

Grumbine, R. E. 1992. *Ghost Bears: Exploring the Biodiversity Crisis.* Island Press, Washington, D.C. This book's general thesis is that the protection of biodiversity depends on large interconnected wildlands. The public's acceptance of such massive changes in land use will require fundamental changes in our value system. This is an important critique of the "species-by-species" approach to conserving biodiversity.

Keiter, R. B. and M. S. Boyce (eds.). 1991. *The Greater Yellowstone Ecosystem: Redefining America's Wilderness Heritage.* Yale University Press, New Haven. Both the Chase and Grumbine books provide critical perspectives on natural resource management. This edited volume contains good examples of the kind of research that is conducted in Yellowstone National Park and the surrounding lands.

Moran, E. F. 1990. *The Ecosystem Approach in Anthropology: From Concept to Practice.* University of Michigan Press, Ann Arbor. The cultural context of ecosystem management is usually left out of most publications that deal with the science of ecological management. Moran is one of the best known of the "ecological anthropologists," and his book provides a good introduction to the cultural context of conservation.

# Management to Meet Conservation Goals
## Applications

*Regardless of whether we wish to protect nature as it is, reconstitute it, correct imbalances, or merely keep options open, will we have the ability to plan such complex exercises, and the techniques to implement them?*

*David Western, 1989*

### How Are Management Decisions Made?

In ideal circumstances, conservation managers would focus their time and efforts on the protection and restoration of biodiversity and would head off crises by good advance planning. The unfortunate reality is that many of the decisions made by conservation managers are made in a rather ad hoc fashion simply because there are so many different kinds of small crises and contingencies to deal with. In a single day, a manager might have to decide the best way to prevent trail erosion, respond to requests from school groups to take nature walks through sensitive natural areas, resolve conflicts between scientists over the location of research plots, file permits to work with a federally listed endangered species, and attend a public hearing concerning the possible impact of a nearby development.

On a day-to-day basis, few managers of large conservation areas or projects have the luxury to contemplate the "big issues" in conservation, such as the ones addressed throughout this book; instead, their days are ruled by a "tyranny of small decisions." Yet, it is these same conservation managers who, in many cases, must create the management programs for conserving critical resources, protecting sensitive species, and identifying areas where research is needed.

How can a conservation manager function in such a confusing and demanding environment? We cannot offer a recipe, a generic solution, to this problem because the constraints vary considerably depending on whether the manager works for a public or a private agency, on the kinds of land use or other agreements in place, or whether the manager is responsible for the multiple resources of a large area or for the conservation of particular species. For example, the manager of a private forested reserve may have considerable freedom to create forest management plans, whereas the manager of a public national forest may have to meet criteria for timber yields and recreation, in which case conservation goals become part of a larger set of competing goals, objectives, and programs. We can, however, offer some general advice on planning management activities, based on experience in both tropical and temperate-zone management, in humid and semi-arid regions, and on many conversations with managers.

The planning process should have several general characteristics. It should be focused on achieving the principal management goals and not try to encompass too much. The process should lead to an adaptive and flexible management plan; that is, there should be periodic evaluations of how well the plan is achieving the goals, whether or not the goals need to be changed, and what modifications to the plan may need to be made. The plan should also develop around and implement the five principles of good management outlined in Chapter 11.

For the sake of illustration, suppose you have been hired to manage a large reserve for a private conservation organization, such as The Nature Conservancy (the same principles would apply to most management scenarios). The following steps should lead to a sound structure on which good management decisions can be based.

1. *Review the mission statement.* Conservation management, whether of a protected reserve, multiple-use public land, or for recovery of endangered species, needs to proceed from clear goals and objectives. The absence of a clearly stated mission can easily lead to management inefficiency and to conflicting programs.

2. *Review the history of the site or program.* Learning as much as possible about the history of a site or program is important for two reasons. First, it is useful to know what changes have taken place in the landscape (Figure 12.1). For example, records for a locality that has an unusually low abundance of moose and elk might reveal the legacy of earlier disease epidemics and sug-

**Figure 12.1** Knowing and understanding the history of a natural area is critical to its protection. (A) In Ciénega Creek, southeastern Arizona, parts of the creek bed are intact and appear as they historically would have, with deeply deposited marsh sediments and a well-developed riparian forest. (B) Other parts of the creek, however, are incised 5–10 m into the sediments due to a history of cattle overgrazing, wood cutting, and other human abuses of the land. Such historical knowledge is crucial for protecting or restoring the landscape, and should be part of management plans. (Photographs by G. K. Meffe.)

(A)

(B)

gest that some efforts might be made to maintain isolated subpopulations to reduce the likelihood of new epidemics. The absence of desert grasses might be explained by a history of overgrazing, and such information would support reducing grazing allotments as part of a management plan for grass restoration. Second, a historical review might reveal important information about how neighboring private landowners perceive the biological reserve or conservation program, and help in enlisting their support.

3. *Identify the major specific problems that require management.* In many cases the problems will be evident, while others will emerge from research. The role of the manager is to identify problems at an early stage while they are still manageable, to determine the essence of each problem, and to develop and implement plans for solving the problem or mitigating its effects. A particularly frustrating issue for managers is that many of the root causes of conservation problems are beyond their control. Thus, they are often left with no options but to offer proximate solutions. A good example is the problem of controlling invasive plants in Everglades National Park, discussed in Chapter 11. The ultimate cause of that problem is the altered hydrology of the Everglades due to water extraction for agricultural and urban consumers, but managers are forced to deal with invaders through proximal solutions such as removal of individual plants. It would help for managers to take an active role in educating the public about root causes of conservation crises; for example, the hydrology of the Everglades is now being improved, due in no small part to the constant efforts of park biologists to educate the public.

4. *Establish a group of formal or informal advisors.* This advisory group should include all relevant points of view: scientists, managers of similar reserves or programs, representatives of appropriate resource management agencies, representatives of conservation advocacy groups, and neighboring landowners. Because the solutions to many conservation problems will involve sociological and economic considerations as well as biology, the smart manager will seek advice from all quarters. The advisory group can be informal, just a directory of people the manager can talk to about particular problems, but it is generally more productive to formalize the advisory group, which tells its members that their advice is important. Many such advisory groups will expect no compensation for their time other than to know they are being taken seriously.

5. *Develop a management plan for the reserve.* The previous four steps should all lead to development of a comprehensive management plan, whose purpose is to define the major goals and objectives to be accomplished and to project the resources needed. Generally, a 5-year time frame is reasonable; anything beyond 5 years for planning purposes is probably speculation. A management plan for a reserve should include planning for the physical plant (such as buildings, roads, and waste disposal), and for budgetary and personnel needs. It should also include zoning for different uses (for example, public use areas, areas for manipulative research, areas for observational research only, wilderness areas, and areas for educational use). All management plans should include milestones for evaluating progress in meeting goals and objectives, and should be reviewed and probably revised on an annual basis.

6. *Develop annual work plans.* Management plans are general planning documents, but they do not specifically tell you what to do during the year to actually implement the plan (such as establish five, 10-ha research grids with marked coordinates, or radio-collar 20 adult bobcats), nor will they tell you what the line items of your annual budget will include. For these pur-

poses, you will need to develop detailed annual work plans. Often these work plans lock the manager into a rigid set of priorities for the year, so they should be developed with considerable thought.

7. *Develop an inventory of resources and a site description.* Various kinds of inventories will be appropriate. For a conservation area, lists of species occurrences and site locales, a reference museum, and photographs and other historical documents of land use and changes will be appropriate. For a species management or recovery program it may suffice to simply collate reports and other "gray literature" that is not broadly available. These inventories will be useful for management purposes, and they will also make the reserve or program more attractive to researchers and conservation courses. The inventories thus serve three possible purposes: to support management decisions, to attract research collaboration, and to allow the reserve or project to contribute to environmental education (another way of addressing root causes of environmental problems).

8. *Identify key areas where research is needed.* Good management of conservation problems involves identifying priority areas where research is needed to support management decisions. The advisory committee, with its interdisciplinary mix and diverse makeup, can be put to good use in formulating research questions. It is also helpful and efficient to develop and maintain good interactions with appropriate universities and agencies where research talent can be found. If seed money is available to attract graduate students, this can be a particularly valuable means to leverage larger research efforts. Managers of large comprehensive areas should make a special effort to write proposals and otherwise seek funds to improve living quarters and laboratories for professional and student researchers, a powerful attractor for conservation scientists. Managers also should be directly engaged in conservation research themselves and not simply see themselves as facilitators for other researchers.

9. *Maintain good relations with the local community.* Managers should develop the mindset that the community is a critical resource, and that long-term successful conservation will depend on having good community support. Inviting community participation on the advisory committee, making the management area available as an outdoor classroom for local schools, and providing nature tours are just a few of the many ways that the reserve or conservation program can become an integral part of the community.

10. *Look for opportunities to develop cooperative agreements for land use and resource sharing.* Examples include developing a memorandum of understanding with a public agency such as the Bureau of Land Management that would allow researchers access to adjacent agency land, or formal or informal agreements with private landowners. These kinds of agreements are important for three reasons. First, management areas are frequently too small to provide all the resources needed to maintain biodiversity (Chapters 9 and 10). Agreements to use surrounding lands as a buffer zone may increase the viability of the management area. Second, agreements with neighboring landowners and managers can be an effective means of reducing "external threats" such as contamination of streams, pesticide drift, and wildfires. Third, entering into land use agreements may provide access to a larger pool of human and physical resources.

Underlying all of these points, however, must be a healthy and rigorous philosophy toward management of biodiversity. "Good management" really is a function of how one defines the goals and directions of the endeavor, and the same management action may be judged positively under one value system and negatively under another. For example, clearcutting old-growth forests is considered very good resource management if the goal is short-term timber production, and the manager who produces more board-feet is commended and rewarded under that value system. Under a value system based in conservation of biodiversity, the same action is considered objectionable and even unconscionable. Thus, like beauty, "good management" is in the eye of the beholder, and depends on the particular philosophical underpinnings and value system. An example of disparate value systems in management is discussed with respect to conservation of desert fishes in Essay 12A by Edwin P. Pister.

Successful conservation management must be applied at different levels of ecological organization, from the population to the landscape, depending on place and circumstance. With this background in developing a sound management decision agenda, we can now look at some specifics of managing at different levels of ecological organization, and the different and sometimes conflicting goals of conservation management.

## ESSAY 12A
# The Importance of Value Systems in Management
## Considerations in Desert Fish Management

Edwin P. Pister, Bishop, California

As one who started his career in 1953 managing game fish populations for the California Department of Fish and Game in the state's vast and heavily tourist-impacted eastern Sierra and desert regions, it has been encouraging to note how, during the ensuing 40 years, the priorities of society have grown more sophisticated in matters relating to conservation. Unfortunately, programs of resource management agencies have been slow in recognizing and responding to the public will.

During the two decades following World War II, most government fisheries management effort in the United States was directed toward satisfying the desires of a nation freed from wartime constraints and eager to explore outdoor recreation. This was the era of huge production trout hatcheries and reservoir management programs. Agency leadership assumed a complacent attitude that such programs would satisfy society's needs forever. All one had to do to accomplish this was build more fish hatcheries, and introduce into the reservoirs any alien game fish (regardless of the source or ecological consequence) that showed promise of improving angling for a while. Into this management scenario entered a cadre of fisheries biologists/managers, emerging in vast numbers from burgeoning fish and wildlife schools and eager to apply their newly learned technologies to satisfying angler demand

and, where this proved to be inadequate, to top off the harvest by calling for yet another hatchery truck. The term "biodiversity," yet unborn, lay dormant in the womb of a society unaware of adverse changes in fish communities that, even at this early date, were beginning to occur throughout the American West. In the context of this essay, the terms "manage" and "conserve" are essentially synonymous. What we are attempting to do now is manage for the conservation of biodiversity.

As one might expect, considering the basic need of fish for water, changes were first noted in the desert areas of North America, where negative biological impacts of water extraction and diversion by humans were soon recognized (Miller 1961). Government agencies in the Southwest (and nationwide) soon found themselves faced with responsibilities for which they were ill-prepared: management and preservation of a native fish fauna with which they were almost totally unfamiliar (or even unaware), known essentially only to academic researchers. Ironically, most agency knowledge of this component of the fauna derived from inventories conducted following chemical poisoning projects designed to eradicate native fishes. Up to that point, nongame fishes had been viewed primarily in the very negative context of being unwanted competitors with economically important, introduced game

species (Pister 1991).

Agencies were caught off-guard from two major perspectives: (1) their knowledge of the biology of many of these species and related ecological interactions was totally inadequate to assure the continued existence of an intact fauna, and (2) few individuals within these agencies were of a philosophical bent that encouraged enthusiasm for nongame management; those that were, were constantly plagued by a question posed by their peers and society: "What good are they?"—a question that, unfortunately, remains with us even today. The infancy of nongame species management is reflected in the fact that when Robert Rush Miller and I wrote a paper in 1971 on the management of the Owens pupfish, it was the first paper ever published in the Transactions of the American Fisheries Society relating to the management of a nongame, or commercially unimportant, species (Miller and Pister 1971).

It was the certain knowledge that government inertia in this respect would persist for at least a decade that caused a group of concerned scientists in 1969 to form the Desert Fishes Council, essentially to "hold the fort" until such time as fully funded management programs for native fishes could be implemented (Pister 1991). At this writing, nearly 25 years later, we still await full implementation, as both state and federal agencies struggle with perpetually underfunded programs in an often futile effort to fulfill their obligations under the provisions of the Endangered Species Act, and to conserve biodiversity within their jurisdictions. Federal suppression of environmental and endangered species programs during the environmental "Dark Ages" of the 1980s, a syndrome from which we are hopefully now emerging, was a major factor impeding development of a concerted national recovery effort.

Native fish faunas are in trouble primarily because of habitat destruction and change and because of introduced predacious and competitive species. Efforts to manage or conserve native fishes to date have taken several directions, chronicled in the Proceedings of the Desert Fishes Council and other publications. They include establishment of small refuges, free from alien species and designed to emulate as closely as possible the evolutionary habitat of the species or species complex, restoration of damaged habitat, artificial rearing facilities such as the Dexter National Fish Hatchery, operated by the U.S. Fish and Wildlife Service near Roswell, New Mexico, and acquisition

and protection of major habitat areas, utilizing an ecosystem integrity approach. In this latter instance managers must often learn to live with the existence of alien fishes and inexorable change due to increasing societal demands for water. Recent research on habitat preferences of desert fishes allows this information to be incorporated into operational plans of water development projects, thus assisting in management and recovery efforts.

The long-term importance of the refuge management approach cannot be overemphasized. If a North American desert fish species is not currently listed as endangered, it will not be long before it reaches that point. From all indications, urban development in the desert will continue indefinitely into the future, and each time a new dwelling is connected to a domestic water supply, it either directly or indirectly impacts an aquatic habitat. Very few desert aquatic habitats today even approach pristine, and the situation continues to deteriorate. We must live with the possibility that much of our desert aquatic fauna may eventually exist only in artificial refuges, or in greatly altered native habi-

tats. The ethics and evolutionary practicality of such a scenario provide much discussion for biologists and philosophers as we enter the next century.

Recovery efforts to date have primarily been holding actions, and very little "recovery" per se has been effected. This rather depressing situation will in all likelihood continue for as long as ever-increasing numbers of people demand an ever-increasing standard of living. We can only hope, before it is too late, that the values inherent in maintaining natural biodiversity will become sufficiently clear, and society will be willing to make the minor sacrifices necessary to retain it. Indiana University's Lynton Caldwell put it this way (Miller 1988):

"The environmental crisis is an outward manifestation of a crisis of mind and spirit. There could be no greater misconception of its meaning than to believe it to be concerned only with endangered wildlife, human-made ugliness, and pollution. These are part of it, but more importantly, *the crisis is concerned with the kind of creatures we are and what we must become in order to survive*" (emphasis added).

## Managing at the Population Level

### Managing for Sustained Yields

Managers of timber, fisheries, and game are interested in maintaining populations that can be logged, fished, or hunted in perpetuity; that is, they are interested in maintaining sustained yields. A sustained yield, whether by people catching fish, lions hunting zebra, or rabbits eating plants, simply means that the harvested individuals are not removed at a rate faster than they can be replaced in the population through reproduction. In practice, this simple relationship becomes complicated and difficult to achieve. This is true for even the most sophisticated harvest schemes.

The difficulty arises because we are seldom interested in taking just a few individuals. In human terms, "yield" implies an economic harvest, whether of commercial fish, recreational game animals, or timber. We usually want to know how close can we come to the **maximum sustained yield** (MSY) without jeopardizing the population. If a population behaved according to the classic logistic equation $dN/dt = rN[1-(N/K)]$ for growth with density-dependent mortality and birth rates, then its growth from a small to a large population would follow an S-shaped curve that is symmetrical around its inflection point (Figure 12.2). The MSY corresponds to the point on the curve that represents the maximum rate of recruitment into the population. For small populations, the individual reproductive rate is high but numbers are few; for high-density populations, crowding lowers individual and population reproductive rates. In this symmetrical growth curve, the maximum rate of recruitment occurs at the inflection point; hence the point of MSY is $K/2$.

So, all one has to do is have a rate of harvest such that the population is

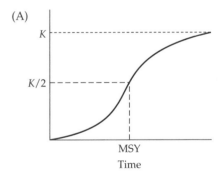

(A)

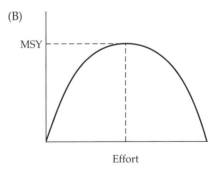

(B)

**Figure 12.2** Logistic growth curve (A) with point of maximum sustained yield, $K/2$, indicated; (B) drawn as a yield-per-effort curve.

kept at $K/2$, no higher and no lower, and you will have achieved MSY. If it is that simple, why do we not have a very clear idea of the MSY for any species? The answer embraces all the complexities of population dynamics. First, populations are not controlled by the deterministic logistic equation. As Hall (1988) has pointed out, only a few artificial laboratory populations appear to follow the logistic growth curve. Second, $K$, the carrying capacity of the environment, is essentially impossible to identify accurately, and because the environment is never constant, it is not a constant value. Third, because there are important sources of environmental stochasticity that influence birth and death rates, the intrinsic rate of increase ($r$) is not a simple function of population density ($N$) and reproductive physiology. Finally, population growth is often strongly influenced by the number of individuals moving into and out of the population, that is, by immigration and emigration. Net migration in any one population is, in turn, influenced by the spatial pattern, the quality of habitats, and population densities in the surrounding landscape.

The foregoing problems indicate that $K/2$ is a moving, and perhaps illusory, target, and the population density that corresponds to MSY becomes a very fuzzy region. If we set our harvest goals too far below the actual value of $K/2$, then we are economically inefficient, that is, we could increase net profit if we harvested more individuals. On the other hand, if our harvest goal is set too far above the real level of MSY, then we may remove too many individuals and put the population at risk of extinction.

In practice, the problems with MSY are even worse. We almost never know the real population size ($N$) but only estimates of $N$, which may be highly inaccurate. In some cases, local populations are maintained by immigrants whose rate of arrival may be independent of the local population density (although their successful colonization may depend on the local population density being neither too high nor too low). Rates of immigration are exceedingly difficult to estimate and are often ignored. However, underestimating significant immigration as a component of $N$ will inflate the apparent birth rate and/or deflate the apparent death rate, thus erroneously raising the estimation of $K/2$. The contribution of the immigration rate is important because the notion of a density that allows MSYs rests on the assumption that, at that density, the population will replace harvested individuals at the maximum rate, but immigration rates may be independent of harvest rates and intrinsic population growth.

Two further properties of many real populations cause particular difficulties for natural resource managers. The first is time lag. All of the population processes described in life tables require time before their effects on population density are fully expressed. Commercial, recreational, and subsistence forms of hunting and fishing are just special forms of mortality that may be specific to particular age or size classes or even to one sex. Because mortality can affect age structure, sex ratios, and social systems, the full population effects of hunting and fishing in any one year may take several years to be expressed, particularly in longer-lived species such as whales or sea turtles. Thus, an increased harvest effort may result in a short-term increase in yield but a sustained decrease over a longer time period. *Management decisions based on short-term responses could be counterproductive in the longer term.*

The second difficult property of populations is the minimum viable population (MVP) size, discussed in Chapter 7. Estimates of MVP have exactly the same sources of uncertainty that are present in estimates of maximum sustained yields. Recall that small populations are more vulnerable to extinction than large populations, due to stochastic environmental events, genetic losses, and in some cases, the low probability of finding mates. If a population is exploited such that density drops below this level, the probability of extinction greatly increases.

With all of the biological uncertainties involved in estimating the population density that results in a MSY, it is not surprising that there have been few instances of management providing long-term sustainable yields. The two most commonly cited examples are certain forms of forest management and commercial fisheries.

In forests managed for timber production, tree density, growth rates, and reproduction can all be managed through various silvicultural methods to produce high yields (Figure 12.3). On United States National Forest lands, trees are cut to meet a mandate for MSY for each harvested species. Thus, for managed temperate zone forests, one would think that the necessary population parameters for determining MSY should be known with considerable precision. Additionally, the long generation time of trees means that tree populations are less susceptible to short-term environmental stochasticity. However, whether or not timber management in national forests is meeting the mandate for maintaining maximum sustained yields is at least debatable. First, few stands have been harvested for more than one or two cutting cycles, so the empirical basis for determining whether or not MSY has been reached is very incomplete. Second, the resource management principle that natural systems can be harvested on a sustainable basis loses much of its meaning if the natural system is transformed into a production system. Silvicultural practices that include intensive site preparation, removal of potentially competing species, replanting with single species, and extensive use of herbicides and fertilizers fundamentally change the natural forest ecosystem. Under these conditions, a forest managed for maximum sustained yield has a closer ecosystem analogy with a wheat field than with a natural forest.

In commercial fisheries, population estimates are far less precise, and significant immigration and recruitment from areas remote from the area of harvest are common. Fisheries management has therefore relied heavily on the use of techniques for estimating population density from partial samples, combined with sophisticated computer modeling. Mistakes are to be expected in this approach, and a major objective is to make management as adaptive as possible so that corrective measures can be taken. For example, different mesh sizes in fishing nets can be used to selectively harvest different age classes in an anchovy fishery (Figure 12.4). Because each age class

(A)

(B)

(C)

**Figure 12.3** (A) High-density loblolly pine monoculture grown for pulpwood; (B) lower density loblolly pine monoculture grown for timber; (C) mixed pine/hardwood system for both wildlife and timber. (Photographs by C. R. Carroll.)

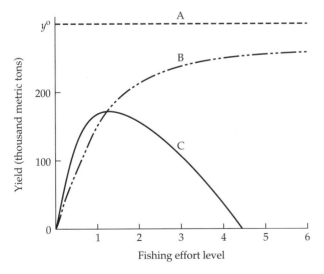

**Figure 12.4** The effects of mesh size of fishing nets on the sustainability of the South African anchovy fishery. Curve A represents the theoretical ultimate maximum sustained yield ($y^o$) that could be attained if it were possible to select any age class for harvest. Curve B represents the effect of harvesting age class 3 and older. Curve C represents a harvest of age class 1 and older. Note that a net mesh size that would release age classes younger than 3 would provide a sustainable fishery (curve B), but a nonselective mesh would harvest the highest immediate yields with the lowest fishing effort (curve C). The addition of more fishing boats has little effect on curve B, but rapidly degrades the nonselective fishery (curve C). (From Getz and Haight 1989.)

makes a characteristic contribution to population growth through age-specific fecundity and mortality rates, it is possible to achieve sustainable yields by using the appropriate mesh size in nets. However, a nonselective mesh size, which captures all age classes, would produce the highest yields with the lowest fishing effort and thus be economically most efficient in the short term, but not sustainable in the long term. Getz and Haight (1989) and Clark (1990) are good sources for an advanced treatment of the use of such models in population harvesting.

However, even for our "best" examples of sustainable use, forests are frequently overcut and fisheries typically depleted and then abandoned. Why does that happen? One might imagine that low economic returns would ensure that populations would not be commercially harvested below this minimum viable level; however, as you will see in Chapter 15, there are many difficulties with a laissez-faire economic approach to the management of biological resources. Furthermore, there is frequently economic and political pressure on the manager to increase short-term yields, even at the expense of long-term sustainability. The consequence of erring on the side of excess harvest rates is that the population may quickly decline and even become locally extinct.

The history of exploitation of the Antarctic blue whale (*Balaenoptera musculus*) illustrates how overexploitation can lead to a decline toward extinction. By the early 1960s, populations of the blue whale had drastically declined. In spite of an international ban on hunting initiated in the early 1970s, populations have not recovered (Small 1971; Clark 1990), and the future of the species remains clouded. There may be some reason for optimism: in the last few years, blue whale sightings off the California coast have increased (Baskin 1993). How much of the increase is due to population growth versus changing migration patterns is, however, unknown. Clark (1990) has convincingly argued that the deliberate overexploitation of biological resources possessing low rates of return—that is, low rates of biological growth—is widespread. He notes that, "If forests, marine mammals, or grazing lands are incapable of replenishing themselves at sufficiently high rates, economically rational owners will tend to overexploit these resources." The economic aspects of this issue are discussed in Chapter 15.

From this brief discussion of population management for sustained yields, we can take two important lessons for management of individual species populations: (1) our ability to maintain a population at a particular level through management is limited by the inherent difficulties in estimating critical population parameters and by the time lags characteristic of biological systems; and (2) where the population is managed as a renewable natural resource for economic gain, there will typically be a conflict between managing for sustained yield and harvesting for the maximum economic return.

### Conflicts in Single-Species Management: Lessons from Game Management

In Chapter 11, we emphasized the limitations of managing for single species, and stressed that management should be focused on how best to maintain the ecological system that supports biodiversity. This does not mean that recovery plans for endangered species or other single-species management efforts are unimportant, but rather that, if we hope to develop proactive approaches to conservation, we will have to develop more holistic goals. Within these holistic goals, single-species management remains an important approach.

Management of single species can lead to maximizing production of a few species without regard to the community/ecosystem in which they occur.

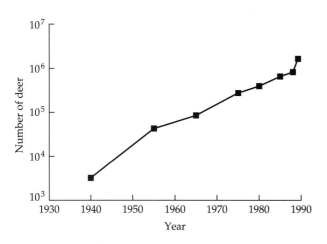

**Figure 12.5**   Populations of white-tailed deer in Georgia have grown exponentially for the past several decades. (From Odum 1988.)

Achieving high densities for one species may cause serious habitat degradation and reduce biodiversity. For example, deer populations can be increased and held at high levels by providing them with special plantings of forage, but the resulting high deer densities may have negative effects on natural vegetation. In Georgia, white-tailed deer populations have grown exponentially for the past several decades (Figure 12.5); throughout much of their range, plants have been directly affected by high deer densities, and a few plants have been affected secondarily as deer modify the habitat (Table 12.1).

The effects of non-native game species on habitats and biodiversity can be particularly harmful. Until the latter part of this century there were few regulations in the United States controlling the transplant of native game species into new geographic ranges or even the introduction of exotic game species. This reflected a common attitude that nature was simply scenery and a source of recreational enjoyment. The consequences of those early unregulated times continue to plague conservation biologists today. Western rainbow trout introduced into eastern hatcheries carried pathogens (furunculosis) devastating to eastern brook trout (Piper et al. 1982). European boar introduced into the United States by private hunting clubs wreak havoc by rooting up large tracts of Hawaiian forests (Stone and Scott 1985) and have

**Table 12.1**
Plant Species Known to Be Affected by Large Deer Populations

| Plants/Species | Effects |
|---|---|
| Yew, white oak, live oak, pin cherry, sugar maple, white ash, yellow birch, eastern hemlock, blackberry, orchids, lilies | Decline when deer density is high |
| Leatherwood, wood sorrel | Indirectly affected by decline in eastern hemlock caused by deer browsing |
| Ferns, black cherry | Abundance increased by deer browsing |
| Tree seedlings | Seedling species diversity decreases |
| Deciduous trees | Affected more than coniferous vegetation by deer browsing |

*Note:* See Carroll 1992 for sources.

virtually eliminated oak regeneration in some localities in the California coastal ranges. Asian Pheasants may displace native Prairie Chickens, Axis deer may displace native deer when forage quality declines, and so on.

In too many cases the ecological and financial costs of eliminating these exotic game species is more than the habitat or the management budgets can bear. The United States National Park Service has forbidden introduction of exotic species into parklands for many years; however, this proscription does not hold for all public lands. In 1977, President Carter signed an executive order that restricted, but did not completely forbid, the introduction of exotic species onto federal lands. Either the Secretary of the Interior or the Secretary of Agriculture can authorize the introduction of exotics if they determine that there will be no negative impacts on native species. Except for certain listed pest or endangered species, private citizens can still introduce exotic, and potentially invasive, species onto their lands.

In spite of the narrow focus of game management studies, many important conceptual contributions and, especially, field techniques have come from single-species studies that may have application to the study and management of rare and/or endangered species. Some of the more significant examples include: mark–recapture and other techniques for estimating population sizes; radiotelemetry for determining movement patterns and habitat utilization; various methods for determining diet from stomach contents and fecal analysis; methods for aging individuals and thereby permitting life table analyses; techniques for assessing the significance of parasites and pathogens; measures of "health" and reproductive status from body fat, hormone titers, and fecal analysis; and the relationship between habitat "quality" and carrying capacity. We have also learned from game studies a very important lesson, the value of native predators, and many contemporary conservation programs now involve predator reintroductions, a topic taken up in Essay 12B by Robert Warren.

---

## ESSAY 12B

# An Emerging Management Tool
## Large Mammal Predator Reintroductions

Robert J. Warren, University of Georgia

Early species transplantation and reintroduction efforts conducted by wildlife managers in North America were designed to restore game animals into areas from which they had been extirpated in the late 19th and early 20th centuries. These early wildlife restoration efforts were funded from hunting license sales and taxes on sporting arms and ammunition. Thus, state and federal wildlife agencies appropriately directed most of their efforts toward reintroducing game species.

Today, with the greater level of interest in nongame, community, and ecosystem-level management, wildlife and conservation biologists are investigating the potential of predator reintroductions in an effort to restore wildlife communities in specific areas. However, the decision and the process whereby one implements a program to reintroduce predators requires more than merely consideration of biological and ecological questions. Of equal importance are public and political questions. In this essay I will present general considerations for a predator reintroduction program by using examples of current mammalian predator reintroduction efforts—three for felid (cat) species and two for canid (dog) species.

One of the more important requirements for successful predator reintroduction is suitable habitat, which in part requires an abundant supply of prey. However, an equally important consideration is the area's degree of isolation. Almost all sites to which predators have been reintroduced or are proposed for reintroduction are large, rather isolated areas of public land, such as national parks or wildlife refuges. An appropriately sized area is obviously important, given the relatively large home range sizes of most wild felids or canids.

However, one must also consider land ownership patterns and land uses surrounding the area proposed for predator reintroduction. Except in the instance of islands, predators are likely to move off the reintroduction site, and may represent a source of problems to surrounding landowners. Some of the red wolves (*Canis rufus*) reintroduced to Alligator River National Wildlife Refuge, North Carolina, had to be recaptured after wandering off the refuge. Indeed, even an island is not capable of ensuring that predators will not leave a reintroduction area. One bobcat (*Felis rufus*) reintroduced to Cumberland Island National Seashore (CINS), Georgia, swam 1–2 miles of salt marsh and open water to return to the mainland.

The next consideration for predator reintroduction is the source of individuals. It is most desirable to translocate wild-trapped individuals from areas that are ecologically similar to the proposed reintroduction area. Such wild-trapped individuals are most likely to be genetically adapted to the reintroduction area, and generally are likely to have a greater chance of successfully establishing themselves than captive-reared individuals. My colleagues and I live-trapped bobcats from coastal Georgia for reintroduction to CINS. We also recruited local fur trappers to assist in the trapping effort by paying them more for an uninjured, live bobcat than the trappers could obtain by selling the animal's pelt. Diefenbach (1992) describes the detailed procedures for housing, handling, and transporting wild-trapped bobcats prior to reintroduction to CINS. In general, wild-trapped individuals should be quarantined for a few weeks and tested serologically to ensure they are free of disease. Davidson and Nettles (1992) describe some of the wildlife disease concerns associated with reintroduction of wild species in North America.

Obviously, a readily available source of individuals from threatened or endangered predator species is not to be found in the wild. Therefore, most threatened or endangered predator reintroduction programs require captive breeding. The 1982 Endangered Species Act Amendments provided for the experimental reintroduction of populations of endangered species. Most red wolf reintroduction efforts to date have been conducted with captive-reared individuals. The recovery effort for Florida panthers (*Felis concolor coryi*) uses, for captive breeding, individuals injured on highways. This recovery effort also includes field research on panthers in southern Florida to obtain the ecological data necessary for the even-

tual reintroduction of captive-reared or wild-trapped panthers to northern Florida. These researchers also have experimentally introduced sterilized, radio-collared mountain lions captured from western Texas into northern Florida (Belden and Hagedorn 1993). The use of surrogate panthers enabled the researchers to determine whether panthers could survive in northern Florida before risking reintroduction of an individual of the endangered subspecies.

Public and political concerns are of paramount importance to any predator reintroduction effort. Stipulations of the National Environmental Policy Act (NEPA; Public Law 91-190) apply to any predator reintroduction on public land. NEPA requires federal agencies to consider the environmental effects (including the human environment) of any proposed action. This usually is accomplished by preparation of an Environmental Assessment (EA) or an Environmental Impact Statement (EIS), which describes the proposed action and its possible environmental effects. These documents must be sent out for public review and comment. Wildlife and conservation biologists should be careful in the preparation of these documents, because public perceptions or misconceptions regarding predators may interfere with the proposed reintroduction efforts. Warren et al. (1990) and Brocke et al. (1990) describe important biopolitical lessons they learned in their dealings with public, political, and media concerns while attempting to reintroduce bobcats and lynx (*Lynx canadensis*), respectively.

The proposed reintroduction of gray wolves (*Canis lupus*) to Yellowstone National Park in Idaho, Montana, and Wyoming has been very controversial. This proposal potentially could affect several federal and state agencies, as well as park visitors and surrounding ranchers. The potential environmental effects of this reintroduction were so great that Congress ordered the U.S. Fish and Wildlife Service (FWS), in consultation with the National Park Service and U.S. Forest Service, to prepare a detailed EIS. The EIS included detailed

evaluations of historical evidence for the gray wolf in the area, sociological and economic effects of wolf reintroduction (this includes public and park visitor attitude surveys), and the management and ecological effects of wolves in the ecosystem (NPS and FWS 1990).

Predator reintroduction programs should not be justified on the basis of restoring control over a particular prey population, because the ecological interactions between most predator and prey populations are very complex. Predators are only one of a myriad of interacting factors that may affect the number of individuals in prey populations in a particular area. The reintroduction of bobcats to CINS was described as a "failure" in some media stories despite the fact that the reintroduced bobcats met the project's criteria of survival and reproduction on the island. Two news articles were published one year after the reintroduction, stating that the original justification for bobcat reintroduction had been to control the white-tailed deer (*Odocoileus virginianus*) population on the island, and that the bobcats had "done little to control the deer population" (Warren et al. 1990).

Finally, it is important that wildlife and conservation biologists evaluate the success of their predator reintroduction efforts. A species reintroduction effort is only successful if it results in a self-sustaining population. Hence, information on survival and reproduction of the reintroduced predators must be obtained. Bobcats reintroduced on CINS were released with radio-transmitter collars. These transmitters revealed the location of females in dens to document kitten production, but also emitted a special signal if the bobcat died. These data on survival and reproduction provided the basis for a computer model that considered inbreeding and loss of genetic diversity, median population persistence time, and whether future supplemental releases of bobcats might be warranted (Diefenbach 1992). In essence, the work on a predator reintroduction project only just begins after the releases have occurred.

## Managing Species as Surrogates for the Larger Community

Because it will not be possible to include all species in management plans, management for biodiversity may be achieved by focusing on management of indicator species that can act as surrogates for the larger community. This strategy requires monitoring populations of, and long-term habitat suitability for, species that are known to be sensitive to habitat fragmentation, pollution, or other stresses that degrade biodiversity. For example, with the growing evidence for widespread decline in amphibian populations, Vitt et al. (1990) suggested that amphibians may be useful indicators of environmental degradation because they may be more sensitive to environmental stresses than are other vertebrates. However, they may be inappropriate indicator species on other grounds. Pechmann et al. (1991) analyzed long-term data sets on amphibian populations in South Carolina and showed that their population densities can fluctuate greatly from year to year, even with no human influences (Figure 12.6). This implies that the population dynamics of at least some amphibians are too "noisy" for them to be good indicators of habitat change; that is, they may respond to environmental events that are insignificant to the larger community. On the other hand, they may be good indicators of normal temporal dynamics of at least a subset of the other species.

Another problem with potential indicator species involves longevity. Long-lived species may persist in an altered habitat for decades, but not reproduce. This occurred with razorback suckers (*Xyrauchen texanus*) in several reservoirs of the Colorado River drainage in Arizona. Adults persisted for 40 years or more in reservoirs after dams were constructed, but there has been no evidence of recruitment (Minckley 1983), making the presence of adults a poor indicator of environmental change. As pointed out in Chapter 11, the choice of appropriate indicator species that can act as surrogates for the larger community is difficult and probably will never be completely success-

**Figure 12.6**  Natural fluctuations in population size of three species of salamanders (A–C) and one species of frog (D) in a temporary pond, Rainbow Bay, in South Carolina from 1979 to 1990. Both breeding females (left axis) and metamorphosing juveniles (right axis) vary greatly annually, and some species disappear from and reappear in the system. Such species may be poor choices as indicator species for the larger system, since their natural, or background, population fluctuations are so large. (From Pechmann et al. 1991.)

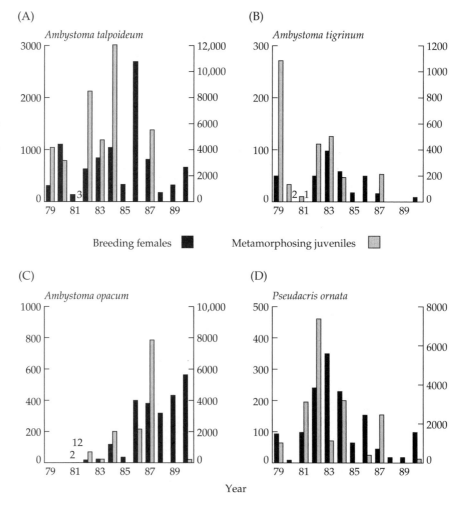

ful. Great caution must be applied, or the concept can be easily misused. This should not be surprising given the complexities and diversities of taxa and life histories that are represented in any habitat.

## Habitat Management

Management at the scale of habitats has been most intensively investigated for forests, deserts, and rangelands; that is, management has emphasized systems that are harvested for timber or grazed by livestock and native ungulates. The history of forest management provides the most comprehensive view of habitat management. Formerly, game management was often part of forest management plans, and multiple-use forest management in some regions was synonymous with production for trees, deer, and turkey. Now, United States federal forests are mandated to manage for nongame biodiversity as well.

The most common private forest management practice in the southeastern United States is conversion of mixed-age hardwoods and pine to a monoculture of even-aged, short-rotation pine, typically loblolly or slash pine (Figure 12.7). These plantations are seldom allowed to grow for more than about 30 years before harvesting. Forest conversion to simple monocultures must have major effects on the diversity of other forest organisms, though investigations of these possible effects have only recently begun.

Once conversion to monoculture has taken place, the rapid successional process that follows also forces changes in forest biodiversity. In a 14-year study of wildlife responses to loblolly pine conversion in Alabama, Johnson (1986) found major effects on selected plants and game animals. Forb and vine cover declined after about the fifth year following pine planting. Populations of quail, raccoon, and opossum all declined in the later years of succession. Interestingly, even though deer forage was poor in the later successional years, deer populations remained high. Highly mobile deer herds were probably helped by the mosaic of conversion plots in the region that were in various stages of succession: the older conversions provided shelter

**Figure 12.7**   A short-rotational pine plantation. The loblolly pines in this photograph from the Georgia Piedmont are approximately 20 feet tall and 5 years old. (Photograph by C. R. Carroll.)

**Figure 12.8** This approximately 70-m tall tree in Costa Rica was toppled during a windstorm. Natural tree-falls in tropical forests create light gaps, which are required by many species of tropical trees for their regeneration. Forest management that mimics light gap dynamics is much preferable to clear-cutting and may be sustainable in the long term. (Photograph by C. R. Carroll.)

but poor food, while younger conversions offered poor shelter but high-quality food. Thus, the regional habitat mosaic maintained deer density.

However, forest management need not be analogous to monoculture crop production. Indeed, some management schemes attempt to use ecological principles to achieve sustained harvest while maintaining natural biodiversity. Polycyclic management is a method of harvesting mature trees from uneven-aged stands. Forest vertical structure has long been known to be an important determinant of forest bird diversity (MacArthur and MacArthur 1961), and the uneven-aged stand structure maintains some of the heterogeneous physical structure found in natural forests.

Another example of forest management compatible with biodiversity maintenance is the use of small strip clear-cuts. This form of management is designed to mimic the natural "gap-phase dynamics" of temperate and tropical forests (Figure 12.8). In unmanaged mature forests, a gap is created when a large tree falls and creates an opening in the canopy. The increase in light penetration allows saplings in the gap to grow rapidly and, until the canopy again begins to close, the gap is filled with small trees, shrubs, and herbaceous plants. Birds and other animals forage in these resource-rich gaps and disperse seeds throughout the forest. Obviously, the frequency and size of gaps will be related to the age distribution and species composition of the forest trees, and gaps in even-aged monoculture plantations will be scarce. The strip clear-cut method, developed in the Palcazú Valley of Peru, is based on ecological principles learned from studies of gap-phase dynamics in natural forests, and is discussed in detail in Chapter 17, Case Study 1. Later in this chapter we will discuss the general significance of disturbance regimes as a management approach for maintaining biodiversity.

In the United States, various forest management schemes have been developed for enhancing game species while still permitting economic return from timber harvests. Typically, these programs are based on pine harvests; they require lower pine planting densities than in maximum yield harvest schemes and include some admixture of hardwoods and understory forbs and shrubs (see Figure 12.3C). For the most part, these methods are designed to improve habitat quality for a few game species, such as deer and turkey, and larger issues of biodiversity are incidental.

The National Forest Management Act of 1976 requires that protection of biodiversity be included in U.S. National Forest management plans. It is likely that management for biodiversity will become mandated for all federal lands. At present, we do not know what the optimal management plan for maintaining biodiversity in any particular forest would look like. In general, the twofold objective will be (1) to produce sustainable management practices that provide for multiple sources of revenue, such as timber, recreation, hunting leases, and other extractive uses; and (2) at the same time to maintain the biological integrity of the forest ecosystem. This is no small task and it is not at all evident that both objectives can be satisfactorily achieved, but some innovative attempts have begun.

One approach gaining acceptance in the southeastern United States is the development of selective harvesting techniques that ultimately generate uneven stands of pine–hardwood mixtures and thereby mimic natural forest structure and, to some extent, tree and understory diversity (Hunter 1990). It is important that such management schemes be based on scales larger than simply management of individual stands. It will be necessary to develop comprehensive management schemes that contain subprograms, applicable to the scale of individual stands, and these subprograms should be integrated at the higher level of regional landscapes. An example of this approach, as developed by Pulliam and his students for Bachman's Sparrow in pine stands, was discussed in Chapter 7.

**Assessing Habitat Quality**

There have been numerous attempts to assess habitat quality for particular species. Probably the most widely practiced method in the United States is the **Habitat Suitability Index (HSI),** which, together with the **Habitat Evaluation Procedures (HEP)** developed by the U.S. Fish and Wildlife Service, has frequently been used to assess habitat. That is, HSI and HEP form the core of a decision-making process for evaluating the aggregate habitat quality of an area. Essay 14A offers a different perspective on biological indices used in management.

The Habitat Suitability Index is a ratio of actual habitat quality to optimal habitat quality, and has many implicit assumptions, not the least of which is that we can accurately and appropriately assess habitat quality for a given species. Optimal habitat is defined as the maximum carrying capacity ($K$) for that type of habitat. The resources of that "optimal" habitat are used as the reference against which resources in the observed habitat are measured. Thus, an HSI of 0.5 means that a unit area of that habitat can support approximately half of the population that could be supported in an optimal habitat.

The Habitat Evaluation Procedure combines measures of habitat quality in terms of numbers of habitat units (HU), where HU = HSI × Area. A comparison of two wetland areas, based on HEP, would compare the total HUs for each wetland. This means that the wetlands could be compared just on the HEP values for duck habitat, or on a community basis where HSIs would be developed for each species. Note that a large wetland with a low HSI could have the same HEP value as a small, but high-quality, wetland because of its size.

The advantage of HEP and similar approaches is that they are flexible and, because they are unitless, can be compared among species and be given additive scores. The HEP approach also has weaknesses: it assumes the existence of an optimal reference habitat, where optimality is defined by density of individuals rather than average reproductive success; it ignores the effects of immigration and spatial distribution of habitats; and it assumes that each resource in the habitat makes an equivalent contribution to the carrying capacity of the habitat. On this last point, a habitat that contained many nest sites might be equivalent (in the rating system) to a habitat that had abundant food. While there are many problems with the use of these indices, they provide some empirical basis for decision making in habitat management, such as in setting priorities for habitat restoration. Loar (1985) provides examples of the application of HEP models.

A more refined use of HSI applied to particularly important species, such as indicator species, keystone species, and other strongly interactive species, may be a useful contribution to management. It is possible to develop sets of habitat suitability indices specifically for indicator species. These indicator-species HSIs might then be useful for setting objective management goals, as implied above. In general, HSI approaches should be based on the relationship of habitat correlates to excess reproduction by a species rather than to simple density of the species. That is, HSI needs to be complementary to habitat source–sink models, as described in Chapter 7.

## Managing at the Community and Ecosystem Levels

Westman (1990) has argued that if the goal of conservation is to save as many species as possible, then it will be necessary to focus research on the structure of the community. Species vary in the number of functional links with other species and in the strength of those links. For some species, such as "keystone species," many strong links exist (Chapters 5 and 8); for other species the links may be few and relatively weak. Management-oriented research should emphasize species that have strong interactions with other species because their loss can result in disproportionate effects on the community. This is an important research objective because, for most systems, we do not know which species are strongly linked and which are only weakly linked to other species. Understanding this hierarchy is an important management objective.

Species or populations are usually not lost from an ecosystem independently of other species. Suites of weakly interactive species may be lost as part of a general process. For example, the loss of one species may be part of a decline of several taxa because the habitat is generally degraded. In other cases, though, direct and indirect relationships among species link their fates. This is especially true with mutualists and with keystone predators and competitors, that is, functionally important species. An example of a quite unusual case of ecosystem management involving an introduced keystone grazer is discussed in Essay 12C by Michael McCoy.

## ESSAY 12C

# Seasonal, Freshwater Marshes in the Tropics
## A Case in which Cattle Grazing Is Not Detrimental

Michael B. McCoy, Universidad Nacional , Costa Rica

You have probably heard about how the cattle industry in Latin American countries contributes to the elimination of tropical rainforests. The uproar over use of "south of the border beef" by American fast-food restaurant franchises is testimony to this concern. This issue involves a land use change that does contribute to the demise of these forests, mainly because alternative, sustainable uses have not been pursued. Humankind is now faced with the challenge of saving these forests. On the other hand, you would be surprised to learn that the opposite problem, cattle *removal*, has resulted in the demise of some seasonal, freshwater marshes in the tropics. In fact, if you want to see waterfowl in the seasonally dry tropics, your best bet is to visit a lowland cattle ranch!

In the 1980s, two internationally renowned tropical wetland ecosystems on opposite sides of the globe lost critical waterfowl habitat after removal of cattle grazing. In both cases, a sincere effort to protect a valuable ecosystem resulted in an unexpected effect with

severe consequences for the birdlife that depended on the resource. One of these marshes is in Keoladeo National Park, south of New Delhi, India (Ali and Vijayan 1986). I herein describe events in the second marsh, Palo Verde in Costa Rica, Central America, where cattle elimination resulted in a massive invasion of cattail (*Typha dominguensis*), which eliminated waterfowl habitat.

The Palo Verde marsh is about 5 km long and 1 km wide, and runs parallel to the Tempisque River about 20 km upstream from its mouth at the Gulf of Nicoya in northwestern Costa Rica (Guanacaste Province). Strong tidal fluctuations stir up riverbed sediment, which is deposited along the bank at high tide. The marsh, isolated from the river by a natural levee, fills with rainwater during the wet season to depths of up to 1.25 m. In December the marsh starts to dry and by April is completely dried out.

Since at least 1923, the marsh and natural levee (1000 ha) were heavily grazed by 10,000 to 15,000 cattle from

November (end of wet season) until March or April. As the upland areas dried and water became scarce, the cattle were brought to the marsh. After decades of grazing by up to 15 cows per hectare, an open marsh resulted, with virtually no tall emergent vegetation, but a diverse flora of about 60 species. During the wet season, large expanses of deeper water were covered only by floating vegetation (*Nymphea*). The undulating marsh floor created shallower islands where low-growing sedges (*Eleocharis mutata*) and small palo verde trees (*Parkinsonia aculeata*) thrived under shorter hydroperiods.

In December, with the onset of strong northeasterly trade winds and cattle in the marsh, the floating vegetation was broken up and pushed toward the shallower areas of sedges, creating open water in the deeper pools and channels. As water levels dropped, bands of exposed soil formed between the open water and the shallower sedgebeds. Shallow, open water near exposed soil was the attractant for the varied bird life that descended upon the marsh at that time.

By the time the marsh completely dried in late March or April, the emergent vegetation in the shallower areas, except the sedgebeds, was grazed to soil level or heavily trampled. This biomass reduction from cattle grazing was so great that there was not enough forage to support cattle again until the following November.

For decades, the marsh was probably the most important wetland in Central America for about 60 species of resident and migratory waterbirds. In 1979 we observed up to 35,000 Black-bellied Whistling Ducks, 25,000 migratory Blue-winged Teal, and many other species of migrants such as Northern Shovelers, American Widgeons, Ring-necked Ducks, and Lesser Scaups during the dry-season concentration (Sánchez et al. 1985). In addition to these migrants, up to 500 resident Muscovy Ducks and several hundred wading birds, such as Wood Storks, Roseate Spoonbills, Great Blue Herons, and three or four pairs of Jabiru Storks (only 40 remain in Costa Rica), were observed in the dry season. Because the marsh was a center of bird and plant diversity and abundance, after expropriation of the cattle ranch, the Board of Directors of the Agrarian Development Institute was motivated to donate the marsh and surrounding forest to the Costa Rican Wildlife Service in 1977 as the first National Wildlife Refuge in Latin America.

One of the first acts of the new administration (Costa Rican Wildlife Service) for this area was elimination of cattle from the refuge in 1980. From that moment on, we observed a rapid transformation of marsh vegetation in this highly productive ecosystem. The small patches of cattail that existed in 1980 were able to fill the open voids until what was once an expanse of 40–50 ha, had grown to cover 95% of the 500-ha marsh by 1988. By moving first into the deeper channels and then into the shallower sedgebeds, the cattails prevented the important interface of shallow, open water and exposed soil from forming during the dry season, resulting in a dramatic decrease in waterbirds during the 1980s. In February of 1988 we counted a peak of only 3000 Black-bellied Whistling Ducks and 500 Blue-winged Teal, and almost no wading birds arrived at the marsh.

To complicate matters, uncontrolled forest fires entered the marsh during the dry seasons of 1982–1985 and 1987. The flames from the dried cattail leaves destroyed virtually all palo verde trees (the only nesting sites for six pairs of Everglade Kites in 1979) and fertilized new cattail growth upon arrival of the wet season. Almost no other vegetation was able to grow in the dense cattail stands.

The elimination of grazing in the upland pastures adjacent to the dry forest was also detrimental. The prolific, 3-m-high African bluestem grass produced dangerous levels of combustible material. With each fire, some trees were felled and the forest was degraded. Over time, the non-native, fire-loving African grass invaded the forest openings and produced more fuel for the next fire, allowing increased forest reduction and bluestem invasion. Forest fires had never been a problem in the area during its ranch days.

The ecosystem's biodiversity thus seems to have been maintained by and benefited from cattle grazing, a rather unusual conclusion. With grazing removal, the diversity of Central America's most important marsh was severely reduced to a nearly 100% homogeneous cattail stand, the largest cattail marsh in the region; it also led to destruction of the tropical dry forest.

Many have asked what the marsh was like before grazing. Unfortunately we do not know. It is possible that this highly dynamic ecosystem was not a good waterfowl site. It is possible that grazing created and maintained an artificial system, but one desirable for waterfowl production. Some have suggested that grazing allowed the cattail to come in. If this is true, the presence of the cattle also kept the cattail in check. This same balance occurs in two similar marshes on the other side of the Tempisque River, where grazing prevents small patches of cattail from expanding.

The formation of large, successional cattail stands has also been a problem for marsh managers in North America. At the Horicon Marsh in Wisconsin, cattail covered only 30% of the area in 1947, but increased to 80% by 1971 (Buele 1979). These stands of dense, nearly impenetrable stems reduced the amount of open water and food-producing plants to the point that waterfowl use declined dramatically.

In 1987 we initiated research to restore the Palo Verde marsh to 1979 conditions. We found that mowing underwater could eliminate cattail stands. Moreover, cuts at soil level in shallow water (15 cm) during the early wet season promoted natural reestablishment of original floating vegetation, and cuts made in deeper water (80 cm) produced little vegetation and mostly open water. As water levels dropped after the opening up of 30 ha by this method, bird response was rapid and definite. For the first time in a decade, that all-important interface of open, shallow water and exposed soil sedgebeds once again formed along the margins in the deeply cut area. Black-bellied Whistling Ducks peaked at 17,000 and Blue-winged Teal at 4000 in 1990. Whistling Ducks used the floating vegetation, as did large wading birds such as White and Glossy Ibis; one pair of nesting Jabiru Storks fed exclusively in this habitat. Wood Storks and Roseate Spoonbills fed in the open water. Most of the original 60 species of plants came back on their own. After further, and modified, cattail control in 1991, Whistling Ducks increased to 20,000, and Blue-winged Teal reached 13,000.

As we open this marsh through mechanical methods, cattle grazing, at least in the dry season, should be reinstated. In addition to maintaining preferred waterfowl habitat, this approach can produce economic gains through modest grazing fees. Perhaps more importantly, neighboring small-scale ranchers can benefit, and the local inhabitants will ultimately determine the fate of this area. Efforts are under way to organize ranchers to not only graze their cattle on the marsh in the dry season, but also to graze the upland pasture during the wet season, thus protecting the dry forest by returning to the traditional grazing system that produced one of the most remarkable habitats in Central America.

---

The rich interactions that higher plants have with animals and microorganisms include some of the best-known examples of mutualisms, including specialist pollination syndromes, such as those of Neotropical orchids and euglossine bees; seed dispersal systems, such as those of elaiosome-bearing

**Figure 12.9** The bullhorn acacia has a close mutualistic relationship with ants, which protect the tree from some herbivores, and in turn receive protection from predators by living in specialized hollow thorns of the acacia. (Photograph by D. H. Janzen.)

seeds that are dispersed by ants (Figure 12.9) or terpene-scented fruits dispersed by bats; and microbial mutualisms, such as those of many legumes and their nitrogen-fixing *Rhizobium* bacteria root associates.

While direct species interaction is most apparent, indirect interactions, in which the interaction between species A and species B influences species C, can also be important. A dramatic example concerns the indirect effects of introducing the predatory Nile perch (see Figure 5.1), into Lake Victoria, Africa. Following the introduction, more than 200 species of endemic fish have disappeared or are threatened with extinction, and the explosive increase of Nile perch is a major factor in this extinction process. As an example of important indirect effects, the decline of algae-eating species may have contributed to recent increases in large blooms of blue-green algae. Bacteria feeding on the algae have depleted oxygen in large areas of the lake and contributed to extensive fish kills (Witte et al. 1992).

Despite the general importance of identifying "strong interactors," we need to remember that ecosystems may be resilient even to the loss of species that have strong links with other species. This can happen when the loss of one species results in compensatory increases in other species that have similar ecological roles. One of the most common trees in the North American eastern deciduous forest was the American chestnut. The prolific fruit production (mast) of chestnuts was dispersed by birds and was important in the diet of turkeys, deer, passenger pigeons, jays, and other animals. Thus, the chestnut was strongly linked to these other species. However, when chestnut blight all but wiped out the chestnut tree in the early part of this century (discussed in Chapter 8), other mast fruiting trees, especially oaks and beeches, increased in abundance. To the extent that the ecological roles of some species are similar, ecosystems are said to contain redundancy. Therefore, an important goal for conservation biologists is to understand the extent to which ecological roles of species add redundancy to ecosystems.

## Managing Ecosystem Processes

Management plans for the maintenance of biodiversity typically focus on higher animals and plants. However, critical ecosystem processes act as the life-support system for biodiversity, and because these processes are vulnerable, their protection should be included in management plans. For example, excess removal of fixed carbon and nitrogen may result from prescribed burning and clearing in logging operations, and from "debris dam" removal from streams (Figure 12.10), as well as through increased microbial respiration following soil disturbance and application of herbicides and fertilizers.

Analogous to keystone species are what might be called **key processes.** An ecosystem's rate of primary and secondary productivity is dependent on a few key biogeochemical processes. The two processes probably having the most general significance are the nitrogen and carbon cycles, although other nutrients may be limiting in particular circumstances; for example, lack of available phosphorus limits plant net productivity in many tropical forests. Nitrogen is the most commonly limiting nutrient in temperate terrestrial systems and is also the nutrient most sensitive to management practices. Nitrogen in the form of nitrates and ammonium is easily leached from soils, volatilized by fires, or converted to gaseous form through microbial processes. Carbon, as respired carbon dioxide, is an indication of the amount of total metabolic energy in flux and storage in the ecosystem. Also, carbon as a structural compound, such as cellulose, is a measure of the total plant biomass of the ecosystem. Nitrogen, phosphorus, and carbon cycles are essentially driven by biological processes in the sense that rates of transfer be-

**Figure 12.10**   Branches, logs, and other woody debris often collect in streams to form "debris dams" as shown in this stream in northwestern New Jersey. These dams retain nutrients, change flow patterns, provide cover for fishes and invertebrates, and are important sites of productivity in stream systems. (Photograph by G. K. Meffe.)

tween the pools of carbon, nitrogen, and phosphorus are determined by biological, especially microbial and higher plant, activities.

The greatest amount of carbon in biological systems is found in living plants, animals, and soil organic matter. The latter is important as a mechanism for cation exchange capacity, soil physical structure (bulk density, gas exchange, infiltration) and water storage. Soil stable aggregates (the union of large carbohydrate compounds with clay particles) are especially important in reducing erosional losses. Thus, while nitrogen is an important nutrient that maintains net productivity, carbon maintains soil fertility as an important structural component.

The so-called "New Forestry" approach to timber management is a good example of recognizing the importance of maintaining these nutrient cycles and protecting biodiversity. This enlightened approach to timber management was developed in the Pacific Northwest at the Andrews Experimental Forest by Jerry Franklin and his colleagues. They place particular emphasis on returning minerals and organic matter to the soil by leaving large amounts of tree limbs and twigs on the ground after tree harvest, reducing erosion by maintaining ground cover, and encouraging wildlife through habitat protection.

### A Caveat: Do We Need to (or Can We) Save All Species?

Not all species are critical to a community; some species can be lost from a habitat with little effect on the abundance or distribution of other species. Such weakly linked species will be difficult and not very cost-effective to include in management plans because they may each require individual attention unless they can be protected under the "umbrella" of habitat-scale management. This raises challenging questions. Should we dismiss species from explicit management consideration unless they can be shown to affect other species? Throughout this book, we argue that utilitarian approaches to nature should be augmented with broader perspectives that embrace other value systems. Have we, in effect, accepted a new version of utility by defining the value of a species in relation to its ecological role in an ecosystem? Or, do species have equal value independent of their ecosystem roles?

## The Landscape Scale

The largest unit of practical concern for managers of ecological systems is the landscape. Game and forest managers have a long history of involvement with landscape-scale issues: some game birds migrate, and waterfowl depend on networks of wetlands; fish may use entire drainage systems and migrate between rivers and oceans; game mammals may have distinct winter and summer habitats. Because natural areas are increasingly small, isolated, and surrounded by lands used to meet economic goals, conservation biologists must also deal with important management problems associated with landscape scales.

The expansion of agricultural, urban, and other economic landscapes affects natural areas and populations in three principal ways. First, natural ecosystems become disrupted, and important linkages may be changed. For example, wetlands do not exist independently of the uplands that supply their water. Therefore, management plans for a wetlands ecosystem will also have to include contingencies to deal with possible impacts from surrounding uplands, such as from chemical-intensive crop production. Second, the fragmentation of natural areas means that edges will become more important (Chapters 9 and 10). In an agricultural setting, the consequences of increasing the boundary/interior ratio of a natural area may be increased problems with establishment of invasive weeds, more nesting bird mortality from generalist predators and scavengers such as raccoons and crows (Wilcove et al. 1986), and more points of entry for agricultural chemicals. As natural areas become very small, boundary effects will reach all parts of the interior (Lovejoy et al. 1986). Third, as natural areas become increasingly distant from one another, local extinction rates may exceed recolonization rates for many species.

Special techniques, such as **remote sensing** and **geographic information systems** (GIS), are typically required for landscape-scale studies. Remote sensing may be based on low-altitude aerial photography or high-altitude satellite imagery (Figure 12.11). The former provides high resolution of rela-

**Figure 12.11**   Both (A) low-altitude aerial photography and (B) high-altitude satellite imagery provide valuable data sets for conservation practices dealing with landscape-scale issues. Both images are of the Savannah River, separating South Carolina (on right) from Georgia. The site in (A) is 3.75 km on a side, and is shown as an inset of the larger image in (B), which is 15.6 km on a side. Note the greater detail in (A), but the better overall landscape perspective in (B). Choosing the correct scale of landscape analysis is a matter of the particular interests and questions in each case. (Photographs courtesy of the Savannah River Ecology Laboratory.)

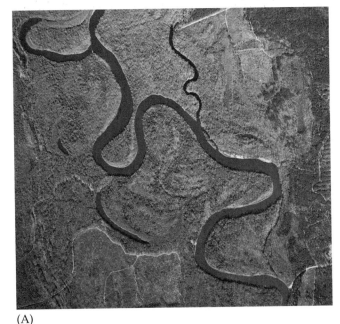

(A)

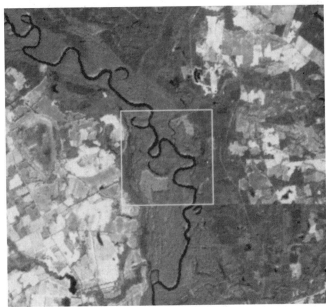

(B)

tively small areas, thereby sacrificing general information over large land-scapes; the latter provides low resolution of relatively large areas, thereby sacrificing detail for broad geographic information. The use of special films and filters allows different portions of the electromagnetic spectrum to be emphasized, and thus permits a focus on particular kinds of information. For example, photographs of landscapes taken with infrared film will show spatial variation in surface temperatures. Vegetation cover can easily be seen in these photographs and can be distinguished from rock, bare soil, or water. A recent international symposium on technology in natural resource management (ASPRS/ACSM/RT 1992) provides a good treatment of the application of GIS and remote sensing to resource conservation.

However, it is important to understand the limits of these techniques. Infrared film will easily detect vegetation, but only if it covers more than about one-third of a pixel, that is, a dot that forms the smallest unit of photographic resolution. Therefore, these photographs will bias vegetation cover by lumping areas of sparse vegetation with areas that lack vegetation. In desert regions, where plant cover is sometimes highly dispersed, infrared photography would fail to detect a substantial fraction of the total vegetation.

Remote sensing is especially useful for detecting major changes in land use, such as deforestation and conversion of forestlands to agriculture (Figure 12.12). Because the reflectance properties of plants vary somewhat by species and physiological condition of the plant, it is possible to correlate conditions on the ground with remote imagery. This technique can be used in detecting habitat degradation such as large changes in plant species composition, or loss of cover from overgrazing. Geostationary satellite imagery can be used to record environmental changes in a particular region over time through sequential photographs.

Computer-based geographic information systems are used to analyze spatially related data sets. GIS can be used, for example, to highlight topo-

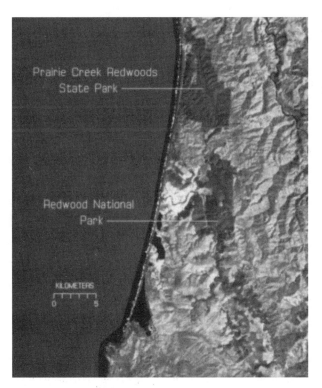

**Figure 12.12**   A satellite image of the northern California coast between Klamath and Trinidad. The remaining old-growth stands of redwoods (*Sequoia sempervirens*) and Douglas fir (*Pseudotsuga menziesii*) in parks appear dark in contrast to brighter areas of secondary forests and pastures. The image was developed using the near infrared reflectance from a Landsat Multi-Spectral Scanner scene obtained on April 8, 1988, and demonstrates the utility of remote sensing for detecting land use changes over time and space. (Photograph courtesy of Savannah River Ecology Laboratory.)

**Figure 12.13** Geographic information system techniques can be used to emphasize topographic features. This figure represents an exaggerated relief of a basin in the Coweeta Hydrologic Laboratory in North Carolina. (Courtesy of Kurt Saari.)

graphic relief, vegetation patterns, or any physical feature that can be displayed from remote sensing data. GIS can be a useful tool for selecting the best locations for reserves by facilitating mapping of centers of species richness, and for improving reserve design by emphasizing physical features, vegetation patterns, habitat delineation, and drainage basins (Figure 12.13).

An important application of GIS is so-called **GAP analysis**, developed by Michael Scott and his colleagues at the University of Idaho (Scott et al. 1987). GAP analysis uses various GIS-developed data bases such as vegetation maps, topography, current distribution of reserves, maps of private and public wildlands, and distribution maps of rare and endangered species. By superimposing these data bases, "gaps" between the distribution of an endangered mammal, for example, potential vegetation zones where it could thrive, and protection of lands necessary for its survival are readily identified. Management efforts are then initiated to fill in these gaps by protecting critical areas. The entire state of Idaho has been studied using GAP analysis, and many other states and various countries have adopted the approach to identify gaps in their biodiversity conservation and land use programs.

All this exciting technology must come with a warning: The products of GIS applications can be quite eye-catching, and it is easy to become seduced by the technology and to forget that GIS is simply a useful tool for answering questions about large spatial scales. To be properly used it must be combined with good ecological knowledge and good decision-making capabilities. Computers hold only data, not the answers to vexing conservation problems. These answers will always need to come from competent and creative conservationists.

## Critical Management Issues

### Conflicts Created by Multiple-Use Management

A difficult but pervasive problem in conservation is how to manage landscapes for both resource extraction and biodiversity protection, so-called multiple use. We will explore this problem by examining public lands, such as national forests, that are used for forestry and grazing, but the problem is more widespread. How can we protect native fish diversity in streams that are managed for sport fishing, or biodiversity on lands managed for deer or quail hunting? How can we protect biodiversity in parklands that are managed for recreation, or wilderness areas where mineral extraction occurs? An insightful perspective on multiple-use conflicts based on personal experience is offered by Edwin P. Pister in Essay 12D.

## ESSAY 12D
# Agency Multiple-Use Conflicts

Edwin P. Pister, Bishop, California

Having conducted my 38-year career within the philosophical and practical insulation of an essentially unilateral California Department of Fish and Game, dichotomies inherent within federal land and resource management departments and their constituent agencies have intrigued and perplexed me. Early on I had naively assumed that such agencies, and the personnel staffing them, were all focused toward a common and righteous goal, and essentially comprised a team directed toward the long-term benefit of the natural resource (and, therefore, the people). I was sadly mistaken! The infighting and budgetary battles within "the system," largely directed by politically driven economic considerations and pushed by Administration priorities in Washington, D.C., were astounding.

My first significant encounter with bureaucratic dichotomies involved five agencies within the U.S. Department of the Interior in the early days of an effort to save the Devil's Hole pupfish (*Cyprinodon diabolis*) in a remote portion of the Nevada desert. Devil's Hole (see Figure 5.2) is a disjunct portion of Death Valley National Monument, administered by the National Park Service, with the endangered fish primarily a responsibility of the U.S. Fish and Wildlife Service. Causing the fish's endangerment was deep well pumping on federal land administered by the Bureau of Land Management under lease to private farming interests, encouraged strongly by the Bureau of Reclamation, which was actively involved in drilling exploratory wells to allow more pumping. A fifth agency of Interior, the U.S. Geological Survey, was monitoring the venture, with its hydrologists confirming our worst fears that if the pumping were allowed to continue unabated, virtually every spring in the biological wonder-

land of Ash Meadows (Nye County, Nevada), along with its highly endemic biota, would be severely affected and ultimately destroyed (Deacon and Williams 1991). It was only after a strong threat of legal action that Secretary of the Interior Walter Hickel called together a Washington-level task force representing all involved agencies, and progress was made to save the fish.

Often we are not so fortunate. Devil's Hole and Ash Meadows were the subject of dramatic events that came and went rather quickly, with the fish ultimately receiving protection by a unanimous decision of the U.S. Supreme Court. Much more cumbersome and damaging to the nation's biodiversity are chronic problems resulting from multiple-use management on public lands throughout the western United States, primarily for extractive activities such as timber harvest, mining, livestock grazing, and energy development. A representative situation, which began for me in 1965 and persists to this day, involves the Inyo National Forest and a series of livestock grazing permits within the Golden Trout Wilderness of the southern Sierra Nevada.

During the 1860s, the meadows of the Kern River Plateau, 2500–3000 m in elevation and underlain by recently formed and very fragile granitic soils, were viewed by livestock operators as a source of quick wealth. Eyewitness accounts during the latter part of the 19th century told of invasions of hundreds of thousands of sheep and cattle that quickly removed the meadow grasses and began watershed degradation that has never fully healed (King 1935). Attempts by fish and wildlife biologists to effect significant reductions in livestock numbers were countered politically by the livestock operators, supported by a Forest Service range lobby eager to re-

tain a budgetary status quo. When the Golden Trout Wilderness was created under the Endangered American Wilderness Act of 1978, Western congressmen made retention of the grazing leases part of the price to be paid to achieve "wilderness" status. Consequently, a wilderness dedicated to California's state fish continually and needlessly suffers severe habitat degradation and riparian damage. Major eroded areas are widespread, riparian growth and undercut banks are virtually nonexistent, the best campsites near water have been reduced to dust bins fouled with cow manure, and one cannot drink safely from the South Fork Kern River (the evolutionary habitat of the golden trout, *Oncorhynchus aguabonita*) without prior filtering or boiling. The habitat change thus effected brought the added ecological problem of favoring an invasion of brown trout (*Salmo trutta*) which, in the early 1970s, nearly succeeded in extirpating the endemic goldens.

Other rare life forms have been similarly affected. A very rare species of sand verbena, *Abronia alpina*, exists on only a few acres of the Plateau and must be fenced by the Forest Service to protect it from cattle. Only recently has some progress been made toward rectifying these problems, utilizing an ecosystem-wide approach involving major adjustments in the cattle operation, fencing of riparian areas, erection of fish barriers, eradication of brown trout, and very costly repair of headcuts and eroded areas (USDA Forest Service 1982a,b).

To make the situation even less acceptable, cattle operations on public lands are often subsidized by taxpayers. The costs of supporting such programs are several times greater than revenues derived from lease fees, and monetary returns to the Forest Service are so minimal that many readers could (and would, if permitted) easily pay them out of their own pockets. Resource abuse under multiple-use management is not restricted to livestock operations. Perhaps even more flagrant is energy development in key recreation areas.

The Inyo National Forest constitutes perhaps the most heavily used (and therefore most important) recreation area in the United States. Located but a half day's drive away for more than 20 million people in metropolitan southern California, the Inyo presently supports more recreational use than Yellowstone, Grand Canyon, and Glacier National Parks combined. Yet, while geothermal features comprise major tourist attractions in Yellowstone, energy projects encouraged by multiple-use management have tapped the Inyo National Forest's geothermal resources (already very popular with tourists), which are gradually and inexorably being reduced, first to subsurface levels and eventually to nothing.

As Ellis (1975) points out in a classic paper describing geothermal development in New Zealand, "After major well production, the hot springs of Wairakei Geyser Valley and Broadlands no longer discharge, and what were once tourist attractions are now gray holes in the ground." When these fears were emphasized to federal decision makers during the environmental review process, they were almost totally ignored, and the plants were built, with accompanying press fanfare from Bureau of Land Management bureaucrats about how multiple-use management was playing a major role in freeing the nation from reliance upon foreign oil! (BLM administers all geothermal leases on federal lands). Absolutely no mention was made of the negative impacts.

Probably nothing is more intransigent than bureaucracy at the policymaking level that takes comfort in the status quo.

At this writing, predictions are indeed proving to be accurate. We are already experiencing "gray holes in the ground," a major trout hatchery operated on geothermally heated water since the 1930s is currently running at less than half capacity because of reduced flows and altered water temperatures, and the lawyers are sharpening their pencils. However, successful legal action would be but a hollow victory. It is unlikely that the geothermal resource will recover within several lifetimes. Considering the limited life expectancy of geothermal projects (30 years at best), even the most loyal, "system-dedicated" federal land manager would now find it difficult to defend such irresponsible development as achieving "the greatest good of the greatest number for the longest time." The underlying (but arguable) utilitarian principle of multiple-use management is a concept that badly needs to be redefined in light of modern ecological thought and understanding (Callicott 1989).

Similar threats are posed by hydroelectric development on the streams that form the basis and backbone of the roadside recreational resource. All this, of course, is simply because multiple-use management is expected, encouraged, and budgeted for on Forest Service and BLM lands, and valuable and irreplaceable resources located thereon are not afforded the protection required by law within the boundaries of a national park. Long-term destruction of publicly owned recreational resources is routinely sanctioned to accommodate private business interests.

What I have pointed out above con-

stitutes only the most obvious of problems created by the monster frequently produced by a combination of politics and multiple-use mandates. To livestock and energy development can be added other extractive uses such as mining and timber harvest. Even though local Forest Service and BLM officials may oppose particularly flagrant projects, they are required to fulfill the congressional mandates that direct their agencies, mandates that may be significantly skewed during pre-project evaluation and planning. Value judgments and resultant employee zeal basic to constructive change are seldom manifested and lie far outside of the training (or career aspirations) of most federal land managers. Many are keenly aware of the case involving John Mumma, Regional Forester from Missoula, Montana, who was fired from his job for refusing to implement timber harvest quotas assigned to him because doing so would have required violation of federal law (Wilkinson 1992).

The public can benefit in the long run from multiple-use management, but much too often politics and blind bureaucracy take precedence over the long-term public interest. It is not multiple use per se that works against the public interest, but questionable management priorities that allow certain favored uses to proceed to the detriment of the overall resource. Williams and Rinne (1992) propose a solution to this long-standing problem by suggesting management for biodiversity within a broader, ecosystem management approach, a concept that offers much hope for federal land managers and, more importantly, the publicly owned resources under their stewardship.

Whether a forest is managed to maximize sustained yield or for some specified economic return, a particular rotational time (the age of the tree at harvest) will be selected and applied to the entire management area. For example, in the southeastern United States pinelands, a rotational time of 30 years is common. The result is that the age structure of the forest is truncated by eliminating the older age classes of trees. In addition, noncommercial tree species are removed and, occasionally, the shrub and herbaceous understory is also removed. At the extreme, when a complex forest ecosystem is transformed into a production system for maximizing board feet of lumber, biodiversity will collapse. Can we avoid the extreme and find an acceptable compromise between narrow economic and broad conservation goals? This is an important question that will confront conservationists more frequently as pressures on our finite land base increase.

A major obstacle to addressing this question is the difficulty that traditional economists and conservationists have in communicating across disciplines. The economist's conventional cost–benefit approach to resource use is measured strictly in market values, and therefore is rejected by conservationists who balk at assigning market values to biodiversity or putting a price tag on species. On the other hand, many traditional economists refuse to recognize any value beyond economic return, or benefits beyond those measured in dollars, and therefore reject conservation arguments. In order to initiate rational discourse between resource economists and conservationists, we need objective measures of the real "costs" of different management decisions, cost measured both in lost revenue and in probabilities of population extinction, loss of genetic diversity, or modified ecosystem function.

Initial steps have been taken by Liu (1992), who coupled the spatial population models described in Chapter 7 with resource economic models used in timber management (Figure 12.14). Liu showed how different management decisions for harvesting pine would affect the probabilities of extinction for Bachman's Sparrow and the annual revenue from tree harvest. More importantly, by coupling these models he showed the probable least-cost ways to achieve reasonable protection for the sparrow while minimizing lost revenue. For example, because these birds require old-growth pine for successful reproduction, some patches of old-growth are a necessary requisite for population viability. Liu's model suggests that the spatial location of the old-growth patches within the pine stand can be as important as adding an additional old-growth patch (Figure 12.15). Similar approaches have been developed for habitat protection for the Northern Spotted Owl in the Pacific Northwest and the Red-cockaded Woodpecker in the southeast. As important as these efforts are, they represent just a beginning to the much more complex task of protecting many species in economic landscapes.

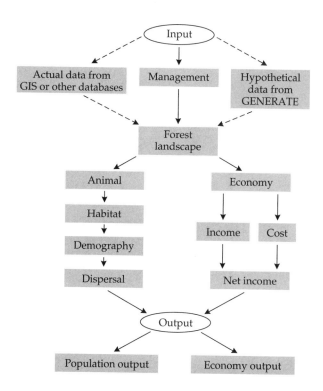

**Figure 12.14**   A flow diagram illustrating the process of simultaneously evaluating the consequences of timber cutting practices in terms of conservation and of economic effects. "GENERATE" is a computer software program that simulates various management scenarios. (From Liu 1992.)

**Figure 12.15**   The location of key habitats can strongly influence population dynamics. In this simulation model, the simple location of old-growth stands in the management area has a strong effect on sparrow populations. (From Liu 1992.)

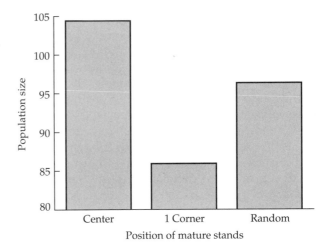

## Mimicking Nature: Disturbance Type, Frequency, Intensity, and Scale

Ecological systems in nature are strongly influenced by stochastic processes, and the disturbance patterns created by these processes are essential for maintaining a region's characteristic biodiversity. It would seem to follow that ecological management should attempt to restore disturbance regimes when they are artificially missing from protected areas. For example, the use of fires in prescribed burns for lowering the risk of catastrophic wildfires and for maintaining characteristic patterns of vegetation is a common and generally accepted management practice that follows this theme (see Essay 12E by Ronald Carroll, Katherine Kirkman, and Larry Landers).

## ESSAY 12E

# The Use of Fire in Habitat Management

C. Ronald Carroll, University of Georgia and
L. Katherine Kirkman and J. Larry Landers (late), J. W. Jones Ecological Research Center

Fire is a significant ecological factor in most terrestrial environments; only barren polar and extreme desert regions are free of its effects. The signature of past fires can be found in charcoal deposits in habitats as varied as dry upland pine forests, lowland swamps, and even the wettest Amazonian rainforests. Although nearly all habitats experience fire at least on rare occasions, there are some regions where fire is a frequent occurrence. Tallgrass prairie, savannas, and chaparral are dependent on the regular occurrence of fire every few years.

When lightning ignites a fire in an extensive habitat such as a large prairie, it may burn for days and cover thousands of hectares; thus, fires need to start in only one or a few places in order to affect large areas. However, when habitats become small and isolated, naturally occurring fires are less frequent. One of the consequences of habitat frag-

mentation is the removal or reduction of fire as an ecological disturbance process. When the frequency of fire declines, ecological changes as fundamental as altered biodiversity and reduced net productivity can occur. Some of the more common consequences of fire removal include the following:

1. In forests and shrublands, woody debris begins to accumulate. Mineral nutrients in the fallen wood, which would normally be returned to the soil as a pulse when the wood is consumed by fire, are returned more slowly during the long process of decomposition. Thus, the rate of nutrient cycling is changed.
2. Because of the accumulation of woody debris, when fires eventually occur, they may be exceptionally hot and kill much of the

vegetation (even fire-tolerant species) and volatilize soil nitrogen. Thus, the soil may be episodically depleted of available nitrogen for plants by catastrophic wildfires.
3. Because some plants are dependent on fire for reproduction, the absence of fire can cause local extinction of these species, or at least alter population and community dynamics. For example, the cones of some pines (e.g., sand pine, *Pinus clausa*) require fire before they open and shed their seeds, a condition known as serotiny. Some perennial herbaceous plants in grasslands, such as wiregrass (*Aristida stricta*), typically flower and fruit extensively after growing-season fires.

4. Some plants are characteristic of early successional areas and may disappear if fires do not create sufficient successional habitat for them. Some of these species, such as cherries, elderberries, and blackberries, produce copious amounts of fruit and are major food sources for frugivorous birds and mammals. Thus, the loss of post-fire early successional habitat could have significant indirect effects on birds and mammals.

5. In tree savannas, such as the longleaf pine savannas of the southeastern United States, fire suppression usually results in woody species invasion and displacement of grasses and other herbaceous species. Animals that are dependent on the savanna, such as gopher tortoises and indigo snakes, may also disappear as a result.

6. In perennial grasslands where grasses form clumps or "bunches," fires are important in maintaining high net productivity. Following a fire, perennial grasslands quickly replace lost biomass and add new growth. In the absence of fire, the senescing grass tillers (stems) shade the clump and reduce photosynthesis.

Fire has been used by humans for thousands of years throughout the tropical and temperate zones to manipulate natural resources by creating grasslands for hunting, opening farmland for agriculture, and driving game into traps. The landscape seen by the first European colonists arriving on the east coast of North America was highly modified by the burning practices of Native Americans who used fire to maintain fields for crops and second growth for hunting (Russell 1976). Fire is also an important management tool for contemporary conservation managers. In order to restore the ecological functions that were formerly provided by natural fires, conservation managers now commonly impose a fire regime technique generally referred to as "prescribed burning." Most commonly, prescribed burns are used to achieve three management goals: stimulating renewed grass growth in perennial grasslands, limiting encroachment of woody vegetation into savannas and mountain balds, and controlling accumulation of woody debris (called reducing "fuel-loads") in forests and shrublands. Even some wetlands, such as waterfowl habitat in Florida and prairie potholes in the midwestern United States, are managed by prescribed burning. Prescribed burning is also the easiest, and perhaps the only feasible, way to create and maintain habitat heterogeneity on large scales. Consequently, prescribed burning can be used to generate the kind of landscape heterogeneity that is necessary to support the metapopulation structure of some populations.

Some rare species are dependent on particular microhabitats that can be created and maintained through prescribed burning. In the longleaf pine savanna, the endangered plant *Schwalbea americana* (Scrophulariaceae) has an extremely narrow environmental requirement. The species is generally restricted to the narrow ecotone (border habitat) between periodically burned upland pine savanna and wetlands. This perennial plant appears to be dependent on fires for flowering.

As you might imagine, it is critical that the ecological system be well understood before prescribed burning is used as a management tool. For example, the species composition of trees invading old meadows in the eastern United States is influenced both by meadow voles (small rodents in the genus *Microtus*) and fire. The voles kill tree seedlings (Ostfeld and Canham 1993), but when vegetation cover is reduced by fire, herbivory decreases and tree seedling survival is greatly enhanced, even when voles are abundant.

Fire can be an extremely useful tool for conservation management, but should only be used as a tool in the context of a thorough understanding of the ecological system. In contrast to the old U.S. Forest Service perspective that fires were always damaging (Figure A) and Smokey Bear's admonition that "Only you can prevent forest fires," conservation biologists must convince the public that fire is a normal ecological process and should be accepted as an important part of the toolkit of conservation management. Fire becomes ecologically dysfunctional when our attempts to suppress fires fail, and catastrophic wildfires ultimately result.

**Figure A** The U.S. Forest Service's outlook on fires is a very anthropocentric, harvest-oriented perspective: every*one* (i.e., people) loses when a forest burns. In fact, many ecosystems are dependent upon periodic fires for their maintenance, and those forests "lose" if fire is suppressed. (Photograph by G. K. Meffe.)

The need to create disturbance regimes is generally inversely related to the size of the management area. In large areas, natural processes such as fires from lightning strikes, tree windthrows from storms, or sediment deposits from floods may maintain the appropriate disturbance regimes, and little or no management intervention may be needed. In small management areas, natural stochastic processes may not occur at the right frequency or scale, and management intervention may be necessary. Even when natural disturbances do occur in small protected areas, their consequences may not be the same as when they occur in large areas. As noted in Chapter 11, the fate of a tree-fall gap is related to the size of the forest. In very small forests surrounded by agricultural lands, the gap may be invaded by weedy species that compete with regenerating forest trees. In eastern United States forests, fragmentation of the rural landscape into small forest patches surrounded by young, second-growth vegetation supports high population densities of white-tailed deer. When a gap is formed in these small forest patches, whether from natural tree-falls and windthrows or through management, excessive browsing by deer can change the normal regenerative process (Table 12.1 gave examples of plants affected by deer browsing).

In practice, finding the level of management intervention that appropriately mimics a natural disturbance regime is difficult. Some of the important questions to address in this regard are:

1. Will the artificially created disturbance patch "behave" like a natural one? The answer will depend on how well management has created within-patch conditions similar to those created by natural disturbances. For example, prescribed burns for maintaining natural vegetation patterns should be done during the normal fire season if possible, and should create the patchy burn patterns seen in lightning-caused fires.

2. Do the patch dynamics depend on particular spatial patterns of other patches? If the patches are too large or too close together they could favor invasion by weedy and other generalist species.

3. Will implementation of disturbance regimes conflict with other parts of the larger management plan? A common conflict that managers face is the need to meet researchers' demands for long-term site security while meeting the need to create habitat disturbances. For example, researchers who are studying long-term population patterns in woodpeckers may agree in principle that fires are an essential part of maintaining normal forest structure, but will object strenuously to any suggestion that their part of the forest be burned while their study is in progress.

The 1988 wildfire that burned much of Yellowstone National Park stimulated considerable interest in landscape-scale management. Many studies illustrate the need for a landscape approach but also point out the difficult compromises that will have to be made. In northern Yellowstone National Park, elk survival during normal and severe winters is thought to be influenced by the pattern of fires. Survival appears to be greater when fires of small or intermediate scale (15% or 30% of the landscape) occur as single blocks rather than as isolated smaller fires (Turner et al. 1992). In the same region, streams such as Cache Creek and its tributaries, which are in heavily burned landscapes, were so strongly affected that biotic recovery may take many years (Minshall and Robinson 1992). Thus, a management strategy to improve elk survival through prescribed burns in large blocks would need to be evaluated in the context of possible increased negative effects on streams in the management area.

### Priorities for Management: Sensitive Natural Areas and Vulnerable Processes

Management requires allocation of limited resources: personnel, time, money, and expertise. Despite limiting resources, management decisions may not have to be so austere as to require triage, abandoning the species and systems least likely to be conserved or the ones most costly to save. However, managers will need to make cost-effective decisions and support priority areas. Fortunately, not all natural areas or the ecological processes contained within them require intensive active management. The following represents a taxonomy of natural areas and ecological processes that are likely to require the most active management to prevent serious resource degradation and local extinction. (For an expanded treatment of these priorities, see Carroll 1992.)

1. *Rare and declining species, habitats, and resources.* Of particular concern are species and natural areas that are rare and are undergoing rapid decline. However, some rare species and unique habitats have a long history of being rare, and may need little management to maintain their integrity, other than ensuring that they continue unaltered by humans.

2. *Small and fragmented habitats.* Fragmentation becomes a severe problem when migration is absent and the habitat quality is too poor or the area too small to sustain viable populations. Small areas may need to have critical resources augmented (e.g., planting fruit-bearing trees for frugivores), while the problem of isolation may have to be addressed through translocating individuals.

3. *Areas that are vulnerable because of location.* This is probably the most common problem that managers face. Areas near large human populations or intensively used lands face an enormous array of possible human impacts, such as stream pollution, wildfires, pesticide drift, and roads.

4. *Systems that have low resilience to perturbations.* These are usually ecosystems such as mountaintops, tundras, tropical forests on oxysols, and deserts that have low net primary productivity and hence recover slowly from disturbances. Because such systems are susceptible to irreversible damage, management must be proactive and preventative.

5. *Keystone species and processes.* Identifying which species have disproportionate effects in the ecosystem is an important research goal in conservation ecology. Management planning for these species should be done with particular care because any mistakes could have large community-wide effects.

These two chapters on management offer only an initial look at the complex, challenging, and sometimes frustrating world of the conservation manager. It should be clear that there are no set prescriptions, no clear and consistent rules by which conservation management actually proceeds. Every situation is unique, and each has its own complications and constraints. The best advise is to obtain as much relevant biological, sociological, economic, and political information as is available regarding a management situation, and act according to your best intuition on behalf of long-term perpetuation of biodiversity. Five real-world examples of conservation management follow in the case studies in Chapter 13. There, you will recognize many of the problems and opportunities that were discussed in more abstract terms in these last two chapters. There, you will see conservation management in action.

## Summary

The world of the conservation manager is challenging and complex. Many decisions on many fronts need to be made on a daily basis, with few opportunities for "cookbook" guidance and easy answers. However, we offer ten key planning activities that are common to most management scenarios, which should provide a basis for strong and informed management of conservation landscapes.

Conservation management proceeds at several spatial scales of interest. At the single-species or populational level, there is a long history of management for sustained yields, especially of game and commercial species. The results of such management are mixed at best, and no good examples of maximum sustained yield of a commercial animal species without eventual collapse exist. Single-species management is also the focus when using species as surrogates, or indicator species, for larger systems. Again, there are few examples of successful management on this basis.

The next level of scale, habitat management, shows promise for conservation if habitat manipulation for biodiversity, and not just for single species of interest, is pursued. Modification of existing habitat-scale practices, especially forest management and harvest techniques, to make them compatible with biodiversity conservation would make important contributions toward conservation at the habitat level.

Conservation at the community, ecosystem, and landscape levels probably offers the most promise for successful biodiversity conservation. Identification and management of critical species or processes, such as keystone species or nutrient cycling, has the promise of great advances in conservation practice. Technological advances such as remote sensing, satellite imagery, and geographic information systems are helping to quickly advance the utility of landscape-level management.

Some critical issues that are commonly faced by the conservation manager include the conflicts inherent in multiple-use management, the problem of mimicking nature by creating or promoting natural disturbances, and the choice of priorities for managing areas and ecological processes from among the many and conflicting demands. We offer suggestions for each of these areas.

## Questions for Discussion

1. What are the various ways that the multiple-use mandate for public lands creates conflicts with the protection of biodiversity? What can be done to resolve these conflicts?

2. An essential management goal is to maintain populations above their minimum levels for viability. Due to limited resources, you cannot determine MVPs for very many species. How will you decide which species to include in the analyses and which to leave out?

3. Some people have criticized the use of geographic information systems and remote sensing as just a fancy way to impress the people who control funding. Can you think of important issues in conservation that can best be addressed using these techniques?

4. For a natural habitat in your area, discuss which species are likely to be keystone species and what is needed to protect their populations.

5. Do you think that legislation is needed to protect landscapes that provide important environmental services, such as flood control, recreational amenities, or urban drinking water? What are some important environmental services in your area that are provided by natural environments?

6. For any habitat you wish to consider, describe how its biodiversity is influenced by natural and anthropogenic disturbances. How can these be approximated by some management method? Discuss this question in terms of type, scale, frequency, and intensity of disturbance.

7. Some ecologists say that the great fire that burned much of the vegetation in Yellowstone National Park a few years ago was natural and should have been left to burn itself out without intervention. Others maintain that the fire was a catastrophe and should have been more aggressively controlled. What is your position on the following question: "Should fires be controlled in national parks?"

8. If many natural areas are too small to support minimum viable populations of their larger and more charismatic species, why shouldn't we sell them and apply the money to other conservation efforts? What conservation value do you see for small reserves?

9. The multiple-use concept that guides much of the management of public lands in the United States and elsewhere often seems unbalanced toward economic development and away from biodiversity protection. How can the concept be modified to better accommodate conservation? Should the concept be abandoned, or is there a place for economic gain from public lands?

## Suggestions for Further Reading

Agee, J. K. and D. R. Johnson (eds.). 1988. *Ecosystem Management for Parks and Wilderness.* University of Washington Press, Seattle. This is a collection of articles that treat conservation management at the "system level" rather than at the level of individual populations. It is a good introduction to both the limitations of and the potential for managing ecosystems rather than individual species.

Ahlgren, C. E. and T. T. Kozlowski. 1974. *Fire and Ecosystems.* Academic Press, New York. Fire is one of the most important and pervasive sources of disturbance in natural ecosystems. This book provides good coverage of fire, both as a natural process that maintains landscape heterogeneity and as a management tool.

Hunter, M. L. 1990. *Wildlife, Forests, and Forestry: Principles of Managing Forests for Biodiversity.* Prentice Hall, Englewood Cliffs, NJ. A good general treatment of modern forest management in the context of conservation of biodiversity.

Mitchell, R. S., C. J. Sheviak and D. J. Leopold. 1990. *Ecosystem Management: Rare Species and Significant Habitats.* Proceedings of the 15th Annual Natural Areas Conference. New York State Museum Bulletin no. 471. Albany, NY. Despite the title, there are only a few articles about ecosystem-level management. This is a good collection of articles illustrating modern techniques and approaches for species and habitat management.

Office of Technology Assessment. 1987. *Technologies to maintain biological diversity.* OTA, Washington, D.C. As the title implies, this is a good overview of the various techniques, tools, and approaches for conserving biodiversity.

Turner, M. G. 1989. Landscape Ecology: The effect of pattern on process. *Annu. Rev. Ecol. Syst.* 20:171–197. This is one of the best reviews of landscape ecology as it relates to functional linkages among ecosystems and the ecological significance of spatial patterns in the landscape. For anyone interested in how heterogeneity in the landscape might influence ecological processes, this remains the best source of information.

# Conservation Management Case Studies

*The land is too various in its kinds, climates, conditions, declivities, aspects, and histories to conform to any generalized understanding or to prosper under generalized treatment.*

*Wendell Berry, 1977*

In Chapters 11 and 12 we developed the important principles of conservation management and discussed how these management principles and methodologies have been applied at scales ranging from individual populations to the landscape. In this chapter, we present five case studies that provide in-depth descriptions of important management issues, which weave in many of the themes and problems discussed in previous chapters.

The first three studies focus on the management of endangered species, or groups of species, and their systems. Black-footed ferrets, sea turtles, and Spotted Owls are all high-profile organisms that have received a great deal of attention in scientific circles and various news media. You will see the various problems and challenges facing managers in these very different scenarios, ranging from the need to understand the biology of secretive species, to altering human behavior in global ecosystems, to the tangled political and legal webs that managers are often caught in.

The last two studies deal with management of conservation areas: one focuses on a single tropical research station and its central mission of biological research and teaching, and the other on management of multiple systems, or conservation units, using the Costa Rican National System of Conservation Areas as a model. Both of these examples illustrate the multitude of management challenges facing anyone wanting to go from the theoretical world of concerns for reserve size, heterogeneity, and context, to the real world of selection and protection of reserves, with its issues of fund-raising, public acceptance, and legal recognition of reserves.

You will probably find that these studies are not very tidy. Management in the real world is usually a far cry from the neat, clear, and sensible layout of topics in textbooks. Messy issues such as lack of funding, conflicts with individuals or groups with different value systems, impacts on people's livelihoods, historical contingencies, and lack of cooperation or understanding by political leaders inflict themselves on the best-laid plans of conservation managers. The answer is to be flexible and adaptive, and to try to understand each management scenario as completely as possible, while keeping the overall goals of the program in mind.

## CASE STUDY 1

### Management of an Endangered Species: The Black-Footed Ferret

Dean E. Biggins, U.S. Fish and Wildlife Service, and
E. Tom Thorne, Wyoming Game and Fish Department

*This is the oldest recovery program for an endangered species in the United States. Among the management lessons illustrated are the need to conserve natural habitat to receive captive-bred individuals, the importance of landowner cooperation, and the need for flexibility in dealing with contingencies such as unexpected disease outbreaks.*

The black-footed ferret (*Mustela nigripes*, Figure 13.1) is a 600–1400-g mustelid (weasel family) whose closest relatives are the European (*M. putorius*) and Siberian (*M. eversmanni*) polecats. The former range of the black-footed ferret coincided with the ranges of the black-tailed (*Cynomys ludovicianus*), Gunnison's (*C. gunnisoni*), and white-tailed (*C. leucurus*) prairie dogs, extending from Saskatchewan to Texas. Despite this large range, ferrets declined precipitously in this century; they were listed as threatened in 1967 under the Endangered Species Preservation Act of 1966, and as endangered under the more comprehensive Endangered Species Act of 1973.

In response, the U.S Fish and Wildlife Service (FWS) established a recovery team in 1974, and in 1978 approved a recovery plan with the objective of maintaining at least one self-sustaining population within each state of the ferrets' former range; however, by the time the plan was adopted, ferrets had declined to near extinction.

### Causes of Decline

The most likely explanation for the decrease of black-footed ferrets is a huge decline in prairie dogs, which constitute about 90% of the ferrets' diet. From 1900 to the present, prairie dog abundances plummeted to about 5%–10% of their former numbers, largely due to agricultural development and extensive poisoning campaigns in the Great Plains, where prairie dogs are considered pests (Figure 13.2). Sylvatic plague, probably introduced to North America at about the turn of the century (Eskey and Haas 1940), also caused massive die-offs of prairie dogs (Barnes 1982).

By the 1940s, black-footed ferret habitat was already severely fragmented, and extirpated colonies of ferrets could no longer be reestablished by normal dispersal from remaining populations (Seal et al. 1989). By the winter of 1985, black-footed ferrets, having been reduced to about 10 known individuals, were probably the rarest mammals in the world.

### Recent History

Only two free-ranging ferret populations have been studied: a low-density population found in Mellette County, South Dakota, in 1964 (Henderson et al. 1969), and a population near Meeteetse, Wyoming, discovered in 1981 by

**Figure 13.1** The black-footed ferret (*Mustela nigripes*) is highly endangered, due largely to habitat loss and intentional extermination of its primary prey, various prairie dog species. (Photograph by D. E. Biggins, U.S. Fish and Wildlife Service.)

(A)

(B)

**Figure 13.2** (A) The black-tailed prairie dog (*Cynomys ludovicianus*) is one of the species critical to ferret survival, but has been actively exterminated by ranching and farming interests. (B) Note the symbolic use of prairie dogs as pests on the sign. (Photographs by D. E. Biggins, U.S. Fish and Wildlife Service.)

the FWS after one was killed by a dog (Schroeder and Martin 1982). A captive breeding effort using the South Dakota population was initiated by the FWS at its Patuxent Wildlife Research Center in Maryland; nine animals were captured between 1972 and 1974 (Anderson and Inkley 1985). Although the project was not successful, the birth of two litters demonstrated that captive breeding was at least possible.

Under the provisions of the Endangered Species Act, FWS asked the Wyoming Game and Fish Department (WGFD) to assume the role of lead agency in managing the Meeteetse ferret population. The WGFD established a Black-footed Ferret Advisory Team (BFAT), consisting of representatives of state and federal wildlife and land management agencies, a key landowner, and the National Wildlife Federation, to provide guidance in recovery of black-footed ferrets in Wyoming (Anderson and Inkley 1985).

BFAT encouraged research on the Meeteetse population, and research teams were fielded by a private consulting firm and the FWS. This research was primarily descriptive in nature, advancing knowledge of ferret life history and ecology, and improving ferret search techniques (Anderson and Inkley 1985; Wood 1986). Documented ferret numbers appeared to increase dramatically from 1982, and by the fall of 1984, approximately 128 animals were recorded in the population (Forrest et al. 1988).

Almost from the time the Meeteetse ferrets were discovered, captive breeding or translocation was recommended by some participants and observers as the primary management approach. In the spring of 1985, WGFD and FWS agreed to capture a small number of ferrets in October 1985. The summer and fall of 1985, however, was a crisis period for the Meeteetse ferrets. In June, sylvatic plague was discovered in prairie dogs in the Meeteetse ferret habitat. This led to predictions of loss of the entire prairie dog complex, and resulted in a massive plague control program in which approximately 80,000 burrows were treated with carbaryl to kill fleas, the plague vector.

By midsummer, ferret numbers appeared to have declined greatly, and controversy erupted when claims were made that agencies were not acting aggressively enough. The cause of continued decline was discovered in October, when six ferrets were captured to initiate the captive breeding program: two of these were infected with canine distemper contracted in the wild. The six animals were not isolated from one another, and all died of distemper. A second effort then led to capture of an additional six animals (Williams et al. 1988).

A few more free-ranging ferrets escaped exposure to canine distemper, and two litters were born at Meeteetse in 1986, but none were born to the six captives. Under conflicting pressure from captive breeding proponents and from those who felt that the few remaining ferrets should be left to their own resources, WGFD and FWS decided in August 1986 to capture all surviving animals because there were not enough to constitute a viable field population. The last of 12 additional ferrets was captured in February 1987. The canine distemper epizootic ultimately led to extirpation of the free-ranging population (Williams et al. 1988). Recovery was now totally dependent on captive propagation to be initiated at WGFD's Sybille Wildlife Research Unit and on reintroduction (Thorne and Oakleaf 1991).

When the emphasis of ferret management shifted in 1986 from free-ranging animals to captive breeding and reintroduction, WGFD prepared a strategic plan for management of black-footed ferrets in Wyoming (WGFD 1987). The plan established objectives for captive breeding and an experimental reintroduction in 1991. It recognized that only 18 animals were available for captive propagation and that some were related, potentially creating genetic problems. A genetic objective of maintaining approximately 90% of the original heterozygosity for 50 years was set; this relatively short time frame was in anticipation of early reintroduction. It required maintaining a captive population of 200 breeding animals, to be subdivided as quickly as possible in order to avoid extinction through catastrophe at a single facility. At least two free-ranging populations were to be established in Wyoming (WGFD 1987).

In 1988, FWS published a revised recovery plan (USFWS 1988), which incorporated WGFD's objectives and placed the ferret program in a national scope. Additional objectives in the recovery plan were to establish at least 10 geographically distinct free-ranging populations with no fewer than 30 adults in any single population and a cumulative total of 1500 adults by 2010. Specific tasks and assignments were identified to accomplish these goals.

The need for outside technical advice was recognized by WGFD and FWS well before captive breeding was initiated, and late in 1985 a Captive Breeding Specialist Group (CBSG) was invited to serve in that role. In 1986, CBSG, WGFD, and FWS cosponsored a workshop on conservation biology of black-footed ferrets, which provided valuable guidance for the early crisis-ridden years of the captive propagation program (Seal et al. 1989). In 1988, the formal relationship with CBSG was terminated in order to shift emphasis to long-term management using an American Association of Zoological Parks and Aquariums Species Survival Plan.

The 1987 breeding season was difficult, but two litters were born in captivity. Too few kits were born in 1987 to allow division of the captive colony, but after the 1988 breeding season, the first and second of six eventual subcolonies were established at cooperating North American zoos.

From the beginning, the captive breeding program encouraged applied research to address specific problems, such as improving fertilization rates through a variety of techniques (such as electroejaculation and artificial insemination), learning to manipulate the female reproductive cycle, sperm characterization and cryopreservation, understanding feeding habits and general behavior, learning about vaccination and disease control, and conditioning ferrets to field conditions (Figure 13.3). The research was generally successful; it not only enhanced the ferret recovery program, but will prove valuable to other captive breeding programs.

The success of the program in 1987 and 1988 fostered optimism that reintroduction would be feasible by 1991. Although WGFD and FWS were already planning for reintroduction at Meeteetse, preparation for reintroduction on a national scale was lacking. In 1987, an Interstate Coordinating Committee (ICC) was organized to address this problem. The ICC is made up of state, federal, and tribal land and wildlife managers who meet yearly to assess availability of reintroduction sites and prioritize them. Meeteetse was preferred as the first reintroduction site, but was rejected because of the ongoing sylvatic plague epizootic. From 1988 to 1992, plague reduced prairie dog numbers at Meeteetse by 80%. Shirley Basin, in southeastern Wyoming, was biologically better suited and became the priority site.

Private landowner acceptance and participation in reintroduction is important for ferret recovery, because many landowners harbor serious concerns about endangered species, such as perceived governmental interference and restrictions on land use (Reading and Kellert 1993). In Wyoming, landowners at Meeteetse and Shirley Basin played key, but cautious, roles in developing cooperative management plans and assuring that reintroduced

(A)

(B)

**Figure 13.3** Captive black-footed ferrets are conditioned to possible field dangers from potential predators, using models such as (A) stuffed owls and (B) a "robo-badger," a remote-controlled, stuffed and motorized badger. Captives must be acclimated to field conditions before being released. (Photographs by D. E. Biggins, U.S. Fish and Wildlife Service.)

**Figure 13.4**   Black-footed ferrets are so rare that technologies and techniques are often worked out on "surrogate" species, such as these Siberian polecats (*Mustela eversmanni*) being used to test release procedures. (Photograph by D. E. Biggins, U.S. Fish and Wildlife Service.)

ferrets and traditional land uses remained compatible. In some states, this facet of reintroduction remains extremely difficult.

Other key factors facilitating reintroduction in 1991 were the development of a cooperative management plan and the designation of the population as "experimental, nonessential" under the provisions of the Endangered Species Act. This designation provided protection for landowners and allowed flexibility on the part of wildlife managers. An animal rights group disagreed with this designation, unsuccessfully suing for a temporary restraining order against reintroduction. The Sierra Club Legal Defense Fund and its client, the Greater Yellowstone Coalition, opposed the "nonessential" designation because they felt reintroduced ferrets should receive full protection; the Wyoming Farm Bureau opposed reintroduction because it felt the ferrets would receive too much protection at the expense of landowners. The compromise, although resulting in a lower level of protection for released ferrets, gained the cooperation of local farmers and ranchers, allowing some level of protection.

Because small, captive-bred mustelids had not previously been reintroduced in a conservation context, FWS and WGFD again sought outside expert advice in the format of a workshop in the spring of 1990. The black-footed ferret reintroduction workshop involved biologists familiar with ferrets or reintroductions of other species. Consensus was not reached on many points, but ideas led to a final protocol (Oakleaf et al. 1991) that involved releasing 4.5-month-old kits from small cages after 10 days of confinement for pre-release observation and acclimation to the site; providing food to the ferrets for as long as they returned to the release cages, and telemetric monitoring of postrelease movement, habitat use, and activity patterns (Figure 13.4). The first reintroduction involved 49 ferrets. Surveys in early spring of 1992 revealed survival of at least 12% over winter, and in July 1992 at least four survivors and two litters born in the wild were found.

In the fall of 1992, 90 more captive-reared ferrets were released at Shirley Basin. Modifications tested in 1992 included changes in release cage design; release of 18 kits reared at Sybille in large outside cages to allow prerelease conditioning in prairie dog burrows; and telemetric monitoring of less than half the released animals. Animals reared in outdoor pens fared better than their cage-reared counterparts; they dispersed less than half as far and were found four times more often in the reintroduction area 30 days after release (Biggins and Godbey 1993).

In both years, most radio-collared ferrets left the release area, one moving more than 50 km in 3 days. Overall survival was at least 20%–25% for 30 days (Oakleaf et al. 1992). Predation, primarily by coyotes (*Canis latrans*), caused 88% of known deaths of radio-collared animals (Biggins and Godbey 1993).

### Roadblocks to Recovery

Low survivorship and high dispersal rates of released ferrets are impairing rapid establishment of populations, but these concerns are being addressed through research into improved rearing and release methods. Two additional biological problems, genetics and diseases, are ominous.

Ferrets from Meeteetse have some of the lowest levels of genetic variation reported for carnivores (Seal et al. 1989). Because of the very small number of founders that contributed to the captive population, inbreeding depression and loss of genetic diversity could become a major problem to the entire program through reduced rates of reproduction and survival. Short of the discovery of a new population, little can be done about inbreeding depression, beyond the present genetic management and careful breeding programs. However, the large number of kits produced quickly in the captive breeding program is cause for optimism. The best way to avoid long-term genetic decline after a bottleneck is to very quickly increase population size (see Chapter 6); that is, to avoid a more prolonged bottleneck.

Diseases present potentially formidable obstacles to recovery. The relative contribution of canine distemper to the historic decline of ferrets is unknown, and it is impossible to predict the effect of this disease on reintroduced populations. However, the existing evidence on canine distemper is disconcerting: (1) it was present during the crash of the Meeteetse population; (2) evidence of it is commonly found in other carnivores sampled at reintroduction sites; and (3) black-footed ferrets are hypersensitive to it. Sylvatic plague has destroyed the reintroduction potential at sites in several states, at least temporarily. Oscillations in prairie dog populations affected by plague make it difficult to predict long-term trends, but at the least they will create periodically severe bottlenecks for ferret populations.

Some major constraints facing ferret recovery are socioeconomic and can be overcome only by the will of the public and their government agencies. Ferret recovery is made difficult by the fact that the species depends upon habitat (the prairie dog community) that society has been attempting to eliminate for nearly 100 years. Acceptance of prairie dogs may improve in the future through education and demonstration by the first few reintroductions that ferrets, prairie dogs, and traditional land uses are compatible. Will enlightenment come soon enough, or will progress be so slow that current momentum is lost and black-footed ferrets become a relict species archived in zoos?

Obtaining sufficient ferret habitat may require the lowering of minimum area criteria established by ICC, and more intensive management of smaller reestablished ferret populations, primarily through periodic addition of captive-reared animals that have greater genetic variation. However, given the rarity of native prairies in the United States (to be discussed in Chapter 14), even small amounts of prairie habitat protected for ferrets could be a substantial gain for that ecosystem.

Captive propagation and reintroduction are expensive. Private funding could help ferret recovery, but understandably, most conservation groups are concentrating on programs in less developed countries where governments do not have adequate resources. It is incumbent upon government agencies to continue to provide funding for full ferret recovery. The infrastructure is in place, and future interruptions or delays in the program due to reduced or diverted funding will only result over the long term in vastly increased overall costs or failure to recover ferrets.

## Conclusions

The ferret program has had its share of conflict and controversy; its real and perceived mistakes, in addition to its successes, will be instructive to other endangered species management programs. The difficulties and costs associated with single-species management, and the advantages of early ecosystem and multispecies management, which have not been applied to ferret recovery until very recently, have been demonstrated by this program. The spin-off benefits alone that can be applied to other recovery programs justify the costs of the ferret recovery effort. These ancillary products of ferret recovery will most certainly aid in conservation of additional small carnivores and other endangered species. They include husbandry techniques; development of natural and artificial reproduction procedures; increased knowledge of sylvatic plague, canine distemper, and other diseases in the natural environment; reintroduction techniques; public education; and protection of a small part of the American prairie ecosystem, which may prevent other species from becoming endangered. Continued success and early completion of recovery goals will allow black-footed ferret recovery to become a positive example for conservationists and governments struggling to protect other endangered species.

## CASE STUDY 2

### Sea Turtle Headstarting and Hatchery Programs

Nat B. Frazer, Savannah River Ecology Laboratory

*Recent declines in sea turtle populations are largely due to coastal development, which destroys nest sites, and adult mortality in fishing and shrimping nets. Recovery of sea turtles requires protection of juveniles through captive-release programs as well as preservation of beach habitat by limiting development. It also requires protecting adults at sea by decreasing mortality from fishing and shrimping.*

As a group, turtles are older than the dinosaurs. They have enjoyed a rich evolutionary history for more than 200 million years, colonizing freshwater, terrestrial, and marine habitats. The two modern families of sea turtles survived whatever factor(s) caused the extinction of the dinosaurs some 65 million years ago. However, human influences threaten their continued existence today. We now must count on swift and effective management action to avoid drastic reduction or elimination of these ancient survivors within one or a few human generations.

Like all other turtles, marine species must lay their eggs on land. Females crawl ashore to dig large holes, into which they deposit about 100 eggs (Figure 13.5). They may lay up to 11 or more such nests in a single year, although most lay only two to four. After covering their eggs with sand, the female returns to the sea. About 2 months after a nest is laid, the eggs hatch, and the hatchlings emerge and crawl down the beach and into the sea, where they may spend one to three decades before reaching maturity.

Sea turtles face natural challenges in both the marine and terrestrial phases of their life cycles, but the most vulnerable stages are the early ones. While eggs incubate buried on the beach, they are vulnerable to numerous predators. In some areas, heavy waves or storms wash away most of the nests before the eggs have a chance to hatch. Even if the nests remain safe, the hatchlings are vulnerable to predation by birds and fish. Only about one in every thousand eggs will survive to become an adult sea turtle. This high infant mortality has led to strong evolutionary pressures selecting for high adult survival and a resulting ability for repeated reproduction (see Essay 7A).

As sea turtles grow larger, fewer predators are able to kill them. Once they reach adult sizes of 1–2 m in length, sharks and people are the only major predators they face at sea. On land, only very large mammalian predators such as panthers are able to kill adult sea turtles easily. Thus, historically in the wild, an adult female was able to return repeatedly to her nesting beach over periods of many years to lay the thousand or more eggs required to replace herself in the population. But suddenly, after outlasting the dinosaurs,

**Figure 13.5**  A nesting loggerhead turtle (*Caretta caretta*). Up to 100 or more eggs are laid in a single nest, covered, and left by the mother. Such nests are highly susceptible to predation by wild and domestic animals, and humans. (Photograph by John Domant; courtesy of Center for Marine Conservation.)

sea turtles face new challenges from human activities that they may not be able to survive.

For thousands of years, people in coastal areas exploited sea turtles for meat, eggs, oil, and tortoiseshell without diminishing turtle populations. But in the late 19th and early 20th centuries, commercial hunting replaced the traditional subsistence take of sea turtles. In some areas, millions of eggs were taken annually from nesting beaches, and thousands of kilograms of tortoiseshell and turtle meat were taken to market from harvesting adult turtles at their breeding sites. More recently, sea turtles have been affected by habitat destruction through massive beachfront development and by inadvertent capture in commercial fishing gear. As a result, all of the eight existing species are considered to be either endangered or threatened with extinction worldwide (Bjorndal 1982).

A number of human activities also affect sea turtles indirectly (National Research Council 1990). Seawalls for beach erosion control may make nesting impossible for sea turtles (Figure 13.6). Beach nourishing operations, in which sand is pumped ashore to offset the effects of erosion, may cover sea turtle nests under several feet of sand if done during the nesting season, making it impossible for the hatchlings to emerge. Artificial lights from beachfront condominiums or parking lots may disorient or discourage adult turtles as they search for nesting sites on shore. Even if nesting is successful, lights may disorient hatchlings, which emerge from their nests at night, interfering with their ability to find the sea and exposing them to predation and desiccation.

Although hunting of sea turtles is now banned in the United States, many turtles are killed inadvertently as a result of human activities (National Research Council 1990). The shrimp trawls that ply the waters of the Gulf of Mexico and the southeastern Atlantic states are estimated to capture and drown 10,000 to 40,000 sea turtles each year (National Research Council 1990). New predators introduced by humans, such as pigs, dogs, or cats, may eat nearly all of the eggs laid on some beaches. Oil spills can kill young turtles at sea, or even on the beach if the oil washes ashore in a nesting area. Plastic bags thrown overboard from boats are mistaken for jellyfish and

**Figure 13.6** Protective seawalls and coastal development, such as this resort on St. Simons Island, Georgia, threaten sea turtle nesting beaches. (Photograph by Faye Frazer.)

**Figure 13.7**   Sea turtles, such as these Atlantic green turtles (*Chelonia mydas*) off the coast of Florida, experience high mortality rates when caught in active or abandoned fishing nets. (Photograph by Lou Erhardt; courtesy of Center for Marine Conservation.)

eaten by adult turtles, who then choke and suffocate. Many turtles become entangled in discarded fishing lines or nets, resulting in drowning or starvation (Figure 13.7). Others are killed by boat propellers in high traffic areas, or by dredging equipment in shipping channels.

With the ongoing destruction of sea turtles and degradation of their nesting habitat, conservationists have sought ways to manage sea turtle populations by mitigating human impacts. Two programs that many believe may help restore populations to former levels of abundance are hatcheries and headstarting.

Hatchery programs are intended to protect eggs from natural or introduced predators, as well as from storms and hurricanes. The programs typically consist of gathering eggs as they are laid on the beach and reburying them in a fenced enclosure (Figure 13.8), or moving them into a building in

**Figure 13.8**   Sea turtle hatchery programs often involve field enclosure of nests to reduce losses to predation, as in this project in Mexico. (Photograph by U.S. Fish and Wildlife Service; courtesy of Center for Marine Conservation.)

which they are reburied in nest boxes. Unlike fish hatcheries, which may be intended to preserve genetic variability for endangered fish species, sea turtle hatcheries usually are local efforts intended to protect only those eggs laid on a particular beach. After the eggs hatch, the hatchlings usually are released onto the same beach on which the nests were laid so that they can crawl into their "native" waters.

There is some genetic evidence that sea turtles may return to nest on their own natal beach (Bowen et al. 1992, 1993), and many sea turtle managers believe that the turtles "imprint" on a particular beach while the eggs are incubating in the sand or when the hatchlings make their initial crawl from the nest to the sea. This would enable the females to return to their own birthplace years later when they mature, just as salmon return to their native stream to lay their eggs. However, no one has actually observed a marked sea turtle hatchling making such a return visit as an adult.

Headstarting projects also start by collecting and hatching eggs, but continue rearing sea turtles in captivity for 9 months to a year (Figure 13.9) until they grow to so-called "dinner plate size." (This does not indicate that they are ready to be *served* on a dinner plate, but only that they have reached that approximate *diameter!*) Managers believe that in this way they can protect the eggs from the high natural mortality rates they normally face while incubating on a beach, and then protect the hatchlings in captivity from the fish, birds, and other predators that otherwise would prey on them during their crucial first year in the ocean. Once the turtles have safely reached "dinner plate size," it is believed that they have outgrown most of their natural predators, and so they are released into the ocean.

**Figure 13.9** "Dinner plate sized" Kemp's ridley sea turtles (*Lepidochelys kempi*) being raised in the National Marine Fisheries Service headstart program in Galveston, Texas. (Photograph by Nat B. Frazer.)

There is little doubt that many sea turtle hatcheries increase the number of young turtles entering the water from some beaches. More than 90% of all eggs laid on some beaches can be destroyed by a combination of predators and heavy storms. In such cases, protecting eggs in a hatchery can safely ensure that the great majority of turtles will hatch out and at least have a chance to enter the ocean.

Hatcheries and headstarting programs also have immense public relations value. Filming the release of thousands of hatchling turtles or hundreds of headstarted yearlings provides attractive and important nature programming for TV news. It also serves to heighten public awareness of the need for funding sea turtle conservation activities. Headstarting facilities and hatcheries can serve the same educational purpose as do zoos and aquariums, giving people a chance to observe and appreciate animals that they otherwise might never see. They also provide potential for scientific work. By holding eggs, hatchlings, or young turtles in captivity, scientists have learned a great deal about the physiology, anatomy, embryology, genetics, evolutionary relationships, diseases, learning, and behavior of sea turtles.

There are, of course, problems that have arisen. For example, collecting eggs in a fenced-in area or a building goes against the ancient advice about "putting all your eggs in one basket." Managers of at least one project wished they had followed this advice when their natural-dune hatchery was inundated by thunderstorms, drowning almost all of the entire year's worth of developing eggs and hatchlings.

Another problem concerns the sex ratio produced. Initially, scientists were unaware that the sex of sea turtles can be determined by incubation temperature: warmer incubation produces female turtles, and cooler temperatures produce males. Imagine the disappointment of the managers of one hatchery program when they realized that they had been producing mostly male turtles for several years—an unintended but potentially disastrous result for management!

Another hard-learned lesson involved moving the eggs. Unlike chicken eggs, which should be turned as they incubate, sea turtle eggs must remain stationary because the embryo attaches to the inside wall of the egg early in development; if the egg is turned after that time, the embryo will die. This is why most sea turtle hatcheries now collect the eggs from natural nests and rebury them within six hours of laying. But untold thousands of eggs were probably killed by early hatchery managers who were not aware of this problem.

In some areas, where destruction of natural nests is high, hatcheries may help to ensure that hatchlings have a better chance of getting into the ocean. In other areas, however, this strategy is not likely to succeed from a management standpoint. For example, at one nesting beach in Australia, up to 85% of the hatchlings may be eaten by fish in the first 10 minutes after they crawl into the ocean (E. Gyuris, unpublished data). Releasing more hatchlings off this beach may be just an exercise in fish feeding rather than sea turtle management.

Still another concern is the long period that may elapse before hatchery or headstart programs result in an observable increase in the number of adult turtles. For example, several hatchery programs have now operated for 30 years or more, with no apparent increase in numbers of nesting female turtles. There is no conclusive evidence that any sea turtle hatchery program ever has resulted in a measurable increase in numbers of adult turtles on the nesting beach. Is this because hatchery programs do not work? Or is it just that sea turtles may require 30 years or more to reach maturity? Perhaps it was the lack of any immediate results from hatchery programs that led some managers to consider trying headstarting.

From the beginning of headstarting projects, some people questioned the value of using an unproven practice as a management technique—for how could we be sure that raising turtles in captivity would even work? In response to this criticism, proponents of headstarting were quick to call it an "experiment." In a counterresponse, critics pointed out that scientific experiments have a "control" group with which the experimental group can be compared. Proponents of headstarting then claimed that they did have a control group of turtles, the wild turtles in the natural habitat. If headstarted turtles could be shown to survive better than wild turtles, then headstarting would be judged a success. Unfortunately, this is easier said than done. Although headstarted turtles can survive and grow once released into the ocean, there is no reliable information on the survival rate of small wild juvenile sea turtles. Because no one knows what is going on in the "control" group, how can we determine whether the "experiment" is a success?

One group of managers who conducted an "experimental" headstarting program with Kemp's ridley sea turtles (*Lepidochelys kempi*) defined success this way: "When a nesting Kemp's ridley can be identified as a head-started animal, the overall project will be a complete success." (Manzella et al. 1988). In other words, as soon as even one headstarted sea turtle crawls up on a beach to nest as an adult, their project would be deemed a success. This would indicate that it is possible for at least some turtles reared in captivity for a year and then released, to survive to adulthood and reproduce. If the problem is defined as simply as that, then their criterion for success is acceptable. But are we simply trying to determine whether turtles can survive in the wild after their release from captivity? Or are we attempting to manage and recover endangered species? These are two very different "experiments."

If headstarting is to be viewed as a possible management technique, an entirely different set of criteria must be used to assess success. A panel of scientists selected by the federal government to evaluate the very same Kemp's ridley headstarting program had this to say about it:

> If headstarting is successful, the proportion of nesting headstarted females should increase relative to the proportion of nonheadstarted nesting females. We consider that a gradual increase in this proportion over a five year period would be an indicator that headstarting is an effective conservation technique. (Wibbels et al. 1989).

In other words, these scientists felt it necessary not only to demonstrate that headstarted turtles *can* survive to adulthood, but that their chances of doing so are *better* than those of naturally wild turtles. Headstarting is of interest primarily because natural sea turtle populations are in decline. Therefore, a successful management program must enhance turtle survival to levels greater than the wild turtles are currently experiencing; otherwise, their populations will not grow. If headstarted turtles did survive better than wild turtles, then we would be able to see a gradual increase in the percentage of headstarted turtles among nesting adults on the beach. Just seeing one headstarted turtle nesting on a beach would not mean that the population was growing.

Are hatcheries and headstarting activities successful management techniques for sea turtles? No one really knows. Unfortunately, not a single sea turtle of any species released from a hatchery or headstarting program has ever been reliably identified coming ashore to nest as an adult. Both proponents and opponents of hatcheries and headstarting programs eagerly await news of such a sighting, for all sea turtle conservationists want the turtles to survive and their populations to expand.

Choosing an appropriate management strategy first depends upon our ability to define the goals of management. Are we attempting to keep in captivity what we are not able to protect in the wild? Or are we attempting to rebuild wild populations to their former levels of abundance? We now know that we can hatch and rear turtles in captivity. What we do not know is whether they will survive any better than their wild counterparts when released into a marine environment that is continually declining in quality. Indeed, some scientists have cautioned against any attempt at management through such relocation, repatriation, or translocation programs unless the problems leading to the original decline of the species have been determined and eliminated (Dodd and Seigel 1991).

Thus, some critics of headstarting and hatchery projects point out that the techniques serve more as palliatives than as cures. For example, headstarting conceivably might result in an immediate increase in the numbers of turtles at sea, but it does nothing to address the causes of their original decline, nor to ensure that the population will grow back to its former levels of abundance. If management efforts are limited to hatcheries and headstarting, turtles will still be disoriented by lights, trapped in fishing gear, and kept from nesting on beaches with seawalls or beach nourishing projects. The so-called "management projects" then become exercises in perpetual crisis management rather than attempts to solve or ameliorate problems.

There is also concern that hatcheries and headstarting programs might give society a false sense of security (Dodd and Seigel 1991). As the public sees the thousands of turtles being released, they may assume that nothing more need be done, such as environmental cleanup or restoration or prevention of additional damage. If translocated turtles are released into the same degraded environment in which their parents and grandparents cannot survive, we will have to continue headstarting and hatchery programs indefinitely into the future, and will not solve the problem; we will be addressing symptoms rather than causes.

**Figure 13.10**   The turtle excluder device, or TED, is effective in releasing sea turtles, such as this Atlantic loggerhead (*Carretta caretta*), inadvertently captured in shrimp trawls. (Photograph by Rex Heron; courtesy of Center for Marine Conservation.)

How we define a problem determines in large part what we are willing to accept as an adequate solution. If we define the problem of the impending extinction of sea turtles simply as there being too few turtles in the ocean, then we are likely to view any management activity that results in there being more turtles (even temporarily) as a solution. But if we define the problem as the lack of suitable habitat in which sea turtles can thrive, we then must address larger issues of managing and protecting the marine and coastal environments. These same arguments apply to virtually any management scenario that involves declining numbers of a species or population. For example, the same problems and questions apply to declining Pacific salmon populations (Meffe 1992).

If we choose to address our management efforts toward reducing human impact on marine and coastal ecosystems, many species other than sea turtles will benefit. For example, nesting shorebirds also are displaced by beachfront development, and porpoises, birds, and seals also are killed by commercial fishing gear.

Fortunately, there are means available for making habitats safer for turtles and other marine life. Most shrimp trawls in U.S. waters now carry turtle excluder devices (TEDs) that allow turtles and other larger animals to escape from nets (Figure 13.10). Beachfront lighting can be modified by placing lights lower to the ground, putting shades on the seaward side of the lights, or changing the color. In some areas, local laws regulate the timing of beach nourishment projects so they do not coincide with the nesting season.

Despite such corrective measures, sea turtle populations continue their decline, and we are driven to managing their populations. Should we continue to operate hatcheries and headstarting programs, even though neither has yet been shown to be effective? Should we abandon them and redirect efforts toward addressing the direct causes of sea turtle decline? If we know that this alternative approach will take many decades to accomplish, should we continue hatchery and headstarting efforts in the meantime? In the face of tightening conservation budgets as government and industry attempt to address deficits and service debt, the controversy concerning how best to spend scarce management funds for sea turtle conservation is sure to continue.

## CASE STUDY 3

## Management of the Spotted Owl: The Interaction of Science, Policy, Politics, and Litigation

Barry R. Noon, U.S. Forest Service, and
Dennis D. Murphy, Stanford University

*Knowledge of scientific methods is not always enough in conservation management. Political pressures, legal proceedings, and policy decisions often dictate success or failure in a management scheme. The Spotted Owl epitomizes the high-visibility struggle that sometimes ensues when protective legislation restricts use of a resource. Success or failure in management often is determined by skills other than ecological knowledge.*

The requisite skills for effective conservation planning, reserve design, or species management entail more than knowledge of the theoretical and applied principles of population and community ecology. These principles, plus an understanding of relevant species' ecologies, life histories, and habitat relationships, are essential components of any effective conservation strategy, but by themselves are insufficient to conserve most of the species about which we are concerned.

The process of developing a scientifically sound conservation strategy defensible to political attacks, likely to be adopted by society, and subsequently implemented, is often the most difficult and least discussed aspect of conservation biology. Many strategies, even those built on a firm foundation of defensible science, will fail if the biologists involved are inept at defending their plan against inevitable criticisms, or are unable to convince decision makers of the true costs to society of failing to implement the conservation actions.

Drawing on our experiences in conservation planning for both the Northern (*Strix occidentalis caurina*) and the California (*S. o. occidentalis*) Spotted Owls, our goals in this case study are to (1) briefly review the logic and methods used to produce scientifically credible plans; (2) focus on the tactics necessary to make a conservation plan resilient to attack; (3) contrast the Northern and California Spotted Owl plans; (4) discuss ways to explicitly address scientific uncertainty and incomplete information; and (5) provide suggestions to decrease the adversarial nature of conservation planning, and increase the influence of scientists and managers in the formulation of natural resource policy.

### The Northern Spotted Owl

Perhaps more than any threatened or endangered species, the Northern Spotted Owl (Figure 13.11) epitomizes the struggle between groups representing disparate value systems in a land of limited resources and unlimited demands. The debate has been oversimplified as a choice between employment and economic vitality on one hand, versus species survival and rich, functioning ecosystems on the other. This dichotomy has provoked lawsuits and intense public and scientific disagreement; with rapidly diminishing options, it led the U.S. Congress and President Clinton to judge the Spotted Owl/timber harvest situation a conflict to be resolved at the highest political levels.

One effort at resolution arose from a 1989 amendment to an appropriations bill, in which Congress directed the U.S. Fish and Wildlife Service, U.S. Forest Service, National Park Service, and Bureau of Land Management to convene an Interagency Spotted Owl Scientific Committee (ISC) to "develop a scientifically credible conservation strategy for the Northern Spotted Owl." As members of the ISC, we struggled to develop a scientific protocol, using the rigor of strong inference (i.e., hypothesis testing, discussed below), that would allow consideration of both biological and nonbiological factors in development of a habitat conservation plan. The strategy developed by the ISC and presented to Congress (Thomas et al. 1990) is not the most recent proposal for resolution of the Northern Spotted Owl conservation crisis (Thomas and Verner 1992). However, the process, logic, and rationale employed has formed the foundation for all subsequent reserve design proposals for the subspecies.

Conservation planning for the Northern Spotted Owl has a long and complex history that reads like the plot of a political novel. Protagonists, antagonists, confrontations, disputes, secret memos, political pressure, litigation, media distortion, and personal attacks have been everyday players and events. Set against this background of political and legal turmoil, our challenge was to bring to the forefront all information pertinent to the preservation of the species and to provide a defensible conservation plan that appropriately considered scientific uncertainty and competing value systems.

**Figure 13.11** The Northern Spotted Owl (*Strix occidentalis caurina*), a focal point of conflicts between endangered species preservation and short-term economic interests. (Photograph by David Johnson.)

### The California Spotted Owl

Concern with, and studies of, the California Spotted Owl are more recent than for the northern subspecies. Consequently, its ecological associations are less well known, and it has not yet accumulated the contentious history of legal, political, and scientific debate that characterizes its northern counterpart.

Scientific and management interest in the California Spotted Owl was largely stimulated by release of the ISC report (Thomas et al. 1990), and by concern that some environmental groups were about to petition the Fish and Wildlife Service to list the California subspecies as threatened. In response, the Forest Service, California Department of Forestry, and other state and federal agencies established a scientific team to evaluate the status of the California subspecies and, if needed, to recommend changes in land management practices. The expectation was that a proactive management response would preclude the need to list this subspecies at a later date.

### Hypotheses Tested and Reserve Design Principles Invoked

To determine whether the Northern and California Spotted Owls were threatened subspecies and in jeopardy due to logging practices, we tested the following null hypotheses:

1. The finite rate of population change ($\lambda$) of owls is $\geq 1.0$ (i.e., the population is growing).
2. Spotted Owls do not differentiate among habitats on the basis of forest age or structure.
3. No decline has occurred in the areal extent of habitat types selected by Spotted Owls for foraging, roosting, or nesting.

*The Northern Spotted Owl.* For the Northern Spotted Owl, the first null hypothesis was rejected based on the observation that $\lambda$ was significantly less than 1.0 at two long-term study sites (Thomas et al. 1990). Subsequent tests of this hypothesis, based on additional study sites and additional years of data (USDI 1992), indicate that populations of resident, territorial females declined significantly, at an estimated rate of 7.5% per year, during the 1985–1991 period. No studies have found areas of stable or increasing populations.

The majority of Northern Spotted Owl habitat studies supported rejection of the second null hypothesis and provided evidence in favor of selection of old-growth forests, or forests that retained the characteristics of old forests (Thomas et al. 1990). The exception to this pattern was in coastal redwood forests of northern California (<7% of the owl's range) where owls are also found in younger forests that retain some residual old-growth components. Since the ISC report, numerous studies have confirmed that Northern and California Spotted Owls prefer old-growth habitat, providing additional falsification of hypothesis 2 (Solis and Gutierrez 1990; Buchanan 1991; Ripple et al. 1991; Bart and Forsman 1992; Blakesley et al. 1992; Carey et al. 1992; Lehmkuhl and Raphael 1993).

The rejection of hypothesis 2 led to the test of hypothesis 3. Based on data from National Forest lands in Oregon and Washington, the ISC found significant declines in the extent of owl habitat, a trend that was projected to continue into the future (Figure 13.12). Additional analyses since the ISC report provide evidence of significant habitat declines in California (McKelvey and Johnston 1992); regionally specific estimates of habitat loss are provided in the Draft Recovery Plan (USDI 1992).

Subsequent development of the conservation strategy was based, in large part, on the results of map-based tests of five basic principles of reserve design (Wilcove and Murphy 1992), stated as falsifiable hypotheses:

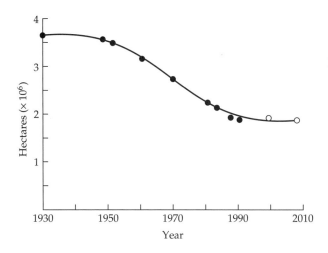

**Figure 13.12** Estimated trend in the areal extent of suitable Northern Spotted Owl habitat in National Forest lands in Oregon and Washington for 1930 to 2010. Estimates beyond 1990 are projections based on National Forest plans.

1. Species that are well distributed across their ranges are less prone to extinction than species confined to small portions of their ranges.
2. Large blocks of habitat containing many individuals of a given species are more likely to sustain that species than are small blocks of habitat with only a few individuals.
3. Habitat patches (blocks) in close proximity are preferable to widely dispersed habitat patches.
4. Contiguous, unfragmented blocks of habitat are superior to highly fragmented blocks of habitat.
5. Habitat between protected areas is more easily traversed by dispersing individuals the more closely it resembles suitable habitat for the species in question.

Particularly relevant to a territorial species with obligate juvenile dispersal, such as the Spotted Owl, was the prediction from theoretical models of sharp thresholds for species extinction (Lande 1987; Thomas et al. 1990; Lamberson et al. 1992; Lamberson et al., in press; see also Chapter 7). One threat arises when the amount of suitable habitat is reduced to such a small fraction of the landscape that the difficulty of finding a territory becomes an insurmountable barrier to the population's persistence. Another occurs if population density is so low that the probability of finding a mate drops below that required to maintain a stable population.

One area of scientific uncertainty relevant to Spotted Owl reserve design was the size and spacing of reserve areas. Existing biogeographic principles were helpful, but too broad for specific application to the Spotted Owl problem. To address this uncertainty, we used computer simulation models, premised on Lande (1987), structured and parameterized in terms of the life history of the Northern Spotted Owl. The ISC determined the goal for conservation to be a 95% certainty of range-wide persistence for 100 years. Given estimates of the current amount of habitat, and its ability to regrow within 100 years, model results suggested that a minimum habitat size for locally stable populations would be a network of blocks, each capable of supporting at least 20 pairs of birds (Figure 13.13; Thomas et al. 1990; Lamberson et al. 1992; Lamberson et al., in press).

*The California Spotted Owl.* Demographic studies have been conducted for long enough to compute estimates of λ for two study populations in the northern Sierra Nevada of California. Estimates of λ for the Sierra Nevada populations were not significantly less than 1.0 (Noon et al. 1992). Even

**Figure 13.13**   Some of the predictions for Spotted Owl persistence upon which management is based come from computer modeling. Shown here are predictions of mean occupancy rates of suitable sites by pairs of Spotted Owls over time for various sizes of cluster (blocks of suitable habitat sites), assuming 60% of the sites within a cluster are suitable. Numbers on the right are total sites per cluster. These results predict that clusters with more individual sites will support more owls.

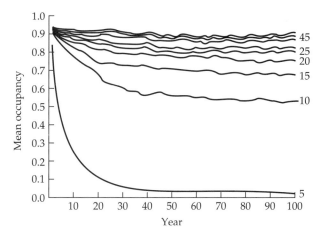

though hypothesis 1 was not rejected for these study populations, Verner et al. (1992) proceeded to test hypothesis 2 because the tests for hypothesis 1 had low power, and the point estimates of λ were less than 1.0 (Noon et al. 1992). Hypothesis 2 was rejected at both the landscape and home-range scale for both Sierra Nevada populations (Gutierrez et al. 1992). At both spatial scales, owls selected stands of large, old trees with closed canopies. This pattern was particularly pronounced in nest and roost stands.

Consistent rejection of hypothesis 2 led to tests of hypothesis 3. Forests in the Sierra Nevada have been markedly affected by human activities within the last 150 years (McKelvey and Johnston 1992). A combination of logging and natural attrition of old-growth forest has led to a decline in the number of large, old trees (particularly pines), broken up the patchy mosaic of the natural forest, and encouraged development of dense understory conifer regeneration. The result has been rather uniform, landscape-wide loss of old-growth forest elements (e.g., large, standing live and dead trees, and large downed logs) strongly associated with the habitat use patterns of Spotted Owls.

Based on current Forest Service land management plans, loss of old-growth forest elements was projected to continue, resulting in forests susceptible to fire disturbance and nearly devoid of large, old trees. Given these projections, Verner et al. (1992) proposed interim (5–10 year) guidelines that both reduced allowable harvest levels and restricted silvicultural activities in habitats selected by Spotted Owls. These restrictions, invoked at a landscape scale, would serve to retain the large tree components in harvested stands in order to greatly accelerate the rate at which these degraded stands would become suitable habitat in the future. The locations of suitable blocks of habitat would shift dynamically across the landscape, but with reduced harvest levels, an adequate amount and distribution of suitable habitat would always be available.

### Why Two Different Conservation Strategies?

At both landscape and home-range scales, the Northern and California Spotted Owls select habitats that retain old-growth forest characteristics. Consequently, timber harvest of old-growth forests, or their components, is responsible for concern over both subspecies' long-term persistence. Given the wide acceptance by the scientific community of the ISC reserve design for the northern subspecies, why was a similar strategy not adopted for the California Spotted Owl? There are several reasons (Verner et al. 1992).

First, during the past 50 years the number and distribution of Northern Spotted Owls may have been reduced by as much as 50% from pre-20th century levels (Thomas et al. 1990). No evidence of similar declines in number or distribution exists for California Spotted Owls, despite the fact that forests in the Sierra Nevada have been logged for the past 100 years. Currently, Spotted Owls in the Sierra Nevada are widely distributed throughout the conifer zone.

Second, the primary silvicultural method in the Pacific Northwest, west of the Cascade crest, was clear-cutting. Because clear-cutting practices have dominated in the Pacific Northwest, particularly over the last 50 years, habitat within the range of the Northern Spotted Owl is either undisturbed and suitable, or cut within the last 50 years and unsuitable. The result has been an island-like distribution of suitable habitat. The ISC opted for a Northern Spotted Owl strategy that clearly differentiated habitat reserves from areas where logging could occur. In contrast, selective tree harvest has been the predominant harvest method over most of the range of the California Spotted Owl (Figure 13.14). Current data indicate that some level of selective harvest does not render habitat unsuitable for owls, at least over the long term. As a result, the current distribution of Spotted Owls in the Sierra Nevada is comparatively uniform in both the conifer zone and adjacent foothill riparian/hardwood forest. Imposing a static reserve design here would leave many owls outside of reserves and vulnerable to habitat loss.

Third, fire is not a major threat to forests west of the Cascade crest in Washington or Oregon (Agee and Edmonds 1992). Despite the fact that fire spreads contagiously, even large contiguous blocks of old-growth forest within this region would face little risk of catastrophic loss. On the other hand, the Sierran mixed conifer forests, where most California Spotted Owls occur, are drier, and given a history of fire exclusion, very prone to catastrophic fires. A habitat reserve strategy there could deal with the uncertainties of logging, but not fire.

Collectively, the above considerations led Verner et al. (1992) to propose an interim landscape-level conservation strategy that would retain the old-growth forest components apparently needed by owls for roosting and nesting. Based on continuing research and adaptive modifications to the interim plan, such a strategy would preserve future options for Spotted Owl management.

**Figure 13.14**  Photos of two forest management types: (A) clear-cutting and (B) selective harvesting. In the latter, an 80-year-old stand of Douglas fir was thinned (selectively harvested) to 50 trees/acre at age 40, and planted with hemlock in the understory. (Photographs by Barry R. Noon and John Tappeiner.)

(A)

(B)

## Issues that Arise after the Conservation Plan Is Put Forward

*Confronting Scientific Uncertainty.* Contentious debate surrounding the value of threatened and endangered species like the Spotted Owl inevitably arises if their conservation is accompanied by significant economic costs. As a result, conservation biologists and their colleagues in forestry, range sciences, and wildlife biology have been swept into public debates that take them from the status of sequestered experts to that of key players in development of public policy. Scientists have been drawn into the land use decision-making process, have been required to defend the merits of their field studies in public forums, and are finding themselves defending their science against often savage criticism.

Scientists are trained to treat facts with doubt and to question their validity, a circumstance that lawyers use to advantage. Uncertainty is inherent in the scientific process because the goal of science is to incrementally reduce levels of uncertainty by subjecting alternative hypotheses to rigorous tests. Thus, scientists do not construct conclusions from data; rather, they construct hypotheses that are tested with further data. They cannot *prove* the truth of an assertion; rather, they fail to disprove that assertion, and thus support it.

Special interest groups employ lawyers and consultants to seek flaws and weaknesses in scientific analyses and data. And in those cases in which no obvious flaws exist, critics will note how little scientists actually know. They exaggerate and misconstrue the inherent, inevitable uncertainty that accompanies the best scientific efforts.

In the courtroom, the tactic used most frequently is to exploit the areas of uncertainty inherent in the scientific process—or worse, to use disinformation and distortion in an attempt to discredit the scientist. Also, critical data that could significantly contribute to problem definition and resolution may be purposely excluded as lawyers manipulate the litigation process so that the critical issues are never put on the table.

A disproportionate amount of criticism of the ISC strategy, both in industry press releases and during litigation, was directed toward the computer simulation models and the inferences drawn from them. Models are ready candidates for commentary because any model simple enough to be operational is necessarily too simple to be completely realistic. Like all simulation models, those used in the conservation assessments of both owl subspecies were characterized by abstractions and simplifying assumptions. And, like all models, they were open to criticism if one demands (unrealistically) that a model be a complete representation of the real world. Because of these perceived weaknesses, the scientists responsible for the models were frequent targets during litigation.

The motivation to discredit both conservation strategies rested on the simple fact that owl protection meant reducing allowable tree harvest. From the timber industry's perspective, access to large-diameter, economically valuable trees on public lands would simply be too restricted. This stipulation, however, was not a consequence of the model results, but was dictated by the habitat associations of the Spotted Owl.

*Burden of Proof in Conservation Debates.* The allocation of burden of proof can often determine the results of decision making. Some entity must assume the responsibility for providing sufficient information to compel a decision maker to adopt a solution. In the Northern Spotted Owl litigation, the strategy of the timber industry, and to some extent the federal agency lawyers, was to put the burden on the scientists to prove an adverse effect of timber harvest on Spotted Owl persistence. In the absence of compelling information and arguments, the lawyers argued, the status quo (high levels of harvest in late seral stage forests) should continue. Failure to make a decision to change management practices for Spotted Owls was a de facto decision to continue current practices.

Federal environmental laws do not require judges to be scientific experts. Rather, the law requires public agencies to fully disclose all pertinent information, and to openly consider competing interpretations of this information. Despite attacks on the credibility and objectivity of the Spotted Owl scientists, these courtroom tactics failed because the judges ruled that existing environmental laws require a full disclosure and analysis of existing data. The analyses provided by the ISC and other scientists provided convincing evidence of risk to the species, thus mandating conservation action. Defensible science and open debate prevailed in the courtroom, and eventually led to more responsible decision making.

*Ethics and Science.* Most people involved in conservation science are motivated by a strong sense of responsibility to the biota and to future generations. Lawyers attempt to label such scientists as "advocates" who are therefore biased, and refuse to recognize that one can support a position in the absence of bias; bias does not necessarily follow from advocacy. Science is not value-free, nor should it be. Environmental science and environmental law have a clear ethical foundation, which is appropriate. "Resource stewardship" is not a buzz phrase but a meaningful expression of responsibility to future generations. Conservation scientists recognize that meeting this responsibility will often come at the expense of maximizing short-term economic gain.

Some scientists involved in the Spotted Owl debates chose not to participate in the normative process to render data scientifically credible (e.g., peer review and publication). Instead, they exploited the uncertainty inherent in the scientific process to justify maintaining the status quo or to obscure reasonable hypotheses. They were often able to stir up doubt, not because a hypothesis was unreasonable, but simply because irrefutable proof was a standard that could not be met.

## Improving the Role of Science in Conservation Policy

The courts have assumed an increasing role in rendering land management decisions based on procedural aspects of law, as well as deciding substantive issues that should be discussed and resolved in other arenas. Because of society's continuing failure to acknowledge that hard choices must be made, and then to move forward and make them, we have lacked an adequate forum and process for environmental problem resolution.

We need to develop alternative strategies for problem resolution, and scientists should be key contributors to this process. The forum for decision making must be expanded to include all affected parties, representing a diversity of perspectives. Given such a forum, behavior must be governed by a set of rigidly enforced ground rules, including: (1) participating parties must treat one another with professional respect; (2) the strength of any argument put on the table should be a function of the information content of the argument; (3) no pertinent data may be withheld or suppressed; and (4) the reliability of the data should be judged by the degree to which they have been exposed to the scientific process of peer criticism and repeated attempts at falsification.

Such a forum for problem resolution would be a significant step toward solving emerging crises in land use and natural resource management. Once solutions were offered, the final responsibility would be to conduct risk assessments to accompany each of the alternative management plans.

Thus, the decision makers would be the final arbiters of which conservation plans were implemented and would be obligated to make known the risks, to both present and future generations, associated with the decisions they made.

Ultimately, the decisions we make as a society regarding management of declining resources come back to a fundamental question: "Does the value gained from the continued existence of a species equal the cost incurred to assure its persistence?" How we respond to this question will determine the fate of many species, including the Spotted Owl.

## CASE STUDY 4

## Management of a Multiple-Function Reserve: The La Selva Biological Station

David B. Clark, La Selva Biological Station

*The La Selva Biological Station is one of the largest and most productive field research centers in the tropics. The author, formerly a co-director of the station, describes a stepwise approach for analyzing the mission and resources of a conservation area, and managing for that mission.*

### Multiple-Function Reserves

Anyone interested in conservation biology quickly becomes involved with areas set aside for various forms of protection. Much of the research on which conservation biology is based is done in protected areas that contain the last remnants of once-extensive communities. Much of the teaching of conservation biology also occurs in these areas. As a teacher, researcher, or interested visitor, you will encounter protected areas throughout your life, and much of this book concerns biological aspects of such areas. This case study addresses how the biological and conservation goals of a reserve are made possible through effective administration and management.

Conservation biologists are frequently called upon to participate in reserve management. Citizens interested in conservation biology also have multiple occasions to affect the management of protected areas. Whatever your eventual career, this study will provide you with insight into how to analyze a given reserve's operations. In the end, the scientific principles of conservation biology have to be put into practice, against a background of economic, political, and other human constraints. Here, we will see ways of analyzing reserve management in its real-world context.

There are thousands of areas around the world set aside for special management for various reasons: public education, protection of flora and fauna, research, professional training, and watershed management are typical rationales. The purposes of some reserves are so narrowly defined that they may serve only a very limited set of objectives. In many others, however, the area is intended to fulfill a variety of functions, which inevitably involve trade-offs. Managing these trade-offs among different functions is an inexact science. Political, economic, and sociological factors all play a role, sometimes in ways never dreamed of by the reserve's founders. Conservation biology emphasizes interrelations among a diversity of disciplines, and management of multiple-function reserves is an excellent example of what this means in practice.

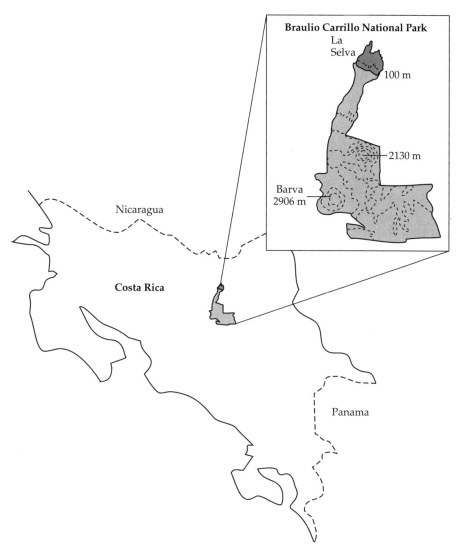

**Figure 13.15** Location of La Selva Biological Station within Costa Rica. The inset shows La Selva in relation to Braulio Carrillo National Park, and the corridor that connects La Selva to the volcanic mountains that form the core of the park.

*La Selva Biological Station: A Multiple-Function Reserve.* The La Selva Biological Station is a reserve owned and managed by the Organization for Tropical Studies (OTS), an international consortium of universities and research institutions (see Essay 16B). The mission of OTS, as defined by its board of directors, is to provide leadership in education, research, and sustainable use of natural resources in the tropics.

La Selva is located in the Atlantic lowlands of the Republic of Costa Rica, an area originally covered by tropical rainforest (Figure 13.15). The station currently consists of about 1500 ha of protected lands (adjacent to Braulio Carrillo National Park) with a diversity of use histories, ranging from pristine lowland tropical rainforest to abandoned cattle pasture (Figure 13.16). From a humble beginning as a few farmhouses in 1968, the physical plant has grown to 22 buildings, including a central dining room, dormitories, researcher housing, and laboratories. The station is now one of the most active sites in the world for teaching and research in lowland rainforest. More than 1100 articles and theses have been published on the flora and fauna of La Selva, and in 1992 station use topped 18,000 person-days.

**Figure 13.16**   The La Selva Biological Station has a variety of intact, tropical lowland habitats that are used for study of ecological processes and conservation practices. (Photographs by C. R. Carroll.)

### Identifying the Mission: What Are the Goals?

The first step in analyzing any reserve is to ask, "What is the mission?" To examine management policies in a rational way, one must first identify and understand their goals. Sometimes these are clearly stated in a "Mission Statement." At other times the goals are never explicitly defined, in which case goal-directed management is difficult. Another common situation is to find a large difference between what a reserve was originally intended to do and what it is currently doing.

La Selva is unusual among multipurpose reserves in that its mission has been clearly defined, with the goals arranged in priority order. These goals are:

1. To promote research and university-level teaching in humid lowland tropical ecosystems.
2. To preserve a diversity of habitats for research, teaching, and conservation.
3. To the extent compatible with goals 1 and 2, educate the general public in tropical biology.

The question, "What is the mission?" can now be answered. La Selva's primary mission is to support academic research and teaching, which necessitates habitat protection. To the extent possible without interfering with the primary mission, it is desirable to incorporate a general public educational component. This is a clear statement of management priorities. Based on La Selva's mission statement, one would expect the majority of the station's programs to focus on enhancing academic research and teaching.

### Defining the Mission: Who Has the Power?

A key step in analyzing any reserve is to examine how its goals were determined. Who made the original decisions? Who now has the power to review and change them?

In the case of La Selva, OTS' overall mission was defined by its governing board of directors. Subsequently, an independent advisory committee named by the president of OTS (the La Selva Advisory Committee, LSAC) formulated La Selva's mission statement. From there the goals were adopted by OTS' board of directors as organizational policy. It is worth noting that the station operated for well over a decade with no formal mission statement. The course of its development was determined mainly by the decisions of OTS' executive director, modified by input from the board of directors, the OTS resident director in Costa Rica, station users, and the LSAC. Since 1980, when David and Deborah Clark became the first full-time directors of La Selva, the station directors have played an important role in decisions affecting La Selva's functions.

A researcher once said that "OTS works by consensus." What he was referring to is the fact that OTS is an academic consortium. Compared with a governmental organization or even many academic departments, OTS' decision-making process is open to input from many sectors. There are also several levels at which policy changes can be initiated: meetings of the board of directors or its executive committee, the LSAC, regular meetings of La Selva station users, and one-on-one interactions between members of these groups.

A key element in this power structure is the LSAC. The committee is named by and reports to the president of OTS. Because the committee is only advisory, OTS' president automatically increases or decreases the committee's role to the extent that she or he accepts the committee's recommendations. Historically, OTS presidents along with the board of directors have usually accepted LSAC's advice, so the committee has had a considerable influence in the development of La Selva. OTS has made a conscious effort to ensure that LSAC is a diverse committee, to avoid domination by any one academic discipline. This diversity is a critical element for maintaining the committee's credibility within and outside of OTS.

## Mission and Management: How Well Do They Correspond?

After asking what a reserve's mission is and how it was established, the next logical step is to see whether current management and development are concordant with the stated purposes of the reserve. For many reasons, there is frequently a large discrepancy between what a reserve is intended to do and what it actually does. Sometimes there are financial constraints: resources simply cannot be found to do what is needed. Sometimes the interests of the managing organization evolve and leave the original mission behind. Sometimes administrators implement a new agenda without fully realizing the change in mission. Administrators are usually the ones who face the financial pressures of reserve management. It can be tempting to move into new, well-funded areas without analyzing how these changes relate to the reserve's mission, and how they may affect its future development.

One way to assess the match between mission and management is to examine the allocation of staff time and financial resources to management activities. Resource commitment should show a logical relation to the mission. If the mission is education, most management activities should relate to educational activities in the reserve. If large disparities are found between goals and management, a reevaluation is in order.

At La Selva, there are 44 full-time staff positions. Most staff work full-time at supporting station use by researchers and students, La Selva's primary audience. Nevertheless, several staffers work part-time with general public visitors (goal 3); altogether this totals about 2 staff positions. Almost no staff time is dedicated to supporting activities not mentioned in the mission statement. In La Selva's case, there is a close match between what the mission statement says the staff should be doing, and how they actually spend their time.

If the mission and staff time commitment are reasonably consistent, the next question is how well the staff uses time and money to carry out their assigned goals. This is considerably more difficult to assess than simple time allocation, as it calls for judgments about quality and efficiency. A first step is to look at the measurable outputs a reserve produces in carrying out its mission: how many water buffalo are protected or how many ecotourists are accommodated. Quantity does not necessarily translate to quality, however, so this approach must be used with caution. A frequently used alternative is to ask a number of experienced observers how reserve X compares with similar reserves. At La Selva this approach is taken in two ways. LSAC is a committee made up of experienced users who regularly compare management of the station with that of other reserves. In addition, much of La Selva's funding comes from externally reviewed foundation grants, applications for which are evaluated by other experienced reserve managers and users. For La Selva to continue operating, the community of biological station managers and field biologists has to be convinced that the station is being run efficiently.

## Reserve Functions and Long-Term Sustainability

*General Considerations.* We have argued that a reserve should have a mission, and that the way the reserve is managed should correspond to that mission. We have sidestepped the question of what constitutes a realistic, worthwhile, and sustainable mission. While this is partially a value judgment, there are some useful generalizations for thinking about the appropriateness of a reserve's mission.

1. *Does the mission fulfill an important need?* This clearly calls for a subjective evaluation. The degree to which a reserve fulfills functions not carried out by other reserves is one measure of its importance. Another index is the actual or potential amount of reserve use by target audiences. Importance in this context is necessarily a relative measure. For example, a county nature center may fulfill a critical need in local environmental education even though the biological resources protected are insignificant.

2. *Is the physical site appropriate to the mission?* For example, if public education is the mission, is there sufficient "clientele" within a reasonable distance of the reserve? The site's physical and biological characteristics should be suitable for the mission (or conversely, the mission should be tailored to the characteristics of the area).

3. *Is the mission biologically sustainable?* The general effects of reserves becoming habitat islands are well known and are discussed elsewhere in this book. This question should be asked of every reserve, even if it may not be answerable. For example, there are numerous small reserves in the United States set aside to protect small populations of rare plants. In most cases the long-term sustainability of these small populations is currently unknown. If biological sustainability is important to the reserve's mission, some way of evaluating sustainability should be sought.

4. *Is the mission likely to be financially sustainable?* Given the vagaries of funding, this question may be unanswerable, especially for nongovernment reserves lacking endowment. If no realistic prospect of obtaining long-term funding to carry out the mission can be foreseen, perhaps the mission should be altered to something more affordable.

5. *Is the mission politically sustainable?* Who supports and who opposes the reserve? Who benefits from the reserve? Political considerations affect most reserves, and are a particular issue in developing countries, where there is frequently no long-term history of protected re-

serve management. Legal structures for ensuring protection are likely to be weak, lacking, or unenforceable. Human pressures on natural resources are almost certain to be higher than in developed countries. There are numerous cases of tropical reserves that have been lost because they were not politically sustainable. What constitutes political sustainability will vary from country to country, but it must be considered when analyzing a given reserve.

*The Case of La Selva.* How does La Selva stack up in terms of its mission and long-term sustainability? First, does the target audience agree that the mission is important? Remembering that La Selva's mission is primarily to serve students and assist researchers, there are several quantitative ways to look at this. In 1991, 69 university courses or adult workshops used the station on 198 days; 239 researchers from the United States, Latin America, and Europe also used the reserve. Total use of the station increased an average of 10% per year over the last decade. In that period the research users of La Selva produced over 700 scientific publications, or about 70 per year. These figures indicate that the target audience of the station, mainly university students and researchers, is using the station in increasing numbers and is also publishing results of their work.

One reason use continues to grow is that, in terms of infrastructure and natural resources, La Selva is well suited for its intended function. The buildings, laboratories, trails, and staff offer researchers and students logistic support matched in only a handful of sites in the humid tropics (Figure 13.17). Protected areas and areas zoned for manipulative, high-impact research are available, as are a broad variety of habitats and land-use histories. La Selva's location in Costa Rica is an additional major advantage. Costa Rica is a stable, democratic republic with a traditionally high regard for education and a welcoming stance toward foreign researchers. Biological resources, infrastructure, and geopolitical location all contribute to La Selva's suitability as an international academic research and teaching center.

Biological sustainability has been a key issue in the development of La Selva. The original reserve was much too small to support an intact lowland

**Figure 13.17** Buildings at La Selva, showing some of the infrastructure at the biological station. (Photograph by Cathy Pringle.)

rainforest flora and fauna. In 1986, years of work by Costa Rican and foreign conservationists came to fruition when Braulio Carrillo National Park was extended to surround the southern borders of La Selva (see Figure 13.15). Currently, the Braulio–La Selva strictly protected core encompasses about 44,000 ha, and is buffered by almost 100,000 ha of other units of the Central Cordillera Biosphere Reserve. Even with this large protected area, three large vertebrates (Harpy Eagle, white-lipped peccary, and giant anteater) seem to have disappeared from the region. Nevertheless, the area currently protected should preserve the majority of taxa in all major groups. Exactly how much biodiversity a medium-sized reserve like Braulio–La Selva will sustain in the long run, however, is not known.

In terms of financial sustainability, La Selva is similar to many NGO-operated reserves in that its long-term economic future rests on several unknowns. La Selva currently receives funds from two major sources: fees charged to users (57% of 1992 revenues), and long-term funding by the United States National Science Foundation (43% of revenues). Neither of these sources is a long-term surety. Nevertheless, the continued increase in La Selva usage and the high level of scientific productivity of the researchers increase the probability that both funding sources will continue on their current courses for at least the medium term. For the long run, OTS is seeking an endowment to provide stable core funding.

Assessing political sustainability is fraught with pitfalls. On several fronts, however, there are reasons to argue that La Selva is likely to continue to operate in a favorable political environment in Costa Rica. OTS has enjoyed good relations with the government of Costa Rica, and in 1987 the consortium signed a letter of agreement formalizing these relations. Costa Rica has historically been open to foreign scientists and students, and this continues to be true. At the local level, OTS has taken active measures to ensure that La Selva is well regarded. La Selva runs a comprehensive environmental education and community relations program that regularly interacts with local children, adults, NGOs, and the county government. In an effort to involve the local community more closely with station operations, OTS taught an intensive course in natural history interpretation to local adults. The alumni of this course are now active in OTS' program of general public education, as well as in research, ecotourism, and environmental education. OTS recently purchased an additional 40-ha buffer strip between the current station and the neighboring town, where a new regional environmental education center aimed at the Costa Rican public will be developed. A key element in its planning is incorporation of local residents as primary personnel in natural history interpretation. While political winds can shift rapidly, OTS is taking substantial and continued care to be a good neighbor at the local and national levels.

## Conclusion: From General Principles to Real-World Decisions

By their very definition, all protected areas are being managed; the success of a reserve depends critically on the nature of this management. This case study discussed general principles for analyzing reserve management, and applied them to one tropical rainforest reserve. This type of mission-oriented analysis of reserve function is relatively new. To form your own opinion of the usefulness of this approach, apply it to the next protected area you come into contact with. Talk to the managers and users and ask them the kinds of questions outlined in this study. You will quickly get a taste of the environmental, political, social and economic pressures that shape the operation of reserves. The type of stepwise analysis advocated here is meant to encourage conservation biologists to recognize the practical complexities of reserve management, and to deal with these realities with rational and effective management.

## CASE STUDY 5

### Management of Conservation Units:
### The Costa Rican National System of Conservation Areas

Christopher Vaughan, Universidad Nacional, Costa Rica

*National planning can contribute to successful management of conservation areas by facilitating the coordination of resource and development agencies, by encouraging participation by private landowners in conservation decision making, and by supporting decentralized, flexible regional planning. Stable, long-term funding is essential so that national planning can be implemented.*

Protected natural areas have traditionally been viewed as islands, independent of and protected from their surroundings. However, natural areas both affect neighboring lands and are affected by external ecological, physical, cultural, and social influences. If protected areas are to survive in the long term, they must be managed complementary to, and not isolated from, the general landscape, and must take into account human influences and needs. Integration of protected areas into regional development plans as multiple-use areas is necessary to obtain maximum sustainable natural resource conservation and production without losing future use options. The case of Costa Rica's attempt to integrate protected areas into regional land use programs is explored here, and the management challenges of such an approach are emphasized.

Few countries worldwide can boast of Costa Rica's recent success in wildland conservation and management. Two decades ago, the country was faced with one of the world's highest population growth rates, a huge international debt, land-hungry rich and poor, the world's highest deforestation rate, and a legal system that promoted deforestation (Leonard 1987). However, visionaries changed political and public opinion, received international financial and political support, and established a world-famous wildlands conservation and management system, which includes 29% of the national territory (14,500 km$^2$) in 78 protected national and private areas.

Before 1990, the majority of these protected areas were managed by four separate government institutions: the National Parks Service, the General Forestry Direction, the Wildlife Service, and the National Indian Affairs Commission. Several private organizations, including the Tropical Science Center and the Organization for Tropical Studies, also owned private reserves. Although wildland areas often shared borders, each institution managed its areas independently, with little effective coordination.

By 1990, it was apparent that the existing wildland system was not accomplishing its principal objectives of maintaining ecological processes and essential natural systems in undisturbed ecosystems/communities, restoring natural processes in disturbed communities, preserving biological diversity, and providing for sustainable use of species and ecosystems. Nine major problems made it difficult to achieve these objectives:

1. Wildland management legislation and institutions were overabundant, posing problems in defining institutional jurisdiction and priorities.

2. Size and shape of protected areas could not guarantee perpetuation of biological processes and biodiversity conservation.

3. Increasing pressures from human activities inside and around protected areas (banana development, cattle ranching, fire, uncontrolled ecotourism, poaching, firewood collection, and deforestation) were causing both biogeographical insularization and local human-related management problems.

4. Limited existing scientific information promoted species and ecosystem protection through isolation, rather than active management through restoration and development of biosphere reserves.

5. Budget and human resources were unstable and even decreased in some years, while wildland surface area and institutional responsibilities increased.

6. Local communities were increasingly hostile to wildland policies, partly because residents had never participated in wildlands decision making.

7. Centralized decision making from the capital city of San José had inhibited local area management.

8. Forest reserves, protected zones, and wildlife refuges were not managed as such.

9. Monitoring of natural and socioeconomic processes was insufficient in the protected wildland areas.

Thus, the disjunct wildlands system and its biological riches were increasingly threatened by human populations wanting to exploit resources to improve their standard of living. Management of the wildlands system was uncoordinated between institutions, which had neither sufficient human and economic resources nor innovative programs to guarantee the system's long-term survival. Biological conservation principles, such as minimum reserve size and active management through restoration ecology, were not being applied.

### An Innovative Approach

A new approach to Costa Rican wildland management was devised by the National Parks Service. Called the National System of Conservation Areas (NSCA), it seemed the best way to achieve the aforementioned wildland objectives, to overcome the many limitations of the existing wildlands system, and to allow the system to evolve within modern Costa Rican society. A law was proposed to the Costa Rican Legislative Assembly in June of 1991, creating NSCA within the Ministry of Natural Resources, Energy, and Mines (MIRENEM). The NSCA would consolidate protected area conservation and management, while orienting wildlands toward satisfying the socioeconomic needs of the local communities, and other national and international interests. Biological conservation concepts would be incorporated in this new system, especially paying attention to minimum population sizes, restoration ecology, and long-term monitoring. Although the law has yet to be approved, MIRENEM nevertheless has implemented many aspects of NSCA.

*NSCA Structure.* NSCA consists of three managerial components: central office headquarters, Satellite Areas, and Conservation Areas. The central office headquarters is the administrative body responsible for managing, regulating, guiding, auditing, and consolidating the Conservation Areas and Satellite Areas. It also sets the guidelines, long-term objectives, and policies for NSCA with the Minister and Vice-Minister of MIRENEM. The Satellite Areas are dispersed protected areas that do not belong to any particular Con-

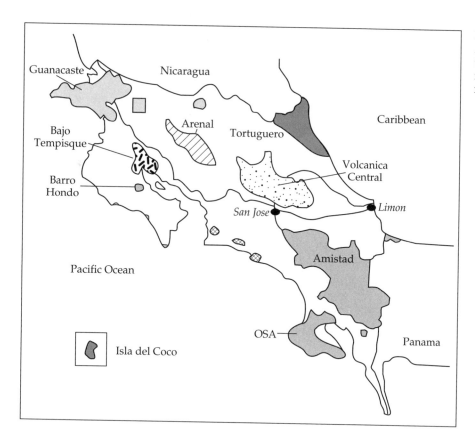

**Figure 13.18** Regional Conservation Areas of Costa Rica. These administrative units are based on ecological and regional influences, including the needs of local people.

servation Area due to their geographic isolation. They also are not integrated from a technical or administrative point of view into any Conservation Area.

The Conservation Areas are groups of contiguous or clustered wildlands that are placed in one of several management categories depending on their characteristics, regional influences, and participation of local inhabitants (Figure 13.18). Each Conservation Area may include one or more core or nucleus areas, consisting of one or more existing wildlands such as national parks, managed for biodiversity conservation, plus surrounding buffer zones for sustainable development activities. Governmental wildlands (forest reserves, wildlife refuges, and protected areas) or private lands adjacent to the core areas serve as buffer zones where, depending on the management criteria, rational, sustainable uses of natural resources are promoted, including controlled timber or firewood extraction, wildlife management, and ecotourism. The establishment of Conservation Areas fits nicely into new governmental policies of regionalization. Each Conservation Area has a regional commission, made up of local community members working with Conservation Area staff, responsible for its own administration and management.

*Governing Concepts.* The principal concepts governing NSCA include the following:

1. Costa Rican wildlands management functions as a system, integrating all wildland categories and areas under one administrative body with uniform general policies.
2. In administrative terms, each Conservation Area functions as a separate entity in technical, financial, and administrative matters, but is dependent on the administrative body for policy, control, and operation facilitation.

3. The unification of different wildlife management categories always includes a core or nucleus area for biodiversity protection and a surrounding buffer area to promote sustainable use of natural resources by local communities.
4. Local community participation is integrated by incorporating the experience and knowledge of residents as members of regional committees and by offering direct benefits to the community through jobs and controlled resource exploitation in the buffer zones.
5. Research and planning are integrated as instruments for management and decision making.
6. International economic and financial support will be continued and augmented for each Conservation Area to encourage investments that assure long-term financial support and reduced dependence on donations and governmental budgets.
7. National mechanisms will be implemented to ensure financial contributions from those who benefit directly or indirectly from the wildland system, with those funds used for NSCA management and maintenance.
8. Human management programs and training will be developed in each Conservation Area to respond to particular needs for specialization, with priority given to local inhabitants.

***An Example of Conservation Area Organization.*** The NSCA unites 71 of the 78 wildlands within seven Conservation Areas: La Amistad, Arenal, Cordillera Volcanica, Tempisque, Guanacaste, Tortuguero, and Osa (see Figure 13.18). Three disconnected marine wildland areas are also considered a Conservation Area. Each Conservation Area has its unique characteristics (Table 13.1), administrative body, and problems to resolve. A detailed summary of one area is presented as an example of how Conservation Areas function.

The Osa Conservation and Sustainable Development Area consists of approximately 160,000 ha in various national wildland areas on the Osa Peninsula in the southern Pacific region of Costa Rica. It is the last remaining large tract of lowland humid tropical forest on Mesoamerica's Pacific coast (Figure 13.19) and protects an immense amount of biological diversity and endemic species. Rainfall varies from 3–4 m per year on the coasts to 5–6 m per year

**Table 13.1**
The Costa Rican National System of Conservation Areas

| Conservation area | No. wildlands | Size (ha) | Special characteristics[a] |
|---|---|---|---|
| La Amistad | 21 | 446,900 | Mi, E, W, I |
| Arenal | 8 | 82,000 | Mi, E, W, G |
| Cordillera Volcanica | 12 | 135,500 | Mi, E, W, G |
| Tempisque | 12 | 21,700 | Mi |
| Guanacaste | 4 | 91,800 | Mi |
| Osa | 10 | 129,000 | M, Mi, G, S |
| Tortuguero | 4 | 123,000 | M, Mi, E, I |
| Marine Parks | 3 | | M |

From Ministerio de Recursos Naturales, Energia y Minas 1992.
[a]E, endemic species; G, geology; I, indigenous groups; M, marine; Mi, migratory species; S, social characteristics; W, watershed protection.

**Figure 13.19** The Osa Peninsula is the largest remaining tract of lowland rainforest in the area, containing huge specimens of trees such as this *Ceiba pentandra*. Holding up the tree is Mario Boza, first director of the Costa Rican National Parks Service. (Photograph by Christopher Vaughan.)

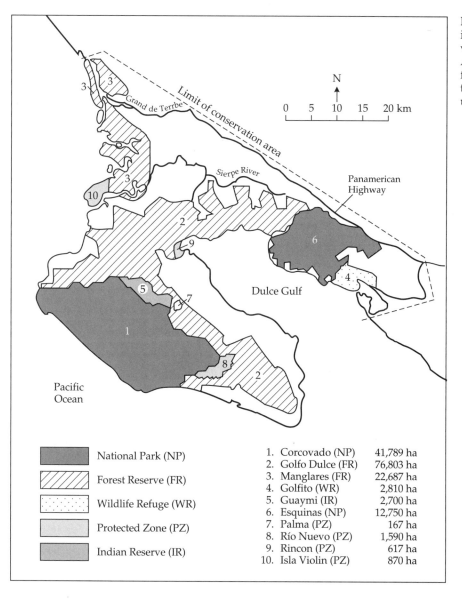

**Figure 13.20** Detailed map of the various units making up the Osa Conservation and Sustainable Development Area. Note the contribution of national forests, Indian lands, parks, and other types of lands with different historical uses.

National Park (NP)

Forest Reserve (FR)

Wildlife Refuge (WR)

Protected Zone (PZ)

Indian Reserve (IR)

| | | |
|---|---|---|
| 1. Corcovado (NP) | 41,789 ha |
| 2. Golfo Dulce (FR) | 76,803 ha |
| 3. Manglares (FR) | 22,687 ha |
| 4. Golfito (WR) | 2,810 ha |
| 5. Guaymi (IR) | 2,700 ha |
| 6. Esquinas (NP) | 12,750 ha |
| 7. Palma (PZ) | 167 ha |
| 8. Río Nuevo (PZ) | 1,590 ha |
| 9. Rincon (PZ) | 617 ha |
| 10. Isla Violin (PZ) | 870 ha |

at the highest points (600 m). This Conservation Area encompasses two national parks, two forest reserves, one mangrove reserve, one wildlife refuge, one Indian reserve, four protected zones and one annex, all created in the last 20 years (Figure 13.20).

The enormous biological richness of the Osa Peninsula has interested scientists for many years. Over 500 species of trees have been identified in Corcovado National Park within Osa, with more than 100 species/ha found in some areas. The Conservation Area is home to 140 mammal, 367 bird, 117 reptile and amphibian, 40 freshwater fish, and at least 6000 insect species. These include endangered large mammals such as the jaguar, cougar, ocelot, and tapir, and one of the largest populations of Scarlet Macaws in Mesoamerica (Vaughan 1981).

Corcovado National Park, the first wildland area created on the Osa Peninsula in 1974 and the cornerstone for the Osa Conservation and Sustainable Development Area, resulted from a land trade with a multinational company, publicity created by the international scientific community, and relocation of several hundred inhabitants from the park area (Vaughan 1981). However, this park was not large enough to protect natural ecosystems on the Osa Peninsula. Exploitation of untouched wilderness increased in the middle 1980s for three reasons: (1) the opening of a year-round highway into the peninsula permitted access for the first time to loggers and squatters; (2) gold deposits found in Corcovado National Park and its expanded areas created a conflict between the government and gold panners; and (3) abandonment of lands controlled by banana companies elsewhere in southwestern Costa Rica caused high levels of unemployment and an exodus to the Osa Peninsula, considered the last frontier in southern Costa Rica.

These colonists had little understanding of the limitations of land use on the peninsula. Poor soils, steep slopes, and high precipitation imposed severe limitations on yields for farmers who practiced slash-and-burn agriculture. Farming destroyed forests and watersheds (Figure 13.21). Uncontrolled hunting, small- to medium-sized gold mining efforts, and small-scale timber operations also detrimentally affected biological communities on the peninsula.

The Osa Conservation and Sustainable Development Area was estab-

**Figure 13.21** Deforestation in Corcovado National Park, such as on this slope for farming, was commonplace before creation of the Park, and threatened the biota of the region. (Photograph by Christopher Vaughan.)

lished in 1990 to avert an ecological disaster while allowing for sustainable human presence on the peninsula. Regional planning is ongoing. The Conservation Area works with local community organizations and NGOs, focusing on finding ways to encourage environmentally sound economic alternatives for the lands surrounding the core areas. At present, the Conservation Area, in cooperation with the Forestry Directorate, National Parks Service, and Mining Directorate, serves as the coordinating agency for formally organized programs in agroforestry, research, ecotourism, protection, land organization, environmental education, and mining.

The "Boscosa project," initiated in 1987, is an example of one of the wildland management programs implemented. A primary goal of the management plan was to maintain forest cover on the Osa Peninsula, including Corcovado National Park and surrounding buffer zones. Several different means have been identified to achieve this goal, including natural forest management, improved agriculture, agroforestry, reforestation, and ecotourism. Extensive socioeconomic surveys and land tenure use and capacity studies were conducted in several communities. An extensive biotic survey was conducted to determine the status of the areas relative to stated goals. A strategy to create and support local organizations to initiate and carry out specific projects was defined and implementation begun. Boscosa has received over $350,000 from several international agencies, especially USAID and the World Wildlife Fund. Funding for the 1992–1996 period is provided by the Costa Rican government, the Swedish government, the Global Environmental Facility, and the Schnitzler Foundation.

### Funding Strategies: A Key to Success

The Costa Rican wildlands system has been successful partly because of its ability to attract international grants and donations, and the willingness of the Costa Rican government to provide financial support. Between 1977 and 1990, both the National Parks Service and the General Forestry Directorate, the organizations that administer most of the wildland areas, operated with a budget of approximately $46 million—$27 million from the Costa Rican government and $19 million from various international funding agencies. Admission fees to national parks have resulted in only $1.1 million in the last 10 years for the NPS.

The National Parks Service discovered years ago that rigid government structures, archaic laws, and administrative regulations created major obstacles to efficient use of financial and human resources. Also, in an uncertain world economy where international aid might cease with the effects of war, recession, and competing projects, the need to secure permanent funding for NSCA was obvious. Several ideas were devised.

*Debt-for-nature swaps.* Debt-for-nature swaps are an innovative way to obtain funds for protecting wildland areas. Unpaid portions of national debt are purchased at real market value (e.g., at 37% of the loan's face value) by conservation organizations. In exchange for canceling the debt, the government agrees to long-term support for a conservation program. Since 1988, Costa Rica has paid off a total of $87,370,000 in debts using donations from organizations and foreign governments for conservation projects. This funding concept is discussed in more detail by Thomas Lovejoy, one of its creators, in Essay 13A.

*The National Park Foundation.* The National Park Foundation and the Neotropical Foundation, NGOs, were created to obtain, channel, and manage funds efficiently. Costa Rican private foundations have several advantages over government agencies, including the fact that many foreign NGOs, foundations, governments, and individuals prefer funds to be managed by local NGOs, so that they are not bound by the Public Administration Law, which delays negotiation and implementation of projects. NGOs also can avoid political entanglements.

*Endowments.* Endowments provide another alternative for guaranteed long-term and consistent funding. They have been called intergenerational transfers or insurance premiums, because present generations sacrifice financial resources to assure future generations sufficient funds to operate Conservation or Satellite Areas. An initial endowment equivalent to 16 times the yearly operation expense of a given Conservation Area, at a 6% interest rate, will finance the Conservation Area's operation expenses indefinitely. This does not include investment and development costs, but donations and entrance and service fees could assist in those areas.

*Trust funds.* Trust funds are managed by state-owned banks following instructions from a board of trustees, similar to procedures used by United States universities. This plan ensures financial freedom to each Conservation Area and reduces administrative costs. Funding plans are set up for each Conservation Area as a separate management unit, and funding is actively pursued by each director and interested people in the local area.

Other funding possibilities are being considered as well. For example, Costa Rica is considering establishing a funding program modeled on the "Golden Eagle" passport issued by the U.S. National Park Service. A "green" passport would be purchased yearly and allow unlimited access to NSCA areas for one year. A two-tiered system, with higher costs for foreign visitors, could be employed to retain local support and attendance in wildland areas.

## ESSAY 13A
# Debt-for-Nature Swaps

Thomas E. Lovejoy, Smithsonian Institution

The underlying concept of debt-for-nature swaps emerged in a *New York Times* article that I authored in 1984. I had come to realize that debt itself is a source of environmental problems through the pressure it puts on governments to generate foreign exchange. Debt also shortchanges government programs such as national park protection, which have less immediacy than those programs addressing social needs of the moment. The temptation to cash in natural resource capital (as by clear-cutting primary forests) to service debt or achieve debt reduction has been and still is great.

My friends in the world of finance largely thought I had taken leave of my senses for some rather ethereal realm, because there was no obvious mechanism for converting a portion of a debt obligation into a conservation product. It was not until after the world of finance had devised a way to convert debt for commercial purposes that it was possible to see a way to do this for

socially useful purposes such as environmental protection. That happened in 1987, when Conservation International, a vibrant, Washington-based conservation organization, achieved the first debt-for-nature swap in Bolivia.

Swaps operate on the principle of buying low in cheap, hard currency and selling high in soft currency. The debt obligations of a sovereign nation to a commercial bank are available at a discount on a secondary market. If the debt load of a country is large relative to its ability to service and repay the debt, the discount will be great. At one point, Peruvian debt sold for two cents on the dollar, and Ecuadorian debt was selling for thirty-three. Basically any entity, including a conservation organization, can acquire such debt.

The leverage comes in redeeming the debt in local currency at an amount close to face value. This arrangement requires the agreement of the nation's central bank or other fiscal authority, and is generally brought about by a

conservation partner in the country. The debt paper is then traded in for currency or some fiscal instrument such as a bond. The proceeds can then be spent on conservation activities.

The monies generated through a debt swap have great versatility; however, they are not generally used to purchase land. Rather, funds typically are used to assist local organizations or governments in offsetting the costs of demarcation and maintenance of natural reserves and parks. They can also be used to construct research stations and nature centers, or for education and training programs. The newly acquired funds are flexible and can be easily directed to satisfying the needs of the particular country and community.

It is important to distinguish between the financial mechanism and the projects it has been used to support. Most of the criticism of debt swaps is in fact misdirected; it has nothing to do with the mechanism itself, but rather with the details of some of the projects that swaps have been used to support.

Another major criticism has been that swaps violate national sovereignty, a misperception that seems to arise out of an emotional response to the actual word "debt." To the contrary, debt-for-nature swaps are impossible unless a central bank agrees and a national conservation organization has been involved. In fact many, if not the majority of all swaps to date have been initiated by local organizations and have merely been facilitated by international conservation organizations. Curiously, the sovereignty issue is rarely raised when swaps are conducted for commercial purposes.

Another frequent criticism is that debt swaps have an inflationary effect on local economies. That is possible, but it is rarely a significant concern. Chile has executed several billion dollars of swaps and is without an inflationary problem, which is a reflection of how well the Chilean economy had been managed in general. Whether there is an inflationary effect really is a function of how well the economy of the nation in question is being managed, and how big the debt swap is relative to the money supply of the nation. Rarely is a swap large enough in that sense to cause problems.

Indeed, debt-for-nature swaps have never been conceived, despite some impressions to the contrary, as *the* solution

to—as opposed to a contribution toward the solution of—a nation's debt problem. What they do achieve is a modest relief of a hard currency obligation, while putting moneys into conservation efforts.

Often, to avoid any concerns about inflation, a central bank will issue an interest-bearing instrument such as a bond. In the case of Ecuador's first swap, bonds were issued for the same length of time as the original debt paper. A great advantage of this sort of mechanism is that it provides financial stability to the effort in question, in essence providing a form of endowment. Inflation becomes a concern in a different sense if the economy is like that of Brazil, where inflation has been a serious presence for as long as almost anyone can remember. This can cause the buying power of the endowment to be rapidly eroded. To guard against this possibility, in a number of cases the bonds are dollar denominated.

To date, something on the order of $200 million of debt has been converted for environmental purposes. While this is a significant sum in the conservation game, it is minuscule relative to the debt that exists. The reason is that in almost all instances, the debt has had to be purchased, which requires conservation organizations with limited resources to come up with the necessary dollars. It has been less advantageous

for banks to donate debt than to sell it on the secondary market. Although occasionally government funds have been made available for purchase (USAID in Madagascar; Sweden's International Development Agency) this has been rare.

Another possibility raised by debt swaps is donations by governments of other governments' debts, which can be used in all the same ways. Generally, governments do not stop to think about the good they might be able to do in this fashion when they are in the process of forgiving outstanding debt. I believe it should become a basic principle when intergovernmental debt forgiveness is being considered to ask whether a portion should be sequestered for an environmental endowment fund of some kind. The Enterprise for the Americas Initiative contained such a provision, and to date several conservation trusts have been set up as a consequence.

The possibility of debt swaps will continue for as long as any nation has a significant debt load. Having been impressed by the variety of packages developed once the general concept and an initial mechanism were available, I fully expect the concept to evolve. I hope, as well, that the notion of pursuing innovative financing for conservation and the environment will continue and even expand.

## Success or Failure?

Although human and economic resources are scarce, and the new law has yet to be approved, NSCA seems to be working. The basic administrative infrastructure is in place in the administrative body and most Conservation Areas. Environmental education, agricultural and scientific research, and environmental monitoring have begun in many conservation areas. Costa Rican wildland areas are increasingly more popular for foreign and Costa Rican ecotourism and scientific use (Figure 13.22), with a 43% increase of visitors with ecological interests between 1991 and 1992. These visitors are attracted because the natural beauty and tropical biota of Costa Rica are accessible and the country is safe for travel due to the stable political system and well-developed infrastructure.

Nationally, there is a strong commitment from government agencies, NGOs, local development agencies, and national development organizations and conservation groups to continue and fortify the NSCA. Many projects have been implemented with support from local communities near or within the Conservation Areas. International support for Costa Rica's conservation efforts has been strong, and the NSCA initiative comes at a time when the world is looking for new approaches to wildlands and surrounding human community management. The pace at which progress has been made is remarkable; this nationwide coordination project, complete with infrastructure and funding, has occurred in three years.

**Figure 13.22** The coastal area of Corcovado National Park, looking at Sirena and Llorona Playas (beaches). Such protected areas are attractive for both tourism and scientific endeavors, and greatly contribute to the local and national economy. (Photograph by Christopher Vaughan.)

Given the support for this project at local, regional, national, and international levels, Costa Rica's track record in conservation, and the technical and scientific capacity of NSCA, the project to consolidate the NSCA should be successfully implemented and should serve as a model for management of diverse and geographically dispersed lands for long-term biodiversity conservation.

***Can the Costa Rican Model be Generalized?*** The key ingredients of the NSCA model that make for successful conservation area management are coordination of agencies, involvement of private landowners, regionalized plans, flexible policy, and long-term support. Can these ingredients be transposed to other tropical countries? In principle, yes, but in practice it will be difficult. Few countries give conservation the priority it is given in Costa Rica, and few tropical countries have the political stability and level of education enjoyed by Costa Rica.

There is perhaps an important lesson here for conservation management in the United States and elsewhere. Coordination by public U.S. agencies does occur, but usually it is due either to the efforts of progressive individuals or to a legal requirement such as the Endangered Species Act. Citizens are usually not brought into the decision-making process, and their input is typically limited to commentary on proposed agency plans or, more forcefully, through initiating legal injunctions that block a state or federal action. Regional planning does occur, but is often constrained by federal guidelines. For example, National Forest management plans are regionalized, but they have to meet federal guidelines for timber harvest. Conservation of biodiversity is not given priority but is simply one of many competing management objectives. Finally, funding and policy often shift with election year cycles. The United States and other developed countries could learn a great deal from Costa Rica about how to develop effective national and regional resource management policy.

## Conclusions

Two important approaches for managing endangered species are illustrated in the case studies on sea turtles, black-footed ferrets, and Spotted Owls. One approach emphasizes critical aspects of the species' population ecology, while the other is more focused on habitat issues.

The black-footed ferret is an extremely endangered specialist predator of prairie dogs, a group of species that was once abundant but now exist in only a few isolated populations. In a last-ditch attempt to save the ferrets, they were brought into a captive breeding program. With virtually none surviving in the wild, a captive breeding and release program seems to be the only solution. But in addition to information on the species' population ecology, critical habitat must be available, including flourishing prairie dog towns.

The ferret case contains some important lessons that are reinforced in the sea turtle study. First and foremost, captive breeding and release programs must be linked with efforts to address the original cause of the species' decline. Species that have become endangered because their habitats are destroyed or degraded obviously cannot be "recovered" by simply releasing captive-bred individuals back into an unsuitable habitat.

Second, contingencies will inevitably arise that call for well-reasoned compromises. For example, population vulnerability analysis tells us that we ought to reestablish ferrets in large populations in order to avoid the stochastic sources of extinction and genetic losses to which small populations are susceptible. However, there was a very real concern over the extreme susceptibility of the ferrets to canine distemper. For this reason, managers chose to reestablish ferrets in several small populations rather than in a single large population. Thus, they chose to accept a somewhat greater risk of stochastic effects in order to lessen the catastrophic risk of disease wiping out all the animals in a single larger population.

Third, a conservation plan to recover and protect an endangered species must be comprehensive, going beyond what can be done by addressing just the population biology of the species. In the case of the ferrets, it was necessary to educate private landowners so that they would stop poisoning prairie dogs and accept the program to reintroduce the ferrets onto their lands. In the case of sea turtles, it is necessary to legislate protection of adults at sea from the dangers of fishing and shrimping operations, and to protect nesting beaches from development.

The Spotted Owl study focused primarily on the importance of habitat protection in management. There are no fundamental problems with the population ecology of owls that are causing their demise; it is clear that protection of old-growth forests is the key to managing the species. In this instance, because of the apparent conflicts between owl ecology and logging, the visibility of endangered species management is higher than in any other case. Political, legal, and policy pressures have greater influence in management of Spotted Owls than possibly any other endangered species.

At the other extreme of management issues is the protection and use of large conservation areas. We have chosen two, both from Costa Rica, to illustrate the wide range of issues that managers of conservation areas must deal with. The La Selva Biological Station is an example of a private conservation area whose mission is focused on education and research. Similar examples in the United States include a large number of private biological field stations, such as the Natural Reserve System of the University of California; nature reserves, such as the lands protected by The Nature Conservancy; field research centers, such as the Joseph W. Jones Ecological Research Center in Georgia, the Savannah River Ecology Laboratory in South Carolina, and the Center for Ecosystem Studies in New York; and the nationwide system of Long Term Ecological Research (LTER) Sites.

In his analysis of the La Selva station, David Clark suggests a stepwise approach for analyzing the degree of fit between the stated mission of the site, its objectives, and site management. Although the La Selva site is discrete, with its multiple functions embraced by teaching and research, its managers still found a strong need to go beyond the boundaries of the reserve to address regional conservation needs. As a result of this "outreach" effort, the station has become involved with local environmental education projects and with programs of other Costa Rican land use agencies in the region. While this is particularly important for La Selva as a field station whose use is dominated by U.S. scientists and students, community outreach and service should be a significant component of the management plan for all conservation sites.

Individual conservation sites cannot be viable in any significant way if they are managed by closing their borders and insulating the site. Individual sites should be integrated into the larger issues of land use, both nationally and regionally. Costa Rica has attempted to do this through a regionalized National System of Conservation Areas in which management decisions on land use around sensitive core natural areas are coordinated and, ideally, kept compatible with conservation goals. The NSCA seems superficially similar to the Biosphere Reserve Concept, in which core natural areas are to be protected with buffer zones in which land use is restricted. NSCA, however, has an administrative structure to implement its goals. Biosphere Reserves are often little more than concepts and paper planning, although the goals are certainly important.

All conservation areas are, to some extent, designed for multiple uses. In rational cases, the multiple uses are complementary or can be at least be made compatible. A difficult and frustrating counterexample is the multiple-use mandate of public lands in the United States, in particular, lands of the U.S. National Forests and the Bureau of Land Management, the two largest federal land agencies. Except in special cases, such as where the Endangered Species Act or wetlands protection legislation restricts public access and limits land use options, conflicts between conservation goals and economic and recreational development are common and unresolved.

The Bureau of Land Management controls approximately 109 million ha, and the Forest Service approximately 77 million ha. Not only is this area significant (more than five times the size of the National Park System), but it includes major ecosystems and surrounds other core sensitive habitats. Clearly, one of the major unresolved conservation management issues is how to protect biodiversity on federal lands mandated for public use. The answer will undoubtedly be some form of zoning that is much more restrictive than at present. If ever the nation's political backbone becomes stiff enough to take on the various vested interests, conservation biologists must be ready to offer management plans grounded in the kinds of experiences illustrated by these case studies, using the principles and methodologies illustrated in the rest of this text.

## Questions for Discussion

1. Black-footed ferrets were reintroduced into the wild in several small, isolated populations. Discuss the possible genetic consequences of this aspect of the recovery plan and the possible implications for the ferrets' long-term susceptibility to canine distemper. What alternative approaches might be possible?

2. There is currently considerable debate about the best way to manage endangered species. At the extremes, one school of thought holds that a species-based approach is essential, while the other school argues that we cannot protect all species so we should shift to an ecosystem-based approach. In the context of the studies presented here, discuss the pros and cons of each approach. Are they mutually exclusive approaches to biodiversity protection?

3. Some conservationists argue that we should continue headstarting projects for sea turtles because the captive turtles provide important opportunities for environmental education. Others argue that we could achieve the same educational effect by displaying a few turtles in zoos or aquariums rather than headstarting hundreds or thousands of turtles each year. What do you think? What are some other factors that bear on this question?

4. Recent computer models of sea turtle conservation options (Crouse et al. 1987) show that protecting the larger juveniles and adults will result in faster recovery of populations than protecting eggs and hatchlings. Because of this, some conservationists argue that we should abandon the unproven hatchery and headstarting projects and concentrate our efforts on protecting the larger, older turtles. Others argue that new turtles can only come from eggs, and that if we abandon protection of early life stages to protect only the older turtles, the species will still go extinct as the older individuals die off from natural causes and are not replaced due to excessive egg and hatchling mortality. What do you think?

5. Compare the Conservation Area approach to multiple use of public lands in Costa Rica with the multiple-use approach taken by the U.S. Bureau of Land Management and the Forest Service. How would each deal with conflict between the need to protect biodiversity and the need to extract economic value from the lands?

6. Recall the Spotted Owl case study. Imagine that you are a biologist who has been invited to present testimony to a Congressional committee concerned about resolving the conflicts between biodiversity protection and local economic growth. How would you respond to the following statement from a Congressional committee member: "My aide tells me that the Spotted Owl also occurs in southern California and that a genetic study showed that the populations were the same [an electrophoretic study that indicated the populations were identical for 29 loci] and the owl doesn't need old-growth forest in southern California. Why can't we just harvest the old-growth forest and let the owl live in southern California?"

7. In the case study of the La Selva Biological Station, David Clark argued that it was important for biologists to contribute to the environmental education needs of the surrounding community. How would you apply your interests and knowledge of conservation ecology to the needs of local environmental education?

## Suggestions for Further Reading

The following suggested readings are meant to supplement the case studies by focusing on management in ecosystems that are not covered in this chapter.

Clausen. B. 1993. A survey of protected areas management by state and provincial Fish and Wildlife Agencies in western states and provinces. *Nat. Areas J.* 13:

204–213. This survey of habitat management programs included agency staff in 13 western states and two provinces. The upside of the survey shows a high level of management activity while the downside suggests that resources are inadequate and declining, and that integration among agencies is weak.

Gibson, D. J., T. R. Seastedt and J. M. Briggs. 1992. Management practices in tallgrass prairie: Large- and small-scale experimental effects on species composition. *J. App. Ecol.* 30:247–255. The authors examine the effects of burning and mowing on community composition in Kansas tallgrass prairie. In addition to their description of grassland management practices, they provide a good discussion of the significance of scale of management.

Hamilton, L. S. 1993. Status and current developments in mountain protected areas. *Mountain Res. and Devel.* 13:311–314. Because of their relatively low productivity and fragile slopes, mountains are particularly vulnerable to mismanagement. At the same time, mountainous regions represent some of the most significant remaining natural habitat and, in a future of climate change, their environmental range may provide important refugia.

Marine Protected Areas. *Oceanus* 36(3), Fall 1993. This issue focuses on marine protected areas, from coastal to oceanic, polar to tropical. The marine environment produces more animal protein than poultry or beef, is the recipient of pollution carried by rivers and sewage systems, and along its coastal fringes is subject to intense development pressures. The need for marine protected areas is evident, but is largely overlooked by the conservation community.

Polis, G. A. (ed.) 1991. *The Ecology of Desert Communities.* University of Arizona Press, Tucson. Most publications that deal with management of desert lands emphasize their use for dryland agriculture or cattle and sheep range; thus, these works have limited usefulness for conservation management. While this book does not dwell on management issues explicitly, it provides a good discussion of the factors (equilibrial and nonequilibrial) that influence desert communities.

Zedler, J. B. and A. N. Powell. 1993. Managing coastal wetlands. *Oceanus* 36(2):19–27. This is a good account of the complexities and uncertainties involved in wetland management. The unexpected outcomes in managing even reasonably intact wetlands should give pause to those who believe that we can re-create them. This is a useful extension of Essay 14B by Zedler.

The following papers, read in combination, provide a good overview of new approaches—and their attendant problems—for management at the scale of large landscapes.

Noss, R. F. 1993. A conservation plan for the Oregon Coast Range: Some preliminary suggestions. *Nat. Areas J.* 13(4):276–290.

Povilitis, T. 1993. Applying the Biosphere Reserve concept to a greater ecosystem: The San Juan Mountain Area of Colorado and New Mexico. *Nat. Areas J.* 13(1):18–28.

# 14

# Ecological Restoration

*The acid test of our understanding is not whether we can take ecosystems to bits on pieces of paper, however scientifically, but whether we can put them together in practice and make them work.*

*A. D. Bradshaw, 1983*

One goal of conservation biology is to preserve biological diversity. Traditionally, this work has been carried out in wilderness or "natural" areas where human influence has been minimal or, as may be the case with some indigenous peoples, in areas where human use has maintained high biological diversity. In recent years, however, a growing number of conservationists have turned their attention to more or less severely altered areas, such as abandoned farm fields, utility corridors, highway rights-of-way, degraded wetlands, eutrophic lakes, ditched and leveed rivers, and even mined lands. Such areas present opportunities to contribute to the conservation of biodiversity not merely by protecting and maintaining populations and communities that persist on such sites, but by enhancing the sites through an active program of ecological restoration.

## What is Ecological Restoration?

Though it was barely recognized as a conservation strategy as recently as a decade ago, and has gained recognition as a discipline only in the past few years, **restoration ecology** is now playing a significant role in the planning and programs of agencies such as the National Park Service and the Army Corps of Engineers, and nongovernment organizations (NGOs) such as The Nature Conservancy, the Audubon Society, and the Sierra Club. Indeed, a new organization committed to restoration ecology, the Society for Ecological Restoration, was created in 1987. Today, restorationists may be said to be in the process of opening up a second conservation frontier; the conservation of biodiversity and other features of the natural landscape in areas written off as a "lost cause" by earlier generations of conservationists.

The term "ecological restoration" is actually one of a family of related terms referring to various approaches to the task of ecological healing or rehabilitation. These include "restoration" itself, as well as rehabilitation, reclamation, re-creation, and ecological recovery, which are defined and discussed in Box 14A. Of these words, the term "restoration" is both the most clearly defined and points toward the most ambitious objectives. This being the case, most of the principles, techniques, and issues relevant to the other forms of ecological rehabilitation work pertain to restoration and can be discussed under this heading. For this reason we confine ourselves to a discussion of restoration.

## Box 14A
## Definitions of Common Terms Used in Restoration Ecology

*Restoration:* The word *restore* means "to bring back . . . into a former or original state" (Webster's New Collegiate Dictionary 1977). Ecological restoration simply means doing that to an ecological system. Restoration is often regarded as a distinctive form of conservation management, differing from "preservation," "conservation," "stewardship," or even "management" itself. There is no sharp distinction among these various forms of manipulation. All of them involve a series of attempts to compensate in a specific, ecologically effective way for alterations typically caused by human activities.

*Rehabilitation:* This is a broad term that may be used to refer to any attempt to restore elements of structure or function to an ecological system, without necessarily attempting complete restoration to any specified prior condition;

for example, replanting of sites to prevent erosion.

*Reclamation:* This term typically refers to rehabilitative work carried out on the most severely degraded sites, such as lands disturbed by open-cast mining or large-scale construction. Though reclamation work often falls short of restoration in the fullest sense (a copy of a native ecosystem is not achieved), it is clearly a necessary step in the process of restoration under such conditions. In a sense it is the first step to restoring a more natural ecosystem. Unfortunately, the disciplines of reclamation and restoration have developed more or less independently, and only recently has significant communication between them occurred.

*Re-creation:* Re-creation attempts to reconstruct an ecosystem, wholesale, on a site so severely disturbed that there is virtually nothing left to restore. The

new system may be modeled on a system located outside the range of the historical system, or may be established under conditions different from those under which it occurred naturally. Such efforts are not restoration in the strictest sense, but they can lead to important insights into the systems involved and the conditions that support them that can be invaluable in restoration efforts (Aber 1987; Jordan et al. 1987).

*Ecological recovery:* Recovery involves letting the system alone, generally in the expectation that it will regain desirable attributes through natural succession. This zero-order approach to restoration may or may not work. It is best regarded as a key *component* of restoration—the contribution of the system itself, as it were. In such cases the restorationist seeks to complement and reinforce natural processes.

To begin our exploration of restoration ecology, some discussion of the characteristics of people who call themselves restorationists is in order.

1. The restorationist acknowledges that the system has been altered in some way as a result of direct or indirect human influences, and makes explicit value judgments about the desirability of reversing this change. This viewpoint is important because it recognizes from the outset something that conservationists have sometimes been tempted to downplay: that human beings, like all other species, are continually interacting with ecosystems, that this is ultimately unavoidable, and that it inevitably alters the ecosystems. This recognition is actually a critical first step toward managing any system in such a way as to conserve its historical qualities.

2. The restorationist makes an explicit commitment to the conservation of a specified system or landscape with specific, historically defined properties. In contrast, rubrics such as "management," "stewardship," and even "conservation" leave room for considerable vagueness in the definition of goals. This is one reason why restoration has proved especially liable to criticism: it promises a particular result that can be objectively judged.

3. The restorationist acknowledges that the return of the system to its historical condition—or its maintenance in the presence of novel in-

fluences—generally involves deliberate manipulations to compensate for those influences. In other words, it is an active as well as a passive process. This viewpoint represents a clear recognition of both the beneficial role humans can play in the recovery of a degraded system, and their responsibility for playing that role.

4. Insofar as possible, the restorationist is also committed to re-creation of the entire system in all its aspects; these include dynamic and functional ecosystem properties as well as concrete elements such as the system's biotic and abiotic components.

## The Role of Ecological Restoration in Conservation

Until recently, protection and management of natural areas have been the major components of conservation practice, while the role of explicit restoration has been minor or nonexistent. There are a number of reasons for this. First, at least in the Western Hemisphere, natural or unaltered areas have been *relatively* plentiful, and conservationists have been preoccupied with attempts to identify them and protect them from undue human influence before they disappear. Second, there is a widely shared feeling that, in some sense, restored systems are intrinsically inferior to their natural counterparts. Third, some feel that true restoration of ecosystems is not possible. Finally, there is a concern that the promise of restoration might be used to undermine arguments for the conservation of existing natural and wild lands. That is, if we have the ability to restore any ecosystem, is there a need to preserve some in situ?

During the past few years several developments have resulted in a growing interest in the practice of restoration, even among those who remain properly skeptical about our ability to produce authentic replicas of historical ecosystems. These include (1) legislation requiring rehabilitation of areas disturbed by certain kinds of mining, as well as restoration or creation of wetlands to compensate for—or "mitigate"—damage to wetlands by activities such as mining or construction (Brenner 1990); (2) increased use of restorative procedures, including use of native vegetation in engineering applications such as utility corridors, rights-of-way, and watercourses (Crabtree 1984); (3) growing interest in native vegetation as an element in ornamental landscapes (Diekelman and Schuster 1982; Smyser 1986); and (4) the sheer level of ecological destruction that has made restoration necessary and attractive.

The decline in opportunities for conservation, as existing natural areas have either been lost or brought under conservation status, has led conservationists to reconsider disturbed areas as objects for conservation action. Similarly, events such as the irruption of animal populations in some protected areas and the catastrophic fires in Yellowstone National Park in the summer of 1988 have drawn the attention of the general public and the professional conservation community alike to the need for more active management, even in protected areas.

In the political arena restoration may be perceived as an alternative to conservation, a very dangerous perspective. In fact, they are not alternatives, but complementary parts of a comprehensive conservation strategy. In a sense, conservation is the objective, while restoration is one means for reaching that goal. Seen in this way, restoration is not an *alternative* to conservation; rather, it is a *subset* of conservation and a means of achieving it—not only under extreme conditions, but in any landscape subject to unwanted influences. The first principle of restoration, borrowed from the medical tradition, is "first, do no harm."

## Some Central Concerns of Restoration Ecology

The value of ecological restoration is the prospect it offers for actually reversing losses, allowing the conservationist to go on the offensive in the struggle to conserve natural landscapes. While initial gains may be modest, the potential of restoration efforts adds a new dimension to the work of designing reserves, and to management and conservation generally. The development and acceptance of restoration leads to conservation that involves ecologically upgrading existing reserves, their expansion and diversification by restoration on adjacent, degraded lands, and even creation of new reserves in heavily developed or other ecologically degraded areas (see, for example, Hughes and Bonnicksen 1990).

Several basic concerns are common to all types of restoration projects. These concerns include the product or goal being strived for, the feasibility of producing an authentic product, the scale of the project, and its costs.

### The Product

The fundamental goal of restoration ecology is to return a particular habitat or ecosystem to a condition as similar as possible to its pre-degraded state (Figure 14.1). It may also involve upgrading habitat for native species—in some cases for a specifically targeted rare species. To achieve any of these goals, some knowledge of the previous, undegraded state is necessary, including knowledge of the structure of the system (the species present and their relative abundances) and its function (the dynamics of biotic and abiotic interactions, including hydrology and nutrient cycling). Of course, for most ecological systems we have only incomplete knowledge of structure and function, but at least some idea of the dominant species present is necessary to develop a "target" for the restored system. The level of knowledge of the former system at least partly determines how closely we can approxi-

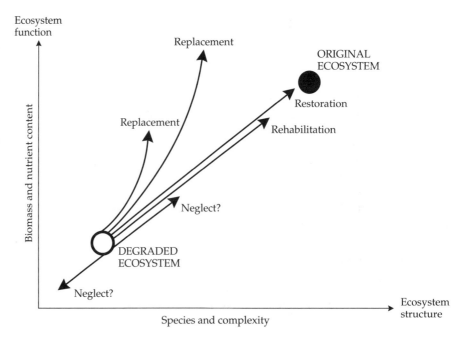

**Figure 14.1** The trajectory of a restoration project may be viewed in terms of ecosystem structure and function. A change in both dimensions occurs upon degradation; the restoration process is an attempt to direct the system back toward the original state. Complete restoration would involve return to that state; partial return, or other trajectories, would result in rehabilitation or replacement by a different system. (Modified from Bradshaw 1984.)

mate it in restoration, and how well we can judge success. One approach to defining the target, an "Index of Biotic Integrity," was developed by James Karr, and is discussed by him in Essay 14A.

The process of restoration actually involves setting the system on a new developmental trajectory toward its particular "target," its former state. How far along that trajectory the system goes depends on a number of things, including the level of knowledge of the previous state; how perturbed the system is; availability of biota for restoration; genetic variation of the biota; the level of alteration of hydrology, soil, and geomorphology; cost and available funding; and political will. Many times the product will not be an exact replica of the former system, but rather will represent a major change in trajectory toward the target.

The design and planning of restoration projects to achieve the product goal can be complex and cover a large variety of problems and issues. The National Research Council (1992) developed a checklist of questions appropriate for restoration projects, including questions to be addressed during project planning and design, during the project itself, and in the post-restoration phase (Table 14.1). Asking such questions helps restorationists to define the product, guide the project toward that product, and evaluate the product and make relevant adjustments.

## Feasibility and Authenticity

Because the process of restoration is guided by its objectives, restorationists have devoted a considerable amount of attention to questions related to how objectives for restoration projects should be defined, how the results can be evaluated, the extent to which restoration can actually be carried out, the quality of restored ecosystems, and the feasibility of carrying out high-quality restoration work on an environmentally significant scale (see for example, Jordan 1990).

Of these questions, the most fundamental relates to the definition of the goals and objectives for restoration projects. It would seem that definition would be simple, but it is often complex and involves difficult decisions and compromises. Ideally, restoration reproduces the entire system in question, complete in all its aspects—genetics, populations, ecosystems, and landscapes. This means not merely replicating the system's composition, structure, and function, but also its dynamics—even allowing for evolutionary as well as ecological change. Thus, one practitioner argued that objectives for restoration projects should be defined as "motion pictures" rather than "snapshots" (Dunwiddie 1992). A limitation here is that objects such as species are generally easier to specify in planning restoration projects—and to monitor when evaluating their success—than are processes such as ecosystem function and community dynamics, to say nothing of evolutionary changes. As a result, there is still a tendency to portray restoration projects in more or less static terms.

This having been said, just how good a job are restorationists able to do, given the current state of the art? How feasible is it to restore authentic ecosystems? Answers differ for each ecosystem type, and depend, of course, on the nature and extent of the influences or degradation involved. A satisfactory answer takes into account not only the *accuracy* of the resulting system—that is, how closely it resembles the model or reference system with respect to ecological parameters such as composition, structure, function, and dynamics—but also its *authenticity* in a larger sense, including consideration of its historical and aesthetic value. Most of these issues have not been investigated in detail, and studies of even the most straightforward ecological pa-

**Table 14.1**
A Checklist of Appropriate Questions for Planning, Conducting, and
Evaluating Restoration Projects

**Project Planning and Design**
1. Has the problem requiring treatment been clearly understood and defined?
2. Is there a consensus on the restoration program's mission?
3. Have the goals and objectives been identified?
4. Has the restoration been planned with adequate scope and expertise?
5. Does the restoration management design have an annual or midcourse correction point in line with adaptive management procedures?
6. Are the performance indicators—the measurable biological, physical, and chemical attributes—directly and appropriately linked to the objectives?
7. Have adequate monitoring, surveillance, management, and maintenance programs been developed along with the project, so that monitoring costs and operational details are anticipated and monitoring results will be available to serve as input in improving restoration techniques used as the project matures?
8. Has an appropriate reference system (or systems) been selected from which to extract target values of performance indicators for comparison in conducting the project evaluation?
9. Have sufficient baseline data been collected over a suitable period of time on the project ecosystem to facilitate before-and-after treatment comparisons?
10. Have critical project procedures been tested on a small experimental scale in part of the project area to minimize the risks of failure?
11. Has the project been designed to make the restored ecosystem as self-sustaining as possible to minimize maintenance requirements?
12. Has thought been given to how long monitoring will have to be continued before the project can be declared effective?
13. Have risk and uncertainty been adequately considered in project planning?

**During Restoration**
1. Based on the monitoring results, are the anticipated intermediate objectives being achieved? If not, are appropriate steps being taken to correct the problem?
2. Do the objectives or performance indicators need to be modified? If so, what changes may be required in the monitoring program?
3. Is the monitoring program adequate?

**Post-Restoration**
1. To what extent were project goals and objectives achieved?
2. How similar in structure and function is the restored ecosystem to the target ecosystem?
3. To what extent is the restored ecosystem self-sustaining, and what are the maintenance requirements?
4. If all natural components of the ecosystem were not restored, have critical ecosystem functions been restored?
5. If all natural components of the ecosystem were not restored, have critical components been restored?
6. How long did the project take?
7. What lessons have been learned from this effort?
8. Have those lessons been shared with interested parties to maximize the potential for technology transfer?
9. What was the final cost, in net present value terms, of the restoration project?
10. What were the ecological, economic, and social benefits realized by the project?
11. How cost-effective was the project?
12. Would another approach to restoration have produced desirable results at lower cost?

From NRC 1992.

rameters defining a successful restoration effort are still in their infancy (Society for Ecological Restoration 1990). Indeed, restoration poses a fundamental challenge to the ecologist—the challenge of identifying those aspects of

## ESSAY 14A
# Measuring Biological Integrity

James R. Karr, University of Washington

To effectively mitigate for or restore degraded habitats, or to protect existing high-quality habitats, one must be able to define the attributes of "normal" habitats as a baseline or model. Otherwise, objective assessment of the success of mitigation or restoration techniques is not possible. One way to do that is to define normal "biological integrity" of systems, and measure deviations from regional expectations.

The phrase "biological integrity" was first used in defining the goal of the Water Pollution Control Act Amendments of 1972: "to restore and maintain the chemical, physical, and biological integrity of the Nation's waters" (U.S. Code, vol. 33, par. 1251[a]). This mandate of the Clean Water Act (CWA) clearly established a legal foundation for protection of aquatic biota. Unfortunately, that vision was not reflected in the implementing regulations supporting the CWA, in part because no generally accepted definition of biological integrity emerged until a decade later (Karr and Dudley 1981).

Integrity implies an unimpaired condition or the quality or state of being complete or undivided. The Clean Water Act defines biological integrity as "the ability to support and maintain a balanced, integrated, adaptive assemblage of organisms having a species composition, diversity, and functional organization comparable to that of natural habitat of the region."

Unfortunately, water resource managers implemented the Act with regulations directed toward reducing release of chemical contaminants (conventional "pollution") with an eye to protection of human health rather than the integrity of biological communities (Karr 1991). As a result, aquatic organisms and aquatic environments have continued their steep and rather frightening declines in recent decades. The water resource crisis extends beyond degradation of water quality (pollution or chemical contamination) to the loss of species, homogenization of the biota, loss of harvestable productivity of aquatic systems, and threats to human health. Current programs are not protecting river resources because society does not see rivers and the landscapes

that they drain in their entirety. Until an integrative perspective dominates our collective conscience, the condition of rivers will continue to decline. In short, we have not been protecting the biological integrity of the nation's waters.

Under Section 305(b) of the CWA, states are required to report the status of water resources within their boundaries; however, a primary focus on chemical conditions results in chronic underreporting of the extent of degradation. In one state, conventional chemical evaluations failed to detect 50% of the impairment of surface waters when compared with the more comprehensive, sensitive, and objective assessment provided by biological evaluations.

Fortunately, recognition of the weaknesses of the chemical contaminants approach is spreading, and state and federal agencies are moving to incorporate sophisticated biological approaches into water quality standards. Historically, numeric chemical criteria were the foundation of these standards. For example, dissolved oxygen (DO) may not fall below 5 mg/l if the designated use of the water body is a coldwater fishery. Recognition of the degraded condition of U.S. waters has, however, stimulated efforts to establish biological criteria—numerical values or narrative expressions that describe the characteristics of an aquatic assemblage.

To implement biological criteria, biologists need formal methods for sampling the biota of streams, evaluating the resulting data, and clearly communicating the results. The complexity of biological systems and the varied impacts of human society require a broadly based, multimetric index that integrates information from individual, population, and assemblage levels. A number of years ago (Karr 1981), I developed such an approach to assessing the quality of water resources, called the index of biotic integrity (IBI). Attributes evaluated include fish species richness, indicator taxa (both intolerant and tolerant of pollution), species and trophic guild relative abundances, and the incidence of hybridization, disease, and anomalies such as lesions, tumors, or fin erosion. The metric values found are compared with the values expected for a relatively undisturbed stream of similar size and geographic region. Each metric is rated 5, 3, or 1 depending on whether its condition is comparable to, deviates somewhat from, or deviates strongly from the expected value. Metric scores are summed to yield an index (based on 12 metrics) that ranges from 12 in areas without fish to 60 in areas with fish faunas equivalent to those in pristine or relatively undisturbed areas. Regional modifications of the IBI have been very successful as long as the met-

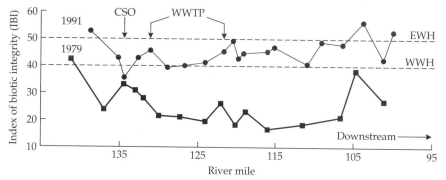

**Figure A** Longitudinal trend in IBI for the Scioto River, Ohio, in an area downstream from Columbus, 1979 and 1991. Locations of wastewater treatment plants (WWTP) and combined sewer overflow (CSO) are indicated by arrowheads. Dashed lines indicate standards for designated uses: WWH, warmwater habitat; EWH, excellent warmwater habitat. IBI below 40 indicates reach does not attain water quality standards under biological criteria. Improvements between 1979 and 1991 are largely due to efforts to reduce the effluent from wastewater treatments plants. Most river reaches do not attain EWH largely because of physical habitat degradation and unresolved chemical contamination.

rics included are selected to retain the general ecological structure of the original IBI (Miller et al. 1988).

Many state agencies have adopted the IBI approach for use in their water management programs. The Ohio Environmental Protection Agency, for example, uses the IBI to establish and maintain use designations for water bodies (Figure A) and in support of their Section 319 Clean Water Act non-point source program, Section 305(b) CWA water quality inventory reports, and National Pollution Discharge Elimination System (NPDES) discharge permits. The conceptual approach of the IBI has now been used with both fish and invertebrates to evaluate a variety of aquatic environments, including large rivers, lakes, estuaries, and reservoirs (Ohio EPA 1988; Lenat 1988; Lyons 1992; Kerans and Karr 1994). The success of efforts to evaluate biological integrity depends less on the taxon selected for sampling and analysis than on the ecological sophistication brought to bear on the development of the analytical approach. Sampling and evaluation of several major taxa is likely to improve the quality of inferences about conditions at a site.

Restoration and mitigation approaches to conservation of biodiversity would benefit by incorporating the concept of biological integrity in order to define baselines of healthy systems and assess sites in an objective, comparative way. An IBI provides an integrative, conceptual framework for evaluating the condition of natural resources and the life-support systems upon which human societies depend, as well as a target for restoration programs.

---

an ecosystem that are most important.

The most extensive work in this area has been conducted on wetlands. Mandated by law in some situations, wetland restoration has become a booming business, but there is concern among conservationists regarding the quality of the resulting systems. In the few cases in which attempts have been made to compare restored systems with their natural counterparts, interpretation of the results vary widely. In one broadly cited study of a tidal marsh that appears to be restored in San Diego Bay, California, the investigators found that, although the restored wetland resembled the reference system with respect to the rate of nitrogen fixation in the root zone, it differed significantly with respect to ten other measures of structure, composition, and function (Zedler and Langis 1991). Essay 14B by Joy Zedler expands on these experiences.

Summing up their impressions of the success of attempts to restore a variety of wetlands, Kusler and Kentula (1990) concluded:

> Total duplication of natural wetlands is impossible due to the complexity and variation in natural as well as created or restored systems and the subtle relationships of hydrology, soils, vegetation, animal life, and nutrients which may have developed over thousands of years in natural systems. Nevertheless, experience to date suggests that some types of wetlands can be approximated and certain wetland functions can be restored, created, or enhanced in particular contexts. It is often possible to restore or create a wetland with vegetation resembling that of a naturally-occurring wetland. This does not mean, however, that it will have habitat or other values equaling those of a natural wetland nor that such a wetland will be a persistent, i.e., long term, feature in the landscape, as are many natural wetlands.

In addition to the work on wetlands, considerable work has been done in evaluating efforts to restore lakes (Cooke et al. 1986) and rivers and streams (Gore 1985). In contrast, evaluations of attempts to restore terrestrial ecosystems are often unsystematic and of limited applicability (Jordan 1990). Most studies address only a few features of the system—typically composition and structural features—rather than the more elusive functional and dynamic attributes. Nevertheless, ecologists' comments on some of the highest quality projects, such as Greene Prairie at the University of Wisconsin Arboretum (Cottam 1987; discussed below) and the estuary of the Salmon River in Oregon (Morlan and Frenkel 1992), suggest that restoration of at least some ecosystems is possible under favorable conditions.

One point that is clear from restoration studies to date is that the feasibility of restoration varies enormously from system to system. Some systems, such as certain tidal wetlands, that have few species of plants and a relatively simple structure have been restored quite readily under favorable conditions. Others, such as peat bogs where the peat has been removed or disturbed, seem refractory to restoration. Thus, it is impossible to provide a general discussion of the restorability of ecosystems. This admission itself represents an important advance in conservation and restoration thinking.

## ESSAY 14B

# Restoring a Nation's Wetlands
## Why, Where, and How?

Joy B. Zedler, San Diego State University

Over the past two centuries, 53% of the wetlands in the contiguous United States have been destroyed, mostly through drainage for agriculture (Dahl 1990). That's an average rate of about 1 acre per minute, for a total loss of over 116 million acres in 200 years. The lower 48 states have only about 100 million acres of wetlands left. No wonder conservation leaders have developed a policy of "no net loss of wetland acreage and function" (The Conservation Foundation 1988). No wonder the National Research Council (1992) has called for restoration of 10 million acres by 2010. This essay considers why, where, and how we should go about meeting this goal.

*Why* wetlands should be restored relates to their many functions that benefit the nation; they are the sponges, kidneys, and supermarkets of the natural landscape. As sponges, they provide flood protection by reducing flood peaks and shoreline erosion. As kidneys, they filter sediments, nutrients, and contaminants from inflowing waters, thereby improving water quality downstream. As supermarkets, they provide the foods for a wide variety of local and migratory animals, plus humans. They are also aesthetically pleasing, and part of the reason that over 160 million Americans spend $14.3 billion each year observing, photographing, and enjoying nature (Duda 1991). Resource agencies and managers agree that wetlands perform critical functions that benefit humankind.

*Where* wetlands should be restored is a more controversial issue. One can argue from various perspectives. Because California has lost the greatest proportion of its historical wetlands (91%), perhaps it should have highest priority. Because Florida has suffered the greatest acreage loss (over 9 million acres; Dahl 1990), the need may be greatest there. On the other hand, Louisiana is currently losing wetlands at the highest rate.

Perhaps the greatest future threat to wetlands lies with coastal wetlands. Only 7% of the nation's remaining wetlands occur along the coast, to which our growing population is moving, bringing increased pressure to develop wetlands. Coastal wetlands are also threatened by rising sea level due to global warming. A 3°C increase in temperature by 2100 is predicted to raise sea level 1 m and to eliminate 65% of the coastal marshes of the contiguous United States (Park et al. 1989). Thus, coastal wetlands may have the greatest need for restoration.

Wetlands can only be replaced where suitable topography and hydrology can be restored. Many wetlands have been ditched or tiled for agriculture but have been only marginally productive; these may well provide the greatest opportunities for wetland restoration at the landscape level (National Research Council 1992).

The most difficult question is *how* wetlands can be restored on a large scale. In some places it is a relatively simple matter of recreating the hydrology that allowed natural wetlands to develop. Drained farmlands can be restored to wetlands by filling ditches or breaking tiles so that runoff can accumulate and saturate the soil. In Florida's Everglades, managers plan to return the Kissimmee River to its historical winding channel by undoing the 93-km straight channel that was cut in the 1960s and which eliminated 45,000 acres of river floodplain wetlands and reduced waterfowl populations by 90%. Forcing the river back into its natural meandering channel will rejuvenate much of its floodplain. This project has high potential for success, since the river channel is still intact and native wetland species occur nearby.

In other places, restoration is more difficult. Southern California's salt marsh restoration attempts may represent the greatest challenge. In the San Diego area, 85% of the original salt marsh is gone, watersheds are greatly modified, streams are dammed, and degraded waters flow into each coastal wetland. Sites are surrounded by urban uses, with no buffer between the wetland and development. Many of southern California's coastal wetland species are considered "sensitive" or threatened with extinction; these include one plant, seven invertebrates, two reptiles, and fourteen birds.

Considerable attention has been given to restoring nesting habitat for one bird on the U.S. endangered species list, the Light-footed Clapper Rail (*Rallus longirostris levipes*). This bird is a year-round resident of southern California salt marshes. As mitigation for damages to natural wetlands caused by highway widening, a new freeway interchange, and a new flood control channel, two marshes have been created at San Diego Bay expressly for Clapper Rails. The first mitigation project was a 12-acre series of islands and channels constructed in 1984. In 1990, an additional 17-acre site was excavated from dredge spoil. To date, rails have not nested at either site.

Some of the inadequacies of these constructed salt marshes, as compared with natural reference marshes, include less abundant epibenthic invertebrates, shorter vegetation, and lower concentrations of soil organic matter and soil nitrogen. From the standpoint of the Clapper Rail, the short stature of the plants is the biggest problem: when the tide rises, the plant canopy is fully submerged, leaving no cover for rails, their nests, or their chicks (Zedler 1993).

A chain of events explains the short

plant canopies at these constructed marshes. The sandy sediments do not retain nutrients well, so nutrients do not accumulate. Nitrogen limits plant growth, especially height. Low organic matter concentrations further limit nitrogen fixation rates and perhaps the invertebrates that help recycle nutrients. Finally, the short vegetation appears to be inadequate for use by beetles (*Coleomegilla fuscilabris*) that consume scale insects (*Haliaspis spartina*), which are native herbivores on the cordgrass vegetation. Scale insect outbreaks further impair cordgrass growth. Experiments to augment soils with both organic matter and nitrogen improved plant growth in the first 2 years, but scale insects reduced plant growth in year 3. Current experiments aim to produce tall plants before scale insect populations can irrupt.

From the problems that have plagued restoration attempts in San Diego Bay, we conclude that we are not yet able to recreate self-sustaining salt marshes or to reestablish self-sustaining populations of our endangered salt marsh birds. It is not yet clear how to guarantee long-term success. Endangered species may well be the most difficult components to restore to wetland ecosystems. Because of their high habitat specificity, they are the first to decline when sites are modified and perhaps the last to return when artificial habitats are created for them.

We know why wetlands need to be restored (to replace hydrologic, water quality, and habitat functions); we have some ideas where the greatest gains can be made in the shortest period of time (marginally productive agricultural lands); and we know how to restore wetlands where sites are not too damaged and where regional biodiversity is not too depleted (restore the hydrology, transplant the native vegetation, and wait for the animal populations to expand into the new habitats). What we cannot yet guarantee is replacement of habitat for the most sensitive species in regions where sites are highly disturbed and populations of critical food web components are no longer abundant. This is where students and researchers can make a difference.

## Scale

The size of a restoration project is a central question that has great bearing on its potential success or failure. Complementing questions about the quality or authenticity of restored ecosystems are questions about the temporal and spatial scales on which restoration can be carried out, and the extent to which restoration efforts can be scaled up without unduly sacrificing quality (Figure 14.2). The National Research Council (1992) gives four considerations to be taken into account in determining the size of a restoration project:

1. The project should be large enough to minimize deleterious effects of boundary conditions and events on internal dynamics.
2. The project should be of a size such that managers can readily add, control, or eliminate, as necessary, disturbances to the system.
3. The project should be large enough so that various effects can be measured to assess project success.
4. The project should be an affordable size.

One might suppose that the best restorations are those conducted on a modest scale, involving relatively labor-intensive procedures. One might also assume that attempts to "scale up" in space or time would necessarily entail compromises in quality. In some cases this is true. At present the best restored prairies, for example, were planted using labor-intensive ("horticul-

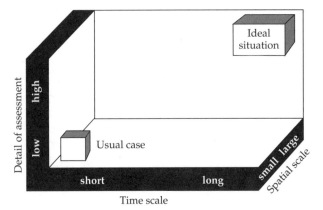

**Figure 14.2**  Temporal and spatial scales of restoration. The ideal situation is to work with a high degree of detail at large spatial scales with a long time scale in mind. More typical cases involve working on smaller temporal and spatial scales, and sacrificing detail. (From NRC 1992.)

**Figure 14.3**  A prairie restoration experiment at the Curtis Prairie, ca. 1985. The highest-quality prairies have been planted using such labor-intensive horticultural methods, and consequently are small in scale. (Photograph courtesy of University of Wisconsin Arboretum.)

tural") methods, and are relatively small (Figure 14.3). Greene Prairie at the University of Wisconsin Arboretum, for example, is only 16 ha. A portion of prairie planted at the Morton Arboretum in suburban Chicago is probably the most meticulously planted prairie anywhere and covers only a few hectares. This area is of higher quality, with respect to the presence and distribution of vascular plants, than portions of the prairie that were added later using less labor-intensive methods. Attempts to scale up to 250 ha in a restored prairie at Fermilab have resulted in further sacrifices in quality. Problems include lower diversity of native species, underrepresentation of rare species or species difficult to propagate or handle, and higher proportions of exotic species.

Observations such as these lead to a certain pessimism regarding the value of restoration in conservation practice. Here the restorationist appears to be caught in a bind between ecological considerations on the one hand and technical and economic limitations on the other. Ecological quality depends, in part, on size: bigger is typically better, owing to various functional and island biogeographic considerations (see Chapter 10). In contrast, scaling projects up, though it may benefit the entire ecosystem, is likely to be carried out at the expense of some system components—at least in the short run.

There are several reasons to suppose it may be possible to restore ecosystems of high ecological quality on a large scale. First is the principle, based on island biogeographic theory, that larger size actually helps. A larger site has a more complete functional infrastructure (a wider range of soils and exposures, more extensive and complete hydrological systems, and so forth), and can support more species. Similarly, large sites have a greater capacity for self-repair than do smaller sites, and will, in effect, pull the restoration effort along more effectively toward the target. Given even a modest effort to ensure the timely introduction of species and the perpetuation of disturbance processes such as burning or grazing over the years, large-scale projects might be expected to improve gradually through what might be called "subsidized succession" until they achieve an even higher quality than more intensively restored, small-scale projects.

A second, related consideration is the realization that an abiotic system that remains either intact or fairly easily repairable, even despite drastic alteration in the biotic components, provides a solid foundation for reassembly of the ecosystem components. An excellent example is the recent discovery by prairie restorationists that simply throwing seed of prairie plants into an old-field sod often results in a prairie with more "conservative" or difficult-to-reintroduce species than does the more laborious and costly traditional method that begins with plowing to set back competing species and open up space for prairie species. The old method disrupts the ecosystem; the newer approach both builds on the existing ecosystem and takes advantage of the rich assortment of establishment possibilities provided by the existing system, even if it is comprised entirely of exotic species (Packard, in press). This work suggests that it may be possible to circumvent the quality–quantity trade-off, allowing restoration of high-quality systems on a large scale.

It is worth noting that restoration projects undertaken on a large scale (hundreds to thousands of hectares) typically involve mainly the reintroduction, removal, or manipulation of ecosystem-scale processes such as burning, grazing, or hydrological processes. Little if any direct manipulation of these communities, through reintroduction of native species or elimination or control of exotics, is possible, given the sheer size of the system. Thus, the restoration of thousands of hectares of tropical dry forest at Guanacaste National Park in Costa Rica (discussed below) has, so far, involved cessation of grazing and burning to reverse the effects of centuries of these practices (Jordan 1987). Likewise, large-scale wetland restoration projects frequently involve little more than restoration of appropriate hydrological regimes—all that is necessary in some cases to ensure gradual recovery of the community.

## Costs

Cost per hectare for restoration is, of course, an important consideration, because it places a price on the ecosystem, linking its ecology with the human economy, and places realistic limits on the scope of projects. Also, cost is one of several considerations that will eventually determine the position of the equilibrium between restored natural systems and other forms of land-use in human-dominated landscapes. A project must be realistically defined within proper financial bounds; an overambitious, overscaled project will soon run out of funding and possibly fail entirely, simply because it went beyond the financial constraints set for it.

Since the costs of restoration projects vary widely, it is impossible to specify in any meaningful way the "going rate" for restoring a hectare of, say, tallgrass prairie or salt marsh. Moreover, costs and fees for projects are often the bases of business competition, discouraging publication of such information, so figures available are likely to be incomplete or otherwise misleading (Guinon 1987). Despite these caveats, a few "ballpark" numbers may help the reader. Thompson (1992) reports that establishing a prairie in Iowa from seed may cost $625 per acre, while maintenance costs are $12–$18 per acre over a 3-year period. Forests, depending on how trees are reestablished, may cost appreciably more.

## The Restoration Process

In a simplistic sense there are two general approaches to restoration, which differ considerably. The first, and most familiar, approach is to restore a disturbed area to its "natural state." However, we seldom know what the "natural" state was—we can only see what exists now. Many sites have undergone an unknown history of use by humans in ways such that we have little idea how they would appear without human influence. Even historical accounts are based on landscapes that may have been altered by prehistoric inhabitants. The second approach to restoration is to create a system that, while it does not mimic the natural situation, has a series of favorable traits that make the area better than it was before restoration. In both cases, either consciously or unconsciously, the restorationist is mimicking the natural process of succession.

Over the last 20 years, ecologists have been attempting to codify the theory underlying succession of natural communities. To an increasing extent the results of this activity have found their way into the literature of applied ecology and restoration, specifically recommending that successional theory be applied to problems of resource management and restoration (Hutnik and Davis 1973; Wali 1979; Bradshaw and Chadwick 1980; Dvorak 1984; Green and Salter 1987; Cairns 1988; Hossner 1988; Redente and DePuit 1988). A careful review of what natural resource managers do suggests that, in most cases, they are actually managing the process of succession to meet a certain goal—often without realizing that they are managing succession.

Most management procedures are designed either to shorten the natural successional sequence (speed up succession) or to hold a community in a particular stage of succession that is considered to have some desirable attributes. For example, the removal of juniper trees to increase cattle forage is, whether recognized or not, an attempt to set back succession and maintain a community dominated by highly productive grasses. Similarly, planting young trees in clear-cuts is an attempt to hasten succession to a forest rather than waiting for natural colonization of a site. The self-conscious use of restoration principles based on natural successional processes should be more economical than trying to plant vegetation and transport animals using methods based on traditional agricultural techniques.

## A Succession Primer

Suppose an ecosystem is disturbed. The exact nature of the disturbance site determines its potential path of recovery, mainly because the disturbance determines what remains to initiate the repair process. In a general sense, no disturbance will completely destroy a site; there usually remain some propagules of plants or animals, some organic matter from the previous ecosystem, or other remnants, as well as the abiotic condition of the site. We can refer to these remnants of the previous system as **residuals** or legacies (Figure 14.4). These residuals are, in essence, the raw materials available to rebuild the ecosystem. Clearly, the type, extent, timing, and intensity of a dis-

**Figure 14.4**  Residual components of the former ecosystem may be critical to restoration efforts. In this extreme case of a residual, a single conifer remains at this site after the eruption of Mount St. Helens in 1980. (Photograph by James A. MacMahon.)

turbance affects the assortment of residuals. Two forest fires in the same forest type can have dramatically different influences on the subsequent trajectory of succession depending on their areal extent, the heat of the fire, the time of year of the burn, and other variables. Similarly, a clear-cutting operation in that same forest type leaves different residuals than the fires.

Soon after disturbance a site is invaded by animals and plants, an invasion that goes on for the life of an ecosystem. In many cases the invaders are quite predictable because they live close to the disturbed area and are specifically adapted for colonizing disturbed sites. However, species that are neither geographically proximate to the site nor specially adapted to disturbance may also be early colonists if they have a high capacity for dispersal and if the site, even in its disturbed state, offers suitable habitat. After the eruption of Mount St. Helens, the early colonizing birds included juncos, ground-nesting birds that can use fallen trees as nest sites. They are not adapted to volcanic landscapes, but the ability to fly got them to the area, and the downed trees offered critical habitat for their breeding.

For both residual species and migrants, the site must offer appropriate conditions for establishing viable populations. Although species may survive a disturbance event, conditions at the site following disturbance may not be conducive to their subsequent breeding and persistence. Similarly, while a migrating species can reach a disturbed site, that does not ensure that conditions will allow it to become established and flourish.

Once established, species interact with one another in all the myriad of biotic interactions that characterize normal ecosystems. Such interactions include predator–prey relations, parasitism, mutualisms, and competition. Under these conditions, some species will flourish while others will simply be "edited" out of the species mix. If one of a pair of true mutualists survives, it cannot persist without its obligatory partner. Similarly, a voracious predator could extirpate a surviving prey population.

As groups of species become established, they often change the conditions of the site. Imagine, if you will, a forested site laid bare by a fire. Plants requiring shade cannot establish themselves or persist. Under such conditions residuals and migrants alike must be sun-tolerant. Species that become established change the light regime, providing conditions for shade-tolerant species that were previously unsuccessful. Similarly, the digging activities of colonizing fossorial mammals, such as pocket gophers (*Thomomys*), may change the residual soil conditions in a way that permits establishment of a different suite of plants than could have occurred without the animals' activities.

Changes in the composition of the system's components will continue until a mixture of species persists and coexists for a long enough period that it is in some sort of equilibrium, often termed the climax. Of course, this "climax" is, in fact, an illusion because the process of succession is always occurring. Species are added to and subtracted from an ecosystem for a variety of reasons all the time. There are constant disturbances of various magnitudes, and new colonists are always arriving. We might perceive little change because our vision of ecosystems is usually dominated by large, long-lived perennial plant species that appear not to change over time. Closer inspection would reveal that many species are highly volatile in their comings and goings. The fact that we may not perceive community composition continually changing can lead to problems in the restoration process. We frequently choose a target ecosystem as a goal for restoration of an area, but that reference system changes over time. Thus, when we try to restore the disturbed site to the condition of the reference system, we are trying to hit a moving target.

**Figure 14.5** In arid regions, establishment of plants is highly dependent on the right sequence of temperature and rainfall. In the Sonoran Desert, wildflowers such as these poppies germinate and bloom only after winters of particularly heavy rainfall; seeds may otherwise lay dormant for years. (Photograph by John Hoffman.)

It should be obvious that each subprocess of succession can dramatically affect the overall outcome and thus change the nature of the evolving ecosystem. It may not be as obvious that these processes are of differing importance in different environments (MacMahon 1981, 1987). It has been proposed, for example, that in arid areas establishment may be more important than some of the other processes, because arid areas have unpredictable abiotic environments (Reith and Potter 1986). Under such conditions the occurrence of the right sequence of temperature and rainfall may not occur each year as predictably as in more mesic sites (Figure 14.5). Thus, while there may be sufficient rain to permit seeds to germinate, the seedlings may not experience subsequent conditions favorable to their establishment, growth, and reproduction. In contrast, very mesic areas such as rainforests may foster rapid growth and establishment of plants. Under these conditions, it is not the establishment phase that is critical, but the fact that plants become established so rapidly that they may preempt a particular site and slow down other aspects of the successional process.

When we attempt to apply our knowledge of succession to the restoration process, we have to be mindful of which processes are key in a particular environment. Although hardly perfect, our knowledge of succession is good enough that the ecological principles can serve as important bases for the restoration process. These principles have been used to restore communities varying from tundra (Cargill and Chapin 1987) to rainforests (Jordan and Farnworth 1982). In fact, three books identify successional theory as the specific basis for restoration strategies (West et al. 1981; Majer 1989; Luken 1990).

## Examples of Restoration Projects

We will now explore several examples of restoration efforts that illustrate different problems, approaches, and scales of activities. The first example is presented in great detail to demonstrate the intricacies often involved in restoration; subsequent examples will be progressively less detailed, instead illustrating the diversity of principles, problems, and opportunities in restoration. These examples together begin to demonstrate the complexities, challenges, and rewards of restoration ecology, and its role in larger conservation issues.

## Restoration Following Mining Activities in Arid Lands

Because energy production and resource use in the United States often involves the mining of coal, uranium, or other minerals in arid areas, the ability to restore sites following such disturbances is of great practical importance. However, because plant establishment is slow and contingent upon a narrow window of climatic conditions, it is difficult and costly to restore lands in arid regions. While the goal of contemporary post-mining restoration includes substrate stabilization, it also includes development of a community characteristic of the area, which will form a self-sustaining system that need not be managed in the future. This requirement for establishment of a persistent desirable ecosystem state implies more work and therefore higher costs.

For this example we will look at a restoration study in an area that underwent surface strip-mining for coal (Parmenter and MacMahon 1983; Parmenter et al. 1985, 1991). The study was conducted on the Pittsburgh and Midway Coal Mining Company's Elkol-Sorenson Mine, located 8 km southwest of Kemmerer, in western Wyoming (2103 m elevation). Precipitation averages 22.6 cm per year, mostly as snow, and is highly variable. May and June are the "wet" months, with approximately 2.5 cm precipitation each. Mean monthly temperatures range from –8°C in January to 17°C in July.

The terrain is characterized by rolling hills, and the presumed native vegetation is shrub-steppe (West 1983). Dominant shrubs in the area include big sagebrush (*Artemisia tridentata*), rabbitbrush (*Chrysothamnus viscidiflorus*), and Gardner's saltbush (*Atriplex gardneri*), with occasional individuals of bitterbrush (*Purshia tridentata*), winterfat (*Ceratoides lanata*), serviceberry (*Amelanchier alnifolia*), and gray horsebrush (*Tetradymia canescens*) (Figure 14.6). A variety of common grasses are found on the site, and the soils are coarse, calcareous loams.

Following the mining process, the first step is to evaluate the state of a site, because not all surface-mined sites are equal. For example, during mining, turning over and mixing of soil horizons can dilute topsoil, expose toxic materials, or dramatically change soil structure. Knowledge of these effects is crucial because the overall potential for restoration often depends on the residual soil properties (Bentham et al. 1992). Along with soil changes comes the question of what plant propagules might be left. These problems were

**Figure 14.6**  Typical vegetation near the Kemmerer mine site. Note the natural clumping of plants. (Photograph by James A. MacMahon.)

(A)                                                          (B)

Figure 14.7    (A) Stored topsoil pile at a coal mine site. (B) Topsoil respread is the first step toward restoration. Saving and replacing such elements of the site is critical to ultimate restoration capabilities. (Photographs by James A. MacMahon.)

recognized early by reclamationists who recommended that, as the topsoil of areas is scraped away, it be removed to storage piles adjacent to the mining sites. When the mined pit is closed and recontoured, the topsoil would then be respread on the surface to act as a fertile seedbed (Figure 14.7).

Initial arrival of plants on mined sites is usually a human-mediated process. The common scenario is for the mining operator to plant seeds or seedlings to initiate and speed up site recovery. The speed of recovery is important so as to minimize soil erosion and to encourage residual seed banks to germinate while still viable. The planted vegetation is intended to stabilize the soil and to provide a source of organic matter that will begin soil regeneration. The intention is that desirable, seeded species will succeed, and that some of the residual species from the stored topsoil may also become reestablished.

This particular study was designed to determine (1) if managing the establishment phase by planting seedlings rather than seeds would permit more rapid restoration of mined lands in arid areas; (2) if planting in dispersion patterns (clumps) and densities characteristic of arid areas would encourage establishment of plants and favorably alter soils; and (3) if providing appropriate architecture of the plant component of the ecosystem would encourage animal reestablishment.

To deal with the problems of the establishment phase in an arid environment, seedlings (grown from seeds collected on an adjacent site) were used rather than attempting to plant seeds (Figure 14.8). Although more expensive than seeding, the extra initial costs of planting would be recovered because the established plants would not have to be irrigated or fertilized, nor would the seedlings as readily fail because of a drought; thus, the site would not require a reseeding effort.

The species selected were three woody perennials: big sagebrush, rabbitbrush, and Gardner's saltbush. One of each of these species formed a "planting unit," an equilateral triangle (40 cm on a side) with one plant at each apex. These were placed in plots representing three dispersion patterns: random, regular, and clumped. Since the goal of restoration was to create a functioning ecosystem that mimicked a reference area, attaining natural plant densities was also important. Native vegetation in the region contains about 16,000 woody plants per hectare. The study used a series of experimental plantings at four different plant densities, each applied to the three dispersion patterns. These densities included values above, equal to, and below the native density.

Figure 14.8    Planting of seedlings at the Kemmerer mining site, using a detailed experimental planting regime. (Photograph by James A. MacMahon.)

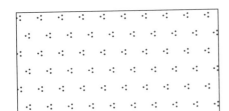

(A)

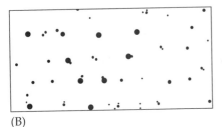

(B)

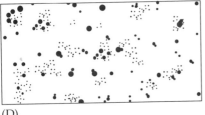

(C)

(D)

**Figure 14.9**    (A) Planting array of triads in a low-density, regular dispersion plot at the Kemmerer site. Each plot is 16 × 32 m. (B) Status of plants in A after 3 years. Positions and sizes of circles indicate actual positions and sizes of plants on the site. (C) Planting array of triads in a high-density, clumped dispersion plot. (D) Status of plants in C after 3 years. Note clumping, the larger sizes of some plants, and more recruitment of new plants from seeds compared with the low-density, regular plantings.

A large suite of measurements of many aspects of the reestablishing community was made, including both meso- and micrometeorology, plant establishment, growth, seed production, the movement, establishment, and effectiveness of mycorrhizal fungi, and recolonization of the site by animals.

Results indicated that, in terms of both survivorship and production of new plants through seeds, plants established in clumps were more successful than those in the regular or random patterns. This can be demonstrated by comparing two extreme planting scenarios. Figure 14.9A shows the planting pattern of triads in a low-density, regular dispersion plot, while Figure 14.9C shows the planting pattern for triads in a high-density, clumped dispersion plot. Figures 14.9B and 14.9D depict the actual size increment and persistence of the plants after 3 years. In the low-density plot, few triads had all three plants surviving, few of the plants had increased appreciably in size, and there was virtually no recruitment of new individuals. In contrast, the higher-density plot had a marked increase in size of plants, a higher proportional survivorship, new recruits, and even coalesced into larger clumps.

A prediction in the study was that planting in clumps would be beneficial because clumps would trap organic matter and the spores of mycorrhizal fungi. This prediction was tested by measuring the establishment rate of the mycorrhizal association, the numbers of mycorrhizal spores in the soil, and the soil organic matter levels. As predicted, all of these measures were higher in clumps than in any other dispersion pattern, and were generally more favorable in the higher densities.

Reestablishment of animals was a more complicated process. Because of limited space on the mine site, plots were a maximum of 0.5 ha; this was too small to accurately measure changes in populations of highly vagile vertebrate species. However, censuses of insects indicated that they recolonized the site rapidly, and cursory observations of vertebrates suggested a better response to clumped sites.

Two main themes emerged from this restoration project. First, the use of seedlings rather than seeds in this arid region resulted in high success rates. A seeding study was conducted simultaneously, and those plots were less successful. Commonly, mine sites such as these need to be reseeded several times before plants are established, but the seedling approach was successful the first time. Second, the clumped pattern of planting fostered establishment of the mycorrhizal association, as well as increasing organic matter in the soil. Thus, this pattern of planting, in itself, enhanced the reaction process and was a major cause of success of plant establishment and subsequent growth. Overall, the use of ecological theory provided a sound and economical basis for restoration.

### Restoration of a Tropical Dry Forest in Guanacaste National Park

Of all tropical forest types, deciduous dry forest has been the most severely affected by human activities (Figure 14.10). On a pantropical scale, these forests have been largely replaced by crops such as sorghum and cotton, and especially by cattle ranching. In Mesoamerica, dry forest formerly extended from the southwestern coast of Mexico south through northwestern Costa Rica and parts of Panama. Today, the forest consists mostly of isolated small remnants that persist in inaccessible sites such as deep ravines. In aerial photographs these forest patches look like tiny islands in a sea of grass and scrub.

Restoring these forests, even on a limited scale, is a formidable problem. First, the conditions that caused the forest losses in the first place must be changed, and this means a fundamental change in land use practices. Second,

(A)                                                        (B)

there must be enough forest nuclei left to act as a source of seeds for restoration. Third, though the animal component of these forest nuclei is greatly different from that of the original forest, it must at the very least contain those animals critical to the survival and expansion of the regenerating forest; that is, the appropriate numbers and kinds of pollinators and seed dispersers.

One of the few places where dry forest exists in nuclei large enough to support ecological conditions prerequisite for restoration is in Guanacaste National Park in northwestern Costa Rica. The 10,700-ha park is located in the lowlands, and spans an altitudinal range from sea level to 317 m. The original forest of this region consisted of canopy trees (dominated by legumes) 20–30 m in height, an understory layer of trees 10–20 m tall, and a shrub layer with many spiny species and woody vines. Two 4-ha forested plots in this region contained 44 and 68 tree species, as compared with two 4-ha plots in the Atlantic rainforest that contained 88 and 112 tree species. In four plots, the 10 most common species made up 45% or more of the total basal area (Hartshorn 1983). Thus, the species richness difference between tropical dry forest and tropical wet forest is the larger number of rare species in the wet forest. As a restoration goal, establishing the 10 most common tree species would represent, at minimum, nearly half of the woody biomass diversity of the dry forest.

Much of the landscape in Guanacaste has been completely converted to pastures, largely monocultures of African grasses. All but a small fraction of the remaining land has been degraded to a savanna-like landscape of a few tree species scattered through weedy fields, to shrubby thickets, or to species-poor second-growth forest. Fire is a key process in degradation, and fire suppression is a critical part of the restoration process. It is important to note that fire is not a significant part of the natural disturbance regime in this region, at least not at the frequency needed to maintain grasslands. Ranchers set fires, typically on an annual basis, to prevent encroachment of tree species on their pastures. In the absence of fire, grass is replaced by native woody species.

For more than a decade, Costa Rican biologists with the National Park System, along with U.S. collaborators, have been restoring the dry forest on these lands by using sound ecological principles and simple techniques. Their management strategy has two tactics: reducing wildfires and enhancing seed dispersal of forest trees. Wildfires had to be eliminated in order to stop the continuing process of forest degradation and exotic grassland enhancement. Seed dispersal had to be enhanced because the remaining forest

**Figure 14.10** (A) Pacific lowland forest at Guanacaste National Park in northwestern Costa Rica, one of the few remaining tracts of intact tropical deciduous dry forest. (B) Most of the Pacific lowland forest has been degraded to poor-quality ranch- or farmlands like this site near Guanacaste National Park. (Photographs by C. R. Carroll.)

(A)

(B)

**Figure 14.11**    (A) If fires can be suppressed in grasslands such as this one, natural and enhanced seed dispersal processes can result in a rapid conversion back to forest. (B) Eight years of fire suppression allowed this young, second-growth forest to develop from a grassland. (Photographs by C. R. Carroll.)

**Figure 14.12**    Horses can effectively disperse the seeds of many forest trees. Emerging from this pile of horse dung is a seedling of a large canopy tree, *Enterolobium cyclocarpum*. (Photograph by D. H. Janzen.)

is fragmented into small and isolated patches, and many of the normal dispersal agents are missing. Alternative, cost-effective ways to move seeds from forest patches into the grasslands had to be found.

The first problem the managers faced, and solved, was gaining management authority over the park land so that public use could be regulated. With this authority, unnecessary roads were closed, campfires and camping locations were restricted, and uncontrolled grazing by cattle was eliminated. In order to reduce wildfires the managers needed to reduce the amount of highly flammable African grasses that make up most of the pastures in the region. Because these grasses can grow more than 2 m high, they can support very hot and rapidly moving fires that penetrate fragmented forests. Along road edges, the grasses were mowed, grazed, or carefully burned to reduce accidental and intentional fires.

Once fire is kept out of the grasslands, the native woody vegetation quickly begins to invade. For example, at one site close to a large forest patch, the grassland was converted to early second-growth forest after only 8 fire-free years (Figure 14.11). However, as the distance between forest patches increases, naturally occurring seed dispersal becomes a limiting factor in the rate of forest restoration. To enhance seed dispersal into grasslands, horses are fed meal containing the seeds of important large forest trees, especially seeds of the "Guanacaste tree" (*Enterolobium cyclocarpum*, Fabaceae). As the horses wander through the grasslands, they deposit seeds in rich piles of manure, a highly cost-effective approach to revegetation (Figure 14.12). As these trees mature, they will become attractive "stopover" stations for other birds and mammals migrating among forest patches. Thus, isolated trees become the foci for additional seed dispersal. Trees that appear to lack effective long-distance seed dispersal, such as the large-seeded legume *Hymenaea courbaril*, are planted manually.

This approach to restoration seems to be working. Areas of the park that only a decade ago were pure expanses of African grass are now healthy secondary forests of native species (Figure 14.13).

Two general lessons about restoration are illustrated by this example. First, degraded tropical forests can be recovered on reasonable time and spatial scales as long as some forest still exists to serve as a source of seed and dispersal agents. Second, once the causes of degradation are understood, relatively simple techniques may be sufficient to initiate the restoration process. In this case, fire suppression, and enhanced seed dispersal, were two key, but simple, techniques for restoration.

(A)

(B)

## Restoration of Native Prairies

Some of the earliest restoration efforts were conducted on the degraded tall-grass prairies of the midwestern United States, begun as Civilian Conservation Corps projects during the depression of the 1930s. Tallgrass prairie had been all but eliminated over its formerly huge range, largely through extensive agriculture. Only tiny remnants existed, often in very small patches where native vegetation was left undisturbed, such as railroad rights-of-way or cemeteries. Although outwardly appearing to be simple systems, prairies actually had quite high plant species diversities, and were spatially heterogeneous systems; restoration efforts over the last half century have attempted to restore some of that diversity.

Prairies have been a focal point of restoration attempts because they lend themselves to experiments on a small scale and in the short term. Prairie patches of less than a hectare can be restored, although restorations orders of magnitude larger have also been attempted or suggested. Few sweeping generalizations can be made about prairie restoration due to great regional and temporal variation in conditions, and each effort has its own set of unique circumstances, including climatic conditions, seed and plant sources, fire history and use in restoration, and planting methods employed (Kline and Howell 1987). Despite the variations involved, there are two basic groups of problems associated with prairie restoration: increasing the populations of native prairie species, and eliminating exotic herbaceous and woody species.

The oldest and probably most famous restoration project involves the Curtis and Greene prairies at the University of Wisconsin Arboretum (Figure 14.14). These sites had been used for crops or pasture for the previous century, and their original vegetation had been almost entirely eliminated. Restoration at the sites began in the 1930s (Cottam 1987). Site preparation for prairie restoration can involve a variety of techniques, depending on local conditions, and several were used at these sites. If the site is entirely taken up by exotic vegetation, then those plants may be eliminated through herbicide use, soil cultivation, or soil sterilization. However, more extreme treatments, such as sterilization, are more destructive to soil organisms, and often result in longer establishment periods for new vegetation and soil organisms. If some desirable vegetation is present, selective raking, soil disking, or burning may eliminate exotic species and open space for natives.

**Figure 14.13**   These satellite images show changes in forest cover at Guanacaste National Park between 1979 (A) and 1985 (B). Forest types are indicated by shading: the lightest shade is young, second growth forest; the medium shade is older, more mature forest; the darkest is swamp forest. Note replacement of light shading in several areas over time. (Courtesy of Elizabeth Kramer.)

(A)

(B)

**Figure 14.14**   (A) Initial efforts by the Civilian Conservation Corps at restoring the Curtis Prairie at the University of Wisconsin Arboretum, ca. 1935; (B) Curtis Prairie as it looked in 1980. (Photographs courtesy of University of Wisconsin Arboretum and Archives.)

Planting techniques also vary. Transplanting of prairie sods, or plants grown individually, has a high success rate, but is costly. Alternatively, if existing prairie is available, it may be mowed late in the season, and the "hay" transferred to the restoration site. Seeds in the hay then seed the new site.

Observations of restored prairies at the Curtis and Greene sites over several decades indicate that these are very dynamic systems, with a great deal of unpredictability in species composition and community structure. Detailed surveys of the prairies every 5 years indicate that community composition at a location changes over time, and that entire communities change locations "in an amoeba-like movement that seems to be a response to the short-term climatic events of years immediately preceding the survey" (Cottam 1987). Such dynamism over a 24-year period is evident in Figure 14.15.

Several classes of questions are relevant to successfully restoring prairies (Kline and Howell 1987) and need further attention. The first involves disturbance. We know that prairies historically experienced disturbances in a dynamic mosaic pattern. How can we develop long-term, relevant disturbance regimes? Historical disturbances included fire, mound-building ants, and the actions of bison. Such disturbances are probably critical in maintaining native species and removing exotics, but what particular disturbance patterns are important?

Second, what is the relevance of population explosions of some plant species? For example, in the Wisconsin prairie projects, a plant called rattlesnake master (*Eryngium yuccifolium*) has completely covered Curtis Prairie, although it is usually abundant (and never dominant) only on mesic native prairies (Cottam 1987). What causes such explosions, will they last, and do they cause declines of other native species?

Third, it is generally recommended that locally adapted strains be used for plantings. But how important is that? Are there advantages to using more distant genetic varieties, perhaps to increase genetic diversity? Should strains from warmer climates be used to anticipate global climate changes? On the other hand, will nonlocal strains have reduced success rates, or conversely, will they outcompete other local species or strains? Obviously, many questions remain regarding the details of prairie restoration.

Since the earliest restoration efforts in the prairie region during the 1930s, many hundreds of projects have been initiated, often by amateurs (Packard and Nelson, in press). Many, developed for educational or orna-

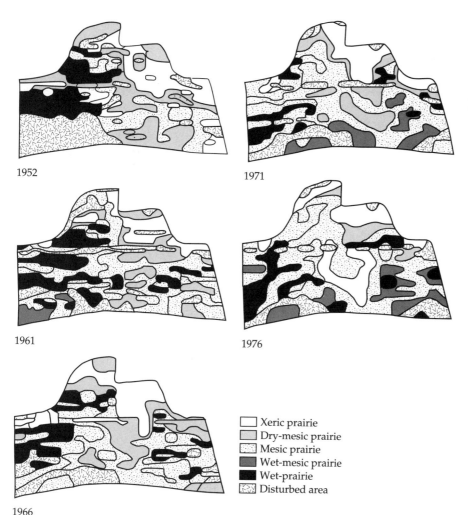

1952

1971

1961

1976

☐ Xeric prairie
◩ Dry-mesic prairie
⊡ Mesic prairie
◼ Wet-mesic prairie
■ Wet-prairie
▨ Disturbed area

1966

**Figure 14.15** The temporal dynamics of prairies as illustrated by the Greene Prairie from 1952 to 1976. Changes were partly due to shifts of species toward more optimal sites, reflecting short-term variations in climate. (From Cottam 1987.)

mental purposes, are small, but projects on the scale of 10 to 20 ha are common. Further development of techniques, including successional restoration (involving seeding directly into existing sod: Packard and Nelson, in press) and the use of customized farm equipment for operations such as seed gathering and planting, have led to a general scaling up of projects in recent years.

A landmark project inside the proton accelerator ring at Fermi National Laboratory in suburban Chicago began in the mid-1970s, and now covers roughly 200 ha (Nelson 1987). The McHenry County Conservation District is now working on a project that will eventually include some 600 ha in northeastern Illinois (Collins, in press), and The Nature Conservancy of Illinois is embarking on its "Chicago Wilderness" project, a program that will restore hundreds of hectares of prairie and other ecosystem types in the Chicago area. A project by the U.S. Fish and Wildlife Service at Walnut Creek, in central Iowa, will eventually include some 2800 ha of prairie, most of it on abandoned farmland (Drobney 1994). Still other projects, such as those on The Nature Conservancy's holdings in Kansas and Nebraska, which employ upgrading of existing prairies, rather than restoration from nothing, involve tracts of many hundreds of hectares.

Of course, even tens of thousands of hectares is still only a small fraction of the millions of hectares of tallgrass prairie that existed in central North

America before European settlement. By the end of the 19th century these prairies had been virtually eliminated from the landscape, especially in the eastern, corn-belt part of the prairie range. Thus, even what appears to be minor progress is highly significant from the perspective of biodiversity conservation. These projects have resulted in reintroduction of prairie to regions from which it had been essentially eradicated, and they provide expanded habitat for hundreds of species of native plants and animals. Some of these species were extremely rare and had been reduced to a tiny fraction of their former range. Many prairie restoration projects now include a number of species on state or federal lists of rare or endangered species. Though no comprehensive figures are available, the work of restorationists during the past three decades has undoubtedly led to a slight increase in prairie acreage in the Midwest, reversing a two-century pattern of decline, and has provided a rich information base on how to restore prairie ecosystems.

### Examples of Aquatic Restoration

Aquatic systems—lakes, streams, rivers, and wetlands—are critical resources in any region, but have a history of abuse throughout the world. Damming, channelization, groundwater pumping, diversion, and use as open sewers are just a few of the many ills experienced by aquatic systems. Fortunately, many of these problems are reversible, often just by removing the particular agent of destruction; others require greater restoration efforts. A few examples will illustrate some of these problems and potential restoration solutions.

Lake Washington is an 87-km$^2$ lake near Seattle, Washington. The lake was affected by raw and treated sewage from Seattle for much of this century, and by 1955, increased phosphorus loads had resulted in large blooms of blue-green algae (*Oscillatoria rubescens*) (NRC 1992), a species not previously found in the lake. The presence of *Oscillatoria* is a classic indicator that water conditions in a lake are rapidly deteriorating (Lehman 1986). Because of sewage releases and resultant heavy algal blooms, water quality continued to deteriorate in Lake Washington, culminating in strong public concern over destruction of this resource. A local government agency was formed, and provided funds to divert sewage releases into the Pacific Ocean at Puget Sound. By 1967, 4 years after diversion began, 99% of the previous sewage input no longer flowed into Lake Washington. The resultant decrease in nutrient loading had rapid effects on the lake: water clarity greatly increased, phosphorus levels declined from 70 to 16 µg/l, and chlorophyll levels (a measure of algal growth) decreased from 35 to 4 µg/l (NRC 1992). Although diversion of sewage from the lake to Puget Sound only seems to redirect the problem elsewhere, in fact the comparatively huge size of that water body makes the additional input of nutrients relatively trivial. The conditions in Lake Washington were improved tremendously simply by removing sewage dumping.

Such eutrophication of water bodies is a common problem in lakes in the United States and around the world. Increased levels of nutrients such as phosphorus and nitrogen from sewage outfalls or agricultural fertilizer runoff stimulate algal growth, fundamentally changing the biological, chemical, and physical conditions of the system. Such waters typically become warm, green, and overproductive. When algal blooms die, they sink to the bottom and decompose; this process depletes the water of oxygen, and the bottom can become anoxic, killing larger organisms such as invertebrates and fish. The restoration approach in such cases is standard and uncomplicated: eliminate the source of extra nutrients. The complications, of course, come in the form of the legal clout and political will necessary to make the changes.

A different type of problem affects many rivers throughout the world: fundamental changes in channel morphology, usually a result of dredging, flood control projects, or agricultural activities in floodplains. Such actions result in unintended changes in river morphology and flow, usually causing greater problems for people than the original river behavior they were intended to change. An example is the San Juan River in southwestern Colorado. In the 1930s, willows along the banks of the San Juan were burned away, and bottomlands along the river were plowed for agriculture. This created an unstable and unnatural channel system broken into several "braids" that meandered across the river valley (NRC 1992). Riverbank soils were badly eroded because willow trees no longer held them in place, adjacent land was washed away, water quality declined, and roads and irrigation projects were damaged.

In an effort to restore the river to former conditions, a hydrologist was called on to study the natural flows of undisturbed rivers in the area and to design a restoration program for the San Juan. He constructed a new river channel, floodplains, and river terraces based on the meander patterns, width-to-depth ratios, and flow patterns of stable streams in the region. He employed so-called "soft engineering" technology, which uses natural materials and heeds natural tendencies of river flows. Rather than building a concrete and steel channel or relying on "riprap" (large rocks used to artificially stabilize the bed), he used natural materials such as tree trunks, boulders, roots, and vegetation to reinforce the new river channel. The new meander pattern has remained stable for 5 years, transports sediments as it should, and handles full flood capacity with no problem. The project demonstrated that understanding natural and predictable riverine flows is key to restoration of a system without use of heavy technology and creation of an artificial state. The "soft" technology will eventually allow the river to return to a more natural state than would artificial materials, at a lower cost.

Finally, wetlands throughout the world have declined extensively in the last few centuries. In the coterminous United States, some 53% of the estimated original extent of wetlands has been lost in the last two centuries (Dahl 1990; Figure 14.16). Swamps, floodplains, bogs, sloughs, marshes, springs, and other wetlands that serve vital ecosystemic functions and are centers of biological diversity have been drained, ditched, pumped, and diked. The obvious restoration action in such cases is to reinstate former hydrological conditions by reestablishing historical water flows. Ditches may be closed, pumping stopped, dikes removed, and so forth.

A potentially limiting and complicating factor in this form of restoration is availability of propagules or immigrants to the newly restored wetland. If only a few years have elapsed since drying, viable seed banks may still exist in the local soils, and the native plant community can become reestablished. If habitat corridors to other wetlands or associated uplands have not been destroyed, then natural migrations may bring wetland animals, such as amphibians and reptiles, back to the system. However, in the absence of natural recolonization, it could be necessary to reestablish the plant community, such as was done in the prairie and arid mine land examples above. Likewise, it could be necessary to bring fish and other invertebrate populations to the site, and even to "inoculate" the system with water and substrate containing invertebrates and microbes from a comparable system.

**Figure 14.16** Wetland distribution in the United States in the 1780s and the 1980s. The percentage of wetland habitat has declined in every state over this 200-year period, and continues in that direction. (From Dahl 1990.)

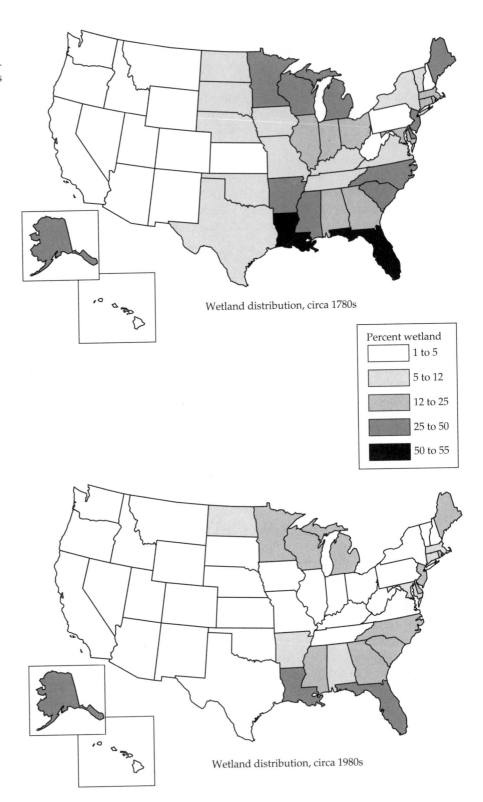

Wetland distribution, circa 1780s

Percent wetland
1 to 5
5 to 12
12 to 25
25 to 50
50 to 55

Wetland distribution, circa 1980s

## General Observations on Restoration

As evidenced by the several examples given, planning and conducting a restoration project requires the consideration of a myriad of site conditions and the selection of appropriate techniques from a huge array of alternatives.

Of special importance is the recognition that the factors addressed in restoration—essentially those factors that limit, constrain, or influence the natural recovery process—vary enormously from system to system (MacMahon 1987). On the prairies, a key limiting factor is typically the genetic material available to the restorationist. The major restoration effort goes into finding and introducing native species in appropriate proportions (while eliminating or excluding exotics), but with relatively little attention being paid to their patterns of distribution. On the shrublands of the arid West, pattern and structure are critical, and the distribution of species, even at the individual level, may be important attributes of the system that are critical to successful restoration efforts. In aquatic systems, restoration may be as simple as eliminating the major source of phosphorus or restoring a natural hydrological pattern, or as complicated as restructuring a stream channel. In a megascale restoration project such as Guanacaste, restoration focuses on eliminating human disturbance regimes and changing land use practices to allow recovery of native vegetation, assisted by intentional seed dispersal of native species.

Other factors, often of a very different nature, come into play when dealing with distinctly different kinds of systems, such as cliffsides, alpine regions, or vernal pool systems. For some systems, especially forests, the sequence of species introductions is a key, and often challenging, concern. In other systems, the particular soil type and structure may determine success or failure. There is literally no end to special considerations, and they are the subject of a growing body of literature. Successful restoration depends on identifying these key limiting factors and dealing with them effectively.

Similar considerations apply to restoration efforts undertaken in systems that have experienced different degrees or kinds of alteration—differences in the disturbance process. Restoration may simply involve rejuvenation of a system that, though altered or degraded in some way, offers basic structure to work with and has not, in the jargon of the auto-body shop, been "totaled." There frequently *is* something to work with—residuals or legacies—even though this is not always obvious. The time and trouble spent identifying and taking advantage of residuals is likely to be repaid later. In fact, recognition of what is available to work with may indeed be the most important single step in successful restoration. Close observation of the system, often over a period of years, may be required. A classic example of this is the work being done locating relict prairies in old cemeteries and along rights-of-way in northeastern Illinois, and then restoring them, principally by judicious hand weeding and reintroduction of fire (Betz and Lamp 1992). In many cases this has led to the recovery of respectable stands of prairie on sites so heavily infested with exotic species that prairie species were suppressed and difficult to find.

Despite such successes there is a tendency to skip this first step in restoration, ignoring what is there and wiping the slate clean, as it were, with plow, ax, or herbicide. Unfortunately, this frequently entails destruction of elements of the functioning ecosystem that can actually provide the best base for the restoration effort. If these elements are removed or destroyed, they may be nearly impossible to reconstruct. An intriguing example of this principle, mentioned previously, is the recent development of successional restoration of prairies, in which, rather than clearing the ground with plow or pesticides, the restorationist merely throws seed of prairie species onto existing sod (Packard, in press). The development of prairie is relatively slow under such conditions, but results suggest that this method favors species that may be difficult to establish on bare-soil sites. Not only is it an easier and cheaper process, but the resulting prairie may also be of higher quality than that achieved by more intensive methods. This method provides a way of avoiding the tradeoff of quality for quantity that, in the past, has limited the value of prairie restoration as a conservation strategy.

This principle obviously has important implications for the practice and application of restoration. Recognizing that even low-key work with relatively intact systems actually *is* restoration will help the practitioner think more clearly about the work at hand, including identification of disturbances, definition of goals and so forth. This approach will also discourage the tendency to hide faulty or unclear thinking and planning behind softer, more ambiguous terms such as "management," "stewardship," or even "preservation."

Our relative neglect of animals in this discussion, to a certain extent, reflects the state of our knowledge, both in research and in the practice of restoration. Most studies tend to concentrate on vegetation, and usually on the most obvious species. Animals can play a vital role in restoration efforts (as was seen in the Guanacaste program), but systematic study of most of them, from a restoration perspective, is still in its infancy. For an introduction to research on animals and other components of the system, the reader should refer to Miller (1987) on soil mycorrhizae, Panzer (1984) on insects in restored prairies, and Green and Salter (1987) and Majer (1989) on animals in general.

Restoration has a valid and important role to play in conservation. The number of degraded ecological systems around the world grows as the number of relatively pristine systems declines. Concentrating only on the latter and ignoring the former throws away tremendous conservation opportunities. Most lands and waters around the globe are degraded to some degree, but many are usable as important conservation areas and buffers for wildlands. Growing attention to these degraded areas as the matrix within which centers of wilderness exist can only serve to enhance overall efforts to stem the loss of biodiversity. Restoration ecology is a key to our conservation future and is likely to be most efficient if conducted using sound ecological and conservation principles.

## Summary

Restoration ecology is simply a tool in the arsenal against biodiversity loss, and not an end unto itself. Protection of natural habitat before it is damaged by humans is the preferred course of action in conservation, but sometimes restoring damaged habitat is a viable and necessary option. Restorationists work in systems that have been damaged or degraded by human action, with the explicit intention of guiding those systems back toward their former, natural state through deliberate manipulation. Restoration ecology has been advanced by a number of factors, including legislation requiring habitat rehabilitation after human damage, increased use of restoration techniques in various engineering applications, a growing interest in native as opposed to exotic vegetation, and increased awareness of ecological destruction worldwide. But restoration runs the political risk of appearing to allow ecological destruction that can be fixed later, a false impression. Restoration is not an alternative to conservation, but a complement to and subset of conservation.

Basic concerns common to all restoration efforts include defining the desired product, determining the feasibility of the project, assessing the authenticity of the results, working at an appropriate and feasible scale, and working within realistic cost constraints. A "target" should be established for any restoration project, which can be based on good knowledge of the pre-disturbance system, knowledge of a similar, undisturbed system, or simply an ecologically more desirable condition than the present, degraded state. The system is then sent on a new developmental "trajectory" toward that state. The feasibility of restoration depends on a myriad of factors, including the present condition of the site (such as level of disturbance, and condition of hydrology and soils), availability of biological materials for restoration (including their genetic diversity), and the cost of restoration and availability of funding. The scale of a project has great bearing on its potential success. In general, quantity sacrifices quality; that is, details cannot usually be tended to as readily in larger projects. The reality of cost also has great bearing on restoration success.

Much of restoration simply involves manipulation of succession, either to speed up the successional process or to halt it in an earlier state. Within this successional context, residuals or legacies of the undegraded system should be identified and used to advantage. Remnants of the former system not only provide raw materials for restoration efforts but also information about the unperturbed state.

We discussed several examples of restoration projects that demonstrated various concerns, challenges, and techniques used in restoration ecology. Collectively, they demonstrate that each restoration project is unique, and each must be designed and conducted for the particular site. As with most of conservation biology, there are no standardized, "cookbook" prescriptions that substitute for good local ecological knowledge.

## Questions for Discussion

1. Imagine that you are given the job of restoring a prairie. What would you need to think about to begin the task? Prepare a list of questions to address regarding what you would need to know and what you would need to do in order to get the prairie restored.

2. Repeat Question 1 for another habitat, such as an estuary that has been degraded by dredging, a small swamp that has been drained for agriculture, or an alpine meadow that has been trampled by cattle and people. How does the list differ from that in Question 1?

3. If you successfully restored the prairie in Question 1, could those same techniques be transferred to another prairie restoration project 50 km away? 500 km away? What are some factors that might have to be considered in modifying the techniques and approach used?

4. How worthwhile is it to attempt a restoration project when you are certainly not guaranteed success? What are some of the ecological and political pitfalls that might be encountered in a failed restoration attempt? How far along the restoration path should one travel, putting time and money into the project? Can you develop some guidelines (ecological, economic, political) that could suggest when to abandon (or not attempt) a restoration project?

## Suggestions for Further Reading

Bradshaw, A. D. and M. J. Chadwick. 1980. *The Restoration of Land: The Ecology and Reclamation of Derelict and Degraded Land.* Blackwell Scientific Publications, Oxford. Two British authors show how a scientific approach to the management of derelict lands can pay substantial dividends in reclaiming land to a useful state. Many examples of work in Great Britain and Australia are given.

Buckley, G. P. (ed.). 1989. *Biological Habitat Reconstruction.* Belhaven Press, London. Topics related to habitat reconstruction, from the viewpoints of over 30 authors, are addressed, including consideration of developing new habitats as well as the ecological principles of habitat reconstruction.

Cairns, J., Jr. (ed.). 1988. *Rehabilitating Damaged Ecosystems.* Vol. I and II. CRC Press, Boca Raton, FL. This pair of volumes, edited by one of the pioneers of restoration ecology, contains a wealth of information concerning the reclamation of sites as disparate as coal slurry ponds and salt marshes. It contains a very readable first chapter by Cairns that lays out some of the problems of restoration ecology.

Jordan, W. R. III, M. E. Gilpin and J. D. Aber (eds.). 1987. *Restoration Ecology: A Synthetic Approach to Ecological Research.* Cambridge University Press, Cambridge. This book was one of the first to invite a group of ecologists to address problems of restoration from theoretical as well as practical viewpoints. It has been used as a textbook in a number of university courses devoted to restoration ecology.

Luken, J. O. 1990. *Directing Ecological Succession.* Chapman and Hall, London. Luken specifically applies successional theory to the problems of management of disturbed lands in a detailed presentation.

Majer, J. D. (ed.). 1989. *Animals in Primary Succession: The Role of Fauna in Reclaimed Lands.* Cambridge University Press, Cambridge. This book deals with the role of animals on reclaimed lands as well as in primary succession in nature. A variety of case studies of reestablishment of fauna on reclaimed lands is presented.

National Research Council (U.S.), Committee on Restoration of Aquatic Ecosystems. 1992. *Restoration of Aquatic Ecosystems: Science, Technology, and Public Policy.* National Academy Press, Washington, D.C. In the short time that this book has been available, it has been hailed as an important statement of how restoration can be accomplished in aquatic systems. It includes restoration case studies of wetlands, lakes, and rivers, as well as a series of general principles that can be applied to any wetlands.

Nilsen, R. (ed.). 1991. *Helping Nature Heal: An Introduction to Environmental Restoration.* A Whole Earth Catalog, Ten Speed Press, Berkeley, CA. The publishers of *The Whole Earth Catalog* provide an extremely readable presentation of environmental restoration theory as well as practice in the United States. While not especially scientific in nature, this book is quite practical and makes restoration more accessible to anyone.

Thompson, J. R. 1992. *Prairies, Forests, and Wetlands.* University of Iowa Press, Iowa City. Thompson addresses the restoration of forests, wetlands, and prairies in Iowa, offering a single perspective on a variety of types of restoration. This is quite a useful approach, given that most people are involved in the restoration of only one type of biotic community.

Wali, M. K. (ed.). 1992. *Ecosystem Rehabilitation.* Vol. 1: *Policy Issues;* Vol. 2: *Ecosystem Analysis and Synthesis.* SPB Academic Publishing, The Hague, The Netherlands. Wali is a pioneer in the area of restoration and reclamation ecology. This work is merely the most recent of a number of edited and original works that Wali has contributed to the field. In this case, the two volumes address policy issues as well as more esoteric scientific aspects of restoration.

# 15

# Ecology, Politics, and Economics

## Finding the Common Ground for Decision Making in Conservation

*The ideas of economists and political philosophers, both when they are right and when they are wrong, are more powerful than is commonly understood. Indeed, the world is ruled by little else. . . . Madmen in authority, who hear voices in the air, are distilling their frenzy from some academic scribbler a few years back.*

*John Maynard Keynes, 1936*

As you have seen throughout this book, planetary biodiversity is in serious jeopardy for a multitude of reasons: habitat destruction, pollutants and pesticides from industrial societies, human population explosions in desperately poor countries, introductions of exotic species, acidic deposition associated with the combustion of fossil fuels, direct exploitation of particular species, and a myriad of other processes. The reasons individuals interact detrimentally with the biosphere vary by culture, the structure of economies, and the social status of the actors. In this chapter, we will explore some of these reasons by focusing on economic and political aspects of decision making in conservation.

Conserving biodiversity requires that people both change how they interact with the biosphere in a great number of ways (see Chapters 16 and 18) and address a plurality of reasons as to why they should do so. Furthermore, the decision to change must be a collective one; people acting individually cannot conserve much biodiversity for their progeny. Given the myriad ways and reasons biodiversity is being lost, finding the common ground for framing and negotiating a collective agreement is proving to be a major challenge.

Discussing and negotiating less destructive modes of human interaction with the biosphere has proven difficult for two reasons. First, the problems involve many different actors in various positions doing different things for a variety of reasons. These differences make it inherently difficult to find common ground for agreement on less destructive modes of interaction. Second, to facilitate analysis and communication, people simplify the complex problem of biodiversity loss in different ways. Some think of it as driven by human population growth, some by our social structure, others by our materialism, still others by our choice of technologies. Each explanation is partially correct, but agreement on the big, complex picture has been stymied by arguments among those who each insist that their limited perspective is better than that of others. Each small, simplified picture of the problem pins the blame differently and suggests a different, simple solution that appeals to different interest groups. In fact, the blame is largely indirect and widely dispersed, and the solutions will be multiple and complex. But, to date, the politics of reducing biodiversity loss has largely been carried out among groups who find particular combinations of simple censure and new directions to be in their own interests.

Reaching a collective understanding of how to conserve biodiversity will require going beyond debate over simple explanations and solutions. For this to occur, those concerned with conserving biodiversity need to become familiar with the variety of simple perspectives being put forward and begin to see how they interrelate. That is the objective of this chapter. The separate perspectives are neither right nor wrong, merely too simple. Surprisingly, the perspectives of those favoring environmental conservation, as well as the views of those favoring greater material consumption, are rooted in the history of economic thought. While conservation biologists are challenging the course of economic development, their perception of the processes of biodiversity loss is driven by historical economic reasoning. Even environmental ethicists argue in the context, or in opposition to the context, of thinking dominated by economic philosophers during the past two centuries. Going beyond these historical, simple positions will be facilitated by understanding their origins. Thus, this chapter stresses the history of economic thought and its philosophical roots.

Conversely, this chapter neither argues for a correct economics nor presents examples of economies or development projects that appropriately conserve biodiversity. A new economics and its integration with environmental understanding is emerging through the collective global discourse on the human predicament. Some insights into these new directions are provided at the end of the chapter and in its three essays. Appropriate economies or development projects, if they have existed in recent history, have had little chance to survive and prove themselves within a global political/economic system designed around and driven by multiple, fractious, historical interpretations of the human–environment relationship.

We, *Homo sapiens,* distinguish ourselves from other species in terms of the nature and extent of our knowledge and the ways in which we use knowledge to devise technologies and organize our activities. We are also the only species to have initiated the wholesale extinction of other species. These distinctions are undoubtedly interrelated. Conserving biodiversity will ultimately depend on our uncovering and transforming the way we think, and recognizing how our thinking guides the politics of social organization, economic activity, and individual behavior.

## Economic Philosophy and the Roots of the Biological Crisis

### Background

Somewhat more than two centuries ago, economics emerged from moral philosophy at a time of great social change and scientific promise (Canterbury 1987; Nelson 1991). Long-standing moral principles with respect to the obligations of individuals to larger social goals were being challenged by the development of markets and by scientific advances that brought new opportunities for personal material improvement and fed great hopes for a plentiful future. Then, in the second half of the 18th century, as today at the end of the 20th, people were concerned that following one's own economic interests might hurt society as a whole. Economists, then as now, argued that markets guided individual behavior, as if by an "invisible hand," toward the common good.

There is a critical difference between the times, however. Historically, material security had been the reward for good moral conduct, but increasingly after the Renaissance it was argued that material security was needed to establish the conditions for moral progress. Scarcity caused greed and even war; scarcity forced people to work so hard that they did not have time to contemplate the Scriptures and live morally. Material progress, in short, was necessary to establish the conditions for moral progress. Thus, two centuries ago, the individual pursuit of materialism was justified on the presumption that once their basic material needs of food, shelter, and clothing were met, people would have the time and conditions to pursue their individual moral and collective social improvement. Today, these earlier concerns with moral and social progress have largely been forgotten while individual materialism for many people has become an end in itself.

Two centuries ago, as now, technological optimists were convinced that the essentials of life would eventually be assured through the advance of human knowledge leading to a mastery of underlying natural laws. The presumption has been that such laws are relatively few and that their mastery will make superfluous our dependence on the particular ways that nature, and people's place therein, evolved. To those concerned only with material well-being, the expectation of such mastery has meant that people do not have to be concerned with long-term scarcities or how their activities otherwise might affect the future (Simon 1981). Over the past two centuries, scientists have touted the goal of eventual mastery of nature and have justified their research on this basis. The belief that scientific progress will inevitably lead to dominion over nature and material plenty is still popularly held and frequently invoked, even by scientists, to support further population increases, technological change, and economic development along their historical, biologically destructive, paths (Simon 1981).

Economic thought evolved in the context of these dominant moral, material, and scientific beliefs and will continue to do so. Reality, however, does not always unfold as expected; the social and environmental problems associated with economic development have dampened earlier ruling beliefs and empowered other interpretations. Thus, today most scientists are more humble, and many—conservation biologists most notably among them—argue that we need to direct the best of our scientific expertise and far more of our educational effort toward learning how to work *with* nature (Ehrenfeld 1981; Meffe 1992). Similarly, environmental ethicists are challenging the vacuity of individual material progress for its own sake, and economic thought is now evolving in this new context as well.

## Adam Smith and the Invisible Hand

Adam Smith (1723–1790), widely recognized as the founder of modern economics, was a moral philosopher. While economics assumed a scientific gloss and a technical application late in the 19th century, ethical issues have always been embedded in its theory. And the key ethical issue has always been whether the pursuit of individual wealth can be in the interest of society as a whole. Smith reasoned, in the tradition of key liberal social philosophers such as Hobbes and Locke, that society is merely the sum of its individuals. If two people who are fully informed of the consequences of their decision choose to enter into an exchange, it is because the exchange makes each of them better off. Appealing to Judeo–Christian images of God, Smith invented the metaphor of the "invisible hand," arguing that markets induced people to behave in the common interest as if they were guided by a higher authority.

Modern economics assumes that society is simply the sum of its individuals, that the social good is the sum of individual wants, and that markets automatically guide individual behavior to the common good. This atomistic–mechanistic view of a social system contrasts sharply with the earlier, more holistic view that community relations define who people are, affect what they want, facilitate collective action, and have a historical continuity of their own. Although Adam Smith was a moral philosopher, his economics made morality less important. For most of history, people's sense of identity developed through living within a community and its moral precepts. Today, this is increasingly less important among either the materially wealthy or aspirants to wealth. Among the multiplicative factors affecting the loss of biodiversity, the role of materialism, as well as its relation to moral behavior, is rarely discussed and is in need of broader, more serious scientific and public discourse.

Certainly the growth of individualism and materialism, and the decline in community and concern with moral conduct associated with modernity, are not Adam Smith's fault, but he did play a decisive role. In an age when Europeans and North Americans were rebelling against the tyranny of church and state, and social philosophers were building theories from the individual up to the society rather than the reverse, Adam Smith argued that markets link individual greed to the common good without coercive social institutions. And ever since Smith, the critical question, one too rarely discussed, has been whether markets really do this as well as he argued and whether communities at various geographic scales are not still necessary (Daly and Cobb 1989; Bellah et al. 1991).

### Thomas Malthus and Population Growth

The Reverend-turned-economist Thomas R. Malthus (1766–1834) explained the prevalence of war and disease as secular, material phenomena rather than acts of God. He argued that human populations were capable of increasing exponentially and would do so as long as sufficient food and other essentials of life were available (Malthus 1963). He further hypothesized that people could expand their food supply only arithmetically through new technologies and expansion into new habitats. Given the geometric potential of population growth and the arithmetic food constraint, population would periodically surpass food supply. At these times, Malthus argued, people would ravage the land, go to war over food, and succumb to disease and starvation. Human numbers would consequently drop to sustainable levels, whence the process would repeat again (Figure 15.1). This simple model was widely used by biological scientists; both Darwin and Wallace acknowledged that Malthus's model was key to their formulation of the theory of natural selection.

Malthus's model is charmingly simple, but subsequent human demographic history generally has not supported it. Yet, periodically and in specific places, Malthus' model has been confirmed, and history may yet

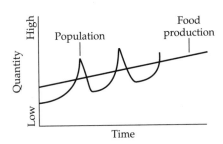

**Figure 15.1** Thomas Malthus's model of population growth and collapse. Collapse occurs when population exceeds food production or carrying capacity.

confirm it globally. Few question whether population must ultimately be stabilized in order to sustain human well-being at a reasonable level. The expansion of human populations into previously unpopulated or lightly populated regions, the intensity with which resources are collected, and the push to increase food production through the modern agrochemical, monocultural techniques that are so harmful to biodiversity are driven over the long run by population increase. The continued rapid rates of population increase in the poorest nations threaten to keep them poor.

Without people, there would be no human-induced biodiversity loss. People working on reducing the rate of population growth, however, are not misanthropes; they are fully aware that population is but one of many interrelated variables. Unfortunately, the full complexities of the interactions of the factors causing biodiversity loss are not consistently communicated, especially through the mass media. Due to incomplete communication and miscommunication, people primarily concerned with the social processes maintaining inequities in access to resources falsely label those primarily concerned with population growth as "neo-Malthusians." As a consequence, effective discourse and action on population is being stymied by misunderstanding and divisive misrepresentation.

Whether or not one finds our demographic history consistent with Malthus's model, it has become a part of human consciousness. This makes it difficult to contemplate, let alone discuss, the issues of population increase and its effects on biodiversity without Malthus's framing becoming central to the discussion. The success of his model stems from its simplicity. But the dynamics of population growth and the ways people depend on the environment are much more complex than Malthus's model. Thus, while Malthus provided us with a powerful model, its simplicity restricts its usefulness for policymaking beyond the obvious prescription that fewer people would probably be better.

### David Ricardo and the Geographic Pattern of Economic Activity

David Ricardo (1772–1823) introduced a second model of how economic activity relates to the environment (Figure 15.2), not because he was concerned with environmental degradation or human survival, but rather because he wished to justify why landlords received a rent from their ownership of land

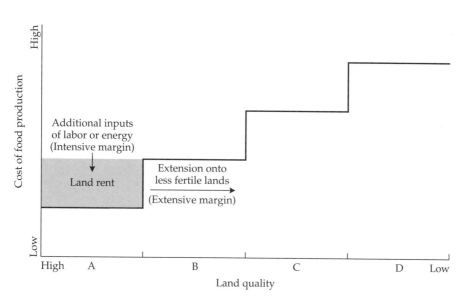

**Figure 15.2**   Ricardo's model of land rent. High quality land (area A) is farmed first, at a low cost. As population, and hence food demand, increases, lower quality land (area B) is brought into production (the extensive margin) at a higher cost, and the higher quality land (area A) experiences a greater return, or land rent. (Note that economists refer to land "rent" as economic return deriving from land or resources; it is not a payment in the sense of housing rent.) Additional inputs of labor or energy may be applied to area A as well, which is the intensive margin; that is, greater production (and return) may be realized by more intensive efforts. As population and demand increase further, areas C and D may be brought into production, with increasing rent on all higher quality land areas.

(Ricardo 1926). Ricardo argued that people would initially farm the land that produced the most food for the least work. As population increased, farming would extend to less fertile soils requiring more labor; economists refer to this additional land as the **extensive margin**. Food prices would have to rise to cover the cost of the extra labor on the less fertile land. This means that the initial land would earn a rent, a return above production cost, because it would now be more valuable. Higher food prices, in turn, would also induce a more intensive use of labor on the better land; economists refer to these additional inputs as the **intensive margin**.

This model shows how increasing population drives people to farm in previously undisturbed areas and how higher food prices lead to intensified efforts, and in modern agriculture, the greater use of fertilizers and pesticides, on prime agricultural lands. This model also provides insights into how fluctuations in food prices can result in the periodic entry and exit of farmers on the extensive margin and in shifts in farming practices on the intensive margin. Ricardo's model also helps us understand why 20% of North American farmland has gone out of production as modern technologies have driven the price of food down. Ricardo's model of the way agricultural activities are patterned on the land in response to population growth and changes in food prices is critical to our understanding of the complex interrelations between human survival and biodiversity.

### John Stuart Mill and the Steady State

John Stuart Mill (1806–1873) was the son of social philosopher James Mill (1773–1836), who also wrote on economics. J. S. Mill is important for having expanded on the linkages between individual behavior and the common good proposed by Adam Smith, arguing that competitive markets are critical to individual liberty. As a social philosopher seriously concerned with liberty, Mill also wrote on the immorality and waste of subjugating women to men. At the same time, he neither saw material prosperity as an end in itself nor foresaw that continuous growth in material well-being was possible. Mill envisioned economies becoming mature and reaching a steady state in which people would be able to enjoy the fruits of their earlier savings, or of their material abstinence necessary for the accumulation of industrial capital. The idea that economies would reach a steady state was consistent both with the Newtonian worldview of the time and with natural phenomena. Change was common, unceasing growth was not, and relatively steady states, rather than random change, were perceived as natural. Contemporary ecological economist Herman Daly argues from Mill for a steady-state economy, in which flows of resources into production and of pollutants back to the environment are fixed at a steady level. Mill's and Daly's visions of a steady-state economy mesh with our understanding of how ecological systems operate (Daly 1991). The steady-state metaphor could become critical to finding common ground for slowing the loss of biological diversity. Essay 15A by Herman Daly extends this argument.

## ESSAY 15A
## Steady-State Economics

Herman E. Daly, The World Bank*

Any system in a steady state is characterized by balanced, opposing forces or fluxes. This does not imply stagnation; indeed, steady-state systems may be highly dynamic internally. For example, as long as the environment does not change in a major way, the species composition of an old-growth forest will remain in a steady state, neither losing nor gaining species overall, although considerable turnover of species may be occurring locally and seasonal changes will occur. Similarly, an economic steady-state system may be highly dynamic, but, on average, the many flows and exchanges are balanced.

The worldview underlying standard economics is that the economy is a system isolated from the natural world, a circular flow of exchange value just between businesses and households. In such an isolated system neither matter nor energy enters or exits, and the system has no relation with its environment; for all practical purposes there *is* no environment. Thus, standard economics ignores the origin of resources and the fate of wastes; they are "external" to the economic system. While this vision may be useful for analyzing exchange between producers and consumers, as well as related questions of price and income determination, it is useless for studying the relation of the economy to the environment. It is as if a biologist's vision of an animal contained a circulatory system, but no digestive tract. The animal would be an isolated system, completely independent of its environment. If it could move it would be a perpetual motion machine.

Whatever flows through a system, entering as input and exiting as output, is called "throughput." Just as an organism maintains its physical structure by a metabolic flow and is connected to the environment at both ends of its digestive tract, so too an economy requires a throughput, which must to some degree both deplete and pollute the environment. As long as the scale of the human economy was very small relative to ecosystems, one could ignore throughput since no apparent sacrifice was involved in increasing it. The economy has now grown to a scale at which this is no longer reasonable.

Standard economics has also failed to make the elementary distinction between *growth* (physical increase in size resulting from accretion or assimilation of materials; a *quantitative* change), and *development* (realization of potentialities, evolution to a fuller, better, or different state; a *qualitative* change). Quantitative and qualitative changes follow different laws. It is clearly possible to have growth without development or to have development without growth.

The usual worldview, the one that supports most economic analysis today, is that the economy is not a subsystem of any larger environment, and is unconstrained in its growth by anything. Nature may be finite, but it is just one sector of the economy, for which other sectors can substitute without limiting overall growth in any important way. If the economy is seen as an isolated system, then there is no environment to constrain its continual growth. But if we see the economy as one subsystem of a larger, but finite and nongrowing, ecosystem, then obviously its growth is limited. The economy may continue to develop qualitatively without growing quantitatively, just as the planet Earth does, but it cannot continue to grow; beyond some point it must approximate a steady state in its physical dimensions.

The worldview from which steady-state economics (Daly 1991) emerges is that the economy, in its physical dimensions, is an open subsystem of a finite, nongrowing, and materially closed total system—the earth-ecosystem or biosphere. An "open" system is one with a "digestive tract," one that takes matter and energy from the environment in low-entropy form (raw materials) and returns it to the environment in high-entropy form (waste). A "closed" system is one in which only energy flows through, while matter circulates within the system. A steady-state economy is an open system whose throughput remains constant at a level that neither depletes the environment beyond its regenerative capacity nor pollutes it beyond its absorptive capacity. A result of steady-state economics is sustainable development, or development without growth—a physically steady-state economy that may continue to develop greater capacity to satisfy human wants by increasing the efficiency of resource use, but not by increasing the resource throughput.

Economic growth is further limited by the complementary relation between manufactured and natural capital. If the two forms of capital were good substitutes for one another, natural capital could be totally replaced by manufactured capital. But, in fact, manufactured capital loses its value without an appropriate complement of natural capital. What good are fishing boats without populations of fish, or sawmills without forests? And even if we could convert the whole ocean into a fishpond, we would still need the natural capital of solar energy, photosynthetic organisms, nutrient recyclers, and so forth. The standard economists' emphasis on substitution while ignoring complementarity in analyzing technical relations among factors of production seems a reflection of their preference for competition (substitution) over cooperation (complementarity) in social relations.

In an empty world, increasing throughput implies no sacrifice of ecosystem services, but in a full world it does. The ultimate cost of increasing throughput is loss of ecosystem services. Throughput begins with depletion of natural stock and ends with pollution, both of which are costs in a full world. Therefore, it makes sense to minimize throughput for any given level of stock. If we recognize that the economy grows by converting ever more of the ecosystem (natural capital) into economy (manufactured capital), then we see that the benefit of that expansion is the extra services from manufactured capital and its cost is the loss of service from reduced natural capital.

The efficiency with which we use the world to satisfy our wants depends on the amount of service we get per unit of manufactured capital, and the amount of service we sacrifice per unit of natural capital lost as a result of its conversion into manufactured capital. This overall *ecological–economic efficiency* is the ratio of manufactured capital services gained (MK) to natural capital services sacrificed (NK), or MK/NK. In an empty world there is no noticeable sacrifice of NK services required by increases in MK, so the denominator is irrelevant. In a full world any increase in MK comes at a noticeable reduction in NK and its services.

The steady-state economic view recognizes that economic systems are not isolated from the natural world, but are fully dependent on ecosystems for the goods and services they provide. Inasmuch as the overall size of the natural world cannot increase (and in fact decreases steadily at the hands of humankind), our economic systems cannot continually increase; they must operate as a steady-state system, one which does not quantitatively grow without bounds, but which can qualitatively develop. The internal workings of the economic machine must fully account for the raw natural materials consumed and the resultant wastes eliminated. The ultimate accounting rules for a realistic economy are the first and second laws of thermodynamics, which are inviolable.

*The views here presented are those of the author and should in no way be attributed to The World Bank.

### Karl Marx and the Ownership of Resources

Karl Marx (1818–1883) addressed, in his multiple critiques of capitalism, how the concentration of land and capital within a small portion of society affected the way economies worked. There is an extensive literature written by scholars influenced by Marx, some of it now addressing the sustainability of development and the way ownership of resources affects the path of development (Redclift 1984; Blaikie and Brookfield 1987). Neoclassical models also readily show how resource ownership affects resource use (Bator 1957). However, for a variety of political reasons, this facet of neoclassical economics was ignored in the West during the Cold War. Indeed, in the United States, economists who were concerned with the **distribution** of ownership of resources were politically disempowered because of their association with a central concern of Marx. Western neoclassical economists, including resource and environmental economists, addressed questions of the **efficient allocation** of resources, leaving their initial distribution among people as given. We now know that the initial distribution of rights to resources and to the services of the environment is critically important to resource and environmental conservation (Howarth and Norgaard 1992).

It has long been known that the way economies allocate resources to different material ends depends on how resources are distributed among people—owned by or otherwise under the control of different individuals—in the first place. Peasants or others who work land and interact with biological resources owned by someone else have little incentive to protect them. Landlords can only counteract this lack of incentive by diverting labor from other productive activities and employing it to monitor and enforce their interests in protection, a diversion that would not be necessary with a more equal distribution of control. Furthermore, especially wealthy landlords may have little interest in protecting any particular land or biological resource for their descendants when they hold land in abundance.

Imagine two countries with identical populations and identical resources allocated by perfect markets. In the first country, rights to resources are distributed among people approximately equally, people have similar incomes, and they consume similar products, perhaps corn, chicken, and cotton clothing. In the second country, rights are concentrated among a few people who can afford luxury goods such as beef, wine, caviar, fine clothes, and ecotourism, while those who have few rights to resources, living nearly on their labor alone, consume only the most basic of goods, such as rice and beans. In each country, markets efficiently allocate resources to the production of products, but the way land is used, the types of products produced, and who consumes them depend on how rights to resources are distributed. Under different distributions of rights, the efficient use of resources is different.

Within the 20th-century global discourse on development policy, many have argued that economic injustices within nations and in the international economic order have limited the development options of poor nations and thereby, in the long run, those of rich nations as well. Similarly, within the late 20th-century global environmental discourse, many are arguing that environmental injustices and the international ecological order limit the possibilities for conservation. The vast majority of the people on the globe still consume very little. The poor are poor for two reasons. First, they do not have sufficient long-term access to resources to meet their ongoing material needs. Second, they are well aware that others consume far more than they do—that their poverty is relative—and they rightfully strive to improve their own relative condition. Striving to meet their material needs and aspirations without the long-term security of adequate resources, the poor have little choice but to use the few resources at their disposal in an unsustainable manner. The poor, excluded from the productivity of the fertile valleys or fossil hydrocarbon resources controlled by the rich, are forced to work land previously left idle because of its fragility and low agricultural productivity: the tropical forests, the steep hillsides, and arid regions.

Environmental justice also speaks to the excessive material and energy consumption of the wealthy 20%–30% of the total population, made up of the middle classes and rich in the Northern industrialized nations as well as the elite in middle-income and poor nations. The global access to resources by the rich means that many of the environmental and resource impacts of their consumption decisions occur at a great distance, beyond their view, beyond their perceived responsibility, and beyond their effective control.

The relationships between unequal access to resources, unsustainability of development generally, and the loss of biodiversity in particular were major themes of the United Nations Conference on Environment and Development held in Rio de Janeiro in June 1992. Rich peoples and political leaders of Northern industrialized countries generally have had some difficulty participating in this discourse and even greater difficulty participating in the design of new global institutions to address the role of inequity in environmental degradation.

Our understanding of the environmental consequences of concentrated ownership and control is rooted in economic thinking, especially that of Karl Marx. Questions of equity are extremely important in the process of biodiversity loss and in the possibilities for conservation. For example, the occupation and ecological transformation of the Amazon has been driven partly by the concentration of land ownership in the more productive regions of Amazonian nations among a few people, and partly by the economic power (and political influence) of the rich that has enabled them to obtain subsidies to engage in large-scale cattle ranching. The ongoing efforts to establish international agreements on the management of biodiversity have been repeatedly forestalled by debate over the ownership and control of biological resources. But this is not simply a debate over fairness. The structure of the global economy and the ways specific economies interact with nature in the future will depend on which nations—the nations of resource origin or those of the Northern commercial interests, the likely discoverers of new uses for biodiversity—receive the "rent" from biological resources.

## A. C. Pigou and Market Failure

Alfred C. Pigou (1877–1959) formally elaborated how costs that are not included in market prices affect the way people interrelate with their environment. Such a cost, or **externality**, is considered external to markets and hence does not affect how markets operate, when in fact it should. Consider, for example, pesticide use in agriculture and the associated loss of biodiversity (Figure 15.3) Normally, as the price of food increases, the **supply**—the quantity of food that farmers are willing to produce—increases. As prices rise, however, the **demand**—the quantity of food that consumers are willing to purchase—decreases. The market reaches equilibrium when the quantity supplied equals the quantity demanded—at price $P_0$ and quantity $Q_0$.

Now, imagine that we could measure the value of the biodiversity that is lost because of pesticide use—currently considered an externality—and add this to the cost of using pesticides to produce food. This would reduce the quantity of food that farmers could produce at a given price, shifting the supply curve, the price of food, and the quantity of food supplied. By including the cost of biodiversity lost due to farmers' decisions to use pesti-

**Figure 15.3**  Model of a market and its distortion due to an external cost. $S_0$ (the supply curve) represents the willingness of farmers to supply food at different prices (P). As the price of food increases, the quantity of food (Q) that farmers are willing to supply increases. D is the demand curve, illustrating that people purchase lesser quantities of food at higher prices. The market reaches equilibrium when $P_0 = Q_0$. If an externality, such as the cost of biodiversity loss resulting from pesticide use, is added to the cost of the food, the price of the food shifts to $P_1$, the quantity of food supplied to $Q_1$, and the supply curve to $S_1$.

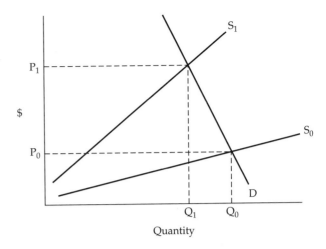

cides, we *internalize* a cost that was previously external to the market, and affect how the market operates. Following the logic of Pigou and numerous environmental economists since, *biodiversity is not adequately protected because its value is not included in the market signals that guide the economic decisions of producers and consumers and thereby the overall operation of the economic system.*

This logic of market failure has led conservationists and some economists to argue that species need to be incorporated into the market system (Hanemann 1988; McNeely 1988; Randall 1988). When it is possible to give private individuals or local communities the rights to use a certain species, exploitation of the resource by others will be averted. This means that the community may benefit from conserving the species and thereby choose to do so; consumers will then pay a higher price, reflecting the costs of managing the species in a more sustainable manner. It is important to keep in mind, however, that incorporating species into the market system might *not* result in their conservation and indeed could even accelerate their extinction. Species within the market system, for example, will not be conserved if their value is expected to grow at less than the rate of interest unless other controls are also placed on their harvest (see the discussion below on the rate of interest).

The processes of biodiversity loss also interact with one another in a larger, reinforcing process of positive **feedbacks**. The degradation of any particular area increases the economic pressure on other areas. For example, the loss of woody species through extensive clear-cutting reduces total carbon fixation and thus reduces opportunities to ameliorate climate change. To bring a system into equilibrium, negative feedbacks are needed. Economics helps us understand why biodiversity is decreasing: few genetic traits, species, or ecosystems have market prices, the negative feedback signals that equilibrate market economies. In market systems, prices increase to reduce the quantity demanded when supplies are low, and drop to increase the quantity demanded when supplies are high, keeping demand and supply in equilibrium. By placing economic values on species, and by including them in market signals, biodiversity loss might be reduced.

The idea that we need to know the economic values of species is compatible with conservationists' understanding that, if the true value of species to society were understood, more species would be conserved. Clearly, if we knew the value of biological resources, we would be in a better position to manage them more effectively. And to the extent that these values could be included in the market system, markets themselves could assist in the conservation of biodiversity. The situation can frequently be improved through amending market signals—for example, by heavily taxing pollution or use of rare species or ecosystems. At the same time, it is important to remember that market values only exist within a larger system of values which for many people includes the preservation of nature as their ethical or religious underpinnings (Sagoff 1988). An alternative view, of the dangers of economically valuing species, is offered by Ehrenfeld (1986).

Even when species or ecosystems cannot be better conserved through the market, knowing their economic value can help convince people and their political representatives that the species or ecosystem deserves protection. Environmental valuation can also improve our analyses of the benefits and costs of development projects that affect biodiversity. Techniques for such valuation include determining—through questionnaires and analyses of people's expenditures to observe interesting environments and particular species—people's willingness to pay to maintain biodiversity (Mitchell and Carson 1989). Essay 15B by Robert Costanza elaborates this perspective.

While several techniques for estimating the value of biodiversity are proving interesting, valuation is by no means an easy task, and estimates should be used cautiously. A major difficulty is related to the systemic nature of economics, ecosystems, and the process of loss. Market systems relate everything to everything else. When the price of oil changes, for example, the price of gasoline changes, the demand for and hence the price of products such as automobiles that use gasoline change, the demand for and hence the price of coal changes, and so on. Prices bring markets to equilibrium, and their flexibility is essential to this task. Similarly, the "right" price for a given species or ecosystem will depend on the availability of a host of other species or ecosystems with which it is interdependent, as well as on the availability of other species and ecosystems that may be substitutes or complements in its use. To think that a species or ecosystem has a single value is to deny both ecosystem and economic system interconnections. Nevertheless, the valuation of genetic diversity, species, and ecosystems can assist us in understanding their importance and conveying this understanding to the public to improve the political process of finding common ground.

## ESSAY 15B
# Valuation of Ecological Systems

Robert Costanza, University of Maryland

The issue of valuation is inseparable from the choices and decisions we have to make about ecological systems. Some argue that valuation of ecosystems is either impossible or unwise, that we cannot place a value on such "intangibles" as human life, environmental aesthetics, or long-term ecological benefits. But, in fact, we do so every day. When we set construction standards for highways, bridges and the like, we value human life—acknowledged or not—because spending more money on construction can save lives. Another frequent argument is that we should protect ecosystems for purely moral or aesthetic reasons, and that we do not need valuations of ecosystems for this

purpose. But there are equally compelling moral arguments that may be in direct conflict with the moral argument to protect ecosystems; for example, the moral argument that no one should go hungry. All we have done is to translate the valuation and decision problem into a new set of dimensions and a new language of discourse, one that, in my view, makes the valuation and choice problem more difficult and less explicit.

So, while ecosystem valuation is certainly difficult, one choice we do *not* have is whether or not to do it. Rather, the decisions we make as a society about ecosystems *imply* valuations. We can choose to make these valuations explicit or not; we can undertake them us-

ing the best available ecological science and understanding or not; we can do them with an explicit acknowledgment of the huge uncertainties involved or not; but as long as we are forced to make choices we are doing valuation. The valuations are simply the relative weights we give to the various aspects of the decision problem.

I believe that society can make better choices about ecosystems if the valuation issue is made as explicit as possible. This means taking advantage of the best information we can muster and making uncertainties about valuations explicit too. It also means developing new and better ways to make good decisions in the face of these uncertainties.

Ultimately, it means being explicit about our goals as a society, in both the short term and the long term. Society has begun to do this with the recent growing consensus that sustainability is the appropriate long-range, global goal (WCED 1987).

## Sustainability and the Valuation of Natural Capital

Sustainability has been variously construed, but one useful definition is the amount of consumption that can be sustained indefinitely without degrading capital stocks—including "natural capital" stocks (Pearce and Turner 1989; Costanza and Daly 1992). Since "capital" is traditionally defined as produced (manufactured) means of production, the term "natural capital" needs explanation. It is based on a more functional definition of capital as "a stock that yields a flow of valuable goods or services into the future." What is functionally important is that the stock yields a flow—whether the stock is manufactured or natural is in this view a distinction between kinds of capital and not a defining characteristic of capital itself. For example, a stock or population of trees or fish provides a flow or annual yield of new trees or fish, a flow that can be sustainable year after year. The sustainable flow is "natural income;" the stock that yields the sustainable flow is "natural capital." Natural capital may also provide services like recycling of waste materials or water catchment and erosion control, which are also counted as natural income. Since the flow of services from ecosystems requires that they function as whole systems, the structure and diversity of the ecosystem is a critical component of natural capital.

To achieve sustainability, we must incorporate natural capital, and the ecosystem goods and services that it provides, into our economic and social accounting and our systems of social choice. In estimating these values we must consider how much of our ecological life-support systems we can afford to lose. To what extent can we substitute manufactured for natural capital, and how much of our natural capital is irreplaceable? For example, could we replace the radiation screening services of the ozone layer if it were destroyed,

or the pollination services of honeybees if they were eliminated?

Because natural capital is not captured in existing markets, special methods must be used to estimate its value. These range from attempts to mimic market behavior using surveys and questionnaires to elicit the preferences of current resource users (i.e., willingness to pay), to methods based on energy analysis of flows in natural ecosystems, which do not depend on current human preferences at all (Farber and Costanza 1987, Costanza et al. 1989). Because of the inherent difficulties and uncertainties in determining these values, we are better off with a pluralistic approach that acknowledges and utilizes these different, independent approaches.

The point that must be stressed is that the economic value of ecosystems is connected to their physical, chemical, and biological role in the long-term, global system—whether the present generation of individuals fully recognizes that role or not. If it is accepted that each species, no matter how seemingly uninteresting or lacking in immediate utility, has a role in natural ecosystems (which *do* provide many direct benefits to humans), it is possible to shift the focus away from our imperfect short-term perceptions and toward the goal of developing more accurate values for long-term ecosystem services. Ultimately, this will require the collaborative construction of dynamic evolutionary models of linked ecological–economic systems that adequately address long-term responses and uncertainties.

## Toward an Ecological Economics

Valuation of natural capital will always involve large uncertainties. How do we make good decisions in the face of this uncertainty? Current systems of direct environmental regulation attempt to directly enforce specific behavior from the top down in an effort to control pollution. They are not very efficient at managing environmental resources for sustainability, particularly in the face of uncertainty about long-term values and impacts. They are inherently reactive rather than proactive. They induce legal confrontation, obfuscation, and government intrusion into business in a way that reduces efficiency. Rather than encouraging long-range technical and so-

cial innovation, they tend to suppress it. They do not mesh well with the market signals that firms and individuals use to make decisions and do not effectively translate long-term global goals into short-term local incentives.

We need to explore promising alternatives to our current command-and-control environmental management systems, and modify existing government agencies and other institutions accordingly. The enormous uncertainty about local and transnational environmental impacts needs to be incorporated into decision making. We also need to better understand the sociological, cultural, and political criteria for acceptance or rejection of policy instruments.

One example of an innovative policy instrument currently being studied is a flexible environmental assurance bonding system designed to incorporate environmental criteria and uncertainty into the market system and to stimulate positive environmental technological innovation (Costanza and Perrings 1990). In addition to paying direct charges for known environmental damages, a company would be required to post an assurance bond equal to the current best estimate of its largest potential future environmental damages; the money would be kept in interest-bearing escrow accounts. The bond (plus a portion of the interest) would be returned if the firm could show that the suspected damages had not occurred or would not occur. If damages occurred, the bond would be used to rehabilitate or repair the environment and to compensate injured parties. Thus, the burden of proof would be shifted from the public to the resource user, and a strong economic incentive would be provided to determine the true costs of environmentally innovative activities and to develop cost-effective pollution control technologies. Ecological economic thinking leads one to conclude that instead of being mesmerized into inaction by scientific uncertainty over our future, we should acknowledge uncertainty as a fundamental part of the system. We must develop better methods to model and value ecological goods and services, and devise policies to translate those values into appropriate incentives. If we continue to segregate ecology and economics, we are courting disaster.

## Common Property Management

Pigou also elaborated what mistakenly came to be popularized as "the tragedy of the commons" (Hardin 1968). Resources used by multiple users

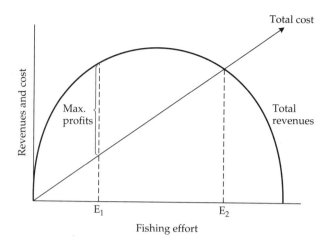

**Figure 15.4** Excessive fishing effort occurs in an open-access fishery because existing fishermen expand their effort and new fishermen enter the fishery beyond level $E_1$, the point of maximum profit. Each fisherman makes a profit by increased fishing up to level $E_2$, where the industry as a whole breaks even (total revenues equal total costs). Further fishing beyond this point is economically counterproductive because costs exceed profits.

without rules governing their use will be overexploited. Both traditional and modern societies typically develop rules for the use of resources held in common. Common ownership itself is not a tragedy; many resources have been successfully managed as commons. The absence or destruction of institutions regulating the use of resources used jointly by people, however, leads to a tragedy. Societies in transition between traditional and modern form frequently experience the tragedy of overuse when neither traditional nor modern forms of common control prevail. Similarly, resources for which access is difficult to restrict, such as the open sea and wildlife that crosses national boundaries, are frequently overexploited (Berkes 1989). The absence or destruction of institutions regulating commons has led to the extinction of diverse species and the genetic impoverishment of many more.

H. Scott Gordon (1954) formulated the problem of common property and open-access resources as shown in Figure 15.4. Imagine an open-access fishery with total costs and total revenues from fishing effort as shown. Profits from the fishery are maximized at level of effort $E_1$, but with unrestricted access, people can put more effort into fishing, until the level $E_2$ is reached, where no profit would be earned from fishing (costs would equal revenue). Additional fishing beyond $E_2$ would not be worth the effort because costs would now exceed revenues. Because more fish are caught at $E_2$, overfishing is more likely to occur in an open-access fishery than in a fishery managed as a commons.

When genetic traits, species, and ecosystems cannot be owned by individuals and incorporated into market systems, common management institutions need to be established or strengthened. In some cases, traditional common property institutions can be maintained in the face of modernization. In other cases, new institutions will be needed. Common property institutions may be communal, regional, national, or global. The health of institutions at all of these levels will be critical to conserving biological diversity. We will return to common properties and the tragedy of the commons in Chapter 18.

### Harold Hotelling and the Efficient Use of Resources over Time

Harold Hotelling (1895–1973) developed a model of efficient resource use over time that helps to explain how species are driven to extinction (Hotelling 1931). According to Hotelling's model, even when market prices fully reflect the value of a biological resource, it will be efficient to exploit a species to extinction or totally degrade an ecosystem if the value of the species or the ecosystem over time is not increasing at least as fast as money deposited in an interest-bearing bank account. Hotelling's logic was distressingly simple. If the value of a biological resource is not increasing as fast as the rate of interest, both individual owners of the resource and society at large are *economically* better off exploiting the resource faster and putting the returns from the exploitation in the bank. Those returns can then be invested in the creation of human-produced capital that earns a return greater than the rate of interest. In this solely economic view, biological resources are a form of natural capital that can be converted into human-produced capital and should be so converted if they do not earn as high a return as human-produced capital.

This argument both describes why economically rational owners of biological resources exploit them to extinction or destruction, and prescribes that they "should" do so. So long as we assume that markets reflect true values, historical and ongoing losses of genetic, species, and ecosystem diversity are efficient and "should" occur. Hotelling's reasoning currently dominates resource economic theory and policy advice from economists. However, in light of the principle of intergenerational equity (discussed below), Hotelling's model is inappropriate for most decisions regarding conservation.

### The Rate of Interest

Hotelling's argument highlights the importance of interest rates in the management of biological resources. If a person can earn an 8% return per year by investing in industrial expansion through stock or bond markets, he or she has little economic incentive to invest in trees that only increase in value at 3% per year, or in the preservation of tropical forests that may have no immediate economic return. By strictly economic logic, biological resources that are not increasing in value as fast as the rate of interest "should" be exploited and the revenues put into industrial capital markets. This logic is a form of "discounting the future." The rate of interest affects how, by economic reasoning, people discount the future. If the rate of interest is 10%, one dollar one year from now is worth only $0.91 today, because one can put $0.91 in the bank today and, earning 10% interest, it will be worth $1.00 next year. The problem is that, at 10% interest, one dollar one decade from now is only worth $0.39 today, two decades from now a mere $0.15 today. Clearly, discounting at 10%, a species has to have a very high value in the distant future to be worth saving today. With a lower rate of interest, it would be discounted less and hence worth more. Thus, lower interest rates appear to favor conservation.

It has long been argued, for example, that trees that grow more slowly than the rate of interest will never be commercial. Imagine that it costs $10.00 to plant a tree seedling, and that the rate of interest is 10%. An entrepreneur has the choice of putting $10.00 in the bank to earn 10% or planting the tree seedling and harvesting it at a later date. Each year, the money in the bank increases in value: to $11.00 at the end of the first year [$10.00 + ($10.00 × 0.1) = $10.00 × 1.1], to $10.00 × $(1.1)^2$ or $12.10 at the end of the second year, to $10.00 × $(1.1)^3$ or $13.31 at the end of the third year, and so on. As long as the value of the tree grows faster than the money in the bank, it is a commercial tree species and it pays to invest in the tree (Figure 15.5). Eventually, of course, the tree begins to grow more slowly, and when it is only growing in value as fast as money in the bank, it pays to cut the tree. But if the tree never grows in value faster than money in the bank, it is a noncommercial tree species, and it never pays to plant the tree in the first place. Slow-growing trees such as teak and many other hardwoods will be cut down and not re-

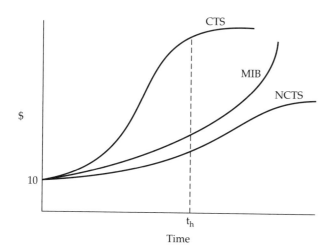

**Figure 15.5**   Commercial tree species (CTS) are those that grow faster in their early years than does money in the bank (MIB). When their rate of return equals or is less than return from MIB, it is, economically, time to harvest ($t_h$). Noncommercial tree species (NCTS) are those that always grow more slowly than money in the bank, and thus are not economically attractive.

planted when interest rates are even moderately high. This has had an enormous effect on development projects. For example, the World Bank considers returns of 15% to be acceptable, and hence has rarely financed timber projects except those with very fast growing species such as eucalyptus. Historically, development aid has financed the replacement of natural forests of mixed species with monocultural forests of fast-growing species based on this understanding of economic efficiency. High interest rates encourage transformation of natural ecosystems toward faster-growing species or other uses of land.

Clearly, interest rates affect the way biological resources are managed, and hence affect the rate and direction of ecosystem transformation and species extinction. Any species or ecosystem that cannot be managed such that it generates a flow of services at a rate greater than the rate of interest should—under economic perspectives—be depleted. Since even many economists find exploitation to extinction rather crass, there has been considerable interest in whether the interest rate produced by private capital markets accurately reflects social interests, and whether, when these interests are factored in, a social rate of interest would not be significantly lower than the private interest rate. Might private capital markets be working imperfectly, generating rates of interest that are too high and hence lead to excessive biodiversity loss (Marglin 1963)? There are good reasons to expect that lower interest rates would generally favor the conservation of biodiversity, though there are some situations in which this would not be the case. This has not been simply an academic argument. The World Bank now realizes how its own evaluation policies have hastened biodiversity loss and, in part for this reason, now has a policy of not financing the transformation of natural forest habitat.

## Preserving Biodiversity as an Option

Many assumptions about the efficient use of resources over time underlie the logic of Hotelling's argument. Assumptions are made about the substitutability of human-produced and natural capital, people's ability to comprehend how the future will unfold, and the appropriateness of current peoples exposing future peoples to the risks of not having biological diversity that they might later find of value. These complications have led economists to argue, given the irreversibility of biodiversity loss (Fisher and Hanemann 1985), that it is appropriate to some extent to maintain biological diversity as an *option* even though narrow economic reasoning suggests otherwise. "Better-safe-than-sorry" reasoning has led to the introduction of the concept of **option value**, an upward adjustment of price to help assure conservation of the resource (Bishop 1978). The quantity analogue to option value is a *safe minimum standard* (see Chapter 2), the setting of a lower limit on the quantity of a resource that must be maintained (Wantrup 1952).

### The Economics of Biodiversity Conservation

The foregoing separate models of the ways people interact with the environment are generally understood among environmental economists and have become a part of the understanding of conservation biologists and environmental policy analysts as well. To the extent that common ground has been found for conservation decision making among people of diverse interests and situations, these models are proving critical to the framing of policies to ameliorate biodiversity loss. Several caveats must be kept in mind, however.

First, these simple economic models and arguments have been presented separately to highlight the special contribution of each to our understanding of the process of biodiversity loss. It is important to keep in mind that the different processes each model emphasizes are interactive. In reality, we are dealing with Malthus's concern with population growth, the patterns of land use suggested by Ricardo's model, the maldistribution of rights to biological resources highlighted by Marxian thinking, the problems of open access and other forms of market failure identified by Pigou, and the questions regarding the appropriateness of interest rates and the quality of information about the future used by economic actors highlighted by Hotelling's model, all at once. Reducing the rate of biodiversity loss will almost always entail multiple instruments for adjusting economic decision making. A single instrument, such as inclusion of the values of biological resources in the economic evaluation of development projects, will rarely be sufficient. Finding common ground has been difficult because people mistakenly think that one explanation and solution is correct and the others are wrong, then argue over which is correct. Different mixes will be correct in different places, but understanding this requires increased sophistication. Furthermore, implementing different mixes of solutions across different areas is much more difficult than imposing one simple solution universally.

Second, environmental economists, conservation biologists, and environmental policy analysts share these understandings of how biodiversity is lost, but the consensus does not extend to economists in general, to policymakers less directly linked to environmental issues, and to most political representatives. Environmental economic understanding is not widespread because the environmental economic models complicate, or raise serious questions about, the general model of neoclassical economics, the role of economics in the policy process, and the possibility of making general policy conclusions. In light of environmental economic models, for example, the general "rule" of economists—government interference in markets and trade should be minimized—does not hold. Most economists still downplay the complexities of the interactions between economies and environmental systems, because if they conceded that such complexities were important, economic analysis would be much more difficult and would result in much more complex economic policies (Figure 15.6). The vast majority of economic theory books, whether beginning or advanced, rarely even refer to environmental complexities as a special problem, let alone as a general problem.

Thus, whatever shared understanding of the process of biodiversity loss exists, it has not provided sufficient common ground for finding a broad political consensus for the conservation of biological diversity. Economics as a

**Figure 15.6** Many economic models ignore real-world complexities and limitations such as resource exploitation or waste disposal. Including such factors would make the models more realistic, but also more complicated.

science of systems is relatively insignificant compared with economics as a collection of rhetorical arguments that support one political ideology or another. Biodiversity is being lost, in part, because most economists, policy analysts, and politicians refuse to admit complexities that confound or blatantly contradict their political economic ideology. In short, the process of loss is intimately related to human beliefs that the world is a relatively simple system that people can control through relatively simple knowledge, is resilient to human impacts, and has infinite potential for human exploitation through new knowledge and technologies. These beliefs are deeply rooted in economic thinking and they blind economists—and thereby politicians—to the more sophisticated economic models that complement biological understanding.

Third, although economic explanations of the process of biodiversity loss are quite helpful, they have serious weaknesses. On the one hand, a concerted effort is needed to bring what is now conventional understanding among environmental economists into the mainstream of economics, policy analysis, and political discourse. On the other hand, our understanding of the process of loss needs further improvement. New directions under way are discussed below.

## New Directions in Economic Thought

### The Rights of Future Generations

Much of conservationists' concern with biodiversity is rooted in concern for our descendants (Partridge 1981; Norton 1986; Weiss 1989; Laslett and Fishkin 1992). Economists have also worried about how economic logic treats future generations, but the formal models economists have advocated for use in the policy process to date have implicitly assumed the existing between-generation distribution of resource rights, as defined by existing property law, government programs, and social mores. These economic models show how the current generation can efficiently exploit resources rather than how resources might be shared more equitably with future generations. Environmental economists, though concerned with the future, have also followed this tradition in economic thinking, false to their own theory, of looking for *the single* most efficient allocation of resources when there are many efficient allocations defined by moral criteria beyond economic values. Moral criteria with respect to our obligation to future generations are especially important. Only recently have economists constructed models that allow them to understand how resources can be both efficiently used now and equitably shared with future generations. These recent models are based on the concept of utility.

**Utility** is defined as personal satisfaction of some economic desire, or the want-satisfying power of goods. If one good (say, a wilderness experience) provides more satisfaction to an individual than another good (say, a day at the local mall), it is said to have higher utility. A major concern of environmental economists is the relationship between satisfying the needs and desires of the present generation and satisfying those of future generations. Because utility has real limits, including resource limits, at the societal level, the limitations form a utility possibility frontier represented as a curve in Figure 15.7. In this conceptual model, the frontier represents the highest utility possibly available to people in future generations, given the utility for people in the current generation.

If collectively we are not at the possibility frontier (say, we are at point *A*), then by improving economic efficiency we can reach a point on the frontier (point *B*) where more desires can be satisfied. But where we fall on the utility frontier curve is critical to future generations. If we do not care about leaving resources for future generations, we will satisfy our current utility close to the *X*-axis; that is, we will use many resources now so that utility to the current generation is very high, while that to future generations is low. To the extent that we are willing to make sacrifices by leaving part of current desires unsatisfied in order to leave resources for future generations, the utility function will move upward along the frontier curve toward the *Y*-axis. The 45° line represents sustainability—the point on the frontier where utility is equally satisfied between the current and future generations.

The models used by economists to date, even in the most recent eco-

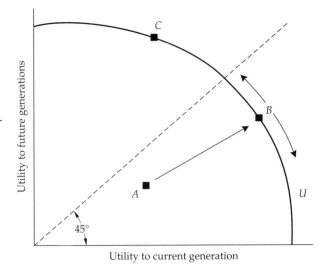

**Figure 15.7**  The concept of utility and its interaction with intergenerational equity. Curve *U* represents the frontier of possible utility; the dashed line at 45° represents the points at which the needs of current and future generations are equally satisfied. A move from point *A* at some distance from the possibility frontier to point *B* on the frontier results in greater efficiency. Points *B* and *C* are both efficient. However, at point *B*, utility to current generations is high, but utility to future generations is low. Moving from point *B* below the 45° line to point *C* above the line represents a redistribution (a change in equity) between generations that promotes sustainability—the situation in which the utility to future generations is equal to or greater than the utility to the current generation.

nomic literature on sustainability, are inappropriate for addressing intergenerational equity. The emphasis has been on internalizing externalities to increase overall efficiency; that is, on moving the economy from a position such as point *A* toward a position such as point *B*. Unfortunately, neither of these is sustainable for future generations—both points fall below the 45° line, and thus satisfy current utility at the expense of future utility. Note that simply transforming nonmarket goods—such as biodiversity—into a quantitative evaluation will not necessarily lead to their sustainable use. Biological resource valuation as currently conducted, for example, derives prices that would move an economy toward point *B*, increasing efficiency, helping future generations relative to point *A*, but not necessarily making the economy sustainable. Wholly new ways of thinking about environmental valuation will be needed; an example is offered in Essay 15C by Michael Balick and colleagues.

With respect to the rate of interest, the intergenerational models have an exciting theoretical result. When the current generation decides to assure assets for future generations, the rate of interest goes down. Economists have been reasoning backward in their search for reasons why interest rates perhaps should be lower in order to protect future generations. When we decide to protect future generations, interest rates *become* lower.

The intergenerational models elaborating the relationship between efficiency and intergenerational equity highlight the need for economic reasoning to work in conjunction with ethical criteria—a larger system of values—exercised through politics. While many economists will continue to argue in political arenas that protecting biological resources for future generations is inefficient, their arguments violate economic logic. There are more efficient and less efficient ways to protect biological resources, but caring about the future is not a matter of economic efficiency alone. Adopting the existing distribution of rights between generations is merely a convention of economic practice; it has no roots in economic theory. Changing this convention is critical to conserving biodiversity.

## ESSAY 15C

# Valuation of Extractive Medicines in Tropical Forests
## Exploring the Linkage to Conservation

M. J. Balick, R. Mendelsohn, R. Arvigo, and G. Shropshire
New York Botanical Garden

The discovery of new pharmaceuticals from tropical forests to add to the war chest of modern medicine is an enticing reason to conserve tropical ecosystems. For example, the importance of the rosy periwinkle (*Catharanthus roseus*) in treating childhood leukemia and Hodgkin's disease is frequently cited in popular and scientific articles about the need for conserving rainforests. But another, perhaps more pressing, argument for conservation is the use of forests as pharmaceutical "factories" to produce local medicines used in primary health care.

New therapies for major diseases such as AIDS or cancer may be living in tropical forests. For various reasons, this potential is unlikely to result in significant conservation in the short term unless carefully constructed mechanisms are adopted. First, the development of a new pharmaceutical product from wild plants is a decade-long process, at best. Plants studied today, if found to be of value in medicine, will only yield royalties many years later, and cannot meet the immediate needs for money to support conservation activities.

Second, only a small fraction of plants studied actually reach the pharmacy shelves. Although there are undoubtedly numerous valuable chemicals to be derived from forests, these are hidden among tens of thousands of species and billions of hectares, and the net value of securing these areas may be small.

Third, when medicines are found, their extraction has historically led to destructive, not sustainable use. *Pilocarpus* species, shrubby trees native to northeastern Brazil, are a case in point. The leaves of the trees are harvested by local people and extracted by chemical companies to yield pilocarpine, a compound used in glaucoma treatment. The leaves have been wild-harvested from northeast Brazil for many decades without concern for continuity of the supply, and vast populations of *Pilocarpus jabo-*

*randi, P. microphylla,* and *P. pinnatifolius* are now extirpated.

Finally, local people traditionally have not benefitted from discoveries of new medicines, and so have little incentive to manage forests to encourage discovery. Recent programs initiated by drug companies and developing countries address these last two points, as will be discussed in Case Study 2 in Chapter 17. However, it remains unclear to what extent these new efforts, while promising, will significantly contribute to global ecosystem conservation.

An additional, and more immediate, incentive for conservation may be the role of tropical forest ecosystems in providing traditional medicines and rural health care where local plants comprise 95% of the ethnopharmacopoeia. The World Health Organization estimates that 2.5–3.5 billion people worldwide use traditional medicines as part of their primary health care program. In Belize, Central America, where we are completing an inventory of ethnobotanical knowledge, up to 75% of the primary health care is provided by traditional healers using plant remedies. Both primary and secondary forests are sources of the plants processed into medicine. In many cases people known as "hierbateros" collect and sell these plants to the "curanderos," or traditional healers, actually providing the health care.

We conducted a series of forest inventories, combining ethnobotanical investigation with studies of the market value of the plants locally used in medicine (Balick and Mendelsohn 1992). We identified two 1-ha plots, one in a 30-year-old forest (plot 1) and another in a 50-year-old forest (plot 2). The two plots yielded 308.6 and 1433.6 kg dry weight, respectively, of medicines whose value could be judged by local market forces. Local herbal pharmacists and healers purchase unprocessed medicine from hierbateros and small farmers at an average price of U.S. $2.80/kg. Multiply-

ing the quantity of medicines found per hectare by this price suggests that clearing a hectare of medicines would yield the collector between $864 and $4014 of gross revenue. Of course, the collector has costs he or she must bear to harvest this material. On a per-hectare basis, harvesting required 25 person-days on plot 1 and 80 person-days on plot 2. Given the local wage of $12/day, the total harvest costs for the plots were $300 and $960 respectively. When these costs are subtracted from gross revenue, the net revenue from clearing a hectare was $564 and $3054 on 1 and 2 respectively. However, the labor costs go back to the local economy, so they are not really lost from the system.

These value estimates of using tropical forests for medicinal plant harvest compare favorably with alternative land uses in the region; for example, milpa (corn, bean, and squash cultivation) in Guatemalan rainforest, yields $288/ha. We also identified commercial products such as allspice, copal, chicle, and construction materials in the plots that could be harvested and added to the medicinal value. Thus, use of at least some areas of rainforest as extractive reserves for medicinal plants appears to be economically justified. A periodic harvest of medicinal plant materials seems a realistic and sustainable method of utilizing the forest. For example, with a 50-ha parcel of forest similar to the second plot analyzed, one could clear one hectare of medicines per year indefinitely.

As a postscript to our original study, the Belize Association of Traditional Healers is now negotiating with the government of Belize to allocate a 2430-ha parcel of land to be used as an extractive reserve for medicinal plants. Its management would be in the hands of the traditional healers and herb gatherers, with input from researchers. Larger-scale experiments aimed at developing sustainable extraction techniques for stems, roots, bark, and tubers would be

carried out in this setting, in collaboration with local people who utilize these plants for health care.

On a global level, there are approximately 3 billion people using wild-harvested medicines. Assuming each person uses $2.50–$5.00 worth of medicine per year, the annual value of this resource could range between $7.5 billion and $15 billion. This is a significant aggregate value, and a large portion of it represents tropical forest species. The entire global pharmaceutical trade is estimated at $80–$90 billion annually. New drugs from tropical forests would have to compete for a substantial share of the modern drug market before they would be as valuable as the natural factory of local medicines. Thus, local rainforest medicines worth billions of dollars today could, if properly managed, have a more immediate effect on conservation than a new drug developed from a plant commercialized a decade from now.

Another issue is the replacement costs (substitution costs) of commercial pharmaceutical products when and if local plant resources become exhausted. The cost of replacing the type of primary health care delivery system now in place would be many times that of the present system; thus, a vast constituency ranging from individuals to governments has a vested interest in maintaining adequate supplies of forest medicines. One of the most effective and least expensive ways of accomplishing this is through in situ conservation of these resources in tropical forests.

We do not wish to underestimate the potential benefits of pharmaceutical drug discovery for tropical forest conservation. However, the importance of traditional medicines from tropical forests is another powerful argument for their conservation. Additional work is needed in order to properly understand and evaluate this issue and, if possible, harness it for maximum benefit to the conservation enterprise.

## Distancing and Economic Globalization

The relationship between the environment and the modern global economy is clearly different than its historical interface with more local or regional economies. While considerable environmental concern has been expressed in hemispheric and global trade negotiations, economics is surprisingly ill equipped to address the effects of globalization of the economy on environmental management. Whether they have dominantly market or centrally directed economics, modern societies exhibit a historical process that is most simply and effectively understood as **distancing**. Increasing specialization distances scientists from one another, impeding a collective scientific consciousness of how we are interacting with nature, let alone how we could. Increasing dependence on modern technologies shifts environmental and social problems from the local and immediate to the distant and future. Increasing specialization in the production process distances industrialists and workers from an overall consciousness of production technologies. Increasing urbanization distances people from the soil and water on which they depend. Increasing globalization distances people from the environmental and social effects of their consumption. Distancing makes it more difficult for people to be environmentally aware and to design, agree to implement, and enforce environmental management strategies.

At the same time, global communication is now nearly instantaneous and affordable for many. Some individuals are acquiring new perceptions of our global environmental predicament and are working to address it through nongovernmental organizations, which are less prone than government agencies to the communication barriers of disciplinary and professional specialization. There is now a discernible tension between bureaucratized but formal channels of power and less bureaucratized, informal channels of global communication and agreement.

The globalization of regional economies has been rationalized by the logic of trade, but falsely so. The logic of trade is simply that when two choosers decide to enter into an exchange, it is because the exchange makes each of them better off. To argue that free trade is good policy, one must also assure that there are no costs and benefits external to those who choose; otherwise, new international institutions must be created to internalize those costs and benefits. Clearly, nations are having sufficient difficulty internalizing externalities nationally; international institutions are inherently more complicated and necessarily weaker. But the false application of the logic of trade to justify globalization is even more fundamental than this. Economists have always assumed that it is individuals and corporations who should be free to choose. Interestingly, the logic of trade is indifferent to whether the choosers are individuals, communities, bioregions, or nations. The logic does not say "individuals (and multinational corporations) should be free to choose, but communities or nations should not." But this is exactly how the logic has been misinterpreted. The association of trade with individualism reflects the dominant premise in modern political thought. It reflects Western culture, not economic logic. The difference between individual and community interest, of course, is intimately tied to the systemic character of environmental systems. Nature cannot readily be divided up and assigned to individuals, hence the failure of markets.

## The Coevolution of Modern Societies

Neither neoclassical nor Marxist economic models are adequate to preserve biodiversity. Each implicitly incorporates assumptions about the interrelationships of science, technology, and materialism that have driven the development and the accelerated biological transformation of the past century. A new, more comprehensive model is needed if we are to find common ground on these larger issues.

Consider development as a process of coevolution among knowledge, values, organization, technology, and the environment (Figure 15.8). Each of these subsystems is related to each of the others, yet each is also changing and affecting change in the others through selection. Deliberate innovations, chance discoveries, and random changes occur in each subsystem and affect, through selection, the distribution and qualities of components in each of the

**Figure 15.8**  A coevolutionary model of development. Social and environmental change can be understood as a process of innovations (mutations) and introductions in various subsystems, and selection among them. Coevolutionary "development" occurs when this process favors the continued well-being of people.

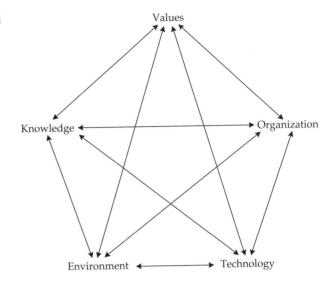

other subsystems. Whether new components prove fit depends on the characteristics of each of the subsystems at the time. With each subsystem putting selective pressure on each of the others, they coevolve in a manner whereby each reflects the others. Thus everything is coupled, yet everything is changing (Norgaard 1994).

In this coevolutionary perspective, environmental subsystems are treated symmetrically with the subsystems of values, knowledge, social organization, and technology. New technologies, for example, exert new selective pressures on species, while newly evolved characteristics of species, in turn, select for different technologies. Similarly, transformations in the biosphere select for new ways of understanding the biosphere. For example, the use of pesticides selects for resistance and secondary pest resurgence, which in turn select both for new pesticides and for more systematic ways of thinking about pest control. Pests, pesticides, pesticide production, pesticide institutions and policy, our understanding of pest control, and the way we value chemicals in the environment demonstrate an incredibly tight and rapid coevolution in the second half of this century.

In the short run, people can be thought of as interacting with the environment in response to market signals or their absence. The coevolutionary model, however, incorporates longer-term evolutionary feedbacks. To emphasize coevolutionary processes is not to deny that people directly intervene in and change the characteristics of environments. The coevolutionary perspective puts its emphasis on the chain of events thereafter—how different interventions alter the selective pressure on and hence the relative dominance of environmental traits which, in turn, select for values, knowledge, organization, and technology, and hence subsequent interventions in the environment.

While a coevolutionary perspective treats changes in the various subsystems symmetrically, we can use this model to address technology in particular. People have interacted with their environments over millennia in diverse ways, many of them sustainable over very long periods, many not. Some traditional agricultural technologies, at the intensities historically employed, probably increased biological diversity. There is general evidence that many traditional technologies, again at the level employed, included biodiversity-conserving strategies as a part of the process of farming. Technology today, however, is perceived as a leading culprit in the process of biodiversity loss. Modern agricultural technologies override nature, but do so only locally and temporarily. They do not "control" nature. Pesticides kill pests, solving the immediate threat to crops. But when a competitively dominant pest is eliminated, other species may quickly become pests. Pesticides also drift away from the farm to interfere with the agricultural practices of other farmers, and pesticides and their by-products accumulate in soil and groundwater aquifers to plague production and human health for years to come. Each farmer strives to control nature on his or her farm in each growing season but creates new problems in other places and times. It is noteworthy that preharvest crop losses due to pests since World War II have remained at about 35%, while pesticide use has increased dramatically (Pimentel 1988).

Similarly, use of fertilizers can reduce the vagaries and limits of relying on nitrogen-fixing bacteria and other soil microorganisms that assist in nutrient uptake, microorganisms that are supported by traditional agricultural practices. But in the process of overriding them, these natural properties of ecosystems are lost while the effects of nitrogen and phosphate pollution in groundwater aquifers and surface waters accumulate. While there is no doubt that modern crop breeding has produced far more productive varieties of rice, wheat, corn, and other grains, these varieties depend on irrigation, fertilization, pesticide technologies, and expansive monocultures, and thus have substantial environmental costs beyond agriculture and over time. The accelerated evolution of plant diseases associated with the monocropping of a limited number of varieties makes further improvements in crop disease resistance necessary. Whether or not modern agriculture can be thought of as less dependent on nature, it is surely more dependent on continual advances in agricultural research.

The contradictions of modern agriculture have stimulated a new interest in how traditional agricultural technologies conserve biodiversity and in the potential for combining modern scientific understanding with traditional techniques (National Research Council 1989). Clearly, people must still interact with the environment: the question is not whether, but how. While modern agriculture certainly causes environmental degradation, it is also clear that it feeds many people who would otherwise have to be supported through the use of more land devoted to agriculture, further threatening biodiversity. Traditional agricultural practices in areas of rapidly increasing population result in the expansion of farming into previously undisturbed regions. Furthermore, with the onset of modern development, the social relations and traditions that conserve resources break down, further hastening environmental degradation.

Beyond modern agriculture, fossil fuel-based technologies support industry, transportation, and thereby the concentration of people in urban areas. While packing people into cities reduces their direct impact on the land, and hence on biodiversity, fossil fuel-based transport, residential heating and cooling, and industry produce the vast majority of carbon dioxide and other greenhouse gases driving climate change. More immediate threats from ongoing air, soil, and water pollution, as well as from accidents such as oil spills, are also inextricably linked to fossil fuel-based technologies.

Improved technologies can increase energy and material efficiency, reducing energy and material flows and thereby the rate of environmental transformation. But technologies that merely reduce the consequences of existing approaches may offer little hope in the longer run. The multiplicative effects of increasing population and materialism on resource use and environmental transformation have outpaced efficiency increases to date.

New technologies that work *with* natural processes rather than overriding them are sorely needed. During the past two centuries, technologies have largely descended from physics, chemistry, and, at best, microbiology; ecologists never had the opportunity to systemically review such technologies. A few agricultural technologies, such as the control of pests in agriculture through the use of other species, have arisen from ecological thinking. But research and technological development in biological pest control was nearly eliminated with the introduction of DDT in agriculture after World War II. Research on and development of agricultural technologies requiring fewer energy and material inputs eventually received considerable support in industrialized countries after the rise in energy prices during the 1970s and the farm financial crises in the United States during the early 1980s. Support for agroecology, however—for technologies based on the management of complementarities among multiple species including soil organisms—is still minimal. Learning how to use renewable energy sources will be a long and difficult process because most of our knowledge has developed to capture the potential of fossil energy. Our universities and other research institutions are still structured around disciplinary rather than systemic thinking (discussed in Chapter 16), and public understanding of the shortcomings of current technologies and the possibilities of ecologically based technologies is weak.

From the coevolutionary perspective, we can now see more clearly how economies have shifted from coevolving with their ecosystems to coevolving around the combustion of fossil hydrocarbons. In this transformation, people were freed from environmental feedbacks of their economic activities that they once experienced relatively quickly as individuals and communities. The feedbacks that remain, however, occur over longer periods and greater distances and are experienced collectively by many peoples, even globally, making them more difficult to perceive and counteract (Norgaard 1994).

By tapping into fossil hydrocarbons, Western societies freed themselves, at least for the short term, from many of the complexities of interacting with environmental systems. With an independent energy source, tractors replaced animal power, fertilizers replaced the interplanting of crops that were good hosts of nitrogen-fixing bacteria, and pesticides replaced the biological controls provided by more complex agroecosystems. Furthermore, inexpensive energy meant that crops could be stored for longer periods and transported over greater distances.

Each of these accomplishments was based on the partial understanding of separate sciences and separate technologies. At least in the short run and "on the farm," separate adjustments of the parts seemed to fit into a coherent, stable whole. Agriculture was transformed from an agroecosystem culture of relatively self-sufficient communities to an agroindustrial culture of many separate, distant actors linked by global markets. The massive changes in technology and organization gave people the sense of having control over nature and being able to consciously design their future while in fact they were merely shifting problems beyond the farm and onto future generations.

The unsustainability of modern societies arises from the fact that development based on fossil hydrocarbons allowed individuals to control their immediate environments for the short run while shifting environmental impacts to broader publics and longer time frames. Working with these collective, longer-term, and more uncertain interrelationships is at least as challenging as trying to control nature had been historically. People's confidence in the sustainability of development is directly proportional to their confidence in our ability to address these new challenges.

The coevolutionary perspective helps us to see that the solution to biodiversity loss is not simply a matter of establishing market incentives to adjust the way we interact with nature. Nor is conservation simply a matter of intergenerational equity. Our values, knowledge, and social organization have coevolved around fossil hydrocarbons. Our fossil fuel-driven economy has not simply transformed the environment; it has selected for individualist, materialist values, favored the development of reductionist understanding at the expense of systemic understanding, and preferred a bureaucratic, centralized form of control that works better for steady-state industrial management than for the varied, surprising dynamics of ecosystem management. The coevolutionary model also points out that our abilities to perceive and resolve environmental problems are severely constrained by the dominant modes of valuing, thinking, and organizing.

### Ecological Economics

Ecology and economics have been separate disciplines throughout their histories. While each has certainly borrowed theoretical concepts from the other, and the two have shared patterns of thinking from other sciences, they have addressed separate issues, utilized different assumptions to reach answers, and supported different interests in the policy process. Indeed, in their popular manifestations as environmentalism and economism, these disciplines have become juxtaposed secular religions, preventing the collective interpretation and resolution of the numerous problems at the intersection of human and natural systems. Many people have understood the importance of bringing these domains of thought together. After numerous experiments with joint meetings between economists and ecologists, the International Society for Ecological Economics (ISEE) was formed in the late 1980s, its journal, *Ecological Economics,* was initiated, and major international conferences of ecologists and economists have been held since. Many ecological economic institutes have been formed around the world, and a significant number of books have appeared with the term *ecological economics* in their titles (e.g., Costanza 1991; Peet 1992).

Ecological economics is not a single new paradigm based in shared assumptions and theory. It represents a commitment among economists, ecologists, and other academics and practitioners to learn from each other, to explore together new patterns of thinking, and to facilitate the derivation and implementation of new economic and environmental policies. To date, ecological economics deliberately has been conceptually pluralistic, even while particular practitioners may prefer one paradigm over another (Norgaard 1989).

Robert Costanza, the founder and first president of ISEE, views ecological economics as encompassing economics and ecology; their existing links are shown in Figure 15.9 (Costanza et al. 1991). Ecological economists are rethinking both ecology and economics, extending the energetic paradigm of ecosystem ecology to economic questions (Hall et al. 1986), and participating in the effort to include environmental values in national economic statistics such as measures of national income (Costanza and Daly 1992). This melding of economics and ecology must proceed if we are to have a realistic chance of developing an environmentally sustainable existence.

## Summary

Those in search of common ground for deciding upon sustainable modes of interacting with the environment largely use patterns of reasoning developed within the history of economic thought. Conservation biologists invoke the population model of Malthus, rely on economic arguments to emphasize

**Figure 15.9** Ecological economics addresses the interactions between economies and ecological sectors. It encompasses conventional economics and ecology as well as environmental and resource economics and impact analysis. The overall system is driven by the sun and dissipates waste heat. (Modified from Costanza et al. 1991.)

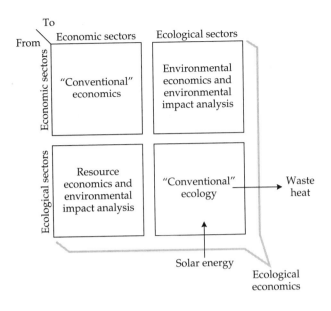

the value of diversity, use economics to design and argue for new social institutions to change individual behavior, and have become entangled in international debates over free trade and global inequity. At the same time, economics more generally remains the bastion of technological optimism and the overseer of the old development agenda. With economic arguments being used both by those who want to change the course of history and by those who want to stay the course, considerable economic sophistication is required to make sense of and constructively participate in the effort to find common ground.

Like the multifaceted, hierarchical systems character of biodiversity itself, the loss of biodiversity has many, nested economic explanations. The politics of framing a more viable future is a cacophony of different voices, of diverse peoples using separate economic arguments to explain their understanding of the world's problems and to articulate their interests. The global political discord is unfamiliar, even frightening, to the untrained ear. We will find common ground when enough people understand how the diverse economic arguments evolved, how they all interrelate, how they all help to explain the human dilemma, and how they all need to be understood together in order to go beyond any one of them individually.

## Questions for Discussion

1. Explore how some of the simple economic explanations interact. How, for example, might population growth and inequity interrelate with each other and with biodiversity loss, externalities, and globalization of the economy?

2. Which specific political interests (e.g., Northern developed vs. Southern undeveloped countries, capitalists vs. laborers) might find which particular economic models more attractive than others?

3. The advantage of market prices is that they adjust to give economic actors appropriate signals under different conditions. What is the significance of this to the valuation of species or ecosystems?

4. If we argue that we should forgo consumption of some resources now in order to save resources for future generations, how can we deal with the following argument that many people raise: technology will create substitutes for the resource, so there is no need to conserve it, and resource scarcity merely increases incentive to find alternative resources.

5. The early development of neoclassical economics was said to be "value-free." Do you think any form of economics can really be "value-free?"

6. Traditional economists sometimes argue that conservationists should not be overly concerned about exploitation of renewable resources because the rate of exploitation will decline as the resource becomes scarce. Discuss this perspective in light of information such as that provided by conservation genetics, the concept of minimum viable populations, and the behavior of nonlinear biological systems.

7. How does Ricardo's model of land use relate to capital–intensive agriculture and fisheries? That is, how does the purchase of expensive equipment such as harvesters or ocean-going fishing boats influence "rent," and thus resource exploitation?

## Suggestions for Further Reading

Bellah, R. N., R. Madsen, W. M. Sullivan, A. Swidler and S. M. Tipton. 1991. *The Good Society.* Alfred A. Knopf, New York. Bellah et al. present an excellent critique of the economic worldview and show how it has broken down many of the important social relationships of communities. The final chapter discusses the conceptual parallels with ecosystem transformation and the importance of reestablishing communities for the protection of natural systems.

Berkes, F. (ed). 1989. *Common Property Resources: Ecology and Community-Based Sustainable Development.* Bellhaven Press, London. Berkes has assembled a lively set of essays on social organization and environmental management in traditional and modern societies. Institutions for the management of common property resources are critically important to the conservation of biodiversity.

Blaikie, P. and H. Brookfield. 1987. *Land Degradation and Society.* Metheun, London. Blaikie and Brookfield, along with numerous additional contributors, develop the paradigm they call "political ecology" and give excellent examples of how inequities prevent good environmental management in developing countries.

Costanza, R. (ed). 1991. *Ecological Economics: The Science and Management of Sustainability.* Columbia University Press, New York. Costanza has compiled the best of the early papers on ecological economics. This volume demonstrates the conceptual diversity and breadth of application of work by this new group of activist–scholars.

Ehrenfeld, D. 1981. *The Arrogance of Humanism.* Oxford University Press, New York. Ehrenfeld's book on the errors wrought by Western science's hopes to control nature has become a classic among biologists. A philosophical treatise that is accessible and informative.

Hall, C. A. S., C. J. Cleveland and R. Kaufman. 1986. *Energy and Resource Quality: The Ecology of the Economic Process.* John Wiley and Sons, New York. Hall et al. provide insightful analyses of the relationships between energy, environmental systems, and the economy. They both critique neoclassical economic thinking and use the best of it along with energetic analysis.

McNeely, J. A. 1988. *Economics and Biological Diversity: Developing and Using Economic Incentives to Conserve Biological Resources.* International Union for the Conservation of Nature and Natural Resources, Gland, Switzerland. McNeely combines sound analysis with numerous applications of economic principles. This book is readily accessible to readers with little or no economic training.

Norton, B. G. (ed). 1986. *The Preservation of Species: The Value of Biological Diversity.* Princeton University Press, Princeton, NJ. An excellent compendium on biodiversity and values with good coverage of economics as well as the way it fits into a larger scheme of environmental and other values.

# 16

# The Role of Institutions and Policymaking in Conservation

*Politics is the art of taking good decisions on insufficient evidence.*
*Lord Kennet*

When all is said and done, and the history of conservation advances and the role of conservation biology is written in coming decades, one thing will stand out clearly: the success of conservation efforts will be measured not in numbers of research grants garnered, nor numbers of students trained, nor papers published, nor amount of money spent by governments, industry, or NGOs on environmental issues, although these will all contribute to success. Rather, success will be measured by how well we succeed in achieving a vision of a world that serves the needs of humans and preserves nature. Success or failure will be determined by whether or not species extinction rates are stabilized and then lowered, by how many truly natural habitats remain, by how many intact ecosystems endure, and by the degree of social justice and equity we have achieved, since these are integral to the conservation of nature. And this, in turn, will be determined not by conservation or ecological theory alone, but by how well that theory, and knowledge, and experience in all forms, are put into practice. Transforming ecological knowledge into public practice is largely the domain of institutions and policymaking.

Regardless of how well we understand the natural world, how sophisticated our theories, how accurate our computer models, how complete our empirical knowledge, or how well we incorporate indigenous knowledge, none of this will be of value if the information is not put into useful practice. All of the information in this book and elsewhere is worthless until it contributes to sound conservation policy and appropriate action. Consequently, policy and the institutions that drive it are the focus of this chapter.

As we begin to address the topics of policy and the institutions that put policy into action, three principles should be kept clearly in mind that should drive our understanding of policy:

1. *The humility principle*: We must recognize and accept the limitations of human knowledge, and as a result the limits of our capacity to manage the planet.
2. *The precautionary principle*: When in doubt (and uncertainty is more the norm than the exception), we must think deeply and move slowly.
3. *The reversibility principle*: We must not make irreversible changes.

We must have the humility to recognize that our knowledge and understanding will always be limited; "completeness," like the Holy Grail, is an unachievable goal. This places an added burden on the scholar/scientist, the activist, the manager, and the policymaker. "Managing Planet Earth," the title of the September 1989 issue of *Scientific American*, is merely a fantasy. We must recognize from the start that our limited capacity to manage nature, even at the smallest scale, makes planetary management unlikely at best, and unwise and perhaps disastrous at worst (Ehrenfeld 1993).

The precautionary principle tells us to be very cautious when making decisions about systems we do not fully understand, which describes our relationship to both the natural and human world. If significant doubt exists regarding a choice to be made, or a technology to be used, the decision should be made with as much caution as possible, and with long-range consequences as fully thought out as we are capable of doing (Figure 16.1). This principle also tells us not to do something that cannot be reversed later on if our decision is wrong. For example, many scientists feel that destruction of tropical forests, in addition to eliminating a great deal of biological diversity, is dangerous because it could change planetary climate patterns. Although this is not certain, the reversibility principle tells us it would be unwise to continue deforestation, as it is largely irreversible.

Before we move further into the policies and institutions that address environmental problems, we must stop and ask what exactly we mean by an environmental "problem," or, for that matter, any type of problem. Because policies and institutions are developed to deal with "problems" of some description, a definition is in order. Most philosophers would argue that a "problem" is not defined by the present and particular situation, but by the distance between the present situation and a vision of a desired state sometime in the future. This formulation emphasizes the importance of defining and envisioning the desired, rather than the present, state. It also emphasizes analysis of where we really are and forces us to distinguish between what is *cause* and what is *symptom*.

Our goal is to try to create systemic change to achieve our larger vision, not simply to focus only on individual events. Therefore, along with its role in defining environmental research (below), there is a value in having environmental researchers working consciously and formally with policymakers and stakeholders to envision a desired state. "Problem," then, is redefined as *the path between the present and the desired state*, and solutions require analysis of how to get from here to there, and working backward from there to here, in order to free our thinking from the potential straightjacket of the present.

You may find parts of this chapter upsetting to your long-held notions about science, conservation, the education process, the policy process, and/or various institutions with which you are often in contact. In this chapter we will challenge the status quo, accepted policies, institutions, and ways of doing business. We have no choice here, for the status quo has not worked well to date. If institutions and environmental policies were succeeding,

"Let's concentrate on technology for a couple thousand years and *then* we can develop a value system."

**Figure 16.1** The precautionary principle would dictate that we be very careful about new technologies or policies affecting the natural world. This creates a need for a well-developed public value system that recognizes the potential hazards of policies that are not well considered. (Modified from an unidentified source.)

there would be no need for this book, or for the field of conservation biology. The mere existence of this field indicates that there is something very wrong with our policies, institutions, and humanity's way of conducting its affairs. To continue along the same institutional and policy paths would merely extrapolate present trends of degradation well into the future. We challenge students and professional scientists alike to question all present conservation practices and policies (including those presented throughout this book) and to ask whether these are the best means of achieving the long-term security of biological diversity and sustainability of the human species. Are systems and institutions working? If not, what needs to be done to achieve appropriate system change? What new practices, policies, and institutions must be developed, replacing the tired solutions that have failed?

## Types of Institutions and Their Roles in Conservation

There are a number of institutions in Western society that directly and indirectly bear on the development and outcome of conservation actions and policies, both locally and throughout the world. Each has the potential to contribute significantly to conservation efforts, or to serve as a barrier to such efforts. As with all human institutions, some are functioning better than others with respect to meeting the joint needs of nature and humankind. As human institutions they must be challenged to meet the needs of present and future generations. Our observations relate directly to the United States and do not attempt to be comprehensive, for to do so would require volumes rather than a chapter. They are meant to provoke thought about institutions with which Western students and scientists are familiar.

### Educational Institutions

There are a number of problems facing universities and other higher educational research institutions that prevent them from being as effective in conservation as they might be. Too often they have cut themselves off from society. There is clearly a place for narrowly defined and elegant disciplinary research driven by the curiosity of researchers, but if universities are truly to be citizens of the communities in which they are located and of the world, they must respond appropriately to the broader social concerns at the intersection of the biotic system and the human system. New incentives are needed, from within and without, that will permit students and scholars to develop competencies that can contribute to this goal.

No one today seriously denies the breadth, depth, and importance of ecological concerns to present and future generations. Yet each year, colleges and universities graduate hundreds of thousands of young men and women who will be active citizens and leaders, but who are totally unaware of, and unschooled in, matters of ecology. Just as these institutions over the years defined certain requirements as to what it means to be an educated individual, so too it is now necessary for colleges and universities to ensure that their graduates are ecologically literate (Orr 1992). David Orr develops this theme in a special, extended Essay (16A).

At the research level, universities have too often defined themselves along narrow disciplinary lines, with little communication among these disciplines. Thus, former biology departments have split into departments of zoology, botany, microbiology, physiology, genetics, molecular biology, and other narrow fields. The very action of dividing life sciences into separate disciplines means that communication among them is stifled, reductionism is encouraged, and, in some very important ways, knowledge is lost. When an environmental issue is then confronted, it is done by groups of disparate specialists who see only a very narrow slice of the overall problem, often in a way that merely advances their particular specialty but does little toward addressing the real problem. This "discipline-defined approach," as opposed to an "issue-defined approach," will be discussed below.

The need for ecological literacy is critical, and the process should begin as early as possible in a student's education. At early ages it is possible to take full advantage of the natural curiosity of young people about the world around them. The environment is both gray and green—both urban and rural—and students should be introduced to ever-widening ecosystem concerns, beginning in their neighborhoods and expanding to the globe. If primary and secondary educational institutions, and all of the other institutions where young people learn (clubs, churches, television, movies, and so forth), do not do this, these students are less likely to cultivate an interest in and appreciation for environmental issues later in life.

## ESSAY 16A
## Liberalizing the Liberal Arts
### From Dominion to Design

David W. Orr, Oberlin College

After reflecting on the state of education in his time, H. L. Mencken concluded that significant improvement required only that the schools be burned down and the professorate be hanged. For better or worse, the suggestion was largely ignored. Made today, however, it might have found a more receptive public ready to purchase the gasoline and rope. Americans, united on little else, seem to be of one mind in believing that their educational system, K through Ph.D., is too expensive, cumbersome, and ineffective. But they are divided on how to go about the task of reform. On one side of the debate are those who argue that the failure is due mostly to the lack of funding for laboratories, libraries, equipment, salaries, and new buildings—a view, not surprisingly, held most avidly by professional educators. On the other side are those, such as Benno Schmidt, the former president of Yale University, who propose to make education over as a business.

Both sides of the debate, nonetheless, agree on the basic aims and purposes of educational institutions, which are, first, to equip our nation with a "world-class" labor force in order to compete more effectively in the global economy, and, second, to provide each individual with the means for maximum upward mobility. In these, the purposes of education both higher and lower, there is great assurance and repose.

### Education from an Ecological Perspective

There are, however, better reasons to rethink education, having to do with the issues of human survival that will dominate the world of the 21st century. Those now being educated will have to do what we, the present generation, have been unable or unwilling to do: stabilize a world population now growing at the rate of over a quarter of a million each day, reduce the emission of greenhouse gases that threaten to change the climate (perhaps disastrously), protect biological diversity now declining at perhaps 100–200 species per day, reverse the destruction of rainforests (both tropical and temperate) now being lost at the rate of 116 mi$^2$ or more each day, and conserve soils being eroded at the rate of 65 million tons per day. They must learn how to use energy and materials efficiently. They must learn how to use solar energy. They must rebuild the economy in order to eliminate waste and pollution. They must learn how to conserve resources for the long term. They must begin the great work of repairing, as much as possible, the damage done to the earth in the past 200 years of industrialization. And they must do all of this while reducing poverty and egregious social inequities. No generation has ever faced a more daunting agenda.

For the most part, however, we are still educating the young as if there were no planetary emergency. It is widely assumed that environmental problems will be solved by technology of one sort or another. Better technology can certainly help, but the crisis is not primarily one of technology. Rather, it is one of mind, and hence one within the minds that develop and use technology. It is first and foremost a crisis of thought, perception, imagination, intellectual priorities, and loyalties. It is ultimately a crisis of education that purports to shape and refine the capacity of minds to think clearly, to imagine what could be and is not, and to act faithfully. Resolution of the great challenges of the next century will require us to reconsider the substance, process, and purposes of education at all levels and to do so, in Yale historian Jaroslav Pelikan's (1992) words, with "an intensity and ingenuity matching that shown by previous generations in obeying the command to have dominion over the planet".

### From Dominion to Design

Liberal arts institutions have a crucial role to play in reshaping education. We cannot know for certain what particular skills the young will need in coming decades, but we know with great certainty that they will need to be liberally educated in the fullest sense in order to do the work of designing households, farms, institutions, communities, corporations, and economies that (1) do not emit heat-trapping gases, (2) operate on renewable energy, (3) conserve biological diversity, (4) use materials and water efficiently, and (5) recycle materials and organic wastes.

The old curriculum was shaped around the goal of extending human dominion over the earth to its fullest extent. The new curriculum will be organized around development of the analytic abilities, ecological wisdom, and practical wherewithal needed for making things that fit in a world of microbes, plants, animals, and entropy: what can be called the "ecological design arts." Ecological design requires the ability to comprehend patterns that connect, which means getting beyond the boxes we call disciplines to see things in their larger context. Ecological design is the careful meshing of human purposes with the larger patterns and flows of the natural world, and the careful study of those patterns and flows to inform human purposes.

Competence in ecological design means incorporating intelligence about how nature works into the way we think, build, and live (Wann 1990). Design applies to the making of nearly everything that directly or indirectly requires energy and materials or that governs their use. When houses, farms, neighborhoods, communities, cities, transportation systems, technologies, energy policies, and entire economies are well designed, they are in harmony with the ecological patterns in which they are embedded. When poorly designed, they undermine those larger patterns creating pollution, higher costs, social stress, and ecological havoc. Bad design is not simply an engineering problem, although better engineering would often help. Its roots go deeper.

Good designs everywhere have certain common characteristics, including right scale, simplicity, efficient use of resources, a close fit between means and ends, durability, redundancy, and resilience. They are often place-specific, or in John Todd's words, "Elegant solutions predicated on the uniqueness of place." Good design also solves more than one problem at a time and promotes (1) human competence instead of addiction and dependence, (2) efficient and frugal use of resources, (3) sound regional economies, and (4) social resilience. Where good design becomes part of the social fabric at all levels, unanticipated positive side effects multiply. When people fail to design with ecological competence, unwanted negative side effects and disasters multiply.

By the evidence of pollution, violence, social decay, and waste all around us we have designed things badly. Why? There are, I think, three primary reasons. The first is that, while energy and land were cheap and the world relatively empty, we simply did not have to master the discipline of good design. We developed extensive rather than intensive economies. Accordingly, cities sprawled, wastes were dumped into rivers and landfills, houses and automobiles got bigger and less efficient, and whole forests were converted into junk mail. Meanwhile, the know-how necessary for a diverse, frugal, intensive economy declined, and words like "convenience" became synonymous with habits of waste.

Second, design intelligence fails when greed, narrow self-interest, and individualism take over. Good design is a community process requiring people who know and value the positive things that bring them together and hold them together. Old Order Amish, for example, refuse to buy combines, not because combines would not make farming easier or more profitable, but because they would undermine the community by depriving people of the opportunity to help their neighbors. This is pound-wise and penny-foolish, the way intelligent design should be. In contrast, American cities with their extremes of poverty and opulence are the products of people who believe that they have little in common with each other. Greed, suspicion, and fear undermine good community and good design alike.

Third, poor design results from poorly equipped minds. Good design can only be done by people who understand harmony, patterns, and systems. Industrial cleverness, on the contrary, is mostly evident in the minutiae of things, not in their totality or in their overall harmony. Good design requires a breadth of view that causes people to ask how human artifacts and purposes fit within a particular culture and place. It also requires ecological intelligence, by which I mean an intimate familiarity with how nature works in a particular place.

A contemporary example of ecological design is to be found in John Todd's "living machines," which are carefully orchestrated ensembles of plants, aquatic animals, technology, solar energy, and high-tech materials that purify wastewater, but without the expense, energy use, and chemical hazards of conventional sewage treatment technology. In Todd's words:

> People accustomed to seeing mechanical moving parts, to experiencing the noise or exhaust of internal combustion engines or the silent geometry of electronic devices, often have difficulty imagining living machines. Complex life forms, housed within strange light-receptive structures, are at once familiar and bizarre. They are both garden and machine. They are alive yet framed and contained in vessels built of novel materials. . . . Living machines bring people and nature together in a fundamentally radical and transformative way (Todd 1991).

Todd's living machines resemble greenhouses filled with plants and aquatic animals. Wastewater enters at one end, purified water leaves at the other. In between, the work of sequestering heavy metals in plant tissues, breaking down toxics, and removing nutrients has been done by an ensemble of organisms driven by sunlight.

Ecological design also applies to the design of public policies. Governmental planning and regulation require large and often ineffective or counterproductive bureaucracies. Design, in contrast, means

> . . . the attempt to produce the outcome by establishing criteria to govern the operations of the process so that the desired result will occur more or less automatically without further human intervention (Ophuls 1977).

In other words, well-designed policies and laws get the big things right, like prices, taxes, and standards for fairness, while preserving a high degree of freedom for people and institutions to respond in different ways. Design focuses on the structure of problems as opposed to their coefficients. For example, the Clean Air Act of 1970 required car manufacturers to install catalytic converters to remove air pollutants. Several decades later, emissions per vehicle are down substantially, but with more cars on the road, air quality is about the same. A design approach to transportation would cause us to think more about creating access to housing, schools, jobs, and recreation that eliminates the need to move lots of people and materials over long distances. A design approach would cause us to reduce dependence on automobiles by building better public transit systems, restoring railroads, and creating bike trails and walkways.

## Implementing Ecological Design in the Institution

What does ecological design have to do with educational institutions? The starting point is to ask how those institutions work within the larger patterns and flows of nature on which they depend for energy, materials, water, food, and into which they discard their wastes. What impact do institutional purchases and operations have on the diversity of life on the earth? Do these institutions have a clear policy to implement state-of-the-art energy efficiency? Do they use nontoxic materials in new construction and renovations? Do they recycle organic wastes and paper? Do they purchase recycled paper and materials? Have they begun to phase out toxic substances in landscaping and maintenance? Do they use their institutional buying power to support local and regional economies? Have they begun to invest their endowments in things that preserve biological diversity and move the world in more sustainable directions? In short, do those same institutions that purport to induct the young into responsible adulthood act responsibly and imaginatively in making decisions that shape the world the young will inherit?

These are difficult and complex questions. But many colleges and universities are making significant progress in redesigning institutional operations to reduce environmental impacts while saving money at the same time. The State University of New York-Buffalo saved $3 million in 1991 by implementing a systematic energy efficiency program. They also significantly reduced the University's contribution to global warming and acid rain. For the same reasons, other institutions are implementing systematic energy policies.

Hendrix College in Conway, Arkansas, is buying as much of its food as possible from local farms, thereby cutting transportation costs, improving the quality of its dining service, helping local farmers, and reducing the environmental impacts of its food service. Dozens of colleges and universities have implemented full-scale recycling programs. The University of Kansas has established an Environmental Ombudsman office to pursue cost-effective environmental reforms throughout the institution. Nationally, the Student Environmental Action Coalition in Chapel Hill and the National Wildlife Federation are helping to organize informed student involvement in issues of campus ecology (Eagan and Orr 1992).

The redesigning of institutional resource flows is a visible sign of an institution's commitment to the future. Done with intelligence and persistence, it can save money, but it also represents a significant educational opportunity. From a student's perspective, global problems appear to be abstract, remote, and mostly unsolvable. They invite apathy, or what's worse, posturing and hypocrisy. Problems in campus resource flows, in contrast, are visible, immediate, and at the right scale to be solved. Participation in projects that aim to improve the fit between the campus and the environment by increasing energy efficiency, closing waste loops, using recycled materials, supporting local economies, and designing low-impact buildings provides students with opportunities to learn the analytic and practical skills of ecological design. Such projects also provide opportunities to learn the realities of how institutions work and how, sometimes, they do not work.

This emphasis on ecological design requires an institution-wide commitment to environmental literacy that crosses discipline boundaries. Charles Knapp, President of the University of Georgia, decreed in 1991 that the university would no longer graduate environmentally illiterate students, and then set forth to develop coursework in a variety of departments to meet that goal. Tufts University has established an Ecological Literacy Institute, a summer program that attracts faculty from all departments. The Institute offers instruction and information about environmental issues and enables faculty to revise courses to include the environment and to develop new courses. There is good reason to extend the goal of environmental literacy to include administrative officials, staff, and trustees as well.

Competence in the ecological design arts finally requires extending the curriculum to include new fields of knowledge such as conservation biology, restoration ecology, ecological engineering, environmental ethics, solar design, landscape architecture, sustainable agriculture, sustainable forestry, energetics, industrial ecology, ecological economics, and least-cost, end-use analysis. A program in ecological design would weave these and similar elements together with the goal of making students smarter about systems and how specific things and processes fit in their ecological context.

Instruction in the ecological design arts aims to develop the habits of mind, analytic skills, and practical competence necessary to solve problems that are insuperable within the context that caused them in the first place. Its inclusion as an integral part of education at all levels is a recognition that the crisis of environment is solvable, but on nature's terms, not our own.

## Governments

Virtually all governmental institutions, whether their focus is local, state, regional, national, or international, suffer from the same problem: they are vertically oriented. Thus, there are agencies that deal separately with education, agriculture, finance and the economy, international affairs, commerce, health and safety, defense, sometimes the environment, and so forth (Figure 16.2). It is a fact, however, that most human and environmental problems are horizontal, and do not fit neatly into the boxes of government. This is especially true of such major concerns as biodiversity protection and human population growth. Each of these problems affects, and is deeply affected by, actions in any of the more traditional areas. These effects are often exacerbated by the fact that, for example, ecosystem concerns are measured in decades and generations, whereas the political "needs" of traditional agencies are often

**Figure 16.2** The federal government of the United States is organized in a vertical fashion around 14 departments that have representatives on the President's Cabinet. Each department is concerned with a particular aspect of human existence, but many issues, including environmental ones, cut across the boundaries of all the departments.

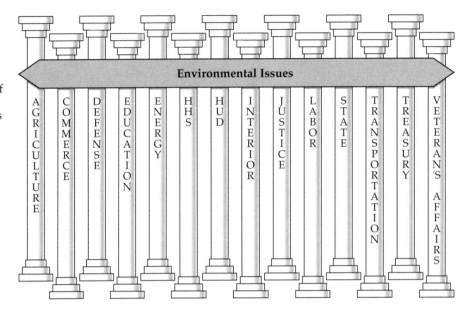

measured in the months and years leading up to the next election.

Processes for adjudicating conflicts between these horizontal concerns and traditional agencies are largely missing. There is an urgent need to find out on whose desk the buck stops, and to ensure that that person can reflect the needs and desires of *both* present and future generations. Unless governmental institutions that concern themselves not with the next quarter, but with the next quarter century, can be developed, ecosystem and human losses will be significant. Political time frames (especially reelection) are much shorter than ecological (let alone evolutionary) time frames; this is a major reason why institutions focus on such short-sighted goals.

Many government agencies also work directly at cross-purposes with other agencies (see Essay 12D). For example, the U.S. Forest Service has, as a major mandate, production of harvestable timber in the billions of board feet per year. At the same time, it and the U.S. Fish and Wildlife Service have a legal obligation to maintain biodiversity that is directly dependent upon those trees. Thus, while the Forest Service cuts old-growth forests, Fish and Wildlife tries to maintain endangered species such as the Spotted Owl and Red-cockaded Woodpecker. Other examples abound. Departments of public health in many states actively raise mosquitofishes (*Gambusia affinis* and *G. holbrooki*) and distribute them in natural water bodies in the mistaken notion that they will eliminate mosquitoes (Courtenay and Meffe 1989), while other agencies simultaneously work to remove mosquitofishes as exotic pests because they are so dangerous to native faunas. The U.S. Department of Agriculture spends large sums of money subsidizing tobacco farmers, while the Department of Health and Human Services also spends large sums educating citizens to the deadly dangers of smoking. Thus, the government inadvertently subsidizes production of lung cancer while promoting higher health care costs. The examples could go on for pages.

It would seem more logical that government agencies, which all fly the same national flag, should all be on the same side, whether in conservation, human health, or any other issue. Horizontal policy consistency seems a reasonable goal, but is difficult to achieve within the vertical structure of government agencies.

Part of the reason that government agencies frequently work at cross-purposes is that there are no fundamental, underlying visions and philosophies that guide all government action in a common direction regardless of political party in power or short-term needs. For example, adopting ecological design principles as the one underlying philosophy of our existence and our vision of the future (see Essay 16A) would clearly dictate how all government agencies should operate. It would also ensure that moneys spent and directions taken by one administration would not be undermined by the different philosophies of the next administration, which are yet again dismantled by the following administration.

Instead, each agency seems to have its own, separate mission, divorced from the missions of other agencies. Witness the decision in November 1993 of the Food and Drug Administration to allow the use of a genetically engineered drug, bovine somatotropin, to increase the amount of milk produced by dairy cows, without taking into account the social and economic effects of the drug's introduction, especially on agriculture: smaller dairy farmers are likely to be forced from their farms as production on larger farms increases. Rather than agencies continuing on a course of aggressively seeking expanded funding and protection of their own policy territories, what is needed is a vision of a desirable future, created in a truly participatory process involving scientists, policymakers, activists, and other stakeholders, that would serve to bring together disparate goals, perspectives, and mandates into a manageable whole.

## Nongovernmental Organizations

It is hard to categorize nongovernmental organizations (NGOs) under one heading. Some are massive, with large budgets and global concerns, like the World Resources Institute, the Environmental and Energy Study Institute, the New York Botanical Garden, and The Nature Conservancy. Others are small and focus on a single community, region, or ecosystem, such as the Oregon Natural Resources Council, the Southwest Network on Environmental and Economic Justice, the Desert Fishes Council, and the Gulf Coast Tenants Organization. Some carry out research with or without a policy focus, and in some respects are indistinguishable from universities. Some, both large and small, are potential consumers of knowledge as they organize and advocate for the environment at community, state, regional, national, or global levels.

The nongovernmental community plays an important role by providing a window on the real world for conservation scientists. NGOs can assist in the process of identifying knowledge needs because they are often in a position to listen to the needs of stakeholders and policymakers more directly than are scientists. As advocates at local, state, national, and even international levels, NGOs serve as policy analysts and policy synthesizers, taking the results of more narrowly defined research and packaging them for various audiences. NGOs are also potentially important employers of graduates in conservation biology, whether their interests are in further research or in the uses of research for social goals.

Increasingly, nongovernmental conservation organizations are working in concert, building coalitions that are contributing to the democratization of the policy process. These coalitions are strengthened through linkages with other organizations that have economic and social concerns, such as jobs and environmental justice. This alliance could contribute to more holistic solutions that meet the needs of nature and humans.

Nongovernmental organizations often play an essential role in experimenting with new approaches to old problems. The Center for Rural Affairs in Walthill, Nebraska, for example, has developed an innovative approach to saving economically viable family farms, preserving communities, and promoting environmentally sound and sustainable agriculture. Funds raised through a unique bond issue will help younger family farmers to buy land from older farmers wishing to retire. The Center will help to develop the farm plans, and will also provide technical assistance for implementing environmentally sound and economically viable farming methods. Preservation of the farms will also contribute to community revitalization.

## Business

Businesses, and the economic frameworks upon which many business decisions are made, present serious challenges to the conservation of biodiversity. So long as the concern of business seems to be the bottom line after the next quarter, rather than after the next quarter century, ecosystem protection is not likely to be given high priority (see Chapter 15). So long as a standing redwood, or an Amazonian rainforest, has no "economic value" until it becomes lumber, nature will be consumed. So long as industrial tragedies (such as the oil spill from the *Exxon Valdez*) and natural tragedies exacerbated by human follies (such as the flooding of the Mississippi River in the summer of 1993) are contributors to the calculation of the nation's gross national product, nature will be shortchanged. So long as waste from production processes is seen as an "externality" and not as a real cost of doing business, the biosphere will lose. Farmer, novelist, and essayist Wendell Berry has defined a community as "a neighborhood of humans in place plus the place itself: its soil, its water, its air, and all the families and tribes of the non-human creatures that belong to it" (Berry 1993). So long as production and place are separated, corporations are likely to have little commitment to place, and as a result, to the humans and ecosystems in place. So long as the market system gives little value either to equity or to ecology, ecosystems will be disadvantaged.

There is little doubt that businesses at all levels can be more environmentally sensitive (Hawken 1993; Figure 16.3). Whether business philosophy and

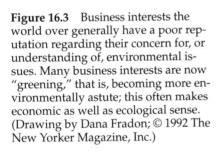

**Figure 16.3** Business interests the world over generally have a poor reputation regarding their concern for, or understanding of, environmental issues. Many business interests are now "greening," that is, becoming more environmentally astute; this often makes economic as well as ecological sense. (Drawing by Dana Fradon; © 1992 The New Yorker Magazine, Inc.)

*"Sir, would you take this latest warning of ecological disaster and pooh-pooh it for me?"*

practice can truly be congruent with conservation remains a great, unanswered question. For the sake of ecosystems and humankind, we must try to ensure that the answer is yes. Unfortunately, however, the evidence to date suggests that the need for institutional and system changes is only vaguely perceived by some, and accepted by fewer. These views are further pursued in Chapter 18 in the section on "the tragedy of the commons."

### Consumers

Obviously, consumer preferences will have an important effect on the conservation of biodiversity. Consumers are subject to what businesses provide. However, they can, have, and will continue to change the way business does business if they can be organized effectively; for example, witness the recent demands for "dolphin-free tuna" and many other environmentally friendly products in the United States (Figure 16.4). This, however, will require a much deeper understanding of the importance of the environment for oneself and one's children. The environment is the basis for all life and all production. The environment cannot be perceived as a special interest, but must be recognized for what it is: the playing field on which all human interests occur. Like businesses, consumers will have to understand the full social costs (as differentiated from prices) of their activities, and ultimately exhibit a willingness to pay those costs (Durning 1992). Until now, businesses and consumers have been getting a free lunch, paid for by the environment.

### Legal Institutions

Much is made of the fact that the United States is a litigious society. However, it is important to understand the roots of the legislative emphasis that has given so much attention to the courts. Environmental regulation did not come about simply because Congress or other legislative bodies wanted to take control. It was a response to the failure on the part of various actors, including businesses, to perform voluntarily in ways that met the needs of the common good. For example, chemical companies were slow to react to the observation of the ozone hole and the need to stop the production of CFCs. The Clean Air Act and international environmental legislation seemed to be the appropriate mechanisms at a given point in time to reduce pollution that was deleterious to the health and safety of the society. Today there are still circumstances in which businesses are fighting regulations when, by meeting them, they would actually reduce their own costs. Understanding and change occur slowly, especially when the time frames are perceived narrowly.

Underlying much of the concern about regulation is the assertion, usually from business, that we are a paranoid society that is too risk-averse. Part of the problem, however, is in the very definition of risk and how we assess it. In the first place, risk is rarely assessed by the people who are exposed to the risk. Secondly, our methods of assessment are at best primitive. We may be able to determine, for example, the relationship of one pollutant to the incidence of one kind of cancer. However, in the real world we are all exposed to a "pollution soup," a variety of pollutants delivered in different concentrations, in different media—air, water, food. In addition, we are all different in physical and genetic characteristics, and therefore react differently to the "pollution soups" we are served. Thus, how can one even approximate a serious assessment of risk? Here, the precautionary principle comes into play: better to be safe than sorry. Ginsburg (1993) addresses such questions in greater detail.

Consider the case of Rose Marie Augustine of South Tucson, Arizona. There are 30 tidy, simple houses on her block in a predominantly Hispanic

**Figure 16.4** Environmentally "friendly" or "green" product lines, such as these paper and cleaning products, are experiencing greater consumer demand and are becoming more available. (Photograph by John Goodman, courtesy of Seventh Generation.)

area. Twenty-eight of the 30 families in those houses have experienced deaths from cancer, or have a cancer patient still living. Their drinking water is believed to have been polluted with the industrial solvent trichloroethylene, TCE, which was used in great quantities by the Hughes Aircraft plant nearby. Scientists who studied this neighborhood did not deny the correlations that were all too obvious, but they were unwilling to assign causation (Lavelle and Coyle 1992). Humility would suggest that we cannot know the cause of the cancers for sure, but common sense argues that the problem is real. Perhaps the question to be asked is whether the scientists who performed the risk assessment would themselves be willing to live next door to Ms. Augustine and drink the water, given the situation they have observed. If not, then how much credence should be given to their findings?

It is often argued that the United States as a whole has become risk-averse, and that we are also afraid of the wrong risks. It is suggested, for example, that we pay too much attention to a chemical that might cause one extra cancer death in 10 million, while allowing cigarette smoking and car driving by the millions, both of which kill people by the hundreds of thousands. There is, of course, legitimacy to this argument. However, what it fails to take into account is the unequal distribution of the risks. Cigarette smoking and driving are volitional—we can choose to do them or not. Exposure to chemicals is, however, disproportionately felt by minorities and the poor. Chemical exposures are imposed upon people rather than subject to their free will and choice (Chavis and Lee 1987; Lavelle and Coyle 1992).

Alternative means of regulation have been proposed, and it is clear that we should explore all avenues to a better system. However, most that have been proposed to date are significantly flawed. For example, to assume that voluntary compliance for the common good will preserve systems is at best naive, given the fact, as already noted, that regulation became necessary in the absence of voluntary compliance. Similarly, while so-called market-based approaches may have some applicability, the market, by failing to deal adequately with both equity and ecology, starts as a flawed instrument.

## Religious Institutions

There has been a long debate among scholars concerning the role that Judeo-Christian teachings have played in humankind's destruction of the environment (see Chapter 2). Do these teachings suggest that we are conquerors of the land—"be fruitful and multiply"—or stewards? Has the Judeo-Christian ethic done more harm or good for the environment?

Whatever the past debate, organized religion in the United States is now beginning to take seriously the challenge of stewardship. Churches and synagogues are preaching on the environment, and there is pressure for church-owned lands to be managed in a sustainable and environmentally sound manner. Theological schools are training seminarians about the interface between religion and the environment. These efforts are all part of a major interfaith program instituted late in 1993 that will underline the injunction to revere God's creation and to protect it (Joint Appeal 1992). Because changes in the underlying value systems of human societies are necessary before any real progress can be made in conservation, perhaps one of our best hopes for changing the human relationship with the earth is progress in religious teachings and values. However, those teachings must move beyond self-salvation for an afterlife to incorporate planetary salvation now.

Examples of such a transformation can be found in rural parts of Latin America and the Philippines, where a religious movement known as "liberation theology" has begun to make connections between poverty and environmental degradation. Clergy in this movement have recognized a common pattern: poor farmers are displaced from relatively fertile lands by highly capitalized commercial agriculture. These displaced farmers often end up either in urban slums or on ecologically fragile and agriculturally marginal lands. Because sustainable agriculture is not possible on these marginal lands, the farmers continue to exploit new lands, usually by cutting forests, inadvertently destroying biodiversity. These experiences have led some clergy to argue that marginalized small farmers and degradation of biodiversity are endpoints of the same process—exploitative economic growth—and they are actively working to change this pattern.

## The Media

American society at the end of the 20th century suffers from "info-glut," a satiation of information. As a result, it is likely that all messages become weakened. In addition, the messages come in small boxes, and the interrelationships among these boxes are hardly ever drawn. For example, during the 1993 New York mayoral election, the front page of *The New York Times* had side-by-side articles on crime and the economy; neither mentioned the other issue, and the linkages between the two were never made.

The range of opinions voiced through the media frequently reflects the needs and positions of the well-to-do, while the needs of the earth are heard only partially, if at all. For example, in 1993 *The New York Times* published three advertorials supporting NAFTA (North American Free Trade Agreement), but the high cost of advertising in these special sections precluded the participation of NGOs opposing NAFTA.

The news media, almost by definition, focus on immediate problems and not on long-term education and trends. Thus, it is difficult to build up the base of knowledge that makes it possible for the citizenry as a whole to understand events in their systemic context. Furthermore, it is not clear whether the plethora of "nature" programs on television, picturing animals and ecosystems near and far, contribute more to the true appreciation of nature and the desire to experience it and save it, or to the passivity of the "couch potato."

When one also considers the decline in literacy and reading in the United States, and the focus on television as our main source of news and information, the problem becomes exacerbated. If it is not visual and quick, the message is unlikely to get through. Many of the changes that are of concern to conservation biology are not of the dramatic sort that lend themselves to this form of public information. And then again, after a while, people may just tire of seeing what they perceive to be the same thing they have seen before. Do all the pretty places and exotic animals eventually begin to look alike?

Another problem with the media relates to scientists themselves. Journalists suggest that scientists do not know how to speak effectively to them and through them to laypeople. When asked a question, scientists may offer reprints of a number of their published papers, rather than explaining their work in understandable terms. Or, perhaps worse, scientists go into a detailed and complicated explanation as if they were speaking to a colleague rather than a communicator. Scientists need to learn how to communicate in ways that maintain the integrity of their thinking without glazing over the eyes of the people they are trying to reach. This can be a great challenge, however. Ecological or economic concepts are generally too complicated for the short "sound bites" that have become the currency of the modern news media. Perhaps the media also need to make strides to change the way they present this type of information to the public.

## Institutional and Policy Challenges for Conservation Biology

Students and professionals in conservation and other scientific fields often slip into a narrow, comfortable, and naive worldview: that conservation (or their particular discipline) is central to public thought, that everyone else cares about the discipline as much as they do, and that if only politicians, bureaucrats, and activists would adopt their perspective, then all would be well. The world is, however, much more complex than that. The public and policymakers usually do care about the issues, but often do not know how to respond to scientists and conservationists, whose frequently contradictory views add confusion rather than confirmation to their perceptions of the actions needed. Consequently, conservation scientists will have to work especially hard to have their knowledge and messages incorporated into society.

Scientific perspectives are suspect to many, especially when the clash of different "experts" leaves the public and policymakers confused. Policy is, and will continue to be, made with or without the input of scientists, regardless of the relevance of their information. Consequently, a number of major challenges related to institutions and policy development face conservation biologists and others interested in contributing to policy through their theoretical and empirical insights. We discuss six of these challenges here.

### Defining Appropriate Environmental Research

Much of ecological and conservation research is rooted in particular scientific disciplines. Geneticists have their domain, as do population biologists, ecophysiologists, landscape ecologists, and so forth. However, real-world environmental issues rarely lend themselves to strict, disciplinary solutions. An environmental issue is not bounded or defined by a particular scientific discipline. Thus, the knowledge needed for the solution of problems needs to be defined by the issue and not by the discipline if it is to contribute effectively to policy formation and implementation.

The difference between a discipline-driven approach and an issue-driven approach is that the former, almost by definition, begins and ends with its own set of tools for dealing with its particular issue. Discipline-driven research usually begins with the curiosity of the investigator, who wants to understand some particular phenomenon. The issue of any particular application or implication other than a deeper understanding of nature, is usually absent. The desire is to "discover" something new, and the audience is usually the investigator's peers.

Presumably, one reason conservation biology began was to somewhat enlarge the tool kit and encompass broader perspectives. Issue-driven research is different than discipline-driven research because it starts with real-world issues and then tries to determine what methods, knowledge, and information might be available or needed to help resolve the problem. For example, rather than asking a discipline-driven question such as "What is the effect of trade on biodiversity?" an issue-driven question might be framed as "What would a trading system look like that valued cultural and biological diversity, equity, and democracy?"

We need to break through disciplinary and interdisciplinary boundaries if we are to make much progress in policy research for conservation. In most cases that research will need to be shifted from a discipline orientation to an issue orientation. A particular environmental issue is not simply the domain of genetics, while another answers to ecosystem ecology or economic theory. Environmental problems are complex and nondisciplinary; the answers should embrace the tools of the appropriate disciplines but not be limited by them. These disciplines go well beyond environmental science and conservation biology, embracing psychology, philosophy, and the humanities, as well as other social sciences and ecological economics. As Wendell Berry (1989) reminds us: "The answers to human problems of ecology are to be found in the economy. And answers to the problems of the economy are to be found in human culture and character."

### Incorporating Broader Sources of Information

The frame of reference for defining environmental issues and the research needed for the amelioration and prevention of environmental assaults should be broadened by listening to people most affected. All stakeholders must have an opportunity to be heard, and all must also listen carefully to the views of others. The issue is not what scientists and researchers believe to be important in some idealized sense, but what is useful and can be used, as identified by several groups:

- people most affected by environmental assaults
- people who have historically maintained sustainable societies
- people who are charged by virtue of election or appointment to make and implement policy
- people who may produce the knowledge to assist and inform the policy process

In the area of conservation there is the issue of who speaks for "the families and tribes of non-human creatures that live in the place," and who speaks for future generations. This is a moral and ethical issue of great importance, for which all stakeholders bear responsibility. However, it is the voice most often lacking, because it is a reflection of values that legitimately may be in conflict. Conservation biologists have a potentially important role to play here. In the absence of these voices, environmental research has a lesser chance of being substantively relevant to the policy process. Appropriate inclusion also increases chances of solutions working politically.

In 1990, the U.S. Environmental Protection Agency's Scientific Advisory Board presented to its Administrator its assessment of the worst environmental problems. It revealed that hazardous and toxic wastes and underground storage tanks, the issues that topped the public agenda, were not on the scientists' list, and that climate change and radon, near the top of the EPA list, were near the bottom in the public's view. Scientists reviewing this discrepancy usually suggest that it reflects a lack of understanding on the part of the public of "real risks," their fears irrationally fanned by activists who pay little attention to "acceptable risk levels." The public most affected by the environmental assaults see the scientists as insensitive and uncaring, and too abstract. They also see the scientists as not subject to the same exposures, so that their research "findings" blind them to the needs of people at risk.

There is an important lesson here: scientists, policymakers, representatives of the public, and the stakeholders most deeply affected and concerned need to be consulted. The "scientific assessment" and the "public assessment" of key problems are both based upon an implicit or explicit analysis of who wins and who loses, of possible tradeoffs, and of opportunity costs. These are important calculations. By definition, however, they are neither value-free nor ethically neutral, though often cloaked in the language of a "value-free" science. They must be reconciled in a democratic society.

If the public is "ill-informed," the scientific community concerned with contributing to the solution of environmental problems bears partial responsibility and has an obligation to work to overcome this alleged ignorance. At the same time, the scientific community has an obligation to listen to the public, and particularly to the people most affected by environmental assaults, often minorities and the poor. Cost-benefit analysis can work only if we are clear on how we measure costs and benefits, taking into account alternative values, especially those that cannot easily be quantified. For example, the value of a human life is usually imputed from projected lifetime earnings, making a poor person "less valuable" than a conservation biologist, who in turn will be less valuable than a Donald Trump or a Michael Jackson. A socially and ethically adjusted cost–benefit analysis can then become the basis for setting priorities for the funding of environmental research. What may appear to be the public's lack of scientific information may in fact be a reflection of different values given to that information, and/or a lack of trust in the purveyor of the information, whether the government, the academy, or business.

### Understanding the Policy Process

There is a tendency among scientists to argue the centrality of scientific information in the policy process. Knowledge is clearly better than ignorance, but "good science" does not necessarily make "good policy." Science may be necessary, but cannot be sufficient, because policymaking is the process of reflecting what we value in a society, which is at heart a matter of ethics and values. Often, the scientist and policymaker have difficulty even communicating at the same level (Figure 16.5).

The question then becomes, what is good science for policy? What is the nature of the knowledge needed and attainable in the time frame available for action? And how can that knowledge best be utilized? Policy to "solve" environmental problems in a democratic society is a process of adjudicating the conflicting values of different legitimate interests in different time frames. Thus, science is not sufficient in and of itself; rather it is, and can only be, one input, albeit an important input, to policy.

To design a policy-relevant conservation agenda, it is essential to take into account the culture of the policy process, recognizing the differences between executive and legislative branches, and between different levels of government. Some aspects of that process are listed here, admittedly painted with a broad brush:

**Figure 16.5** The scientist and policymaker often have problems communicating with each other. Their backgrounds, vital interests, and goals often differ enough so that they work toward very different ends, and may even have problems communicating simple ideas. (Modified from Byerly 1989.)

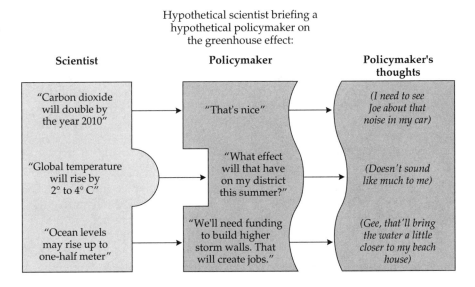

Hypothetical scientist briefing a hypothetical policymaker on the greenhouse effect:

**Scientist**

"Carbon dioxide will double by the year 2010"

"Global temperature will rise by 2° to 4° C"

"Ocean levels may rise up to one-half meter"

**Policymaker**

"That's nice"

"What effect will that have on my district this summer?"

"We'll need funding to build higher storm walls. That will create jobs."

**Policymaker's thoughts**

*(I need to see Joe about that noise in my car)*

*(Doesn't sound like much to me)*

*(Gee, that'll bring the water a little closer to my beach house)*

- There are usually no institutional structures for effectively integrating economic, environmental, and political concerns.
- No one is in charge, but there are lots of people involved in dealing with pieces of the problem.
- Policymakers, more often than not, have plenty of information (although perhaps not enough from the scientist's viewpoint), often conflicting, and plenty of demands for action, also conflicting.
- Policymakers do not want more problems; they want silver bullets, or quick answers, for those problems (which is an approach fraught with danger).
- Information for policymakers is usually imperfect, and there is often little or no organized demand for specific information by policymakers.
- Information, when requested, is often not available in the time frame needed, or in a form that is usable or useful.
- Scientists disseminate their work through publications, papers at conferences, and the mailing of reprints, but rarely place great emphasis on increasing the utilization of their findings by policymakers.
- Scientists often want to provide information on what interests them, rather than what may be needed.
- Requests for information from policymakers are often quite sincere; frequently, however, such requests are excuses for postponing action.
- Requests for information from policymakers are often framed in ways that make it difficult for scientists to respond effectively; there are differences of culture and too few opportunities to overcome those cultural differences.
- Policymakers generally perceive global change as small, barely perceptible, somewhere else, and/or far in the future, and they perceive the demands on them as a need for action in response to a specific event, here and now.
- Policymakers, as a corollary to the above, first deal with pressing problems with short-term solutions, putting off the long-term, recognizing that the first law of politics is to get reelected.
- Bureaucrats in academia, government, and nongovernmental organizations, especially in larger organizations, are extremely sensitive to the explicit and implicit incentive systems of the organizations in which they work, reacting more to those incentives than to the statements of outsiders or to larger value systems (see Byerly 1989).

It is clear that the policy process is not linear, and it is certainly not pretty. In that sense it is very human, and often differs from textbook models. "Muddling through" is the way one observer described it some years ago. It is necessary to involve scientists and other relevant parties in the policy process throughout, both as listeners and as speakers, to increase the likelihood that the results of their research will be used and the best policy decisions will be made. The link between policy and science is pursued further in Box 16A.

---

# BOX 16A
# Improving the Link Between Policy and Science

C. R. Carroll

---

Rational people would agree that sound public policy for conservation should be based on good conservation science.

However, there are two fundamental weaknesses in the linkage between the policy and the science of conservation.

First, the diversity of conservation issues and the inherent dynamic characteristics of biological systems are difficult to address in natural resource public policy, which tends to be both static and generalized. Thus, public policy needs to become more adaptive and more system-specific. That is, policy should be designed to change progressively in response to new information and environmental conditions.

While public policy themes should derive from a coherent philosophy and generalized principles, the manner in which those themes are implemented in real time and space should be tailored to specific issues or particular ecological systems. By way of illustration, a public policy philosophical perspective might value biodiversity protection over other competing land uses. The general principles used to support that protection might include such things as penalty-based proscriptions against any removal or killing of endangered species. What right-thinking conservationist could object to that policy? However, it could happen that such a policy against removing endangered species could act as a disincentive to biodiversity protection. An obvious case is one in which such a rigid policy might inhibit research that is needed to develop a recovery plan for the species, research, for example, that might require that some individuals be removed and translocated to experimental areas. Conservationists must find ways to work more closely with policymakers so that public policy better reflects biological realities.

The second fundamental weakness in the linkage between conservation policy and science that must be addressed is the relatively weak predictive power of conservation biology. We are able to show what will happen only if current conditions remain unchanged; that is, we can make simple deterministic projections. We can sometimes show what might happen, in a probabilistic sense, if the system is changed in particular ways. We can develop simulation models that show, for example, the probability that a small population will survive for a specified span of time. The point of this is not that ecology is poor science but that *weak predictability is an inherent property of complex system behavior*. Biological systems are complex and will always present us with surprises and unexpected behavior. Not only are multiple interactions, age- and sex-related traits, and phenotypic variation characteristic of biological systems, but the species components also evolve, and the whole is influenced by environmental stochasticity. By comparison, physicists and engineers have it easy! Even where intense efforts have been made to develop predictive management models—as in optimal fisheries management, in which we know a great deal about the conditions required for sustained yields—public policy has not reflected the biological reality. Regulatory policies designed to help sustain fisheries have not prevented most of

them from collapsing from overexploitation (Ludwig et al. 1993).

There are two messages here. First, we need to do more work on understanding the behavior of complex systems so that, while we may never be able to predict endpoints with great precision, we will at least be able to say which ones are more likely than others. Second, we must learn how to better communicate to policymakers and the general public the important, but arcane, fact that processes in the natural world are best described as a series of conditional probabilities. We do not live in the "balance of nature;" we do live in a complex world of uncertainty, risk, and environmental change. Our public policy toward biodiversity protection must become more adaptive and flexible. Therefore, rather than asking biologists and resource managers to make untenable predictions, such as maximum sustained yields or minimum viable populations, resource policymakers should be asking biologists and resource managers the following two general questions. For renewable natural resources, we should ask, "If we want to be able to extract economic value from this resource for the next 50 years or so, how should we change our extraction practices?" For biodiversity protection, we should ask, "If we want this ecological system to be functional 50 years from now, how should we change our conservation programs?"

## The Nature of Knowledge in Environmental Policymaking

There is a need for more and better interactions among scientists and the users—real and potential—of scientific knowledge: policymakers, activists and organizers, and affected citizens. These interactions can help determine the nature of the knowledge that will be useful and used in the solution of environmental problems in an appropriate time frame. The primary foci in policy are political, economic, administrative, and organizational, and, under the best of circumstances, moral and ethical. This, in turn, will greatly influence the nature of the scientific knowledge that will be usable and utilized in the policy process. As David Orr (1991) has observed, "As important as research is, the lack of it is not the limiting factor in the conservation of biological diversity."

*Integrating Politics, Economics, and Administration.* To achieve environmentally sensitive policy we must have political will to effect change: to stop, to conserve, to restore, to prevent. This process must take into account the claims of the various stakeholders who may lose, as well as those who may gain, from a particular policy position. For example, many Brazilian policymakers and politicians are fully aware of the social, ecological, and economic absurdity of destroying tropical Amazonian rainforests. It is not a need for new knowledge that keeps them from acting in line with their understanding; it is a lack of political will, based on their analysis of the political pressures upon them, and on their own desire to get reelected or reappointed.

Policy problems are economic in the sense that over the years we have conscientiously avoided paying attention to real costs. The food and fiber sector of the United States economy is a $700 billion per year enterprise. But we do not take into account an approximate additional $250 billion of environmental and social "externalities" involved in the production, distribution and processing of food- and fiber-related products (Viederman, unpublished data). This is but one example of the ways that neoclassical economics fails to take account of nature as a source of capital and as a sink for the wastes of the productive system.

From the narrow disciplinary perspective, we find ourselves in the situation of identifying so-called side effects and by-products. For example, in economics there is the well-known concept of externalities, which, simply put, are those effects that economists choose not to address (Chapter 15). In the real world, however, there are no such things as side effects or by-products, which are only fictions created by too narrow a paradigm; there can only be effects and products. For example, when your doctor prescribes an antibiotic to treat an infection and informs you that a "side effect" might be nausea, to the doctor the nausea is a side effect because you are perceived only as the infection. To you, however, the nausea is very much an effect.

Efforts to achieve solutions to environmental problems require adjudication of conflicts among values and political needs that are exacerbated by inadequate or cumbersome administrative structures and organizational arrangements. Thus, for example, the U.S. Secretary of the Interior, as head of both the Bureau of Land Management and the Fish and Wildlife Service, has conflicting mandates to use and to preserve nature's resources. Similarly, the number of committees in Congress responsible for preparing agricultural legislation makes coordination among them almost impossible. The Carnegie Commission on Science, Technology, and Government (n.d.) estimates that there are at least 16 federal agencies and departments involved in policies and activities related to the greenhouse effect (Table 16.1).

As David Ehrenfeld has observed,

> Rarely is expert knowledge sufficient for analysis, prediction and management of a given [environmental] situation. This is because in order to limit the number of variables they have to contend with, experts make the assumption that the systems they are working with are closed. Real-life systems are hardly ever closed. . . . The reductionist methods of science, which can work extremely well in closed systems, tend to break down under the open-endedness imposed by biological complexity and by the interacting complexities of political, economic and social systems. (Ehrenfeld 1991)

***Developing an Issue-Driven Science.*** A new scientific methodology, an "issue-driven" science, will be needed to address the realities of conservation problems. It will not pretend to be either value-free or ethically neutral, although it will certainly need to remain objective and unbiased in its approaches, and continue to be based on rigorous hypothesis testing. The scientific enterprise in this new paradigm will have to accept the world as it is, rather than try to recreate it in ways that are more susceptible to its research needs. The circumstances that demand this new paradigm, as Funtowicz and Ravetz (1991) have observed, are that "facts are uncertain, values in dispute, stakes high and decisions urgent." As a result, the new paradigm will focus attention on the qualitative assessment of the quantitative data available, recognizing that uncertainty exists. It will also extend the peer community involved in assessment to all stakeholders, as the only way to arrive at decisions that are both scientifically sound and politically tenable.

**Table 16.1**
United States Federal Agencies Involved in Various Aspects of Policies and Activities Related to the Greenhouse Effect

| Policy/activity | EOP | DOE | EPA | NOAA | DOC | STATE | AG | DOI | NASA | USTR | TRE | NSF | DOT | FEMA | DOD | JUST |
|---|---|---|---|---|---|---|---|---|---|---|---|---|---|---|---|---|
| Conduct periodic assistance | x | x | x | x | x | x | x | x | x | x | x | x | x | x | x | |
| Increase stockpiles | | | | | | | x | x | | | | | | x | | |
| Identify adaptive business opportunities | | x | | | x | | x | | | x | | | | | | |
| Develop insurance/emergency warning systems | | | x | x | x | x | x | | x | | | | | x | | |
| Manage ecosystems strategy | | x | | | | | | x | | | | | | | | |
| Civil works/build infrastructure/ water and coastal zones | | | | | x | | x | x | | | | | | | | |
| Promote agricultural research | | | | | | | x | x | | | | | | | | |
| Promote energy conservation/efficiency | | x | x | | x | | | x | | | | | x | | | |
| Promote solar energy | | x | | | x | | | | | | | | | | | |
| Promote natural gas | | x | | | | | | x | | | | | | | | |
| Promote nuclear energy | | x | | | | x | | | | | | | | | | |
| Introduce carbon tax | x | x | x | | x | | | x | | x | x | | x | | | x |
| Improve land use | | x | | | | | x | x | | | | | | | | |
| Expand hydropower | | x | x | | | | | x | | | | | | | | |
| Develop biomass energy | | x | x | | | | | x | | | | | | | | |
| Reduce coal use | | x | | | x | | | x | x | | | | | | | |
| Adopt ambient greenhouse gas standards | | x | x | x | | | | | x | | | | | | | |
| Promote reforestation | | x | | | | x | x | x | | | | | | | | |
| Explore geoengineering | | x | x | x | x | | | | | | | x | | | | |
| Research weather modification | | | x | x | x | x | x | | x | | | | | | x | |
| Liability/compensation: Domestic | | x | x | | x | | x | x | | x | x | | | | | |
| International | | | | | | | | | | | | | | | | x |
| Conduct international negotiation | x | x | x | x | | x | | | x | x | x | x | | | x | |

From Carnegie Commission on Science, Technology, and Government Task Force on Environment and Energy (no date).
[a]EOP, Executive Office of the President; DOE, Department of Energy; EPA, Environmental Protection Agency; NOAA, National Oceanic & Atmospheric Association; DOC, Department of Commerce; STATE, Department of State; AG, Department of Agriculture; DOI, Department of the Interior; NASA, National Aeronautics & Space Administration; USTR, United States Trade Representative; TRE, Department of the Treasury; NSF, National Science Foundation; DOT, Department of Transportation; FEMA, Federal Emergency Management Agency; DOD, Department of Defense; JUST, Department of Justice.

An "issue-driven" science will therefore begin with a problem orientation that is nondisciplinary or transdisciplinary, recognizing at the outset that the situation is fraught with uncertainties. This orientation distinguishes it from curiosity-driven science, in which the effort is to minimize uncertainties. In this respect the new paradigm can be called "postnormal," to differentiate it from the scientific paradigm that is now considered "normal." The characteristics of this postnormal paradigm will include:

- Pragmatism and plurality: use of tools and conceptual frameworks appropriate to the solution of the problem, rather than being limited by the tools and conceptual frameworks of a particular discipline

- Acceptance of uncertainty as a given: asking questions about the real world that at present we do not know how to answer
- A focus on data quality rather than data completeness
- Use of a systems approach that is comprehensive, holistic, global, long-term, and contextual
- Incorporation of an explicit concern for future generations, sustainability, and equity
- A concern for dynamics, process, nonequilibrium, heterogeneity, and discontinuity
- Social as well as individualistic points of view
- Concern for the processes through which the behaviors of individuals and institutions change

The ongoing training and research efforts to develop a new ecological economics, for example, are reflective of the approaches of an "issue-driven, postnormal" science.

## The Nature of the University and the Problems of Research

What are the criteria for assessing the capability of universities and other organizations to be effective providers of the training and research needed for environmental policymaking? Among others, the future requirements for good conservation research and policy are a transdisciplinary, issue-driven approach, a systems orientation, and flexibility.

By and large, universities are not presently organized to effectively carry out research and training along the lines of the paradigm described above. The guild system of the disciplines has a stranglehold on effective change, particularly at the more prestigious institutions. Investigator-initiated, peer-reviewed research is not likely to solve the world's problems by itself. Cross-disciplinary barriers in universities and elsewhere must be brought down so that effective, issue-driven research can be promoted. An example of this approach is the Organization for Tropical Studies (OTS), a university-based education program that crosses disciplinary barriers. OTS is discussed by its executive director, Donald Stone, in Essay 16B.

Derek Bok, who retired in 1992 from the presidency of Harvard University, observed:

> Our universities excel in pursuing the easier opportunities where established academic and social priorities coincide. On the other hand, when social needs are not clearly recognized and backed by adequate financial support, higher education has often failed to respond as effectively as it might, even to some of the most important challenges facing America. Armed with the security of tenure and time to study the world with care, professors would appear to have a unique opportunity to act as society's scouts to signal impending problems long before they are visible to others. Yet rarely have members of the academy succeeded in discovering emerging issues and bringing them vividly to the public attention. What Rachel Carson did for risks to the environment, Ralph Nader for consumer protection, Michael Harrington for problems of poverty, Betty Friedan for women's rights, they did as independent critics, not as members of a faculty. Universities will usually continue to respond weakly unless outside support is available and the subjects involved command prestige in academic circles (Bok 1990).

Universities often reward reductionism, which is contrary to most needs of the environment. For example, in many disciplines, elegance is more honored than relevance. Traditional concerns, such as taxonomy, are put on the waste heap for more "exciting" and certainly more lucrative ventures such as molecular biology. The university incentive system, especially within the traditional departmental structure, does not reward knowledge generation of the sort needed for policy. This is especially true for younger faculty members without tenure, who accept considerable risk in entering what is perceived to be the "softer" field of environmental policy research. Interdisciplinary efforts are usually the first to go in times of budget stringency. It is also true for graduate students who want to assist nongovernmental organizations in dealing with "real-world" problems, only to be thwarted by their academic advisers because the topic chosen allegedly does not lend itself to "good science," defined as a discipline-driven approach.

## ESSAY 16B
# OTS as an Institution for Conservation Education

Donald E. Stone, Organization for Tropical Studies

Slides, videos,and engaging professors can make class exciting at times. However, there is no substitute for the real thing when it comes to seeing nature at work, and more particularly, to gaining insight into the dynamics of nature. It is these building blocks of conservation education that the Organization for Tropical Studies, Inc. (OTS) stresses in its hands-on programs in Costa Rica to promote an understanding of the complexities of tropical ecosystems, and to engage in dialogue as to how these ecosystems can be sustainably managed.

Understanding the nature and strength of the OTS programs in the broadly defined area of conservation requires an appreciation of the institution itself. Its origin is a once-upon-a-time story dating back to the early 1960s, when most of the world viewed tropical rainforests as an unlimited cache of timber and biological diversity. OTS was formed by a small consortium of United States universities and the Universidad de Costa Rica to engage in "training, research and the wise use of natural resources in the tropics." Over the past 30 years the consortium has grown to nearly 50 institutions, and has continued to maintain its operational base in Costa Rica, where it provides training for graduate students and policymakers and maintains field station facilities used by researchers from throughout the world. Quite simply, OTS is a world-class convener of field-oriented courses and facilitator of tropical research.

Precisely what OTS does in conservation education is best viewed in terms of its three principal audiences, namely, graduate students, policymakers, and the Costa Rican community. The graduate student audience, which is the prime justification for consortium membership, is served by courses on *Tropical Biology: An Ecological Approach* and *Tropical Managed Ecosystems*, and their Spanish equivalents, *Ecología de Poblaciones* and *Agroecología*. From time to time, OTS offers specialty courses in various areas of biology, the most recent of which are *Agroforestry* and *Tropical Diversity and Conservation*. Policymakers in the United States are reached by a short course in *Interdependence: Economic Development and Environmental Concerns in Tropical Countries*, whereas the Latin American constituency, consisting mainly of mid-level government officials, is served by *Principios Ecológicos para Toma de Decisiones y el Manejo de los Recursos Naturales en America Latina*. The Costa Rican community is a highly diverse audience reached by environmental education materials and methodologies developed by OTS through workshops and by working with our field station neighbors in programs best described as community relations.

This diversity of audiences may at first glance seem to transcend OTS' mission in training and research, and indeed it does in some ways, but the realities of operating an international consortium place a special premium on observing the common courtesies expected of guests in a foreign country. Indeed, our more recent involvement in environmental education has forced OTS to reconsider the appropriate interface between basic and applied sciences and the appropriate role for an academic institution like OTS to take in technology transfer and community outreach. This is a dynamic and complex issue and no hard and fast rules have been developed. One thing that is clear, however, is that OTS must play on its strengths and continue to exercise an international leadership role in conservation education.

What makes OTS' approach to conservation education so unique can best be appreciated by examining a typical course, *Tropical Biology: An Ecological Approach*. This course is designed for graduate students in their formative years of choosing a dissertation research problem. Some 20 to 22 competitively selected participants are thrust into the field to experience a contrasting range of ecosystems, from sea level to 3000 m, from deciduous dry to evergreen wet forest, and from pristine to highly manipulated landscapes. The pace and focus over the eight-week term are intense and unrelenting from dawn to dusk, seven days a week. The principal instructors, called coordinators, and a graduate teaching assistant establish the intellectual framework and set the tone for the course, but the pace and rigor are maintained throughout by inviting a series of scientists to share their knowledge at one or more field sites. In a two-month course stationed at five or six sites, it is not uncommon for the students to be exposed to the expertise of a dozen or more world-class scientists.

So what does the OTS experience add up to when the exhilaration wears off? For most participants it becomes a unique reference point against which to judge future studies and experiences in the temperate zone, and for a few it becomes the cornerstone for future research in tropical biology. For graduate students cum educators, the tropical experience permeates their future teaching (alas, all too often with slides of pristine forest shown long after they have succumbed to the pressures of development!). For graduate students cum policymakers in the private or public sector, their future decisions regarding natural resources will have a personal frame of reference. And for all alumni there is the enviable opportunity to be invited back as a distinguished faculty participant. In a sense, it is this aspect of recruitment that nourishes the sustainability of the institution and permits progressive updating of our teachings in conservation education.

## The Sufficiency of Knowledge and Some Roles for Environmental Research

Knowledge measured by the canons of a "normal" science is rarely adequate for environmental problem solving, but policy action cannot be postponed in the hope that "complete" information will become available. In all conservation endeavors, use should be made of all available knowledge, and when the time frame for decision making permits it, new research should be undertaken, guided by the needs of the policy process, not those of the researcher. An additional, and often overlooked necessity is the assessment of the possible political, social, environmental, cultural, and economic consequences of the policy action in order to avoid doing harm.

We often have enough information to make informed decisions with respect to conservation. However, much of it is not used because it is in forms that are not always valued by the scientific community—for example, indigenous knowledge—or because it is the product of persons working outside the "normal" scientific system—for example, nonprofit or advocacy organizations. Even if there is no impending disaster, there are many problems, such as global warming and ozone depletion, where the windows of opportunity are narrowing and action would best be taken now, based on the best available information. Prudence may be more important than certitude. As has been observed, "it is better to be approximately right, than precisely wrong."

Nothing stated above should be taken to suggest that science—particularly a new, issue-driven science—does not have a critical role to play in policy, for it does. Such a science will not only ask the traditional questions—what do we need to know?—but will also recognize the limits of our capacity to know and to manage something as complex as the biosphere and human behavior. As such, it will also seek to minimize what harm we might do.

Here we list only a few of the important ways in which science can contribute to the solution of environmental problems; others easily may be added.

*Early warning systems* need to be developed to identify environmental problems before they become severe. The work of early researchers on global warming and the ozone hole are good examples, although the initial cool reception of their work underscores the problems of researchers who are ahead of their colleagues. Attention should also be directed to the development of "vital signs" that can signal issues on the horizon. What constitutes appropriate measures of real change is a key issue.

*Technology assessment* needs to be developed in order to better understand the anticipated and unanticipated political, social, economic, cultural, and ecological consequences of technological development over the short, medium, and long term. Technologies tend to develop more quickly than does our ability or motivation to question their appropriateness or desirability. Today's problems are all too often yesterday's solutions.

*Research for ameliorating the consequences of environmental assaults and developing benign technologies to restore natural systems* is of high priority, particularly research using nature as its model. Todd's (1988) work on solar aquatic treatment of wastewater, discussed in Essay 16A, is a good example. By imitating the way nature cleans dirty water—using various life-forms that ingest the organic material in sewage—Todd's system purifies municipal wastewater and sewage without using chemicals and without creating significant amounts of hazardous sludge products. The system also requires considerably less energy and money than conventional treatment facilities.

*Psychological and organizational research* is necessary to understand how to encourage needed environmental behavioral change in individuals and institutions. More information and changes in values and attitudes are important, but are not sufficient for behavior change. How can changes in consumption patterns be encouraged? Why does it take us so long to adjust to the inevitable global limitations that face us?

*Agroecological and farming systems research* is needed to assist farmers in the different climatic zones who wish to make the transition to a sustainable agriculture that is also economically viable and helps to revitalize rural communities.

*Conceptualization and implementation of an "ecological economics"* that will marry ecology and the economy, taking into account nature as resource and as sink. Among the issues of importance are the development of socio-economic-ecological accounting systems that combine qualitative and quantitative measures.

## Conclusions

Moving from the elegance of science in its traditional and normal form to the messy world of politics, policy, program, and management is difficult for many. Not all conservation biologists need to be working in the trenches of policy. All, however, should be aware of policy needs and of the relationships of policy and science that we have tried to lay out here. Scientists have dual roles as scientists and citizens. Their goal should be not only to create knowledge, but to see that the knowledge is used to protect the very subjects of their study, the species and ecosystems of the world.

Some conservation biologists in university settings will take personal risks to their careers to make the leap. This is an unfortunate necessity, given the status of many of the institutions that we have discussed. We can hope that many institutions will begin processes of change: to train people differently (and better) for policy purposes, and to encourage, or at least recognize as equally valid, the needs of relevance and elegance.

The world of policy presents a real challenge to the conservation biologist. It requires incorporating in greater detail than would otherwise be the case the nature of other human systems as they are affected by and affect the ecosystems that are at the heart of conservation biology. Individually, the ecosystem and the human system are each extraordinarily complex; any effort to combine the two into one system is daunting. If we accept the limits of our knowledge, and as a result the limits of our capacity to "manage the planet," if we become more comfortable with uncertainty and are willing to assess our actions in order to avoid harm as best we can, then there is yet hope for us all.

## Summary

If conservation biology is to be successful in its ultimate mission of biodiversity protection, its concepts and models must be transformed into rational policies that reflect our knowledge of human influences on the natural world. This transformation is the realm of institutions and policymaking.

The principles of humility, precaution, and reversibility should guide policymaking with respect to the environment. This requires new ways of defining problems, and changes in the way many institutions conduct business. The fact that the status quo is not working toward improved environments for humans or most other species on earth is a strong argument for change.

A number of institutions have direct bearing on our ultimate success or failure at conservation of biodiversity. These include educational institutions, governments at all levels, NGOs, businesses, consumers, legal institutions, religious institutions, and the media. All can contribute in various ways to promotion of reasonable conservation progress, or can impede that progress to the detriment of all. The policymaking process presents numerous challenges for conservation biology. These challenges include defining appropriate and useful environmental research programs, using broad information bases to define environmental issues and research agendas, understanding the policy process, and developing an issue-driven science to provide better input to policy. The world of policy and institutions can be messy, but it is critical that conservation biologists participate in it. If they do not, the decisions that most affect conservation will be made by those perhaps least qualified to do so. The creation of conservation knowledge will only be of real utility when it is transformed into policy action.

## Questions for Discussion

1. In what ways do you feel that your training in conservation biology—including this text—could be better organized to increase your opportunities to contribute to public policy now and in the future?

2. Who defines the priorities, sets the agendas, and frames the problems for research? What, for example, are the sources of funding for research at your university, and how might they influence the nature of the research being done?

3. How does scientific research and scientific knowledge influence policy?

4. What alternative structures might provide a firmer base of science for public policy?

5. How can we balance the need for objective science and the need for subjective judgment in the policy process?

6. In determining the most important issues for scientific research for policy, who speaks for nature? Who are the surrogate stakeholders for nature? Who speaks for future generations? Who are their stakeholders?

7. How do stakeholders become a part of the process of identifying research needs and using research results? How can a better balance be achieved between the research needs perceived by researchers and by the public?

8. What changes in policies, practices, and institutions are needed to conserve biodiversity and sustain humanity? What new institutions and systems are needed?

9. What is your vision of a sustainable future that preserves ecological integrity while enhancing economic security and democracy?

10. Is conservation biology an issue-driven science?

## Suggestions for Further Reading

Benedict, R. 1991. *Ozone Diplomacy: New Directions in Safeguarding the Planet.* Harvard University Press, Cambridge, MA. The author, chief United States negotiator of the Montreal Protocol on Substances that Deplete the Ozone Layer, combines science, politics, economics, and diplomacy in his portrayal of how the agreement came to be accepted.

Carnegie Commission on Science, Technology, and Government, Task Force on Environment and Energy. (n.d.) *E³: Organizing for Environment, Energy, and the Economy in the Executive Branch of the U.S. Government.* The Carnegie Commission, New York. One of a series of reports from a high-level commission emphasizing the needs for research for policy and suggesting mechanisms to increase its utilization.

Funtowicz, S. O. and J. R. Ravetz. 1990. *Uncertainty and Quality in Science for Policy.* Kluwer, Dordrecht, Netherlands. In response to the need for a method of expressing judgments of uncertainty and quality in science for policy, the authors present a notational system that is convenient, robust, and nuanced.

Ludwig, D., R. Hilborn and C. Winters. 1993. Uncertainty, resource exploitation, and conservation: Lessons from history. *Science* 260:17. The title tells it all in this critique of the status quo of resource exploitation.

National Research Council, Commission on Life Sciences, Committee on Environmental Research. 1993. *Research to Protect, Restore, and Manage the Environment.* National Academy Press, Washington, D.C. A review of federal support for research on the environment, and a proposal for reorganizing the research effort to make it more effective in supporting policy. It tends to focus more on what scientists have to offer than what the policy process needs, being insufficiently critical of what does not work.

Rubin, E. S., L. B. Lave and M. G. Morgan. 1992. *Keeping Climate Research Relevant.* Issues in Science and Technology, VIII, no. 2. A serious critique of federal support for research on acid rain and its failure to provide policy-relevant information in a timely fashion.

# 17

# Sustainable Development Case Studies

*The first step toward a sustainable human future must be to break the grip that the growth myth retains on our thinking and institutions. Growth-centered development is itself inherently unsustainable. Sustainability does not depend on ending human progress, only on abandoning the myth that erroneously equates such progress with growth.*

*David C. Korten, 1991–1992*

In the 1980s, the concept of **sustainable development** emerged as the means by which biodiversity and natural ecosystems would be saved while enabling humanity to continue to prosper. The concept was first promoted by the *World Conservation Strategy* (IUCN/UNEP/WWF 1980), a global conservation blueprint that grew from the United Nations Conference on the Human Environment, held in Stockholm in 1972. This was followed by *Our Common Future*, the so-called Brundtland Commission Report (World Commission on Environment and Development 1987), a document adopted by many governments and global institutions as a guide to environmentally compatible development. Its most recent successor is *Caring for the Earth: A Strategy for Sustainable Living* (IUCN/UNEP/WWF 1991). All of these documents promote sustainable development as a reasoned means of balancing the demands of nature and people.

But what exactly is sustainable development? Does it mean the same thing to everyone? Is it a legitimate alternative to continued outright destruction of nature? Does it hold the answer to the many conservation problems faced today and in the future? These and many other questions surround sustainable development, and many remain unanswered.

Sustainable development has been defined in various ways. The earlier reports, the *World Conservation Strategy* and the Brundtland Commission report, were anthropocentric: they largely focused on human aspirations and well-being, with the natural environment providing the means by which this was to be accomplished (Robinson 1993). For example, the concept of development used in the *World Conservation Strategy* emphasized that we should "satisfy human needs and improve the quality of human life" (quotes taken from Robinson 1993). Conservation of biodiversity would ensure that we "yield the greatest sustainable development to present generations while maintaining its potential to meet the needs and aspirations of future generations." The Brundtland Commission report of 1987 modified this only slightly to define sustainable development as that which "seeks to meet the needs and aspirations of the present without compromising the ability to meet those of the future." Finally, the most recent global document, *Caring for the Earth*, defines sustainable development as "improving the quality of human life while living within the carrying capacity of supporting ecosystems."

In all of these cases sustainable development is defined entirely around one species, *Homo sapiens*, and promotes continued economic prosperity. All of these definitions are utilitarian—they perceive the environment as merely the means to an end (human happiness), rather than having inherent good apart from human gain. The definitions do not promote biological diversity other than as a means toward human happiness and well-being. This is perhaps not surprising, since humans wrote these definitions. However, the definitions may not go far enough in recognizing the extraordinary complexities of nature and the diversity of life-forms, in addition to the services they provide to humanity. They also tend not to recognize the fundamental, underlying problems that create a need for sustainability in the first place. For example, Korten (1991–1992) observed that "The [Brundtland] report's key recommendations—a call for the world's economic growth to rise to a level five to ten times the current output and for accelerated growth in the industrial countries to stimulate demand for the products of poor countries—fundamentally contradicted its own analysis that growth and overconsumption are root causes of the problem. Where ecological reality conflicted with perceived political feasibility, the latter prevailed."

Obviously, human population growth and inequitable environmental demands must both be addressed in a realistic definition. Perhaps a more enlightened definition of sustainable development was offered by Viederman (1992):

> A sustainable society is one that ensures the health and vitality of human life and culture *and* of nature's capital, for present and future generations. Such a society acts to *stop* the activities that serve to destroy human life and culture and nature's capital, and to encourage those activities that serve to *conserve* what exists, *restore* what has been damaged, and *prevent* future harm.

In this case, although humanity still takes center stage, as perhaps it should in a definition of development, it more broadly recognizes the role and rights of the remainder of the world and places limits on human activities relative to that world. We offer a definition of sustainable development that goes even further, and also acknowledges the inherent worth of biodiversity apart from its benefits to humanity. Thus, we define truly sustainable development as *human activities conducted in a manner that respects the intrinsic value of the natural world, the role of the natural world in human well-being, and the need for humans to live on the income from nature's capital rather than on the capital itself.*

There is a most critical distinction to be made between sustainable *growth* and sustainable *development*. Growth is a *quantitative* increase in the size of a system; development is a *qualitative* change in its complexity and configuration. An economic, social, political, or biophysical system can develop without growing, and thus can be sustainable. It can also grow in size without developing or maturing; this is *not* sustainable development. "Sustainable growth" is a self-contradictory term—an oxymoron. Continued, indefinite growth on this planet or any subset of the planet is a physical impossibility.

Eventually, limits of some type (space, food, waste disposal, energy) must be reached; the point at which that will happen is the only aspect open to debate. "Sustainable *development*," however, is the issue of concern. Can we make *qualitative* changes in complexity and configuration within existing human systems that do not place increasing *quantitative* demands on natural systems, and are in fact compatible with their continued existence?

If we are to attain such a goal, we must first understand the patterns of human behavior and desires that brought us to this crisis in the first place. These have been outlined by Viederman (1992), from whom we borrow and modify:

1. We have consistently failed to accept the fact that the economic system is an open system in a finite biosphere. The economic system is not a closed system, separate from the biosphere, as most traditional economists would have us believe (see Essay 15A); it requires inputs from and exports to living ecosystems, which impose real limits at both ends. Additionally, much of our attention has focused on resource constraints and substitutability, rather than sink constraints—the disposal of wastes.

2. We have consistently failed to recognize that the environment is the basis for all life, including our own, and all production. The natural world should not be merely another special interest competing for our attention, but the playing field upon which all interests compete (recall the "ecological theater" of Chapter 1).

3. We have continued to exhibit a disdain for nature, and a belief that we can master and control it (called by Ehrenfeld [1981] the "arrogance of humanism").

4. We do not question our uncritical acceptance of technology as the answer to all problems, despite a multitude of examples of today's problems being yesterday's solutions. This "techno-arrogance" (Meffe 1992) results in a disdain for the "natural" and a love of the "technical."

5. We have not distinguished between growth and development, perhaps due to our belief in technology as savior. Likewise, we fail to recognize that growth will not automatically lead to equity and justice within and among nations; that is, an "economic trickle down" effect is unlikely and unfair, and simply an excuse for a few to amass personal wealth at the expense of many.

6. We mistakenly have placed our faith in market systems as the principal mechanism for realizing social goods, such as economic sustainability and justice. Yet, in its failure to value nature's capital or human health, the market system has failed to deal adequately with that which we seek to protect: human life and culture, and nature's capital.

7. We have failed to consider the needs of, and our obligations to, future generations. This must be at the core of any conceptualization of sustainability.

These "sources of unsustainability" as Viederman calls them, help to explain how we have arrived at the precarious position we occupy today. They also imply that changes are needed in each of these areas to attain sustainability for the good of humanity and the natural world. Viederman (1992) guides us further by providing seven *principles of sustainability*:

1. Nature should be understood to be an irreplaceable source of knowledge, from which we can learn potential solutions to some of our problems.

2. We should understand that issues of environmental deterioration and human oppression and violence are linked in analysis and action. Gender and racial oppression, and efforts to dominate nature have a common root.
3. Humility must guide our actions. Good stewardship begins with restraint.
4. We must appreciate the importance of "proper scale." Place and locality are the foundation for all durable economies, and must be the starting point of action to deal with our problems. Solutions are local and scale-dependent.
5. Sufficiency must replace economic efficiency. The earth is finite, and that fact must be accepted in order for humanity to adopt limits. Living within our needs on a planetary scale does not mean a life of sacrifice, but of greater fulfillment. We must distinguish between "needs" and "wants."
6. Community is essential for survival. The "global community" should reflect and encourage diversity while being interdependent.
7. Biological and cultural diversity must be preserved, defended, and encouraged.

With these guidelines setting up the basis of sustainable development, we will examine six case studies of potential sustainability. They will illustrate the principles and problems discussed thus far, and show the complexities inherent in managing interacting systems of humans and nature. We say "potential" sustainability because none of these have yet been proven in the long term, as none have existed for very long. All offer some promise of maintaining natural systems while satisfying human needs, if properly managed. Afterward, we will offer some cautionary comments and alternative perspectives on sustainable development.

## CASE STUDY 1

### Sustainable Tropical Forestry

Gary S. Hartshorn, World Wildlife Fund

*Limited sustainable use of tropical forests can be carried out if the natural dynamics of the particular forest under consideration are well understood, and if local people are included in the planning and have a stake in successful management.*

Despite growing national and global concerns about tropical deforestation, forests still dominate landscapes over much of the humid lowland tropics. For example, most of the forest-rich countries have more than one-third of their national territory still in forest cover (Table 17.1). Just ten countries account for 70% of our planet's remaining tropical forests, covering an area about the size of the United States. Yet, global loss of tropical forests continues at an ever-increasing rate; an area of tropical forest the size of the state of South Carolina was lost in 1992 (WRI 1992).

Many countries rich in tropical forests have made significant efforts to create a national system of protected areas. However, few forest-rich countries have exceeded the IUCN recommendation of a minimum of 10% of the country in protected areas (WRI 1992; Dinerstein and Wikramanayake 1993). Unprotected forests are usually available for development, but traditional de-

**Table 17.1**
Status of Tropical Forests in Ten Forest-Rich Countries

| Rank | Country | Remaining forests (km²) | Percent cover | Annual loss (km²) | Percent loss/yr |
|------|---------|------------------------|---------------|-------------------|-----------------|
| 1 | Brazil | 3,560,200 | 42 | 13,800 | 0.5 |
| 2 | Zaire | 1,039,300 | 44 | 1,820 | 0.2 |
| 3 | Indonesia | 1,038,950 | 69 | 10,000 | 0.5 |
| 4 | Peru | 669,800 | 52 | 2,700 | 0.4 |
| 5 | India | 513,610 | 16 | 480 | 0.3 |
| 6 | Bolivia | 431,400 | 41 | 870 | 0.2 |
| 7 | Colombia | 382,000 | 33 | 8,200 | 1.8 |
| 8 | Mexico | 362,500 | 18 | 10,000 | 1.3 |
| 9 | Venezuela | 306,200 | 34 | 1,250 | 0.4 |
| 10 | Myanmar | 259,410 | 38 | 6,000 | 0.2 |

From data recalculated from WRI 1992.

velopment is virtually synonymous with deforestation. Without major progress in the sustainable use of tropical forests, it is unlikely that unprotected or unmanaged forests will survive well into the 21st century. Thus, the challenge of finding and testing techniques for using tropical forests economically and sustainably, without destroying their ecological functions and the millions of species they harbor, is not only enormous, but extremely urgent. We do not have the luxury of conducting a decade or two of experimental research before recommending how to sustainably use tropical forests.

## Theoretical Basis for Tropical Forest Management

While conducting field research on the demography of a dominant tropical tree species in Costa Rica in the early 1970s, I noticed a high incidence of large canopy trees falling and creating gaps in the old-growth canopy. Having read the classic literature on the antiquity and extreme stability of tropical forests, the slow growth rates of most tropical trees, and the dearth of natural regeneration, I feared that my study forest was literally collapsing. However, my own monitoring of tree-fall frequency and of the rebuilding of forest structure in gaps led to the revisionist conclusion that this tropical forest was extremely dynamic (Hartshorn 1978). Other studies at several sites caused a surprising change in our thinking about tropical forests, revealing that canopy gaps are important foci for natural regeneration and rebuilding of these very dynamic forests. Detailed observations of hundreds of tree species in the La Selva old-growth forest in Costa Rica indicated that about 50% of the native tree species are dependent on gaps for successful regeneration (Hartshorn 1980).

The frequent occurrence of gaps in the forest canopy due to tree-falls and the surprisingly high number of species dependent on gaps for successful regeneration support the intermediate disturbance theory of community diversity (see Figure 10.3). Just as has been shown for the marine intertidal zone, frequent disturbance in tropical forests prevents competitive exclusion of many species by the actual or putative dominant species. In pragmatic terms, tree species dependent on gaps in the forest canopy are able to grow rapidly and close the gap from beneath (Pickett 1983; Brokaw 1985; Uhl et al. 1988). When these gap species attain the canopy (in as short a period as 10–20 years) they may become reproductive long before slower-growing, shade-tolerant tree species can reach the canopy.

Such gap-phase or patch dynamics are also important to other groups or guilds of species, as well as to overall community functions. For example, shade-intolerant understory plants commonly colonize forest gaps and provide a patchy nectar source for hummingbirds. Young gap-phase forest patches also attract mixed-species flocks of insectivorous birds characteristic of the primary forest understory. Even more intriguing is the strong fidelity of some flightless grasshoppers to young gaps in the primary forest (Braker 1991). It is clear that undisturbed old-growth tropical forest is extremely dynamic due to the high frequency of tree-falls and the rapid rebuilding of forest structure. These dynamic processes create a heterogeneous community that is patchy in time as well as space. The stochastic occurrence of intermediate levels of disturbance in tropical forests is a key reason for the persistence of their very high levels of biotic diversity (Hartshorn 1980; Menges 1992).

As concerns about tropical deforestation gained momentum in the 1970s, there was a growing frustration that forest management offered little hope for the survival of tropical forests. The primary ecological bases for this perception were the almost universal failures to obtain acceptable natural regeneration of commercial species and the extremely slow growth rates of most tropical trees. A key element of these failures was the narrow focus on just a few of the most valuable and preferred timber species, such as the mahoganies, ebonies, and rosewoods.

The serendipitous presentation of four key papers at a 1976 symposium (Ashton 1978; Hartshorn 1978; Oldeman 1978; Whitmore 1978) opened the door to visionary thinking about tropical forest dynamics. It occurred to me that a cause of poor natural regeneration could be that a single tree-fall gap might not be large enough to promote seedling establishment or juvenile growth of the preferred species. Furthermore, the high tree species richness of most tropical forests may drastically reduce the probabilities of successful seedling establishment under stochastic ecological processes. I thus proposed simulating gap-phase dynamics by creating long, narrow strip clearcuts as a forest management technique (Hartshorn 1979, 1981, 1989).

### Yánesha Forestry Cooperative: The Palcazú Project

The strip-cut technique of tropical forest management has been pioneered by the Yánesha Forestry Cooperative (COFYAL) in the Central Selva region of Peruvian Amazonia. With major funding from the U.S. Agency for International Development (USAID), the Palcazú Project was initially designed as a typical rural development project based on agricultural colonization of the forest, facilitated by construction of a road into the Palcazú Valley. Because of U.S. Congress regulations in the Foreign Assistance Act, USAID was required to do an environmental assessment of the proposed development project before signing a loan agreement with the Peruvian government. That comprehensive, multidisciplinary assessment stated in very clear terms that agricultural development of the Palcazú Valley would fail due to excessively high rainfall (ca. 7000 mm/yr) and infertile soils.

I concluded that production forestry was the only viable development option for the valley and recommended that the strip-cut technique be tested as a forest management model. A companion social-soundness analysis of the proposed project noted that the project area's human population was about 60% Amuesha Indians, a small tribe of Arawakan Indians now largely confined to the Palcazú Valley. As a consequence of these environmental and social assessments, USAID required the Peruvian government to officially recognize and legally title all Amuesha native community lands in the Palcazú Valley as a condition for disbursement of funds; this was necessary because typically, Indians in Peru do not hold title to their lands. Eleven native communities' land claims were accepted in the central and southern sectors of the lower Palcazú Valley (300–500 m elevation).

It took two years of technical assistance and political advocacy to create the Yánesha Forestry Cooperative, founded by five native communities and 70 individual Amuesha Indians. COFYAL is the first Indian forestry cooperative in South America. Its objectives are: (1) to provide a source of employment for members of the native communities; (2) to manage the communities' natural forests for sustained yield of forest products; and (3) to protect the cultural integrity of the Yánesha (Amuesha) people. Though political strife in Peru has occasionally disrupted or slowed COFYAL activities, the cooperative has grown in its number of native community and individual members, including women.

Strip cuts are the cornerstone of the COFYAL management system for production forestry (Figure 17.1). Commercial strips are 30–40 m wide (about 10–15 m wider than the diameter of an average tree-fall gap) and of variable length depending on topography and logistics; in practice, strips are usually in the range of 100–300 m long. In contrast to traditional forest felling, in which only the largest trees are felled and land on top of standing smaller trees, strip cutting begins with a machete cleaning of the understory (all stems smaller than 5 cm). Harvesting begins with small pole-sized stems and proceeds through ever-larger trees. Each cut tree is immediately delimbed and hauled off the strip, so worker and oxen mobility on the strip is not seriously impeded by the crowns of felled trees.

COFYAL technicians classify forest that is suitable for timber management and identify the size and boundary of each production stand, including the location of all strips, hauling roads, and areas to be excluded from harvesting—such as steep slopes, streamside buffer areas, and swampy lands. Once all the strips to be harvested are determined and located on the ground, the harvesting cycles and sequence are assigned to maximize the persistence of mature or advanced regrowth forest bordering any recently harvested strip. For example, a four-cycle spatial harvesting sequence of strips is . . . |1|3|2|4|1| . . . , while a six-cycle harvest sequence is . . .

**Figure 17.1** A demonstration strip in Peru 6 months after cutting. Note the intact adjacent forest and lack of erosion at the strip site. (Photograph by Gary S. Hartshorn.)

**Figure 17.2**  A strip-cut site after 28 months of regeneration. Note the size of saplings and the presence of a thick herbaceous layer. (Photograph by Gary S. Hartshorn.)

|1|3|5|2|4|6|1| . . . . In either repetitive series, all parallel strips of the same number are harvested before cutting strips of the next higher number. Depending on the size of the production stand, it may take 6–10 years to complete one cycle of strip cuts. We are projecting a 30–40-year rotation between harvesting any given strip. Again, this surgical insertion of a narrow strip in the matrix of forest is fundamentally different from the classic advancement of the agricultural frontier that cuts entire patches of forest to create ever-larger treeless fields or pastures.

The principal ecological purpose of strip-cutting in tropical forests is to promote natural regeneration of native tree species. Detailed inventories of natural regeneration of trees on two demonstration strips cut in 1985 (Figure 17.2) indicate superb regeneration and growth of hundreds of tree species (Hartshorn 1988, 1989; Hartshorn and Pariona 1993). Because harvested strips are not burned or used for agricultural crops, about 13% of the trees regenerating in a strip are exclusively from stump sprouts and the rest are from natural seed germination, stump sprouts, or both. The high tree species richness on the regenerating strips includes many individuals of the valuable heavy hardwoods, which are purportedly slow-growing. However, silvicultural interventions occur every 3–5 years to control aggressive, sun-loving lianas and to reduce competition among trees. If COFYAL members prefer to enrich a strip with a highly preferred tree or to favor particular individuals in the regenerating strip, these silvicultural treatments are acceptable.

COFYAL has a timber processing complex on land ceded to the cooperative by the Shiringamazú native community. Timber processing facilities include a sawmill with a small bandsaw and a portable circular saw, a portable steel kiln for converting scrap wood to charcoal, and a network of 44 PresCaps® that fit over the butt ends of logs (5–30 cm diameter) and use hydraulic pressure to replace the sap with chemicals for preserving posts and poles (Figure 17.3).

Local processing of wood enables COFYAL to harvest most of the timber on a strip cut, averaging 250 m$^3$/ha. The pole preservation facility uses trees normally too small for sawmilling. Local production of sawn wood enables COFYAL to market many more species of trees than would be acceptable as logs at national sawmills; some of the woods are of sufficiently high quality

**Figure 17.3** The pole preservation facility of the Yánesha Forestry Cooperative (COYFAL). Here, wood from the areas that were strip-cut is made into finished products, providing further employment to local citizens. (Photograph by Gary S. Hartshorn.)

that COFYAL exports modest quantities to specialty markets such as musical instrument makers and wood artisans in the United States and the United Kingdom. Sales of processed wood brought in $30,000 (U.S.) in 1991. Profits were distributed to community and individual members, who used the cash to build schools and health posts, hire resident teachers, and improve housing.

Appropriate technologies are used by COFYAL wherever they are cost-effective and environmentally sound. For example, oxen are used to extract logs from the strip cuts. Though slower from a volume production perspective, oxen logging does far less damage to the fragile forest soil than does heavy machinery such as skidders, bulldozers, or tractors. Oxen drag the logs to a patio at the end of a strip along a graveled road, where a flatbed truck or tractor and wagon haul logs to the processing center. Where logistically feasible, a winch mounted on a truck is used to extract logs from the proximal part of a strip cut.

The strip-cut model for tropical forest management is being tested in other countries, including Bolivia, Costa Rica, and Ecuador. Preliminary observations indicate that, as in the Palcazú Valley, narrow strip cuts promote outstanding natural regeneration of native tree species. Thus, the strip-cut model appears to be an increasingly robust technique for sound ecological management of complex tropical forests. In the race to find ways and techniques to use tropical forests without destroying them, many more projects like COFYAL must be tested and expanded to larger commercial scales.

As has been amply demonstrated by the COFYAL project, however, it is not sufficient just to have an environmentally sound management system. Sustainable development must also be integrated across disciplines. Unless these initiatives and projects are economically viable, socially responsible, politically acceptable, and ecologically sound, they have little chance of being sustainable, but more likely will be added to the long list of failed development projects. Tropical forests *can* be managed on a sustained-yield basis for timber or non-timber forest products, while protecting biotic habitats and ecological services, generating adequate economic returns to local communities, promoting local well-being, and providing politically acceptable models for sustainable development.

## CASE STUDY 2

# Costa Rica's INBio: Collaborative Biodiversity Research Agreements with the Pharmaceutical Industry

Ana Sittenfeld and Renata Villers
Instituto Nacional de Biodiversidad, Costa Rica

*Sustainability can arise from better understanding of local or regional biodiversity resources and their value to humanity at large. These resources are becoming better appreciated by drug companies and other industries, who are beginning to pay for the rights to use natural products found in developing countries. Such moneys are being turned back into conservation of these biotic resources, thereby sustaining them in the long term.*

Located in Central America on a narrow land bridge between South and North America, Costa Rica has a varied topography and climate and contains some of the world's richest biodiversity for its small size (Wille 1991). Some 4% of the world's terrestrial species can be found within the country's 51,000-km$^2$ territory, smaller than the state of West Virginia. Between 1966 and 1989 some 28% of Costa Rica's forests were removed (Repetto 1992). However, concerned for the survival of its natural resources, social and political forces within the country succeeded in also setting aside more than 25% of the country's territory over two decades in an integrated system of protected government and private conserved wild lands (Janzen and INBio 1992).

The sociopolitical climate of Costa Rica has contributed to the country's favorable climate for biological exploration and conservation. Since the elimination of the country's army in 1949, Costa Rica has enjoyed a stable society with high standards of health and education, conducive to developing an ambitious national biodiversity conservation project. Even though the country has made considerable progress in protecting large in situ areas of biological diversity, the remaining challenge is to put these resources to work for society and to contribute to their own upkeep costs.

### Costa Rica's National Institute of Biodiversity (INBio)

INBio (Instituto Nacional de Biodiversidad), established in 1989, is located in Santo Domingo, Heredia, Costa Rica. It operates on the philosophy that, unless wild biodiversity can be made economically and intellectually valuable, society is unlikely to continue to pay its high maintenance costs and resist the political pressures that lead to its destruction. To put this philosophy into practice INBio is conducting a national biodiversity inventory. In addition to its wide array of programs related to intellectual uses of biodiversity (such as education and science), INBio is working with major pharmaceutical and other industry participants, along with universities and independent research organizations, to collaboratively explore and conserve the tremendous biological wealth of Costa Rica. Although INBio enjoys collaborative agreements with major research centers and universities, we focus this case study on INBio's pioneering efforts to explore and conserve biodiversity in collaboration with the pharmaceutical industry.

INBio's collaborative research agreements with the pharmaceutical industry reverse a centuries-old tradition of the industry freely extracting raw plant and animal material from tropical countries for shipment to laboratories and companies in the North, with no economic return to the country of origin. Instead, these agreements call for adding value to biological materials by generating knowledge about their ecology and taxonomy, and for carrying out some processing and research inside Costa Rica. Agreements are typically structured with direct fees for services (sample collection, processing, identification, resupply) and funding for direct conservation activities, including national park maintenance funds, as well as royalty payments to conservation if commercialization is successful.

The National Biodiversity Inventory (NBI), expected to take 10 years and cost over $70 million (1992 dollars) is intended to encompass all major taxa and will involve broad national and international participation. With an estimated half million wild species to inventory, the NBI Division at INBio will determine the identity and distribution of species, begin to accumulate data on their biology and ecology, and assure that they are correctly identified, so that Costa Rica can begin to use its biodiversity in a systematic and sustainable fashion.

Given the country's lack of trained taxonomists, INBio pioneered the "parataxonomist" concept to carry out its inventory. Parataxonomists are individuals drawn from local communities and rural branches of government who receive an initial six-month intensive training course run by INBio, with follow-up courses (Figure 17.4). This training provides them with the basics in biology, taxonomy, and fieldwork. Subsequently they assume paid positions to carry out the important work of collecting and initial cataloging of tens of thousands of species.

**Figure 17.4**  An INBio parataxonomist collecting plants in the field. (Photograph courtesy of INBio.)

Working out of 28 biodiversity field offices within the conservation areas around the country, the parataxonomists work with a team of Costa Rican specimen and information curators at INBio, as well as in collaboration with a network of international specialists (Figure 17.5). Specimens and other field data flow into INBio, where information is recorded in INBio's growing biodiversity computer data bases and processed into the collections of the National Biodiversity Inventory with the collaboration of an international network of taxonomists. All information on the identities, geographic distributions, and natural history of species is in the public domain.

To facilitate management and manipulation of the accumulating data bases of species and conservation information, INBio is collaborating with the Intergraph Corporation, a world leader in computer-aided graphics, to jointly design and develop a computerized Biodiversity Management Information System capable of handling traditional Geographic Information Systems, text, and numbers. The design and management of this new system is the task of the recently formed Division of Biodiversity Information Management at INBio. The Institute is also in the process of making its biodiversity information available to a larger cross-section of society within and outside Costa Rica through the newly established Division of Biodiversity Information Distribution.

## Biodiversity Prospecting

Biodiversity prospecting, a critical component of INBio's overall biodiversity conservation strategy, is the systematic search for, and development of, new sources of chemical compounds, genes, micro- and macroorganisms, and other economically valuable products from nature (Eisner 1989; Sittenfeld and Villers 1993). The dual objectives of INBio's Biodiversity Prospecting Division are to generate income in support of the country's conservation activities and to promote the country's sustainable economic development by facilitating biodiversity-intensive, market-driven research and development, with results capable of being transferred to the private and other sectors. To achieve these objectives, INBio enters into collaborative research agreements

**Figure 17.5**  An INBio curator at work at a microscope, identifying species collected in the field. (Photograph courtesy of INBio.)

with universities, research organizations, industry, and appropriate governmental agencies inside and outside the country in order to combine INBio's inventory knowledge and collection abilities with their skills to transform wild species into valuable tools for research and industry.

**Pharmaceutical Collaborative Research**

An estimated 25% of all U.S. prescription drugs are said to contain at least one compound derived from plants alone (Principe 1991). If microorganisms from environmental samples were added, the percentage would be much higher. Despite the relative importance of these natural sources of leading drug compounds, natural products research poses many challenges (Principe 1991), including: (1) difficulty in re-collecting the same material earlier supplied; (2) difficulty in obtaining the same biological activity as the first time from a species that is re-collected; and (3) difficulty with structural elucidation and synthesis of the molecules found in nature, which tend to be more complex than artificial ones. Given these inherent problems, many drug companies chose to get out of natural products research in the 1970s and 1980s, imagining that synthetic compounds and rational drug design could replace the need for testing materials from nature.

In the 1990s, major technological advances in drug screening techniques and improved biological knowledge have created a resurgence of interest in drugs derived from nature (Bull et al. 1992; Sittenfeld and Villers 1993). Improved biochemical isolation and characterization techniques are making natural drug research more productive (Fox 1991; Steele and Stowers 1991). Coupled with these improvements in screening technology is the recognition that humanity's ability to replicate the chemical diversity of nature through synthetic compounds is limited. In contrast to programs that begin with screening of synthetic compounds, natural products screening offers templates from nature for the subsequent development and optimization of drug candidates, even though the resultant drug compounds are typically synthetic. For all of these reasons, the pharmaceutical industry as a whole is returning to natural products as a source of promising drug leads (McAllister 1991).

INBio's approach to exploring and conserving biological diversity differs substantially from traditional materials collection and supply agreements. By linking systematic biological inventories and prospecting to sustainable development, INBio is able to offer a higher level of security in the resupply of biological materials for research, while returning funds to contribute to the long-term conservation of the same resources. Following a positive test result, INBio can return to its data bases for information on the location, time of year, and ecological conditions under which the initial sample was found, thereby introducing more security into the drug discovery process. Taxonomically driven data searches can also be conducted to reveal other species of the same taxonomic group that may contain similar or more powerful biological or chemical properties of interest.

Nevertheless, the road to discovery and development of commercial drugs is long and hard (Vagelos 1991). The ratio of synthetic compounds explored to final drug compounds approved—the "hit ratio"—has been conservatively placed at one in ten thousand (Stix 1993). For natural products in which one plant or insect extract represents over a hundred compounds, the figures are expected to be better. However, meaningful estimation of hit ratios for natural products is difficult given recent changes in technology and the development of institutions like INBio that offer greater biochemical diversity with better chances of resupply than available in the past. Average financial costs for the development of one successful commercial drug have been estimated at $231 million (1987 dollars) with an average time interval from discovery to market approval of 12 years (DiMasi et al. 1991). For their effort, drug companies have achieved up to $1 billion in sales for break-through drugs, but much less for average drugs (Goldberg et al. 1992).

## The INBio/Merck Agreement

In the first such agreement of its kind, INBio sought and gained a $1 million collaborative agreement with Merck & Co. (Roberts 1992; Blum 1993). According to the terms of the initial two-year agreement (renewable at the discretion of both parties) Merck will receive from INBio a limited number of well-identified and documented environmental samples (plant and insect extracts) for use in its drug discovery process (Hiebert 1993). INBio has agreed not to provide these samples to any other organization for use in health or agricultural screening during this two-year period of initial evaluation, in order to give Merck an opportunity to study them. All samples come from national parks or other kinds of conservation areas.

To assist INBio in assuring the quality of the materials it supplies, Merck helped to establish an extraction lab within the University of Costa Rica and donated the equipment needed. The project also benefits from the involvement of Costa Rican University scientists, some of whom will receive training in Merck's laboratories. As part of the compensation for the materials, services, and scientific know-how provided by INBio, 10% of the company's million dollar payment has been donated by INBio to the Costa Rican National Park Fund to help defray the direct costs of biodiversity upkeep. The remainder supports the in-country science and processing infrastructure that produces the samples and continues the biodiversity inventory for all kinds of users. If there is commercialization, then under the contract INBio signed with the Costa Rican Ministry of Natural Resources, Energy, and Mines, 50% of the royalties will go to the Costa Rican national system of conservation areas, and the remainder will be used to continue the INBio process.

## Future Challenges

As INBio moves forward with the pharmaceutical industry to collaboratively explore and conserve Costa Rican biodiversity, it faces a number of pointed challenges. Principal among these are the need to manage public expectations regarding drug research results, the need to find funding for ongoing conservation activities within INBio and the conservation areas themselves, and the need to recognize that wild biodiversity must become a sustainable generator of income if it is to survive.

As the president of one small pharmaceutical company put it: "If you read the popular press and listen to what is being said by enthusiastic conservationists, you would think that drugs grow on trees in the rainforest, just waiting for pharmaceutical companies to come and pluck them off." Both INBio and Merck know that it will be many years before drug compounds can be found and receive marketing approval. No one at either organization expects drug results within the initial two-year agreement period, but this is the amount of time that both organizations need to learn how to optimally collaborate. With all of the public interest the agreement has generated, both organizations are concerned that without early discoveries, the public may well lose its enthusiasm and retract some of its support for needed long-term efforts to conserve tropical biodiversity.

Obtaining funding for conservation activities also presents a challenge for INBio. The national inventory alone is expected to cost more than $70 million over a 10-year period. As of yet INBio has not formally begun the large-scale national inventory, and is instead carrying out pilot inventory projects that focus on specific biota. Plants compose an estimated 2% of the terrestrial species in Costa Rica, and nearly 80% have already been described. However, arthropods, on which INBio is placing a stronger emphasis, make up nearly 73% of Costa Rican wildlife and less than 20% have been described. Nor does INBio see the full support of the Costa Rican conservation areas coming from the pharmaceutical industry's use of biological diversity within these regions. INBio tries to remind people that this is only one approach. Other sources of self-supporting income for sustainable economic development and the conservation areas must also be tapped, such as agreements with other industries, environmental management, and profits from ecotourism, recently one of the country's major sources of foreign exchange.

## CASE STUDY 3

## Sustainable Development in African Game Parks

Richard F. W. Barnes, University of California, San Diego

*Reserves designed to protect game or other species must include local citizenry in their planning and must incorporate their traditional lifestyles into the reserve if they are to be sustainable. Reserves cannot be "locked away" from humans; they can provide sustainable means of sustenance and thus receive critical local support.*

Many Westerners will be surprised to learn that protected areas are often an unpopular institution in Africa. This is largely because protected areas are an alien concept, based on the American ideal of national parks, which has been uncritically transplanted into the African context (Harmon 1987). The first African national park was created in 1925 in the Belgian Congo (now Zaire). Since then the African protected area system has expanded; protected land in many African countries now exceeds 5%–10% of the national area (Table 17.2). Most African parks were established as ecological islands protected from the surrounding people, whose needs were ignored. However, over the last two decades conservationists have been forced by the growing conflict between parks and local communities to rethink the way in which protected areas should be managed. They are working to reconcile the goals of conservation with the need to enhance the welfare of the surrounding communities.

This case study will discuss the general issue of economics and African protected areas, and then examine three parks that illustrate the problems of conservation and sustainable development. These examples span the continent from east to west and cover a range of habitats, from semiarid to humid, from lowland to montane, and from the sparsest human populations to the most dense.

### Valuation of Protected Areas

As has been brought out previously in this book, many positive values can arise from the establishment of a park, including conservation of biological diversity, maintenance of genetic resources, protection of representative ecosystems or unique landscapes or features, protection of endangered species of plants or animals, and opportunities for scientific research. However, only a few benefits of parks are perceived as advantageous by local people; principal among these are stabilization of water catchments, ecotourism, recreation, education of local citizenry, and the setting aside of areas to secure

**Table 17.2**
Examples of Investments of Land That Some
African Countries Have Made in Protected Areas

| Country | Percentage of country covered by protected areas | |
|---|---|---|
| | National parks | All protected areas |
| *West Africa* | | |
| Senegal | 5.2 | 11.4 |
| Côte d'Ivoire | 5.5 | 6.2 |
| Burkina Faso | 1.8 | 9.6 |
| *Central Africa* | | |
| Gabon | 0.0 | 6.3 |
| Zaire | 3.6 | 5.1 |
| Chad | 0.3 | 0.4 |
| *East Africa* | | |
| Uganda | 3.5 | 20.5 |
| Tanzania | 4.1 | 14.6 |
| Rwanda | 12.4 | 13.6 |
| *Southern Africa* | | |
| Zambia | 8.5 | 29.8 |
| Botswana | 15.1 | 17.2 |
| Namibia | 10.9 | 13.5 |

From IUCN 1993.

for future generations a sample of their cultural heritage. Unfortunately, the most important effects of parks, as far as most Africans are concerned, are often negative: opportunity costs (due to prevention of cultivation or grazing in the park) and crop damage caused by animals from the park.

The economic benefits of tourism are often given as the principal justification for game parks in Africa, and tourism is often the most profitable land use in areas of low rainfall or poor soils. For example, the total revenue from Amboseli National Park was estimated by Western and Henry (1979) to be about forty times the potential income from farming the same land. Each lion in the park was estimated to be worth $27,000 per year in tourist revenue. Similarly, Brown (1989) estimated that the game-viewing value of elephants was worth between $22 million and $30 million to Kenya's economy. Furthermore, tourism stimulates the economy and provides other employment.

On the other hand, the balance sheet may show a net loss. The central and local governments must make heavy initial investments (roads, airports, hotels) to attract tourists, which may not be balanced by later receipts from game viewing. Often, a large percentage of the profits go to foreign companies such as airlines or hotel operators (Pullan 1984). Ordinary citizens living around the park and suffering the costs imposed by it often receive nothing unless special provisions are made.

Emphasizing only the economic benefits of a park can be counterproductive. Governments may be persuaded to overdevelop infrastructure such as roads and hotels and so spoil the features the park was intended to protect. If the park loses money, justification for its existence disappears, or if another activity is shown to be more profitable, then it may replace the park. Tourism is a fickle industry; it depends on stable political conditions in the host country, healthy economies in the countries from which the tourists come, and cheap travel. Rather than concentrating on tourism, it is better to include tourism as only one of several uses for a park. It is better if other benefits accrue to local citizens from the existence of a park.

### Three Examples of Protected Areas

*Ruaha National Park, Tanzania.*    Ruaha (Figure 17.6, park 1), Tanzania's second largest national park, covers 10,300 km² and is part of a huge wilderness with a wealth of plant, bird, and mammal life. Scattered through this vast area of woodland and bushland were small settlements where local people lived by subsistence hunting and farming. During the 1940s a long period of drought resulted in crop failures and the people asked to be moved away.

Redistribution of people from inside the protected area to new villages beyond its periphery had unforseen consequences. Suddenly human pressures within the park were relaxed. There was no hunting, no human disturbance, no harassment of elephants as they came to water. With unrestricted access to water in the dry season, calf mortality decreased, resulting in a steady increase in the elephant population (Barnes 1983).

In the mid-1950s, the long drought ended with 15 years of good rains, and elephants benefited. Meanwhile, the human population outside the park expanded and drove elephants into the park. Elephants eat trees, and by the mid-1960s the Tanzania National Park (TNP) authorities were worried about woodland changes caused by burgeoning elephant numbers, a scenario common to many parks in eastern and southern Africa in the 1960s and 1970s. Authorities were faced with the dilemma of whether or not to cull thousands of elephants in parks established for their protection.

Ironically, the fate of the Ruaha elephants was decided not by the TNP authorities, but by the combined effects of the world ivory trade and Tanzania's economic recession. In the 1970s the economies of the western Pacific Rim, especially Japan, were developing rapidly, and the demand for luxuries such as ivory increased (Barbier et al. 1990). Furthermore, financial uncertainties caused by the oil price shock of 1973 caused some investors to turn

**Figure 17.6**   Map of Africa showing the sites mentioned in the text: 1: Ruaha National Park, Tanzania; 2: M'Passa Biosphere Reserve, Gabon; 3: Parc National des Virungas (PNV), Rwanda; 4: Zakouma National Park, Chad; 5: Kakum National Park, Ghana.

to ivory as a wealth store, in the same way that people invest in art or gold. The demand for ivory drove up its price and triggered a surge of ivory poaching that swept across the African continent.

Tanzania was in a deep recession at the time. Fuel was available only on the black market in small quantities and at high prices. Spare parts were unobtainable, so park vehicles ground to a halt. Park guards carried old, bolt-action rifles for which there was little ammunition, while the ivory poachers had automatic weapons from wars in Uganda, Angola, and Mozambique. Under such conditions, who can blame the impoverished villagers around the park for turning to ivory poaching? Between 1977 and 1984 about 60% of the Ruaha elephants were killed (Barnes and Kapela 1991). Thus, the elephants were culled, not by TNP, but by citizens stimulated by national and international economic forces.

The intense harassment by poachers forced elephants to concentrate in the area around park headquarters, resulting in accelerated habitat change: conversion of woodland to bushland to open grassland, and loss of shady riverine groves of acacia trees. These areas changed more as a result of the illegal cull than they would have done otherwise. A legal cull would have been conducted more evenly or in areas where elephant densities were a particular problem, and would have avoided the adverse effects of elephant concentration and overbrowsing. Thus, one could argue that the Japanese public and global economics played a greater role in the management of Ruaha National Park than did the TNP authorities. The point is, although Ruaha is one of East Africa's largest and remotest national parks, it is dominated by human pressures, not just inside and adjacent to the park itself, but even on the other side of the globe.

How does the park influence the local people and has it contributed to the local economy? Its negative effects include crop raiding by elephants, and a ban on honey gathering and hunting in the park and fishing in the Great Ruaha River. A large force of paramilitary game guards is needed to enforce prohibitions on illegal entry into the park. Benefits come from employment opportunities in the park (in the tourist hotel, or as guards, mechanics, and clerks) and the contribution of employees' wages to the local economy. The park staff spends much of its money in the villages close to the park, where many have built houses and married. Even so, the park's effect on the local economy is modest. But there are moves afoot to make it part of a wilderness multiple land use program that will involve, among other things, a wildlife utilization scheme.

*M'Passa Biosphere Reserve, Gabon.*   The M'passa Biosphere Reserve (Figure 17.6, park 2) was created in the early 1970s as an example of the rich rainforest of northeastern Gabon. Much valuable research in rainforest ecology has been conducted there. Unfortunately, those involved in siting the reserve neglected to consult the local people. The boundaries of the reserve enclose a large area of forest close to several villages on the road west of Makokou (Figure 17.7). Consequently, the nearby villagers woke up one day to find that their former hunting grounds were now out of bounds. These people relied on hunting and fishing as their sole source of protein, for there are no cattle in the rainforest and very few goats. Inevitably, the villagers developed an intense bitterness toward the reserve. The reserve was also within 10 km of the provincial capital of Makokou, and many of those residents had also hunted in the reserve.

From the perspective of the local people, every aspect of the reserve was negative and they drew no benefits from it. Strange foreign scientists, many from the former colonial power, roamed through the forests in which resi-

**Figure 17.7**   The M'Passa Biosphere Reserve, showing the surrounding villages and the nearby town of Makokou.

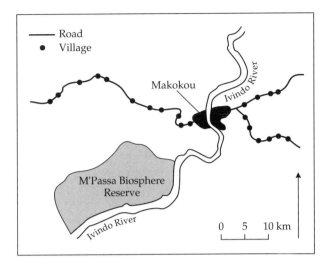

dents had traditionally hunted, but from which they were now banned. Residents reacted by simply ignoring reserve boundaries and continuing to hunt as before. By 1987 the much-studied monkeys and antelopes had been shot and eaten, and cultivators were about to encroach upon the reserve. The reserve has failed because the local people were not involved in either its planning or its management.

*Virunga National Park, Rwanda.*   The Virunga Volcanoes straddle the frontiers of Rwanda, Uganda, and Zaire (Figure 17.6, park 3). Their montane forest and high-altitude plant communities form an island habitat surrounded by dense human cultivation. The Rwandan side is protected by the Parc National des Virungas (PNV), which covers about 200 km². Rwanda is one of the poorest countries in the world. Its human population density is the highest on the continent, about 270 people per km², growing at over 3% per annum; around the PNV the human population density is even higher.

The forests play a vital hydrologic role, absorbing moisture during rains and releasing it as streamflow during the dry season. Weber (1987) believes that this hydrologic function is the most important feature of the volcanoes for the local people. After part of the forest was felled in 1968 for agriculture, some streams ceased flowing in the dry season.

The volcanoes have become famous as the realm of the mountain gorilla (*Gorilla gorilla berengei*). Gorilla numbers dropped from about 450 in 1960 to 270 in 1973 as the forests were felled or degraded by cattle grazing. The first efforts on the Rwandan side to protect the gorillas were based on the notion that the park had to be defended against the native hordes outside. Protection was confrontational, and some gorillas may have been shot in revenge for the brutal tactics used to dissuade poachers.

Nevertheless, these tactics bought time until a more enlightened approach was adopted. In 1979 a consortium of international conservation organizations launched the Mountain Gorilla Project (MGP) on the Rwandan side of the volcanoes. The MGP worked on the principle that the park, the volcanoes, the natural communities, and the local people were all part of a larger system that required an integrated management approach.

The conservation program had three main components. First, park protection was improved. The number of park guards was increased, they were reequipped, and the system of patrolling was reorganized. Second, ecotourism based on gorillas was initiated with the aim of improving the financial viability of the park (Figure 17.8). A number of gorilla groups were ha-

**Figure 17.8** Mountain gorillas are an important component of park protection in Rwanda. In addition to a high recognition factor, and nearly universal desire for their protection, gorillas also generate income for the local economy through ecotourism. (Photograph © Peter Veit/DRK Photo.)

bituated to allow one visit per day, for one hour, by six tourists. Third, conservation education was initiated. A mobile unit toured the villages and schools around the park, giving lectures and showing films. This effort was expanded to include the whole country and to cover environmental education in its broadest sense.

The MGP has been a spectacular success. Poaching declined, and gorillas on the Rwandan side reproduced better than those on the Zaire side, where there was no MGP. No gorillas have been killed by poachers since 1984, and gorilla numbers have increased to about 300. Furthermore, despite fears that regular tourist visits would disturb the gorilla groups, those groups visited by tourists have the highest rates of reproduction.

Attitudes of the local people toward the park have changed as they see the prosperity that tourism has brought to themselves, the district, and the nation. The revenues from tourism rose from about U.S. $10,000 in 1979 to about U.S. $230,000 in 1984. Tourism, attracted by the gorillas, is now Rwanda's second largest foreign exchange earner.

Sadly, much of this progress was reversed when rebels launched an attack from Uganda in 1990. The rebel and government armies have both occupied the Virunga forests, but so far both sides have avoided killing gorillas; they may realize that once the civil war is over, gorillas will again be part of Rwanda's economy.

### A New Age in African Wildlife Conservation

The Ruaha case illustrates a number of important lessons. First, even a huge, remote park can be dominated by human pressures from outside, including pressures at a national and international scale. Second, some of Ruaha's problems arose because the people moved out. People have long been part of the African landscape, and parks without human residents may experience backlashes. Third, if incentives are great enough, then even a paramilitary guard force may not be able to defend the park from local people. Fourth, it is impossible to protect high-value species like elephants and rhinos over large areas with the resources typically available to conservation authorities, and without the involvement of the local populace. In order to be effective, protection must be concentrated on a small area. In other words, large parks are virtually unprotectable.

This being the case today, what will the situation be in 25 years, when human pressures outside the park will have more than doubled? The old "defensive" approach to park management cannot succeed in the long term. This was dramatically illustrated by M'Passa, which has been a conservation disaster. M'Passa shows how the failure to involve local people in the creation and management of a park generates attitudes that eventually destroy it. M'Passa is typical of the colonial approach to wildlife conservation in Africa: define a rich wildlife area, declare it protected, remove indigenous people, and prevent them from reentering.

But this is changing. Conservation projects that in years past would have been narrow-minded and focused just on the park are now being conceived as wide-ranging multidisciplinary exercises involving not just the park but surrounding human populations. For example, in Chad, the European Community is financing rehabilitation of the Zakouma National Park (Figure 17.6, park 4). The overall objective is to integrate the park into the regional economy and improve the standard of living of people living around the park. Socioeconomic surveys will be conducted first to determine the needs of the local communities, and then programs for improving education, health, nutrition, water supply, and employment opportunities will be developed.

Another broad-ranging project to integrate a park into the regional economy is being planned for Kakum National Park in southern Ghana (Figure 17.6, park 5). The Kakum forest plays an important hydrologic role because it contains the headwaters of the rivers supplying nearby coastal towns, but it is surrounded by a dense human population that practices subsistence agriculture. The project will work with local people to reduce the negative effects of the park (such as crop raiding by elephants) and to improve standards of living. Tourists will provide a market for fruits and vegetables grown by the local villagers and stimulate the local economy.

Another major change in conservation philosophy is the notion of giving greater control of wildlife resources to local people. After all, if natural areas and wildlife are part of the African heritage, then Africans must have a say in the decisions about how those areas operate. This most imaginative step in the evolution of wildlife management has developed in southern Africa, where several schemes involving participation of local communities have been established. In Zimbabwe the Department of National Parks and Wildlife has set up the CAMPFIRE scheme (Communal Areas Management Programme For Indigenous Resources), based on the principle that rural populations should take responsibility for wildlife on their land and draw a direct benefit from management of those resources.

These schemes can bring about a revolution in people's attitudes toward wildlife. In the Nyaminyami district of northern Zimbabwe the local people have suffered for years from elephants that ravage their crops. The CAMPFIRE program in that area has twin goals. One is to reduce the elephant damage by shooting persistent crop raiders, dividing up the area into specified land use categories such as cultivation, pasture, and wildlife, and constructing electric fences where necessary. The second goal is to raise revenues for elephant management through a combination of game viewing and safari hunting. In only its first year of operation, the district generated a profit of over a quarter of a million dollars. Such revenues are used for community projects and for cash payments to each household. In many poor areas of Zimbabwe residents received a $200 payment, which exceeded their normal annual income; such a payment serves to emphasize the value of wildlife.

### Conclusions

Before independence, many parks were established as ecological islands protected from local people. The influence of the colonial period on conservation continued for a long time. As a result, many Africans associated protected areas with colonialism, and many government wildlife agencies were viewed as organs of repression. But this strategy was failing, and of necessity park managers had to take account of local people. Now the idea is to integrate parks into local and regional economies. The old dichotomy of protected and nonprotected areas is breaking down, and more flexible approaches to park management are being adopted as parks become elements within a mosaic of different land uses.

Africa is changing rapidly. As more rural Africans realize the power of the vote, unpopular game parks and wildlife legislation left over from the colonial era will be swept away. Those parks that survive will be those that the local people perceive as offering tangible benefits. These will be the truly sustainable ventures in wildlife conservation.

## CASE STUDY 4

### The Role of Ecotourism in Sustainable Development

Robert Mendelsohn, Yale University

*Ecotourism is emerging as a popular approach to protecting natural areas throughout the world. However, to be sustainable, ecotourism must provide reasonable economic benefits locally and nationally, and must avoid damaging the natural areas on which it depends. By itself, ecotourism is not the answer to environmental destruction, but if carried out properly, and in concert with other protective measures, it can contribute to sustainable and economically rewarding use of natural areas.*

It is well known that ecosystems throughout the world, especially tropical forests, are being degraded and converted to alternative uses at rapid rates. What is less clear is whether this is in the long-term best interests of each nation and the world as a whole. The immediate benefits of converting land so as to reap market goods such as crops and livestock are easy to measure, and alluring to poor nations. The long-term costs associated with losing vast natural holdings, in contrast, are more elusive. They include the difficult-to-quantify biodiversity and ecological effects, as well as lost economic opportunities that may have been available in natural ecosystems. Analysts concerned about whether further deforestation is desirable argue that these elusive costs now exceed the more readily measured conversion benefits.

However, before conservation arguments can hold much sway in land use decisions, and therefore contribute to sustainable use of the land, the value of natural ecosystems must be quantified and supported. In particular, if there are economic benefits to retaining natural ecosystems, they must be brought to the fore and placed alongside the touted benefits of conversion to other uses. Conservation is more likely to succeed in places where it is in the economic interest of local decision makers to retain natural areas. The search for quantifiable economic benefits associated with natural forests is thus an urgent and critical task.

Current research has identified three sources of economic benefits associ-

**Figure 17.9** Ecotourism is a rapidly growing economic venture in many areas of the world. Here, an ecotourist photographs a sea lion (*Zalophus californianus*) on Seymour Island in the Galápagos. To minimize the effect on the environment, visitors are restricted to a trail marked by white stakes, and a park naturalist must accompany each group. (Photograph by Tim M. Berra.)

ated with natural forests: timber, non-timber forest products, and ecotourism. Timber use has limited appeal for conservation, given its historical patterns of clear-cutting and subsequent land conversion. Although alternative timber practices are being developed (see Case Study 1), they have not yet demonstrated widespread economic utility. Non-timber forest products have potential appeal, as discussed elsewhere in this text (see especially Essay 15C). Here, we explore the potential of ecotourism as an incentive for conservation of natural areas.

Ecotourism is a large and rapidly growing industry in many countries and regions, especially in the tropics. For example, in 1988, approximately 15 million tourists visited Latin and Central America, and many of these came to see the flora and fauna of natural areas (Figure 17.9). Visitor records from select ecotourism destinations show steadily growing attendance over the last decade (see Harrison 1992). For example, in Belize, visitation grew from 99,000 in 1987 to 215,442 in 1991 (Belize Tourist Board 1992). Similar increases have been observed in Costa Rica. In Argentina, there is a huge tourist demand to see a single species, the Magellanic Penguin; thousands of tourists now come to view a huge colony of 200,000 penguins (Figure 17.10). This dramatic increase in tourism strongly implies that the demand for intact temperate and tropical marine and forest ecosystems is growing.

Ecotourism promises to be an important part of larger sustainable development programs because ecotourism can be a strong motivation to conserve natural sites. People use wild areas for a wide variety of nonconsumptive purposes, including casual nature walks, bird watching, whale watching, other wildlife viewing, photography, nature education, and canoeing and kayaking. Ecotourists also spend large sums of money on their pursuits. For example, at just one national park in Ontario, Canada, bird watchers at the peak of the spring birding season, 24 days in May, spent $3.8 million; $2.1 million of this was spent locally (Figure 17.11). Thus, ecotourism has tremendous economic potential for local sustainable development.

However, ecotourism as a truly sustainable development strategy faces three challenges. First, it must be decided which lands are suitable for ecotourism and which should be used for alternative purposes. Second, ecotourism must be made profitable at the national and local levels. Third, in order to be sustainable, ecotourism must be conducted in a manner that is not damaging to the natural sites it is trying to protect.

**Figure 17.10** Magellenic Penguins are a major tourist attraction at Punta Tomba, Argentina. Huge numbers of the birds (A) have drawn increasing numbers of human visitors (B), who are willing to pay to see these spectacular aggregations. (A, photograph by Dee Boersma; B, modified from Boersma et al. 1990.)

(A)

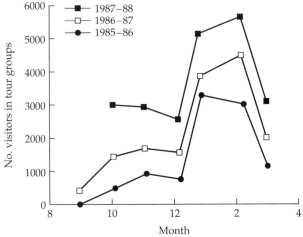

(B)

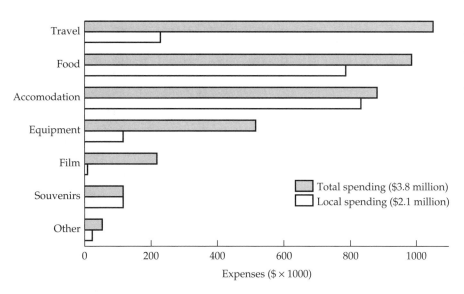

**Figure 17.11** The money generated by ecotourism can be significant. Bird-watchers at Point Pelee National Park, Ontario, spent $3.8 million from May 1 through May 24, 1987, the peak of bird-watching season. With the exception of travel costs, the bulk of that money was spent locally. (From Hvengaard et al. 1989.)

### Which Lands Are Suitable for Ecotourism?

It is largely unknown how much land, or which lands, should be set aside for ecotourism. Early studies and initial development have focused on unique natural sites supporting high-profile species such as lemurs (Maille and Mendelsohn 1993), elephants (Brown and Henry 1989), or grizzly bears (Clayton and Mendelsohn 1993), or on ecosystems with obvious public appeal such as tropical rainforests (Tobias and Mendelsohn 1991) or marine coral reefs (Svendsen et al. 1993). Places that are rare and have special characteristics that people value highly have been successfully developed for ecotourism. More common and abundant sites do not have the same appeal to visitors and cannot generate the same interest or income per hectare.

Ecotourism may also be successful near high-density cities. For example, the million-acre Pinelands National Reserve in southern New Jersey is developing as a major ecotourism region for the crowded cities of the Northeast such as New York and Philadelphia. Local residents in southern New Jersey are protecting their rivers and lands, and developing ecotourist activities such as bird watching, whale watching, and boat tours. Muir Woods near San Francisco also serves as an important escape from that populous area.

These insights into what ecotourists are looking for suggest that ecotourism is likely to result in isolated, specialized reserves scattered around the world, rather than vast protected tracts. Consequently, ecotourism will function as a sustainable development strategy only in concert with other protective measures. Scattered, specialized ecotourism reserves would have the effect of protecting some (though not all) of the larger and more interesting vertebrates from extinction. However, they would not be extensive enough to protect the broader diversity of plants and animals that is currently being destroyed by land conversion. Also, ecotourism may not bring in enough revenue to support the large areas that megafauna require for sustainability. Ecotourism thus has a role in conservation because it can contribute to protecting species the public values the most. However, that role is limited; ecotourism's positive effects fade quickly as one moves from key, high-profile reserves to surrounding areas.

### How Can Ecotourism Be Made Profitable?

Ecotourism currently generates substantial rewards for tourists: seeing exotic animals and plants close up, and experiencing a sense of wildness. For ecotourism to be effective as a conservation strategy, however, the land use decision makers at the site must find ecotourism economically valuable; it must provide at least as high a standard of living as would alternative, and more destructive, uses of the land. This requires two steps that are typically not yet in place: the sites must generate revenue from the tourists, and this revenue must be distributed to the people who will either preserve or destroy the local landscape.

At most ecotourism sites, tourist access is presently either free or involves a minimal charge. Foreign tourists who appear to have a high desire to visit these sites are being charged a very low price. Since many tourists are willing to pay more than they are being charged, tourists are currently the main beneficiaries of these sites. For example, at sites in Madagascar, foreign tourists are willing to pay between $275 and $360 per trip to see lemurs (Maille and Mendelsohn 1993). In Belize, it is estimated that foreign tourists are willing to pay about $350 per trip to dive on the coral reefs (Svendsen et al. 1993). These amounts are beyond travel or other costs associated with getting to the sites, yet presently, fees are only a few dollars in each place.

With little or no revenue being collected, ecotourism is not providing an incentive for local people to protect the resources. In countries such as Madagascar and Belize, fees in the range of $100 to $200 per person could be charged to visit the country for ecotourism purposes. Multiplying by the number of visitors in each case yields potential annual revenues in the millions of dollars.

In order to link such revenues with conservation, another goal must be accomplished: the local people who are likely to convert the land to alternative uses must benefit directly from the tourist revenue being collected. If central bureaucracies in the nation's capital collect all the revenue, the local people will still have no incentive to protect the reserve. In contrast, if local people share in the benefits of a reserve, they are far more likely to protect the reserve and this source of income.

Efforts must also be undertaken to win the cooperation of people who reside in the vicinity of reserves, which can be done in a number of ways. For example, local people could be granted exclusive rights to harvest resources in the reserve. Alternatively, the reserve could offer local services such as health care, employment, and education as incentives for protection and cooperation.

The need to charge higher fees for ecotourism reinforces the earlier point that sites have to be relatively scarce for ecotourism to work. If people establish a reserve in an ordinary forest and then charge high fees, tourists will simply go to alternative sites in nearby forests. There is little potential ecotourism revenue in common sites, limiting the role of ecotourism as an approach to sustainable development.

### Can Ecotourism Avoid Damaging Natural Areas?

In order to be sustainable in the long term, ecotourism must avoid damaging natural areas, and areas used for ecotourism must function as true reserves. As discussed in Chapter 10, if the reserves are too small, they may not be effective for species or ecosystem protection. If reserves begin to resemble islands surrounded by a matrix of land used for conflicting purposes, the species being protected will have small population sizes and may not be able to migrate to other protected areas, and ecosystem processes may begin to break down. Issues such as minimal numbers of breeding pairs and insufficient territory sizes become critical in very small reserves, threatening the viability of the reserve as a whole.

Few species of conservation interest benefit from contact with humans. Species that prefer more privacy may keep themselves hidden and thus offer little viewing potential. Ecotourists may spend large amounts of money to actually see these animals; if the animals remain hidden, the tourists' experience could be poor, and discourage further investment. This could result in only "human-adapted" systems being supported by ecotourism. In some cases reserve managers could establish viewing sites to overcome this problem. For example, the reserve could establish hidden viewing shelters near water holes or other places that large, charismatic vertebrates are likely to visit. Another approach is to zone the area for ecotourist activities. For example, many tourists are interested in seeing colorful birds, which are often most common or observable along forest edges. It is then possible to restrict forest interiors to very limited ecotourist access, and focus activities along less ecologically sensitive edges and clearings.

Another problem is that sites can be overused, causing ecological degradation, and thus also degrading the tourism experience; that is, sites can be "too successful" (Figure 17.12). Sites need to be carefully managed to minimize the effects of high-density use. For example, boardwalks can be built to sustain short, but heavily used, nature trails. Networks of trails can be built in more remote areas to disperse visitors. Total numbers of visitors may need to be limited on an annual or seasonal basis. Economically, this would have the effect of increasing the demand for the experience, the prices charged, and thus the revenues obtained.

**Figure 17.12** Many popular areas for ecotourists and outdoor enthusiasts, such as Grand Canyon National Park, are under great pressure from human visitation, and require special effort for protection because of this heavy use. (Photograph © Tom Bean/DRK Photo.)

### Conclusions

Ecotourism can make an important contribution to sustainable development throughout the world, particularly in developing tropical regions. Coupled with a mechanism to collect and distribute revenues from this activity, ecotourism can become an active force for conservation and sustainability. If practiced carefully and managed with the interests of the local site and local people in mind, ecotourism can be a sustainable source of income that will promote the conservation of many unique habitats throughout the world. However, it has only limited potential to protect natural areas, and must be conducted in ways that minimize threats of degradation from tourist activities.

## CASE STUDY 5

### The Sian Ka'an Biosphere Reserve Project

Francisco J. Rosado-May, Universidad de Quintana Roo, Mexico

*Sustainability can arise from careful incorporation of human activities into large expanses of protected land designed as biosphere reserves. Zoning and control of these activities, if properly managed, can allow protection of large vertebrate species and ecological processes while accruing human economic benefits from the area. However, the results often do not live up to these lofty goals.*

### What Is a Biosphere Reserve?

The concept of **biosphere reserves** as a method of sustainable development was launched in the early 1970s by the UNESCO Man and the Biosphere Program (MAB). In contrast to typical national parks or other nature reserves, the biosphere reserve concept allows human habitation within a reserve. Rather than isolating natural areas and protecting them from humans, biosphere reserves carefully incorporate, at least in theory, limited and sustainable human activities into the planning and management of the area.

In contrast to many natural areas that are selected on the basis of spectacular aesthetics or species of special interest, a biosphere reserve must represent a typical, biotically important terrestrial or coastal site. A goal of the MAB program is to include representatives of all 193 identified biogeographic provinces of the earth in a biosphere reserve system (Tangley 1988). Nearly 300 biosphere reserves exist worldwide today.

According to one of the creators of the concept, Michel Batisse (1986), biosphere reserves should meet three interacting goals: conservation, training, and development. The conservation role is typical: reserves should encompass areas large enough to ensure maintenance of genetic, species, habitat, and ecosystem diversity over time. The training role includes education, research, and information exchange, done in a carefully planned manner so there are no significant perturbations to the reserve. Reserves may be used, for example, as sites for study of long-term global climate or biogeochemistry changes. Development is the most innovative and controversial role. Limited human activities compatible with conservation are allowed, but they raise serious questions about how to achieve sustainability.

The three roles of a biosphere reserve are realized by the designation of three geographic regions within a reserve (see Figure 10.22). A **core zone** is a natural, protected area in which only nondisruptive research, such as environmental monitoring, is allowed. Often, core zones are preexisting protected areas such as national parks or nature preserves. A **buffer zone** surrounds or adjoins the cores, and only activities compatible with the protection and preservation of the cores are allowed there. Examples include natural history tourism, education and training, low-impact manipulative research, and traditional land uses such as low-intensity agriculture or extraction of renewable natural products. Both of these zones should have clearly defined borders and legal protection. Beyond the buffer zone is a **transition zone**, which has no clear limits. It includes human settlements and economic activities compatible with conservation and preservation of the reserve ecosystems. We will focus on one such biosphere reserve, Sian Ka'an, in Quintana Roo, Mexico.

### The Sian Ka'an Biosphere Reserve

In January 1986, the Sian Ka'an Biosphere Reserve (SKBR), the fifth such reserve in Mexico, was created by presidential decree. SKBR encompasses about 10% of the state of Quintana Roo, on the Yucatán Peninsula (Figure 17.13), and its boundaries are determined mostly by the presence of surrounding small communities. The word Sian Ka'an comes from the Maya language and means "where the sky is born." Many local residents are Mayan, and their influences are felt throughout the area.

The decree completed only the first step toward conserving the diversity of tropical ecosystems, both terrestrial and aquatic, included in the 528,147 ha of the reserve. The Sian Ka'an reserve is made up of 33% periodically flooded coastal vegetation, 29% tropical forest, 21% marine bays, 8% shrubs, dunes, and secondary growth, 5% coral reefs, and 4% fresh water such as lagoons and sinkholes (Figure 17.14).

There are three core zones in Sian Ka'an—Muyil, Cayo Culebras, and Uaimil—in which no development is allowed. About 95% of the 800 or so human inhabitants of the reserve live along the coastal area outside of the core zones. The reserve contains two bays, Ascención Bay and Espiritu Santo

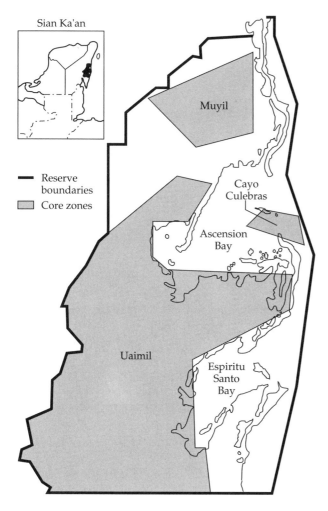

Bay, with several small islands, mostly covered by several mangrove species. The water in these bays is nutrient rich, and is responsible for high productivity and an active and successful lobster fishery. The reserve also contains part of the world's second longest barrier reef.

A number of factors interacted in the formation of the reserve: (1) Sian Ka'an would help meet the MAB goal of establishing reserves in area representative of the earth's biogeographical provinces; (2) based on the National Plan for Development, the Mexican government and people were interested in establishing protected areas; (3) Quintana Roo's central–eastern area was sparsely populated and included several ecosystems worthy of protection; (4) about 99% of the land was federally owned, permitting easier designation of reserve territory; (5) the ecosystems involved were in fairly pristine condition due to limited access to the area; consequently, there was little concern about major human disturbance; (6) Quintana Roo had a research center (Centro de Investigaciones de Quintana Roo, CIQRO), that could provide scientific expertise for management decisions; and (7) a Mexican citizen, Gonzalo Halffter, played an important role as president of MAB's International Coordinating Council. Halffter's plan was for residents to be the main protectors of, and the first to receive benefits from, the reserve. In addition, there would be close interactions among CIQRO, nongovernmental organizations, and federal, state, and local governments regarding decision making in reserve administration. Thus, Sian Ka'an was established.

(A)

(B)

**Figure 17.14**   Some natural habitats of Sian Ka'an. (A) A freshwater sinkhole. (B) A typical landscape of dunes, mangroves, and shrubs along the coastal zone. (Photographs by Francisco J. Rosado-May.)

### Sian Ka'an and the Goals of Biosphere Reserves

*Conservation.*   Biological and ecological information for SKBR is sketchy but is being added to constantly. Studies conducted thus far have mostly concentrated on identifying species composition in the various environments or identifying major habitat types (Navarro L. and Robinson 1990). Species lists have been developed for a number of groups ranging from algae, bryophytes, zooplankton, and ferns to corals, insects, earthworms, birds, mammals, and crustaceans. The reserve includes at least 1200 species of vascular plants, 339 bird species (including migrants and aquatic species), and several endangered vertebrates, including jaguars, pumas, tapirs, manatees, and three sea turtle species (Tangley 1988).

According to Olmsted and Duran (1990), the vegetation has been classified into three different types of tropical forests, four different swamp communities, dunes, and hardwood hammocks. Most of these studies have not outlined species distributions, nor do they discuss ecological information on species or conservation implications. This type of work remains to be completed.

*Training.*   An organization called "Amigos de Sian Ka'an" is helping to achieve the training goals of the reserve. They organize nature tours for tourists that arrive from Cancun (220 km away) and sponsor applied research on resource use in the reserve. Projects include a study of the spiny lobster fishery (a major source of income), sustainable harvest of palms, and a model farm to demonstrate intensive agriculture on small parcels of land (Tangley 1988). They also are developing public education programs such as brochures and exhibits, and publish a regular newsletter about the reserve. The reserve also has facilities such as the Santa Teresa station, at which interested people can stay for as long as needed for teaching or research.

*Development.*   The impact of human activities has been poorly studied to date, and much work remains to be done. Socioeconomic studies have been conducted mostly by César Dachary and Arnaiz Burne (1989) on the human population living in Sian Ka'an and their economic activities. Seven farms were identified within the reserve, and 67 human settlements are located along the coast, with much of their economic base coming from the sea.

There is an obvious need to move forward with further studies in SKBR in all three areas. Now that species inventories are being completed, ecological processes and mechanisms need to be addressed. For example, there is little information on species interactions or keystone elements of the biota.

Education and controlled tourism need to be developed as economic bases for local communities. There is little information for proposing informed quotas for fishing or other development activities, or for establishing a carrying capacity for permanent inhabitants or tourists. Much work remains to be done to meet the broad goals of a biosphere reserve as set out by MAB.

### How Is Sian Ka'an Doing?

Eight years after the decree, SKBR illustrates several problems with and opportunities for the biosphere reserve approach:

- Along the coastal zone, there used to be a landscape dominated by coconut plantations (Figure 17.15A). In the northern half of the reserve, coconuts nearly disappeared due to a lethal yellowing disease caused by a mycoplasma and transmitted by an insect. Initial efforts to stop the spread of the disease failed, and some erosion occurred. Now natural vegetation recovery is proceeding and the sandy dunes are again being protected (Figure 17.15B).

- Managers have yet to define the sizes and locations of the most critical habitats within the reserve, identify which species are most in danger, or develop appropriate management programs for core areas. The defined limits of the core zones seem to simply follow patterns established by private property ownership and previous human settlements, rather than reflecting ecological criteria. Whether or not these are the best ecological boundaries remains unknown. Sensitive ecosystems such as coral reefs are not included in the core areas, with the exception of a small portion near the Cayo Culebra zone.

- The most important economic activity within the reserve is lobster harvesting, followed by fishing. Studies are being conducted by David Miller of the State University of New York, Cortland on lobster ecology and recruitment, which could serve to establish harvest limits based on population size and recruitment. Fishermen are very aware of the importance of this resource to them and their descendants.

- Administration of the reserve needs attention. The federal government, via the Social Development Secretary, still holds much control over the reserve. However, the state government is very interested in having reserve management under its control.

- Sian Ka'an faces pollution problems, deforestation, and unauthorized hunting, and there are not enough personnel to enforce the laws. Legal

**Figure 17.15** (A) An example of a coastal coconut plantation, many of which have succumbed to lethal yellowing disease. Such plantations, or other types of farming that replace them, make the coast susceptible to erosion. (B) Where former coconut plantations have been abandoned, vegetation recovers to species typical of dunes, reducing erosion. (Photographs by Francisco J. Rosado-May.)

(A)

(B)

(A)

(B)

**Figure 17.16** Development of a resort complex near the Muyil core zone of Sian Ka'an threatens the integrity of the reserve. (A) One of at least three large buildings under construction at the resort. (B) Power lines are being cut through the forests to provide electricity for the resort. (Photographs by Francisco J. Rosado-May.)

protection of reserves is only as good as enforcement on the ground. There is also a large resort being built very close to the Muyil core zone, in violation of the intent of the reserve (Figure 17.16).

- The federal authorities recently promoted and formed a council to make decisions regarding reserve management (Diario de Quintana Roo 1992; Segoviano Martínez 1992). According to news reports, there were irregularities in this process, but at least on paper, there are representatives of each of the sectors involved in the reserve: private, municipal, inhabitants, NGOs, research institutes, and federal and state government.

- There is also concern about contamination from garbage and crude oil carried by marine currents from the heavy traffic in the Caribbean Sea. To the north, a tourist megaproject called The Corridor Cancun–Tulum has been slowly but surely increasing tourism and development. To the south, the interest in tourism is also growing and resorts are developing. To the east, the *ejidos* (land ownerships established in Mexico by President Lazaro Cardenas) have mined the forest for chewing gum latex, timber, and construction material. Recently, due to overexploitation of other areas, there has been interest in obtaining railroad ties from the reserve. The present municipal administration of Felipe Carrillo Puerto has expressed an interest in developing ecotourism to bring income to the area; its present economy depends largely on state and federal aid. Studies that describe and quantify these various pressures are sorely needed.

### Is Sian Ka'an a Good Example of Sustainable Development?

In order to answer this question, we must establish a working definition of sustainable development. The definition that should be used at Sian Ka'an is "dynamic equilibrium between three factors involved in determining the structure and function of ecosystems: ecological factors, technological factors, and social-economic-political factors." The key here is the "dynamic equilibrium." In order to reach a common ground to achieve the same level of understanding, all those involved should be aware that although ecologists define boundaries of ecosystems for study purposes, there are strong connections between ecosystems. A perturbation of one ecosystem can have significant effects on others; thus, ecology should be the common bridge between the various people involved in sustainable projects. Usually business people and developers work under the assumption that natural resources are, by definition, renewable. This vision of nature is often wrong, and economies based on this premise are usually not sustainable.

Sian Ka'an and other biosphere reserves offer a challenge and an opportunity for humans to reach a dynamic equilibrium with nature. Although there have been major advances in Sian Ka'an toward the goals set for biosphere reserves, there remains a great deal of work ahead, and many challenges to be overcome before the Sian Ka'an Biosphere Reserve is truly a good example of sustainability. Grumbine (1992) offered a more sobering view of biosphere reserves in general, one that illustrates the huge tasks ahead:

> Though today there are over 266 biosphere reserves in seventy nations, it did not take long for the concept to run aground. Most such reserves were simply laid over existing national parks, cores without the intended buffer zones. Conflicts were avoided, but so was integrated land management. After almost twenty years few biosphere reserves fit the idealized pattern, and there were none with fully integrated human communities. Though conceived as a global network to protect examples of worldwide biodiversity, only 1.6 percent of global ecosystem types are represented. . . . Overall, this first model of management beyond administrative boundaries suffers from nebulous goals that offer something for everybody. The hard questions are left unanswered. Biosphere reserves may yet have a future, but they are not the panacea that some wish them to be.

# CASE STUDY 6

## The Greater Yellowstone Ecosystem

Mark S. Boyce, University of Wyoming

*To anyone concerned about the conservation of nature the very name Yellowstone is like a battle cry. This is where it all started; Yellowstone was the first wilderness set aside for a national park, and it remains an inspiration and the confirmation that dreams can be made to come true.*

> H. R. H. Prince Phillip *(quoted in Sutton and Sutton 1972)*

***The next step up in sustainability from biosphere reserves is protection and management of even larger expanses of land as intact ecosystems. Sustainability at the ecosystem level is a laudable goal and the ultimate form of protection, but it faces many obstacles. Local people and their lifestyles must be accounted for, previous resource exploitation must be reduced and controlled, and tourism must be limited.***

One approach to sustainable development is to set aside large tracts of land as reserves, but allow a combination of human economic activities within the reserves. Activities such as moderate grazing, extraction of minerals, timber removal, agriculture, and tourism can all be compatible with biodiversity protection, if done properly. If the set-aside area is large enough to encompass entire ecosystems, then an integrated approach to resource management may be developed. One example that begins to approach this ideal is the Greater Yellowstone Ecosystem (GYE) in the United States.

Since its establishment as the world's first national park in 1872, Yellowstone has been a paradigm of nature preservation. Today, Yellowstone National Park and the adjacent wild lands frequently serve as proving grounds for changing perspectives in resource management, exemplified by recent debates over fire management policy, ungulate population control, and wolf reintroduction. The pivotal issue in these debates usually is how human development can interact with our attempts to preserve a large ecosystem. It is not yet clear that we understand ecological processes well enough to accomplish sustainable development in the context of ecosystem preservation. But there are few places remaining in the world where we have a better opportunity to make it work than in the GYE.

### Ecological Issues

The GYE encompasses an area of some 60,000 km$^2$ in the Rocky Mountains of Wyoming, Idaho, and Montana, with most lands managed by the Forest Service and the National Park Service (Figure 17.17). The area is high in elevation (1,500–4,200 m) with a short growing season, low to moderate productivity, and relatively low species diversity. The GYE is well known for its natural beauty, spectacular geothermal features, and a fauna rich in large mammals including elk (*Cervus elaphus*), moose (*Alces alces*), mule deer (*Odocoileus hemionus*), pronghorn (*Antilocapra americana*), bison (*Bison bison*), bighorn sheep (*Ovis canadensis*), black bear (*Ursus americanus*), and of course, the threatened grizzly bear (*Ursus horribilis*). Few endemic species of conservation significance occur in the area, exceptions being the Ross bentgrass (*Agrostis rossiae*) restricted to the Upper Geyser Basin of Yellowstone National Park, and the Jackson Lake sucker (*Chasmistes muriei*), which is presumed extinct.

Because of its low species diversity and relatively few threatened or endangered species, the GYE would not rank high as a site on which to focus

**Figure 17.17** The Greater Yellowstone Ecosystem. Note the relationship of Yellowstone and Grand Teton National Parks (dark shading) to various surrounding national forests, wildlife refuges, and other wild lands (light shading).

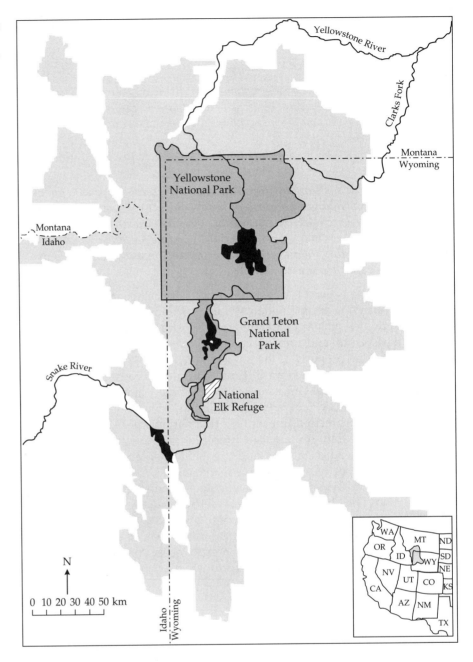

attention for the preservation of biodiversity. Rather, the value of the GYE lies in its relatively intact status, affording a unique opportunity to protect a large, major ecosystem. In practice, however, the strongest motivation for conservation in the GYE is the protection of aesthetic wilderness values.

*Ecological Process Management.* National parks can serve a valuable function as ecological baseline preserves. Natural areas can be managed with a minimum of human interference in order to document change through time relative to other areas where human influence is greater. Such management usually implies a "hands-off" policy, and ecological processes are allowed to take their course unimpeded. Sometimes this is insufficient, and because of prior human disturbances or influences occurring beyond the boundary of the park, intervention may be necessary to restore natural ecological processes to the landscape. This approach is known as ecological process management.

The legal boundaries of Yellowstone National Park established by Congress in 1872 (see Figure 17.17) do not coincide with ecological processes governing nature in Yellowstone. For example, large numbers of elk, mule deer, and bison regularly cross park boundaries to find winter ranges outside the park. Wildfires cross boundaries with total disregard for agency jurisdictions. Even ecosystem boundaries may be arbitrary, and a number have been proposed for the GYE (Patten 1991). But to capture a geographic unit that makes any biological sense requires extending the boundaries of Yellowstone onto national forest lands on all sides. Transcending these agency boundaries to accomplish ecological process management has proved difficult in many instances.

At least in spirit, ecological process management prevails in the national parks of the GYE. Although lands adjacent to Yellowstone National Park are mostly Wilderness Areas, Congress has imposed constraints that preclude ecological process management as a priority in national forests. In particular, the Forest Service must provide multiple-use options for resources occurring in national forests, even if the uses conflict.

*Fire Ecology and Management.*   During the summer of 1988, approximately one-half of Yellowstone National Park was burned by wildfires. Large-area fires are typical of the Yellowstone area, but occur at low frequency, with major large fires every 350 years (Romme and Despain 1989). Fire is clearly an integral part of the forest ecosystems throughout the Rocky Mountains, and one may envisage the Yellowstone landscape as comprising a dynamic, ever-changing mosaic of burned and unburned areas. Fire maintains aspen (*Populus tremuloides*) communities, and enhances wildlife habitats. Recognition of the ecological importance of fire formed the basis for "let-burn" policies, established in the early 1970s, for natural fires in wilderness regions of Yellowstone and the adjacent national forests.

But people fear fires and their destructive capabilities. Political objections to the fires of 1988 resulted in challenges to the fire management policies of the Forest Service and the Park Service. Despite extensive reviews, the fire management policies of the National Park Service and Forest Service have remained largely intact. Yet, strict constraints have been imposed that reduce the chances that wildfires could burn out of control as they did in 1988. Nevertheless, given the low frequency of large fires in the GYE, we have several centuries to wait for a more enlightened administration.

*Ungulate Management.*   Elk and bison populations have increased to near carrying capacity, and in some areas the consequences of herbivory on vegetation are pronounced. Willow (*Salix* spp.) and aspen are browsed extensively, resulting in changes in vegetation communities, especially on winter ranges. However, such plant–herbivore dynamics are expected to change vegetation communities, and probably have done so for millennia.

Range managers argue that allowing native ungulates to heavily graze ranges in Yellowstone reflects a double standard because comparable grazing levels by domestic livestock outside the park would be unacceptable to federal land management agencies. However, managers in the National Park Service have quite a different charge—fostering native species—from those in the U.S. Bureau of Land Management and the Forest Service, who are required to manage for multiple use, including cattle grazing. Claims of "overpopulation" and "overgrazing" by native ungulates on Yellowstone's ranges appear vacuous—the presence of cattle is not ecologically or ethically equivalent to the presence of native ungulates. Recreational users of public lands in the West are becoming increasingly intolerant of heavy livestock grazing.

**Figure 17.18** Bison may damage fences and other agricultural developments and may carry brucellosis, which can infect domestic livestock. (Photograph by Mark S. Boyce.)

A substantial fraction of bison and elk carry brucellosis, a bacterial disease, causing another ungulate management concern in the GYE (Figure 17.18). The disease is contagious to livestock and can cause ranchers substantial economic losses because infected cattle must be destroyed. No practical methods have been devised for controlling the disease other than seasonally minimizing the contact between wildlife and domestic livestock. Thus, wildlife dispersal out of the park is viewed as a threat by the livestock industry, and they have leveraged Yellowstone National Park into destroying bison as they migrate into Montana during winter. Curiously, such draconian measures have not been implemented for the Jackson elk herd, despite the fact that 40% of the cow elk carry the disease.

There are no easy solutions to ungulate population problems in the GYE. The public finds it unacceptable to kill wildlife inside park boundaries, and enjoys having abundant ungulate populations for viewing. Certain conservation groups have argued that eliminating livestock grazing on public lands in the GYE would resolve most conflicts, but this is an impolitic proposal in a region so traditionally dominated by ranching interests, and would violate the current multiple-use mandate of the Forest Service.

*Wolf Recovery.* Wolves were fairly common in the GYE until they were extirpated by U.S. Government hunters and trappers during the 1920s. Ungulate numbers would be reduced by wolves (Boyce 1992), so wolf reintroduction could reduce some of the perceived problems caused by elk and bison "overpopulation." Indeed, our ability to restore natural ecological processes throughout the GYE is seriously compromised by the absence of wolves from the system.

But proposals to restore wolves to the GYE are deplored by local ranchers, who fear that wolves will prey on their livestock, and by those who fear that wolves will compete with hunters for game. Furthermore, the mining industry opposes wolf recovery because the presence of yet another sensitive/threatened species might further restrict public lands available to them for development. Thus, proposals to release wolves in Yellowstone National Park have been met with strong political resistance.

One proposal has been to release wolves into Yellowstone as an "experimental population," giving federal agencies authority to control the population when needed. However, new wolf sightings in the GYE during 1992 suggest that wolves may have dispersed naturally to the area from northern Montana, thereby eliminating the need for human intervention. Natural recolonization of the GYE will afford greater protection for the wolves since they will retain full protection under the Endangered Species Act.

### Development Issues

Traditionally, commodity extraction, including both mining and renewable resource development, has been an important component of the economy of the GYE. Gradually, demands for development in the GYE are shifting to include construction of vacation homes, ski resorts, tourism facilities, and new roads and trails to facilitate access (Figure 17.19). Whereas commodity development has always been an issue primarily involving the national forests in the GYE, recreational facilities are also being developed within the national parks.

**Figure 17.19**  Ski lift at Teton Village west of Jackson, Wyoming, an example of recreational development in the Greater Yellowstone Ecosystem. (Photograph by Mark S. Boyce.)

*Commodity Development in National Forests.*  Because of its multiple-use mandate, the Forest Service is obligated to provide opportunities for mining, timber harvest, and grazing in national forests. However, endangered species legislation gives the Forest Service license to place certain areas off limits for incompatible uses if they might jeopardize habitats for threatened or endangered species. For example, in the GYE, the Shoshone and Custer National Forests have banned oil and gas exploration and development on prime grizzly bear habitat. In Bridger-Teton National Forest, oil and gas leases may be granted in grizzly bear habitat or on steep slopes, but no surface occupancy by oil rigs is allowed. Still, throughout most of the GYE, oil and gas exploration is permitted and is frequently at odds with wildlife and recreational uses of the area.

In the same year that Yellowstone was designated a national park, Congress also passed the mining law of 1872, encouraging hard-rock mining on public lands. In the GYE mining primarily for gold and palladium occurs in the spectacular Beartooth Mountains north of Yellowstone National Park in Custer National Forest. Modern gold-mining techniques involve bathing ore in a cyanide bath, which carries the risk of chemical spills that could devastate stream biota.

In contrast to mineral extraction, logging and grazing are potentially sustainable uses of the national forests. Yet neither is particularly profitable in the GYE, and in many cases these uses may conflict with wildlife habitat and recreational values. Every national forest in the GYE loses money on its timber program (O'Toole 1991), and cattle ranching is declining in the area despite the low fees charged for grazing on federal lands.

Conflicts between cattle and elk on winter range were responsible for the establishment of the National Elk Refuge near Jackson, Wyoming (Figure 17.20), where some 7500 elk are provisioned with alfalfa each year in lieu of their natural winter forage. More than 44% of the GYE's public lands are open to cattle and sheep grazing, resulting in competition with native wildlife, degradation of riparian habitats, and conflicts with predators. One-fifth of the grizzly bear deaths in the GYE have been linked to conflicts with domestic sheep grazing.

Despite these problems with livestock grazing in the GYE, there is much local support for ranching. The rugged lifestyle of the cowboy adds flavor to the tourism experience in the GYE, and ranching is viewed by the public as being less in conflict with natural resources than are other forms of development. Many of the problems with livestock grazing in the GYE could be resolved by more conscientious grazing management on public lands—a responsibility of the Forest Service.

**Figure 17.20** Winter feeding of elk at the National Elk Refuge is justified because livestock ranching and the town of Jackson, Wyoming displaced elk from traditional winter ranges. (Photograph by Mark S. Boyce.)

Resistance to ecosystem management on the part of the Forest Service may also relate to the fact that its financing comes partly from timber sales. O'Toole (1991) argues that greater attention to noncommodity interests could be secured if recreational users of the national forests were charged a user fee, which the Service could then use to support its management programs.

*Recreation Based Development.* The GYE is gradually changing to a recreation based economy, which would appear more benign than a commodity based economy (Figure 17.21). But recreational uses are not without consequences to the ecological integrity of the ecosystem. For example, in recent years snowmobiling has become a popular recreational activity in Yellowstone during winter. Roads used by snowmobiles become snowpacked, creating corridors for movement of snowbound bison, resulting in shifts in their distribution. Conflicts with humans occur when these movements take bison beyond the boundaries of the park. We do not yet know the ramifications to the bison population, but it appears that snowmobile corridors have substantially increased available winter range.

One might argue that virtually any development will alter the system, and therefore that the best management for the GYE would be to minimize human visitation and use. Yet, much of the support for conservation of Yellowstone comes from people who have enjoyed their experiences in the area. Therefore it is unrealistic to envision extreme protection; rather, a balance between preservation and development is needed.

### Striking the Balance

Because ecosystem boundaries cross agency jurisdictions, any attempt to manage the GYE will require interagency coordination. Yet, attempts at cooperative planning by federal and state agencies in the GYE have been blocked by political pressures driven by development interest groups.

Nevertheless, it would appear that the transition to an ecosystem management philosophy is happening throughout the GYE, despite lobbying pressures. It seems obvious that priority for management in the GYE should be given to recreational and tourism values, simply because of their overwhelming economic importance in the area. This transition has already led

**Figure 17.21** A horse corral maintained for a trail ride concession within Grand Teton National Park. Development is often required to support recreational use within national parks. (Photograph by Mark S. Boyce.)

to the closing of sawmills, abandonment of grazing leases, and restrictions on mining and oil and gas exploration in certain areas. Yet, incentives for development persist, and ensuring that it is done properly will require vigilance on the part of environmental organizations.

Ecologists have argued that there is value in maintaining ecosystem structure and function, but such values seem esoteric to many people. From a pragmatic perspective, perhaps Yellowstone's greatest value is as one of America's great playgrounds. In 1992 Yellowstone hosted over 3 million visitors. Maintaining its wilderness character and avoiding tawdry development has secured the GYE's attraction for recreation and tourism. Consequently, ecosystem protection in the GYE can be justified economically.

But to keep the GYE *pristine* would extract a cost. Resources left unexploited in the GYE to protect ecosystem structure and wilderness values there will be exploited somewhere else. It would be tragic if these resources were to come from tropical regions where diversity is greater but environmental regulations are more lax. Perhaps nature conservation priorities need reevaluation in the context of a global human population now at 5.5 billion people and growing rapidly. Should the utilitarian justification for preservation of genetic resources take precedence? If so, preserving the GYE may be a poor choice.

The way we manage Yellowstone will be a model of conservation and sustainability for the rest of the world. One alternative that we might foster is a model of preservation, that is, showing that we are willing to make sacrifices to protect large areas for ecosystem and wilderness values. Another alternative is to demonstrate that sustainable development can be achieved by integrating commodity uses and recreation while still preserving biological diversity. Yellowstone will have greater global relevance if it is the latter conservation paradigm that we develop.

## General Conclusions

These six studies demonstrate various aspects of and opportunities for sustainable development, and the many problems encountered in implementing it. These and similar approaches around the globe seem to offer some promise for conservation of biodiversity and natural systems, but not everyone is impressed by their potential. Many skeptics feel that sustainable development is a camouflaged, "politically correct" approach to further and perpetual economic growth and continued, but less overt, environmental destruction under the guise of conservation. Ecological economist Herman Daly has said that sustainable development "should be rejected as a bad oxymoron" (quoted in Hardin 1993). Donald Mann, president of Negative Population Growth, Inc., said that "The concept of sustainable development is little more than a gigantic exercise in self-deception," because advocates really mean "sustainable economic growth," which, in a limited world, he termed "a thundering oxymoron if ever there was one" (quoted in Hardin 1993).

Herman Daly furthermore pointed out that Norwegian Prime Minister Brundtland, chair of the Brundtland Commission, "insisted that global economic growth must increase by a factor of 5 to 10 to make so-called 'sustainable development' possible. The amount of global pollution generated if the world turnover of nature's bounty were to become 5 to 10 times greater than it is now should give pause to even the most 'optimistic' of anticonservatives." Few economists have bothered to say a word against Brundtland's "optimistic" remedy for the world's ills. Natural scientists, however, delight in quoting the words of Kenneth Boulding, former president of the American Economic Association: "Only madmen and economists believe in perpetual exponential growth." (Hardin 1993). So, can sustainable development really work, or is it merely a ploy by economists to justify continued development? Let's take a look at the "down side" of these issues for a moment.

Some argue that there has never been a case of successful sustainability over the long term; the resource has inevitably been overexploited. This is particularly apparent in commercial fishing, in which the concept of maximum sustained yield (MSY) has driven policy for decades. Under this concept, harvest is done at a rate such that the exploited population is maintained at a level of maximum production (see Figure 12.2). Although this makes sense in theory, in reality it has often resulted in loss of fisheries after a period of overexploitation (Larkin 1977). It is impossible to accurately estimate the point of maximum yield; that point changes over time and space, and no known population grows according to a logistic curve, as assumed by the model. If the sometimes considerable uncertainties involved in estimating MSY curves are not taken into account, these are dangerous models to use for predicting sustainability.

Beyond fishery failures, why have such models of sustainability not worked thus far? Ludwig et al. (1993) offer these common features of our failures at sustainability:

1. Wealth or the prospect of wealth generates political and social power that is used to promote unlimited exploitation of resources.
2. Scientific understanding and consensus is hampered by the lack of controls and replicates, so that each new problem involves learning about a new system.
3. The complexity of the underlying biological and physical systems precludes a reductionist approach to management. Optimum levels of exploitation must be determined by trial and error.
4. Large levels of natural variability mask the effects of overexploitation. Initial overexploitation is not detectable until it is severe and often irreversible.

They go on to say:

It is more appropriate to think of resources as managing humans than the converse: the larger and the more immediate the prospects for [economic] gain, the greater the political power that is used to facilitate unlimited exploitation. The classic illustrations are gold rushes [or old-growth forests]. Where large and immediate gains are in prospect, politicians and governments tend to ally themselves with special interest groups in order to facilitate the exploitation.

In a response to Ludwig et al. (1993), Rosenberg et al. (1993) indicated that multiple examples of sustained fisheries do exist, but many failures have indeed occurred. These failures, they argue, are less a function of inadequate scientific understanding than of frequent "... failure of resource managers to follow scientific advice." Resource managers, they say, have frequently ignored scientific evidence and allowed higher harvest levels than are sustainable. Thus, attaining truly sustainable development seems as much a problem in changing human behavior and value systems as it is a biological or ecological problem. Unless human value systems change globally, and political and economic power no longer favors overexploitation, the prospects for sustainability appear dim. Ludwig et al. (1993) offer five principles of effective management that would help promote truly sustainable development:

> 1. Include human motivation and responses as part of the system to be studied and managed. . . . 2. Act before scientific consensus is achieved. Calls for additional research may be mere delaying tactics. . . . 3. Rely on scientists to recognize problems, but not to remedy them. The judgement of scientists is often heavily influenced by their training in their respective disciplines, but the most important issues involving resources and the environment involve interactions whose understanding may involve many disciplines. . . . 4. Distrust claims of sustainability. Because past resource exploitation has seldom been sustainable, any new plan that involves claims of sustainability should be suspect. One should inquire how the difficulties that have been encountered in past resource exploitation are to be overcome. . . . 5. Confront uncertainty. Once we free ourselves from the illusion that science or technology (if lavishly funded) can provide a solution to resource or conservation problems, appropriate action becomes possible.

We do not offer these counter-perspectives to discourage a drive toward sustainable development or to denigrate the concept. Indeed, several of the case studies incorporated these points, and a truly sustainable global society, combined with a stable (zero growth) human population, seems the only real hope for avoiding the massive biological extinctions and ecosystem collapses discussed in earlier chapters. Instead, we caution that blind acceptance of the sustainable development approach can be dangerous to conservation interests because there are so many potential problems and pitfalls, and because the concept can be abused to the benefit of further growth. Healthy skepticism, combined with honest attempts to balance the needs of natural systems against actual, long-term human needs, seems the most sensible approach.

Sustainable development certainly is possible, and may be the best hope for conservation of global biodiversity. However, three things must change radically if this is to be achieved. First, the value systems that lie at the core of the human fabric and drive our collective behaviors need to change drastically (discussed in Chapter 18). In wealthy, developed countries, long-term global sustainability must replace short-term personal gain as the primary human motivation. People must learn to value the environmental services provided by natural ecosystems, to understand the relationship between ecosystem protection and their long-term economic security, to reduce excessive resource exploitation, and to raise their appreciation of their natural heritage. Second, the growth-oriented economic systems that drive human existence must be replaced by equilibrium-oriented, ecological–economic systems that accept natural limits to our artificial economies. Finally, human population growth must slow, stop, and eventually reverse; toward this goal, sustainable development projects must contain internal incentives to limit population growth. These topics are addressed more fully in the final chapter.

## Questions for Discussion

1. Keeping in mind the difference between "growth" and "development," do you think global economies need to expand in order to maintain a state of sustainable development? If they continually expand, *is* it sustainable development?

2. Many claims of sustainability are, under the surface, false. What criteria might you use to judge sustainability?

3. Consider this scenario: a major United States building supply franchaise contracts with a South American consortium to provide mahogany doors in a sustainable fashion. Mahogany trees are carefully managed in cooperatives so that relatively few are harvested annually, at or below the replacement rate, keeping the resource sustainable. The world market is then limited to the doors that can be made from this amount of mahogany and no more, keeping both price and demand high. Is this scenario in fact sustainable? How might a "cheater" external to the system prosper and thereby destroy the process?

4. Discuss some of the potential problems with possible ecotourism ventures near you. What issues would need to be addressed to ensure that ecotourism would be sustainable and not damaging to natural areas?

5. Some conservationists have proposed "extractive reserves" (i.e., non-timber harvest of forest products) as good models of economic and ecological sustainability. What are some potential extractive reserve products in your region? Discuss the limitations of extractive reserves. Under what circumstances might they be sustainable?

6. One of the keys to long-term sustainability is a stable or declining human population. However, declining populations do not simply change in numbers, but also in age structure and geographic distribution. What implications might these changes have for sustainable development? Think about issues such as taxes, trade, leisure time, health, resource demand, and tourism.

## Suggestions for Further Reading

Daly, H. E. and J. B. Cobb, Jr. 1989. *For the Common Good: Redirecting the Economy Toward Community, the Environment, and a Sustainable Future.* Beacon Press, Boston. Daly and Cobb identify the logical fallacies of economics as currently practiced, show how economics works against community and ecological sustainability, and provide excellent suggestions for the development of a new, ecologically and humanly more sensible, economics.

Goodland, R., H. Daly and S. El Serafy (eds.). 1991. *Environmentally Sustainable Economic Development: Building on Brundtland.* Working paper, The World Bank, Washington, D. C. This is a critique of the principles laid out by *Our Common Future* (the Brundtland report) for sustainability. It helps to expose the fallacies of continued economic growth as the answer to sustainability.

Korten, D. C. 1991–1992. Sustainable development. *World Policy Journal* 9:157–190. This is an outstanding analysis of sustainable development and the problems in economic institutions that promote unsustainability. Korten provides an astute perspective on traditional economics, global lending policies, and human attitudes, all of which need to be overhauled in order to move toward sustainability.

# 18

# Meeting Conservation Goals in an Uncertain Future

*It is often said today that 'what we need are more facts.' Actually we already have more facts than we know how to interpret or how to use wisely. What we need most is the wisdom which facts ought to generate but often, unfortunately, do not.*

*Joseph Wood Krutch, 1962*

We have now come a long way in our journey into the principles of conservation biology, but the most difficult task remains: transduction of conservation knowledge into human lifestyle changes that are consistent with what we know about the natural world and our effects on it. The challenges facing the human species are legion, but none is greater than getting the majority of humanity to recognize the conservation problems facing the world, admit that they are serious problems, and commit to vastly changing the human condition in appropriate ways. As a species, we have barely begun that effort. Much of the necessary knowledge, ecological and otherwise, to accomplish the task is in place. What remains is a "buy-in" from *Homo sapiens* to live up to its moniker of "wise man." This is perhaps the greatest challenge in the history of humanity.

Momentous changes are needed in the way that humanity conducts its business and relates to the natural world if the principles of conservation biology are even to be given a chance to work. We will discuss some of those necessary changes in this chapter, with the hope of clearly identifying areas in which we can make major and relatively rapid advances toward conservation of biodiversity. But the changes are not trivial, and the resistance will be great. Thomas Berry (1988) stated this succinctly: "We must be clear concerning the *order of magnitude* of the changes that are needed. We are not concerned here with some minor adaptations, but with the most serious transformation of human–earth relations that has taken place at least since the classical civilizations were founded." Indeed, an entirely new way of thinking must be explored and adopted if biodiversity and the quality of human existence are to remain high. Such visions for a changing future are presented in Essay 18A, by Frederick Ferré in his view of the "postmodern world."

## ESSAY 18A
# The Postmodern World

Frederick Ferré, University of Georgia

If we think of the "modern" world as beginning in the 17th century, the period when a distinctly modern science was founded by Galileo, Descartes, and Newton, we can appreciate how rapidly we are leaving that world behind. The modern framework of ideas, despite nearly three centuries of triumph, has proved no longer adequate for our best scientific thinking, and the technological society shaped by these ideas is no longer satisfactory for life on this fragile planet.

We cannot be certain about what is coming next, once the current transition from the modern world's ideas, attitudes, technologies, and institutions is complete. For this reason we haltingly (and uninformatively) call the new era we are entering "postmodern." But if we look at the main ways in which modern ideas—both in the abstract and as incarnated in the structures of modern civilization—have failed us, and if we look along the vector of the new ideas that are gradually growing up to replace them, we may be able to speculate with some hope on the general character of the rising postmodern world.

The main features of modern scientific thinking were (1) its stress on quantities over qualities, (2) its tendency to break problems into ever smaller parts (reductionism), and (3) its firm rejection of explanations involving purpose (or mind) in nature.

First, all the founders of modern science were opponents of the ancient and medieval emphases on thinking qualitatively about things. Instead, they translated qualities like heat and color into attributes that could be measured and counted and turned into mathematical formulae. The process began in astronomy with Kepler's laws of motion, and in physics with Galileo's studies of falling bodies and Newton's experiments on the refraction of light. Only the numerable could be precisely known; therefore (it was too quickly concluded), only the quantitative could be "really real" or fundamentally important. This devotion to the quantifiable has resulted in rapid progress in all the fields in which qualities could be safely ignored, particularly in physics. But as the civilization built on these scientific attitudes grew rich and powerful—both quantitative measures—issues of quality seemed less and less to matter. The "bottom line" for the effective rulers of this civilization became a quantitative one. Quality, in personal lives, in environment, became a matter of "mere value judgments," and was relegated to the bottom of the priority list. But real human beings occupy a world of experienced qualities. Failure to nurture quality leads to the anger, despair, and violence all too familiar in the waning years of the modern world.

Second, typical modern thought rests on an assumption that problems are best solved by analysis: cutting them up into ever-smaller questions for individual solution. As modern science sought to give all its explanations in terms of littlest parts, it also encouraged specialization in smaller and smaller units of subject matter. Thus, modern civilization has at its foundations the assumption that reality is just a conglomeration of material particles and that ideal knowledge is more and more about less and less. When characteristically engineered modern technologies are introduced into the tangled web of causes and effects in nature, however, we find that "side effects" like climate change and ozone holes mock our compartmentalized ways of thinking and threaten us in potentially catastrophic ways.

Third, modern scientific thinking defined itself as determined to avoid ancient ways of explaining phenomena by including reference to real goals in nature. The modern way was to restrict explanation to quantified formulae dealing with prior causes only. Modern thinking, as a result, has had a hard time finding a place for itself in the real world. If there are no goals in nature, but humans have goals, then it seems that humans are not in nature. If there are no qualities except in our minds, where are our minds? The modern civilization that was built on these ideas has increasingly isolated and alienated humankind from the world of physics and even of biology. Hillsides became resources; animals turned into commodities.

In all these ways the modern world-view has fallen short. It has institutionalized the neglect of quality, the disregard for the subtler connectedness of things, and the alienation of humanity from nature. If we look, instead, at the direction in which new thinking is taking us, we find that in all these respects a postmodern consensus is developing. This is true not only for many disillusioned writers and artists but also for many scientists. The fact that some fields of science itself are becoming distinctly postmodern may encourage us to hope that whole new institutions and technologies grounded in new ways of thinking, now to be described, may be achieved in a postmodern world.

Although one could look to fundamental changes in physics, chemistry, and systems theory for postmodern elements, the science leading most obviously toward the postmodern reform is ecology. Ecology does not abandon quantitative, analytical tools, of course. It is not a premodern science, urging return to obscurity and imprecision; it is, rather, a new science incorporating, yet going beyond, the typical modern sciences. Although it uses modern quantitative analysis as a tool, it is rooted in the recognition of quality as a vital feature of the world it studies. Ecology can and must recognize the qualitative differences between healthy and damaged ecosystems. Its repertoire is wide, and includes "number crunching," but its "bottom line" is not numbers. Its postmodern goal is understanding life thriving in an environment.

Ecology also deals essentially in complexity and connection. Although it uses simplification (modeling) as a tool along the way, it recognizes that ecological systems are interconnected wholes made up of organisms that are themselves interconnected wholes. Reductive, overspecialized "tunnel vision" is ruled out by both the subject matter and the goals of ecology. In a world like ours, in which there are no "side effects" except those relative to our ignorance or neglect, ecology teaches us to look carefully on all sides before concluding that our technological interventions in nature are safe.

Ecology, if attended to, also overcomes the alienation of humanity from the rest of nature. Not only are we reminded of our connection to everything else, we are also shown to be part of a continuous, evolving organic world of interactive goals. Animals have interests, too; every species, not only *Homo sapiens*, has a good-of-its-kind. It is in the long-term interest of species to maintain the health of the complex whole in which thriving can be sustained.

The postmodern world is not yet here, but the modern world is visibly failing and new possibilities are coming to light. One possible future would be a world organized around the ideas and attitudes of ecology, the bellwether postmodern science. Such a world would nurture the human hunger for quality: for beauty, balance, creative advance. Its technologies and institutions would embody the recognition of the subtle, often surprising connections between disparate things, emphasizing the benefits of interdisciplinary thinking in education and the joys of cooperative pluralism in global culture. In such a world we would find methods of transportation and housing, heating and cooling, farming and manufacture, that respect the natural order, organic and inorganic. It would allow the human race to join the web of life as a significant participant rather than an exploiting tyrant. Such a postmodern world seems to be on its way; but it could use our help in being born.

---

In this concluding chapter we offer some guidance to help you find your way through the confusion, uncertainty, and challenges of the future. We emphasize two general approaches: tangible actions that can be taken to reduce uncertainty and risk in the short term, and major societal changes we should encourage that will provide the necessary conditions for conserving biodiversity in the long term. The fate of biodiversity depends on how well we, as a species, can adopt and incorporate these ideas.

## The Nature and Centrality of Uncertainty

We live in a world characterized by many forms of uncertainty. Death, taxes, the final exam, and the sun rising and setting are examples of deterministic processes and events that we can count on with great certainty, but most of our decisions, either as citizens or professional conservation biologists, are made in a climate of some uncertainty and risk. We know that we live in a probabilistic world where we must assess the odds of alternative conservation decisions, do the best we can, and try to minimize the adverse effects of consequences we did not intend. The success of this text will be measured somewhat by the extent to which you are now able to understand the complexity that characterizes much of conservation biology, determine and evaluate competing conservation decisions, and take actions to reduce the risk and consequences of failure.

The three great variables that influence uncertainty and risk are (1) the quality, depth, and breadth of information available; (2) the complexity and nonlinearity of the processes whose outcome we are trying to predict; and (3) how far into the future we wish to carry our predictions. It is critically important for the long-term prospects of conserving biodiversity that you come to terms with how you are going to make decisions now in order to improve the future. If you do not, if you become paralyzed by the seemingly overwhelming odds against success, then you have simply made a different kind of decision that will affect the future: a decision to do nothing.

## Responding to Short-Term Economic Change

Nobody has a very clear idea of what the economies of the world will look like in a hundred years, although we can say with certainty that we will be closer to nature's finite limits and may have exceeded some, unless our appetite for consuming the world's natural resources substantially decreases.

**Figure 18.1**  Our imaginary corporation, "BioPro, Inc.," like any service industry, has four major concerns: we must get people to value our service, we must manage and develop our business, we must invest our income, and we must shape public policy to enhance our industry.

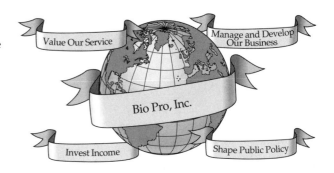

In the shorter run, say over periods of several years to a decade, we can look at recent history as our best guide to the future. Thus, we can expect to see a global economy that is growing slowly, with some countries and regions doing better than others. The quality-of-life gap between poorer countries, such as many in Africa, and the richer industrialized countries will continue to expand. Within individual countries, frequent recessional periods will force the retrenchment of public programs, including those that support conservation of biodiversity. This is the uncertain economic environment of the future. As conservation biologists, what are our options for securing resources to maintain critical conservation programs and advance the principles of conservation?

An analogy may help. Imagine that conservation biology is like a service industry, such as insurance sales, and the service we are selling is called "biodiversity protection." How do we simultaneously protect our industry, which we will call "BioPro, Inc.," from adverse economic events and encourage its development? We would probably pursue four general strategies (Figure 18.1). First, we would encourage people to value our service. Second, we would look for better ways to manage and develop our business. Third, we would look for the best investment of our income. And fourth, we would help to shape public policy so that our industry would receive incentives for continued growth and development. As you can imagine, this analogy would quickly break down if we followed it too far, but we simply ask, as conservationists, can we pursue similar strategies?

### Increasing the Perceived Value of Conservation Biology

The most effective thing we can do is convince as many people as possible to share our conviction that conserving biodiversity is an important value and that, in various ways, public support will maintain this value. As individual professionals, we should make two commitments for strengthening public support: to formal and to informal environmental education. First, we should each find some means for actively contributing to environmental education in schools, especially at the elementary and secondary levels (Figure 18.2). If your reaction to this suggestion is "I don't know anything about teaching children and adolescents, I'm a research scientist!," your protest is without merit. The potential range of contributions to environmental education is so large that even the most entrenched researcher can find something useful to offer. Probably the most generally useful contribution we can make is through helping teachers develop curricular materials, such as case studies for teaching, photographic slides and films, simple experimental designs, or just by serving as resource contacts. More active involvement could include anything from leading an occasional field trip to visiting classrooms and telling students what conservation ecologists do and why it is important.

**Figure 18.2** Education of children regarding nature and conservation is an easy and rewarding activity. The natural curiosity and open minds of children make them wonderful recipients for conservation education. Here, a member of the Savannah River Ecology Laboratory Environmental Outreach Program discusses snakes and their ecological roles with an eager group of elementary school students. (Photograph by David Scott.)

Informal public education is also important, and the two best ways to communicate with the public are through popular "nature" articles and books, and through contact with print and broadcast journalists. Scientists, with some famous exceptions, tend to shy away from journalists, perhaps feeling that they will not understand what scientists do and therefore the science will neither be appreciated nor correctly interpreted. Sometimes these concerns are valid, but because journalists are our bridge to the public, we can ill afford not to work with them. Besides, when communication has broken down, there is fault on both sides: the journalist may not understand what the scientist is saying, and the scientist may have become too lazy or too preoccupied with his or her arcane work to communicate effectively to the public. The importance to conservation of public communication is elaborated further by Laura Tangley in Essay 18B.

We must remember that the public supports the work of scientists through taxes, and it is simply unethical to deliberately keep the public ignorant of this work. The vast majority of the public may in fact be uninterested in what you do as a scientist, but they have a right to know, and we, as scientists, have an obligation to make an effort at communicating on their terms. This can only help in improving the value of our "product."

## ESSAY 18B
# The Importance of Communicating with the Public

Laura Tangley, Conservation International

In the fall of 1992, the Brazilian journal *Goeldiana Zoologia* published a paper describing a new primate species, the Rio Maues marmoset (*Callithrix mauesi*). Like most reports in obscure scientific journals, this one would have gone virtually unnoticed if not for one thing: one of the three primatologists who described the new species, Russell Mitter-

meier, was president of a conservation organization.

On the day the report was published, the organization, Conservation International, sent out a press release on *Callithrix mauesi*. Within a few weeks, stories about the marmoset appeared in more than 500 magazines and newspapers, reaching an audience of at least 36

million worldwide.

More important, these 36 million people also learned about the conservation significance of the finding. "The discovery of a new primate species attests to the vast diversity of life on earth that remains unknown to us," said Mittermeier in the press release. "It also shows how ignorant we still are of our fellow species—even fairly well-studied groups like our closest relatives, the primates." The release went on to discuss the importance of biodiversity, the species extinction crisis, and the significance of the Amazon to protecting global biodiversity.

To Mittermeier, a conservation biologist, communicating the significance of this scientific discovery was at least as important as the discovery itself. After all, the conservation biologist is a new breed of scientist that cares deeply about saving, as well as studying, earth's plants, animals, and ecosystems. It was in fact biologists—including Mittermeier, E. O. Wilson of Harvard University, Peter Raven of the Missouri Botanical Garden, Paul Ehrlich of Stanford University, Norman Myers of Oxford University, and Daniel Janzen of the University of Pennsylvania, among many others—who first brought the biodiversity crisis to the attention of policymakers and the public.

Today, continued vigilance in science and conservation communication remains critical. Solving our most serious environmental problems, including pollution, overpopulation, deforestation, and species extinctions, will require that both the government and the private sector invest considerable amounts of time, effort, and money, something that is possible only if there is broad awareness and support by the public.

Similarly, public *mis*information can thwart conservation efforts. The best-known recent example has been the controversy surrounding the old-growth forests of the United States Pacific Northwest. This controversy, which has been depicted far too often as an issue of logging jobs versus the Spotted Owl, is in fact much more complicated. Although it is true that many jobs

have been lost in the logging industry in recent years, the major causes—including increased automation and the practice of exporting raw logs as opposed to finished wood products—stem from economics, not conservation. An even more important point missed by the public throughout this controversy is that the forests themselves—not just the owl—are at stake. The primary forests of the United States, which once blanketed 385 million ha of the nation, have now been reduced to scattered remnants. The largest remaining blocks of old-growth forest are in the Pacific Northwest.

These ancient, complex ecosystems support hundreds of plant and animal species. Some of these species, including the Spotted Owl, live nowhere else on earth. Old-growth forests also ensure water quantity and quality, protect salmon fisheries and other economically important resources, and earn the region millions of dollars a year in tourism and recreation. So while important in its own right, the Spotted Owl is much more: the bird has become a symbol of the nation's last old-growth forests and the many services they provide.

Of course, mailing out a press release would have done little to prevent the misunderstanding surrounding the Spotted Owl, which was fueled in part by timber industry efforts to deliberately mislead the public. In addition, most biologists are in no position—or have no desire—to become so directly involved with the press. But this does not mean these scientists lack opportunities to communicate with the public.

Conservation biologists who care about the species and habitats they study should take advantage of every opportunity to share their knowledge and concern. When writing journal arti-

cles, for example, scientists should always explain the conservation implications of their work. If possible, they should include photographs or drawings of the species and ecosystems they study to bring their work to life. For those who like to write, submitting an article to a popular publication is an even better way to communicate with the public. Certainly it will experience broader readership than it would in a scientific journal.

In addition, conservation biologists should make themselves available to journalists who work on environmental stories for newspapers, magazines, radio, or television. Better still, they could offer to hold briefings for reporters who have access to large audiences, and keep those journalists up to date on new developments. Whenever possible, they should describe the species, ecosystems, and research involved in their projects in terms that the general public can understand.

Another good way to reach large audiences is to write editorials for newspapers and magazines. A particularly good time to do this is whenever the public's interest—and the interest of editors—has been piqued by some political or other kind of controversy.

Beyond these specific ideas, conservation biologists should simply be aware at all times of the importance of communicating with the public. Take every opportunity that arises to talk to students, friends, and family about conservation. Better still, invite people to visit your study site with you, or another natural area. As any biologist who cares about conservation knows, there is nothing better than direct experience in the field to awaken a lifelong love and concern for earth's biodiversity.

## Improving Conservation Management and Development

A business that is operating under increased financial pressure cannot tolerate the luxury of inefficient operations and unnecessary management. The primary goal of conservation biology is the preservation of biodiversity, including the potential for adaptive responses to environmental change, over the long run. Therefore, the metric by which we should judge the institutions of conservation—including the management and effectiveness of their operations—is their contribution to the protection of biodiversity.

We can roughly divide institutions into two classes, based on whether their mandate is direct protection, such as through land purchases and environmental law, or indirect protection, through research and education. Direct protection is the purview of individuals, private organizations, and some public agencies. Individuals may directly protect biodiversity through land protection and good stewardship, conservation easements, living bequests, and donations to other organizations. Private organizations may protect biodiversity through land purchases (e.g., The Nature Conservancy) or through support of conservation management (e.g., World Wildlife Fund). Public agencies, such as the nongame parts of natural resource agencies, may directly support biodiversity protection, and are also the instrument through which laws protecting biodiversity are implemented.

Indirect protection is usually the domain of educational institutions, and ranges from environmental education in the elementary grades through research and training at the university level. Increasingly, private stewardship organizations are supporting research (the Andrew W. Mellon Foundation has supported research in plant ecology) and training (the Jessie Smith Noyes Foundation has sponsored training programs for Latin American conservation biologists). Significant research and training is also conducted by public agencies; for example, the U.S. Fish and Wildlife Service, through its Western Hemisphere program, has supported research and training in Latin America.

How can we judge the effectiveness of such a multitude of programs? This broad question has to be divided into two smaller questions. First, do the goals of the programs really directly or indirectly improve the protection of biodiversity? Second, do the organizations have an effective program for achieving their goals? With regard to the first question, some institutions with conservation programs have goals only marginally related to the protection of biodiversity. Some examples include public agencies whose multiple-use mandates seriously compromise their ability to protect biodiversity. This is the central problem of protecting public resources as "commons," which we discuss in depth later in this chapter. Private stewardship organizations that are excessively focused on single-species protection may not represent the best allocation of scarce resources. Major lending agencies, such as large private banks, that compromise biodiversity protection in economic development projects may give little more than lip service to protection.

With regard to the second question, it is often difficult to gauge the effectiveness of conservation programs unless they have conducted programmatic evaluations, but it is possible to make some general observations. For example, other things being similar, a school that offers a few isolated units on environmental education is likely to be less effective than one that incorporates environmental education through all grade levels and courses. Public agencies that allocate large fractions of their budget and personnel to supporting game, recreational, and resource extraction interests, and only token support to biodiversity protection, are unlikely to be very effective protectors of biodiversity. Unfortunately, most United States natural resource agencies fall into this category, much to the frustration of the often excellent conservation biologists who work for them.

Finally, one way to evaluate the effectiveness of private stewardship organizations is to examine the proportion of their funds that are spent on programmatic activities versus administrative support or other fund-raising efforts. However, private stewardship organizations cannot be evaluated by the general formulas that might be applied to other "charitable" organizations. For example, the discovery that a charity associated with a particular religion has a low fund-raising cost in comparison with a secular conservation organization simply says that the religious charity has a "captive clientele" that requires relatively less effort for fund raising. It is more reasonable to compare similar conservation organizations with one another, comparing their public records of the ratio of programmatic funds to other overhead funds.

**Improving Investment**

We do not usually sell our conservation services for money, except as consultants, and so conservation biology as a service does not have investment income in the way other for-profit service industries do. However, because biodiversity protection has social value, we have access to funds from private donors, corporations, development banks, private foundations, international agencies, and governmental institutions. How can we best use those funds?

Most of the funds are made available only for restricted uses that match the interests of donors, or to meet the programmatic goals of foundations and public institutions. As conservation biologists, we have two options: either work actively to reshape the agendas of the donors and institutions so that they meet the most important needs of conservation biology, or try to find the best fit between our interests and the interests of the source of support for our work.

The latter approach is not necessarily as vulgarly opportunistic as it might appear. Perhaps because we have been doing an effective job of environmental education, the individuals and private and public agencies that support conservation biology are now far more knowledgeable and sophisticated about biodiversity protection than they were just a few years ago. Therefore, finding a match between an important conservation project and a source of potential support is not nearly as difficult now as it used to be.

It is also possible to reshape the agendas of the various donor and institutional sources supporting conservation programs. This is not an easy task because the setting of priorities for support is usually the product of considerable analysis and possibly some internal constraints. Consider first how a private foundation might set its priorities for supporting programs in conservation. A private foundation working from a restricted endowment or trust may be precluded from certain areas of activity, such as family planning and birth control, by the terms used to create the endowment or trust. Given the areas that are appropriate, the program directors of the foundation may consult with knowledgeable people outside the foundation to determine important areas that need support. With these priorities in mind, the program directors may look at what other foundations and public sources are doing and then choose to support some important kinds of programs that are currently underfunded. Usually, a board of directors of the foundation will then have to decide whether or not to approve the choices made by the program directors and what level of support should be made available. Still, by writing focused articles on the role of foundations and by cultivating interactions with program directors, it is possible to effect changes.

It is more difficult to reshape the agendas of public agencies because their priorities are usually compromises between what they should be, based on ecological reasoning, and what can receive political backing. During the Reagan and Bush Administrations, for example, support for programs that encouraged family planning and birth control was actively discouraged and, in some cases, simply not allowed. The best chance for reshaping the agendas of public agencies is through the public affairs offices or programs of professional societies such as the Society for Conservation Biology and the Ecological Society of America, and through NGOs, such as the World Wildlife Fund and The Nature Conservancy.

While change may be slow and difficult to achieve, it is not impossible, and some recent successes can be cited. As recently as the late 1980s, support for biodiversity protection was nearly nonexistent in U.S. foreign assistance programs for developing nations. Now, biodiversity protection has become an active part of such programs to the extent that it is the norm for the U.S.

Agency for International Development to include biodiversity support as part of each country's portfolio of programs. Similarly, the U.S. Endangered Species Act of 1973 and subsequent amendments to the Act have prohibited federal programs from jeopardizing threatened or endangered species and have authorized the federal departments of Commerce and Interior to protect and recover these vulnerable species. In large part, the improvement in federal program support for biodiversity protection is the result of collective efforts made by nongovernmental organizations and professional conservation societies.

## Developing Policy Incentives

We need better ways for public policy to create economic incentives for biodiversity protection. Usually public policy influences biodiversity protection in two ways, both of which are negative: through punitive legislation that assesses fines or jail sentences when environmental laws are broken, and, usually inadvertently, by offering disincentives for protection. Examples of the latter include the mandate for multiple use of U.S. national forests—which places biodiversity protection on the same level as recreational use of off-road vehicles—and the undervaluing of grazing fees for cattle using public lands. Clearly, we need to eliminate such disincentives in public policy and find more innovative and flexible *positive* incentives for biodiversity protection.

One example of an innovative and positive economic incentive is the idea of a flexible environmental assurance bonding system (Costanza 1991), as discussed in Chapter 15. Such a system would encourage environmental technological innovation by incorporating environmental criteria and future uncertainty into the marketplace. Under this plan, development loans would require that the borrower take out a long-term bond against any environmental damage that might be caused by the project in the future. If damage occurred, then the bond and accrued interest could be used to repair the damage. If no damage occurred, then the value of the bond and some of the interest would return to the borrower. The hope is that the cost of the bond would encourage developers to be more cautious about projects and to pursue more environmentally benign forms of development. Obviously, the value of the bond must be high enough to provide the necessary economic incentive for borrowers to change their ways; also, the real cost of repairing any future damage must be accurately reflected by the face value and accrued interest of the bond.

It is in innovative ways such as these that the conservation community—"BioPro, Inc."—must respond to short-term economic uncertainties and vagaries. It should be obvious that there is room for many more new perspectives and contributions in this area.

## Responding to Long-Term Planetary Environmental Change

Any reading of either the long-term paleontological history of the earth or of its shorter-term history since the beginning of the Pleistocene must convey a sense of changing environments. In Chapter 4, we reviewed the most important of these environmental changes and showed how they influenced contemporary patterns of conservation, especially through the creation of centers of high endemism such as Madagascar. Other chapters emphasized two related points. First, species distributions have changed markedly over the past 12,000 years or so, largely in response to changing climate. Second, community composition has not been constant, but rather, species have migrated largely independently of other species.

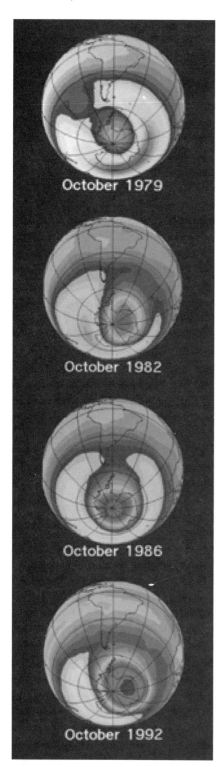

**Figure 18.3** Although local patterns of atmospheric ozone depletion are difficult to predict, there is little doubt that ozone is being depleted to dangerously low levels over some parts of the earth. Note the changes in shape and size of the ozone hole over the South Pole over a 13-year period.

There is every reason to believe that the earth will continue to change in the future and that these changes will continue to influence biodiversity patterns and processes. However, as we emphasized in our chapters on biodiversity losses, reserve design, and conservation management, there are now two new considerations that will profoundly affect our attempts to conserve biodiversity for future generations. The first is that human effects on the environment, primarily through habitat destruction and degradation, are accelerating the rate of extinction. The second is that increased fragmentation and isolation of natural habitat has greatly limited the possibilities for long-distance migration. Historically, species have responded to climate change by migrating, albeit over many generations, to more favorable regions. Fragmentation and isolation have largely foreclosed that option.

Of course we have no oracle to guide our conservation programs very far into the next millennium, but if we take the next hundred years as a reasonable time frame for conservation planning, there are some broad environmental changes that we can anticipate and whose effects we should be able to mitigate through careful planning now. There seems little doubt that global climate patterns are going to change significantly over the next hundred years. Our rampant industrialized economies continue to pollute the atmosphere to such an extent that ozone is being depleted over polar regions, and the heat balance of the globe is possibly being altered (Figure 18.3).

The engine for climate change is in place, but there is great uncertainty over how the climate will change in any particular locality (Box 18A). There are basically three options for conservation planning, given this degree of uncertainty. First, the design for reserves should include an array of climate refugia, such as permanent water sources should the climate become drier, or a greater altitudinal range should the temperature change. Second, there should be larger-scale planning for corridor connections that will allow animals and plants more opportunity to migrate, as was discussed in several chapters and essays. The third option is to plan for more active management of populations and reserves in order to minimize the effects of climate change. In the latter case, management programs may include anything from introducing new food sources, to maintaining high levels of heterozygosity and thereby preserving adaptability, to translocating populations to more favorable regions. It is up to individual conservation biologists and their agencies to develop locally workable ideas to mitigate the effects of an altered climate.

We should also realize that local climate change may not represent a drastic alteration from current patterns but may still be large enough to have some effect on population dynamics. How should we plan for uncertain change at this level? There are several general strategies worth considering. First, we may consider doing nothing beyond what is needed to meet existing problems. This approach would make sense if we had reason to believe that the system was likely to be resilient to moderate climate change; that is, that there might be some reshuffling of relative species abundances but no species would be put at special risk of extinction. This neutral strategy might apply, for example, to communities whose member species are adapted to highly variable climates, such as species of the Great Plains of North America.

Second, in cases in which we think peripheral populations might suffer greater extinction rates, we should think of approaches that both decrease probabilities of local extinction and enhance recolonization following extinction. That is, our planning efforts should reflect the need to maintain sensitive populations well above their lower limits of viability, as well as considering source–sink dynamics and the "rescue effect" of metapopulation structure as discussed in Chapter 7. Such a strategy might involve maintain-

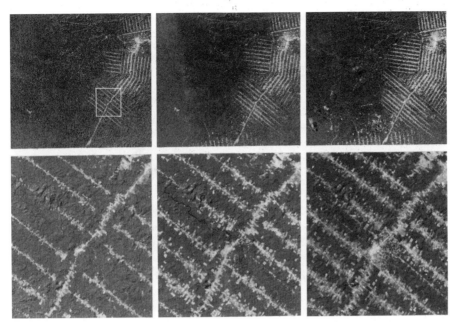

**Figure 18.4**   Progressive habitat loss is demonstrated by development in and destruction of the Amazon Basin in Brazil. These six Landsat satellite images of central Rondonia show progressive forest destruction from 1976 (left), 1978 (middle) and 1981 (right). In each case, a 185 × 185 km block is shown on the top, and an inset of 30 × 30 km is on the bottom. Uncut forest is dark, and cleared areas are light. Note progressive deforestation in only five years. (Photographs courtesy of Thomas A. Stone, Woods Hole Research Center.)

ing well-protected core habitat both as a source of migrants and as a hedge against stochastic sources of extinction, and satellite habitat both as a sink to absorb excess migrants and as a hedge against density-dependent sources of catastrophic mortality such as disease. The core–satellite model of reserve design may be the most cost-effective way to plan for moderate, but uncertain, climate change.

The other very predictable long-term environmental change is continued loss of natural areas and degradation of all habitat types. With the exception of some limited restoration activities, habitat destruction is a one-way street; we are destroying vast amounts of natural areas every year and creating no new ones to replace them (Figure 18.4). This pattern must be considered in all conservation planning. All protected areas become increasingly important as fewer such areas exist, and their management becomes more critical. Perhaps a good working rule is to remove from consideration any further destruction or degradation of any remaining natural areas, especially those with real wilderness characteristics.

## BOX 18A
## Scenarios for Global Climate Change
### A Summary

Many scenarios have been developed for global climate change, based on a variety of computer models. The details of these models vary greatly, depending on the assumptions used and the level of detail investigated, but together the models paint a somewhat unified picture of likely global change patterns. These are as follows:

1. All models show substantial changes in climate when $CO_2$ concentrations are doubled, even though the changes vary from model to model on a subcontinental scale.

2. The results from models become less reliable at smaller scales, so predictions for smaller than continental regions should be treated with great caution. The continents warm more than the oceans. Temperature increases in southern Europe and central North America are greater than the global mean and are accompanied by reduced precipitation and soil moisture in summer. The Asian summer monsoon is intensified.

3. Changes in the day-to-day variability of weather are uncertain. However, episodes of high temperature will become more fre-

quent in the future simply due to an increase in the mean temperature. There is some evidence of a general increase in convective precipitation.

4. The direct effect of deforestation on global mean climate is small. The indirect effects (through changes in the $CO_2$ sink) may be more important. However, tropi-

cal deforestation may lead to substantial local effects, including a reduction of about 20% in precipitation.

5. Improved predictions of global climate change require better treatment of processes affecting the distribution and properties of clouds, ocean–atmosphere interactions, convection, sea ice, and

transfer of heat and moisture from the land surface. Increased model resolution will allow more realistic predictions of global-scale changes, and some improvement in the prediction of regional climate change.

(From Intergovernmental Panel on Climate Change 1990.)

## Responding to the Demographic Imperative

The first paragraph and first figure of this book focused on human population growth, and for good reason. The human global population is currently growing at about 1.7% per year (World Population Prospects 1990); if this growth rate continues, then today's population of about 5.5 billion will double to 11 billion in about 41 years, an ominous threat. Several trends are masked by these aggregate statistics. The good news is that the growth rate of the world's population is expected to decline. Although the average growth rate was 1.73% in the late 1970s and 1.74% during the 1980s, the rate is expected to decline to 1.63% during the period 1995–2000 (World Population Prospects 1990). Today's annual population growth rate is less than what it was only 10 years ago, and for the industrialized parts of the world at least, low growth rates may be a long-term demographic feature.

But the bad news is that, though global growth rates are slowing, they are still positive. Thus, each year during 1975–1980, about 74 million people were added to our finite globe, 88 million during each year of the late 1980s, and, even with a lower population growth rate, we will add about 98 million people each year during the last half of the 1990s. To put that number in perspective, this means that *each year* for the rest of this decade we will be adding to the planet more than one-third the existing population of the United States. At the current size of the human population, and with our destructive capabilities, *any* positive growth rate is cause for concern. Additionally, the countries that continue to experience high population growth rates are typically tropical or other developing countries that are home to a large fraction of the world's biodiversity (Table 18.1).

Fortunately, economies are generally improving in developing nations (with the exception of many African countries) and this is, of course, a welcome change from the debilitating poverty that has been their legacy. However, economies that are growing are also making increasing demands on natural resources. Because birth rates are inversely correlated with per capita gross national product, we would expect to see a country's birth rate decline as its economy improves. Indeed, the developing countries in Asia and Latin America have shown striking decreases in their population growth rates. If we compare the growth rates expected during 1995–2000 with the growth rates of the late 1980s, Colombia's growth rate will decline from 1.97% to 1.70%, and Malaysia's from 2.64% to 1.85%. For the regions as a whole, South America's rate will decrease from 2.01% to 1.71%, and Asia's from 1.87% to 1.68%, but Africa's will change imperceptibly, from 2.99% to 2.98% (World Resources Institute 1992).

By itself, population size is a misleading and simplistic index of concern for the human presence on earth. A more complete and realistic view of our effects must include not just numbers, but total impacts. The impact of humanity on the earth and its resources is a function of at least its population

**Table 18.1**
Countries with the Highest Fertility Rates (Average Number of Children per Woman)

| Country | Total fertility rate | Population growth rate (%/yr) | Approx. doubling time (yrs) |
|---------|---------------------|------------------------------|-----------------------------|
| Kenya | 8.0 | 3.9 | 17.9 |
| Afghanistan | 7.6 | 2.6 | 26.9 |
| Jordan | 7.4 | 3.7 | 18.9 |
| Tanzania | 7.1 | 3.5 | 20.0 |
| Zambia | 7.0 | 3.5 | 20.0 |
| Saudi Arabia | 6.9 | 3.1 | 22.6 |
| Ethiopia | 6.7 | 2.3 | 30.4 |
| Senegal | 6.7 | 2.8 | 25.0 |
| Nigeria | 6.6 | 2.8 | 25.0 |
| Pakistan | 6.6 | 2.9 | 24.1 |
| Sudan | 6.5 | 2.8 | 25.0 |
| Zimbabwe | 6.5 | 3.5 | 20.0 |
| Iran | 6.3 | 3.2 | 21.8 |
| Bangladesh | 6.2 | 2.7 | 25.9 |
| Zaire | 6.1 | 3.1 | 22.6 |

Modified from Population Reference Bureau 1987.

size, times a measure of the average consumption of resources (an index of affluence, times a measure of the effects of the technologies used to attain that affluence. Ehrlich and Ehrlich (1990) refer to this as

$$I = P \times A \times T$$

in which overall impact (*I*) is a function of population size (*P*), times the per capita level of affluence (*A*), times the environmental disruptiveness of the technologies used (*T*).

The *I = PAT* approach indicates that we need to focus on more than simply population size. A large total impact may arise from many people, or a high consumptive standard of living, or damaging technologies, or combinations of all three. For example, a small, industrially based country could have a much greater global impact on the environment than a similar-sized country that has a mixed, less resource-consumptive economy.

This relationship between population size, affluence, and technologies means that a developed country such as the United States, with the highest level of affluence in the world and many environmentally damaging technologies, cannot expand its population at all if it does not wish to increase its environmental impact, or if it wants to retain a high standard of living. *Any* expansion of such a population has a larger environmental impact than that of any other country. Conversely, there is little hope that a country like China, India, or many other developing nations will ever have a significantly higher standard of living for all its citizens unless it either reduces its population drastically or has huge and irreversible effects on the environment.

The *I = PAT* perspective is critical because it more realistically balances the environmental influences of various cultures than does population size alone. The countries of western Europe, for example, with stable populations, and the United States, with only a modestly expanding population, cannot simply point fingers at developing countries with high population growth rates and blame them for environmental damage when the overall impacts of the developed nations are probably much higher. According to Ehrlich and Ehrlich (1990), the total impact of a baby born in the United States is "twice that of one born in Sweden, 3 times one born in Italy, 13 times one born in Brazil, 35 times one in India, 140 times one in Bangladesh or Kenya, and 280 times one in Chad, Rwanda, Haiti, or Nepal." Thus, not only are decreased population growth rates desirable in developing nations, but population shrinkage and acceptance of limits to affluence are called for in the richer, developed nations.

Unfortunately, not everyone understands or accepts the population, affluence, and technology relationship. Hardin (1993) relates that "in 1984, ecologists were astounded at the official position taken by the United States [under the Reagan administration] at the U.N. conference on population and the environment in Mexico City; our spokesman said that 'population growth is neutral.' This was also the position taken by the Vatican. All other delegations supported the default position, $I = PAT$." It is incumbent upon all knowledgeable persons to educate humanity of the dangers inherent in such denialist views.

What are we to make of population trends with regard to our long-term chances of protecting global biodiversity? On balance, we should recognize that 10 or 20 years ago we thought that the world's population picture today would be worse than it actually is. Some nations have been able to achieve drastic reductions in their population growth rates (Table 18.2). This change alone should provide some optimism that beneficial demographic shifts can happen rather quickly, and we should feel encouraged to participate in helping to make further improvements. But this optimism may simply reflect our inabilities to develop accurate demographic models and predictions; perhaps the coming decades will have *higher* growth rates than predicted. Uncertainty looms large once again.

The effect of probable population and economic trends is likely to be a mixed bag: some trends may have positive effects on conservation while others will be negative. For example, if a tropical country's economy is growing simply because it is selling more timber, then the consequences for biodiversity obviously are not improved. However, if the economy is improving because the country is investing more in service industries or manufacturing—in the production of "value-added" goods—it is possible that less pressure may be put on forests as the primary source of foreign exchange. Furthermore, to the extent that economic advance requires better-educated workers, there is a twofold effect on population growth. Family size is inversely related to level of education; as the level of education increases, average family size decreases (World Development Report 1992). Also, the process of acquiring education and training is a major commitment of time that tends to delay marriage and to increase the average age at first childbearing. These two factors, smaller family size and older parents, act as a powerful brake on population growth rates.

However, three assumptions must be met before a country's growing economy can lead to declining birth rates. First, the engine for economic growth must come from activities that require improved education and training rather than exploitation of natural capital. Second, the economic transformation must include both rural and urban sectors of the country. Third, and most important, women must fully participate in the transformation, in the form of education and empowerment to make reproductive and other decisions.

**Table 18.2**
Countries with the Greatest Reductions in Fertility Rates (Average Number of Children per Woman) from 1960 to 1987

| Country | Total fertility rate | | |
| | 1960 | 1987 | Percent change |
|---|---|---|---|
| Singapore | 6.3 | 1.6 | −75 |
| Taiwan | 6.5 | 1.8 | −72 |
| South Korea | 6.0 | 2.1 | −65 |
| Cuba | 4.7 | 1.8 | −62 |
| China | 5.5 | 2.4 | −56 |
| Chile | 5.3 | 2.4 | −55 |
| Colombia | 6.8 | 3.1 | −54 |
| Costa Rica | 7.4 | 3.5 | −53 |
| Thailand | 6.6 | 3.5 | −47 |
| Mexico | 7.2 | 4.0 | −44 |
| Brazil | 6.2 | 3.5 | −44 |
| Malaysia | 6.9 | 3.9 | −43 |
| Indonesia | 5.6 | 3.3 | −41 |
| Turkey | 6.8 | 4.0 | −41 |
| Tunisia | 7.3 | 4.5 | −38 |
| Sri Lanka | 5.9 | 3.7 | −37 |
| India | 6.2 | 4.3 | −31 |
| Philippines | 6.6 | 4.7 | −29 |
| Peru | 6.6 | 4.8 | −27 |
| Egypt | 6.7 | 5.3 | −21 |

From Brown et al. 1988.

**Figure 18.5** Positive changes in local economies can have critical demographic consequences. The illusion of economic success in cities can attract rural poor in search of a better life, but may instead result in suburban slums, such as this shantytown on the edge of Rio de Janeiro, Brazil. (Photograph UPI/Bettman.)

Increasingly, conservation ecologists are participants in international economic development projects. The protection of biodiversity now is frequently a requirement that countries must meet before they are eligible to receive development loans from multinational banks, such as the World Bank, or assistance from other countries. Thus, it is important that conservation ecologists consider the probable human demographic consequences of economic development projects. It would be hypocritical to bring a conservation biologist into a development project to ensure biodiversity protection when the nature of the project encouraged local population growth. Unfortunately, some well-meaning economic development projects do just that.

Consider the following scenario. In the lowlands of a tropical country, a small farming and logging community receives foreign assistance targeted to meet two objectives: help farmers move away from chemical dependency in their farming practices, and improve the livelihood of loggers by building a small mill so they will receive more value for the trees they cut. These are worthy objectives, but unless the details are carefully thought through, success could backfire: short-term economic improvement could result in increased local population growth—either through higher reproductive rates or immigration from surrounding areas—that would undermine both long-term economic development and biodiversity protection.

In general, improving local economies can have adverse demographic consequences in two ways. Most obviously, migrants will be attracted from poorer areas (Figure 18.5). Less obviously, some types of development may offer incentives to have more children. Why would families opt to have more children? Very simply, the history of human demography in poor countries carries two powerful messages. First, parents have children as a form of insurance, because children are expected to provide for the needs of their parents when aged. Second, parents tend to have children as long as each additional child is a positive economic asset to the family by increasing the family's labor pool (Figure 18.6).

This economic appraisal should not imply that parents in developing countries do not also love their children and make decisions for reasons other than economics. Whether parents limit the number of their children

**Figure 18.6** These Honduran children contribute to the family economy by gathering fuelwood, weeding cotton fields, and tending the family's livestock and gardens. (Photograph by C. R. Carroll.)

also will depend on their access to birth control materials and knowledge. Still, family economics is a powerful incentive that influences family size. For example, in rural Pakistan, each male child makes a positive economic contribution to the family. By the time a male child is 6 he is self-supporting, by age 12 he is a positive contributor to the family's economy, and by 22 he has already "paid back" the entire cost of his rearing and the cost of a sister of equal age (Murdoch 1980). Under those economic conditions, why would a family wish to limit the number of children?

Conservation ecologists should look for socially acceptable disincentives to population growth as an integral part of the planning of any development process. In general, these brakes on population growth will involve gender equity (the full involvement of women in economic and social development), improved education and training of the participants, and improved livelihoods that do not require converting the family into a labor pool.

Clearly, population growth must be slowed, stopped, and eventually reversed. How quickly these changes can or should be made is the subject of considerable policy debate. If changes are forced through draconian population control programs, the result may more likely be a political revolution than a demographic one, as Indian politicians discovered when citizens overwhelmingly rejected the austere population programs of Indira Gandhi and voted out the ruling party. Furthermore, it is not just increased numbers of people that are of concern; it is their pattern of consumption as well. In these terms, the addition of one more North American has a far greater negative impact on the earth's resources than the birth of a child in rural India, Sudan, or any other developing country. As conservation biologists we must look at the human demographic consequences of economic development projects; as responsible citizens we must also take a global perspective. The problems of human population growth are further developed in Essay 18C by Paul Ehrlich.

---

## ESSAY 18C
# The Bottom Line
## Human Population Control

Paul R. Ehrlich, Stanford University

---

As you learned in earlier chapters, humanity needs biodiversity as a source of foods, medicines, industrial products, and aesthetic pleasures. Even more important, microorganisms, plants, and animals are working parts of natural ecosystems that supply civilization with an array of critical services without which our economies would collapse. It is ironic, then, that human beings, in order to support themselves over the short term, are destroying natural ecosystems and the biodiversity they contain. We are paving ecosystems over, plowing them under, overgrazing, logging, flooding, draining, and poisoning them, and subjecting them to increased levels of ultraviolet-B radiation. In various ways we are changing their composition, structure, and extent so as to make them less hospitable to other organisms. In addition, anthropogenic modification of the atmospheric balance of gases is now raising the distinct possibility that climates will change at rates far in excess of the abilities of natural systems to adjust without massive extinctions of populations and species.

The large contribution to this destruction made by human population growth is easily demonstrated using the equation $I = P \times A \times T$. Unfortunately, there is no completely satisfactory statistic gathered by governments on per capita impact ($A \times T$). The best surrogate available as an index of each individual's destructive impact on ecosystems is per capita energy use, and therefore a society's impacts are best measured by its total energy use. Although it is an imperfect measure (among other things it tends to underestimate somewhat the impacts of the poorest societies), energy use so clearly is heavily involved in most environmentally damaging activities that employing it as a surrogate for them makes good sense.

Since 1850, worldwide energy use (and thus, roughly, $I$) has increased some 20-fold. In the same period, the human population ($P$) has increased about 5-fold, and per capita energy use ($A \times T$) about 4-fold. So population growth, by this measure, accounts for some 5/9 (about 55%) of the growth in environmental impact over the last 140 years.

Similar considerations show that, because of their very high per capita impacts, the rich nations account for roughly 70% of the environmental destruction now occurring. Nonetheless, continuing rapid population growth and substantial plans for development in poor nations indicate that their share of the blame may soon escalate. For example, if China and India should both choose to fuel future development with their abundant coal reserves, each could soon be adding more $CO_2$ to the atmosphere than the United States could remove by ceasing to use coal (now almost 25% of U.S. energy supply). That would happen, even under highly optimistic assumptions about success in controlling their population growth, before either China or India had achieved 15% of U.S. per capita energy consumption—just because of the gigantic size of those nations' populations.

Loss of biodiversity, however, may at first glance not seem as well indexed by energy statistics as is environmental deterioration overall. Because of the large-scale invasion of species-rich tropical forests by landless farmers, the greatest loss of *species* diversity is occurring in the poor nations. But energy-profligate rich nations bear indirect responsibility for their landlessness, and often contribute to other causes of tropical deforestation. Moreover, critical diversity of natural populations is being rapidly lost in the developed countries as habitats are altered and destroyed. Most important, rich nations are making the largest contribution to the massive threats to biodiversity posed by global warming and ozone depletion.

The growing human population also competes for resources very directly with populations of other animals. For instance, today the global human population of some 5.5 billion is collectively using, co-opting, or destroying about 40% of terrestrial net primary production—the basic food source of all land animals. That is not a cheering statistic when one realizes that 95 million people are added to the planet each year, 260,000 each day, 11,000 each hour.

One of the critical jobs for conservation biologists, then, is to press, wherever possible, for the halting and then reversing of population growth, reduction of wasteful consumption, and development and deployment of more benign technologies. In other words, conservation biologists must work to reduce all three components of *I*: *P, A,* and *T.* Properly inventorying biodiversity, designing and establishing appropriate reserves, enhancing non-reserve areas, and monitoring the results will fail to protect biodiversity in the long run unless the scale of the human enterprise is brought under control. To that end, conservation biologists should document as thoroughly as possible the ways in which *P, A,* and *T* promote the loss of biodiversity.

In overconsuming nations like the United States, it is critical to reduce birth rates to a level at which the population will soon stabilize and begin a slow decline. In rich nations that are still growing, probably all that is needed to get average family sizes well under two children is an intensive educational program explaining how large families hurt the chances for future generations to have decent lives. Italy and Spain are leading the way with average family sizes of 1.3 children.

In poor nations, the problems are more difficult to address, but a great deal is known about ways of reducing family sizes. One of the keys is education, human rights, equal opportunities, and adequate health care for women and their children. So conservation biologists would do well to support the liberation of women, something that would be socially desirable even if it did not produce a salutary reduction in family size.

Ways of reducing per capita consumption and ameliorating the effects of technologies are clear in principle but often rather difficult to achieve in practice. Many politicians and economists are under the impression that a continual increase in consumption is necessary to keep economic systems healthy. Fortunately, there is a new school of ecological economists who understand that goal to be physically impossible, and who are examining ways of designing economic systems not dependent on perpetual growth. Conservation biologists can work with these economists on such things as assigning monetary values to ecosystem services so that the importance of biodiversity can be better integrated into political decision making.

Ecological economists are also searching for ways to "get the prices right" so that, for example, the social and environmental costs of using fossil fuels (especially in internal combustion engines) are "internalized" in the price of the fuels. If that happened, relatively biodiversity-friendly technologies such as solar power would become economically attractive.

Dramatically reducing the *A* and *T* factors of the $I = PAT$ equation can be done in a decade or so. Humanely halting population growth and eventually reducing population size by lowering birth rates below death rates will take many decades. Considering the intense competition that already exists for space and energy between human populations and most other organisms, efforts to preserve biodiversity and natural ecosystems are doomed to fail in the end unless the growth and impact of the human population are brought under control.

## The Tragedy of the Commons

Many, perhaps most, environmentally destructive practices come from misuse of common resource pools for private gain, what Garrett Hardin (1968) called "the tragedy of the commons." A tragedy of the commons potentially occurs whenever a common, publicly "owned" resource (such as land, oceans, or clean air) is used for private gain without tight internal or external controls on that use, controls that are designed to ensure long-term sustainability. Often the resource is overused and may be destroyed. This pattern has also been termed "commonized costs, privatized profits" by Hardin (1993). That is, costs are shared publicly among many (commonized), while profits are realized by a few (privatized).

The classic example of the tragedy of the commons involves a publicly owned grazing land (a "commons"), used by, say, 10 different herdsmen to graze their sheep. Suppose the land can support 100 sheep in a sustainable manner, but will be degraded over the long term if significantly more than 100 sheep graze. Also, more sheep means less grass for each individual sheep, and thus a lower growth rate for all. If the system is uncontrolled, herdsman A may decide that he would like to graze 15 sheep. The costs associated with this action (commons degradation, and slightly less grass for each sheep because of those 5 extra grazers) are incurred by all 10 herdsmen (including A), but all the profits from the extra sheep go only to herdsman A. Thus, it benefits A, at least in the short term, to "cheat" and graze extra sheep. Herdsman B then realizes this and decides to add 10 more of his sheep to the commons, thus also realizing a larger personal profit, while spreading the costs among all 10 herdsmen. Herdsmen C, D, and E wake up to this, and, well, you get the picture. The land is terribly overgrazed, and eventually the grazing ecosystem collapses, but short-term profits increase for those who overexploit the system.

What are some tragedies of the commons occurring today? They are too numerous to enumerate and occur virtually everywhere a publicly owned, unregulated resource exists. National forests, ocean fisheries, and grazing on rangelands are frequently cited as examples. Timber companies in the United States—often subsidized with taxpayer dollars through road building by the U.S. Forest Service and encouraged by public policies—clear-cut national forests, which are owned by all citizens, at high profits to the companies. The costs—such as lost opportunities to visit wilderness areas, lost ecosystem services, and subsidies paid through taxation—are commonized, or spread across all citizens, but collectively are high: the owners lose millions of hectares of primary forest and wilderness areas that will not return for several generations, if at all, and pay tax moneys to do it. The immediate (and privatized) profits to the companies are huge, but short-lived, because these forests are being depleted. The same pattern occurs with ocean fisheries ("owned" by everyone but exploited for profit by a few), which are easily overexploited, or western U.S. public rangeland, where grazing fees are much lower than on privately owned lands, and overgrazing is consequently very common. Some of these ranches, incidentally, are owned by large corporations, not struggling "cowboys" trying to make a living.

Regarding rangeland grazing, Hardin (1993) relates the following: "A stockman in the western United States can raise his cattle either on private land or on government land managed by the Forest Service. In Idaho, as of 1990, the grazing fee on public land was only one-fifth what it was on private land. We can assume that a private land-owner sets his fee to cover the true cost of maintaining the carrying capacity of the land indefinitely. Obviously the government is not following this prudent rule. In direct costs, the Forest Service paid out $35 million for maintaining grazing lands, the costs being offset by only $11 million taken in as fees. Who paid the deficit? Taxpayers, of course. Costs were commonized while the profits (from the sale of beef) were privatized to the stockmen."

Other tragedies of the commons occur with respect to pollution and toxification of the environment. By releasing wastes into the air, rivers, or oceans (common resources "owned" by all citizens) the polluter profits by cheap or free disposal of wastes (Figure 18.7), while all citizens pay the costs, either of cleanup or of living in polluted areas. The same principle even applies to irresponsible automobile owners who do not fix "smoking" cars: The owners benefit (by saving repair bills) while spreading costs (more pollutants) among the general population. As long as the costs of polluting are lower

**Figure 18.7** Air pollution, as seen in this view of Athens, Greece, is an example of the tragedy of the commons. Clean air, a common resource, is destroyed by a few for profit, while many pay the health and economic costs. (Photograph © M. P. Kahl/DRK Photo.)

than the costs of responsible behavior toward the commons, then heavy pollution will continue.

One solution is to eliminate the practice of free exploitation of publicly owned resources for private gain, and have all public costs paid by those who privately benefit. Not only does this seem eminently fair, but history bears out the recommendation. Hardin (1968) states that "the commons, if justifiable at all, is justifiable only under conditions of low-population density. As the human population has increased, the commons has had to be abandoned in one aspect after another." Commons have become increasingly limited and protected throughout human history: we restricted food gathering by enclosing farms, and have restricted hunting and fishing to certain areas at certain times, within certain numerical limits. Restrictions on waste materials have increased throughout human history, resulting in more and stronger laws controlling pollution and treatment of wastes. However, some commons, such as rangeland and forests, have remained unregulated or poorly regulated, and that is of major concern to conservationists.

The full costs of exploitation must be transferred from the commons "owners" to the commons users. One way to accomplish this is to heavily tax users and fine abusers of common resources. Higher and unsubsidized grazing fees on rangelands, heavy taxes on and no subsidies for timber companies using publicly owned land, and severe fines for intentional or even accidental pollution are examples of necessary policy changes needed to reduce tragedies of commons use. Of course, such actions face stiff opposition from the users, who are used to welfare subsidies for their activities. As of this writing, the Clinton/Gore administration is attempting to raise grazing fees to more accurately represent the true public costs of grazing cattle on western rangeland in the United States; however, this is being vehemently resisted by powerful ranchers and their political representatives. Likewise, cutting of old-growth forests is being restricted, again with outcries from those personally benefiting from exploiting a common resource essentially free of charge. And polluting industries have always fought regulation of and fines for their activities. However, the true costs of use of common resources must be paid by the users if those resources are not to be overexploited for privatized, short-term gain at a price of commonized, long-term costs.

## Five Major Actions Needed to Conserve Biodiversity

The problems and challenges facing humanity with respect to conserving biological diversity can seem overwhelming, and consequently their solutions can appear diffuse and ineffective. However, we believe that concentration on five areas of effort could focus conservation problems and their potential solutions; attention to these areas would result in major advances toward conserving biodiversity and developing a sustainable human society, compatible with the natural world, that supports humans at a reasonable standard of living. We identify the following five actions as most critical and most likely to have the greatest impact in the short term, and especially the long term. There are certainly other areas of endeavor that would also help in reversing the destructive trends evident today, but these five seem pervasive and most able to result in real progress.

1. *First stabilize, then reverse human population growth.* The first and overriding major action to take must be a fundamental change in patterns of human population growth and impact if we are to avoid major and disastrous losses of biodiversity and increasing levels of human misery. Regardless of advances in any other areas, including scientific information or policy development, the human population juggernaut must be slowed and stopped. If not, it would appear that growth of this one species will continue to destroy, at an accelerating rate, natural habitats and ecosystem functions. We believe that, eventually, most conservation advances will be lost if the human population grows to the currently predicted levels of 12 to 15 billion by the end of the 21st century.

2. *Protect tropical forests and other centers of biodiversity.* We know that the bulk of biological diversity occurs in tropical forests and a few other hot spots around the globe. Many of these are relatively small areas whose protection would conserve levels of biodiversity far out of proportion to their size. Even large regions such as the Amazon basin represent only a small percentage of the total land area of the earth. Immediate protection of these areas and their biological treasures is necessary to save as many pieces as possible. This would not only keep millions of species in existence, but also would help to retain the ecosystem functions of these regions, as well as their role in controlling global climate patterns. But there are many practical problems in protection, and local perspectives must be included if protection is to succeed. One of these perspectives, that of Latin American countries, is offered in Essay 18D by Garo Batmanian.

## ESSAY 18D

# A Latin American Perspective on the Future of Conservation and Development

Garo Batmanian, World Wildlife Fund

The Latin American and Caribbean (LAC) region is of utmost importance for biodiversity conservation. Forests still cover approximately 50% of LAC territory, and Brazil, Mexico, Colombia, Ecuador, and Peru are among the nine megadiversity countries of the world (Mittermeier et al. 1992). The region includes a vast range of ecosystems from the cold deserts of Patagonia to the lush jungles of the Amazon. LAC countries are a real key to future global biodiversity preservation.

However, the LAC region has many problems that threaten this biodiversity: a growing human population of more than 350 million, an average annual per capita income of U.S. $1500–$3000, and regional foreign debt of U.S. $400 billion. Most of its exports are primary commodities. The ratio of many LAC countries' import/export balance is over 2.75:1.00, which is one of the indicators used by The World Bank for severe indebtedness. Furthermore, sanitation, literacy levels, and access to health services are typically poor region-wide.

Consequently, most LAC countries feel pressure to occupy new, previously undisturbed areas to accommodate a growing population, to generate revenue for debt reduction, and to improve basic public services such as schools, sewage systems, and health centers. The Amazon region, although previously considered to be marginal land with difficult access, provides just such an area for many new settlements.

When questioned about the environmental damages from these settlements, officials often point to the conflict between feeding their people and protecting the environment. Although there is no single solution, there are two main concepts that together can address this problem as we move toward the future: protection of conservation units and sustainable use of renewable natural resources.

## Protection of Conservation Units

Public concern about rapid deforestation in Latin American countries has led to pressure for preservation of large portions of land for the sake of global ecological health. However, LAC countries perceive this approach as a threat to their national sovereignty, because they would relinquish rights to use those areas for their own economic needs.

The Brazilian Amazon has about 13 million ha of federally protected areas (National Parks, Biological Reserves, Ecological Reserves, and Ecological Stations), in addition to 15 million ha in National Forests and Extractive Reserves. None of these protected areas has resolved its land tenure situation, or has comprehensive management, or has an adequate number of trained personnel, or has sufficient infrastructure; they are all "paper parks." A similar situation occurs throughout the LAC region, so creating many new protected areas under these circumstances would be futile. Most LAC countries do not have sufficient financial resources, nor the technical knowledge, to effectively manage their protected areas. Moreover, the revenues generated by tourism would usually not cover maintenance costs.

Multilateral development banks, such as The World Bank, and bilateral development agencies, such as the U.S. Agency for International Development (USAID) and the U.K. Overseas Development Agency (ODA), could fund comprehensive projects to effectively implement these conservation units. For example, one such project in Peru, the Manu Biosphere Reserve, is a joint effort of Peru, USAID, and several NGOs. Ideally, endowment funds should be created to help provide long-term sustainability for such conservation units. Debt-for-nature swaps (discussed in Essay 13A) are another tool that can finance these activities without further increasing the economic burdens on the LAC countries.

## Sustainable Use of Renewable Resources

Most current practices of land and natural resource use in the LAC region are directly imported from developed countries, and are generally inappropriate for the environmental, cultural, or economic situations in LAC countries. Thus, the current development models for the wildland areas in LAC are ecologically and socially unsustainable. For example, some pastures created in the Amazon for cattle grazing are so degraded that their eventual regeneration is questionable. Moreover, those pastures provide fewer jobs to the local population and cause more environmental damage than the traditional land use of gathering forest products combined with small shifting cultivation practices.

Several approaches can help to reduce losses of biodiversity and rates of environmental degradation. These approaches provide incentives for sustainable use of natural resources rather than for clearing existing vegetation to gain other uses of the land.

### Patrimony

Much has been said about the potential use of tropical species for the treatment of AIDS, cancer, and other diseases. However, the countries containing these valuable species ordinarily derive no benefit from their discovery, thus providing little incentive to preserve the areas in their natural state. One possible solution, extractive reserve agreements with pharmaceutical companies, was discussed in Case Study 2 in Chapter 17.

### Marketing and Processing Local Products

A number of products used throughout the world, such as latex and rubber, many types of nuts, waxes, and fibers, come from tropical regions. The existing economic system provides most of the profit from these products to a series of middlemen, processing plant owners, and traders, while the forest dwellers who extract them receive little compensation. Most of the final value of the product is added in processing. Consequently, many forest dwellers and farmers sell or abandon their areas to loggers or ranchers and move to shantytowns.

Changes are needed to increase benefits to forest dwellers and small farmers, encouraging them to remain in the area while conserving the environment. One of the most promising efforts has been made by rubber tappers in the Brazilian Amazon. Like most forest dwellers, rubber tappers have no legal rights to their traditional land. Recently, rubber tappers organized themselves, presented their problems to the Brazilian public and government, and were instrumental in having the government establish protected Extractive Reserves where rubber tappers or other forest dwellers live. However, in order to sufficiently increase their income, these communities must increase their productivity and add value locally by performing the basic processing of the product. Rubber tappers in the state of Acre, Brazil, are processing and packing Brazil nuts in a low-technology plant, thus increasing their income about threefold. The main challenge now is to design resource management plans that would establish sustainable use practices to increase the local population's income without further damaging the environment.

### Identifying Sustainably Produced Commodities

Worldwide awareness of tropical wildland destruction has affected international trade of various products, especially timber. Although most developed countries now have regulations limiting or prohibiting importation of such products, these practices are not necessarily contributing to forest protection. Regional decision makers and businesses argue that these areas still must generate economic benefits for their countries. Therefore, if the standing forest seems to have no economic value, further deforestation will ensue. A better approach would be to encourage those countries to use their natural resources sustainably. The International Tropical Timber Organization (ITTO) is proposing guidelines to certify sustainable forest practices. Operations that comply with such guidelines would receive some form of "green label" similar to those already in use for organically grown products. This initiative would be acceptable to local governments, encouraging them to change their own policies to comply. It would reward those who sustainably manage forests by facilitating trade, while encouraging other producers to improve currently unsustainable management practices.

## Cleared Areas and Agroforestry Systems

There are millions of hectares of cleared and abandoned land in the LAC region under little or no economic use. Their rehabilitation to productive levels would decrease pressure for clearing new areas, while improving local economies and ecosystem health.

A promising approach for restoring degraded lands is agroforestry. Coffee, cacao, palm trees, papaya, and other tree crops can be successfully produced in tropical regions in association with cassava, rice, or beans. These systems can also include valuable timber species. Moreover, several native species such as cashew (*Anacardium occidentale*), guarana (*Aullinia cupana*), and cupuassu (*Theobroma grandiflorum*) are adapted to low soil fertility conditions, and can do well in degraded areas.

Such practices are not well known locally, and existing policies still encourage establishment of large plantations and pastures. To change this pattern, technical assistance and extension service is needed, while policies throughout the LAC region should be altered to enable small farmers to receive loans and other incentives for establishing agroforestry systems in areas already cleared.

The future of the LAC region and its biodiversity largely depends on reasonable and attractive alternatives to current destructive practices. Assistance from developed countries, *offered within the cultural and ecological constraints of the region,* is needed to make significant changes and offer hope for biodiversity in tropical regions well into the next century.

---

**3. *Develop a more global perspective of earth's resources, while solving problems locally wherever possible.*** Most humans have a tendency to think locally and in immediate time frames; that is, they discount things that are far away in time or space (Chapter 15). This is understandable; immediate needs such as food, shelter, and comfort dominate our senses, and they must be satisfied before we can contemplate larger temporal and spatial scales. However, we also have the ability as a species to think abstractly and understand patterns and trends over space and through time. We can understand and appreciate that global trends in resource use, natural habitat destruction, species loss, and so forth are ultimately detrimental to humanity and transcend political boundaries. Unfortunately for our long-term well-being, we often act as though political boundaries will protect us from the various forms of destruction now occurring, even though some problems, such as global warming, air and water pollution, and ozone depletion by definition are global.

The NIMBY ("Not In My Back Yard") phenomenon is a good example of this way of thinking; this is a common behavior wherein we tolerate some forms of destruction as long as they are far removed in time or space. ("Put it somewhere, but not in *my* backyard"). But we need to overcome such time and space biases, look beyond local problems, and realize that destruction elsewhere or later is just as bad as destruction here and now.

Globalization of problems, that is, accepting that on a finite planet, any problem, no matter where it occurs, should be of concern to all, is a key to reversing trends in environmental destruction. However, this does not mean that all problems should be *solved* globally. Hardin (1993) argues forcefully that any environmental or social problem that *can* be solved locally *should* be addressed that way, and not be approached in a global manner. Solutions to those problems that are truly global, of course, should be developed globally. He uses the analogy of potholes in roads. There are problems with potholes in roads all over the world, but this does not argue for creation of a "Global Pothole Authority" to develop solutions. The solutions need to emerge locally, within the constraints and opportunities peculiar to each nation and each location. Likewise, solutions to many conservation problems, although they may be common through many parts of the world, should first be solved through local means whenever possible, with the participation of local people who best understand the problem and the potential solutions. But concern for all environmental problems must transcend political boundaries and become part of the operating consciousness of all humans. "Think globally, act locally" is more than just a catchy slogan for bumper stickers.

**4. Develop ecological (steady-state) economics to replace growth economics.** We cannot envision a bright future for humanity and the natural world if we retain an economy that requires continual and perpetual growth in order to sustain itself. Growth is a fundamental assumption of virtually all current political and economic systems, but expansion in size *in perpetuity* on a finite planet is logically unrealistic. As discussed in Chapter 17, continued expansion in size must eventually be abandoned and replaced by an equilibrium economy that functions in a steady-state environment (Daly 1991). Regardless of the rate, *any* positive economic expansion and increase in use of nonrenewable resources must eventually reach limits and exhaust supplies. High expansion rates incur limits sooner, slow rates later, but *limits will be reached*. This logical fact seems lost on most traditional economists, politicians, and laypeople, but that must change. The frenzied economic exploitation of our planet, what Ehrlich and Ehrlich (1990) call "The One-Time Bonanza," is destined to end eventually.

**5. Change human value systems to reflect ecological reality.** Implicit in and necessary for all four of the above suggestions is a requisite and major change in human value systems (one perspective is elaborated by Eric Katz in Essay 18E). If fundamental changes do not take place in the way humans perceive their world and the value of natural systems, then we see little reason for optimism that biodiversity conservation will be effective and humanity can live sustainably. Changes in value systems could be manifest in several ways.

---

**ESSAY 18E**

# A New Vision
## Humans and the Value of Nature

Eric Katz, *New Jersey Institute of Technology*

---

Many suggested answers to our environmental problems fall into two categories: innovations in science and technology, or changes in governmental, industrial, and social policies to deal with pollution and other environmental destruction. For philosophers, both kinds of choices—scientific development and implementation of policy—miss the real point. Neither an appeal to science nor adjustments in social policy go deep enough into the underlying cause of the environmental crisis: *an inappropriate set of values concerning the human relationship with the natural world.* Traditional values have failed. The solution to the environmental crisis is development of a new set of values, a new vision of the human relationship with nature. What is required is a radical reinterpretation of the human place in the natural world.

In analyzing the human relationship with the natural environment, the traditional perspective, at least in Western civilization, is that of an anthropocentric individualism. The entire natural world is evaluated in human terms. What is good for human beings, what human beings deserve—these are the primary considerations in the development of human knowledge and human society. Science is modeled after the vision of Francis Bacon to dominate and subdue the secrets of the natural world, to bend them to our will to make life more comfortable. And within the realm of social policy, the vision of the good society is based on the political philosophy of John Locke. Locke argued that man must cultivate the wild, untamed common land of the earth to claim it as private property and thus to improve it for the increase of human happiness and justice. The traditional value system results in an environmental policy that seeks to maximize human benefit. Nature is to be used wisely—conserved, preserved, and restored—so that humanity can reap the highest amount of good.

Is there anything wrong with the human race attempting to maximize its gain and increase its happiness? Is there a problem with the value system of anthropocentrism? Yes: it is possible to discern three fundamental mistakes in the traditional Western worldview.

The first mistake is the idea of anthropocentrism itself. The traditional value system considers human good to be the goal of all human activity. This perspective is clearly a remnant of pre-Copernican thought; it creates a value system based on an incorrect scientific notion of the geocentric universe. Since Copernicus, we know that the earth is not the center of the physical universe, but we have yet to understand the corollary moral point: humans are not the center of the moral universe. Our value system and worldview should not reflect a belief in our own centrality. Environmental policies need not focus on the exclusive and primary importance of humanity. The natural world exists independently from human beings, though not from our influence and power.

The second mistake is the notion of individualism, the belief that the world is a vast arena of interacting individuals. The 17th-century empiricists conceived of the world on the model of a billiard table, with billiard balls constantly moving, colliding, and interacting. Our notions of cause and effect relationships are derived from this picture of the collision of hard and discrete individual entities. Individualism is also the hallmark of the major Western political and ethical systems. We hold the rights of individual human beings to be fundamental, regardless of the form of government or the economic system.

But the belief in discrete individuals is actually a claim not supported by contemporary science. The world is actually a dynamic flow of process and change; it is not constituted by static individuals. The lessons of ecological science and conservation biology apply this insight to the interactions of humans and the natural world. The individual entity is not the central unit of concern; rather, the focus is on populations, habitats, and ecosystems. Our view of the world is holistic, not individualistic.

The third and final mistake is the most subtle, the most difficult to discern in our basic worldview: it is the idea of domination. Throughout our policies and activities, humans attempt to control the world. Our political and social systems attempt to control other humans; our science and technology at-

tempt to dominate the natural world. If the purpose of science is to "predict and control" the natural world, then we try to make ourselves the masters of the universe. For pragmatic reasons alone, we ought to abandon this perspective, since we have done such a poor job. One way to view the contemporary environmental crisis is that it is the reaction to our inadequate attempts to predict and control—one meaning of David Ehrenfeld's (1981) "arrogance of humanism." But we ought to reject the idea of control for moral reasons as well—it is more ethical to permit all entities the freedom to flourish in their natural states. All beings are not tools for the satisfaction of human desires. Once we reject anthropocentrism, we reject domination also, and recognize that it is not the purpose of the natural world to be the victim of the human drive for power and domination.

An analysis of these three mistakes in the traditional Western value system suggests a new vision, a new perspective, on the human relationship with the natural world. By rejecting anthropocentrism, individualism, and domination, we can create a worldview that is non-anthropocentric, holistic, and liberating. This vision will be infused with a concern for an autonomous nonhuman natural world, a world that is unfolding and developing toward its own

self-realization. The interrelated systems of the natural world will have meaning and value free of the domination and interests of humanity.

This new vision has enormous implications for practical environmental policy. It amounts to an almost magical change in the evaluation of nature's role in human life. At the very least, the natural world will be seen as an equal partner in the development of the good life. This new vision requires that we respect the processes and systems of nature, that we extend to them our basic understanding of moral obligations, that we develop a direct moral concern for the nonhuman world. In practical terms, it will require a much greater emphasis on the preservation of whole ecological systems and habitats.

Philosophy not only teaches us that our scientific descriptions of the world and our policies of action are shaped by our values; it also demonstrates that the world itself is determined by our concepts, our vision, our perspective on the fundamental nature of reality. Do we have the courage to admit the errors of the traditional worldview, to adopt a new vision, a new meaning of value, for the natural world? I believe that humanity must discover this courage. We have a moral obligation to recognize the value of a natural world freed of human domination.

---

First, the human species needs to accept limits—limits to growth, limits to personal wealth at public cost, and limits to planetary dominance. We as a species currently use some 40% of the primary production on the planet (Vitousek et al. 1986), with the figure rising as our numbers and technological prowess increase. Any system of logic indicates that there are natural limits to how much production we can co-opt, and how much energy we can produce, even apart from conservation concerns. Yet, the prevailing approach to limits has been arrogance, an attitude that prevails through much of at least Western thought. This "techno-arrogance" (Meffe 1992), expressed as a frontier, "conquer nature" mentality, assumes that any challenges nature presents us can and should be overcome through our collective engineering abilities.

A rather astounding and illustrative example of this attitude concerns the 1991 and subsequent eruptions of Mt. Unzen in Japan. Rather than moving people and living within the natural constraints of volcanic activity, the Japanese government actually plans to reengineer the effects of volcanic eruptions with a series of dams, earth-retaining structures, and deep channels (Amato 1993). The same approach has guided the largely failed attempts in the United States to control river flows through dams and levees; that failure was evident in the Mississippi River floods of 1993 (Figure 18.8), which resulted in many billions of dollars of damage, to be paid by taxpayers (communized costs) to individuals who have benefited from living in floodplains (privatized profits).

Second, we need to replace "bottom line," short-term thinking with a long-term perspective that includes concern for intergenerational equity. By continually eroding natural capital in the interests of current financial gain and increased standards of living, we may be condemning future generations to lifestyles constrained by extremely limited resources and highly degraded ecosystems.

Third, we need to replace anthropocentrism with biocentrism. The present concept of the centrality and superiority of the human species to all others automatically places the 5 to 100 million other species, plus their collective ecosystems, in a tenuous position at best. Whenever there is a question of human gain versus conservation of nature, the former is likely to prevail. Ironically, this ultimately runs counter to human benefit, because loss of these systems will be devastating to the rapidly increasing human population. Biocentrism is, after all, in the best, and most selfish, interests of humanity.

Finally, we need to adopt and incorporate "ecological design principles" into all facets of human existence. As David Orr discussed in Essay 16A, we are at the dawn of a new way of thinking; we will by necessity have to replace our "control of nature" mentality with a "cooperate with nature" way of doing business. This must be done by replacing our industrial civilization—a "conquer nature" mentality—with an ecological design civilization—a "learn from and cooperate with nature" mentality. This transition is discussed in depth by Berry (1988).

Good ecological design, and the other changes in human value systems, must ultimately become part of the human psyche, and the accepted and common way of conducting the business of human existence on the planet. A "business as usual" approach that continues the prevailing outlooks and methods of the past several centuries, while making modest alterations to placate environmentalists, is unlikely to last long in a world where natural resources are rapidly degrading while the human population is simultaneously rapidly expanding. There seems little choice here.

Good conservation for both humanity and nature comes down to nothing less than a revolution in human thought, on par with the social changes wrought by the Industrial Revolution or struggles for racial equality. Such revolutions are not easy, quick, or painless, but they are necessary and inevitable. Human ethics and value systems are certain to change and become more sophisticated over time. Our values must evolve in the direction of sustainability and cooperation with, rather than conquest and destruction of, nature, if humankind is to continue to experience the rich rewards of living on a biologically complex and unique planet. Over 3 billion years of the history of life, and the future of conscious human thought and achievement, are at stake.

**Figure 18.8** Damage from the Mississippi River flood of 1993 is a consequence of our "conquer nature" mentality. Many communities that developed in natural and expansive floodplains were supposed to be protected by huge levees and other engineering marvels designed to "control" the river's behavior. In this case they did not work, and nature won. The more important question now is whether we will have learned anything from this. (Photograph by Reuters/Bettman.)

## Summary

Transduction of the principles of conservation biology into actions that reflect our cumulative knowledge may be the greatest challenge in the history of humanity. Major changes are needed in the way that the human species interacts with the planet, changes in human behavior as large as any in our history.

Conservation biology faces a number of challenges. It must operate within uncertainties of all kinds, including uncertain economic environments. To succeed, conservation biologists must convince the public that our science has value to all; we must improve the way that conservation is managed and develops; we must improve funding opportunities for conservation work; and we must influence policy development in positive ways. Conservation biologists also must work within certain long-term global environmental changes of uncertain magnitude and direction. The best we can do is plan for likely contingencies based on current knowledge.

The human "demographic imperative" is so overriding that all other success or failure may derive from it. Simply put, human population growth and increasing overall impact on the planet must be slowed, stopped, and reversed. Analysis of human impact must include not just population numbers, but effects from levels of affluence and consequences of technological development; total impact is thus a function of population size, affluence, and technology. Several countries have reversed disastrous population trends in little more than a decade, demonstrating that it can be done.

One of the major forms of destructive practice that has led to so much environmental degradation is the so-called "tragedy of the commons." Tragedies of the commons frequently occur when a commonly "owned" resource such as air, water, or wilderness is exploited for private gain at little to no expense to the individual, and is unregulated or poorly regulated. In these situations, the resources are typically overexploited to the benefit of a few, but the costs are spread among many. A solution is to have the costs of using these resources internalized to the users, rather than spread among public "owners."

We believe that five major actions on the part of humanity are needed to conserve biodiversity in the long term. First, the human population growth problem must be dealt with squarely and quickly. Second, tropical forests and other hot spots of biological diversity must be protected from further destruction. Third, we must develop a more global perspective on the earth's resources, but solve problems locally wherever possible; all environmental insults, regardless of where or when they occur, should be treated as here and now. Fourth, we must replace growth-oriented economics with ecological, or steady-state, economics, which recognizes limits to natural resources and sinks. Finally, human value systems must change to reflect ecological realities. Humans need to accept limits, replace short-term, myopic thinking with long-term perspectives that include intergenerational equity, replace anthropocentrism with biocentrism, and incorporate ecological design principles as we move from an industrial age to an ecological age. Updated and appropriate value systems are, when all is said and done, the best hope for conservation of biological diversity.

## Questions for Discussion

1. Consider these two positions. (A) The expected environmental effects of global change are so great that we must take extreme measures now to protect biodiversity in the future. (B) The uncertainty surrounding global climate change is so great that any measures we take now should be minimally intrusive and reversible. Compare these positions. Do you favor either one? Why?

2. Examine a series of development projects of The World Bank that have a component of biodiversity protection, with the following two questions in mind: What are the likely demographic consequences of each project? What set of demographic questions should be included as part of the general process of evaluating projects for support?

3. Eugene P. Odum has commented that "poverty is no friend of the environment." In what ways does economic impoverishment lead to environ-

mental degradation? Conversely, how does economic wealth contribute to the same?

4. Select some important concept or issue in conservation biology that you believe the average citizen should understand. Develop a plan for introducing this concept or issue into elementary and secondary schools through curricular enhancement.

5. How would educating the general public about this issue differ from your plan in Question 4?

6. How about actually implementing the plan from Question 4? If you do not do it, who will?

7. The political reality is that the U.S. presidency usually changes hands every four to eight years, and priorities for biodiversity protection also change. Discuss some creative ways to address major problems in conservation that require long-term solutions when the political support for policy implementation is ephemeral. We develop treaties and trade agreements with other countries, and these treaties survive elections; can we develop an analogue—domestic treaties—to protect our natural heritage? Are there existing models to work from?

8. Discuss the future of conservation biology. Where do you think the field is heading? Where do you see the largest advances? Where do you think you could make the best contributions, given your own talents, interests, and experiences?

## Suggestions for Further Reading

Berry, T. 1988. *The Dream of the Earth.* Sierra Club Books, San Francisco. A visionary perspective on where humanity has been and where it is going with respect to the planet and the universe. Berry argues that we are moving into the fifth age of humanity, an ecological age, and are now in a very difficult transition period from the industrial age. Somewhat heavy reading, but a great mind expander.

Hardin, G. 1993. *Living within Limits: Ecology, Economics, and Population Taboos.* Oxford University Press, New York. An outstanding update of Hardin's thoughts on human population growth and the human condition. Hardin exposes a number of myths and fallacies in the population problem in a frank and firm manner. He faces head-on a number of controversial and challenging topics such as immigration policy and the tragedy of the commons.

Kareiva, P. M., J. G. Kingsolver and R. B. Huey (eds.). 1993. *Biotic Interactions and Global Change.* Sinauer Associates, Sunderland, MA. These chapters focus on the implications of global warming and $CO_2$ enrichment, and cover a broad range of biological responses from the population through the community levels, including evolutionary considerations.

Orr, D. W. 1992. *Ecological Literacy: Education and the Transition to a Postmodern World.* State University of New York Press, Albany. An absolutely outstanding series of essays that will shape your own vision of the future. Orr argues persuasively that the core of human education should be ecology and our relationship with the natural world. He also has very perceptive insights into sustainability and the need for a transformation to a postmodern existence. A "must read."

Tobin, R. 1990. *The Expendable Future.* Duke University Press, Durham, NC. An excellent critical analysis of United States policies on biodiversity protection and how priorities are developed to support (or thwart) implementation of the policies.

Western, D. and M. Pearl. 1989. *Conservation for the Twenty-first Century.* Oxford University Press, New York. This is an outstanding collection of papers on conservation biology that takes a hard look at future trends and likely scenarios. It also stresses conservation management, human values, planning, and the developed world. Western and Pearl provide a much broader perspective than the typical conservation biology volume.

# Glossary

[Listed after each entry is the chapter number in which the term is highlighted and discussed.]

**Allele**   One of a pair of genes at a particular genetic locus. Chapters 4 and 6.

**Allopatric**   Describes two or more populations or species that occur in geographically separate areas. *See* also Sympatric.   Chapter 3.

**Allozyme**   One of several possible forms of an enzyme that is the product of a particular allele at a given gene locus. Chapter 6.

**Anthropocentric**   Any human-oriented perspective of the environment, but usually used to emphasize a distinction between humans and nonhumans. For example, assessing a tropical forest in terms of its potential timber value would be an exclusively anthropocentric perspective.   Chapter 1.

**Area/perimeter ratio**   The ratio of internal area to edge habitat of a region. The area/perimeter ratio is an indication of the amount of interior habitat with respect to edge habitat, and may indicate potential success of a reserve in protecting interior species.   Chapter 10.

**Background Extinction Rate**   Historical rates of extinction due to environmental causes not influenced by human activities, such as the rate of species going extinct because of long-term climate change.   Chapter 1.

**Bayesian statistics**   A branch of modern statistics that bases statistical inferences and decisions on a combination of information derived from observation or experiment and from prior knowledge or expert judgment. The approach contrasts with classical statistics, which regards only the data from observations or experiments as useful for estimation and inference.   Chapter 11.

**Biodiversity**   The variety of living organisms considered at all levels, from genetics through species, to higher taxonomic levels, and including the variety of habitats and ecosystems.   Chapter 1.

**Biological species concept (BSC)**   A species concept based on reproductive isolation, which defines a species as groups of actually or potentially interbreeding populations, which are reproductively isolated from other such groups.   Chapter 3.

**Biome**   A large, regional ecological unit, usually defined by some dominant vegetative pattern, such as the coniferous forest biome.   Chapter 4.

**Biophilia**   A term coined by E. O. Wilson to describe humans' seemingly innate, positive attitudes about, and love for, nature and natural diversity.   Chapters 1 and 10.

**Biosphere reserve**   A concept of reserve design in which a large tract of natural area is set aside, containing an inviolate core area for ecosystem protection, a surrounding buffer zone in which nondestructive human activities are permitted, and a transition zone in which human activities of greater impact are permitted. Three goals of a biosphere reserve are conservation, training (education), and sustainable human development compatible with conservation.   Chapter 17.

**Buffer zone**   An area in a reserve surrounding the central core zone, in which nondestructive human activities such as ecotourism, traditional (low-intensity) agriculture, or extraction of renewable natural products, are permitted. Chapter 17.

**Cladistic**   Pertaining to branching patterns. A system of classification based on historical (chronological) sequences of divergence from a common ancestor.   Chapter 3.

**Cladogram**   A diagram of cladistic relationships. An estimate or hypothesis of true genealogical relationships among species or other groupings.   Chapter 3.

**Coadapted gene complex**   A concept in which particular gene combinations, presumably acting in concert through a long association, function particularly well together. Chapter 6.

**Cohesion species concept**   A species concept based on intrinsic cohesion mechanisms, such as gene flow and natural selection, that results in species cohesion (contrast with species isolation in BSC).   Chapter 3.

**Commons**   Originally referred to lands in medieval Europe that were owned by townships rather than by private individuals. Now used to include any exploitable resource that is not privately owned. Sometimes applied to so-called "open resources" that are neither privately owned nor regulated by a country or agency.   Chapter 1.

**Conservation Biology**   An integrative approach to the protection and management of biodiversity that uses appropriate principles and experiences from basic biological fields such as genetics and ecology, from natural resource management fields such as fisheries and wildlife, and from social sciences such as anthropology, sociology, philosophy, and economics.   Chapter 1.

**Core zone**   Within a larger protected reserve or park, an area of critically important habitat in which development and other kinds of disruptive activities are prohibited.   Chapter 17.

**Critical habitat**   According to U.S. Federal law, the ecosystems upon which endangered and threatened species depend.   Chapter 3.

**Cryptic species**   Distinct species that show little to no outward morphological differences, and thus are difficult to distinguish. Also called "sibling species."   Chapter 3.

**Deep ecology**   An environmental philosophy that believes in inherent rights of nature, and a human existence that does minimal damage to natural systems.   Chapter 2.

**Demand**   The aggregate desire for economic goods and services. The quantity of a good or service that consumers are willing to purchase at different prices. Demand involves the relationship between quantity and price. Chapter 15.

**Deme**   A randomly interbreeding (panmictic) local population.   Chapter 6.

**Demographic bottleneck**   A significant, usually temporary, reduction in genetically effective population size, either from a population "crash" or a colonization event by a few founders.   Chapter 6.

**Demographic uncertainty**   Chance populational events, such as sex ratios or the act of finding a mate, that influence survival in small populations.   Chapter 7.

**Density-dependent factors**   Life history or population parameters that are a function of population density.   Chapter 7.

**Density-independent factors**   Life history or population parameters that are independent of population density. Chapter 7.

**Distancing**   An economic term that refers to the process of specialization creating alienation (distance) of people from each other, from the means of production of essential goods and services, and from the environment. Chapter 15.

**Distribution**   An economic term referring to the pattern of ownership of resources. The way in which natural resources and other assets are initially assigned among different owners.   Chapter 15.

**Ecological release**   Habitat expansion or density increase of a species when one or more competing species are not present.   Chapter 4.

**Ecological species concept**   A species concept based on adaptive zones used by organisms.   Chapter 3.

**Edge effect**   (1)The negative influence of a habitat edge on interior conditions of a habitat, or on species that use interior habitat. (2) The effect of adjoining habitat types on populations in the edge ecotone, often resulting in more species in the edge than in either habitat alone.   Chapter 9.

**Efficient allocation**   An economic term that refers to the market's ability to match resources with material ends. The apportionment of resources to the production of different goods and services.   Chapter 15.

**Electrophoresis**   A process by which gene products of an individual organism are separated by an electrical field in a gel medium and then stained so that they may be identified and classified. Used to infer genotypes in populations.   Chapter 6.

**Endangered species**   According to U.S. Federal law, a species is endangered if it is in imminent danger of extinction throughout all or a significant portion of its range.   Chapter 3.

**Endemic**   Any localized process or pattern, but usually applied to a highly localized or restrictive geographic distribution of a species.   Chapter 4.

**Environmental modification**   Modification of the phenotype as a result of environmental influences on the genotype.   Chapter 6.

**Environmental uncertainty**   Unpredictable sources of density-independent mortality, such as an early snowstorm, that jeopardize the survival of a small population by pushing it below its minimum viable population size. Chapter 7.

**Equilibrium**   A state reached when the population birth rate and immigration is equal to mortality and emigration. Also applied to species changes in a community or to any other ecological process in which rate of increase equals rate of decrease, resulting in a steady state.   Chapter 1.

**Evolutionarily significant unit (ESU)**   A population that is reproductively isolated from other conspecific population units, and represents an important component in the evolutionary legacy of the species.   Chapter 6.

**Evolutionary species concept (ESC)**   A species concept based on historical ties, and phenotypic cohesions and discontinuities.   Chapter 3.

**Evolutionary-Ecological Land Ethic**   A philosophical approach to conservation derived from the evolutionary and ecological perspective, first advanced by Aldo Leopold. In this perspective, nature is seen not as a collection of independent parts, to be used as needed, but as an integrated system of interdependent processes and components, in which the disruption of some components may greatly affect others. This ethic is the philosophical foundation for modern conservation biology.   Chapter 1.

**Extensive margin**   Refers to low-quality agricultural lands in which increased inputs do not produce greater net economic returns per unit land area; rather economic returns are increased by increasing land area.   Chapter 15.

**Externality**   A cost, usually in terms of environmental degradation, that results from an economic transaction but is not included as a debit against economic returns. Chapter 15.

**Feedback**   Refers to a system whose output modifies input to the system. Prices play this role in market systems. Chapter 15.

**Fencerow scale**   With respect to corridors, the connection of habitat patches by narrow rows of habitat, usually effective only for small, edge-tolerant species.   Chapter 10.

**Fitness**   The relative contribution of an individual's genotype to the next generation in context of the population gene pool. Relative reproductive success.   Chapters 4 and 6.

**Founder effect**   The principle that the founders of a new population carry only a random fraction of the genetic diversity found in the larger, parent population.   Chapter 6.

**Founder model**   A rapid speciation scenario in which a small, isolated population, such as a few colonists on an island, undergoes rapid divergence from its parent population. Also called quantum speciation.   Chapter 3.

**Fragmentation**   The disruption of extensive habitats into isolated and small patches. Fragmentation has two negative components for biota: loss of total habitat area, and smaller, more isolated remaining habitat patches.   Chapter 9.

**Fundamental Theorem of Natural Selection**   The basic theorem of population genetics, which states that the rate of evolutionary change in a population is proportional to the amount of genetic diversity (specifically, additive genetic variance) available in the population.   Chapter 6.

**Gaia hypothesis**   A model of planetary dynamics postulating a tight interrelationship between life processes and conditions on earth that support life. Feedback mechanisms are proposed by which biological processes modify the physical and chemical conditions that are appropriate for the biological processes. In the extreme viewpoint, the Gaia hypothesis holds that the earth is a superorganism. Now usually refers to the belief that biotic processes are the major regulators of physical processes.   Chapter 2.

**GAP analysis**   The use of various remote sensing data sets to build overlaid sets of maps of various parameters (e.g., vegetation, soils, protected areas, species distributions) to identify spatial gaps in species protection and management programs.   Chapter 12.

**Gene flow**   The uni- or bi-directional exchange of genes between populations due to migration of individuals and subsequent successful reproduction in the new population.   Chapter 6.

**Gene locus**   The site on a chromosome occupied by a specific gene.   Chapter 6.

**Gene pool**   The sum total of genes in a sexually reproducing population, or deme.   Chapter 6.

**Genetic drift**   Random gene frequency changes in a small population due to chance alone.   Chapter 3.

**Genetically effective population size ($N_e$)**   The size of an idealized population that would have the same rate of increase in inbreeding, or decrease in genetic diversity through drift, as the population in question. The functional size of a population, in a genetic sense, based on numbers of actual breeding individuals and the distribution of offspring among families. $N_e$ is typically smaller than the census size of the population.   Chapter 6.

**Genotype**   The entire genetic constitution of an organism, or the genetic composition at a specific gene locus or set of loci.   Chapter 6.

**Geographic information system (GIS)**   A computerized system of organizing and analyzing any spatial array of data and information.   Chapter 7.

**Geographic variation**   Change in a species' trait over distance or among different distinct populations. Measurable character divergence among geographically distinct populations, often, though not necessarily, the result of local selection.   Chapter 3.

**Gradual allopatric speciation**   The process of species formation by which a population is split into two or more subpopulations by a geographic barrier, followed by evolutionary divergence until one or more of the populations become distinct species.   Chapter 3.

**Habitat Evaluation Procedures (HEP)**   A method developed by the U.S. Fish and Wildlife Service for evaluating the quality of wildlife habitat. A general class of appraisal systems to judge habitat availability and quality for a given species. An HEP combines a habitat quality measure, such as an HSI, with areal extent or availability of the habitat.   Chapter 12.

**Habitat or ecosystem management**   A management focus that de-emphasizes individual species, focusing instead on maintaining habitat or ecosystem quality, including ecological processes important in maintaining the characteristic biodiversity of an area.   Chapter 11.

**Habitat Suitability Index (HSI)**   A relative index developed by the U.S. Fish and Wildlife Service to compare a habitat against an "ideal" optimal habitat.   Chapter 12.

**Hardy-Weinberg equilibrium**   The stability of gene frequencies expected in a sexual, diploid population when a number of assumptions are met, including random mating, a large population, and no migration, mutation or selection.   Chapter 6.

**Heterozygosity**   A measure of the genetic diversity in a population, as measured by the number of heterozygous loci across individuals.   Chapters 4 and 6.

**Heterozygous**   The situation in which an individual has two different alleles at a given gene locus.   Chapter 6.

**Hierarchical gene diversity analysis**   An approach to defining population genetic structure for a species in nature that defines components of total genetic diversity in a spatially hierarchical fashion.   Chapter 6.

**Homozygous**   The situation in which an individual has two of the same alleles at a given gene locus.   Chapter 6.

**Hot spot**   A geographic location characterized by unusually high species richness, often of endemic species.   Chapter 4.

**I = PAT**   An equation describing the total impact of humans on natural systems as a function of population size (P), level of affluence (A), and technological sophistication employed (T).   Chapter 18.

**Inbreeding**   The mating of individuals who are more closely related than by chance alone.   Chapter 6.

**Inbreeding depression**   A reduction in fitness and vigor of individuals as a result of increased homozygosity through inbreeding in a normally outbreeding population.   Chapter 6.

**Incipient species**   A population or group of populations in the process of speciating. Also called semispecies.   Chapter 3.

**Indicator species**   A species used as a gauge for the condition of a particular habitat, community, or ecosystem. A characteristic, or surrogate species for a community or ecosystem.   Chapter 11.

**Inherent value**   *See* Intrinsic value.   Chapter 2.

**Instrumental value**   The worth of an entity as judged by its utility or usefulness to humans.   Chapter 2.

**Intensive margin**   Refers to high-quality agricultural lands in which increased inputs produce greater net economic returns per unit land area.   Chapter 15.

**Intermediate disturbance hypothesis**   An hypothesis, with good empirical support, that maximum species richness in many systems occurs at an intermediate level (intensity or frequency, or both) of natural disturbance.   Chapter 10.

**Intrinsic value**   The worth of an entity independent from external circumstances or its value to humans; value judged on inherent qualities of an entity rather than value to other entities.   Chapter 2.

**Key process**   An ecosystem analog of a keystone species; a critical ecosystem function that controls broad ecosystem characteristics. Nitrogen or phosphorus cycling, for example, may be key processes in given ecosystems.   Chapter 12.

**Key species management**   Management directed toward maintaining keystone species or other ecologically or politically important species as a surrogate for managing for all species in a system.   Chapter 11.

**Keystone species**   Species that have a disproportionately large effect on other species in a community.   Chapter 5.

**Land-bridge island**   Areas that are presently island habitats, but were formerly connected to the mainland during periods of lower ocean levels. Land-bridge islands tend to lose species over time in a process called "relaxation." Chapter 9.

**Landscape mosaic scale**   With respect to corridors, the connection of major landscape features using broad habitats, including representation of interior habitat, as corridors. Chapter 10.

**Line corridor**   A simple, narrow corridor consisting of all edge habitat, usually connecting small habitat patches. Chapter 10.

**Locus**   *See* Gene locus.   Chapter 6.

**Mass extinction**   The extinction of large numbers of taxa during a relatively brief geologic time frame, such as the extinction of dinosaurs at the end of the Cretaceous Period.   Chapter 5.

**Maximum sustained yield (MSY)**   The largest harvest level of a renewable resource that can be sustained over a period of many generations. Harvest of a natural population at the population size representing the maximum rate of recruitment into the population, based on a logistic growth curve.   Chapter 12.

**Metapopulation**   A network of semi-isolated populations with some level of regular or intermittent migration and gene flow among them, in which individual populations may go extinct but then be recolonized from other populations.   Chapters 6 and 7.

**Minimum dynamic area**   The smallest area necessary for a reserve to have a complete, natural disturbance regime in which discrete habitat patches may be colonized from other patches within the reserve.   Chapter 10.

**Minimum viable population size**   The smallest isolated population size that has a specified percent chance of re maining extant for a specified period of time in the face of foreseeable demographic, genetic, and environmental stochasticities, plus natural catastrophes.   Chapter 6.

**Mobile Link Species**   Mobile keystone species who influence the survival or reproductive success of other species through their movement over a geographic area; e.g., highly specific pollinators.   Chapter 5.

**Monetizing**   The process of placing monetary value on typically non-monetary goods and processes such as biological material or ecological processes. The process of converting values to economic units.   Chapter 2.

**Monomorphic**   Description of a population in which nearly all individuals have the same genotype at a given locus. Chapter 6.

**Monophyletic**   Derivation of two or more taxa from a single, common ancestor.   Chapter 3.

**Multiple Use Concept**   Refers to the simultaneous and compatible use of public land and water resources by different interest groups. For example, U.S. public law requires that national forests be open to recreational use, timber extraction, mining or other concessions, and biodiversity protection. In reality, the activities of the various interest groups generally conflict, and are often incompatible with biodiversity protection.   Chapter 1.

**MUM**   Acronym for "Multiple Use Module," consisting of a central, protected core area surrounded by buffer zones of increasing human use further from the core.   Chapter 10.

**Mutation**   A spontaneous change in the genotype of an organism at the gene, chromosome, or genomic level. Mutations usually refer to alterations to new allelic forms, and represent new material for evolutionary change.   Chapter 6.

**Mutualism**   An interspecific relationship in which both organisms benefit, frequently a relationship of complete dependence. Examples include flower pollination and parasite cleaning.   Chapter 8.

**Natural catastrophe**   A major environmental cause of mortality, such as a volcanic eruption, that can affect the probability of survival for both large and small populations. Chapter 7.

**Natural selection**   A process by which differential reproductive success of individuals in a population results from differences in one or more hereditary characteristics. Natural selection is a function of genetically based variation in a trait, fitness differences (differential reproductive success) among individuals possessing different forms of that trait, and inheritance of that trait by offspring. Chapter 6.

**Nested subset**   A pattern of species biogeographic distribution in which larger habitats contain the same subset of species in smaller habitats, plus new species found only in the larger habitat. Common species are found in all habitat sizes, but some species are found only in progressively larger habitats.   Chapter 9.

**Network**   A reserve system connecting multiple nodes and corridors into a landscape that allows material and energy flow among the various components.   Chapter 10.

**Node**   An area with unusually high conservation value that may serve as one center of a regional conservation network.   Chapter 10.

**Nominalist** A school of thought that questions the existence of species as real and natural groupings. Considers "species" to be a human-made concept. Chapter 3.

**Nonequilibrium** A condition in which rate of increase does not equal rate of decrease. In nonequilibrial population growth, environmental stochasticity disrupts the equilibrium. Chapter 1.

**Option value** An economic term that refers to assigning a value to some resource whose consumption is deferred to the future. Chapter 15.

**Overdominance** The condition in which a heterozygote at a given locus has higher fitness than either homozygote. Also called heterozygote superiority. Chapter 6.

**Panmictic** Random breeding among individuals of a population. Chapter 6.

**Paradigm** An established pattern of thinking. Often applied to a dominant ecological or evolutionary viewpoint, e.g., during earlier decades the dominant paradigm held that communities were shaped by equilibrial processes. Chapter 1.

**Patch dynamics** A conceptual approach to ecosystem and habitat analysis that emphasizes dynamics of heterogeneity within a system. Diverse patches of habitat created by natural disturbance regimes are seen as critical to maintenance of diversity. Chapter 10.

**Phenetic** Pertaining to phenotypic similarities, such as a phenetic classification system. Based on numerical measurements of individuals and mathematical analyses of morphological discontinuities. Chapter 3.

**Phenotype** The physical expression (outward appearance) of a trait of an organism, which may be due to genetics, environment, or an interaction of the two. Chapter 6.

**Phylogenetic species concept (PSC)** A species concept based on branching, or cladistic relationships among species or higher taxa. The PSC presents a hypothesis of the true genealogical relationship among species, based on the concept of shared, derived characteristics (synapomorphies). Chapter 3.

**Phylogeographic** Evolutionary relationships among species populations based on geographic relationships and historical gene flow patterns. Chapter 6.

**Plasticity** Genetically based, environmentally induced variation in characteristics of an organism. Chapter 3.

**Plesiomorphic** An evolutionarily primitive character shared by two or more taxa. *See* Synapomorphic. Chapter 3.

**Pluralist** A school of thought which holds that species concepts should vary with the taxon under consideration. Many different species definitions would be employed. Chapter 3.

**Point richness** The number of species found at a single point in space. Chapter 4.

**Polymorphic** Description of a population in which individuals have two or more genotypes at a given locus. Chapter 6.

**Polyploidy** Possessing more than two complete sets of chromosomes. Chapter 3.

**Population viability analysis (PVA)** A comprehensive analysis of the many environmental and demographic factors that affect survival of a population, usually applied to small populations at risk of extinction. Chapter 7.

**Populational** A philosophical perspective that embraces and recognizes variation in classes of objects. Objects, including species, are seen as belonging to a changing class of entity with inherent trait variation. Also called the evolutionary perspective. *See* Typological. Chapter 3.

**Quantitative genetics** The study of phenotypic traits that are influenced by multiple genetic and environmental factors (polygenic traits). Chapter 6.

**Quantum speciation** *See* Founder model. Chapter 3.

**Recognition species concept** A species concept based on reproductive mechanisms that facilitate gene exchange, or a field for gene recombination. Chapter 3.

**Regional scale** With respect to corridors, the largest scale of activity, in which major swaths of habitat connect regional networks of reserves. Chapter 10.

**Relaxation** The loss of species on land-bridge islands following separation from the mainland or the loss of species during any process of habitat fragmentation and isolation. Chapter 9.

**Remote sensing** Any technique for analyzing landscape patterns and trends using low altitude aerial photography or satellite imagery. Any environmental measurement that is done at a distance. Chapter 12.

**Rescue effect** The recolonization of a habitat when a subpopulation of a metapopulation has gone locally extinct. Chapter 7.

**Residuals** In restoration ecology, the remnants of natural systems that can provide the building blocks for system restoration or rehabilitation. Chapter 14.

**Resource Conservation Ethic** A philosophical approach to conservation derived from the views of forester Gifford Pinchot, based on the utilitarian philosophy of John Stuart Mill. Nature is seen as a collection of natural resources, to be used for "the greatest good of the greatest number for the longest time." Chapter 1.

**Restoration ecology** The process of using ecological principles and experience to return a degraded ecological system to its former or original state. Chapter 14.

**Romantic-Transcendental Conservation Ethic** A philosophical approach to conservation derived from the writings of Emerson, Thoreau, and Muir, in which nature is seen in a quasi-religious sense, and as having uses other than human economic gain. This ethic strives to preserve nature in a wild and pristine state. Chapter 1.

**Secondary extinctions** Loss of a species as a direct or indirect result of loss of another species. Chapter 8.

**Sentient** Capable of feeling or perception. Refers to a state of self-awareness among organisms, usually applied only to vertebrates. Chapter 2.

**Sibling species** *See* Cryptic species. Chapter 3.

**Sink** A habitat in which local mortality exceeds local reproductive success for a given species. Chapter 7.

**Sink population** A population in a low-quality habitat in which birth rate is generally less than the death rate and population density is maintained by immigrants from source populations. Chapter 7.

**SLOSS** An acronym for "single large or several small," reflecting a debate that raged for several years asking whether, all else being equal, it was better to have one large reserve or several small reserves of the same total size. Chapter 10.

**Source** A habitat in which local reproductive success exceeds local mortality for a given species. Chapter 7.

**Source and sink dynamics** Spatial linkage of population dynamics such that high-quality habitats (sources) provide excess individuals that maintain population density, through migration, in low-quality habitats (sinks). Chapter 7.

**Source population** A population in a high-quality habitat in which birth rate greatly exceeds death rate and the excess individuals leave as migrants. Chapter 7.

**Spatially-explicit population model** A population model, especially a simulation model, that takes space, differences in habitat quality, and inter-habitat movement into consideration. Chapter 7.

**Speciation** Any of the processes by which new species form. Chapter 3.

**Species diversity** Usually synonymous with "species richness," but may also include the proportional distribution of species. Chapter 4.

**Species problem** Ambiguity of the species category and definition. The species problem—what species definition(s) to use, and what constitutes species—has been with us for decades and is unlikely to be completely resolved in the near future. Chapter 3.

**Species richness.** The number of species in a region, site, or sample. Chapter 4.

**Stewardship** Management of natural resources that conserves them for future generations. Usually used to distinguish from short-term, utilitarian management objectives. Chapter 1.

**Stochastic** Any random process, such as mortality due to weather extremes. Chapter 1.

**Strip corridor** A broad corridor consisting of some interior habitat and intact and functioning communities. Chapter 10.

**Succession** The natural, sequential change of species composition of a community in a given area. Chapter 8.

**Supply** The aggregate amount of goods or services available to satisfy economic needs or wants. The quantity of a good or service which producers are willing to sell at different prices. Supply involves the relationship between quantity and price. Chapter 15.

**Sustainable Development** There is considerable debate over the meaning of this term. Most generally it refers to attempts to meet economic objectives in ways that do not degrade the underlying environmental support system. In Chapter 17, we define it as "human activities conducted in a manner that respects the intrinsic value of the natural world, the role of the natural world in human well-being, and the need for humans to live on the income from nature's capital rather than the capital itself." Chapters 1 and 17.

**Sympatric** A description of two or more populations or species that occur in the same geographic area. *See* also Allopatric. Chapter 3.

**Synapomorphic** An evolutionarily derived or advanced character shared by two or more taxa. *See* Plesiomorphic. Chapter 3.

**Synergistic Interaction** An interaction that has more than additive effects, such as the joint toxicity of two compounds being greater than their combined, independent toxicities. Chapter 5.

**Threatened species** According to U.S. Federal law, a species is threatened if it is likely to become endangered in the foreseeable future. Chapter 3.

**Tragedy of the commons** An idea, set forth primarily by Garrett Hardin, that unregulated use of a common, public resource for private, personal gain, will result in overexploitation and destruction of the resource. Chapter 2.

**Transition zone** An area of a reserve surrounding a buffer zone, usually with indistinct boundaries, in which human activities such as selective logging, fishing, or other sustainable pursuits, are permitted. Chapter 17.

**Typological** A philosophical perspective that embraces existence of a "type," or perfect form, of objects. Objects, including species, are seen as belonging to a relatively fixed class of entity in which individual variation is viewed as an imperfection. *See* Populational. Chapter 3.

**Utilitarian** A philosophical term applied to any activity that produces a product useful to humans, typically in some economic sense. Also used to describe a system of values which is measured by its contribution to human well-being, usually in terms of health and economic standard of living. Chapter 1.

**Utilitarian value** *See* Instrumental value. Chapter 2.

**Utility** The "want-satisfying" power of goods; personal satisfaction received through an economic gain. Chapter 15.

**Vicariance** The process of a continuously distributed biota becoming separated by an intervening geographic event (such as mountain uplift or river flow), or extinction of intervening populations, resulting in subsequent independent histories of the fragmented biotas, and possible speciation events. Chapter 4.

**Zoning** An important component of reserve design which controls human activities within and adjacent to conservation reserves so that reserve function may be protected while some human activities, including economic benefit, may take place. Chapter 10.

# Bibliography

The numbers in brackets identify the chapter(s) in which the reference is cited.

Abel, N. and P. Blaikie. 1986. Elephants, people, parks and development: The case of the Luangwa Valley, Zambia. *Environ. Mgmt.* 10:735–751. [10]

Abele, L. G. and E. F. Connor. 1979. Application of island biogeographic theory to refuge design: Making the right decision for the wrong reasons. In R. M. Linn (ed.), *Proceedings of the First Conference on Scientific Research in the National Parks,* Vol. I. pp. 89–94. USDI National Park Service, Washington, D.C. [9]

Abugov, R. 1982. Species diversity and phasing of disturbance. *Ecology* 63:289–293. [4]

Ackery, P. R. and R. I. Vane-Wright. 1984. *Milkweed Butterflies: Their Cladistics and Biology.* Cornell University Press, Ithaca, NY. [4]

Adams, L. W. and A. D. Geis. 1983. Effects of roads on small mammals. *J. Appl. Ecol.* 20:403–415. [9]

Agee, J. K. and R. L. Edmonds. 1992. Forest protection guidelines for the Northern Spotted Owl. College of Forest Resources, University of Washington, Seattle, WA. Unpublished draft. [13]

Aiken, W. 1984. Ethical issues in agriculture. In T. Regan (ed.), *Earthbound: New Introductory Essays in Environmental Ethics,* pp. 247–288. Random House, New York. [2]

Ali, S. and V. S. Vijayan. 1986. *Keoladeo National Park Ecology Study: Summary Report 1980–1985.* Bombay Natural History Society, Bombay, India. [12]

Allee, W. C., A. E. Emerson, O. Park, T. Park and K. P. Schmidt. 1949. *Principles of Animal Ecology.* Saunders, Philadelphia. [7]

Allen, W. H. 1988. Biocultural restoration of a tropical forest. *BioScience* 38:156–161. [10]

Allendorf, F. W. 1983. Isolation, geneflow, and genetic differentiation among populations. In C. M. Schonewald-Cox, S. M. Chambers, B. MacBryde and L. Thomas (eds.), *Genetics and Conservation: A Reference for Managing Wild Animal and Plant Populations,* pp. 51–65. Benjamin/Cummings, Menlo Park, CA. [6]

Allendorf, F. W. and R. F. Leary. 1986. Heterozygosity and fitness in natural populations of animals. In M. E. Soulé (ed.), *Conservation Biology: The Science of Scarcity and Diversity,* pp. 57–76. Sinauer Associates, Sunderland, MA. [6]

Allendorf, F. W., R. B. Harris and L. H. Metzgar. 1991. Estimation of effective population size of grizzly bears by computer simulation. In *Proceedings of the Fourth International Congress of Systematics and Evolutionary Biology,* pp. 650–654. Fourth Dioscorides Press, Portland, OR. [6]

Alverson, W. S., D. M. Waller and S. L. Solheim. 1988. Forests too deer: Edge effects in northern Wisconsin. *Conserv. Biol.* 2:348–358. [9]

Amato, I. 1993. Mt. Unzen be dammed! *Science* 261:827. [18]

Ames, R. T. 1992. Taoist ethics. In L. Becker (ed.), *Encyclopedia of Ethics,* pp. 1126–1230. Garland Press, New York. [2]

Andersen, A. N. 1983. Species diversity and temporal distribution of ants in the semi-arid mallee region of northwestern Victoria. *Aust. J. Ecol.* 8:127–137. [4]

Andersen, R. A. 1992. Diversity of eukaryotic algae. *Biodiv. and Conserv.* 1:267–292. [4]

Anderson, S. H. and D. B. Inkley, (eds.). 1985. *Black-Footed Ferret Workshop Proceedings.* Wyoming Game and Fish Department, Cheyenne. [13]

Andren, H. and P. Angelstam. 1988. Elevated predation rates as an edge effect in habitat islands: Experimental evidence. *Ecology* 69:544–547. [9]

Andrewartha, H. G. and L. C. Birch. 1984. *The Ecological Web.* University of Chicago Press, Chicago. [7]

Antonovics, J., A. D. Bradshaw and R. G. Turner. 1971. Heavy metal tolerance in plants. *Adv. Ecol. Res.* 7:1–85. [3]

Arrhenius, O. 1921. Species and area. *J. Ecol.* 9:95–99. [4]

Arthington, A. H. and L. N. Lloyd. 1989. Introduced poeciliids in Australia and New Zealand. In G. K. Meffe and F. F. Snelson, Jr. (eds.), *Ecology and Evolution of Livebearing Fishes* (Poeciliidae). Prentice Hall, Englewood Cliffs, NJ. [8]

Ashley, M. V., D. J. Melnick and D. Western. 1990. Conservation genetics of the black rhinoceros (*Diceros bicornis*), I: Evidence from the mitochondrial DNA of three populations. *Conserv. Biol.* 4:71–77. [3]

Ashton, P. 1978. Crown characteristics of tropical trees. In P. B. Tomlinson and M. H. Zimmermann (eds.), *Tropical Trees as Living Systems.* pp. 591–615. Cambridge University Press, London. [17]

ASPRS/ACSM/RT 92. 1992. *The Third International Symposium on Advanced Technology in Natural Resource Management,* Washington, D.C. Vol. 5, *Resource Technology.* American Society for Photogrammetry and Remote Sensing and American Congress on Surveying and Mapping, Bethesda, Maryland. [12]

Avise, J. C. 1989. A role for molecular genetics in the recognition and conservation of endangered species. *Trends Ecol. Evol.* 4:279–281. [3,6]

Avise, J. C. and seven others. 1987. Intraspecific phylogeography: The mitochondrial DNA bridge between population genetics and systematics. *Annu. Rev. Ecol. Syst.* 18:489–522. [6]

Avise, J. C. and R. M. Ball. 1990. Principles of genealogical concordance in species concepts and biological taxonomy. *Oxford Surv. Evol. Biol.* 7:45–67. [6]

Avise, J. C. and W. S. Nelson. 1989. Molecular genetic relationships of the extinct dusky seaside sparrow. *Science* 243:646–648. [6]

Balick, M. J. and R. Mendelsohn. 1992. Assessing the economic value of traditional medicines from tropical rain forests. *Conserv. Biol.* 6:128–130. [15]

Ball, G. H. 1922. Variation in fresh-water mussels. *Ecology* 3:93–121. [3]

Balla, S. A. and K. F. Walker. 1991. Shape variation in the Australian freshwater mussel *Alathyria jacksoni* Iredale (Bivalvia, Hyriidae). *Hydrobiologica* 220:89–98. [3]

Ballard, W. B. and T. Spraker. 1979. Unit 13 wolf studies: Alaska Department of Fish and Game Projects W-17-9 and W-17-10 Progress Report. [10]

Bambach, R. K. 1986. Phanerozoic marine communities. In D. M. Raup and D. Jablonski (eds.), *Patterns and Processes in the History of Life,* pp. 407–428. Dahlem Konferenzen 1986. Springer-Verlag, Berlin. [8]

Barbier, E. B., J. C. Burgess, T. M Swanson and D. W. Pearce. 1990. *Elephants, Economics, and Ivory.* Earthscan Publications, London. [17]

Barnes, A. M. 1982. Surveillance and control of bubonic plague in the United States. *Symp. Zool. Soc. Lond.* 50:237–270. [13]

Barnes, R. F. W. 1983. The elephant problem in Ruaha National Park, Tanzania. *Biol. Cons.* 26:127–148. [17]

Barnes, R. F. W. and E. B. Kapela. 1991. Found ivory records reveal changes in the Ruaha elephant population caused by poaching. *Afr. J. Ecol.* 29:289–294. [17]

Barr, J. 1972. Man and nature: The ecological controversy and the Old Testament. *Bull. John Rylands Library* 55:9–32. [2]

Bart, J. and E. D. Forsman. 1992. Dependence of Northern Spotted Owls on old-growth forests in the western USA. *Biol. Conserv.* 37:95–100. [13]

Baskin, Y. 1992. Africa's troubled waters. *BioScience* 42:476–481. [5]

Baskin, Y. 1993. Blue behemoth bounces back. *BioScience* 43:603–605. [12]

Batisse, M. 1986. Developing and focusing the biosphere reserve concept. *Nature Res.* 22:1–10. [17]

Bator, F. 1957. The simple analytics of welfare maximization. *Am. Econ. Rev.* 47:22–59. [15]

Beaver, R. A. 1979. Host specificity of temperate and tropical animals. *Nature* 281:139–141. [4]

Beier, P. 1993. Determining minimum habitat areas and habitat corridors for cougars. *Conserv. Biol.* 7:94–108. [7]

Belden, R. C. and B. W. Hagedorn. 1993. Feasibility of translocating panthers into northern Florida. *J. of Wildl. Mgmt.* 57:388–397. [12]

Belize Tourist Board. 1992. *Visitor Statistics 1987–1991.* Immigration and Nationality Services of Belize. [17]

Bellah, R. N., R. Madsen, W. M. Sullivan, A. Swidler and S. M. Tipton. 1991. *The Good Society.* Alfred A. Knopf, New York. [15]

Belovsky, G. E. 1987. Extinction models and mammalian persistence. In M. E. Soulé (ed.), *Viable Populations for Conservation,* pp. 35–57. Cambridge University Press, Cambridge. [10]

Bennitt, R., J. S. Dixon, V. H. Cahalane, W. W. Chase and W. L. McAtee. 1937. Statement of policy. *J. Wildl. Mgmt.* 1:1–2. [1]

Bentham, H., J. A. Harris, P. Birch and K. C. Short. 1992. Habitat classification and soil restoration assessment using analysis of soil microbiological and physico-chemical characteristics. *J. Appl. Ecol.* 29:711–718. [14]

Berg, R. Y. 1975. Myrmecochorus plants in Australia and their dispersal by ants. *Aust. J. Bot.* 23:475–508. [4]

Berkes, F. (ed.). 1989. *Common Property Resources: Ecology and Community-Based Sustainable Development.* Bellhaven Press, London. [15]

Berry, T. 1988. *The Dream of the Earth.* Sierra Club Books, San Francisco. [18]

Berry, W. 1977. *The Unsettling of America.* Sierra Club Books, San Francisco. [13]

Berry, W. 1989. The futility of global thinking. *Harper's Magazine,* September, 16–22. [16]

Berry, W. 1993. Decolonizing rural America. *Audubon Magazine,* March/April, 100–105. [16]

Bettenay, E. 1984. Origin and nature of the sandplains. In J. S. Pate and J. S. Beard (eds.), *Kwongan: Plant Life of the Sandplain,* pp. 51–68. University of Western Australia Press, Nedlands. [4]

Betz, R. F. and H. F. Lamp. 1992. Species compositions of old settler savanna and sand prairie cemeteries in northern Illinois and northwestern Indiana. In D. Smith and C. A. Jacobs (eds.), *Proceedings of the 12th North American Prairie Conference,* pp. 79–87. University of Northern Iowa, Cedar Falls. [14]

Bibby, C. J. and eight others. 1992. *Putting Biodiversity on the Map: Priority Areas for Global Conservation.* International Council for Bird Preservation, Cambridge. [5]

Biggins, D. E. and J. Godbey. 1993. *Influence of Pre-Release Experience on Reintroduced Black-Footed Ferrets* (Mustela nigripes). U.S. Fish and Wildlife Service, NERC, Fort Collins, CO. [13]

Billington, H. L. 1991. Effect of population size on genetic variation in a dioecious conifer. *Conserv. Biol.* 5:115–119. [6]

Bischof, L. L. 1992. Genetics and elephant conservation. *Endangered Species Update* 9:1–8. [6]

Bishop, R. C. 1978. Endangered species and uncertainty: The economics of a safe minimum standard. *Am. J. Agric. Econ.* 60:10–18. [2,15]

Bjorndal, K. A. 1982. *Biology and Conservation of Sea Turtles.* Smithsonian Institution Press, Washington, D.C. [13]

Blaikie, P. and H. Brookfield. 1987. *Land Degradation and Society.* Methuen, London. [15]

Blake, J. G. 1991. Nested subsets and the distribution of birds on isolated woodlots. *Conserv. Biol.* 5:58–66. [9]

Blake, J. G. and J. R. Karr. 1984. Species composition of bird communities and the conservation benefit of large versus small forests. *Biol. Conserv.* 30:173–187. [9]

Blakesley, J. A., A. B. Franklin and R. J. Gutierrez. 1992. Spotted Owl roost and nest site selection in Northwestern California. *J. Wildl. Mgmt.* 56:388–392. [13]

Blockstein, D. E. and H. B. Tordoff. 1985. Gone forever—a contemporary look at the extinction of the Passenger Pigeon. *Amer. Birds* 39:845–851. [7]

Blum, E. 1993. Making biodiversity conservation profitable: A case study of the Merck-INBio agreement. *Environment* 35:17–45. [17]

Bodhi, B. Foreword. In *Buddhist Perspectives on the Ecocrisis,* pp. i–x. Buddhist Publication Society, Kandy, Sri Lanka. [2]

Boersma, P. D., D. L. Stokes and W. Conway. 1990. *Punta Tomba Management Plan.* New York Zoological Society, New York. [17]

Bok, D. 1990. *Universities and the Future of America.* Duke University Press, Durham, NC. [16]

Bond, W. 1983. On alpha-diversity and the richness of the Cape flora: A study in southern Cape fynbos. In F. J. Kruger, D. T. Mitchell and J. U. M. Jarvis (eds.), *Mediterranean-Type Ecosystems: The Role of Nutrients,* pp. 337–356. Springer-Verlag, Berlin. [4]

Boone, J. L., J. Laerm and M. H. Smith. 1993. Taxonomic status of *Peromyscus gossypinus anastasae* (Anastasia Island cotton mouse). *J. Mammal.* 74:363–375. [6]

Bormann, F. H. and G. E. Likens. 1979. *Pattern and Process in a Forested Ecosystem.* Springer-Verlag, New York. [9]

Botkin, D. B. 1990. *Discordant Harmonies: A New Ecology for the Twenty-First Century.* Oxford University Press, New York. [1,2]

Botkin, D. B. and M. J. Sobel. 1975. Stability in time-varying ecosystems. *Am. Nat.* 109:625–646. [10]

Bowen, B. W., J. C. Avise, J. I. Richardson, A. B. Meylan, D. Margaritoulis and S. R. Hopkins-Murphy. 1993. Populations structure of loggerhead turtles (*Caretta caretta*) in the northwestern Atlantic Ocean and Mediterranean Sea. *Conserv. Biol.* 7:834–844. [13]

Bowen, B. W., A. B. Meylan and J. C. Avise. 1991. Evolutionary distinctiveness of the endangered Kemp's Ridley sea turtle. *Nature* 352:709–711. [6]

Bowen, B. W., A. B. Meylan, J. P. Ross, C. J. Limpus, G. H. Balazs and J. C. Avise. 1992. Global population structure and natural history of the green turtle (*Chelonia mydas*) in terms of matriarchal phylogeny. *Evolution* 46:865–881. [13]

Boyce, M. S. 1992. Population viability analysis. *Annu. Rev. Ecol. Syst.* 23:481–506. [7,10]

Boyce, M. S. 1992. Wolf recovery for Yellowstone National Park: A simulation model. In D. R. McCullough and R. H. Barrett (eds.), *Wildlife 2001: Populations,* pp. 123–138. Elsevier Applied Science, London. [17]

Bradshaw, A. D. 1983. The reconstruction of ecosystems. *J. Appl. Ecol.* 10:1–17. [14]

Bradshaw, A. D. 1984. Ecological principles and land reclamation practice. *Landscape Planning* 11:35–48. [14]

Bradshaw, A. D. and M. J. Chadwick. 1980. *The Restoration of Land: The Ecology and Reclamation of Derelict and Degraded Land.* Blackwell Scientific Publications, Oxford. [14]

Braker, H. E. 1991. Natural history of a neotropical gap-inhabiting grasshopper. *Biotropica* 23:41–50. [17]

Bratton, S. P. 1993. *Christianity, Wilderness and Wildlife: The Original Desert Solitaire.* University of Scranton Press, Scranton, PA. [2]

Brenner, F. J. 1990. Mine reclamation: Opportunity for critical habitat development. In *Ecosystem Management: Rare Species and Significant Habitats,* pp. 235–238. New York State Museum Bulletin 471. [14]

Brisbin, I. L. 1968. The Passenger Pigeon: A study in the ecology of extinction. *Modern Game Breeding* 4:13–20. [6]

Brittingham, M. C. and S. A. Temple. 1983. Have cowbirds caused forest songbirds to decline? *BioScience* 33:31–35. [9]

Brocke, R. H., K. A. Gustafson and A. R. Major. 1990. Restoration of lynx in New York: Biopolitical lessons. *Trans. N. Am. Wildlife and Natural Resources Conference* 55:590–598. [12]

Brody, A. J. and M. P. Pelton. 1989. Effects of roads on black bear movements in western North Carolina. *Wildl. Soc. Bull.* 17:5–10. [9]

Brokaw, N. L. V. 1985. Treefalls, regrowth, and community structure in tropical forests. In S. T. A. Pickett and P. S. White (eds.), *The Ecology of Natural Disturbance and Patch Dynamics*, pp. 53–69. Academic Press, Orlando, FL. [17]

Brothers, T. S. and A. Springarn. 1992. Forest fragmentation and alien plant invasion of central Indiana old-growth forests. *Conserv. Biol.* 6:91–100. [9]

Brower, L. P. and S. B. Malcolm. 1991. Animal migrations: Endangered phenomena. *Am. Zool.* 31:265–276. [4]

Brown, G. 1989. The viewing value of elephants. In S. Cobb (ed.), *The Ivory Trade and the Future of the African Elephant.* Ivory Trade Review Group, Oxford. [17]

Brown, G. and W. Henry. 1989. *The Economic Value of Elephants.* LEEC Paper 89–12, London. [17]

Brown, J. H. and A. Kodric-Brown. 1977. Turnover rates in insular biogeography: Effect of immigration on extinction. *Ecology* 58:445–449. [7,9]

Brown, L. R. and 12 others. 1988. *State of the World: A Worldwatch Institute Report on Progress Toward a Sustainable Society.* W. W. Norton, New York. [18]

Brown, L. R., C. Flavin and H. Kane. 1992. *Vital Signs.* W. W. Norton, New York. [18]

Brown, P., R. Wilson, R. Loyn and N. Murray. 1985. The Orange-Bellied Parrot — An RAOU conservation statement. RAOU Report no. 14. Royal Australian Ornithology Union, Moonee Ponds, Victoria. [6]

Browne, J. 1983. *The Secular Ark: Studies in the History of Biogeography.* Yale University Press, New Haven. [9]

Brubaker, L. B. 1988. Vegetation history and anticipating future vegetation change. In J. K. Agee and D. R. Johnson (eds.), *Ecosystem Management for Parks and Wilderness*, pp. 42–58. University of Washington Press, Seattle. [2,8]

Buchanan, J. B. 1991. Spotted Owl nest site characteristics in mixed conifer forests of the eastern Cascade Mountains, Washington. M.S. Thesis, University of Washington, Seattle. [13]

Buechner, M. 1987. Conservation in insular parks: Simulation models of factors affecting the movement of animals across park boundaries. *Biol. Conserv.* 41:57–76. [10]

Buele, J. D. 1979. *Control and management of cattails in southeastern Wisconsin wetlands.* Wisconsin Department of Natural Resources Technical Bulletin no. 112. [12]

Bull, A. T., M. Goodfellow and H. Slater. 1992. Biodiversity as a source of innovation in biotechnology. *Annu. Rev. Microbiol.* 46:219–252. [17]

Bunt, J. S. 1975. Primary productivity of marine ecosystems. In H. Leith and R. H. Whittaker (eds.), *Primary Productivity of the Biosphere*, pp. 169–215. Springer-Verlag, New York. [4]

Burgess, H. 1986. The emergency condition of the Veddas. Letter to the directors, World Wildlife Fund, Washington, D.C. [10]

Burgess, R. L. and D. M. Sharpe (eds.). 1981. *Forest Island Dynamics in Man-Dominated Landscapes.* Springer-Verlag, New York. [9]

Burkey, T. V. 1989. Extinction in nature reserves: The effect of fragmentation and the importance of migration between reserve fragments. *Oikos* 55:75–81. [9]

Byerly, R. Jr. 1989. The Policy Dynamics of Global Change, *Earthquest*, Spring, pp. 11–13, 24. [16]

Cairns, J., Jr. (ed.). 1988. *Rehabilitating Damaged Ecosystems*, Vols. I and II. CRC Press, Boca Raton, FL. [14]

Callicott, J. B. 1986. On the intrinsic value of nonhuman species. In B. G. Norton (ed.), *The Preservation of Species: The Value of Biological Diversity*, pp. 138–172. Princeton University Press, Princeton, NJ. [2]

Callicott, J. B. 1987a. The conceptual foundations of the land ethic. In J. B. Callicott (ed.), *Companion to A Sand County Almanac: Interpretive and Critical Essays*, pp. 186–217. University of Wisconsin Press, Madison. [2]

Callicott, J. B. 1987b. The philosophical value of wildlife. In D. Decker and G. Goff (eds.), *Valuing Wildlife: Economic and Social Perspectives*, pp. 214–221. Westview Press, Boulder, CO. [2]

Callicott, J. B. 1989. *In Defense of the Land Ethic: Essays in Environmental Philosophy.* State University of New York Press, Albany. [2,12]

Callicott, J. B. 1990. Whither conservation ethics? *Conserv. Biol.* 4:15–20. [1]

Callicott, J. B. 1992. Can a theory of moral sentiments support a genuinely normative environmental ethic? *Inquiry* 35:183–198. [2]

Callicott, J. B. 1994. *Earth's Insights: A Multicultural Survey of Ecological Wisdom.* University of California Press, Berkeley.[2]

Calvert, W. H. and L. P. Brower. 1986. The location of monarch butterfly (*Danaus plexippus* L.) overwintering colonies in Mexico in relation to topography and microclimate. *J. Lepid. Soc.* 40:164–187. [4]

Campbell, F. 1991. The appropriations history. In K. A. Kohm (ed.), *Balancing on the Brink of Extinction: The Endangered Species Act and Lessons for the Future*, pp. 134–146. Island Press, Washington, D.C. [3]

Campbell, N. A. 1987. *Biology.* Benjamin/Cummings, Menlo Park, CA. [3]

Canterbury, E. R. 1987. *The Making of Economics*, 3rd ed. Wadsworth, Belmont, CA. [15]

Carey, A. B., J. A. Reid and S. P. Horton. 1992. Northern Spotted Owls: Influence of prey base and landscape character. *Ecol. Monogr.* 62:223–250. [13]

Cargill, S. M. and F. S. Chapin III. 1987. Application of successional theory to tundra restoration: A review. *Arct. Alp. Res.* 19:366–372. [14]

Carlson, A. and G. Aulen. 1992. Territorial dynamics of an isolated White-Backed Woodpecker (*Dendrocoposd leucotos*) population. *Conserv. Biol.* 6:450–458. [9]

Carlton, J. T., G. J. Vermeij, D. R. Lindberg, D. A. Carlton and E. Dudley. 1991. The first historical extinction of a marine invertebrate in an ocean basin: The demise of the eelgrass limpet *Lottia alveus*. *Biol. Bull.* 180(1):72–80. [4]

Carnegie Commission on Science, Technology, and Government, Task Force on Environment and Energy. n.d. $E^3$: *Organizing for Environment, Energy, and the Economy in the Executive Branch of the U.S. Government.* The Carnegie Commission, New York. [16]

Caro, T. M. 1993. Behavioral solutions to breeding cheetahs in captivity: Insights from the wild. *Zoo. Biol.* 12:19–30. [6]

Caro, T. M. and M. K. Laurenson. 1994. Ecological and genetic factors in conservation: A cautionary tale. *Science* 263:485–486. [6]

Carroll, C. R. 1990. The interface between natural areas and agroecosystems. In C. R. Carroll, J. H. Vandermeer and P. M. Rosset (eds.), *Agroecology*, pp. 365–384. Biological Resource Management Series. McGraw-Hill, New York. [1,10]

Carroll, C. R. 1992. Ecological management of sensitive natural areas. In P. L. Fiedler and S. Jain (eds.), *Conservation Biology: The Theory and Practice of Nature Conservation, Preservation and Management*, pp. 347–372. Chapman and Hall, New York. [12]

Case, T. J. and M. L. Cody. 1987. Testing theories of island biogeography. *Am. Sci.* 75:402–411. [5]

Caughley, G. 1976. The elephant problem: An alternative hypothesis. *East Afr. Wildl. J.* 14:265–283. [10]

César Dachary, A. and S. M. Arnaiz Burne. 1989. *Sian Ka'an, el Hombre y su Economláia.* Centro de Investigaciones de Quintana Roo, Chetumal, Q. Roo, México. [17]

Chambers, S. M. 1983. Genetic principles for managers. In C. M. Schonewald-Cox, S. M. Chambers, B. MacBryde and L. Thomas (eds.), *Genetics and Conservation: A Reference for Managing Wild Animal and Plant Populations*, pp. 15–46. Benjamin/Cummings, Menlo Park, CA. [6]

Chappel, C. 1990. Contemporary Jaina and Hindu responses to the ecological crisis. Paper presented at the 1990 meeting of the College Theological Society, Loyola University, New Orleans. [2]

Charlesworth, B. 1980. *Evolution in Age Structured Populations.* Cambridge University Press, New York. [7]

Charnov, E. L. 1990. On evolution of age at maturity and adult lifespan. *J. Evol. Biol.* 3:139–144. [7]

Chavis, B. F., Jr. and C. Lee. 1987. *Toxic Wastes and Race in the United States: A National Report on the Racial and Socio-Economic Characteristics of Communities with Hazardous Waste Sites.* Commission for Racial Justice, United Church of Christ, New York. [16]

Chen, J. and J. F. Franklin. 1990. Microclimatic pattern and basic biological responses at the clearcut edges of old-growth Douglas fir stands. *Northwest Environ. J.* 6:424–425. [9]

Chen, J., J. F. Franklin and T. A. Spies. 1992. Vegetation responses to edge environments in old-growth Douglas fir forests. *Ecol. Applic.* 2:387–396. [9]

Clark, C. W. 1973. Profit maximization and the extinction of animal species. *J. Polit. Econ.* 81:950–961. [2]

Clark, C. W. 1990. *Mathematical Bioeconomics.* John Wiley & Sons, New York. [12]

Clausen, J., D. D. Keck and W. M. Heisey. 1940. *Experimental Studies on the Nature of Species. I. Effects of Varied Environments on Western North American Plants.* Publication 520, Carnegie Institution of Washington, Washington, D.C. [3]

Clayton, C. and R. Mendelsohn. 1993. The value of watchable wildlife: A case study of McNeil River. *J. Environ. Mgmnt.* 39:101–106. [17]

Clebsch, E. E. C. and R. T. Busing. 1989. Secondary succession, gap dynamics, and community structure in a southern Appalachian cove forest. *Ecology* 70:728–735. [9]

Club of Earth. 1990. *Loss of Biodiversity Threatens Human Future.* Department of Biological Sciences, Stanford University, Stanford, CA. [5]

Cody, M. L. 1975. Towards a theory of continental species diversity: Bird distributions over Mediterranean habitat gradients. In M. L. Cody and J. M. Diamond (eds.), *Ecology and Evolution of Communities,* pp. 214–257. Belknap Press of Harvard University Press, Cambridge, MA. [4,10]

Cody, M. L. 1986. Structural niches in plant communities. In J. Diamond and T. J. Case (eds.), *Community Ecology,* pp. 381–405. Harper & Row, New York. [4]

Cogger, H. G. 1979. *Reptiles and Amphibians of Australia.* A. H. and A. W. Reed, Sydney. [8]

Colinvaux, P. A., M. Bush, M. K-Liu, P. E. De Oliveira, M. Riedinger and M. C. Miller. 1989. Amazonia without refugia: Vegetation and climate of the Amazon basin through a glacial cycle. Proceedings of the International Symposium on Global Changes in South America during the Quaternary. São Paulo, Brazil. [8]

Collins, B. S., K. P. Dunne and S. T. A. Pickett. 1985. Responses of forest herbs to canopy gaps. In S. T. A. Pickett and P. S. White (eds.), *The Ecology of Natural Disturbance and Patch Dynamics,* pp. 218–234. Academic Press, Orlando, FL. [6]

Collins, E. In press. Prairie restoration at Glacial Park. *Rest. Mgmt. Notes.* [14]

Conant, R. 1975. *A Field Guide to Reptiles and Amphibians of Eastern and Central North America,* 2nd ed. Houghton Mifflin Co., Boston. [3]

Congdon, J. D., A. E. Dunham and R. C. van Loben Sels. 1993. Delayed sexual maturity and demographics of Blanding's turtles (*Emydoidea blandingi*): Implications for conservation and management of long-lived organisms. *Conserv. Biol.* 7:826–833. [7]

Connell, J. H. 1975. Some mechanisms producing structure in natural communities. In M. L. Cody and J. M. Diamond (eds.), *Ecology and Evolution of Communities,* pp. 460–490. Belknap Press of Harvard University Press, Cambridge, MA. [4]

Connell, J. H. 1978. Diversity in tropical rain forests and coral reefs. *Science* 199:1302–1310. [4,10]

Connell, J. H. 1983. On the prevalence and relative importance of interspecific competition: Evidence from field experiments. *Am. Nat.* 122:661–696. [4]

Connell, J. H. and E. Orias. 1964. The ecological regulation of species diversity. *Am. Nat.* 111:1119–1144. [4]

Connor, E. F. and E. D. McCoy. 1979. The statistics and biology of the species–area relationship. *Am. Nat.* 113:791–833. [9]

Cooke, G. D., E. B. Welch, S. A. Peterson and P. R. Newroth. 1986. *Lake and Reservoir Restoration.* Butterworth, Boston. [14]

Cooperrider, A. 1991. Reintegrating humans and nature: Introduction. In W. Hudson (ed.), *Landscape Linkages and Biodiversity,* pp. 141–148. Island Press, Washington, D.C. [11]

Cornell, H. V. 1985. Species assemblages of cynipid gall wasps are not saturated. *Am. Nat.* 126:565–569.

Costanza, R. 1991. Assuring sustainability of ecological economic systems. In R. Costanza (ed.), *Ecological Economics,* pp. 331–343. Columbia University Press, New York. [18]

Costanza, R. (ed.). 1991. *Ecological Economics: The Science and Management of Sustainability.* Columbia University Press, New York. [15]

Costanza, R., H. E. Daly and J. A. Bartholomew. 1991. Goals, agenda, and policy recommendations for ecological economics. In R. Costanza (ed.), *Ecological Economics: The Science and Management of Sustainability,* pp. 1–21. Columbia University Press, New York. [15]

Costanza, R. and H. E. Daly. 1992. Natural capital and sustainable development. *Conserv. Biol.* 6:37–46. [15]

Costanza, R., S. C. Farber and J. Maxwell. 1989. The valuation and management of wetland ecosystems. *Ecol. Econ.* 1:335–362. [15]

Costanza, R. and C. Perrings. 1990. A flexible assurance bonding system for improved environmental management. *Ecol. Econ.* 2:57–76. [15]

Coston-Clements, L., L. R. Settle, E. E. Hoss and F. A. Cross. 1991. *Utilization of the Sargassum habitat by Marine Invertebrates and Vertebrates: A Review.* NOAA Technical Memorandum NMFS-SEFSC-296. [7]

Cottam, G. 1987. Community dynamics on an artificial prairie. In W. L. Jordan III, M. E. Gilpin and J. D. Aber (eds.), *Restoration Ecology,* pp. 257–270. Cambridge University Press, Cambridge. [14]

Courtenay, W. R., Jr. and G. K. Meffe. 1989. Small fishes in strange places: A review of introduced poeciliids. In G. K. Meffe and F. F. Snelson, Jr. (eds.), *Ecology and Evolution of Livebearing Fishes (Poeciliidae),* pp. 319–331. Prentice Hall, Englewood Cliffs, NJ. [8]

Cox, G. W. and R. E. Ricklefs. 1977. Species diversity, ecological release, and community structuring in Caribbean land bird faunas. *Oikos* 29:60–66. [4]

Crabtree, A. F. (ed.). 1984. *Proceedings of the Third International Symposium on Environmental Concerns in Rights-of-Way Management,* Mississippi State University. [14]

Cracraft, J. 1983. Species concepts and speciation analysis. In R. F. Johnston (ed.), *Current Ornithology,* Vol. 1, pp. 159–187. Plenum Press, New York. [3]

Cracraft, J. 1992. The species of the birds-of-paradise (Paradisaeidae): Applying the phylogenetic species concept to a complex pattern of diversification. *Cladistics* 8:1–43. [3]

Crouse, D. T., L. B. Crowder and H. Caswell. 1987. A stage-based population model for loggerhead sea turtles and implications for conservation. *Ecology* 68:1412–1423. [7,13]

Crow, J. F. and M. Kimura. 1970. *An Introduction to Population Genetic Theory.* Harper & Row, New York. [6]

Crozier, R. H. 1992. Genetic diversity and the agony of choice. *Biol. Conserv.* 61:11–15. [3,6]

Currie, D. J. and V. Paquin. 1987. Large-scale biogeographical patterns of species richness of trees. *Nature* 329:326–327. [4]

Curtis, J. T. 1956. The modification of mid-latitude grasslands and forests by man. In W. L. Thomas (ed.), *Man's Role in Changing the Face of the Earth,* pp. 721–736. University of Chicago Press, Chicago. [9]

Cutler, A. 1991. Nested faunas and extinction in fragmented habitats. *Conserv. Biol.* 5:496–505. [9]

Dahl, T. E. 1990. *Wetlands losses in the United States 1780s to 1980s.* U.S. Department of the Interior, Fish and Wildlife Service, Washington, D.C. [14]

Daly, H. 1991. *Steady-State Economics,* 2nd ed. Island Press, Washington, D.C. [15,18]

Daly, H. E. and J. B. Cobb, Jr. 1989. *For the Common Good: Redirecting the Economy Toward Community, the Environment, and a Sustainable Future.* Beacon Press, Boston. [15]

Dansereau, P. 1957. Description and recording of vegetation on a structural basis. *Ecology* 32:172–229. [4]

Darlington, P. J. 1957. *Zoogeography: The Geographical Distribution of Animals.* Wiley, New York. [5,9]

Darwin, C. R. 1859. *On The Origin of Species by Means of Natural Selection.* John Murray, London. [3,7]

Darwin, C. R. 1904. *The Descent of Man and Selection in Relation to Sex.* J. A. Hill and Company, New York. [2]

Dasmann, R. F. 1959. *Environmental Conservation.* John Wiley & Sons, New York. [1]

Dasmann, R. F. 1988. Biosphere reserves, buffers, and boundaries. *BioScience* 38:487–489. [10]

Daugherty, C. H., A. Cree, J. M. Hay and M. B. Thompson. 1990. Neglected taxonomy and continuing extinctions of Tuatara (*Sphenodon*). *Nature* 347:177–179. [3,6]

Davidson, W. R. and V. F. Nettles. 1992. Relocation of wildlife: Identifying and evaluating disease risks. *Trans. N. Am. Wildlife and Natural Resources Conference* 57:466–473. [12]

Davidson, J. and H. G. Andrewartha. 1948a. Annual trends in a natural population of *Thrips imaginis* (Thysanoptera). *J. Anim. Ecol.* 17:193–199. [7]

Davidson, J. and H. G. Andrewartha. 1948b. The influence of rainfall, evaporation and atmospheric temperature on fluctuations in the size of a natural population of *Thrips imaginis* (Thysanoptera). *J. Anim. Ecol.* 17:200–222. [7]

Davies, S. 1987. *Tree of Life: Buddhism and Protection of Nature*. Buddhist Perception of Nature Project, Hong Kong. [2]

Davis, G. M. and M. Mulvey. 1993. *Species status of Mill Creek* Elliptio. SRO-NERP-22, Savannah River Site, Aiken, SC. [3]

Davis, M. B. 1981. Quaternary history and the stability of forest communities. In D. C. West, H. H. Shugart and D. B. Botkin (eds.), *Forest Succession: Concepts and Application*, pp. 132–153. Springer-Verlag, New York. [8,9]

Davis, M. B. 1983. Holocene vegetational history of the eastern United States. In H. E. Wright, Jr. (ed.), *Late-Quaternary Environments of the United States*, Vol. II, *The Holocene*. pp. 166–181. University of Minnesota Press, Minnesota. [3]

Davis, M. B. 1986. Climatic instability, time lags, and community disequilibrium. In J. Diamond and T. J. Case (eds.), *Community Ecology*, pp. 269–284. Harper & Row, New York. [8]

de Boer, L. E. M. 1982. Karylogical problems in breeding owl monkeys, *Aotus trivirgatus*. *Int. Zoo Yearb.* 22:119–124. [6]

de Candolle, A. P. A. 1874. *Constitution dans le règne végétal de groupes physiologiques applicables à la géographie ancienne et moderne*. Archives des Sciences Physiques et Naturelles, Geneva, Switzerland. [4]

Deacon, J. E. and M. S. Deacon. 1979. Research on endangered fishes in national parks with special emphasis on the Devil's Hole pupfish. In R. M. Lin (ed.), *Proceedings of the First Conference on Scientific Research in the National Parks*, pp. 9–19. U.S. National Park Service, Transactions and Proceedings, Series 5, Washington, D.C. [6]

Deacon, J. E. and C. D. Williams. 1991. Ash Meadows and the legacy of the Devil's Hole pupfish. In W. L. Minckley and J. E. Deacon (eds.), *Battle against Extinction: Native Fish Management in the American West*, pp. 69–91. University of Arizona Press, Tucson. [10,12]

Del Tredici, P., H. Ling and G. Yang. 1992. The *Gingkos* of Tian Mu Shan. *Conserv. Biol.* 6(2):202–209. [2]

Delcourt, P. A. and H. R. Delcourt. 1987. *Long-Term Forest Dynamics of the Temperate Zone*. Springer-Verlag, New York. [8]

Den Boer, P. J. 1970. On the significance of dispersal power for populations of carabid beetles (Coleoptera, Carabidae). *Oecologia* 4:1–28. [9]

Denniston, C. 1978. Small population size and genetic diversity: Implications for endangered species. In S. A. Temple (ed.), *Endangered Birds: Management Techniques for Preserving Threatened Species*, pp. 281–289. University of Wisconsin Press, Madison. [6]

Desert Fishes Council. *Proceedings of the Annual Symposium*, Vols. 1–24. Desert Fishes Council, Bishop, CA. [12]

Diamond, J. M. 1972. Biogeographic kinetics: Estimation of relaxation times for avifaunas of Southwest Pacific islands. *Proc. Nat. Acad. Sci. U.S.A.* 69:3199–3203. [9]

Diamond, J. M. 1975. The island dilemma: Lessons of modern biogeographic studies for the design of natural preserves. *Biol. Conserv.* 7:129–146. [9]

Diamond, J. M. 1976. Island biogeography and conservation: Strategy and limitations. *Science* 193:1027–1029. [9]

Diamond, J. M. 1984a. Historic extinctions: A rosetta stone for understanding prehistoric extinctions. In P. S. Martin and R. G. Klein (eds.), *Quaternary Exinctions: A Prehistoric Revolution*, pp. 824–862. University of Arizona Press, Tucson. [8]

Diamond, J. M. 1984b. "Normal" extinctions of isolated populations. In M. H. Nitecki (ed.), *Extinctions*, pp. 191–246. University of Chicago Press, Chicago. [8]

Diamond, J. 1989. Overview of recent extinctions. In M. Pearl and D. Western (eds.), *Conservation for the Twenty-First Century*, pp. 37–41. Oxford University Press, New York. [6]

Diamond, J. M. 1989. The present, past and future of human-caused extinction. *Philos. Trans. R. Soc. London B* 325:469–478. [5]

Diamond, J. 1992. *The Third Chimpanzee: The Evolution and Future of the Human Animal*. Harper Perennial, New York. [1]

Diamond, J. M. and R. M. May. 1976. Island biogeography and the design of natural reserves. In R. M. May (ed.), *Theoretical Ecology: Principles and Applications*, pp. 163–186. W. B. Saunders, Philadelphia. [9]

Diario de Quintana Roo. 1992. Reflexiones. 12-11-92, secciáon nuestro estado, p. 1. Chetumal, Quintana Roo, México. [17]

Diefenbach, D. R. 1992. The reintroduction of bobcats to Cumberland Island, Georgia: Validation of the scent-station survey technique and analysis of population viability. Ph.D. Dissertation, University of Georgia, Athens. [12]

Diekelman, J. and R. Schuster. 1982. *Natural Landscaping: Designing with Native Plant Communities*. McGraw-Hill, New York. [14]

DiMasi, J. A., R. W. Hansen, H. G. Grabowski and L. Lasagna. 1991. Cost of innovation in the pharmaceutical industry. *J. Health Econ.* 10:107–142. [17]

Dinerstein, E. and G. F. McCracken. 1990. Endangered greater one-horned rhinoceros carry high levels of genetic variation. *Conserv. Biol.* 7:39–52. [3]

Dinerstein, E. and E. Wikramanayake. 1993. Beyond "hotspots": How to prioritize investments in biodiversity in the Indo-Pacific region. *Conserv. Biol.* 7:53–65. [17]

Dobzhansky, Th. 1970. *Genetics of the Evolutionary Process*. Columbia University Press, New York. [3]

Dodd, C. K. 1990. Effects of habitat fragmentation on a stream-dwelling species, the flattened musk turtle *Sternotherus depressus*. *Biol. Conserv.* 54:33–45. [9]

Dodd, C. K. Jr. and R. A. Seigel. 1991. Relocation, repatriation, and translocation of amphibians and reptiles: Are they conservation strategies that work? *Herpetologica* 68:1412–1423. [13]

Dodson, C. H. and A. H. Gentry. 1991. Biological extinction in Western Ecuador. *Ann. Mo. Bot. Gard.* 78:273–295. [5]

Donoghue, M. J. 1985. A critique of the biological species concept and recommendation for a phylogenetic alternative. *The Bryologist* 88:172–181. [3]

Dorf, E. 1976. Climate changes of the past and present. In C. A. Ross (ed.), *Paleobiogeography*, pp. 384–412. Benchmark Papers in Geology, 31. Dowden, Hutchinson and Ross, Stroudsburg, PA.[10]

Drake, J. A., H. A. Mooney, F. di Castri, R. H. Groves, F. J. Kruger, M. Rejmanek and M. Williamson (eds.). 1989. *Biological Invasions: A Global Perspective*. John Wiley & Sons, New York. [8]

Drobney, P. 1994. Prairie restoration project at Walnut Creek, Iowa. *Rest. Mgmt. Notes*. In press. [14]

Dubinsky, Z. (ed.). 1990. *Coral Reefs*. Ecosystems of the World, Vol. 25. Elsevier, Amsterdam. [5]

Duda, M. D. 1991. *A Bridge to the Future: The Wildlife Diversity Funding Initiative. A Needs Assessment for the Fish and Wildlife Conservation Act*. Western Association of Fish and Wildlife Agencies. [14]

Dunham, A. E. 1993. Population responses to environmental change: Physiologically structured models, operative environments, and population dynamics. In P. M. Kareiva, J. S. Kingsolver and R. B. Huey (eds.), *Biotic Interactions and Global Change*, pp. 95–119. Sinauer Associates, Sunderland, MA. [7]

Dunning, J. B., B. J. Danielson and H. R. Pulliam. 1992. Ecological processes that affect populations in complex landscapes. *Oikos* 65:169–175. [9]

Dunning, J. B. and B. D. Watts. 1990. Regional differences in habitat occupancy by Bachman's Sparrow. *Auk* 107:463-472. [7]

Dunwiddie, P. W. 1992. On setting goals: From snapshots to movies and beyond. *Rest. Mgmt. Notes.* 10(2):116–119. [14]

Durning, A. 1992. *How Much is Enough? The Consumer Society and the Future of the Earth*, W. W. Norton, New York. [16]

Dvorak, A. J. (tech. ed.). 1984. *Ecological Studies of Disturbed Landscapes: A Compendium of the Results of Five Years of Research Aimed at the Restoration of Disturbed Ecosystems*. U.S. Department of Energy, NTIS, Springfield, VA. [14]

Eagan, D. and D. Orr (eds.). 1992. *The Campus and Environmental Responsibility.* Jossey-Bass Publishers, San Francisco. [16]

Eagar, R. M. C. 1978. Shape and function of the shell: A comparison of some living and fossil bivalve molluscs. *Biol. Rev.* 53:169–210. [3]

East, R. 1981. Species–area curves and populations of large mammals in African savanna reserves. *Biol. Conserv.* 21:111–126. [10]

Ebenhard, T. 1988. Introduced birds and mammals and their ecological effects. *Swed. Wildl. Res.* 13:1–107. [8]

Echelle, A. A. 1991. Conservation genetics and genetic diversity in freshwater fishes of western North America. In W. L. Minckley and J. E. Deacon (eds.), *Battle Against Extinction: Native Fish Management in the American West,* pp. 141–153. University of Arizona Press, Tucson. [6]

Echelle, A. A., A. F. Echelle and D. R. Edds. 1987. Population structure of four pupfish species (Cyprinodontidae: Cyprinodon) from the Chihuahuan Desert region of New Mexico and Texas: Allozymic variation. *Copeia* 1987(3):668–681. [6]

Echelle, A. F., A. A. Echelle and D. R. Edds. 1989. Conservation genetics of a spring-dwelling desert fish, the Pecos gambusia, *Gambusia nobilis* (Poeciliidae). *Conserv. Biol.* 3:159–169. [6]

Ehrenfeld, D. W. 1970. *Biological Conservation.* Holt, Rinehart and Winston, New York. [1]

Ehrenfeld, D. W. 1976. The conservation of non-resources. *Am. Sci.* 64:660–668. [2]

Ehrenfeld, D. W. 1981. *The Arrogance of Humanism.* Oxford University Press, New York. [15,17,18]

Ehrenfeld, D. W. 1988. Why put a value on biodiversity? In E. O. Wilson and F. M. Peter (eds.), *Biodiversity,* pp. 212–216. National Academy Press, Washington, D.C. [2,15]

Ehrenfeld, D. W. 1991. Environmental protection: The experts' dilemma. *Report from the Institute for Phiolo;ophy and Public Policy* 11(2):8–12. [16]

Ehrenfeld, D. W. 1991. The management of diversity: A conservation paradox. In F. H. Bormann and S. R. Kellert (eds.), *Ecology, Economics, Ethics: The Broken Circle,* pp. 26–39. Yale University Press, New Haven. [6,11]

Ehrenfeld, D. W. 1993. *Beginning Again: People and Nature in the New Millennium.* Oxford University Press, Oxford. [16]

Ehrlich, P. R. 1961. Has the biological species concept outlived its usefulness? *Syst. Zool.* 10:167–176. [3]

Ehrlich, P. R. 1986. *The Machinery of Nature.* Simon and Schuster, New York. [5]

Ehrlich, P. R. 1986. Extinction: What is happening now and what needs to be done. In D. K. Elliott (ed.), *Dynamics of Extinction,* pp. 157–164. John Wiley & Sons, New York. [3]

Ehrlich, P. R. and A. H. Ehrlich. 1981. *Extinction: The Causes and Consequences of the Disappearance of Species.* Random House, New York. [5]

Ehrlich, P. R. and A. H. Ehrlich. 1990. *The Population Explosion.* Simon & Schuster, New York. [18]

Ehrlich, P. R. and R. W. Holm. 1963. *The Process of Evolution.* McGraw-Hill, New York. [3]

Ehrlich, P. R. and H. A. Mooney. 1983. Extinction, substitution, and ecosystem services. *BioScience* 33:248–254. [10]

Ehrlich, P. R. and D. D. Murphy. 1987. Conservation lessons from long-term studies of checkerspot butterflies. *Conserv. Biol.* 1:122–131. [6,7,10]

Ehrlich, P. R., D. D. Murphy, M. C. Singer, C. B. Sherwood, R. R. White and I. L. Brown. 1980. Extinction, reduction, stability and increase: The responses of checkerspot butterfly (*Euphydryas*) populations to the California drought. *Oecologia* 46:101–105. [7]

Ehrlich, P. R. and E. O. Wilson, 1991. Biodiversity studies: Science and policy. *Science* 253:758–762. [5]

Eisner, T. 1989. Prospecting for nature's chemical riches. *Issues Sci. Technol.,* Winter 89–90, 31–34. [17]

Elliot, R. 1992. Intrinsic value, environmental obligation and naturalness. *Monist* 75:138–160. [2]

Ellis, A. J. 1975. Geothermal systems and power development. *Am. Sci.* 63(5):510–521. [12]

Elton, C. S. 1946. Competition and the structure of ecological communities. *J. Anim. Ecol.* 15:54–68. [8]

Elton, C. S. 1949. Population interspersion: an essay on animal community patterns. *J. Ecol.* 37:1-23. [7]

Elton, C. S. 1973. The structure of invertebrate populations inside tropical rainforest. *J. Animal Ecol.* 42:55–104. [5]

Endler, J. A. 1973. Gene flow and population differentiation. *Science* 179:243–250. [6]

Endler, J. A. 1986. *Natural Selection in the Wild.* Princeton University Press, Princeton, NJ. [6]

Endler, J. A. 1989. Conceptual and other problems in speciation. In D. Otter and J. Endler (eds.), *Speciation and its Consequences,* pp. 625–648. Sinauer Associates, Sunderland, MA. [3]

Errington, P. L. and F. N. Hamerstrom, Jr. 1937. The evaluation of nesting losses and juvenile mortality of the ring-neck pheasant. *J. Wildl. Mgmt.* 1:3–20. [1]

Erwin, T. L. 1988. The tropical forest canopy: The heart of biotic diversity. In E. O. Wilson and F. M. Peter (eds.), *Biodiversity,* pp. 123–129. National Academy Press, Washington, D.C. [2,4]

Erwin, T. L. 1991. How many species are there?: Revisited. *Conserv. Biol.* 5:330–333. [5]

Eskey, C. R. and V. H. Haas. 1940. Plague in the western part of the U.S. *U.S. Public Health Bulletin* no. 254. [13]

Estes, J. A. and J. F. Palmisano. 1974. Sea otters: Their role in structuring nearshore communities. *Science* 185:1058–1060. [8]

Ewel, J. J. 1986. Invasibility: Lessons from South Florida. In H. A. Mooney and J. A. Drake (eds.), *Ecology of Biological Invasions of North America and Hawaii,* pp. 214–230. Springer-Verlag, New York. [8]

Faaborg, J. 1979. Qualitative patterns of avian extinction on Neotropical land-bridge islands: Lessons for conservation. *J. Appl. Ecol.* 16:99–107. [9]

Faeth, S. H. and E. F. Connor. 1979. Supersaturated and relaxing island faunas: A critique of the species–age relationship. *J. Biogeogr.* 6:311–316. [9]

Fahrig, L. and G. Merriam. 1985. Habitat patch connectivity and population survival. *Ecology* 66:1762–1768. [9]

Faith, D. P. 1992. Conservation evaluation and phylogenetic diversity. *Biol. Conserv.* 61:1–10. [3,6]

Falconer, D. S. 1981. *Introduction to Quantitative Genetics,* 2nd ed. Longman, New York. [6]

Falk, D. A. and K. E. Holsinger, (eds.). 1991. *Genetics and Conservation of Rare Plants.* Oxford University Press, New York. [6]

Farber, S. and R. Costanza. 1987. The Economic Value of Wetlands Systems. *J. Environ. Mgmt.* 24:41–51. [15]

Farnsworth, N. R. 1988. Screening plants for new medicines. In E. O. Wilson and F. M. Peter (eds.), *Biodiversity,* pp. 83–97. National Academy Press, Washington, D.C. [2]

Feder, H. M. 1966. Cleaning symbiosis in the marine environment. In S. M. Henry (ed.), *Symbiosis,* pp. 327–380. Academic Press, New York. [8]

Fenchel, T. 1975. Character displacement and coexistence in mud snails (Hydrobiidae). *Oecologia* 20:19–32. [8]

Ferreras, P., J. J. Aldama, J. F. Beltran and M. Delibes. 1992. Rates and causes of mortality in a fragmented population of Iberian lynx *Felis pardina* Temminck, 1824. *Biol. Conserv.* 61:197–202. [9]

Finlayson, B. J. and K. M. Verrue. 1982. Toxicities of copper, zinc and cadmium mixtures to juvenile chinook salmon. *Trans. Amer. Fish. Soc.* 111:645–650. [11]

Fisher, A. C. and M. Hanemann. 1985. Endangered species: The economics of irreversible damage. In D. O. Hall, N. Myers and N. S. Margaris (eds.), *Economics of Ecosystem Management,* pp. 129–138. W. Junk, Dordrecht. [15]

Fisher, R. A. 1930. *The Genetical Theory of Natural Selection.* Clarendon Press, Oxford. [6]

Food and Agricultural Organization. 1981. *Tropical Forest Resources Assessment Project.* FAO, Rome. [5]

Food and Agricultural Organization. 1988. *An Interim Report on the State of Forest Resources in Developing Countries.* FAO, Rome. [5]

Food and Agriculture Organization. 1993. *Tropical Forest Resources Assessment.* FAO, Rome. [5]

Foose, T. J. 1983. The relevance of captive populations to the conservation of biotic diversity. In C. M. Schonewald-Cox, S. M. Chambers, B. MacBryde and L. Thomas (eds.), *Genetics and Conservation: A Reference for Managing Wild Animal and Plant Populations,* pp. 374–401. Benjamin/Cummings, Menlo Park, CA. [6]

Forcan, P. 1979. A world order for whales. In T. Wilkes (ed.), *Project Interspeak*, pp. 77–82. Graphic Arts Center, Portland, OR. [2]

Foreman, D., J. Davis, D. John, R. Noss and M. Soulé. 1992. The Wildlands Project Mission Statement. *Wild Earth* Special Issue:3–4.[3,10]

Forman, R. T. T. 1990. Ecologically sustainable landscapes: The role of spatial configuration. In I. S. Zonneveld and R. T. T. Forman (eds.), *Changing Landscapes: An Ecological Perspective*, pp. 173–198. Springer-Verlag, New York. [10]

Forman, R. T. T. l992. Landscape corridors: From theoretical foundations to public policy. In D. A. Saunders and R. J. Hobbs, (eds.), *Nature Conservation 2: The Role of Corridors*, pp. 71–84. Surrey Beatty, Chipping Norton, Australia. [10]

Forman, R. T. T. l993. *Landscape and Regional Ecology*. Cambridge University Press, Cambridge. [10]

Forman, R. T. T. and M. Godron. 1986. *Landscape Ecology*. John Wiley & Sons, New York. [7,9,10]

Forman, R. T. T. and P. N. Moore. l99l. Theoretical foundations for understanding boundaries in landscape mosaics. In A. J. Hansen and F. di Castri, (eds.), *Landscape Boundaries: Consequences for Biodiversity and Ecological Flows*, pp. 236–258. Springer-Verlag, New York. [10]

Forman, R. T. T., A. E. Galli and C. F. Leck. l976. Forest size and avian diversity in New Jersey woodlots with some land use implications. *Oecologia*. 26:1–8. [10]

Forrest, S. C., D. E. Biggins, L. Richardson, T. W. Clark, T. M. Campbell III, K. A. Fagerstone and E. T. Thorne. 1988. Population attributes for the black-footed ferret (*Mustela nigripes*) at Meeteetse, Wyoming, 1981–1985. *J. Mammal.* 69:261–273. [13]

14th Dalai Lama (Tenzin Gyatso). 1992. A Tibetan Buddhist perspective on spirit in nature. In S. C. Rockefeller and J. C. Elder (eds.), *Spirit and Nature: Why the Environment is a Religious Issue*, pp. 109–123. Beacon Press, Boston. [2]

Fox, B. W. 1991. Medicinal plants in tropical medicine. 2. Natural products in cancer treatment from bench to the clinic. *Trans. R. Soc. Trop. Med. Hyg.* 85:22–25. [17]

Fox, W. 1990. *Toward a Transpersonal Ecology: Developing New Directions for Environmentalism*. Shambala, Boston. [2]

Fox, W. 1993. What does the recognition of intrinsic value entail? *Trumpeter* 10:101. [2]

Frankel, O. H. 1983. The place of management in conservation. In C. M. Schonewald-Cox, S. M. Chambers, B. MacBryde and L. Thomas (eds.), *Genetics and Conservation: A Reference for Managing Wild Animal and Plant Populations*, pp. 1–14. Benjamin/Cummings, Menlo Park, CA. [6]

Frankel, O. H. and M. E. Soulé. 1981. *Conservation and Evolution*. Cambridge University Press, Cambridge. [1,6,10]

Franklin, I. R. 1980. Evolutionary change in small populations. In M. E. Soulé and B. A. Wilcox (eds.), *Conservation Biology: An Evolutionary-Ecological Perspective*, pp. 135–139. Sinauer Associates, Sunderland, MA. [6]

Franklin, J. F. and R. T. T. Forman. 1987. Creating landscape patterns by forest cutting: Ecological consequences and principles. *Landscape Ecol.* 1:5–18. [9,10]

Frazer, N. B. 1983. Survivorship of adult female loggerhead sea turtles, *Carretta caretta*, nesting on Little Cumberland Island, Georgia, USA. *Herpetologica* 39:436–447. [7]

Frazer, N. B. 1984. A model for assessing mean age-specific fecundity in sea turtle populations. *Herpetologica* 40:281–291. [7]

Frazer, N. B. 1992. Sea turtle conservation and halfway technology. *Conserv. Biol.* 6:179–184. [7]

Freed, L. A., S. Conant and R. C. Fleischer. 1988. Evolutionary ecology and radiation of Hawaiian passerine birds. *Trends Ecol. Evol.* 2:196–202. [8]

Freeman, M. III. 1979. *The Benefits of Environmental Improvements*. Resources for the Future, Washington, D.C. [17]

Freemark, K. E. and H. G. Merriam. 1986. Importance of area and habitat heterogeneity to bird assemblages in temperate forest fragments. *Biol. Conserv.* 36:115–141. [9]

Freemuth, J. C. 1991. *Islands Under Siege: National Parks and the Politics of External Threats*. University Press of Kansas, Lawrence. [10]

Fujita, R. M., M. S. Epstein, T. J. Goreau and K. Gjerde. 1992. *A Guide to Protecting Coral Reefs*. United Nations Environment Programme, Nairobi, Kenya. [5]

Funtowicz, S. O. and J. R. Ravetz. 1991. A New Scientific Methodology for Global Environmental Issues. In R. Costanza (ed.), *Ecological Economics: The Science and Management of Sustainability*, pp. 137–152. Columbia University Press, New York. [16]

Futuyma, D. J. 1986. *Evolutionary Biology*, 2nd ed. Sinauer Associates, Sunderland, MA. [3,4]

Game, M. and G. F. Peterken. 1984. Nature reserve selection strategies in the woodlands of Central Lincolnshire, England. *Biol. Conserv.* 29:157–181. [10]

Garland, T. and W. G. Bradley. 1984. Effects of a highway on Mojave Desert rodent populations. *Am. Midl. Nat.* 111:47–56. [9]

Gaston, K. J. 1991. The magnitude of global insect species richness. *Conserv. Biol.* 5:283–296. [2]

Gates, D. M. 1993. *Climate Change and Its Biological Consequences*. Sinauer Associates, Sunderland, MA. [10]

Gates, J. E. and L. W. Gysel. 1978. Avian nest dispersion and fledgling success in field-forest ecotones. *Ecology* 59:871–883. [9]

Gee, J. H. R. and Giller, P. S. 1987. *Organization of Communities Past and Present*, pp. 21–82. Blackwell Scientific Publications, Oxford. [10]

Geist, V. 1971. *The Mountain Sheep*. University of Chicago Press, Chicago. [5]

Gentry, A. H. 1986. Endemism in tropical versus temperate plant communities. In M. E. Soulé (ed.), *Conservation Biology: The Science of Scarcity and Diversity*, pp. 153–181. Sinauer Associates, Sunderland, MA. [9]

Gentry, A. H. 1988. Changes in plant community diversity and floristic composition of environmental and geographical gradients. *Ann. M. Bot. Gar.* 75:1–34. [4]

Gentry, A. H. 1992. Tropical forest biodiversity: Distributional patterns and their conservational significance. *Oikos* 63:19–28. [5]

Georgiadis, N. and A. Balmford. 1992. The calculus of conserving biological diversity. *Trends Ecol. Evol.* 7:321–322. [3]

Gerrodette, T. and W. G. Gilmartin. 1990. Demographic consequences of changed pupping and hauling sites of the Hawaiian monk seal. *Conserv. Biol.* 4:423–430. [7]

Getz, W. M. and R. G. Haight. 1989. *Population Harvesting*. Monographs in Population Biology no. 27. Princeton University Press, Princeton, NJ. [12]

Ghiselin, M. T. 1974. A radical solution to the species problem. *Syst. Zool.* 23:536–544. [2]

Gibbs, J. P. and J. Faaborg. 1990. Estimating the viability of ovenbird and Kentucky warbler populations in forest fragments. *Conserv. Biol.* 4:193–196. [9]

Gilbert, L. E. 1980. Food web organization and conservation of neotropical diversity. In M. E. Soulé and B. A. Wilcox, (eds.), *Conservation Biology: An Evolutionary-Ecological Perspective*, pp. 11–34. Sinauer Associates, Sunderland, MA. [5]

Gilpin, M. and I. Hanski, (eds.). 1991. *Metapopulation Dynamics: Empirical and Theoretical Investigations*. Academic Press, San Diego. [11]

Gilpin, M. E. and M. E. Soulé. 1986. Minimum viable populations: Processes of species extinction. In M. E. Soulé (ed.), *Conservation Biology: The Science of Scarcity and Diversity*, pp. 19–34. Sinauer Associates, Sunderland, MA. [6,7]

Ginsburg, R. 1993. Quantitative Risk Assessment and the Illusion of Safety. *New Solutions*, Winter, 8–15. [16]

Goldberg R., E. Anderson, J. Auwater and E. Stacey. 1992. *INBio/Merck Agreement: Pioneers in Sustainable Development*. Harvard Business School Case N1-593-015. [17]

Goldschmidt, T., F. Witte and J. Wanink. 1993. Cascading effects of the introduced Nile perch on the detritivorous/phytoplanktivorous species in the sublittoral areas of Lake Victoria. *Conserv. Biol.* 7:686–700. [5]

Goodpaster, K. E. 1978. On being morally considerable. *J. Philos.* 75:308–325. [2]

Gordon, H. S. 1954. The economic theory of a common property resource. *J. Polit. Econ.* 62:124–142. [15]

Gore, A., Jr. *Earth in the Balance: Ecology and the Human Spirit*. Penguin Books, New York. [3]

Gore, J. A. (ed.). 1985. *The Restoration of Rivers and Streams: Theories and Experiences*. Butterworth, Boston. [14]

Gould, S. J. 1989. *Wonderful Life: The Burgess Shale and the Nature of History*. W. W. Norton, New York. [4]

Graham, R. W. 1986. Response of mammalian communities to environmental changes during the late Quaternary. In J. Diamond and T. J. Case (eds.), *Community Ecology*, pp. 300–313. Harper & Row, New York. [8,10]

Grant, V. 1957. The plant species in theory and practice. In E. Mayr (ed.), *The Species Problem*. pp. 39–80. AAAS Publication 50. [3]

Grassle, J. F. 1989. Species diversity in deep-sea communities. *Trends Ecol. Evol.* 4:12–15. [4]

Grassle, J. F. 1991. Deep-sea benthic biodiversity. *BioScience* 41: 464–469. [4,5]

Grassle, J. F., P. Lasserre, A. D. MacIntyre and G. C. Ray. 1991. Marine biodiversity and ecosystem function: A proposal for an international research program. Biology International Special Issue no. 23. International Union for Biological Sciences, Paris, France. [5]

Grassle, J. F. and N. J. Maciolek. 1992. Deep-sea species richness: Regional and local diversity estimates from quantitative bottom samples. *Am. Nat.* 139:313–341. [4,5]

Green, G. M. and R. W. Sussman. 1990. Deforestation history of the eastern rain forests of Madagascar from satellite images. *Science* 248:212–215. [5]

Green, J. E. and R. E. Salter. 1987. *Methods for Reclamation of Wildlife Habitat in the Canadian Prairie Provinces*. Prepared for Environment Canada and Alberta Recreation, Parks and Wildlife Foundation by the Delta Environmental Management Group Ltd., Edmonton, Alberta. [14]

Greenslade, P. J. M. and P. Greenslade. 1984. Soil surface insects of the Australian arid zone. In H. G. Cogger and E. E. Cameron (eds.), *Arid Australia*, pp. 153–176. Australian Museum, Sydney. [4]

Greenstone, M. H. 1984. Determinants of web spider species diversity: Vegetation structural diversity vs. prey availability. *Oecologia* 62:299–304. [4]

Greig, J. C. 1979. Principles of genetic conservation in relation to wildlife management in Southern Africa. *S. Afr. Tydskr. Naturnav.* 9:57–78. [6]

Grier, N. M. 1920. Morphological features of certain mussel shells found in Lake Erie, compared with those of the corresponding species found in the drainage of the upper Ohio. *Ann. Carnegie Mus.* 13(2):145–182. [3]

Griffith, B., J. M. Scott, J. W. Carpenter and C. Reed. 1989. Translocation as a species conservation tool: Status and strategy. *Science* 245:477–480. [6]

Griffith, M. A. and T. T. Fendley. 1982. Pre- and post-dispersal movement behavior of subadult bobcats on the Savannah River Plant. In S. D. Miller and D. D. Everett (eds.), *Cats of the World*, pp. 277–289. National Wildlife Federation, Washington, D.C. [10]

Groom, M. J. and N. Schumaker. 1993. Evaluating landscape change: Patterns of worldwide deforestation and local fragmentation. In P. M. Kareiva, J. G. Kingsolver and R. B. Huey (eds.), *Biotic Interactions and Global Change*, pp. 24–44. Sinauer Associates, Sunderland, MA. [5]

Grover, H. D. 1990. Global climate change and planetary health. In *Proceedings of the Fourth National Environmental Health Conference*, pp. 93–108. San Antonio, Texas. [10]

Grumbine, R. E. 1990. Viable populations, reserve size, and federal lands management: A critique. *Conserv. Biol.* 4:127–134. [10]

Grumbine, R. E. 1992. *Ghost Bears: Exploring the Biodiversity Crisis*. Island Press, Washington, D.C. [1,3,17]

Guha, R. 1989a. Radical American environmentalism: A Third World critique. *Environ. Ethics* 11:71–83. [2]

Guha, R. 1989b. *The Unquiet Woods: Ecological Change and Peasant Resistance in the Himalaya*. University of California Press, Berkeley. [2]

Guinon, M. 1987. No free lunch. *Rest. Mgmt. Notes* 7(2):56. [14]

Gutierrez, R. J. and eight others. 1992. In *The California Spotted Owl: A Technical Assessment of Its Current Status*, pp. 79–147. General Technical Report PSW-GTR-133. Albany, California: Pacific Southwest Research Station, Forest Service, U.S. Department of Agriculture. [13]

Haffer, J. 1969. Speciation in Amazonia forest birds. *Science* 165: 131–137. [4]

Haig, S. M., J. D. Ballou and S. R. Derrickson. 1990. Management options for preserving genetic diversity: Reintroduction of Guam rails to the wild. *Conserv. Biol.* 4:290–300. [6]

Haila, Y. 1990. Toward an ecological definition of an island: A northwest European perspective. *J. Biogeogr.* 17:561–568. [9]

Haila, Y., I. K. Hanski and S. Raivio. 1993. Turnover of breeding birds in small forest fragments: The "sampling" colonization hypothesis corroborated. *Ecology* 74:714–725. [9]

Hairston, N. G., F. E. Smith and L. B. Slobodkin. 1960. Community structure, population control and competition. *Am. Nat.* 94: 421–425. [4]

Hall, C. A. S. 1988. An assessment of several of the historically most influential theoretical models used in ecology and of the data provided in their support. *Ecological Modeling* 43:5–31. [12]

Hall, C. A. S., C. J. Cleveland and R. Kaufman. 1986. *Energy and Resource Quality: The Ecology of the Economic Process*. John Wiley & Sons, New York. [15]

Halle, F. R., A. A. Oldemann and P. B. Tomlinson. 1978. *Tropical Trees and Forests: An Architectural Analysis*. Springer-Verlag, Berlin. [4]

Hanemann, W. M. 1988. Economics and the preservation of biodiversity. In E. O. Wilson and F. M. Peter (eds.), *Biodiversity*, pp. 193–199. National Academy Press, Washington, D.C. [2,15]

Hansen, A. J., D. L. Urban and B. Marks. 1992. Avian community dynamics: The interplay of landscape trajectories and species life histories. In A. J. Hansen and F. di Castri (eds.), *Landscape Boundaries: Consequences for Biodiversity and Ecological Flows*, pp. 170–195. Springer-Verlag, New York. [10]

Hanski, I. 1989. Metapopulation dynamics: Does it help to have more of the same? *Trends Ecol. Evol.* 4:113–114. [7]

Hansson, L. 1991. Dispersal and connectivity in metapopulations. In M. E. Gilpin and I. Hanski (eds.), *Metapopulaton Dynamics: Empirical and Theoretical Investigations*, pp. 89–103. Linnaean Society of London and Academic Press, London. [9]

Hardin, G. 1968. The tragedy of the commons. *Science* 162:1243–1248. [2,15,18]

Hardin, G. 1993. *Living Within Limits: Ecology, Economics, and Population Taboos*. Oxford University Press, New York. [17,18]

Hardt, R. A. and R. T. T. Forman. 1989. Boundary form effects on woody colonization of reclaimed surface mines. *Ecology* 70:1252–1260. [10]

Harley, J. L. and S. E. Smith. 1983. *Mycorrhizal Symbiosis*. Academic Press, New York. [8]

Harmon, D. 1987. Cultural diversity, human subsistence, and the national park ideal. *Environ. Ethics* 9:147–158. [17]

Harner, R. F. and K. T. Harper. 1976. The role of area, heterogeneity, and favorability in plant species diversity of pinyon-juniper ecosystems. *Ecology* 57:1254–1263. [9]

Harris, L. D. 1984. *The Fragmented Forest: Island Biogeography Theory and the Preservation of Biotic Diversity*. University of Chicago Press, Chicago. [9,10]

Harris, L. D. and K. Atkins. 1991. Faunal movement corridors in Florida. In W. E. Hudson (ed.), *Landscape Linkages and Biodiversity*, pp. 117–134. Island Press, Washington, D.C. [10]

Harris, L. D. and P. B. Gallagher. 1989. New initiatives for wildlife conservation: The need for movement corridors. In G. MacKintosh (ed.), *Preserving Communities and Corridors*, pp. 11–34. Defenders of Wildlife, Washington, D.C. [9]

Harris, L. D. and G. Silva-Lopez. 1992. Forest fragmentation and the conservation of biological diversity. In P. L. Fiedler and S. K. Jain (eds.), *Conservation Biology: The Theory and Practice of Nature Conservation, Preservation, and Management*, pp. 197–237. Chapman and Hall, New York. [9]

Harris, L. D. and R. D. Wallace. 1984. Breeding bird species in Florida forest fragments. *Proc. Annu. Conf. Southeastern Assoc. Fish Wildl. Agencies* 38:87–96. [9]

Harris, R. B. and F. W. Allendorf. 1989. Genetically effective population size of large mammals: Assessment of estimators. *Conserv. Biol.* 3:181-191. [6]

Harrison, D. (ed.). 1992. *Tourism and the Less Developed Countries*. Bellhaven Press, London. [17]

Harrison, R. L. 1992. Toward a theory of inter-refuge corridor design. *Conserv. Biol.* 6:293–295. [10]

Harrison, S. 1991. Local extinction in a metapopulation context: An empirical evaluation. *Biol. J. Linn. Soc.* 42:73–88. [9]

Harrison, S., D. D. Murphy and P. R. Ehrlich. 1988. Distribution of the Bay checkerspot butterfly, *Euphydryas editha bayensis*: Evidence for a metapopulation model. *Am. Nat.* 132:360–382. [6,9]

Hartl, D. L. and A. G. Clark. 1990. *Principles of Population Genetics.* 2nd ed. Sinauer Associates, Sunderland, MA. [6]

Hartshorn, G. S. 1978. Tree falls and tropical forest dynamics. In P. B. Tomlinson and M. H. Zimmermann (eds.), *Tropical Trees as Living Systems,* pp. 617–638. Cambridge University Press, New York. [17]

Hartshorn, G. S. 1979. *Preliminary management plan for Sarapiquí.* Unpublished report to USAID/San José. Tropical Science Center, San José, Costa Rica. [17]

Hartshorn, G. S. 1980. Neotropical forest dynamics. *Biotropica* 12:23–30. [17]

Hartshorn, G. S. 1981. *Forestry potentials in the Palcazú Valley, Peru.* Unpublished report to USAID/Lima. JRB Association, McLean, VA. [17]

Hartshorn, G. 1983. Plants. In D. H. Janzen (ed.), *Costa Rican Natural History,* pp. 118–183. University of Chicago Press, Chicago. [14]

Hartshorn, G. S. 1988. *Natural regeneration of trees on the Palcazáu demonstration strips.* USDA Forest Service report, Washington, D.C. [17]

Hartshorn, G. S. 1989. Application of gap theory to tropical forest management: Natural regeneration on strip clear-cuts in the Peruvian Amazon. *Ecology* 70:567–569. [17]

Hartshorn, G. S. 1992. Forest loss and future options in Central America. In J. M. Hagan and D. W. Johnston (eds.), *Ecology and Conservation of Neotropical Migrant Landbirds,* pp. 13–19. Smithsonian Institution Press, Washington, D.C. [9]

Hartshorn, G. S. and W. Pariona A. 1993. Ecological forest management in the Peruvian Amazon: The Yánesha forestry cooperative in the Palcazú valley. In C. Potter and J. Cohen (eds.), *Perspectives on Biodiversity,* pp. 151–166. AAAS Press, Washington, D.C. [17]

Hassell, M. P. 1978. *The dynamics of arthropod predator-prey systems.* Monographs in Population Biology, no. 13. Princeton University Press, Princeton, NJ. [7]

Hawken, P. 1993. *The Ecology of Commerce.* Harper Collins, New York. [16]

Hawksworth, D. L. 1991a. The fungal dimension of biodiversity: Magnitude, significance and conservation. *Mycol. Res.* 95: 641–655. [4]

Hawksworth, D. L. (ed.). 1991b. *Improving the Stability of Names: Needs and Options.* Koeltz Scientific Books, Koenigstein. [4]

Hedrick, P. W. and P. S. Miller. 1992. Conservation genetics: Techniques and fundamentals. *Ecol. Applic.* 2:30–46. [6]

Heinselman, M. L. 1973. Fire in the virgin forests of the Boundary Waters Canoe Area, Minnesota. *Quat. Res.* 3:329–382. [10]

Henderson, F. R., P. F. Springer and R. Adrian. 1969. *The black-footed ferret in South Dakota.* South Dakota Department of Game, Fish and Parks, Technical Bulletin 4. [13]

Henderson, M. T., G. Merriam and J. Wegner. 1985. Patchy environments and species survival: Chipmunks in an agricultural mosaic. *Biol. Conserv.* 31:95–105. [9]

Hickey, L. J. 1984. Changes in the angiosperm flora across the Cretaceous-Tertiary boundary. In W. A. Bergren and J. A. van Couvering (eds.), *Catastrophes and Earth History,* pp. 279–313. Princeton University Press, Princeton, NJ. [5]

Hiebert, K. 1993. The Merck-INBio agreement conserving forest and discovering new medicines. *Concordare,* Winter 1993, 5. [17]

Hinegardner, R. 1976. Evolution of genome size. In F. J. Ayala (ed.), *Molecular Evolution,* pp. 179–199. Sinauer Associates, Sunderland, MA. [5]

Hobbs, R. J. and L. F. Huenneke. 1992. Disturbance, diversity, and invasion: Implications for conservation. *Conserv. Biol.* 6:324–337. [10]

Hof, J. G. and M. G. Raphael. 1993. Some mathematical programming approaches for optimizing timber age class distributions to meet multispecies wildlife population objectives. *Can. J. Forest Res.* 23:829–834. [11]

Hof, J. G. and L. A. Joyce. 1992. Spatial optimization for wildlife and timber in managed forest ecosystems. *Forest Sci.* 38:489–508. [11]

Holdridge, L. R. 1967. *Life Zone Ecology.* Tropical Science Center, San José, Costa Rica. [4]

Holsinger, K. E. 1993. The evolutionary dynamics of fragmented plant populations. In P. M. Kareiva, J. G. Kingsolver, and R. B. Huey (eds.), *Biotic Interactions and Global Change,* pp. 198–216. Sinauer Associates, Sunderland, MA. [5]

Hopkins, R. A., M. J. Kutilek and G. L. Shreve. 1982. Density and home range characteristics of mountain lions in the Diablo Range of California. In S. D. Miller and D. D. Everett (eds.), *Cats of the World,* pp. 223–235. National Wildlife Federation, Washington, D.C. [10]

Hossner, L. R. (ed.). 1988. *Reclamation of Surface-Mined Lands,* Vols. I and II. CRC Press, Boca Raton, FL. [14]

Hotelling, H. 1931. The economics of exhaustible resources. *J. Polit. Econ.* 39:137–175. [15]

Houghton, R. A., D. S. Lefkowitz and D. L. Skole. 1991. Changes in the landscape of Latin America between 1850 and 1985. I. Progressive loss of forests. *For. Ecol. Mgmt.* 38:143–172. [5]

House of Representatives. 1973. Report no. 412, 93rd Congress, 1st Session. [3]

Howard, L. O. and W. F. Fiske. 1911. The importation into the United States of the parasites of the gypsy moth and the brown-tailed moth. *Bull. U.S. Bur. Entomol.* no. 91. [7]

Howarth, F. G. 1985. Impacts of alien land arthropods and molluscs on native plants and animals in Hawaii. In C. P. Stone and J. M. Scott (eds.), *Hawaii's Terrestrial Ecosystems: Preservation and Management,* pp. 149–179. Cooperative National Park Resources Study Unit, University of Hawaii, Honolulu. [10]

Howarth, R. B. and R. B. Norgaard. 1992. Environmental valuation under sustainable development. *Am. Econ. Rev.* 82:473–477. [15]

Hudson, W. E. (ed.). 1991. *Landscape Linkages and Biodiversity.* Island Press, Washington, D.C. [3]

Hughes, G. H. and T. M. Bonnicksen (eds.). 1990. *Restoration '89: The New Management Challenge.* Proceedings of the first annual meeting of the Society for Ecological Restoration. Society for Ecological Restoration, Madison, WI. [14]

Hull, D. L. 1976. Are species really individuals? *Syst. Zool.* 25:174–91. [2]

Hull, D. L. 1978. A matter of individuality. *Phil. of Sci.* 45:335–360. [2]

Hummel, M. 1990. *A Conservation Strategy for Large Carnivores in Canada.* World Wildlife Fund Canada, Toronto. [10]

Hunter, M. L. 1990. *Wildlife, Forests, and Forestry: Principles of Managing Forests for Biodiversity.* Prentice Hall, Englewood Cliffs, NJ. [12]

Hunter, M. L., G. L. Jacobson and T. Webb. 1988. Paleoecology and the course-filter approach to maintaining biological diversity. *Conserv. Biol.* 2: 375–385. [10]

Hutchinson, G. E. 1965. *The Ecological Theater and the Evolutionary Play.* Yale University Press, New Haven. [1]

Hutnik, R. J. and G. Davis (eds.). 1973. *Ecology and Reclamation of Devastated Land,* Vols. 1 and 2. Gordon and Breach, New York. [14]

Hvengaard, G. T., J. R. Butler and D. K. Krystofiak. 1989. Economic values of bird watching at Point Pelee National Park, Canada. *Wildlife Society Bulletin* 17:526–531. [14]

Intergovernmental Panel on Climate Change (eds. J. T. Houghton, G. J. Jenkins and J. J. Ephramus). 1990. *Climate Change: The IPCC Scientific Assessment.* Cambridge University Press, Cambridge. [5,18]

Intergovernmental Panel on Climate Change (eds. J. T. Houghton, B. A. Callander and S. K. Barney). 1992. *Climate Change 1992: The Supplementary Report to the IPCC Scientific Assessment.* Cambridge University Press, New York. [5]

IUCN. 1993. *World Conservation Strategy.* Gland, Switzerland. [17]

IUCN/UNEP/WWF. 1980. *World Conservation Strategy: Living Resource Conservation for Sustainable Development.* Gland, Switzerland. [17]

IUCN/UNEP/WWF. 1991. *Caring for the Earth: A Strategy for Sustainable Living.* Gland, Switzerland. [17]

Jablonski, D. 1986. Background and mass extinctions: The alteration of macroevolutionary regimes. *Science* 231:129–133. [5]

Jablonski, D. 1991. Extinctions: A palaeontological perspective. *Science* 253:754–757. [5]

Jacobson, S. K. 1990. Graduate education in conservation biology. *Conserv. Biol.* 4:431–440. [1]

Janos, D. P. 1980. Mycorrhizae influence tropical succession. *Biotropica* (Suppl.) 12:56–64. [8]

Janzen, D. H. 1975. *Ecology of Plants in the Tropics.* Edward Arnold Publishers Ltd., London. [5]

Janzen, D. H. 1983. No park is an island: Increase in interference from outside as park size decreases. *Oikos* 41:402–410. [9,10]

Janzen, D. H. 1986. The eternal external threat. In M. E. Soulé (ed.), *Conservation Biology: The Science of Scarcity and Diversity,* pp. 286–303. Sinauer Associates, Sunderland, MA. [9,10,11]

Janzen, D. H. and INBio. 1992. A North-South perspective on science in the management, use, and economic development of biodiversity. In Sandlund, O. T., K. Hindar and A. H. D. Brown (eds.), *Conservation of Biodiversity for Sustainable Development,* pp. 27–54. Scandanavian University Press, Oslo. [17]

Johns, A. D. 1985. Selective logging and wildlife conservation in tropical rain forest: Problems and recommendations. *Biol. Conserv.* 31:355–375. [5]

Johnson, K. G. 1986. *Responses of Wildlife to Large Scale Even-Aged Silvicultural Practices.* Alabama Department of Conservation. Final report, Project no. W-35. [12]

Johnson, L. E. 1991. *A Morally Deep World: An Essay on Moral Significance and Environmental Ethics.* Cambridge University Press, Cambridge. [2]

Johnson, M. P. and P. H. Raven. 1973. Species number and endemism: The Galapagos Archipelago revisited. *Science* 179:893–895. [9]

Johnson, M. P. and D. S. Simberloff. 1974. Environmental determinants of island species numbers in the British Isles. *J. Biogeogr.* 1:149–154. [9]

Johnson, N. K. 1975. Controls on number of bird species on montane islands in the Great Basin. *Evolution* 29:545–567. [9]

Johnson, R. G. and S. A. Temple. 1990. Nest predation and brood parasitism of tallgrass prairie birds. *J. Wildl. Mgmt.* 54:106–111. [9]

Johnson, R. I. 1970. The systematics and zoogeography of the Unionidae (Mollusca: Bivalia) of the southern Atlantic slope region. *Bull. Mus. Comp. Zool.* 140:263–450. [3]

Joint Appeal by Religion and Science for the Environment. 1992. *A Directory of Environmental Activities and Resources in the North American Religious Community.* National Religious Partership on the Environment, New York. [16]

Jones, H. L. and J. Diamond. 1976. Short-term-base studies of turnover in breeding bird populations on the California Channel Islands. *Condor* 78:526–549. [7]

Jordan, C. F. 1986. Local effects of tropical deforestation. In M. E. Soulé (ed.), *Conservation Biology: The Science of Scarcity and Diversity,* pp. 410–426. Sinauer Associates, Sunderland, MA. [5]

Jordan, C. F. and E. G. Farnworth. 1982. Natural vs. plantation forests: A case study of land reclamation strategies for the humid tropics. *Environ. Mgmt.* 6:485–492. [14]

Jordan, W. R. III. 1987. Making a user-friendly national park for Costa Rica—A visit with Daniel Janzen. *Rest. Mgmt. Notes* 5(2):72–75. [14]

Jordan, W. R. III (ed.). 1990. Standards for restoration and management projects. In G. H. Hughes and T. M. Bonnicksen (eds.), *Restoration '89: The New Management Challenge,* Proceedings of the first annual meeting of the Society for Ecological Restoration, pp. 301–337. Society for Ecological Restoration, Madison, WI. [14]

Jordan, W. R. III, M. E. Gilpin and J. D. Aber. 1987. Restoration ecology: Ecological restoration as a technique for basic research. In W. L. Jordan III, M. E. Gilpin and J. D. Aber (eds.), *Restoration Ecology: A Synthetic Approach to Ecological Research,* pp. 3–22. Cambridge University Press, Cambridge. [14]

Kadr, A. B. A. B. , A. L. T. E. S. A. Sabbagh, M. A. S. A. Glenid and M. Y. S. Izzidien. 1983. *Islamic Principles for the Conservation of the Natural Environment.* International Union for the Conservation of Nature and Natural Resources, Gland, Switzerland. [2]

Kale, H. W. 1983. Distribution, habitat, and status of breeding Seaside Sparrows in Florida. In T. L. Quay, J. B. Funderburg, Jr., D. S. Lee, E. F. Potter and C. S. Robbins (eds.), *The Seaside Sparrow, Its Biology and Management,* pp. 41–48. Occasional Papers of the North Carolina Biological Survey, North Carolina State Museum of Natural History, Raleigh, NC. [7]

Kant, I. 1959. *Foundations of the Metaphysics of Morals.* Library of Liberal Arts, New York. [2]

Kareiva, P. M., J. G. Kingsolver and R. B. Huey. (eds.). 1992. *Biotic Interactions and Global Change.* Sinauer Associates, Sunderland, MA. [10]

Karr, J. R. 1981. Assessment of biotic integrity using fish communities. *Fisheries* 6(6):21–27. [14]

Karr, J. R. 1982. Avian extinction on Barro Colorado Island, Panama: A reassessment. *Am. Nat.* 119:220–239. [5]

Karr, J. R. 1982. Population variability and extinction in the avifauna of a tropical land bridge island. *Ecology* 63:1975–1978. [9]

Karr, J. R. 1990. Avian survival rates and the extinction process on Barro Colorado Island, Panama. *Conserv. Biol.* 4:391–397. [5]

Karr, J. R. 1991. Biological integrity: A long-neglected aspect of water resource management. *Ecol. Appl.* 1:66–84. [14]

Karr, J. R. and D. R. Dudley. 1981. Ecological perspective on water quality goals. *Environ. Mgmt.* 5:55–68. [14]

Kauffman, E. G. and O. H. Walliser. (eds.). 1990. *Extinction Events in Earth History.* Springer-Verlag, New York. [5]

Kauffman, L. 1992. Catastrophic change in species-rich freshwater ecosystems: The lessons of Lake Victoria. *BioScience* 42(11):846–858. [5]

Keast, A. 1961. Bird speciation on the Australian continent. *Bull. Mus. Comp. Zool.* 123:305–495. [4]

Keeton, W. T. 1972. *Biological Science.* 2nd ed. W. W. Norton, New York. [3]

Kellert, S. R. 1984. Wildlife values and the private landowner. *Am. Forests* 90(11):27–28, 60–61. [3]

Kendeigh, S. C. and fifteen others. 1950–1951. Nature sanctuaries in the United States and Canada: A preliminary inventory. *Living Wilderness* 15(35):1–45. [10]

Kerans, B. L. and J. R. Karr. 1994. Development and testing of a benthic index of biotic integrity (B-IBI) for rivers of the Tennessee Valley. *Ecol. Appl.* In press. [14]

Keynes, J. M. 1936. *The General Theory of Employment, Interest, and Money.* Harcourt Brace, New York.

Kimura, M. and J. F. Crow. 1963. The measurement of effective population number. *Evolution* 17:279–288. [6]

King, C. 1935. *Mountaineering in the Sierra Nevada.* W. W. Norton, New York. [12]

Kinne, O. (ed.). 1971. *Maine Ecology: A Comprehensive, Integrated Treatise on Life in Oceans and Coastal Waters.* Vol. I. Wiley Interscience. [4]

Kirk, D. 1975. *Biology Today,* 2nd ed. Random House, New York. [3]

Klein, B. C. 1989. Effects of forest fragmentation on dung and carrion beetle communities in central Amazonia. *Ecology* 70:1715–1725. [9]

Kline, V. M. and E. A. Howell. 1987. Prairies. In W. R. Jordan III, M. E. Gilpin and J. D. Aber (eds.), *Restoration Ecology,* pp. 75–83. Cambridge University Press, Cambridge. [14]

Knoll, A. H. 1984. Patterns of extinction in the fossil record of vascular plants. In M. H. Nitecki (ed.), *Extinctions,* pp. 21–68. University of Chicago Press, Chicago. [5]

Knoll, A. H. 1986. Patterns of change in plant communities through geological time. In J. Diamond and T. J. Case (eds.), *Community Ecology,* pp. 126–141. Harper & Row, New York. [8]

Koblentz-Mishke, O. J., V. V. Volkovinsky and J. G. Kabanova. 1970. Plankton primary productivity of the world ocean. In W. S. Wooster (ed.), *Scientific Exploration of the South Pacific,* pp. 183–193. National Academy of Sciences Press, Washington, D.C. [4]

Koehn, R. K. and S. E. Shumway. 1982. A genetic/physiological explanation for differential growth rate among individuals of the American oyster, *Crassostrea virginica* (Gmelin). *Marine Biol. Lett.* 3:35–42. [6]

Koehn, R. K., W. J. Diehl and T. M. Scott. 1988. The differential contribution by individual enzymes of glycolysis and protein catabolism to the relationship between heterozygosity and growth rate in the coot clam *Mulinia lateralis.* *Genetics* 118:121–130. [6]

Köppen, W. 1884. Die Wärmezonen der Erde, nach Dauer der Heissen, Gemässigten und Kalten Zeit, und nach der Wirkung der Wärme auf die Organische Welt betrachtet. *Meterolog. Zeit.* 1:215–226. [4]

Korten, D. C. 1991–1992. Sustainable development. *World Policy J.* 9:157–190. [17]

Krebs, C. J. 1985. *Ecology: The Experimental Analysis of Distribution and Abundance.* 3rd ed. Harper & Row, New York. [8]

Krebs, C. J. 1988. *The Message of Ecology.* Harper & Row, New York. [8]

Kruckeberg, A. 1985. *California Serpentines: Flora, Vegetation, Geology, Soils and Management Problems.* University of California Publications in Botany no. 78. [4]

Kruger, F. J. 1981. Seasonal growth and flowering rhythms: South African heathlands. In R. L. Specht (ed.), *Heathlands and Related Shrublands*, pp. 1–4. (Ecosystems of the World, Vol. 9B). Elsevier, Amsterdam. [4]

Kruger, F. J. and H. C. Taylor. 1979. Plant species diversity in Cape fynbos: Gamma and delta diversity. *Vegetatio* 41:85–93. [4]

Kuhn, T. S. 1972. *The Structure of Scientific Revolutions.* 2nd ed. University of Chicago Press, Chicago. [1]

Kusler, J. A. and M. E. Kentula (eds.). 1990. *Wetland Creation and Restoration: The Status of the Science.* Island Press, Washington, D.C. [14]

Lack, D. 1947. *Darwin's Finches.* Cambridge University Press, Cambridge. [6,8]

Lack, D. 1976. *Island Biology: Illustrated by the Land Birds of Jamaica.* Blackwell Scientific Publications, Oxford. [9]

Laerm, J., J. C. Avise, J. C. Patton and R. A. Lansman. 1982. Genetic determination of the status of an endangered species of pocket gopher in Georgia. *J. Wildl. Mgmt.* 46:513–518. [6]

Lamberson, R. H., B. R. Noon, C. Voss and K. S. McKelvey. 1994. Reserve design for territorial species: The effects of patch size and spacing on the viability of the Northern Spotted Owl. *Conserv. Biol.* In press. [13]

Lamberson, R. H., R. McKelvey, B. R. Noon and C. Voss. 1992. The effects of varying dispersal capabilities on the population dynamics of the Northern Spotted Owl. *Conserv. Biol.* 6:505–512. [13]

Lamont, B. B., A. J. M. Hopkins and R. J. Hnatiuk. 1984. The Flora — Composition, Diversity and Origins. In J. S. Pate and J. S. Berd (eds.), *Kwongan: Plant Life of the Sandplain*, pp. 27–50. University of Western Australia Press, Nedlands. [4]

Lande, R. 1987. Extinction thresholds in demographic models of territorial populations. *Am. Nat.* 130:624–635. [7,13]

Lande, R. 1988. Genetics and demography in biological conservation. *Science* 241:1455–1460. [6,10]

Larkin, P. A. 1977. An epitaph to the concept of maximum sustained yield. *Trans. Amer. Fish. Soc.* 106:1–11. [17]

Laslett, P. and J. S. Fishkin (eds.). 1992. *Justice between Age Groups and Generations.* Yale University Press, New Haven. [15]

Laurance, W. F. 1990. Comparative responses of five arboreal marsupials to tropical forest fragmentation. *J. Mammal.* 71:641–653. [9]

Laurance, W. F. 1991. Edge effects in tropical forest fragments: Application of a model for the design of nature reserves. *Biol. Conserv.* 57:205–219. [9]

Lavelle, M. and M. Coyle. 1992. Unequal protection: The racial divide in environmental law. *Nat. Law J. Spec. Invest.*, September 21, s1–s12. [16]

Lawton, J. H. and K. C. Brown. 1986. The population and community ecology of invading insects. *Phil. Trans. R. Soc. Lond.* 314:607–617. [8]

Lea, I. 1827–1874. Observations on the genus *Unio.* Privately published, Philadelphia, PA. [3]

Leary, R. F., F. W. Allendorf and K. L. Knudsen. 1983. Developmental stability and enzyme heterozygosity in rainbow trout. *Nature* 301:71–72. [6]

Leberg, P. L. 1991. Influence of fragmentation and bottlenecks on genetic divergence of wild turkey populations. *Conserv. Biol.* 5:522–530. [6,9]

Leck, C. F. 1979. Avian extinctions in an isolated tropical wet-forest preserve, Ecuador. *Auk* 96:343–352. [9]

Lehman, J. T. 1986. Control of eutrophication in Lake Washington. In G. H. Orians et al. (eds.), *Ecological Knowledge and Environmental Problem-Solving*, pp. 301–312. National Academy Press, Washington, D.C. [14]

Lehmkuhl, J. F. and M. G. Raphael. 1993. Habitat pattern around Northern Spotted Owl locations on the Olympic Penisula, Washington. *J. Wildl. Mgmt.* 57:302–315. [13]

Lenat, D. R. 1988. Water quality assessment of streams using a qualitative collection method for benthic macroinvertebrates. *J. N. Am. Benthic Soc.* 7:222–233. [14]

Leonard, J. 1987. *Natural Resources and Economic Development in Central America.* International Institute for Environment and Development, Washington, D.C. [13]

Leopold, A. 1933. *Game Management.* Charles Scribner's Sons, New York. [11]

Leopold, A. 1939. A biotic view of land. *J. Forestry* 37:727–730. [11]

Leopold, A. 1949. *A Sand County Almanac and Sketches Here and There.* Oxford University Press, New York. [1,2,8]

Leopold, A. 1953. *Round River: From the Journals of Aldo Leopold.* Oxford University Press, New York. [2]

Levin, D. A. 1979. The nature of plant species. *Science* 204:381–384. [3]

Levin, D. A. and W. L. Crepet. 1973. Genetic variation in *Lycopodium lucidulum*: A phylogenetic relic. *Evolution* 27:622–632. [6]

Levins, R. 1966. Strategy of model building in population biology. *Am. Sci.* 54:421–431. [7]

Levins, R. 1969. Some demographic and genetic consequences of environmental heterogeneity for biological control. *Bull. Entomol. Soc. Am.* 15:237–240. [7]

Levinton, A. and R. I. Bowman (eds.). 1981. *Patterns of Evolution in Galápagos Organisms.* Special Publication, AAAS, Pacific Division. [6]

Lewis, M. 1978. Acute toxicity of copper, zinc and managnese in single and mixed salt solutions to juvenile longfin dace, *Agosia chrysogaster. J. Fish. Biol.* 13:695–700. [11]

Lindburg, D. G., B. S. Durrant, S. E. Millard and J. E. Oosterhuis. 1993. Fertility assessment of cheetah males with poor quality semen. *Zoo Biol.* 12:97–103. [6]

Lindenmayer, D. B. and H. A. Nix. 1993. Ecological principles for the design of wildlife corridors. *Conserv. Biol.* 7:627–630. [10]

Liu, J. 1992. ECOLECON: A spatially-explicit model for ecological economics of species conservation in complex forest landscapes. Ph.D. dissertation, University of Georgia, Athens. [7,12]

Liu, J., J. B. Dunning and H. R. Pulliam. A spatially-explicit model of animal population dynamics on a changing landscape: the Bachman's Sparrow at the Savannah River Site. Unpubl. manuscript. [7]

Livingstone, D. A. 1975. Late quaternary climate change in Africa. *Annu. Rev. Ecol. Syst.* 6:249–280. [4]

Livingstone, D. A. and T. van der Hammen. 1978. Paleogeography and paleoclimatology. In *Tropical Forest Ecosystems*, pp. 61–90. UNESCO/UNEP/FAO. [4]

Loar, J. M. 1985. *Application of habitat evaluation models in Southern Appalachian trout streams.* Publication 2383. Oak Ridge National Laboratory, Environmental Science Division. [12]

Lodge, D. M. 1993. Species invasions and deletions: community effects and responses to climate and habitat change. In P. M. Kareiva, J. G. Kingsolver and R. B. Huey (eds.), 1993. *Biotic Interactions and Global Change*, pp. 367–387. Sinauer Associates, Sunderland, MA. [8]

Long, J. 1981. *Introduced Birds of the World.* David and Charles, London. [8]

Lord, J. M. and D. A. Norton. 1990. Scale and the spatial concept of fragmentation. *Conserv. Biol.* 4:197–202. [9]

Lorimer, C. G. 1989. Relative effects of small and large disturbances on temperate forest structure. *Ecology* 70:565–567. [9]

Lovejoy, T. E. 1980. A projection of species extinctions. In Council on Environmental Quality, *The Global 2000 Report to the President: Entering the Twenty-First Century*, pp. 328–331. U.S. Government Printing Office, Washington, D.C. [5]

Lovejoy, T. E. and H. O. R. Shubart. 1980. The ecology of Amazonian development. In F. Barbira-Scazzacchio (ed.), *Land, People and Planning in Contemporary Amazonia*, pp. 21–26. Cambridge University Press, Cambridge. [5]

Lovejoy, T. E. and ten others. 1986. Edge and other effects of isolation on Amazon forest fragments. In M. E. Soulé (ed.), *Conservation Biology: The Science of Scarcity and Diversity*, pp. 257–285. Sinauer Associates, Sunderland, MA. [9,12]

Lovelock, J. 1988. *The Ages of Gaia: A Biography of Our Living Earth*. W. W. Norton, New York. [2]

Ludwig, D. R. Hilborn and C. Walters. 1993. Uncertainty, resource exploitation, and conservation: Lessons from history. *Science* 260:17, 36. [16,17]

Lugo, A. E. 1988. Estimating reductions in the diversity of tropical forest species. In E. O. Wilson and F. M. Peter (eds.), *Biodiversity*, pp. 58–70. National Academy Press, Washington, D.C. [5]

Luken, J. O. 1990. *Directing Ecological Succession*. Chapman and Hall, London. [14]

Lyons, J. 1992. *Using the Index of Biotic Integrity (IBI) to Measure Environmental Quality in Warmwater Streams of Wisconsin*. General Technical Report NC-149. U.S. Forest Service, Minneapolis, MN. [14]

MacArthur, R. H. 1964. Environmental factors affecting bird species diversity. *Am. Nat.* 98:387–397. [4]

MacArthur, R. H. 1972. *Geographical Ecology: Patterns in the Distribution of Species*. Princeton University Press, Princeton, NJ. [9]

MacArthur, R. H. and J. MacArthur. 1961. On bird species diversity. *Ecology* 42:594–598. [4,12]

MacArthur, R. H. and E. O. Wilson. 1963. An equilibrium theory of insular zoogeography. *Evolution* 17:373–387. [9]

MacArthur, R. H. and E. O. Wilson. 1967. *The Theory of Island Biogeography*. Princeton University Press, Princeton, NJ. [4,5,7,9]

MacArthur, R. H., H. E. Recher and M. L. Cody. 1966. On the relation between habitat selection and species diversity. *Am. Nat.* 100:319–332. [4]

MacKinnon, J. and K. MacKinnon. 1986a. *Review of the Protected Areas System in the Afrotropical Realm*. International Union for the Conservation of Nature and Natural Resources, Gland, Switzerland. [5]

MacKinnon, J. and K. MacKinnon. 1986b. *Review of the Protected Areas System in the Indo-Malayan Realm*. International Union for the Conservation of Nature and Natural Resources, Gland, Switzerland. [5]

MacMahon, J. A. 1979. North American deserts: Their floral and faunal components. In R. A. Perry and D. W. Goodall (eds.), *Arid Land Ecosystems: Structure, Functioning and Management*, Vol. 1. pp. 21–82. Cambridge University Press, Cambridge. [10]

MacMahon, J. A. 1981. Successional processes: Comparisons among biomes with special reference to probable roles of and influences on animals. In D. C. West, H. H. Shugart and D. B. Botkin (eds.), *Forest Succession: Concept and Application*, pp. 277–304. Springer-Verlag, New York. [14]

MacMahon, J. A. 1987. Disturbed lands and ecological theory: An essay about a mutualistic association. In W. R. Jordan III, M. E. Gilpin and J. D. Aber (eds.), *Restoration Ecology: A Synthetic Approach to Ecological Research*, pp. 221–237. Cambridge University Press, Cambridge. [14]

Mader, H. J. 1984. Animal habitat isolation by roads and agricultural fields. *Biol. Conserv.* 29:81–96. [9]

Mader, H. J., C. Schell and P. Kornacker. 1990. Linear barriers to movements in the landscape. *Biol. Conserv.* 54:209–222. [9]

Maille, P. and R. Mendelsohn. 1993. Valuing Ecotourism in Madagascar. *J. Environ. Mgmt.* 38:213–218. [17]

Majer, J. D. (ed.). 1989. *Animals in Primary Succession: The Role of Fauna in Reclaimed Lands*. Cambridge University Press, Cambridge. [14]

Malthus, T. 1963. *Principles of Population*. Reprint. Richard D. Irwin, Homewood, IL. [15]

Manzella, S. A., C. W. Caillouet, Jr. and C. T. Fontaine. 1988. Kemp's Ridley, *Lepidochelys kempi*, sea turtle head start tag recoveries: Distribution, habitat, and method of recovery. *Mar. Fish. Rev.* 50:24–32. [13]

Marcot, B. G. and R. Holthausen. 1987. Analyzing population viability of the Spotted Owl in the Pacific Northwest. *Trans. N. Am. Wildl. Nat. Res. Conf.* 52:333–347. [7]

Marglin, S. A. 1963. The social rate of discount and the optimal rate of investment. *Q. J. Econ.* 77:95–112. [15]

Margules, C. R. and M. P. Austin (eds.). 1992. *Nature Conservation: Cost Effective Biological Survey and Data Analysis*. CSIRO, Melbourne, Australia. [10]

Margules, C. R., A. J. Higgs and R. W. Rafe. 1982. Modern biogeographic theory: Are there any lessons for nature reserve design? *Biol. Conserv.* 24:115–128. [9]

Marks, G. C. and T. T. Kozlowski. 1973. *Ectomycorrhizae*. Academic Press, New York. [8]

Marquis, R. L. and H. E. Braker. 1994. Plant-herbivore interactions: Diversity, specificity, and impact. In L. A. McDade, K. S. Bawa, H. A. Hespenheide and G. S. Hartshorn (eds.), *LaSelva: Ecology and Natural History of a Neotropical Rainforest*, pp. 261–281. University of Chicago Press, Chicago. [4]

Martin, P. 1973. The discovery of America. *Science* 179:969–974. [1]

Martin, P. S. and R. G. Klein (eds.). 1984. *Quaternary Extinctions: A Prehistoric Revolution*. University of Arizona Press, Tucson. [1,5]

Mary, F. and G. Michon. 1987. When agroforestry drives back natural forests: A socio-economic analysis of a rice-agroforest system in Sumatra. *Agroforestry Systems* 5:27–55. [1]

Maxson, L. R. and A. C. Wilson. 1974. Convergent morphological evolution detected by studying proteins of tree frogs in the *Hyla eximia* species group. *Science* 185:66–68. [6]

May, R. M. 1975. *Stability and Complexity in Model Ecosystems*. 2nd ed. Princeton University Press, Princeton, NJ. [4]

May, R. M. 1988. How many species are there on earth? *Science* 241:1441–1449. [4]

May, R. M. 1990. Taxonomy as destiny. *Nature* 347:129–130. [3]

May, R. M. 1992a. Bottoms up for the oceans. *Nature* 357:278–279. [5]

May, R. M. 1992b. How many species inhabit the Earth? *Sci. Am.* 267:42–48. [5]

Mayr, E. 1942. *Systematics and the Origin of Species*. Columbia University Press, New York. [3]

Mayr, E. 1959. Darwin and the evolutionary theory in biology. In *Evolution and Anthropology: A Centennial Appraisal*, pp. 409–412. The Anthropological Society of Washington, Washington, D.C. [3]

Mayr, E. 1963. *Animal Species and Evolution*. Belknap Press of Harvard University Press, Cambridge, MA. [3]

Mayr, E. 1969. *Principles of Systematic Zoology*. McGraw-Hill, New York. [3]

Mayr, E. 1982. *The Growth of Biological Thought: Diversity, Evolution and Inheritance*. Harvard University Press, Cambridge, MA. [3,5]

McAllister, D. 1991. Estimating the pharmaceutical value of forests, Canadian and tropical. *Can. Biodiv.* 1:16–25. [17]

McDonald, K. A. and J. H. Brown. 1992. Using montane mammals to model extinctions due to global change. *Conserv. Biol.* 6:409–415. [10]

McKelvey, K. S. and J. D. Johnston. 1992. Historical perspectives on the forests of the Sierra Nevada and the Transverse Ranges of Southern California: Forest conditions at the turn of the century. In J. Verner et al., *The California Spotted Owl: A Technical Assessment of Its Current Status*, pp. 225–246. General Technical Report PSW-GTR-133. Albany, California: Pacific Southwest Research Station, Forest Service, U.S. Department of Agriculture. [13]

McKelvey, K., B. R. Noon and R. H. Lamberson. 1993. Conservation planning for species occupying fragmented landscapes: The case of the Northern Spotted Owl. In P. M. Kareiva, J. G. Kingsolver and R. B. Huey (eds.), *Biotic Interactions and Global Change*, pp. 424–450. Sinauer Associates, Sunderland, MA. [7,11]

McKibben, B. 1989. *The End of Nature*. Anchor Books, New York. [1]

McKitrick, M. C. and R. M. Zink. 1988. Species concepts in ornithology. *Condor* 90:1–14. [3]

McNeely, J. A. 1988. *Economics and Biological Diversity: Developing and Using Economic Incentives to Conserve Biological Resources*. International Union for the Conservation of Nature and Natural Resources, Gland, Switzerland. [15]

Meadows, D. H. 1990. Biodiversity: The key to saving life on earth. *Land Stewardship Letter* (Summer):4–5. [2]

Meffe, G. K. 1992. Techno-arrogance and halfway technologies: Salmon hatcheries on the Pacific coast of North America. *Conserv. Biol.* 6:350–354. [11,13,15,17,18]

Meffe, G. K. and R. C. Vrijenhoek. 1988. Conservation genetics in the management of desert fishes. *Conserv. Biol.* 2:157–169. [6]

Meine, C. 1992. Conservation biology and sustainable societies: A historical perspective. In M. Oelschlaeger (ed.), *After Earth Day: Continuing the Conservation Effort*, pp. 37–65. University of North Texas Press, Denton. [2,11]

Menges, E. 1990. Population viability analysis for an endangered plant. *Conserv. Biol.* 4:52–62. [7]

Menges, E., D. M. Waller and S. C. Gawler. 1986. Seed set and seed predation in *Pedicularis furbishiae*, a rare endemic of the St. John River, Maine. *Am. J. Bot.* 73:1168–1177. [7]

Menges, E. S. 1992. Stochastic modeling of extinction in plant populations. In P. L. Fiedler and S. K. Jain (eds.), *Conservation Biology: The Theory and Practice of Nature Conservation Preservation and Management*, pp. 253–275. Chapman and Hall, New York. [17]

Merriam, G. 1991. Corridors and connectivity: Animal populations in heterogeneous environments. In D. A. Saunders and R. J. Hobbs (eds.), *Nature Conservation 2: The Role of Corridors*, pp. 133–142. Surrey Beatty, Chipping Norton, Australia. [9]

Merriam, G., M. Kozakiewicz, E. Tsuchiya and K. Hawley. 1989. Barriers as boundaries for metapopulations and demes of *Peromyscus leucopus* in farm landscapes. *Landscape Ecol.* 2:227–235. [9]

Milewski, A. V. and W. J. Bond. 1982. Convergence of myrmecochory in mediterranean Australia and South Africa. In R. C. Buckley (ed.), *Ant-Plant Interactions in Australia*, pp. 89–98. Junk, The Hague. [4]

Miller, D. L. and thirteen others. 1988. Regional applications of an index of biotic integrity for use in water resource management. *Fisheries* (Bethesda) 13(5):12–20. [14]

Miller, R. M. 1987. Mycorrhizae and succession. In W. R. Jordan III, M. E. Gilpin and J. D. Aber (eds.), *Restoration Ecology: A Synthetic Approach to Ecological Research*, pp. 205–220. Cambridge University Press, Cambridge. [14]

Miller, R. R. 1961. Man and the changing fish fauna of the American Southwest. *Papers Mich. Acad. Sci. Arts Lett.* 46:365–404. [12]

Miller, R. R. and E. P. Pister. 1971. Management of the Owens pupfish, *Cyprinodon radiosus*, in Mono County, California. *Trans. Am. Fish. Soc.* 100:502–509. [12]

Miller, R. R., J. D. Williams and J. E. Williams. 1989. Extinctions of North American fishes during the past century. *Fisheries* 14(6):22–38. [5]

Miller, T. 1988. *Living in the Environment*. Preface. Wadsworth Biology Series. Wadsworth Publishing. Belmont, CA. [12]

Mills, L. S., M. E. Soulé and D. F. Doak. 1993. The keystone-species concept in ecology and conservation. *BioScience* 43:219–224. [8]

Minckley, W. L. 1983. Status of the razorback sucker, *Xyrauchen texanus* (Abbott), in the lower Colorado River. *Southwest. Nat.* 28:165–187.

Minckley, W. L. and J. E. Deacon (eds.). 1991. *Battle against Extinction: Native Fish Management in the American West*. University of Arizona Press, Tucson. [5,6,8]

Minckley, W. L., G. K. Meffe and D. L. Soltz. 1991. Conservation and management of short-lived fishes: The cyprinodontoids. In W. L. Minckley and J. E. Deacon (eds.), *Battle Against Extinction: Native Fish Management in the American West*, pp. 247–282. University of Arizona Press, Tucson. [10]

Ministerio de Recursos Naturales, Energia y Minas. 1992. *Sistema Nacional de Areas de Conservacíon*. Ministerio de Recursos Naturales, Energia y Minas, San José, Costa Rica. [13]

Minshall, G. W. and C. T. Robinson. 1992. Effects of the 1988 wildfires on stream systems of Yellowstone National Park. In G. E. Plumb and H. J. Harlow (eds.), *University of Wyoming National Park Service Research Center, 16th Annual Report*, pp. 191–198. Laramie, WY. [12]

Mitchell, R. C. and R. T. Carson. 1989. *Using Surveys to Value Public Goods: The Contingent Valuation Method*. Resources for the Future, Washington, D.C. [15]

Mittermeier, R. A., T. Werner, J. C. Ayres and G. A. B. da Fonseca. 1992. O Pais da Megadiversidade. *Ciencia Hoje* 14:20–27. [18]

Mitton, J. B. and M. C. Grant. 1984. Associations among protein heterozygosity, growth rate, and developmental homeostasis. *Annu. Rev. Ecol. Syst.* 15:479–499. [6]

Mladenoff, D. J., M. A. White, J. Pastor and T. R. Crow. 1993. Comparing spatial pattern in unaltered old-growth and disturbed forest landscapes. *Ecol. Applic.* 3:294–306. [9]

Mohsin, A. K. M. and M. A. Ambok. 1983. *Freshwater Fishes of Peninsular Malaysia*. University Pertanian Malaysia Press, Kuala Lumpur. [5]

Moldenke, A. R. and J. D. Lattin. 1990. Dispersal characteristics of old-growth soil arthropods: The potential for loss of diversity and biological function. *Northwest Environ. J.* 6:408–409. [9]

Monastersky, R. 1993. The deforestation debate. *Sci. News* 144:26–27. [5]

Mooney, H. A. 1988. Lessons from Mediterranean-climate regions. In E. O. Wilson and F. M. Peter (eds.), *Biodiversity*, pp. 157–165. National Academy Press, Washington, D.C. [5]

Mooney, H. A. and J. A. Drake. (eds.). 1986. *Ecology of Biological Invasions of North America and Hawaii*. Springer-Verlag, New York. [8]

Morlan, J. C. and R. E. Frenkel. 1992. The Salmon River estuary. *Rest. Mgmt. Notes* 10(1):21–23. [14]

Morrison, P. H. 1990. *Ancient Forests in the Olympic National Forest: Analysis From a Historical and Landscape Perspective*. The Wilderness Society, Washington, D.C. [9]

Morrison, P. H. and F. J. Swanson. 1990. *Fire History and Pattern in a Cascade Range Landscape*. PNW-GTR-254. USDA Forest Service, Portland, OR. [9]

Moulton, M. P. 1985. Morphological similarity and the coexistence of congeners: An experimental test with introduced Hawaiian birds. *Oikos* 44:301–305. [8]

Moulton, M. P. 1993. The all-or-none pattern in introduced Hawaiian passeriforms: The role of competition sustained. *Am. Nat.* 141:105–119. [8]

Moulton, M. P. and S. L. Pimm. 1983. The introduced Hawaiian avifauna: Biogeographical evidence for competition. *Am. Nat.* 121:669–690. [8]

Moulton, M. P. and S. L. Pimm. 1985. The extent of competition in shaping an experimental avifauna. In J. Diamond and T. Case (eds.), *Community Ecology*, pp. 80–97. Harper & Row, New York. [8]

Moulton, M. P. and S. L. Pimm. 1986. Species introductions to Hawaii. In H. Mooney and J. A. Drake (eds.), *Ecology of Biological Invasions of North America and Hawaii*, pp. 231–249. Springer-Verlag, Berlin. [8]

Moulton, M. P. and S. L. Pimm. 1987. Morphological assortment in introduced Hawaiian passerines. *Evol. Ecol.* 1:113–124. [8]

Moyle, P. B. and R. A. Leidy. 1992. Loss of biodiversity in aquatic ecosystems: Evidence from fish faunas. In P. L. Fiedler and S. K. Jain (eds.), *Conservation Biology: The Theory and Practice of Nature Conservation, Preservation, and Management*, pp. 127–169. Chapman and Hall, New York. [9]

Mueller-Dombois, D. 1987. Natural dieback in forests. *BioScience* 37:575–583. [9]

Murdoch, W. W. 1980. *The Poverty of Nations*. The Johns Hopkins University Press, Baltimore, MD. [18]

Murphy, D. D. 1991. Invertebrate conservation. In K. A. Kohm (ed.), *Balancing on the Brink of Extinction: The Endangered Species Act and Lessons for the Future*, pp. 181–198. Island Press, Washington, D.C. [3]

Murphy, D. D. and B. R. Noon. 1991. Coping with uncertainty in wildlife biology. *J. Wildl. Mgmt.* 55:773–782. [13]

Murphy, D. D. and B. R. Noon. 1992. Integrating scientific methods with habitat conservation planning for the Northern Spotted Owl. *Ecol. Applic.* 2:3–17. [13]

Murphy, D. D. and S. B. Weiss. 1988. Ecological studies and the conservation of the Bay checkerspot butterfly, *Euphydryas editha bayensis*. *Biol. Conserv.* 46:183–200. [9]

Murphy, D. D., K. E. Freas and S. B. Weiss. 1990. An environment-metapopulation approach to population viability analysis for a threatened invertebrate. *Conserv. Biol.* 4:41–51. [7,10]

Murrey, J. 1967. *The Elephant People*. Oxford University Press, New York. [10]

Myers, N. 1979. *The Sinking Ark: A New Look at the Problem of Disappearing Species*. Pergamon Press, Oxford. [5]

Myers, N. 1981. A farewell to Africa. *Internat. Wildl.* 11 (Nov/Dec.): 36, 40, 44, 46. [2]

Myers, N. 1983. *A Wealth of Wild Species*. Westview Press, Boulder, CO. [2]

Myers, N. 1985. A look at the present extinction spasm. In R. J. Hoage (ed.), *Animal Extinctions: What Everyone Should Know*, pp. 47–57. Smithsonian Institution Press, Washington, D.C. [5]

Myers, N. 1986. Tackling mass extinction of species: A great creative challenge. The Horace M. Albright Lecture in Conservation, University of California, Berkeley. [5]

Myers, N. 1988. Threatened biotas: "Hot spots" in tropical forests. *The Environmentalist* 8:187–208. [4,5]

Myers, N. 1989. *Deforestation Rates in Tropical Countries and Their Climatic Implications*. Friends of the Earth, Washington, D.C. [5]

Myers, N. 1990a. The biodiversity challenge: Expanded hot-spots analysis. *The Environmentalist* 10(4):243–256. [4,5]

Myers, N. 1990b. Mass extinctions: What can the past tell us about the present and the future? *Global and Planetary Change* 82:175–185. [5]

Myers, N. 1992a. *Future Operational Monitoring of Tropical Forests: An Alert Strategy*. Joint Research Centre, Commission of the European Community, Ispra, Italy. [5]

Myers, N. 1992b. *The Primary Source*. W. W. Norton, New York. [5]

Myers, N. 1992c. Synergisms: Joint effects of climate change and other forms of habitat destruction. In R. L. Peters and T. E. Lovejoy (eds.), *Consequences of the Greenhouse Warming to Biodiversity*, pp. 344–354. Yale University Press, New Haven. [5]

Naess, A. 1989. *Ecology, Community, and Lifestyle*. Cambridge University Press, Cambridge. [2]

Naiman, R. J., J. M. Melillo and J. M. Hobbie. 1986. Ecosystem alteration of boreal forest streams by beaver (*Castor canadensis*). *Ecology* 67:1254–1269. [8]

National Park Service and U.S. Fish and Wildlife Service. 1990. *Yellowstone wolf questions—A digest*. Extracts from *Wolves for Yellowstone? A report to the U.S. Congress*. YELL-560. Yellowstone National Park, WY. [12]

National Research Council. 1980. *Research Priorities in Tropical Biology*. National Academy of Sciences, Washington, D.C. [5]

National Research Council. 1990. *Decline of the Sea Turtles: Causes and Prevention*. National Academy Press, Washington, D.C. [13]

National Research Council. 1992. *Restoration of Aquatic Ecosystems: Science, Technology, and Public Policy*. National Academy Press, Washington, D.C. [14]

National Research Council. *Statement to the Committee on Environmental Research*, January 15, 1992. [17]

National Research Council (NRC), Committee on Restoration of Aquatic Ecosystems. 1992. *Restoration of Aquatic Ecosystems: Science, Technology, and Public Policy*. National Academy Press, Washington, D.C. [14]

Nature Conservancy (UK). 1984. *Nature Conservation in Great Britain*. Nature Conservancy Council, Shrewsbury. [5]

Navarro L. D. and J. G. Robinson (eds.). 1990. *Diversidad Biológica en la Reserva de la Biósfera de Sian Ka'an Quintana Roo, México*. Centro de Investigaciones de Quintana Roo, Chetumal, Q. Roo, México. [17]

Nei, M. 1973. Analysis of gene diversity in subdivided populations. *Proc. Natl. Acad. Sci. U.S.A.* 70:3321–3323. [6]

Nei, M. 1975. *Molecular Population Genetics and Evolution*. North-Holland, Amsterdam. [6]

Nelson, H. L. 1987. Prairie restoration in the Chicago area. *Rest. Mgmt. Notes* 5(2):60–67. [14]

Nelson, M. E. and L. D. Mech. 1987. Demes within a northeastern Minnesota deer population. In B. D. Chepko-Sade and Z. T. Halpin (eds.), *Mammalian Dispersal Patterns*, pp. 27–40. University of Chicago Press, Chicago. [10]

Nelson, R. H. 1991. *Reaching for Heaven on Earth: The Theological Meaning of Economics*. Rowman and Littlefield, Savage, MD. [15]

Nelson, R. K. 1983. *Make Prayers to the Raven: A Koyukon View of the Northern Forest*. University of Chicago Press, Chicago. [2]

Nevo, E. 1978. Genetic variation in natural populations: Patterns and theory. *Theor. Pop. Biol.* 13:121–177. [6]

Newmark, W. D. 1985. Legal and biotic boundaries of western North American national parks: A problem of congruence. *Biol. Conserv.* 33:197–208. [10]

Newmark, W. D. 1987. A land-bridge island perspective on mammalian extinctions in western North American parks. *Nature* 325:430–432. [10]

Newmark, W. D. 1987. Animal species vanishing from U.S. parks. *Internat. Wildl.* 17:1–25. [4]

Newmark, W. D. 1991. Tropical forest fragmentation and the local extinction of understory birds in the eastern Usambara Mountains, Tanzania. *Conserv. Biol.* 5:67–78. [9]

Nilsson, S. G. 1986. Are bird communities in small biotope patches random samples from communities in large patches? *Biol. Conserv.* 38:179–204. [9]

Nixon, K. C. and Q. D. Wheeler, 1992. Measures of phylogenetic diversity. In M. Novacek and Q. D. Wheeler (eds.), *Extinction and Phylogeny*, pp. 216–234. Columbia University Press, New York. [3]

Noon, B. R., K. S. McKelvey, D. W. Lutz, W. S. LaHaye, R. J. Gutierrez and C. A. Moen. 1992. Estimates of demographic parameters and rates of population change. In J. Verner et al., *The California Spotted Owl: A Technical Assessment of Its Current Status*, pp. 175–186. General Technical Report PSW-GTR-133. Albany, California: Pacific Southwest Research Station, Forest Service, U.S. Department of Agriculture. [13]

Norgaard, R. B. 1989. The case for methodological pluralism. *Ecol. Econ.* 1:37–57. [15]

Norgaard, R. B. 1994. *Development Betrayed: The End of Progress and a Coevolutionary Visioning of the Future*. Routledge, London. [15]

Norse, E. A. (ed.). 1993. *Global Marine Biological Diversity: A Strategy for Building Conservation into Decision Making*. Island Press, Washington, D.C. [4]

Norton, B. G. (ed.) 1986. *The Preservation of Species: The Value of Biological Diversity*. Princeton University Press, Princeton, NJ. [15]

Norton, B. G. 1987. *Why Preserve Natural Variety?* Princeton University Press, Princeton, NJ. [2]

Norton, B. G. 1991. *Toward Unity among Environmentalists*. Oxford University Press, New York. [2]

Norton, D. A. 1991. *Trilepidea adamsii*: An obituary for a species. *Conserv. Biol.* 5:52–57. [7]

Noss, R. F. 1981. The birds of Sugarcreek, an Ohio nature reserve. *Ohio J. Sci.* 81:29–40. [9]

Noss, R. F. 1983. A regional landscape approach to maintain diversity. *BioScience* 33:700–706. [7,9]

Noss, R. F. 1987. Corridors in real landscapes: A reply to Simberloff and Cox. *Conserv. Biol.* 1:159–164. [10]

Noss, R. F. 1990. Indicators for monitoring biodiversity: A hierarchical approach. *Conserv. Biol.* 4:355–364. [4,9]

Noss, R. F. 1991. Effects of edge and internal patchiness on avian habitat use in an old-growth Florida hammock. *Natural Areas J.* 11:34–47. [9]

Noss, R. F. 1991. Landscape connectivity: Different functions at different scales. In W. E. Hudson (ed.), *Landscape Linkages and Biodiversity*, pp. 27–39. Island Press, Washington, D.C. [10]

Noss, R. F. 1992. The wildlands project: Land conservation strategy. *Wild Earth* (Special Issue):10–25. [3,10]

Noss, R. F. and L. D. Harris. 1986. Nodes, networks, and MUMs: Preserving diversity at all scales. *Environ. Mgmt.* 10:299–309. [10]

Noss, R. F. and L. D. Harris. 1986. Habitat connectivity and the conservation of biological diversity: Florida as a case history. In *Proceedings of the 1989 Society of American Foresters National Convention*, Spokane, WA. pp. 131–135. Society of American Foresters, Bethesda, MD. [9]

Nowak, R. M. and J. L. Paradiso. 1983. *Walker's Mammals of the World*. 4th ed. Johns Hopkins University Press, Baltimore, MD. [10]

Oakleaf, B., B. Luce, E. T. Thorne and D. Biggins. 1991. *Black-Footed Ferret Reintroduction in Wyoming: Project Description and Protocol*. Wyoming Game and Fish Department, U.S. Fish and Wildlife Service and Bureau of Land Management, Cheyenne. [13]

Oakleaf, B., B. Luce, E. T. Thorne and S. Torbit (eds.). 1992. *Black-Footed Ferret Reintroduction in Shirley Basin, Wyoming; 1991 Annual Completion Report*. Wyoming Game and Fish Department, Cheyenne. [13]

O'Brien, S. J. and nine others. 1985. Genetic basis for species vulnerability in the cheetah. *Science* 227:1428–1434. [6]

O'Brien, S. J., D. E. Wildt, D. Goldman, C. R. Merril and M. Bush. 1983. The cheetah is depauperate in genetic variation. *Science* 221:459–462. [6]

Odum, E. P. 1953. *Fundamentals of Ecology.* W. B. Saunders, Philadelphia, PA. [2]

Odum, E. P. 1988. *Kellogg Task Force, Physical Resources.* Institute of Ecology, University of Georgia. [12]

Odum, E. P. 1989. Input management of production systems. *Science* 243:177–182. [9]

Odum, E. P. 1993. *Ecology and Our Endangered Life-Support Systems.* 2nd ed. Sinauer Associates, Sunderland, MA. [1,5]

Ogutu-Ohwayo, R. 1990. The decline of the native fishes of lakes Victoria and Kyoga (East Africa) and the impact of introduced species, especially the Nile Perch, *Lates niloticus* and the Nile Tilapia, *Oreochromis niloticus. Environ. Biol. Fishes* 27:81–96. [5]

Ohio Environmental Protection Agency. 1988. *Biological Criteria for the Protection of Aquatic Life.* Ohio EPA, Division of Water Quality Monitoring and Assessment, Surface Water Section, Columbus, OH. [14]

Oldeman, R. A. A. 1978. Architecture and energy exchange of dicotyledonous trees in the forest. In P. B. Tomlinson and M. H. Zimmermann (eds.), *Tropical Trees as Living Systems,* pp. 535–560. Cambridge University Press, London. [17]

Olmsted, I. and R. Duran. 1990. Vegetacion de Sian Ka'an. In D. Navarro L. and J. G. Robinson (eds.), *Diversidad Biológica en la Reserva de la Biósfera de Sian Ka'an Quintana Roo, México,* pp. 1–12. Centro de Investigaciones de Quintana Roo, Chetumal, Q. Roo, México. [17]

O'Neill, R. V. and eleven others. 1988. Indices of landscape pattern. *Landscape Ecol.* 1:153–162. [9]

Opdam, P., D. van Dorp and C. J. F. ter Braak. 1984. The effect of isolation on the number of woodland birds in small woods in the Netherlands. *J. Biogeogr.* 11:473–478. [9]

Ophuls, W. 1977. *Ecology and the Politics of Scarcity.* W. H. Freeman, San Francisco. [16]

Opler, P. A. 1978. *Insects of American Chestnut: Possible Importance and Conservation Concern.*The American Chestnut Symposium. West Virginia University Press, Morgantown, WV. [8]

Orians, G. H. and W. E. Kunin. 1991. Ecological uniqueness and loss of species. In G. H. Orians, G. M. Brown, W. E. Kunin and J. E. Swierzbinski (eds.), *The Preservation and Valuation of Biological Resources,* pp. 146–184. University of Washington Press, Seattle. [4]

Orr, D. W. 1991. Politics, conservation, and public information. *Conserv. Biol.* 5:10–12. [16]

Orr, D. W. 1992. *Ecological Literacy: Education and the Transition to a Postmodern World.* State University of New York Press, Albany. [16]

Ortmann, A. E. 1920. Correlation of shape and station in fresh water mussels (*Naiades*). *Proc. Am. Phil. Soc.* 59(4):269–312. [3]

Ostfeld, R. S. and C. D. Canham. 1993. Effects of meadow vole density on tree seedling survival in old fields. *Ecology* 74:1792–1801. [12]

O'Toole, R. 1991. Recreation fees and the Yellowstone forests. In R. B. Keiter and M. S. Boyce (eds.), *The Greater Yellowstone Ecosystem: Redefining America's Wilderness Heritage,* pp. 41–48. Yale University Press, New Haven. [17]

Otte, D. and J. A. Endler (eds.). 1989. *Speciation and Its Consequences.* Sinauer Associates, Sunderland, MA. [3]

Oxley, D. J., M. B. Fenton and G. R. Carmody. 1974. The effects of roads on populations of small mammals. *J. Appl. Ecol.* 11:51–59. [9]

Pace, F. 1991. The Klamath corridors: Preserving biodiversity in the Klamath National Forest. In W. E. Hudson (ed.), *Landscape Linkages and Biodiversity,* pp. 105–116. Island Press, Washington, D.C. [10]

Packard, S. In press. Successional restoration. In S. Packard and H. L. Nelson (eds.), *Prairie Restoration.* Island Press, Washington, D.C. [14]

Packard, S. and H. L. Nelson. (eds.). In press. *Prairie Restoration.* Island Press, Washington, D.C. [14]

Paine, R. T. 1966. Food web complexity and species diversity. *Am. Nat.* 100:65–75. [8]

Paine, R. T. 1969. The *Pisaster-Tegula* interaction: Prey patches, predator food preference, and intertidal community structure. *Ecology* 50:950–961. [8]

Paine, R. T. 1974. Intertidal community structure: Experimental studies on the relationship between a dominant competitor and its principal predator. *Oecologia* 15:93–120. [4]

Paine, R. T., J. T. Wootton and P. D. Boersma. 1990. Direct and indirect effects of Peregrine Falcon predation on seabird abundance. *Auk* 107:1–9. [8]

Panzer, R. 1984. *The Prairie Insect Fauna of the Chicago Region.* Sixth Illinois Prairie Workshop. pp. 1–6. [14]

Park, R., M. Trehan, P. Mausel and R. Howe. 1989. The effects of sea level rise on U.S. coastal wetlands. In J. B. Smith and D. A. Tirpak (eds.), *The Potential Effects of Global Climate Change on the United States,* Appendix B, *Sea level rise,* pp. 1–55. U.S. Environmental Protection Agency, Washington, D.C. [14]

Parmenter, R. R. and J. A. MacMahon. 1983. Factors determining the abundance and distribution of rodents in a shrub-steppe ecosystem: The role of shrubs. *Oecologia* 59:145–156. [14]

Parmenter, R. R., J. A. MacMahon and C. A. B. Gilbert. 1991. Early successional patterns of arthropod recolonization on reclaimed Wyoming strip mines: The grasshoppers (Orthoptera: Acrididae) and allied faunas (Orthoptera: Gryllacrididae, Tettigoniidae). *Environ. Entomol.* 20:135–142. [14]

Parmenter, R. R., J. A. MacMahon, M. E. Waaland, M. M. Stuebe, P. Landres and C. M. Crisafulli. 1985. Reclamation of surface coal mines in western Wyoming for wildlife habitat: A preliminary analysis. *Reclam. Reveg. Res.* 4:93–115. [14]

Partridge, E. (ed.). 1981. *Responsibility to Future Generations: Environmental Ethics.* Prometheus Books, Buffalo, NY. [15]

Paterson, H. E. H. 1985. The recognition concept of species. In E. S. Vrba (ed.), *Species and Speciation,* pp. 21–29. Transvaal Museum Monograph no. 4, Pretoria. [3]

Patten, D. T. 1991. Defining the Greater Yellowstone ecosystem. In R. B. Keiter and M. S. Boyce (eds.), *The Greater Yellowstone Ecosystem: Redefining America's Wilderness Heritage,* pp. 19–26. Yale University Press, New Haven. [17]

Patterson, B. D. 1987. The principle of nested subsets and its implications for biological conservation. *Conserv. Biol.* 1:323–334. [9]

Pearce, D. W. and R. K. Turner. 1989. *Economics of Natural Resources and the Environment.* Wheatsheaf, Brighton. [15]

Pechmann, J. H., D. E. Scott, R. D. Semlitsch, J. P. Caldwell, L. J. Vitt and J. W. Gibbons. 1991. Declining amphibian populations: The problem of separating human impacts from natural fluctuations. *Science* 253:892–895. [7,12]

Peet, J. 1992. *Energy and the Ecological Economics of Sustainability.* Island Press, Washington, D.C. [15]

Pelikan, J. 1992. *The Idea of the University: A Reexamination.* Yale University Press, New Haven. [16]

Peterson, G. L. and A. Randall (eds.). 1984. *Valuation of Wildland Benefits.* Westview Press, Boulder, CO. [2]

Peters, R. L. and J. D. S. Darling. 1985. The greenhouse effect and nature reserves. *BioScience* 35:707–717. [9,10]

Petraitis, P. S. , R. E. Latham and R. A. Niesenbaum. 1989. The maintenance of species diversity by disturbance. *Q. Rev. Biol.* 64:418–464. [1,10]

Petterson, B. 1985. Extinction of an isolated population of the Middle Spotted Woodpecker *Dendrocopos medius* (L.) in Sweden and its relation to general theories on extinction. *Biol. Conserv.* 32:335–353. [9]

Pianka, E. R. 1966. Latitudinal gradients in species diversity: A review of concepts. *Am. Nat.* 100:33–46. [4]

Pianka, E. R. 1967. On lizard species diversity: North American flatland deserts. *Ecology* 48:333–351. [10]

Pianka, E. R. 1986. *Ecology and Natural History of Desert Lizards.* Princeton University Press, Princeton, NJ. [4]

Pickett, S. T. A. 1983. Differential adaptation of tropical tree species to canopy gaps and its role in community dynamics. *Trop. Ecol.* 24:68–84. [17]

Pickett, S. T. A. and J. N. Thompson. 1978. Patch dynamics and the design of nature reserves. *Biol. Conserv.* 13:27–37. [10]

Pickett, S. T. A., V. T. Parker and P. L. Fiedler. 1992. The new paradigm in ecology: Implications for conservation biology above the species level. In P. L. Fiedler and S. K. Jain (eds.), *Conservation Biology: The Theory and Practice of Nature Conservation Preservation and Management,* pp. 65–88. Chapman and Hall, New York. [1,10]

Picton, H. D. 1979. The application of insular biogeographic theory to the conservation of large mammals in the northern Rocky Mountains. *Biol. Conserv.* 15:73–79. [10]

Pimentel, D. (ed.). 1988. *World Food, Pest Losses, and the Environment.* Westview Press, Boulder, CO. [15]

Pimentel, D. 1991. Diversification of biological control strategies in agriculture. *Crop Protection* 10:243–253. [5]

Pimm, S. L. 1991. *The Balance of Nature? Ecological Issues in the Conservation of Species and Communities.* University of Chicago Press, Chicago. [6,8]

Pimm, S. L., H. L. Jones and J. Diamond. 1988. On the risk of extinction. *Am. Nat.* 132:757–785. [7,8,9]

Pinchot, G. 1947. *Breaking New Ground.* Harcourt, Brace, New York. [1]

Piper, R. G., I. B. McElwain, L. E. Orme, J. P. McCraren, L. G. Fowler and J. R. Leonard. 1982. *Fish Hatchery Management.* U.S.D.I. Fish and Wildlife Service, Washington, D.C. [12]

Pister, E. P. 1991. Desert Fishes Council: Catalyst for change. In W. L. Minckley and J. E. Deacon (eds.), *Battle Against Extinction: Native Fish Management in the American West,* pp. 55–68. University of Arizona Press, Tucson. [12]

Pister, E. P. 1993. Species in a bucket. *Natural History* 102:14–19. [11]

Plotkin, M. J. 1988. The outlook for new agricultural and industrial products from the tropics. In E. O. Wilson and F. M. Peter (eds.), *Biodiversity,* pp. 106–116. National Academy Press, Washington, D.C. [2]

Poinar, G. O. 1983. *The Natural History of Nematodes.* Prentice-Hall, Englewood Cliffs, NJ. [4]

Population Reference Bureau. 1987. *World Population Data Sheet.* Population Reference Bureau, Washington, D.C. [18]

Power, D. M. 1972. Numbers of bird species on the California Islands. *Evolution* 26:451–463. [9]

Power, M. E. and W. J. Matthews. 1983. Algae-grazing minnows (*Campostoma anomalum*), piscivorous bass (*Micropterus* spp.), and the distribution of attached algae in a small prairie-margin stream. *Oecologia* 60:328–332. [8]

Power, M. E., W. J. Matthews and A. J. Stewart. 1985. Grazing minnows, piscivorous bass and stream algae: Dynamics of a strong interaction. *Ecology* 66:1448–1456. [8]

Prance, G. T. 1982. Forest refuges: Evidence from woody angiosperms. In G. T. Prance (ed.), *Biological Diversification in the Tropics,* pp. 137–158. Columbia University Press, New York. [4]

Preston, F. W. 1960. Time and space and the variation of species. *Ecology* 41:611–627. [9]

Preston, F. W. 1962. The canonical distribution of commonness and rarity. *Ecology* 43:185–215, 410–432. [9]

Principe, P. P. 1991. Valuing the biodiversity of medicinal plants. In O. Akerete, V. Heywood and H. Synge (eds.), *The Conservation of Medicinal Plants,* pp. 79–124. Cambridge University Press, Cambridge. [17]

Pryor, L. D. and L. A. S. Johnson. 1971. *A Classification of the Eucalyptus.* Australian National University, Canberra. [4]

Pullan, R. A. 1984. The use of wildlife as a resource in the development of Zambia. In Ooi Jin Bee (ed.), *Natural Resources in Tropical Countries,* pp. 267–325. Singapore University Press, Singapore. [17]

Pulliam, H. R. 1983. Ecological community theory and the coexistence of sparrows. *Ecology* 64:45–52. [7]

Pulliam, H. R. 1988. Sources, sinks, and population regulation. *Am. Nat.* 132:652–661. [7,9]

Pulliam, H. R. 1992. Incorporating concepts from population and behavioral ecology into models of exposure to toxins and risk assessment. In R. Kendall and T. Lacher (eds.), *The Population Ecology and Wildlife Toxicology of Agricultural Pesticide Exposure,* pp. 13–26. Lewis Publishers, Chelsea, MI. [7]

Pulliam, H. R. 1994. Sources and sinks. In O. E. Rhodes, R. K. Chesser and M. H. Smith (eds.), *Spatial and Temporal Aspects of Population Processes.* In press. [7]

Pulliam, H. R. and B. J. Danielson. 1991. Sources, sinks, and habitat selection: a landscape perspective on population dynamics. *Am. Nat.* 137:S50–S66. [7]

Pulliam, H. R., J. B. Dunning, Jr. and J. Liu. 1992. Population dynamics in a complex landscape: A case study. *Ecol. Applic.* 2:165-177. [7]

Rabinowitz, D., S. Cairns and T. Dillon. 1986. Seven forms of rarity and their frequency in the flora of the British Isles. In M. E. Soulé, (ed.), *Conservation Biology: The Science of Scarcity and Diversity,* pp. 182–204. Sinauer Associates, Sunderland, MA. [5,9]

Ralls, K. and J. Ballou. 1983. Extinction: Lessons from zoos. In C. M. Schonewald-Cox, S. M. Chambers, B. MacBryde and L. Thomas (eds.), *Genetics and Conservation: A Reference for Managing Wild Animal and Plant Populations,* pp. 164–184. Benjamin/Cummings, Menlo Park, CA. [6]

Ralls, K. and J. Ballou. 1986. Captive breeding programs for populations with a small number of founders. *Trends Ecol. Evol.* 1:19-22. [6]

Randall, A. 1986. Human preferences, economics, and the preservation of species. In B. G. Norton (ed.), *The Preservation of Species: The Value of Biological Diversity,* pp. 79–109. Princeton University Press, Princeton, NJ. [2]

Randall, A. 1988. What mainstream economists have to say about the value of biodiversity. In E. O. Wilson and F. M. Peter (eds.), *Biodiversity,* pp. 217–223. National Academy Press, Washington, D.C. [2,15]

Ranney, J. W., M. C. Bruner and J. B. Levenson. 1981. The importance of edge in the structure and dynamics of forest islands. In R. L. Burgess and D. M. Sharpe (eds.), *Forest Island Dynamics in Man-Dominated Landscapes,* pp. 67–95. Springer-Verlag, New York. [9]

Ratti, J. T. and K. P. Reese. 1988. Preliminary test of the ecological trap hypothesis. *J. Wildl. Mgmt.* 52:484–491. [9]

Raunkaier, C. 1934. *The Life Forms of Plants and Statistical Plant Geography.* Clarendon Press, Oxford. [4]

Raup, D. M. 1988. Diversity crises in the geological past. In E. O. Wilson and F. M. Peter (eds.), *Biodiversity,* pp. 51–57. National Academy Press, Washington, D.C. [5]

Raup, D. M. 1991a. *Extinction: Bad Genes or Bad Luck?* W. W. Norton, New York. [5]

Raup, D. M. 1991b. A kill curve for Phanerozoic marine species. *Paleobiology* 17(1):37–48. [5]

Raven, P. H. 1988. Our diminishing tropical forests. In E. O. Wilson and F. M. Peter (eds.), *Biodiversity,* pp. 119–122. National Academy Press, Washington, D.C. [2,5]

Raven, P. H. 1990. The politics of preserving biodiversity. *BioScience* 40(10):769–774. [5]

Raven, P. H., L. R. Berg and G. B. Johnson. 1993. *Environment.* Saunders College Publishing, New York. [5]

Raven, P., R. Norgaard, C. Padoch, T. Panayotou, A. Randall, M. Robinson and J. Rodman. 1992. *Conserving Biodiversity: A Research Agenda for Development Agencies.* National Academy Press, Washington, D.C. [2]

Ray, G. C. and J. F. Grassle. 1991. Marine biological diversity. *BioScience* 41:453–457. [5]

Reading, R. P. and S. R. Kellert. 1993. Attitudes toward a proposed reintroduction of black-footed ferrets (*Mustela nigripes*). *Conserv. Biol.* 7:569–580. [13]

Redclift, M. 1984. *Development and the Environmental Crisis: Red or Green Alternatives.* Methuen, London. [15]

Redente, E. F. and E. J. DePuit. 1988. Reclamation of drastically disturbed rangelands. In P. T. Tueller (ed.), *Vegetation Science Applications for Rangeland Analysis and Management,* pp. 559–584. Kluwer Academic Publishers, Dordrecht, The Netherlands. [14]

Redford, K. H. 1992. The empty forest. *BioScience* 42:412–422. [1]

Redford, K. H., A. Taber and J. A. Simonetti. 1990. There is more to biodiversity than the tropical rain forests. *Conserv. Biol.* 4:328–330. [5]

Reffalt, W. The endangered species lists: Chronicles of extinction? In K. A. Kohm (ed.), *Balancing on the Brink of Extinction: The Endangered Species Act and Lessons for the Future,* pp. 77–85. Island Press, Washington, D.C. [3]

Regan, T. 1983. *The Case for Animal Rights.* University of California Press, Berkeley. [2]

Reh, W. and A. Seitz. 1990. The influence of land use on the genetic structure of populations of the common frog *Rana temporaria.* *Biol. Conserv.* 54:239–249. [9]

Reid, W. V. and K. R. Miller. 1989. *Keeping Options Alive: The Scientific Basis for Conserving Biodiversity.* World Resources Institute, Washington, D.C. [5]

Reith, C. C. and L. D. Potter. (eds.). 1986. *Principles and Methods of Reclamation Science.* University of New Mexico Press, Albuquerque. [14]

Repetto, R. 1992. Accounting for environmental assets. *Sci. Am.* 266:94–100. [17]

Reznick, D. N. and H. Bryga. 1987. Life-history evolution in guppies (*Poecilia reticulata*): 1. Phenotypic and genetic changes in an introduction experiment. *Evolution* 41:1370–1385. [3]

Reznick, D. N., H. Bryga and J. A. Endler. 1990. Experimentally induced life-history evolution in a natural population. *Nature* 346:357–359. [3]

Ricardo, D. 1926. *Principles of Political Economy and Taxation.* Reprint. Everyman, London. [15]

Rice, B. and M. Westoby. 1983. Species richness at tenth-hectare scale in Australian vegetation compared to other continents. *Vegetatio* 52:129–140. [4]

Ricklefs, R. 1987. Community diversity: Relative roles of local and regional processes. *Science* 235:167–171. [4]

Ricklefs, R. 1990. *Ecology,* 3rd. ed. W. H. Freeman, San Francisco. [5]

Ricklefs, R. and D. Schluter (eds.). 1993. *Species Diversity in Ecological Communities: Historical and Geographical Perspectives.* University of Chicago Press, Chicago.

Ripple, W. J., G. A. Bradshaw and T. A. Spies. 1991. Measuring forest landscape patterns in the Cascade Range of Oregon, USA. *Biol. Conserv.* 57:73–88. [9]

Ripple, W. J., D. H. Johnson, K. T. Hershey and E. C. Meslow. 1991. Old-growth and mature forests near Spotted Owl nests in western Oregon. *J. Wildl. Mgmt.* 55:316–318. [13]

Robbins, C. S., D. K. Dawson and B. A. Dowell. 1989. Habitat area requirements of breeding forest birds of the Middle Atlantic states. *Wildl. Monogr.* 103:1–34. [9]

Robbins, L. W., D. K. Tolliver and M. H. Smith. 1989. Nondestructive methods for obtaining genotypic data from fish. *Conserv. Biol.* 3:88–91. [6]

Roberts, L. 1992. Chemical prospecting: Hope for vanishing ecosystems? *Science* 256:1142–1143. [17]

Robinson, S. K. 1992a. *Effects of Forest Fragmentation on Migrant Songbirds in the Shawnee National Forest.* Report to Illinois Department of Energy and Natural Resources. Illinois Natural History Survey, Champaign, IL. [9]

Robinson, S. K. 1992b. Population dynamics of breeding Neotropical migrants in a fragmented Illinois landscape. In J. M. Hagan and D. W. Johnston (eds.), *Ecology and Conservation of Neotropical Migrant Landbirds,* pp. 408–418. Smithsonian Institution Press, Washington, D.C. [9]

Robinson, J. G. 1993. The limits to caring: Sustainable living and the loss of biodiversity. *Conserv. Biol.* 7:20–28. [17]

Rogers, L. L. 1987. Factors influencing dispersal in the black bear. In B. D. Chepko-Sade and Z. T. Halpin (eds.), *Mammalian Dispersal Patterns,* pp. 75–84. University of Chicago Press, Chicago. [10]

Rojas, M. 1992. The species problem and conservation: What are we protecting? *Conserv. Biol.* 6:170–178. [3]

Rolston, H. 1988. *Environmental Ethics: Duties to and Values in the Natural World.* Temple University Press, Philadelphia, PA. [2]

Romme, W. H. and D. G. Despain. 1989. Historical perspectives on the Yellowstone fires, 1988. *BioScience* 39:695–699. [17]

Rood, J. P. 1987. Dispersal and intergroup transfer in the dwarf mongoose. In B. D. Chepko-Sade and Z. T. Halpin (eds.), *Mammalian Dispersal Patterns,* pp. 85–103. University of Chicago Press, Chicago. [10]

Root, T. 1988. Energy constraints on avian distributions and abundances. *Ecology* 69:330–339. [7]

Rosenberg, A. A., M. J. Fogarty, M. P. Sissenwine, J. R. Beddington and J. G. Sheperd. 1993. Achieving sustainable use of renewable resources. *Science* 262:828–829. [17]

Russell, H. S. 1976. *A Long Deep Furrow: Three Centuries of Farming in New England.* University Press of New England, Hanover, NH. [1,12]

Ryman, N. and F. Utter (eds.). 1987. *Population Genetics and Fishery Management.* University of Washington Press, Seattle. [6]

Sagoff, M. 1980. On the preservation of species. *Columbia J. Environ. Law* 7:33–76. [2]

Sagoff, M. 1988. *The Economy of the Earth: Philosophy, Law, and the Environment.* Cambridge University Press, Cambridge. [2,15]

Samson, F. B. 1983. Minimum viable populations — A review. *Nat. Areas J.* 3(3):15–23. [9]

Sánchez, J., J. M. Rodríguez and C. Salas. 1985. Distribución, ciclos reproductivos y aspectos ecológicos de aves acuáticas. In E. Guier (ed.), *Investigaciones sobre Fauna Silvestre de Costa Rica,* pp. 83–102. Editorial de la Universidad Estatal de Distancia, San José, Costa Rica. [12]

Sanders, H. L. 1968. Marine benthic diversity: A comparative study. *Am. Nat.* 102:243–282. [4]

Sanders, H. L. and R. R. Hessler. 1969. Ecology of the deep-sea benthos. *Science* 163:1419–1424. [4]

Santiapillai, C. 1992. Asian rhino specialist group. *Species* 18:55. [3]

Santos, T. and J. L. Tellaria. 1992. Edge effects of nest predation in Mediterranean fragmented forests. *Biol. Conserv.* 61:1–5. [9]

Sarich, V. M. 1977. Rates, sample sizes, and the neutrality hypothesis for electrophoresis in evolutionary studies. *Nature* 265:24–28. [6]

Saunders, D. A. 1989. Changes in the avifauna of a region, district, and remnant as a result of fragmentation of native vegetation: The Wheatbelt of Western Australia. A case study. *Biol. Conserv.* 50:99–135. [9]

Saunders, D. A., R. J. Hobbs and C. R. Margules. 1991. Biological consequences of ecosystem fragmentation: A review. *Conserv. Biol.* 5:18–32. [9,10]

Savidge, J. A. 1987. Extinction of an island avifauna by an introduced snake. *Ecology* 68:660–668. [8]

Scheuer, J. H. 1993. Biodiversity: Beyond Noah's Ark. *Conserv. Biol.* 7:206–207. [3]

Schneider, S. H. 1993. Scenarios of global warming. In P. M. Kareiva, J. G. Kingsolver and R. B. Huey (eds.), *Biotic Interactions and Global Change,* pp. 9–23. Sinauer Associates, Sunderland, MA. [5,18]

Schoener, T. W. 1983. Field experiments on interspecific competition. *Am. Nat.* 122:240–285. [4]

Schonewald-Cox, C. M. 1983. Conclusions: Guidelines to management: A beginning attempt. In C. M. Schonewald-Cox, S. M. Chambers, B. MacBryde and L. Thomas (eds.), *Genetics and Conservation: A Reference for Managing Wild Animal and Plant Populations,* pp. 414–445. Benjamin/Cummings, Menlo Park, CA. [10]

Schonewald-Cox, C. M. and J. W. Bayless. 1986. The boundary model: A geographical analysis of design and conservation of nature reserves. *Biol. Conserv.* 38:305–322. [10]

Schonewald-Cox, C. M., S. M. Chambers, B. MacBryde and L. Thomas (eds.). 1983. *Genetics and Conservation: A Reference for Managing Wild Animal and Plant Populations.* Benjamin/Cummings, Menlo Park, CA. [1,6]

Schowalter, T. D. 1988. Forest pest management: A synopsis. *Northwest Environ. J.* 4:313–318. [9]

Schroeder, M. H. and S. J. Martin. 1982. Search for the black-footed ferret succeeds. *Wyo. Wildl.* 46(7):8–9. [13]

Scott, J. M., B. Csuti, J. D. Jacobi and J. E. Estes. 1987. Species richness. *BioScience* 37:782–788. [12]

Scott, J. M., S. Mountainspring, F. L. Ramsey and C. B. Kepler. 1986. *Forest Bird Communities on the Hawaiian Islands: Their Dynamics, Ecology and Conservation.* Cooper Ornithological Society, Berkeley, CA. [8]

Scudder, G. G. E. 1974. Species concepts and speciation. *Can. J. Zool.* 52:1121–1134. [3]

Seal, U. S. 1985. The realities of preserving species in captivity. In R. J. Hoage (ed.), *Animal Extinctions: What Everyone Should Know,* pp. 71–95. Smithsonian Institution Press, Washington, D.C. [6]

Seal, U. S., E. T. Thorne, M. A. Bogan and S. H. Anderson (eds.). 1989. *Conservation Biology and the Black-Footed Ferret.* Yale University Press, New Haven. [6]

Segoviano Martínez, J. 1992. Polimicos planteamientos del comité "la puerta del cielo." *Diario Por Esto,* Mérida, Yucatán, 12-12-92, sección Quintana Roo, p. 5. [17]

Sepkoski, J. J., Jr. 1984. A kinetic model of Phanerozoic taxonomic diversity. III. Post-Paleozoic families and mass extinctions. *Paleobiology* 10:246–267. [4]

Sepkoski, J. J., Jr. 1988. Alpha, beta, or gamma: Where does all the diversity go? *Paleobiology* 14:221–234. [5]

Sepkoski, J. J., Jr. and D. M. Raup. 1986. Periodicity in marine extinction events. In D. K. Elliott (ed.), *Dynamics of Extinction*, pp. 3–36. John Wiley & Sons, New York. [4]

Servheen, C. 1985. The grizzly bear. In R. L. Di Silvestro (ed.), *Audubon Wildlife Report*, pp. 400–415. National Audubon Society, New York. [6]

Shafer, C. L. 1991. *Nature Reserves: Island Theory and Conservation Practice.* Smithsonian Institution Press, Washington, D.C. [5]

Shaffer, M. L. 1981. Minimum population sizes for species conservation. *BioScience* 31:131–134. [7]

Shaffer, M. L. 1983. Determining minimum viable population sizes for the grizzly bear. *International Conference on Bear Research and Management* 5:133–139. [7]

Shaffer, M. L. 1987. Minimum viable populations: Coping with uncertainty. In M. E. Soulé (ed.), *Viable Populations for Conservation*, pp. 69–86. Cambridge University Press, Cambridge. [7]

Shaffer, M. L. 1990. Population viability analysis. *Conserv. Biol.* 4:39–40. [7]

Shaffer, M. L. and F. B. Sampson. 1985. Population size and extinction: A note on determining critical population sizes. *Am. Nat.* 125:144–152. [6]

Sheldon, A. L. 1987. Rarity: Patterns and consequences for stream fishes. In W. J. Matthews and D. C. Heins (eds.), *Community and Evolutionary Ecology of North American Stream Fishes*, pp. 203–209. University of Oklahoma Press, Norman. [5]

Shelford, V. E. 1933. Ecological Society of America: A nature sanctuary plan unanimously adopted by the Society, December 28, 1932. *Ecology* 14:240–245. [10]

Sherry, T. W. and R. T. Holmes. 1988. Habitat selection by breeding American Redstarts in response to a dominant competitor, the Least Flycatcher. *Auk* 105:350–364. [11]

Sherwin, W. B., N. D. Murray, J. A. M. Graves and P. R. Brown. 1991. Measurement of genetic variation in endangered populations: Bandicoots (Marsupialia: Peramelidae) as an example. *Conserv. Biol.* 5:103–108. [6]

Shiva, V. 1989. *Staying Alive: Women, Ecology and Development.* Zed Books, London. [2]

Sieving, K. E. 1992. Nest predation and differential insular extinction among selected forest birds of central Panama. *Ecology* 73:2310–2328. [5]

Signor, P. W. 1990. The geological history of diversity. *Annu. Rev. Ecol. Syst.* 21:509–539. [4,5]

Simberloff, D. 1981. Community effects of introduced species. In H. Nitecki (ed.), *Biotic Crises in Ecological and Evolutionary Time*, pp. 53–81. Academic Press, New York. [8]

Simberloff, D. 1986. Are we on the verge of a mass extinction in tropical rain forests? In D. K. Elliott (ed.), *Dynamics of Extinction*, pp.165–180. Wiley, New York. [5]

Simberloff, D. 1988. The contribution of population and community biology to conservation science. *Annu. Rev. Ecol. Syst.* 19:473–511. [9]

Simberloff, D. 1991. *Review of Theory Relevant to Acquiring Land.* Report to Florida Department of Natural Resources. Florida State University, Tallahassee. [9]

Simberloff, D. and L. G. Abele. 1976. Island biogeography theory and conservation practice. *Science* 191:285–286. [9]

Simberloff, D. and L. G. Abele. 1982. Refuge design and island biogeographic theory: Effects of fragmentation. *Am. Nat.* 120:41–50. [9]

Simberloff, D. and J. Cox. 1987. Consequences and costs of conservation corridors. *Conserv. Biol.* 1:63–71. [9]

Simberloff, D. and J. L. Martin. 1991. Nestedness of insular avifaunas: Simple summary statistics masking species patterns. *Ornis Fennica* 68:178–192. [9]

Simberloff, D. S., J. A. Farr, J. Cox and D. W. Mehlman. 1992. Movement corridors: Conservation bargains or poor investments? *Conserv. Biol.* 6:493–504. [10]

Simon, J. L. 1981. *The Ultimate Resource.* Princeton University Press, Princeton, NJ. [15]

Simpson, B. B. and J. Haffer. 1978. Speciation patterns in the Amazonian forest biota. *Annu. Rev. Ecol. Syst.* 9:497–518. [4]

Simpson, G. G. 1961. *Principles of Animal Taxonomy.* Columbia University Press, New York. [3]

Singer, P. 1975. *Animal Liberation: A New Ethics for Our Treatment of Animals.* The New York Review, New York. [2]

Singhvi, L. M. n.d. *The Jain Declaration on Nature.* Federation of Jain Associations of North America, Cincinnati, OH. [2]

Sittenfeld, A. and R. Villers. 1993. Exploring and preserving biodiversity in the tropics: The Costa Rican Case. *Current Opinions in Biotechnology*, 4:280–285. [17]

Skole, D. and C. Tucker. 1993. Tropical deforestation and habitat fragmentation in the Amazon: Satellite data from 1978–1988. *Science* 260:1905–1910. [5]

Slatkin, M. 1987. Gene flow and the geographic structure of natural populations. *Science* 236:787–792. [6]

Slobodkin, L. B. and D. E. Dykhuizen. 1991. Applied ecology, its practice and philosophy. In J. Cairns, Jr. and T. V. Crawford (eds.), *Integrated Environmental Management*, pp. 63–70. Lewis Publs. Boca Raton, FL. [11]

Small, G. 1971. *The Blue Whale.* Columbia University Press, New York. [12]

Small, M. F. and M. L. Hunter. 1988. Forest fragmentation and avian nest predation in forested landscapes. *Oecologia* 76:62–64. [9]

Smith, A. T. and M. M. Peacock. 1990. Conspecific attraction and the determination of metapopulation colonization rates. *Conserv. Biol.* 4:320–327. [9]

Smith, H. M. 1899. The mussel fishery and pearl-button industry of the Mississippi River. *Bull. U.S. Fish Comm.* 18:289–314. [3]

Smyser, C. A. 1986. *Nature's Design: A Practical Guide to Natural Landscaping.* Rodale Press, Emmaus, PA. [14]

Snelson, F. F., Jr., S. H. Gruber, F. L. Murru and T. H. Schmid. 1990. Southern stingray, *Dasyatis americana*: Host for a symbiotic cleaner wrasse. *Copeia* 1990(4):961–965. [8]

Society for Ecological Restoration. 1990. *The Sistine Ceiling debate.* Tape-recording of a symposium on the authenticity of restored ecosystems. Society for Ecological Restoration, Madison, WI. [14]

Solis, D. M. and R. J. Gutierrez. 1990. Summer habitat ecology of Northern Spotted Owls in northwestern California. *Condor* 92:739–784. [13]

Soulé, M. E. 1980. Thresholds for survival: Maintaining fitness and evolutionary potential. In M. E. Soulé and B. A. Wilcox (eds.), *Conservation Biology: An Ecological-Evolutionary Perspective*, pp. 151–169. Sinauer Associates, Sunderland, MA. [6]

Soulé, M. E. 1985. What is conservation biology? *Bioscience* 35:727–734. [1,2]

Soulé, M. E. 1986. Conservation biology and the "real world." In M. E. Soulé (ed.), *Conservation Biology: The Science of Scarcity and Diversity*, pp. 1–12. Sinauer Associates, Sunderland, MA. [1]

Soulé, M. E. (ed.). 1986. *Conservation Biology: The Science of Scarcity and Diversity.* Sinauer Associates, Sunderland, MA. [6]

Soulé, M. E. (ed.). 1987. *Viable Populations for Conservation.* Cambridge University Press, New York. [5,7]

Soulé, M. E. 1991. Conservation: Tactics for a constant crisis. *Science* 253:744–750. [5]

Soulé, M. E. 1991. Theory and strategy. In W. E. Hudson (ed.), *Landscape Linkages and Biodiversity*, pp. 91–104. Island Press, Washington, D.C. [10]

Soulé, M. E. and K. Kohm (eds.). 1989. *Research Priorities for Conservation Biology.* Island Press, Washington, D.C. [8]

Soulé, M. E. and D. Simberloff. 1986. What do genetics and ecology tell us about the design of nature reserves? *Biol. Conserv.* 35:19–40. [10]

Soulé, M. E. and B. A. Wilcox (eds.). 1980. *Conservation Biology: An Evolutionary-Ecological Perspective.* Sinauer Associates, Sunderland, MA. [1,7]

Soulé, M. E. and B. A. Wilcox. 1980. Conservation biology: Its scope and its challenge. In M. E. Soulé and B. A. Wilcox (eds.), *Conservation Biology: An Evolutionary-Ecological Perspective*, pp. 1–8. Sinauer Associates, Sunderland, MA. [5]

Sousa, W. P. 1984. The role of disturbance in natural communities. *Annu. Rev. Ecol. Syst.* 15:353–391. [10]

Specht, R. L. and E. J. Moll. 1983. Mediterranean-type heathlands and sclerophyllous shrublands of the world: An overview. In F. J. Kruger, D. T. Mitchell and J. U. M. Jarvis (eds.), *Mediterranean-Type Ecosystems: the Role of Nutrients*, pp. 41–65. (Ecological Studies No. 43). Springer-Verlag, Berlin. [4]

Stacey, P. B. and M. Taper. 1992. Environmental variation and the persistence of small populations. *Ecol. Appl.* 2:18–29. [7]

Stangel, P. W., M. R. Lennartz and M. H. Smith. 1992. Genetic variation and population structure of Red-cockaded Woodpeckers. *Conserv. Biol.* 6:283–292. [6]

Stanley, S. M. 1981. *The New Evolutionary Timetable*. Basic Books, New York. [5]

Steele, B. D. and M. D. Stowers. 1991. Techniques for selection of industrially important microorganisms. *Annu. Rev. Microbiol.* 45:89–106. [17]

Stenseth, N. C. 1984. The tropics: Cradle or museum? *Oikos* 43:417–420. [5]

Stevens, G. C. 1989. The latitudinal gradient in geographical range: How so many species coexist in the tropics. *Am. Nat.* 133:240–256. [5,7]

Stiassny, M. L. J. 1992. Phylogenetic analysis and the role of systematics in the biodiversity crisis. In N. Eldridge (ed.), *Systematics, Ecology, and the Biodiversity Crisis*, pp. 109–120. Columbia University Press, New York. [3]

Stiassny, M. L. J. and M. C. C. DePinna. In press. Basal taxa and the role of cladistic patterns in the evaluation of conservation priorities: A view from freshwater. In P. Forey, C. J. Humphries and R. I. Vane-Wright (eds.), *Systematics and Conservation Evaluation.* (Systematics Association Special Volume Series.) [3]

Stix, G. 1993. Back to roots: Drug companies forage for new treatments. *Sci. Am.* 268:142–143. [17]

Stone, C. P. and J. M. Scott (eds.). 1985. *Hawaii's Terrestrial Ecosystems: Preservation and Management.* Cooperative National Park Resources Study Unit, University of Hawaii, Honolulu. [12]

Sturt, G. 1923. *The Wheelwright's Shop*. Cambridge University Press, Cambridge. [16]

Sutton, A. and M. Sutton. 1972. *Yellowstone: A Century of the Wilderness Idea*. Macmillan, New York. [17]

Svendsen, E., R. Mendelsohn and A. Davis. 1993. *The Ecotourism Value of Marine Diving Areas*. Yale School of Forestry and Environmental Studies, New Haven. [17]

Sward, S. 1990. Secretary Lujan and the squirrels: Interior chief calls Endangered Species Act "too tough." *San Francisco Chronicle*, May 12. [3]

Swihart, R. K. and N. A. Slade. 1984. Road crossing in *Sigmodon hispidus* and *Microtus ochrogaster*. *J. Mammal.* 65:357–360. [9]

Tangley, L. 1988. A new era for biosphere reserves. *BioScience* 38:148–155. [17]

Tangley, L. 1988. Beyond national parks. *BioScience* 38:146–147. [10]

Taylor, P. W. 1986. *Respect for Nature: A Theory of Environmental Ethics.* Princeton University Press, Princeton, NJ. [2]

Temple, S. A. 1986. Predicting impacts of habitat fragmentation on forest birds: A comparison of two models. In J. Verner, M. L. Morrison and C. J. Ralph (eds.), *Wildlife 2000: Modeling Habitat Relationships of Terrestrial Vertebrates*, pp. 301–304. University of Wisconsin Press, Madison. [9]

Temple, S. A. and J. R. Cary. 1988. Modeling dynamics of habitat-interior bird populations in fragmented landscapes. *Conserv. Biol.* 2:340–347. [9]

Templeton, A. R. 1989. The meaning of species and speciation: A genetic perspective. In D. Otte and J. A. Endler (eds.), *Speciation and Its Consequences*, pp. 3–27. Sinauer Associates, Sunderland, MA. [3]

Templeton, A. R. 1990. The role of genetics in captive breeding and reintroduction for species conservation. *Endangered Species Update* 8:14–17. [11]

Templeton, A. R. 1994. Translocation as a conservation tool. In R. Szaro (ed.), *Biodiversity in Managed Landscapes: Theory and Practice*. Oxford University Press, New York. In press. [6]

Templeton, A. R. and B. Read. 1984. Factors eliminating inbreeding depression in a captive herd of Speke's gazelle (*Gazella spekei*). *Zoo Biol.* 3:177–199. [6]

Terborgh, J. 1973. On the notion of favorableness in plant ecology. *Am. Nat.* 107:481–501. [4]

Terborgh, J. 1974. Preservation of natural diversity: The problem of extinction prone species. *BioScience* 24:715–722. [9]

Terborgh, J. 1986. Keystone plant resources in the tropical forest. In M. E. Soulé (ed.), *Conservation Biology: The Science of Scarcity and Diversity*, pp. 330–344. Sinauer Associates, Sunderland, MA. [5,8]

Terborgh, J. 1988. The big things that run the world: A sequel to E. O. Wilson. *Conserv. Biol.* 2:402–403. [5]

Terborgh, J. and B. Winter. 1980. Some causes of extinction. In M. E. Soulé and B. A. Wilcox (eds.), *Conservation Biology: An Evolutionary-Ecological Perspective*, pp. 119–134. Sinauer Associates, Sunderland, MA. [5,9]

Terborgh, J. and B. Winter. 1983. A method for siting parks and reserves with special reference to Columbia and Ecuador. *Biol. Conserv.* 27:45–58. [9]

The Conservation Foundation. 1988. *Protecting America's Wetlands: An Action Agenda.* The Conservation Foundation, Washington, D.C. [14]

Thomas, C. D. 1990. What do real population dynamics tell us about minimum viable population sizes? *Conserv. Biol.* 4:324–327. [7]

Thomas, J. W., E. D. Forsman, J. B. Lint, E. C. Meslow, B. R. Noon and J. Verner. 1990. *A Conservation Strategy for the Northern Spotted Owl.* U.S. Government Printing Office, Washington D.C. 1990-791-171/20026. [7,13]

Thomas, J. W. and J. Verner. 1992. Accomodation with socio-economic factors under the Endangered Species Act — More than meets the eye. Trans. 57th North American Wildlife Natural Resources Conference. 57:627–641. [13]

Thompson, J. R. 1992. *Prairies, Forests, and Wetlands*. University of Iowa Press, Iowa City. [14]

Thorne, E. T. and B. Oakleaf. 1991. Species rescue for captive breeding: Black-footed ferret as an example. *Symp. Zool. Soc. London* 62:241–261. [13]

Thorne, R. F., B. A. Prigge and J. Henrickson. 1981. A flora of the higher ranges and Kelso Dunes of the eastern Mojave Desert in California. *El Aliso* 10:71–186. [10]

Tilman, D. 1982. *Resource Competition and Community Structure.* Princeton University Press, Princeton, NJ. [4]

Tilman, D. 1985. The resource ratio hypothesis of succession. *Am. Nat.* 125:827–852. [4]

Tobias, D. and R. Mendelsohn. 1991. Valuing Ecotourism in a Tropical Rain-Forest Reserve. *Ambio* 20, 91–93. [17]

Todd, J. 1988. Solar aquatic wastewater treatment. *BioCycle* 29:38–40. [16]

Todd, J. 1991. Ecological engineering, living machines and the visionary landscape. In C. Etnier and B. Guterstam (eds.), *Ecological Engineering for Wastewater Treatment*, pp. 335–343. Bokskogen, Gothenburg, Sweden. [16]

Traverse, A. 1988. Plant evolution dances to a different beat: Plant and animal evolutionary mechanisms compared. *Hist. Biol.* 1:277–301. [5]

Trexler, M. C. and L. H. Kosloff. 1991. International implementation: The longest arm of the law? In K. A. Kohm (ed.), *Balancing on the Brink of Extinction: The Endangered Species Act and Lessons for the Future*, pp. 114–133. Island Press, Washington, D.C. [3]

Trüper, H. G. 1992. Prokaryotes: An overview with respect to biodiversity and environmental importance. *Biodiver. Conserv.* 1:227–236. [4]

Tscharntke, T. 1992. Fragmentation of *Phragmites* habitats, minimum viable population size, habitat suitability, and local extinction of moths, midges, flies, aphids, and birds. *Conserv. Biol.* 6:530–536. [9]

Turgeon, D. D. and nine others. 1988. *Common and Scientific Names of Aquatic Invertebrates from the United States and Canada: Mollusks.* American Fisheries Society Special Publication 16. [3]

Turnbull, C. 1972. *The Mountain People.* Simon & Schuster, New York. [10]

Turner, J. R. G. 1971. Two thousand generations of hybridisation in a *Heliconius* butterfly. *Evolution* 25:471–482. [3]

Turner, M. G. 1989. Landscape ecology: The effect of pattern on process. *Annu. Rev. Ecol. Syst.* 20:171–197. [7,9]

Turner, M. G. and C. L. Ruscher. 1988. Changes in landscape patterns in Georgia, USA. *Landscape Ecol.* 1:241–251. [9]

Turner, M. G., G. J. Arthaud, R. T. Engstrom, S. J. Hejl and J. Liu. 1994. Usefulness of spatially-explicit population models in land management. *Ecol. Appl.*, In press. [7]

Turner, M. G., V. H. Dale and R. H. Gardner. 1989. Predicting across scales: theory development and testing. *Landscape Ecol.* 3:245–252. [7]

Turner, M. G. and R. H. Gardner, (eds.), 1991. *Quantitative Methods in Landscape Ecology.* Springer-Verlag, New York. [10]

Turner, M. G., W. W. Hargrove, R. H. Gardner and W. H. Romme. Effects of fire on landscape heterogeneity in Yellowstone National Park, Wyoming. Unpubl. manuscript. [7]

Turner, M. G., Y. Wu, S. M. Pearson, W. H. Romme and L. L. Wallace. 1992. Landscape-level interactions among ungulates, vegetation, and large-scale fires in northern Yellowstone National Park. In G. E. Plumb and H. J. Harlow (eds.), *University of Wyoming National Park Service Research Center, 16th Annual Report,* pp. 206–211. Laramie, WY. [12]

Uhl, C. and R. Buschbacher. 1985. A disturbing synergism between cattle ranch burning practices and selective tree harvesting in Eastern Amazon. *Biotropica* 17:265–268. [5]

Uhl, C., K. Clark, N. Dezzeo and P. Maquirino. 1988. Vegetation dynamics in Amazonian treefall gaps. *Ecology* 69:751–763. [17]

U.S. Department of the Interior. 1990. *Endangered and Threatened Species Recovery Programs.* U.S. Fish and Wildlife Service, Washington, D.C. [3]

U.S. Department of the Interior. 1992. *Recovery Plan for the Northern Spotted Owl.* Unpublished report. [13]

U.S. Fish and Wildlife Service. 1988. *Black-Footed Ferret Recovery Plan.* U.S. Fish and Wildlife Service, Denver, CO. [13]

U.S. Fish and Wildlife Service. 1988. *Endangered Species Act of 1973. As Amended Through the 100th Congress.* U.S. Department of the Interior, Washington, D.C. [3]

USDA Forest Service. 1982a. *Golden Trout Wilderness Management Plan, Inyo and Sequoia National Forests.* USDA Forest Service, San Francisco. [12]

USDA Forest Service. 1982b. *Golden Trout Habitat and Wilderness Restoration on the Kern Plateau, Inyo National Forest.* USDA Forest Service, San Francisco. [12]

Vagelos, R. 1991. Are prescription drug prices high? *Science* 252:1080–1084. [17]

Van Devender, T. R. 1986. Climatic cadences and the composition of Chihuahuan Desert communities: The late Pleistocene packrat midden record. In J. Diamond and T. J. Case (eds.), *Community Ecology,* pp. 285–299. Harper & Row, New York. [8]

Van Dorp, D. and P. F. M. Opdam. 1987. Effects of patch size, isolation and regional abundance on forest bird communities. *Landscape Ecol.* 1:59–73. [9]

Van Riper, C. III and J. M. Scott. 1979. Observations on distribution, diet, and breeding of the Hawaiian thrush. *Condor* 81:65–71. [8]

Van Valen, L. 1976. Ecological species, multispecies, and oaks. *Taxon* 25:233–239. [3]

Vane-Wright, R. I., C. J. Humphries and P. H. Williams. 1991. What to protect? Systematics and the agony of choice. *Biol. Conserv.* 55:235–254. [3,6]

Vaughan, C. 1981. Parque Nacional Corcovado: Plan de Manejo y Desarrollo. Editorial of the Universidad Nacional, Costa Rica. [13]

Verner, J., K. S. McKelvey, B. R. Noon, R. J. Gutierrez, G. I. Gould, Jr. and T. W. Beck. 1992. *The California Spotted Owl: A Technical Assessment of Its Current Status.* U.S. Forest Service General Technical Report PSW-GTR-133. Pacific Southwest Research Station, Albany, CA. [7,13]

Vickerman, K. 1992. The diversity and ecological significance of Protozoa. *Biodiv. Conserv.* 1:334–341. [4]

Viederman, S. 1992. Public Policy: Challenge to Ecological Economics. Unpublished manuscript. [17]

Vietmeyer, N. 1986a. Exotic edibles are altering America's diet and agriculture. *Smithsonian* 16(9):34–43. [2]

Vietmeyer, N. 1986b. Lesser-known plants of potential use in agriculture and forestry. *Science* 232:1379–1384. [2]

Vitousek, P. M., P. R. Ehrlich, A. H. Ehrlich and P. A. Matson. 1986. Human appropriation of the products of photosynthesis. *BioScience* 36:368–373. [18]

Vitousek, P. M. and L. R. Walker. 1989. Biological invasion by *Myrica faya* in Hawaii: Plant demography, nitrogen fixation, ecosystem effects. *Ecol. Monogr.* 59:247–265. [8]

Vitt, L. J., J. P. Caldwell, H. M. Wilbur and D. C. Smith. 1990. Amphibians as harbingers of decay. *BioScience* 40: 418. [12]

von Humboldt, A. 1806. *The Physiognomy of Plants.* English ed., London, 1849. [4]

von Wantrup, S. C. 1952. *Resource Conservation: Economics and Politics.* Agricultural Experiment Station, University of California, Berkeley. [15]

Vrijenhoek, R. C. 1989a. Genotypic diversity and coexistence among sexual and clonal lineages of *Poeciliopsis.* In D. Otte and J. A. Endler (eds.), *Speciation and Its Consequences,* pp. 386–400. Sinauer Associates, Sunderland, MA. [6]

Vrijenhoek, R. C. 1989b. Population genetics and conservation. In M. Pearl and D. Western (eds.), *Conservation for the Twenty-First Century,* pp. 89–98. Oxford University Press, New York. [6]

Vrijenhoek, R. C., M. E. Douglas and G. K. Meffe. 1985. Conservation genetics of endangered fish populations in Arizona. *Science* 229:400–402. [6]

Wagner, F. H. 1989. American wildlife management at the crossroads. *Wild. Soc. Bull.* 17:354–360. [11]

Wali, M. K. (ed.). 1979. *Ecology and Coal Resource Development.* Vols. 1 and 2. Pergamon Press, New York. [14]

Wallace, A. R. 1863. On the physical geology of the Malay archipelago. *J. R. Geogr. Soc.* 33:217–234. [2]

Wallace, A. R. 1878. *Tropical Nature and Other Essays.* Macmillan, London. [4]

Wallin, J. E. 1989. Bluehead chub (*Nocomis leptocephalus*) nests used by yellow fin shiners (*Notropis lutipinnis*). *Copeia* 1989(4):1077–1080. [8]

Wann, D. 1990. *Biologic: Environmental Protection by Design.* Johnson, Boulder, CO. [16]

Waples, R. S. 1991. Definition of "species" under the Endangered Species Act: Application to Pacific salmon. NOAA Technical Memorandum NMFS F/NWC-194. National Marine Fisheries Service, Seattle, WA. [3,6]

Warnock, G. J. 1971. *The Object of Morality.* Methuen, London. [2]

Warren, R. J., M. J. Conroy, W. E. James, L. A. Baker and D. R. Diefenbach. 1990. Reintroduction of bobcats on Cumberland Island, Georgia: A biopolitical lesson. *Trans. N. Am. Wild. and Nat. Res. Conf.* 55:580–589. [12]

Watt, A. S. 1947. Pattern and process in the plant community. *J. Ecol.* 35:12–22. [9]

WCED. 1987. *Our Common Future: Report of the World Commission on Environment and Development.* Oxford University Press, Oxford. [15]

Weber, A. W. 1987. Socioecological factors in the conservation of afromontane forest reserves. In J. S. Marsh and R. A. Mittermeier (eds.), *Primate Conservation in Tropical Rain Forest,* pp. 205–229. Alan R. Liss, New York. [17]

*Webster's New Collegiate Dictionary.* 1977. G. & C. Merriam Co., Springfield, MA. [14]

Weiss, E. B. 1989. *In Fairness to Future Generations: International Law, Common Patrimony, and Intergenerational Equity.* Transnational Publishers, Ardsley-on-Hudson, NY. [15]

Werner, E. E., G. G. Mittlebach, D. J. Hall and J. F. Gilliam. 1983. Experimental tests of optimal habitat use in fish: The role of relative habitat profitability. *Ecology* 64:1525–1539. [7]

West, D. C., H. H. Shugart and D. B. Botkin (eds.). 1981. *Forest Succession: Concept and Application.* Springer-Verlag, New York. [14]

West, N. E. 1983. Western intermountain sagebrush steppe. In N. E. West (ed.), *Ecosystems of the World,* Vol. 5. pp. 351–374. Elsevier, Amsterdam. [14]

Western, D. 1989. Overview. In D. Western and M. C. Pearl (eds.), *Conservation for the Twenty-First Century,* pp. xi–xv. Oxford University Press, New York. [12]

Western, D. 1989. Why manage nature? In D. Western and M. C. Pearl (eds.), *Conservation for the Twenty-First Century*, pp. 133–137. Oxford University Press, New York. [10]

Western, D. and W. R. Henry. 1979. Economics and conservation in Third World National parks. *BioScience* 29:414–418. [17]

Western, D. and M. C. Pearl (eds.). 1989. *Conservation for the Twenty-First Century*. Oxford University Press, New York. [5]

Westman, W. E. 1990. Managing for biodiversity. *BioScience* 40:26–33. [12]

Westoby, M., K. French, L. Hughes, B. Rice and L. Rodgerson. 1991. Why do more plant species use ants for dispersal on infertile compared with fertile soils? *Aust. J. Ecol.* 16:445–455. [4]

Wheelwright, N. T. 1983. Fruits and the ecology of resplendent quetzals. *Auk* 100:286–301. [9]

Whitcomb, R. F., C. S. Robbins, J. F. Lynch, B. L. Whitcomb, M. K. Klimkiewicz and D. Bystrak. 1981. Effects of forest fragmentation on avifauna of the eastern deciduous forest. In R. L. Burgess and D. M. Sharpe (eds.), *Forest Island Dynamics in Man-Dominated Landscapes*, pp. 125–213. Springer-Verlag, New York. [9,10]

White, L. W. 1967. The historical roots of our ecologic crisis. *Science* 155:1203–1207. [2]

White, P. S. and S. P. Bratton. 1980. After preservation: Philosophical and practical problems of change. *Biol. Conserv.* 18:241–255. [10]

White, P. S. and S. T. A. Pickett. 1985. Natural disturbance and patch dynamics: an introduction. In S. T. A. Pickett and P. S. White (eds.), *The Ecology of Natural Disturbance and Patch Dynamics*, pp. 3–13. Academic Press, Orlando, FL. [10]

Whitmore, T. C. 1978. Gaps in the forest canopy. In P. B. Tomlinson and M. H. Zimmermann (eds.), *Tropical Trees as Living Systems*, pp. 639–655. Cambridge University Press, London. [17]

Whittaker, R. H. 1956. Vegetation of the Great Smoky Mountains. *Ecol. Monogr.* 26:1–80. [9]

Whittaker, R. H. 1970. *Communities and Ecosystems.* Macmillan, New York. [4]

Whittemore, A. T. and B. A. Schaal. 1991. Interspecific gene flow in sympatric oaks. *Proc. Nat. Acad. Sci. U.S.A.* 88:2540–2544. [3]

Wibbels, T., N. Frazer, M. Grassman, J. Hendrickson and P. Pritchard. 1989. *Blue Ribbon Panel Review of the National Marine Fisheries Service Kemp's Ridley Headstart Program*. Southeast Regional Office, National Marine Fisheries Service, Miami, FL. [13]

Wiens, J. A. 1977. On competition and variable environments. *Am. Sci.* 65:590–597. [4]

Wiens, J. A. 1985. Vertebrate response to environmental patchiness in arid and semiarid ecosystems. In S. T. A. Pickett and P. S. White (eds.), *The Ecology of Natural Disturbance and Patch Dynamics*, pp. 169–193. Academic Press, Orlando, FL. [9]

Wiens, J. A. 1989. *The Ecology of Bird Communities.* Vol. 2. *Processes and Variations.* Cambridge University Press, New York. [9]

Wilcove, D. S. 1985. Nest predation in forest tracts and the decline of migratory songbirds. *Ecology* 66:1211–1214. [9]

Wilcove, D. S. 1987. From fragmentation to extinction. *Nat. Areas J.* 7:23–29. [5]

Wilcove, D. S., C. H. McLellan and A. P. Dobson. 1986. Habitat fragmentation in the temperate zone. In M. E. Soulé (ed.), *Conservation Biology: The Science of Scarcity and Diversity*, pp. 237–256. Sinauer Associates, Sunderland MA. [9,10,12]

Wilcove, D. S., M. McMillan and K. C. Winston. 1993. What exactly is an endangered species? An analysis of the U.S. Endangered Species list: 1985–1991. *Conserv. Biol.* 7:87–93. [3]

Wilcove, D. and D. Murphy. 1991. The Spotted Owl controversy and conservation biology. *Conserv. Biol.* 5:261–262. [13]

Wilcox, B. A. 1980. Insular ecology and conservation. In M. E. Soulé and B. A. Wilcox (eds.), *Conservation Biology: An Ecological-Evolutionary Perspective*, pp. 95–117. Sinauer Associates, Sunderland, MA. [9]

Wilcox, B. A. and D. D. Murphy. 1985. Conservation strategy: The effects of fragmentation on extinction. *Am. Nat.* 125:879–887. [9,10]

Wildt, D. E. and seven others. 1987. Reproductive and genetic consequences of founding isolated lion populations. *Nature* 329:328–331. [6]

Wiley, E. O. 1978. The evolutionary species concept reconsidered. *Syst. Zool* 27:17–26. [3]

Wilkinson, C. F. 1992. *Crossing the Next Meridian: Land, Water, and the Future of the West.* Island Press, Washington, D.C. [12]

Wille, C. 1991. Central America: Biodiversity at stake. In C. L. Cardieux (ed.), *Wildlife Extinction*, pp. 174–182. Stone Wall Press, Washington, D.C. [17]

Williams, C. B. 1943. Area and number of species. *Nature* 152:264–267. [9]

Williams, E. S., E. T. Thorne, M. J. G. Appel and D. W. Belitsky. 1988. Canine distemper in black-footed ferrets (*Mustela nigripes*) from Wyoming. *J. Wildl. Dis.* 24:385–398. [13]

Williams, G. C. 1966. *Adaptation and Natural Selection.* Princeton University Press, Princeton, NJ. [3]

Williams, J. D., M. L. Warren, K. S. Cummings, J. L. Harris and R.J. Neves. 1993. Conservation status of freshwater mussels of the United States and Canada. *Fisheries* 18(9):6–22. [3]

Williams, J. E., J. E. Johnson, D. A. Hendrickson, S. Contraras-Balderas, J. D. Williams, M. Navarro-Mendoza, D. E. McAllister and J. E. Deacon. 1989. Fishes of North America, endangered, threatened, or of special concern, 1989. *Fisheries* 14(6):2–38. [5]

Williams, J. E. and J. N. Rinne. 1992. Biodiversity management on multiple-use federal lands: an opportunity whose time has come. *Fisheries* 17(3):4–5. [12]

Williams, P. H., C. J. Humphries and R. I. Vane-Wright. 1991. Measuring biodiversity: Taxonomic relatedness for conservation priorities. *Aust. Syst. Bot.* 4:665–679. [3]

Williams, P. H., R. I. Vane-Wright and C. J. Humphries. In press. Measuring biodiversity for choosing conservation areas. In J. LaSalle (ed.), *Hymenoptera and Biodiversity.* CABI, Sheffield. [3]

Williamson, M. 1981. *Island Populations.* Oxford University Press, New York. [5]

Willis, E. O. 1974. Populations and local extinctions of birds on Barro Colorado Island, Panama. *Ecol. Monogr.* 44:153–169. [9]

Wilson, E. O. 1971. *The Insect Societies.* Harvard University Press, Cambridge, MA. [5]

Wilson, E. O. 1984. *Biophilia.* Harvard University Press, Cambridge, MA. [1,2,10]

Wilson, E. O. 1985. The biological diversity crisis. *BioScience* 35:700–706. [2]

Wilson, E. O. 1985. The biological diversity crisis: A challenge to science. *Issues Sci. Tech.* 2:20–25. [5]

Wilson, E. O. 1985. Time to revive systematics. *Science* 230:1227. [3,6]

Wilson, E. O. 1987. The little things that run the world (the importance and conservation of invertebrates). *Conserv. Biol.* 1:344–346. [3,8]

Wilson, E. O. 1988b. Conservation: The next hundred years. In D. Western and M. C. Pearl (eds.), *Conservation for the Twenty-First Century*, pp. 3–7. Oxford University Press, New York. [5]

Wilson, E. O. 1988. The current state of biological diversity. In E. O. Wilson and F. M. Peter (eds.), *Biodiversity*, pp. 3–18. National Academy Press, Washington, D.C. [1,3]

Wilson, E. O. 1989. Threats to biodiversity. *Sci. Am.* 261:108–117. [5]

Wilson, E. O. 1992. *The Diversity of Life.* Belknap Press of Harvard University Press, Cambridge, MA. [3,4,5]

Wilson, E. O. and W. H. Bossert 1971. *A Primer of Population Biology.* Sinauer Associates, Sunderland, MA. [6]

Wilson, E. O. and F. M. Peter (eds.). 1988a. *Biodiversity.* National Academy Press, Washington, D.C. [5]

Wilson, E. O. and E. O. Willis. 1975. Applied biogeography. In M. L. Cody and J. M. Diamond (eds.), *Ecology and Evolution of Communities*, pp. 522–534. Belknap Press of Harvard University Press, Cambridge, MA. [9]

Witt, S. C. 1985. *Briefbook: Biotechnology and Genetic Diversity.* CSI, San Francisco. [5]

Witte, F., T. Goldschmidt, P. C. Goudswaard, W. Ligtvoet, M. J. P. Van Oijen and J. H. Wanink. 1992. Species extinction and concommittant ecological changes in Lake Victoria. *Netherlands J. Zool.* 42:214–332.

Wolfe, S. H., J. A. Reidenauer and D. B. Means. 1988. *An Ecological Characterization of the Florida Panhandle.* Biological Report 88(12). U.S. Fish and Wildlife Service, National Wetlands Research Center, Slidell, LA. [9]

Wood, S. L. (ed.). 1986. *The Black-footed Ferret.* Great Basin Naturalist Memoirs no. 8. Brigham Young University, Provo, UT. [13]

Woodruff, D. S. 1989. The problems of conserving genes and species. In M. Pearl and D. Western (eds.), *Conservation for the Twenty-First Century*, pp. 76–88. Oxford University Press, New York. [6]

Woodruff, D. S. 1992. *Biodiversity: Conservation and Genetics.* Proc. 2nd Princess Chulabhorn Congress of Scientific Technology, Bangkok. [6]

Woodruff, D. S. 1993. Non-invasive genotyping of primates. *Primates* 34:333–346. [6]

Wootton, T. J. and D. A. Bell. 1992. A metapopulation model of the Peregrine Falcon in California: Viability and management strategies. *Ecol. Applic.* 2:307–321. [7,11]

World Commission on Environment and Development. 1987. *Our Common Future.* Oxford University Press, Oxford. [17]

World Conservation and Monitoring Centre. 1992. *Global Biodiversity: State of the Earth's Living Resources.* Chapman & Hall, London. [4]

World Development Report. 1992. *Development and the Environment.* The World Bank. Oxford University Press, New York. [18]

World Population Prospects. 1990. United Nations Population Division, New York. [18]

World Resources Institute. 1991. *World Resources Report 1991–1992: A Guide to the Global Environment.* Oxford University Press, New York. [5]

World Resources Institute. 1992. *World Resources 1992–1993: A Report by the World Resources Institute in Collaboration with the United Nations Environment Programme and the United Nations Development Programme.* Oxford University Press, New York. [17,18]

Wright, S. 1969. *Evolution and the Genetics of Populations.* Vol. 2, *The Theory of Gene Frequencies.* University of Chicago Press, Chicago. [6]

Wright, S. 1978. *Evolution and the Genetics of Populations.* Vol. 4, *Variability Within and Among Natural Populations.* University of Chicago Press, Chicago. [6]

Wyoming Game and Fish Department (WGFD). 1987. *A Strategic Plan for the Management of Black-footed Ferrets in Wyoming.* Wyoming Game and Fish Department, Cheyenne. [13]

Yeatman, C. W., D. Kafton and G. Wilkes (eds.). 1984. *Plant Genetic Resources: A Conservation Imperative.* AAAS, Washington, D.C. [5]

Yoakum, J. and W. P. Dasmann. 1971. Habitat manipulation practices. In R. H. Giles, (ed.), *Wildlife Management Techniques*, pp. 173–231. The Wildlife Society, Washington, D.C. [9]

Zedler, J. B. and R. Langis. 1991. Comparisons of constructed and natural salt marshes of San Diego Bay. *Rest. Mgmt. Notes* 9(1):21–25. [14]

Zedler, J. B. 1993. Canopy architecture of natural and planted cordgrass marshes: Selecting habitat evaluation criteria. *Ecol. Appl.* 3:123–138. [14]

Zouros, E. and D. W. Foltz. 1987. The use of allelic isozyme variation for the study of heterosis. In M. C. Rattazzi, J. G. Scandalics and G. S. Whitt (eds.), *Isozymes*, pp. 1–59. Current Topics in Biological and Medical Research 13. Alan R. Liss, New York. [6]

# Index

**ABOUT THE BOOK**

Typography:   Cover type; Optima
                      Text type; Palatino
Editor:   Andrew D. Sinauer
Project Editor:   Kathaleen Emerson
Copy Editor:   Norma Roche
Production Manager:   Christopher Small
Book Production:   Peter Irvine
Book Design:   Christopher Small
Cover Design:   Christopher Small and Peter Irvine
Cover Photograph:   Daniel Dancer
Composition:   Peter Irvine and Sinauer Associates
Cover Manufacture:   John P. Pow Co.
Book Manufacture:   Courier Companies, Inc.